Autodesk 3ds Max 2017 A Comprehensive Guide

(17th Revised and Updated Edition)

Sham Tickoo
Professor
Purdue University Northwest
Hammond, Indiana, USA

Contributing Authors
Tickoo Institute of Emerging Technologies (TIET)
Gurgaon, India

CADCIM Technologies
Indiana, USA

BPB PUBLICATIONS

ISBN: 978-93-86551-13-9
17th Revised and Updated Edition
(For distribution in SAARC countries only)

Limits of Liability and Disclaimer of Warranty

The information contained in this book is the best of Author's & Publisher's knowledge. We are committed to serve students with best of our knowledge and resources. We have taken utmost care and attention while editing and printing of this book but Author and Publisher should not be held responsible for errors, omissions and any other unintentional mistake that might have crept in. However, errors brought to our notice shall be gratefully acknowledged and attended to.

All trademarks referred to in the book are acknowledged as properties of their respective owners. This book is written solely for the benefit and guidance of the students.

Distributors

COMPUTER BOOK CENTRE
12, Shrungar Shopping Centre
M.G. Road
BENGALURU–560001
Ph: 25587923/25584641

DECCAN AGENCIES
4-3-329, Bank Street
HYDERABAD-500195
Ph: 24756967/24756400

MICRO MEDIA
Shop No. 5, Mahendra Chambers
150 DN Rd. Next to Capital Cinema
V.T (C.S.T.) Station
MUMBAI-400001

BPB BOOK CENTRE
376 Old Lajpat Rai Market
DELHI-110006
Ph: 23861747

INFOTECH
G-2, Sidhartha Building, 96 Nehru Place
NEW DELHI-110019
Ph: 26438245

BPB PUBLICATIONS
20, Ansari Road, Darya Ganj
New Delhi-110002
Ph: 23254990/23254991

Published by Manish Jain for BPB Publications, 20 Ansari Road, Darya Ganj
New Delhi-110002 and Printed Repro India Pvt. Ltd, Mumbai

DEDICATION

To teachers, who make it possible to disseminate knowledge to enlighten the young and curious minds of our future generations

To students, who are dedicated to learning new technologies and making the world a better place to live in

SPECIAL RECOGNITION

A special thanks to Mr. Denis Cadu and the ADN team of Autodesk Inc. for their valuable support and professional guidance to procure the software for writing this textbook

THANKS

To employees of CADCIM Technologies and Tickoo Institute of Emerging Technologies (TIET) for their valuable help

Note

If you are a faculty member, you can register by clicking on the following link to access the teaching resources: ***http://www.cadcim.com/Registration.aspx***. The student resources are available at ***http://www.cadcim.com***.

Table of Contents

Chapter 2: Standard Primitives

Chapter 3: Extended Primitives

Chapter 5: Splines and Extended Splines

Chapter 6: Modifying Splines

Chapter 7: Materials and Maps

Chapter 8: Modifying 3D Mesh Objects

Chapter 9: Graphite Modeling Technique

Chapter 10: NURBS Modeling

Chapter 11: Compound Objects

Chapter 7: Materials and Maps

Chapter 8: Modifying 3D Mesh Objects

Chapter 9: Graphite Modeling Technique

Chapter 10: NURBS Modeling

Chapter 11: Compound Objects

Chapter 12: Modifiers

Chapter 13: Lights and Cameras

Chapter 14: Animation Basics

Chapter 15: Systems, Hierarchy, and Kinematics

Chapter 16: Rigid Body Dynamics and Helpers

CHAPTERS FOR FREE DOWNLOAD

In this text book three chapters have been given for free download. You can download these chapters from our website *www.cadcim.com*. To download these chapters follow the given path: *Textbooks> Animation and Visual Effects > 3ds Max > Autodesk 3ds Max 2017: A Comprehensive Guide > Chapters for Free Download* and then select the chapter name from the **Chapters for Free Download** drop-down. Click the **Download** button to download the chapter in the PDF format.

This page is intentionally left blank

This page is intentionally left blank

Preface

Autodesk 3ds Max 2017

Autodesk 3ds Max is developed by Autodesk Inc., provides powerful tools for 3D modeling, animation, rendering, dynamics, and compositing. This enables game developers, visual effects artists, architects, designers, engineers, and visualization specialists to create stunning artwork. Additionally, the intuitive user interface and workflow tools of 3ds Max 2017 have made the job of design visualization specialists easier.

Autodesk 3ds Max 2017: A Comprehensive Guide textbook aims at harnessing the power of Autodesk 3ds Max for modelers, animators, and designers. The textbook caters to the needs of both the novice and the advanced users of 3ds Max. Keeping in view the varied requirements of the users, the textbook first introduces the basic features of 3ds Max 2017 and then gradually progresses to cover the advanced 3D models and animations. In this textbook, two projects based on the tools and concepts covered in the book have been added to enhance the knowledge of users.

This book will help you unleash your creativity, thus helping you create stunning 3D models and animations. The textbook will help the learners transform their imagination into reality with ease. Also, it takes the users across a wide spectrum of animations through progressive examples, numerous illustrations, and ample exercises.

The main features of this textbook are as follows:

- **Tutorial Approach**
  The author has adopted the tutorial point-of-view and the learn-by-doing theme throughout the textbook. About 36 real-world 3D animation and 3D modeling projects have been used as tutorials in the textbook. This enables the readers to relate these tutorials to the real-world models. In addition, there are about 48 exercises based on the real-world projects.

- **Tips and Notes**
  Additional information related to various topics is provided to the users in the form of tips and notes.

- **Learning Objectives**
  The first page of every chapter summarizes the topics that will be covered in that chapter. This will help the users to easily refer to a topic.

- **Self-Evaluation Test, Review Questions, and Exercises**
  Every chapter ends with a Self-Evaluation Test so that the users can assess their knowledge of the chapter. The answers to Self-Evaluation Test are given at the end of the chapter. Also, the Review Questions and Exercises are given at the end of each chapter and they can be used by the Instructors as test questions and exercises.

- **Heavily Illustrated Text**
  The text in this book is heavily illustrated with about 1500 diagrams and screen captures.

Symbols Used in the Textbook

Note
The author has provided additional information to the users about the topic being discussed in the form of notes.

Tip
Special information and techniques are provided in the form of tips that helps in increasing the efficiency of the users.

This symbol indicates that the command or tool being discussed is new.

This symbol indicates that the command or tool being discussed is enhanced in the current release.

Formatting Conventions Used in the Textbook

Please refer to the following list for the formatting conventions used in this textbook.

- Names of tools, buttons, options, renderer, rollouts, and tabs are written in boldface.

  Example: The **Select and Move** tool, the **Render** button, the **Modify** tab, **NVIDIA mental ray** renderer, the **Common Parameters** rollout, and so on.

- Names of dialog boxes, drop-downs, drop-down lists, spinners, areas, edit boxes, check boxes, and radio buttons are written in boldface.

  Example: The **Render Setup** dialog box, the **Look in** drop-down, the **Length** spinner, the **Bend** area, the **Angle** edit box, **Real-World Map Size** check box, the **Cube** radio button, and so on.

- Values entered in spinners are written in boldface. — Example: Enter **10** in the **Length** spinner.

- Names of the files are italicized. — Example: *c02_tut1.max*

- The methods of invoking a tool/option from menu bar, toolbar, or the shortcut keys are given in a shaded box.

> **Menu bar:** Rendering > Render
> **Toolbar:** Main Toolbar > Render Production
> **Keyboard:** SHIFT + Q

Naming Conventions Used in the Textbook

Tool

If you click on an item in a panel of the ribbon and a command is invoked to create/edit an object or perform some action, then that item is termed as **tool**.

For example:
Select and Move tool, **Select and Link** tool, **Angle Snap Toggle** tool
Render Setup tool, **Select and Rotate** tool, **Align** tool

If you click on an item in a panel of the ribbon and a dialog box is invoked wherein you can set the properties to create/edit an object, then that item is also termed as **tool**.

For example:
Material Editor tool, **Render Setup** tool

Flyout

A flyout is an icon-based menu that contains tools with similar type of functions. Figure 1 shows the **Snap Toggle** flyout. The buttons having a small triangle at their lower right corner contain a flyout. Press and hold such a button; a flyout will be displayed, refer to Figure 1.

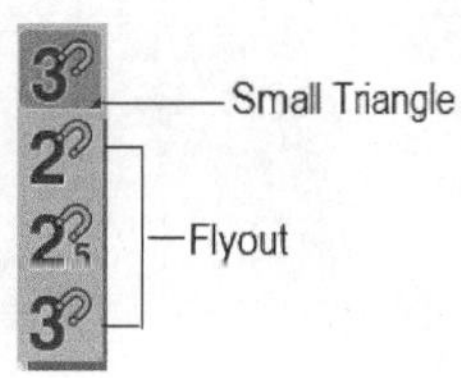

***Figure 1** The **Snap Toggle** flyout*

Right-click Menus

In Autodesk 3ds Max, the right-click menus provide quick access to the commonly used commands that are related to the current selection of an object. When you right-click on an object, a quad menu is displayed, as shown in Figure 2. Some of the options in the quad menu have an arrow on their right side. If you move the mouse on these options, a cascading menu will be displayed, refer to Figure 2. But, if you right-click in the viewport, a shortcut menu will be displayed, refer to Figure 3.

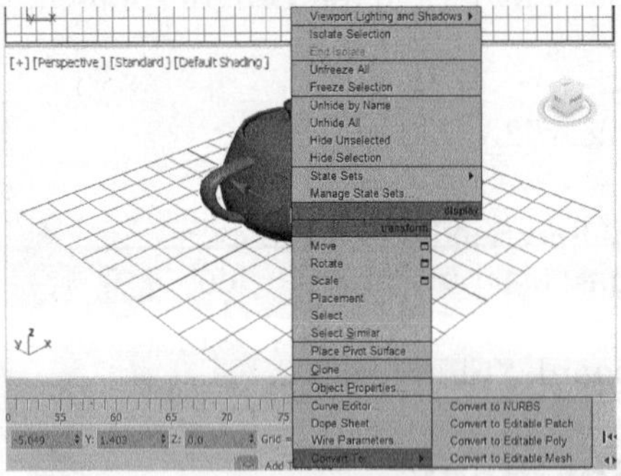

Figure 2 The Quad menu and the cascading menu

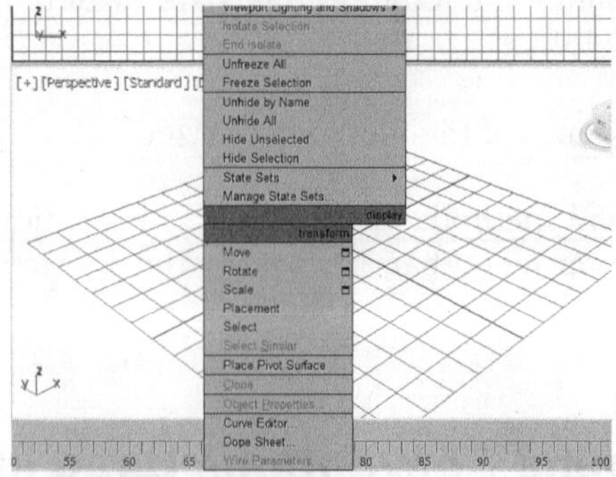

Figure 3 The shortcut menu displayed on right-clicking in the viewport

Button

The item in a dialog box that has a 3D shape is termed as **Button**. For example, **OK** button, **Cancel** button, **Render** button, and so on, refer to Figure 4.

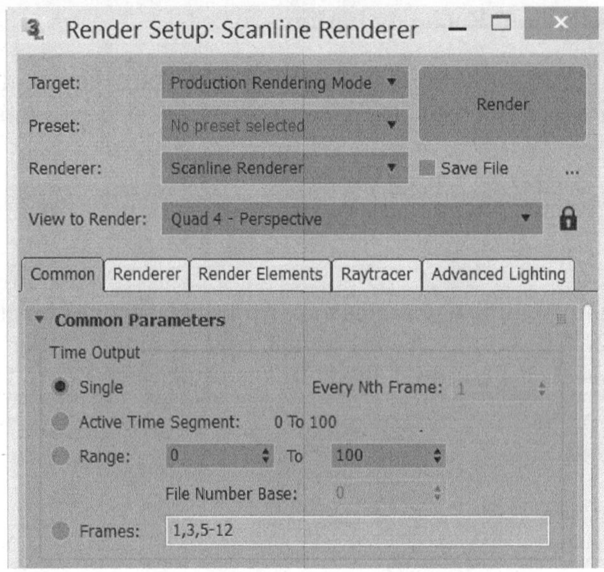

*Figure 4 The **Render** button in the **Render Setup:Scanline Renderer** dialog box*

Dialog Box

In this textbook, different terms are used to indicate various components of a dialog box; refer to Figure 5 for different terminologies used in a dialog box.

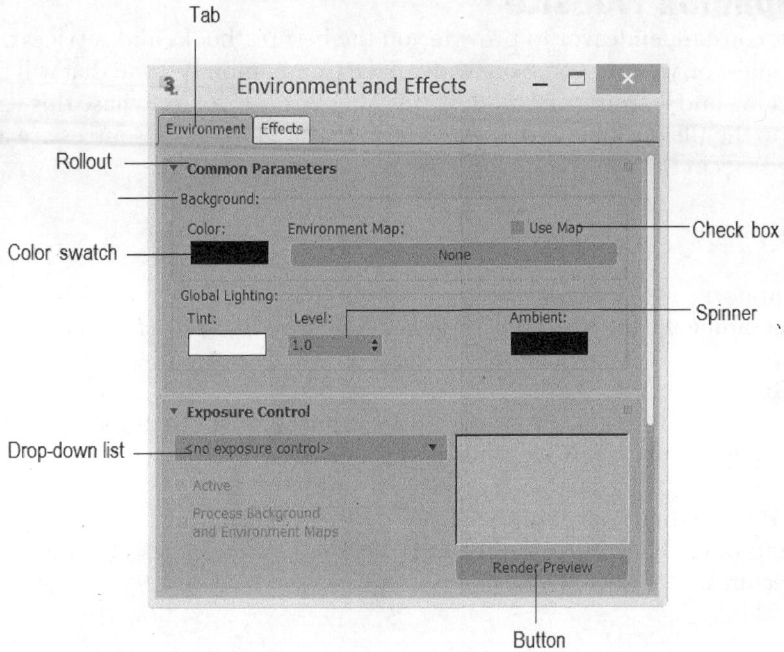

Figure 5 Different terminologies used in a dialog box

Drop-down List

A drop-down list is the one in which a set of options are grouped together. You can set various parameters using these options. You can identify a drop-down list with a down arrow on it. For example, **Reference Coordinate System** drop-down list, **Modifier List** drop-down list, and so on; refer to Figure 6.

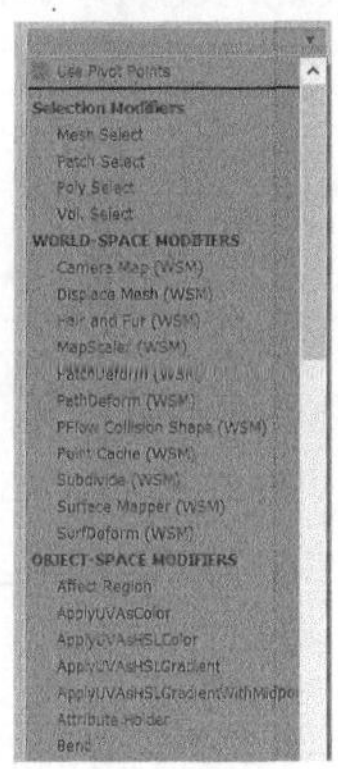

Figure 6 Selecting an option from the ***Modifier List*** *drop-down list*

Free Companion Website

It has been our constant endeavor to provide you the best textbooks and services at affordable price. In this endeavor, we have come out with a Free Companion Website that will facilitate the process of teaching and learning of Autodesk 3ds Max 2017. If you purchase this textbook, you will get access to the files on the Companion website. The following resources are available for faculty and students in this website:

Faculty Resources

- **Technical Support**
  You can get online technical support by contacting *techsupport@cadcim.com.*

- **Instructor Guide**
  Solutions to all the review questions and exercises in the textbook are provided to help the faculty members test the skills of the students.

- **PowerPoint Presentations**
  The contents of the book are arranged in PowerPoint slides that can be used by the faculty for their lectures.

- **3ds Max Files**
  The 3ds Max files used in illustration, tutorials, and exercises are available for free download.

- **Rendered Images**
  If you do an exercise or tutorial, you can compare your rendered output with the one provided in the CADCIM website.

- **Additional Resources**
  You can access additional learning resources by visiting *http://3dsmaxexperts.blogspot.com*.

- **Colored Images**
  You can download the PDF file containing color images of the screenshots used in this textbook from CADCIM website.

Student Resources

- **Technical Support**
  You can get online technical support by contacting *techsupport@cadcim.com.*

- **3ds Max Files**
  The 3ds Max files used in illustrations and tutorials are available for free download.

- **Rendered Images**
  If you do an exercise or tutorial, you can compare your rendered output with the one provided in the CADCIM website.

- **Additional Resources**
  You can access additional learning resources by visiting *http://3dsmaxexperts.blogspot.com.*

- **Colored Images**
  You can download the PDF file containing color images of the screenshots used in this textbook from CADCIM website.

If you face any problem in accessing these files, please contact the publisher at ***sales@cadcim.com*** or the author at ***stickoo@pnw.edu*** or ***tickoo525@gmail.com***.

Stay Connected

You can now stay connected with us through Facebook and Twitter to get the latest information about our textbooks, videos, and teaching/learning resources. To stay informed of such updates, follow us on Facebook ***(www.facebook.com/cadcim)*** and Twitter (@cadcimtech). You can also subscribe to our YouTube channel ***(www.youtube.com/cadcimtech)*** to get the information about our latest video tutorials.

This page is intentionally left blank

Chapter 1

Introduction to Autodesk 3ds Max 2017

Learning Objectives

After completing this chapter, you will be able to:

- *Understand the Autodesk 3ds Max interface components*
- *Use controls for creating or modifying objects*
- *Use and customize hotkeys in Autodesk 3ds Max*
- *Customize the colors of the scene elements*

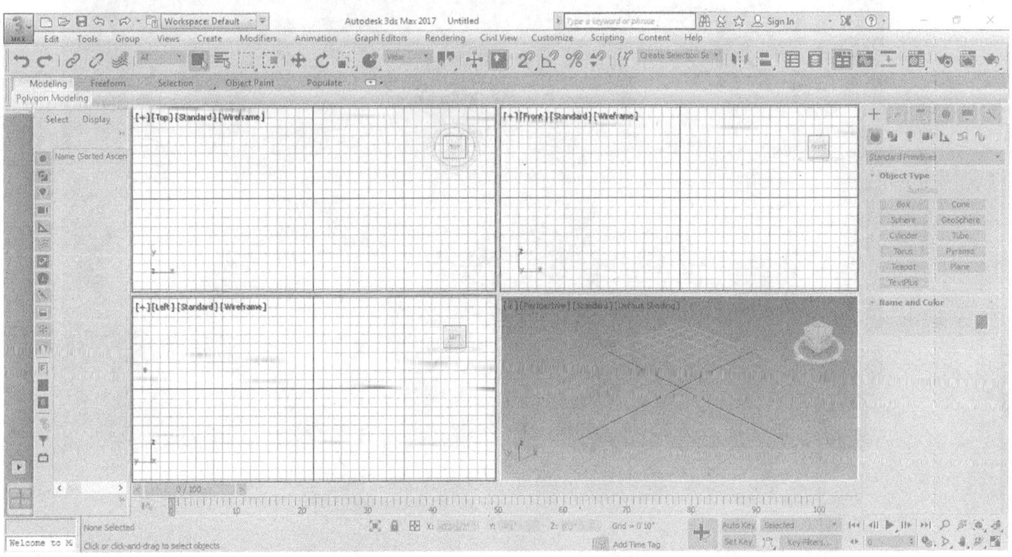

INTRODUCTION TO Autodesk 3ds Max 2017

Welcome to the world of Autodesk 3ds Max, an advanced application that is used to create still or animated 3D models and objects. With the help of this application, you can create realistic scenes by modifying objects, applying maps and materials to a scene, assigning environment to a scene, adding lights and cameras, and so on. Before working with Autodesk 3ds Max, you should have the basic knowledge of various tools and commands available in this software. In this chapter, you will learn the basic features of Autodesk 3ds Max.

GETTING STARTED WITH Autodesk 3ds Max

First, you need to install Autodesk 3ds Max 2017 on your computer. On installing the software, the **3ds Max 2017** shortcut icon will be created automatically on the desktop. Double-click on this icon to start Autodesk 3ds Max. Alternatively, you can start Autodesk 3ds Max from the Start menu. To do so, click the **Start** button from the taskbar to display the Start menu and then choose **All Apps > Autodesk > 3ds Max 2017**, refer to Figure 1-1.

Figure 1-1 Starting Autodesk 3ds Max 2017 from the taskbar

The system will prepare to start 3ds Max 2017 by loading all the required files. If you are running 3ds Max 2017 for the first time, the **Data collection and use** dialog box will be displayed, as shown in Figure 1-2, and you will be prompted to join this program. Select the **I agree to data collection in desktop products for Autodesk analytics programs** check box and then choose the **OK** button to join the program. If you do not wish to join the program, then clear this check box. On joining this program, Autodesk will gather product feature usage and system information to improve 3ds Max and to personalize the working features of the application. This entire information helps Autodesk to improve 3ds Max. You can also invoke the **Data collection and use** dialog box by choosing **Help > Speak Back > Desktop Analytics Program** from the menu bar.

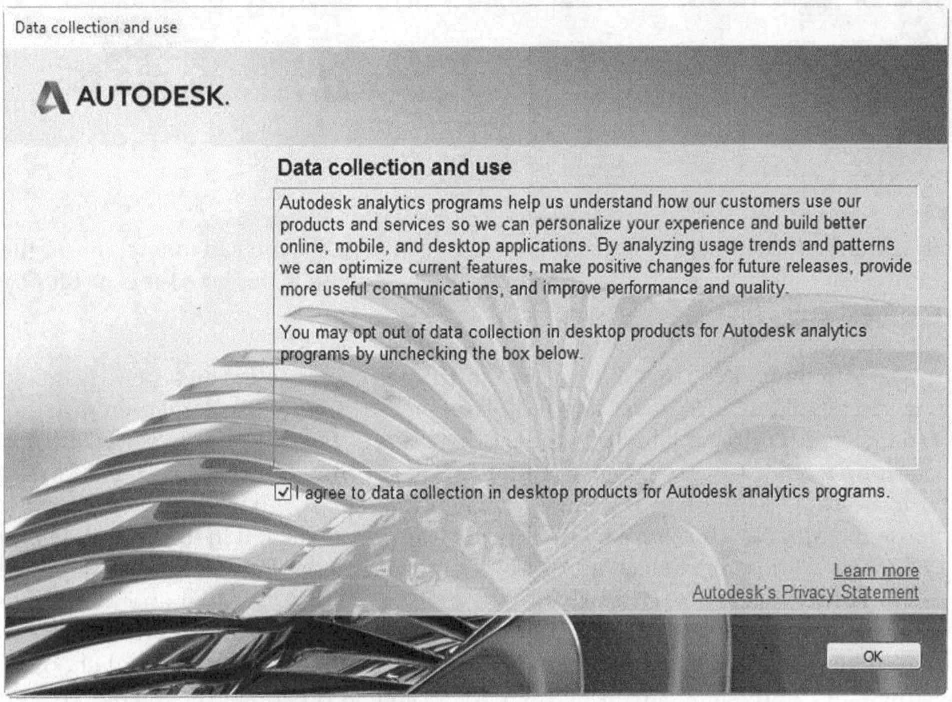

Figure 1-2 The **Data collection and use** *dialog box*

After all the required files are loaded, the 3ds Max interface will be displayed along with the Welcome Screen, refer to Figure 1-3. There are three tabs in the Welcome Screen: **Learn**, **Start**, and **Extend**. These tabs are discussed next.

Learn

In this tab, if you hover the mouse pointer at the top right corner of the Welcome screen, a layer will flip over and a button **Start new or open a file**, will be displayed. Choose this button to create a new file or open an existing one. This tab provides access to video tutorials that are helpful in learning the basics of 3ds Max. To start a tutorial, select one of the options in the **More 1-Minute Movies** drop-down list available on the left in the Welcome screen; the corresponding tutorial will be displayed in a separate window. Also, links for more learning resources such as 3ds Max Learning Channel, Autodesk Learning Path, What's New, and Sample Scenes are provided in this tab.

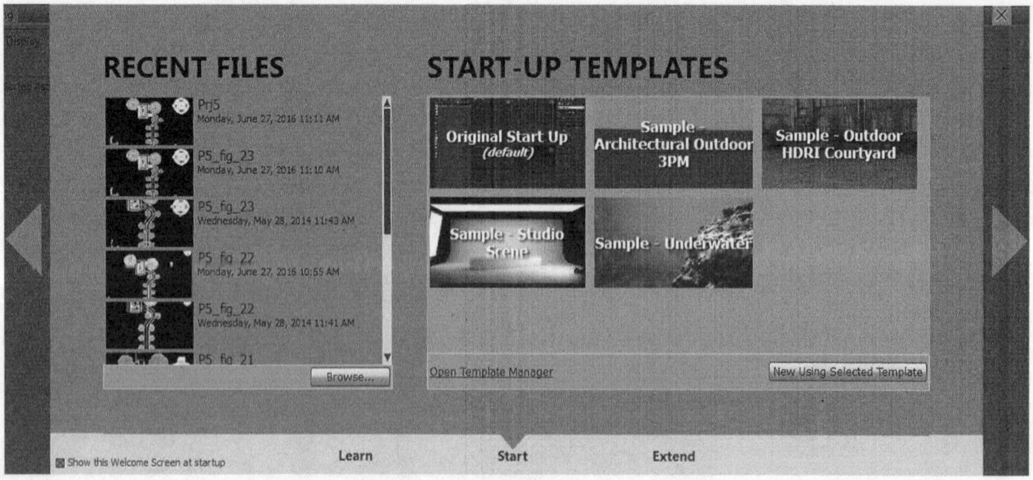

Figure 1-3 *The Welcome screen*

Start

This tab is chosen by default in the Welcome screen. In this tab, you can open a recent file from the list of recent files. Choose the **Browse** button located below the list of recent files to open file other than recent files.

Various start-up templates are also provided in this tab. You can create a new scene by using these start-up templates. To create a new template, first set up the scene and then save the scene at desired location. The default location to save this file is *C:\Program Files\Autodesk\3ds Max 2017\en-US\StartupTemplates*. Choose **Open Template Manager** from the **START - UP TEMPLATES** area of the Welcome screen; the **Template Manager** dialog box will be displayed. In this dialog box, choose the **Add New** button; a template will be added on the left in the **Template Manager** dialog box. Now, choose the **Select** button corresponding to the **Project Folder** parameter, the **Browse For Folder** dialog box is displayed. Navigate to the project folder and then choose the **OK** button. Next, choose the **Select** button corresponding to the **Scene File** parameter; the **Open File** dialog box is displayed. Select the *.max* file that is saved earlier and choose **Open**. Change the name of the template using the field located at the top of the dialog box and then choose the **Done** button.

Extend

This tab contains links that can be used to access Autodesk Exchange store and to Autodesk resources such as Autodesk 360 and Autodesk Area. The **Autodesk 3ds Max Asset Library** and the **Download Vegetation** button in this tab are used to download assets.

STARTING A NEW FILE IN Autodesk 3ds Max

To start a new file in Autodesk 3ds Max, choose the **Application** button at the top left corner of the interface; the **Application** menu will be displayed. Next, choose **New > New All** from the **Application** menu; a new file will be displayed in the 3ds Max interface. The new file will clear all the contents of the current file. Alternatively, press the CTRL+N keys; the **New Scene** dialog box will be displayed, as shown in Figure 1-4. By default, the **New All** radio button is selected in this dialog box. Choose the **OK** button; a new file will be displayed.

You can also reuse the objects from the current scene in the new scene. Select the **Keep Objects** radio button in the **New Scene** dialog box to keep only the objects from the current scene for the new file. However, on selecting this radio button, all the animation keys and links between the objects will be cleared. To keep the objects and the links between them, select the **Keep Objects and Hierarchy** radio button. However, in this case, the animation keys will be deleted.

Before starting a new scene in Autodesk 3ds Max, it is recommended to reset Autodesk 3ds Max and start afresh. By doing so, you will be able to reset all settings for the new scene. To reset Autodesk 3ds Max, choose **Reset** from the **Application** menu; the **3ds Max** message box will be displayed, as shown in Figure 1-5. The message box will ask if you really want to reset 3ds Max. Choose the **Yes** button; the 3ds Max will be reset.

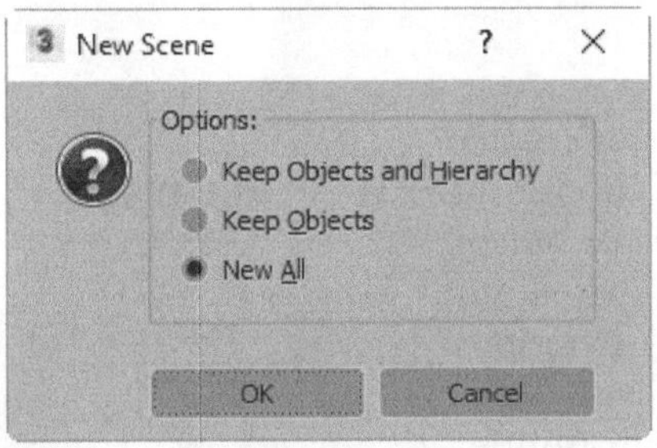

*Figure 1-4 The **New Scene** dialog box*

*Figure 1-5 The **3ds Max** message box*

Autodesk 3ds Max INTERFACE COMPONENTS

The 3ds Max interface screen consists of different components, as shown in Figure 1-6. These components are discussed next.

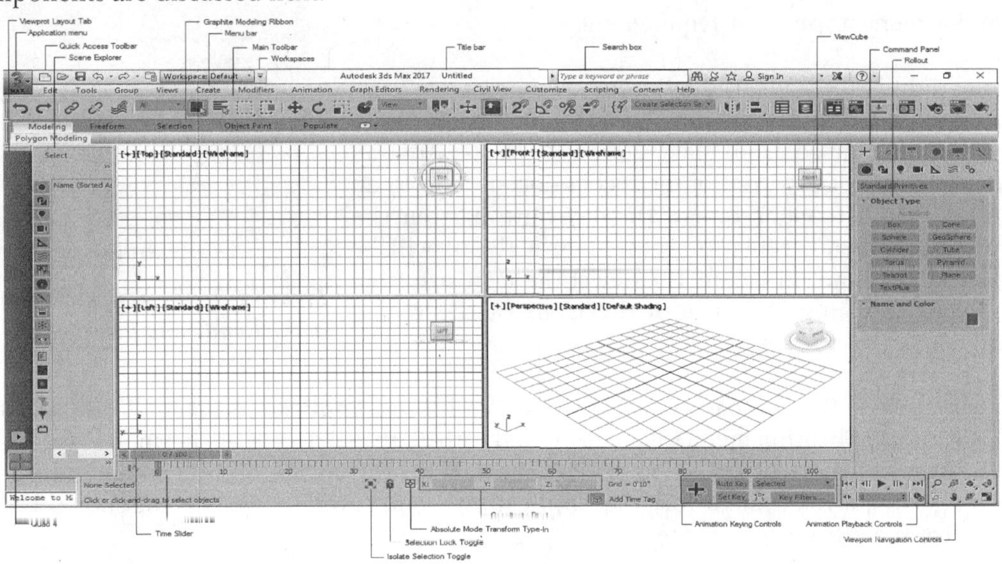

Figure 1-6 Different screen components of Autodesk 3ds Max interface screen

Menu Bar

The menu bar is located just below the title bar, refer to Figure 1-6 and contains various pull-down menus. Some of the pull-down menus are standard window menus such as **Edit**, **Help**, and so on while others are 3ds Max pull-down menus such as **Create**, **Modifiers**, **Animation**, **Graph Editors**, **Rendering**, **Customize**, and so on. The title of each pull-down menu indicates the purpose of commands in the menu. When you choose one of the menu titles, Autodesk 3ds Max displays the corresponding pull-down menu. Each menu consists of a collection of commands. In a pull-down menu, the dots after a command indicate that a dialog box will be displayed on choosing that command. An arrow next to a command indicates that a cascading menu will be displayed on placing the cursor on that command. For some of the commands in the pull-down menus, the keyboard shortcuts are displayed on their right side, as shown in Figure 1-7.

Application Menu

The **Application** menu is used to manage the files created in 3ds Max. To display the **Application** menu, choose the **Application** button on the top left of the 3ds Max screen. Figure 1-8 displays the **Application** menu. This menu comprises the most commonly used file management options. The **Send to** option provides interoperability with other Autodesk applications such as Softimage, MotionBuilder, Maya, and Mudbox. When you choose the **Send to** option from the **Application** menu, a cascading menu will be displayed. Choose the desired option from the cascading menu; a submenu will be displayed with the following options: **Send as New Scene**, **Update Current Scene**, **Add to Current Scene**, and **Select Previously Sent Objects**. You can choose the option from this menu as per your requirement.

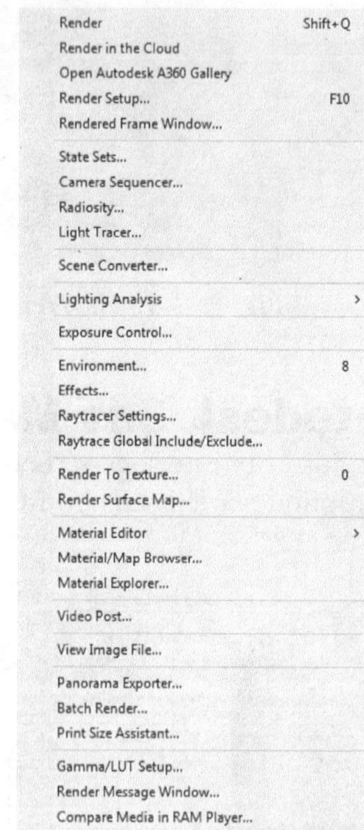

***Figure 1-7** The keyboard shortcuts in the **Rendering** pull-down menu*

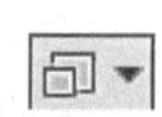

On the right in the menu is the **Recent Documents** page that provides information about the files that were previously saved in 3ds Max, refer to Figure 1-8. You can change the size of the icons of the recent documents. To do so, choose the Icon or Image Display button from the **Application** menu, refer to Figure 1-8; a flyout will be displayed, as shown in Figure 1-9. Select the icon size from the flyout to change the size of the icons of the recent documents.

You can also use the keyboard shortcuts to work with the **Application** menu. To do so, press ALT+F; the **Application** menu will be displayed with all the shortcuts, as shown in Figure 1-10. Next, press the shortcut key as per your requirement; the corresponding command will be executed. Now, if you again invoke the **Application** menu, it will not display the shortcuts. You can repeat the process to view the shortcuts again.

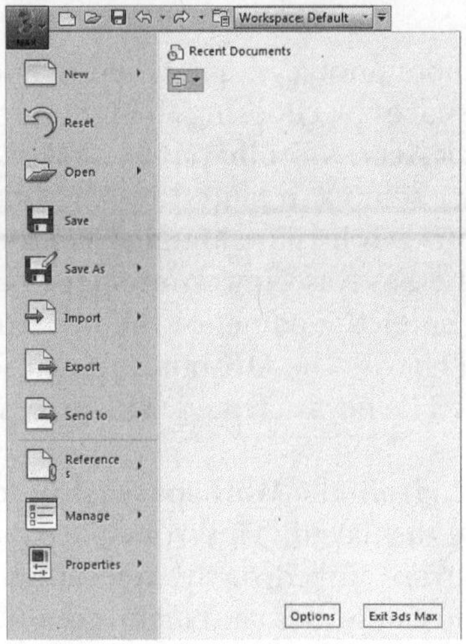

*Figure 1-8 Partial view of the **Application** menu*

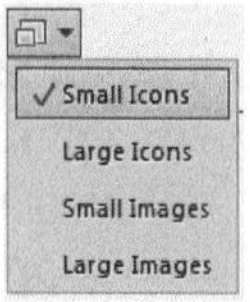

Figure 1-9 Flyout displayed on choosing the Icon or Image Display button

Quick Access Toolbar

The **Quick Access Toolbar** comprises of the most commonly used file management buttons, as shown in Figure 1-11. These buttons are also available in the **Application** menu. Apart from the commonly used buttons, the **Quick Access Toolbar** also contains the **Redo Scene Operation** and **Undo Scene Operation** buttons.

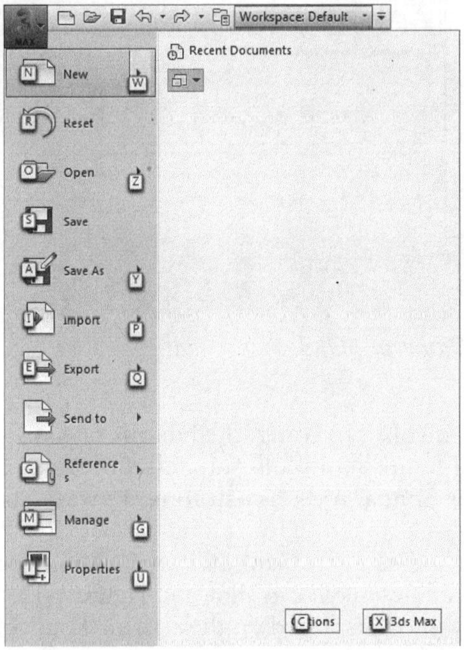

*Figure 1-10 The **Application** menu with the shortcuts*

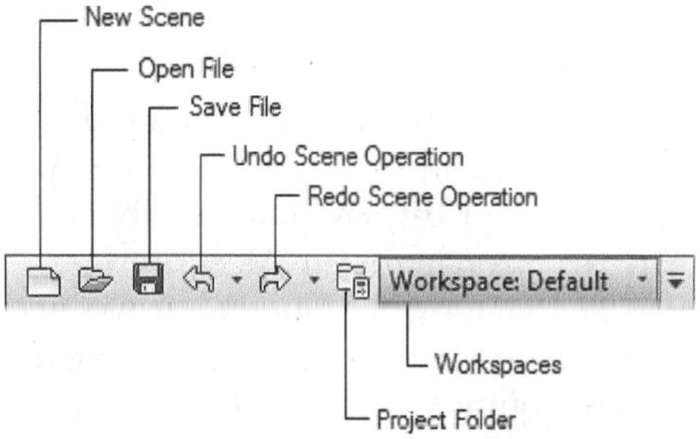

*Figure 1-11 The **Quick Access Toolbar***

Workspaces

The workspace includes toolbars, menus, the ribbon, hotkeys, quad menus, and viewport layout presets. You can switch between different workspaces by choosing the required option from the **Workspaces** drop-down list located on the **Quick Access Toolbar**, refer to Figure 1-11. To create a new workspace, you need to change the interface setup as required and then choose the **Manage Workspaces** option from the **Workspaces** drop-down list; the **Manage Workspaces** dialog box will be displayed. In this dialog box, choose the **Save as New Workspace** button; the **Create New Workspace** dialog box will be displayed. Enter the name for the workspace in the **Name** text box in the **New Workspace** area and then choose the **OK** button to close the dialog box. Next, close the **Manage Workspaces** dialog box. The newly created workspace will be active now.

Select the **Default with Enhanced Menus** option from the **Workspaces** drop-down list; the 3ds Max interface with the enhanced menus will be displayed. This workspace consists of features such as improved layout, detailed tooltips that are linked to the relevant help topics in the documentation, drag and drop support for menu categories, and menu commands search using keyboard. Figure 1-12 shows the enhanced **Lighting/Cameras** pull-down menu.

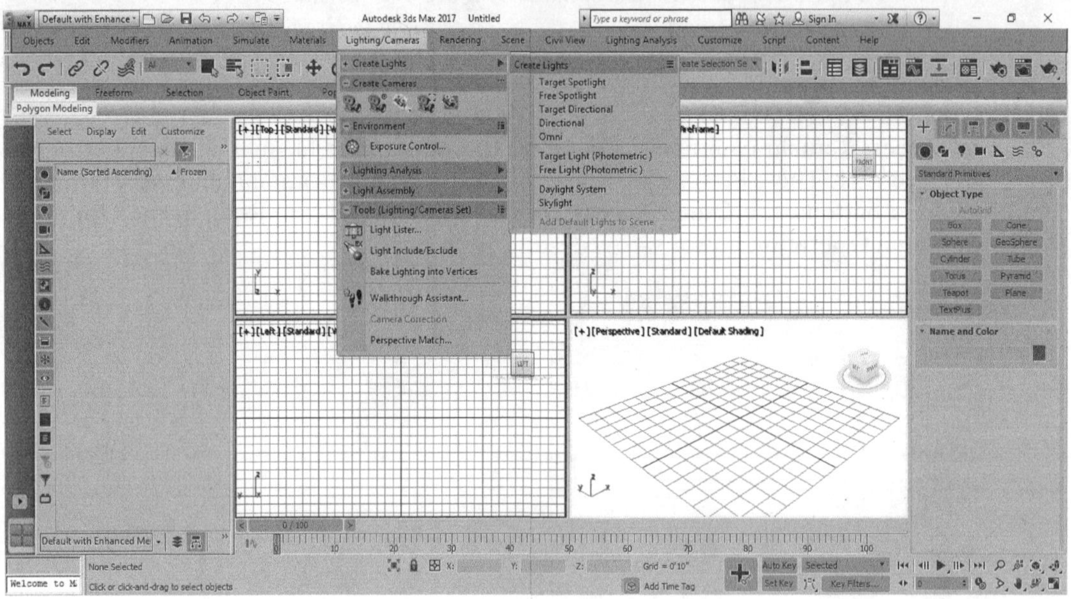

*Figure 1-12 The enhanced **Lighting/Cameras** pull-down menu displayed*

Toolbars

In Autodesk 3ds Max, various commands can be invoked by using the buttons or tools in the toolbars. By default, only the **Main Toolbar** will be displayed on Autodesk 3ds Max screen. However, you can display other toolbars such as **Snaps**, **Axis Constraints**, **Extras**, **MassFX Toolbar**, and so on in the 3ds Max interface. Also, you can move, resize, and undock them based on your requirements. To display these toolbars, right-click in the blank area on the **Main Toolbar**; a shortcut menu will be displayed with the names of all toolbars, as shown in Figure 1-13. Next, choose the required toolbar; the chosen toolbar will be displayed on the screen. Also, you can hide any of the displayed toolbars by choosing its label from the shortcut menu.

The **Main Toolbar** provides quick access to many tools and dialog boxes such as **Select and Link**, **Unlink Selection**, **Select Object**, **Material Editor**, and so on. This toolbar is docked just below the menu bar. You will learn more about the tools available in various toolbars in the later chapters.

Command Panel

By default, the **Command Panel** is docked on the right in the 3ds Max screen. There are six tabs in the **Command Panel**: **Create**, **Modify**, **Hierarchy**, **Motion**, **Display**, and **Utilities**, as shown in Figure 1-14. Most of the 3ds Max modeling and animation tools are placed in these tabs. The tools in the **Command Panel** are used to create, modify, and animate the objects. Each tab has several rollouts that can be expanded or collapsed. These tabs in the **Command Panel** are discussed next.

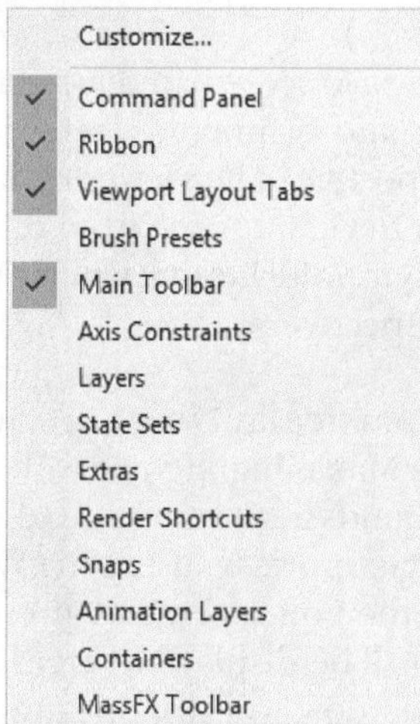

Figure 1-13 The shortcut menu displayed to view the hidden toolbars

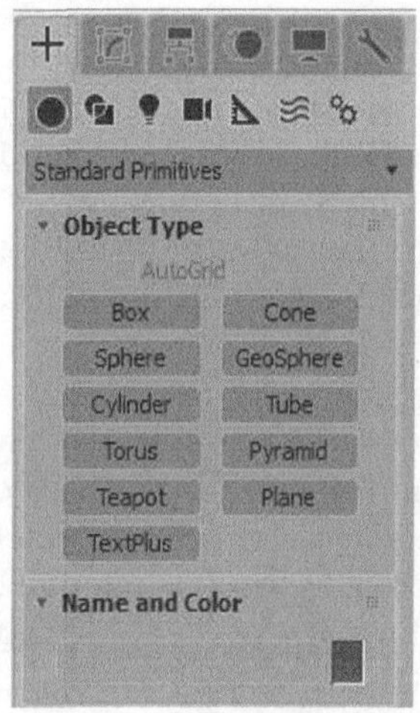

Figure 1-14 The ***Command Panel***

The **Create** tab is chosen by default. The tools in the **Create** tab are used to create objects, cameras, lights, and so on.

The **Modify** tab is used to modify the selected objects by modifying their parameters, applying various modifiers, and editing the mesh as well as polygonal and patch objects.

The **Hierarchy** tab is used to control the links in the hierarchy, joints, and inverse kinematics.

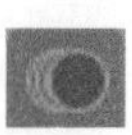

The **Motion** tab is used to control the animation controllers and trajectories.

The **Display** tab is used to hide and unhide the objects in the viewports.

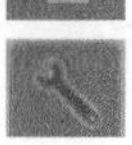

The **Utilities** tab is used to access various utility programs.

Note

*You can undock the **Command Panel** and **Main Toolbar** and place them anywhere on the screen. To do so, move the cursor at the top of the **Main Toolbar**; the cursor will change into an arrow with two overlapping rectangles. Now, press and hold the left mouse button and drag the **Main Toolbar** to the desired location. Double-click on the **Main Toolbar** to dock it back to its default position.*

Scene Explorer

The Scene Explorer is used to view, select, filter, and sort objects. It is also used to rename, delete, group, freeze, and hide objects. The Scene Explorer is by default docked on the left in the default workspace, refer to Figure 1-6. It is discussed in detail in Chapter 2.

Viewports

When you start Autodesk 3ds Max, the default interface screen appears. This interface consists of four equal sized viewports surrounded by tools and commands, refer to Figure 1-6. These viewports are labeled as Top, Front, Left, and Perspective. The viewports in Autodesk 3ds Max are used to create 3D scenes. Also, they enable you to view a scene from different angles. When you create an object in the viewport, the Top, Front, and Left viewports will display the top, front, and left orthographic views of the object, respectively.

You can loop between viewports to make a particular viewport active by using the WINDOWS+SHIFT keys. The active viewport in 3ds Max is highlighted with a yellow border. Only one viewport can remain active at a time. All commands and actions in 3ds Max are performed in the active viewport. You can switch between the viewports by using the WINDOWS + SHIFT keys. However, if only one viewport is maximized, then on repeatedly pressing the WINDOWS + SHIFT keys, a window with available viewports will be displayed, refer to Figure 1-15. When the WINDOWS + SHIFT keys are released, the window will disappear and the viewport you have chosen will become active.

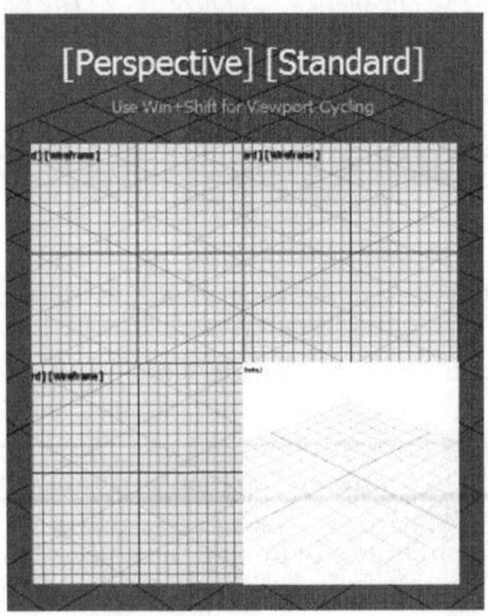

Figure 1-15 Selecting a viewport to make it active

You can modify the size of the viewports by dragging the intersection of the viewports on the splitter bars. To restore the original layout, right-click on the intersection of the dividing lines; a shortcut menu will be displayed, as shown in Figure 1-16. Choose the **Reset Layout** option from the shortcut menu; the viewports will be restored to their default size.

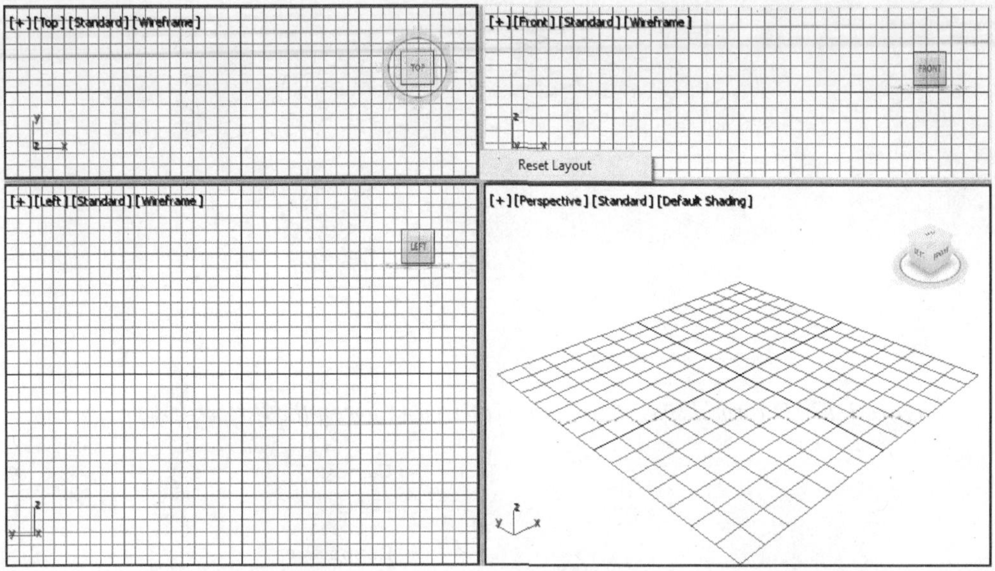

***Figure 1-16** Choosing the **Reset Layout** option from the shortcut menu*

On the bottom left corner of each viewport, there is a world-space tripod, as shown in Figure 1-17. The world-space tripod has three axes, X, Y, and Z, which are displayed in red, green, and blue colors, respectively. The tripod always refers to the world coordinate system, regardless of the local coordinate system. ViewCube is placed at the top right corner of the viewport, refer to Figure 1-17. The ViewCube provides visual feedback of the current orientation of the viewport.

Note

The ViewCube will not be visible in the camera and light viewport.

It is important to note that the Local coordinate system defines local position of an object in a scene whereas the World coordinate system uses fixed axes to define the position of all the objects in the world space. Each viewport has a grid placed in it, refer to Figure 1-17. It is like a graph paper in which all the lines intersect each other at right angles. You can modify the spacing in the grids. The grids in all viewports act as an aid to visualize the spacing and distance while creating objects. Also, they are used as a construction plane to create and align the objects. You can also use the grids as a reference system while using the snap tools to align the objects. You can also hide the grid in the viewport. To do so, press the G key; the grid will disappear from the viewport. To make the grid visible, press G again.

At the top left corner of each viewport, there are four viewport labels: General viewport label, Point of view (POV) viewport label, Settings viewport label, and Shading viewport label, refer to Figure 1-18. When you click on any of the viewport labels, the corresponding flyout will be displayed, as shown in Figure 1-19. The options in these shortcut menus are used to modify various aspects of the active viewport.

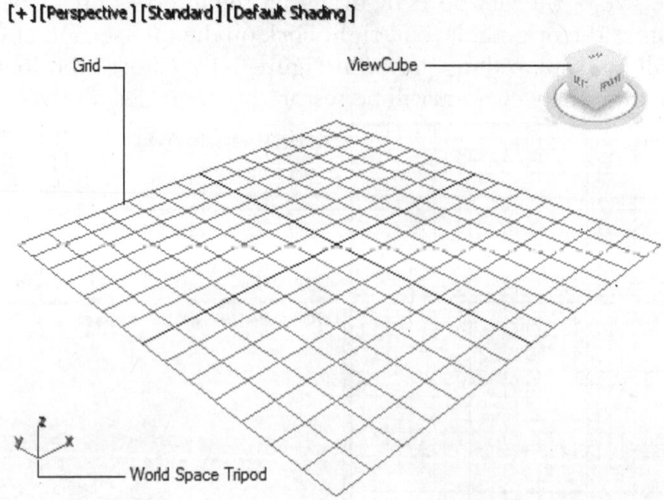

Figure 1-17 *The world space tripod, grid, and ViewCube in the Perspective viewport*

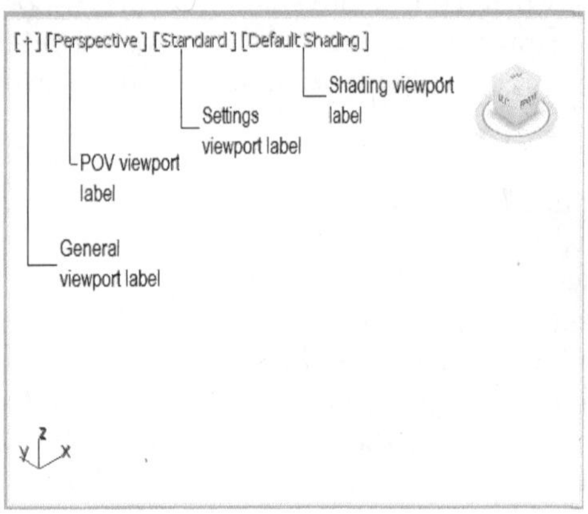

Figure 1-18 *The viewport labels in the Front viewport*

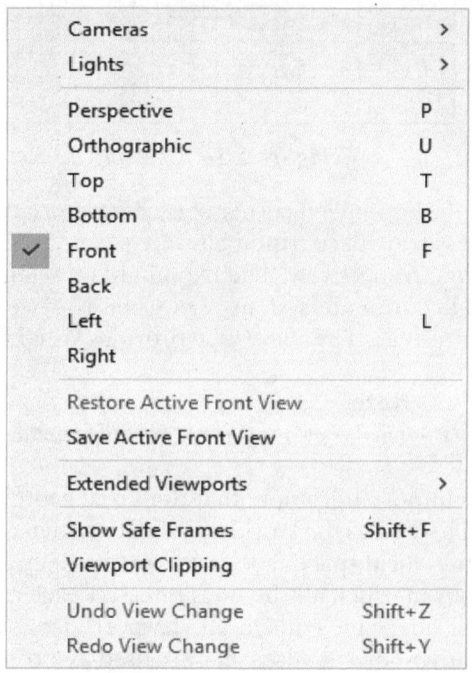

Figure 1-19 *The flyout displayed on clicking the POV viewport label*

You can configure the active viewport by using the options in the General viewport label menu. Choose the **Configure Viewports** option from this menu; the **Viewport Configuration** dialog box will be displayed. Various options in this dialog box can be used to configure the viewports. You already know that four equally sized viewports are displayed on the screen. However, you can change the viewport configuration based on your requirement. To change the basic configuration of the viewports, choose the **Layout** tab of the **Viewport Configuration** dialog box, refer to Figure 1-20. In the **Layout** tab, you can specify the division method of the viewports. There are 14 types of configurations displayed at the top in the tab. Select the required configuration and then choose the **OK** button; the viewports will be displayed according to the configuration that you have selected in the **Viewport Configuration** dialog box.

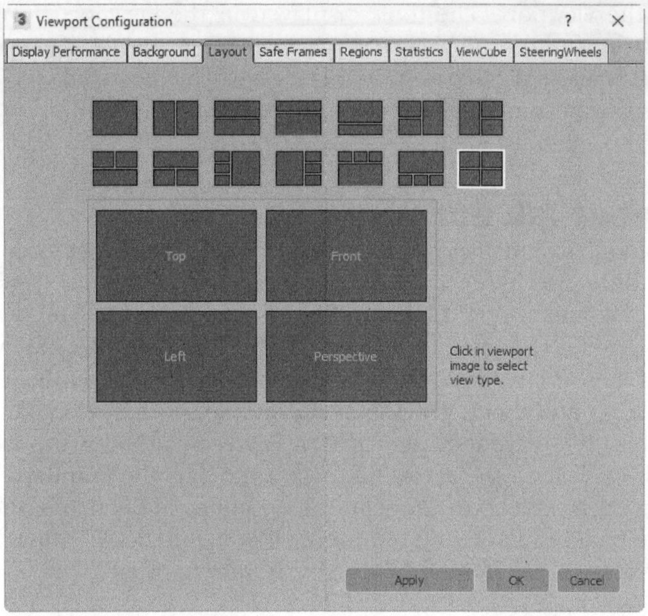

*Figure 1-20 The **Layout** tab of the **Viewport Configuration** dialog box*

Note
The viewport configuration specifies how the viewports will be arranged on the screen.

You can change the default viewport to any other viewport type available such as Bottom, Right, and so on, by using the options in the POV viewport label menu. To do so, click on the POV viewport label; a flyout will be displayed. Choose the viewport that you want to display. Using the Settings viewport label, you can change the display quality in viewports as well as lighting, shadows, and material settings. Different types of shading types that can be defined using the Settings Viewport label are: **Default shading**, **Facets**, **Flat color**, **Bounding Box**, **Clay**, and so on. However, some other shading types are available in the cascading menu of the **Stylized** option, refer to Figure 1-21. These shading types are **Graphite**, **Color Pencil**, **Ink**, and so on. You can choose any one of the options to change the shading.

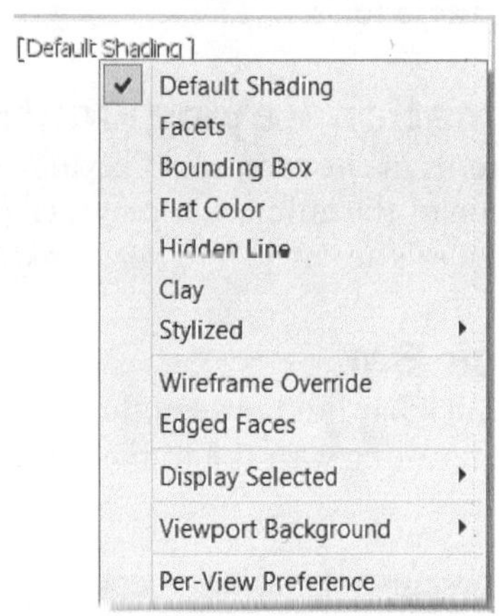

Figure 1-21 The flyout displayed on clicking the Shading viewport label

Viewport Navigation Controls

There are various tools available at the bottom right corner of the Autodesk 3ds Max screen, as shown in Figure1-22. These tools are known as viewport navigation controls and they are used to control the display and navigation of the viewport. The tools displayed in the viewport navigation controls depend on the viewport selected. For example, if the Camera viewport is selected, its corresponding tools will be displayed in the viewport navigation control. These tools are discussed in detail in the later chapters.

***Figure 1-22** The viewport navigation controls*

Viewport Layout Tab Bar

The Viewport Layout tab bar enables you to store multiple viewport setups in a single scene. You can switch between different viewport setups with a click. To display the viewport layout tab bar, right-click in the blank area on the **Main Toolbar**; a shortcut menu will be displayed with the names of all toolbars, refer to Figure 1-13. Next, choose the **Viewport Layout Tabs** option; the Viewport Layout tab bar will be displayed on the screen. To dock it on the left of the viewports, right-click on its title bar and choose **Dock > Left** from the shortcut menu displayed. By default, there is a single tab at the bottom of the bar that represents the startup layout. To add more layout tabs to the bar, click on the arrow button on the bar; the **Standard Viewport Layouts** flyout will be displayed. Next, choose the required option from the flyout; the chosen layout tab will be added to the bar. To remove a tab from the bar, right-click on the tab; a shortcut menu will be displayed. Next, choose **Delete Tab** from the shortcut menu.

Animation Playback Controls

The tools in the animation playback controls are displayed on the left side of the viewport navigation controls, refer to Figure 1-23. These tools are used to control the animation in the active viewport. Also, you can set the total number of frames, animation length, and other settings of the animation using these tools.

***Figure 1-23** The animation playback controls*

Animation Keying Controls

The tools in the animation keying controls are displayed on the left side of the animation playback controls, refer to Figure 1-24. These tools are used to enter or exit different animation modes.

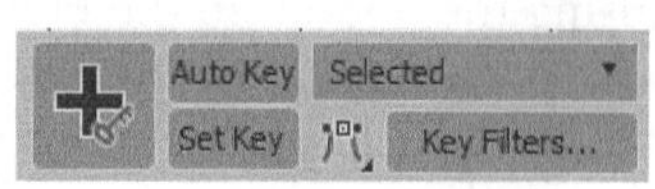

***Figure 1-24** The animation keying controls*

Track Bar

The track bar lies between the time slider and the status bar, refer to Figure 1-25. It displays a timeline along with the frame numbers.

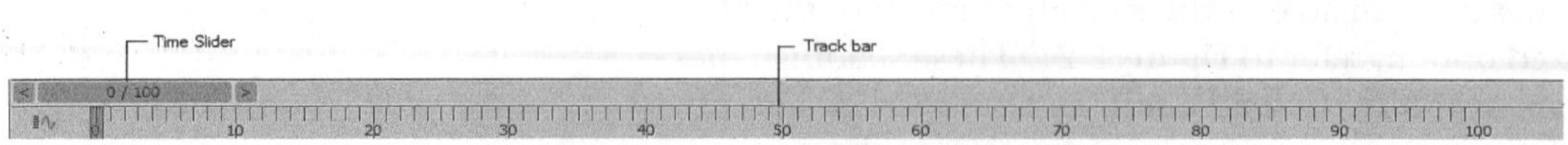

***Figure 1-25** The track bar and the time slider*

Time Slider

The time slider displays the current frame and the total number of frames in the current time segment, refer to Figure 1-25. You can view the animation at each frame by dragging the time slider. The time segment is the total range of frames that you can access using the time slider. By default, it ranges from 0 to 100. You can set the range using the **Time Configuration** dialog box, about which you will learn in the later chapters.

Status Bar

There are various tools in the status bar that provide information about the scene and the active command, as shown in Figure 1-26. The prompt line, which is located at the bottom of the screen, displays information about the active command or tool. On top of the status bar, a text box known as the status line is available. This status line displays the number of currently selected objects (current selection set). The **Selection Lock Toggle** tool on the right side of the status bar is used to lock the selection set. The Coordinate display/transform type-in area displays the X, Y, and Z coordinates of the cursor or the currently selected object. The Coordinate display/transform type-in area can also be used to enter transform values while moving, scaling, or rotating the selected object(s).

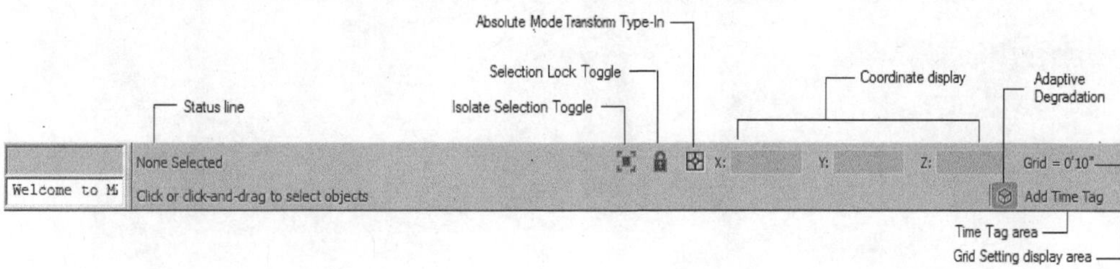

Figure 1-26 The status bar

The Grid setting display area is placed on the right of the Coordinate display area. It displays the size of the grid. The time tag area located below the grid setting display area is used to assign the text labels at any point of time in your animation. Click on the time tag area; a flyout with the **Add Tag** and **Edit Tag** options will be displayed. Use these options to add or edit the text labels at any point of time in your animation.

The **Adaptive Degradation** button placed on the right of the prompt line is used to improve the viewport performance in a complex scene by decreasing the visual fidelity of some of the objects temporarily. This results in smoother viewport motions and object transformations in such scenes. It also improves viewport quality incrementally, depending on the availability of processing time. To activate this feature, right-click on the **Adaptive Degradation** button; the **Viewport Configuration** dialog box will be displayed, as shown in Figure 1-27. The **Display Performance** tab is chosen by default in this dialog box. Now, change the settings in the **Display Performance** tab based on your requirement and choose the **OK** button.

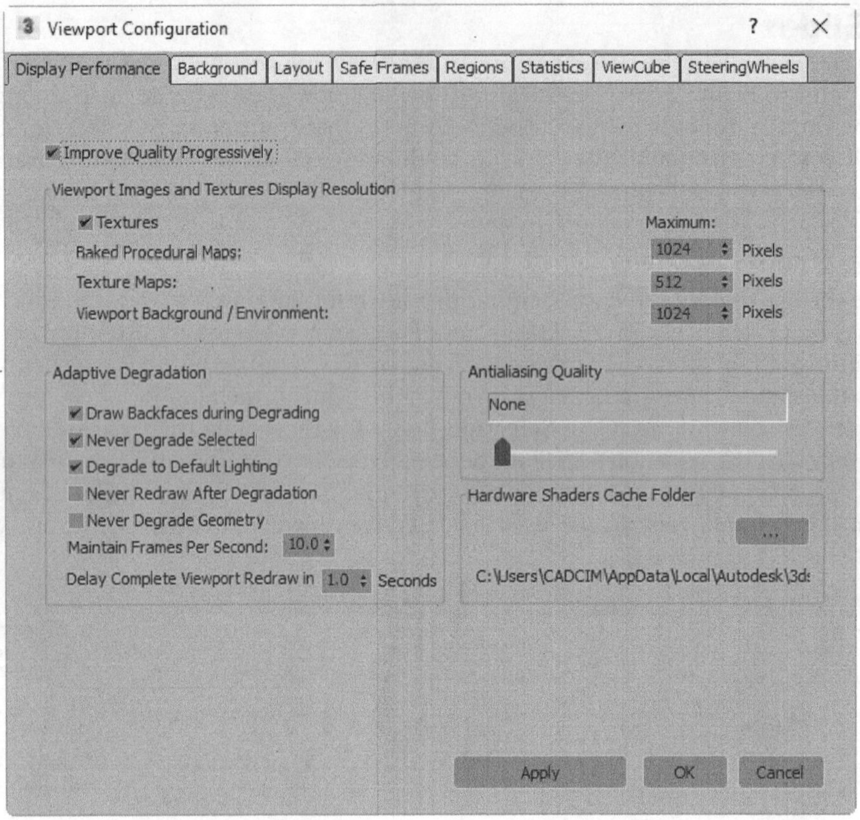

Figure 1-27 The ***Viewport Configuration*** *dialog box*

MAX CREATION GRAPH

Max Creation Graph uses node based Max Creation Graph Editor. Using this editor, you can create customized tools which are used to create various geometrical shapes, create modifiers, specify render settings, create utilities, and so on. To open Max Creation Graph Editor, choose **Scripting > Max Creation Graph Editor** from the menu bar; the **Max Creation Graph-Untitled** window will be displayed, as shown in Figure 1-28. This window has menu bar at the top and four panels: **Available Nodes/Operators**, **Operator Desription**, **Main Graph Window**, and **Message Log**. All these panels in the **Max Creation Graph-Untitled** window can be resized, undocked, and closed.

The **Available Nodes/Operators** panel consists of a number of nodes and operators under various categories. These categories are **3ds Max Camera**, **3ds Max Shapes**, **Array**, **Geometry - Bounding Box**, **Geometry - Deformers**, and so on. Click on the arrow at the left of the category name to expand it. The **Operator Description** panel provides detailed information of selected operator/node in the **Available Nodes/Operators** panel.

The **Main Graph Window** panel is used to connect various nodes and operators. You need to drag the nodes and operators from the **Available Nodes/Operators** panel to the **Main Graph window** panel. These nodes and operators has input and/or output connector(s) to create a network of nodes and operators. This network is then evaluated using the commands in the menu bar to create customized tools. The **Message Log** panel displays messages for the network created in the **Main Graph Window** panel once it is evaluated.

On creating the network of nodes and operators, you need to evaluate it and save it at the default location with desired name to use it as a customized tool in 3ds Max interface.

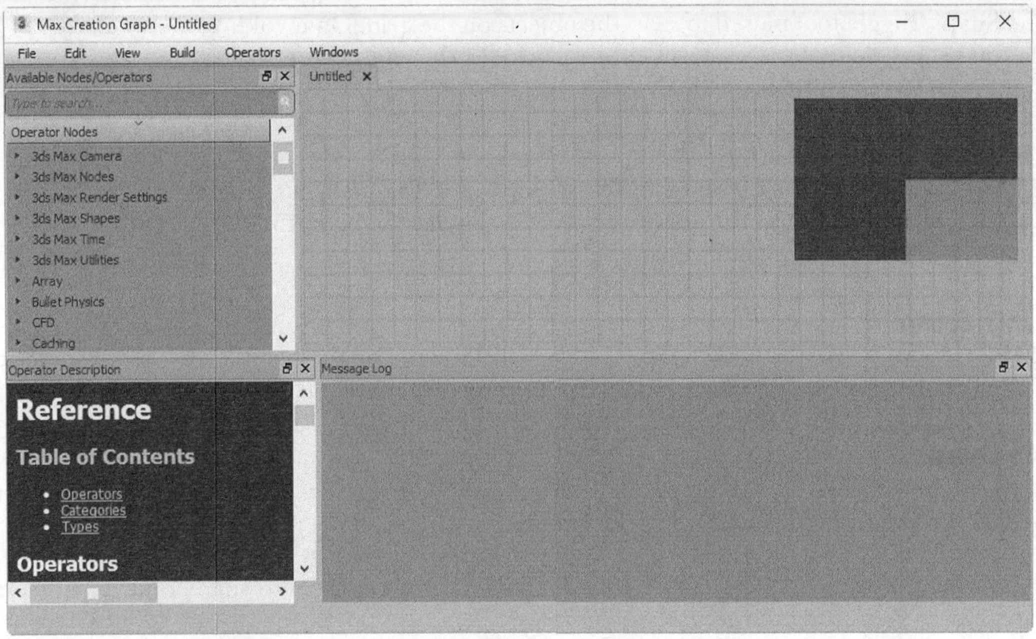

*Figure 1-28 The **Max Creation Graph - Untitled** window*

SNAPS SETTINGS

Snaps restrict the movement of the cursor to a specific part of an object or grid. There are four buttons available for snap settings in the **Main Toolbar**: **Snaps Toggle**, **Angle Snap Toggle**, **Percent Snap Toggle**, and **Spinner Snap Toggle**. If you right-click on the **Snaps Toggle**, **Angle Snap Toggle**, or **Percent Snap Toggle** button, the **Grid and Snap Settings** dialog box will be displayed, as shown in Figure 1-29. In this dialog box, you can select different parts of the objects or grid where the cursor will snap to. You can turn the snap command on and off by pressing the S key or by choosing the **Snaps Toggle** tool. If you choose and hold the **Snaps Toggle** tool, a flyout will be displayed. This flyout contains the **2D Snap**, **2.5 Snap**, and **3D Snap** tools, which can be chosen to snap the cursor.

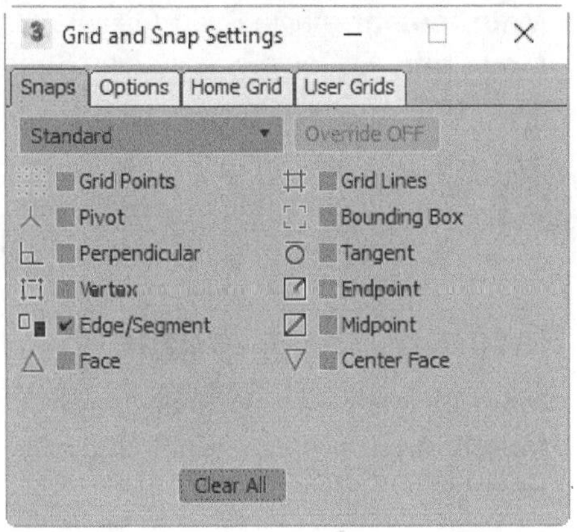

*Figure 1-29 The **Grid and Snap Settings** dialog box*

Snaps Toggle

Main Toolbar: Snaps Toggle
Menu bar: Tools > Grids and Snaps > Snaps Toggle
Keyboard: S

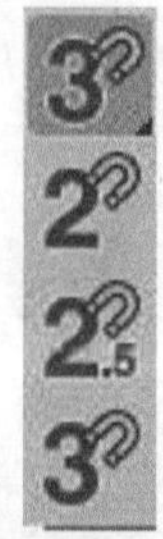

Figure 1-30 The ***Snaps Toggle*** *flyout*

The **Snaps Toggle** tool is used to snap the objects on the grid. On invoking the **Snaps Toggle** tool, a flyout will be displayed, as shown in Figure 1-30. This flyout has three tools which are discussed next.

2D Snap

If you choose the **2D Snap** tool from the **Snaps Toggle** flyout, then the cursor snaps to the active grid in two dimensions, X and Y. The Z-axis is not taken into consideration.

2.5D Snap

If you choose the **2.5D Snap** tool from the **Snaps Toggle** flyout, then the cursor snaps to the vertices and edges of the objects projected on the active grid.

3D Snap

If you choose the **3D Snap** tool from the **Snaps Toggle** flyout, then the cursor snaps to any object in 3D space using the **3D Snap** tool.

On moving the gizmo or snap handle, this axis center will act as the start snap point. This feature also helps in increasing the accuracy of snaps.

Angle Snap Toggle

Main Toolbar: Angle Snap Toggle
Menu bar: Tools > Grids and Snaps > Angle Snap Toggle
Keyboard: A

The **Angle Snap Toggle** tool enables you to rotate an object in angular increments. The increment value is specified in the **Angle** spinner of the **Grid and Snap Settings** dialog box. By default, the value in the **Angle** spinner is set to 5.0.

Percent Snap Toggle

Main Toolbar: Percent Snap Toggle
Menu bar: Tools > Grids and Snaps > Percent Snap Toggle
Keyboard: CTRL+SHIFT+P

The **Percent Snap Toggle** tool enables you to scale an object in percent increments. The increment value can be specified in the **Percent** spinner of the **Grid and Snap Settings** dialog box. By default, the value set in the **Percent** spinner is set to 10.0.

Spinner Snap Toggle

Main Toolbar: Spinner Snap Toggle

The **Spinner Snap Toggle** tool is used to set the single increment or decrement value for all the spinners in Autodesk 3ds Max. By default, the increment or decrement value is set to 1. To set the increment value, right-click on the **Spinner Snap Toggle** tool; the **Preference Settings** dialog box will be displayed. In this dialog box, choose the **General** tab, if it is not already chosen. Now, in the **Spinners** area, set a value in the **Snap** spinner, refer to Figure 1-31.

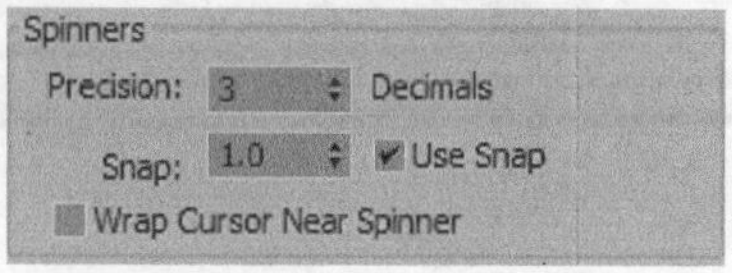

*Figure 1-31 The **Spinners** area in the **Preference Settings** dialog box*

Also, select the **Use Snap** check box and then choose the **OK** button; the **Spinner Snap Toggle** tool in the **Main Toolbar** is chosen. Now, when you use any spinner in 3ds Max, the value will increase or decrease according to the value that you have specified in the **Preference Settings** dialog box.

UNITS SETUP

The units setup in 3ds Max is used to specify the units that help in measuring the geometry in a scene. You can change the settings for units by using the **Customize** pull-down menu. To do so, choose **Customize > Units Setup** from the menu bar; the **Units Setup** dialog box will be displayed, as shown in Figure 1-32. By default, the **Generic Units** radio button is selected in the **Display Unit Scale** area in this dialog box. You can select any other radio button as per the requirement from the **Display Unit Scale** area of this dialog box and then choose the **OK** button; the limits in all the spinners in 3ds Max will be modified accordingly.

Setting Grid Spacing

To set the spacing between the visible grids in the viewports, choose **Tools > Grids and Snaps > Grid and Snap Settings** from the menu bar; the **Grid and Snap Settings** dialog box will be displayed. Choose the **Home Grid** tab in this dialog box, as shown in Figure 1-33. In the **Grid Dimensions** area, set the value in the **Grid Spacing** spinner to specify the size of the smallest square of the grid. The value in the spinners will be measured in the units that you specify in the **Units Setup** dialog box. Set the value in the **Major Lines every Nth Grid Line** spinner to specify the number of squares between the major lines in the grid. Set the value in the **Perspective View Grid Extent** spinner to specify the size of the home grid in the Perspective viewport. Note that the default grid displayed in the viewports on starting 3ds Max is known as the home grid.

In the **Dynamic Update** area, the **Active Viewport** radio button is selected by default. It is used to update the active viewport according to the new values of the **Grid and Snap Settings** dialog box. Select the **All Viewports** radio button to update all viewports simultaneously according to the new values that you set in the spinners of the **Grid and Snap Settings** dialog box.

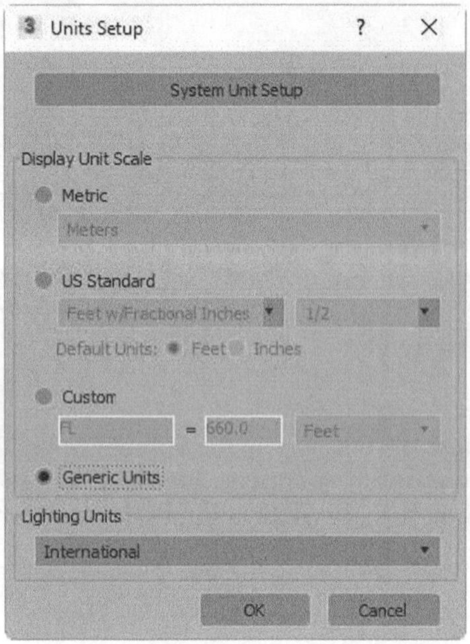

*Figure 1-32 The **Units Setup** dialog box*

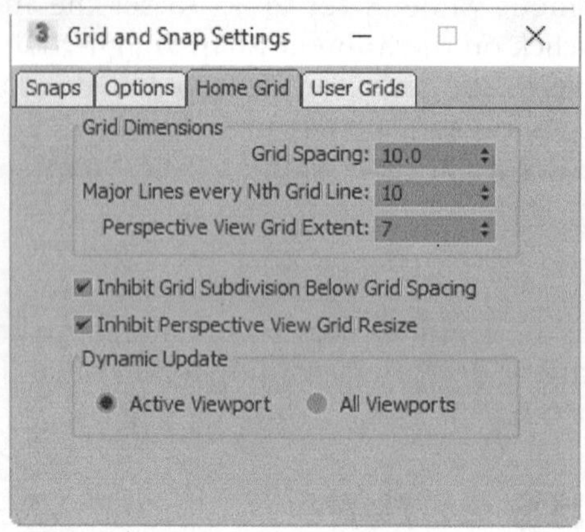

*Figure 1-33 The **Home Grid** tab chosen in the **Grid and Snap Settings** dialog box*

UNDO AND REDO TOOLS

Quick Access Toolbar:	Undo Scene Operation or Redo Scene Operation
Menu bar:	Edit > Undo or Redo
Keyboard:	CTRL+Z (Undo) or CTRL+Y (Redo)

The **Undo** tool is used to revert the last actions performed while creating or modifying a model in Autodesk 3ds Max. To undo an action, choose the **Undo Scene Operation** tool from the **Quick Access Toolbar** or press the CTRL+Z keys. You need to choose the **Undo Scene Operation** tool repeatedly till all the previously performed actions are reversed. To reverse a number of actions at a time, click on the arrow with the **Undo Scene Operation** tool in the **Quick Access Toolbar**; a list of actions will be displayed, refer to Figure 1-34. Move the cursor over the number of actions that you want to reverse; the actions will be selected and then click. By default, you can reverse your actions up to 20 times. If you want to change this number, choose **Customize > Preferences** from the menu bar; the **Preference Settings** dialog box will be displayed. By default, the **General** tab is chosen in this dialog box. In the **Scene Undo** area, set the new value in the **Levels** spinner, as shown in Figure 1-35.

The **Redo** tool is used to revert the last actions performed by the **Undo** tool. To redo an action, choose the **Redo Scene Operation** tool from the **Quick Access Toolbar** or press the CTRL+Y keys. You need to choose the **Redo Scene Operation** tool repeatedly till you want to reverse the actions performed earlier. To reverse a number of actions at a time, click on the arrow of the **Redo Scene Operation** tool in the **Quick Access Toolbar**; a list of last actions will be displayed. Move the cursor over the number of actions that you want to reverse; the actions will be selected. Next, click on the list; the selected action will be displayed.

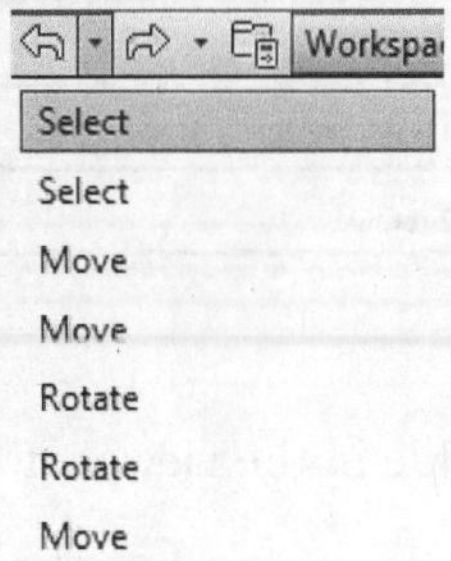

Figure 1-34 The list of actions displayed

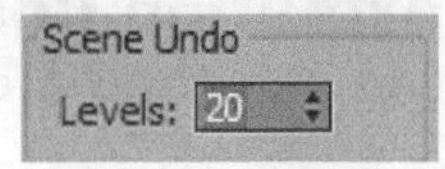

Figure 1-35 The ***Scene Undo*** *area in the* ***Preference Settings*** *dialog box*

HOLD AND FETCH TOOLS

Menu bar: Edit > Hold or Fetch
Keyboard: CTRL+H (Hold) or ALT+CTRL+F (Fetch)

Sometimes you may want to perform experiments on a scene. In such as a case you need to hold the scene. The **Hold** tool is used to hold a scene and to save the work done in a temporary file with the name *maxhold.mx*.

The file is saved at the location *\Documents\3dsmax\autoback*. To perform an experiment in a scene, choose the **Hold** tool from the **Edit** menu or press the CTRL+H keys. Next, if you need to go back to the previous command, choose the **Fetch** tool from the **Edit** menu or press ALT+CTRL+F; the **About to Fetch. OK?** dialog box will be displayed, as shown in Figure 1-36. Choose the **Yes** button; the scene with the previous command will be displayed. In this way, you can go back to a series of commands using the **Hold** tool.

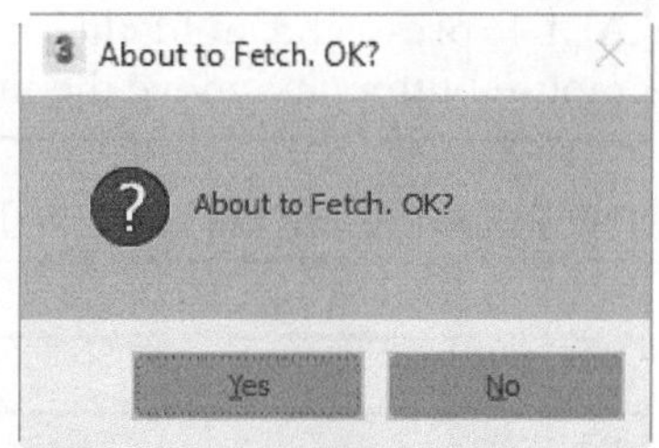

Figure 1-36 The ***About to Fetch. OK?*** *dialog box*

Note

When you use the ***Fetch*** *tool in a scene, the history of the actions performed so far will be deleted. As a result, you cannot undo or redo the actions performed before invoking this tool.*

HOT KEYS

In 3ds Max, you can use the hot keys to choose some of the commonly used tools and commands. These keys are known as the hot keys. You can work faster and more efficiently using the hot keys. The major hot keys and their functions are listed next.

Main Toolbar

The hot keys that can be used to invoke the tools available in the **Main Toolbar** are given next:

H	Invokes the **Select From Scene** dialog box
S	Invokes the **Snaps Toggle** tool
A	Invokes the **Angle Snap Toggle** tool

CTRL+SHIFT+P	Invokes the **Percent Snap Toggle** tool
M	Invokes the **Material Editor** dialog box
SHIFT+Q	Invokes the **Render Production** tool

Viewport Navigation Controls

The hot keys that can be used to invoke the tools available in the viewport navigation controls are given next:

ALT+CTRL+Z	Performs the action of the **Zoom Extents** tool
ALT+W	Invokes the **Maximize Viewport Toggle** tool
ALT+Z	Invokes the **Zoom** tool
CTRL+W	Invokes the **Zoom Region** tool
CTRL+P	Invokes the **Pan View** tool
Scroll the middle mouse button	Zooms in or out the active viewport
CTRL+R	Invokes the **Orbit** tool
SHIFT+Z	Used to undo the **Zoom** or **Pan** command actions
ALT+ press and hold the middle mouse button and move the mouse	Performs the actions of the **Orbit** tool

The following hot keys are used to change the POV viewport labels:

V	Invokes the viewport quad menu
T	Invokes the Top viewport
F	Invokes the Front viewport
L	Invokes the Left viewport
P	Invokes the Perspective viewport
B	Invokes the Bottom viewport
U	Invokes the Orthographic viewport

Animation Playback Controls

The hot keys that can be used to invoke the tools available in the animation playback controls are given next:

N	Invokes the **Auto Key** tool
Home	Go to start frame
End	Go to end frame
/ (backslash)	Plays animation
ESC	Stop the animation
, (comma)	Go to previous frame
. (period)	Go to next frame

Customizing the Hot Keys

In 3ds Max, you can create your own keyboard shortcuts. To do so, choose **Customize > Customize User Interface** from the menu bar; the **Customize User Interface** dialog box will be displayed, as shown in Figure 1-37. In this dialog box, the **Keyboard** tab is chosen by default. Next, select a command from the **Group** and **Category** drop-down lists; a list of corresponding actions will be displayed just below the **Category** drop-down list. Now, select one of the actions from the list and then enter the key that you want to assign to the selected action in the **Hotkey** text box. Next, choose the **Assign** button; the key is assigned to the selected action.

CUSTOMIZING THE COLORS OF THE USER INTERFACE

3ds Max allows you to modify the colors of the interface. You can modify the colors for almost every element in the interface. To modify the colors, choose **Customize > Customize User Interface** from the menu bar; the **Customize User Interface** dialog box will be displayed. Choose the **Colors** tab from this dialog box, refer to Figure 1-37. Next, select the category of the interface element from the **Elements** drop-down list; the list of the corresponding elements will be displayed just below the **Elements** drop-down list. Now, select one of the elements from the list and click on the **Color** swatch on the right of the **Elements** drop-down list; the **Color Selector** dialog box will be displayed. Select a new color and choose the **OK** button to close the **Color Selector** dialog box.

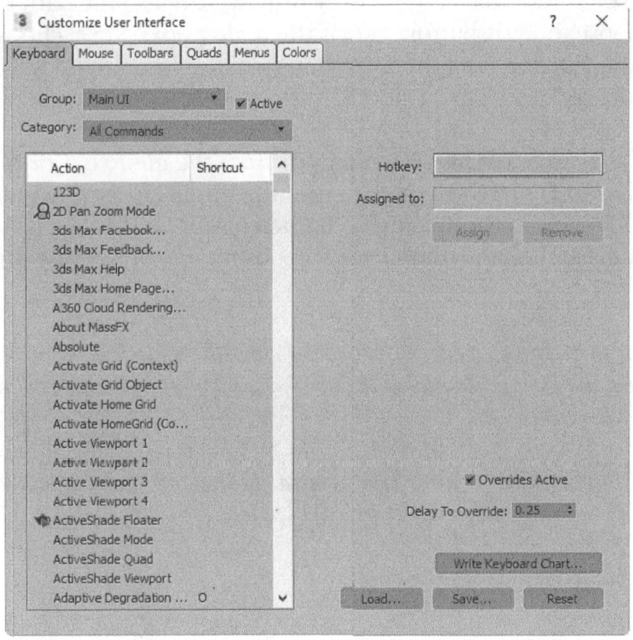

Figure 1-37 The ***Customize User Interface*** *dialog box*

To reset the new color to the default one, click on the **Reset** button located next to the **Color** color swatch. You can also reset all the changes you made to colors. To do so, choose the **Reset** button at the bottom of the **Customize User Interface** dialog box; the **Revert Color File** message box will be displayed, as shown in Figure 1-38. Choose the **Yes** button; the default colors will be displayed in the color swatches.

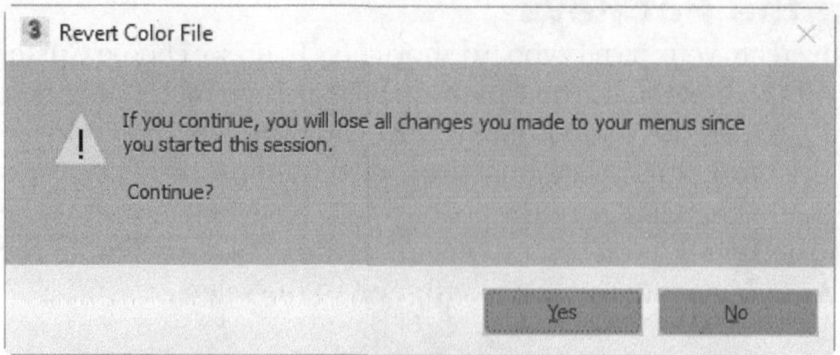

Figure 1-38 The ***Revert Color File*** *message box*

HELP PREFERENCES

When you choose **Help > Autodesk 3ds Max Help** from the menu bar, the 3ds Max help will be displayed. If you want to open help from a local drive, you need to download it from *http://www.autodesk.com/3dsmax-helpdownload-enu* and then install it on your system. Next, choose **Customize > Preferences** from the menu bar; the **Preference Settings** dialog box will be displayed. Choose the **Help** tab in this dialog box, refer to Figure 1-39. Select the **Local Computer/ Network** radio button from the **Help Location** area and then choose the **Browse** button; the **Browse For Folder** dialog box will be displayed. Select the path where you have saved the file and then choose the **OK** button to exit the dialog box. Next, choose the **OK** button in the **Preference Settings** dialog box; the dialog box will be closed. Now, you can access the help from your local drive.

If you choose **Help > Search 3ds Max Commands** from the menu bar or press X, a search field will be displayed, refer to Figure 1-40. Next, enter the initial characters of a command; a list of command names that contain the specified characters will be displayed, refer to Figure 1-41. Now, you can execute the desired command by choosing it from the list displayed.

Note

For the printing purpose, this textbook will follow the white background. However, for better understanding and clear visualization, at various places this textbook will follow other color schemes as well.

In addition, the ***Shaded*** *shading type is used throughout the textbook in all screen captures. Moreover, at some places in figures, grids will be hidden for better understanding and visualization.*

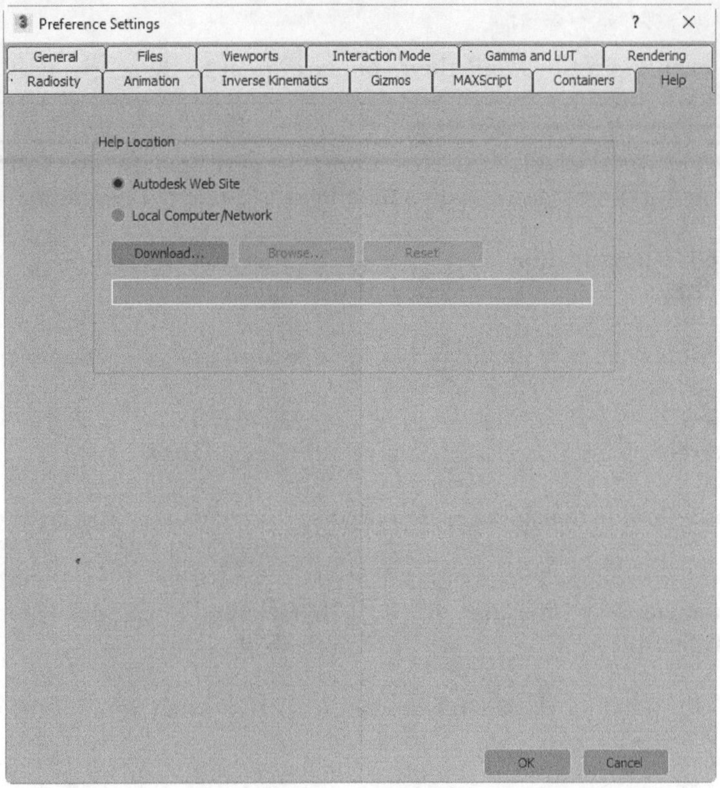

***Figure 1-39** The **Help** tab chosen in the **Preference Settings** dialog box*

***Figure 1-40** The search field*

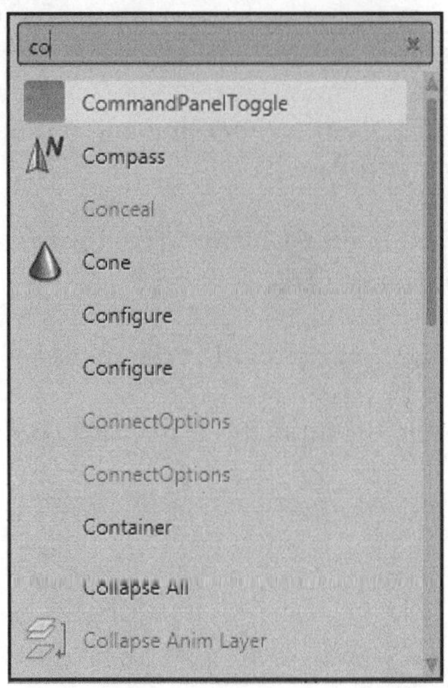

***Figure 1-41** List of commands displayed on entering first few characters*

Self-Evaluation Test

Answer the following questions and then compare them to those given at the end of this chapter:

1. Which of the following buttons is used to improve the performance of a viewport in a complex scene by temporarily decreasing the visual fidelity of some of the objects?

   (a) **Adaptive Degradation** (b) **Time Configuration**
   (c) **Auto Key** (d) All of these

2. Which of the following tabs should be chosen to control the animation controllers?

   (a) **Motion** (b) **Display**
   (c) **Hierarchy** (d) None of these

3. Which of the following dialog boxes is used to set the spacing in the grids displayed in the viewports?

   (a) **Customize User Interface** (b) **Grid and Snap Settings**
   (c) **Units Setup** (d) All of these

4. The __________ provides visual feedback of the current orientation of the viewport.

5. The __________ is located at the bottom of the screen and displays the information about the active command or tool.

6. The __________ provides access to video tutorials that are helpful in learning the basics of 3ds Max.

7. Most of the 3ds Max modeling and animation tools can be chosen from the tabs located in the **Command Panel**. (T/F)

8. The default interface of 3ds Max consists of three equal sized viewports surrounded by tools and commands. (T/F)

9. In 3ds Max, you can modify the colors of almost every element in the interface. (T/F)

10. The tools in the animation playback controls are used to control the display of a viewport. (T/F)

Review Questions

Answer the following questions:

1. Which of the following combinations of keys is used to choose the **Pan** tool?

   (a) CTRL+P (b) SHIFT+Z
   (c) CTRL+A (d) CTRL+W

2. The __________ is located between the time slider and the status bar.

3. The __________ tool located on the right of the status bar is used to lock a selection set.

4. The Viewport Layout tab bar enables you to store multiple viewport setups in a single scene. (T/F)

5. Snapping restricts the movement of the cursor to a specific part of an object or grid. (T/F)

6. The options in the General viewport label menu are used for defining the type of shadings displayed in the viewport. (T/F)

Answers to Self-Evaluation Test

1. a, **2.** a, **3.** b, **4.** ViewCube, **5.** prompt line, **6.** Welcome Screen, **7.** T, **8.** F, **9.** T, **10.** F

2

Standard Primitives

Learning Objectives

After completing this chapter, you will be able to:

- *Understand viewport navigation controls*
- *Understand selection techniques*
- *Understand Scene Explorer/Layer Explorer*
- *Create standard primitives*
- *Render a still image*
- *Change the background color of a scene*

INTRODUCTION

In this chapter, you will learn to create the default 3D objects called standard primitives. These geometric primitives are parametric objects. You will also learn about viewport navigation controls and selection techniques.

VIEWPORT NAVIGATION CONTROLS

Enhanced

The tools at the lower right corner of the Autodesk 3ds Max screen are known as viewport navigation controls. These tools are used to control the display and navigation of the viewport.

To adjust the view of an object in a viewport, you need to be familiar with the tools in the viewport navigation controls area. Note that some of the tools mentioned below are available in a flyout which will be displayed when you click on the arrow on the lower right corner of the tool icon. These tools are discussed next.

The **Zoom** tool is used to increase or decrease the magnification in the active viewport. You can zoom in by pressing the left mouse button and dragging the cursor up. Similarly, you can zoom out by pressing the left mouse button and then dragging the cursor down.

The **Zoom All** tool is the same as the **Zoom** tool with the only difference that this tool zooms the display in all the four viewports simultaneously.

The **Zoom Extents** tool is used to view all objects in the active viewport.

The **Zoom Extents Selected** tool is used to view all selected objects in the active viewport.

The **Zoom Extents All** tool is the same as the **Zoom Extents** tool with the only difference that this tool is used to view all objects in all viewports.

The **Zoom Extents All Selected** tool is the same as the **Zoom Extents Selected** tool with the only difference that this tool is used to view all selected objects in all viewports.

The **Zoom Region** tool is used to define the area to be magnified and viewed in the current viewport. The area to be magnified is specified by a rectangle created by dragging the cursor. The **Zoom Region** tool is not available in the Camera viewport.

The **Field-of-View** tool is available only in the Perspective and Camera viewports. It is used to change the field of view of the scene in these viewports. More the field of view of a camera more will be the visibility of the scene, and vice-versa.

The **Pan View** tool is used to pan the scene in the viewport. This tool enables you to display the contents of the viewport that are outside the display area without changing the magnification of the current viewport.

The **2D Pan Zoom Mode** tool is available in Perspective and Camera viewports only. On invoking this tool you can pan and zoom the scene outside the rendering frame. In other words, the position of the camera does not change when you pan or zoom in the scene. If the **2D Pan Zoom Mode** tool is chosen, an additional viewport label appears on the right of the other viewport labels.

The **Walk Through** tool is available in Perspective and Camera viewports only. It allows you to navigate through these viewports by pressing a set of shortcut keys. On invoking this tool, the cursor changes into a circle with a dot at its center. Press the arrow keys to navigate through the viewport. On pressing the arrow keys, the cursor shows a directional arrow indicating the navigation direction.

The **Orbit** tool is used to rotate the viewport around its view center. This enables you to see three-dimensional (3D) view of the objects in the Perspective viewport. You can also rotate the Top, Front, and Left viewports. But in such cases, the respective viewport becomes the Orthographic viewport.

The **Orbit Selected** tool is the same as the **Orbit** tool with the only difference that it is used to rotate the viewport around the center of the current selection.

The **Orbit SubObject** tool is the same as the **Orbit** tool with the only difference that it is used to rotate the viewport around the center of the current sub-object selection.

The **Orbit Point of Interest** tool uses the location of the cursor as the center of rotation. The point of interest remains at the same position in the viewport while the view rotates around its center.

The **Maximize Viewport Toggle** tool is used to maximize the active viewport so that you can view only the active viewport instead of all the four viewports.

The **Dolly Camera** tool is available in Camera viewport only. It is used to move the camera toward and away from the target. If the camera passes through the target, the camera flips 180 degrees and moves away from its target.

The **Dolly Target** tool is only available if viewport's camera is a target camera. This tool is used to move the target of the camera toward and away from it. If the target passes through the camera to the other side, the camera view will be reversed. Otherwise, there will be no visual change in the camera viewport.

The **Dolly Camera + Target** tool is only available if viewport's camera is a target camera. This tool is used to move both the camera and its target.

The **Roll Camera** tool is available in Camera viewport only. It rotates the target camera about its line of sight, and rotates a free camera about its local Z axis.

SELECTION TECHNIQUES

In 3ds Max, you can select objects using various tools such as **Select Object**, **Select by Name**, **Select and Move**, and so on. These tools are discussed next.

Select Object Tool

Quad Menu:	Select
Main Toolbar:	Select Object
Keyboard:	Q

The **Select Object** tool is used to select one or more objects in the viewport. To select an object, choose this tool and move the cursor over the object; the cursor will convert into a selection cursor. Next, press the left mouse button; the object will be selected. To select more than one object at a time, hold the CTRL key and select the objects that you want to add to the selection. To remove an object from the selection, press and hold the ALT key and then click on the object that you want to remove from the selection.

Select by Name Tool

Menu bar:	Edit > Select By > Name
Main Toolbar:	Select by Name
Keyboard:	H

The **Select by Name** tool is used to select an object from the list of objects in the scene. When you choose the **Select by Name** tool from the **Main Toolbar**, the **Select From Scene** dialog box will be displayed. If there are some components in the scene, then those components will be displayed in this dialog box, as shown in Figure 2-1. Now, select an object in the list and choose the **OK** button. Alternatively, you can double-click on the object name in the list to select it. You can also select more than one object by holding the SHIFT or CTRL key. The buttons at the top of the dialog box are used to filter the objects in the list.

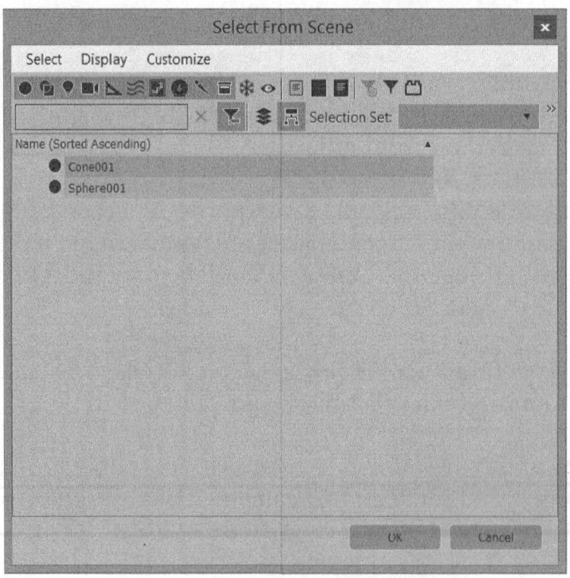

*Figure 2-1 The **Select From Scene** dialog box*

Select and Move Tool

Quad Menu:	Move
Main Toolbar:	Select and Move
Keyboard:	W

The **Select and Move** tool is used to select and move the objects in the viewports. You can move an object by selecting it and then dragging the mouse along the X, Y, or Z axis. You can also move the selected object in the XY, YZ, or ZX plane. To move the selected object along one of the axes, choose this tool and then select the object; the move gizmo will be displayed. Move the cursor over the axis along which you want to move the object, press the left mouse button, and then drag the cursor. Similarly, to move the object in one of the planes, move the cursor over the plane displayed between the two axes; the plane will be highlighted in yellow. Next, press the left mouse button and drag the cursor.

Select and Rotate Tool

Quad Menu:	Rotate
Main Toolbar:	Select and Rotate
Keyboard:	E

The **Select and Rotate** tool is used to rotate the objects in the viewport along the X, Y, or Z axis. To rotate the object along one of the axes, choose the **Select and Rotate** tool, and then select the object; a rotate gizmo will be displayed along with the X, Y, and Z axes. Next, move the cursor over the axes along which you want to rotate the object, press the left mouse button, and then drag the cursor. When you rotate the object, a transparent slice will be displayed which will provide a visual representation of the direction and the degree of rotation, refer to Figure 2-2. Also, you can view the degree of rotation in the X, Y, and Z axes in the coordinates displayed in the Coordinate display area at the bottom of the screen.

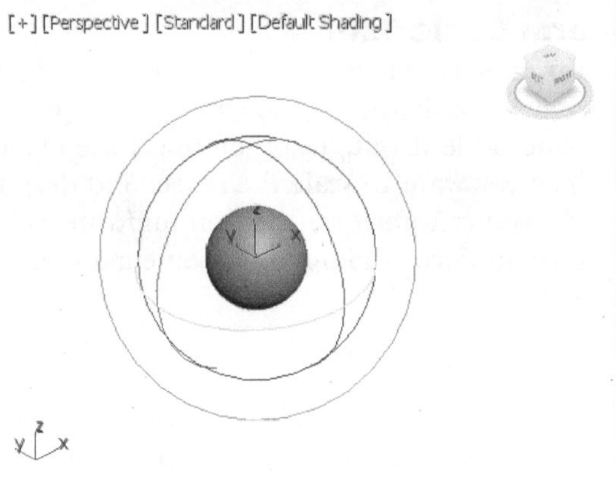

***Figure 2-2** The circular gizmo in the Perspective viewport displayed while rotating the object*

Select and Scale Tools

Quad Menu:	Scale
Main Toolbar:	Select and Scale
Keyboard:	R

There are three types of tools that are used to scale an object. These tools are available in the Select and Scale flyout and are discussed next.

Select and Uniform Scale

The **Select and Uniform Scale** tool is used to scale the objects proportionally along the three axes. To scale an object uniformly along all the three axes, choose the **Select and Uniform Scale** tool from the **Main Toolbar** and select the object; the scale gizmo will be displayed, as shown in Figure 2-3. Move the cursor to the center of the gizmo and make sure its central portion is highlighted, refer to Figure 2-3. Next, drag the cursor up or down to scale the selected object. You can also perform non-uniform scaling using this tool. To do so, move the cursor over the axis along which you want to scale the object, refer to Figure 2-4, and then drag the cursor. Similarly, you can perform non-uniform scaling along the XY, YZ, or ZX plane by selecting the required plane and then dragging that plane, refer to Figure 2-5.

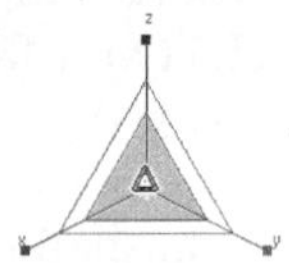

Figure 2-3 The scale gizmo for uniform scaling

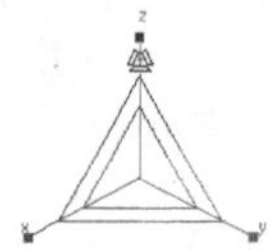

Figure 2-4 Selecting the Z-axis for non-uniform scaling

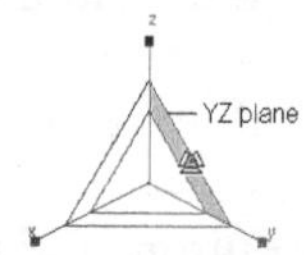

Figure 2-5 Selecting the YZ plane for non-uniform scaling

Select and Non-uniform Scale Tool

The **Select and Non-uniform Scale** tool is used to scale an object along a particular axis or plane non-uniformly. To scale the object, choose the **Select and Non-uniform Scale** tool from the Select and Scale flyout, and then select the object. Move the cursor over the X, Y, or Z axis along which you want to scale the object and drag the cursor to modify the shape of the object. Similarly, you can perform the non-uniform scaling along the XY, YZ, or ZX plane. You can also perform uniform scaling in the same manner, as described in the **Select and Uniform Scale** tool.

Select and Squash Tool

The **Select and Squash** tool is used to stretch and squash the object along the selected axis. To squash the object along one of the axes, choose the **Select and Squash** tool and select the object. Move the cursor over the axis along which you want to squash it. Next, drag the cursor. Similarly, you can squash the selected object along the XY, YZ, or ZX plane. To do so, move the cursor over the plane displayed between the two axes and drag the cursor to squash the object along that plane.

Note

*By default, the color of the X-axis, the Y-axis, and the Z-axis of the transform gizmos is red, green, and blue, respectively. When you move the cursor over any one of these axes, it gets activated and turns yellow. You can see the colors of these axes displayed at the bottom left corner of each viewport. Also, the colored axes are displayed while selecting an object using the **Select and Move**, **Select and Rotate**, or **Select and Scale** tool. Figures 2-6, 2-7, and 2-8 show the move gizmo, rotate gizmo, and scale gizmo, respectively.*

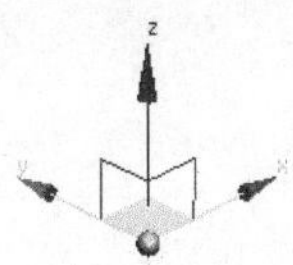

Figure 2-6 *The move gizmo*

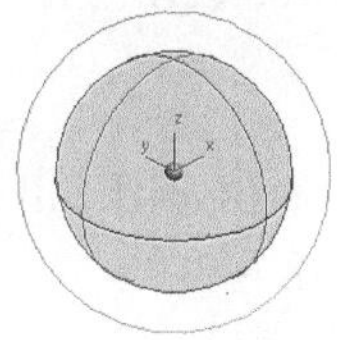

Figure 2-7 *The rotate gizmo*

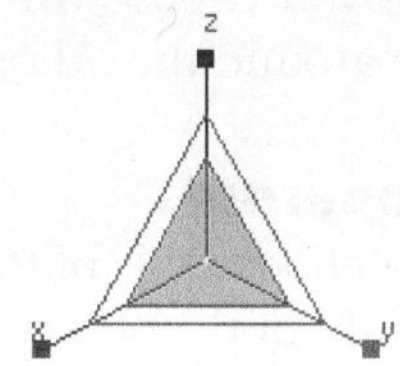

Figure 2-8 *The scale gizmo*

Select and Place Tool

This tool is used to position and orient an object with respect to another object. The placed object changes its orientation according to the shape of the object on which it is placed. Figure 2-9 shows the placement of the objects in the Perspective viewport. To place an object on another object, choose the **Select and Place** tool from the **Select and Place** flyout from the **Main Toolbar** and then drag the object onto the other object. On achieving the required orientation of the object, release the left mouse button; the selected object will be aligned with the target object the Z axis, as shown in Figure 2-10.

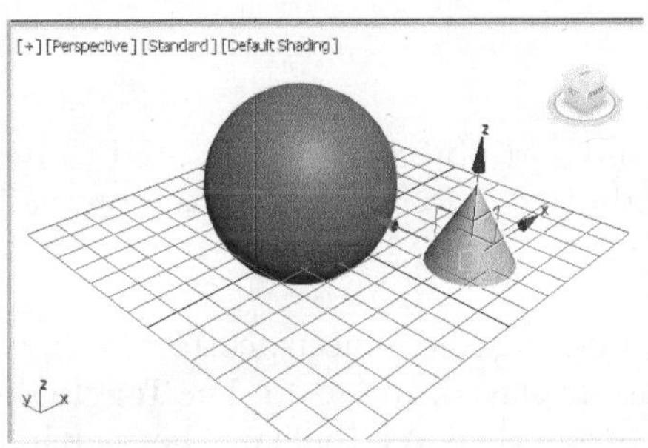

Figure 2-9 *The placement of the objects in Perspective viewport*

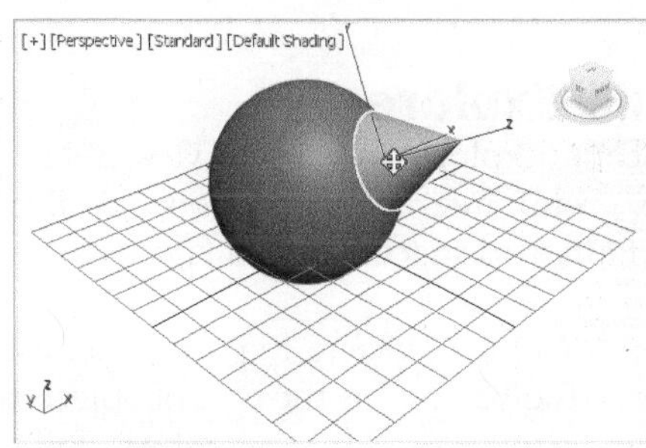

Figure 2-10 *The selected object aligned with other object*

To modify placement settings of the object, right-click on the **Select and Place** tool; the **Placement Settings** dialog box will be displayed, refer to Figure 2-11. The options in this dialog box are discussed next.

Select and Rotate Tool

Choose this button to rotate the object around the axis specified in the **Object Up Axis** area. You can also choose the **Select and Rotate** tool from the **Select and Place** flyout in the main toolbar to rotate the object.

Use Base as Pivot
If you choose this button, the base of the object to be placed will act as the pivot point of the object. This is useful when the pivot is not located at the base of the object.

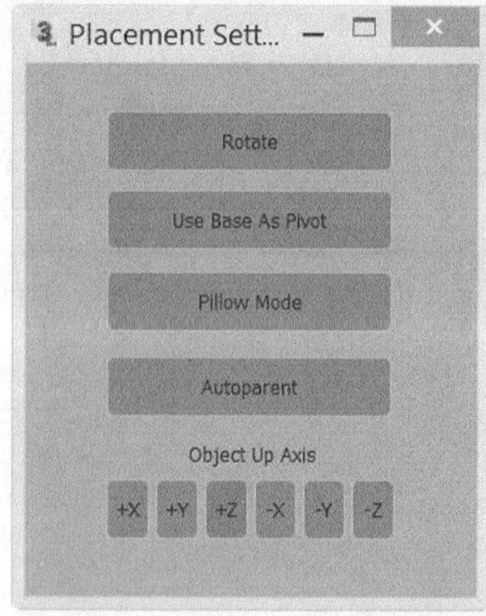

Figure 2-11 The Placement Settings dialog box

Pillow Mode
When you choose this button, the object to be placed will move around the other object without intersecting it.

Autoparent
If you choose this button, the object to be placed will act as the child of the object on which it is being placed.

Object Up Axis Area
The **+Z** button is chosen by default in this area. As a result, the orientation of the object will be along the z axis. To change the axis of orientation of the object, you need to choose the required button from this area.

SCENE MANAGEMENT
The Scene Explorer and Layer Explorer are used to manage complex scenes in an efficient manner. The Scene Explorer can be switched to Layer Explorer. These explorers are discussed next.

Scene Explorer
The Scene Explorer is used to view, select, filter, and sort objects. It is also used to rename, delete, group, freeze, and hide objects. By default, the Scene Explorer is docked on the left in the default workspace, refer to Figure 2-12.

The options in the Scene Explorer menu bar are used to select objects, customize the Scene Explorer Toolbar, define the type of objects for the list displayed, and so on. The **Toggle Display Toolbar** button is used to toggle the visibility of the Scene Explorer Toolbar. The Search field is used to search an object from the list of objects and thereby adding a filter to the list of objects. The **Remove Filter** button is used to remove the applied filter.

The Scene Explorer Toolbar is located on the left in the Scene Explorer. The buttons in this toolbar are used to list specific type of objects in the Scene Explorer such as lights, shapes, cameras, and so on.

If some of the buttons on the right of the **Toggle Display Toolbar** button are not visible, click on the double arrow located at the upper right corner or resize the Scene Explorer to make them visible. These buttons are discussed next.

The **Lock Cell Editing** button is used to lock the editing of the cells in the Scene Explorer. The **Pick Parent** button is used to select or change parent of the selected object. The **Select Children** button is used to select all the child objects and layers of the selected parent object.

Alternatively, if you double-click on the parent object in the Scene Explorer, the parent object and all its child objects will be selected.

When you right-click in the area displaying a list of objects, a quad menu will be displayed. The options in this quad menu are used to rename object, freeze object, and so on. The name of the workspace used in the scene is displayed in the field located at the bottom of the Scene Explorer. When you click on the arrow at the right of this field, a flyout will be displayed, as shown in Figure 2-13. The options in this flyout are used to convert the Scene Explorer to Property Explorer, Light Explorer, and so on. Figure 2-14 shows the Property Explorer. The **Sort By Layer** button is used to switch the Scene Explorer to Layer Explorer.

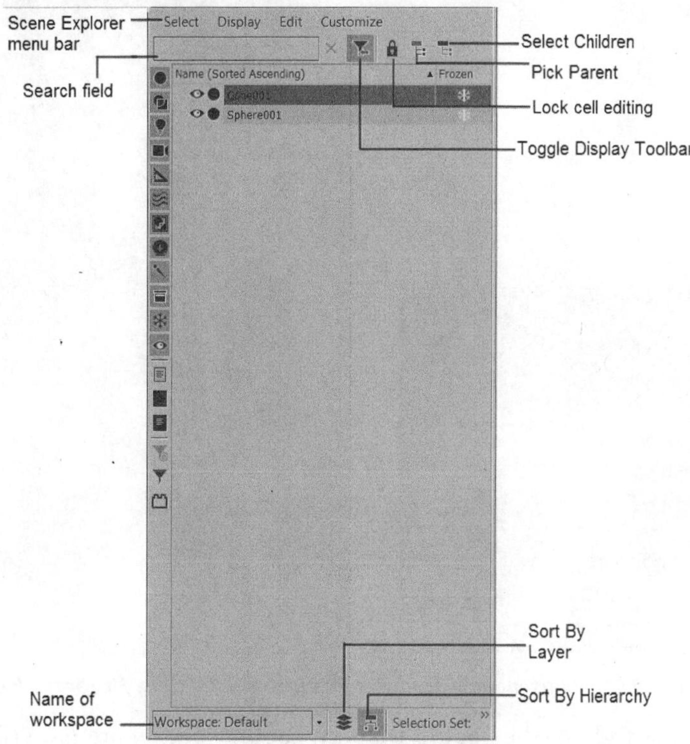

*Figure 2-12 The **Scene Explorer***

The Layer Explorer is discussed next.

Layer Explorer

The Layer Explorer will be displayed in the interface on choosing the **Sort By Layer** button in the Scene Explorer, refer to Figure 2-12. Alternatively, click on the arrow on the right of the field located at the bottom of the Scene Explorer, a flyout will be displayed. Choose the Layer Explorer from the flyout displayed, refer to Figure 2-13. By default, the Layer Explorer is displayed with a **0 (default)** layer, as shown in Figure 2-15. You can create any number of layers in the Layer Explorer by using the **Create New Layer** button. To add an object to the newly created or existing layer, expand the **0 (default)** layer and then select the object from the list of objects in the Layer Explorer and right-click on it; a quad menu will be displayed, refer to Figure 2-16. Choose **Add Selection To > New Parent (pick)** from the quad menu and select the desired layer from the list of layers displayed; the selected object is transferred to the selected layer. You can also create new layer and add the selected object to it by using the quad menu. To do so, select the object from the list of objects displayed. Next, right-click on it and then choose **Add Selected To > New Layer** from the quad menu displayed; a new layer will be created and the selected object will be added to it. To rename a layer, right-click on it and choose **Rename** from the quad menu displayed.

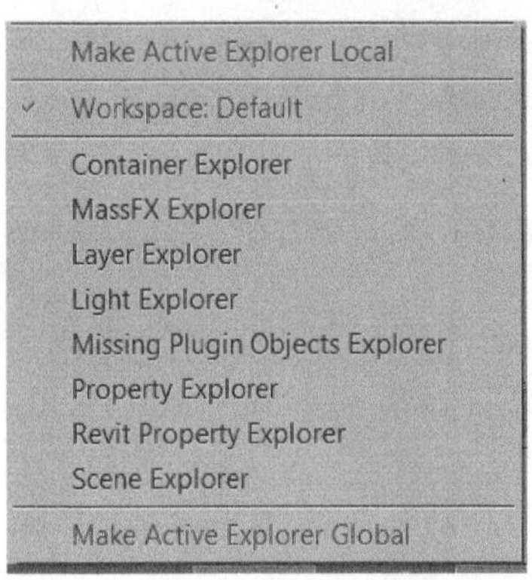

Figure 2-13 The flyout displayed

*Figure 2-14 The **Property Explorer***

If the buttons on the right of the **Toggle Display Toolbar** button are not visible in the Layer Explorer, click on the double arrow located at the upper right corner or resize the Layer Explorer to make them visible. These buttons are discussed next.

The **Create New Layer** button is used to create a new layer. The **Make Selected Layer Active** button is used to change the selected layer to an active layer.

To add an object to the active layer, select the object and choose the **Add to Active Layer** button.

Managing Local and Global Scene Explorers

There are two types of scene explorers in Autodesk 3ds Max 2017: global and local. Local scene explorers can be used in current scene only whereas global scene explorers can be used in any scene. By default, all the scene explorers are global. To change a global scene explorer to a local scene explorer, click on the arrow on the right of the field available at the bottom of the

Scene Explorer; a flyout will be displayed, refer to Figure 2-13. Next, choose the **Make Active Explorer Local** option from the flyout. Similarly, to change a local scene explorer to a global scene explorer, choose the **Make Active Explorer Global** option from the flyout.

To manage various local explorers like Scene Explorer, Revit Property Explorer, and so on, choose **Tools > Manage Local Explorers** from the menu bar; the **Manage Local Scene Explorers** dialog box will be displayed, refer to Figure 2-17. Using this dialog box, you can load a Scene Explorer into a scene. To do so, choose the **Load** button; the **Load Scene Explorer** dialog box will be displayed. Select the desired Scene Explorer from this dialog box and choose **Open**; the Scene Explorer will be opened in the current scene as a local Scene Explorer and will be added to the dialog box. You can also rename or delete local Scene Explorer(s) using this dialog box. To save a local Scene Explorer, choose the **Save** button; the **Save Scene Explorer** dialog box will be displayed. Next, enter the desired name in the **File name** text box and choose **Save**; the Scene Explorer will be saved with the desired name.

Figure 2-15 *The* ***Layer Explorer***

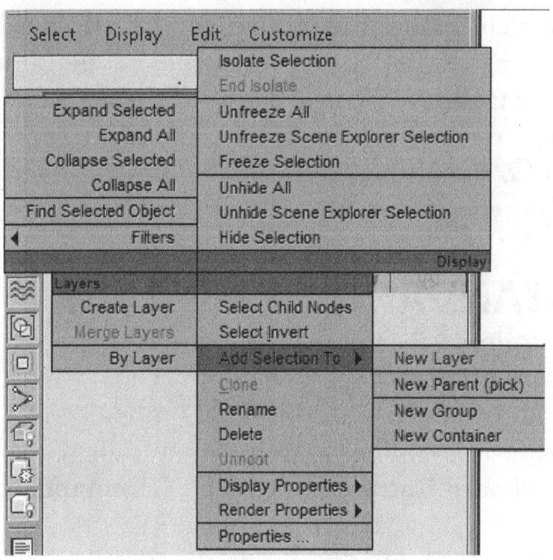

Figure 2-16 *The quad menu*

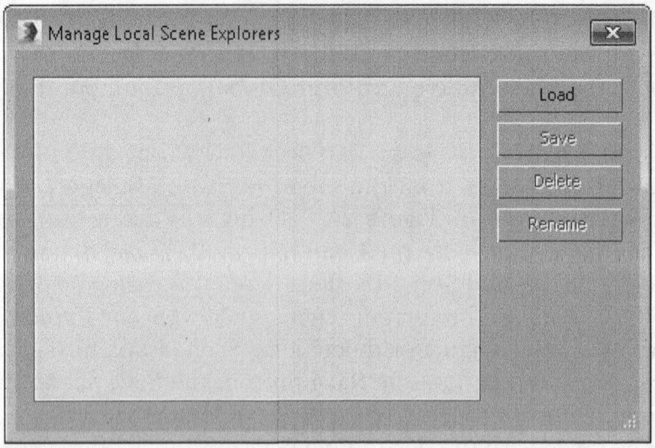

*Figure 2-17 The **Manage Local Scene Explorers** dialog box*

AXIS CONSTRAINTS TOOLBAR

The buttons in the **Axis Constraints** toolbar are used to specify the axis or plane along which the transformation would be restricted. The transformation includes movement, rotation, and scaling of an object. The **Axis Constraints** toolbar is not displayed by default in the interface. To display it, right-click in the blank area on the **Main Toolbar**; a shortcut menu will be displayed. Choose **Axis Constraints** from the shortcut menu; the toolbar will be displayed on the screen, as shown in Figure 2-18. Now, choose one of the buttons available in the **Axis Constraints** toolbar to perform the transformation along the selected axis. You can use the F5, F6, and F7 function keys to invoke the **X**, **Y**, and **Z** constraints, respectively. To toggle between the **XY**, **YZ**, and **XZ** axes, you can use the F8 function key.

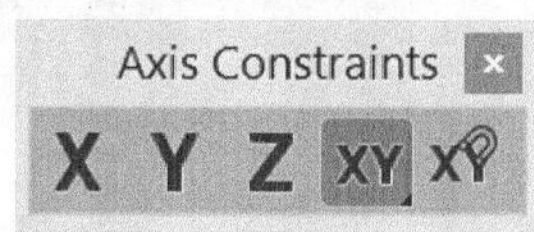

*Figure 2-18 The **Axis Constraints** toolbar*

STANDARD PRIMITIVES

Autodesk 3ds Max has several basic three-dimensional geometric shapes which are known as standard primitives such as box, cone, sphere, cylinder, torus, tube, and so on. You can use these primitives to create simple 3D models such as a table, box, chair, and so on. All the standard primitives can be created dynamically using the mouse or by specifying the parameters in the **Keyboard Entry** rollout of the **Command Panel**.

To create the standard primitives, choose **Create > Geometry** in the **Command Panel**. By default, the **Standard Primitives** option is selected in the drop-down list below the **Geometry** button. Now, activate the viewport in which you want to create the primitives.

Next, choose the corresponding tool from the **Object Type** rollout. In the following section, you will learn to create and modify the standard primitives using various tools available in the **Object Type** rollout.

Creating a Box

Menu bar:	Create > Standard Primitives > Box
Command Panel:	Create > Geometry > Standard Primitives > Object Type rollout > Box

To create a box, activate the viewport by clicking in it. Next, choose the **Box** tool from the **Object Type** rollout; the **Name and Color**, **Creation Method**, **Keyboard Entry**, and **Parameters** rollouts will be displayed, as shown in Figure 2-19. Press and hold the left mouse button in the viewport to specify the first corner of the box and then drag the cursor to define the length and width of the box. Release the left mouse button to get the desired length and width. Now, move the cursor up or down to define the height of the box. Click after you get the desired height; the box will be created, as shown in Figure 2-20.

Note

1. To view all the rollouts, position the cursor over any of the rollouts until you see the pan icon (hand). Next, press and hold the left mouse button and drag the cursor in the rollout.

2. This arrow sign on the left side of the rollout head indicates that the rollout is collapsed and the arrow sign indicates that the rollout is expanded.

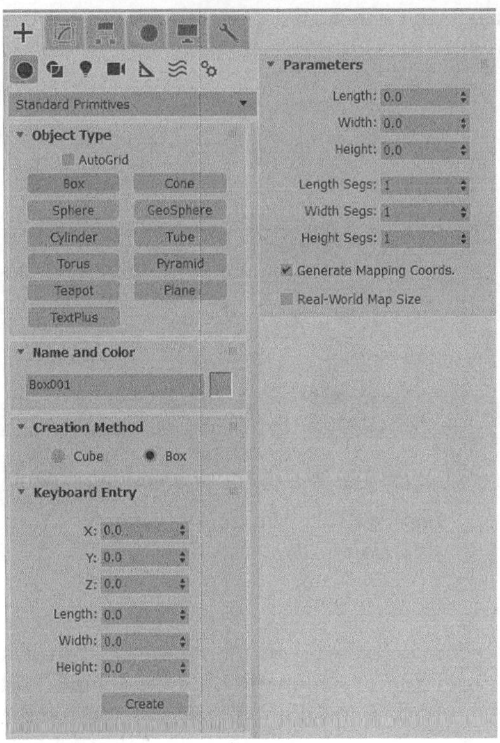

Figure 2-19 *Various rollouts to create a box*

Figure 2-20 *A box displayed in the viewport*

Tip
If you are creating a standard primitive that requires multiple steps, you can pan or orbit the viewport between the steps. To pan the viewport, drag the cursor with the middle-mouse button or mouse wheel held down. To rotate the viewport, press and hold the ALT key and then drag the cursor with middle-mouse button or mouse wheel held down.

Various rollouts used to create and modify the box are discussed next.

Name and Color Rollout

In Autodesk 3ds Max, a specific name and color is automatically assigned to the newly created box. To modify this name, expand the **Name and Color** rollout. Enter a new name in the text box available in this area and then press ENTER. To change the color of the box, choose the color swatch on the right side of the text box; the **Object Color** dialog box will be displayed, as shown in Figure 2-21. Choose a new color from this dialog box; the selected color will be displayed in the **Current Color** color swatch. Now, choose the **OK** button; the new color will be assigned to the box.

To customize a color, choose the **Add Custom Colors** button in the **Object Color** dialog box; the **Color Selector: Add Color** dialog box will be displayed, as shown in Figure 2-22. Now, customize a new color in this dialog box and choose the **Add Color** button; the new color will be displayed in one of the color swatches in the **Custom Colors** area of the **Object Color** dialog box. Next, choose the **OK** button; the new color will be assigned to the box.

Note
The options in the ***Name and Color*** *rollout are same for all the standard primitives.*

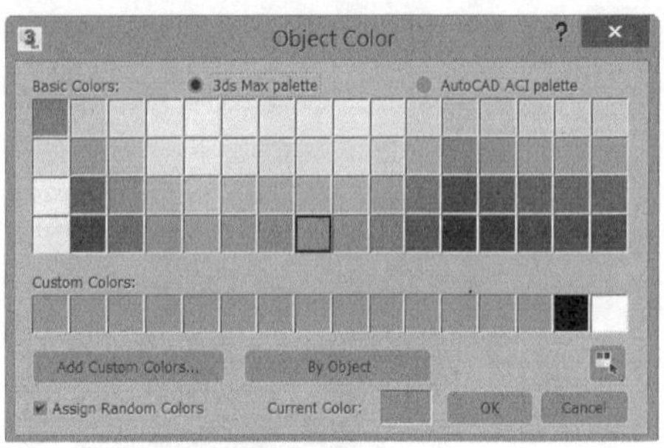

Figure 2-21 The ***Object Color*** *dialog box*

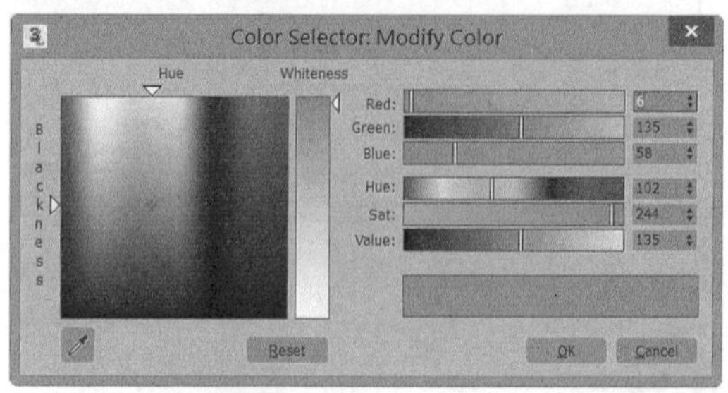

Figure 2-22 The Color Selector: Add Color *dialog box*

Creation Method Rollout

The options in this rollout are used for creating the box dynamically using the mouse. By default, the **Box** radio button is selected. As a result, you can create a box having different length, width, and height. Select the **Cube** radio button to create a box of equal length, width, and height.

Keyboard Entry Rollout

This rollout is used to create a box by entering the parameters in the **Keyboard Entry** rollout using the keyboard. The **Length**, **Width**, and **Height** spinners are used to specify the length, width, and height of the box, respectively. The **X**, **Y**, and **Z** spinners are used to specify the position of the box in the viewport along the axes of the home grid or of a grid object. By default, the value in these spinners is 0, therefore, the object will be created at the center of the home grid or of a grid object in the viewport. The **Create** button in the **Keyboard Entry** rollout is used to create a box in the viewport of specified dimensions.

Note

1. The grid object is a type of helper object which can be created by you if required.

2. The ***Keyboard Entry*** *rollout for all the standard primitives is used to create the corresponding primitive by entering the parameters. The method of creating all primitives is the same as already discussed. The only difference is the type and number of parameters entered.*

Parameters Rollout

After creating the box, you can modify its dimensions using the **Parameters** rollout. The **Length**, **Width**, and **Height** spinners are used to specify the length, width, and height, respectively of the box. The **Length Segs**, **Width Segs**, and **Height Segs** spinners are used to define the number of divisions or segments along each axis of the object. By default, the **Generate Mapping Coords.** check box is selected. As a result, mapping coordinates are created automatically with a projection appropriate to the shape of the box. You can select the **Real-World Map Size** check box to correct the scale of the texture mapped materials that are applied to the box. This option allows you to create a material and specify the actual width and height of a 2D texture map in the **Material Editor**.

Note

After creating a primitive in the viewport if you right-click in the viewport to exit the tool, the ***Parameters*** *rollout will disappear from the* ***Create*** *tab. In such a case, to modify the parameters of the primitive, make sure the primitive is selected in the viewport and then choose the* ***Modify*** *tab in the* ***Command Panel****; the* ***Parameters*** *rollout will be displayed in the* ***Modify*** *tab.*

Creating a Sphere

Menu bar:	Create > Standard Primitives > Sphere
Command Panel:	Create > Geometry > Standard Primitives > Object Type rollout > Sphere

To create a sphere, activate a viewport by clicking on it and choose the **Sphere** tool from the **Object Type** rollout; the **Name and Color**, **Creation Method**, **Keyboard Entry**, and **Parameters** rollouts will be displayed, as shown in Figure 2-23. Press and hold the left mouse button to specify the center of the sphere and then drag the cursor to define the radius of the sphere. Release the left mouse button; the sphere of the specified radius will be created, as shown in Figure 2-24. Note that the sphere will be displayed in all viewports.

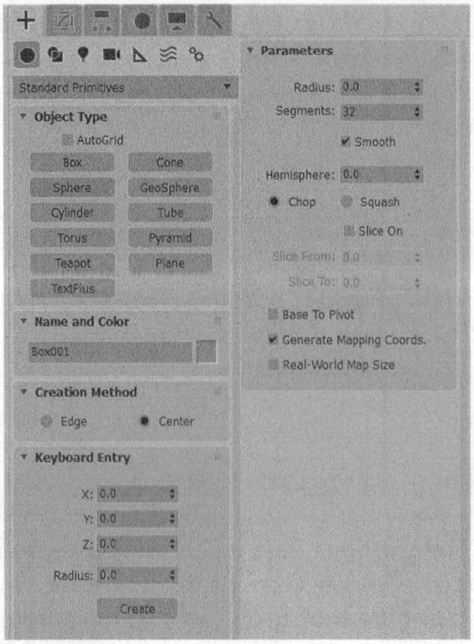

Figure 2-23 *Various rollouts to create a sphere*

Figure 2-24 *A sphere displayed in the viewport*

Various rollouts used to create and modify the sphere are discussed next.

Creation Method Rollout

The options in this rollout are used for creating a sphere dynamically. By default, the **Center** radio button is selected in this rollout. As a result, the starting point is at the center of the sphere. You can select the **Edge** radio button to set the starting point on an edge at the surface of the sphere.

Parameters Rollout

The options in this rollout are used to modify the parameters of the sphere. The **Radius** and **Segments** spinners are used to specify the radius and divisions, respectively for the sphere. By default, the **Smooth** check box is selected, therefore, the sphere appears smooth. If this check box is cleared, it will give a faceted appearance to the sphere. The **Hemisphere** spinner is used to create a partial sphere. By default, the **Chop** radio button is selected. As a result, the starting point is at the center of the sphere. If you select the **Squash** radio button, the hemisphere will have the same number of vertices and faces as in the complete sphere. On selecting the **Slice On** check box, the **Slice From** and **Slice To** spinners will be enabled. Set the values in the **Slice From** and **Slice To** spinners to specify the start and end angle to create a partial sphere. By default, the pivot point of the sphere is located at its center. If you select the **Base To Pivot** check box, then the pivot point of the sphere will be at its base.

Creating a GeoSphere

Menu bar: Create > Standard Primitives > GeoSphere
Command Panel: Create > Geometry > Standard Primitives > Object Type rollout > GeoSphere

The **GeoSphere** tool creates a more regular surface than the **Sphere** tool. To create a geosphere, activate the required viewport and choose the **GeoSphere** tool from the **Object Type** rollout; the **Name and Color**, **Creation Method**, **Keyboard Entry**, and **Parameters** rollouts will be displayed, as shown in Figure 2-25. Press and hold the left mouse button to specify the center of the geosphere and then drag the cursor to define the radius of the geosphere. Next, release the left mouse button to get the desired radius; a geosphere will be created, as shown in Figure 2-26.

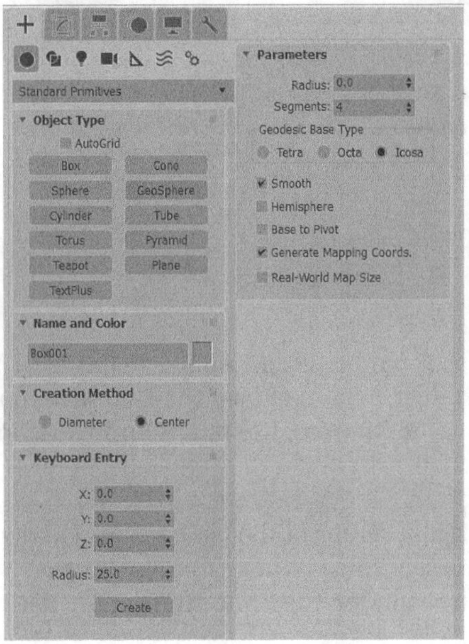

Figure 2-25 Various rollouts to create a geosphere

Figure 2-26 A geosphere displayed in the viewport

Various rollouts used to create and modify the geosphere are discussed next.

Creation Method Rollout

The options in this rollout are used for creating a geosphere dynamically. By default, the **Center** radio button is selected. As a result, the starting point is at the center of the geosphere. You can select the **Diameter** radio button to specify the first point on an edge at the surface of the geosphere.

Parameters Rollout

The options in this rollout are used to modify the geosphere. The **Radius** and **Segments** spinners are used to specify the radius and divisions, respectively for the geosphere. By default, the **Icosa** radio button is selected in the **Geodesic Base Type** area. As a result, the surface of the geosphere will consist of 20-sided polygons and equilateral triangles, as shown in Figure 2-27. You can select the **Tetra** radio button in the **Geodesic Base Type** area; the resulting surface will consist of tetrahedrons and triangular faces, as shown in Figure 2-28. Similarly, if you select the **Octa** radio button, you will get a surface consisting of octagons and triangular faces, as shown in Figure 2-29. By default, the **Smooth** check box is selected. As a result, it makes hemisphere smooth. On selecting the **Hemisphere** check box, one half of the geosphere will be created. If the **Base to Pivot** check box is selected, it will shift the pivot point of the geosphere to the base.

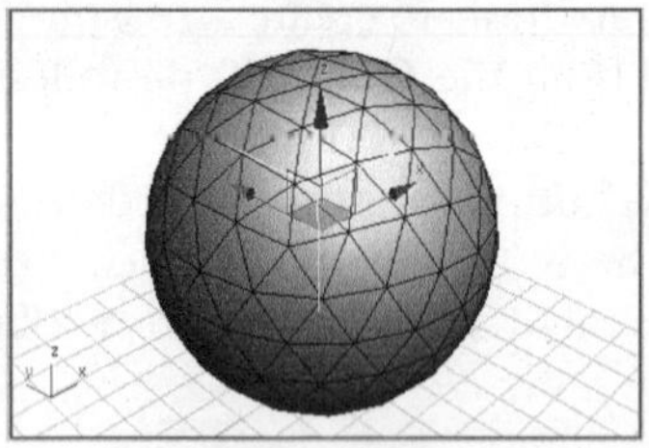

***Figure 2-27** The geosphere displayed on selecting the **Icosa** radio button*

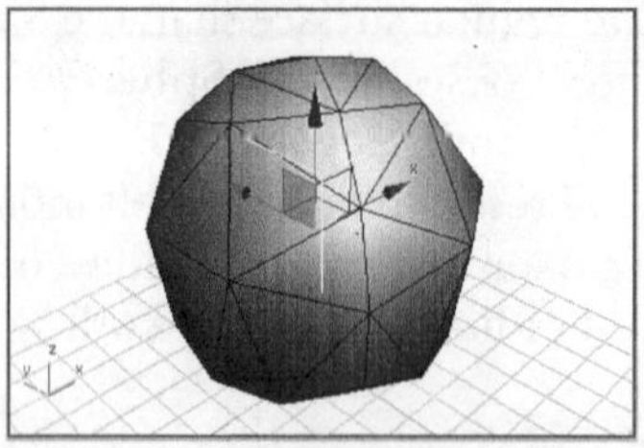

***Figure 2-28** The geosphere displayed on selecting the **Tetra** radio button*

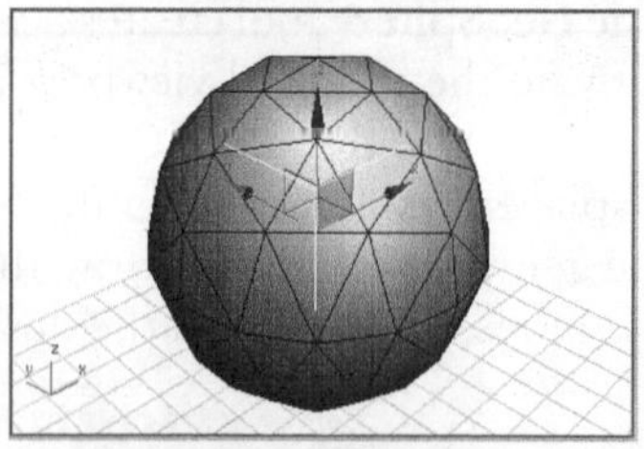

***Figure 2-29** The geosphere displayed on selecting the **Octa** radio button*

Creating a Cylinder

Menu bar:	Create > Standard Primitives > Cylinder
Command Panel:	Create > Geometry > Standard Primitives > Object Type rollout > Cylinder

The **Cylinder** tool is used to create a cylinder that can be sliced along its major axis. To create a cylinder, activate the required viewport by clicking in it and choose the **Cylinder** tool from the **Object Type** rollout; the **Name and Color**, **Creation Method**, **Keyboard Entry**, and **Parameters** rollouts will be displayed, as shown in Figure 2-30.

Press and hold the left mouse button to specify the center of the base of the cylinder and then drag the cursor to define the radius of the cylinder. Release the left mouse button. Next, move the cursor up or down to define the height of the cylinder. Click after you get the desired height; a cylinder will be created, as shown in Figure 2-31.

Various rollouts used to create and modify the cylinder are discussed next.

Creation Method Rollout

The options in this rollout are the same as those discussed in the **Sphere** tool.

Parameters Rollout

The options in this rollout are used to modify the cylinder. The **Radius** spinner is used to set the radius of the cylinder. The **Height** spinner is used to specify the height for the cylinder. The value in the **Height Segments** spinner defines the number of segments along the height of the cylinder. The value in the **Cap Segments** spinner specifies the number of segments at the top and the bottom of the cylinder. The value in the **Sides** spinner specifies the number of sides on the cylinder. Different shapes of the cylinder can be created by entering different values in the **Sides** spinner. By default, the **Smooth** check box is selected, therefore, the cylinder appears smoother. The **Slice On** check box is the same as described in the **Sphere** tool.

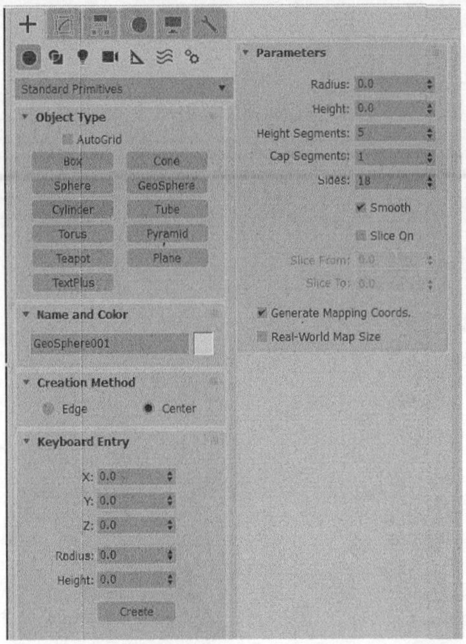

Figure 2-30 Various rollouts to create a cylinder

Figure 2-31 A cylinder displayed in the viewport

Creating a Cone

Menu:	Create > Standard Primitives > Cone
Command Panel:	Create > Geometry > Standard Primitives > Object Type rollout > Cone

The **Cone** tool is used to create upright or inverted round cones. To create a cone, activate the viewport and then choose the **Cone** tool from the **Object Type** rollout; the **Name and Color**, **Creation Method**, **Keyboard Entry**, and **Parameters** rollouts will be displayed, as shown in Figure 2-32.

Press and hold the left mouse button to specify the center of the base of the cone and then, drag the cursor to define radius 1 for base of the cone. Release the left mouse button and move the cursor up or down to define the height of the cone. Next, click to get the desired height. Move the cursor up or down again and click to define radius 2 of the cone; a cone will be created, as shown in Figure 2-33.

Various rollouts used to create and modify the cone are discussed next.

Creation Method Rollout

The options in this rollout are the same as those discussed in the **Sphere** tool.

Parameters Rollout

The **Radius 1** and **Radius 2** parameters are used to create pointed or flat-topped cones by specifying the first and second radii for the cone. The **Height** spinner is used to specify the height of the cone. If you specify a negative value for the **Height** spinner, the cone will be created below the construction plane.

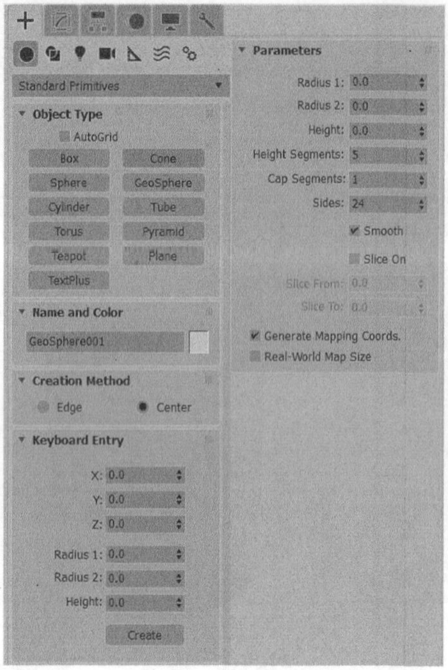

Figure 2-32 *Various rollouts to create a cone*

Figure 2-33 *A cone displayed in the viewport*

Creating a Tube

Menu bar:	Create > Standard Primitives > Tube
Command Panel:	Create > Geometry > Standard Primitives > Object Type rollout > Tube

The **Tube** tool is used to create round and prismatic tubes. The tube primitive is similar to the cylinder primitives with a hole in it. To create a tube, activate the required viewport and choose the **Tube** tool from the **Object Type** rollout; the **Name and Color**, **Creation Method**, **Keyboard Entry**, and **Parameters** rollouts will be displayed, as shown in Figure 2-34.

Press and hold the left mouse button to specify the center of the tube and then drag the cursor to define the first radius of the tube. It can be the inner or the outer radius of the tube. Next, release the left mouse button, move the cursor, and then click to define the second radius. Next, move the cursor up or down and click to get the desired height of the tube; a tube will be created, as shown in Figure 2-35.

Various rollouts used to create and modify the tube are discussed next.

Creation Method Rollout

The options in this rollout are the same as those discussed in the **Sphere** tool.

Parameters Rollout

The options in this rollout are used to modify the tube. The **Radius 1** and **Radius 2** spinners are used to specify the inner and outer radii of the tube. The larger value represents the outer radius while the smaller value represents the inner radius. The **Height** spinner is used to specify the height of the tube. If you specify negative value for this parameter, the tube will be created below the construction plane. The other options in this rollout are the same as those described in the **Cylinder** tool.

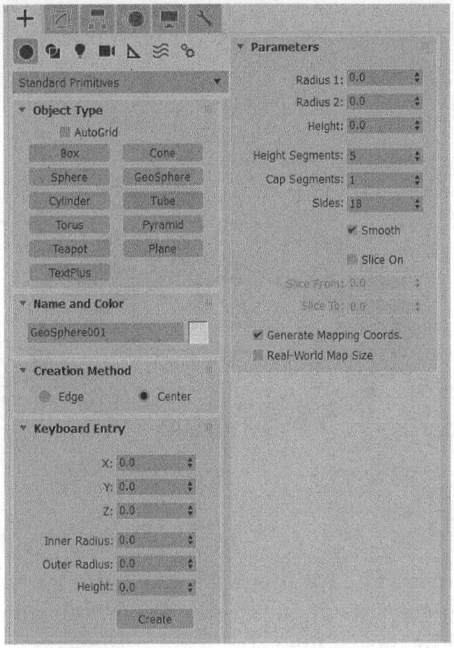

Figure 2-34 Various rollouts to create a tube

Figure 2-35 A tube displayed in the viewport

Creating a Torus

Menu bar:	Create > Standard Primitives > Torus
Command Panel:	Create > Geometry > Standard Primitives > Object Type rollout > Torus

The **Torus** tool is used to create doughnut like shapes. To create a torus, activate the required viewport and choose the **Torus** tool from the **Object Type** rollout; the **Name and Color**, **Creation Method**, **Keyboard Entry**, and **Parameters** rollouts will be displayed, as shown in Figure 2-36.

Press and hold the left mouse button to specify the center of the torus and then drag the cursor to define the radius of the torus. Release the left mouse button and then drag the cursor to adjust the radius of the circular cross-section of the torus. Click to get the desired radius; a torus will be created, as shown in Figure 2-37.

Various rollouts used to create and modify the torus are discussed next.

Creation Method Rollout

The options in this rollout are the same as those discussed in the **Sphere** tool.

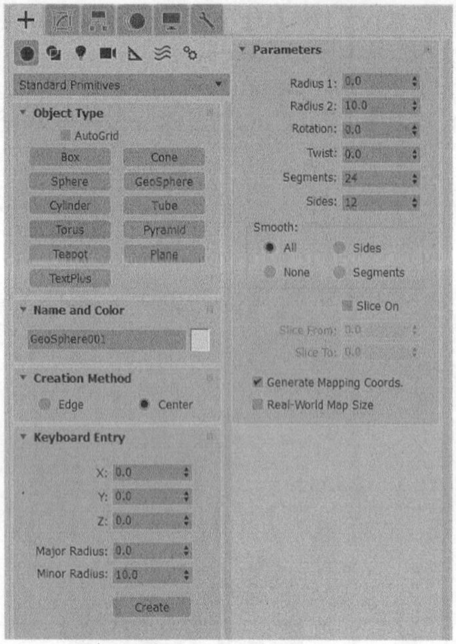

Figure 2-36 Various rollouts to create a torus

Figure 2-37 A torus displayed in the viewport

Parameters Rollout

The options in this rollout are used to modify the torus. The **Radius 1** spinner is used to specify the radius for the ring of the torus. Therefore, you can specify the distance from the center of the torus to the center of the cross-sectional circle in this spinner. By default, the value of the **Radius 2** spinner is set to 10. This spinner specifies the radius of the cross-sectional circle. The value in the **Rotation** spinner defines the degree of rotation of the circular cross-section of the torus. The value in the **Twist** spinner specifies how much the circular cross-section of the torus can be twisted. The **Segments** spinner defines the number of segments around the circumference of the torus. The **Sides** value specifies the number of sides in the circular cross-section of the torus. In the **Smooth** area of the **Parameters** rollout, there are four radio buttons. By default, the **All** radio button is selected. As a result, smoothness is applied to all surfaces of the torus. You can select the **Sides** radio button to apply smoothness between adjacent segments. If you select the **Segments** radio button, smoothness is applied to the segments individually. It results in the formation of ring-like segments along the torus. Select the **None** radio button, if you do not want to apply smoothness to the torus. The function of the **Slice On** check box is the same as described for the **Sphere** tool.

Creating a Pyramid

Menu bar:	Create > Standard Primitives > Pyramid
Command Panel:	Create > Geometry > Standard Primitives > Object Type rollout > Pyramid

To create a pyramid, activate the viewport and choose the **Pyramid** tool from the **Object Type** rollout; the **Name and Color**, **Creation Method**, **Keyboard Entry**, and **Parameters** rollouts will be displayed, as shown in Figure 2-38.

Press and hold the left mouse button to specify the first corner of the pyramid and then drag the cursor to define the width and depth of the pyramid. Release the left mouse button and drag the cursor upward. Click after you get the desired height; a pyramid will be created, as shown in Figure 2-39.

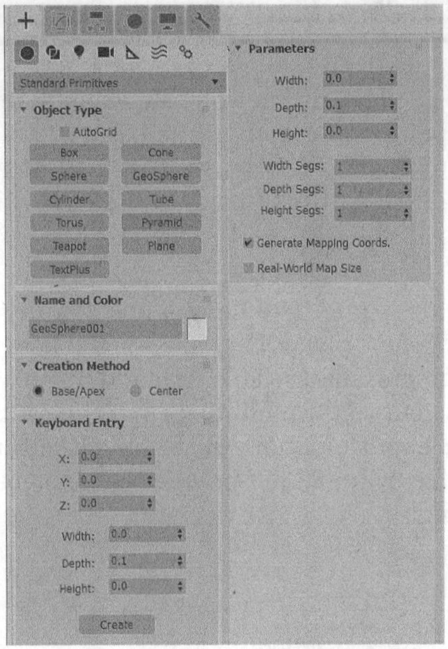

Figure 2-38 Various rollouts to create a pyramid

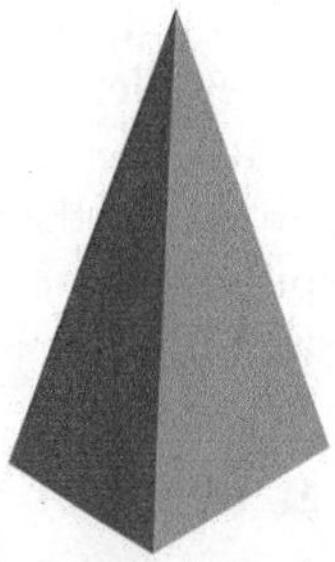

Figure 2-39 A pyramid displayed in the viewport

Various rollouts used to create and modify the pyramid are discussed next.

Creation Method Rollout

The options in this rollout are used for creating a pyramid dynamically. By default, the **Base/Apex** radio button is selected. As a result, the first point is specified as the first corner of the base of the pyramid. You can select the **Center** radio button to specify the first point as the center of the base of the pyramid.

Parameters Rollout

The options in this rollout are used to modify the pyramid. The **Width**, **Depth**, and **Height** spinners are used to specify the width, depth, and height, respectively of the pyramid. The values in the **Width Segs**, **Depth Segs**, and **Height Segs** spinners define the number of segments on the corresponding sides of the pyramid.

Creating a Plane

Menu bar:	Create > Standard Primitives > Plane
Command Panel:	Create > Geometry > Standard Primitives > Object Type rollout > Plane

To create a plane, activate the required viewport and then choose the **Plane** tool from the **Object Type** rollout; the **Name and Color**, **Creation Method**, **Keyboard Entry**, and **Parameters** rollouts will be displayed.

Press and hold the left mouse button to specify the first corner of the plane and then drag the cursor to define the length and width of the plane. Release the left mouse button; a plane will be created, as shown in Figure 2-40.

Various rollouts used to create and modify the plane are discussed next.

Creation Method Rollout

The options in this rollout are used for creating a plane dynamically. By default, the **Rectangle** radio button is selected. As a result, the first point is specified as the corner of a rectangular plane. You can select the **Square** radio button to specify the first point as the center of a square plane. Note that in the case of a square plane, the length and width of the plane will be equal.

Parameters Rollout

The options in this rollout are used to modify the plane. The **Length** and **Width** spinners are used to specify the length and width, respectively of the plane. The values in the **Length Segs** and **Width Segs** spinners define the number of segments along the length and width of the plane, respectively. The **Render Multipliers** area is used to set the multipliers for rendering. The **Scale** spinner is used to specify the value by which the length and width will be multiplied at rendering. The **Density** spinner is used to specify the value by which the number of segments along the length and width will be multiplied at rendering.

Creating a Teapot

Menu bar:	Create > Standard Primitives > Teapot
Command Panel:	Create > Geometry > Standard Primitives > Object Type rollout > Teapot

To create a teapot, activate the required viewport and choose the **Teapot** tool from the **Object Type** rollout; the **Name and Color**, **Creation Method**, **Keyboard Entry**, and **Parameters** rollouts will be displayed.

Press and hold the left mouse button to define the center of the bottom face and then drag the cursor to define the radius of the teapot. Release the left mouse button after you get the desired radius; a teapot will be created with the pivot point at the center of its base, as shown in Figure 2-41.

Figure 2-40 *A plane displayed in the viewport*

Figure 2-41 *A teapot displayed in the viewport*

Various rollouts used to create and modify the teapot are discussed next.

Creation Method Rollout

The options in this rollout are the same as those discussed in the **Sphere** tool.

Parameters Rollout

The options in this rollout are used to modify the teapot. The **Radius** spinner is used to specify the overall size of the teapot. Therefore, it specifies the distance from the center of the teapot to the body parameter. The **Segments** spinner is used to specify the number of divisions in each quadrant of the body. By default, the **Smooth** check box is selected. Therefore, all parts of the teapot will be smoothened. A teapot has four parts: body, handle, spout, and lid. If you want to remove any one of the parts, clear the check box corresponding to that part in the **Teapot Parts** area of the **Parameters** rollout. You can also use different parts of a teapot individually to make another object. For example, you can use the handle of the teapot for creating a coffee mug.

RENDERING A STILL IMAGE

Menu bar:	Rendering > Render
Toolbar:	Main Toolbar > Render Production
Keyboard:	SHIFT + Q

Rendering is a process of generating a 2D image from a 3D scene. It shows the lighting effects, materials applied, background, and other settings that you have applied to the scene. The basic rendering for a still scene is discussed next while the advance rendering for the animated scenes will be discussed in the later chapters.

To render a still image, activate the viewport and choose the **Render Setup** tool from the **Main Toolbar**; the **Render Setup: Default Scanline Renderer** dialog box will be displayed. The **Common** tab is chosen by default in this dialog box. In the **Common Parameters** rollout, make sure that the **Single** radio button is selected in the **Time Output** area. This will enable you to render a single frame at a time. In the **Output Size** area, set the parameters or use the default ones and then choose the **Render** button at the lower right corner in the dialog box; the rendered image will be displayed in the **Perspective, frame 0, Display Gamma:2.2, RGBA Color16 Bits/Channel (1:1)** window, as shown in Figure 2-42.

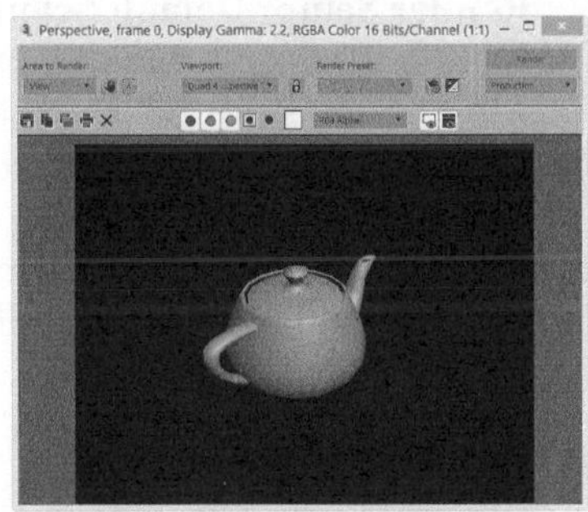

*Figure 2-42 The **Perspective, frame 0, Display Gamma 2.2,RGBA Color16 Bits/Channel (1:1)** window*

Here, **Perspective** refers to the name of the viewport that you have selected at rendering and **frame 0** refers to the number of frame that has been rendered.

Note

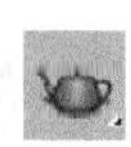

*1. To render a view quickly, choose the **Render Production** tool from the **Main Toolbar** or press the F9 key.*

2. In 3ds Max 2017, you can upload resources to Autodesk A360 cloud and render a scene using the A360 cloud rendering service. This service produces quality renderings in A360 cloud space in considerably less time and you can continue working on your computer even if the rendering is going on in A360 cloud space. To enable the A360 cloud rendering mode, choose the ***Render Setup*** *tool from the* ***Main Toolbar****; the* ***Render Setup: Default Scanline Renderer*** *dialog box will be displayed. In this dialog box, select* ***A360 Cloud Rendering Mode*** *from the* ***Target*** *drop-down list.*

To save the rendered image, choose the **Save Image** button in the **Perspective, frame 0, Display Gamma:2.2, RGBA Color 16 Bits/Channel (1:1)** window; the **Save Image** dialog box will be displayed. Now, select the type of image format from the **Save as type** drop-down list and enter the name of the image in the **File name** text box. Next, browse to the folder where you want to save the scene and choose the **Save** button; a dialog box will be displayed. You can adjust the settings for the file format you have chosen in this dialog box. Use the default settings and choose the **OK** button; the image file will be saved at the selected location.

Note

In later chapters, the ***Perspective, frame 0, Display Gamma:2.2, RGBA Color16 Bits/Channel (1:1)*** *window is referred to as the* ***Rendered Frame*** *window.*

Quicksilver Hardware Renderer

By default, a 3ds Max scene is rendered using the Scanline renderer. However, if you choose the Quicksilver hardware renderer, you can achieve various rendering styles such as wireframe rendering, clay rendering, non-photorealistic rendering, and so on. To do so, you need to follow the steps given next.

1. Activate any of the viewport and choose the **Render Setup** tool from the **Main Toolbar**; the **Render Setup: Default Scanline Renderer** dialog box will be displayed. The **Common** tab is chosen by default in this dialog box.

2. Select the **Quicksilver Hardware Renderer** option from the **Renderer** drop-down list. Alternatively, collapse the **Common Parameters** rollout in this tab and expand the **Assign Renderer** rollout. In this rollout, choose the **Choose Renderer** button at the right of the **Production** text box; the **Choose Renderer** dialog box will be displayed. Select the **Quicksilver Hardware Renderer** option and choose the **OK** button to exit the **Choose Renderer** dialog box. Notice the change in the **Render Setup** dialog box.

3. Choose the **Renderer** tab; various rollouts will be displayed, refer to Figure 2-43. In the **Visual Style** area of the **Visual Style & Appearance** rollout, various options are available in the **Rendering Level** drop-down list, as shown in Figure 2-44.

4. To change the rendering style, you can select the required option from the **Rendering Level** drop down list. Next, choose the **Render** button at the upper right corner of the dialog box; the rendered image will be displayed as per the option selected in the drop-down list.

Note

In 3ds Max 2017, the mental ray and iray renderers are not part of the standard install package. You need to install them separately. To install these, naviagte to the following folder and then install the renderers. After installation, restart 3ds Max.

NVIDIA iray Renderer

The NVIDIA iray renderer creates physically accurate renderings by tracing the light paths. The performance of the renderer can be improved if the system is equipped with a graphics card having a CUDA (Compute Unified Device Architecture) enabled Graphic Processing Unit (GPU).

When you change the current renderer to the NVIDIA iray renderer using the **Render Setup** dialog box, the **iray**, **Advanced Parameters**, **Displacement Parameters**, **Hardware Resources**, and **Motion Blur** rollouts will be displayed in the **Render Setup** dialog box. The procedure to change the renderer has been explained in detail in the previous section. Figure 2-45 shows the **iray** rollout in the **Render Setup** dialog box. It has three radio buttons namely: **Time**, **Iterations**, and **Unlimited**. By selecting the **Time** radio button, you can specify the duration of the rendering. By selecting the **Iterations** radio button, you can specify the number of iterations (passes) to be computed before showing the final render. If the **Unlimited** radio button is selected, rendering will continue for indefinite time and stops when satisfactory quality of rendering is achieved. The rendering done by the iray renderer appears more grainy in the first few passes. The graininess decreases as you increase the number of passes. The NVIDIA iray renderer renders glossy reflections and self illuminating objects with much more precision as compared to the other renderers. However, this renderer supports only certain materials, maps, and shader types.

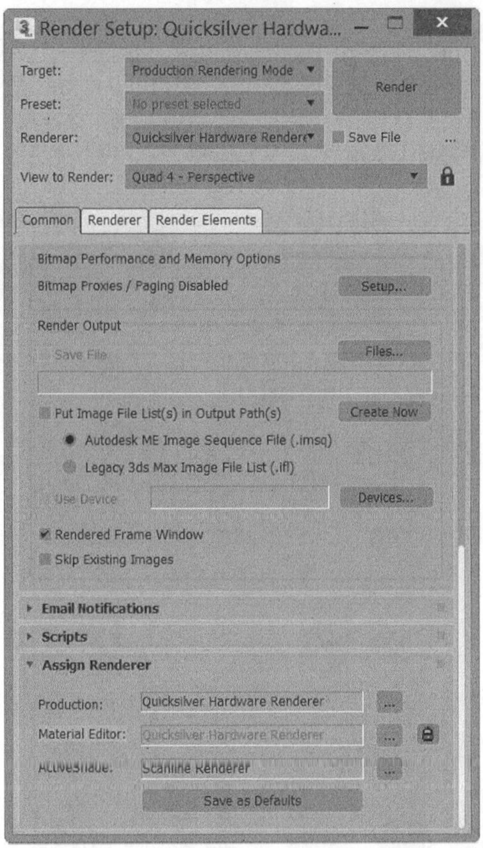

*Figure 2-43 The **Render Setup: Quicksilver Hardware Renderer** dialog box*

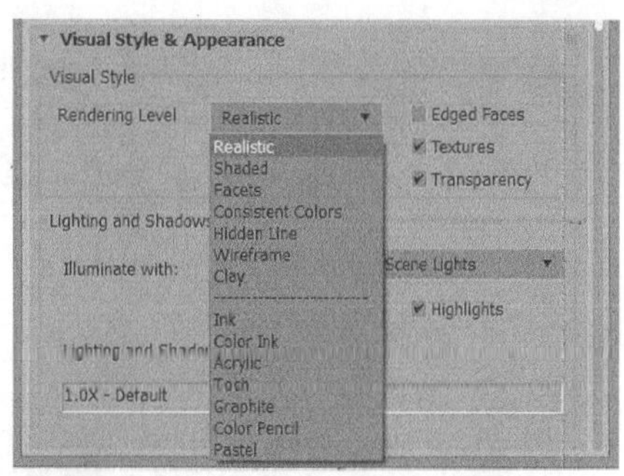

*Figure 2-44 The **Rendering Level** drop-down list*

ART Renderer

The Autodesk Raytracer(ART) renderer is used to create the photo-real images and videos. The ART renderer is used for scenes lit with image-based lighting (IBL). This renderer is used for exterior scene, architectural interiors with daylight, and product renders with HDR studio lighting images. This renderer also includes an image noise filter that can reduce render times, and improve the quality of the rendering. When you change the current renderer to the ART renderer using the **Render Setup** dialog box, the **Rendering Parameters** and **Filtering** rollouts will be displayed in the **ART Renderer** tab of the **Render Setup: Art Renderer** dialog box.

Changing the Background Color

Menu bar:	Rendering > Environment
Keyboard:	8

By default, the background color of the final output is black at the time of rendering. To change the background color, choose **Rendering > Environment** from the menu bar; the **Environment and Effects** dialog box will be displayed, as shown in Figure 2-46. In this dialog box, the **Environment** tab is chosen by default. The **Common Parameters**, **Exposure Control**, and **Atmosphere** rollouts will be displayed under this tab. In the **Common Parameters** rollout, the **Background** area is used to change the background color of the scene on rendering. In the **Background** area, choose the color swatch corresponding to the **Color** parameter; the **Color Selector: Background Color** dialog box will be displayed. Select a new color and choose the **OK** button. Next, close the **Environment and Effects** dialog box; the background will display the new color on rendering.

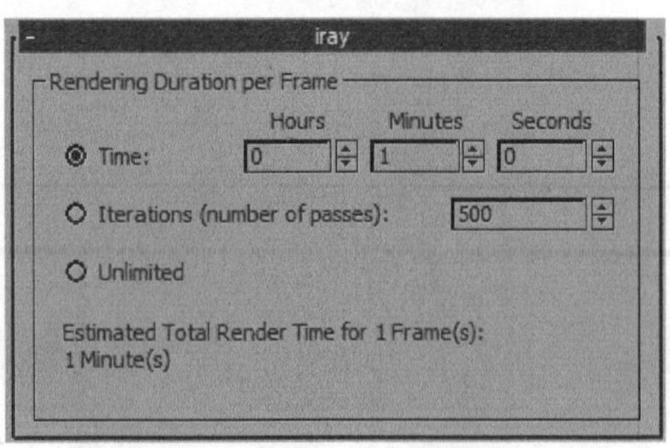

*Figure 2-45 The **iray** rollout in the **Render Setup** dialog box*

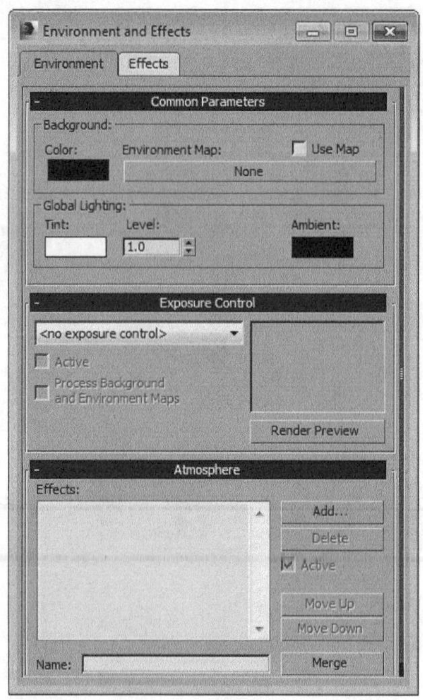

*Figure 2-46 The **Environment and Effects** dialog box*

TUTORIALS

Tutorial 1

In this tutorial, you will create 3D model of a coffee table and chairs, as shown in Figure 2-47, by using the standard primitives. **(Expected time: 30 min)**

Figure 2-47 The model of coffee table and chairs

The following steps are required to complete this tutorial:

a. Create the project folder.
b. Create top of the coffee table.
c. Create legs of the coffee table.
d. Create base of the coffee table
e. Create chairs.
f. Change background color of the scene.
g. Save and render the scene.

Creating the Project Folder

Before starting a new scene, it is recommended that you create a project folder. Creating a project folder helps you keep all the files of a project in an organized manner. Open the Windows Explorer and browse to the *Documents* folder. In this folder, create a new folder with the name *3dsmax2017*. The *3dsmax2017* folder will be the main folder and it will contain all the project folders that you will create while doing tutorials of this textbook. Now, you will create first project folder for Tutorial 1 of this chapter. To do so, you need to follow the steps given next:

1. Start Autodesk 3ds Max 2017.

2. If 3ds Max is already running, you need to reset it. To do so, choose **Reset** from the **Application** menu. If the current work is not saved, the **Autodesk 3ds Max 2017** message box is displayed. Next, choose the desired option from this message box; the **3ds Max** message box is displayed. Choose the **Yes** button from the message box; a new screen is displayed with default settings.

Note

*The **Reset** option is used to reset 3ds Max settings such as viewport configuration, snap settings, the **Material Editor** dialog box, background image, and so on. It also restores the startup defaults.*

3. Choose the **Application** button; the **Application** menu is displayed. Next, choose **Manage > Set Project Folder** from it; the **Browse For Folder** dialog box is displayed.

4. In the **Browse For Folder** dialog box, navigate to *\Documents\3dsmax2017*. Next, choose the **Make New Folder** button to create a new folder with the name *c02_tut1*. Next, choose the **OK** button to close the **Browse For Folder** dialog box.

5. Choose **Save** from the **Application** menu; the **Save File As** dialog box is displayed.

Note

*The scenes created in 3ds Max are saved with the .max extension. As the project folder is already created, the path \Documents\3dsmax2017\c02_tut1\scenes is displayed in the **Save in** drop-down list of the **Save File As** dialog box.*

Tip

*After setting the project when you open or save a scene, 3ds Max uses the **scenes** folder inside the project folder by default.*

6. Enter **c02tut1** in the **File name** edit box and then choose the **Save** button to close the dialog box.

Note

1. When you start 3ds Max, the last project that you have worked with is opened and an empty scene is created with the name Untitled.

*2. You can also save a scene in old versions (2013 to 2017) of 3ds Max. To do so, select the desired option from the **Save as type** drop-down in the **Save File As** dialog box.*

3. It is recommended that you frequently save the files while you are working on them by pressing the CTRL+S keys.

Autodesk 3ds Max creates a backup of the scene and saves changes periodically. In case of system failure, you can open the auto backup scene file and continue working on it. If you have not created the project folder on Windows 7, the default path to save the auto backup file is as follows: *C:\users\<username>\My Documents\3dsmax\autoback*. However, if you have created the project folder, the backup file will be saved in the *autoback* subfolder of the project folder. When 3ds Max is saving a file, the information, "**Autosave in progress... (Press ESC to cancel)**" is displayed in the prompt line at the bottom of the interface. If the size of the file is too large and it is taking time to save, you can press ESC to interrupt the saving process. You can also set the number of autoback files, their names, and backup time interval. To do so, choose **Customize > Preferences** from the menu bar; the **Preferences Settings** dialog box will be displayed. Next, choose the **Files** tab and then set the options as required in the **Auto Backup** area of dialog box.

Creating Top of the Coffee Table

In this section, you will create the top of the coffee table using the **Cylinder** tool and the **Tube** tool.

1. Choose **Create > Geometry** from the **Command Panel**; **Standard Primitives** is displayed in the drop-down list below the **Geometry** button. Also, the **Object Type** rollout is displayed in the **Command Panel**. Next, choose the **Tube** tool from the **Object Type** rollout.

2. Activate the Top viewport. Expand the **Keyboard Entry** rollout from the **Command Panel**. and enter the values in this rollout, as given next.

   Inner Radius : **60**　　Outer Radius : **80**　　Height: **4.2**

   Choose the **Create** button; a tube with the name *Tube001* is created in the viewports.

3. In the **Parameters** rollout, enter **48** in the **Sides** spinner; *Tube001* is displayed in the viewports, as shown in Figure 2-48.

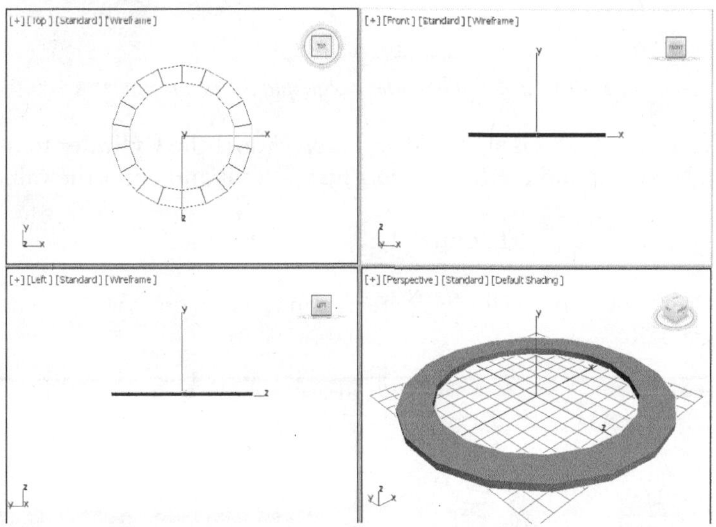

***Figure 2-48** The Tube001 displayed in viewports*

4. Choose the color swatch in the **Name and Color** rollout to change the color of *Tube001*; the **Object Color** dialog box is displayed. Now, using this dialog box, modify the color of *Tube001* to light brown.

5. Create another tube in the Top viewport by using the method described earlier. Enter the following values in the **Keyboard Entry** rollout:

   Z: **-0.5**　　Inner Radius : **60**　　Outer Radius . **40**
   Height: **4.2**

   Tube002 is displayed in the viewports, refer to Figure 2-49. In the **Parameters** rollout, enter **48** in the **Sides** spinner. Also, change the color of *Tube002* to light brown.

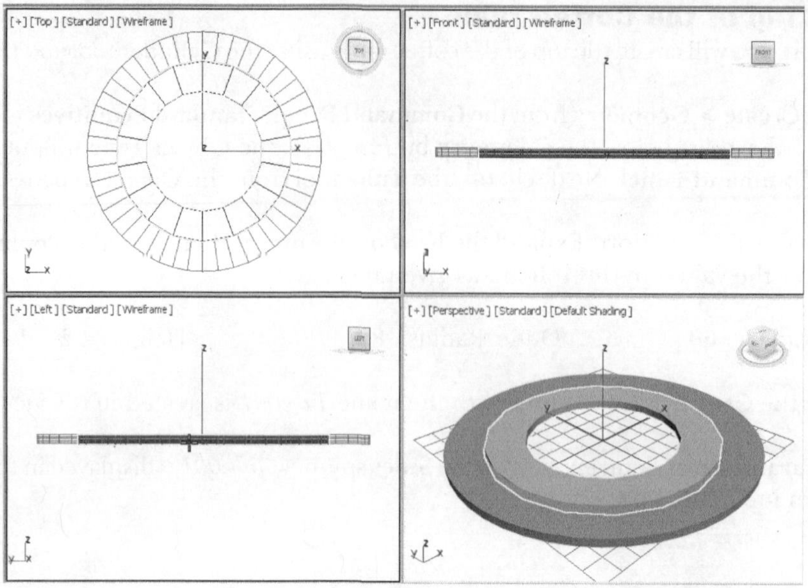

Figure 2-49 The Tube002 displayed in viewports

6. Make sure the Top viewport is activated and then choose the **Cylinder** tool from the **Object Type** rollout. Next, expand the **Keyboard Entry** rollout and enter the values as given next:

   Radius: **40** Height: **4.2**

   Choose the **Create** button; a cylinder is created in the viewports with the name *Cylinder001*, refer to Figure 2-50.

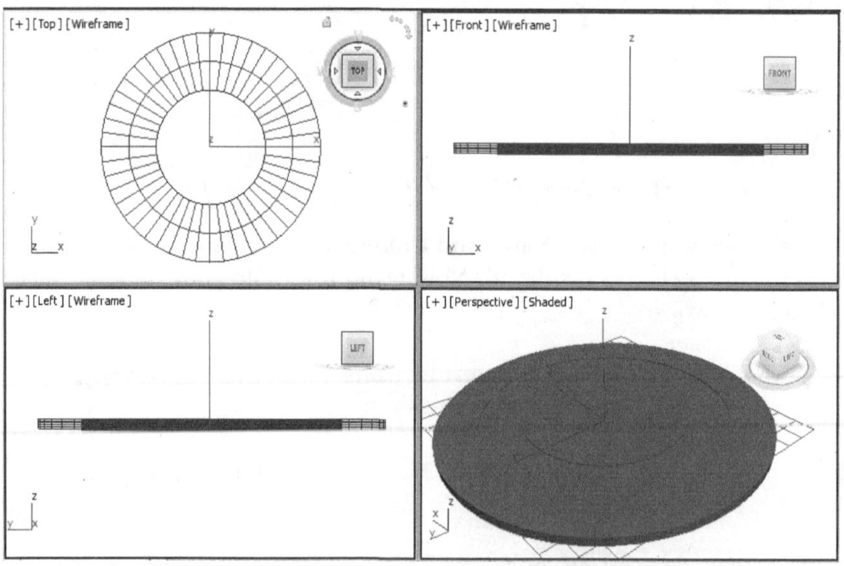

Figure 2-50 The Cylinder001 displayed in the viewports

7. In the **Parameters** rollout, enter **48** in the **Sides** spinner. Also, change the color of *Cylinder001* to light brown.

8. Select *Tube001*, *Tube002*, and *Cylinder001* from the Scene Explorer and right-click; a quad menu is displayed. Choose **Add Selection To > New Group** from it; the **Group** dialog box is displayed. Enter **top** in this dialog box and choose **OK**; the *top* group is created with 3 objects in it.

Creating the Legs of the Coffee Table

In this section, you will create a leg of the table using the **Cylinder** tool and then clone it to create remaining legs..

1. Create cylinder in the Top viewport and enter the following values in the **Parameters** rollout:

   Radius: **5**　　　　　　Height: **150**

2. In the **Name and Color** rollout, enter **leg001** and press ENTER; the object is renamed. Next, change the color of *leg001* to light brown.

3. Align *leg001* with *Tube001* in viewports using the **Select and Move** tool, as shown in Figure 2-51.

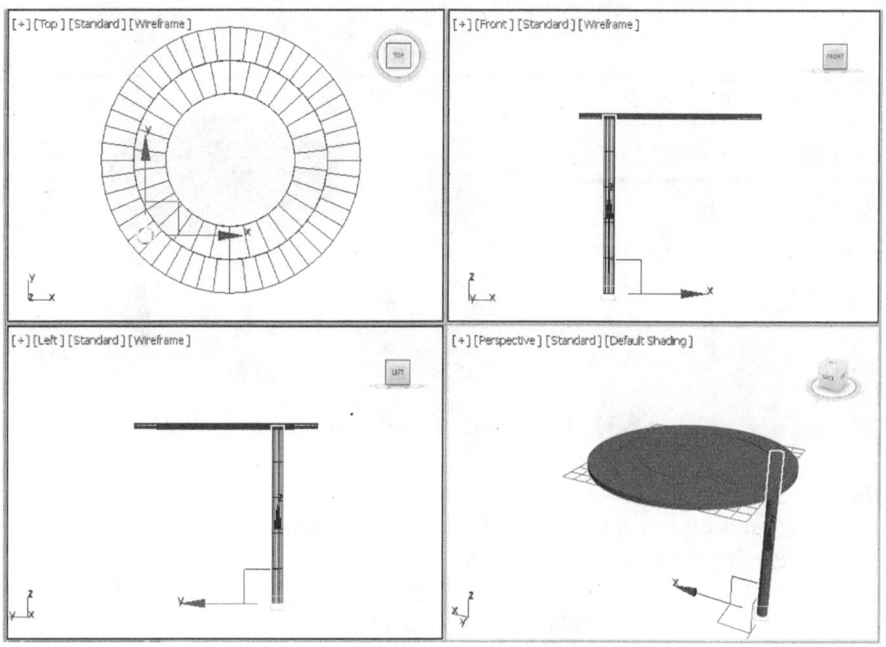

Figure 2-51 *The leg001 aligned in viewports*

Next, you will create copies of *leg001*.

4. Activate the Top viewport and make sure *leg001* is selected. Next, move the cursor over the Y axis, press and hold the SHIFT key, and drag *leg001* upward. Now, release the left mouse button and the SHIFT key; the **Clone Options** dialog box is displayed, as shown in Figure 2-52.

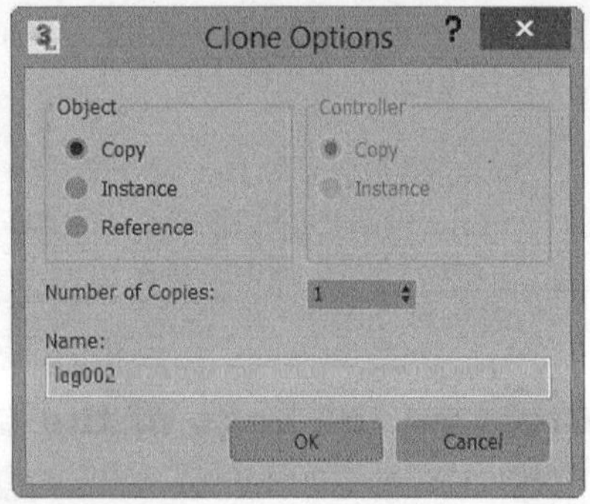

*Figure 2-52 The **Clone Options** dialog box*

5. Make sure the **Copy** radio button is selected in the **Object** area and 1 is displayed in the **Number of Copies** spinner of the **Clone Options** dialog box. Next, choose the **OK** button; *leg002* is created. Align *leg002* in the viewports, as shown in Figure 2-53.

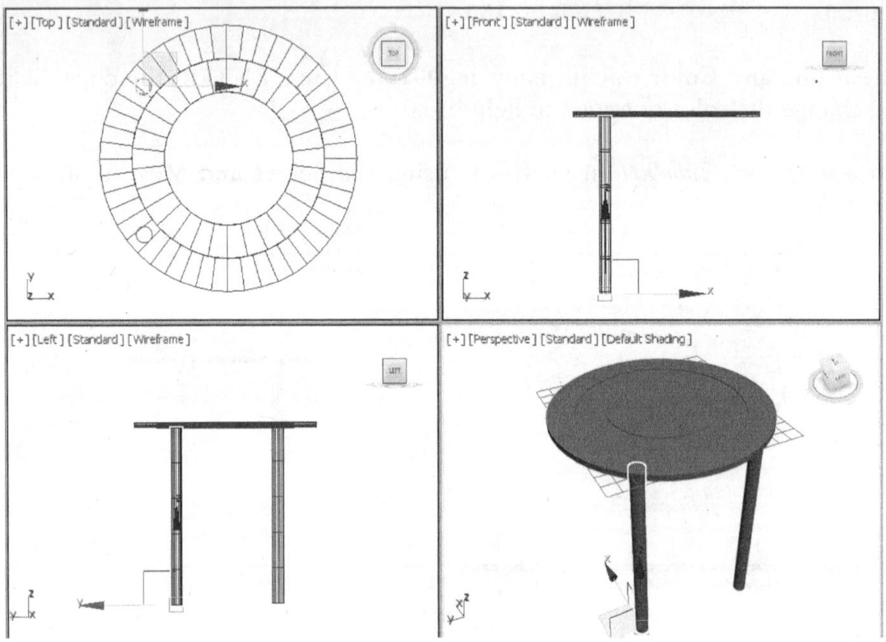

Figure 2-53 The leg002 created after cloning leg001

Note

1. The cloned objects when created, if are not named, get automatically named in a sequence starting from the original object.

2. You can also clone an object by holding the SHIFT key while rotating or scaling it.

6. Select *leg001* and *leg002* from the Scene Explorer. In the Top viewport, move the cursor over the X axis, press and hold the SHIFT key, and drag *leg001* and *leg002* toward right until the value in the **X** spinner of the Coordinate display at the bottom of the screen becomes around **106**. Release the left mouse button and the SHIFT key; the **Clone Options** dialog box is displayed.

7. Make sure the **Copy** radio button is selected in the **Object** area and 1 is displayed in the **Number of Copies** spinner of the **Clone Options** dialog box. Next, choose the **OK** button; *leg003* and *leg004* are created, refer to Figure 2-54.

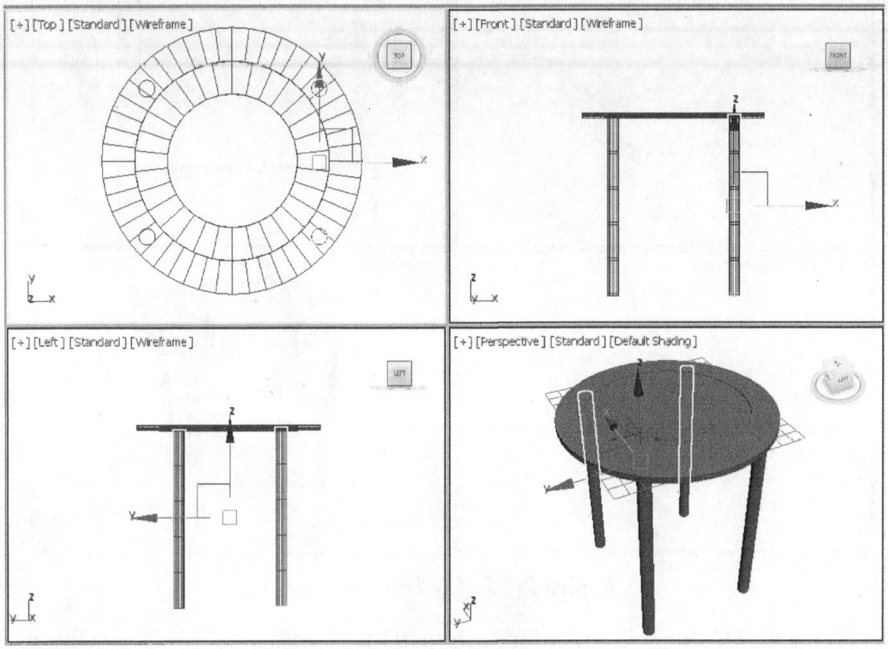

Figure 2-54 *The leg003 and leg004 created*

8. Select *leg001*, *leg002*, *leg003*, and *leg004* from the Scene Explorer and group them under the name *legs* as discussed earlier.

Creating Base of the Coffee Table

In this section, you will create base of the table by using the **Cylinder** tool.

1. Make sure the Top viewport is activated and then choose the **Cylinder** tool from the **Object Type** rollout. Next, expand the **Keyboard Entry** rollout and enter the values as given next:

   Z: **-125** Radius: **60** Height: **4.2**

   Choose the **Create** button; a cylinder is created in the viewports with the name *Cylinder002*.

2. Rename it as *base01* and assign light brown color to it, refer to Figure 2-55.

   Next, you will create supports for *base01*.

3. Activate the Front viewport. Next, choose the **Cylinder** tool from the **Object Type** rollout.

4. Expand the **Keyboard Entry** rollout and enter the values as given next:

   Radius: **4** Height: **140**

Choose the **Create** button; a cylinder is created in the viewports with the name *Cylinder002*.

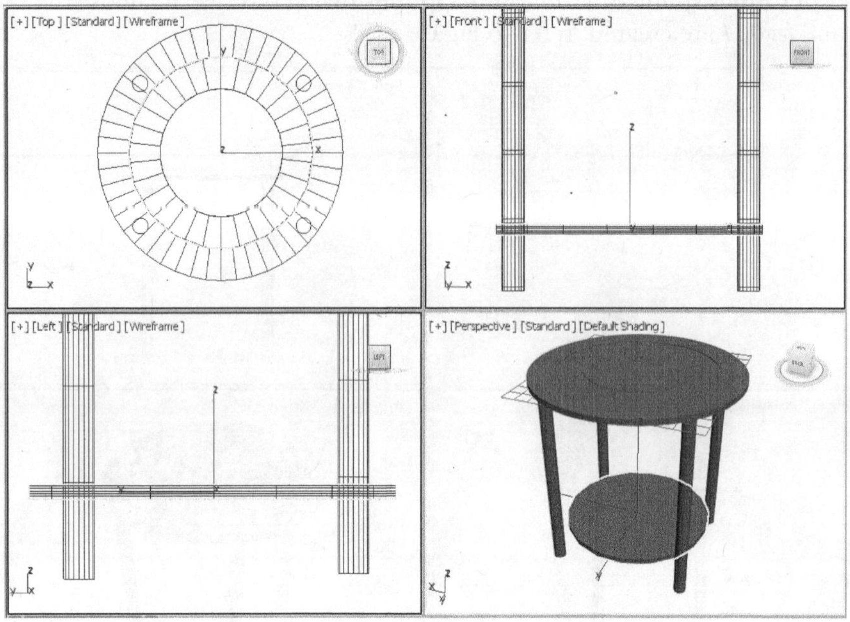

Figure 2-55 *The base01 created*

5. In the **Name and Color** rollout, enter **support01** and press ENTER; the cylinder is named as *support01*. Also, change the color of *support01* to light brown.

6. Align *support01* using the **Select and Move** and **Select and Rotate** tools from the **Main Toolbar**, as shown in Figure 2-56.

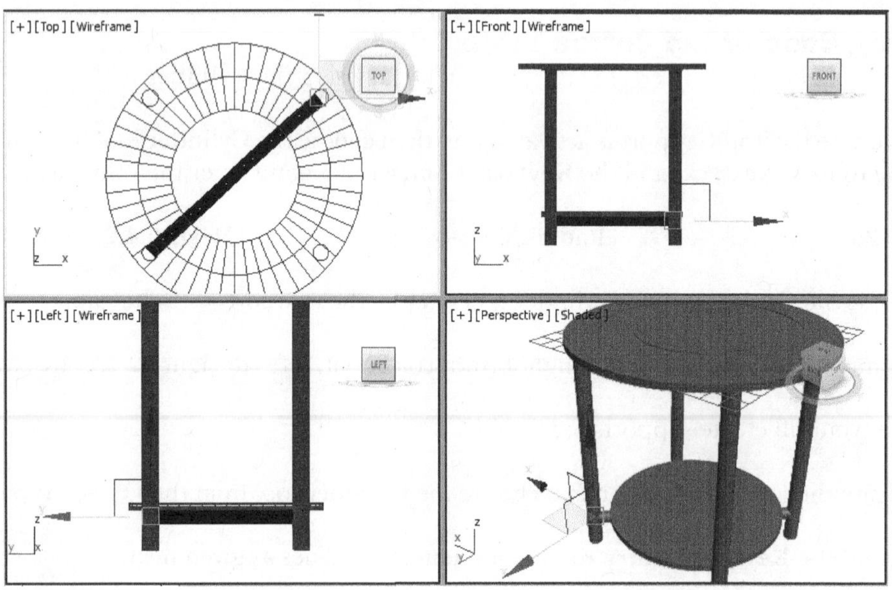

Figure 2-56 *Alignment of support01 in viewports*

7. In the Top viewport, copy *support01* by using the **Clone Options** dialog box as described earlier; *support002* is created. Now, align it with *base01* using the **Select and Move** and **Select and Rotate** tools, refer to Figure 2-57.

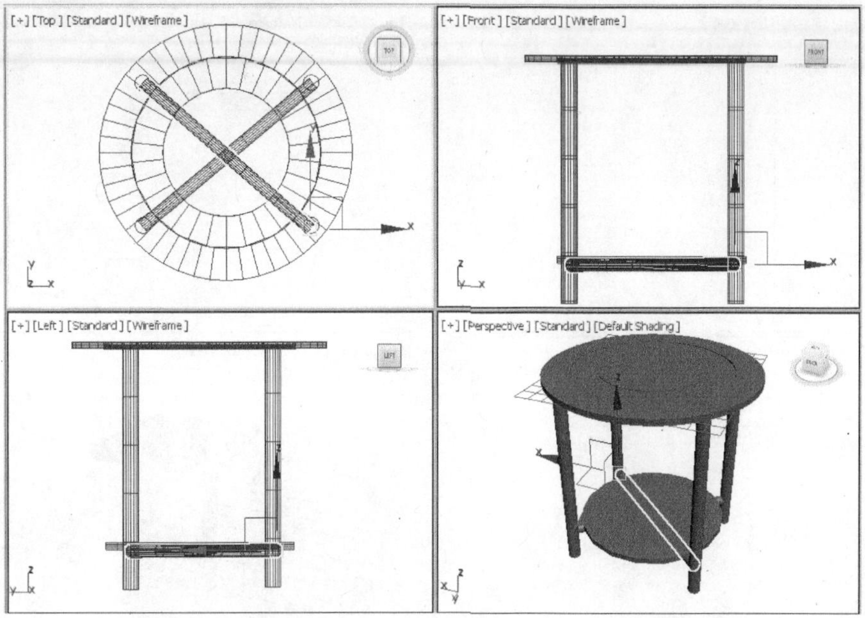

***Figure 2-57** Alignment of support002 with base01*

8. Select *base01*, *support01*, and *support002* from the Scene Explorer and group them under the name *base* as discussed earlier.

9. Select *base*, *top*, and *legs* groups from the Scene Explorer and group them under the name *table* as discussed earlier.

Creating Chair

In this section, you will create chair using the **Box** tool.

1. Select *table* from the Scene Explorer and right-click; a quad menu is displayed. Choose **Hide Selection** from it; *table* is hidden.

2. Activate the Top viewport. Next, choose the **Box** tool from the **Object Type** rollout and create a box. Now, choose the **Modify** tab from the **Command Panel**.

3. Rename the box as *base*. In the **Parameters** rollout, enter the values as given next:

   Length: **60** Width: **58** Height: **5**

   Next, you will create legs of the chair.

4. Repeat step 2 to create one more box. In the **Parameters** rollout, enter the values as given next:

Length: **5** Width: **5** Height: **55**

5. Rename the box as *leg01*. Next, align *leg01* with *base,* as shown in Figure 2-58.

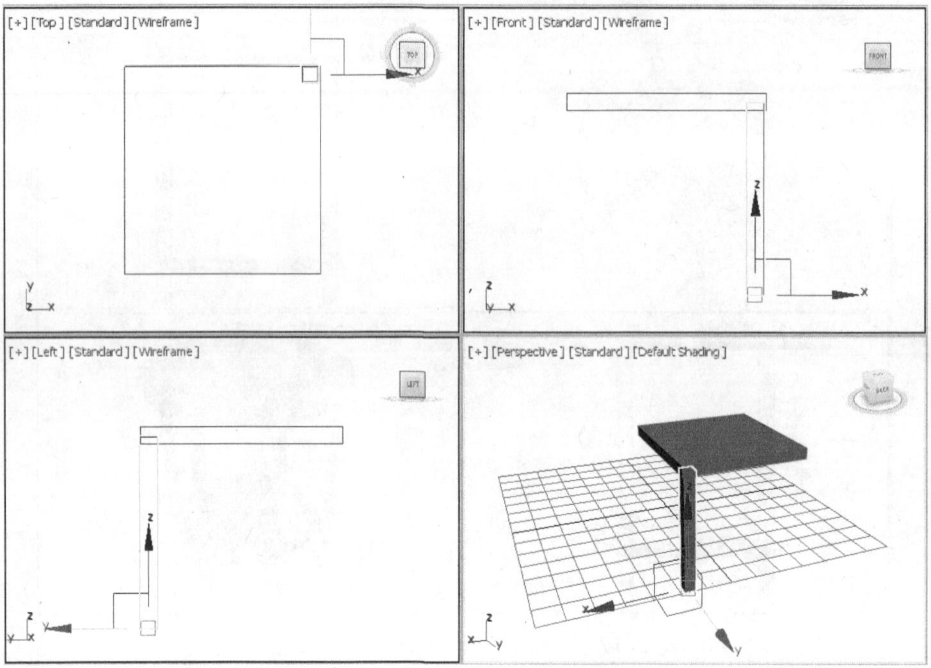

Figure 2-58 *Alignment of leg01 with base*

6. Create 3 copies of *leg01* as discussed earlier and align them, as shown in Figure 2-59.

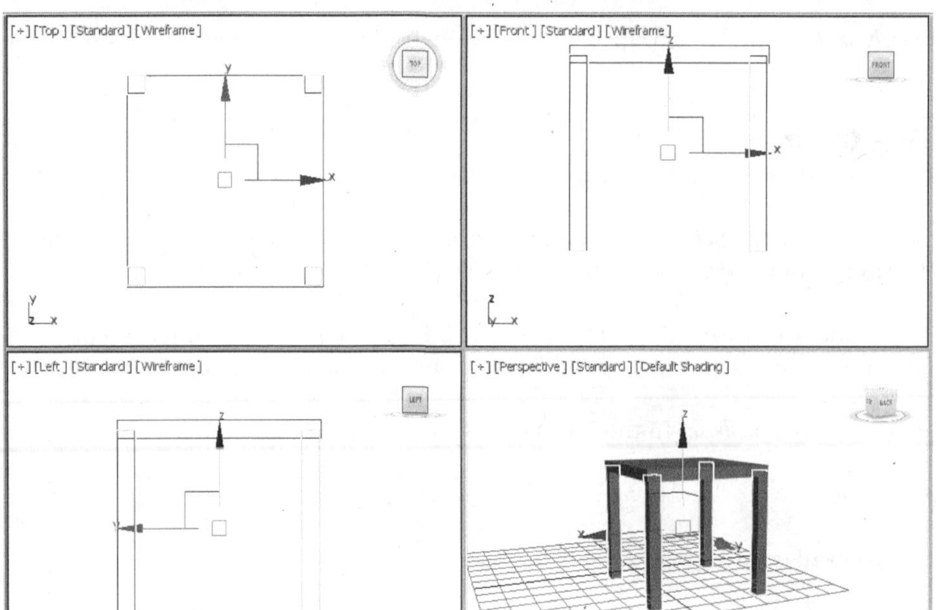

Figure 2-59 *Alignment of legs with base*

7. Select all the legs from the Scene Explorer and group them with the name *legs*.

   Next, you will create back of the chair.

8. Activate the Front viewport. Next, choose the **Box** tool from the **Object Type** rollout and create a box. Now, choose the **Modify** tab from the **Command Panel**.

9. In the **Parameters** rollout, enter the values as given next:

   Length : **9.5**   Width : **65**

10. Rename the created object as *back1*. Next, align it with *base*, refer to Figure 2-60.

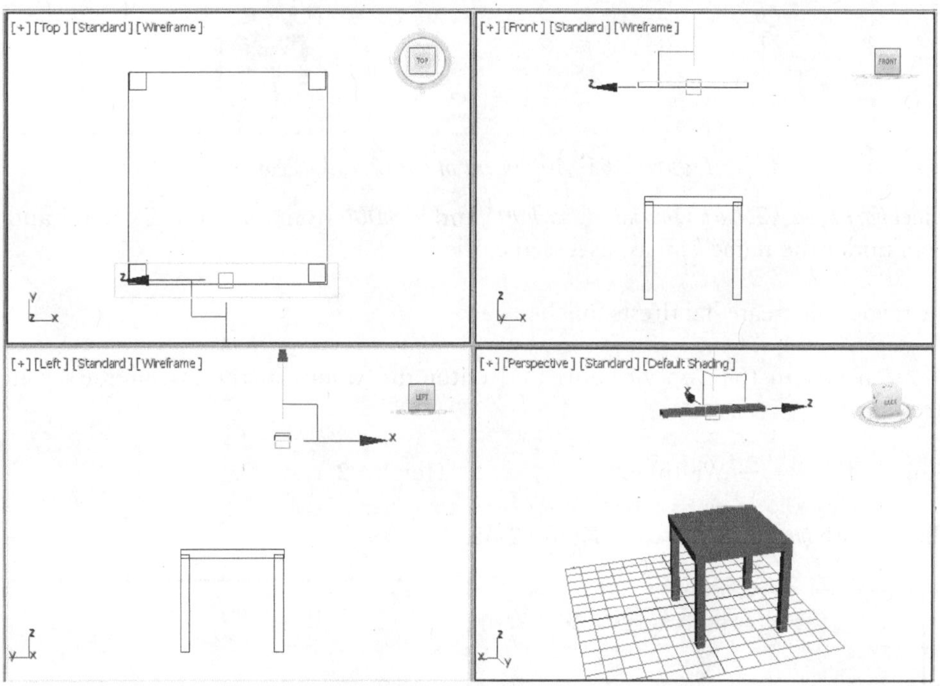

Figure 2-60 *Alignment of back1 with base*

   Note that you may need to adjust the position of *back1* at the time of alignment of objects in step 14.

11. Repeat step 8 to create one more box.

12. In the **Parameters** rollout, enter the values as given next:

   Length : **62**   Width : **5.5**   Height: **3.5**

13. Rename it as *back2*. Next, create 4 copies of *back2* and align them with *base* using the **Select and Move** and **Select and Rotate** tools, refer to Figure 2-61. Also, align *back1* with all these parts, as shown in Figure 2-61.

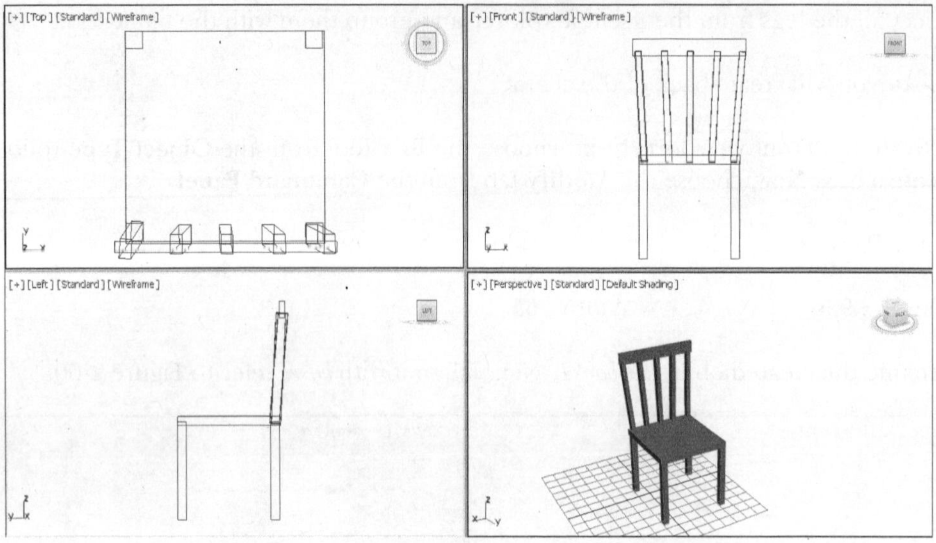

Figure 2-61 *Alignment of back2 and its copies*

14. Select *back1*, *back2*, *back3*, *back004*, *back005* and *back006* from the Scene Explorer and group them under the name *back* as discussed earlier.

    Next, you will create handrests for the chair.

15. Create a box in the Top viewport and enter the values in the **Parameters** rollout, as given next:

    Length: **45** Width: **5.2** Height: **2**

    Align it with *back2*, as shown in Figure 2-62.

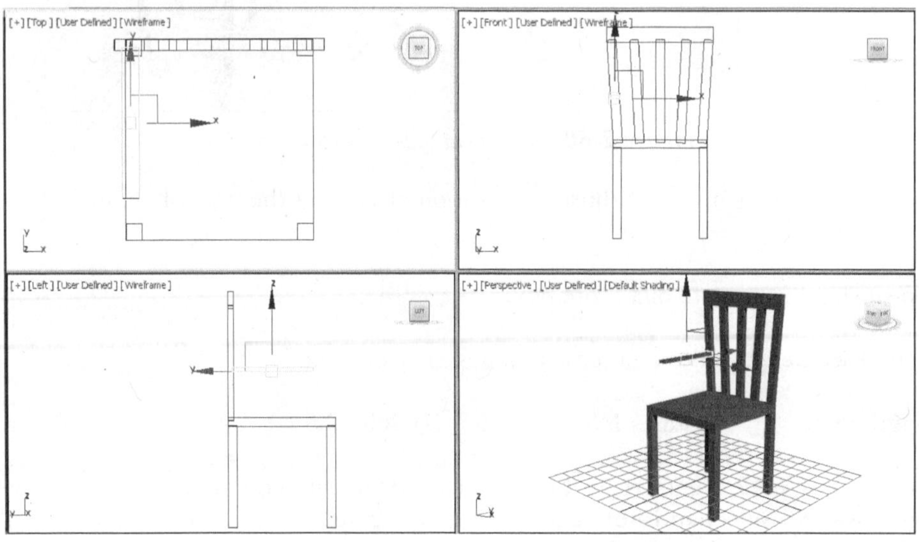

Figure 2-62 *Alignment of box with back2*

16. Create one more box in the Top viewport and enter the values in the **Parameters** rollout, as given next and then align it with the box created in step 16, as shown in Figure 2-63:

    Length: **25** Width: **5.2** Height: **2**

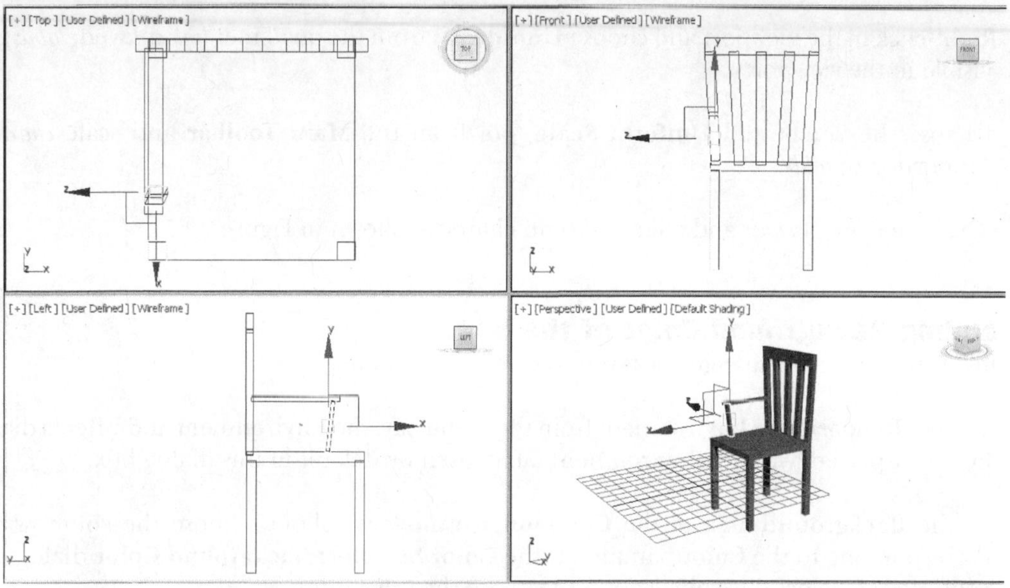

Figure 2-63 *Alignment of box in the viewports*

17. Create a copy of both the boxes created above and align them with *base,* as shown in Figure 2-64.

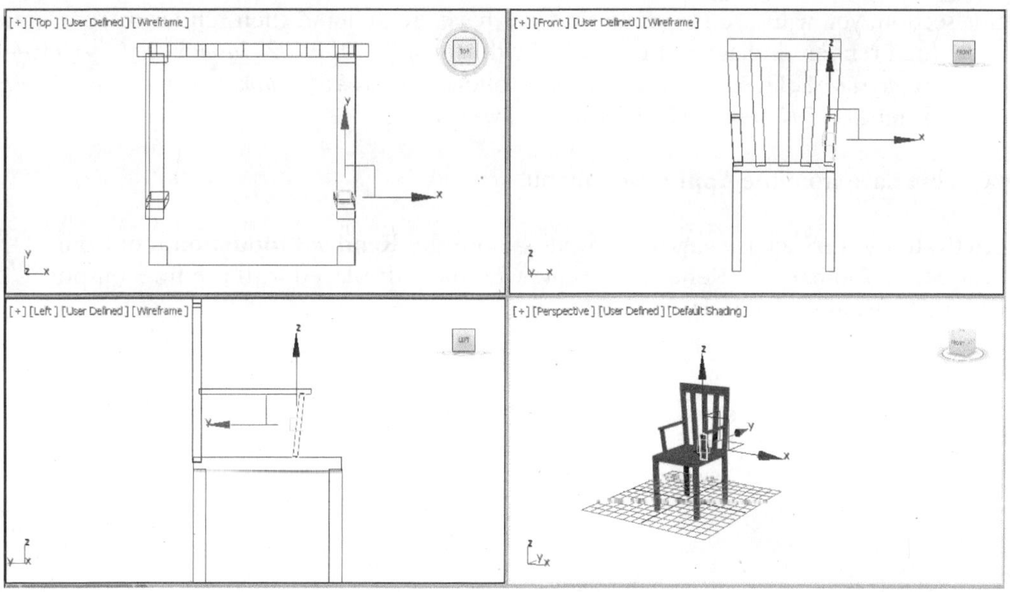

Figure 2-64 *Alignment of boxes in the viewports*

18. Create a group of four boxes created in above steps under the name *handrest.*

19. Select *back, base, legs,* and *handrest* from the Scene Explorer and group them with the name *chair.*

20. Right-click in the viewport and choose **Unhide All** from the quad menu displayed; *table* gets visible in the viewports.

21. Choose the **Select and Uniform Scale** tool from the **Main Toolbar** and scale *chair* in proportion to *table.*

22. Create a copy of *chair* and align *table* and chairs, as shown in Figure 2-65.

Changing Background Color of the Scene

In this section, you will change background color of the scene.

1. Choose **Rendering > Environment** from the menu bar; the **Environment and Effects** dialog box is displayed with the **Environment** tab chosen by default in this dialog box.

2. In the **Background** area of the **Common Parameters** rollout, choose the color swatch corresponding to the **Color** parameter; the **Color Selector: Background Color** dialog box is displayed. Select the white color and choose the **OK** button.

3. Close the **Environment and Effects** dialog box.

Saving and Rendering the Scene

In this section, you will save the scene that you have created and then render it. You can also view the final rendered image of this model by downloading the *c02_3dsmax_2017_rndr.zip* file from *www.cadcim.com.* The path of the file is as follows: *Textbooks > Animation and Visual Effects > 3ds Max > Autodesk 3ds Max 2017: A Comprehensive Guide*

1. Choose **Save** from the **Application** menu.

2. Activate the Perspective viewport. Next, choose the **Render Production** tool from the **Main Toolbar**; the **Rendered Frame** window is displayed with the final output of the table, as shown in Figure 2-65.

Figure 2-65 The final output after rendering

Tutorial 2

In this tutorial, you will create 3D model of a park bench, as shown in Figure 2-66, using the standard primitives. **(Expected time: 90 min)**

The following steps are required to complete this tutorial:

a. Create the project folder.
b. Create horizontal back supports.
c. Group horizontal back supports.
d. Create horizontal seat supports.
e. Group horizontal Seat Supports
f. Create vertical back supports.
g. Create rivets for the horizontal back support.
h. Align rivets .
i. Create right side rivets.
j. Rotate the back support.
k. Create leg supports.
l. Create rivets for the seat support.
m. Create legs of the park bench.
n. Save and render the scene.

Figure 2-66 The model of a park bench

Creating the Project Folder

Create a new project folder with the name *c02_tut2* at *\Documents\3dsmax2017* and then save the file with the name *c02tut2*, as discussed in Tutorial 1.

Creating Horizontal Back Supports

In this section, you need to create horizontal back supports of the park bench.

1. Activate the Top viewport. Choose **Create > Geometry** in the **Command Panel**; **Standard Primitives** is displayed in the drop-down list. Next, choose the **Box** tool from the **Object Type** rollout; various rollouts are displayed in the **Command Panel**.

2. Expand the **Keyboard Entry** rollout and set the values as given below:

   Length: **1.5** Width: **124** Height: **6.03**

3. Choose the **Create** button from the **Keyboard Entry** rollout; a box is created in the viewports, refer to Figure 2-67

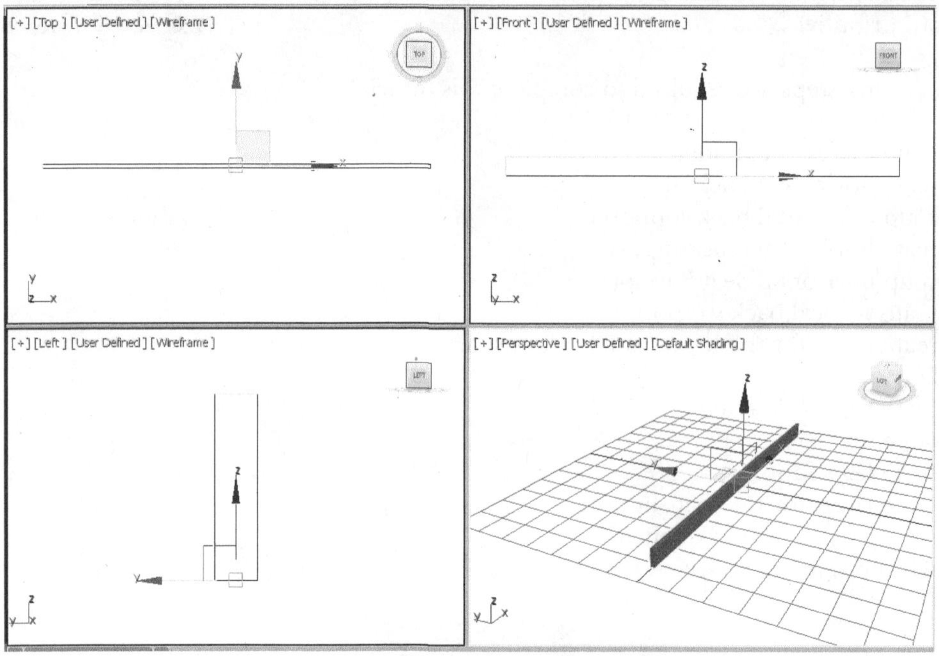

***Figure 2-67** A box created*

4. In the **Name and Color** rollout, name the box as *horizontal back support001* and press the ENTER key.

5. Choose the color swatch from the **Name and Color** rollout; the **Object Color** dialog box is displayed. Now, using this dialog box, modify the color of *horizontal back support001* to light brown. Choose the **OK** button to close the **Object Color** dialog box.

Next, you need to create copies of *horizontal back support001*.

6. Activate the Front viewport. Choose the **Select and Move** tool from the **Main Toolbar** and make sure that *horizontal back support001* is selected. Next, move the cursor over the Y axis. Press and hold the SHIFT key and the left mouse button. Now, drag *horizontal back support001* upward until the value in the **Y** spinner in the Coordinate display becomes around **8.0**. Release the left mouse button and the SHIFT key; the **Clone Options** dialog box is displayed. 

7. In the **Clone Options** dialog box, make sure the **Copy** radio button is selected. Set the value in the **Number of Copies** spinner to **4**. Choose the **OK** button; four boxes having same dimensions are created and are automatically named as *horizontal back support002*, *horizontal back support003*, *horizontal back support004*, and *horizontal back support005*.

8. Choose the **Zoom Extents All** tool from the viewport navigation controls; the horizontal back supports are displayed in the viewports, as shown in Figure 2-68. 

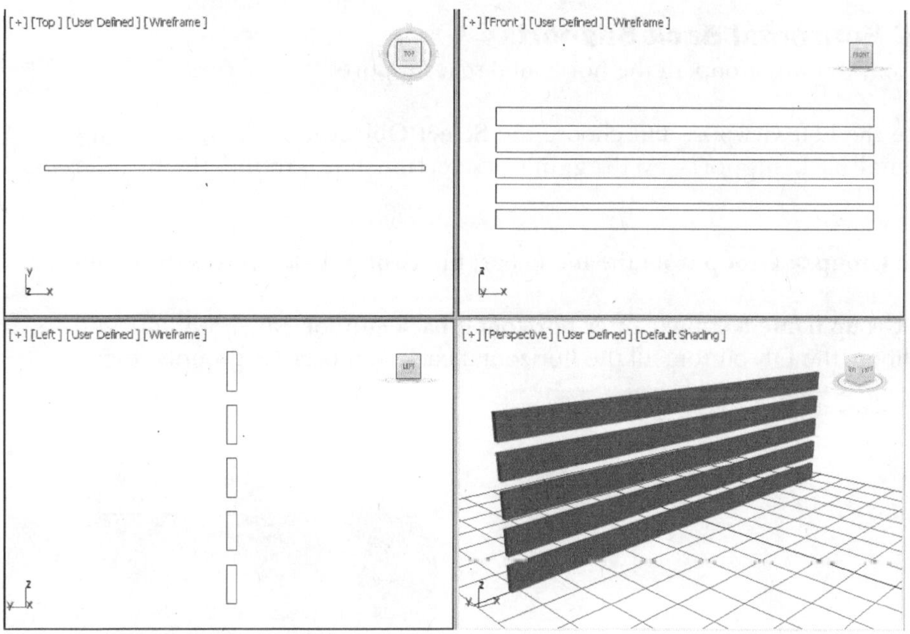

Figure 2-68 *Horizontal back supports displayed in viewports*

Next, you need to rotate *horizontal back support005*.

9. Activate the Left viewport and select *horizontal bach support005*. Next, right-click on the **Select and Rotate** tool in the **Main Toolbar**; the **Rotate Transform Type-In** dialog box is displayed. 

10. In the **Absolute:World** area, set the value **-10** in the **X** spinner, as shown in Figure 2-69 and then press the ENTER key; *horizontal back support005* gets rotated, refer to Figure 2-70. Now, close the **Rotate Transform Type-In** dialog box.

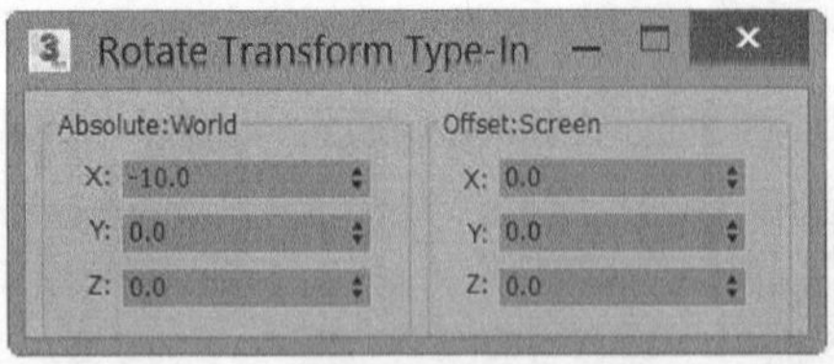

***Figure 2-69** The **Rotate Transform Type-In** dialog box*

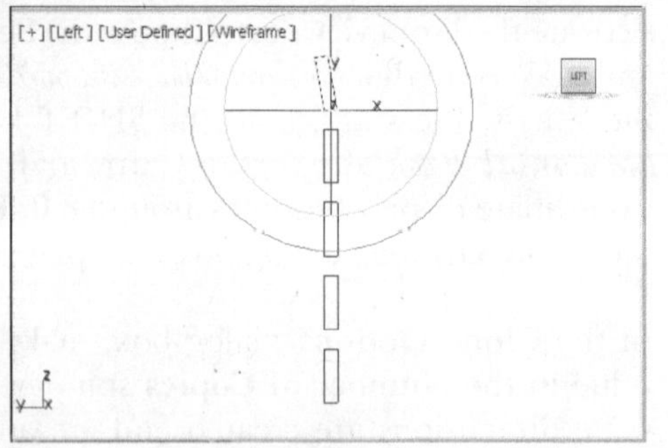

***Figure 2-70** The horizontal back support005 geometry after being rotated in the Left viewport*

11. Click anywhere in the viewport to deselect *horizontal back support005*.

Grouping Horizontal Back Supports

In this section, you will group all the horizontal seat supports.

1. Activate the Left viewport and choose the **Select Object** tool. Now, select all the horizontal back supports by dragging a selection box around them, refer to Figure 2-71.

2. Choose **Group > Group** from the menu bar; the **Group** dialog box is displayed.

3. In the **Group name** text box, enter **horizontal back support**, as shown in Figure 2-72 and then choose the **OK** button; all the horizontal back supports are grouped together.

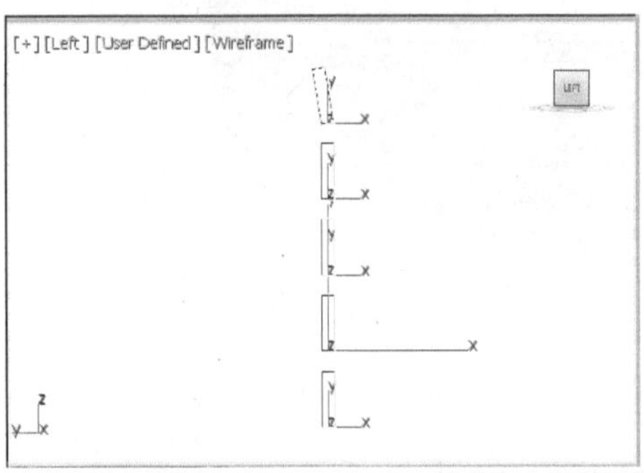

***Figure 2-71** All horizontal back supports selected simultaneously*

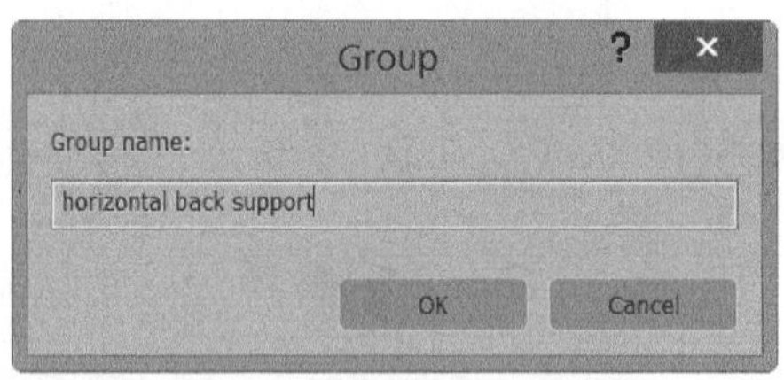

***Figure 2-72** The **Group** dialog box*

Creating Horizontal Seat Supports

In this section, you will create horizontal seat supports.

1. Activate the Top viewport and choose the **Box** tool from the **Object Type** rollout.

2. Expand the **Keyboard Entry** rollout and set the values as follows:

   Length: **6.03** Width: **124** Height: **1.5**

3. Choose the **Create** button from the **Keyboard Entry** rollout; a box is created in the viewports.

4. In the **Name and Color** rollout, name the box as *horizontal seat support001*.

5. Use the color swatch to assign the same color to *horizontal seat support001* that you assigned to *horizontal back support*.

6. Choose the **Select and Move** tool from the **Main Toolbar** and align *horizontal seat support001* with *horizontal back support* in the viewports, refer to Figure 2-73.

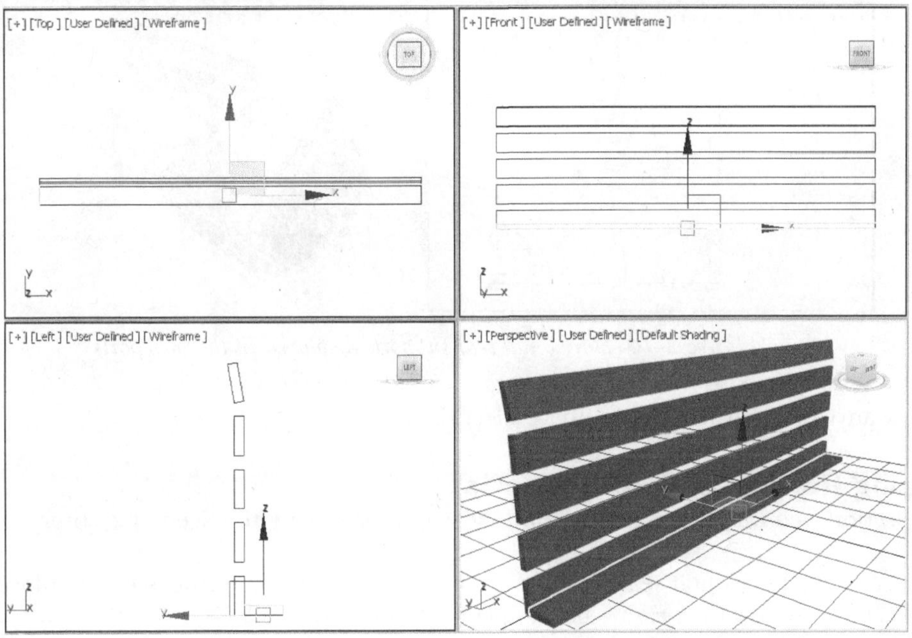

Figure 2-73 *Alignment of horizontal seat support001 in viewports*

Next, you need to create four copies of *horizontal seat support001*.

7. Activate the Top viewport and make sure *horizontal seat support001* is selected. Next, place the cursor over the vertical axis. Press and hold the SHIFT key and drag *horizontal seat support001* downward until the value in the **Y** spinner in the Coordinate display becomes around **-7.5**. Release the left mouse button and the SHIFT key; the **Clone Options** dialog box is displayed.

8. In the **Clone Options** dialog box, make sure the **Copy** radio button is selected. Set the value in the **Number of Copies** spinner to **4** and choose the **OK** button; four boxes having same dimensions are created and are automatically named as *horizontal seat support002*, *horizontal seat support003*, *horizontal seat support004*, and *horizontal seat support005*.

9. Choose the **Zoom Extents All** tool; all the objects are displayed in the viewports, as shown in Figure 2-74.

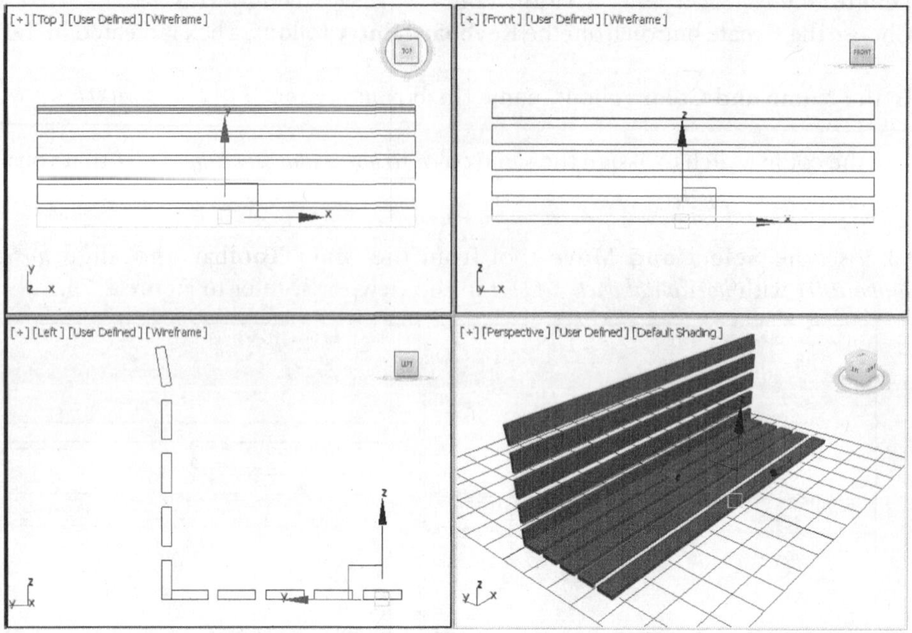

Figure 2-74 Horizontal seat supports displayed in the viewports

10. Click anywhere in the viewport to deselect the objects.

Grouping Horizontal Seat Supports

In this section, you will group all horizontal seat supports using the Scene Explorer.

1. Select all the horizontal seat supports from the list displayed in the Scene Explorer using the CTRL key and then right-click; a quad menu is displayed.

2. Choose **Add Selected to > New Group** from this quad menu; the **Group** dialog box is displayed.

3. In the **Group name** text box, enter **horizontal seat support** and then choose the **OK** button.

Creating Vertical Back Supports

In this section, you will create vertical back supports of the park bench.

1. Activate the Top viewport. Choose **Create > Geometry** in the **Command Panel**; **Standard Primitives** is displayed in the drop-down list. Next, choose the **Cylinder** tool in the **Object Type** rollout.

2. In the **Keyboard Entry** rollout, set the values as follows:

   X: **-60** Y: **1.5** Z: **0.0**
   Radius: **1.0** Height: **38.0**

3. Now, choose the **Create** button in the **Keyboard Entry** rollout; a cylinder is created in the viewports, as shown in Figure 2-75.

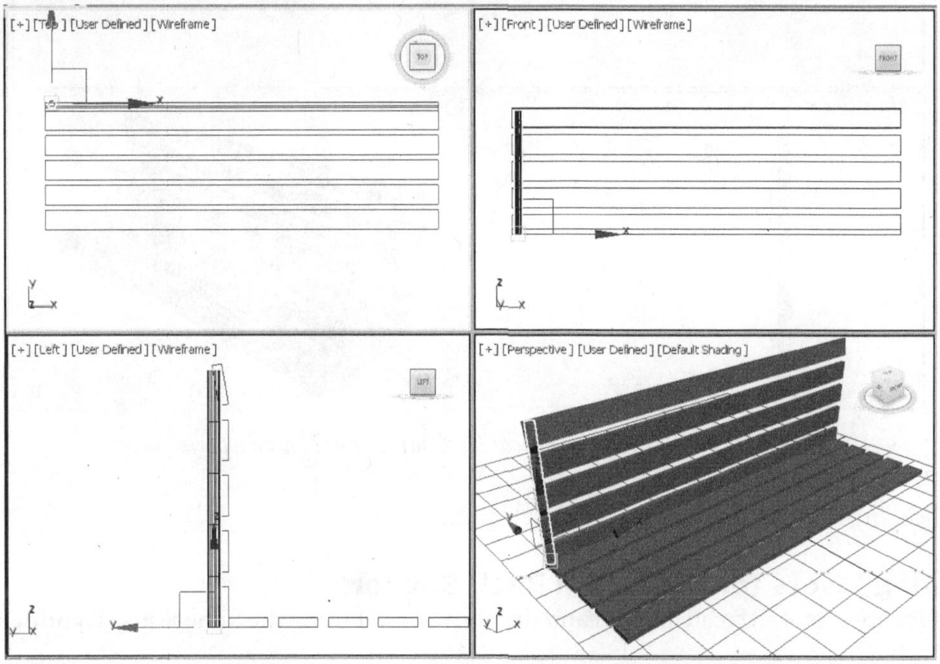

Figure 2-75 *The vertical back support001 geometry in viewports*

4. In the **Name and Color** rollout, name the cylinder as *vertical back support001* and press the ENTER key.

5. Change the color of *vertical back support001* to black.

   Next, you need to create a copy of *vertical back support001*.

6. Activate the Front viewport by middle-clicking in it. Choose the **Select and Move** tool and move the cursor over the horizontal axis. Press and hold the SHIFT key and the left mouse button, and then drag *vertical back support001* to the right side to align it on the right side of *horizontal back support*, as shown in Figure 2-76. Release the left mouse button and the SHIFT key; the **Clone Options** dialog box is displayed.

7. In the **Clone Options** dialog box, make sure the **Copy** radio button is selected and 1 is displayed in the **Number of Copies** spinner. Next, choose the **OK** button; *vertical back support002* is created having same dimensions as *vertical back support001*, refer to Figure 2-76.

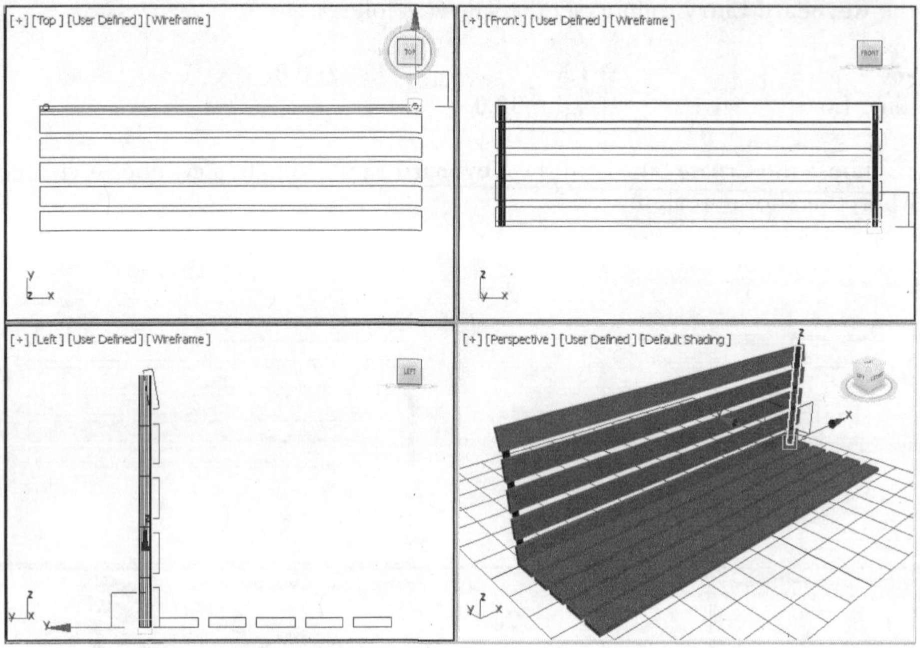

Figure 2-76 The vertical back support002 in viewports

8. Click anywhere in the viewport to deselect the objects.

Creating Rivets for Horizontal Back Support

In this section, you will create the cap and the body of rivet using the **Sphere** and **Cylinder** tools.

1. Activate the Top viewport and choose **Create > Geometry** in the **Command Panel**; **Standard Primitives** is displayed in the drop-down list. Next, choose the **Sphere** tool in the **Object Type** rollout.

2. In the **Keyboard Entry** rollout, set the value **0.8** in the **Radius** spinner and choose the **Create** button; a sphere is created.

3. In the **Parameters** rollout, make sure that the **Smooth** check box and the **Chop** radio button are selected. Enter the value **0.5** in the **Hemisphere** spinner.

4. Name the sphere as **cap** and assign black color to it.

   Next, you need to create a cylinder for the body of the rivet.

5. In the **Command Panel**, choose **Create > Geometry > Standard Primitives**. Next, choose the **Cylinder** tool from the **Object Type** rollout.

6. In the **Keyboard Entry** rollout, set the values as follows:

   X: **0** Y: **0** Z: **0**

Radius: **0.241** Height: **3.5**

7. Choose the **Create** button from the **Keyboard Entry** rollout; a cylinder is created.

8. Name the cylinder as **body** and assign black color to it.

9. Activate the Left viewport and select *cap* and *body* simultaneously from the Scene Explorer by holding the CTRL key; *cap* and *body* are selected in the viewports.

10. Choose the **Zoom Extents All Selected** tool to increase the magnification of the selected objects in the viewports. 

11. Next, align *cap* and *body* of the rivet in the Left viewport using the **Select and Move** tool, as shown in Figure 2-77.

Note
You may need to use the ***Zoom*** *and* ***Pan View*** *tools to align cap and body of the rivet.*

Next, you need to group *body* and *cap* to create the rivet.

12. Select *cap* and *body* of the rivet in the Scene Explorer and group them as *rivet001*.

13. Choose the **Zoom Extents All** tool and move *rivet001* in the Left viewport to visualize it properly, as shown in Figure 2-78.

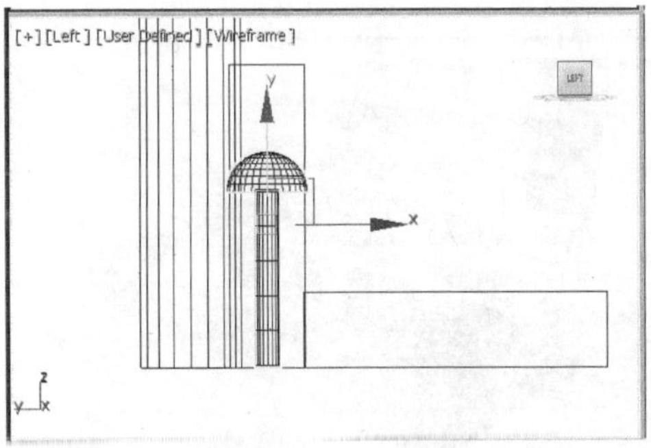

Figure 2-77 *Alignment of cap and body*

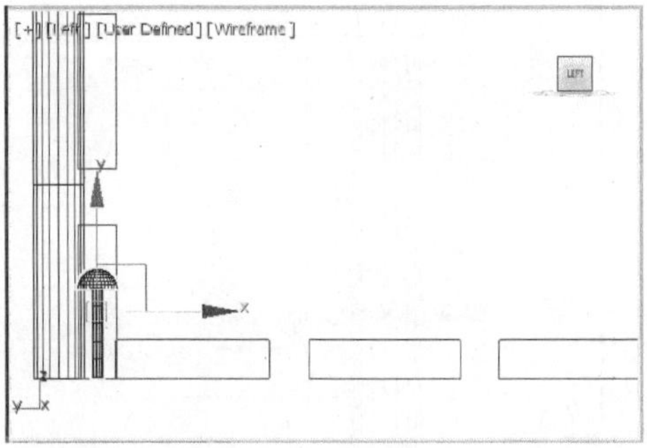

Figure 2-78 *The rivet001 group in the Left viewport*

Aligning Rivets

In this section, you will align the rivets.

1. In the Left viewport, select *rivet001* and right-click on the **Select and Rotate** tool; the **Rotate Transform Type-In** dialog box is displayed. Also, a circular gizmo along with the X, Y, and Z axes is displayed. 

2. In the **Offset:Screen** area of the **Rotate Transform Type-In** dialog box, enter **-90** in the **Z** spinner and press ENTER; *rivet001* gets rotated, as shown in Figure 2-79. Now, close the **Rotate Transform Type-In** dialog box.

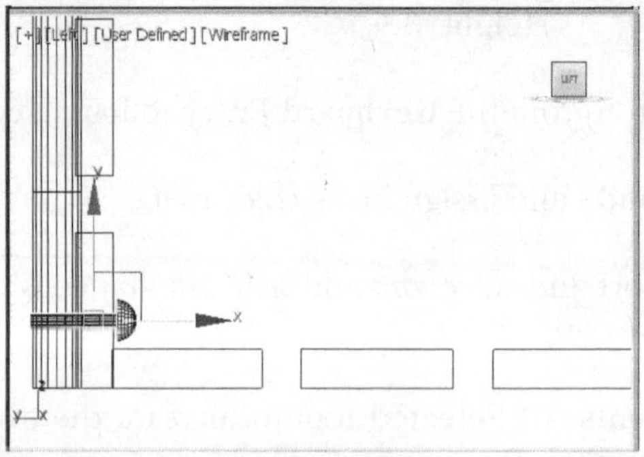

Figure 2-79 Rotating rivet001 in the Left viewport

3. Choose the **Select and Move** tool and align *rivet001* with *horizontal back support* in the viewports, as shown in Figure 2-80.

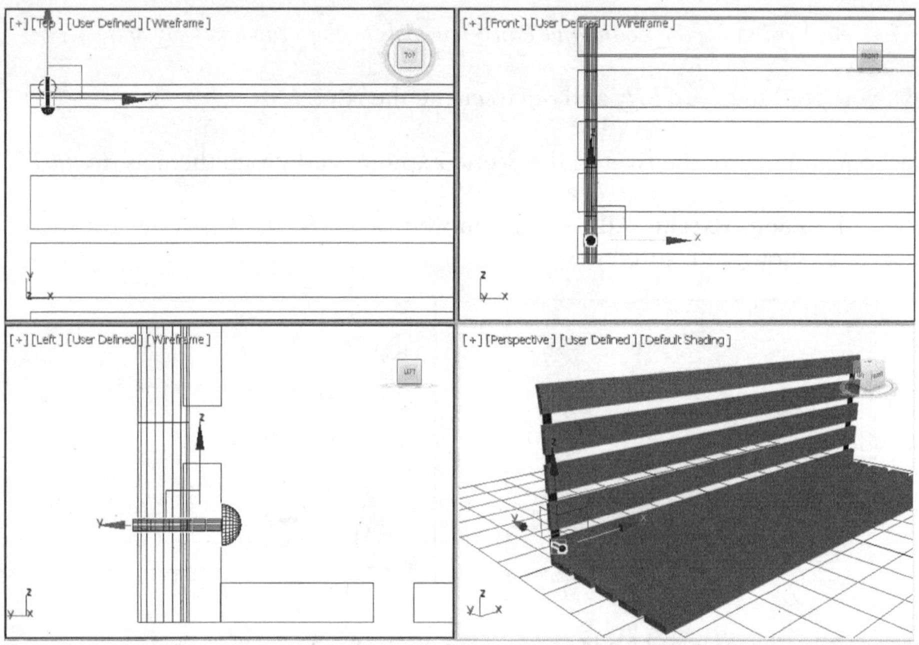

Figure 2-80 Alignment of rivet001 with horizontal back support

4. In the Left viewport, select *rivet001* using the **Select and Move** tool and move the cursor over the vertical axis. Now, create 4 copies of *rivet001*. These copies are automatically named as *rivet002*, *rivet003*, *rivet004*, and *rivet005*. Align them in the Left viewport, refer to Figure 2-81.

5. Select the uppermost rivet and choose the **Select and Rotate** tool. Now, rotate the uppermost rivet by using the outermost ring of the **Select and Rotate** tool in the counterclockwise direction until the value in the **X** spinner in the coordinate display becomes **-15**, refer to Figure 2-82. Next, align it using the **Select and Move** tool.

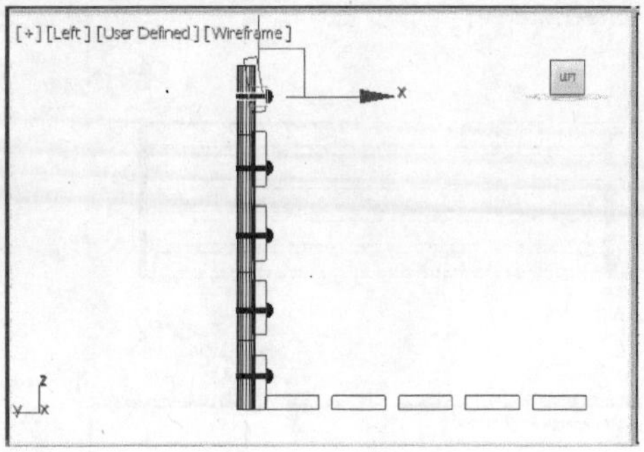

Figure 2-81 *Alignment of rivets in the Left viewport*

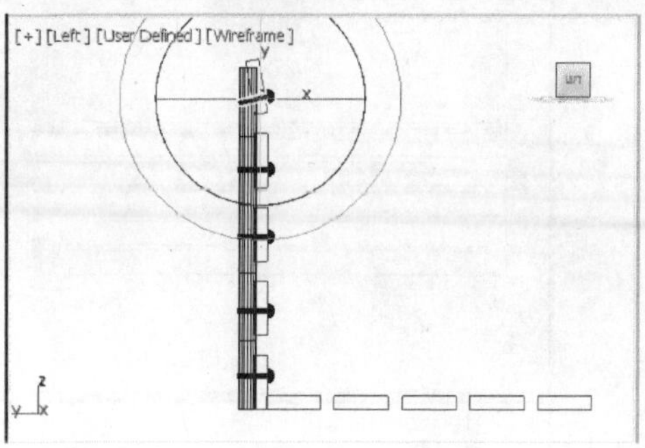

Figure 2-82 *Rotating uppermost rivet*

6. Press and hold the CTRL key and select all the rivets from the Scene Explorer and group them as *left side rivets*. Click anywhere in the viewport to deselect the objects.

Note
To change the viewport without deselecting the objects, middle-click in that viewport; the objects will remain selected.

Creating Right Side Rivets

In this section, you will copy *left side rivets* for creating right side rivets.

1. Select *left side rivets* in the Front viewport using the **Select and Move** tool and move the cursor over the horizontal axis. Next, press and hold the SHIFT key and the left mouse button, and then drag the mouse toward the right side. Release the left mouse button and the SHIFT key exactly over *vertical back support002* on the right side; the **Clone Options** dialog box is displayed.

2. In the **Clone Options** dialog box, make sure the **Copy** radio button is selected. In the **Name** text box, enter **right side rivets** to modify the name of the group and choose **OK**; *right side rivets* group is displayed, as shown in Figure 2-83.

   Now, you need to select *horizontal back support, vertical back support001, vertical back support002, left side rivets,* and *right side rivets*.

3. Select *horizontal back support, vertical back support001, vertical back support002, left side rivets,* and *right side rivets* using the CTRL key from the Scene Explorer and then group them as *back support* as described earlier.

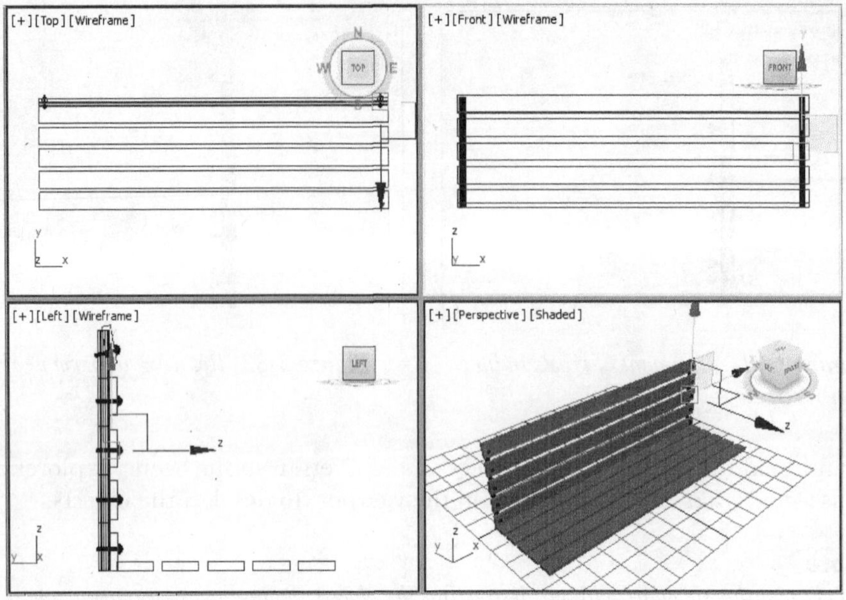

Figure 2-83 The right side rivets group displayed in viewports

Rotating the Back Support

In this section, you will rotate the back support.

1. Select *back support* in the Left viewport and choose the **Select and Rotate** tool; a circular gizmo is displayed.

2. Move the cursor over the Z-axis, which is blue in color; the Z-axis turns yellow and becomes active. Now, press the left mouse button and drag the cursor counterclockwise to rotate the back support until the value in the **Z** spinner in the coordinate display becomes around **10**. Release the left mouse button; the *back support* group gets rotated, as shown in Figure 2-84.

3. Choose the **Select and Move** tool and align *back support* with *horizontal seat support*, as shown in Figure 2-85.

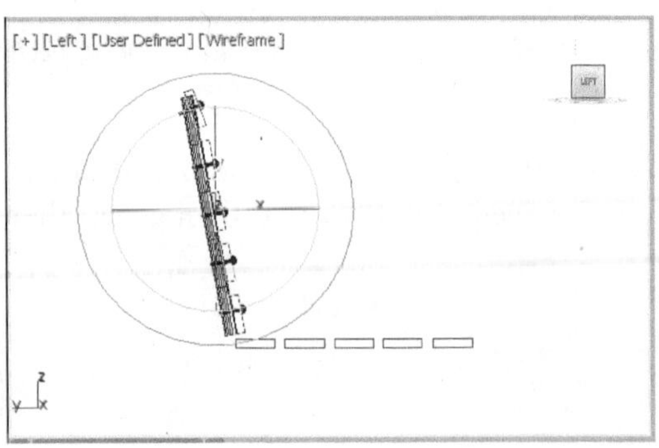

Figure 2-84 The back support after being rotated in the Left viewport

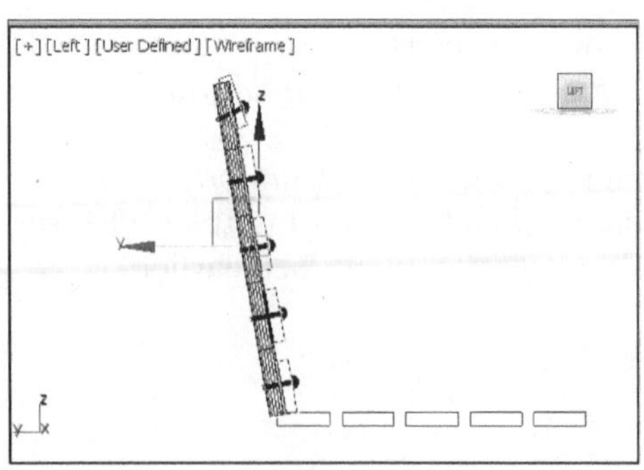

Figure 2-85 Alignment of back support in the Left viewport

Creating Leg Supports

In this section, you will create leg support.

1. Activate the Top viewport and choose **Create > Geometry** in the **Command Panel**; the **Standard Primitives** is displayed in the drop-down list. Next, choose the **Box** tool in the **Object Type** rollout.

2. In the **Keyboard Entry** rollout, set the parameters as follows:

   Length: **36.677** Width: **9.0** Height: **2.8**

3. Choose the **Create** button from the **Keyboard Entry** rollout; the box is created.

4. Name the box as *leg support001* and change its color to black.

5. Choose the **Select and Move** tool and align *leg support001* to the extreme left and below *horizontal seat support* in all viewports, refer to Figure 2-86.

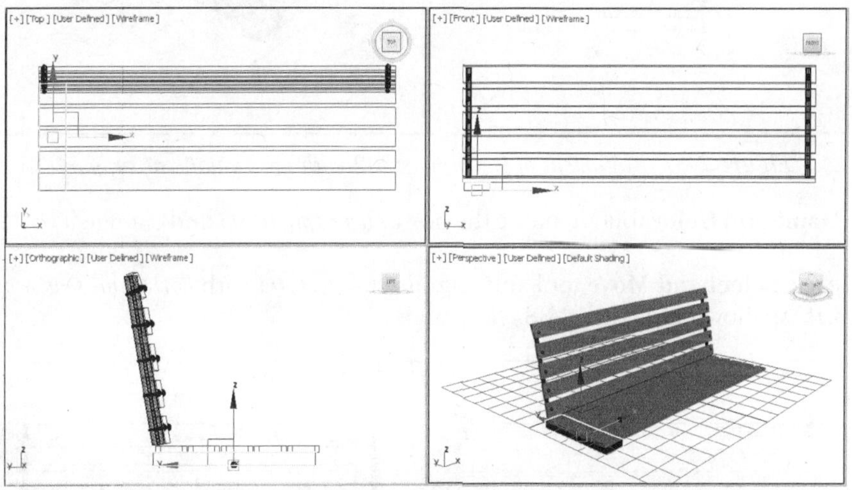

Figure 2-86 *Alignment of leg support001 with horizontal seat support*

   Next, you need to copy *leg support001* to create the leg support on the right side of *horizontal seat support.*

6. Activate the Top viewport by middle-clicking in it and create a copy of *leg support001* as described earlier. It is automatically named as *leg support002.*

7. Choose the **Select and Move** tool and align *leg support002* to *horizontal seat support* in all viewports, as shown in Figure 2-87.

   Next, you need to create another box for other leg supports.

8. Activate the Top viewport and create a box using the values as follows:

Length: **9.0** Width: **124** Height: **2.8**

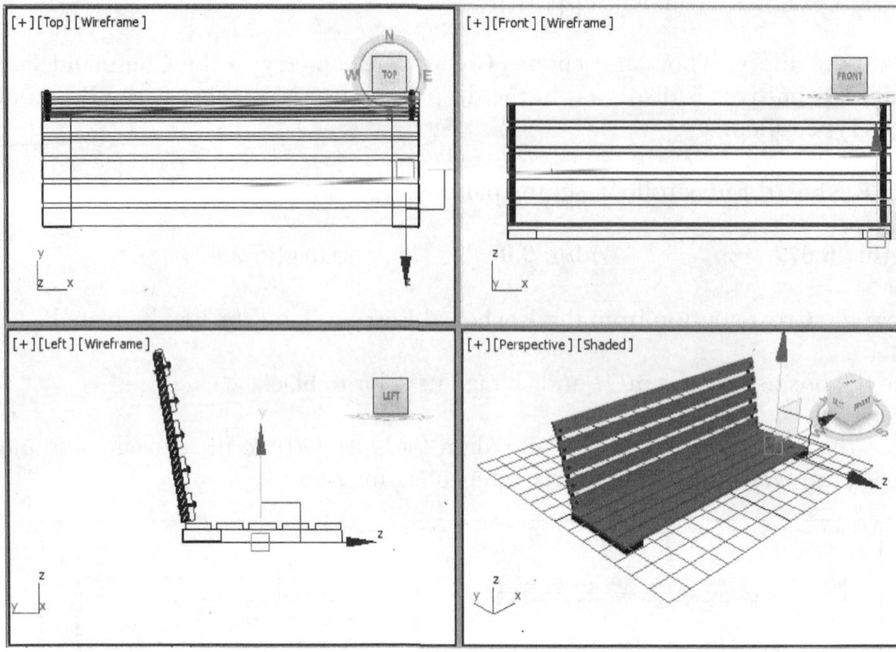

Figure 2-87 *Alignment of leg support002 with horizontal seat support*

9. In the **Name and Color** rollout, name the box as *leg support003* and change its color to black.

10. Choose the **Select and Move** tool and align *leg support003* with *horizontal seat support* in the viewports, as shown in Figure 2-88.

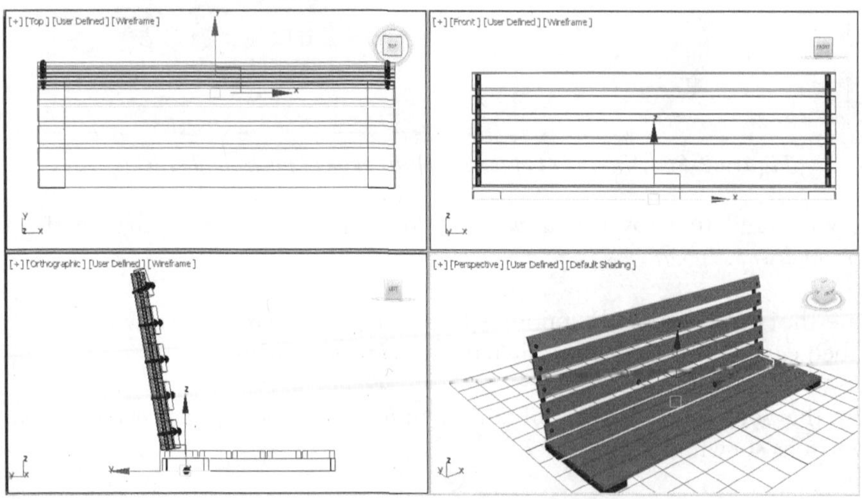

Figure 2-88 *Alignment of leg support003 with horizontal seat support in the viewports*

Note

You need to use the ***Orbit*** *tool to view leg support003 properly in the Perspective viewport.*

11. Create a copy of *leg support003* in the Top viewport; it is automatically named as *leg support004*.

12. Choose the **Select and Move** tool and align *leg support004* with *horizontal seat support* in all the viewports, refer to Figure 2-89.

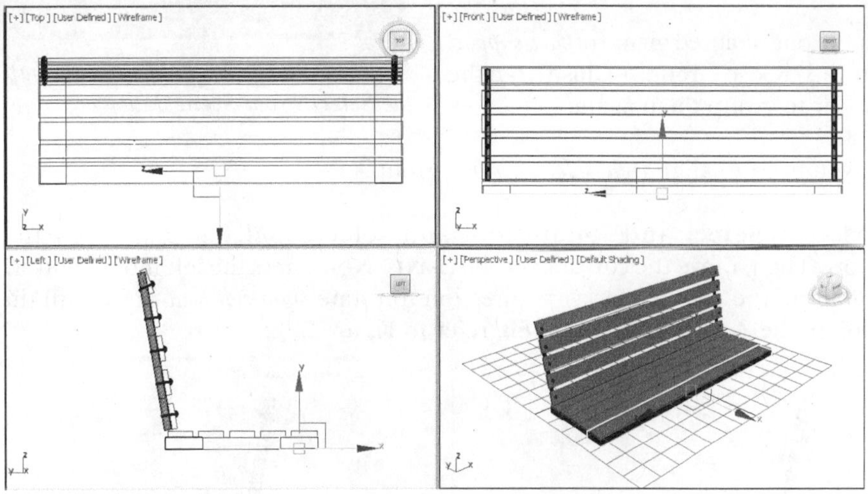

Figure 2-89 *Alignment of leg support004 in viewports*

Creating Rivets for the Seat Support

To create the rivets for *horizontal seat support*, you need to copy *right side rivets*. As you already know that *right side rivets* are grouped under *back support,* therefore first you need to open this group to access them independently. After opening, *back support* group will be ungrouped temporarily and you can transform the objects within it independently.

1. Activate the Left viewport and select *back support*.

2. Choose **Group > Open** from the menu bar; *back support* is now ungrouped temporarily. Also, a pink colored bounding box is displayed around *back support*.

3. Choose the **Select By Name** tool; the **Select From Scene** dialog box is displayed.

4. In the **Select From Scene** dialog box, select *right side rivets* and choose the **OK** button, refer to Figure 2-90.

5. Make sure *right side rivets* group is still selected. Now, create a copy of *right side rivets* and name it as *right side seat rivets*, as shown in Figure 2-91.

6. Make sure that *right side seat rivets* group is selected and choose **Group > Detach** from the menu bar; *right side seat rivets* group is detached from *back support* group.

7. Select the pink colored gizmo of *back support* group and choose **Group > Close** from the menu bar to group them again.

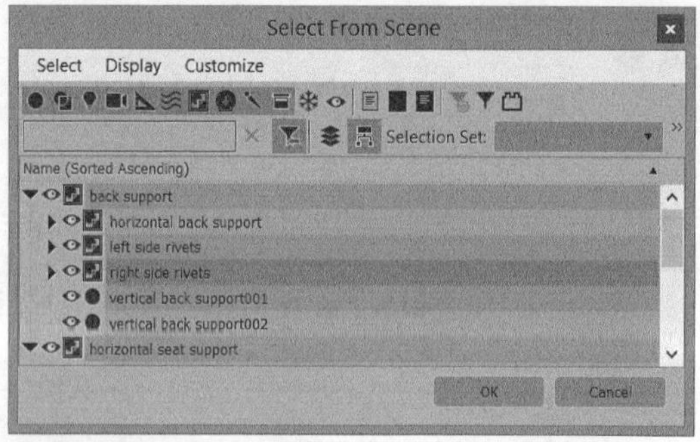

***Figure 2-90** The right side rivets group selected in the **Select From Scene** dialog box*

Next, you need to align *right side seat rivets* group.

8. Choose the **Select and Rotate** tool and select *right side seat rivets* in the Left viewport. Then, move the cursor over the Z-axis. Now, press the left mouse button and drag the cursor in the counterclockwise direction to rotate *right side seat rivets* until the angle of rotation in the **Z** spinner becomes **80**, refer to Figure 2-92.

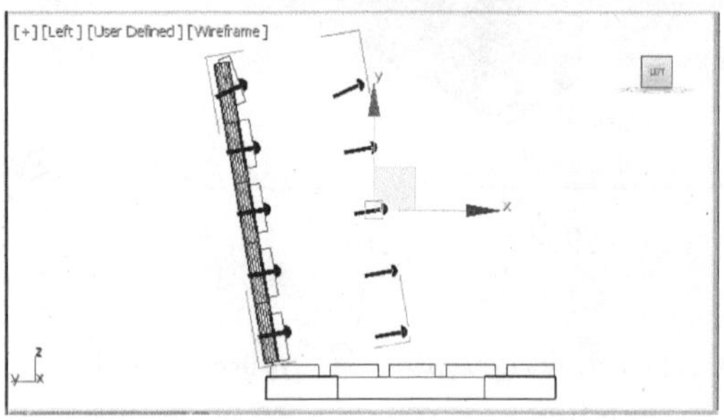

***Figure 2-91** The right side seat rivets group in the Left viewport*

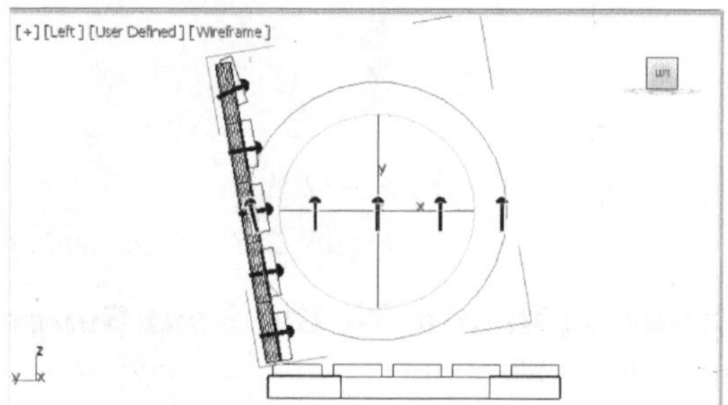

***Figure 2-92** Rotating the right side seat rivets group in the Left viewport*

9. Choose the **Select and Move** tool. Now, move the cursor over the vertical axis and then drag the mouse downward to align *right side seat rivets* with *horizontal seat support*, as shown in Figure 2-93.

   Next, you need to align the rivet (which is near the horizontal back support) to the horizontal seat support.

10. Make sure *right side seat rivets* group is selected and choose **Group > Open** from the menu bar to ungroup them temporarily.

11. Select the rivet which is near *horizontal back support* and choose the **Select and Rotate** tool. Move the cursor over the Z-axis. Now, press the left mouse button and drag the cursor in the clockwise direction to rotate it until the angle of rotation in the **Z** spinner in the coordinate display becomes around **-15**, refer to Figure 2-94.

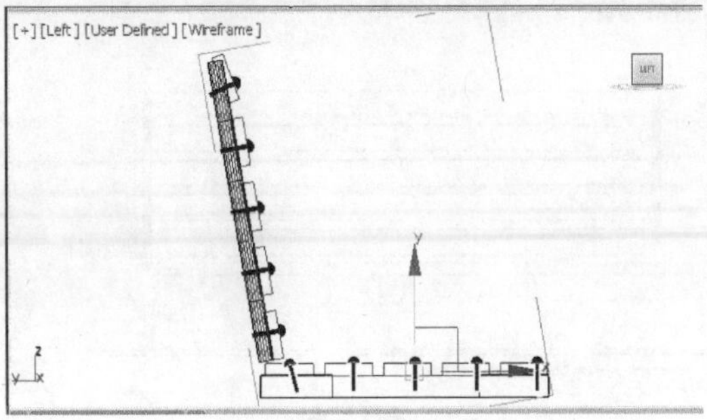

Figure 2-93 Alignment of right side seat rivets in the Left viewport

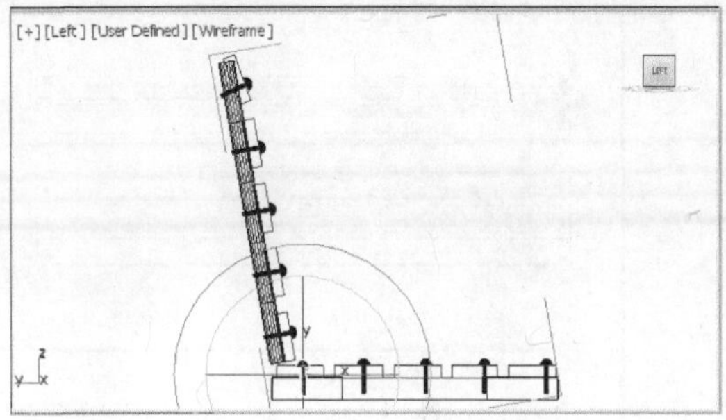

Figure 2-94 Rotating rivet in the Left viewport

12. Choose the **Select and Move** tool and align all the rivets of *right side seat rivets* group with *horizontal seat support*, as shown in Figure 2-95.

13. Make sure that one of the rivets of *right side seat rivets* group is selected and choose **Group > Close** from the menu bar to group them again.

    Next, you need to copy *right side seat rivets* to create rivets on the left side of *horizontal seat support*.

14. Activate the Top viewport and create a copy of *right side seat rivets*. Name the new group as *left side seat rivets*.

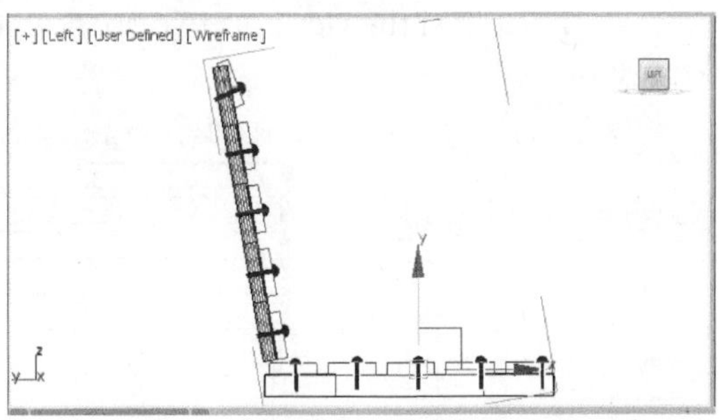

Figure 2-95 Alignment of right side seat rivets in the Left viewport

15. Align *left side seat rivets* using the **Select and Move** tool in the viewports, as shown in Figure 2-96.

Creating Legs of the Park Bench

In this section, you will create legs of the park bench.

1. Activate the Top viewport and choose **Create > Geometry** in the **Command Panel**; **Standard Primitives** is displayed in the drop-down list. Next, choose the **Box** tool in the **Object Type** rollout.

2. In the **Keyboard Entry** rollout, set the values as follows:

   Length: **4.0** Width: **3.0** Height: **26.88**

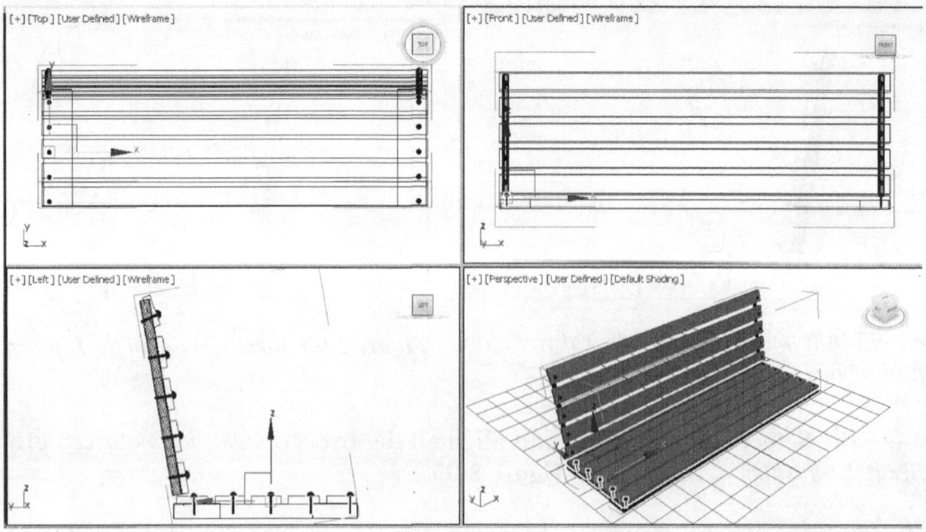

Figure 2-96 Alignment of left side seat rivets in viewports

3. Choose the **Create** button from the **Keyboard Entry** rollout; a box is created.

4. In the **Name and Color** rollout, name the box as *leg001*. Also, change its color to black.

5. Choose the **Select and Move** tool and align *leg001* with *leg support001* in the viewports, refer to Figure 2-97. You need to adjust the viewport to display all the objects properly using the **Zoom** and **Pan View** tools.

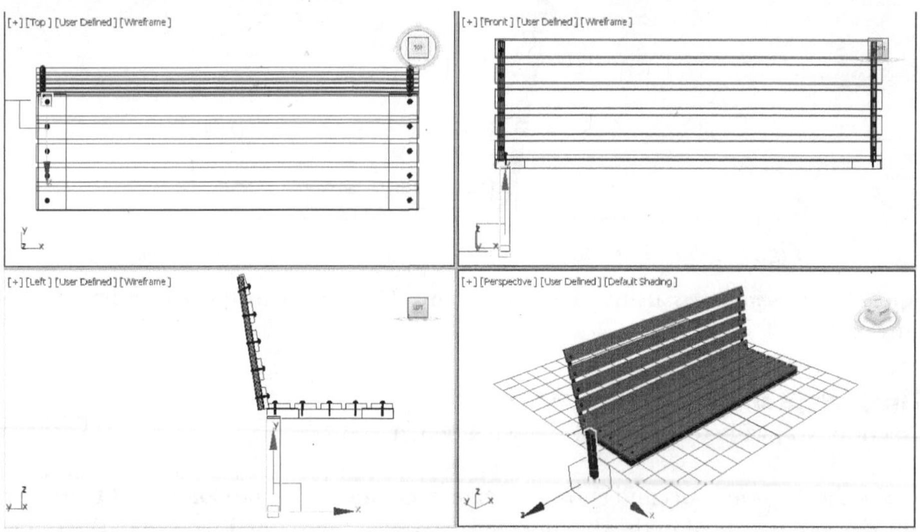

Figure 2-97 Alignment of leg001 in viewports

6. Create three copies of *leg001* to create three more legs. These are automatically named as *leg002*, *leg003*, and *leg004*.

7. Choose the **Select and Move** tool and align *leg002*, *leg003*, and *leg004* in the viewports, as shown in Figure 2-98.

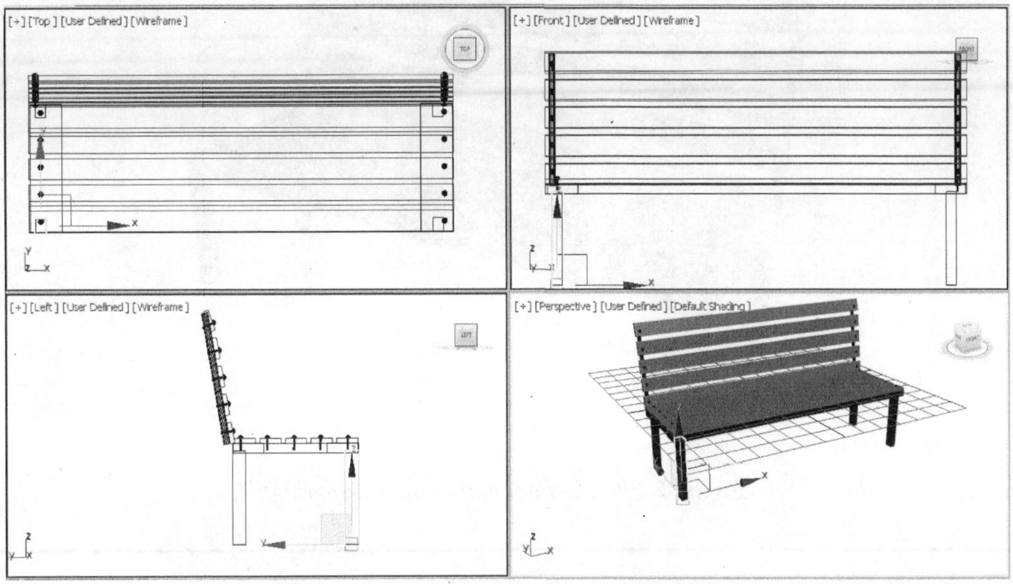

Figure 2-98 *Alignment of legs in viewports*

8. Choose the **Zoom Extents All** tool. Next, modify the view in the Perspective viewport using the **Orbit** tool.

Saving and Rendering the Scene

In this section, you will save and render the scene. You can also view the final rendered image of this scene by downloading the *c02_3dsmax_2017_rndr.zip* file from *www.cadcim.com.* The path of the file is as follows: *Textbooks > Animation and Visual Effects > 3ds Max > Autodesk 3ds Max 2017: A Comprehensive Guide*

1. Change the background color of the scene to white as discussed in Tutorial 1.

2. Choose **Save** from the **Application** menu.

3. Activate the Perspective viewport. Next, choose the **Render Production** tool from the **Main Toolbar**; the **Rendered Frame** window is displayed. This window shows the final output of the scene, refer to Figure 2-99.

Figure 2-99 The final output after rendering

Self-Evaluation Test

Answer the following questions and then compare them to those given at the end of this chapter:

1. Which of the following tools is used to rotate an object in the active viewport?

   (a) **Zoom Extents All** (b) **Orbit**
   (c) **Pan** (d) All of these

2. Which of the following tools is used to select an object from the list of objects that are currently present in the scene?

   (a) **Select Object** (b) **Select and Move**
   (c) **Select by Name** (d) **Select and Rotate**

3. Which of the following rollouts is available when you choose the **Box** tool?

   (a) **Name and Color** (b) **Creation Method**
   (c) **Parameters** (d) All of these

4. Which of the following objects is not a standard primitive?

   (a) Pyramid (b) Geosphere
   (c) Torus Knot (d) Torus

5. To stretch and squash an object, you need to choose the _________ tool from the **Main Toolbar**.

6. You can use the __________ rollout to change the name and color of an object.

7. You can use the __________ rollout to modify the dimensions of an object.

8. The __________ tool is used to move through the viewport.

9. On starting 3ds Max, a screen with three viewports will be displayed. (T/F)

10. You can create any standard primitive dynamically as well as by entering the parameters in the **Keyboard Entry** rollout. (T/F)

11. The options in the **Creation Method** rollout are used only when you create an object using the keyboard. (T/F)

Review Questions

Answer the following questions:

1. Which of the following tools is used to display all objects in the viewports?

   (a) **Zoom** (b) **Pan**
   (c) **Zoom Extents All** (d) **Orbit**

2. Which of the following tools is used to move an object along the X, Y, or Z axis?

   (a) **Select Object** (b) **Select and Move**
   (c) **Select by Name** (d) All of these

3. You need to choose the __________ tool and press and hold the __________ key to select more than one object simultaneously in a viewport.

4. While creating the clone of an object, you need to hold the CTRL key and drag the object. (T/F)

5. To change the background color of a scene, you need to choose **Rendering > Environment** from the menu bar. (T/F)

6. A geosphere is smoother than a sphere. (T/F)

7. The **Zoom Region** tool is used to adjust the view of all objects in the viewports to display them properly. (T/F)

8. You need to choose the **Render Production** tool from the **Main Toolbar** to render a view without using the **Render Setup** dialog box. (T/F)

9. You can use individual parts of a teapot to make a new object. (T/F)

10. You can choose **Reset** from the **Application** menu to reset all settings of 3ds Max. (T/F)

EXERCISES

The rendered output of the models used in the following exercises can be accessed by downloading the *c02_3dsmax_2017_exr.zip* from *www.cadcim.com*. The path of the file is as follows: *Textbooks > Animation and Visual Effects > 3ds Max > Autodesk 3ds Max 2017: A Comprehensive Guide*

Exercise 1

Create the model shown in Figure 2-100 using your own dimensions.

(Expected time: 15 min)

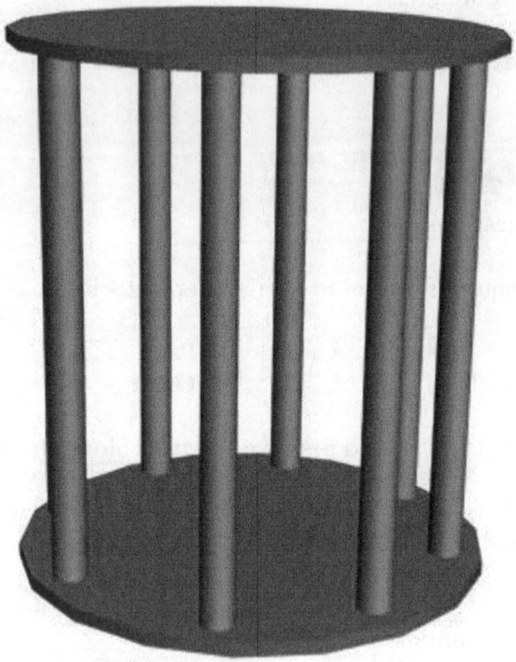

Figure 2-100 *The model to be created in Exercise 1*

Exercise 2

Create the nut model shown in Figures 2-101 and 2-102 using your own dimensions.

(Expected time: 15 min)

Figure 2-101 The model of a nut (view 1)

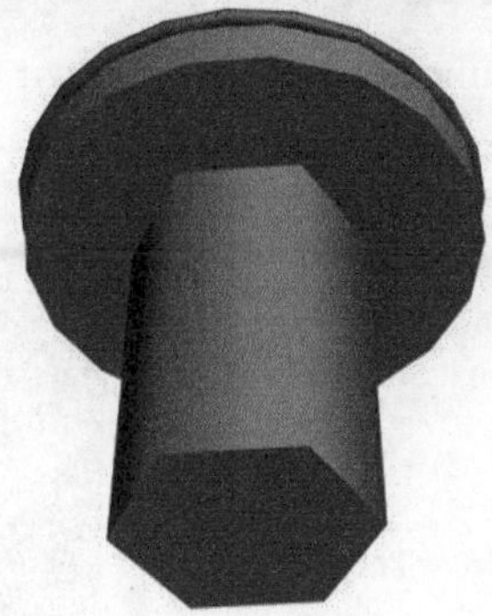

Figure 2-102 The model of a nut (view 2)

Exercise 3

Create the model of a table shown in Figure 2-103 using your own dimensions.

(Expected time: 15 min)

Figure 2-103 The model of a table

Exercise 4

Create the model of a table shown in Figure 2-104 using your own dimensions.

(Expected time: 25 min)

Figure 2-104 *The model of a table*

Answers to Self-Evaluation Test

1. b, **2.** c, **3.** d, **4.** c, **5. Select and Squash**, **6. Name and Color**, **7. Parameters 8. Walk Through**, **9.** F, **10.** T, **11.** F

3

Extended Primitives

Learning Objectives

After completing this chapter, you will be able to:

- *Understand Bend modifier*
- *Understand Taper modifier*
- *Create and edit extended primitives*

INTRODUCTION

In this chapter, you will learn to create complex 3D shapes using extended primitives. Also, you will learn in detail the usage of the Bend and Taper modifiers and different snap controls.

MODIFIERS

In 3ds Max, modifiers are used to apply various types of functions or effects on an object. There are different types of modifiers that perform different functions about which you will learn in the later chapters. In this section, you will learn about the **Bend** and **Taper** modifiers.

Bend Modifier

The **Bend** modifier is used to bend an object upto 360 degrees along the X, Y, or Z axis. To apply the **Bend** modifier on an object, select the object and choose **Modifiers > Parametric Deformers > Bend** from the menu bar. Alternatively, you can select the object in the viewport and choose the **Modify** tab from the **Command Panel**; the **Modifiers List** drop-down list will be displayed. Select **OBJECT-SPACE MODIFIERS > Bend** from the **Modifier List** drop-down list; the **Bend** modifier will be displayed in the modifier stack, refer to Figure 3-1. Also, the **Parameters** rollout will be displayed in the Modify panel, as shown in Figure 3-2. The areas in the **Parameters** rollout are discussed next.

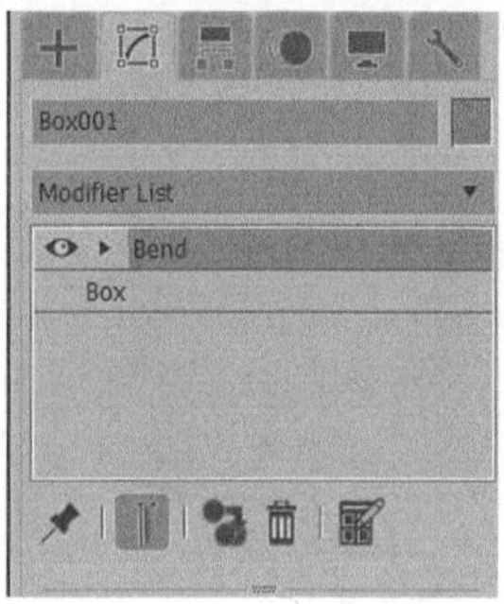

*Figure 3-1 The **Bend** modifier displayed in the modifier stack*

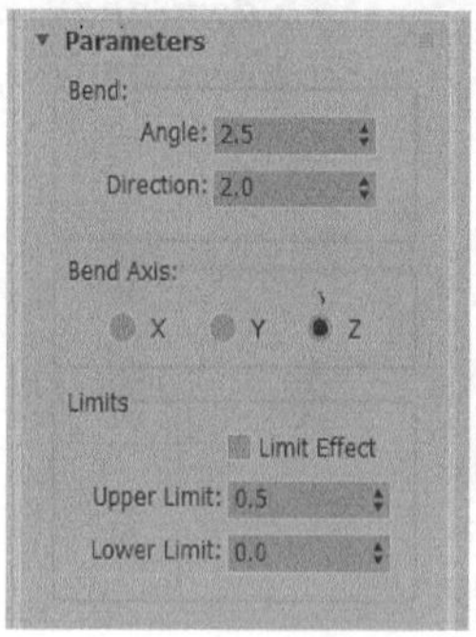

*Figure 3-2 The **Parameters** rollout of the **Bend** modifier*

Bend Area

The options in the **Bend** area are used to set the parameters to bend an object. The **Angle** spinner is used to define the angle of the bend along the X, Y, or Z axis. The **Direction** spinner is used to define the direction of the bend.

Bend Axis Area

The options in the **Bend Axis** area is used to define the axis, which needs to be bent. By default, the Z radio button is selected. As a result, the object will be bent about the Z axis. You can also select the X or Y radio button. Note that the axis to be bent should be local to the bend gizmo instead of the selected object.

Limits Area

The options in the **Limits** area are used to apply constraints to the bend effect. Select the **Limit Effect** check box to make the options in this area active. By default, value in the **Upper Limit** and **Lower Limit** spinners is zero. The **Lower Limit** and **Upper Limit** spinners are used to specify the bending limits of the modifier from its center point.

Taper Modifier

The **Taper** modifier is used to taper an object by scaling it on both ends. After applying this modifier, one side of the object will be scaled up and another will be scaled down. To apply the **Taper** modifier, choose **Modifiers > Parametric Deformers > Taper** from the menu bar; the **Taper** modifier will be displayed in the modifier stack, refer to Figure 3-3. Also, the **Parameters** rollout will be displayed in the Modify panel, as shown in Figure 3-4. The areas in this rollout are discussed next.

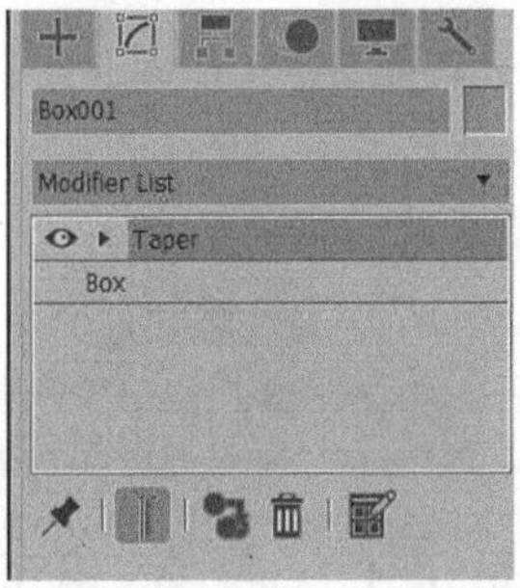

*Figure 3-3 The **Taper** modifier in the modifier stack*

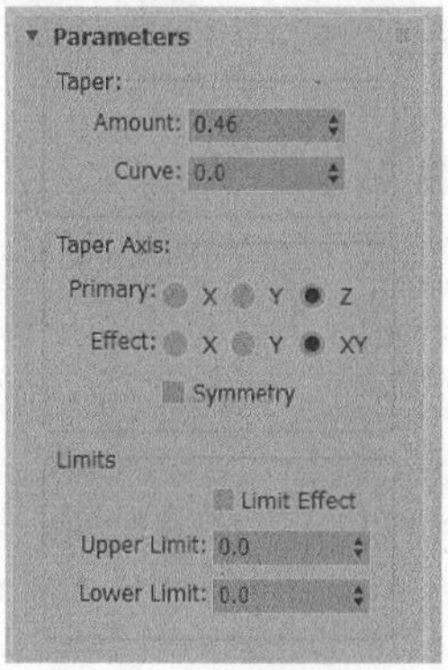

*Figure 3-4 The **Parameters** rollout of the **Taper** modifier*

Taper Area

The options in the **Taper** area is used to set the parameters for scaling the shape of an object. The **Amount** spinner in the **Taper** area is used to define the amount of taper. The **Curve** spinner is used to define the curve applied to the gizmo, and it helps in creating different shapes of the taper. You can set the values of the **Amount** and **Curve** spinners from -10.0 to 10.0.

Taper Axis Area

The Primary group in the **Taper** Axis area is used to define the central axis of the taper. By default, the Z radio button is selected in the **Primary** group. As a result, the Z axis is used as the central axis for the taper. You can also specify the X or Y axis as the central axis for the taper by selecting the X or Y radio button in the Primary group. The **Effect** group is used to define the direction of the taper from the primary axis. By default, the XY radio button is selected in the **Effect** group. As a result, the direction of the taper will be along the XY plane. You can also specify the direction of taper along the X or Y axis by selecting the X or Y radio button from the **Effects** group. The radio buttons in the **Effect** group change according to the selection of the primary axis. You can select the **Symmetry** check box in this area to create a symmetrical taper around the primary axis.

Limits Area

The options in this area are same as discussed in the **Bend** modifier.

EXTENDED PRIMITIVES

In 3ds Max, there are some complex 3D geometric shapes, which can be used to create 3D objects. These shapes are known as extended primitives. The extended primitives are chamfer box, spindle, hedra, and so on.

To create an extended primitive, you need to choose **Create > Geometry** from the **Command Panel**; a drop-down list will be displayed with the **Standard Primitives** option selected by default. Now, select the **Extended Primitives** option from the drop-down list. Activate the viewport in which you want to create the primitives and then choose the corresponding tool from the **Object Type** rollout. In this section, you will learn to create and modify the extended primitives using various tools available in the **Object Type** rollout.

Creating a Hedra

Menu bar:	Create > Extended Primitives > Hedra
Command Panel:	Create > Geometry > Extended Primitives > Object Type rollout > Hedra

To create a hedra, activate the viewport and make sure that the **Extended Primitives** option is selected from the drop-down list in the **Command Panel**. Now, choose the **Hedra** tool from the **Object Type** rollout; the **Name and Color** and **Parameters** rollouts will be displayed, as shown in Figure 3-5. Now, press and hold the left mouse button in the viewport to define the center point of the hedra, and then drag the cursor to define its radius. Release the left mouse button to get the required radius; a hedra will be created, as shown in Figure 3-6.

Various rollouts used to create and modify the hedra are discussed next.

Tip

If you are creating an extended primitive that requires multiple steps, you can pan or orbit the viewport in between the steps. To pan the viewport, drag the cursor with the middle-mouse button or mouse wheel held down. To rotate the viewport, press and hold the ALT key and then drag the cursor with middle-mouse button or mouse wheel held down.

Note

1. The options in the ***Name and Color*** *rollout of all the extended primitives are same as those discussed in the* ***Box*** *tool of Chapter 2.*

2. After creating an extended primitive if you right-click in the viewport to exit the tool, the ***Parameters*** *rollout will disappear from the* ***Create*** *tab. In such a case, to modify the parameters of the primitive, select the primitive in the viewport and choose the* ***Modify*** *tab from the* ***Command Panel****; the* ***Parameters*** *rollout will be displayed.*

Parameters Rollout

The parameters in this rollout are discussed next.

Family Area

The options in the **Family** area are used to define various types of hedra, refer to Figure 3-7. By default, the **Tetra** radio button is selected which is used to create a tetrahedron. You can select the **Cube/Octa** radio button to create a cube or octahedron. Note that the hedra created will depend on the value entered in the spinners in the **Family Parameters** area. If you select the **Dodec/Icos** radio button, a dodecahedron or icosahedron is created. Select the **Star1** and **Star2** radio buttons to create two different star-like polyhedra.

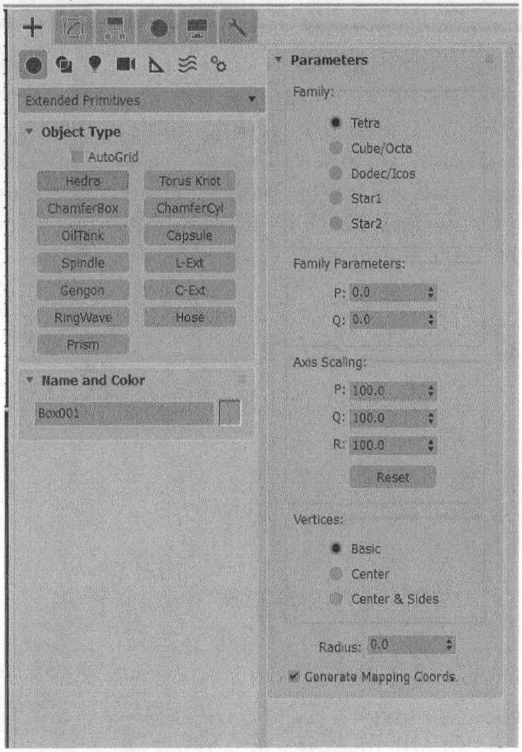

Figure 3-5 *Various rollouts to create a hedra*

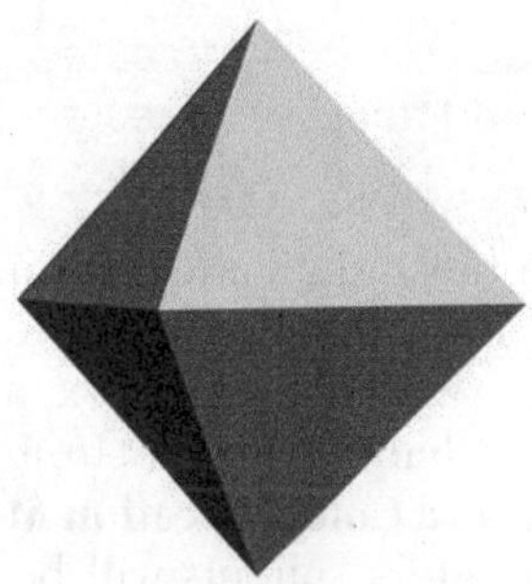

Figure 3-6 *A hedra displayed in the viewport*

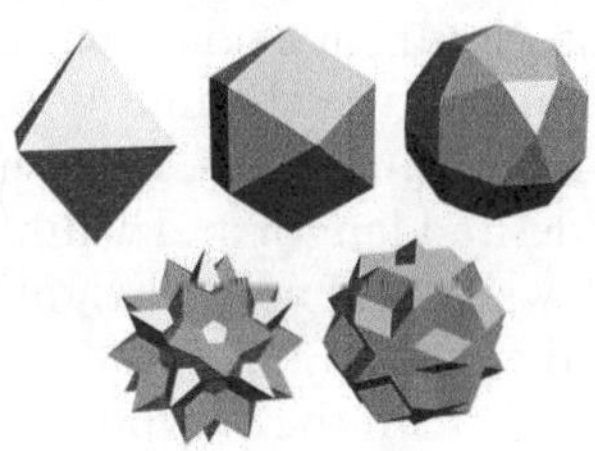

Figure 3-7 *Five basic shapes of hedra*

Family Parameters Area

The two spinners in this area, **P** and **Q**, are used to modify the vertices and faces of a polyhedron. They are related to each other and their combined value can be equal to or less than 1.0. When you set maximum values in P and Q spinners, one parameter represents all vertices while the other represents all facets.

Axis Scaling Area

A polyhedron can have three shapes of polygonal facets: triangle, square, and pentagon.

The **P**, **Q**, and **R** spinners in this area control the axis of reflection for one of the facets of a polyhedron. By default, the value in these spinners is 100. If you change the values in these spinners, they will push the facets in the object or out of the object. On choosing the **Reset** button, the values in these spinners will be reset to 100.

Vertices Area

The options in the **Vertices** area determine the internal geometry of each face of a polyhedron. By default, the **Basic** radio button is selected. As a result, facets are not subdivided and thus have minimum vertices. On selecting the **Center** radio button, an additional vertex is created at the center of each facet. If you select the **Center** and **Side** radio buttons, a vertex is created at the center of each facet and at the edges of all the facets. To see the internal edges, you need to convert the polyhedron object into the **Edit Mesh** or **Edit Poly** modifier. You will learn about the **Edit Mesh** modifier in the later chapters.

Radius

The **Radius** spinner is used to modify the radius of a polyhedron.

Creating a Chamfer Box

Menu bar:	Create > Extended Primitives > Chamfer Box
Command Panel:	Create > Geometry > Extended Primitives > Object Type rollout > ChamferBox

A chamfer box is similar to a box in the standard primitives with the only difference is that it has beveled or rounded edges. To create a chamfer box, activate the viewport and choose the **ChamferBox** tool from the **Object Type** rollout; the **Name and Color**, **Creation Method**, **Keyboard Entry**, and **Parameters** rollouts will be displayed, as shown in Figure 3-8.

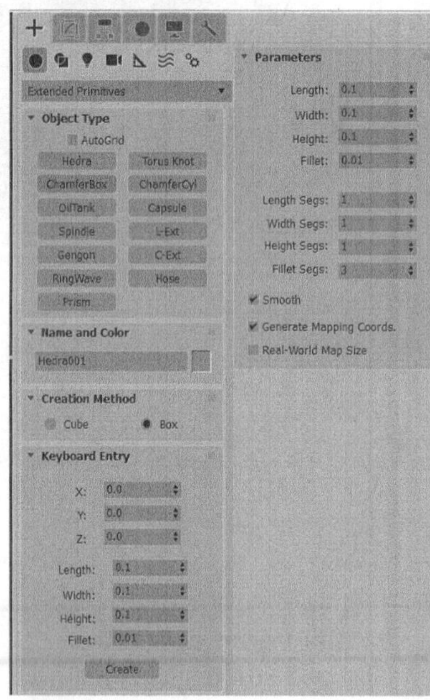

Figure 3-8 Various rollouts to create a chamfer box

Now, press and hold the left mouse button at a point in the viewport for defining the first corner of the chamfer box, and drag the cursor to define its length and width. Release the left mouse button to get the desired length and width. Next, move the cursor up or down to define its height, and click on the viewport to get the desired height. Move the cursor to define the fillet and click on the viewport to get the fillet or chamfer; a chamfer box will be created, as shown in Figure 3-9.

Various rollouts used to create and modify a chamfer box are discussed next.

Creation Method Rollout

There are two radio buttons in this rollout. By default, the **Box** radio button is selected. As a result, a chamfer box is created with individual settings for length, width, and height. You can select the **Cube** radio button to create a chamfer box of equal length, width, and height.

Parameters Rollout

The options in this rollout are used to modify the chamfer box. The **Length**, **Width**, and **Height** spinners are used to specify the length, width, and height, respectively, of a chamfer box. The **Fillet** spinner is used to bevel the edges of a chamfer box. Higher the value of the Fillet spinner, more refined will be the fillet on the edges of a chamfer box. The **Length Segs**, **Width Segs**, and **Height Segs** spinners are used to define the number of segments along the length, width, and height, respectively of a chamfer box. The **Fillet Segs** spinner is used to specify the number of segments in the fillet of a chamfer box.

By default, the **Smooth** check box is selected. As a result, the chamfer box will be smooth at rendering, as shown in Figure 3-9. If this check box is cleared, a chamfer box with beveled edges will be created, as shown in Figure 3-10.

Figure 3-9 *A chamfer box with rounded edges*

Figure 3-10 *A chamfer box with beveled edges*

Creating a Chamfer Cylinder

Menu bar:	Create > Extended Primitives > Chamfer Cylinder
Command Panel:	Create > Geometry > Extended Primitives > Object Type rollout > ChamferCyl

The chamfer cylinder is similar to the cylinder in the standard primitives. The only difference is that the chamfer cylinder has beveled or rounded edges. To create a chamfer cylinder, activate the viewport and choose the **ChamferCyl** tool from the **Object Type** rollout; the **Name and Color**, **Creation Method**, **Keyboard Entry**, and **Parameters** rollouts will be displayed.

Next, press and hold the left mouse button at a point in the viewport for defining the center of the base of the cylinder and then drag the cursor to define its radius. Release the left mouse button and move the cursor up or down to define its height. Click on the screen to get the desired height and move the cursor to define the fillet. Again, click on the screen to get the desired fillet; a chamfer cylinder will be created, as shown in Figure 3-11.

Various rollouts used to create and modify a chamfer cylinder are discussed next.

Creation Method Rollout

The options in this rollout are the same as those discussed while creating the sphere in Chapter 2.

Parameters Rollout

The options in this rollout are used to modify a chamfer cylinder. The **Radius** spinner is used to set the radius of a chamfer cylinder. The **Height** spinner is used to set the height of a chamfer cylinder. The **Fillet** spinner is used to bevel the top and bottom cap edges of a chamfer cylinder. Higher the value of the Fillet spinner, more refined will be the fillet along the cap edges of a chamfer cylinder. The **Height Segs** spinner is used to define the number of segments along the height of a chamfer cylinder. Similarly, the **Fillet Segs** spinner is used to define the number of segments in the fillet area of a chamfer cylinder. The **Sides** spinner specifies the number of sides of a chamfer cylinder. The **Cap Segs** spinner is used to define the number of segments on each end of the cylinder. By default, the **Smooth** check box is selected. As a result, it creates a chamfer cylinder with rounded edges. If this check box is cleared, a chamfer cylinder with beveled edges will be created, as shown in Figure 3-12. The options available on selecting the **Slice On** check box are the same as those discussed in Chapter 2.

Figure 3-11 *A chamfer cylinder displayed in the viewport*

Figure 3-12 *A chamfer cylinder with beveled edges*

Creating a Capsule

Menu bar:	Create > Extended Primitives > Capsule
Command Panel:	Create > Geometry > Extended Primitives > Object Type rollout > Capsule

To create a capsule, activate the viewport and choose the **Capsule** tool from the **Object Type** rollout; the **Name and Color**, **Creation Method**, **Keyboard Entry**, and **Parameters** rollouts will be displayed.

Now, press and hold the left mouse button in the viewport to specify the center of the first face and drag the cursor to define the radius of the capsule. Release the left mouse button and move the cursor up or down to define the height of the capsule. Click on the screen to get the desired height; a capsule will be created, as shown in Figure 3-13.

Figure 3-13 *A capsule displayed in the viewport*

Various rollouts used to create and modify the capsule are discussed next.

Creation Method Rollout

The options in this rollout are the same as those discussed in the previous chapter.

Parameters Rollout

The options in this rollout are used to modify the dimensions of the capsule. The **Radius** and **Height** spinners specify the radius and height of the capsule, respectively. By default, the **Overall** radio button is selected. As a result, the caps will also be included in the overall height of the capsule. However, if you select the **Centers** radio button, the height of the caps is not included in the overall height of the capsule. The **Sides** spinner specifies the number of sides around the capsule. The **Height Segs** spinner defines the number of segments along the height of the capsule. By default, the **Smooth** check box is selected, therefore the surface of the capsule will be smooth at rendering. The options available on selecting the **Slice On** check box are the same as those discussed in the previous chapter.

Creating a Spindle

Menu bar:	Create > Extended Primitives > Spindle
Command Panel:	Create > Geometry > Extended Primitives > Object Type rollout > Spindle

A spindle is a type of cylinder with conical caps. To create a spindle, activate the viewport and choose the **Spindle** tool from the **Object Type** rollout; the **Name and Color**, **Creation Method**, **Keyboard Entry**, and **Parameters** rollouts will be displayed. Now, press and hold the left mouse button in the viewport to specify the center of the first face and drag the cursor to define the radius of the spindle. Release the left mouse button and move the cursor up or down to define the height of the spindle. Click in the viewport to get the desired height and move the cursor again to define the height of the conical caps. Next, click in the viewport again; a spindle will be created, as shown in Figure 3-14.

Figure 3-14 *A spindle displayed in the viewport*

Various rollouts used to create and modify the spindle are discussed next.

Creation Method Rollout

The options in this rollout are the same as those discussed in the previous chapter.

Parameters Rollout

The options in this rollout are used to modify the dimensions of the spindle. The **Radius** and **Height** spinners are used to set the radius and height, respectively of the spindle. The **Cap Height** spinner is used to set the height of the caps. By default, the **Overall** radio button is selected. The functions of the **Overall** and **Centers** radio buttons are same as discussed for the capsule. The **Blend** spinner is used to bevel the top and bottom caps. The rest of the parameters are same as of the other extended primitives.

Creating an L-Ext

Menu bar:	Create > Extended Primitives > L-Extrusion
Command Panel:	Create > Geometry > Extended Primitives > Object Type rollout > L-Ext

The L-Ext or L-Extrusion is an L-shaped object. To create an L-Ext, activate the viewport and choose the **L-Ext** tool from the **Object Type** rollout; the **Name and Color**, **Creation Method**, **Keyboard Entry**, and **Parameters** rollouts will be displayed.

Now, press and hold the left mouse button in the viewport and drag the cursor to define the overall length and width of the object. Release the left mouse button and move the cursor up or down to define the height of the L-Ext. Click in the viewport to get the desired height. Move the cursor again to define the thickness of the L-Ext and click in the viewport; an L-Ext will be created, as shown in Figure 3-15.

Figure 3-15 *An L-Ext displayed in the viewport*

Various rollouts used to create and modify the L-Ext are discussed next.

Creation Method Rollout

There are two radio buttons in this rollout. By default, the **Corners** radio button is selected. As a result, the L-Ext is created from one corner to another. You can select the **Center** radio button to create the L-Ext from its center to the outward direction.

Parameters Rollout

The options in this rollout are used to modify the L-Ext. The **Side Length** spinner is used to define the side length of the L-Ext. The **Front Length** spinners are used to define the front length of the L-Ext. Similarly, the **Side Width** and **Front Width** spinners specify the overall width of the L-Ext. The **Height** spinner is used to specify the height of the L-Ext. The **Side Segs** and **Front Segs** spinners are used to define the number of vertical segments on the sides of the L-Ext. The **Width Segs** spinner specifies the number of segments on the width or thickness of the L-Ext whereas the **Height Segs** spinner specifies the number of segments along the height of the L-Ext.

Creating a Gengon

Menu bar:	Create > Extended Primitives > Gengon
Command Panel:	Create > Geometry > Extended Primitives > Object Type rollout > Gengon

To create a gengon, activate the viewport and choose the **Gengon** tool from the **Object Type** rollout; the **Name and Color**, **Creation Method**, **Keyboard Entry**, and **Parameters** rollouts will be displayed. Now, press and hold the left mouse button in the viewport and drag the cursor to define the radius of the object. Release the left mouse button and move the cursor up or down to define the height of the gengon. Click in the viewport to get the desired height and move the cursor again to define the size of the fillet of the gengon. Next, click in the viewport; a gengon will be created, as shown in Figure 3-16.

Figure 3-16 *A gengon displayed in the viewport*

Various rollouts used to create and modify the gengon are discussed next.

Creation Method Rollout

The options in this rollout are the same as those discussed in the Sphere tool of the previous chapter.

Parameters Rollout

The options in this rollout are used to modify the dimensions of gengon. The **Sides** spinner is used to specify the sides of the gengon. Higher the value of the sides of the gengon, more circular will be the gengon. The **Radius** spinner is used to specify the radius of the gengon. The **Fillet** spinner is used to bevel the corners of the gengon. The **Height** spinner is used to specify the height of the gengon. The **Side Segs**, **Height Segs**, and **Fillet Segs** spinners are used to define the segments on the sides, height, and fillet of the gengon respectively.

Creating a RingWave

Menu bar:	Create > Extended Primitives > RingWave
Command Panel:	Create > Geometry > Extended Primitives > Object Type rollout > RingWave

A ringwave is a ring-shaped object that can have irregular inner and outer edges which can be animated. To create a ringwave, activate the viewport and choose the **RingWave** tool from the **Object Type** rollout; the **Name and Color** and **Parameters** rollouts will be displayed.

Now, press and hold the left mouse button on a point in the viewport to specify the center of the ringwave and drag the cursor to define its outer radius. Release the left mouse button and move the cursor to define the inner radius of the ringwave. Click in the viewport to get the desired radius of the object; a ringwave will be created, as shown in Figure 3-17.

Figure 3-17 *A ringwave displayed in the viewport*

Tip

After creating the ringwave, you can view its in-built animation by dragging the time slider on the track bar or by choosing the ***Play Animation*** *button from the animation playback controls.*

The rollouts used to create and modify the ringwave are discussed next.

Parameters Rollout

The options in this rollout are used to modify the ringwave. The areas in this rollout are discussed next.

RingWave Size Area

In the **RingWave Size** area, the **Radius** spinner is used to define the outer radius of the ringwave. The **Radial Segs** spinner specifies the number of segments between the inner and outer surfaces along the circumference of the ringwave. The **Ring Width** spinner is used to specify the width of the inner ring.The **Sides** spinner is used to specify the number of sides around the circumference of the ringwave. The **Height** spinner is used to specify the height of the ringwave and the **Height Segs** spinner specifies the number of segments along its height.

RingWave Timing Area

The options in the **RingWave Timing** area are used to animate the ringwave. The ringwave grows from the value 0 to the value specified in the **Radius** spinner of the **RingWave Size** area. Select the **No Growth**, **Grow and Stay**, or **Cyclic Growth** radio button to define the pattern of the ringwave growth. The values in the **Start Time**, **Grow Time**, and **End Time** spinners are used to specify the number of frames at which the ring wave starts appearing, reaches to its full size, and disappears, respectively.

By default, the **No Growth** radio button is selected. As a result, the ringwave will not grow over the time. It just appears at the frame number specified in the **Start Time** spinner and disappears after the frame number specified in the **End Time** spinner. You can select the **Grow and Stay** radio button to animate a single growth cycle. In this case, the ringwave starts growing at the frame number specified in the **Start Time** spinner, grows up to its maximum radius in the number of frames specified in the **Grow Time** spinner, and disappears at the frame number specified in the **End Time** spinner. If you select the **Cyclic Growth** radio button, the ringwave animates repeatedly. In this case, the ringwave will start to grow from the specified frame in the **Start Time** spinner. Its radius will grow till the specified frame in the **Grow Time** spinner. This cycle of start and grow of the ring wave will continue upto the specified frame in the **End Time** spinner.

Outer Edge Breakup Area

The options in the **Outer Edge Breakup** area are used to change the shape of the outer edge of the ringwave and define the breakup of the outer edge. To activate the options in this area, you need to select the **On** check box. The **Major Cycles** spinner specifies the number of major waves around the outer edge of the ringwave. The **Width Flux** spinner specifies the size of the major wave in percentage. The **Crawl Time** spinner specifies the number of frames in which a single major wave moves around the outer circumference of the ringwave.

The **Minor Cycles** spinner are used to define the number of small and random-sized waves in each major wave. The **Width Flux** spinner specifies the size of the smaller waves in percentage. The **Crawl Time** spinner specifies the number of frames in which a single minor wave moves around its respective major wave.

Inner Edge Breakup Area

The options in the **Inner Edge Breakup** area are used to change the shape of the inner edge of the ringwave. Also, it defines the breakup of the inner edge. To activate the options in this area, you need to select the **On** check box. The **Inner Edge Breakup** area has the same options for defining the inner edge of the ringwave as those discussed in the **Outer Edge Breakup** area for defining the outer edge of the ringwave.

Surface Parameters Area

The **Texture Coordinates** and **Smooth** check boxes are selected by default in the **Surface Parameters** area. The **Texture Coordinates** check box is used to define the required coordinates for the mapped-material on the ringwave. The **Smooth** check box is used to smoothen the ringwave.

Creating a Hose

Menu bar:	Create > Extended Primitives > Hose
Command Panel:	Create > Geometry > Extended Primitives > Object Type rollout > Hose

A hose is an extended primitive that can link two objects. I t reacts to the movement of linked objects. To create a hose, activate the viewport and choose the **Hose** tool from the **Object Type** rollout; the **Name and Color** and **Hose Parameters** rollouts will be displayed. Now, press and hold the left mouse button in the viewport to specify the center of the hose and drag the cursor to define its radius. Release the left mouse button and move the cursor up or down to define the height of the hose. Click on the screen to get the desired height of the hose; a hose will be created, as shown in Figure 3-18.

Figure 3-18 *A hose displayed in the viewport*

The rollouts used to create and modify a hose are discussed next.

Hose Parameters Rollout

The options in this rollout are used to modify the hose. The different areas in this rollout are discussed next.

End Point Method Area

In the **End Point Method** area, the **Free Hose** radio button is selected by default. As a result, a free hose is created which is not bound to other objects. You can modify the height of the free hose by setting the value in the **Height** spinner in the **Free Hose Parameters** area. If you want to bind the hose with two objects, then you need to select the **Bound to Object Pivots** radio button in the **End Point Method** area. On selecting this radio button, the options in the **Binding Objects** area will be enabled.

Binding Objects Area

The options in this area are used to bind two objects to the hose at the pivot point of these objects. The **Pick Top Object** button in the **Binding Objects** area is used to bind the object with the top of the hose. The **Pick Bottom Object** button in this area is used to bind the object with the bottom of the hose. When you select the objects for the top and bottom of the hose, the name of these objects will be displayed in the **Top** and **Bottom** labels. The value in the **Tension** spinner is used to control the tension between the bend in the hose and the top or bottom objects.

Common Hose Parameters Area

In the **Common Hose Parameters** area, the **Segments** spinner specifies the number of segments along the length of the hose. By default, the **Flex Section Enable** check box is selected. As a result, the **Starts**, **Ends**, **Cycles**, and **Diameter** spinners will be enabled. The values in all these spinners are a percentage of the values of the main hose. The value in the **Starts** spinner specifies the point where the flex section starts along the hose. The value in the **Ends** spinner specifies the point where the flex section ends. The **Cycles** spinner is used to define the number of cycles in the flexible section. To display all the cycles properly, the number of segments should be more. The **Diameter** spinner is used to specify the secondary diameter of the flexible section.

Smoothing Area

By default, the **All** radio button is selected in this area. As a result, the entire hose is smoothened. You can select the **Sides** radio button to smoothen only the sides of the hose. If you select the **None** radio button, it creates a faceted surface of the hose. You can also select the **Segments** radio button to apply smoothness on the inner section of the hose.

By default, the **Renderable** and **Generate Mapping Coords** check boxes are selected in this area. The **Renderable** check box is used to view the hose on rendering. The **Generate Mapping Coords** check box is used to automatically assign the mapping coordinates to an object.

Hose Shape Area

The options in the **Hose Shape** area are used to define the basic shape of the hose. By default, the **Round Hose** radio button is selected. As a result, a circular cross-section is created. If the **Round Hose** radio button is selected, the **Diameter** and **Sides** spinners will be activated. The **Diameter** spinner specifies the diameter of the hose. The **Sides** spinner specifies the number of sides of the hose.

Select the **Rectangular Hose** radio button to create a rectangular hose; the **Width**, **Depth**, **Fillet**, **Fillet Segs**, and **Rotation** spinners below this radio button will be activated. The **Width** and **Depth** spinners are used to define the width and depth of the hose, respectively. The **Fillet** spinner specifies the value by which the cross-section corners of the hose get rounded. The value in the **Fillet Segs** spinner should be higher in order to view the fillet. The value in the **Rotation** spinner rotates the hose around its local Z-axis.

If you select the **D-Section Hose** radio button, a D-shaped hose is created. Also, the **Width**, **Depth**, **Round Sides**, **Fillet**, **Fillet Segs**, and **Rotation** spinners below this radio button will be activated. The **Width** and **Depth** spinners in the **D-Section Hose** radio button are used to define the width and depth of the hose, respectively. The value in the **Round Sides** spinner specifies the total number of segments along the rounded side of the D-shaped hose. The **Fillet** spinner specifies the value by which the square corners of the cross-section get rounded. The value in the **Fillet Segs** spinner should be higher to view the fillet. The value in the **Rotation** spinner rotates the D-shaped hose around its local Z-axis.

TUTORIALS

Tutorial 1

In this tutorial, you will create a 3D model of a couch, as shown in Figure 3-19, by using the extended primitives. **(Expected time: 30 min)**

The following steps are required to complete this tutorial:

a. Create the project folder.
b. Create seat support.
c. Create back support.
d. Create left side of the couch.
e. Create right side of the couch.

f. Create base of the couch.
g. Save and render the scene.

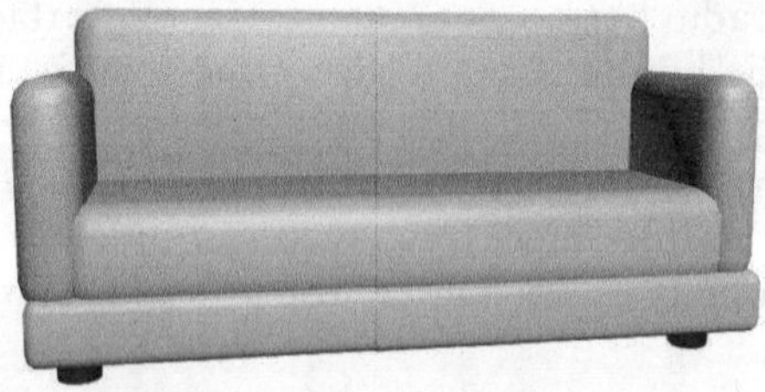

Figure 3-19 The model of a couch

Creating the Project Folder

Create a new project folder with the name *c03_tut1 at \Documents\3dsmax2017* and then save the file with the name **c03tut1**, as discussed in Tutorial 1 of Chapter 2.

Creating Seat Support

In this section, you will use the **ChamferBox** tool to create seat support of the couch.

1. Activate the Top viewport. Choose **Create > Geometry** from the **Command Panel**. In this panel, by default, the **Standard Primitives** option is displayed in the drop-down list. Select the **Extended Primitives** option from the drop-down list and choose the **ChamferBox** tool from the **Object Type** rollout.

2. Expand the **Keyboard Entry** rollout and set the parameters as follows:

   Length: **62.342** Width: **155.575** Height: **22.222** Fillet: **6.0**

3. Choose the **Create** button; a chamfer box is created, as shown in Figure 3-20.

4. In the **Parameters** rollout, set the **Fillet Segs** spinner to 3.0.

5. In the **Name and Color** rollout, enter **seat support** as the name of the chamfer box and press ENTER. Also, use the color swatch to modify the color of *seat support* by entering the values as given below:

   Red: **225** Green: **143** Blue: **87**

Creating Back Support

In this section, you will create a chamfer box primitive to create back support of the couch.

1. Make sure that the Top viewport is activated and the **ChamferBox** tool is chosen.

2. In the **Keyboard Entry** rollout, set the parameters as follows:

   Length: **15.413** Height: **48.089**

Also, make sure the value in the Fillet spinner is 6.0.

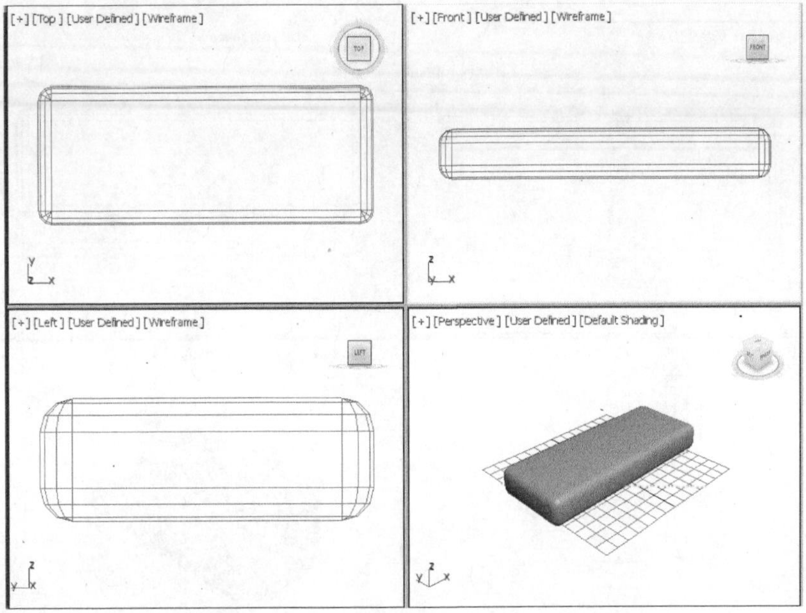

***Figure 3-20** A chamfer box created for seat support*

3. Choose the **Create** button; another chamfer box is created.

4. In the **Name and Color** rollout, enter **back support** as the name of the new chamfer box and press ENTER.

5. Assign the same color to *back support* that was assigned to *seat support*.

6. In the **Parameters** rollout, make sure the value in the **Fillet Segs** spinner is **3.0**.

7. Choose the **Zoom Extents All** tool to display the objects to their extent in all viewports.

   Next, you need to align *back support* with *seat support*.

8. Choose the **Select and Move** tool select *back support* if it is not selected, and move it in the viewports to align it with *seat support*, as shown in Figure 3-21.

Creating Left Side of the Couch

In this section, you will create a chamfer box for left side of the couch.

1. Activate the Top viewport by middle clicking in it and choose the **ChamferBox** tool. Now, in the **Keyboard Entry** rollout, set the values in the respective spinners as given next:

   X: **-80.0** Length: **62.323** Width: **14.506**
   Height: **48.895**

Also, make sure the value in the Fillet spinner is 6.0. Use the default values for other parameters.

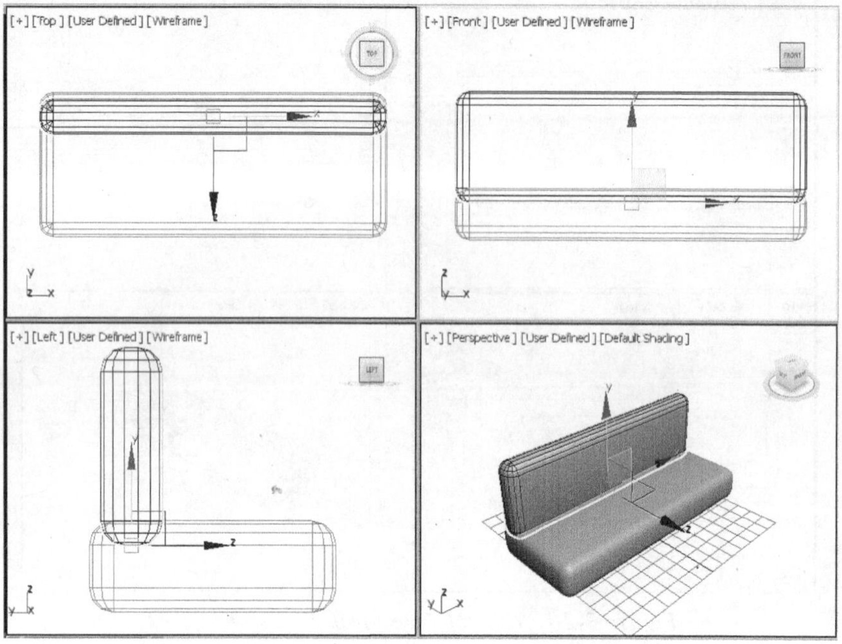

Figure 3-21 *Alignment of back support with seat support*

2. Choose the **Create** button; another chamfer box is created, as shown in Figure 3-22.

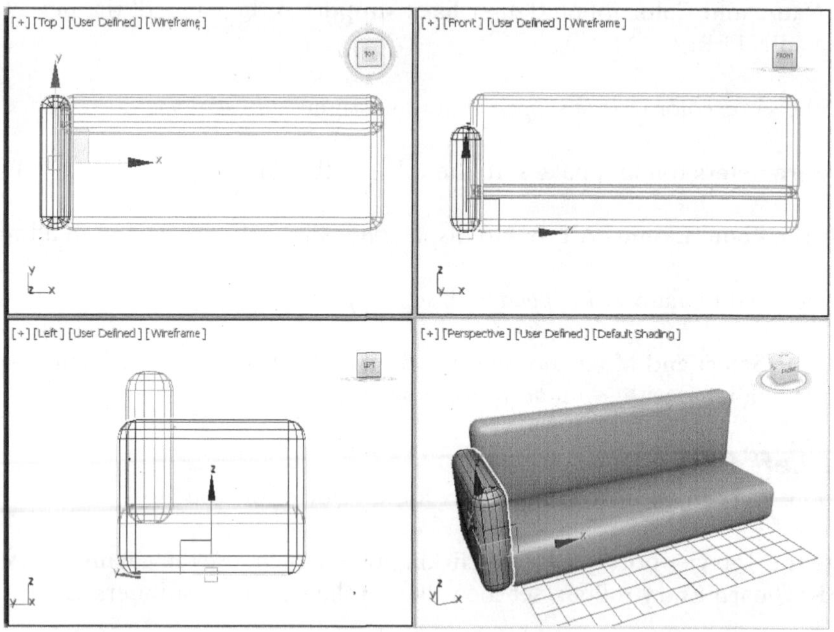

Figure 3-22 *The another chamfer box displayed in the viewports*

3. In the **Parameters** rollout, make sure that the value in the **Fillet Segs** spinner is **3.0**.

4. In the **Name and Color** rollout, enter **left side** and press the ENTER key. Assign the same color to *left side* that you assigned to *seat support*.

Creating Right Side of the Couch

To create right side of the couch, you need to copy *left side* of the couch.

1. Activate the Top viewport. Make sure *left side* is selected.

2. Choose the **Select and Move** tool. Next, move the cursor over the horizontal axis; it turns yellow. Press and hold the SHIFT key and the left mouse button, and then drag the cursor toward the right side of the couch until the value in the **X** spinner in the coordinate display becomes about 159. Release the left mouse button and the SHIFT key; the **Clone Options** dialog box is displayed.

3. In the **Clone Options** dialog box, make sure that the **Copy** radio button is selected and the value in the **Number of Copies** spinner is set to **1**. In the **Name** text box, enter **right side** and choose **OK**; *right side* of the couch is displayed, as shown in Figure 3-23.

Creating Base of the Couch

To create base of the couch, you need to create another chamfer box.

1. Activate the Top viewport and choose the **ChamferBox** tool. In the **Keyboard Entry** rollout, set the following parameters:

   X: **0** Z: **-12.0** Length: **62.782**
   Width: **172.0** Height: **15.0** Fillet: **6.0**

   Make sure **0** is entered in the **Y** spinner.

2. Choose the **Create** button; another chamfer box is created, as shown in Figure 3-24.

3. In the **Name and Color** rollout, enter **base** as the name of the chamfer box and press the ENTER key.

4. Assign the same color to *base* that you assigned to *seat support*.

5. Make sure the Top viewport is activated and then choose the **ChamferCyl** tool. In the **Keyboard Entry** rollout, set the following parameters:

   Radius: **5.0** Height: **5.0** Fillet: **1.0**

   Choose the **Create** button; a chamfer cylinder is created.

6. In the **Name and Color** rollout, enter **support1** and press the ENTER key. Assign black color to it. Next, align it at the bottom left corner of *base*, as shown in Figure 3-25.

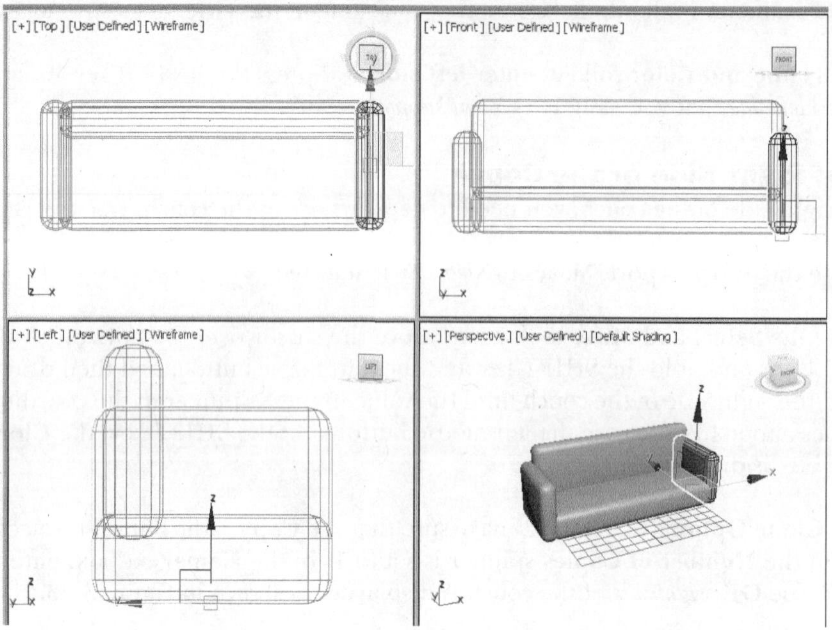

***Figure 3-23** The right side geometry displayed in the viewports*

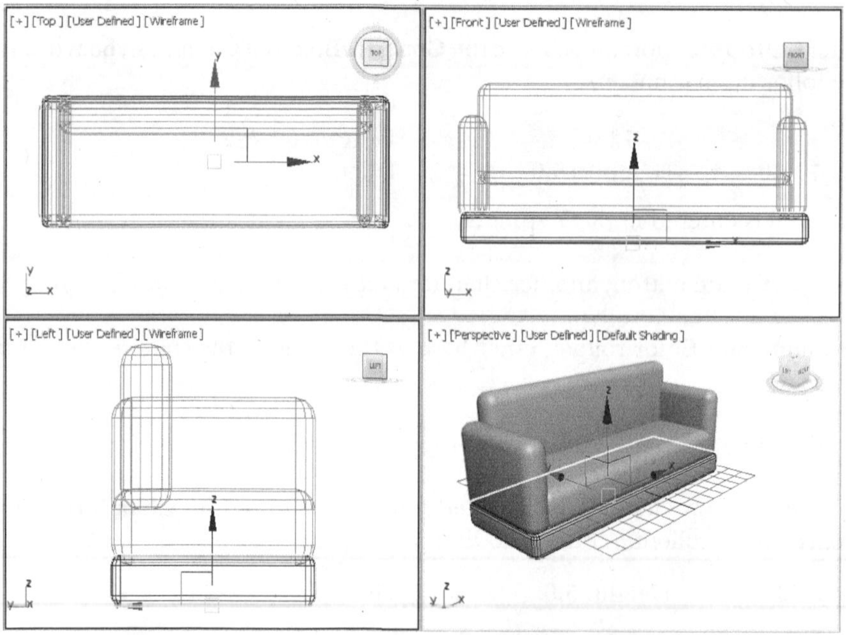

***Figure 3-24** The base geometry displayed in the viewports*

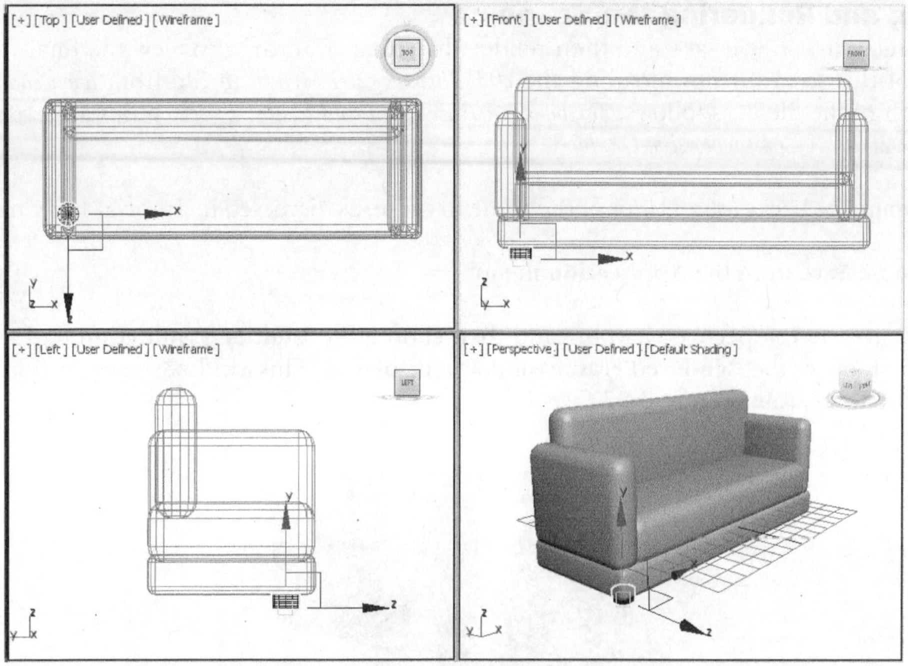

Figure 3-25 *The support1 geometry aligned in the viewports*

7. Create three copies of *support1* as discussed earlier and align them, as shown in Figure 3-26.

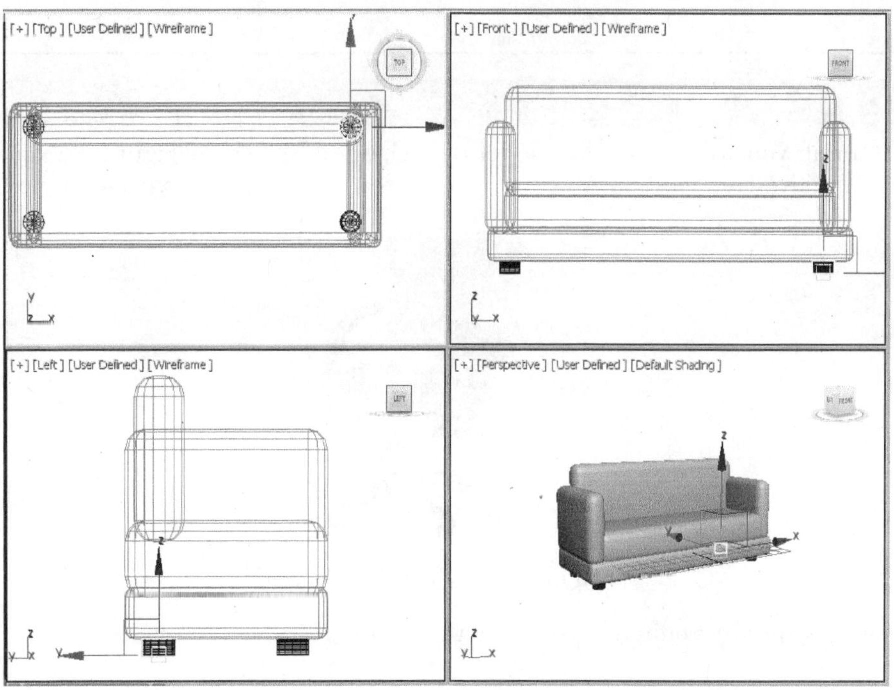

Figure 3-26 *All supports aligned in viewports*

Saving and Rendering the Scene

In this section, you will save and then render the scene. You can also view the final rendered image of this scene by downloading the *c03_3dsmax_2017_rndr.zip* file from *www.cadcim.com*. The path of the file is as follows: *Textbooks* > *Animation and Visual Effects* > *3ds Max* > *Autodesk 3ds Max 2017: A Comprehensive Guide*

1. Change the background color of the scene to white, as discussed in Tutorial 1 of Chapter 2 .

2. Choose **Save** from the **Application** menu.

3. Activate the Perspective viewport and then choose the **Render Production** tool from the main toolbar; the **Rendered Frame** window is displayed. This window shows the final output of the scene, refer Figure 3-27.

Figure 3-27 *The final output after rendering*

Tutorial 2

In this tutorial, you will create the model of a chair, as shown in Figure 3-28, using the extended primitives and modifiers. **(Expected time: 40 min)**

Figure 3-28 *The model of a chair*

The following steps are required to complete this tutorial:

a. Create the project folder.
b. Create seat support.
c. Create back support.

d. Create spring support.
e. Create leg support.
f. Create legs.
g. Create the rollers for legs.
h. Create right hand support.
i. Create left hand support.
j. Save and render the scene.

Creating the Project Folder

Create a new project folder with the name *c03_tut2* at *\Documents\3dsmax2017* and then save the file with the name **c03tut2**, as discussed in Tutorial 1 of Chapter 2.

Creating Seat Support

In this section, you need to create a chamfer box primitive to create seat support of the chair.

1. Activate the Top viewport. Choose **Create > Geometry** from the **Command Panel**; the **Standard Primitives** option is displayed by default in the drop-down list. Select the **Extended Primitives** option from the list and then choose the **ChamferBox** tool from the **Object Type** rollout.

2. Expand the **Keyboard Entry** rollout and set the values as follows:

   Length: **90.0** Width: **100.0** Height: **17.0**
   Fillet: **10.0**

3. Choose the **Create** button; a chamfer box is created.

4. Make sure the chamfer box is selected. In the **Parameters** rollout, set the value **10** in the **Fillet Segs** spinner; the chamfer box is modified, as shown in Figure 3-29.

5. In the **Name and Color** rollout, enter **seat support** as the name of the chamfer box and press ENTER.

6. Use the color swatch to modify the color of *seat support* by entering the values as follows:

   Red: **88** Green: **199** Blue: **225**

Creating Back Support

In this section, you will use the **ChamferBox** tool from the extended primitives to create back support for the chair.

1. Activate the Front viewport and make sure that the **ChamferBox** tool is chosen.

2. Expand the **Keyboard Entry** rollout and set the values as follows:

   X: **0.0** Y: **65.0** Z: **-65.0** Length: **90.0**
   Width: **100.0** Height: **19.633** Fillet: **10.0**

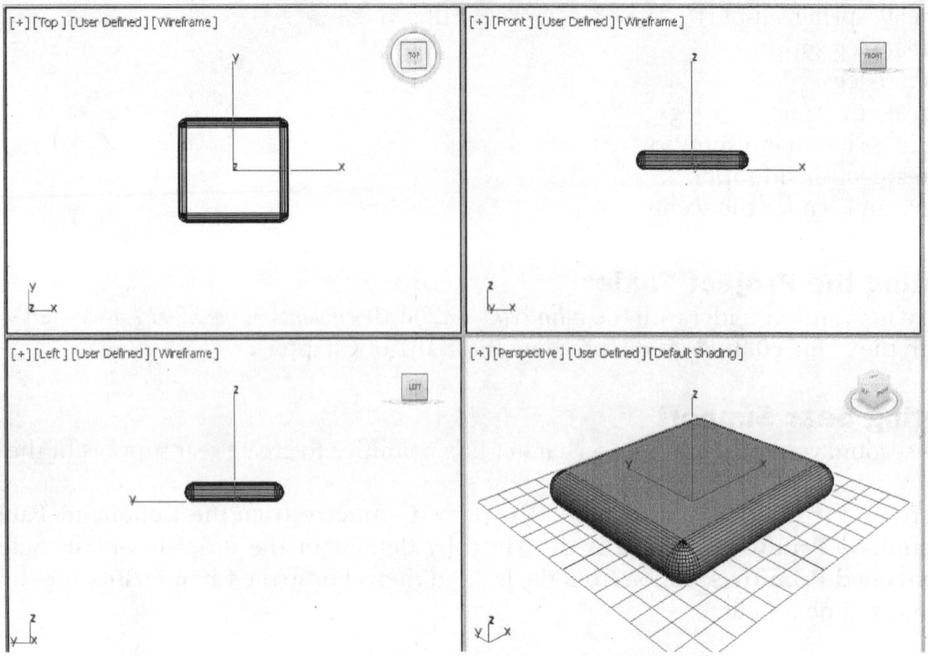

Figure 3-29 The chamfer box created for seat support of the chair

3. Choose the **Create** button; a chamfer box is created. In the **Parameters** rollout, make sure the value in the **Fillet Segs** spinner is **10** and enter **back support** as the name of the chamfer box in the **Name and Color** rollout, refer to Figure 3-30.

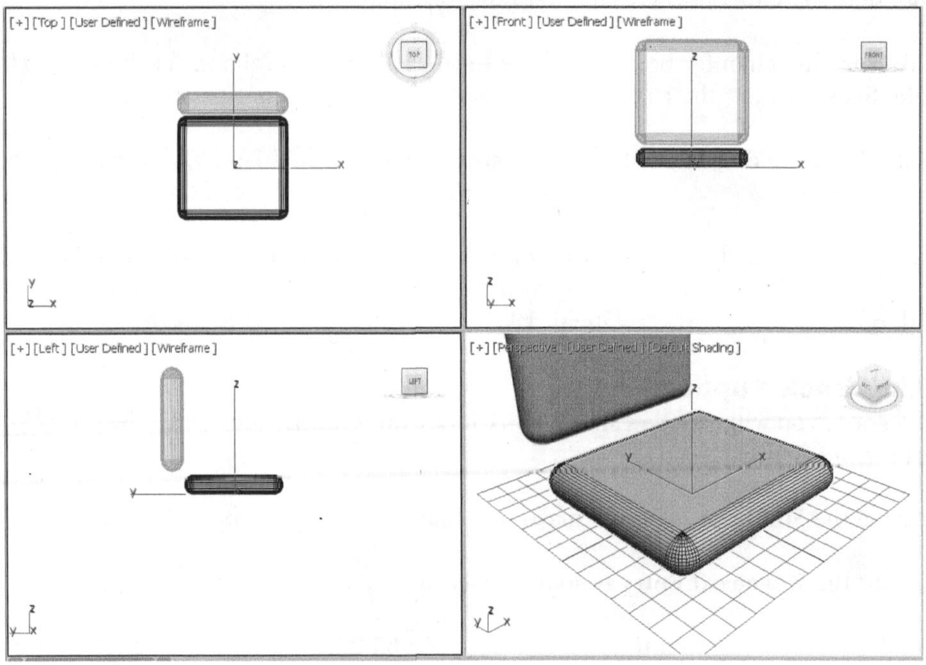

Figure 3-30 The back support geometry in viewports

4. Choose the color swatch and assign the same color to *back support* that you assigned to *seat support*.

5. Choose the **Zoom Extents All** tool to display the objects properly in all viewports.

   Next, you need to create the spring support to join *seat* and *back support*.

Creating Spring Support

In this section, you will create spring support by using the **Hose** tool from the extended primitives.

1. Activate the Top viewport. Choose **Create > Geometry** from the **Command Panel**. Make sure that the **Extended Primitives** option is selected in the drop-down list and then choose the **Hose** tool from the **Object Type** rollout.

2. In the Top viewport, press and hold the left mouse button and drag the cursor to specify the radius of the hose, and then release the left mouse button. Next, move the cursor up to specify the height of the hose and click on the viewport; a hose is created.

3. In the **Name and Color** rollout, enter **spring support** as the name of the hose and press ENTER. Also, modify the color of *spring support* to black.

4. In the **Hose Parameters** rollout, set the values of *spring support* as follows:

   End Point Method Area
   Make sure that the **Free Hose** radio button is selected.

   Free Hose Parameters Area
   Height: **25.815**

   Common Hose Parameters Area
   Cycles: **9**
   Use the default values for the other options in this area.

   Smoothing Area
   Make sure the **All** radio button is selected.

   Hose Shape Area
   Make sure the **Round Hose** radio button is selected.

   Diameter: **15.0** Sides: **8**

   After setting the values in the **Hose Parameters** rollout, align *spring support* in the viewports, as shown in Figure 3-31.

   Next, you will apply the **Bend** modifier to *spring support* to join *seat* and *back support*.

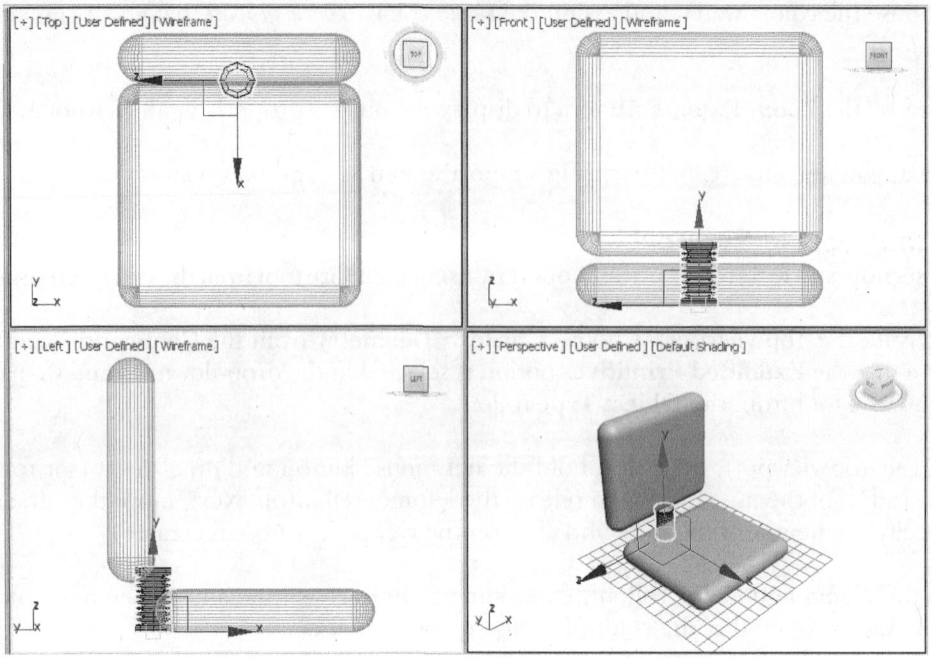

Figure 3-31 The spring support geometry in viewports

5. Make sure *spring support* is selected and then choose **Modifiers > Parametric Deformers > Bend** from the menu bar; the **Bend** modifier is displayed in the modifier stack. Also, the **Parameters** rollout is displayed in the **Modify** tab.

6. In the **Parameters** rollout of the **Bend** modifier, set the values as follows:

   Bend Area
   Angle: **90.0** Direction: **90**

   Bend Axis area
   Make sure the **Z** radio button is selected.

7. After entering the values, *spring support* is displayed, as shown in Figure 3-32.

   Next, you will align *spring support*.

8. Activate the Left viewport and make sure that *spring support* is selected. Choose the **Zoom Extents Selected** tool; *spring support* is zoomed in the Left viewport, as shown in Figure 3-33.

9. Right-click on the **Select and Rotate** tool; the **Rotate Transform Type-In** dialog box is displayed. In the **Offset: Screen** area, set **90** in the **Z** spinner and press ENTER; *spring support* is rotated, as shown in Figure 3-34. Now, close the **Rotate Transform Type-In** dialog box.

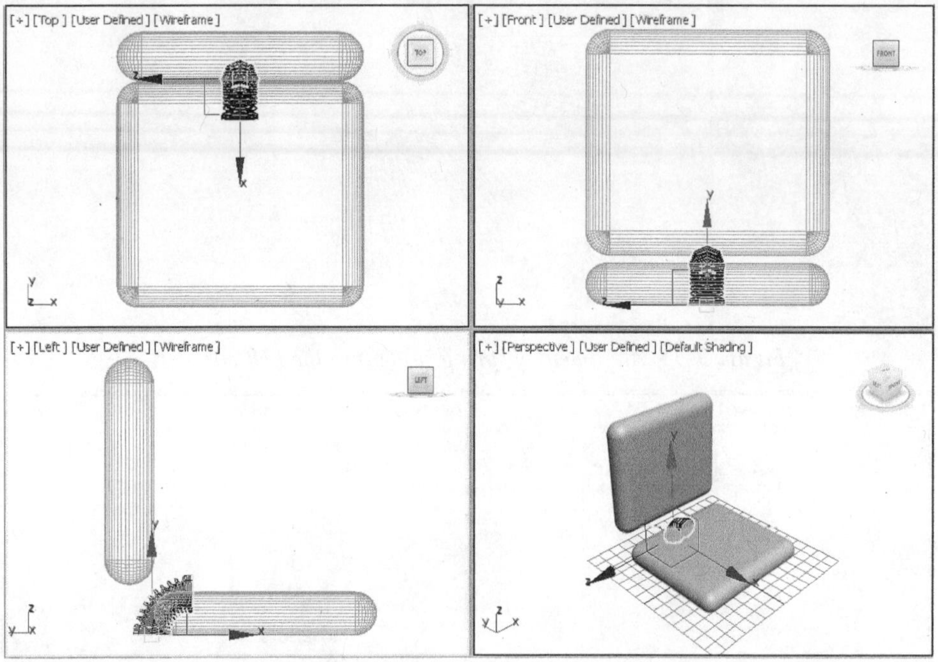

***Figure 3-32** The spring support geometry after applying the **Bend** modifier*

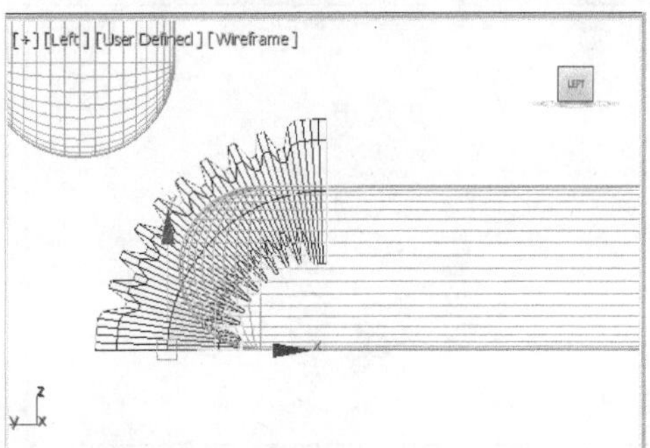

***Figure 3-33** The spring support geometry zoomed in the Left viewport*

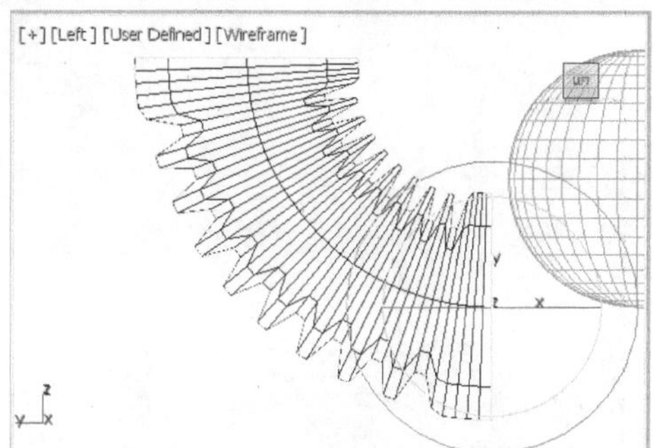

***Figure 3-34** The spring support geometry rotated in the Left viewport*

10. Choose the **Select and Move** tool and align *spring support*, as shown in Figure 3-35.

11. Choose the **Zoom Extents All** tool to display all the objects properly in the viewports, refer to Figure 3-36.

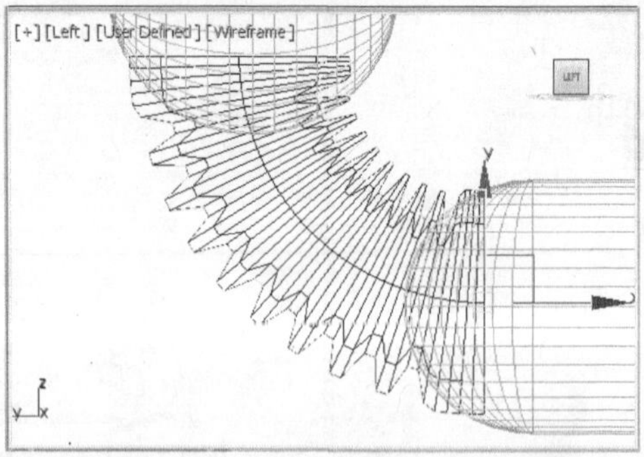

Figure 3-35 Alignment of spring support in the Left viewport

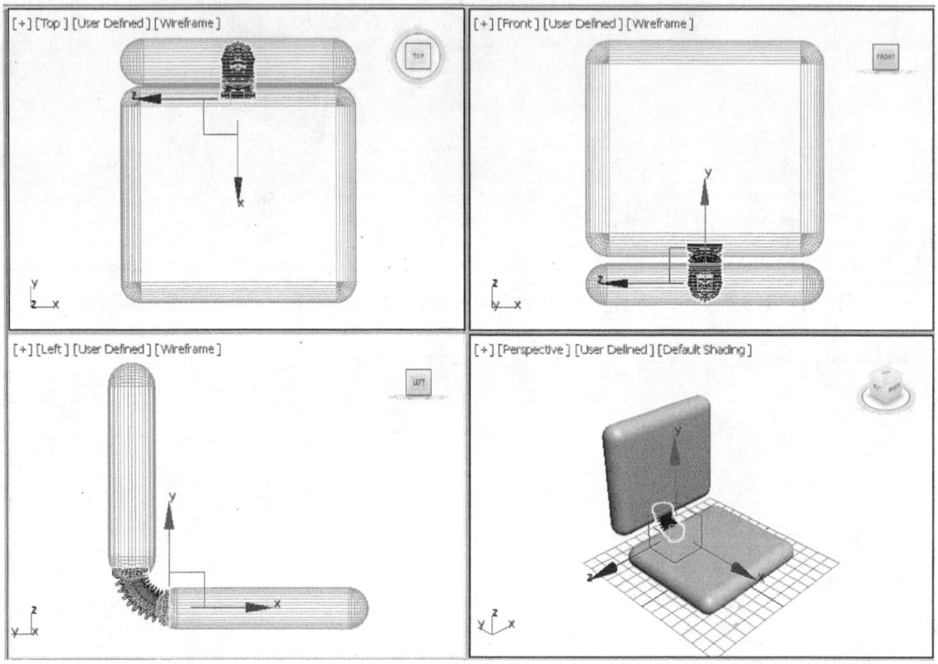

Figure 3-36 Alignment of spring support in the viewports

Creating Leg Support

Now, you need to create leg support. You will use the **Hose** tool from the extended primitives to create it.

1. Activate the Top viewport and then create a hose object as discussed earlier.

2. In the **Name and Color** rollout, enter **leg support** as the name of the hose and press ENTER. Also, modify the color of *leg support* to black.

3. In the **Hose Parameters** rollout, set the values of *leg support* as follows:

   End Point Method Area

Make sure that the **Free Hose** radio button is selected.

Free Hose Parameters Area
Height: **42.0**

Common Hose Parameters Area
Make sure that the **Flex Section Enable** check box is selected.

Starts: **22.0** Ends: **82.0**
Cycles: **10**

Make sure the value in the Diameter spinner is **-20.0**.

Smoothing Area
Make sure the **All** radio button is selected.
Hose Shape Area
Make sure the **Round Hose** radio button is selected.

Diameter: **17.0** Sides: **8**

4. Choose the **Select and Move** tool and align *leg support* in the viewports, as shown in Figure 3-37.

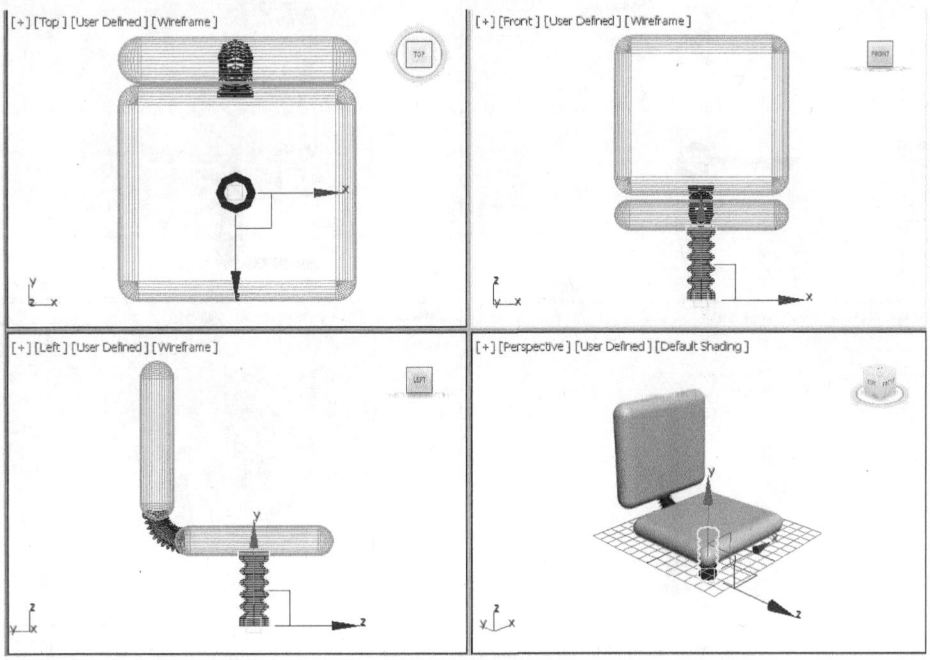

Figure 3-37 Alignment of leg support in the viewports

Creating Legs

In this section, you will use the **ChamferBox** tool from **Extended Primitives** to create legs of the chair.

1. Activate the Top viewport and choose the **ChamferBox** tool.

2. Expand the **Keyboard Entry** rollout and set the values as follows:

   X: **-29** Y: **0.0** Z: **-42.0** Length: **5.748**
   Width: **44.0**. Height: **7.0** Fillet: **2.0**

3. Choose the **Create** button; a chamfer box is created.

4. Make sure the chamfer box is selected. In the **Parameters** rollout, set the values as follows:

   Length Segs: **10** Width Segs: **10** Height Segs: **10**

   Make sure the value in the Fillet Segs is **10**.
   After entering the values, the chamfer box is modified.

5. In the **Name and Color** rollout, enter **leg01** as the name of the chamfer box and press ENTER. Also, modify its color to black.

6. Choose the **Select and Move** tool and align *leg01* with *leg support* in the viewports, as shown in Figure 3-38.

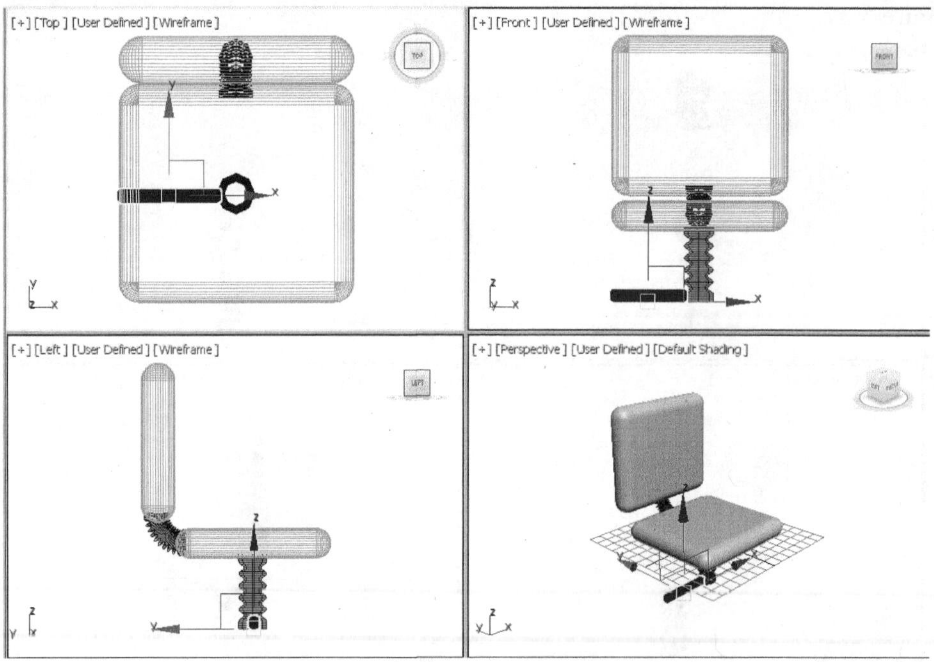

Figure 3-38 *Alignment of leg01 in the viewports*

Now, you need to apply the **Taper** modifier to *leg01* to taper it.

7. Make sure that *leg01* is selected, and then choose the **Zoom Extents All Selected** tool; *leg01* is zoomed in all viewports, as shown in Figure 3-39.

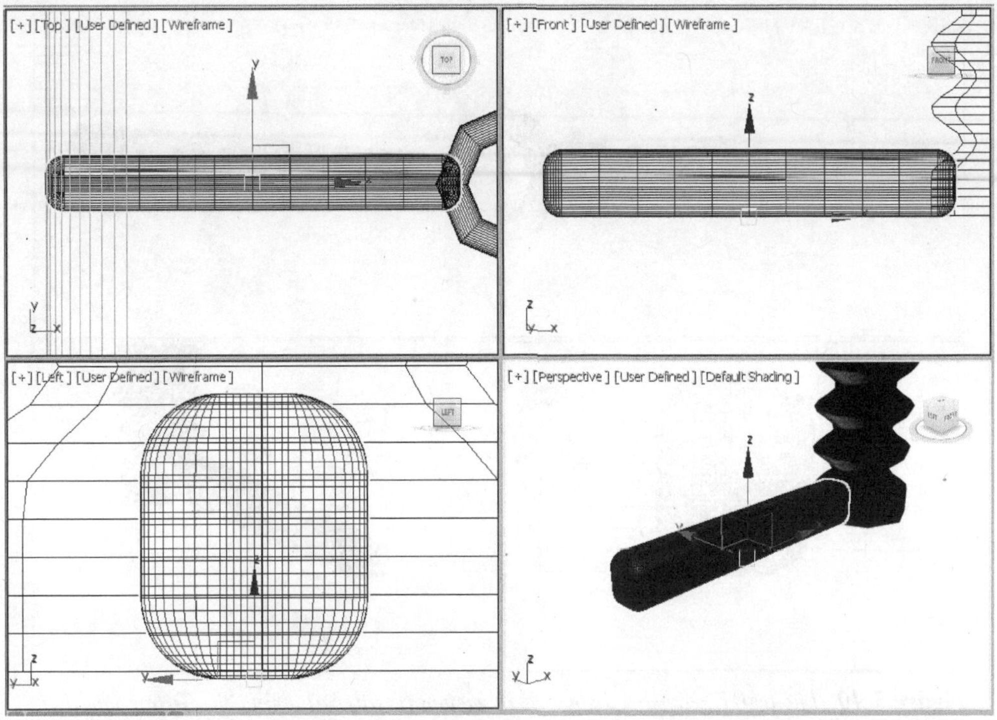

*Figure 3-39 The leg01 geometry after invoking the **Zoom Extents All Selected** tool*

8. Choose **Modifiers > Parametric Deformers > Taper** from the menu bar; the **Taper** modifier is displayed in the modifier stack. Also, the **Parameters** rollout is displayed in the Modify tab.

9. In the **Parameters** rollout of the **Taper** modifier, set the values as given below:

   Taper Area
   Amount: **0.53**

   Taper Axis Area
   Select the **X** radio button in the **Primary** group and make sure the **ZY** radio button is selected in the **Effect** group.

10. After entering the values, *leg01* is tapered, as shown in Figure 3-40.

Next, you need to create rollers.

Creating the Rollers for Legs

In this section, you will create rollers. You will use the chamfer box and chamfer cylinder primitives to create them.

1. Activate the Top viewport and choose the **ChamferBox** tool.

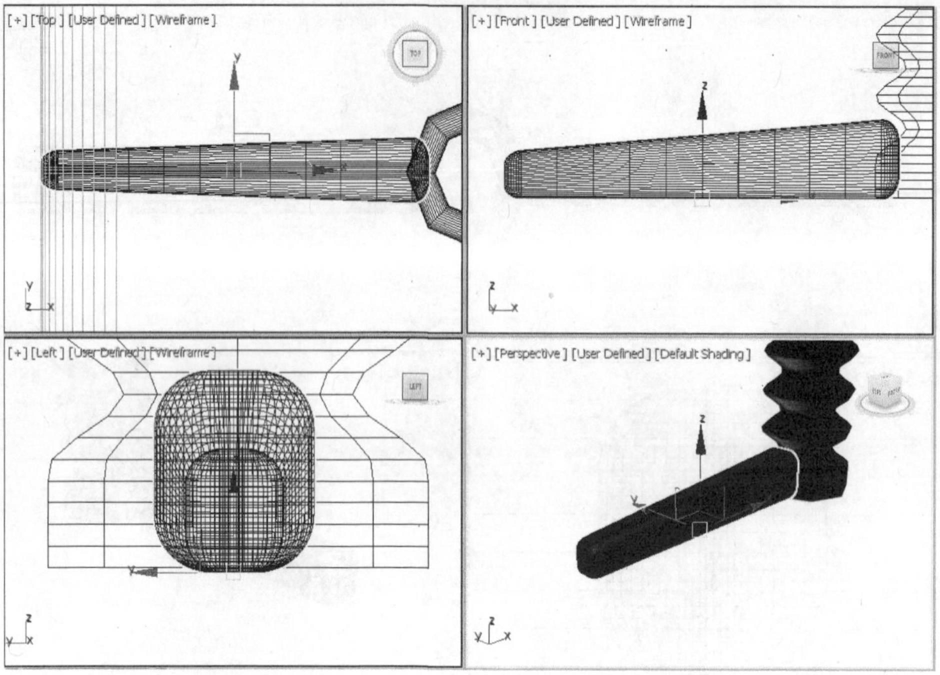

Figure 3-40 The leg01 geometry displayed in viewports after applying the ***Taper*** *modifier*

2. Expand the **Keyboard Entry** rollout and set the values as follows:

   X: **-40** Y: **0.0** Z: **-20.0** Length: **7.032**
   Width: **14.816** Height: **1.799** Fillet: **1.0**

3. Choose the **Create** button; a chamfer box is created.

4. Make sure that the chamfer box is selected. In the **Parameters** rollout, make sure the value in the Length Segs, Width Segs, Height Segs, and Fillet Segs spinners is **10**.

5. In the **Name and Color** rollout, enter **box01** as the name of the chamfer cylinder. Also, modify its color to black.

Note
To view box01 in viewports, you need to adjust the view by invoking the ***Zoom*** *and* ***Pan View*** *tools.*

Next, you will apply the **Bend** modifier to *box01*.

6. Choose **Modifiers > Parametric Deformers > Bend** from the menu bar; the **Bend** modifier is displayed in the modifier stack. Also, the **Parameters** rollout is displayed in the Modify panel.

7. In the **Parameters** rollout of the **Bend** modifier, set the values as follows:

   Bend Area
   Angle: **173.5**

Bend Axis Area
Select the **X** radio button.

8. After applying the **Bend** modifier, *box01* is displayed, as shown in Figure 3-41.

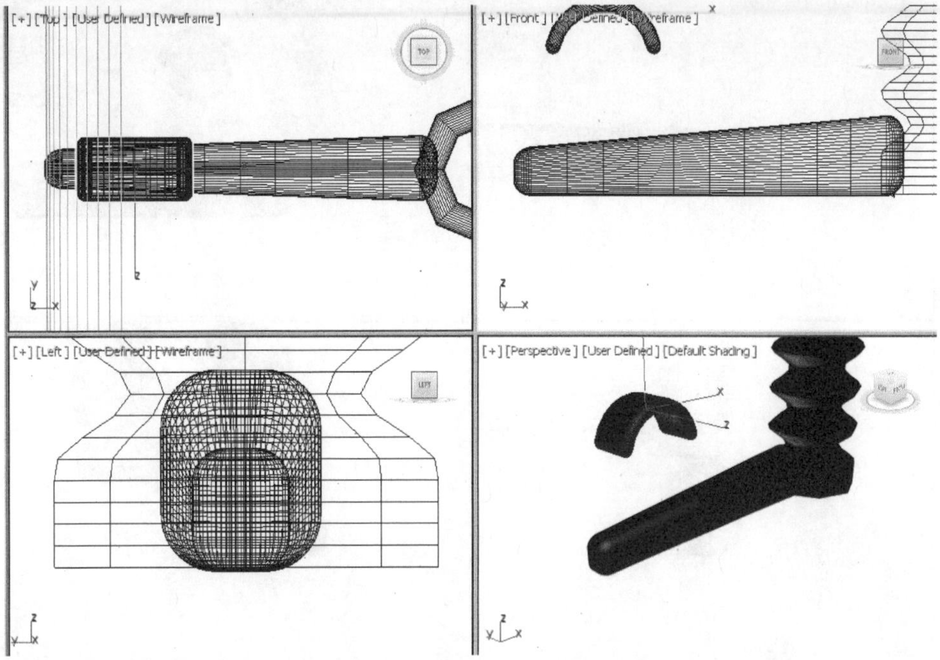

*Figure 3-41 The box01 geometry displayed in viewports after applying the **Bend** modifier*

Next, you need to create a chamfer cylinder.

9. Make sure the **Extended Primitives** option is selected in the drop-down list of the **Command Panel**. Now, choose the **ChamferCyl** tool from the **Object Type** rollout.

10. Activate the Top viewport and expand the **Keyboard Entry** rollout. Set the values as follows:

X: **-40**	Y: **0.0**	Z: **-20.0**
Radius: **5.0**	Height: **7.0**	Fillet: **1.0**

11. Choose the **Create** button; a chamfer cylinder is created.

12. Make sure the chamfer cylinder is selected. In the **Parameters** rollout, set the values as follows:

Height Segs: **10**	Fillet Segs: **10**	Cap Segs: **11**

Make sure the value in the **Sides** spinner is **12** and the **Smooth** check box is selected.

13. In the **Name and Color** rollout, enter **cylinder01** as the name of the chamfer box and press ENTER. Also, modify its color by specifying the values as follows:

Red: **151** Green: **151** Blue: **151**

14. Align *cylinder01* with *box01* in the viewports using the **Select and Rotate** and **Select and Move** tools, refer to Figure 3-42.

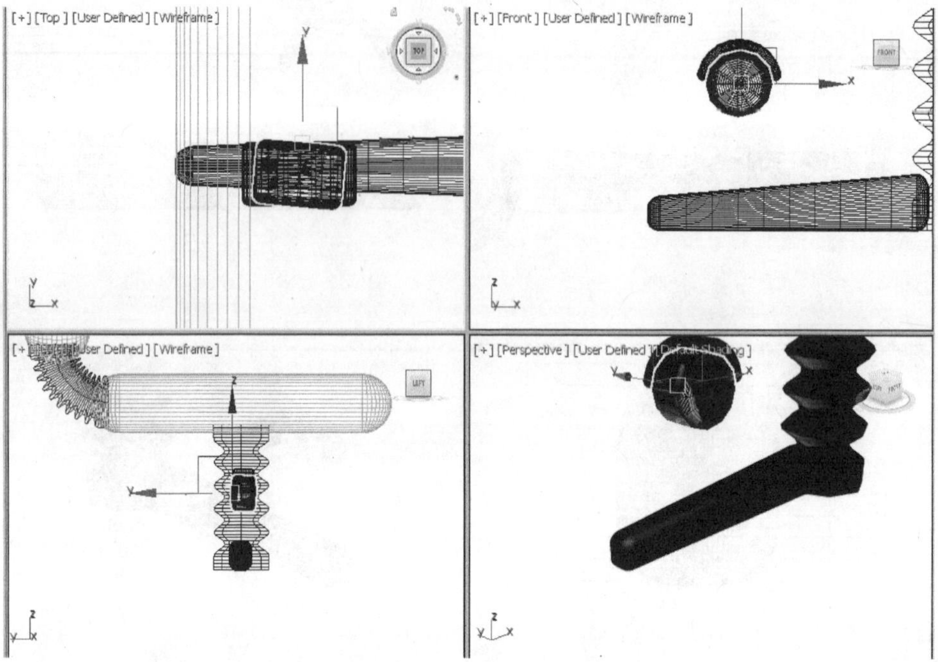

Figure 3-42 Alignment of cylinder01 with box01 in viewports

Next, you need to group *cylinder01* and *box01*.

15. Select *cylinder01* and *box01* from the Scene Explorer and right-click; a quad menu is displayed. Choose **Add Selected to > New Group** from the quad menu; the **Group** dialog box is displayed.

16. Enter **roller01** in the **Group name** text box and choose the **OK** button; the group is named as *roller01*.

17. Using the **Select and Move** and **Select and Rotate** tools, align *roller01* with *leg01* in all viewports, as shown in Figure 3-43.

18. Group *leg01* and *roller01* as *f_leg01* as done earlier.

19. Choose the **Zoom Extents All** tool to view all the objects in the viewports.

Next, you need to create other legs for the chair using the same dimensions. To do so, you need to copy *f_leg01*.

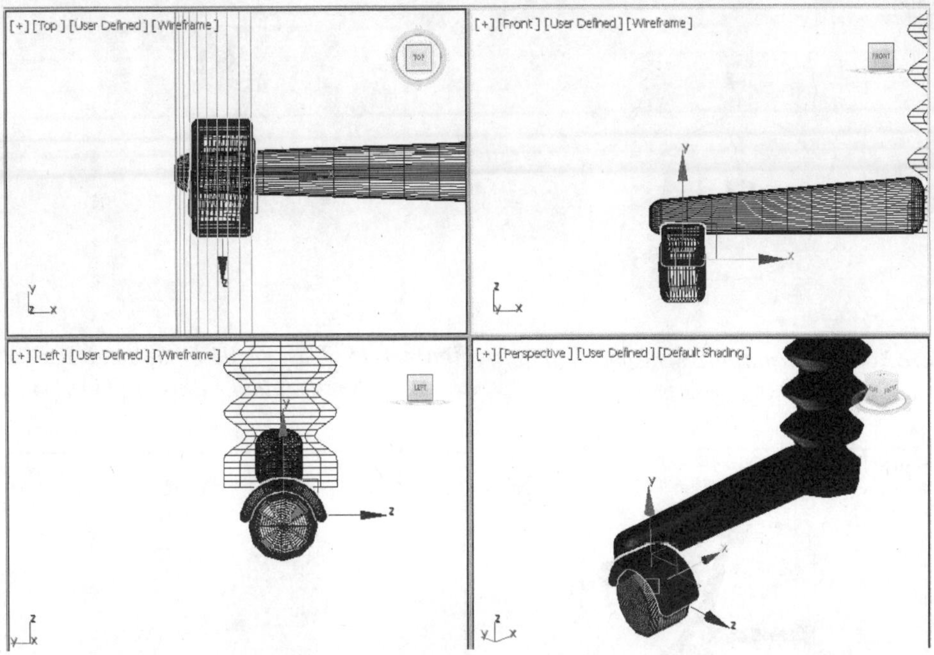

***Figure 3-43** Alignment of roller01 with leg01 in viewports*

20. Activate the Top viewport and make sure *f_leg01* is selected. Now, choose the **Hierarchy** tab from the **Command Panel.** In the **Pivot** tab, choose the **Use Working Pivot** button in the **Working Pivot** rollout; a gizmo is displayed at the center of the scene.

    Also, the **USE WP** text is displayed below the viewport label in the viewports.

    The working pivot point enables you to rotate *f_leg01* about an arbitrary and persistent point in the scene without affecting the original pivot point of the object.

21. Activate the Top viewport and then choose the **Select and Rotate** tool; a circular gizmo is displayed, as shown in Figure 3-44.

22. Move the cursor over the Z-axis that is blue in color; it get highlighted in yellow color. Now, press and hold the SHIFT key as well as the left mouse button and drag the cursor until the value in the **Z** spinner in the coordinate display becomes about **-72**, refer to Figure 3-45. Release the left mouse button; the **Clone Options** dialog box is displayed. Make sure that the **Copy** radio button is selected. Set **4** in the **Number of Copies** spinner. Choose the **OK** button; *f_leg002, f_leg003, f_leg004,* and *f_leg005* are displayed in the viewports, as shown in Figure 3-46.

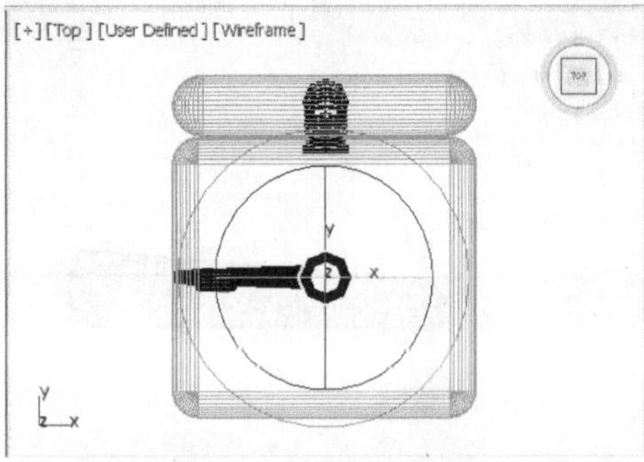

Figure 3-44 *A circular gizmo displayed at the location of the working pivot point*

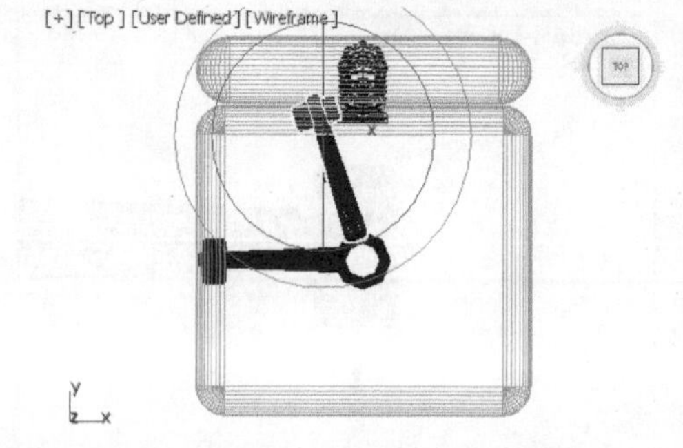

Figure 3-45 *The f_leg01 group rotated about* **-72** *degrees with respect to the working pivot point*

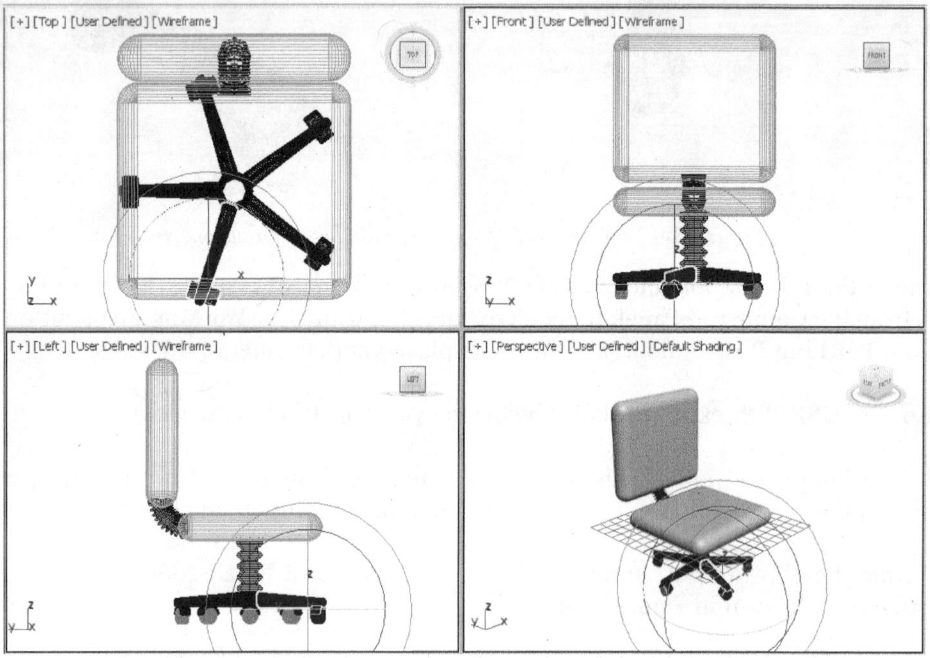

Figure 3-46 *The f_leg002, f_leg003, f_leg004, and f_leg005 in viewports*

23. Deactivate the **Use Working Pivot** button by choosing it again in the **Working Pivot** rollout; the cursor moves to its original position. Also, the USE WP text disappears from the viewport label in the viewports.

Creating Right Hand Support

In this section, you will use the **Box** tool from **Standard Primitives** to create right hand support of the chair.

1. Activate the Top viewport and choose **Create > Geometry** from the **Command Panel**. Now, select the **Standard Primitives** option from the drop-down list. Also, choose the **Box** tool from the **Object Type** rollout.

2. Expand the **Keyboard Entry** rollout and set the values as follows:
   Length: **5.515** Width: **9.0** Height: **55.0**

3. Choose the **Create** button; a box is created.

4. In the **Parameters** rollout, set the values as given below:

   Length Segs: **15** Width Segs: **15** Height Segs: **15**

> **Note**
> *The more the number of segments in an object, the smoother will be its surface when you apply a modifier to it.*

5. In the **Name and Color** rollout, enter **right hand support01** as the name of the box and press ENTER. Also, change its color to black.

   Next, you need to apply the **Bend** modifier to *right hand support01* to give it the shape of a hand rest.

6. Make sure that *right hand support01* is selected and then apply the **Bend** modifier to it as discussed earlier.

7. In the **Parameters** rollout of the **Bend** modifier, set the parameters as follows:

   Bend Area
   Angle: **107.5** Direction: **270.0**
   Bend Axis Area

   Make sure the **Z** radio button is selected.

8. Align *right hand support01* in all viewports, as shown in Figure 3-47.

   Next, you need to create the second part of *right hand support01*. To do so, you need to copy *right hand support01*.

9. Activate the Top viewport, select *right hand support01,* and then create its copy; the copy is automatically named as *right hand support002*.

10. In the **Parameters** rollout of the **Bend** modifier, set the values as follows:

    Bend Area
    Angle: **90** Direction: **180**

    Bend Axis Area
    Make sure the **Z** radio button is selected.

    Limits Area
    Select the **Limit Effect** check box.
    Upper Limit: **18.0**

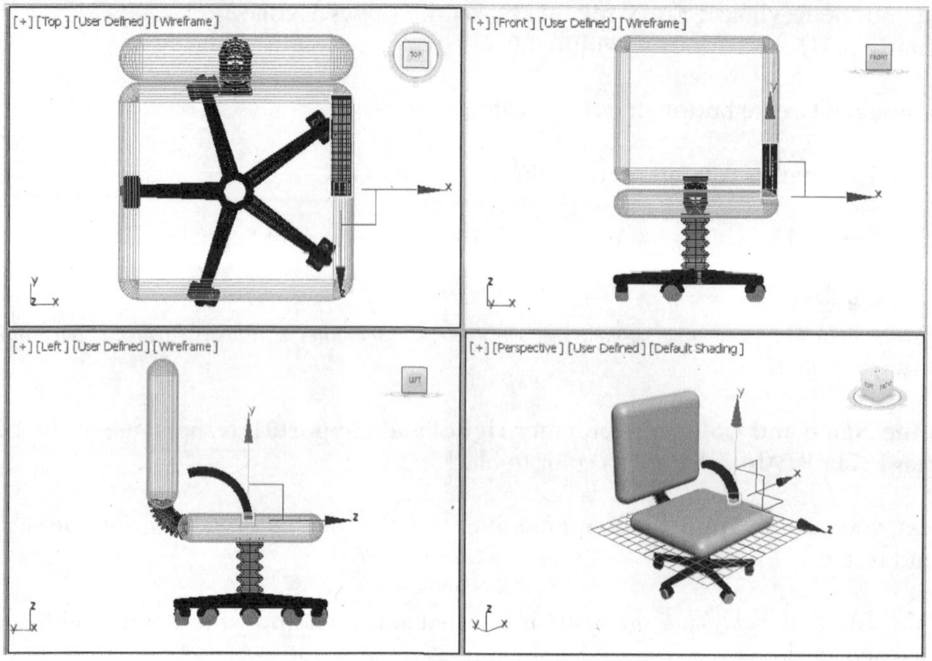

Figure 3-47 Alignment of right hand support01 in viewports

11. After entering the values, *right hand support002* is modified, as shown in Figure 3-48.

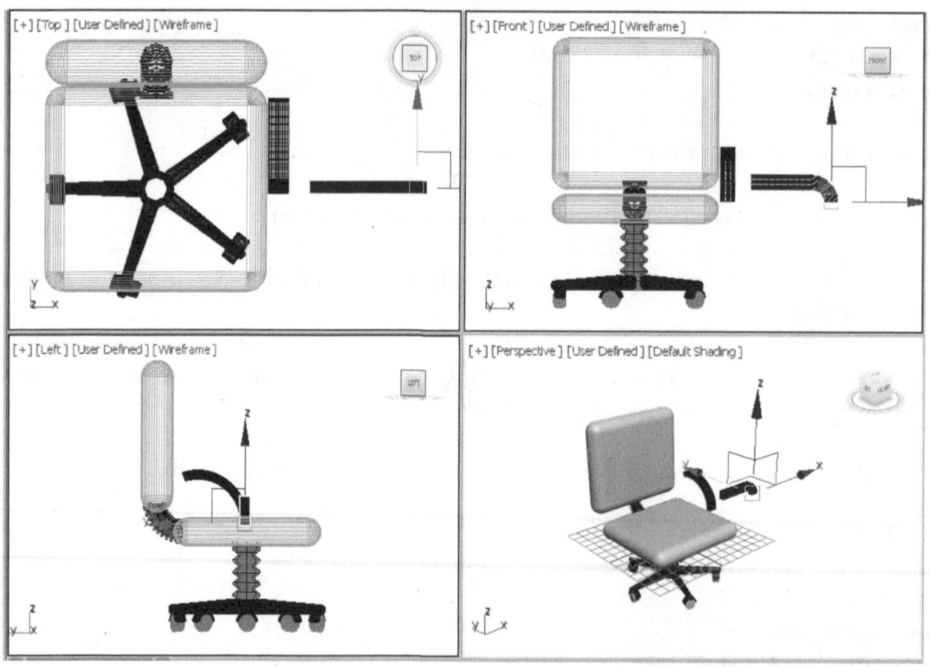

Figure 3-48 *The right hand support002 geometry after modifying the values of the* ***Bend*** *modifier*

12. Align *right hand support002* in viewports using the **Select and Move** and **Select and Rotate** tools, as shown in Figure 3-49.

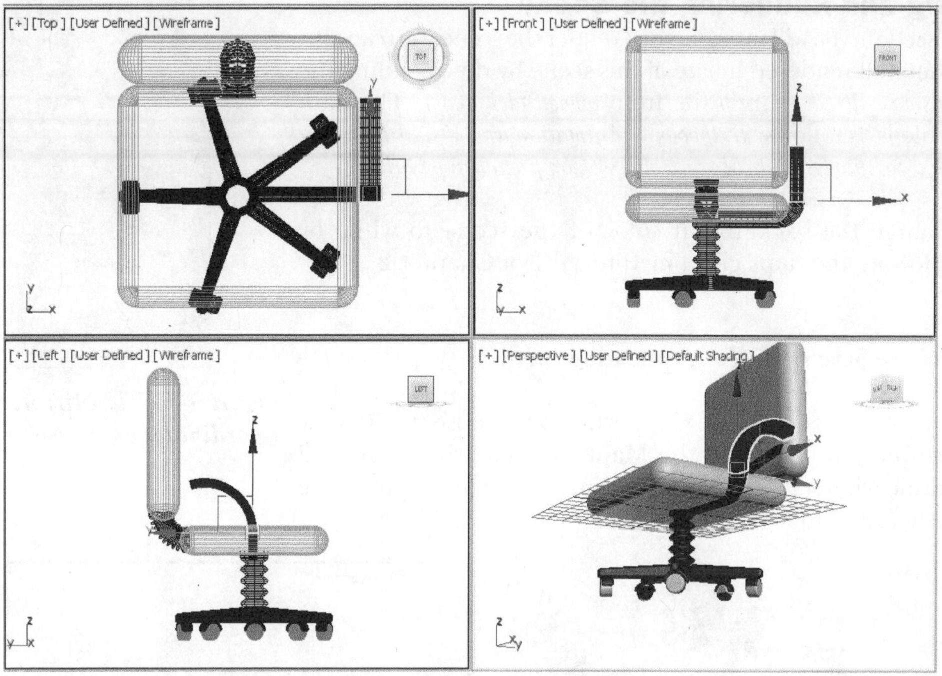

Figure 3-49 *Alignment of right hand support002 in viewports*

Note

You can use the ***Orbit*** *tool in the Perspective viewport to view the proper alignment of right hand support002 in viewports.*

13. Select *right hand support01* and *right hand support002* and group them as *right hand support*.

14. Choose the **Zoom Extents All** tool to view all the objects in the viewports.

Creating Left Hand Support

In this section, you will create a copy of *right hand support* to create a support for the left hand.

1. Activate the Top viewport, select *right hand support*.

2. Choose the **Mirror** tool from the **Main Toolbar**; the **Mirror: Screen Coordinates** dialog box is displayed, as shown in Figure 3-50.

3. In this dialog box, make sure that the **X** radio button is selected in the **Mirror Axis** area and set -81.4 in the **Offset** spinner. Next, select the **Copy** radio button in the **Clone Selection** area and then choose the **OK** button.

   Figure 3-51 shows *left hand support* in the viewports.

Saving and Rendering the Scene

In this section, you will save and then render the scene. You can also view the final rendered image of this scene by downloading the *c03_3dsmax_2017_rndr.zip* file from *www.cadcim.com*. The path of the file is as follows: *Textbooks > Animation and Visual Effects > 3ds Max > Autodesk 3ds Max 2017: A Comprehensive Guide*

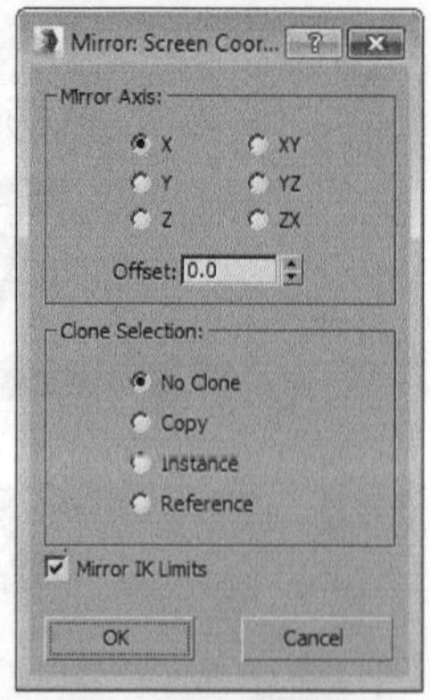

***Figure 3-50** The **Mirror: Screen Coordinates** dialog box*

1. Change the background color of the scene to white by following the steps given in Tutorial 1 of Chapter 2 .

2. Choose **Save** from the **Application** menu.

3. Activate the Perspective viewport. Next, choose the **Render Production** tool from the **Main Toolbar**; the **Rendered Frame** window is displayed showing the final output of the scene, refer to Figure 3-52.

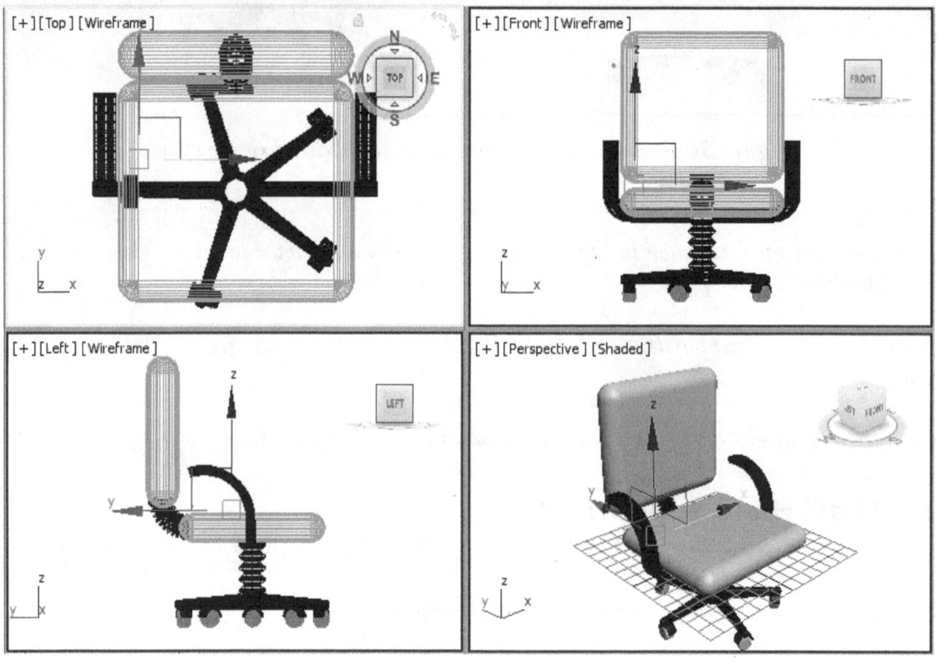

***Figure 3-51** The left hand support geometry in viewports*

Figure 3-52 The final rendered output

Self-Evaluation Test

Answer the following questions and then compare them to those given at the end of this chapter:

1. Which of the following modifiers is used to bend an object along its axis?

   (a) **Bend** (b) **Taper**
   (c) **Percent Snap Toggle** (d) None of these

2. Which of the following tools in the extended primitives does not have the **Creation Method** and **Keyboard Entry** rollouts?

   (a) **RingWave** (b) **Hedra**
   (c) **Hose** (d) All of these

3. Which of the following radio buttons is selected by default in the **RingWave Timing** area of the **Parameters** rollout?

   (a) **No Growth** (b) **Cyclic Growth**
   (c) **Grow and Stay** (d) None of these

4. Which of the following spinners is used to bevel the top and bottom cap edges of a chamfer cylinder?

   (a) **Sides** (b) **Fillet**
   (c) **Cap Segs** (d) **Fillet Segs**

5. The value in the __________ spinner in the **Bend** area of the Bend modifier is used to define the angle of bend along the X, Y, or Z axis.

6. The options in the _________ area are used to change the shape of the outer edge of the ringwave and define the breakup of the outer edge.

7. The _________ spinner in the **Taper** area of the **Taper** modifier is used to define the amount of taper.

8. In the **RingWave Size** area, the **Radius** spinner is used to define the outer radius of the ringwave. (T/F)

9. You cannot modify the height of the free hose by setting the value in the **Height** spinner in the **Free Hose Parameters** area. (T/F)

10. The options in the **Inner Edge Breakup** area are used to change the shape of the inner edge of the ringwave. (T/F)

Review Questions

Answer the following questions:

1. Which of the following command sequences is followed to create a **Hedra** from the **Command Panel**?

(a) **Create > Extended Primitives > Hedra**
(b) **Create > Geometry > Extended Primitives > Object Type** rollout **> Hedra**
(c) **Create > Standard Primitives > Hedra**
(d) **Create > Shape > Extended Primitives > Object Type** rollout **> Hedra**

2. Which of the following radio buttons is selected by default in the **Family** area of the **Parameters** rollout while creating a **Hedra**?

(a) **Tetra** (b) **Star1**
(c) **Star2** (d) **Dodec/Icos**

3. Which of the following three shapes of the polygonal facets of a polyhedron can have in the **Axis Scaling** area?

(a) triangle, square, and rectangle (b) triangle, square, and octagon
(c) triangle, square, and pentagon (d) triangle, square, and hexagon

4. Which of the following spinners is used to specify the number of segments in the fillet of a chamfer box?

(a) **Fillet** (b) **Width Segs**
(c) **Height Segs** (d) **Fillet Segs**

5. Which of the following is an extended primitives?

(a) **Capsule** (b) **Chamfer Box**
(c) **Chamfer Cylinder** (d) All of these

6. In the **Parameters** rollout of the **Taper** modifier, the **Primary** area is used to define the __________ axis and the **Effect** area is used to define the __________ from the primary axis.

7. In the **Limits** area of the **Parameters** rollout of the **Bend** modifier, the default value in the **Upper Limit** and **Lower Limit** spinner is __________.

8. In the **Parameters** rollout of the chamfer cylinder, the **Slice On** check box is used to specify the start and end angle of the chamfer cylinder. (T/F)

9. The **Taper** modifier is used to bend an object in angular increments. (T/F)

10. In the **Family Parameters** area of the **Parameters** rollout of the hedra, the combined value of the **P** and **Q** spinners can be either equal to or less than 1.0. (T/F)

EXERCISES

The rendered output of the models used in the following exercises can be accessed by downloading the *c03_3dsmax_2017_exr.zip* from *www.cadcim.com*. The path of the file is as follows: *Textbooks > Animation and Visual Effects > 3ds Max > Autodesk 3ds Max 2017: A Comprehensive Guide*

Exercise 1

Create the model of a stool shown in Figure 3-53 using your own dimensions.

(Expected time: 30 min)

Figure 3-53 *The model of a stool*

Exercise 2

Create the models shown in Figures 3-54 and 3-55 by using your own dimensions.

(Expected time: 30 min)

Figure 3-54 The model of a table

Figure 3-55 The model of a chair

Answers to Self-Evaluation Test

1. a, **2.** d, **3.** a, **4.** b, **5. Angle**, **6. Outer Edge Breakup**, **7 Amount**, **8.** T, **9.** F, **10.** T

4

Working with Architectural Objects

Learning Objectives

After completing this chapter, you will be able to:

- *Use the Mirror and Align tools*
- *Create AEC extended objects*
- *Create doors and windows*

INTRODUCTION

In this chapter, you will learn to create the default objects and patch grids in 3ds Max. Also, you will learn to use the **Mirror** and **Align** tools while modeling the objects with the help of various primitives and default objects. In addition, you will learn to create doors and windows.

MIRROR TOOL

Menu bar: Tools > Mirror
Main Toolbar: Mirror

The **Mirror** tool is used to mirror or clone the selected object about the center of the current coordinate system. You can also move the object while mirroring its orientation. To mirror an object, select it in a viewport and choose the **Mirror** tool from the **Main Toolbar**; the **Mirror** dialog box will be displayed, refer to Figure 4-1. Set the parameters in this dialog box and choose the **OK** button to mirror the objects. The two areas in this dialog box are discussed next.

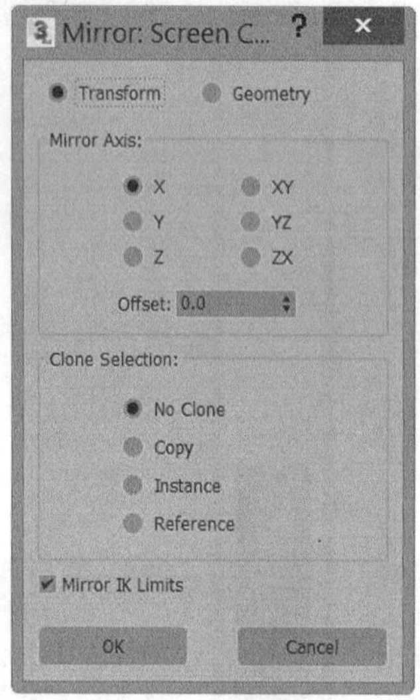

Figure 4-1 The ***Mirror*** *dialog box*

Mirror Axis Area

Select the **X**, **Y**, **Z**, **XY**, **YZ**, or **ZX** radio button in the **Mirror Axis** area to define the direction of the object while mirroring. By default, the **X** radio button is selected. The value in the **Offset** spinner defines the distance of the mirrored object from the original one.

Clone Selection Area

The **Clone Selection** area is used to define the type of clone created by the **Mirror** tool. By default, the **No Clone** radio button is selected in this area. As a result, the selected object is mirrored but not retained. Select the **Copy** radio button to retain the selected object after mirroring. You can also change the position of the copied object by entering the required value in the **Offset** spinner in the **Mirror Axis** area. Select the **Instance** radio button to mirror the selected object as an instance. Select the **Reference** radio button to mirror a reference of the selected object to a specified position.

An instance is a type of clone in which the changes are reflected when they are made in the original object. Also, if you make any change in the instanced object, then it will transfer to the original object.

A reference object is similar to an instance object with the only difference that the changes made in the reference object are not reflected in the original object.

ALIGN TOOL

Menu bar:	Tools > Align > Align
Main Toolbar:	Align
Keyboard:	ALT + A

The **Align** tool enables you to align the current object with the target object. To align an object using the **Align** tool, select the current object and then choose the **Align** tool from the **Main Toolbar**; the shape of the cursor will change, as shown in Figure 4-2. Move the cursor over the target object in the viewport and click on it; the **Align Selection (X)** dialog box will be displayed, refer to Figure 4-3. Here, **X** refers to the name of the target object. You need to use the options in the **Align Selection (X)** dialog box to align the objects. Various areas and options in this dialog box are discussed next.

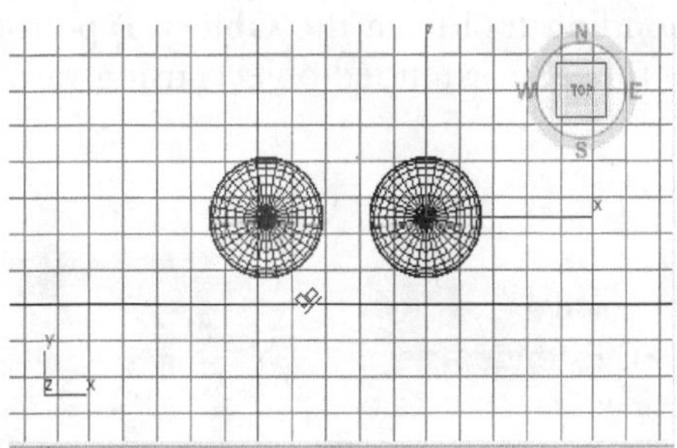

Figure 4-2 The align cursor in the Top viewport

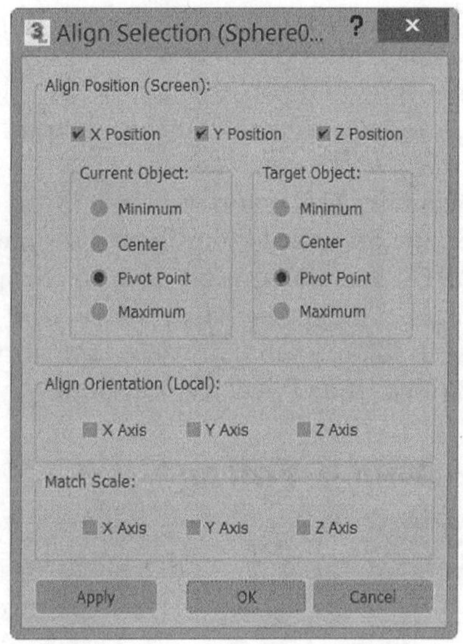

*Figure 4-3 The **Align Selection (Sphere002)** dialog box*

Align Position Area

You can select the check box(es) in this area to specify the axis along which you want to align the object.

Current Object/Target Object Group

The **Minimum**, **Center**, **Pivot Point**, or **Maximum** radio button in the **Current Object** and **Target Object** groups can be selected to specify different points on the current and target objects to be used for alignment.

Align Orientation Area

You can select the check box(es) in this area to specify the axis or axes about which you want to align the orientation. By default, all check boxes are cleared.

Match Scale Area

You can select the check box(es) in this area to match the scale axes values between the current and target object.

Note

1. You should try different combinations of axes in the ***Align Position*** *area. Also, try using different options in the* ***Current Object*** *and* ***Target Object*** *areas to notice the difference.*

2. If the objects have not been scaled before, the ***Match Scale*** *area will not change the size of the objects.*

AEC EXTENDED PRIMITIVES

In 3ds Max, there are some in-built objects such as trees, railings, walls, and so on, which are known as AEC extended objects. The AEC extended objects are used in the architectural, engineering, and construction fields. All AEC extended objects can be created dynamically by using the mouse or by entering the parameters in the **Keyboard Entry** rollout.

To create an AEC extended object, you need to choose **Create > Geometry** in the **Command Panel**; the **Standard Primitives** option will be displayed by default in the drop-down list. Select the **AEC Extended** option from the drop-down list and activate the viewport in which you want to create the objects. Next, choose the corresponding tool from the **Object Type** rollout. In this section, you will learn to create and modify the AEC extended objects using various tools available in the **Object Type** rollout.

Creating a Foliage

Menu bar:	Create > AEC Objects > Foliage
Command Panel:	Create > Geometry > AEC Extended > Object Type rollout > Foliage

To create a foliage or a tree, activate the viewport in which you want to create it. Next, choose the **Foliage** tool from the **Object Type** rollout; the **Name and Color**, **Keyboard Entry**, **Favorite Plants**, and **Parameters** rollouts will be displayed, as shown in Figure 4-4.

Figure 4-4 *Various rollouts to create a tree*

In the **Favorite Plants** rollout, double-click on a tree; the selected tree will be displayed in the viewports. One of the sample trees is shown in Figure 4-5. Alternatively, you can create a tree by dragging it from the **Favorite Plants** rollout to the desired location in the viewport. Also, you can select one of the trees from the **Favorite Plants** rollout and then click in the viewport at the desired location to place it. You need to choose the **Zoom Extents All** tool to view the entire tree in the viewports.

Various rollouts used to create and modify the tree are discussed next.

Note

*1. The options in the **Name and Color** rollout are the same for all AEC extended objects.*

*2. The **Keyboard Entry** rollout is used to create various objects by entering the parameters using the keyboard. The method of creating these objects is the same as discussed earlier in Chapter 2. However, the railing object cannot be created using the keyboard, therefore, it does not have the **Keyboard Entry** rollout.*

Favorite Plants Rollout

The **Favorite Plants** rollout has a palette consisting of a list of default trees to create them in the viewport. By default, the **Automatic Materials** check box is selected. It is used to assign the default material to the trees. If you clear this check box and create a tree, then the tree created will not show any material. Also, the default color will be displayed in it. Choose the **Plant Library** button below the **Automatic Materials** check box; the **Configure Palette** dialog box will be displayed. This dialog box is used to provide information such as **Name**, **Fav.**, **Scientific Name**, **Type**, **Description**, and **# Faces** about all the default trees in the **Favorite Plants** rollout. You can also use this dialog box to remove or add a particular plant from the palette in the **Favorite Plants** rollout. To do so, select the name of a plant from the **Configure Palette** dialog box and choose the **Remove from Palette** button; the status in the **Fav.** column will change to **no**. Now, choose the **OK** button; the removed plant will not be displayed in the **Favorite Plants** rollout. Similarly, to display a plant in the **Favorite Plants** rollout, select the name of the plant from the **Configure Palette** dialog box, and then choose the **Add to Palette** button; **no** will switch to **yes** in the **Fav.** column. Next, choose the **OK** button to save the changes.

*Figure 4-5 A tree created using the **Foliage** tool*

Note

*To modify the default material of the trees, you need to use the **Material Editor** dialog box, which will be discussed in detail in the later chapters.*

Parameters Rollout

The options in this rollout are used to modify the tree created using the **Foliage** tool. To do so, select the tree and choose the **Modify** tab in the **Command Panel**; the **Parameters** rollout will be displayed, as shown in Figure 4-6. Enter a new value in the **Height** spinner to modify the height of the tree. The value in the **Density** spinner varies from 0.0 to 1.0 and is used to specify the amount of leaves and flowers in the tree. The value in the **Pruning** spinner varies from -0.1 to 1.0 and is used to reduce the branches of the tree, refer to Figures 4-7 and 4-8.

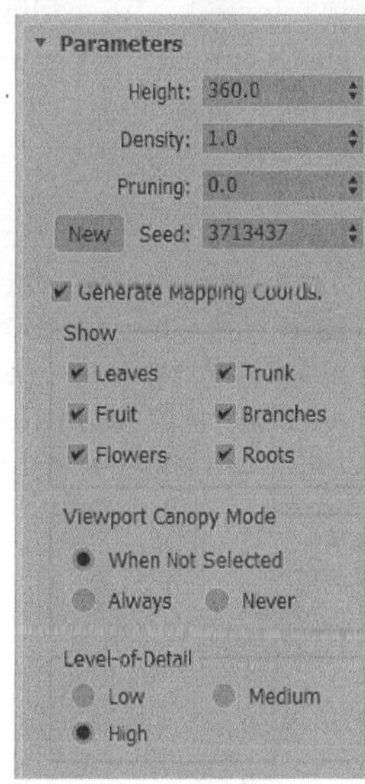

*Figure 4-6 The **Parameters** rollout*

Choose the **New** button to view the variation in the placement of leaves, branches, and the angle of trunk of the selected plant. If you choose the **New** button, the value in the **Seed** spinner changes accordingly, showing the possible variation in the selected tree. By default, the **Generate Mapping Coords** check box is selected. It is used to apply default mapping coordinates to the plant. The other areas in the **Parameters** rollout are discussed next.

*Figure 4-7 A tree with the **0** value in the **Pruning** spinner*

*Figure 4-8 A tree with the **0.5** value in the **Pruning** spinner*

Show Area

The options in this area are used to display leaves, trunk, fruits, branches, flowers, and roots. Select the check boxes to display the corresponding parts of a tree.

Note

*The **Show** area will display only those options which are relevant to the selected tree. For example, if you select a tree that does not have flowers, the **Flowers** check box will not be available.*

Viewport Canopy Mode Area

The options in this area are used to display the plant in the canopy mode in the viewports. The canopy of a plant is a type of covering area which covers the outermost parts of the tree such as leaves, branches, and trunk. By default, the **When Not Selected** radio button is selected. This radio button is used to display the tree in canopy mode in the viewport, when the tree is not selected. Select the **Always** radio button to display the tree always in the canopy mode, whether it is selected or not. Select the **Never** radio button to display the tree without canopy mode.

Level-of-Detail Area

This area is used to define how a tree will be displayed at the time of rendering. Select the **Low** radio button to display the lowest detail of a tree. It renders the tree in the canopy mode, as shown in Figure 4-9. Select the **Medium** radio button to render the tree with less number of faces in the branches and trunk, as shown in Figure 4-10. By default, the **High** radio button is selected. It is used to render the tree with all its faces in the branches and trunk. It will provide the highest detail of a tree, as shown in Figure 4-11.

Figure 4-9 The tree with low level of detail at rendering

Figure 4-10 The tree with medium level of detail at rendering

Figure 4-11 The tree with high level of detail at rendering

Creating a Railing

Menu bar:	Create > AEC Objects > Railing
Command Panel:	Create > Geometry > AEC Extended > Object Type rollout > Railing

To create a railing, activate the viewport in which you want to create it and then choose the **Railing** tool from the **Object Type** rollout; the **Name and Color**, **Railing**, **Posts**, and **Fencing** rollouts will be displayed. Now, press and hold the left mouse button on the left side of a viewport and then drag the cursor to the right side to specify the length of the railing. Release the left mouse button to set the length. Now, move the cursor up to specify the height of the railing and click on the screen; the railing will be created in the viewports, refer to Figure 4-12. You may need to use the **Zoom Extents All** tool to view the entire railing.

Various rollouts used to modify the railing are discussed next.

Railing Rollout

The **Pick Railing Path** button is used to create railing paths using the splines. To create a railing according to the railing path or the spline, first create a spline and a railing in the viewport. Next, select the railing and choose the **Modify** tab in the **Command Panel** and then choose the **Pick Railing Path** button in the **Railing** rollout and move the cursor over the spline in the viewport; the pick cursor will be displayed. Next, click on the spline; the railing will be aligned to the spline. Now, set a value in the **Segments** spinner to specify the number of segments in the railing. Select the **Respect Corners** check box to put the corners in the railing to match the corners of the railing path. The **Segments** spinner and the **Respect Corners** check box will be activated only if you create a railing using the railing path. The value in the **Length** spinner specifies the length of the railing. The areas in the **Railing** rollout are discussed next.

Top Rail Area

The top rail is the topmost part of the railing, refer to Figure 4-12. The options in the **Top Rail** area are used to modify the top rail. The **Profile** drop-down list is used to define the cross-section shape of the top rail. Select the **Round** or the **Square** option from the drop-down list to make the top rail round or square, respectively. Select the **none** option to remove the top rail from the railing. The values entered in the **Depth**, **Width**, and **Height** spinners specify the depth, width, and height of the top rail, respectively, refer to Figure 4-13.

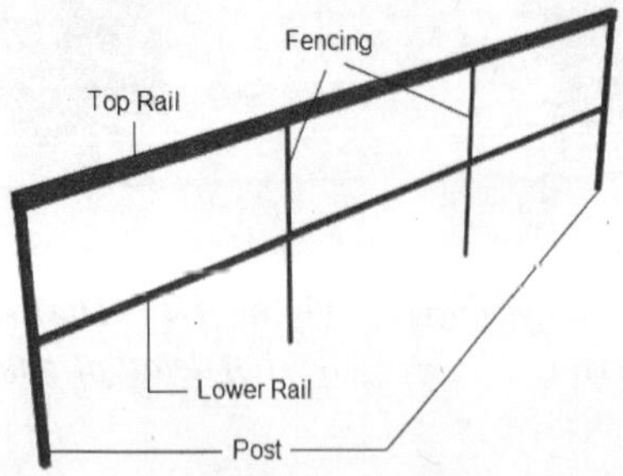

Figure 4-12 The railing with different parts labeled

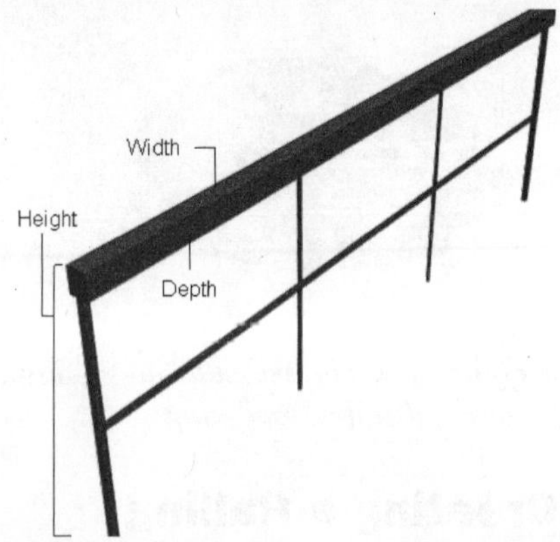

Figure 4-13 The railing with different dimensions

Lower Rail(s) Area

The lower rail is placed below the top railing, refer to Figure 4-12. The options in the Lower Rail area are used to modify the lower rail of the railing. The options in the **Profile** drop-down list are used to define the shape of the cross-section of the lower rail. Select the **Round** or **Square** option from the drop-down list to make the lower rail round or square, respectively. Select the **none** option to remove the lower rail from the railing. The value in the **Depth** spinner specifies the depth of the rail, whereas the value in the **Width** spinner specifies the width of the lower rail. Choose the **Lower Rail Spacing** button on the left side of the **Lower Rail(s)** area; the **Lower Rail Spacing** dialog box will be displayed. In this dialog box, select the **Count** check box, if it is not already selected. The value in the spinner on the right of this check box specifies the number of lower rails in the railing. Choose the **Close** button to close the dialog box.

Posts Rollout

The posts are the left and right supports of the railing, refer to Figure 4-12. The options in the **Posts** rollout are used to modify them. Most of the options in this rollout are the same as those discussed in the **Lower Rail(s)** area of the **Railing** rollout, except the **Extension** spinner. The value in the **Extension** spinner is used to extend the posts of the railing from the bottom of the top rail, as shown in Figure 4-14.

Fencing Rollout

The fencing is placed in between the posts of the railing, refer to Figure 4-12. The options in the **Fencing** rollout are used to modify it. The options in the **Type** drop-down list define the type of fencing in the railing. If you select the **(none)** option in the **Type** drop-down list, the fence will not be displayed and the options in the **Picket** and **Solid Fill** areas will become inactive. If you select the **Pickets** option in the **Type** drop-down list, then the pickets will be displayed in between the posts, as shown in Figure 4-15. Also, the **Picket** area will be activated in this rollout. If you select the **Solid Fill** option in the **Type** drop-down list, then the solid box type shape will be displayed in between the posts, as shown in Figure 4-16. Also, the **Solid Fill** area will be activated. The areas in the **Fencing** rollout are discussed next.

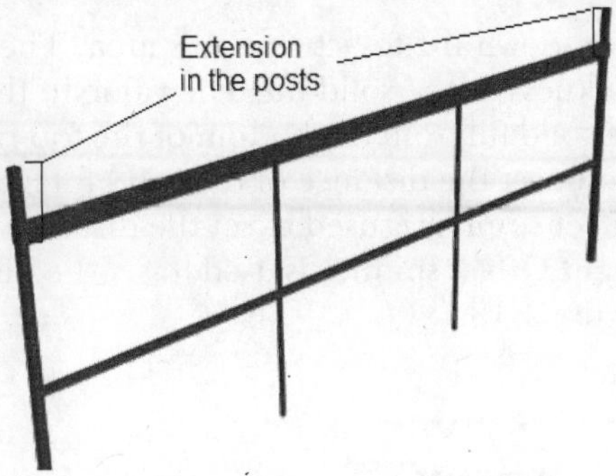

Figure 4-14 The railing with the extension in the posts

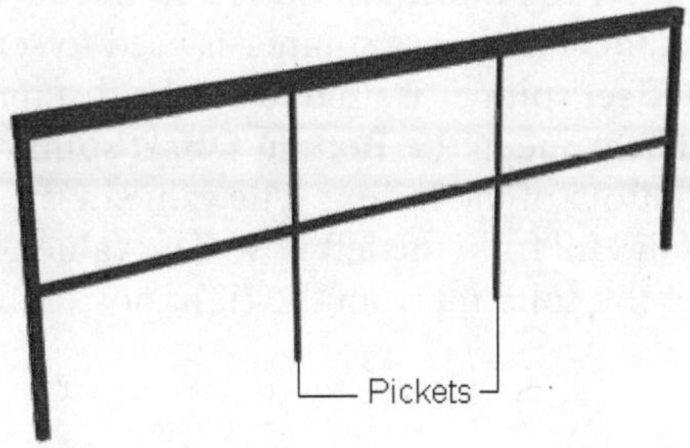

Figure 4-15 The railing with the picket type of fencing

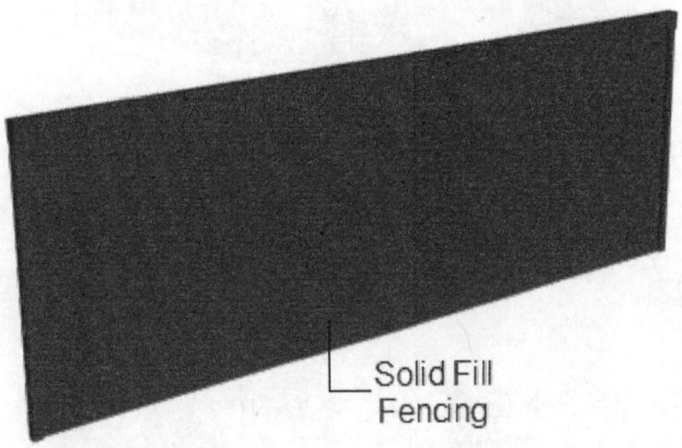

Figure 4-16 The railing with the solid fill type of fencing

Picket Area

You need to select the **Pickets** option from the **Type** drop-down list to activate this area. The **Profile**, **Depth**, **Width**, and **Extension** options in this area are the same as those discussed in the **Posts** rollout. The value in the **Bottom Offset** spinner is used to set the height of the picket from the bottom of the railing, refer to Figure 4-17.

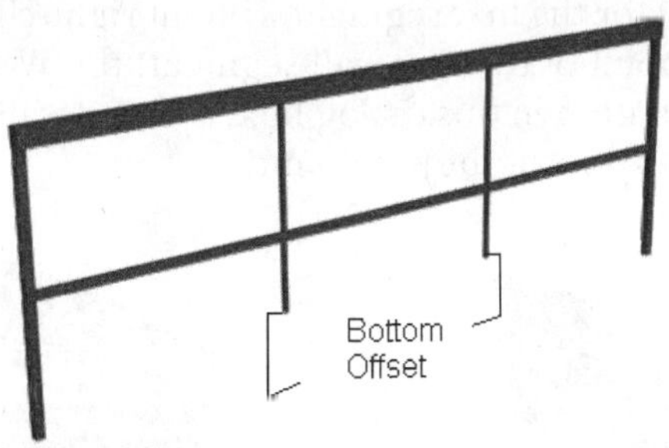

Figure 4-17 The bottom offset in the picket fencing

Solid Fill Area

Select the **Solid Fill** option from the **Type** drop-down list to activate this area. The value in the **Thickness** spinner is used to set the thickness of the solid fill. The value in the **Top Offset** spinner is used to set the distance of the solid fill from the bottom of the top railing. The value in the **Bottom Offset** spinner is used to set the distance of the solid fill from the bottom of the railing. The value in the **Left Offset** spinner is used to set the distance of the solid fill from the left post. The value in the **Right Offset** spinner is used to set the distance of the solid fill from the right post, refer to Figure 4-18.

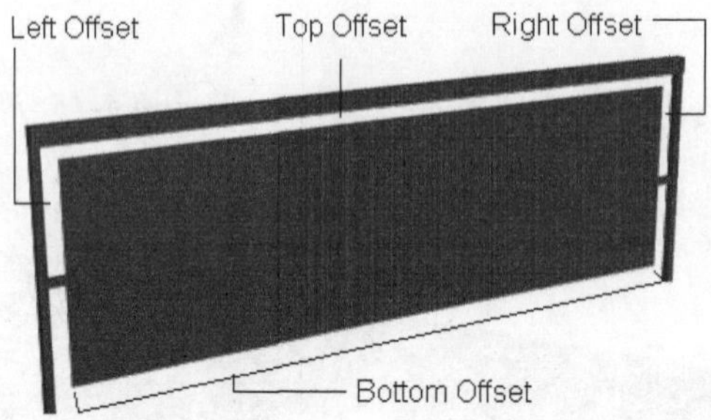

Figure 4-18 Various offsets in the solid fill fencing

Creating a Wall

Menu bar:	Create > AEC Objects > Wall
Command Panel:	Create > Geometry > AEC Extended > Object Type rollout > Wall

To create a wall, activate the Top viewport and then choose the **Wall** tool from the **Object Type** rollout; the **Name and Color**, **Keyboard Entry**, and **Parameters** rollouts will be displayed. Now, in the **Parameters** rollout, set the width and height by entering values in the **Width** and **Height** spinners, respectively. Next, click on the left of the Top viewport to create the starting point of the wall. Drag the cursor to the right to define the length of the wall and then click on the screen. Now, right-click to exit the command; a wall segment will be created, as shown in Figure 4-19. If you want to create another segment of the wall in continuation, then you need to repeat the same procedure as followed for the first segment without right-clicking. Next, to create a closed wall, click on the starting point of the first wall segment; the **Weld Point?** message box will be displayed. Choose the **Yes** button in this dialog box; a closed wall will be displayed, as shown in Figure 4-20. Next, right-click to exit the command.

Figure 4-19 The wall segment displayed

Figure 4-20 A closed wall displayed

Various rollouts used to modify the wall are discussed next.

Keyboard Entry Rollout

This rollout is used to create a wall by entering the parameters in the **Keyboard Entry** rollout. To do so, expand the **Keyboard Entry** rollout. Enter the values in the **X**, **Y**, and **Z** spinners to specify the position of the starting point of the wall segment in the viewport along the axes of the home grid or a grid object. Now, choose the **Add Point** button to add a point. Repeat the same procedure to create another segment. Next, choose the **Close** button to create a closed wall. Choose the **Finish** button to end the creation of the wall.

The **Pick Spline** button is used to create wall using the splines. To create a wall according to the wall path or the spline, first create a spline in the viewport. Next, choose the **Wall** tool from the **Object Type** rollout, and then choose the **Pick Spline** button in the **Keyboard Entry** rollout. Next, move the cursor over the spline in the viewport; the pick cursor will be displayed. Next, click on the spline; the wall will be created and aligned to the spline.

Note

The procedure of creating a spline is discussed in detail in Chapter 5.

Parameters Rollout

In this rollout, enter the values in the **Width** and **Height** spinners to define the width and height of the wall, respectively. The **Justification** area in the **Parameters** rollout is discussed next.

Justification Area

The options in this area are used to align the wall to its baseline. The baseline is the line between the front and back sides of a wall and it is equal to the thickness of the wall. By default, the **Center** radio button is selected in this area and is used to align the wall at the center of its baseline. Select the **Left** radio button to align the wall at the left edge of its baseline. Select the **Right** radio button to align the wall at the right edge of its baseline.

Edit Object Rollout

Select one of the walls in the viewport and choose the **Modify** tab in the **Command Panel**; the **Edit Object** rollout will be displayed. In this rollout, the **Attach** button is used to attach multiple walls to each other in the scene. To do so, choose the **Attach** button; the button will be highlighted. Now, move the cursor over the wall in the viewport; the pick cursor will be displayed. Next, click on the wall to be attached with the selected wall; the walls will get attached to each other. When you select another wall, it will automatically take the same material as that of the selected wall. Choose the **Attach Multiple** button; the **Attach Multiple** dialog box will be displayed with a list of all the walls in the viewport. From the list, select the multiple walls that you want to get attached by pressing and holding the CTRL key. Next, choose the **Attach** button; multiple walls will be attached to the selected wall.

CREATING DOORS

In 3ds Max, there are three tools to create the in-built doors. These tools are **Pivot**, **Sliding**, and **BiFold**. You can use these doors while creating houses, offices, rooms, and so on. To create doors, you need to choose **Create > Geometry** from the **Command Panel**; the **Standard Primitives** option will be displayed in the drop-down list. Select the **Doors** option from the drop-down list and activate the viewport in which you want to create the doors. Next, choose the corresponding tool from the **Object Type** rollout. In this section, you will learn to create and modify different types of doors using various tools available in the **Object Type** rollout.

Creating a Pivot Door

Menu bar:	Create > AEC Objects > Pivot Door
Command Panel:	Create > Geometry > Doors > Object Type rollout > Pivot

The pivot door is joined or hinged only on one side. To create a pivot door, choose the **Pivot** tool from the **Object Type** rollout; the **Name and Color**, **Creation Method**, **Parameters**, and **Leaf Parameters** rollouts will be displayed.

Activate the Top viewport and press and hold the left mouse button on the left of the viewport. Now, drag the cursor to the right of the viewport and release the left mouse button to define the width. Next, move the cursor up or down to define the depth of the door and click on the screen to set the depth. Now, again move the cursor up or down to define the height of the door. Click on the screen; the pivot door will be created in all viewports, refer to Figure 4-21.

Figure 4-21 The pivot door created in the viewport

Various rollouts used to create and modify the pivot door are discussed next.

Creation Method Rollout

The options in this rollout are used to create the pivot door dynamically. You can create the pivot door using any of the two methods that are discussed next.

Width/Depth/Height

To create the door using this method, make sure the **Width/Depth/Height** radio button is selected. Now, first you need to define the width and depth of the door and then you need to move the cursor to define the height, as discussed earlier while creating the pivot door dynamically.

Width/Height/Depth

To create the door using this method, you need to select the **Width/Height/Depth** radio button. Now, first you need to specify the width and height of the door, and move the cursor to specify the depth. To do so, press and hold the left mouse button on the left side of the viewport, drag the cursor to the right of the viewport to specify the width of the pivot door, and release the left mouse button. Next, move the cursor up to define the height of the door and click on the screen to set the height. Next, move the cursor up or down to specify the depth of the door. Click in the viewport; the pivot door will be created in all viewports.

Parameters Rollout

The options in this rollout are used to modify the pivot door. Select the pivot door and choose the **Modify** tab in the **Command Panel**; the **Parameters** and **Leaf Parameters** rollouts will be displayed. Enter the new values in the **Height**, **Width**, and **Depth** spinners to modify the height, width, and depth of the pivot door, respectively. Select the **Double Doors** check box to create two pivot doors, one on the left and other on the right, as shown in Figure 4-22. Select the **Flip Swing** check box to change the direction of swing of the door. Select the **Flip Hinge** check box to change the placement of the joint or the hinge of the pivot door on the opposite side. When you select the **Double Doors** check box, the **Flip Hinge** check box becomes inactive. The value in the **Open** spinner is used to specify the amount in degree to which the door will open, refer to Figure 4-23. The **Frame** area in the **Parameters** rollout is discussed next.

Figure 4-22 A double pivot door

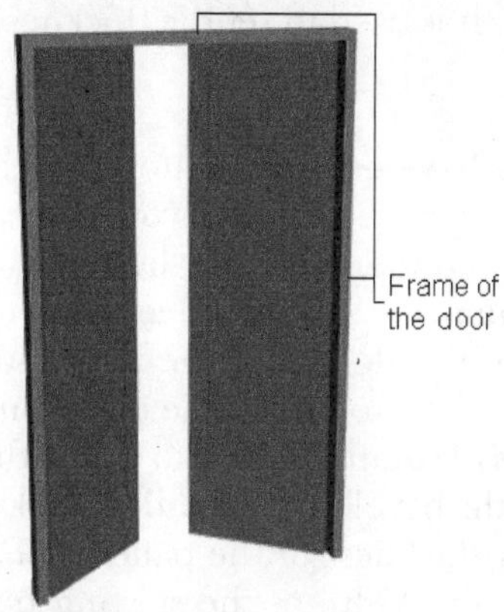

Figure 4-23 An opened double door

Frame Area

The options in this area are used to modify the frame of the pivot door. By default, the **Create Frame** check box is selected. If you clear the **Create Frame** check box, then the other options in this area will become inactive. Also, the frame will not be displayed in the door. Enter the values in the **Width** and **Depth** spinners to specify the width and depth of the frame of the pivot door, respectively. The value in the **Door Offset** spinner specifies the location of the door in reference to the frame.

Leaf Parameters Rollout

This rollout is used to modify the leaf of a door. Set a new value in the **Thickness** spinner to modify the thickness of the leaf of the door. Enter a new value in the **Stiles/Top Rail** spinner to modify the frame of the door leaf on the top, left, and right side, as shown in Figure 4-24. Set a value in the **Bottom Rail** spinner to modify the frame at the bottom of the door leaf. The value in the **# Panels Horiz** spinner specifies the horizontal panels on the leaf of the door. The value in the **# Panels Vert** spinner specifies the vertical panels on the leaf of the door. The value in the **Muntin** spinner is used to specify the width of the gap between the panels of the door leaf.

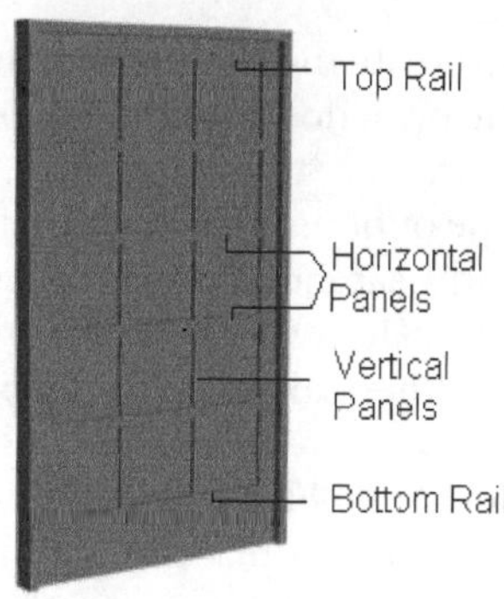

Figure 4-24 The modified door leaf

The **Panels** area in the **Leaf Parameters** rollout is discussed next.

Panels Area

The options in this area are used to modify the panels on the door leaf. The three radio buttons in this area are discussed next.

None

Select the **None** radio button; the panels will not be displayed in the door leaf.

Glass

Select the **Glass** radio button to create the glass panels. Also, the **Thickness** spinner will be activated. It is used to set the thickness of the glass panel.

Beveled

Select the **Beveled** radio button to create the beveled panels, as shown in Figure 4-25. When you select the **Beveled** radio button, the options under this radio button will be activated. The **Bevel Angle** spinner is used to define the angle between the outer surface of the door and the panel surface. The **Thickness 1** spinner is used to define the outer thickness of the panel. The **Thickness 2** spinner is used to define the thickness of the starting point of the bevel. The **Middle Thick** spinner is used to define the inner thickness of the panel. The **Width 1** spinner is used to define the width of the starting point of the bevel and the **Width 2** spinner is used to define the inner width of the panel.

Figure 4-25 *A door with the beveled panels*

Creating a Sliding Door

Menu bar:	Create > AEC Objects > Sliding Door
Command Panel:	Create > Geometry > Doors > Object Type rollout > Sliding

A sliding door has two door components, one is fixed, whereas the other slides or moves over the fixed component to open. To create a sliding door, choose the **Sliding** tool from the **Object Type** rollout; the **Name and Color**, **Creation Method**, **Parameters**, and **Leaf Parameters** rollouts will be displayed.

To create the sliding door, follow the same procedure as you did for the pivot door; a sliding door will be created, as shown in Figure 4-26.

The options in the **Name and Color**, **Creation Method**, **Parameters**, and **Leaf Parameters** rollouts are the same as discussed in the pivot door. However, some options in the **Parameters** rollout are different and these are discussed next.

Select the **Flip Front Back** check box to choose the component that you want to place in the front. Select the **Flip Side** check box to change the fixed component to the sliding component.

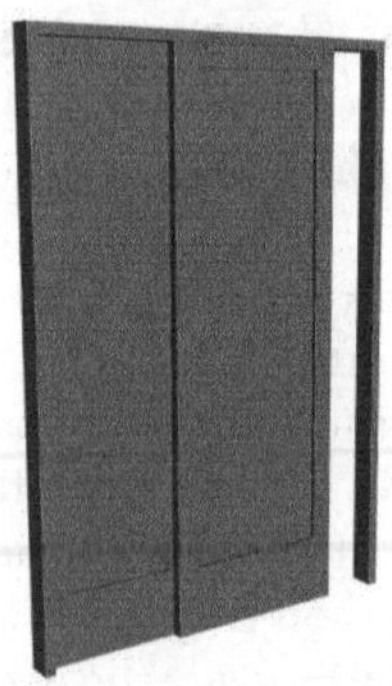

Figure 4-26 *A sliding door*

Creating a BiFold Door

Menu bar:	Create > AEC Objects > BiFold Door
Command Panel:	Create > Geometry > Doors > Object Type rollout > BiFold

The bifold door has two door components and two joints in it. To create the bifold door, choose the **BiFold** tool from the **Object Type** rollout; the **Name and Color**, **Creation Method**, **Parameters**, and **Leaf Parameters** rollouts will be displayed in the**Command Panel**. Now, create a bifold door dynamically using the same method as discussed for creating the pivot door; a bifold door will be created, as shown in Figure 4-27.

Figure 4-27 *A bifold door*

The options in the **Name and Color**, **Creation Method**, **Parameters**, and **Leaf Parameters** rollouts are the same as those discussed for the pivot door.

CREATING WINDOWS

In 3ds Max, there are six tools to create different types of default windows such as **Awning**, **Casement**, and so on. You can use these windows at various places for architectural designs.

To use these tools for creating the windows, choose **Create > Geometry** in the **Command Panel**; the **Standard Primitives** option will be displayed in the drop-down list. Now, select the **Windows** option from this drop-down list; various tools will be displayed in the **Object Type** rollout. In this section, you will learn to create various types of windows using these tools.

Creating an Awning Window

Menu:	Create > AEC Objects > Awning Window
Command Panel:	Create > Geometry > Windows > Object Type rollout > Awning

An awning window has one or more cases that are joined at its top. To create an awning window, choose the **Awning** tool from the **Object Type** rollout; the **Name and Color**, **Creation Method**, and **Parameters** rollouts will be displayed.

Activate the Top viewport and press and hold the left mouse button on the left side of the viewport, drag the cursor to the right side to specify the width of the window, and release the left mouse button. Next, move the cursor up or down to define the depth of the window and click on the screen. Now, move the cursor up or down to specify the height of the window. Click on the screen; the awning window will be created in all viewports, refer to Figure 4-28. The options in the **Name and Color** and **Creation Method** rollouts are the same for all windows as those discussed in the pivot door.

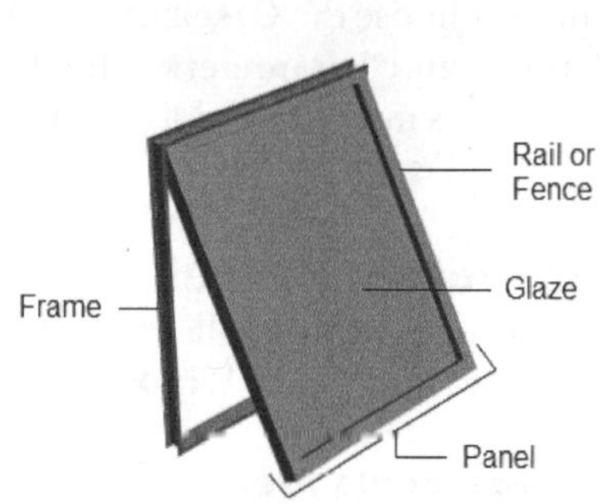

Figure 4-28 *An awning window*

Parameters Rollout

The options in this rollout are used to modify the awning window. Select the awning window and choose the **Modify** tab in the **Command Panel**; the **Parameters** rollout will be displayed. Enter new values in the **Height**, **Width**, and **Depth** spinners to modify the height, width, and depth, respectively of the awning window. The areas in the **Parameters** rollout are used to modify the window. These areas are discussed next.

Frame

The options in this area are used to modify the frame of the window. Enter a value in the **Horiz. Width** spinner to set the width of the horizontal (top and bottom) frames of the window. Enter a value in the **Vert. Width** spinner to set the width of the vertical (left and right) frames of the window. Similarly, enter a value in the **Thickness** spinner to set the overall thickness of the frame of the window.

Glazing

The **Thickness** spinner in this area is used to set the thickness of the glaze or the glass of the window.

Rails and Panels

This area is used to modify the panel of the window. Enter a value in the **Width** spinner to set the width of the fence in the panel. Enter a value in the **Panel Count** spinner to set the number of panels in the window, as shown in Figure 4-29.

Figure 4-29 An awning window with two panels

Open Window

The **Open** spinner in this area is used to open the window. Its value will be in percentage.

Creating a Casement Window

Menu bar:	Create > AEC Objects > Casement Window
Command Panel:	Create > Geometry > Windows > Object Type rollout > Casement

A casement window has one or more cases that are joined on the sides. To create the casement window, choose the **Casement** tool from the **Object Type** rollout; the **Name and Color**, **Creation Method**, and **Parameters** rollouts will be displayed. Create a casement window dynamically using the same method as discussed for creating the awning window. A casement window is shown in Figure 4-30.

Parameters Rollout

The options in this rollout are the same as those discussed for the **Awning** tool, except the **Casement** and **Open Window** areas. These areas are discussed next.

Casements Area

The options in this area are used to modify the panel of the window. Enter a value in the **Panel Width** spinner to set the width of the fence in the panel. By default, the **One** radio button is selected to create one panel in the window. If you want to create two panels in the window, as shown in Figure 4-31, you need to select the **Two** radio button.

Figure 4-30 *A casement window*

Figure 4-31 *A casement window with two panels*

Open Window Area

The **Open** spinner in this area is used to open the window. Its value will be in percentage. Select the **Flip Swing** check box to swap the swinging of the panel of the window.

Creating a Fixed Window

Menu bar:	Create > AEC Objects > Fixed Window
Command Panel:	Create > Geometry > Windows > Object Type rollout > Fixed

A fixed window cannot be opened. To create a fixed window, choose the **Fixed** tool from the **Object Type** rollout; the **Name and Color**, **Creation Method**, and **Parameters** rollouts will be displayed. Next, activate the Top viewport and follow the same method as discussed for creating the awning window; a fixed window will be created, as shown in Figure 4-32.

Parameters Rollout

The options in this rollout are the same as those discussed in the **Awning** tool, except the **Rails and Panels** area. This area is discussed next.

Rails and Panels Area

This area is used to modify the panel of the window. Enter a value in the **Width** spinner to set the width of the fence in the panel. Set a value in the **#Panels Horiz** spinner to define the number of horizontal divisions in the panel. Similarly, set a value in the **#Panels Vert** spinner to define the number of vertical divisions in the panel. On selecting the **Chamfered Profile** check box, the rails are chamfered between the glazed panels, refer to Figure 4-33.

Figure 4-32 *A fixed window*

Figure 4-33 *A fixed window with horizontal and vertical divisions*

Creating a Pivoted Window

Menu bar:	Create > AEC Objects > Pivoted Window
Command Panel:	Create > Geometry > Windows > Object Type rollout > Pivoted

A pivoted window has only one panel that is joined at the middle of the frame. When you open this window, it will swing around the horizontal axis. To create a pivoted window, activate the viewport and choose the **Pivoted** tool from the **Object Type** rollout; the **Name and Color**, **Creation Method**, and **Parameters** rollouts will be displayed. Now, follow the same method as discussed while creating the awning window; a pivoted window will be created, as shown in Figure 4-34.

Parameters Rollout

Most of the options in this rollout are the same as discussed for the **Awning** tool, except the **Rails** and **Pivots** areas. These areas are discussed next.

Rails Area

This area is used to modify the panel of the window. Enter a value in the **Width** spinner to set the width of the fence in the panel.

Pivots Area

When you open the window, by default it rotates about the horizontal axis. To rotate the window about the vertical axis, select the **Vertical Rotation** check box; the window will be vertically rotated, as shown in Figure 4-35.

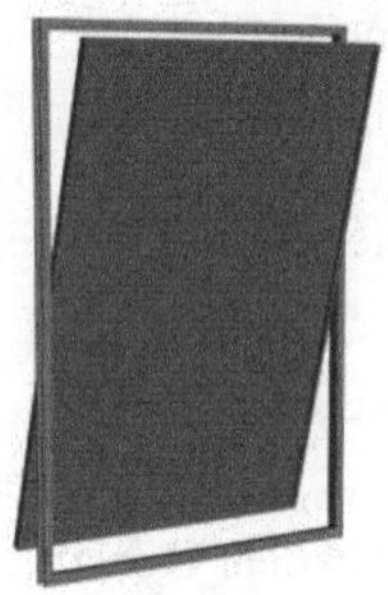

Figure 4-34 *A pivoted window rotated around the horizontal axis*

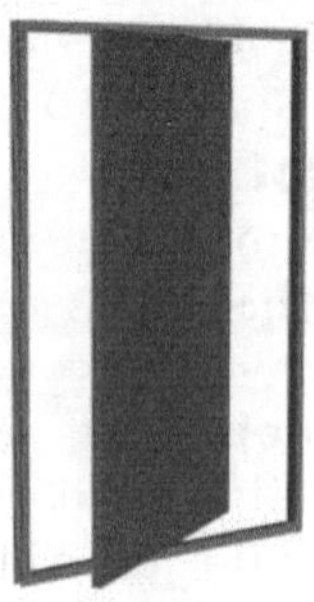

Figure 4-35 *A pivoted window rotated around the vertical axis*

Creating a Projected Window

Menu bar:	Create > AEC Objects > Projected Window
Command Panel:	Create > Geometry > Windows > Object Type rollout > Projected

A projected window has three panels in which the top one remains still and the other two swing in the directions opposite to each other. To create a projected window, activate the viewport and choose the **Projected** tool from the **Object Type** rollout; the **Name and Color**, **Creation Method**, and **Parameters** rollouts will be displayed. Now, follow the same method as discussed while creating the awning window; a projected window will be created, as shown in Figure 4-36.

Parameters Rollout

Most of the options in this rollout are the same as discussed for the **Awning** tool, except the **Rails and Panels** area. This area is discussed next.

Figure 4-36 *A projected window*

Rails and Panels Area

This area is used to modify the panel of the window. Set the value in the **Width** spinner to specify the width of the fence in the panel. Set the value in the **Middle Height** spinner to define the height of the middle panel relative to the frame of the window. Similarly, set the value in the **Bottom Height** spinner to define the height of the bottom panel relative to the frame of the window.

Creating a Sliding Window

Menu bar:	Create > AEC Objects > Sliding Window
Command Panel:	Create > Geometry > Windows > Object Type rollout > Sliding

A sliding window has two panels in which one remains still and the other one slides to open. To create a sliding window, activate the viewport and choose the **Sliding** tool from the **Object Type** rollout; the **Name and Color**, **Creation Method**, and **Parameters** rollouts will be displayed.

Now, create a sliding window dynamically by using the same method as discussed while creating the awning window; a sliding window will be created, as shown in Figure 4-37.

Parameters Rollout

Most of the options in this rollout are the same as those discussed for the **Awning** tool, except the **Rails and Panels** and **Open Window** areas. These areas are discussed next.

Rails and Panels Area

This area is used to modify the panel of the window. Set the value in the **Rail Width** spinner to set the width of the fence in the panel. Set the value in the **#Panels Horiz** spinner to define the number of horizontal divisions in the panel. Set the value in the **#Panels Vert** spinner to define the number of vertical divisions in the panel. On selecting, the **Chamfered Profile** check box, the rails between the glazed panels will be chamfered, as shown in Figure 4-38.

Open Window

The **Open** spinner in this area is used to open the window and its value will be in percentage. By default, the **Hung** check box is selected. As a result, the panel slides in the vertical direction. Clear the **Hung** check box to slide the panel in the horizontal direction, refer to Figure 4-39.

CREATING STAIRS

In 3ds Max, there are four tools that are used to create different types of default stairs such as **LType Stair**, **Spiral Stair**, and so on. To invoke these tools, choose **Create > Geometry** in the **Command Panel**; the **Standard Primitives** option will be displayed in the drop-down list. Now, select the **Stairs** options from the drop-down list; various tools will be displayed in the **Object Type** rollout. In this section, you will learn to create various types of stairs using these tools.

Figure 4-37 The sliding window

Figure 4-38 The sliding window with two horizontal and vertical chamfered divisions

Figure 4-39 The sliding window with the horizontal sliding

Creating L-Type Stairs

Menu bar:	Create > AEC Objects > L-Type Stair
Command Panel:	Create > Geometry > Stairs > Object Type rollout > L-TypeStair

The L-type stairs have two stairways that are joined at right angles to each other. To create the L-type stairs, choose the **L-Type Stair** tool from the **Object Type** rollout; the **Name and Color**, **Parameters**, **Carriage**, **Railings**, and **Stringers** rollouts will be displayed.

Now, activate the Top viewport. Press and hold the left mouse button on the left side of the viewport, drag the cursor to the right side of the viewport to specify the length of the first stairway of the stairs, and then release the left mouse button. Next, move the cursor up or down to define the length of the second stairway of the stairs and then click on the screen. Now, move the cursor up to specify the overall height of the stair and then click on the screen; the L-type stairs will be created in the viewport, as shown in Figure 4-40.

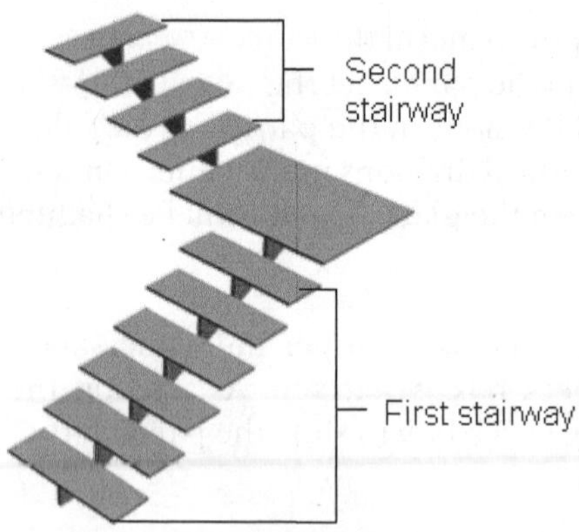

Figure 4-40 The L-type open stairs created

Various rollouts used to create and modify the L-type stairs are discussed next.

Parameters Rollout

The options in this rollout are used to modify the L-type stairs. To do so, select the L-type stairs and choose the **Modify** tab in the **Command Panel**; the **Parameters**, **Carriage**, **Railings**, and **Stringers** rollouts will be displayed. The **Parameters** rollout has a number of options which can be used to modify the stairs. These options are discussed next.

Type Area

The options in this area are used to define the type of stairs. By default, the **Open** radio button is selected, and therefore the stairs with open steps are created. Select the **Closed** radio button to create the stairs with closed steps, as shown in Figure 4-41. Select the **Box** radio button to create a support for the steps of the stairs, as shown in Figure 4-42.

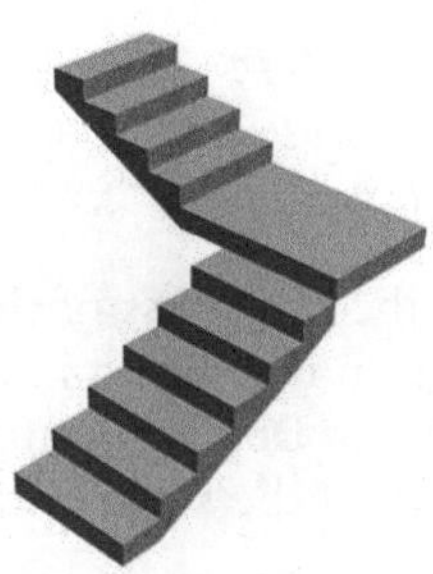

Figure 4-41 The L-type closed stairs

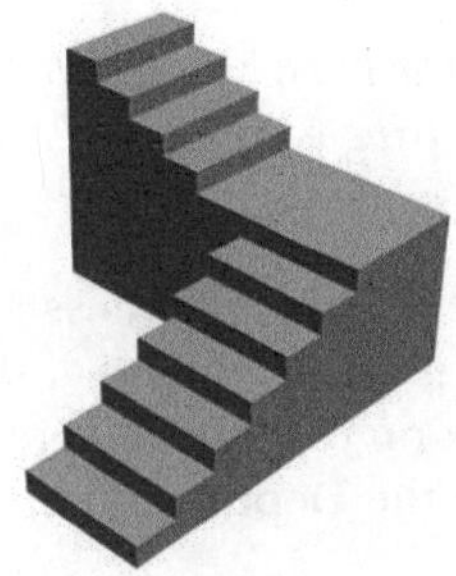

Figure 4-42 The L-type box stairs

Generate Geometry Area

The options in this area are used to modify the stairs by incorporating the geometry shapes. Select the **Stringers** check box to create the left and right support for the steps of the stairs. Select the **Carriage** check box to create support for the steps of the stairs. Select the **Left** and **Right** check boxes in the **Handrail** group to create the left and right handrails, as shown in Figure 4-43.

Layout Area

The options in this area are used to modify the dimensions of the stairs. Enter a value in the **Length 1** spinner to set the length of the first stairway. Similarly, enter a value in the **Length 2** spinner to set the length of the second stairway. The value in the **Width** spinner is used to set the width of the overall steps in the stairs. Enter a value in the **Angle** spinner to set the angle between the second stairway and the landing of the stairs. Figure 4-44 shows an L-Type stair with its **Angle** value set to zero.

Rise Area

There are three spinners in this area. These spinners are controlled by choosing the buttons available on their left side. When you choose one of the buttons, the spinner on the right side of that button becomes inactive. You can modify only two spinners at a time. Enter a value in the **Overall** spinner to define the height of stairways. The **Riser Ht** spinner is used to set the height of the risers in the stairs. The **Riser Ct** spinner is used to set the number of risers in the stairs. The riser is the gap between the steps in a stairway.

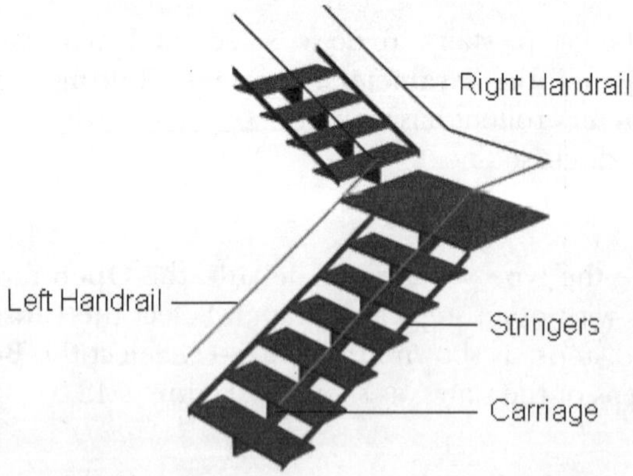

Figure 4-43 The L-Type stairs with handrails, carriage, and stringers

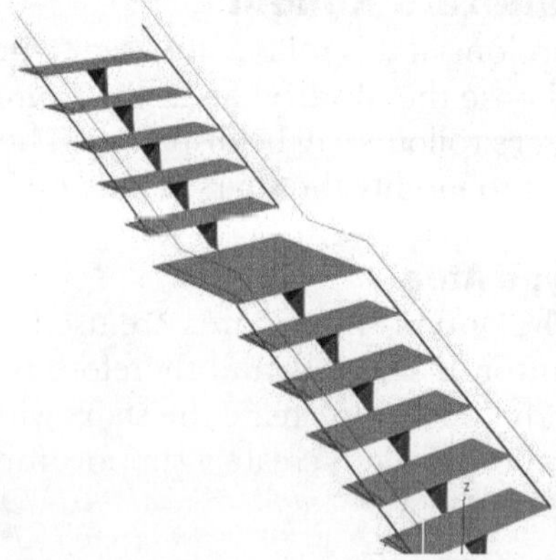

Figure 4-44 The L-Type stairs with ***Angle*** *value set to zero*

Steps Area

Enter a value in the **Thickness** spinner to modify the thickness of the steps of the stairs. This spinner is activated only if the **Open** radio button is selected in the **Type** area. Select the check box on the left side of the **Depth** spinner; the **Depth** spinner will become active. Set a value in the **Depth** spinner to modify the depth of the steps of the stairs.

Carriage Rollout

To activate the options in this rollout, make sure the **Carriage** check box in the **Generate Geometry** area of the **Parameters** rollout is selected. In the **Parameters** area of the **Carriage** rollout, enter a value in the **Depth** spinner to set the depth of the carriage. Enter a value in the **Width** spinner to set the width of the carriage. Choose the **Carriage Spacing** button just below the **Width** spinner; the **Carriage Spacing** dialog box will be displayed. Select the **Count** check box, if it is not already selected. The value in the spinner on the right side of the **Count** check box specifies the number of carriages in the stairs. The **Spring from Floor** check box in this rollout is used to control the starting point of the carriage from the floor. Set the required value and then choose the **Close** button to close the dialog box.

Railings Rollout

To activate the options in this rollout, you need to select one of the **Handrail** check boxes in the **Generate Geometry** area of the **Parameters** rollout. Enter a value in the **Height** spinner to set the height of the railing from the steps of the stairs. The **Offset** spinner is used to set the offset of the railing from the ends of the steps. The value in the **Segments** spinner is used to set the number of segments in the railing. The more the number of segments, smoother will be the railing. The value in the **Radius** spinner is used to set the radius of the railing.

Stringers Rollout

To activate the options in this rollout, you need to select the **Stringers** check box in the **Generate Geometry** area of the **Parameters** rollout. Enter a value in the **Depth** spinner to set the distance of the stringers from the floor. The value in the **Width** spinner is used to set the width of the stringers. The **Offset** spinner is used to set the distance of the stringers from the steps. The **Spring from Floor** check box is used to control the starting point of the stringers from the floor.

Creating Spiral Stairs

Menu bar:	Create > AEC Objects > Spiral Stair
Command Panel:	Create > Geometry > Stairs > Object Type rollout > Spiral Stair

The spiral stairs have a spiral shaped staircase. To create the spiral stairs, choose the **Spiral Stair** tool from the **Object Type** rollout; the **Name and Color**, **Parameters**, **Carriage**, **Railings**, **Stringers**, and **Center Pole** rollouts will be displayed. To create the spiral stairs dynamically, activate the Top viewport. Next, click on a point in the viewport to specify the center of the spiral stair, hold the left mouse button, and drag it downward to specify the radius and width. Release the left mouse button and move the cursor up or down to specify the overall rise in the height. Then, click on the screen; the spiral stairs will be created in the viewport. Different types of spiral stairs are shown in Figures 4-45 through 47.

Figure 4-45 *The spiral stairs*

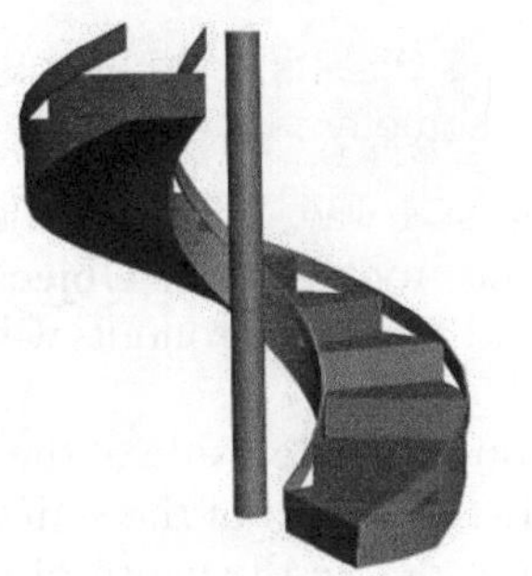

Figure 4-46 *The closed spiral stairs*

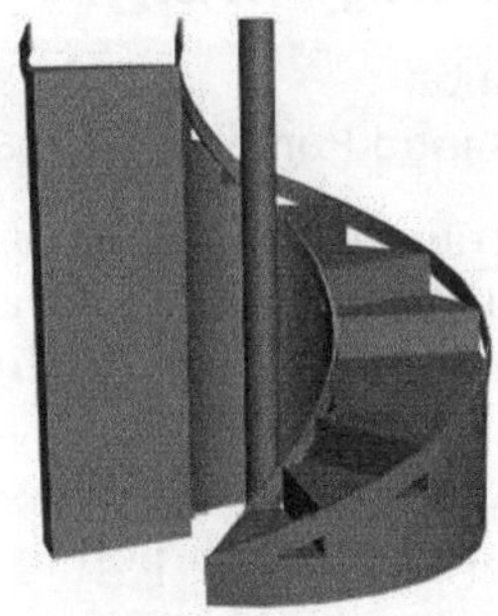

Figure 4-47 *The spiral box stairs*

Note

*The options in the **Carriage**, **Railings**, and **Stringers** rollouts for the **Spiral Stair**, **Straight Stair**, and **U-Type Stair** tools will be same as discussed for the **L-Type Stair tool**.*

Parameters Rollout

In this rollout, the **Type**, **Rise**, and **Steps** areas are the same as discussed for the **L-Type Stair** tool. However, the **Generate Geometry** and **Layout** areas are different and these areas are discussed next.

Generate Geometry

The options in this area are used to modify the stairs by incorporating the geometry shapes. Select the **Stringers** check box to create the left and right supports for the steps of the stairs. Select the **Carriage** check box, if it is not already selected to create support for the steps of the stairs. Select the **Center Pole** check box to create a pole at the center of the stairs, refer to Figure 4-45. Select the **Inside** and **Outside** check boxes in the **Handrail** area to create the handrails on both sides.

Layout

The options in this area are used to modify the dimensions of the stairs. Select the **CCW** radio button, if not already selected, to rotate the stairs in the counterclockwise direction. Select the **CW** radio button to rotate the stairs in the clockwise direction. Enter a value in the **Radius** spinner to set the radius of the spiral stairs. Enter a value in the **Revs** spinner to set the number of revolutions of the stairs. The value in the **Width** spinner is used to set the width of the spiral stairs.

Center Pole Rollout

To activate the options in this rollout, you need to select the **Center Pole** check box in the **Generate Geometry** area of the **Parameters** rollout. In the **Parameters** area of the **Center Pole** rollout, set a value in the **Radius** spinner to set the radius of the center pole. Set the value in the **Segments** spinner to set the number of segments of the center pole. Select the check box on the left side of the **Height** spinner to activate it and set the value in this spinner to define the height of the pole.

Creating Straight Stairs

Menu bar:	Create > AEC Objects > Straight Stair
Command Panel:	Create > Geometry > Stairs > Object Type rollout > Straight Stair

The straight stairs have only one stairway. To create the straight stairs, activate the Top viewport and choose the **Straight Stair** tool from the **Object Type** rollout; the **Name and Color**, **Parameters**, **Carriage**, **Railings**, and **Stringers** rollouts will be displayed.

Press and hold the left mouse button on the left side of the viewport and drag the cursor to the right side of the viewport to specify the length of the stairs. Release the left mouse button and then move the cursor up or down to define the width of the stairs and click on the screen to set the width. Next, move the cursor up or down to specify the height of the stairs. Click in the viewport; the straight stairs will be created in all viewports, as shown in Figure 4-48. You can also create the closed and box straight stairs in the same way as described in the L-type stairs, refer to Figures 4-49 and 4-50.

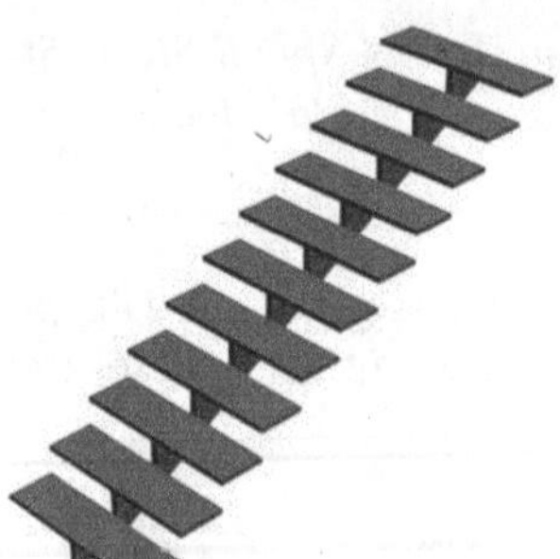

Figure 4-48 The straight stairs

Figure 4-49 The straight closed stairs

Figure 4-50 The straight box stairs

Parameters Rollout

In this rollout, all areas are same as discussed in the **L-Type Stair** tool, except the **Layout** area and this area is discussed next.

Layout Area

The options in this area are used to modify the dimensions of the stairs. The value in the **Length** spinner is used to set the length and the value in the **Width** spinner is used to set the width of the stairs.

Creating U-Type Stairs

Menu bar:	Create > AEC Objects > U-Type Stair
Command Panel:	Create > Geometry > Stairs > Object Type rollout > U-TypeStair

The U-type stairs have two stairways parallel to each other in U shape. To create the U-type stairs, activate the Top viewport and choose the **U-Type Stair** tool from the **Object Type** rollout; the **Name and Color**, **Parameters**, **Carriage**, **Railings**, and **Stringers** rollouts will be displayed.

Next, press and hold the left mouse button on the left side of the viewport, drag the cursor to the right side to specify the length of the stairs, and then release the left mouse button. Now, move the cursor up to define the width of the stairs and the distance between the two stairways. Click on the screen to set the width. Next, move the cursor up or down to specify the rise of the stairs. Click on the screen; the U-type stairs will be created in all viewports. Different U-type stairs are shown in Figures 4-51 through 53.

Figure 4-51 *The U-type stairs*

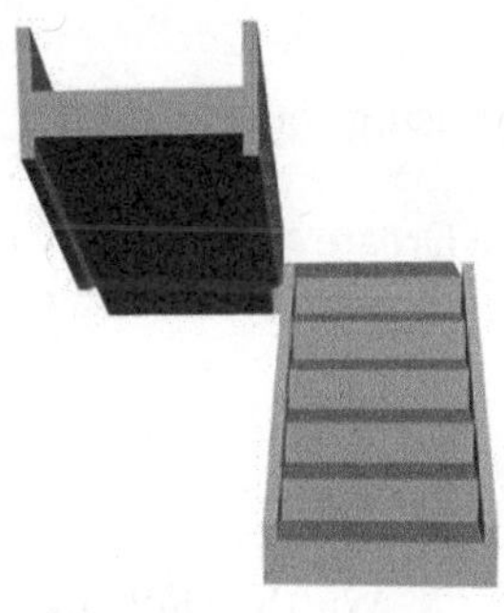

Figure 4-52 *The U-type closed stairs*

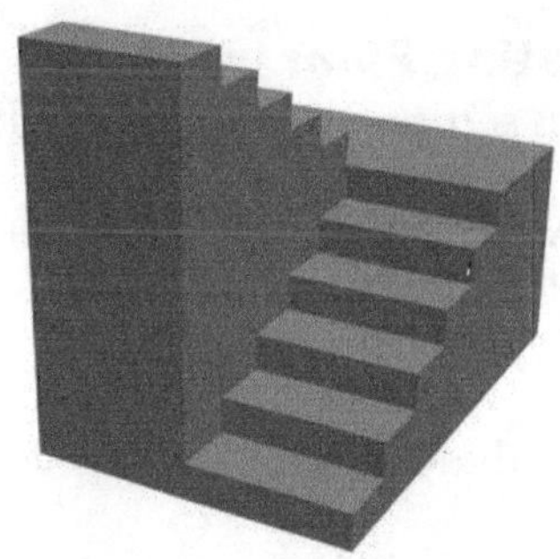

Figure 4-53 *The U-type box stairs*

TUTORIALS

Tutorial 1

In this tutorial, you will create a nature scene, as shown in Figure 4-54, using the AEC extended objects and standard primitives. **(Expected time: 30 min)**

The following steps are required to complete this tutorial:

a. Create the project folder.
b. Create floor.

c. Create railings.
d. Create trees.
e. Create gate.
f. Save and render the scene.

Figure 4-54 The nature scene

Creating the Project Folder

Create a new project folder with the name *c04_tut1* at *\Documents\3dsmax2017* and then save the scene with the name *c04tut1*, as discussed in Tutorial 1 of Chapter 2.

Creating Floor

In this section, you will create a floor using the **Plane** tool.

1. Activate the Top viewport. Choose **Create > Geometry** in the **Command Panel**; the **Standard Primitives** option is displayed in the drop-down list. Choose the **Plane** tool from the **Object Type** rollout.

2. In the **Keyboard Entry** rollout, set the parameters as follows:

   Length: **1485.0** Width: **1605.15**

3. Choose the **Create** button from the **Keyboard Entry** rollout; a plane is displayed in viewports. Now, choose the **Zoom Extents All** tool to display the entire plane in the viewports.

4. In the **Name and Color** rollout, enter **floor**; the plane is named as *floor*.

5. Use the color swatch in the **Name and Color** rollout to modify the color of *floor* to green.

6. Activate the Perspective viewport and set the view using the **Zoom** and **Orbit** tools, as shown in Figure 4-55.

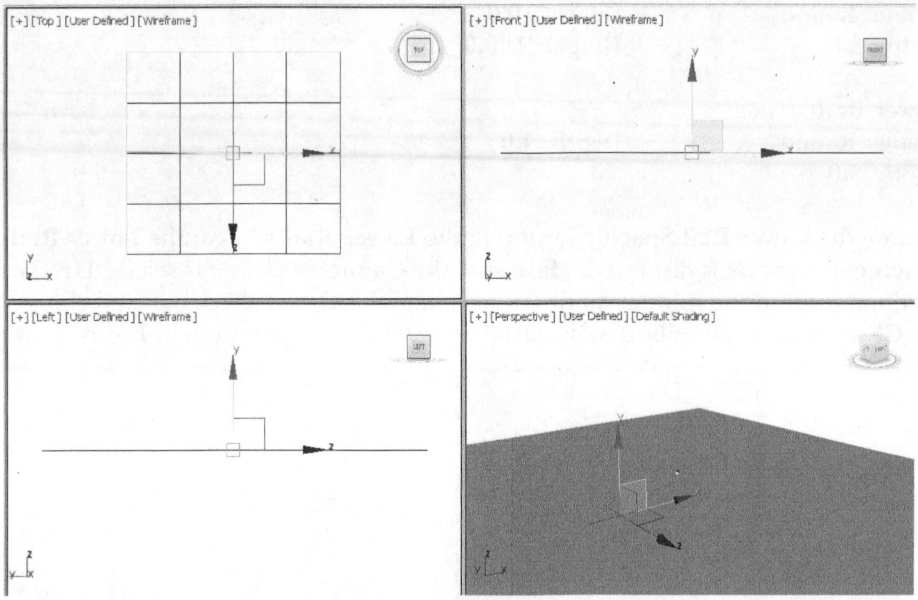

*Figure 4-55 The floor geometry after using the **Zoom** and **Orbit** tools*

Creating Railings

In this section, you will create railings around *floor* using the **Railing** tool.

1. Choose **Create > Geometry** in the **Command Panel**; a drop-down list is displayed below the **Geometry** button. Select the **AEC Extended** option from the drop-down list and then choose the **Railing** tool from the **Object Type** rollout.

2. Activate the Top viewport. Next, move the cursor to the upper left corner of *floor*, press and hold the left mouse button, and drag the cursor to the upper right corner of *floor* to specify the length of the railing. Release the left mouse button to set the length, and then move the cursor up to specify the height of the railing. Click on the viewport; a railing is created.

3. In the **Name and Color** rollout, enter **railing01** and press ENTER.

4. Use the color swatch to modify the color of *railing01* and enter the values as follows:

   Red: **177** Green: **88** Blue: **26**

5. Make sure *railing01* is still selected. Choose the **Modify** tab in the **Command Panel**; the **Railing**, **Posts**, and **Fencing** rollouts are displayed.

6. In the **Railing** rollout, set the parameters as follows:

   Length: **1400.0**

   Top Rail area

Profile: **Round** Depth: **10.0**
Width: **3.0** Height: **100.0**

Lower Rail(s) area
Profile: **Round** Depth: **4.0**
Width: **3.0**

7. Choose the **Lower Rail Spacing** button in the **Lower Rail(s)** area; the **Lower Rail Spacing** dialog box is displayed. Make sure the **Count** check box is selected. Next, set the value **3** in the spinner on the right side of the **Count** check box and choose the **Close** button; the railing is displayed in all viewports, as shown in Figure 4-56.

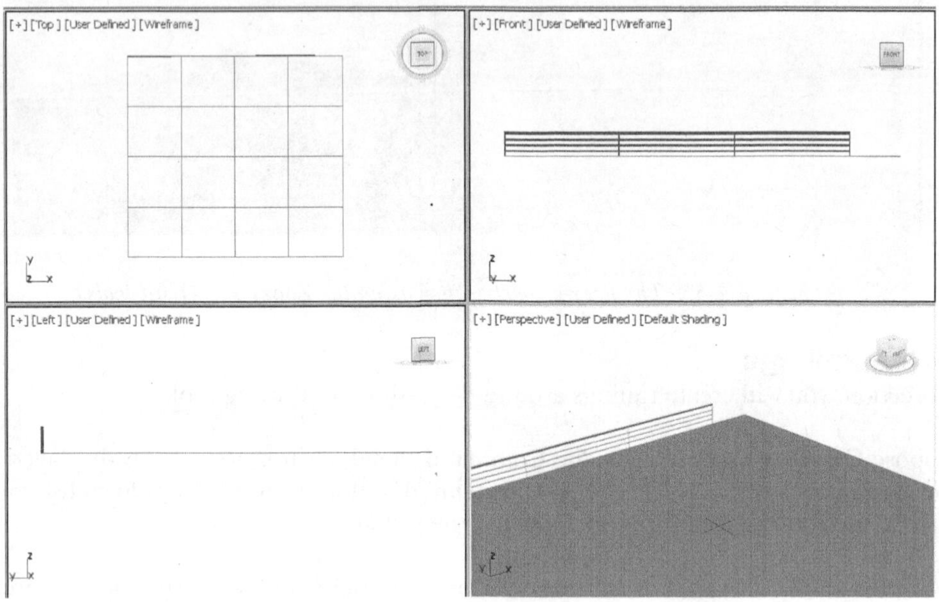

Figure 4-56 The railing01 displayed in viewports

8. In the **Posts** rollout, set the values as follows:

Profile: **Round** Depth: **7.0**
Width: **5.0** Extension: **2.0**

9. Choose the **Post Spacing** button in the **Post** rollout; the **Post Spacing** dialog box is displayed. Make sure the **Count** check box is selected. Next, set the value **4** in the spinner on the right side of the **Count** check box and choose the **Close** button.

10. In the **Fencing** rollout, select **(none)** from the **Type** drop-down list.

Note
If you want to add fencing to the railing, then select the type of fencing from the **Type** *drop-down list and set the parameters in the respective area.*

11. Make sure *railing01* is selected in the Top viewport. Now, choose the **Select and Move** tool from the **Main Toolbar** and align the railing manually, as shown in Figure 4-57.

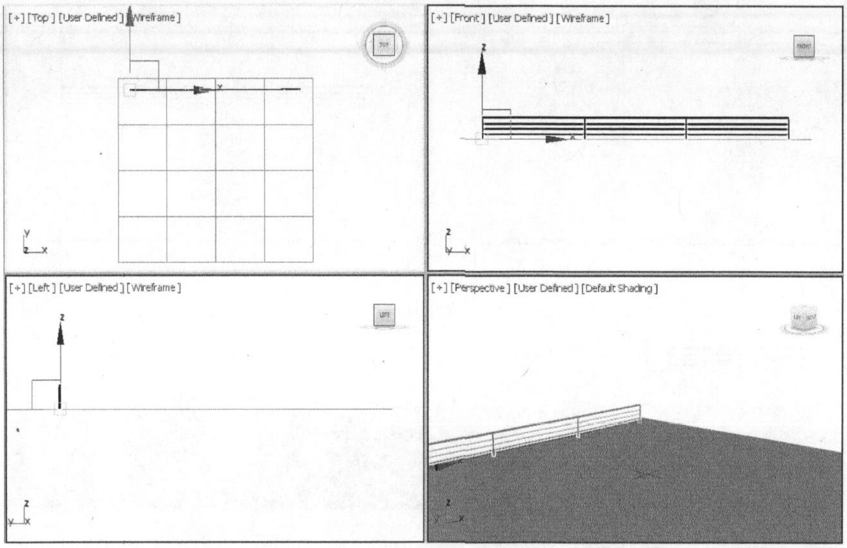

Figure 4-57 *The railing01 geometry in viewports after aligning it in the Top viewport*

Next, you need to create one more railing.

12. Activate the Top viewport and choose the **Railing** tool. Create one more railing at the right angle of *railing01* using the same method as discussed for creating *railing01*, refer to Figure 4-58.

Note
When you create another railing, all the dimensions of railing01, except the length and height, will be taken automatically.

13. In the **Name and Color** rollout, enter **railing02**.

14. Assign the same color to *railing02* as was assigned to *railing01*.

15. Make sure *railing02* is selected. Next, choose the **Modify** tab in the **Command Panel**; the **Railing**, **Post**, and **Fencing** rollouts are displayed.

16. In the **Railing** rollout, set the parameters as follows:
Length: **600.0**

Top Rail area
Height: **100.0**

17. Choose the **Select and Move** and **Select and Rotate** tools and align *railing02* in the viewports, as shown in Figure 4-58.

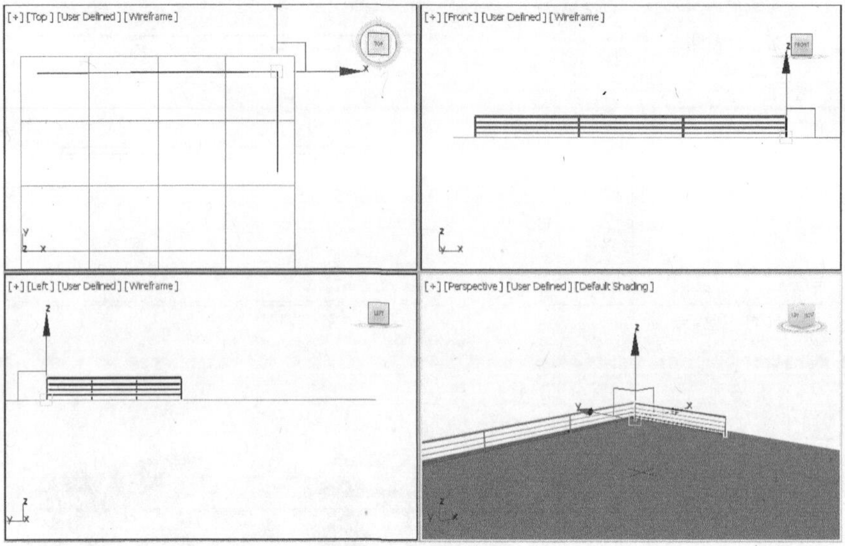

Figure 4-58 *The railing02 geometry in viewports after alignment*

Next, you need to copy *railing02*.

18. Activate the Top viewport. and make sure *railing02* is selected. Next, place the cursor over the vertical axis. Press and hold the SHIFT key and drag *railing02* downward until the value in the **Y** spinner in the Coordinate display becomes around **-601**. Release the left mouse button and the SHIFT key; the **Clone Options** dialog box is displayed.

19. In the **Clone Options** dialog box, make sure the **Copy** radio button is selected. Set the value in the **Number of Copies** spinner to **1** and enter *railing03* in the **Name** text box. Next, choose the **OK** button; *railing 03* is created, as shown in Figure 4-59.

20. Activate the Top viewport and select *railing03*. Choose the **Select and Rotate** tool, move the cursor over the Z-axis, and rotate it to -45 degrees in the clockwise direction, as shown in Figure 4-60.

Note

*While rotating railing03, choose the **Angle Snap Toggle** tool from the **Main Toolbar** to measure the angle of rotation in increments.*

Now, you need to create the fourth railing.

21. Activate the Top viewport and create another railing starting from the endpoint of *railing03*.

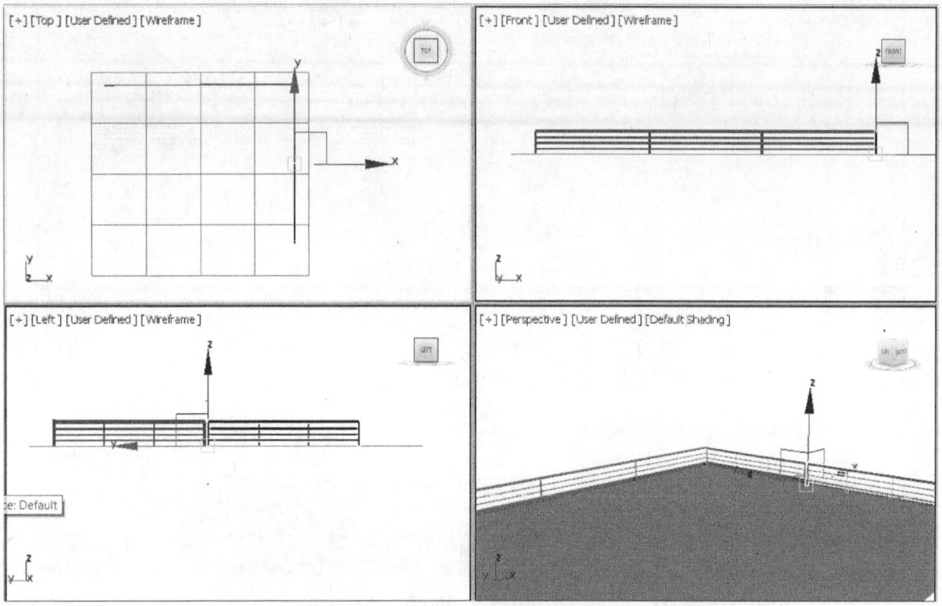

***Figure 4-59** The railing03 geometry after alignment*

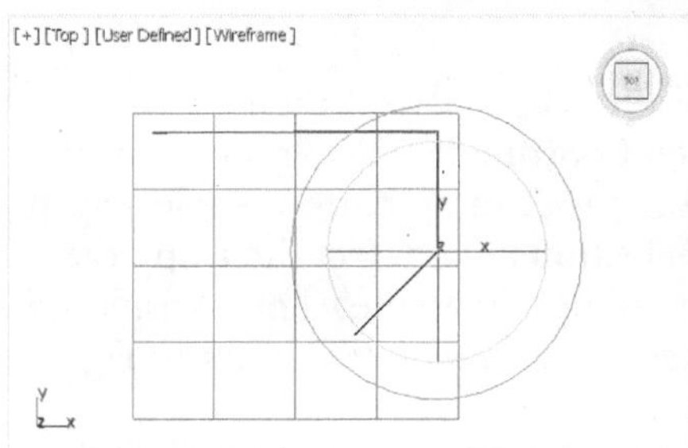

***Figure 4-60** The railing03 geometry rotated in the Top viewport*

22. In the **Name and Color** rollout, enter **railing04**.

23. Assign the same color to *railing04* as was assigned to *railing01*.

24. Make sure *railing04* is selected. Choose the **Modify** tab in the **Command Panel**; the **Railing**, **Post**, and **Fencing** rollouts are displayed.

25. In the **Railing** rollout, set the parameters as follows:

    Length: **325.0**
    Top Rail area
    Height: **100.0**

26. Make sure *railing04* is aligned in the viewports, as shown in Figure 4-61.

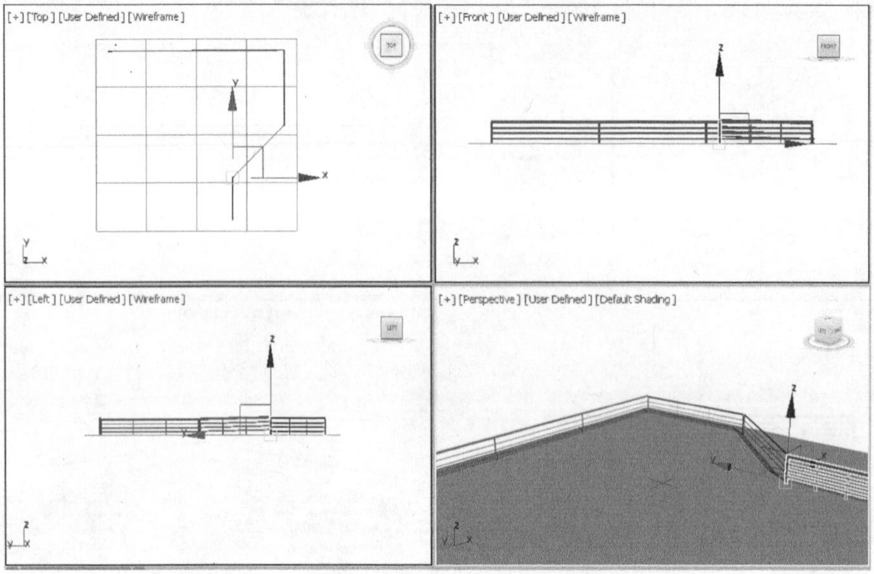

Figure 4-61 *The railing04 geometry aligned in viewports*

27. Select *railing02*, *railing03*, and *railing04* from the Scene Explorer; three railings are selected in the viewports.

28. Make sure the Top viewport is activated and then choose the **Mirror** tool from the **Main Toolbar**; the **Mirror: Screen Coordinates** dialog box is displayed. In the **Mirror Axis** area of this dialog box, make sure the **X** radio button is selected. In the **Offset** spinner, set the value **-980**. In the **Clone Selection** area, select the **Copy** radio button and choose the **OK** button; the copy of all the railings created earlier is displayed and they are automatically named as *railing005*, *railing006*, and *railing007*, refer to Figure 4-62.

29. Adjust the view in the Perspective viewport using the tools in the viewport navigation controls, refer to Figure 4-62.

Creating Trees

In this section, you will create trees using the **Foliage** tool.

1. Choose **Create > Geometry** in the **Command Panel**; a drop-down list is displayed below the **Geometry** button. Select the **AEC Extended** option from the drop-down list and then choose the **Foliage** tool from the **Object Type** rollout.

2. Activate the Top viewport. In the **Favorite Plants** rollout, double-click on **Generic Palm**; the tree is created and displayed in all viewports.

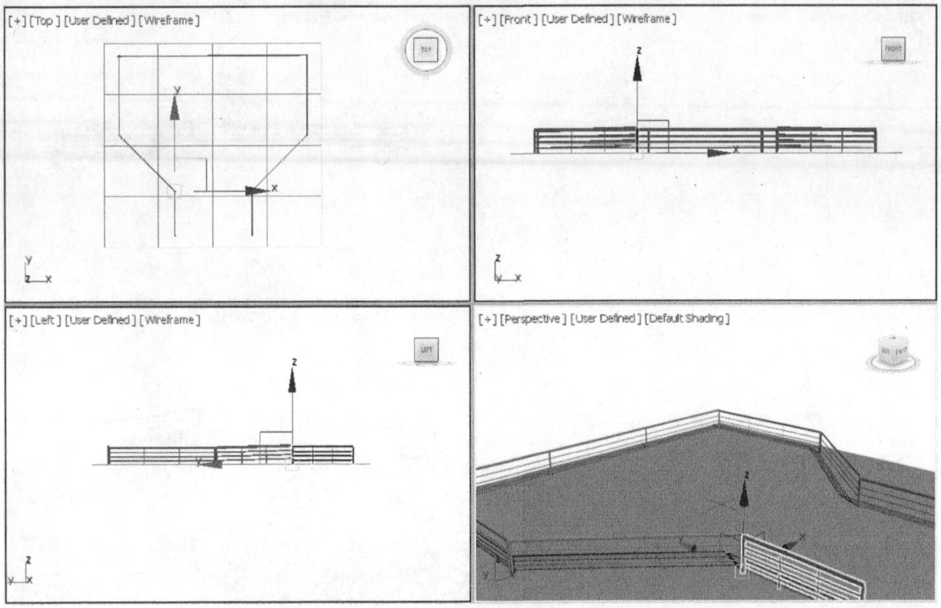

Figure 4-62 *The railings geometry displayed in viewports*

> **Note**
>
> *If the **Generic Palm** tree is not displayed in the palette of the **Favorite Plants** rollout, then choose the **Plant Library** button at the bottom of the rollout; the **Configure Palette** dialog box is displayed. Double-click on the **Generic Palm** tree; the **yes** option is displayed in the **Fav.** column indicating that the tree will be available in the palette. Next, choose the **OK** button.*

3. In the **Name and Color** rollout, enter **tree01**; the tree is named as *tree01*.

4. Make sure *tree01* is still selected. Choose the **Modify** tab in the **Command Panel**; the **Parameters** rollout is displayed.

5. In the **Parameters** rollout, set the following parameters:

   Height: **300.0**
   Use the default values for other options.

6. In the Top viewport, choose the **Select and Move** tool and move *tree01* toward *railing01* in all viewports, as shown in Figure 4-63.

7. Create multiple copies of *tree01* in the Top viewport and align them using the **Select and Move** tool, as shown in Figure 4-64.

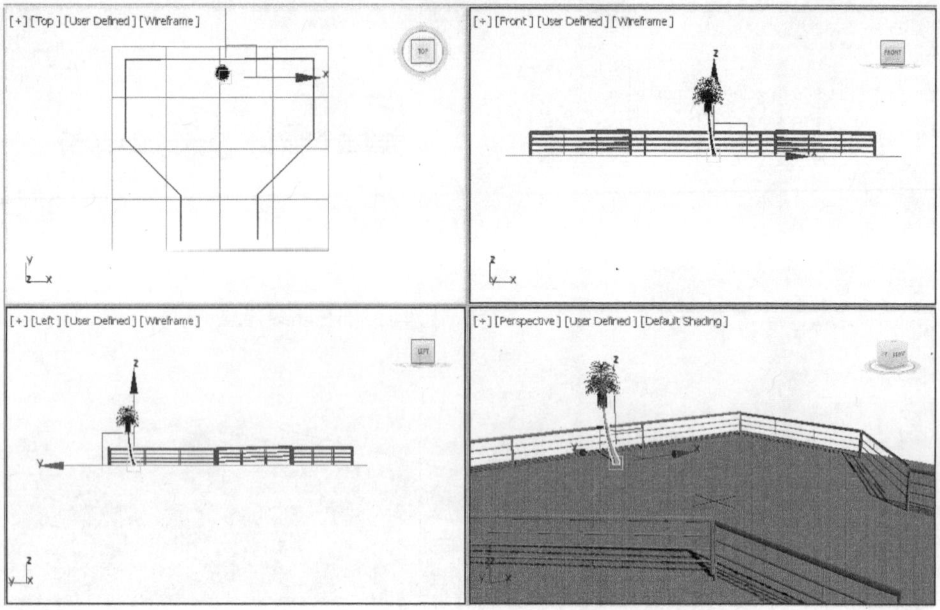

Figure 4-63 *Alignment of tree01 in viewports*

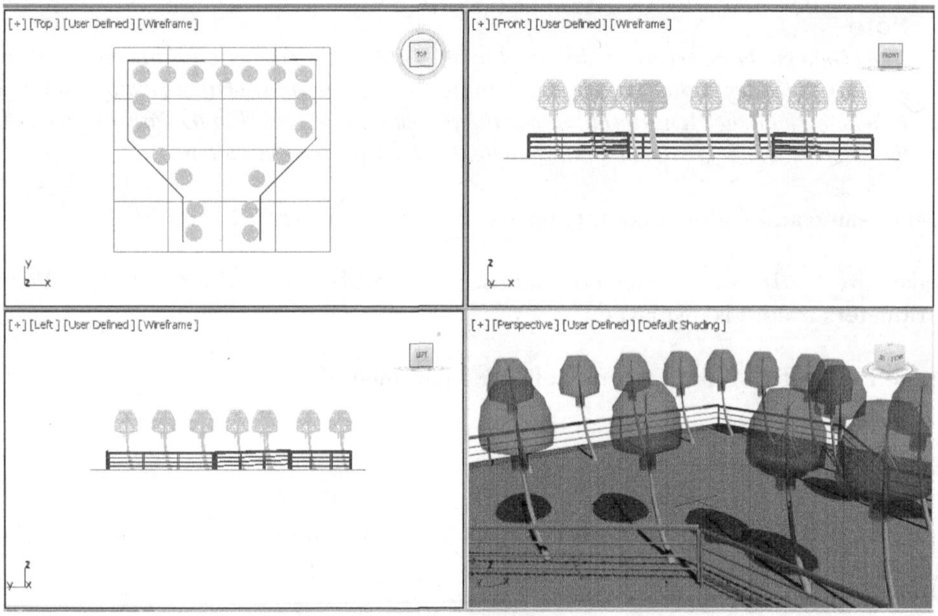

Figure 4-64 *Multiple copies of tree01 created and aligned in viewports*

Creating the Gate

In this section, you will create the gate using the **Pivot** and the **Cylinder** tools.

1. Choose **Create > Geometry** in the **Command Panel**; a drop-down list is displayed below the **Geometry** button. Select the **Doors** option from the drop-down list and then choose the **Pivot** tool from the **Object Type** rollout.

2. Activate the Top viewport and press and hold the left mouse button on the left of the viewport. Now, drag the cursor to the right of the viewport and release the left mouse button to define the width. Next, move the cursor up to define the depth of the door and click on the screen to set the depth. Now, again move the cursor up to define the height of the door. Click on the screen; the pivot door is created in all viewports.

3. In the **Name and Color** rollout, enter **gate**.

4. Use the color swatch to modify the color of *gate* and enter the values as follows:

   Red: **49** Green: **13** Blue: **6**

5. In the **Parameters** rollout, set the following parameters:

   Height: **92** Width: **532** Depth: 9.234
   Open: **20**

   Also, select the **Double Doors** and **Flip Swing** check boxes.

6. In the **Leaf Parameters** rollout, set the following parameters:

   Thickness: **7.7** Stiles/Top Rail: **6.48** Bottom rail: **13.44**
   #Panels Horiz.: **6** #Panels Vert.: **4**

7. In the **Panels** area, select the **Beveled** radio button and then set the following parameters:

   Thickness 1: **0.74** Thickness 2: **1.96** Middle Thick.: **0.991**
   Width 1: **4.871** Width 2: **1.364**

8. Align *gate* using the **Select and Move** and **Select and Rotate** tools, as shown in Figure 4-65. Make sure that there is equal space at both sides of *gate* to place the rods to be created later.

9. In the **Parameters** rollout, set **0** in the **Open** spinner to close *gate*.

   Next, you will create rods at both sides of *gate*.

10. Activate the Top viewport. Make sure the **Geometry** button is chosen in the **Command Panel**. Next, select **Standard Primitives** from the drop-down list located below it. Now, choose the **Cylinder** tool from the **Object Type** rollout.

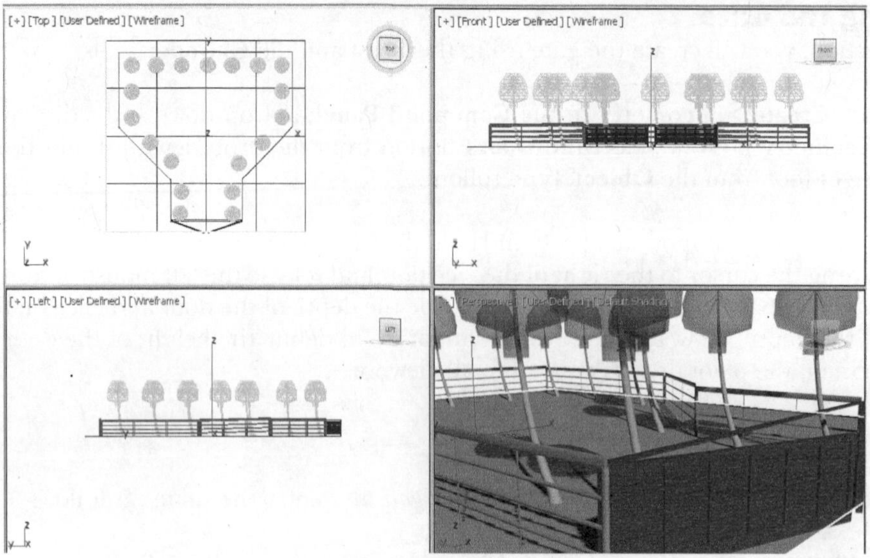

Figure 4-65 The gate geometry aligned in viewports

11. In the **Keyboard Entry** rollout, set the parameters as follows:

    Radius: **2.4** Height: **94**

    Choose the **Create** button; a cylinder is created.

12. In the **Name and Color** rollout, enter **rod1**. Also, assign black color to it.

13. Align *rod1* in the viewports, as shown in Figure 4-66.

14. Create a copy of *rod1* as done earlier and align it, as shown in Figure 4-67.

    Next, you will create handles for *gate*.

15. Activate the Top viewport. Choose **Create > Geometry** in the **Command Panel**. Make sure that the **Standard Primitives** option is selected in the drop-down list and then choose the **Cylinder** tool from the **Object Type** rollout.

16. In the **Keyboard Entry** rollout, set the parameters as follows:

    Radius: **1.5** Height: **35**

    Choose the **Create** button; a cylinder is created.

17. In the **Name and Color** rollout, enter **handle1** and press ENTER. Also, assign black color to it.

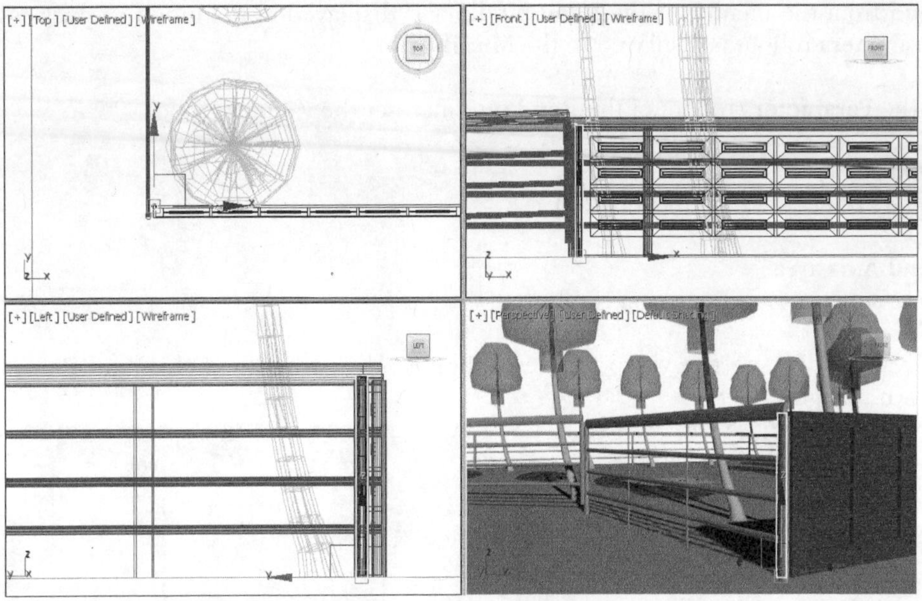

Figure 4-66 The rod1 geometry aligned in viewports

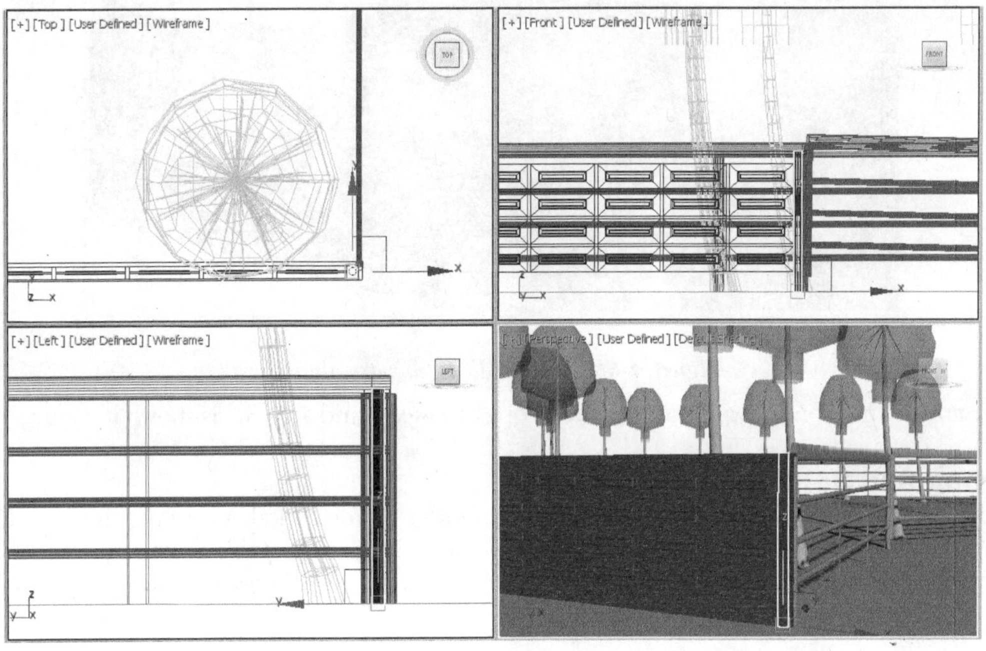

Figure 4-67 The rod2 geometry aligned in viewports

18. Make sure *handle1* is selected. In the **Parameters** rollout, set **15** in the **Height Segments** spinner.

    Next, you will apply the **Bend** modifier to *handle1*.

19. Make sure *handle1* is selected and then choose **Modifiers > Parametric Deformers >**

Bend from the menu bar; the **Bend** modifier is displayed in the modifier stack. Also, the **Parameters** rollout is displayed in the **Modify** tab.

20. In the **Parameters** rollout of the **Bend** modifier, set the values as follows:

    Bend Area
    Angle: **180** Direction: **270**

    Bend Axis area
    Make sure the **Z** radio button is selected.

21. Activate the Perspective viewport. Next, align *handle1* using the **Select and Place** tool, as shown in Figure 4-68.

Figure 4-68 *The handle1 geometry aligned*

22. Activate the Front viewport and create a copy of *handle1* and align it, as shown in Figure 4-69.

Saving and Rendering the Scene

In this section, you will save the scene and then render it. You can also view the final rendered image of this scene by downloading the *c04_3dsmax_2017_rndr.zip* file from *www.cadcim.com*. The path of the file is as follows: *Textbooks > Animation and Visual Effects > 3ds Max > Autodesk 3ds Max 2017: A Comprehensive Guide*

1. Change the background color of the scene to light blue, as discussed in Tutorial 1 of Chapter 2, using the following parameters:

    Red: **145** Green: **241** Blue: **244**

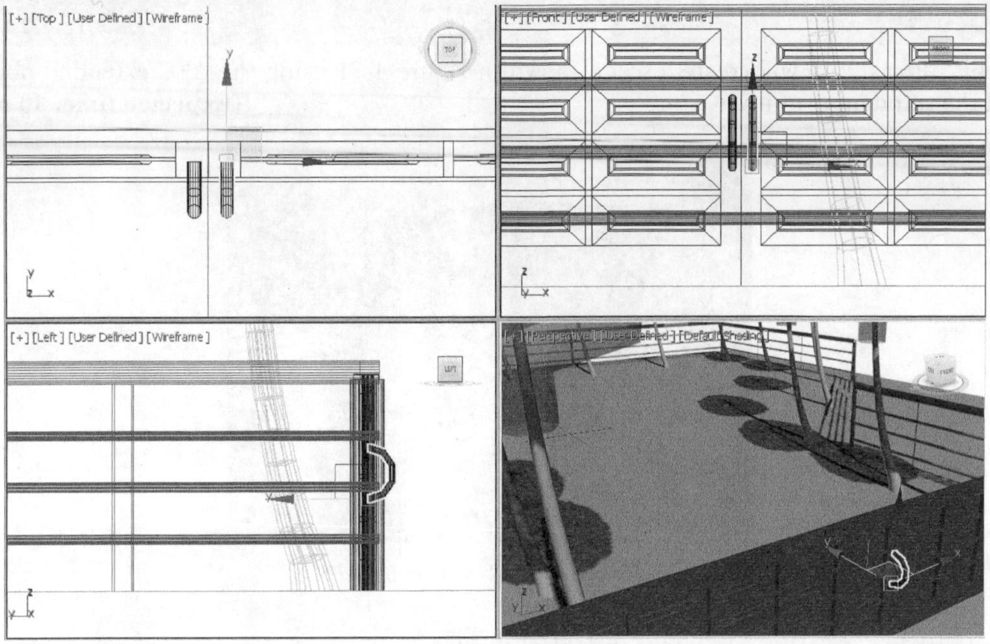

Figure 4-69 The copy of handle1 aligned

2. Choose **Save** from the **Application** menu.

3. Set the render view the Perspective viewport and choose the **Render Production** tool from the **Main Toolbar**; the **Rendered Frame** window is displayed. This window shows the final output of the scene, refer to Figure 4-70.

Figure 4-70 The final output after rendering

Tutorial 2

In this tutorial, you will create a scene shown in Figure 4-71 using the AEC extended objects and the standard primitives. **(Expected time: 30 min)**

Figure 4-71 The room model

The following steps are required to complete this tutorial:

a. Create the project folder.
b. Create the floor.
c. Create railings.
d. Create the room.
e. Create the window.
f. Create the foot support.
g. Create the door.
h. Create trees.
i. Save and render the scene.

Creating the Project Folder

Create a new project folder with the name *c04_tut2* at *\Documents\3dsmax2017* and then save the file with the name *c04tut2*, as discussed in Tutorial 1 of Chapter 2.

Creating the Floor

Start Autodesk 3ds Max and reset it as described earlier; a new screen with default settings is displayed. Next, you need to use the **Plane** tool from **Standard Primitives** to create the floor of the scene.

1. Activate the Top viewport and choose **Create > Geometry** in the **Command Panel**; the **Standard Primitives** option is displayed in the drop-down list. Choose the **Plane** tool from the **Object Type** rollout.

2. In the **Keyboard Entry** rollout, set the parameters as follows:

   Length: **1100.0** Width: **1200.0**

3. Choose the **Create** button from the **Keyboard Entry** rollout; a plane is created in all viewports. Choose the **Zoom Extents All** tool to display the entire plane in all viewports.

4. In the **Name and Color** rollout, enter **floor**; the plane is named as *floor*.

5. Modify the color of the floor by using the following values:

   Red: **61** Green: **135** Blue: **6**

6. Activate the Perspective viewport and press the G key to hide grids in it. Also, set the view using the **Zoom** and **Orbit** tools, as shown in Figure 4-72.

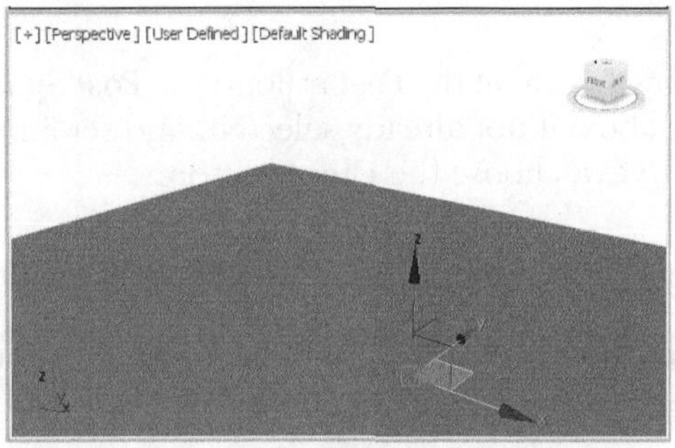

***Figure 4-72** The floor geometry in the Perspective viewport*

Creating Railings

In this section, you will create railings around *floor* using the **Railing** tool.

1. Activate the Top viewport and create a railing starting from the upper left corner of *floor* to its upper right corner.

2. In the **Name and Color** rollout, enter **railing01**.

3. Use the color swatch and change the color of *railing01* by entering the values as follows:

   Red: **177** Green: **88** Blue: **27**

4. Make sure *railing01* is still selected. Choose the **Modify** tab in the **Command Panel**; the **Railing**, **Post**, and **Fencing** rollouts are displayed.

5. In the **Railing** rollout, set the values as follows:

   Length: **1200.0**

   Top Rail area
   Profile: **Round** Depth: **15.0**
   Width: **13.0** Height: **100.0**

Lower Rail(s) area
Profile: **Round** Depth: **7.0** Width: **7.0**

6. Choose the **Lower Rail Spacing** button in the **Lower Rail(s)** area; the **Lower Rail Spacing** dialog box is displayed. Select the **Count** check box, if it is not already selected, and set the value **3** in the spinner on the right side of the **Count** check box and choose the **Close** button.

7. In the **Posts** rollout, set the values as follows:

   Profile: **Round** Depth: **10.0**
   Width: **5.0**

8. Choose the **Post Spacing** button in the **Post** rollout; the **Post Spacing** dialog box is displayed. Select the **Count** check box, if not already selected, and set **5** in the spinner on the right of the **Count** check box. Next, choose the **Close** button.

9. In the **Fencing** rollout, select **(none)** from the **Type** drop-down list.

10. Choose the **Select and Move** tool and align *railing01* in viewports, as shown in Figure 4-73.

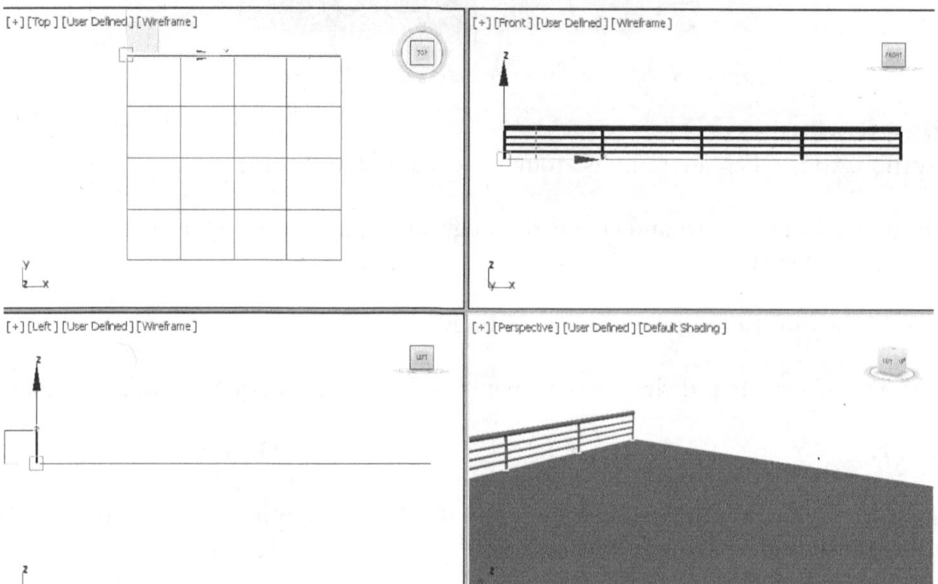

Figure 4-73 *The railing01 geometry in viewports after alignment*

11. Create other railings to surround *floor* keeping same dimension, except the length. Also, activate the Perspective viewport and set the view using the **Pan**, **Zoom**, and **Orbit** tools, as shown in Figure 4-74.

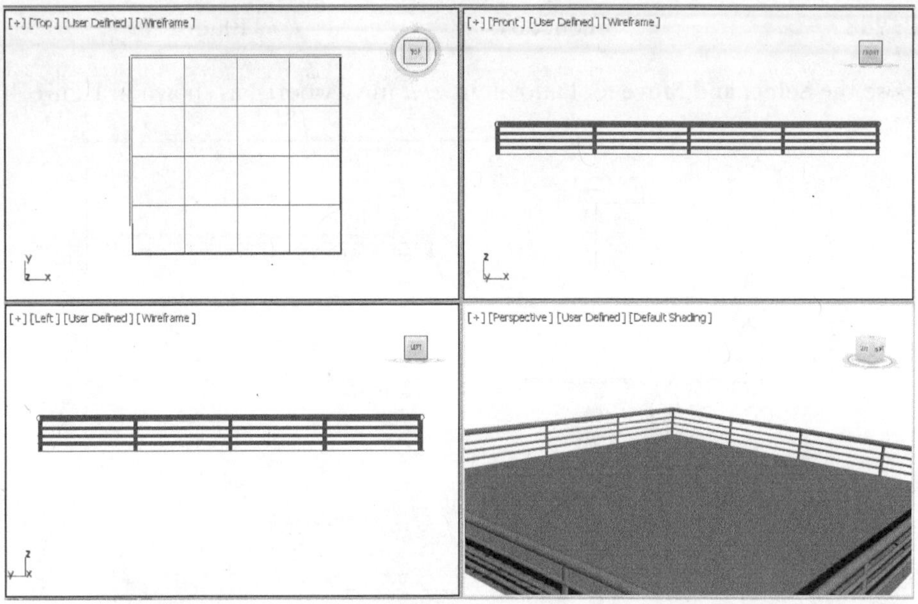

Figure 4-74 *The railings geometry displayed in viewports*

Creating the Room

In this section, you will create the walls of the room using the **Wall** tool.

1. Activate the Top viewport. Choose **Create > Geometry** in the **Command Panel**; a drop-down list is displayed below the **Geometry** button. Select the **AEC Extended** option from the drop-down list and then choose the **Wall** tool from the **Object Type** rollout.

2. In the **Parameters** rollout of the wall, set the values as follows:

   Width: **5.0** Height: **230.0**

3. Click on the upper left side of *floor* to specify the starting point of the wall. Drag the cursor toward the right to define the length, and then click on the viewport; a wall segment is created. In continuation, create another segment of the wall at the right angle of the first segment. Repeat the same procedure to create a wall of rectangular shape. Now, click on the starting point of the first wall segment; the **Weld Point?** message box is displayed. Choose the **Yes** button to weld the end points of the wall. Next, right-click to end the creation of the wall.

Note

*You can modify the wall using the tools in the **Select and Uniform Scale** flyout in the **Main Toolbar**.*

4. In the **Name and Color** rollout, enter **wall** and press the ENTER key.

5. Use the color swatch and change the color of *wall* by entering the values as follows:

   Red: **248** Green: **231** Blue: **120**

6. Choose the **Select and Move** tool and align *wall* in viewports, as shown in Figure 4-75.

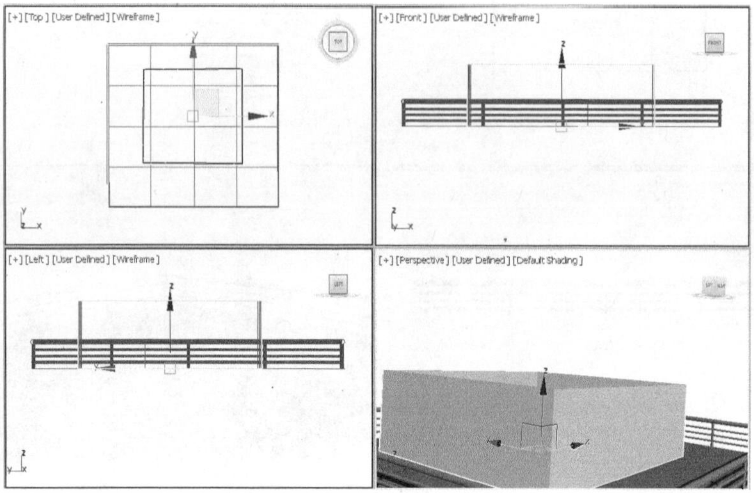

Figure 4-75 *The wall geometry displayed in viewports*

7. Select **Standard Primitives** from the drop-down list below the **Geometry** button. Choose the **Box** tool from the **Object Type** rollout to create the roof of *wall.*

8. Activate the Top viewport and create a box.

9. In the **Name and Color** rollout, enter **roof**.

10. Change the color of *roof* by entering the values as follows:

    Red: **143** Green: **225** Blue: **87**

11. In the **Parameters** rollout, set the values in the **Length** and **Width** spinners to cover the upper portion of the wall. Set the value **5.0** in the **Height** spinner.

12. Choose the **Select and Move** tool and align *roof* at the top of the wall in all viewports, refer to Figure 4-76.

13. Create a copy of *roof* as discussed earlier. Next, rename it as *room floor* and align it with *floor.*

Note

You may need to change the length and width of room floor to align it with floor.

14. Change the color of *room floor* to dark brown.

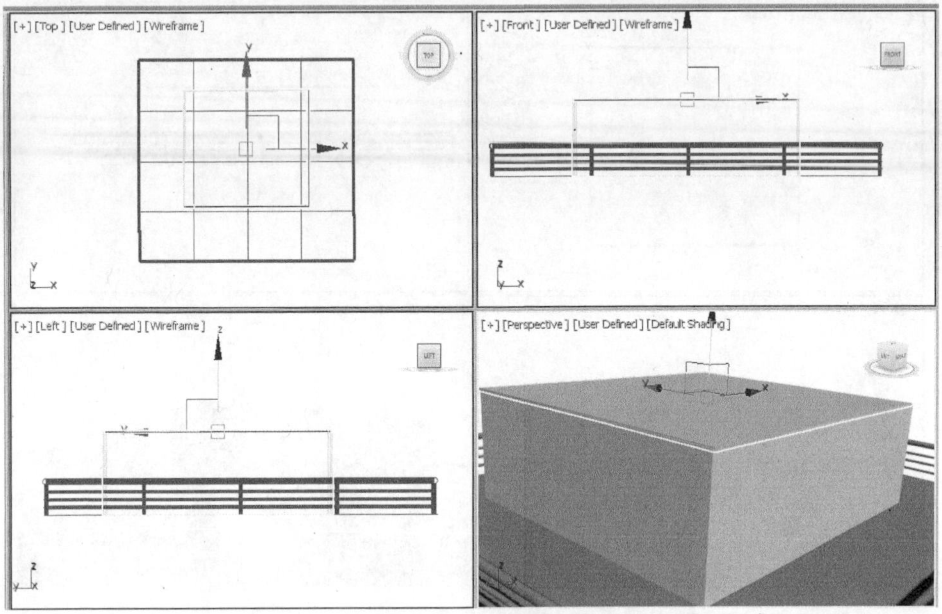

Figure 4-76 The roof geometry in viewports after alignment

15. Activate the Front viewport and select *roof*.

16. Choose the **Mirror** tool from the **Main Toolbar**; the **Mirror: Screen Coordinates** dialog box is displayed. In the **Mirror Axis** area of this dialog box, select the **Y** radio button. Next, set the value in the **Offset** spinner to **10**. In the **Clone Selection** area, select the **Copy** radio button and choose the **OK** button; *roof001* is displayed at the top of *roof*.

17. In the **Name and Color** rollout, modify the name as *roof fencing*.

18. Use the color swatch to change the color of *roof fencing* by entering the values as follows:

    Red: **243** Green: **93** Blue: **47**

    Make sure *roof fencing* is still selected.

19. Right-click on the **Select and Uniform Scale** tool; the **Scale Transform Type-In** dialog box is displayed. Now, in the **Offset: Screen** area, set the value **105** and press ENTER; *roof fencing* is scaled, as shown in Figure 4-77. Close the dialog box.

    Next, you need to create fencing for the corners of *wall*.

20. Activate the Top viewport and choose the **Box** tool. In the **Keyboard Entry** rollout, set the values as follows:

    Length: **6.0** Width: **1.0** Height: **230.0**

21. Choose the **Create** button; a box is displayed in the viewports.

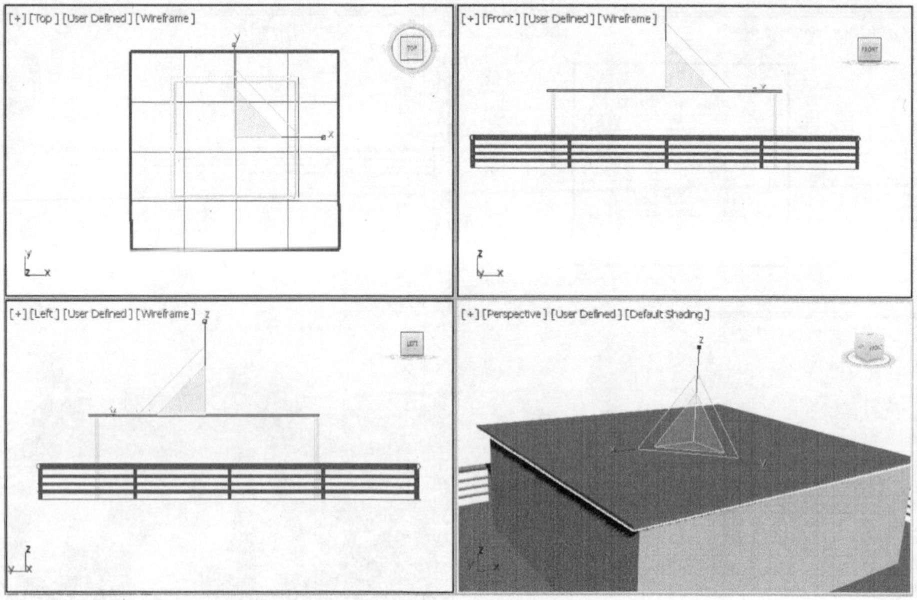

Figure 4-77 *The roof fencing geometry after scaling in the Front viewport*

Note

You may need to adjust the height of the box created, if you have modified the size of the wall earlier.

22. In the **Name and Color** rollout, enter **fc01**; the box is named as *fc01*.

23. Assign the same color to *fc01* that was assigned to *roof fencing*.

24. Choose the **Select and Move** tool and align *fc01* with *wall*, as shown in Figure 4-78.

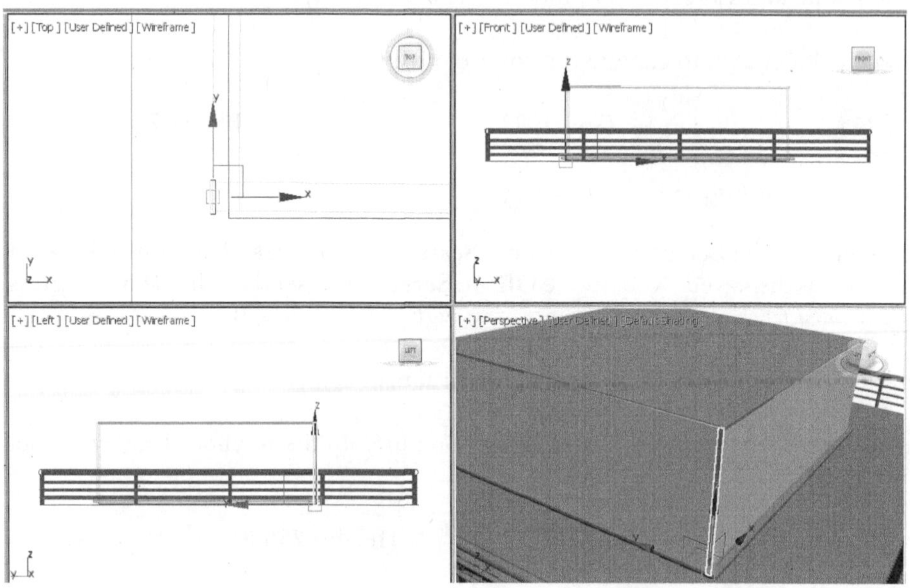

Figure 4-78 *The fc01 geometry in the Top viewport after alignment*

25. Make sure *fc01* is selected in the Top viewport and choose the **Select and Rotate** tool. Now, press and hold the SHIFT key, move the cursor over the Z-axis, and rotate it until the value in the **Z** spinner in the coordinate display becomes **90**. Now, release the mouse button; the **Clone Options** dialog box is displayed. Make sure the **Copy** radio button is selected in the **Objects** area and 1 is displayed in the **Number of Copies** spinner. Next, choose the **OK** button in this dialog box; a copy of *fc01* is created and gets rotated. It is automatically named as *fc002*.

26. Choose the **Select and Move** tool and align *fc002* with *wall*, as shown in Figure 4-79.

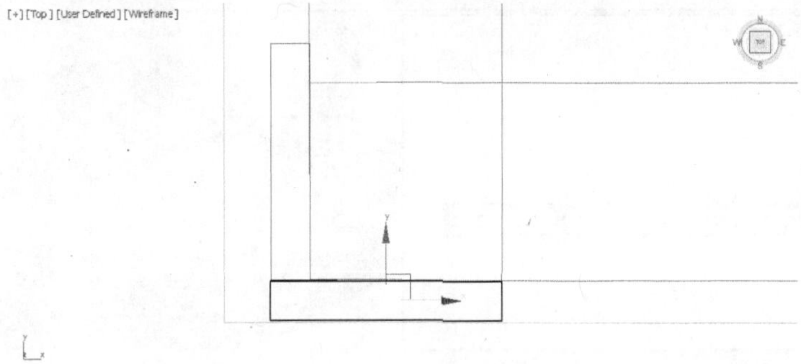

Figure 4-79 *The fc002 geometry in the Top viewport after alignment*

27. Select both *fc01* and *fc002* by pressing and holding the CTRL key and group them as *fencing01*.

28. Select *fencing01* and create its three copies. The copies are automatically named as *fencing002*, *fencing003*, and *fencing004*. Now, align them at the corners of *wall* using the **Select and Rotate** and **Select and Move** tools, refer to Figure 4-80. Also, you can use the **Zoom** tool to view the corners of *wall*.

29. Choose the **Maximize Viewport Toggle** tool to view the four viewports, as shown in Figure 4-80.

Note

*You can also use the **Mirror** tool to create copies of fencing01.*

Creating the Window

In this section, you will create a window by using the **Awning** tool.

1. Activate the Top viewport and select *wall* from the Scene Explorer. Next, choose **Create > Geometry** in the **Command Panel**; a drop-down list is displayed. Select the **Windows** option from the drop-down list and then choose the **Awning** tool from the **Object Type** rollout.

2. Press and hold the left mouse button and click on the left side of *wall*. Drag the cursor downward to specify the width of the window and then release the left mouse button. Next, move the cursor to the left to define the depth of the window, and then click on the viewport. Now, move the cursor to the left to specify the height of the window and then click on the viewport; an awning window is created in the viewports.

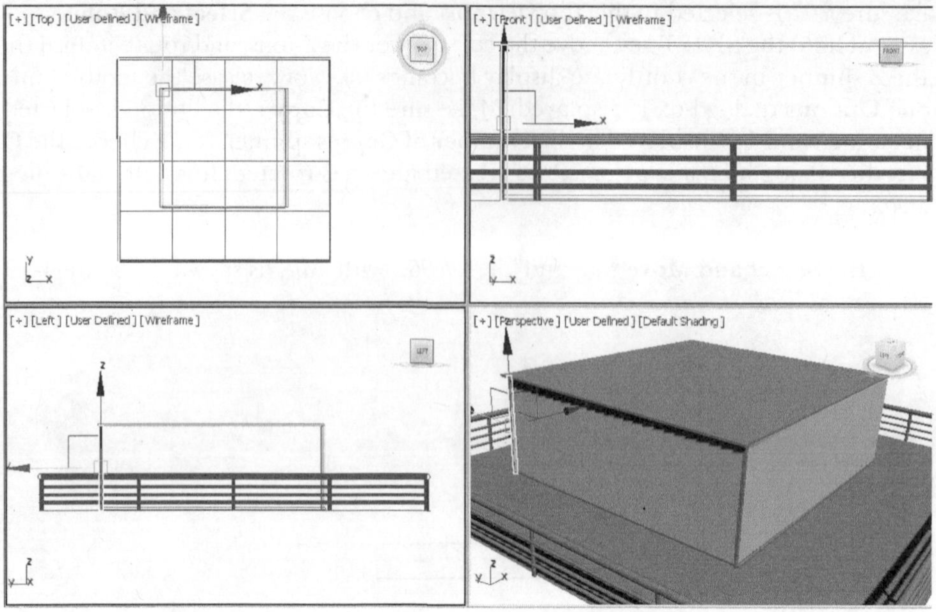

Figure 4-80 The fencing geometry at the four corners of wall in viewports

3. In the **Name and Color** rollout, enter **window**; the window is named as *window*.

4. Use the color swatch to change the color of *window* by entering the following values:

   Red: **135** Green: **59** Blue: **8**

5. Make sure *window* is selected. Choose the **Modify** tab in the **Command Panel**; the **Parameters** rollout is displayed.

6. In the **Parameters** rollout, set the values as follows:

   Height: **148.826** Width: **106.116** Depth: **10.0**

   Frame area
   Horiz. Width: **8.94** Vert. Width: **8.94** Thickness: **0.5**

   Glazing area
   Thickness: **0.25**

   Rails and Panels area
   Width: **14.554** Panel Count: **3**

   Open Window area
   Open: **25**

   You may need to adjust the height, length, and width of *window* according to *wall* size in your scene.

7. Use the **Select and Move** tool to align *window* with *wall* in the viewports, as shown in Figure 4-81.

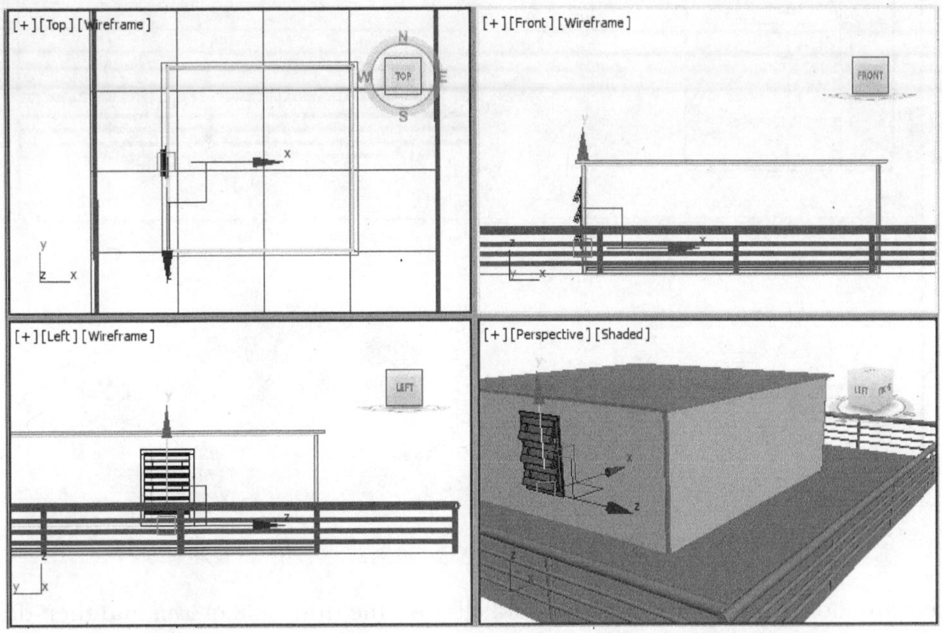

Figure 4-81 *The window geometry in viewports after alignment*

Creating the Foot Support

In this section, you will create a box primitive to create the foot support.

1. Activate the Top viewport and create a box. Next, choose the **Modify** tab.

2. In the **Parameters** rollout, set the values as follows:

   Length: **157.098** Width: **135.743** Height: **10.0**

3. In the **Name and Color** rollout, enter **foot support** and press ENTER.

4. Use the color swatch to change the color of the foot support by entering the values as follows:

   Red: **241** Green: **249** Blue: **200**

5. Align *foot support* with the front side of *wall* in viewports, as shown in Figure 4-82.

Creating the Door

In this section, you will create a door by using the **Pivot** tool.

1. Activate the Top viewport and select *wall* from the Scene Explorer. Next, choose **Create > Geometry** in the **Command Panel**; a drop-down list is displayed below the **Geometry** button. Select the **Doors** option from the list and choose the **Pivot** tool from the **Object Type** rollout.

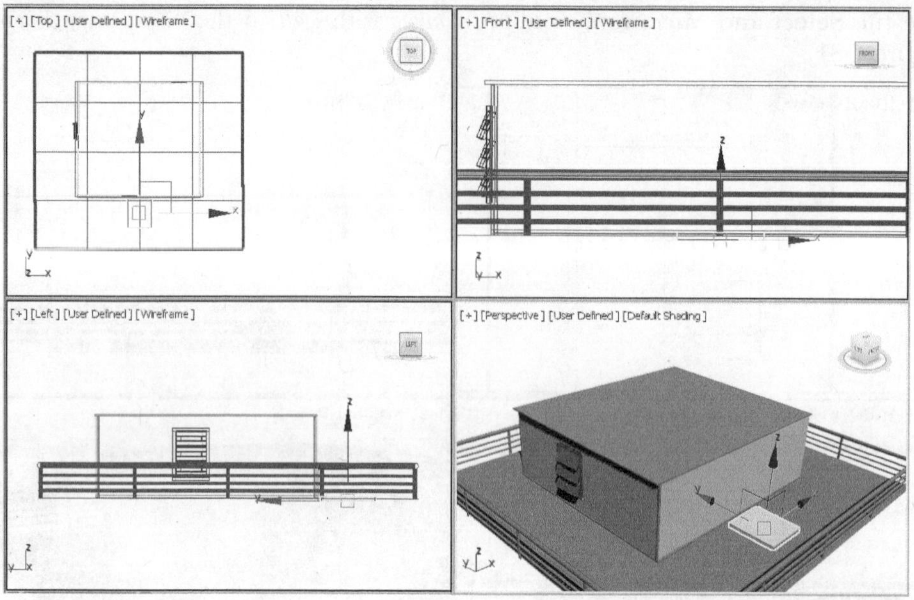

***Figure 4-82** The foot support geometry in viewports after the alignment*

2. Press and hold the left mouse button and click on the front side of *wall* and then drag the cursor to the right to specify the width of the door, and then release the left mouse button. Next, move the cursor upward to define the depth of the door, and then click on the viewport. Now, move the cursor upward again to specify the height of the door and then click on the viewport; the pivot door is created in the viewports.

3. In the **Name and Color** rollout, enter **door** as the name of the pivot door and assign it the same color that was assigned to *window*.

4. Make sure *door* is still selected. Choose the **Modify** tab in the **Command Panel**; the **Parameters** and **Leaf Parameters** rollouts are displayed.

5. In the **Parameters** rollout, select the **Flip Swing** check box and set the values as follows:

   Height: **200.0** Width: **120.341** Depth: **12.0**
   Open: **30**

6. In the **Frame** area of the **Parameters** rollout, make sure the **Create Frame** check box is selected and the values **2.0**, **1.0**, and **0.0** are specified for the **Width**, **Depth**, and **Door Offset** spinners, respectively.

   You may need to set the height and width of the door according to the size of *wall* in your scene.

7. In the **Leaf Parameters** rollout, make sure the value **2.0** is specified in the **Thickness** spinner and then set the remaining values in the rollout as follows:

Bottom Rail: **20.0** # Panels Horiz: **3** # Panels Vert: **4**
Muntin: **3.265** Stiles/Top Rail: **10**

8. In the **Panels** area of the **Leaf Parameters** rollout, select the **Beveled** radio button and make sure the value **45** is specified in the **Bevel Angle** spinner.

Thickness 1: **9.46** Thickness 2: **10.0** Middle Thick: **3.0**
Width 1: **3.0** Width 2: **3.0**

9. Align *door* in all viewports, as shown in Figure 4-83.

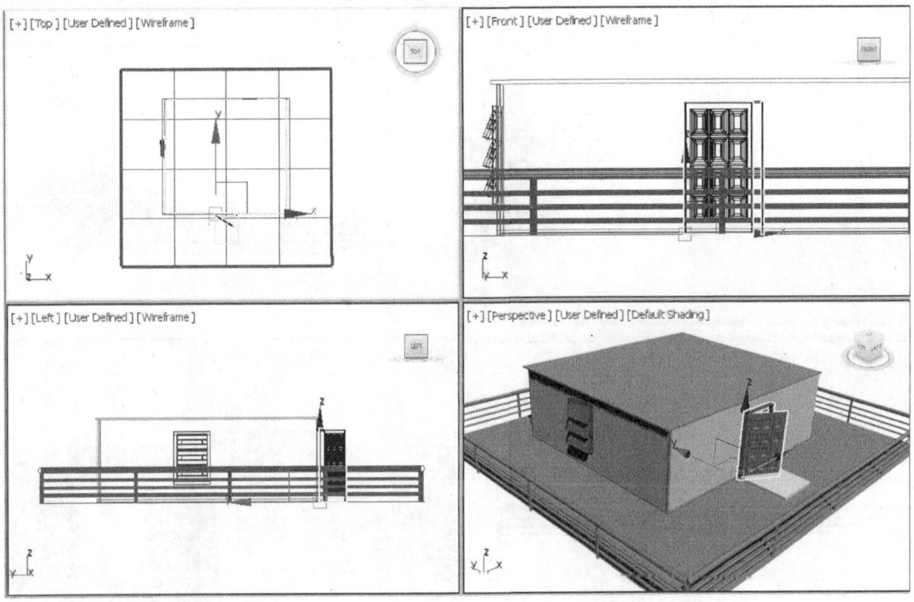

Figure 4-83 *The door geometry in viewports after alignment*

Creating the Trees

In this section, you will create trees by using the **Foliage** tool from **AEC Extended**.

1. Choose **Create > Geometry** in the **Command Panel**; a drop-down list is displayed. Select the **AEC Extended** option and choose the **Foliage** tool from the **Object Type** rollout.

2. Activate the Top viewport. Double-click on the **Banyan tree** in the **Favorite Plants** rollout; a tree is displayed in all viewports.

3. In the **Name and Color** rollout, enter **tree01** as the name of the tree.

4. Make sure *tree01* is still selected. Choose the **Modify** tab in the **Command Panel**; the **Parameters** rollout is displayed.

5. In the **Parameters** rollout, set the values as follows:

   Height: **120.0**

   Level-of-Detail area
   Select the **Medium** radio button.

   Use the default values for other options.

6. Choose the **Select and Move** tool and align *tree01* in the Top viewport, as shown in Figure 4-84.

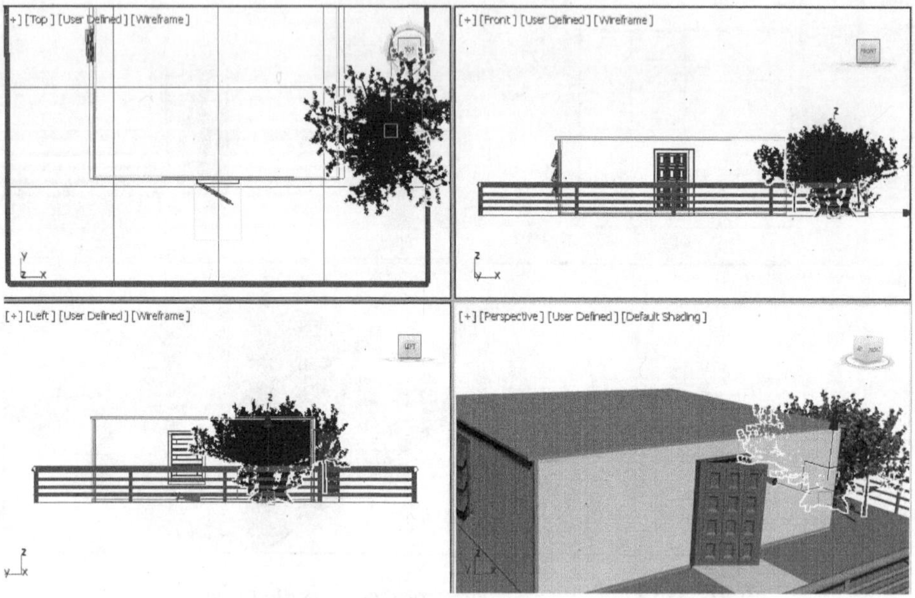

***Figure 4-84** The tree01 geometry displayed in viewports after alignment*

Now, you need to create another tree.

7. Activate the Top viewport. Choose the **Create** tab in the **Command Panel** and make sure the **Foliage** tool is chosen. Now, double-click on the **American Elm** tree from the **Favorite Plants** rollout; the tree is displayed in all viewports.

8. In the **Name and Color** rollout, enter **tree02** as the name of the new tree.

9. Choose the **Modify** tab in the **Command Panel**; the **Parameters** rollout is displayed.

10. In the **Parameters** rollout, set the values as follows:

Height: **300.0**

Use the default values for other options.

11. Choose the **Select and Move** tool and align *tree02* in the viewports, as shown in Figure 4-85.

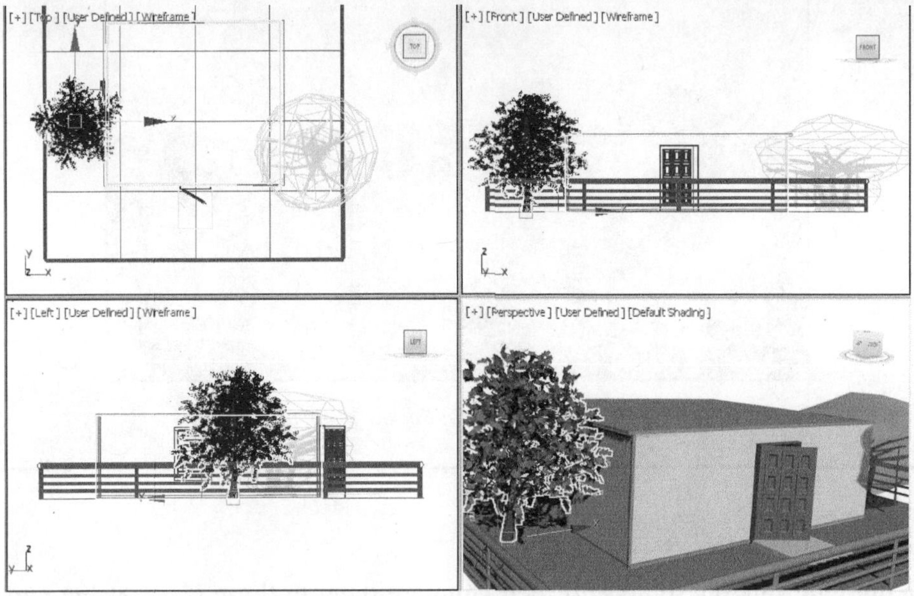

Figure 4-85 The tree02 geometry in viewports after the alignment

Saving and Rendering the Scene

In this section, you will save the scene and then render it. You can also view the final rendered image of this scene by downloading the *c04_3dsmax_2017_rndr.zip* file from *www.cadcim.com*. The path of the file is as follows: *Textbooks* > *Animation and Visual Effects* > *3ds Max* > *Autodesk 3ds Max 2017: A Comprehensive Guide*

1. Change the background color of the scene to light blue, as discussed in Tutorial 1 of Chapter 2, using the following parameters:

   Red: **145** Green: **241** Blue: **244**

2. Choose **Save** from the **Application** menu.

3. Activate the Perspective viewport. Next, choose the **Render Production** tool from the **Main Toolbar**; the **Rendered Frame** window is displayed. This window shows the final output of the scene, refer to Figure 4-86.

Figure 4-86 The final output of the scene at rendering

Self-Evaluation Test

Answer the following questions and then compare them to those given at the end of this chapter:

1. Which of the following tools is a part of the **Object Type** rollout for the **AEC Extended** objects?

   (a) **Foliage** (b) **Railing**
   (c) **Wall** (d) All of these

2. Which of the following tools is used to create doors?

   (a) **Awning** (b) **Bifold**
   (c) **Projected** (d) **Fixed**

3. Which of the following tools is used to create windows?

   (a) **Pivot** (b) **Railing**
   (c) **Casement** (d) **Bifold**

4. Which of the following tools is used to create stairs?

   (a) **Straight Stair** (b) **U-Type Stair**
   (c) Both (a) and (b) (d) None of these

5. To activate the **Align** tool, you need to press the __________ keys.

6. The __________ button in the **Favorite Plants** rollout of the **Foliage** tool in **AEC Extended** is used to give information about all the default trees.

7. You can increase the number of lower rails in the railing by entering a value in the __________ spinner of the __________ dialog box.

8. The **Mirror** tool is used to clone an object about the center of the selected coordinate system. (T/F)

9. You can change the default material of the plants that you create using the tools given in **Create > Geometry > AEC Extended > Foliage > Favorite Plants** rollout. (T/F)

10. The **Align** tool is used to align the current object with the target object. (T/F)

Review Questions

Answer the following questions:

1. Which of the following tools is used to create spiral stairs?

   (a) **L-Type Stair** (b) **Straight stair**
   (c) **U-Type Stair** (d) None of these

2. Which of the following rollouts is used to modify the panels of the doors?

   (a) **Name and Color** (b) **Parameters**
   (c) **Leaf Parameters** (d) **Creation Method**

3. When you select the stair in the viewport and choose the **Modify** tab in the **Command Panel**, the __________, __________, __________, and __________ rollouts are displayed.

4. An instance of an object is a clone in which the changes are reflected when they are made in the original object. (T/F)

5. You can create default trees in the viewports by invoking the **Foliage** tool from the **AEC Extended** drop-down list. (T/F)

EXERCISE

The rendered output of the models used in the following exercise can be accessed by downloading the *c04_3dsmax_2017_exr.zip* from *www.cadcim.com*. The path of the file is as follows: *Textbooks > Animation and Visual Effects > 3ds Max > Autodesk 3ds Max 2017: A Comprehensive Guide*

Exercise 1

Create the model shown in Figure 4-87 using the dimensions of your choice.

(Expected time: 15 min)

Figure 4-87 *The model for Exercise 1*

Answers to Self-Evaluation Test

1. d, **2.** b, **3.** c, **4.** c, **5.** ALT+A, **6. Plant Library**, **7. Count**, **Lower Rail Spacing**, **8.** T, **9.** T, **10.** T

5

Splines and Extended Splines

Learning Objectives

After completing this chapter, you will be able to:

- *Use the AutoGrid option*
- *Create splines*
- *Create extended splines*

INTRODUCTION

3ds Max has several basic 2D geometric shapes known as splines and extended splines. They are used to create 3D objects, 3D surfaces, and paths for lofting and creating animation. All splines and extended splines can be created dynamically by using the mouse or by entering the parameters in the **Keyboard Entry** rollout. In this chapter, you will learn about splines and extended splines.

AutoGrid

The **AutoGrid** option helps you to create an object on the surface of another object by generating a temporary grid on it. You can use this option by selecting the **AutoGrid** check box, which is available in the **Object Type** rollout of all object categories such as **Geometry**, **Shapes**, **Lights**, **Cameras**, and so on in the **Create** panel of the **Command Panel**. When you choose a tool from the **Object Type** rollout, the **AutoGrid** check box becomes active.

Choose **Create > Geometry** in the **Command Panel**; the **Standard Primitives** option will be displayed in the drop-down list. Now, choose the **Sphere** tool and create a sphere in the Perspective viewport, refer to Figure 5-1. Choose the **Torus** tool; the **AutoGrid** check box located at the top of the **Object Type** rollout will be activated. Select this check box; the gizmo will be displayed in the viewport along with the cursor to specify the position of the torus. Click on the top of the sphere in the Perspective viewport; a temporary grid will be created in the Perspective viewport. Now, drag the cursor; the torus will be created on the surface of the sphere, as shown in Figure 5-2.

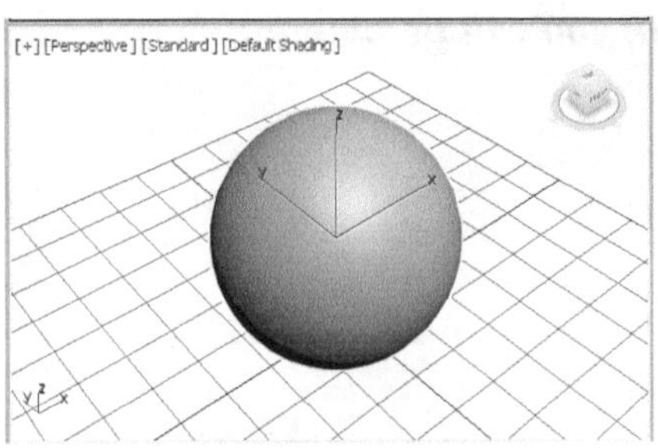

Figure 5-1 *The sphere created*

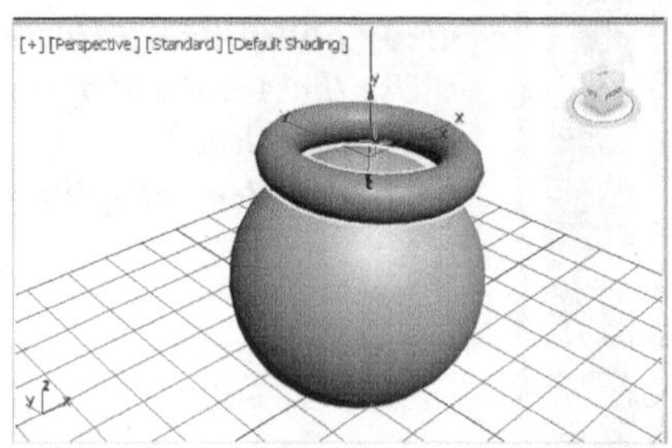

Figure 5-2 *The torus created after selecting the **AutoGrid** check box*

Note

The temporary grid will be visible only in the Perspective viewport.

CREATING SPLINES

To create splines, choose **Create > Shapes** in the **Command Panel**; the **Splines** option will be displayed in the drop-down list below the **Shapes** button. Now, activate the viewport in which you want to create the spline by clicking on it and then choose the corresponding tool from the **Object Type** rollout. In this section, you will learn to create and modify the splines and extended splines using the various tools available in the **Object Type** rollout.

Note

*By default, the **Start New Shape** check box is selected in the **Object Type** rollout. This check box enables you to create new shapes separately in the viewport using different tools such as **Line**, **Circle**, **Arc**, and so on available in the **Object Type** rollout. If you clear this check box and then create new shapes, the newly created shapes will be added to the current shape in the viewport. However, the **Section** shape is an exception.*

Creating a Line Spline

Menu bar:	Create > Shapes > Line
Command Panel:	Create > Shapes > Splines > Object Type rollout > Line

To create a line spline, activate the viewport and then choose the **Line** tool from the **Object Type** rollout; various rollouts will be displayed, as shown in Figure 5-3.

To create a line spline dynamically, click in the Top viewport to specify the first vertex or the start point of the line. Now, move the cursor to define the distance between the first and the second vertex, and click on the viewport to create the second vertex. Again, move the cursor and click to create additional vertices. Next, right-click to end the command; an open line spline will be created, as shown in Figure 5-4. To create a closed line spline, instead of right-clicking at the end, click on the first vertex; the **Spline** message box will be displayed, as shown in Figure 5-5. Choose the **Yes** button; a closed line spline will be created, as shown in Figure 5-6.

You can also create a line spline using another method. Click in the viewport to specify the first vertex and then move the cursor to define the distance between the first and the second vertex. Now, press and hold the left mouse button and drag the cursor to create additional vertices; a line spline with a bezier vertex and smooth curve will be created. The bezier vertex is controlled by two points on both endpoints, which help in modifying the curve of the line.

While creating a line spline, if you click in the viewport to create additional vertices, they will become corner vertices, as shown in Figure 5-7. But, if you click and drag to create additional vertices, the curve between the vertices will be smooth and the vertices will be bezier, as shown in Figure 5-8, depending on the options selected from the **Drag Type** and **Initial Type** areas of the **Creation Method** rollout.

Various rollouts used to create and modify a line are discussed next.

Rendering Rollout

The options in this rollout are used to toggle the shape renderability in the viewports and rendered output. It is also used to specify the cross-section settings and apply coordinates. These options are discussed next, refer to Figure 5-9.

Enable In Renderer

By default, the line spline created by you is not visible at the time of rendering. Select the **Enable In Renderer** check box to render spline as 3D mesh.

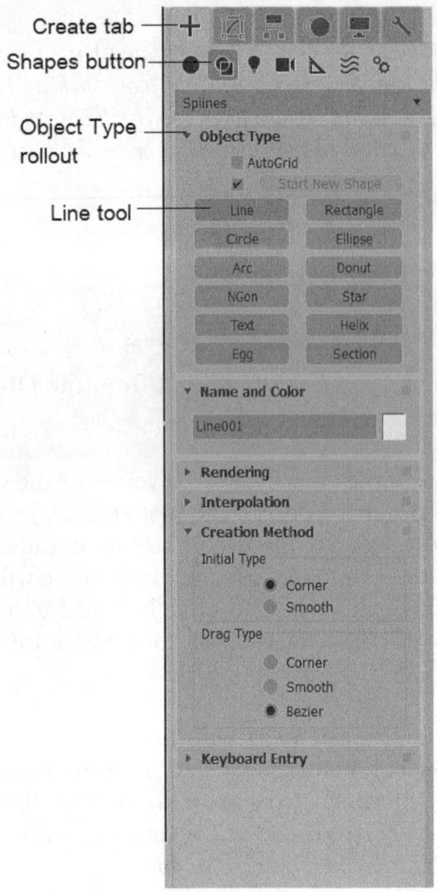

Figure 5-3 Various rollouts displayed to create and modify a line spline

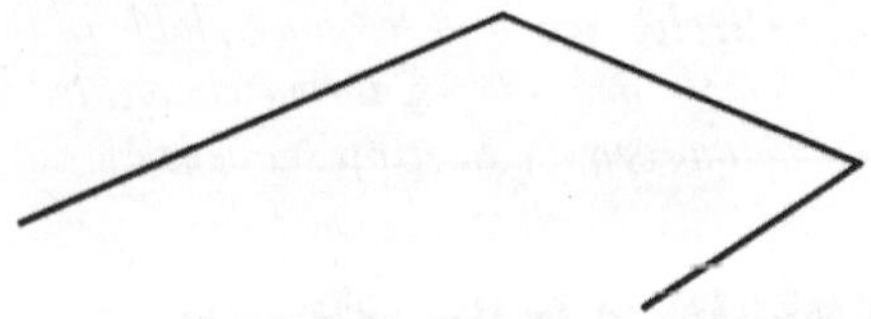

Figure 5-4 An open line spline created

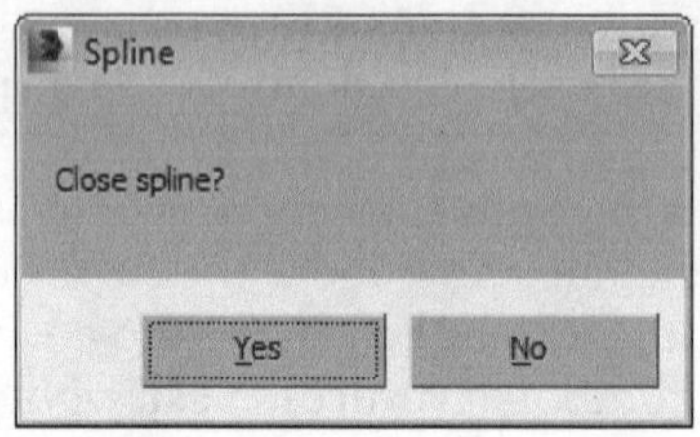

*Figure 5-5 The **Spline** message box*

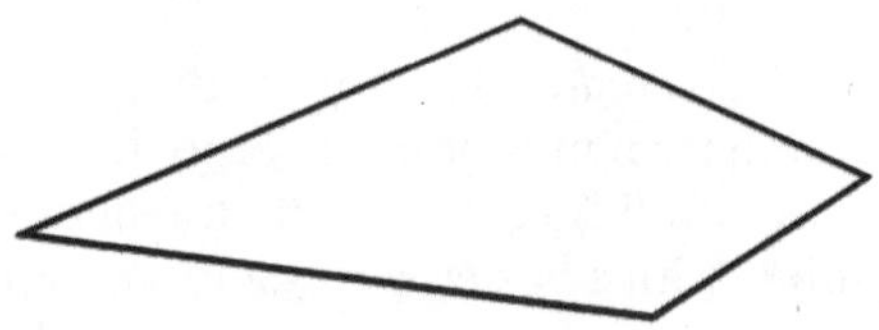

Figure 5-6 A closed line spline

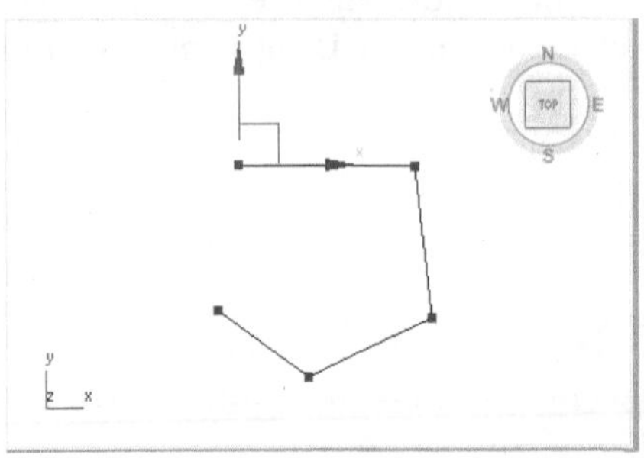

Figure 5-7 A line with corner vertices

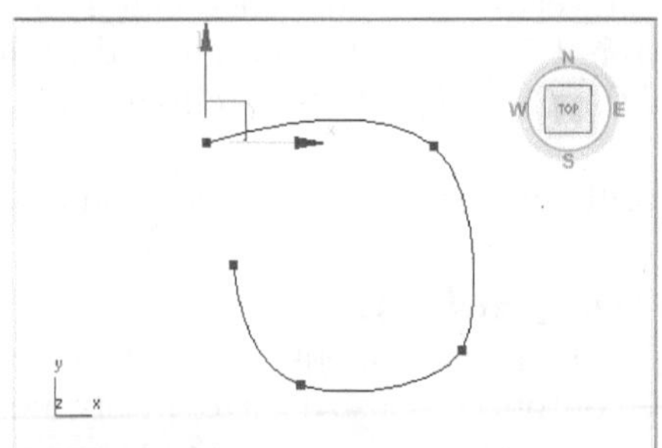

Figure 5-8 A line spline with bezier vertex and smooth curve

Enable In Viewport

Select the **Enable In Viewport** check box to make the line visible as 3D mesh in the viewport. The **Use Viewport Settings** check box is used to set different rendering parameters and display the mesh generated in the viewport. It is activated only when the **Enable In Viewport** check box is selected. On selecting the **Use Viewport Settings** check box; the **Viewport** radio button will be activated. Select this radio button and modify the parameters such as **Thickness** and **Sides** in the respective spinners; the line will be displayed as a 3D mesh in the viewport according to the parameters you set.

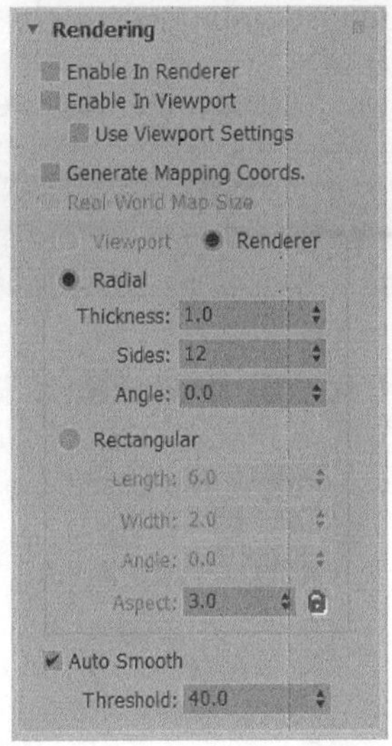

Figure 5-9 The ***Rendering*** *rollout*

Viewport

This radio button will be activated only if the **Use Viewport Settings** and **Enable In Viewport** check boxes are selected. It is used to specify the dimension and shape of the line in the viewport using the **Radial** or **Rectangular** radio button, respectively.

Renderer

This radio button is used to specify the dimension and shape of the line on rendering, using the **Radial** or **Rectangular** radio button. Note that you can view the modifications in the line at rendering, only if the **Enable In Renderer** check box is selected.

Radial

This radio button is used to display the shape with a circular cross-section. The **Thickness** spinner is used to set the thickness of the line. Similarly, the **Sides** spinner is used to set the number of faces along with the cross-section of the line. The value in the **Angle** spinner is used to set the position of the cross-section of the line by rotating it.

Rectangular

This radio button is used to display the shape as rectangular mesh. You can set the length and width of the line in the **Length** and **Width** spinners, respectively. The **Angle** spinner is used to set the position of the cross-section of the line by rotating it. The **Aspect** spinner is used to set the constant ratio of width to length. Choose the lock icon on the right side of the **Aspect** spinner to lock the constant ratio of width to length. Now, if you set the value in the **Length** or the **Width** spinner, the values will be set in both the spinners simultaneously.

Auto Smooth

By default, the **Auto Smooth** check box is selected. It is used to smoothen the angle between the line segments depending upon the value set in the **Threshold** spinner. The value in the **Threshold** spinner is used to set the threshold angle in degrees.

Interpolation Rollout

The options in the **Interpolation** rollout, are used to define how a line will be created, refer to Figure 5-10. The number of segments between each vertex on the line are called steps. The value in the **Steps** spinner defines the number of steps between each vertex on the line. Larger the value in the **Steps** spinner, smoother will be the line.

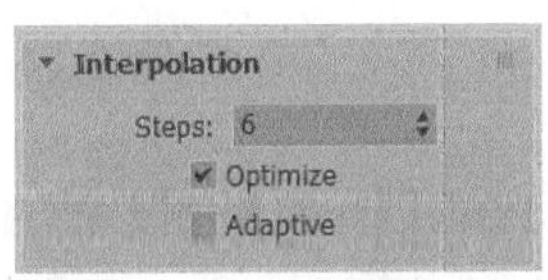

Figure 5-10 The ***Interpolation*** *rollout*

By default, the **Optimize** check box is selected, which helps you to remove the unwanted steps on the straight line, and you can set the number of steps by entering the value in the **Steps** spinner. If you select the **Adaptive** check box, it will automatically set the number of steps to create a smooth line. The **Optimize** check box and the **Steps** spinner will also become inactive.

Note

*The options in the **Name and Color**, **Rendering**, and **Interpolation** rollouts are same for all splines and extended splines in Autodesk 3ds Max.*

Creation Method Rollout

The options in this rollout are used while creating a line dynamically. The two areas in this rollout are discussed next.

Initial Type Area

The options in this area are used to define the type of vertex when you click on the viewport to create it. By default, the **Corner** radio button is selected. As a result, a sharp point is created and the line between the two corner vertices becomes straight. You can select the **Smooth** radio button to create a smooth and non-adjustable curve between the two vertices.

Drag Type Area

The options in this area are used to define the type of vertex of the spline while dragging the cursor in the viewport. By default, the **Bezier** radio button is selected which creates a smooth adjustable curve with bezier vertices. You can modify the shape of the curve using the two control points of these bezier vertices. The **Corner** and **Smooth** radio buttons perform the same functions as described in the **Initial Type** area.

Keyboard Entry Rollout

The options in this rollout are used to create a line by entering the parameters in the **Keyboard Entry** rollout, refer to Figure 5-11. The **X**, **Y**, and **Z** spinners are used to specify the position of the first vertex of the line along the axes of the home grid or a grid object. The **Add Point** button is used to create the vertex at the location specified in the X, Y, and Z coordinates in the viewport.The **Close** button is used to create a closed line and the **Finish** button is used to create an open line.

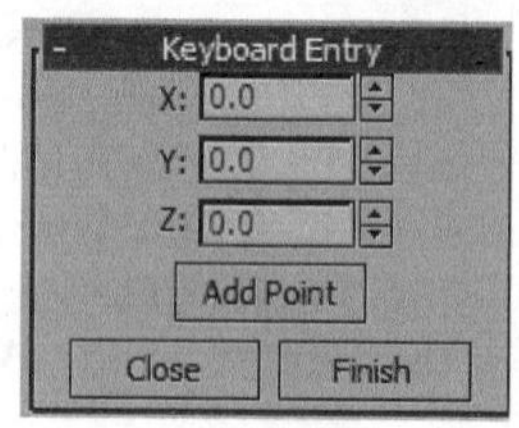

*Figure 5-11 The **Keyboard Entry** rollout*

Note

*The **Keyboard Entry** rollout for all the splines and extended splines is used to create the corresponding spline by entering the parameters using the keyboard. The method of creating all splines is same as discussed above with the only difference in the type and number of parameters entered for various splines and extended splines.*

Creating a Rectangular Spline

Menu bar:	Create > Shapes > Rectangle
Command Panel:	Create > Shapes > Splines > Object Type rollout > Rectangle

To create a rectangular spline, activate the viewport in which you want to create it and then choose the **Rectangle** tool from the **Object Type** rollout; the **Name and Color**, **Rendering**,

Interpolation, **Creation Method**, **Keyboard Entry**, and **Parameters** rollouts will be displayed, as shown in Figure 5-12. Click at the upper left corner of the viewport and hold the left mouse button and then drag the cursor to the lower right corner of the viewport. Next, release the left mouse button to set the length and width values; a rectangular spline will be displayed in the viewport, as shown in Figure 5-13.

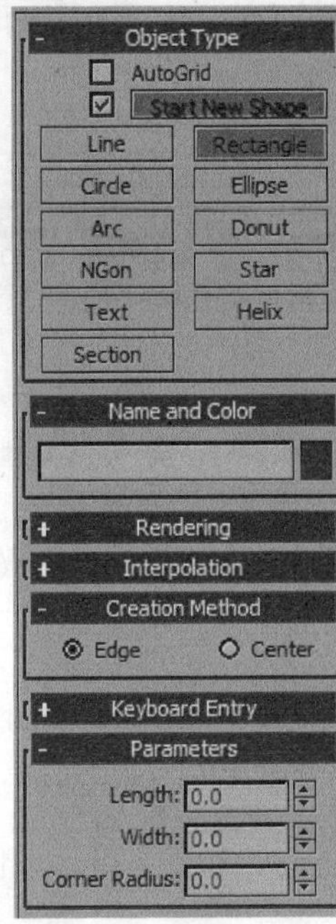

***Figure 5-12** Various rollouts to create and modify a rectangular spline*

Note

You can also create a square spline, as shown in Figure 5-14, using the same method as described above. The only difference in this case is that you need to hold the CTRL key while dragging the cursor.

Various rollouts used to create and modify the rectangular spline are discussed next.

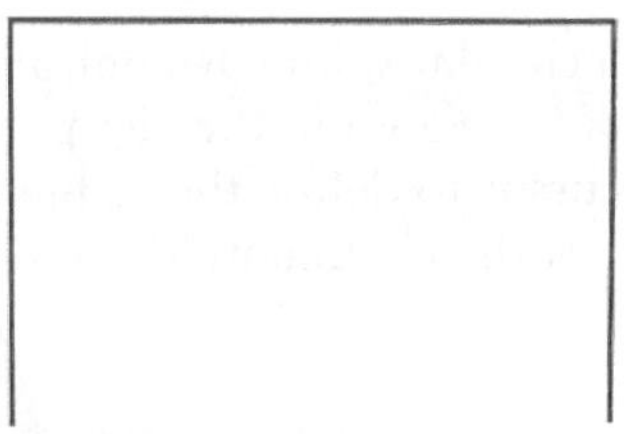

***Figure 5-13** A rectangular spline*

***Figure 5-14** A square spline*

Creation Method Rollout

The options in this rollout are used to create a rectangle. By default, the **Edge** radio button is selected. As a result, a point is created in the viewport. Press and hold the left mouse button on this point and drag the cursor to define the diagonal corner of the shape. This distance between the two corner points will be the diagonal of the rectangle. You can select the **Center** radio button to create a point at the center of the rectangle and then drag the cursor to specify the distance between the center and its corner.

Parameters Rollout

The options in this rollout are used to modify the rectangularspline. The **Length** spinner is used to specify the length of the rectangular spline along the local Y axis. The **Width** spinner is used to specify the width of the rectangular spline along the local X axis. The **Corner Radius** spinner is used to create round corner for the rectangular spline, refer to Figure 5-15.

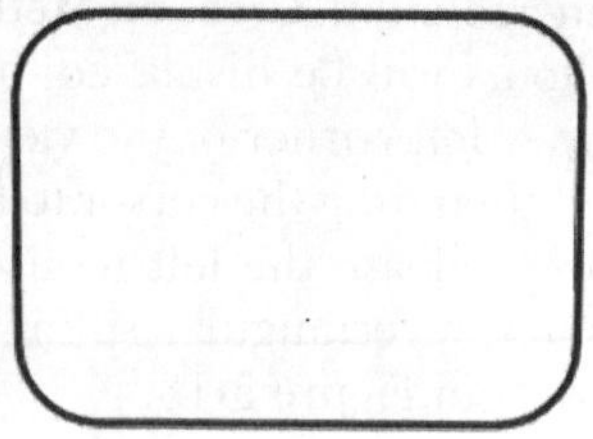

Figure 5-15 A rectangle with corner radius

Creating a Circular Spline

Menu bar:	Create > Shapes > Circle
Command Panel:	Create > Shapes > Splines > Object Type rollout > Circle

To create a closed circular spline, activate the viewport in which you want to create it and then choose the **Circle** tool from the **Object Type** rollout; various rollouts will be displayed. Next, press and hold the left mouse button and then drag the cursor. Next, release the left mouse button to set the radius of the circle; a circular spline will be created in the viewport, as shown in Figure 5-16.

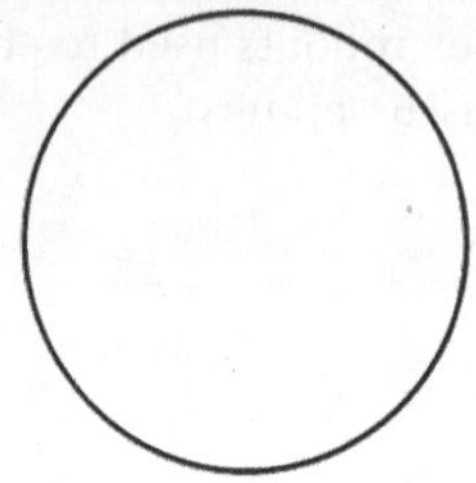

Figure 5-16 A circular spline

Various rollouts used to create and modify the circular spline are discussed next.

Creation Method Rollout

The options in this rollout are used while creating a circular spline dynamically. By default, the **Center** radio button is selected. As a result, a point is created in the viewport. Press and hold the left mouse button on this point and drag the cursor to define the radius of the circle. You can select the **Edge** radio button to specify a point of the circumference of the circle and then drag the cursor to define the radius of the circle.

Parameters Rollout

The options in this rollout are used to modify the circular spline. The **Radius** spinner is used to modify the radius of the circular spline.

Creating an Elliptical Spline

Menu bar:	Create > Shapes > Ellipse
Command Panel:	Create > Shapes > Splines > Object Type rollout > Ellipse

To create an elliptical spline, activate the viewport in which you want to create it and then choose the **Ellipse** tool from the **Object Type** rollout; the **Name and Color**, **Rendering**, **Interpolation**, **Creation Method**, **Keyboard Entry**, and **Parameters** rollouts will be displayed. Next, press and hold the left mouse button and then drag the cursor. Now, release the left mouse button to set the length and width; an elliptical spline will be created in the viewport, as shown in Figure 5-17.

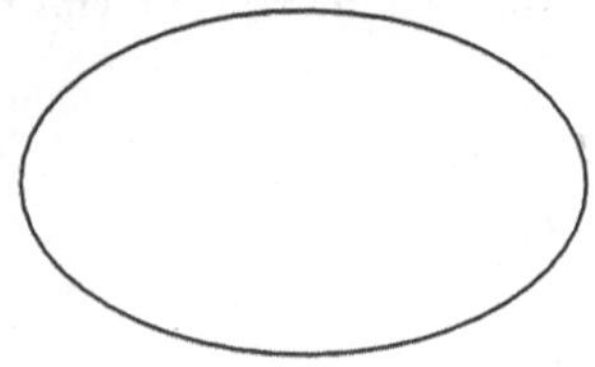

Figure 5-17 An elliptical spline

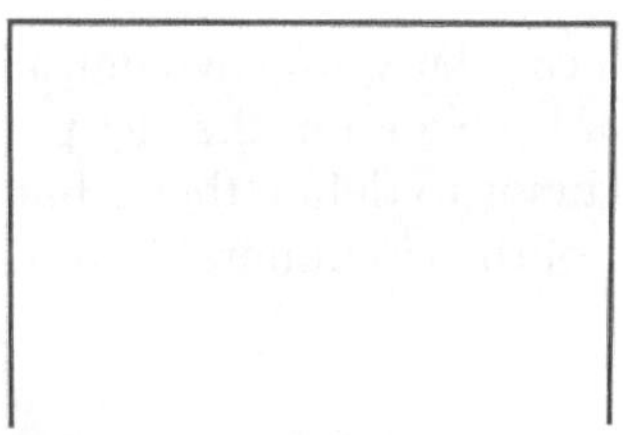

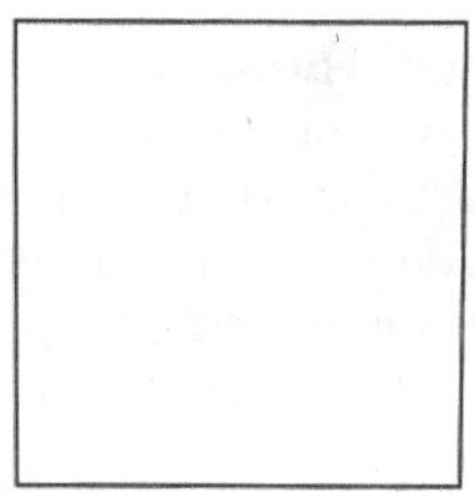

Note

You can also create a circular spline using the same method as discussed earlier. The only difference in this case is that you need to hold the CTRL key while dragging the cursor.

Various rollouts used to create and modify the ellipse are discussed next.

Creation Method Rollout

The options in this rollout are used while creating an elliptical spline dynamically. These options are the same as those discussed earlier.

Parameters Rollout

The options in this rollout are used to modify the elliptical spline. The **Length** spinner is used to define the length of the elliptical spline along the local Y axis. The **Width** spinner is used to define the width of the elliptical spline along the local X axis.

Creating an Arc Spline

Menu bar:	Create > Shapes > Arc
Command Panel:	Create > Shapes > Splines > Object Type rollout > Arc

To create an arc spline, activate the viewport in which you want to create it and then choose the **Arc** tool from the **Object Type** rollout; the **Name and Color**, **Rendering**, **Interpolation**, **Creation Method**, **Keyboard Entry**, and **Parameters** rollouts will be displayed. Various rollouts used to create and modify an arc are discussed next.

Creation Method Rollout

You can create an arc using two methods depending on the selection of the radio button in the **Creation Method** rollout. By default, the **End-End-Middle** radio button is selected. As a result, the first two points are created as the two endpoints of an arc and on dragging the cursor in the viewport, the third and fourth points are created between the two endpoints on the arc. You can select the **Center-End-End** radio button to specify the first point as the center of the arc, and then drag the cursor to specify the two endpoints of the arc. These methods are discussed next.

End-End-Middle Method

To create an arc using this method, activate the Top viewport and make sure that the **End-End-Middle** radio button is selected in the **Creation Method** rollout. Next, press and hold the left mouse button and drag the cursor to define the two endpoints of the arc. Release the left mouse button and move the mouse up or down to define the third and fourth point between the two endpoints on the arc, refer to Figures 5-18 and 5-19. Click on the viewport; an arc spline will be created, as shown in Figure 5-20.

Figure 5-18 *Creating an arc using the* ***End-End-Middle*** *method (step-1)*

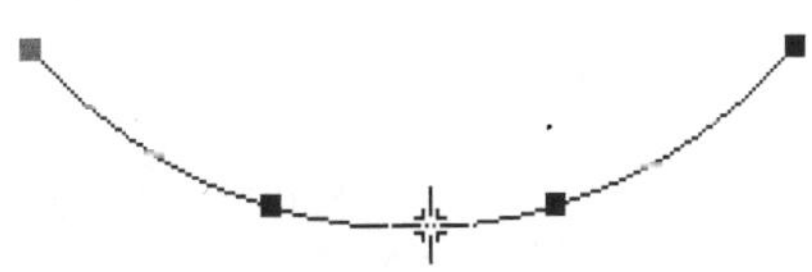

Figure 5-19 *Creating an arc using the* ***End-End-Middle*** *method (step-2)*

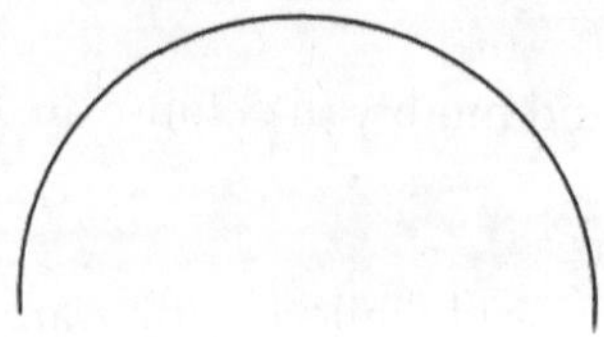

Figure 5-20 An arc spline

Center-End-End Method

To create an arc using this method, activate the Top viewport and select the **Center-End-End** radio button in the **Creation Method** rollout. Press and hold the left mouse button to specify the center point of an arc and drag the cursor to specify the first endpoint of the arc. Now, release the mouse button and move the cursor up or down to specify the second endpoint of the arc, refer to Figures 5-21 and 5-22. Click in the viewport; an arc will be created.

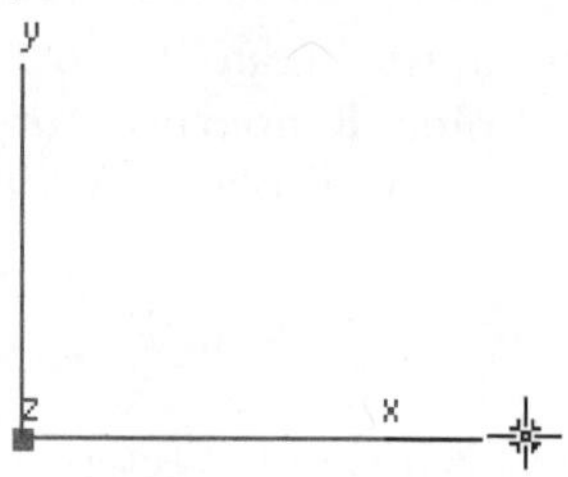

*Figure 5-21 Creating an arc using the **Center-End-End** method (step-1)*

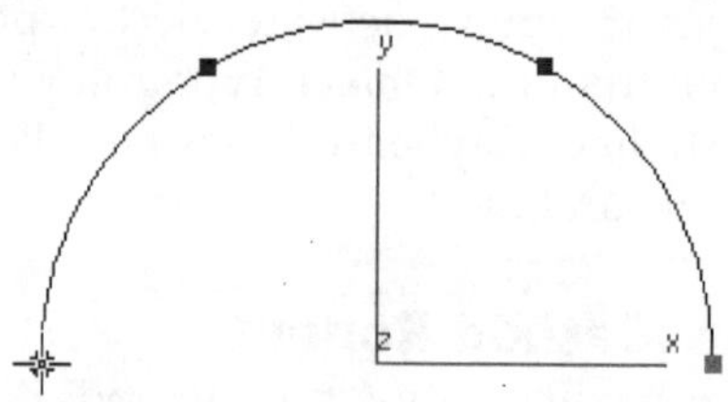

*Figure 5-22 Creating an arc using the **Center-End-End** method (step-2)*

Parameters Rollout

The options in this rollout are used to modify an arc. The **Radius** spinner is used to specify the radius of the arc. The **From** spinner is used to specify the start point of the arc as an angle measured from the local positive X axis. The **To** spinner is used to specify the end point of the arc as an angle measured from the local positve X axis. The **Pie Slice** check box is used to create straight segments from the endpoints of the arc to the radial center, creating a closed pie slice arc, as shown in Figure 5-23. The **Reverse** check box is used to reverse the direction of the arc spline and to place the first vertex at the opposite end of an open arc. To view the reversed direction, you need to convert it into an editable spline object about which you will learn in later chapters.

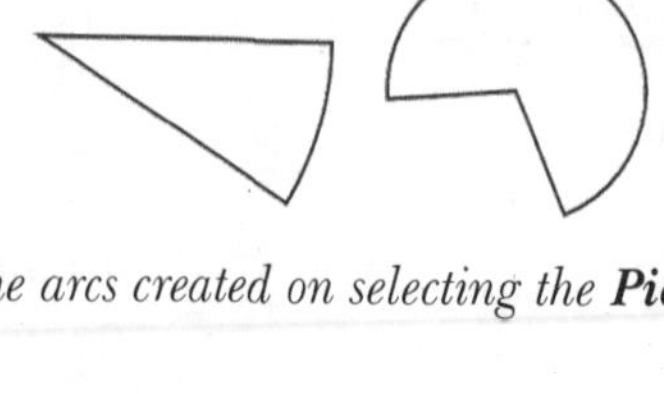

*Figure 5-23 The arcs created on selecting the **Pie Slice** check box*

Creating a Donut Spline

Menu bar:	Create > Shapes > Donut
Command Panel:	Create > Shapes > Splines > Object Type rollout > Donut

The **Donut** tool is used to create a closed spline with two concentriccircles known as donut. To create a donut spline, activate the viewport in which you want to create it and then choose the **Donut** tool from the **Object Type** rollout; the **Name and Color**, **Rendering**, **Interpolation**, **Creation Method**, **Keyboard Entry**, and **Parameters** rollouts will be displayed. Press and hold the left mouse button and drag the cursor. Next, release the left mouse button to set the radius 1. Now, drag the cursor again to define the radius 2 of the second circle and then click in the viewport; a donut spline will be created in the viewport, as shown in Figure 5-24.

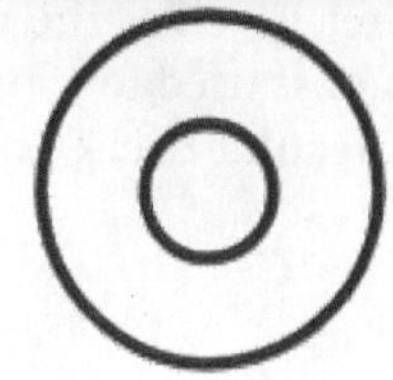

Figure 5-24 *A donut spline*

Various rollouts used to create and modify the donut spline are discussed next.

Creation Method Rollout

The options in this rollout are used while creating a donut spline dynamically. These are the same as discussed earlier while creating a rectangular spline.

Parameters Rollout

The options in this rollout are used to modify the donut. The **Radius 1** spinner is used to define the radius of the first circle of the donut and the **Radius 2** spinner is used to define the radius of the second circle of the donut.

Creating an NGon Spline

Menu bar:	Create > Shapes > NGon
Command Panel:	Create > Shapes > Splines > Object Type rollout > NGon

The **NGon** tool is used to create a closed spline with three or more number of sides known as NGon. To create an NGon spline, activate the viewport in which you want to create it and then choose the **NGon** tool from the **Object Type** rollout; the **Name and Color**, **Rendering**, **Interpolation**, **Creation Method**, **Keyboard Entry**, and **Parameters** rollouts will be displayed.

Next, press and hold the left mouse button and then drag the cursor. As you drag the cursor, the radius value of NGon will be displayed in the **Radius** spinner of the **Parameters** rollout. Release the left mouse button to set the radius of the NGon spline; an NGon spline will be created in the viewport, as shown in Figure 5-25.

Various rollouts used to create and modify the NGon spline are discussed next.

Creation Method Rollout

The options in this rollout are used while creating the NGon dynamically. These are the same as discussed earlier while creating a rectangular spline.

Parameters Rollout

The options in this rollout are used to modify the NGon spline. The **Radius** spinner is used to specify the radius of the NGon. By default, the **Inscribed** radio button is selected which specifies the radius of the NGon from its center to its corners. You can select the **Circumscribed** radio button to specify the radius of the NGon from the center to the midpoint of its sides. The **Sides** spinner specifies the number of sides of the NGon, refer to Figure 5-26. The **Corner Radius** spinner is used to round the corners of the NGon in degrees, refer to Figure 5-27. If you select the **Circular** check box, it creates a circular NGon.

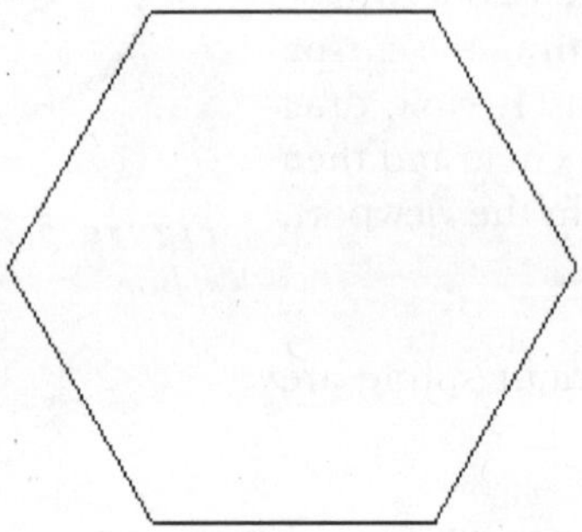

Figure 5-25 An NGon spline

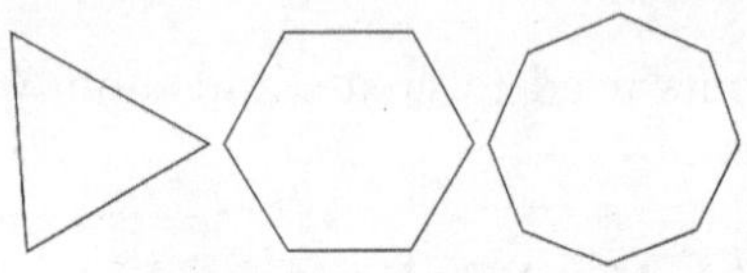

Figure 5-26 The NGons with 3, 6, and 8 number of sides

> **Note**
> *Create a circle and an NGon with same radius and place them in the viewport, as shown in Figure 5-28. Select the NGon and choose the* ***Modify*** *tab in the* ***Command Panel****. In the* ***Parameters*** *rollout, select the* ***Inscribed*** *and* ***Circumscribed*** *radio buttons one by one to notice the difference between them, refer to Figures 5-28 and 5-29.*

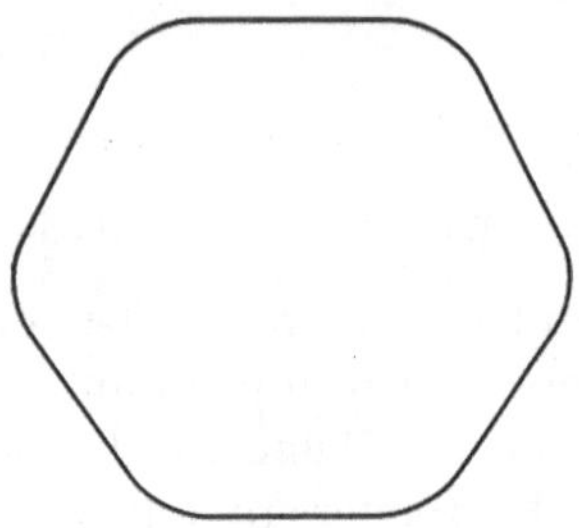

Figure 5-27 The NGon with round corners

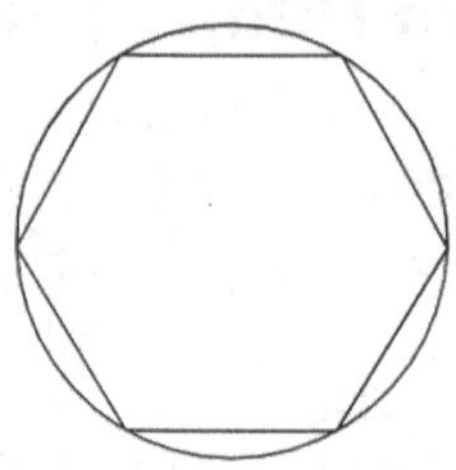

Figure 5-28 An NGon after selecting the ***Inscribed*** radio button

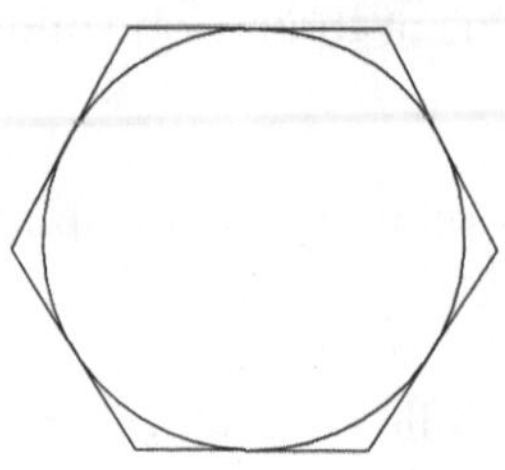

Figure 5-29 An NGon after selecting the ***Circumscribed*** radio button

Creating a Star Spline

Menu bar:	Create > Shapes > Star
Command Panel:	Create > Shapes > Splines > Object Type rollout > Star

The **Star** tool is used to create a star-shaped closed spline with three or more number of points. To create a star spline, activate the viewport in which you want to create it and then choose the **Star** tool from the **Object Type** rollout; various rollouts will be displayed.

Press and hold the left mouse button and then drag the cursor. Next, release the left mouse button and then drag the cursor again inside or outside to define the second radius of the star. Now, click on the viewport; a star spline will be created in all viewports, as shown in Figure 5-30.

Various rollouts used to create and modify the star are discussed next.

Parameters Rollout

The options in this rollout are used to modify a star. To do so, select the star and choose the **Modify** tab in the **Command Panel**; the **Parameters** rollout will be displayed. The **Radius 1** spinner is used to specify the radius of the first set of vertices of the star. The **Radius 2** spinner is used to specify the radius of the second set of vertices of the star. The **Points** spinner is used to specify the number of points in the star, refer to Figure 5-31. The **Distortion** spinner is used to rotate the inner points around the center of the star, refer to Figure 5-32. The **Fillet Radius 1** and **Fillet Radius 2** spinners are used to round the inner and outer points of the star, as shown in Figure 5-33.

Figure 5-30 *A star spline*

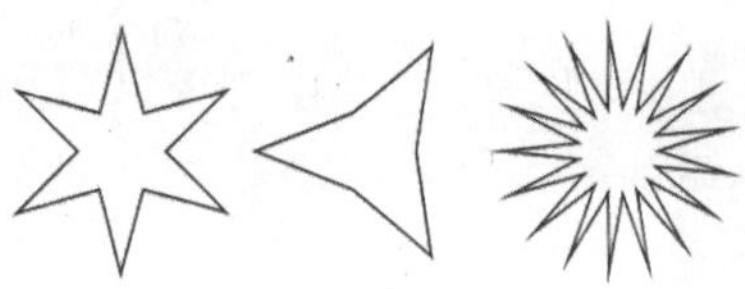

Figure 5-31 *The star splines with different number of points*

Figure 5-32 *A star after setting the value in the **Distortion** spinner*

Figure 5-33 *A star after setting the values in the **Fillet Radius 1** and **Fillet Radius 2** spinners*

Creating a Text Spline

Menu bar:	Create > Shapes > Text
Command Panel:	Create > Shapes > Splines > Object Type rollout > Text

The **Text** tool is used to create a spline in the text shape. To create a text spline, activate the viewport in which you want to create it and then choose the **Text** tool from the **Object Type** rollout; various rollouts will be displayed. To create the text dynamically, type the text in the Text text box of the **Parameters** rollout. Next, activate the Front viewport and click on it; the text will be displayed in the viewports, refer to in Figure 5-34.

Various rollouts used to create and modify the text are discussed next.

Parameters Rollout

The options in this rollout are used to modify the text. At the top of Parameters rollout, a **Font** drop-down list is displayed. You can modify the font type of the text in the viewport by selecting the font from this drop-down list. The ***I*** and **U** buttons are used to italicize and underline the text, respectively. The alignment buttons placed on the right of the **U** button are used for the proper alignment of the text, refer to Figure 5-35. The **Size** spinner is used to modify the size of the text. The **Kerning** spinner is used to set the distance between the letters. If the text is written in two lines, then the **Leading** spinner is used to set the distance between these lines. The **Text** text box is used to enter the text that you want to display in the viewport. By default, the text in the text box is MAX Text.

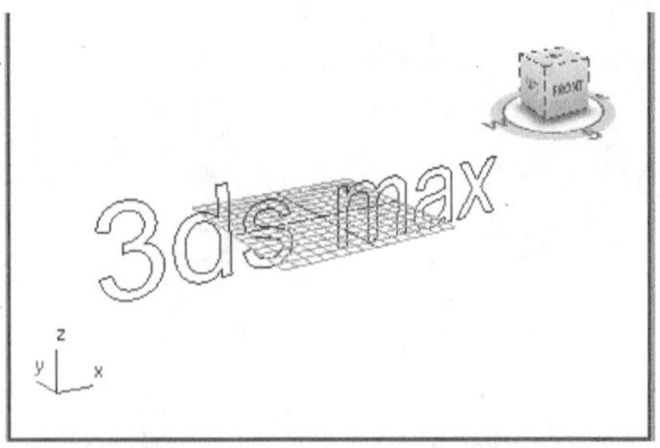

Figure 5-34 The text in the viewport

Figure 5-35 Alignment buttons

Update Area

The **Update** area is used to make modifications in the text using various rollouts in the **Modify** panel. On doing so, the text will automatically be updated in the viewport. The **Manual Update** check box in this area, which is used for manual update of the text in the viewport. The **Update** button is used to view the updated output in the viewports for manual update.

Creating a Helix Spline

Menu bar:	Create > Shapes > Helix
Command Panel:	Create > Shapes > Splines > Object Type rollout > Helix

The **Helix** tool is used to create a spline with spirals. To create a helix spline, activate the viewport in which you want to create it and then choose the **Helix** tool from the **Object Type** rollout; the **Name and Color**, **Rendering**, **Creation Method**, **Keyboard Entry**, and **Parameters** rollouts will be displayed. Press and hold the left mouse button and then drag the cursor. Next, release the left mouse button and then drag the cursor up or down to define the height of the helix. Now, click on the viewport and move the cursor up or down to set the second radius of the endpoint. Again, click on the viewport; a helix spline will be created in viewports, as shown in Figure 5-36.

Various rollouts used to create and modify the helix are discussed next.

Creation Method Rollout

The options in this rollout are used while creating a helix dynamically. These are the same as discussed earlier.

Parameters Rollout

The options in this rollout are used to modify the helix. The **Radius 1** spinner is used to specify the radius for the start point of the helix. The **Radius 2** spinner is used to specify the radius for the end point of the helix. The **Height** spinner is used to specify the height of the helix. The **Turns** spinner is used to specify the number of turns between start and end points of the helix. The **Bias** spinner forces the turns of the helix to accumulate toward its start or end point. By default, the value in the **Bias** spinner is 0, which evenly distributes the turns between the start and end points, refer to Figure 5-37. It varies from -1 to +1. The -1 value forces the turns to accumulate toward the start point of the helix and +1 value forces the turns to accumulate toward the endpoint of the helix, as shown in Figures 5-38 and 5-39. By default, the **CW** radio button is selected. As a result, the helix turns clockwise. You can select the **CCW** radio button to turn the helix counterclockwise.

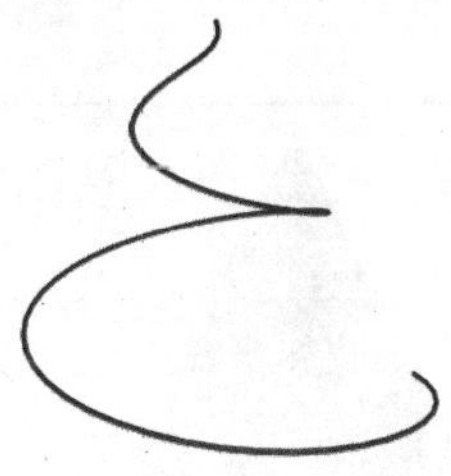

Figure 5-36 A helix spline

*Figure 5-37 The helix spline with three turns and zero value in the **Bias** spinner*

*Figure 5-38 The helix spline with three turns and +1 value in the **Bias** spinner*

*Figure 5-39 The helix spline with three turns and -1 value in the **Bias** spinner*

Creating a Section Spline

Menu bar:	Create > Shapes > Section
Command Panel:	Create > Shapes > Splines > Object Type rollout > Section

The **Section** tool is used to create a special type of spline that appears like a bisected rectangle. It generates shape based on a cross-sectional space through mesh objects. To create a section spline, activate the viewport in which you want to create it and then choose the **Section** tool from the **Object Type** rollout; the **Name and Color**, **Section Parameters**, and **Section Size** rollouts will be displayed.

Press and hold the left mouse button and then drag the cursor. Next, release the left mouse button to set the length and width of the section spline; a section spline will be created in the viewport, as shown in Figure 5-40.

Various rollouts used to create and modify the section spline are discussed next.

Section Parameters Rollout

The options in this rollout are used to create a new shape, based on the cross-section where the section spline slices the objects, refer to Figure 5-41. If you move the section spline on an object, the **Create Shape** button in the **Section Parameters** rollout will be activated. Choose this button; the **Name Section Shape** dialog box will be displayed, as shown in Figure 5-42. In the **Name** text box, enter the name of the new shape and choose the **OK** button; a new shape will be created. This new shape will be editable and will have vertex, segment, and spline sub-objects. You will learn to edit these types of splines in later chapters. The areas in the **Section Parameters** rollout are discussed next.

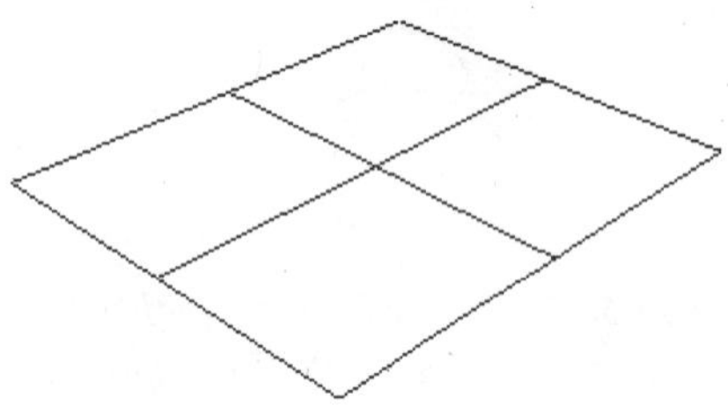

Figure 5-40 *A section spline*

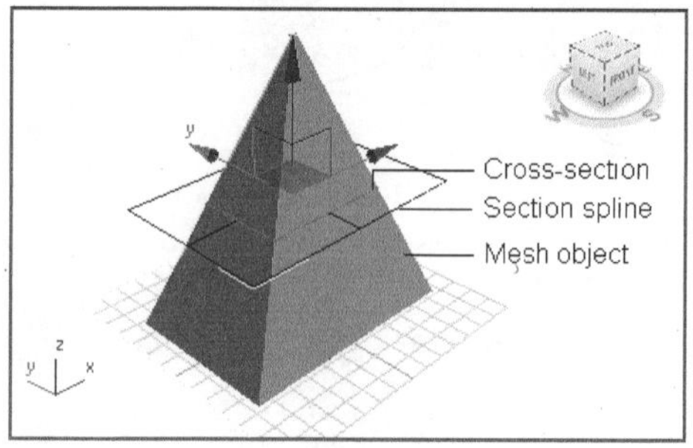

Figure 5-41 *The cross-section of the section spline according to the object*

Update Area

This area has three radio buttons to specify when the cross-section will be updated. By default, the **When Section Moves** radio button is selected. As a result, the cross-section will be updated while moving the section spline. The **When Section Selected** radio button in this area is used to update the cross-section when you select the section shape, but not when you move it. After selecting this radio button, you need to choose the **Update Section** button to update it. If you select the **Manually** radio button, it updates the cross-section manually by choosing the **Update Section** button.

Section Extents Area

The radio buttons in this area are used to define the extent of cross-section created by the section spline. By default, the **Infinite** radio button is selected. As a result, the section plane will be infinite in all directions and it will generate the cross-section for all the objects that passes through the plane, as shown in Figure 5-43. The **Section Boundary** radio button is used to generate the cross-section only for the objects that are touched by the boundary or are inside the section plane. When you select the **Off** radio button; the cross-section will not be displayed and the **Create Shape** button will be deactivated.

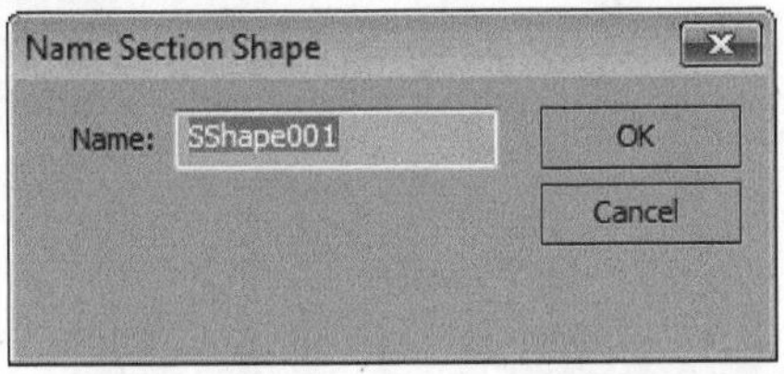

*Figure 5-42 The **Name Section Shape** dialog box*

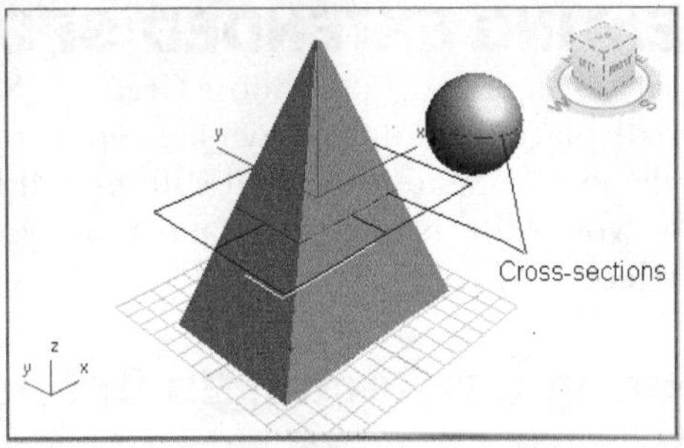

*Figure 5-43 The cross-sections generated in both the objects in their planes on selecting the **Infinite** radio button*

By default, the color of the cross-section in a section spline is yellow. If you want to change it, choose the color swatch at the bottom of the **Section Extents** area; the **Color Selector** dialog box will be displayed. Select the new color and choose the **OK** button; the new color will be displayed in the color swatch.

Section Size Rollout

The options in this rollout are used to modify the overall size of the rectangular section spline. The **Length** and **Width** spinners are used to modify the size of the rectangular section spline.

Creating an Egg Spline

Menu bar:	Create > Shapes > Egg
Command Panel:	Create > Shapes > Splines > Object Type rollout > Egg

The **Egg** tool is used to create an egg shaped spline. To do so, activate the viewport in which you want to create it and then choose the **Egg** tool from the **Object Type** rollout; various rollouts will be displayed.

Press and hold the left mouse button and then drag the cursor.Next, release the left mouse button and then drag the cursor to define the thickness of the egg shaped spline; an egg spline will be created in the viewport, as shown in Figure 5-44.

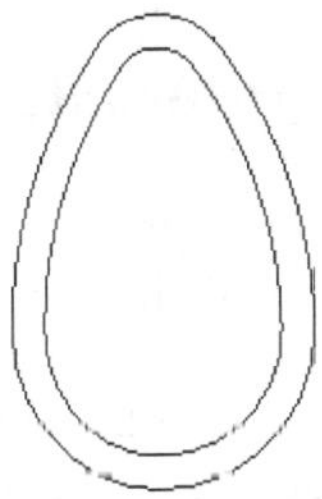

Figure 5-44 An egg spline

Various rollouts used to create and modify the egg are discussed next.

Parameters Rollout

The options in this rollout are used to modify the egg spline. The **Length** spinner is used to set the length of the egg spline. The **Width** spinner is used to set the width of the egg spline. By default, the **Outline** check box is selected. As a result, an additional egg shaped outline is created. The **Thickness** spinner is activated only when the **Outline** check box is selected. This spinner is used to set an outline between the main egg and its outline. The **Angle** spinner is used to set the angle of the egg spline along the local Z axis.

CREATING EXTENDED SPLINES

To create extended splines, choose **Create > Shapes** in the **Command Panel**; the **Splines** option will be displayed in a drop-down list. Select the **Extended Splines** option from the drop-down list; all tools to create extended splines will be displayed in the **Object Type** rollout. In this section, you will learn to create and modify extended splines using various tools available in the **Object Type** rollout.

Creating a WRectangle Spline

Menu bar:	Create > Extended Shapes > WRectangle
Command Panel:	Create > Shapes > Extended Splines > Object Type rollout > WRectangle

The WRectangle spline is a closed spline with two concentric rectangles. To create a **WRectangle** spline, choose the **WRectangle** tool from the **Object Type** rollout; the **Name and Color**, **Rendering**, **Interpolation**, **Creation Method**, **Keyboard Entry**, and **Parameters** rollouts will be displayed.

Press and hold the left mouse button and then drag the cursor. Next, release the left mouse button to set the length and width, and then move the cursor to define the thickness or the inner rectangle. Now, click on the viewport; a WRectangle spline will be created in the viewport, as shown in Figures 5-45.

Various rollouts used to create and modify the WRectangle are discussed next.

Note

*The options in the **Creation Method** rollout for all extended splines are same as described earlier in this chapter.*

Parameters Rollout

The options in this rollout are used to modify the WRectangle spline. The **Length**, **Width** and **Thickness** spinners are used to specify the height, width, and thickness of the WRectangle spline, respectively. By default, the **Sync Corner Fillets** check box is selected. As a result, the corners of the outer rectangle are controlled using the **Corner Radius 1** spinner. If you clear this check box, it will control the radius of the corners of both the concentric rectangles through the **Corner Radius 1** and **Corner Radius 2** spinners, refer to Figure 5-46. The **Corner Radius 1** spinner is used to specify the radius of the four corners of the outer rectangle.

The **Corner Radius 2** spinner is activated only when the **Sync Corner Fillets** check box is cleared. This spinner is used to specify the radius of the four corners of the inner rectangle.

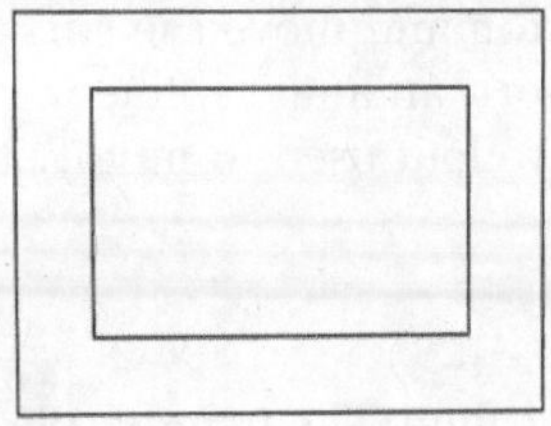

Figure 5-45 A WRectangle spline

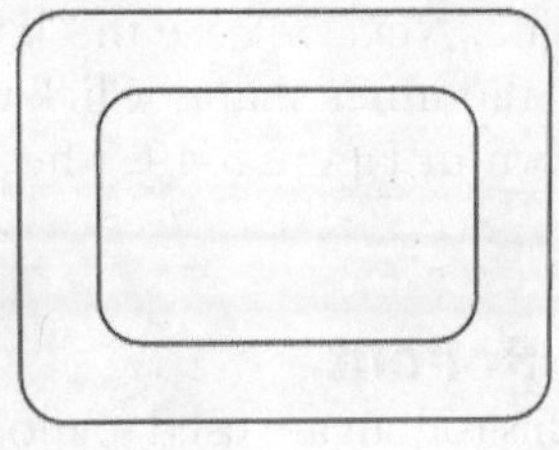

Figure 5-46 The WRectangle spline with corner radius

Creating a Channel Spline

Menu bar:	Create > Extended Shapes > Channel
Command Panel:	Create > Shapes > Extended Splines > Object Type rollout > Channel

The channel spline is a C-shaped closed spline. To create a channel spline, activate the viewport in which you want to create it and then choose the **Channel** tool from the **Object Type** rollout; various rollouts will be displayed.

Now, press and hold the left mouse button and drag the cursor to set the length and width of the channel. Next, release the left mouse button and move the cursor to define the thickness or the inner shape. Click on the viewport; a channel spline will be created in the viewport, as shown in Figure 5-47.

Parameters Rollout

The options in this rollout are used while creating a channel dynamically. These options are the same as those discussed in the **WRectangle** tool. The channel spline with the corner radius is shown in Figure 5-48.

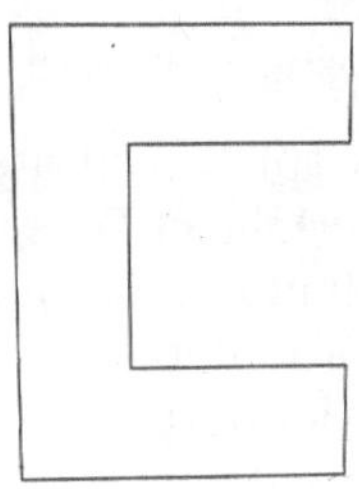

Figure 5-47 A channel spline

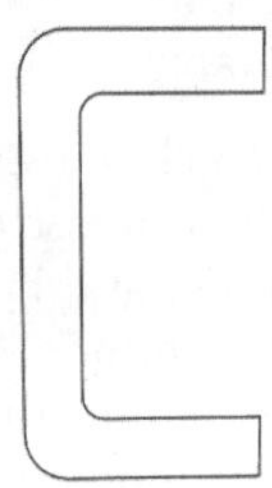

Figure 5-48 The channel spline with corner radius

Creating an Angle Spline

Menu bar:	Create > Extended Shapes > Angle
Command Panel:	Create > Shapes > Extended Splines > Object Type rollout > Angle

The angle spline is an L-shaped closed spline. To create an angle spline, activate the viewport in which you want to create it and then choose the **Angle** tool from the **Object Type** rollout; various rollouts will be displayed.

Next, press and hold the left mouse button and drag the cursor to set the length and width of the angle spline. Next, release the left mouse button and move the cursor inside to define the thickness or the inner shape. Click on the viewport; an angle spline will be created in the viewport, as shown in Figure 5-49. The **Parameters** rollout used to modify the angle spline is discussed next.

Parameters Rollout

The options in this rollout are used to modify an angle spline. The **Length**, **Width** and **Thickness** spinners are used to specify the length, width, and thickness of the angle spline, respectively. By default, the **Sync Corner Fillets** check box is selected. As a result, the radius of the corners of the outer shape are controlled through the **Corner Radius 1** spinner. If you clear this check box, it will control the radius of the corners of inner and outer shapes through the **Corner Radius 1** and **Corner Radius 2** spinners, as shown in Figure 5-50. The **Corner Radius 1** spinner is used to set the external radius between the vertical and horizontal lines of the angle. The **Corner Radius 2** spinner is used to set the internal radius between the vertical and horizontal lines of the angle. The **Edge Radii** spinner is used to define the radius of the edges of the legs of the L-shaped spline, as shown in Figure 5-51.

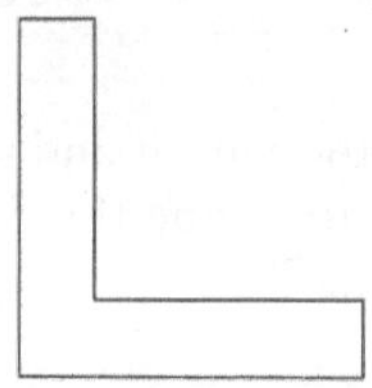

Figure 5-49 An angle spline

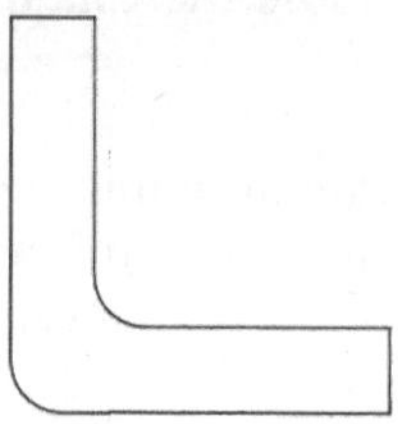

Figure 5-50 The angle spline with corner radius

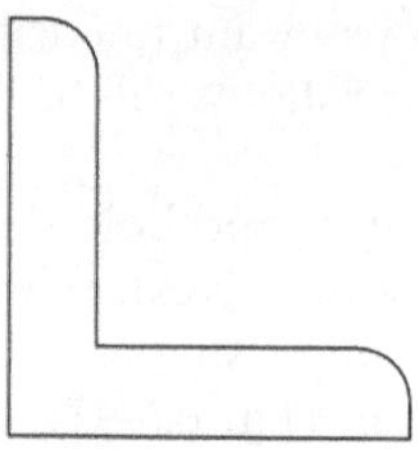

Figure 5-51 An angle spline with edge radii

Creating a Tee Spline

Menu bar:	Create > Extended Shapes > Tee
Command Panel:	Create > Shapes > Extended Splines > Object Type rollout > Tee

The tee spline is a T-shaped closed spline. To create a tee spline, activate the viewport in which you want to create it and then choose the **Tee** tool from the **Object Type** rollout; various rollouts will be displayed. Next, press and hold the left mouse button and drag the cursor to set the length and width of the tee spline. Now, move the cursor to define the thickness and click on the viewport; a T-shaped tee spline will be created in the viewport, as shown in Figure 5-52. The **Parameters** rollout used to modify the tee spline is discussed next.

Parameters Rollout

The options in this rollout are used to modify the tee spline. The **Length**, **Width**, and **Thickness** spinners are used to specify the length, width, and thickness of the angle spline, respectively. The **Corner Radius** spinner is used to round the corners between the horizontal and vertical shapes, as shown in Figure 5-53.

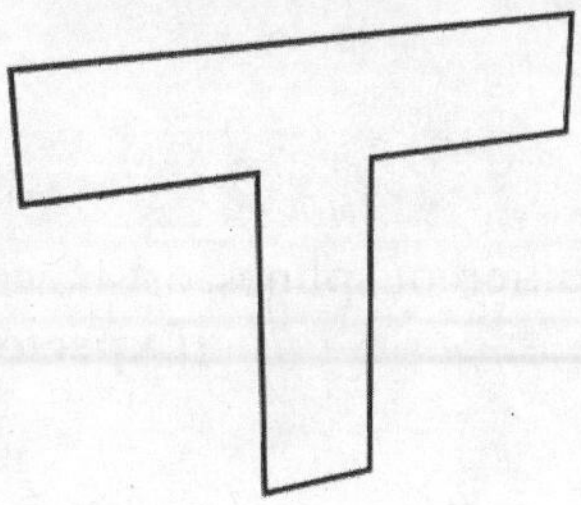

Figure 5-52 A T-shaped tee spline

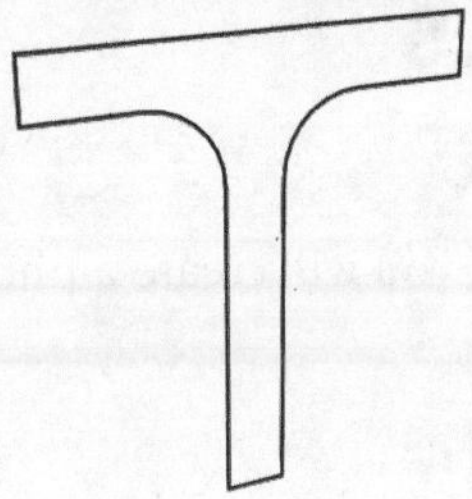

Figure 5-53 A tee spline with corner radius

Creating a Wide Flange Spline

Menu bar:	Create > Extended Shapes > Wide Flange
Command Panel:	Create > Shapes > Extended Splines > Object Type rollout > Wide Flange

The wide flange spline is an I-shaped closed spline. To create a wide flange spline, activate the viewport in which you want to create it and then choose the **Wide Flange** tool from the **Object Type** rollout; various rollouts will be displayed. Next, press and hold the left mouse button and drag the cursor to set the length and width of the wide flange spline. Next, move the mouse to define the thickness and click on the viewport; an I-shaped wide flange spline will be created in the viewport, as shown in Figure 5-54.

The **Parameters** rollout used to modify the wide flange spline is discussed next.

Parameters Rollout

The options in this rollout are used to modify a wide flange spline. The **Length**, **Width**, and **Thickness** spinners are used to specify the length, width and thickness of the wide flange spline. The **Corner Radius** spinner is used to round the corners between the horizontal and vertical shapes of the wide flange spline, as shown in Figure 5-55.

Figure 5-54 An I-shaped wide flange spline

Figure 5-55 The wide flange spline with corner radius

TUTORIALS

Tutorial 1

In this tutorial, you will create a photo frame using different splines, as shown in Figure 5-56.
(Expected time: 45 min)

Figure 5-56 The model of a photo frame

The following steps are required to complete this tutorial:

a. Create the project folder.
b. Create the base.
c. Create the inner rectangular frame.
d. Create the outer rectangular frame.
e. Create joints.
f. Create spiral design.
g. Create text.
h. Save and render the scene.

Creating the Project Folder

Create a new project folder with the name *c05_tut1* at *\Documents\3dsmax2017* and then save the file with the name **c05tut1**, as discussed in Tutorial 1 of Chapter 2.

Creating the Base

In this section, you will create the base of the photoframe using the **Plane** tool.

1. Make sure the Front viewport is activated. Choose **Create > Geometry** in the **Command Panel**. In this panel, Standard Primitives is displayed in the drop-down list located below it. Next, choose the **Plane** tool from the **Object Type** rollout.

2. In the **Keyboard Entry** rollout, set the parameters as follows:

   Length: **111.7** Width: **81.5**

   Choose the **Create** button; a plane is created in the viewports, as shown in Figure 5-57.

3. In the **Name and Color** rollout, enter the name base. Also change its color to white.

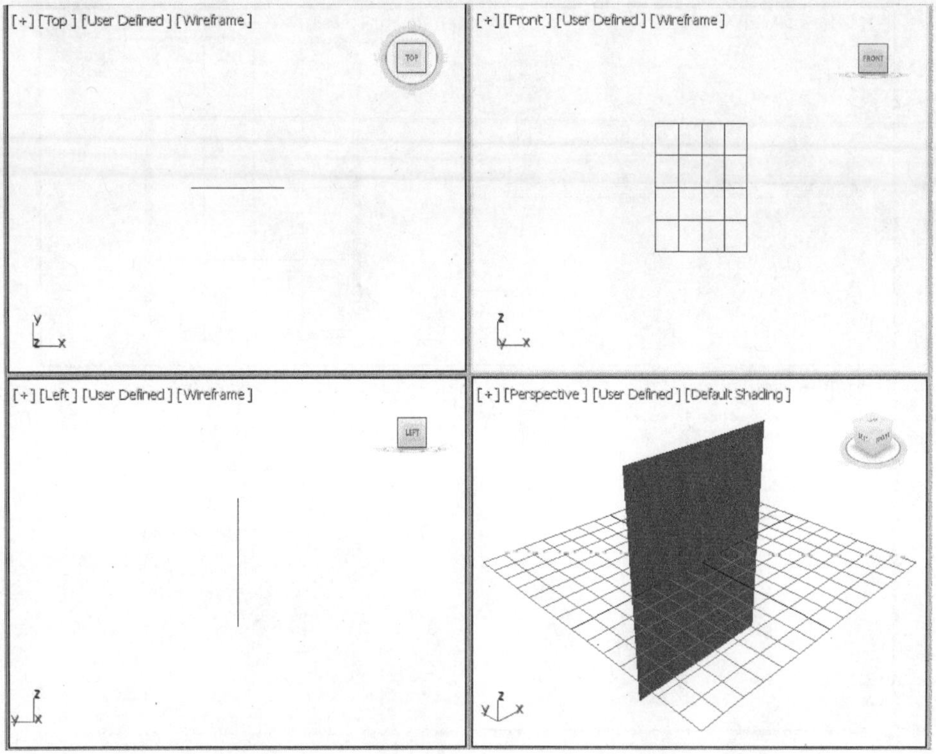

Figure 5-57 The plane created in viewports

Creating the Inner Rectangular Frame

In this section, you will create inner rectangular frame using the **Rectangle** tool.

1. Make sure the Front viewport is active. Choose **Create > Shapes** in the **Command Panel**; the **Splines** option is displayed in the drop-down list. Next, choose the **Rectangle** tool from the **Object Type** rollout.

2 Expand the **Keyboard Entry** rollout and specify the parameters as follows:

   Length: **115.2**   Width: **85.2**   Corner Radius: **10**

3. Now, choose the **Create** button; a rectangle is displayed in the viewports.

4. In the **Rendering** rollout, select the **Enable In Renderer** and **Enable In Viewport** check boxes. Make sure that the **Radial** radio button is selected. Next, set the value **3.5** in the **Thickness** spinner. Figure 5-58 shows the rectangle displayed in the viewports.

5. In the **Name and Color** rollout, enter the name **inner frame** and press the ENTER key. and use the color swatch to change its color by using the following values:

   Red: **248**   Green: **58**   Blue: **0**

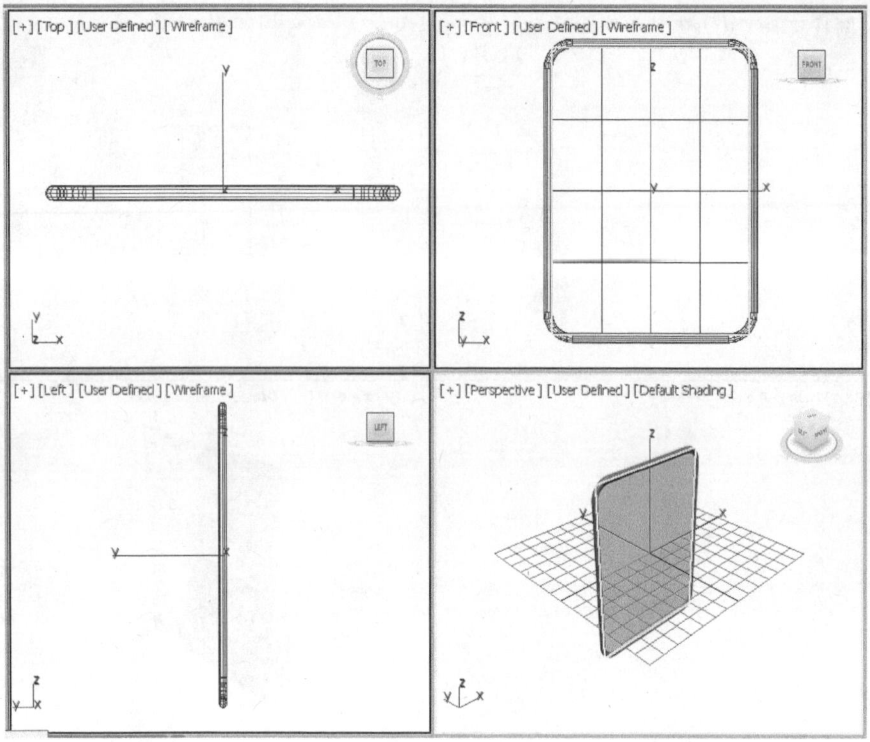

Figure 5-58 The rectangle displayed in the viewports

Creating the Outer Rectangular Frame

In this section, you will create outer rectangular frame using the **Rectangle** tool.

1. Make sure the **Rectangle** tool is chosen from **Create > Shapes > Splines > Object Type** rollout in the **Command Panel**.

2. Make sure the Front viewport is activated. Next, expand the **Keyboard Entry** rollout and set the parameters as follows:

   Length: **143** Width: **107** Corner Radius: **10**

3. Choose the **Create** button; the rectangle is displayed in the viewports, as shown in Figure 5-59.

4. In the **Name and Color** rollout, enter the name **outer frame**. Also, assign the same color to it that you assigned to *inner frame*. Choose the **Zoom Extents All** tool from the viewport navigation controls to view all objects in all the viewports properly.

Creating Joints

In this section, you will create joints between *inner frame* and *outer frame* using the Line tool.

1. Make sure the Front viewport is active. Next, choose the **Line** tool from **Create > Shapes > Splines > Object Type** rollout from the **Command Panel**.

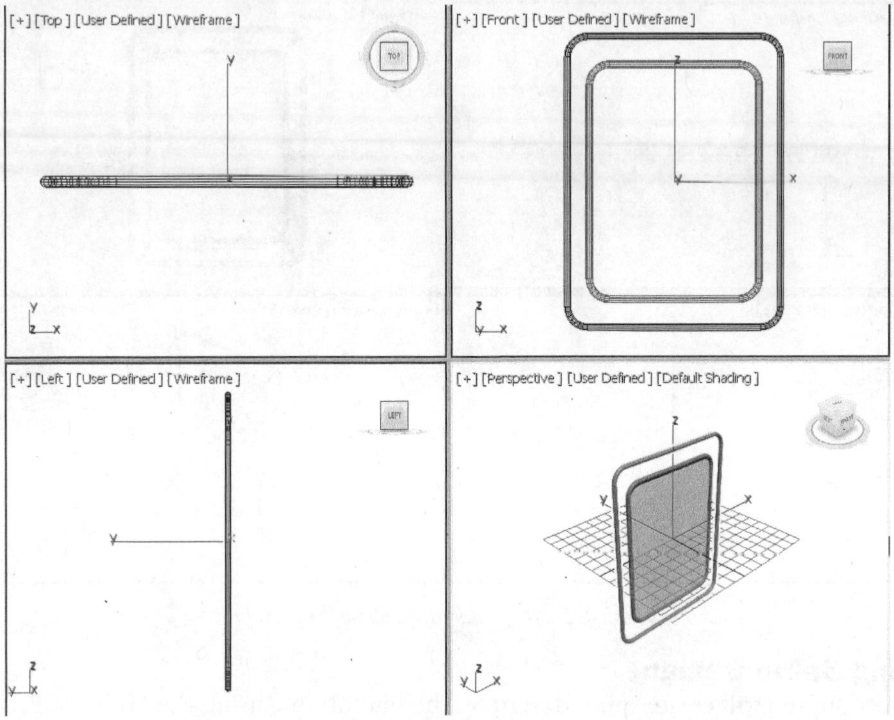

Figure 5-59 The rectangle displayed in the viewports

2. Click in the viewport at the upper left corner of inner frame and create a line upto the upper left corner of outer frame, as shown in Figure 5-60.

3. In the **Rendering** rollout, set **3** in the **Thickness** spinner.

4. In the **Name and Color** rollout, enter the name **joint1** and assign the same color to it that you assigned to *inner frame*. Figure 5-61 shows *joint1* in the Front viewport.

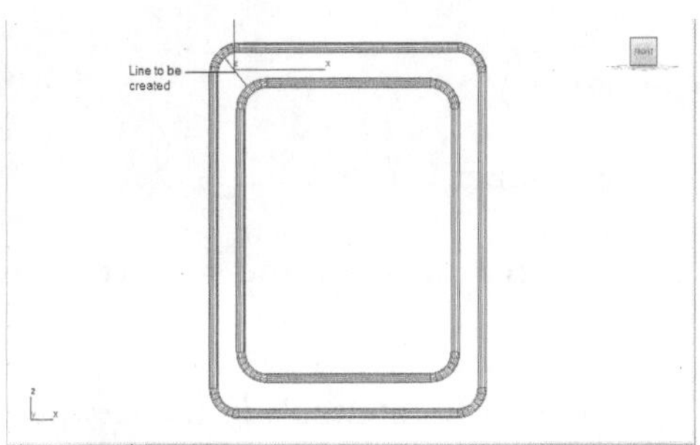

***Figure 5-60** The line to be created in the Front Viewport*

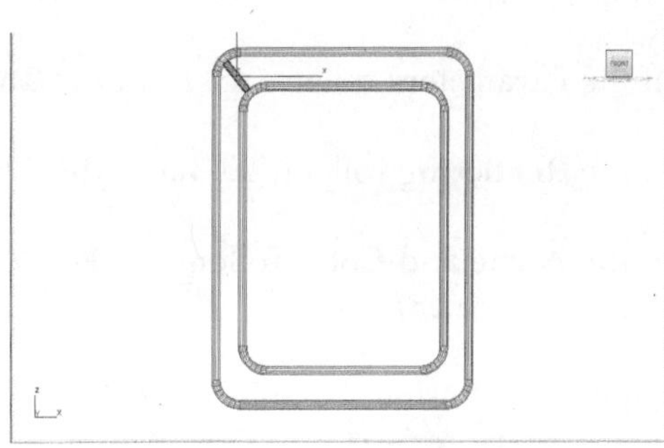

***Figure 5-61** The joint1 geometry in the Front Viewport*

5. Create three copies of *joint1*. Now, align the copied joints in the viewports using the **Select and Rotate** and **Select and Move** tools, as shown in Figure 5-62.

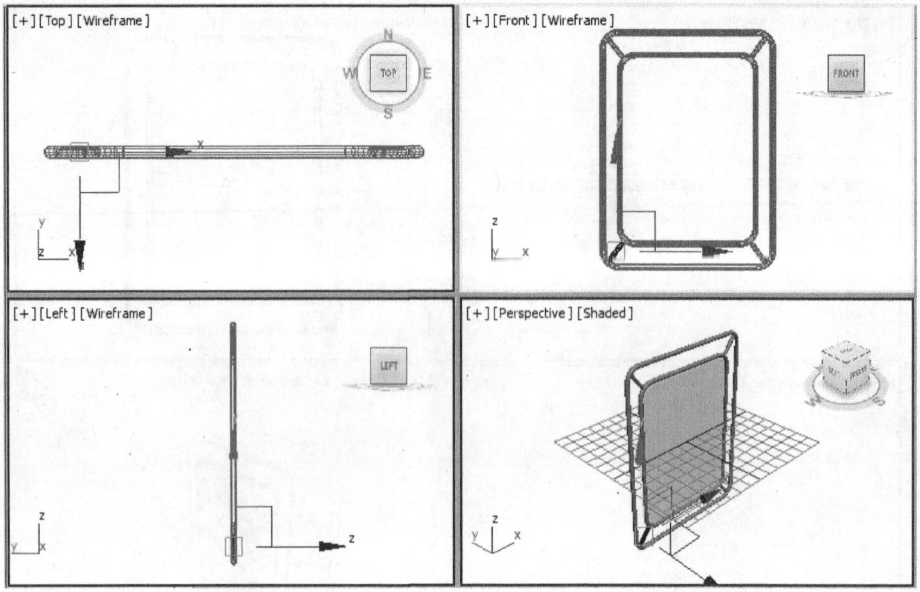

Figure 5-62 All joints aligned in the viewports

Creating Spiral Design

In this section, you will create spiral design on the photoframe using the **Helix** tool.

1. Activate the Left viewport. Choose the **Helix** tool from **Create > Shapes > Splines > Object Type** rollout in the **Command Panel.**

2. In the **Keyboard Entry** rollout, set the following parameters:

   Radius 1: **2.0** Radius 2: **2.0** Height: **100**

   Choose the **Create** button; a helix is created.

3. In the **Parameters** rollout, set **10** in the **Turns** spinner.

4. In the **Rendering** rollout, set **3.5** in the **Thickness** spinner.

5. In the **Name and Color** rollout, enter the name **design1**. Assign it the same color as was assigned to *inner frame*.

6. Align *design1* using the **Select and Move** and **Select and Rotate** tools in the viewports, as shown in Figure 5-63.

7. Create a copy of *design1* and align it, as shown in Figure 5-64.

8. Activate the Top viewport. Choose the **Helix** tool from **Create > Shapes > Splines > Object Type** rollout in the **Command Panel.**

9. In the **Keyboard Entry** rollout, make sure the value in the **Radius 1** and **Radius 2** spinners is set to **2**. Set **132** in the **Height** spinner.

Choose the **Create** button; a helix is created.

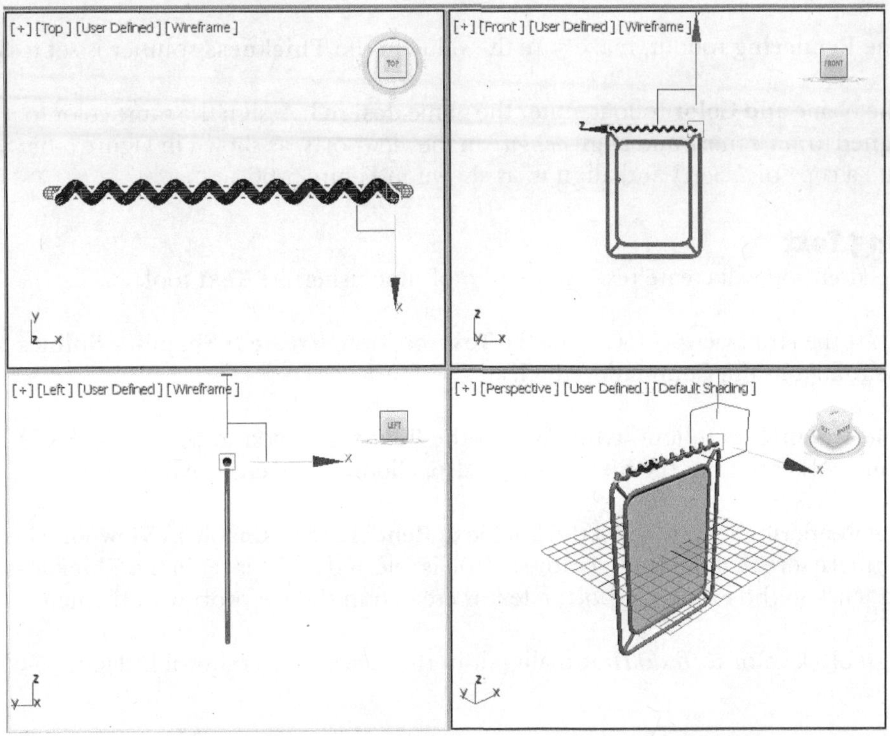

***Figure 5-63** The design1 geometry aligned in the viewports*

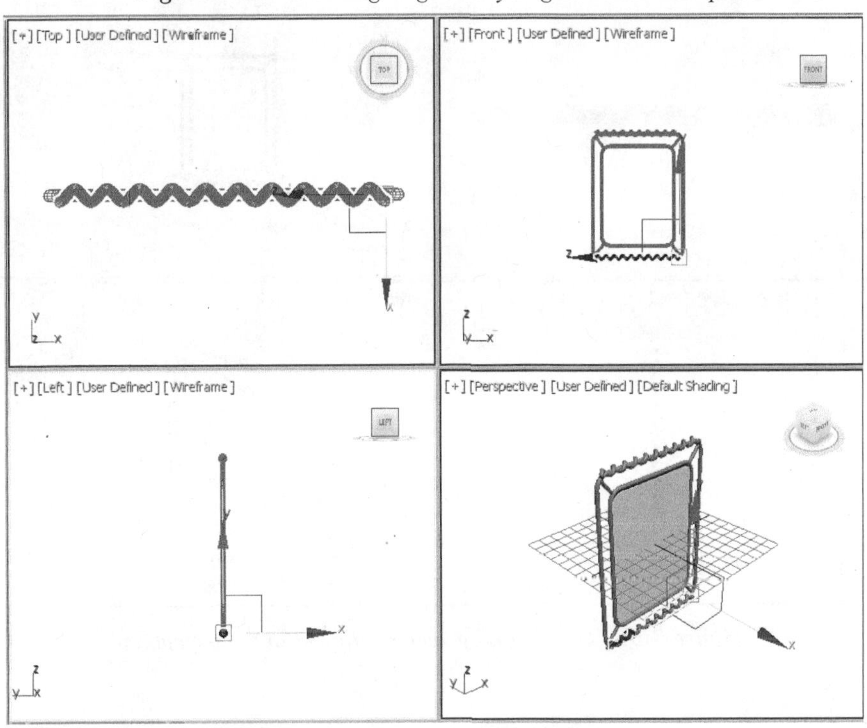

***Figure 5-64** The copy of design1 aligned in the viewports*

10. In the **Parameters** rollout, set **15** in the **Turns** spinner.

11. In the **Rendering** rollout, make sure the value in the **Thickness** spinner is set to **3.5**.

12. In the **Name and Color** rollout, enter the name **design3**. Assign the same color to it that you assigned to *inner frame* and align *design3* in the viewports, as shown in Figure 5-65. Similarly, create a copy of *design3* and align it, as shown in Figure 5-66.

Creating Text

In this section, you will create text on the photoframe using the **Text** tool.

1. Activate the Front viewport. Choose the **Text** tool from **Create > Shapes > Splines > Object Type** rollout in the **Command Panel**.

2. In the **Parameters** rollout, type **Your** in the **Text** text box and press ENTER. Next, type **Picture**. Also set **25** in the **Size** spinner. Also, choose the **Center Align** button.

3. In the **Rendering** rollout, select the **Enable in Renderer** and **Enable in Viewport** check boxes. Also, make sure that the **Radial** radio button is selected and 1 is set in the **Thickness** spinner. Next, click in the **Front** viewport; a text is created in the viewport with the name *Text001*.

4. Assign black color to *Text001* and align it in the viewports, as shown in Figure 5-67.

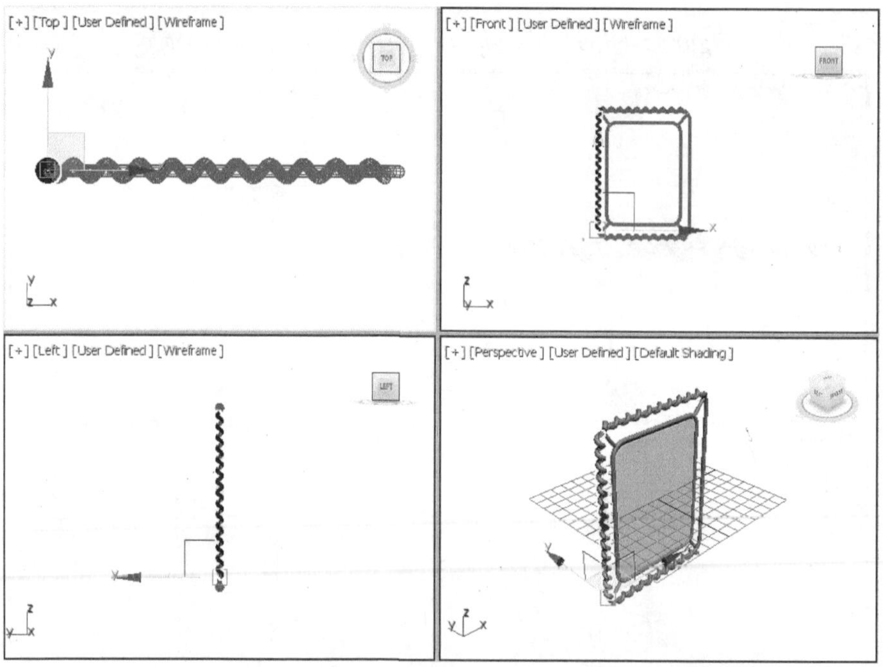

***Figure 5-65** The design3 geometry aligned in the viewports*

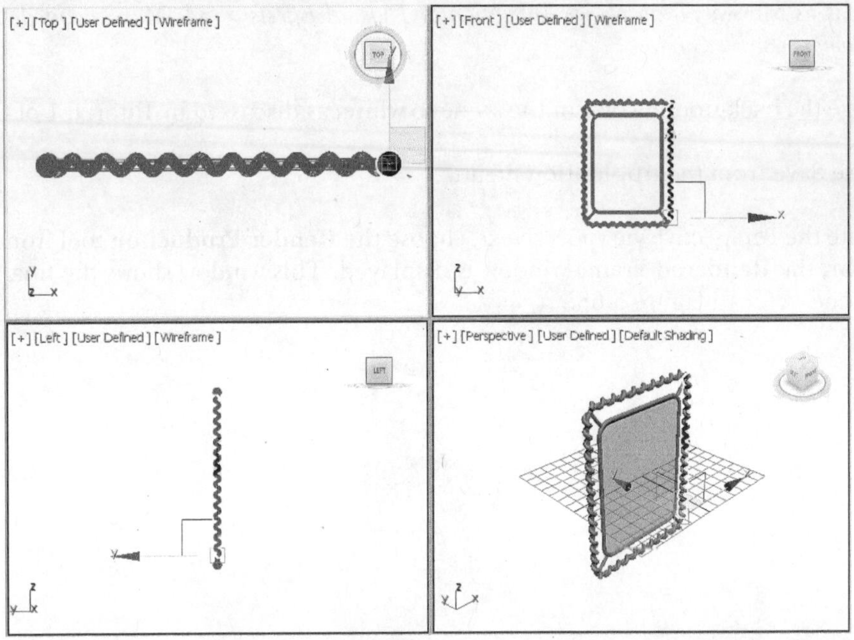

Figure 5-66 The copy of design3 geometry aligned in the viewports

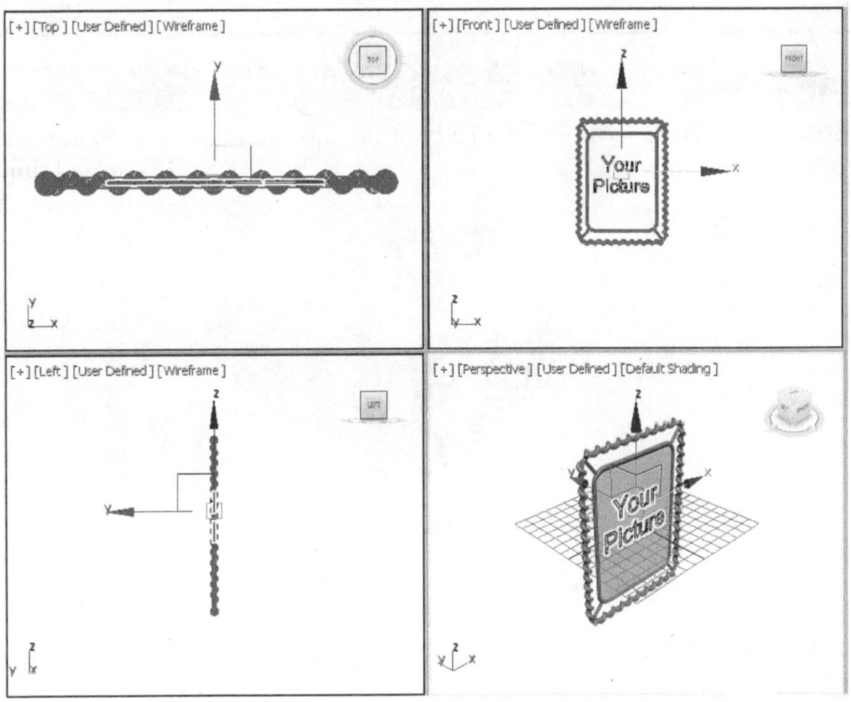

Figure 5-67 Text001 aligned in the viewports

Saving and Rendering the Scene

In this section, you will save and render the scene. You can also view the final rendered image of this scene by downloading the *c05_3dsmax_2017_rndr.zip* file from *www.cadcim.com*. The path of the file is as follows: *Textbooks > Animation and Visual Effects > 3ds Max > Autodesk 3ds Max 2017: A Comprehensive Guide*

1. Change the background color of the scene to white, as discussed in Tutorial 1 of Chapter 2.

2. Choose **Save** from the Application menu.

3. Activate the Perspective viewport. Next, choose the **Render Production** tool from the Main Toolbar; the **Rendered Frame** window is displayed. This window shows the final output of the scene, refer to Figure 5-68.

Figure 5-68 *The final output after rendering*

Tutorial 2

In this tutorial, you will create the model of a book, as shown in Figure 5-69, using splines and extended splines. **(Expected time: 15 min)**

Figure 5-69 *The model of a book*

The following steps are required to complete this tutorial:

a. Create the project folder.
b. Create a book.
c. Create the spiral binding of the book.
d. Create the text on the book.
e. Save and render the scene.

Creating the Project Folder

Create a new project folder with the name *c05_tut2* at*\Documents\3dsmax2017* and then save the file with the name **c05tut2**, as discussed in Tutorial 1 of Chapter 2.

Creating a Book

In this section, you will create a book using the **Hose** tool from **Extended Primitives**.

1. Activate the Top viewport. Choose **Create > Geometry** in the **Command Panel** and then select **Extended Primitives** from the drop-down list displayed below the **Geometry** button. Now, choose the **Hose** tool from the **Object Type** rollout.

2. In the Top viewport, press and hold the left mouse button and drag the cursor to define the radius of the hose. Next, release the left mouse button and move the cursor up to define the height of the hose. Now, click on the viewport to get the desired height; a hose is created.

3. Name the hose as *book* in the **Name and Color** rollout and change its color by entering the values as follows:

   Red: **153** Green: **228** Blue: **214**

4. Choose the **Modify** tab in the **Command Panel**. In the **Free Hose Parameters** area of the **Hose Parameters** rollout, set the value **29.798** in the **Height** spinner. Next, in the **Common Hose Parameters** area of the **Hose Parameters** rollout, make sure the **Flex Section Enable** check box is selected. Use default values for other options.

5. In the **Hose Shape** area of the **Hose Parameters** rollout, select the **Rectangular Hose** radio button and then set the values **144.927** and **210.827** in the **Width** and **Depth** spinners, respectively. Use the default values for other options.

6. Choose the **Zoom Extents All** tool to view *book* in viewports, as shown in Figure 5-70.

Creating the Spiral Binding of the Book

In this section, you will create the helix spline for creating the spiral binding of the book.

1. Activate the Front viewport and choose **Create > Shapes** in the **Command Panel**. Make sure that **Splines** is selected in the drop-down list displayed below the **Shapes** button. Now, choose the **Helix** tool from the **Object Type** rollout.

2. Expand the **Keyboard Entry** rollout and enter the values as follows:

   Radius 1: **17.0** Radius 2: **17.0** Height: **205.0**

3. Choose the **Create** button; a helix shape is created in the viewports.

4. Name the helix as *spiral binding* and change its color by entering the values as follows:

   Red: **6** Green: **134** Blue: **6**

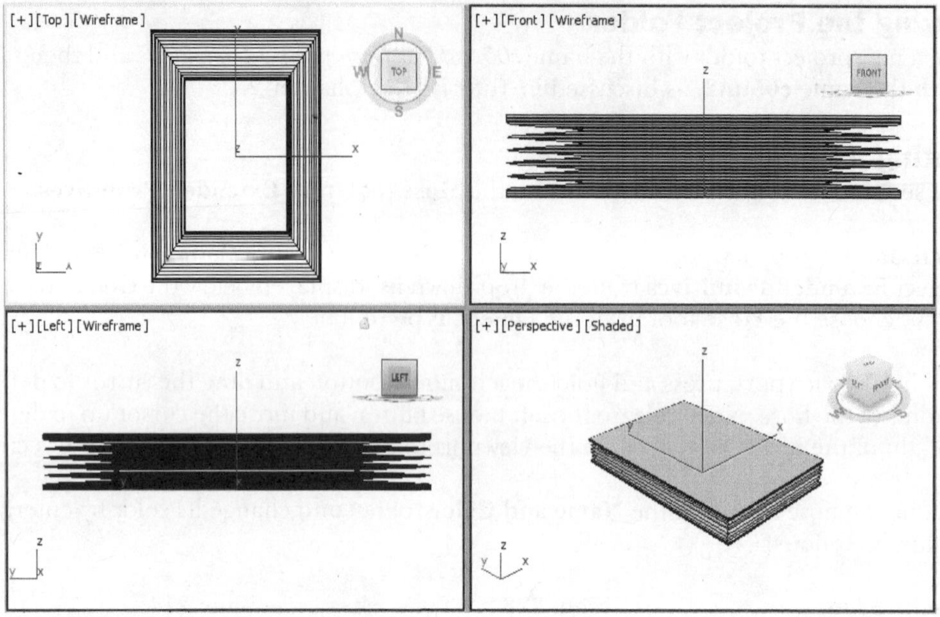

Figure 5-70 The book geometry after invoking the ***Zoom Extents All*** *tool*

5. Choose the **Modify** tab in the **Command Panel** and then in the **Rendering** rollout, select the **Enable In Renderer** and **Enable In Viewport** check boxes. Make sure the **Radial** radio button is selected and then set the value **1.5** in the **Thickness** spinner. Next, in the **Parameters** rollout, set the value **17.0** in the **Turns** spinner. Choose the **Select and Move** tool and align *spiral binding* with *book* in the viewports, as shown in Figure 5-71.

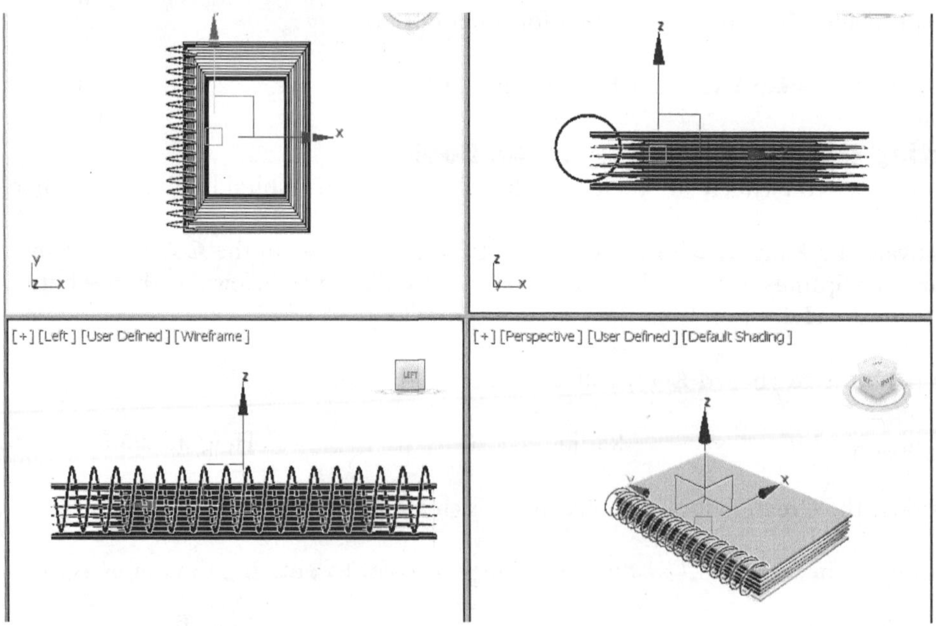

Figure 5-71 Alignment of spiral binding with book in the viewports

Creating the Text on the Book

In this section, you will use the **Text** tool to create the text on the book.

1. Choose **Create > Shapes** from the **Command Panel**; the **Splines** option is selected in the drop-down list. Now, choose the **Text** tool from the **Object Type** rollout. Also, select the **AutoGrid** check box in the **Object Type** rollout.

2. In the **Parameters** rollout of the **Text** tool, type **CADCIM** in the **Text** text box and press ENTER. Next, type **3ds Max** and click in the Perspective viewport; the text is displayed in the viewports.

3. Name the text as *text01* and change its color by entering the values as follows:

   Red: **6** Green: **134** Blue: **6**

4. Choose the **Modify** tab in the **Command Panel** and then select the **Monotype Corsiva** font type from the drop-down list located at the top of the **Parameters** rollout. Next, choose the center align button and enter the values as follows:

   Size: **23** Kerning: **1.0** Leading: **1.0**

5. Choose the **Select and Move** tool and align *text01* in viewports, refer to Figure 5-72.

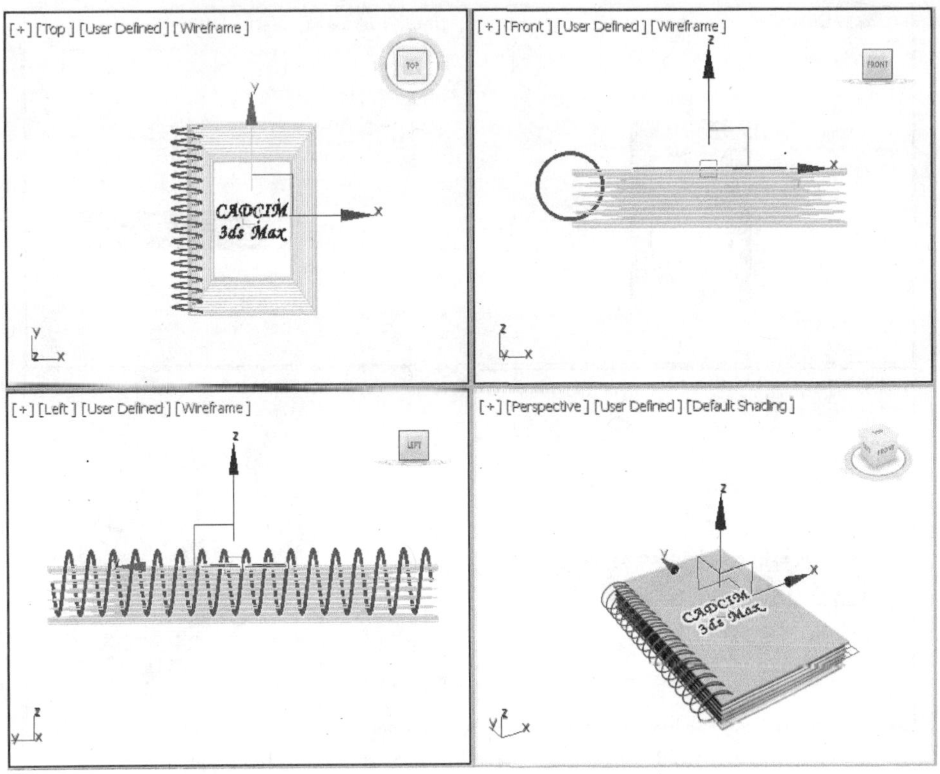

Figure 5-72 Alignment of text01 on book in viewports

Next, you need to create a rectangular design over the text.

6. Make sure that the **Splines** option is selected in the drop-down list of the **Command Panel**. Choose the **Rectangle** tool from the **Object Type** rollout. Make sure the **AutoGrid** check box is still selected.

7. Activate the Perspective viewport. Click at the upper left corner of *book*, hold the left mouse button, and then drag the cursor to the lower right corner of *book*. Next, release the left mouse button to set the length and width; a rectangular spline is created in the viewports.

8. Name the rectangle as *rectangular design* and change its color by entering the values as follows:

   Red: **6** Green: **134** Blue: **6**

9. Choose the **Modify** tab in the **Command Panel**. In the **Rendering** rollout, set the value **1.0** in the **Thickness** spinner. Next, set the parameters in the **Parameters** rollout as follows:

   Length: **126.581** Width: **87** Corner Radius: **10.0**

10. Choose the **Select and Move** tool and align *rectangular design* in the viewports, as shown in Figure 5-73.

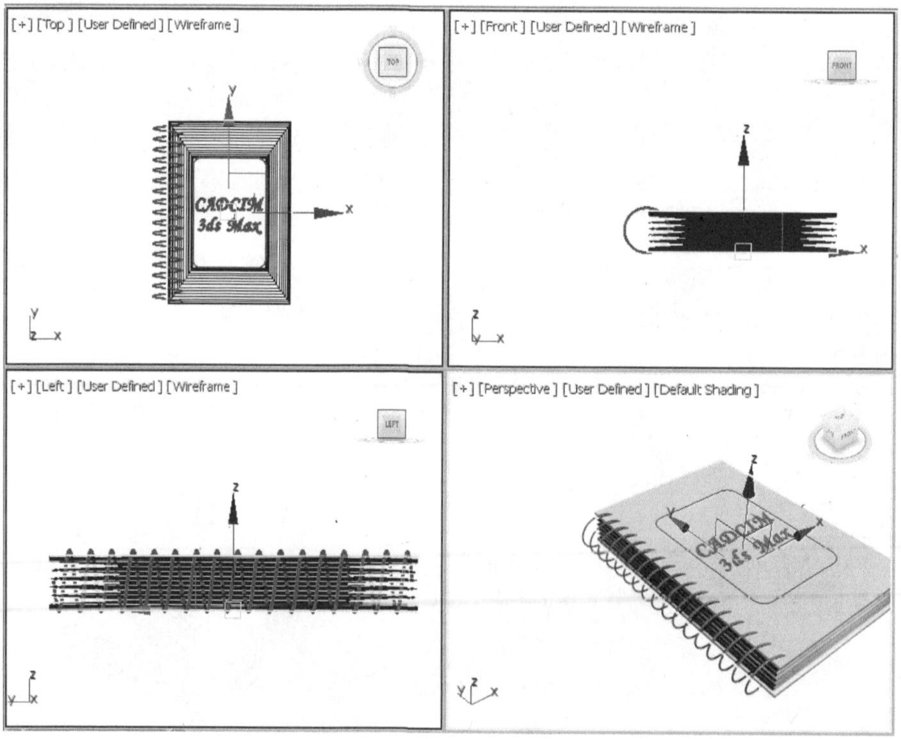

Figure 5-73 *Alignment of rectangular design in the viewports*

Saving and Rendering the Scene

In this section, you will save the scene and then render it. You can also view the final rendered image of this scene by downloading the *05_3dsmax_2017_rndr.zip* file from *www.cadcim.com*. The path of the file is as follows: *Textbooks > Animation and Visual Effects > 3ds Max > Autodesk 3ds Max 2017: A Comprehensive Guide*

1. Change the background color of the scene to white, as discussed in Tutorial 1 of Chapter 2.

2. Choose **Save** from the **Application** menu.

3. Activate the Perspective viewport. Next, choose the **Render Production** tool from the **Main Toolbar**; the **Rendered Frame** window is displayed, showing the final output of *book*, refer to Figure 5-74. Next, close this window.

Figure 5-74 *The final output after rendering*

Self-Evaluation Test

Answer the following questions and then compare them to those given at the end of this chapter:

1. Which of the following check boxes is selected by default in the **Object Type** rollout while creating shapes?

   (a) **AutoGrid** (b) **Start New Shape**
   (c) **Use Viewport Settings** (d) **Real-World Map Size**

2. Which of the following rollouts is used to modify the shape of a donut spline?

   (a) **Object Type** (b) **Interpolation**
   (c) **Rendering** (d) **Parameters**

3. Which of the following keys is used to create a square spline using the **Rectangle** tool?

   (a) CTRL (b) F10
   (c) SHIFT (d) None of these

4. The **AutoGrid** check box in the **Object Type** rollout helps you create an object on the __________ of another object by generating a __________ on it.

5. The __________ spinner in the **Parameters** rollout of the **Text** tool is used to set the distance between the letters of the text.

6. The **Pie Slice** check box is used to create a line from the start point to the center of the arc. (T/F)

7. On selecting the **Start New Shape** check box in the **Object Type** rollout of splines, you can add a new shape to the current shape in the viewport. (T/F)

8. In Autodesk 3ds Max, the options in the **Rendering** and **Interpolation** rollouts are same for all splines. (T/F)

Review Questions

Answer the following questions:

1. Which of the following options is available in the drop-down list when you choose the **Shapes** button in the **Create** tab of the **Command Panel**?

   (a) **Splines** (b) **Extended Splines**
   (c) **NURBS Curves** (d) All of these

2. Which of the following tools is not a part of the **Extended Splines**?

   (a) **Tee** (b) **Channel**
   (c) **Angle** (d) **NGon**

3. Which of the following methods is used to create an arc dynamically?

   (a) **End-End-Middle** (b) **Center-End-End**
   (c) both (a) and (b) (d) None of these

4. You need to select the __________ and the __________ check boxes in the __________ rollout to make the splines visible as 3D mesh in the viewport and at rendering.

5. In the **Section Parameters** rollout of the **Section** tool, the __________ button is used to create a new section spline where the cross-section cuts the object.

6. The **Renderer** radio button in the **Rendering** rollout is used to modify the parameters of a line at rendering. (T/F)

7. The **Pie Slice** check box in the **Parameters** rollout of the **Arc** tool is used to create a line from each endpoint to the center of an arc. (T/F)

EXERCISES

The rendered output of the models used in the exercises can be accessed by downloading the *c05_3dsmax_2017_exr.zip* file from *www.cadcim.com*. The path of the file is as follows: *Textbooks* > *Animation and Visual Effects* > *3ds Max* > *Autodesk 3ds Max 2017: A Comprehensive Guide*

Exercise 1

Create the model of a grid shown in Figure 5-75 using your own dimensions.

(Expected time: 15 min)

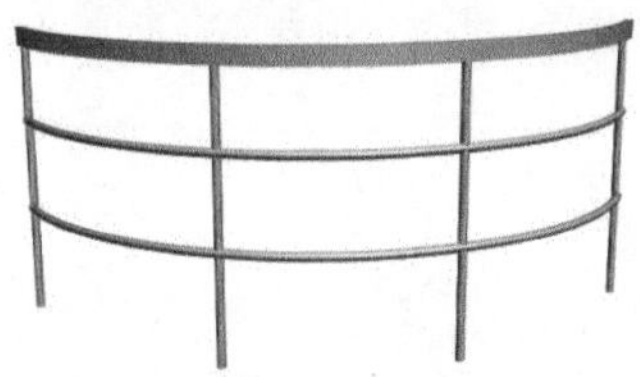

Figure 5-75 *The model of a grid*

Exercise 2

Create the model of a Christmas tree using AEC extended objects and decorate it using various spline objects, as shown in Figure 5-76. **(Expected time: 20 min)**

Figure 5-76 *The Christmas tree model*

Exercise 3

Create the model of an entrance shown in Figure 5-77 using your own dimensions.

(Expected time: 20 min)

Figure 5-77 The model of an entrance

Answers to Self-Evaluation Test

1. b, **2.** d, **3.** a, **4.** surface, temporary grid, **5. Leading**, **6.** F, **7.** F, **8.** T

6

Modifying Splines

Learning Objectives

After completing this chapter, you will be able to:

- *Adjust the pivot point of an object*
- *Use the Lathe modifier to modify objects*
- *Modify shapes*
- *Use editable spline objects*

INTRODUCTION

In this chapter, you will learn to modify shapes such as splines and extended splines at advanced level. Also, you will learn about the pivot point and the **Lathe** modifier.

PIVOT POINT

The pivot point of an object represents the local center and its local coordinate system. When you transform an object, the pivot point acts like a center. To adjust the pivot point of an object, select the object in the viewport and then choose the **Hierarchy** tab in the **Command Panel**. By default, the **Pivot** tab is chosen in the **Hierarchy** tab, as shown in Figure 6-1. You can set the position of the pivot point of an object using the rollouts displayed in the **Pivot** tab. Some of the rollouts in the **Pivot** tab are discussed next.

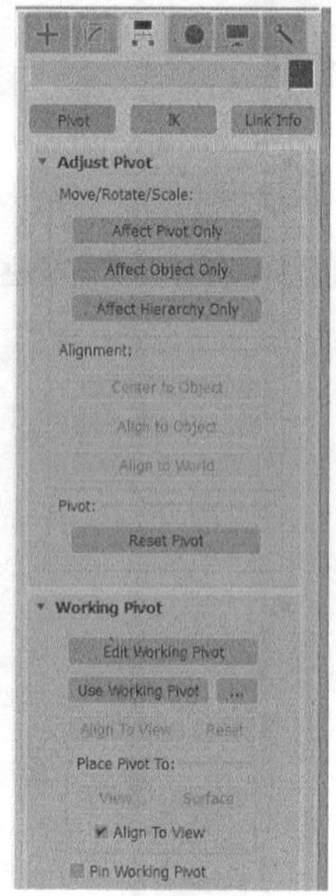

***Figure 6-1** The **Pivot** tab chosen in the **Hierarchy** tab*

Adjust Pivot Rollout

The options in this rollout are used to adjust the position and orientation of the pivot point of an object. The areas in this rollout are discussed next.

Move/Rotate/Scale Area

There are three buttons in this area, **Affect Pivot Only**, **Affect Object Only**, and **Affect Hierarchy Only**. These buttons are used to specify the part of an object that will be affected while performing the functions such as rotation, movement, and so on.

The **Affect Pivot Only** button is used to affect the pivot point of the selected object. To affect the pivot point, choose the **Affect Pivot Only** button; the pivot point of the selected object will be displayed in the viewport, refer to Figure 6-2. Now, you can adjust the position of the pivot point by moving or rotating it. Also, you can use the **Align** tool from the **Main Toolbar** to align the pivot point.

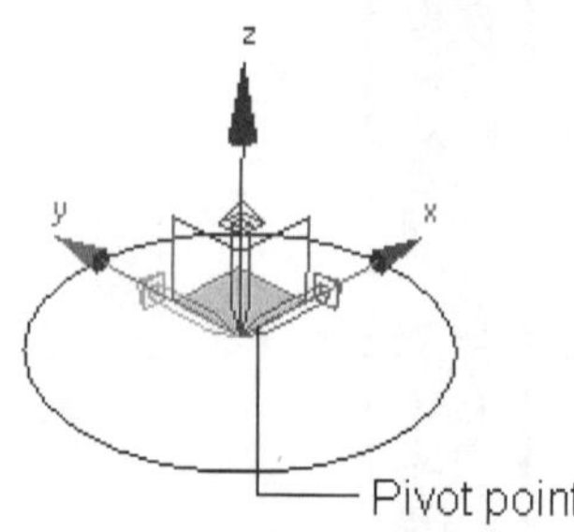

***Figure 6-2** The pivot point of a circle*

> **Note**
> *Scaling has no effect on the pivot of an object.*

The **Affect Object Only** button is used to affect only the selected object. It means that transforms are applied only to the selected object and do not affect the pivot point of the object. On choosing the **Affect Object Only** button, the pivot point of the object will be displayed in the viewport. You can adjust the position of the object according to the pivot point by moving, rotating, and aligning the object.

The **Affect Hierarchy Only** button is used to affect the hierarchy of the objects by rotating or scaling the position of the pivot point. But, the pivot point will not be affected. Select the object in the viewport, choose the **Affect Hierarchy Only** button, and then use the **Select and Scale** or the **Select and Rotate** tool to view the effects on the hierarchy of the objects. You will learn about creating the hierarchy in the later chapters.

Note

When you choose the buttons in the ***Move/Rotate/Scale*** *area of the* ***Adjust Pivot*** *rollout, it is recommended to exit the command after adjusting the position of the pivot point or the object. To exit the command, you need to choose the activated button again.*

Alignment Area

The options in this area depend on the selection of buttons in the **Move/Rotate/Scale** area.

If you choose the **Affect Pivot Only** button in the **Move/Rotate/Scale** area, the **Center to Object**, **Align to Object**, and **Align to World** buttons will be activated in the **Alignment** area. Choose the **Center to Object** button to align the pivot point to the center of the object. Choose the **Align to Object** button to transform the pivot to align with the object's transformation matrix axes. Choose the **Align to World** button to transform the pivot to align it with the world coordinate axes.

If you choose the **Affect Object Only** button in the **Move/Rotate/Scale** area, the **Center to Pivot**, **Align to Pivot**, and **Align to World** buttons will be activated in the **Alignment** area. Choose the **Center to Pivot** button to align the center of the object to its pivot point. Choose the **Align to Pivot** button to transform the object to align its transformation matrix axes with the pivot point. Choose the **Align to World** button to transform the object to align its transformation matrix axes with the world coordinate axes.

If you choose the **Affect Hierarchy Only** button in the **Move/Rotate/Scale** area, then the options in the **Alignment** area will be deactivated.

Pivot Area

The **Reset Pivot** button in this area is used to reset the position of the pivot point of the object.

Working Pivot Rollout

You can use the working pivot to transform the objects without affecting their main pivot point at the object or the sub-object level. For example, you can rotate an object in a scene about an arbitrary point without affecting its own pivot point.

Note

A scene has only one working pivot along with the gizmo, which is independent of other objects in the scene, as shown in Figure 6-3.

You can modify the position of the working pivot. To do so, choose the **Edit Working Pivot** button; the working pivot will be displayed at the center of the scene, refer to Figure 6-3. Also, the *EDIT WP* text will be displayed below each viewport label. You can modify the position of the working pivot by moving it.

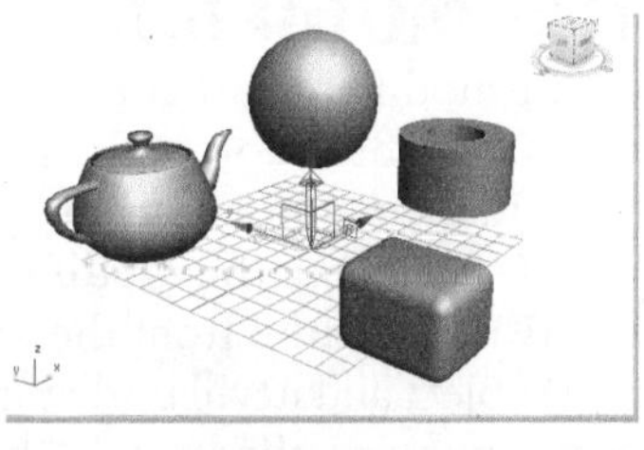

Figure 6-3 *The working pivot along with the gizmo in the scene*

If you choose the **Use Working Pivot** button and select any of the objects from the scene, then a transform gizmo will be displayed at the location of the working pivot, refer to Figures 6-4 and 6-5. Also, the USE WP text will be displayed below each viewport label. Now, the objects or the sub-objects in the scene will be transformed according to the working pivot.

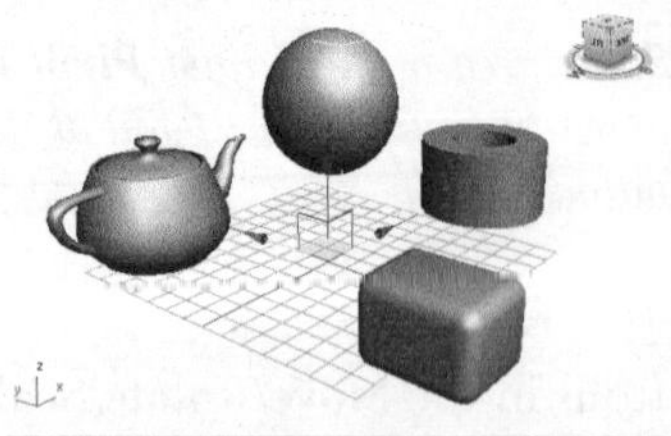

Figure 6-4 The move transform gizmo displayed

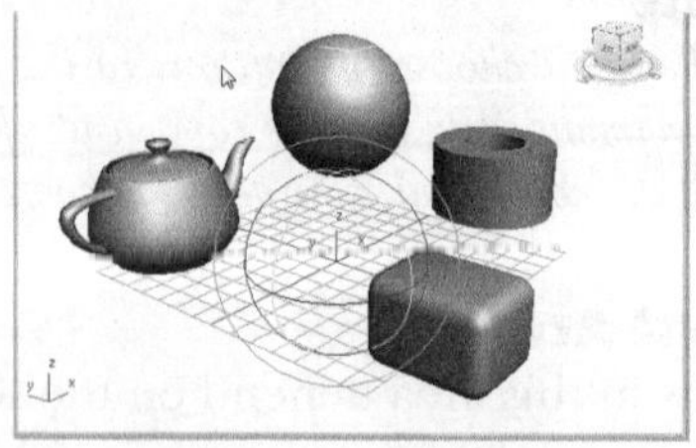

Figure 6-5 The rotate transform gizmo displayed

The **Align To View** button is activated when the **Edit Working Pivot** and **Use Working Pivot** buttons are chosen. The **Align To View** button is used to reorient the working pivot of the XY plane parallel to the active view plane and to orient the X and Y axes parallel to the edges of the viewport.

The **Reset** button in the **Working Pivot** rollout is used to move the working pivot to a location where the pivot of the selected object is placed. If there are more than one objects selected in the viewport, then the working pivot will move to the pivot position of the last selected object.

Place Pivot To Area

The options in this area are used to position the working pivot using the mouse. This enables to set the working pivot quickly on the viewport. To position the working pivot, choose the **View** button, move the cursor in the viewport, and click on any location; the working pivot will be placed accordingly. Next, right-click to exit the command. Alternatively, you can choose the **Surface** button and move the cursor in the viewport. Now, click on the surface of any of the objects in the scene to place the working pivot on the surface. You can also click on the active grid to place the working pivot on it.

The **View** button is used to position the working pivot in the screen space without changing its depth in the screen. The **Surface** button is used to position the working pivot on a surface. If there is no surface present in the scene, then the construction plane will be created in the viewport at the point you click on. By default, the **Align To View** check box is selected. As a result, the working pivot is aligned automatically to the surface or viewport.

LATHE MODIFIER

The **Lathe** modifier is a shape modifier and is used to create 3D objects by rotating shapes about their axes. The direction of the axis of revolution depends on the pivot point of the shape. To apply the **Lathe** modifier on a shape, create a shape in the Front viewport and select it, as shown in Figure 6-6. Choose the **Modify** tab in the **Command Panel** and then select **OBJECT-SPACE MODIFIERS > Lathe** from the **Modifier List** drop-down list; the 2D shape will be converted into a 3D object and it will be displayed in the viewports, refer to Figure 6-7. When you apply the **Lathe** modifier on a shape, it will be displayed in the modifier stack. The **Parameters** rollout will be displayed below the modifier stack. You will learn more about this modifier in Chapter 12.

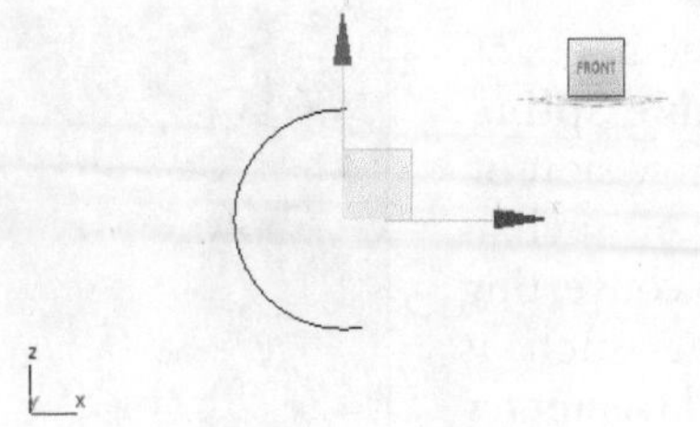

Figure 6-6 An arc displayed in the Front viewport

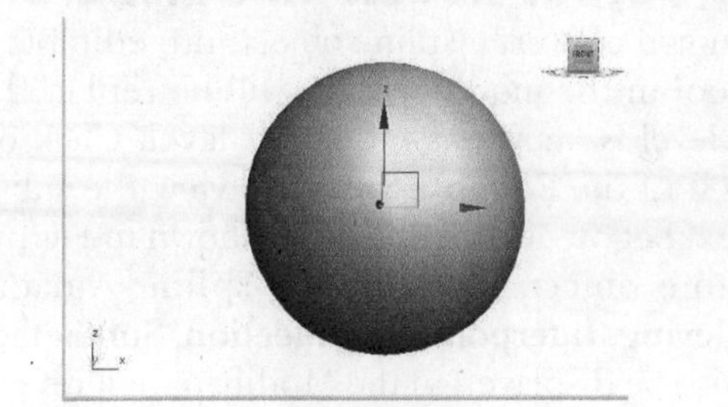

*Figure 6-7 The arc converted into a 3D object after applying the **Lathe** modifier*

MODIFYING THE SHAPES

To modify the shapes in 3ds Max, first create a shape using the tools from **Create > Shapes > Splines/Extended Splines > Object Type** rollout in the **Command Panel** as discussed earlier. Next, select the shape in the viewport and choose the **Modify** tab in the **Command Panel**; the Modify panel will be displayed with various rollouts. Now, you can modify the shapes using one of the following methods:

1. By entering new parameters in the rollouts displayed in the Modify panel. You have already learned about it in the previous chapters.

2. By applying a modifier from the **Modifier List** drop-down list. You will learn about applying modifiers in later Chapters.

3. By converting the shapes into editable splines, which is discussed next.

Converting the Shapes into Editable Splines

You can modify all the spline and extended spline shapes at advanced level by converting them into editable spline objects. The editable spline objects provide the sub-object levels of the shape. These sub-object levels help you to select the sub-objects of the shape in the viewport. You can convert a shape into an editable spline using one of the following methods:

- Create a shape and then select it in the viewport. Next, right-click on the shape; a quad menu will be displayed. Choose the **Convert To** option; a cascading menu will be displayed. Choose **Convert to Editable Spline**; the shape will be converted into editable spline.

- Create a shape and then select it in the viewport. Choose the **Modify** tab in the **Command Panel**. In the modifier stack, right-click on the name of the tool; a shortcut menu will be displayed. Choose the **Editable Spline** option; the shape will be converted into an editable spline.

- Create a shape and then choose the **Modify** tab in the **Command Panel**. Click on the **Modifier List** drop-down list in the **Command Panel** and select **Editable spline** from it; the **Editable Spline** modifier will be applied to the shape in the modifier stack.

Sub-object Levels in Editable Spline

When you convert a spline object into editable spline, the name of the tool in the modifier stack will be replaced by **Editable Spline**. This level is known as the object level. Click on the arrow sign on the left of the **Editable Spline** to view the sub-object levels such as **Vertex**, **Segment**, and **Spline**, as shown in Figure 6-8. On converting a spline object into editable spline, various rollouts such as **Rendering**, **Interpolation**, **Selection**, **Soft Selection**, and **Geometry** will also be displayed in the Modify panel, refer to Figure 6-8. These sub-object levels and rollouts are discussed next.

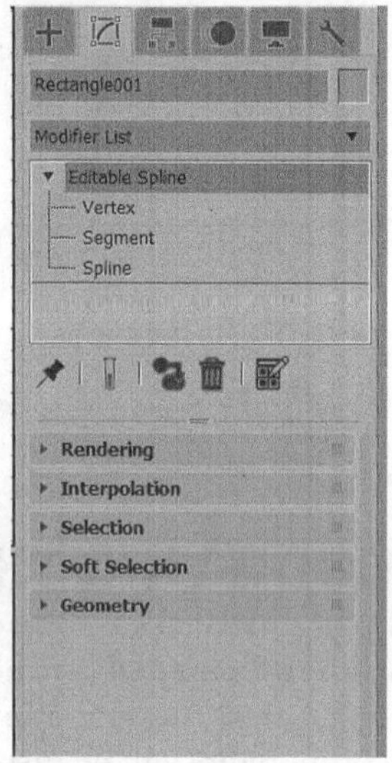

Figure 6-8 *The sub-object levels and rollouts displayed*

Sub-object Levels

The sub-object levels help you to modify the object by moving, rotating, and scaling the sub-objects. To do so, select one of the sub-object levels in the modifier stack; it will be activated and turn yellow. Also, it will prompt you to select the corresponding sub-objects in the viewport. You can select a sub-object in the viewport by clicking on it. If you want to add more sub-objects, then hold the CTRL key and click on the sub-objects that you want to add. You can also drag a selection box around the sub-objects to select them simultaneously. These sub-objects are discussed next.

Vertex

The vertex is a point on the spline. To modify an object using vertices, select the **Vertex** sub-object level; the white and yellow colored vertices of the spline will be displayed in the viewports, refer to Figure 6-9. The yellow colored vertex is the first vertex or the starting point of the spline, refer to Figure 6-9.

There are various types of vertices such as bezier, corner, smooth, and bezier corner vertices, which depend on the type of spline. You can convert a vertex into a bezier, corner, smooth, or bezier corner vertex. To do so, select a vertex in the viewport and right-click on it; a quad menu will be displayed, as shown in Figure 6-10. Choose the type of vertex from the quad menu, refer to Figure 6-10; the vertex will change based on the option chosen from the quad menu.

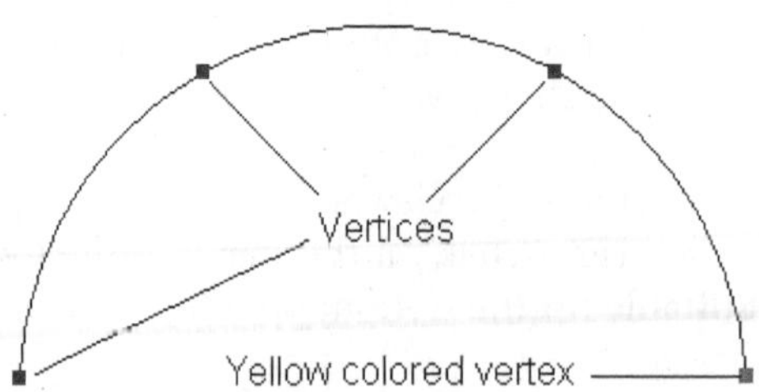

Figure 6-9 *The vertices of an arc spline displayed after selecting the* ***Vertex*** *sub-object level*

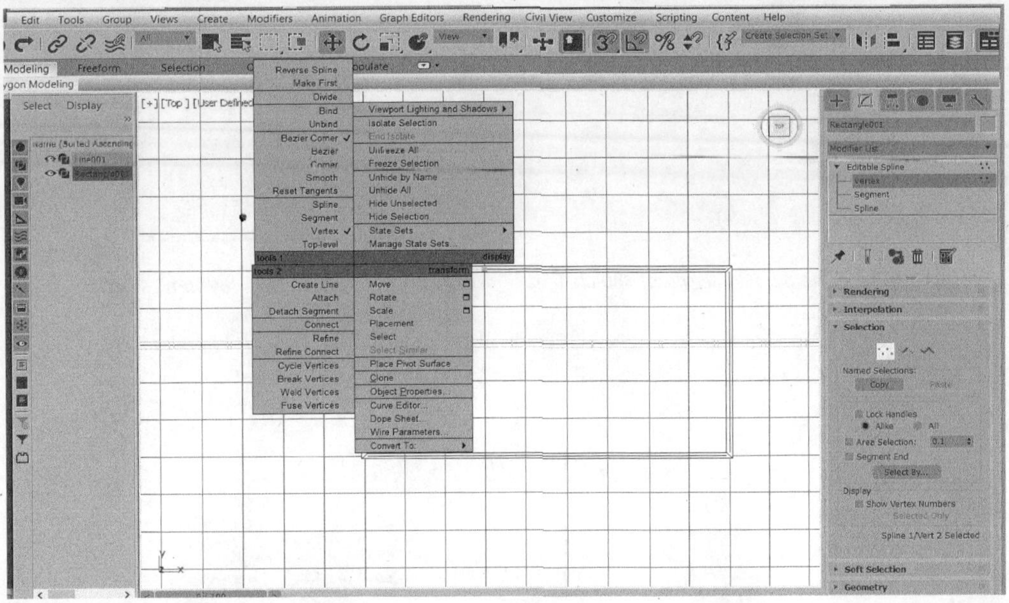

Figure 6-10 Various types of vertices in a quad menu

The bezier vertex has bezier handles on both sides of the vertex for adjusting the shape of the spline. The smooth vertex is used to smoothen the curve of the spline. The corner vertex is used to make the corners of the spline. The bezier corner vertex also has bezier handles and is used to adjust the shape of the spline independently on both the sides, refer to Figure 6-11.

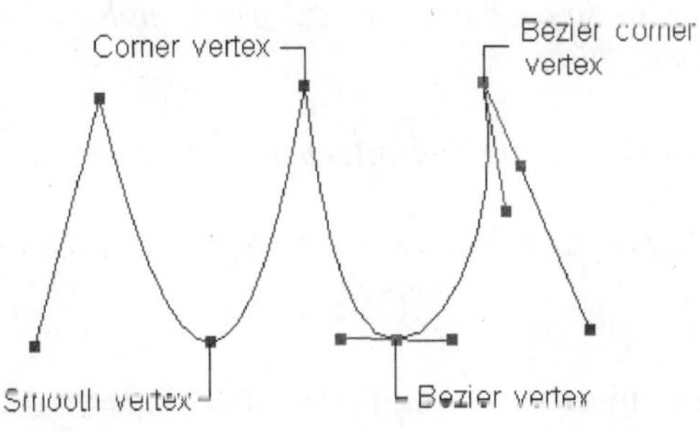

Figure 6-11 Various types of vertices in a line spline

Segment

The segment is a line or a curve between two vertices. To modify an object through segments, you need to select the **Segment** sub-object level. On doing so, you will be prompted to select the segments of the object, refer to Figures 6-12 and 6-13.

Spline

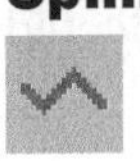

A spline consists of all the adjacent segments of an object. To modify an object using the spline, you need to select the **Spline** sub-object level. On doing so, you will be prompted to select all the adjacent segments of the object, as shown in Figure 6-14.

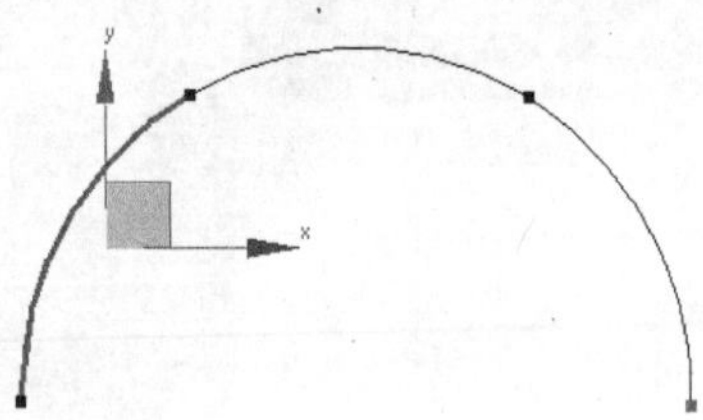

Figure 6-12 The curved segment selected in an arc spline

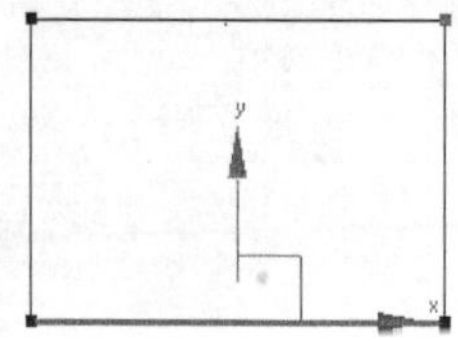

Figure 6-13 The line segment selected in a rectangular spline

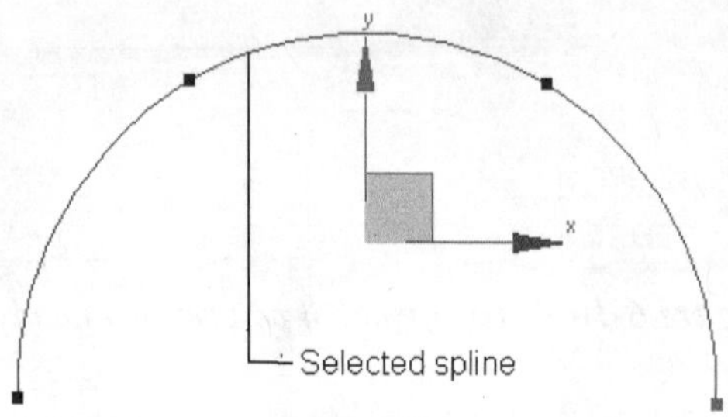

Figure 6-14 The spline selected in an arc

Note

*1. By default, the **Line** spline has all the sub-object levels and rollouts. So, you do not need to convert it into editable spline.*

*2. The options in the **Rendering** and **Interpolation** rollouts are same as described in Chapter 5.*

*3. The **Surface Properties** rollout will not be displayed at the **Vertex** sub-object level.*

Rollouts

When you convert a spline object into an editable spline object, various rollouts will be displayed below the modifier stack in the Modify panel. You can modify the spline objects at sub-object levels using these rollouts. These rollouts are discussed next.

Selection Rollout

At the top of the **Selection** rollout, there are three buttons, **Vertex**, **Segment**, and **Spline**, refer to Figure 6-15. These buttons are used to select the sub-objects of a spline and have been discussed in the previous section. Choose one of the buttons to make it active. It is same as selecting the sub-object level in the modifier stack. The check boxes in the **Display** area are used to display the vertex numbers in the viewport. When you select the **Show Vertex Numbers** check box, the vertex numbers will be displayed in the viewport, as shown in Figure 6-16. Select the **Selected Only** check box to display the vertex number only for the selected vertex.

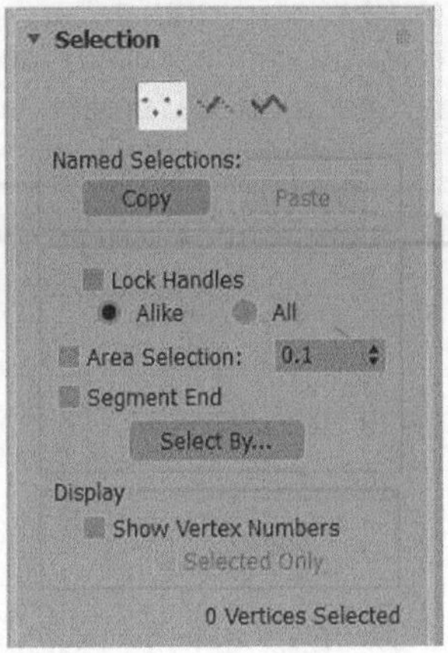

*Figure 6-15 The **Selection** rollout*

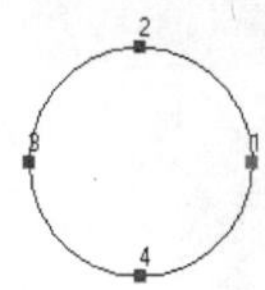

*Figure 6-16 The vertex numbers displayed on selecting the **Show Vertex Numbers** check box*

Soft Selection Rollout

The options in this rollout allow you to soft-select the objects. You can select the **Use Soft Selection** check box to activate the options in this rollout. When you select the sub-objects of an object in the viewport, it shows the falloff in different color combinations. The influence of the colored zone is determined by the value in the **Falloff** spinner. The shape of the falloff is controlled by the value in the **Pinch** and **Bubble** spinners.

Geometry Rollout

The options in this rollout are used to edit the spline at the object and sub-object levels, refer to Figure 6-17. These options are discussed next.

Create Line

The **Create Line** button is used to add a line spline to the selected spline. To do so, select the editable spline object in the viewport and choose the **Modify** tab; all the rollouts will be displayed in the Modify panel. Now, choose the **Create Line** button in the **Geometry** rollout; the button will be activated. Move the cursor in the viewport; its shape will change, as shown in Figure 6-18. Create a new line; it will automatically be attached to the selected spline. Next, right-click in the viewport or choose the **Create Line** button again to exit the command. The **Attach** button is used to attach another spline to the selected spline. When you choose the **Attach Mult.** button, the **Attach Multiple** dialog box will be displayed. It contains the list of all other splines in the scene. Select the shapes in the dialog box that you want to attach and then choose the **Attach** button to attach the shapes.

The **Reorient** check box, next to the **Attach** and **Attach Mult.** buttons, is used to align the local coordinate system of the attached spline with the local coordinate system of the selected spline.

Insert

The **Insert** button is used to insert additional vertices in the splines to create new segments. To do so, select the editable spline object in the viewport and choose the **Modify** tab; all rollouts will be displayed in the Modify panel. Now, choose the **Insert** button in the **Geometry** rollout; it will get activated. Next, move the cursor over the spline; the shape of the cursor will change, as shown in Figure 6-19. Then, click to create a new vertex and move the cursor to place it. Again, move the cursor and click in the viewport to place the new vertices on the spline and right-click to exit the command.

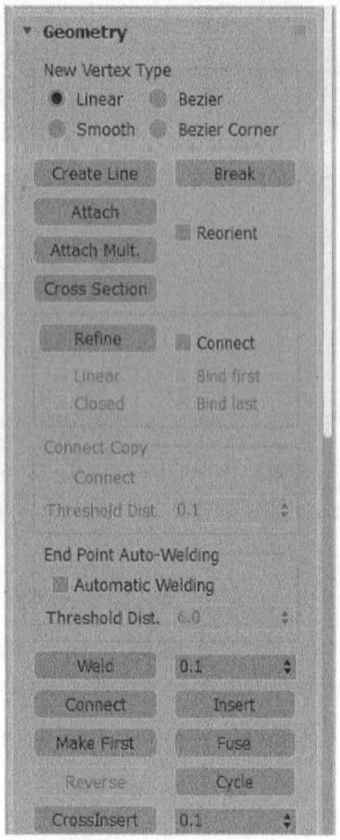

*Figure 6-17 Partial view of the **Geometry** rollout*

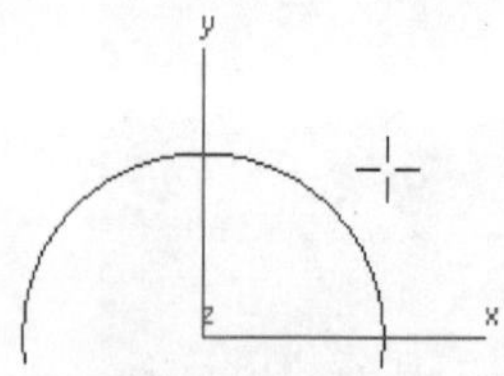

*Figure 6-18 The cursor displayed in the viewport on choosing the **Create Line** button*

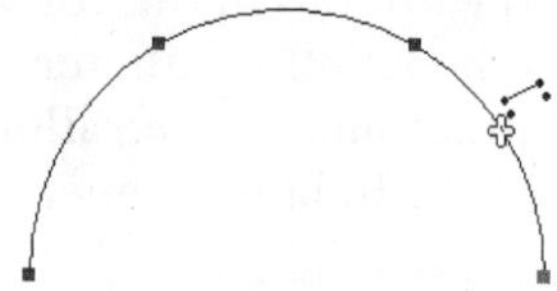

*Figure 6-19 The cursor displayed after choosing the **Insert** button*

Break

The **Break** button is available for the **Vertex** and **Segment** sub-object levels. It is used to break a spline at the selected point. If you select the **Vertex** sub-object level, then select one or more vertices in the viewport to break the spline. Next, choose the **Break** button in the **Geometry** rollout; the spline will split at the selected point. Similarly, if you select the **Segment** sub-object level, then choose the **Break** button and click on a point on the selected spline to break it. To view the split splines, select the **Spline** sub-object level in the modifier stack.

Refine and Connect

The **Refine** button and the **Connect** check box are available for the **Vertex** and the **Segment** sub-object levels. The **Refine** button is used to add new vertices to the selected spline. To add new vertices, choose the **Refine** button and move the cursor over the selected spline; the cursor for refining the spline will be displayed. Then, click on a point to add a new vertex. You can repeatedly click on the spline to create more than one vertex. Next, right-click or choose the **Refine** button again to exit the command.

The **Connect** check box on the right of the **Refine** button is used to connect the new vertices by a segment. To do so, select the **Connect** check box, choose the **Refine** button, and then move the cursor over the selected spline; the cursor for refining will be displayed. Now, click on a point to add a new vertex and then click again to create another vertex. Next, right-click to exit the command; a segment will be created to join the two new vertices, as shown in Figure 6-20.

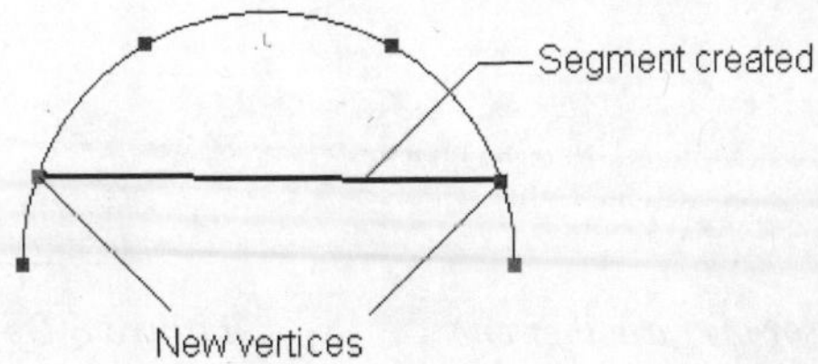

*Figure 6-20 The new vertices and the segment created using the **Refine** button and the **Connect** check box*

Note

*If you insert a vertex using the **Refine** button, then the curve shape of the selected spline will not change. But, if you insert the vertex using the **Insert** button, then the curve shape will change.*

Weld

The **Weld** button is available only for the **Vertex** sub-object level. It is used to join the selected vertices into a single vertex. To do so, select the editable spline object in the viewport and then select the **Vertex** sub-object level; the **Weld** button will be available in the **Geometry** rollout. Next, select the vertices that you want to join together in the viewport and choose the **Weld** button; the vertices will be joined together to create a vertex. The spinner on the right side of the **Weld** button is used to specify the distance between the vertices that can be welded. If the value in the spinner is less than the distance between the vertices, then the vertices will not be welded.

Connect

The **Connect** button is available only for the **Vertex** sub-object level. It is used to connect two end vertices of a spline by creating a segment in between the vertices, refer to Figure 6-21. To do so, select the editable spline object in the viewport. Next, select the **Vertex** sub-object level in the modifier stack, and then choose the **Connect** button in the **Geometry** rollout. Next, move the cursor over one of the end vertices of the spline; the shape of the cursor will change, refer to Figure 6-22. Now, press and hold the left mouse button and drag it to move the cursor over another end vertex; the shape of the cursor will change again and a dotted line will be generated, as shown in Figure 6-23. Now, release the left mouse button; a segment will be created joining the end vertices, as shown in Figure 6-24

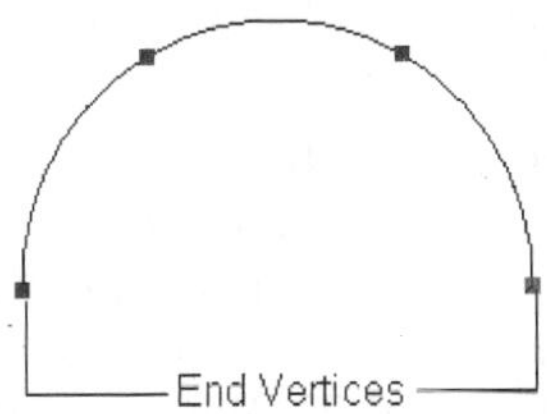

Figure 6-21 The end vertices in an arc spline

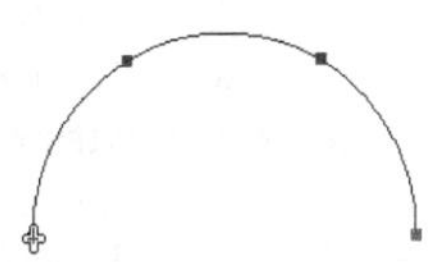

Figure 6-22 The cursor over one of the end vertices

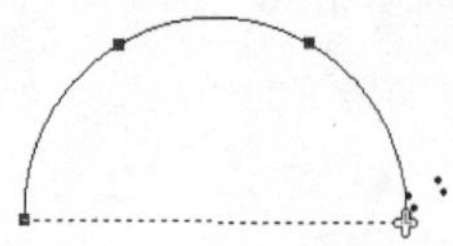

Figure 6-23 The cursor over another end vertex and the dotted line displayed

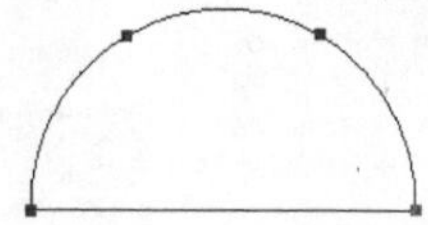

Figure 6-24 The end vertices connected with a segment

Make First

The **Make First** button is used to make any vertex of the spline as its first vertex or the starting point. To do so, select a vertex of the spline in the viewport and choose the **Make First** button in the **Geometry** rollout; the selected vertex will turn yellow and become the first vertex of the spline.

Note

In an open spline such as line, arc, and so on, only the end vertex can be the first vertex.

Fuse

The **Fuse** button is used to move all the selected vertices of a spline to their average center. Select the vertices of a spline in the viewport, as shown in Figure 6-25, and then choose the **Fuse** button in the **Geometry** rollout; the selected vertices will fuse together at their average center, as shown in Figure 6-26.

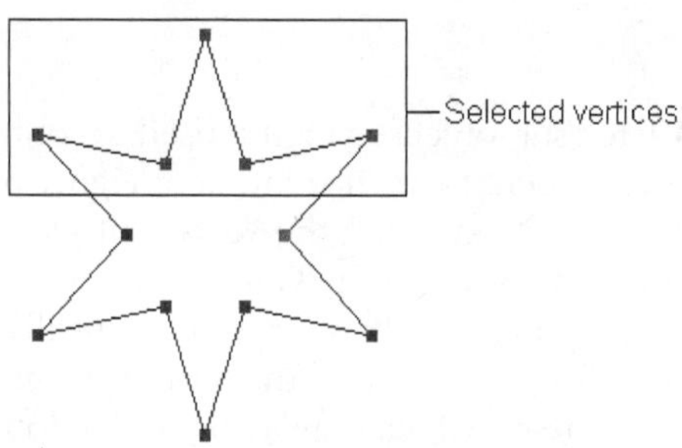

Figure 6-25 The selected vertices inside the rectangular area

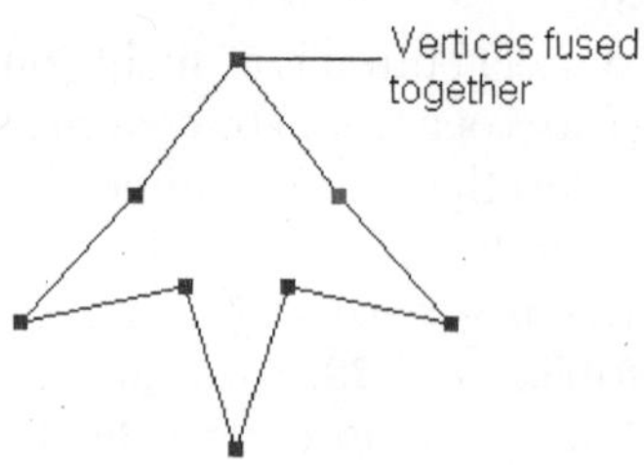

Figure 6-26 The selected vertices fused at their average center

Fillet

The **Fillet** button is used to create round corners in a spline by creating two new vertices. Create a star spline, refer to Figure 6-27. Next, choose the **Fillet** button in the **Geometry** rollout and move the cursor over a vertex; the shape of the cursor will change, as shown in Figure 6-28. Now, press the left mouse button and drag the cursor up; the new vertices with a round corner will be displayed, as shown in Figure 6-29. When you drag the cursor to fillet the vertex, the value of fillet will also be displayed in the spinner on the right side of the **Fillet** button. You can also perform this command by selecting a vertex and entering the value for the fillet in this spinner.

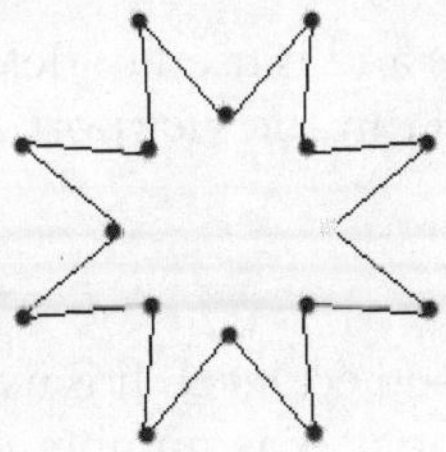

Figure 6-27 The star spline

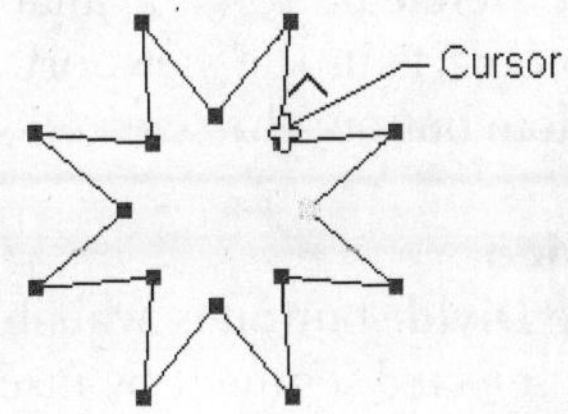

Figure 6-28 The changed shape of cursor displayed after moving the cursor over the selected vertex

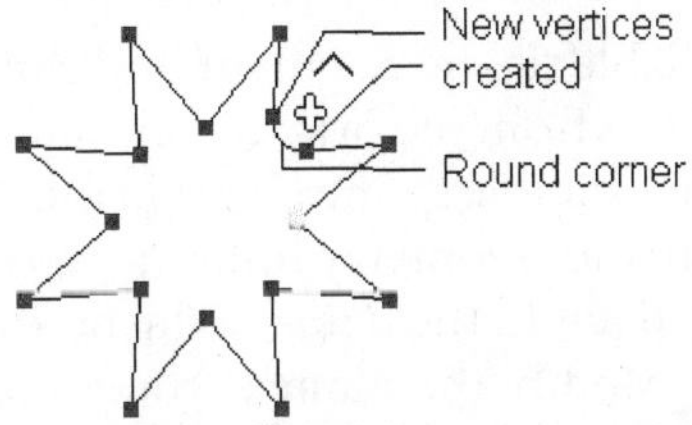

Figure 6-29 The two new vertices and the round corner displayed

Chamfer

The **Chamfer** button is used to create bevel corners in a spline by creating two new vertices. To do so, select the corner vertex of an editable spline object in the viewport. Next, choose the **Chamfer** button in the **Geometry** rollout and move the cursor over the selected vertex; the shape of the cursor will change. Now, press the left mouse button and drag the cursor up; the new vertices with a beveled corner will be displayed, as shown in Figure 6-30. Next, release the left mouse button. You can also chamfer by selecting a vertex and entering the value for the chamfer in this spinner.

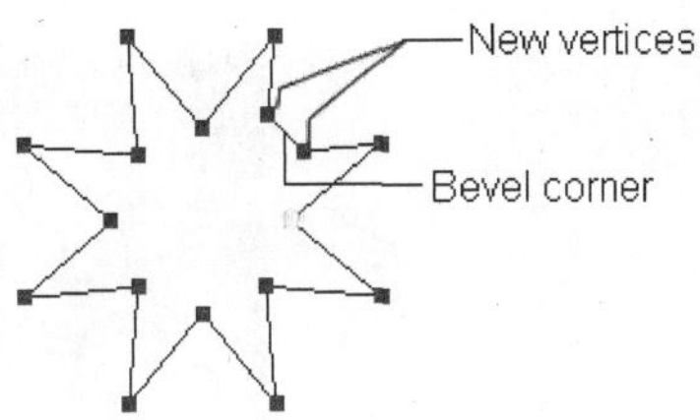

Figure 6-30 The new vertices with a beveled corner

Hide and Unhide All

The **Hide** and **Unhide All** buttons are available for all sub-object levels in the editable spline object. The **Hide** button is used to hide the selected sub-object in the viewport. The **Unhide All** button is used to show all hidden sub-objects in the viewport. To hide the sub-objects of the editable spline object, select them in the viewport and choose the **Hide** button in the **Geometry** rollout. Similarly, to unhide the hidden sub-objects, choose the **Unhide All** button in the **Geometry** rollout.

Delete

The **Delete** button is available at all the sub-object levels and is used to delete the selected sub-objects in the viewport. To do so, select a sub-object in the viewport and choose the **Delete** button; the selected sub-object will be deleted.

Divide

The **Divide** button is available only for the **Segment** sub-object level. It is used to subdivide the selected segment by inserting a number of vertices on it. The number of vertices to be inserted can be set in the spinner on the right side of the **Divide** button. To subdivide a selected segment, select the **Segment** sub-object in the viewport, as shown in Figure 6-31. Next, choose the **Divide** button; the selected segment will be sub-divided, refer to Figure 6-32.

Detach

The **Detach** button is available at the **Segment** and **Spline** sub-object levels. It is used to detach the selected sub-objects from the original one and create a new shape. To do so, select one or more segments of the editable spline object in the viewport, refer to Figure 6-33. Next, choose the **Detach** button in the **Geometry** rollout; the **Detach** dialog box will be displayed, as shown in Figure 6-34. By default, the name of the new shape will be displayed as *Shape001* in the **Detach as** text box. Modify the name if you want and then choose the **OK** button; the detached segment will now behave like a new independent shape, refer to Figure 6-35.

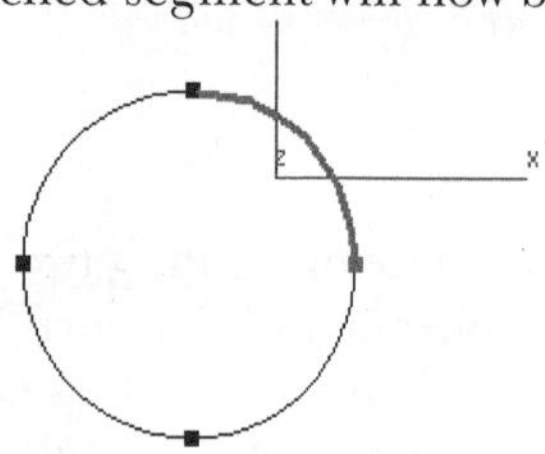

Figure 6-31 *A segment selected in the circle spline*

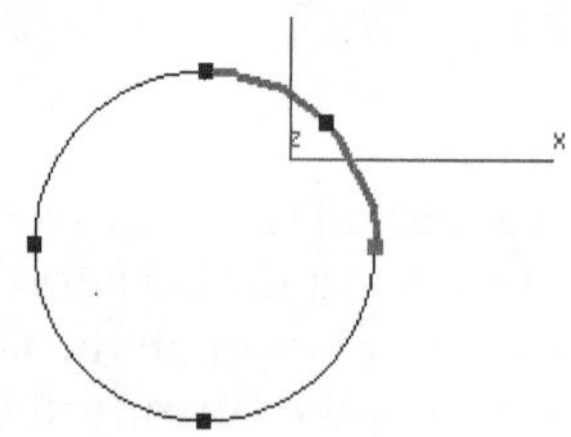

Figure 6-32 *The selected segment sub-divided after using the **Divide** button*

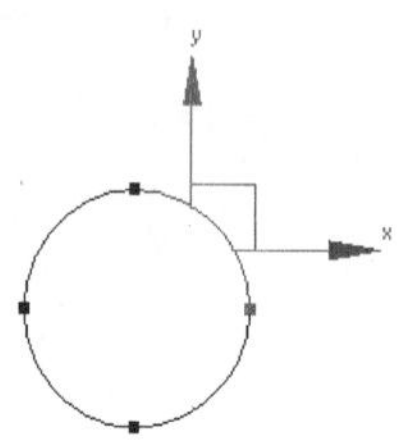

Figure 6-33 *A segment sub-object selected in the circle spline*

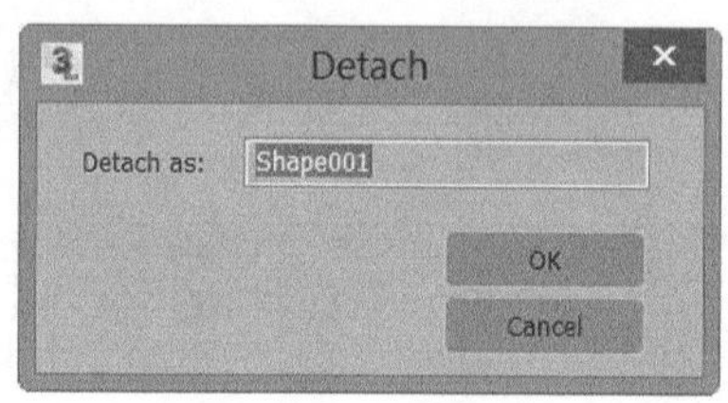

Figure 6-34 *The **Detach** dialog box*

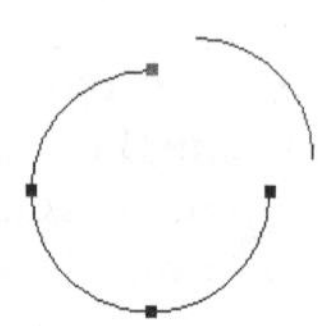

Figure 6-35 *The detached segment as a new independent shape*

Reverse

The **Reverse** button is available only at the **Spline** sub-object level. It is used to reverse the direction of the spline. To do so, select the editable spline object in the viewport, select the **Spline** sub-object level in the modifier stack, and then select the spline in the viewport, as shown in Figure 6-36. Now, choose the **Reverse** button in the **Geometry** rollout; the direction of the selected spline will get reversed, as shown in Figure 6-37. To view the reversed direction, you need to select the **Show Vertex Numbers** check box in the **Display** area of the **Selection** rollout.

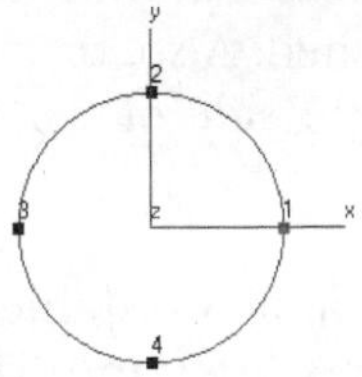

Figure 6-36 The spline selected in a circle

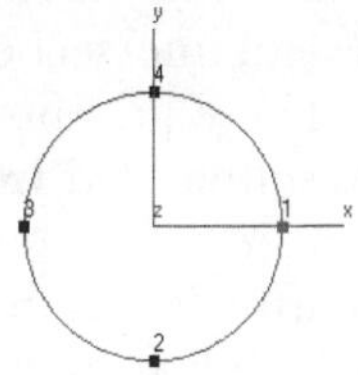

*Figure 6-37 The reversed direction of the selected spline after choosing the **Reverse** button*

Outline

The **Outline** button is available only at the **Spline** sub-object level. It is used to create a copy of the spline at a distance that you enter in the spinner on the right side of the **Outline** button. To do so, select the spline of the editable spline object in the viewport. Next, choose the **Outline** button; the button will be activated. Next, move the cursor over the selected spline; the shape of the cursor will change, as shown in Figure 6-38. Now, press and hold the left mouse button and move the cursor up or down over the selected spline to create a copy of the spline which behaves like its outline, as shown in Figure 6-39. Now, release the left mouse button. Also, right-click in the viewport or choose the **Outline** button again to exit the command.

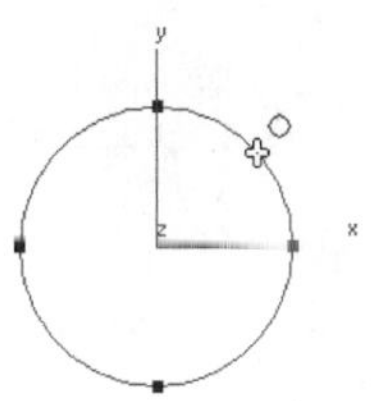

*Figure 6-38 The shape of the cursor changed after choosing the **Outline** button*

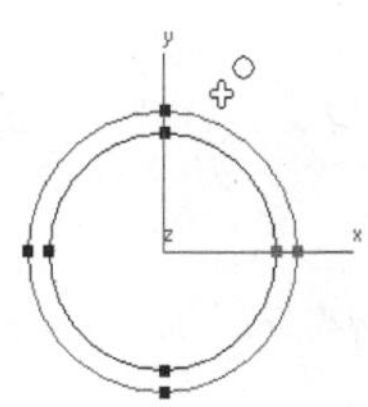

Figure 6-39 A copy of the spline created as an outline of the selected spline

Note

*If you use the **Outline** button for an open spline such as arc, line, and so on, then the copied spline will be attached to the selected spline. Also, the resultant spline will be a closed one, refer to Figures 6-40 and 6-41.*

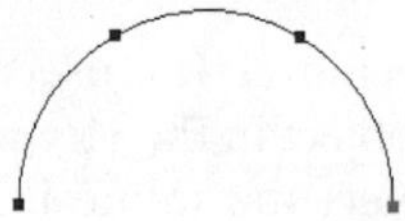

Figure 6-40 *An open arc spline*

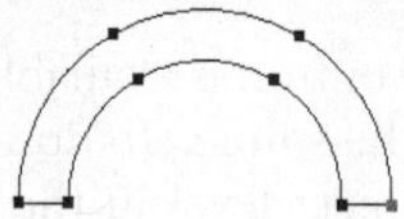

Figure 6-41 *The closed spline after using the* ***Outline*** *button on the open spline*

Boolean

The **Boolean** button is available only in the **Spline** sub-object level. You can choose this button to create complex shapes from two spline objects. Note that these two spline objects should be closed, intersect each other, and should be attached. Also, they should be in the same plane. There are three buttons available on the right side of the **Boolean** button, **Union**, **Subtraction**, and **Intersection**.

The **Union** button is used to remove the overlapping portion of two splines and to create a single spline by combining them, refer to Figures 6-42 and 6-43. The **Subtraction** button is used to subtract the overlapping portion of the second spline from the selected spline and remove the extra portion of the second spline, as shown in Figure 6-44. The **Intersection** button is used to remove the non-overlapping portion of the splines and retain the overlapping portion of the splines, as shown in Figure 6-45.

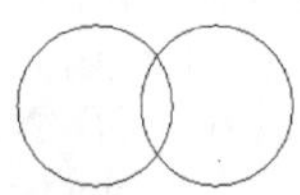

Figure 6-42 *The two attached splines overlapping each other*

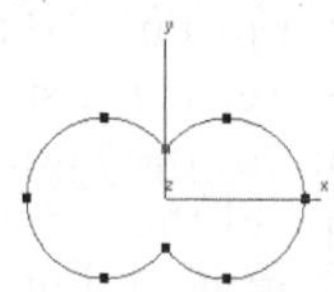

Figure 6-43 *The union boolean final output*

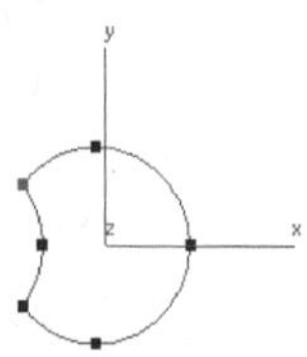

Figure 6-44 *The subtraction boolean final output*

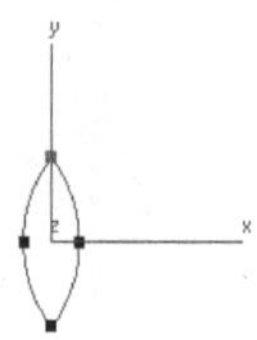

Figure 6-45 *The intersection boolean final output*

To perform the boolean operation, create two splines and convert them into editable splines and then attach them using the **Attach** button as discussed earlier. Next, select the **Spline** sub-object level in the modifier stack. Now, choose one of the boolean type buttons on the right side of the **Boolean** button in the **Geometry** rollout and then choose the **Boolean** button and move the cursor over the attached splines; the cursor will get changed. Click on the overlapping area; the splines will be modified to form a single spline on the basis of the boolean type button chosen.

Mirror

The **Mirror** button is available only at the **Spline** sub-object level. It is used to move the selected spline in a particular direction. There are three buttons on the right side of the **Mirror** button, **Mirror Horizontally**, **Mirror Vertically**, and **Mirror Both**. These buttons are used to define the direction of movement of the spline. To mirror a spline, select the editable spline in the viewport and then select the **Spline** sub-object level in the modifier stack. Specify the direction of movement of the spline by choosing one of the buttons on the right side of the **Mirror** button. Next, choose the **Mirror** button; the spline will move in the specified direction, refer to Figures 6-46 through 6-48.

Select the **Copy** check box below the **Mirror** button to create a copy of the spline while mirroring, as shown in Figures 6-49 through 6-51. Select the **About Pivot** check box to mirror the spline according to the pivot point of the spline.

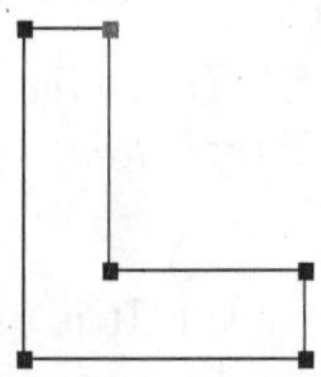

__Figure 6-46__ The angle extended spline created to mirror

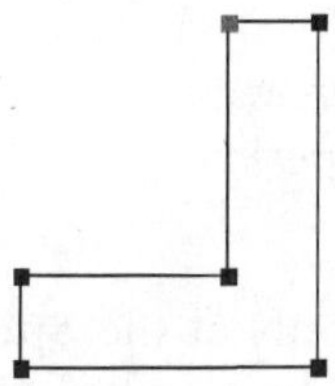

__Figure 6-47__ The spline mirrored horizontally

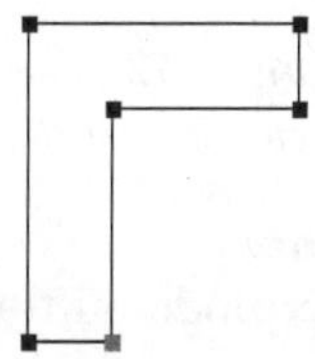

__Figure 6-48__ The spline mirrored vertically

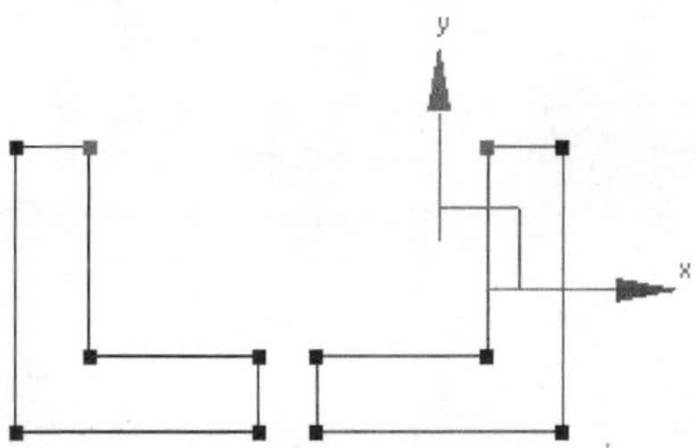

__Figure 6-49__ The spline mirrored horizontally after selecting the __Copy__ check box

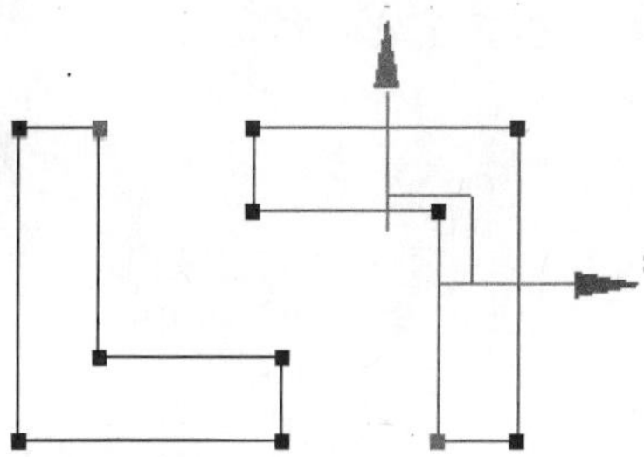

__Figure 6-50__ The spline mirrored on both the sides after selecting the __Copy__ check box

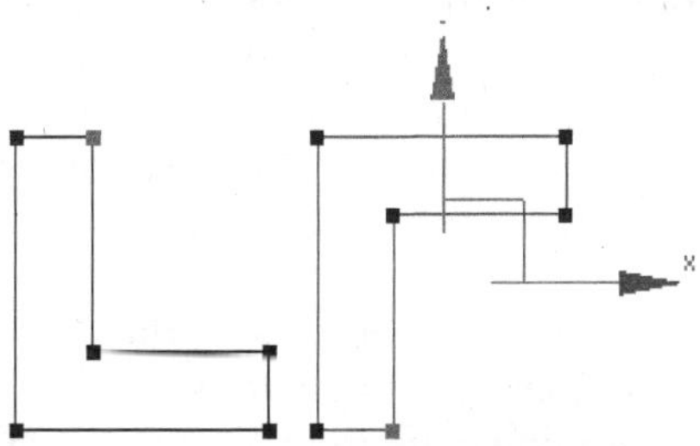

__Figure 6-51__ The spline mirrored vertically after selecting the __Copy__ check box

Trim

The **Trim** button is available only at the **Spline** sub-object level. It is used to remove the overlapping segments of the two attached splines. To do so, create two splines, convert them into editable splines, and then attach them using the **Attach** button as described earlier, refer to Figure 6-52. Next, select the **Spline** sub-object level in the modifier stack. Choose the **Trim** button in the **Geometry** rollout and move the cursor over the overlapping segments of the attached splines; the cursor shape will get changed, as shown in Figure 6-52. Now, click on the overlapping segments to remove them, refer to Figure 6-53.

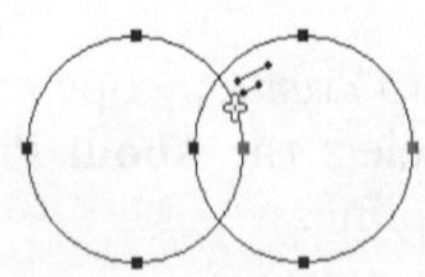

Figure 6-52 The two attached splines and the cursor over the overlapping segments

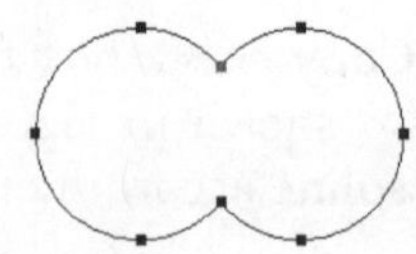

*Figure 6-53 The splines after using the **Trim** button*

Explode

The **Explode** button is available only at the **Spline** sub-object level. It is used to break a spline into a number of splines. The number of broken splines depends on the number of segments of the spline. To break a spline into a number of splines, select the editable spline in the viewport and select the **Spline** sub-object level in the modifier stack. Next, choose the **Explode** button; the spline will be broken into a number of splines, refer to Figures 6-54 and 6-55.

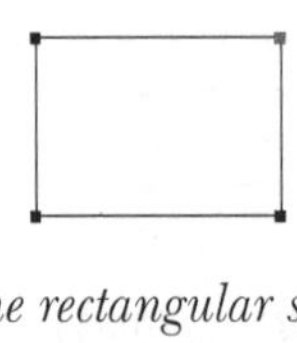

Figure 6-54 The rectangular spline for explosion

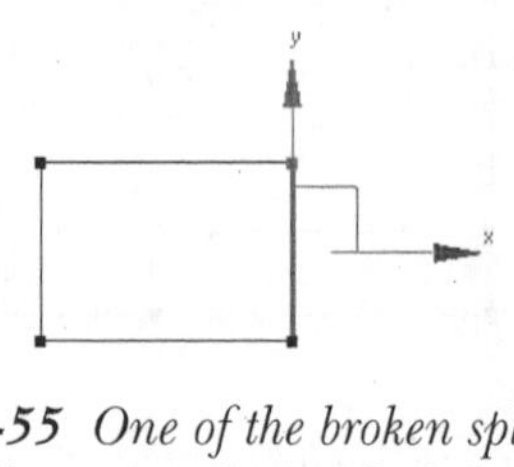

*Figure 6-55 One of the broken splines selected after using the **Explode** button*

There are two radio buttons in the **To** area below the **Explode** button, **Splines** and **Objects**. These buttons are used to select the type of explosion of the spline. By default, the **Splines** radio button is selected, which enables you to break the spline into a number of splines that will be attached together. On selecting the **Objects** radio button, the new splines will be created but they will behave as independent shapes.

Select the **Objects** radio button and then choose the **Explode** button to explode the spline; the **Explode** dialog box will be displayed, as shown in Figure 6-56. Enter a name in the **Object Name** text box and choose the **OK** button; all new shapes will be named according to the name entered in the **Object Name** text box.

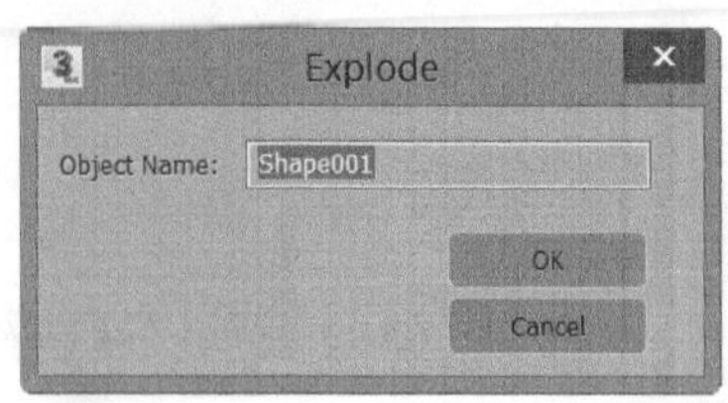

*Figure 6-56 The **Explode** dialog box*

Display Area

The **Display** area will be only active in the **Vertex** and **Segment** sub-object levels. In this area, the **Show selected segs** check box is cleared. As a result, the selected segments will be displayed in the **Segment** sub-object level only. But, if you select the **Show selected segs** check box, the selected segments will be displayed in red color at the **Vertex** sub-object level also.

TUTORIALS

Tutorial 1

In this tutorial, you will create a model of a street lamp, as shown in Figure 6-57, by converting 2D splines into 3D mesh objects. **(Expected time: 25 min)**

Figure 6-57 *The model of a street lamp*

The following steps are required to complete this tutorial:

a. Create the project folder.
b. Create the pole.
c. Create support for side lamps.
d. Create the base for side lamps.
e. Create lamps.
f. Save and render the scene.

Creating the Project Folder

Create a new project folder with the name *c06_tut1* at *\Documents\3dsmax2017* and then save the file with the name *c06tut1*, as discussed in Tutorial 1 of Chapter 2.

Creating the Pole

In this section, you will create a pole using the **Line** tool and the **Lathe** modifier.

1. Activate the Front viewport and choose **Create > Shapes** from the **Command Panel**. The **Splines** option is selected by default in the drop-down list below the **Shapes** button. Now, choose the **Line** tool from the **Object Type** rollout.

2. In the **Creation Method** rollout, select the **Smooth** radio button in both the **Initial Type** and **Drag Type** areas.

3. Click at the bottom middle point of the Front viewport to create the first vertex or the start point of the line spline. Now, create a curve, refer to Figure 6-58. Next, right-click to end creating the line spline.

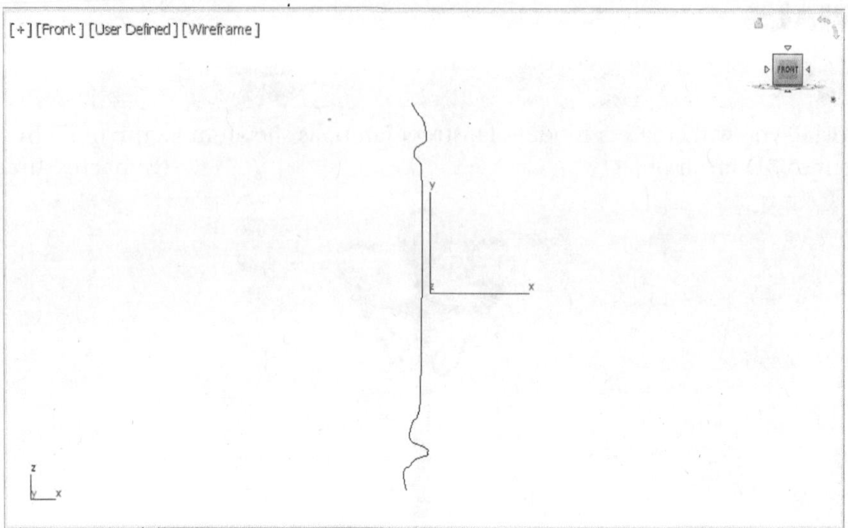

Figure 6-58 The line spline created for glass

To get the shape shown in Figure 6-58, you may need to modify the shape of the line spline by following the step given next:

4. Make sure that the line spline is selected in the viewport and choose the **Modify** tab in the **Command Panel**. Now, select the **Vertex** sub-object level in the modifier stack; all the vertices of the line spline are displayed in the viewport. Next, select the vertices in the viewport one by one and modify the shape by moving them as per requirement. After getting the required shape, select the **Vertex** sub-object level in the modifier stack again to deactivate it.

Next, you need to apply the **Lathe** modifier to convert the 2D spline into a 3D mesh object.

5. Make sure that the line spline is selected in the viewport and choose **Modifiers > Patch/ Spline Editing > Lathe** from the menu bar; the 2D line spline is converted into the 3D mesh object. Also, the **Parameters** rollout is displayed in the Modify panel.

6. In the **Parameters** rollout, select the **Flip Normals** check box.

7. Name the new 3D object as *pole*. Also, change its color to black. Next, click on the **Modifier List** drop-down list and select **Shell** from it; the **Shell** modifier is applied to *pole*.

8. In the **Parameters** rollout, set **0.5** in the **Inner Amount** spinner; *pole* is displayed in the Perspective viewport, as shown in Figure 6-59.

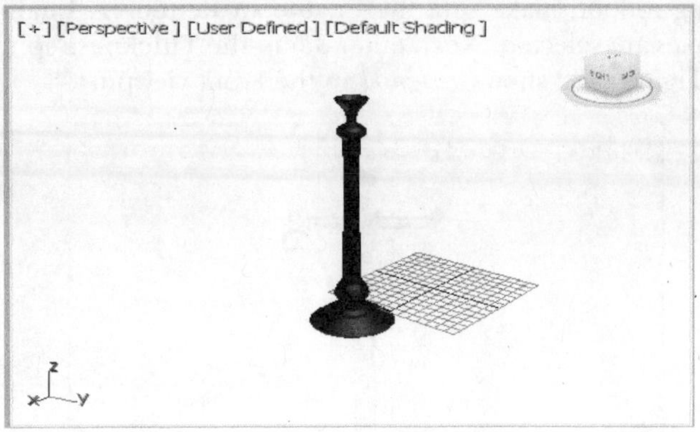

***Figure 6-59** The pole displayed in the Perspective viewport*

Creating Support for Sidelamps

In this section, you will create support for sidelamps using the **Line** tool.

1. Activate the Front viewport and choose **Create > Shapes** from the **Command Panel**. The **Splines** option is selected by default in the drop-down list below the **Shapes** button. Now, choose the **Line** tool from the **Object Type** rollout.

2. In the **Creation Method** rollout, select the **Corner** radio button from the **Initial Type** and **Drag Type** areas and create a line in the Front viewport, as shown in Figure 6-60.

3. In the **Rendering** rollout, select the **Enable In Renderer** and **Enable In Viewport** check boxes. Make sure the **Radial** radio button is selected and enter the values as follows:

   Thickness: **7.0** Sides: **12** Angle: **0.0**

   The line is modified, as shown in Figure 6-61. Name it as *support01*.

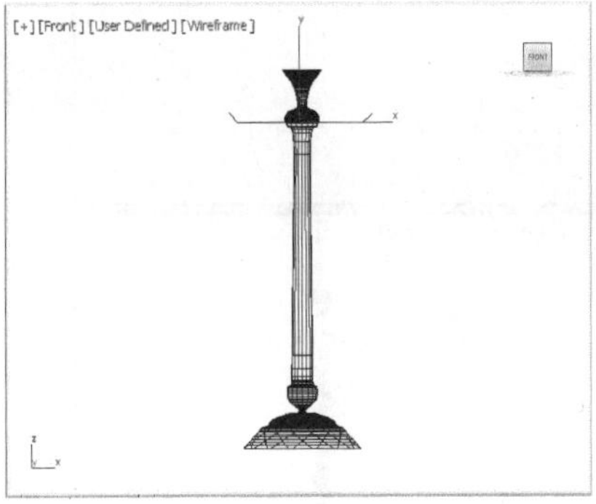

***Figure 6-60** The line created*

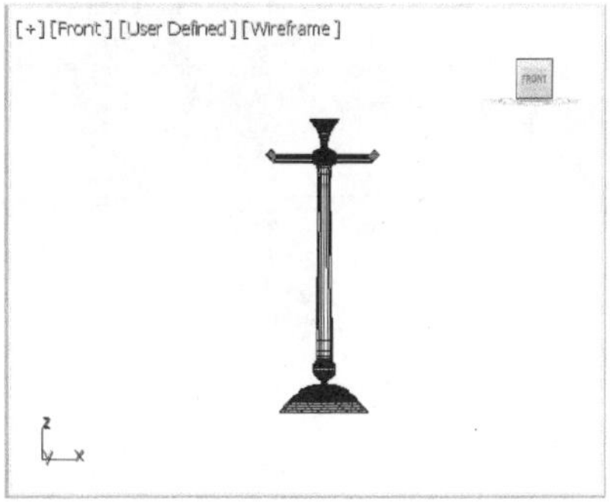

***Figure 6-61** The line modified*

4. Choose the **Line** tool from the **Object Type** rollout. Next, in the **Creation Method** rollout, select the **Smooth** radio button from the **Initial Type** and **Drag Type** areas and create a line in the Front viewport, refer to Figure 6-62.

5. In the **Rendering** rollout, make sure the **Enable In Renderer**, **Enable In Viewport**, and **Radial** check boxes are selected. Next, enter **3.5** in the **Thickness** spinner. Next, name the line as *design01*.Figure 6-62 shows *design01* in the Front viewport.

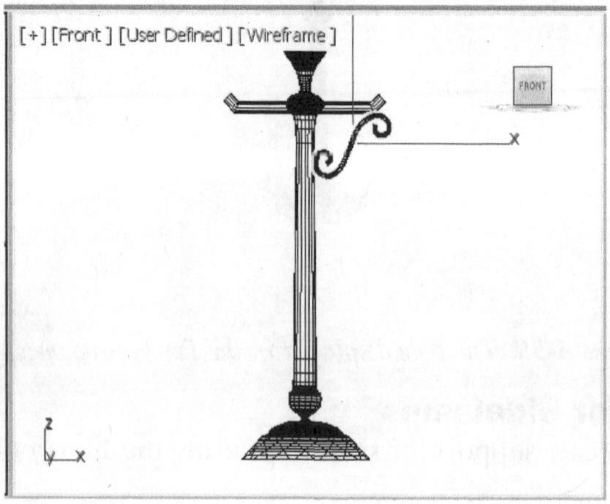

Figure 6-62 *The design01 in the Front viewport*

Note

*When you set the parameters for a spline in the **Rendering** rollout, their values remain unchanged on creating another spline. Therefore, the new spline automatically takes the same parameters unless you change them.*

6. Create a copy of *design01* and name it as *design02*. Next, align *design01* and *design02* in all viewports using the **Select and Move** and **Select and Rotate** tools, as shown in Figure 6-63.

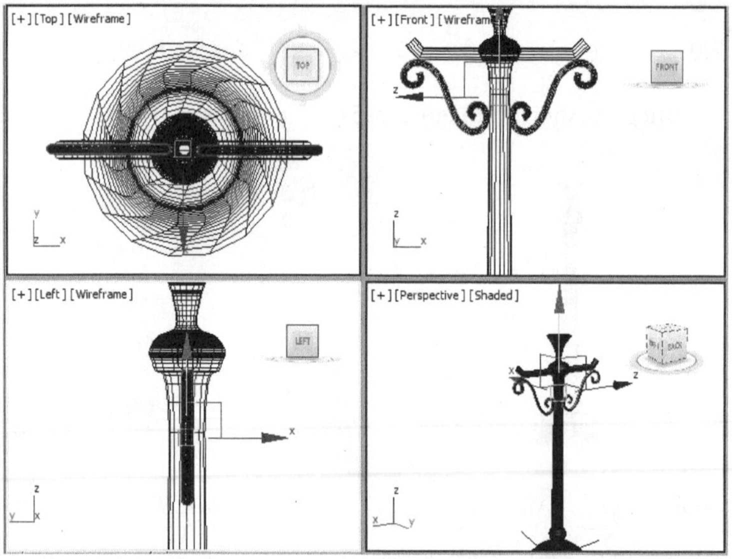

Figure 6-63 *The design01 and design02 aligned*

Creating the Base for Sidelamps

In this section, you will create the base for sidelamps using the **Line** tool.

1. Choose the **Line** tool from the **Object Type** rollout. Next, in the **Creation Method** rollout, select the **Smooth** radio button from the **Initial Type** and **Drag Type** areas.

2. In the **Rendering** rollout, clear the **Enable In Renderer** and **Enable In Viewport** check boxes and create a new line in the Front viewport, refer to Figure 6-64.

3. Rename the new line as *base01*. Apply the **Lathe** and **Shell** modifiers to *base01* as discussed earlier. Figure 6-65 shows *base01* in the Front viewport.

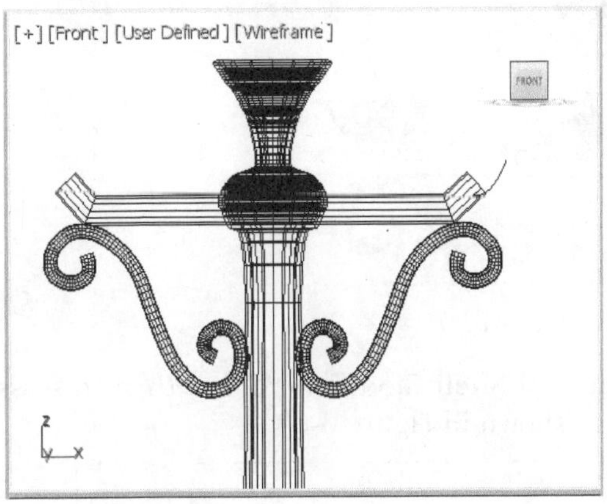

Figure 6-64 *New line created*

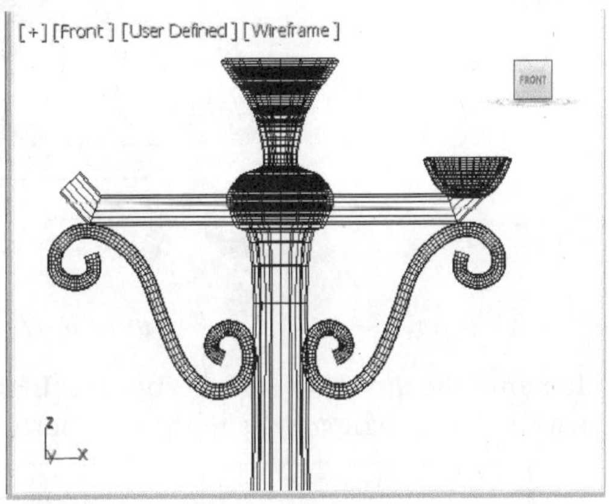

Figure 6-65 *The base01 in the Front viewport*

4. Create a copy of *base01* with the name *base02* and align it in the viewports, as shown in Figure 6-66.

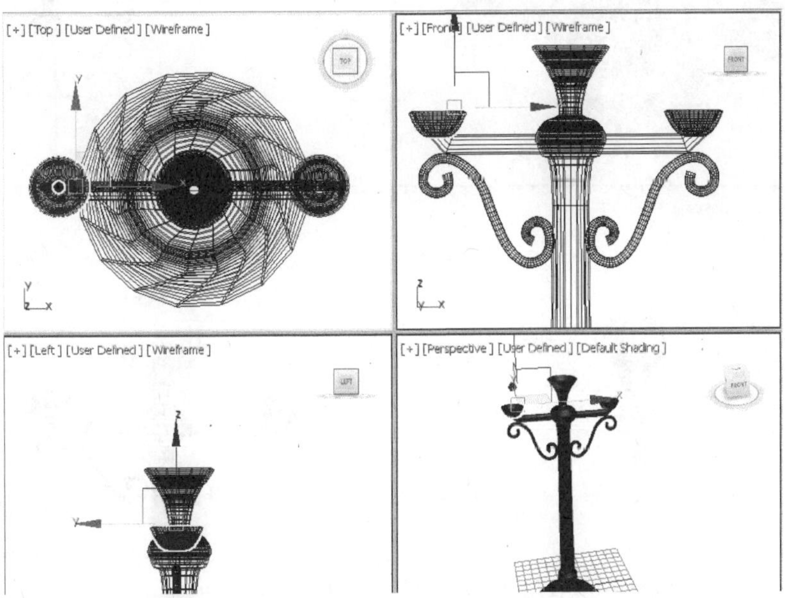

Figure 6-66 *The base02 aligned in the viewports*

Creating Lamps

In this section, you will create lamps using the **Arc** and **Sphere** tool.

1. Choose the **Arc** tool from the **Object Type** rollout. Next, create the arc in the Front viewport, as shown in Figure 6-67.

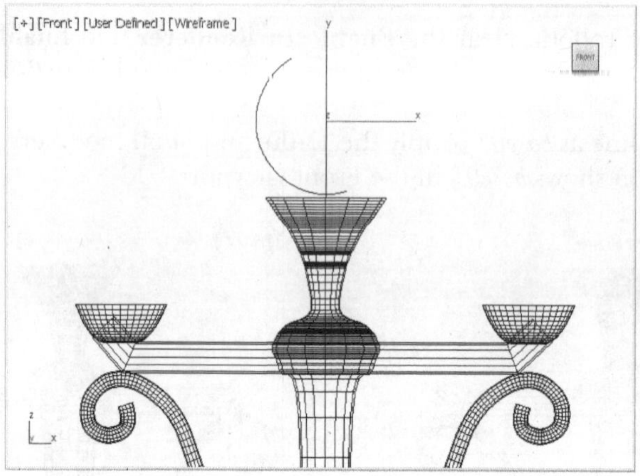

Figure 6-67 *An arc created*

2. Rename the arc as *dome01*. Apply the **Lathe** and **Shell** modifiers to *dome01* as discussed earlier. Next align *dome01* in the viewports, as shown in Figure 6-68.

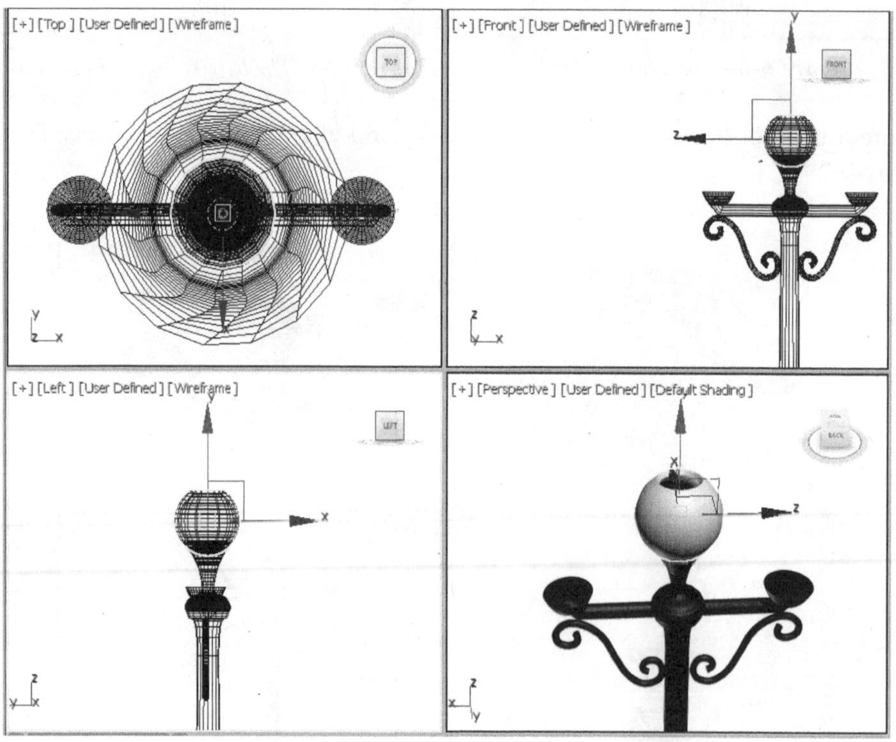

Figure 6-68 *The dome01 aligned in the viewports*

3. Create a copy of *base01* with the name *top01*. Next, make sure that *top01* is selected and right-click on the **Select and Uniform Scale** tool; the **Scale Transform Type-In** area is displayed. In this area, enter **60** in the **Y** spinner of the **Absolute: Local** area; *top01* is scaled.

4. Align *top01* in the viewports, as shown in Figure 6-69.

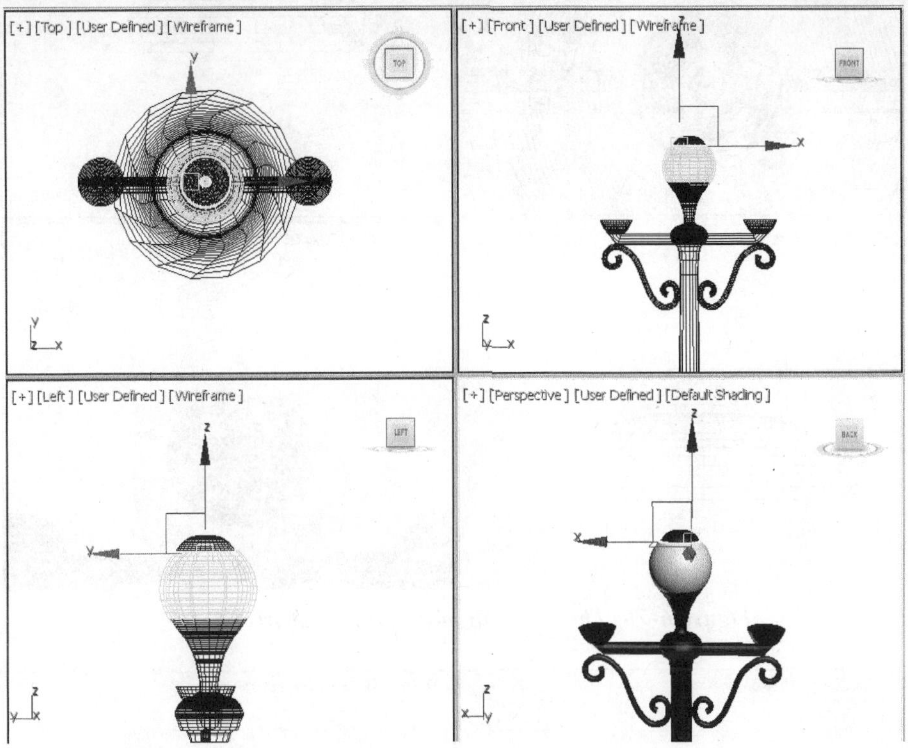

Figure 6-69 *The top01 aligned in the viewports*

5. Activate the Top viewport. Next, choose **Create > Geometry** from the **Command Panel**. Next, choose the **Sphere** tool from the **Object Type** rollout.

6. Expand the **Keyboard Entry** rollout. Next, enter **3.5** in the **Radius** spinner and choose the **Create** button; a sphere is created. Rename it as *top02*.

7. Choose the **Modify** tab from the **Command Panel**. Next, enter **0.6** in the **Hemisphere** spinner of the **Parameters** rollout.

8. Assign black color to *top02* and align it in the viewports, as shown in Figure 6-70.

9. Select *dome01*, *top01*, and *top02* from the Scene Explorer and group them as *lamp01*. Next, create 2 copies of *lamp01* with the name *lamp02* and *lamp03* and align them, as shown in Figure 6-71.

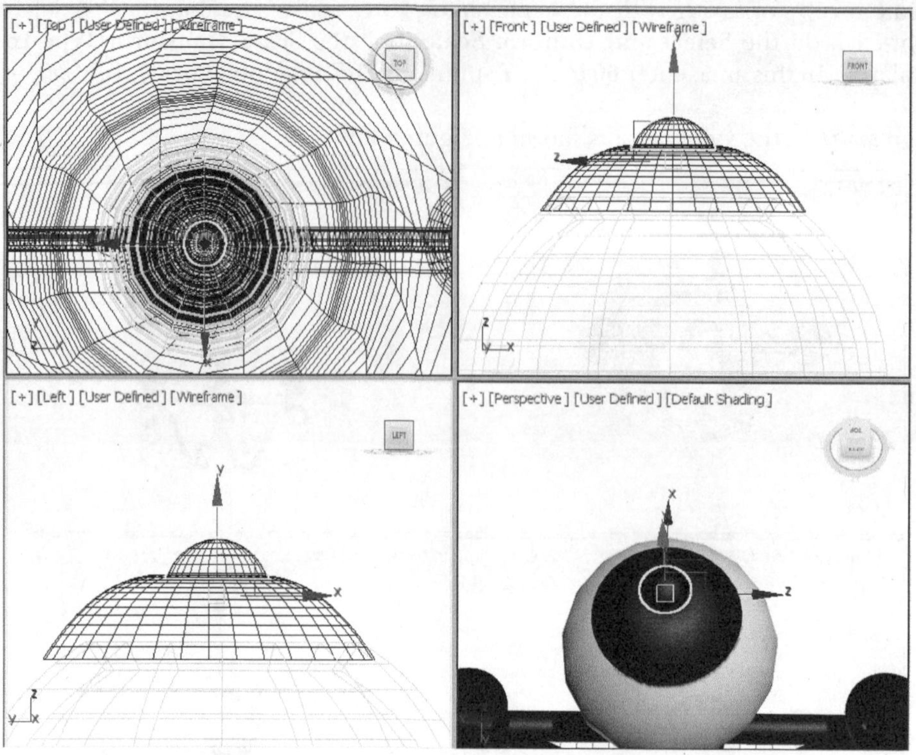

Figure 6-70 The top02 aligned in the viewports

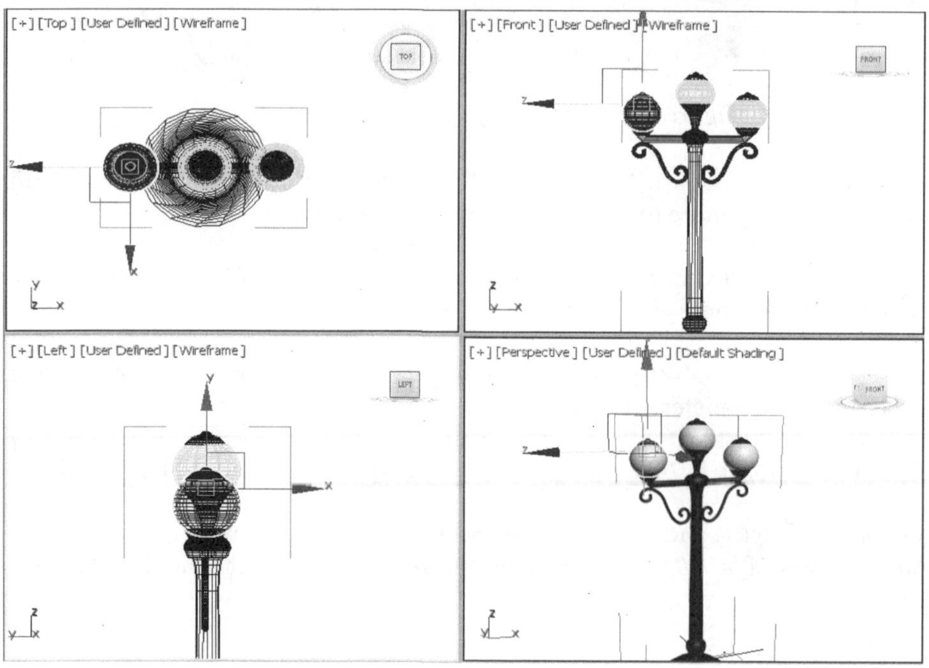

Figure 6-71 The lamp02 and lamp03 aligned in the viewports

10. Select all objects in the scene and group them as *street lamp*.

Saving and Rendering the Scene

In this section, you will save the scene and then render it. You can view the final rendered image of this scene by downloading the *c06_3dsmax_2017_rndr.zip* file from *www.cadcim.com*. The path of the file is as follows: *Textbooks > Animation and Visual Effects > 3ds Max > Autodesk 3ds Max 2017: A Comprehensive Guide*

1. Change the background color of the scene to white, as discussed in Tutorial 1 of Chapter 2. Next, choose **Save** from the **Application** menu.

2. Activate the Perspective viewport. Next, choose the **Render Production** tool from the **Main Toolbar**; the **Rendered Frame** window is displayed. This window shows the final output of the scene, refer to Figure 6-72.

Figure 6-72 *Final output of the street lamp after rendering*

Tutorial 2

In this tutorial, you will create the model of a vase with flower plant, by converting a 2D spline into a 3D mesh object, as shown in Figure 6-73. **(Expected time: 25 min)**

The following steps are required to complete this tutorial:

a. Create the project folder.
b. Create a line spline for the vase.

c. Apply the **Lathe** modifier.
d. Assign the material to the vase.
e. Create a stand for the vase.
f. Save and render the scene.

Figure 6-73 *The model of a vase with flower plant*

Creating the Project Folder
Create a new project folder with the name *c06_tut2* at *\Documents\3dsmax2017* and then save the file with the name *c06tut2*, as discussed in Tutorial 1 of Chapter 2.

Creating a Line Spline for the Vase
In this section, you will create a shape similar to the half portion of the vase using the **Line** tool.

1. Activate the Front viewport and choose **Create > Shapes** in the **Command Panel**; the **Splines** option is selected by default in the drop-down list below the **Shapes** button. Now, choose the **Line** tool from the **Object Type** rollout.

2. In the **Creation Method** rollout, select the **Corner** radio button in both the **Initial Type** and **Drag Type** areas.

3. Create a line spline as discussed in Tutorial 1. This spline should be similar to the half portion of the vase, refer to Figure 6-74.

4. Choose the **Modify** tab and select the **Vertex** sub-object level in the modifier stack; all vertices of the line spline are displayed in the viewport. Next, select the vertices one by one in the viewport and modify the shape by moving them to get a perfect shape.

Applying the Lathe Modifier
In this section, you will apply the **Lathe** modifier to convert the 2D spline into the 3D mesh object.

1. Select the first vertex of the spline in the Front viewport, as shown in Figure 6-75.

2. Choose **Modifiers > Patch/Spline Editing > Lathe** from the menu bar; the 2D line spline is converted into a 3D mesh object.

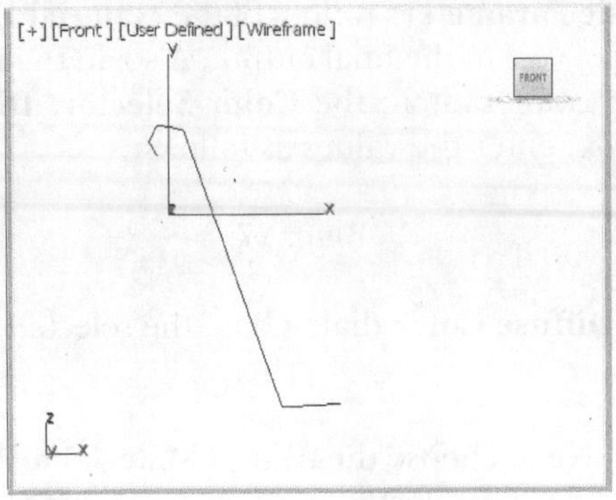

Figure 6-74 *A line spline created for the vase*

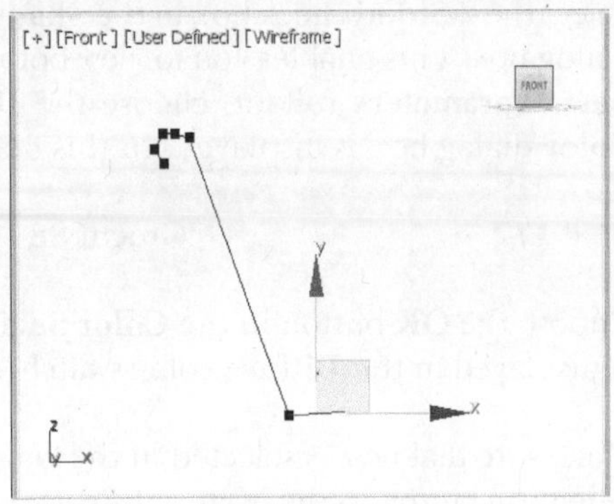

Figure 6-75 *The first vertex of the line spline selected in the Front viewport*

3. Name the new 3D mesh object as *vase*. Also, click anywhere in the viewport to deselect the *vase*.

4. Choose the **Zoom Extents All** tool; the entire *vase* is displayed in the viewports, as shown in Figure 6-76.

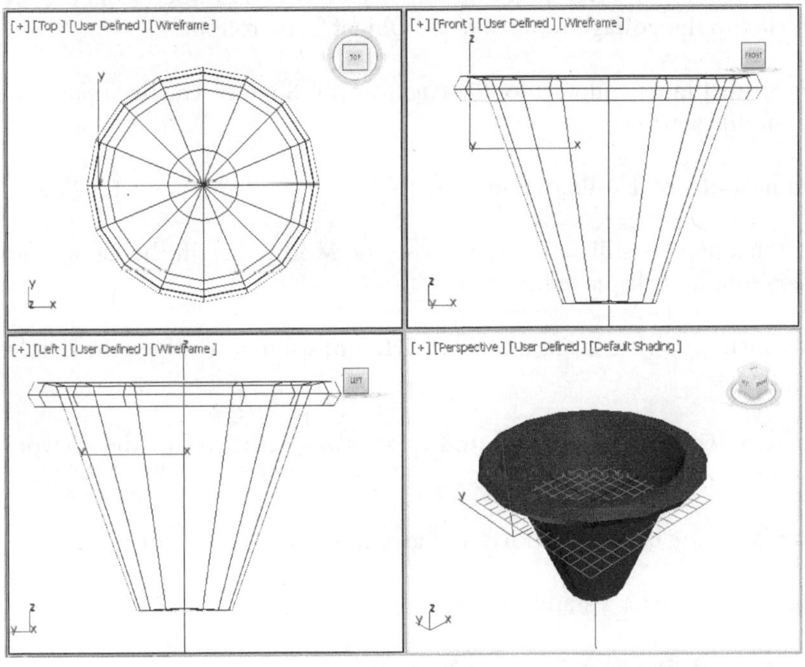

Figure 6-76 *The vase geometry after applying the* ***Lathe*** *modifier*

Assigning Material to Vase

In this section, you will assign the material to *vase* using the **Material Editor** tool as discussed in Tutorial 1 of this chapter.

1. Choose **Rendering > Material Editor > Compact Material Editor** from the menu bar; the **Material Editor** dialog box is displayed.

2. Select the **2-Sided** check box in the **Shader Basic Parameters** rollout of the **Material Editor** dialog box. This enables you to view both sides of *vase* in the final output. Also, in the **Blinn Basic Parameters** rollout, choose the **Diffuse** color swatch; the **Color Selector: Diffuse Color** dialog box is displayed. In this dialog box, enter the values as follows:

   Red: **177** Green: **88** Blue: **27**

   Choose the **OK** button in the **Color Selector: Diffuse Color** dialog box; the selected color is displayed in the **Diffuse** color swatch.

3. Make sure that *vase* is selected in the viewports. Next, choose the **Assign Material to Selection** button in the **Material Editor** dialog box; the selected material is assigned to *vase* in the viewport. Next, choose the **Show Shaded Material in Viewport** button in the same dialog box to view the material in viewport. Next, close the **Material Editor** dialog box.

   Next, you need to use the **Foliage** tool to put a plant in *vase*.

4. Activate the Top viewport. Choose **Create > Geometry** in the **Command Panel**; a drop-down list is displayed below the **Geometry** button. Select **AEC Extended** from the drop-down list and then choose the **Foliage** tool from the **Object Type** rollout.

5. In the **Favorite Plants** rollout, double-click on the **Society Garlic** foliage; the foliage is displayed in the viewports.

6. In the **Name and Color** rollout, name the foliage to *plant* and press ENTER.

7. Make sure that *plant* is still selected. Choose the **Modify** tab in the **Command Panel**; the **Parameters** rollout is displayed.

8. In the **Parameters** rollout, set a value in the **Height** spinner to adjust the height of the *plant* according to *vase*.

9. Choose the **Select and Move** tool and align *plant* with *vase* in the viewports, refer to Figure 6-77.

10. Select *plant* and *vase* in the viewports and group them as *flower vase*.

   Next, you need to create a stand for *flower vase*.

Creating a Stand for the Flower Vase

In this section, you will create a stand for *flower vase*.

1. Select *flower vase* and right-click on it; a quad menu is displayed. Choose the **Hide Selection** option from it; *flower vase* disappears temporarily from the viewports. Now, you can work easily in the viewports.

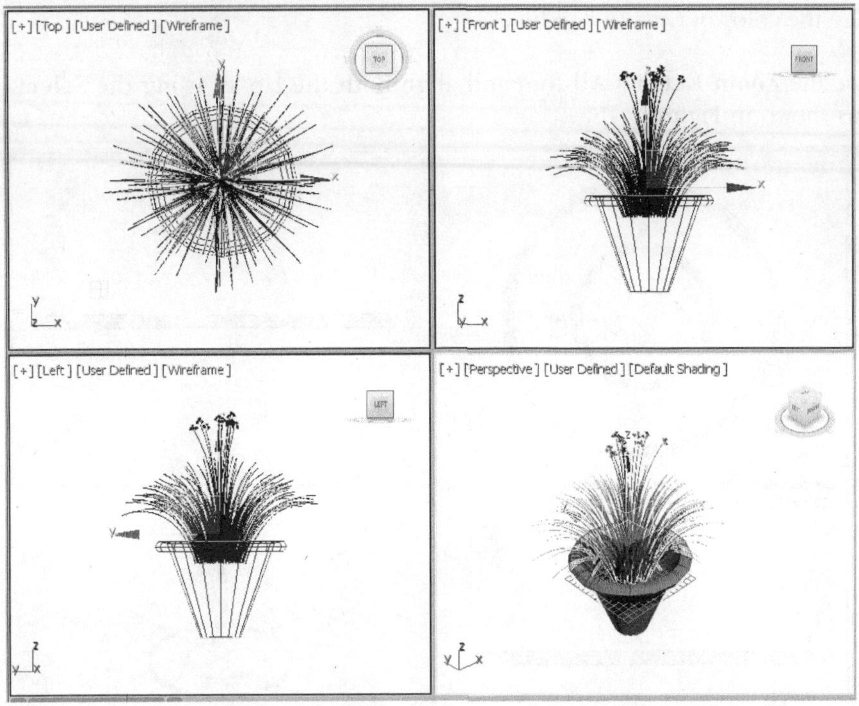

Figure 6-77 *Alignment of plant with vase in viewports*

2. Activate the Top viewport. Choose **Create > Shapes** in the **Command Panel**; the **Splines** option is selected by default in the drop-down list below the **Shapes** button. Now, choose the **Circle** tool from the **Object Type** rollout and create a circular spline.

3. In the **Parameters** rollout, set the radius of the circle to **11.662** in the **Radius** spinner.

   You may need to modify the radius according to the scene in the later section.

4. Expand the **Rendering** rollout and select the **Enable In Renderer** and **Enable In Viewport** check boxes. Select the **Radial** radio button, if it is not already selected. Also, make sure that the **Auto Smooth** check box is selected. Now, enter the values as follows:

   Thickness: **2.0** Sides: **15** Angle: **0.99**

5. The circular spline is automatically named as *Circle001*. Now, change its color by entering the values as follows:

   Red: **193** Green: **193** Blue: **193**

6. Create another circle in the Top viewport. It is automatically named as *Circle002*.

7. In the **Parameters** rollout, set the radius value of *Circle002*. This radius should be double the radius of *Circle001*.

8. Change the color of *Circle002* to black.

9. Choose the **Zoom Extents All** tool and align both the circles using the **Select and Move** tool, as shown in Figure 6-78.

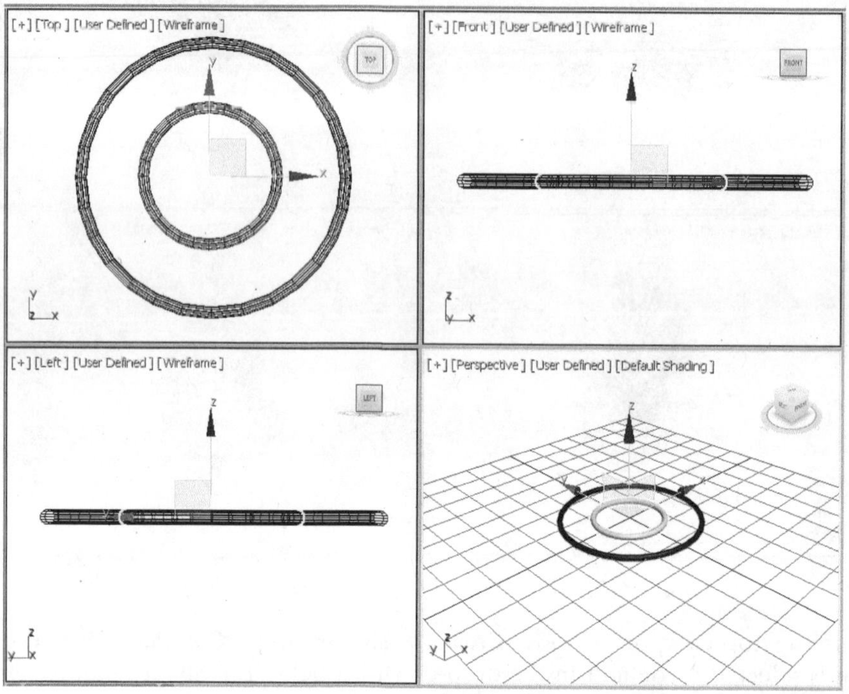

Figure 6-78 Alignment of the circles in viewports

10. Choose the **Line** tool from **Create > Shapes > Splines > Object Type** rollout.

11. In the **Creation Method** rollout, select the **Corner** radio button in the **Initial Type** and **Drag Type** areas.

12. Activate the Top viewport. Next, create four line splines to join both the circles, as shown in Figure 6-79.

13. Assign black color to all line splines.

14. Select the line splines and both the circles in any viewport by dragging a selection box around them, and then group them as *upper portion*.

15. Select *upper portion* and hide it temporarily as described earlier.

    Next, you need to create the legs for the stand using the **Line** tool.

16. Activate the Front viewport. Next, choose the **Line** tool from **Create > Shapes > Splines > Object Type** rollout.

17. In the **Creation Method** rollout, select the **Smooth** radio button in both the **Initial Type** and **Drag Type** areas.

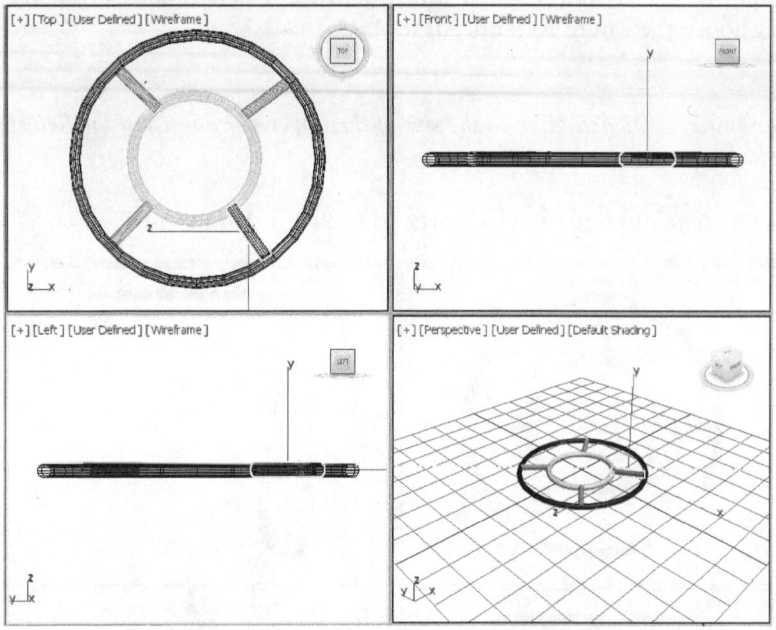

Figure 6-79 *The line splines created to join both the circles*

18. Create a line spline in the Front viewport, as shown in Figure 6-80. It uses the same parameters from the **Rendering** rollout that you had set earlier.

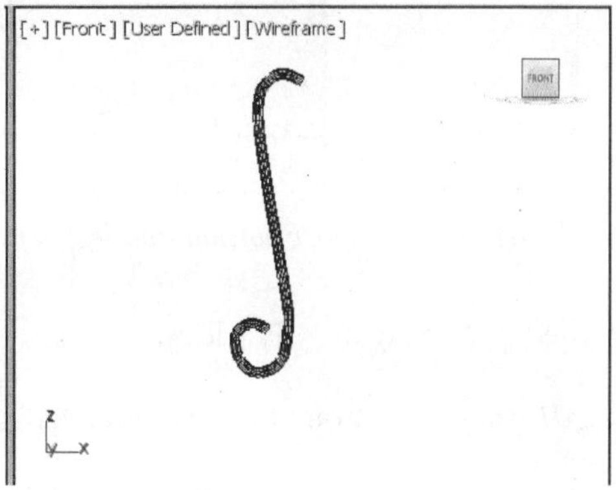

Figure 6-80 *The line spline for the leg of stand*

19. In the **Rendering** rollout, make sure that the **Enable In Renderer** and **Enable In Viewport** check boxes are selected. Select the **Rectangular** radio button and enter the values as follows:

Length: **2.0** Width: **1.5** Angle: **0.0**

20. Name the line spline as *leg01* and change its color to black.

21. Right-click in any of the viewports; a quad menu is displayed. Choose the **Unhide by Name** option; the **Unhide Objects** dialog box is displayed. Select *upper portion* from the list given in this dialog box and choose the **Unhide** button; *upper portion* is now displayed in the viewport. Choose the **Zoom Extents All** tool.

Note
You can resize leg01 according to the size of the upper portion using the ***Select and Uniform Scale*** *tool.*

22. Align *upper portion* and *leg01* in viewports, as shown in Figure 6-81.

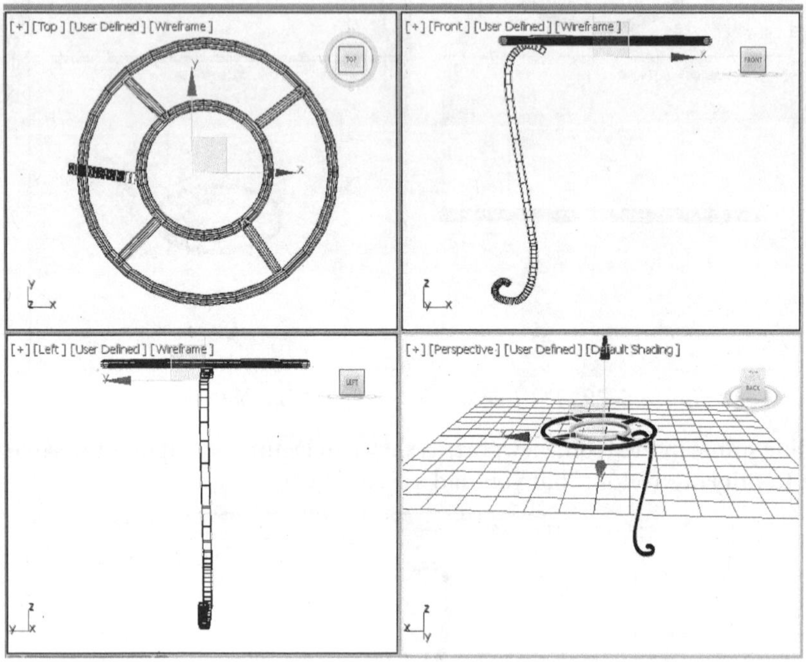

Figure 6-81 *Alignment of upper portion and leg01 in viewports*

Next, you need to copy the *leg01* to create other legs.

23. Create three copies of *leg01*; they are automatically named as *leg002*, *leg003*, and *leg004*.

24. Align *leg01*, *leg002*, *leg003*, and *leg004* using the **Select and Move** and **Select and Rotate** tools, as shown in Figure 6-82.

25. Select all the objects in the viewport and group them as *vase stand*.

26. Right-click on the viewport; a quad menu is displayed. Choose the **Unhide All** option; all the hidden objects are displayed in the viewports.

27. Align *flower vase* and *vase stand* and choose the **Zoom Extents All** tool, refer to Figure 6-83.

Note

You can adjust the size of the flower vase according to the size of the vase stand using the ***Select and Uniform Scale*** *tool.*

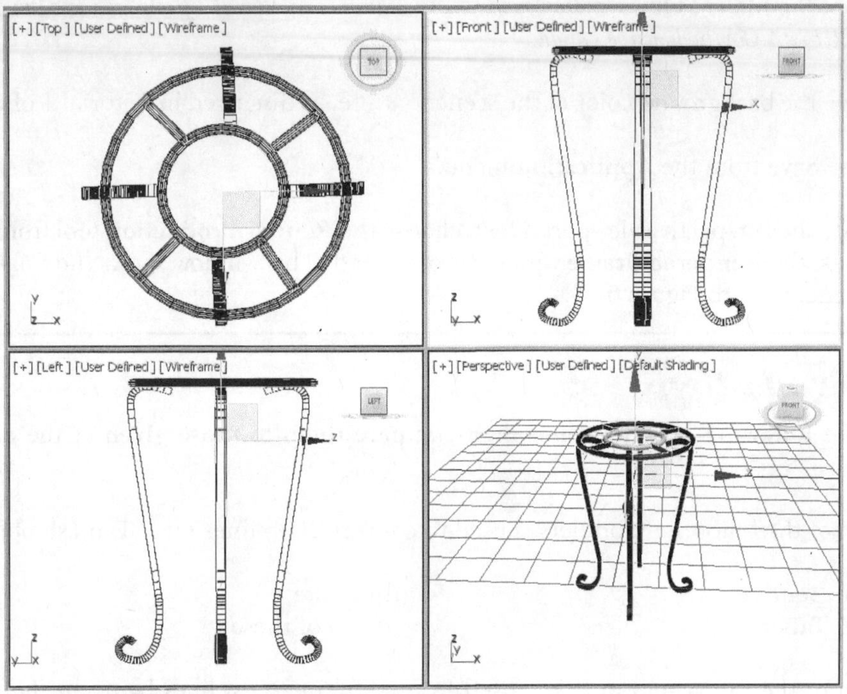

Figure 6-82 *Alignment of leg01, leg002, leg003, and leg004 in viewports*

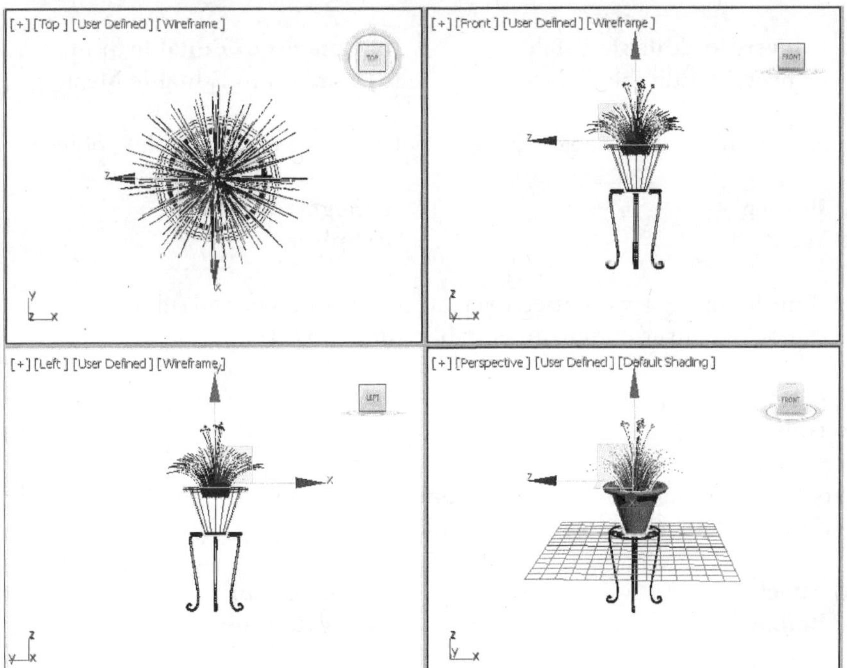

Figure 6-83 *Alignment of flower vase and vase stand in viewports*

Saving and Rendering the Scene

In this section, you will save the scene and then render it. You can also view the final rendered image of this model by downloading the *c06_3dsmax_2017_rndr.zip* file from *www.cadcim.com*. The path of the file is as follows: *Textbooks > Animation and Visual Effects > 3ds Max > Autodesk 3ds Max 2017: A Comprehensive Guide*

1. Change the background color of the scene to white, as discussed in Tutorial 1 of Chapter 2.

2. Choose **Save** from the **Application** menu.

3. Activate the Perspective viewport. Next, choose the **Render Production** tool from the **Main Toolbar**; the **Rendered Frame** window is displayed. This window shows the final output of the scene, refer to Figure 6-73.

Self-Evaluation Test

Answer the following questions and then compare them to those given at the end of this chapter:

1. Which of the following modifiers is used to convert 2D splines into 3D mesh objects?

   (a) **Bend** (b) **Lathe**
   (c) **Taper** (d) All of these

2. Which of the following options is used to modify the 2D splines by using the sub-object levels?

   (a) **Convert to Editable Patch** (b) **Convert to Editable Spline**
   (c) **Convert to Editable Poly** (d) **Convert to Editable Mesh**

3. Which of the following sub-object levels is not a part of editable spline objects?

   (a) **Border** (b) **Segment**
   (c) **Vertex** (d) **Spline**

4. Which of the following tools is used to create a spline that has all sub-object levels by default and need not be converted into an editable spline object?

   (a) **Circle** (b) **Line**
   (c) **Helix** (d) **Star**

5. Which of the following buttons in the **Geometry** rollout is used to create a new line that will automatically get attached to a selected spline?

   (a) **Attach** (b) **Attach Mult.**
   (c) **Refine** (d) **Create Line**

6. The __________ button in the **Geometry** rollout is used to add new vertices to a selected spline in the viewport.

7. The __________ button in the **Geometry** rollout is used to join multiple vertices into a single vertex.

8. The __________ button in the **Geometry** rollout is used to make a vertex of a spline as the first vertex.

9. The pivot point of an object represents its local center. (T/F)

10. The **Weld** button is used to move all selected vertices of a spline to their average center. (T/F)

Review Questions

Answer the following questions:

1. Which of the following buttons in the **Geometry** rollout of an editable spline object is used to create round corners in the spline by creating two new vertices?

   (a) **Fillet** (b) **Fuse**
   (c) **Chamfer** (d) All of these

2. Which of the following buttons in the **Geometry** rollout of an editable spline object is used to sub-divide the selected segment?

   (a) **Refine** (b) **Insert**
   (c) **Divide** (d) All of these

3. Which of the following buttons in the **Geometry** rollout of an editable spline object is used to separate the selected sub-objects from the original one and create a new shape?

   (a) **Attach** (b) **Delete**
   (c) **Detach** (d) **Divide**

4. The **Weld** button is available only for the __________ sub-object level.

5. The __________ button is used to create the outline of an object.

6. The __________ button is used to break up a spline into a number of splines.

7. The **Reverse** button is used to display the number of vertices in the viewport. (T/F)

8. To perform the boolean operation, the two splines must be closed, attached, and also must intersect each other. (T/F)

9. The **Mirror** button is used to create a copy of the spline. (T/F)

10. To attach multiple objects simultaneously to a selected object, you need to choose the **Attach Mult.** button in the **Geometry** rollout. (T/F)

EXERCISES

The rendered output of the models used in the Exercise 1 to Exercise 5 can be accessed by downloading the *c06_3dsmax_2017_exr.zip* from *www.cadcim.com*. The path of the file is as follows: *Textbooks > Animation and Visual Effects > 3ds Max > Autodesk 3ds Max 2017: A Comprehensive Guide*

Exercise 1

Create a pair of cocktail glasses, as shown in Figure 6-84, using your own dimensions.

(Expected time: 15 min)

Figure 6-84 *The pair of cocktail glasses*

Exercise 2

Create a set of vases, as shown in Figure 6-85, using your own dimensions.

(Expected time: 15 min)

Figure 6-85 *Set of vases*

Exercise 3

Create a candle stand, as shown in Figure 6-86, using your own dimensions.

(Expected time: 15 min)

Figure 6-86 A candle stand

Exercise 4

Create a pair of glasses, as shown in Figure 6-87, using your own dimensions.

(Expected time: 15 min)

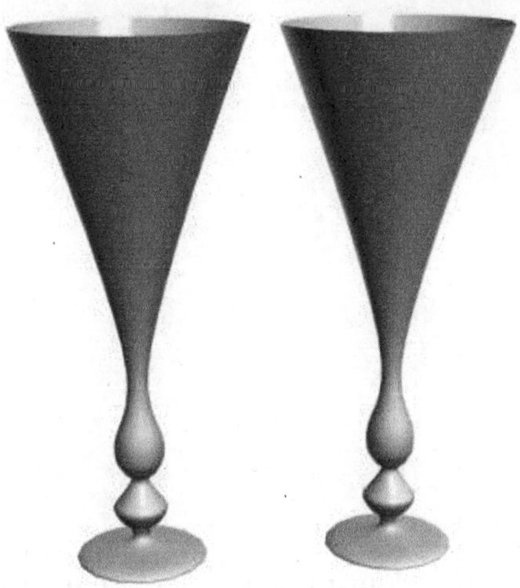

Figure 6-87 The pair of glasses

Exercise 5

Create a pair of glasses, as shown in Figure 6-88, using your own dimensions.

(Expected time: 15 min)

Figure 6-88 *The pair of glasses*

Answers to Self-Evaluation Test

1. b, **2.** b, **3.** a, **4.** b, **5.** d, **6. Refine**, **7. Weld**, **8. Make First**, **9.** T, **10.** F

7

Materials and Maps

Learning Objectives

After completing this chapter, you will be able to:

- *Use the Material Editor dialog box*
- *Understand the types of materials and maps*
- *Create materials and maps*
- *Assign materials to objects*

INTRODUCTION

In this chapter, you will learn to assign various materials and maps to the objects in a scene to make it more realistic. Materials are used to describe the reflection or transmission of light of an object. Maps are used to simulate texture, and apply designs, reflection, refraction, and other effects. To assign materials and maps, you need to use the **Material Editor** tool from the **Main Toolbar**, which is discussed next.

MATERIAL EDITOR

Menu bar:	Rendering > Material Editor > Compact/Slate Material Editor
Main Toolbar:	Material Editor flyout > Compact/Slate Material Editor
Keyboard:	M

In 3ds Max, there are two types of material editors, Slate Material Editor and Compact Material Editor. You can use any of these material editors to create new materials and maps, modify the existing materials, apply these new materials and maps to the models in the scene, and create a new environment for the scene. The Slate Material Editor uses nodes and wiring to graphically display the design of the materials created by you. The Compact Material Editor is easy and stripped down version of Slate Material Editor.

To create a new material, press the M key; the **Slate Material Editor** dialog box will be displayed, as shown in Figure 7-1. Next, if you choose **Modes > Compact Material Editor** from the material editor menu bar, the **Material Editor** dialog box will be displayed, as shown in Figure 7-2. The title bar of the **Material Editor** dialog box displays the name and number of the current material, which gets changed depending on the material that you select. The **Material Editor** dialog box is divided into various areas, refer to Figure 7-2. These areas are discussed next.

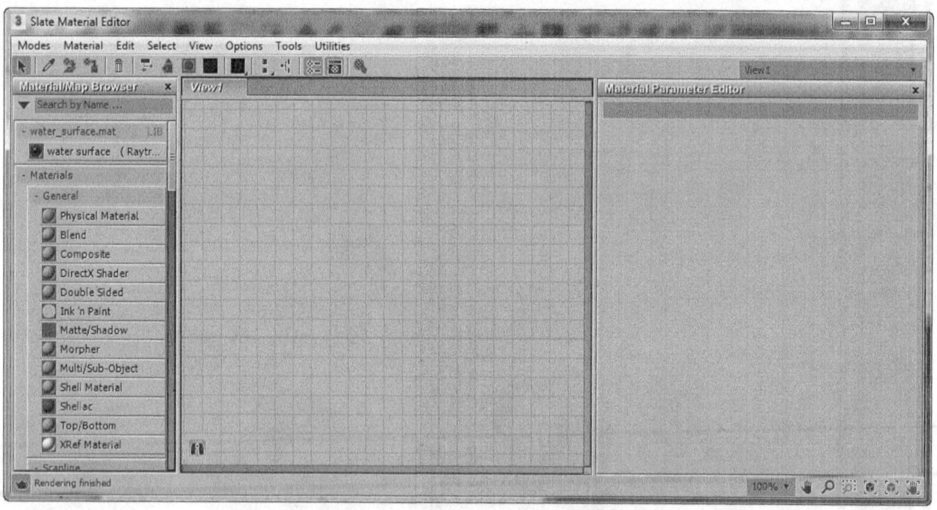

*Figure 7-1 The **Slate Material Editor** dialog box*

Note

*When you press the M key, the material editor that you opened last in 3ds Max will be displayed. However, if you press the M key for the first time in 3ds Max, then the **Slate Material Editor** will be displayed.*

INTRODUCTION

In this chapter, you will learn to assign various materials and maps to the objects in a scene to make it more realistic. Materials are used to describe the reflection or transmission of light of an object. Maps are used to simulate texture, and apply designs, reflection, refraction, and other effects. To assign materials and maps, you need to use the **Material Editor** tool from the **Main Toolbar**, which is discussed next.

MATERIAL EDITOR

Menu bar: Rendering > Material Editor > Compact/Slate Material Editor
Main Toolbar: Material Editor flyout > Compact/Slate Material Editor
Keyboard: M

In 3ds Max, there are two types of material editors, Slate Material Editor and Compact Material Editor. You can use any of these material editors to create new materials and maps, modify the existing materials, apply these new materials and maps to the models in the scene, and create a new environment for the scene. The Slate Material Editor uses nodes and wiring to graphically display the design of the materials created by you. The Compact Material Editor is easy and stripped down version of Slate Material Editor.

To create a new material, press the M key; the **Slate Material Editor** dialog box will be displayed, as shown in Figure 7-1. Next, if you choose **Modes > Compact Material Editor** from the material editor menu bar, the **Material Editor** dialog box will be displayed, as shown in Figure 7-2. The title bar of the **Material Editor** dialog box displays the name and number of the current material, which gets changed depending on the material that you select. The **Material Editor** dialog box is divided into various areas, refer to Figure 7-2. These areas are discussed next.

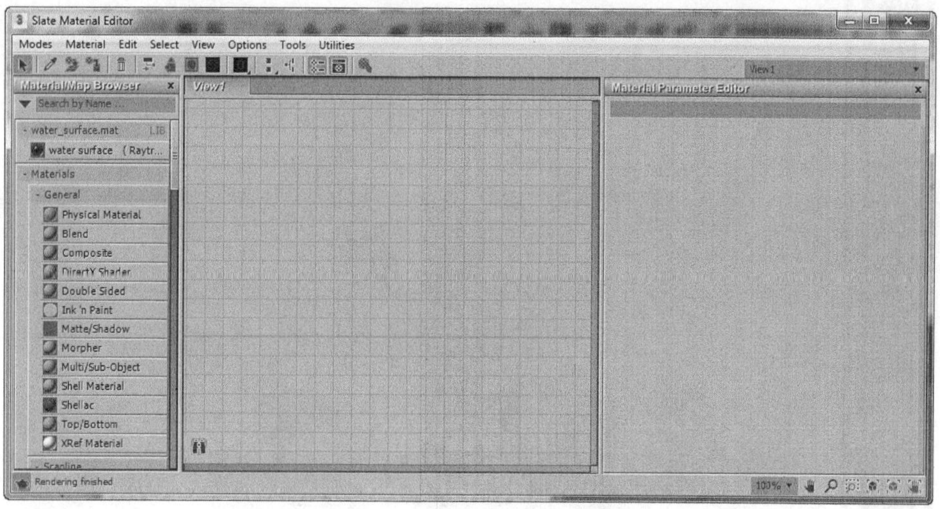

*Figure 7-1 The **Slate Material Editor** dialog box*

Note

*When you press the M key, the material editor that you opened last in 3ds Max will be displayed. However, if you press the M key for the first time in 3ds Max, then the **Slate Material Editor** will be displayed.*

7

Materials and Maps

Learning Objectives

After completing this chapter, you will be able to:

- *Use the Material Editor dialog box*
- *Understand the types of materials and maps*
- *Create materials and maps*
- *Assign materials to objects*

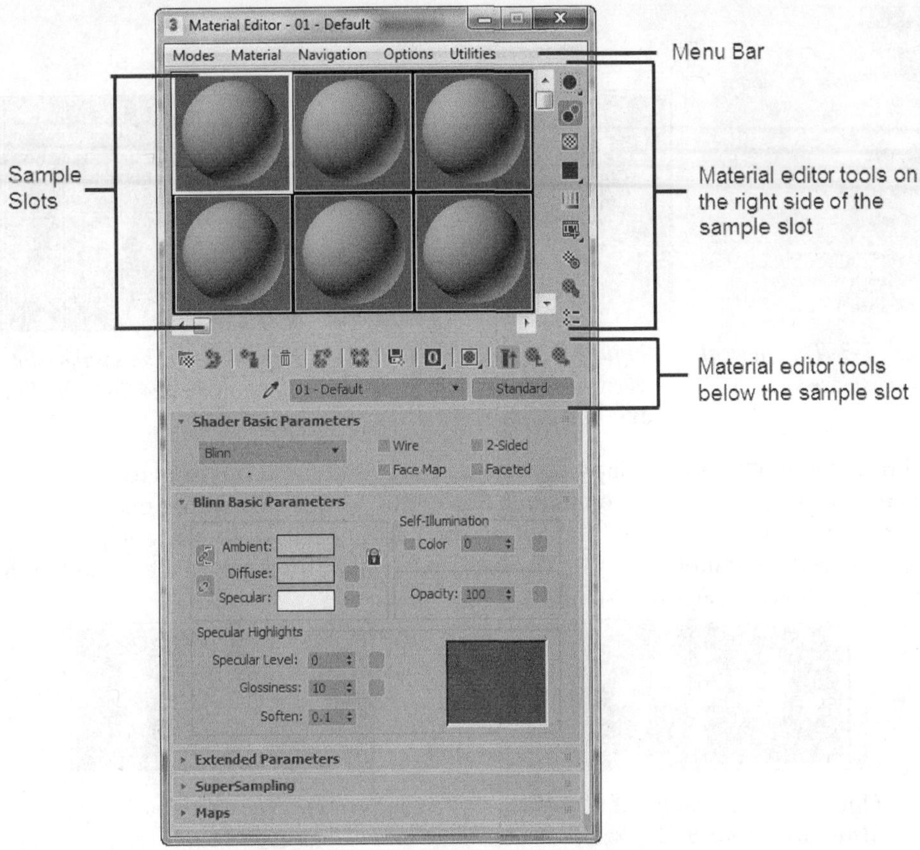

*Figure 7-2 The **Material Editor** dialog box*

Menu Bar

The menu bar is located at the top of the **Material Editor** dialog box. It consists of various pull-down menus such as **Material**, **Navigation**, and so on. The options in these pull-down menus are used to choose various tools. These tools can also be invoked using the options available below as well as on the right side of the sample slots in the **Material Editor** dialog box, refer to Figure 7-2.

Sample Slots

The sample slots in the **Material Editor** dialog box are used to preview the material or the maps that are assigned to the objects in the viewport. By default, there are 6 slots which can be extended to 24 slots and each sample slot represents a single material or map. To view other sample slots, move the scroll bar available on the right, and just below the sample slots. You can also increase the number of visible sample slots. To do so, select one of the sample slots; it will be surrounded by a white colored boundary and will get activated. Next, right-click on the active sample slot; a shortcut menu will be displayed, as shown in Figure 7-3. By default, the **3x2 Sample Windows** option is chosen in the shortcut menu. Next, choose the required option; the number of visible sample slots will be increased accordingly, refer to Figures 7-4 and 7-5.

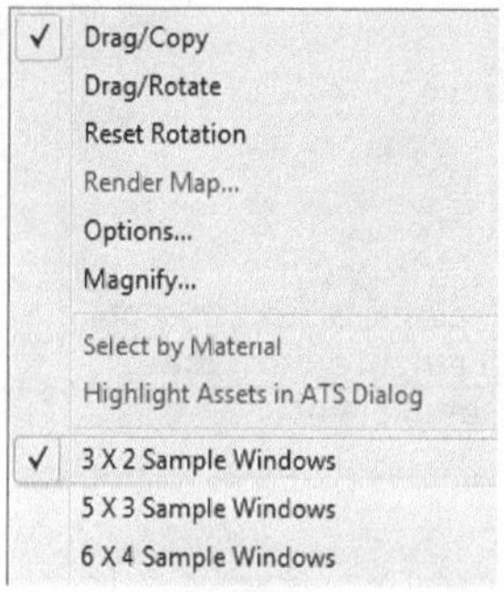

Figure 7-3 The shortcut menu displayed

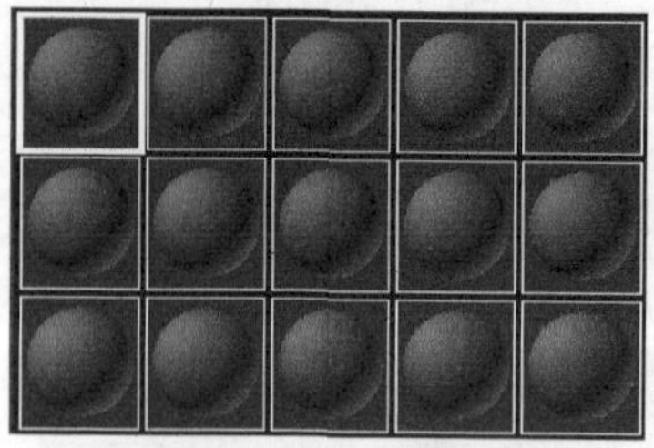

*Figure 7-4 The sample slots after choosing the **5x3 Sample Windows** option*

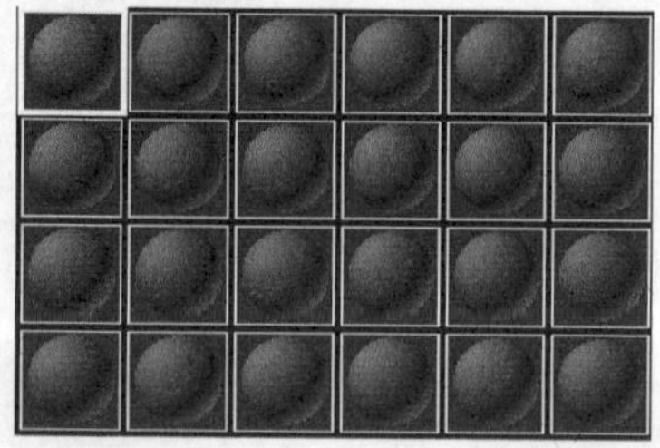

*Figure 7-5 The sample slots after choosing the **6x4 Sample Windows** option*

In the shortcut menu, the **Drag/Copy** option is chosen by default. It is used to copy the material or the map from one sample slot to another. Select the sample slot, whose material or map you want to copy. Next, press and hold the left mouse button on it, drag it to another sample slot, and then release the left mouse button; the same material or the map will be copied to the other sample slot, as shown in Figures 7-6 and 7-7.

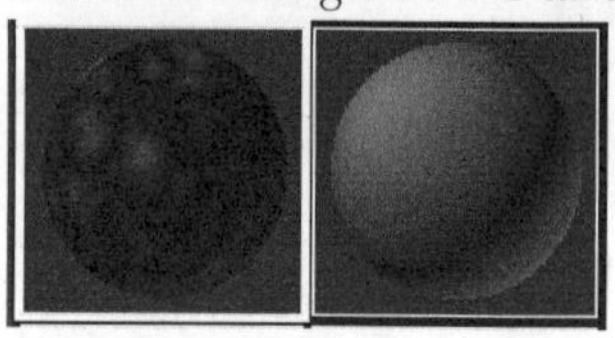

*Figure 7-6 Two sample slots in the **Material Editor** dialog box*

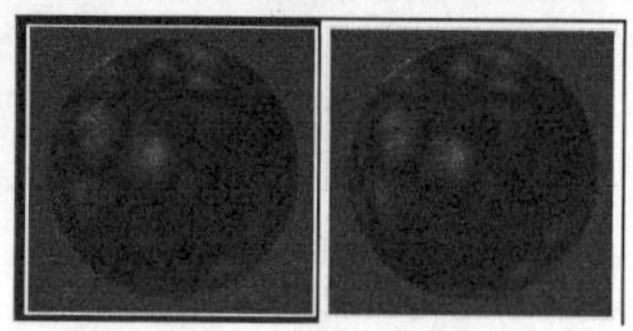

Figure 7-7 The map/material of one sample slot copied to the other

On choosing the **Drag/Rotate** option in the shortcut menu, the shape of the cursor will change. Now, you can view the material map on the sample slot by rotating it. The **Reset Rotation** option in the shortcut menu is used to reset the sample slot to its default orientation. By default, the **Render Map** option in the shortcut menu is not activated. It will be activated on assigning a map to the sample slot. This option is used to render the map in the selected sample slot by creating a bitmap or an *avi* file (if the map is animated). When you choose the **Options** option, the **Material Editor Options** dialog box will be displayed. The options in this dialog box are used to modify the sample slots.

Choose the **Magnify** option; the selected sample slot will be displayed in an enlarged window, as shown in Figure 7-8. Alternatively, double-click on the selected sample slot to display it in an enlarged window. To resize the window, move the cursor at the bottom of the window; the cursor will change to a double-headed arrow. Now, drag the cursor to resize the window.

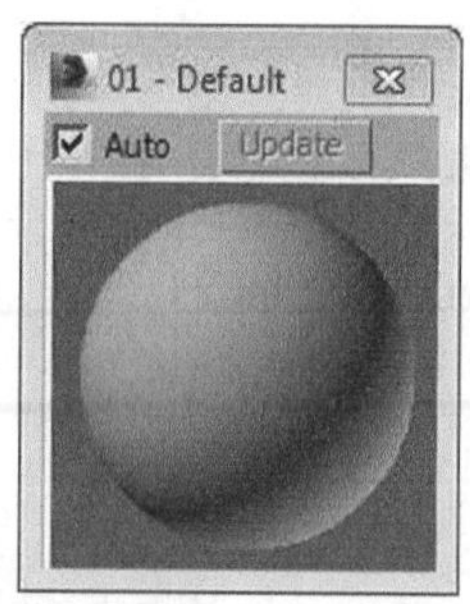

Figure 7-8 The sample slot displayed in a separate window

Material Editor Tools

The material editor tools are used to modify the default settings of the selected sample slot, and apply the materials or the maps to the objects. These tools are available below as well as on the right side of the sample slots in the **Material Editor** dialog box. The most commonly used tools are discussed next.

Get Material

Material Editor Menu:	Material > Get Material
Material Toolbar:	Get Material
Keyboard:	G

The **Get Material** tool is used to get a material or a map for the selected sample slot. Materials affect the color, opacity, glossiness, and other physical properties of objects.

To get a material, select one of the sample slots to activate it. Choose the **Get Material** tool available below the sample slots; the **Material/Map Browser** dialog box with a list of materials and maps will be displayed, as shown in Figure 7-9.

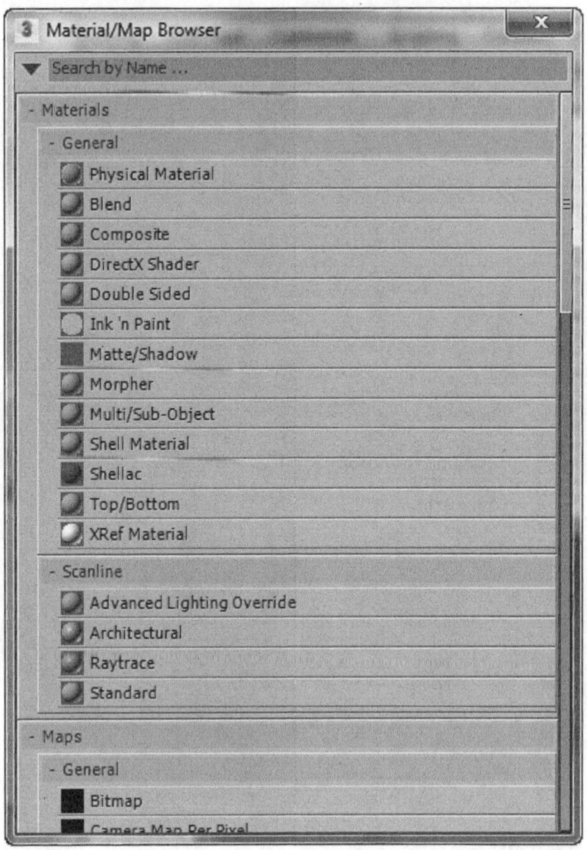

***Figure 7-9** Partial view of the rollouts in the **Material/Map Browser** dialog box*

You can collapse and expand this list as required. Now, double-click on one of the materials or maps from the list; the default material will be replaced by the new material or map. Also, the new material will be displayed on the sample slot in the **Sample Slots** rollout of the **Material/ Map Browser** dialog box. The **Material/Map Browser** dialog box is discussed next.

Note

*The shortcut key G mentioned above will work only if the **Keyboard Shortcut Override Toggle** tool in the **Main Toolbar** is activated and the **Material Editor** dialog box is displayed.*

Material/Map Browser

The **Material/Map Browser** dialog box is used to select different types of materials and maps from the lists displayed in it. Various options in this dialog box are discussed next.

Search by Name: The **Search by Name** text box is located on the top of this dialog box. It is used to search and select the name of the materials or the maps. For example, enter the alphabet **d** in this text box; a drop-down list of all the materials and maps starting with the alphabet d will be displayed, as shown in Figure 7-10. You can double-click on the required material or map; it will be displayed on the selected sample slot. Now, choose the **Clear Results** button on the right side of the text box; the drop-down list will be cleared.

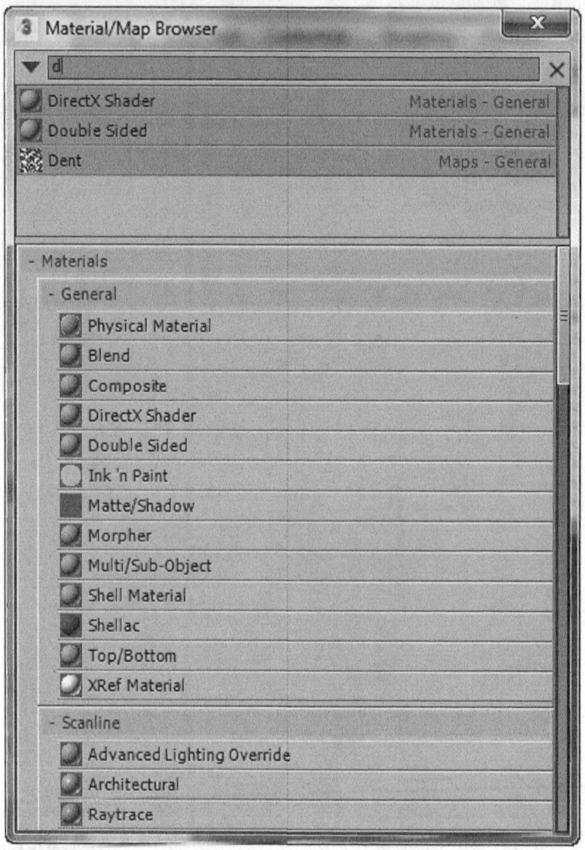

***Figure 7-10** The drop-down list displayed after entering the alphabet **d** in the text box*

Material/Map Browser Options: The **Material/Map Browser Options** button is located on the left of the **Search by Name** text box. Choose the **Material/Map Browser Options** button; a flyout with various options will be displayed, as shown in Figure 7-11. The options in this flyout are used to manage the **Material/Map Browser** dialog box based on the requirement. Also, these options will help you to create new material library, manage Autodesk material library, and so on. These options are discussed next.

The **New Group** option is used to create a new group and add it to the **Material/Map Browser** dialog box. Choose the **New Group** option from the flyout; the **Create New Group** dialog box will be displayed, as shown in Figure 7-12. Type a name of your choice in the text box and then choose the **OK** button; a new group with the specified name will be displayed in the **Material/Map Browser** dialog box. You can expand and collapse the group as required.

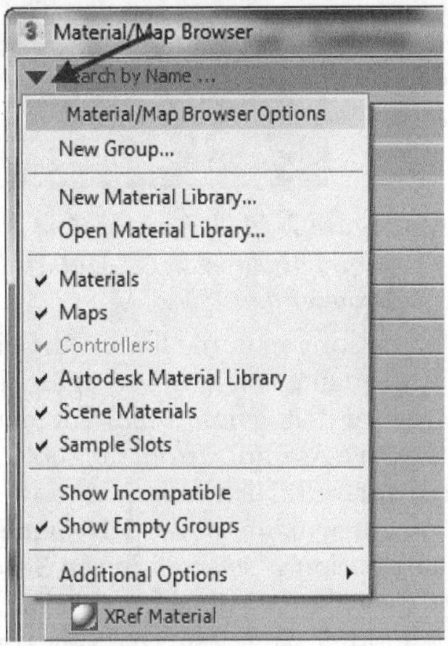

***Figure 7-11** The flyout displayed after choosing the **Material/Map Browser Options** button*

***Figure 7-12** The **Create New Group** dialog box*

When you install 3ds Max, the material libraries will automatically get installed in your system in the *.mat* format. To select the material library of your choice, choose the **Open Material Library** option from the shortcut menu; the **Import Material Library** dialog box will be displayed. Navigate to the location C:*Program Files\Autodesk\3ds Max 2017\materiallibraries*; the material libraries will be displayed in the **Import Material Library** dialog box, as shown in Figure 7-13. Next, select the required material library and choose the **Open** button; all materials of the selected material library will be displayed in the **Material/Map Browser** dialog box, refer to Figure 7-14.

You can also create a new library to put all materials and maps defined in the sample slots of the current file. To create a new library, choose the **New Material Library** option from the shortcut menu; the **Create New Material Library** dialog box will be displayed, as shown in Figure 7-15. Type a name in the text box and choose the **Save** button, a new library with the specified name will be displayed in the **Material/Map Browser** dialog box. Next, you can put the materials defined in the sample slots to the new library using the **Put To Library** tool in the **Material Editor** dialog box.

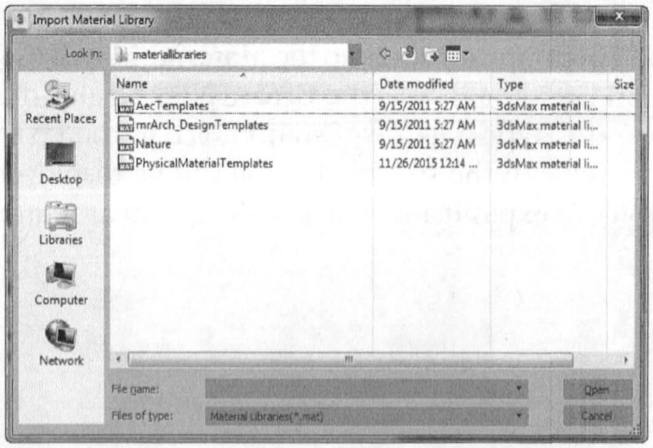

*Figure 7-13 The **Import Material Library** dialog box*

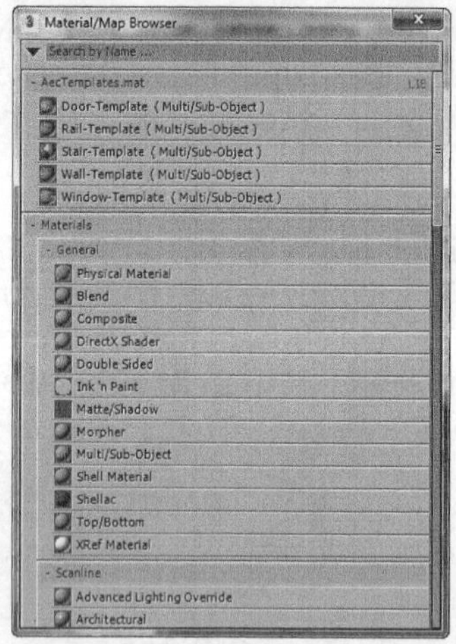

*Figure 7-14 The materials of the selected library displayed in the **Material/Map Browser** dialog box*

When you create a new material library or open an existing material library, the library will have a name and location assigned to it. To modify the name and location, right-click on the title bar of the new library in the **Material/Map Browser** dialog box; a shortcut menu will be displayed, as shown in Figure 7-16. Now, choose the **Save As** option from the shortcut menu; the **Export Material Library** dialog box will be displayed. Next, navigate to the location where you want to save the new library. Also, type a new name in the **File name** text box and make sure that the **Material Libraries (*.mat)** option is selected in the **Save as type** drop-down list. Now, choose the **Save** button; the new library will be saved at the specified location. You can use the newly created library in another scene. Alternatively, you can use the **Rename Group** option from the shortcut menu to change the name of the library.

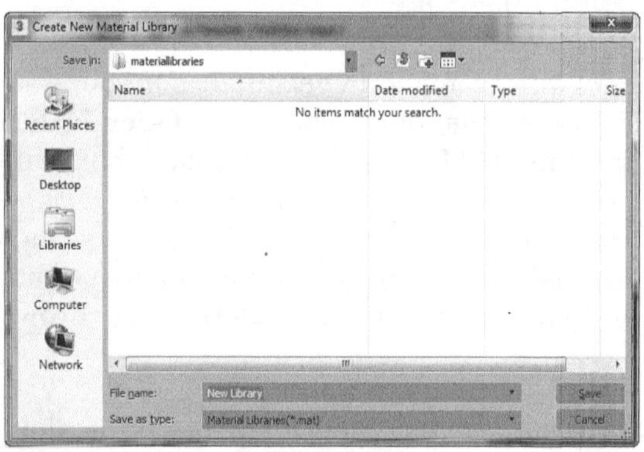

*Figure 7-15 The **Create New Material Library** dialog box*

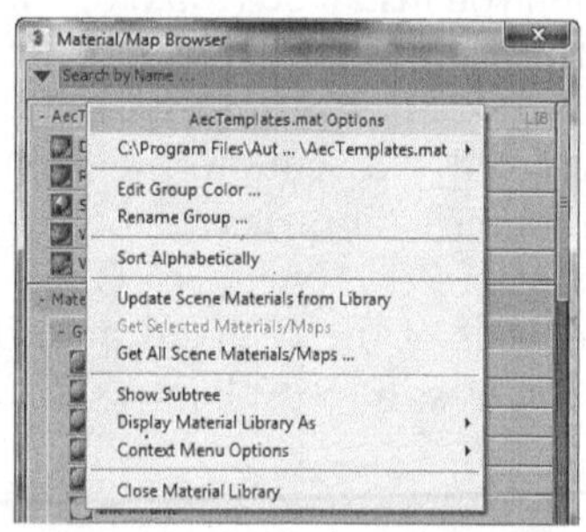

Figure 7-16 The shortcut menu displayed

There are various rollouts such as **Materials**, **Maps**, **Scene Materials**, and **Sample Slots** in the **Material/Map Browser** dialog box. You can toggle the display of these groups by choosing the respective option from the shortcut menu.

You can also reset the **Material/Map Browser** dialog box to its default appearance. Choose the **Additional Options** option from the flyout; a cascading menu will be displayed. Now, choose the **Reset Material/Map Browser** option; the **Reset Material/Map Browser** message box will be displayed. Choose the **Yes** button from this message box; the **Material/Map Browser** dialog box will be reset to its default appearance.

Note

*When you right-click on a material or map in the **Material/Map Browser** dialog box, a shortcut menu will be displayed. On choosing the **Copy to** option from this shortcut menu, a cascading menu will be displayed. You can copy the material or map to a temporary material library or to a new material library using the options available in this cascading menu.*

Assign Material to Selection

Material Editor Menu:	Material > Assign to Selection
Toolbar:	Assign Material to Selection

The **Assign Material to Selection** button is used to assign the material or map from the active sample slot to the selected object in the viewport. On choosing the **Assign Material to Selection** button, the active sample slot will be surrounded by four triangles at corners, as shown in Figure 7-17.

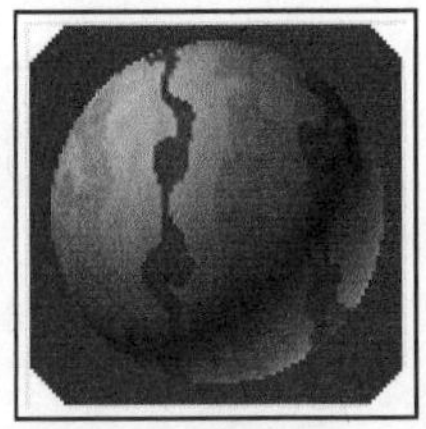

Figure 7-17 The triangles displayed on a sample slot

For assigning a material to the selected object in the viewport, select the sample slot and then select the object on which you need to assign the material in the viewport. Next, choose the **Assign Material to Selection** button in the **Material Editor** dialog box to assign the material to the selected object in the scene. You can also select more than one object to assign the same material to all of them. Alternatively, you can drag the material from the sample slot to the selected objects in the viewport to assign materials to them. You need to choose the **Show Shaded Material in Viewport** button in the **Material Editor** dialog box to view the assigned material in the viewport. You will learn more about this tool later in the chapter.

Reset Map/Mtl to Default Settings

Toolbar:	Reset Map/Mtl to Default Settings

The **Reset Map/Mtl to Default Settings** tool is used to reset the values that were assigned to the map or material in the active sample slot using various rollouts displayed in the **Material Editor** dialog box.

Put to Library

Material Editor Menu:	Material > Put to Library
Toolbar:	Put to Library

The **Put to Library** tool is used to add the selected material to the temporary library or the library created. To do so, select the sample slot that has the material that you want to add to the library. Next, choose the **Put to Library** tool. If you have created a new library, a flyout is displayed, refer to Figure 7-18a. Choose the desired option from the flyout;

the **Put to Library** dialog box will be displayed, as shown in Figure 7-18b. If a new library is not created then the **Put to Library** dialog box will be displayed directly. In the **Name** text box, enter a new name for the material and then choose the **OK** button; the material will be saved in the specified library.

Figure 7-18a The flyout displayed

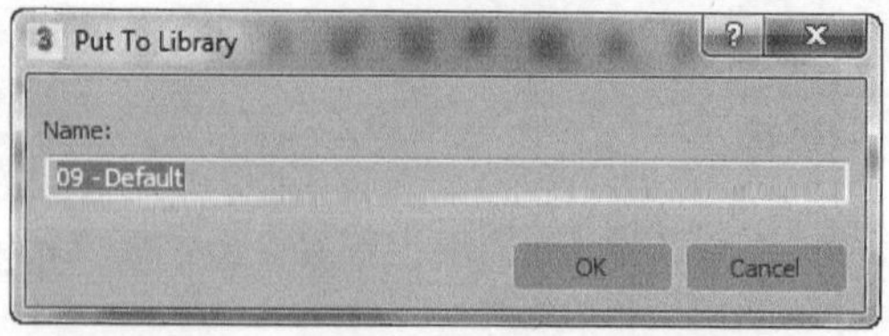

*Figure 7-18b The **Put to Library** dialog box*

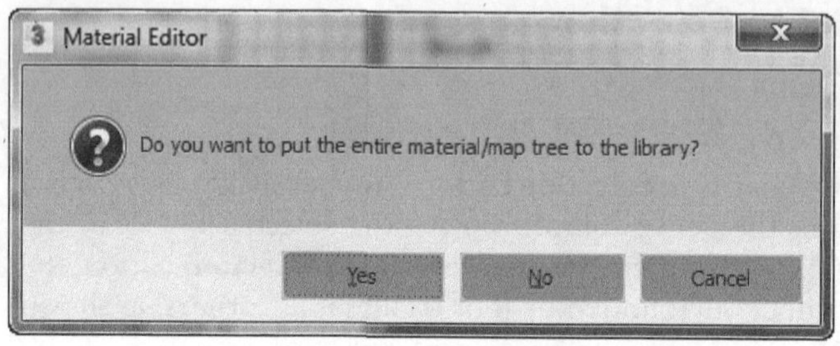

*Figure 7-19 The **Material Editor** message box*

If you are in the sub-level of the material and you invoke the **Put to Library** tool, the **Material Editor** message box will be displayed, as shown in Figure 7-19. In this message box, you will be prompted to specify if you want to put the entire material/map tree to the library. Choose the **Yes** option from the message box; the **Put to Library** dialog box will be displayed. As described earlier, in the **Name** text box, enter a new name of the material and choose the **OK** button; the material will be saved in the temporary library. Also, the material will be displayed in the **Temporary Library** rollout of the **Material/Map Browser** dialog box.

Show Shaded Material in Viewport

Toolbar: Show Shaded Material in Viewport

The **Show Shaded Material in Viewport** button is used to display the material or map assigned to the selected object in the viewport. To do so, select the object in the viewport and assign a material to it and then choose the **Show Shaded Material in Viewport** button; the material will be displayed on the selected object in the viewport.

Go to Parent

Material Editor Menu: Navigation > Go to Parent
Toolbar: Go to Parent

The **Go to Parent** tool is used to go one level up in the current material.

Go Forward to Sibling

Material Editor Menu:	Navigation > Go Forward to Sibling
Toolbar:	Go Forward to Sibling

The **Go Forward to Sibling** tool is used to go to the next map or material at the same level for the current material. This tool is active in compound materials such as **Composite** material, **Blend** material, and so on. These materials are discussed later in the chapter.

Sample Type

Toolbar:	Sample Type

On choosing the **Sample Type** tool, a flyout will be displayed. This flyout consists of three options: sphere, cylinder, and cube. These options are used to choose the geometry type to be displayed in the active sample slot. By default, the material will be displayed on a spherical sample slot.

Backlight

Material Editor Menu:	Options > Backlight
Toolbar:	Backlight
Keyboard:	L

The **Backlight** tool is chosen by default. It is used to add the backside light to the active sample slot, refer to Figures 7-20 and 7-21.

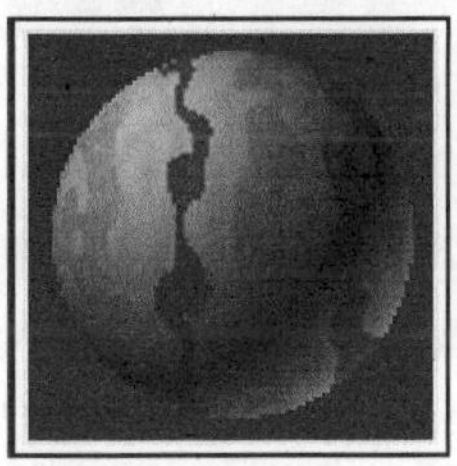

Figure 7-20 The effect of the ***Backlight*** *tool in the sample slot*

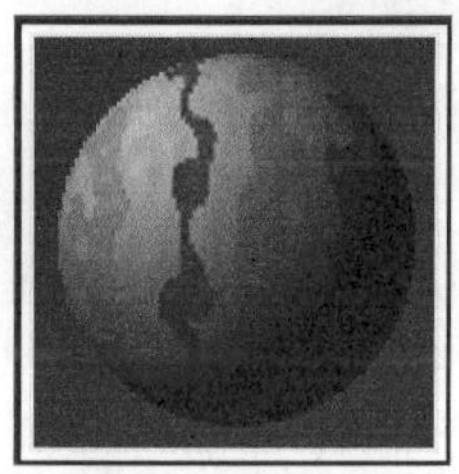

Figure 7-21 The sample slot without the backlight effect

Background

Material Editor Menu:	Options > Background
Toolbar:	Background
Keyboard:	B

The **Background** tool is used to add a multicolored background to the active sample slot, refer to Figures 7-22 and 7-23. The multicolored background is useful for transparent materials.

*Figure 7-22 The sample slot with the **Background** tool invoked*

*Figure 7-23 The sample slot without invoking the **Background** tool*

Sample UV Tiling

Toolbar: Sample UV Tiling

On choosing the **Sample UV Tiling** tool, a flyout will be displayed. This flyout has four options: 1x1, 2x2, 3x3, and 4x4. On selecting any of these tiling patterns, the object in the viewport will not be affected. The selected tiling pattern will be displayed only in the active sample slot, refer to Figures 7-24, 7-25, and 7-26.

Figure 7-24 The 1x1 sample UV tiling in a cube sample slot

Figure 7-25 The 2x2 sample UV tiling in a cube sample slot

Figure 7-26 The 3x3 sample UV tiling in a cube sample slot

Pick Material From Object

The **Pick Material From Object** tool is used to pick the material from the object in the viewport and apply it to the active sample slot. To do so, select the sample slot to activate it and choose the **Pick Material From Object** tool; the shape of the cursor will be changed to the shape of an eye dropper. Now, move the cursor over the object in the viewport from which you want to pick the material and click on it; the selected sample slot will display the same material.

You can change the name of the material of each sample slot by entering a new name in the **Material Name** drop-down list on the right of the **Pick Material From Object** tool. The **Material Type** button on the right of the **Material Name** drop-down list displays the name of the material that is selected from the **Material/Map Browser** dialog box, refer to Figure 7-27.

MATERIALS

In this section, you will learn about the **Material Editor** tool that helps you to create materials and assign them to the objects to make them more realistic. The materials assigned to the objects give the best results with lights, about which you will learn in the later chapters. In 3ds Max, you can create and assign various materials to the objects using the **Material Editor** tool from the **Main Toolbar**.

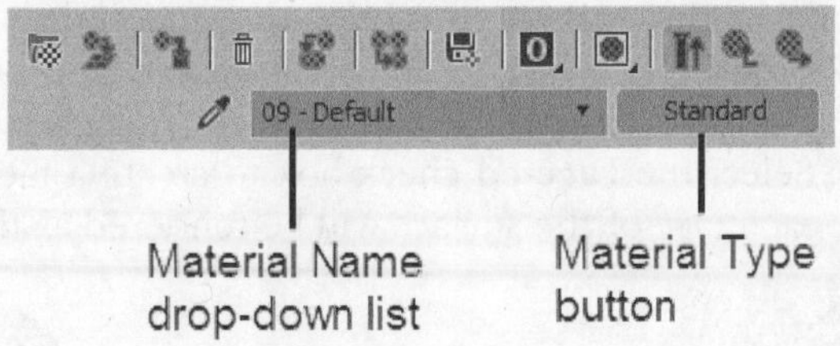

Figure 7-27 The ***Material Name*** *drop-down list and the* ***Material Type*** *button*

Choose the **Material Editor** tool from the **Main Toolbar**; the **Material Editor** dialog box will be displayed. Now, choose the **Material Type** button on the right side of the **Material Name** drop-down list, refer to Figure 7-27; the **Material/Map Browser** dialog box will be displayed. Next, expand the **Materials > General** rollout, if it is not already expanded. In this list, there are some materials that can combine other materials in them. These are known as Compound materials. The Compound materials in this list are **Blend**, **Composite**, **Double-Sided**, **Morpher**, **Multi/Sub-Object**, **Shellac**, and **Top/Bottom**. Select the material as per your requirement from the list and then choose the **OK** button; the name of the selected material will be displayed on the **Material Type** button in the **Material Editor** dialog box. Also, the rollouts related to that material will be displayed in the **Material Editor** dialog box. The material can be modified by using the parameters available in these rollouts. The most commonly used materials are discussed next.

Note

You can also get the default materials using the ***Get Material*** *tool in the* ***Material Editor*** *dialog box, as discussed earlier in this chapter.*

Standard Material

By default, the **Standard** material is selected in the **Material Editor** dialog box. Various rollouts are also displayed below the **Material Type** button to create new materials or modify the properties of the current material. The most commonly used rollouts are discussed next.

Shader Basic Parameters Rollout

The options in this rollout are used to specify the shading types and other properties for the material, refer to Figure 7-28.

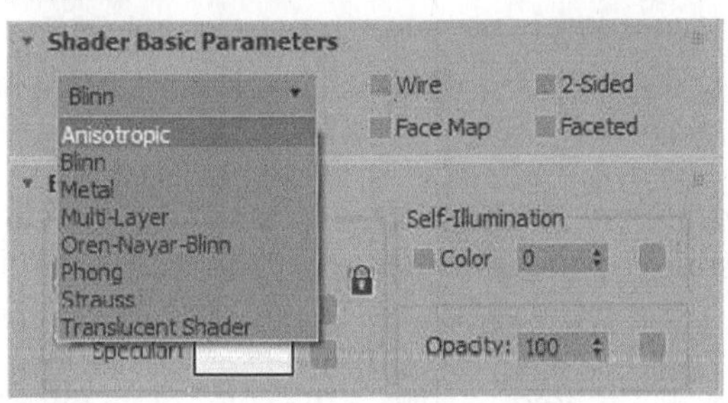

Figure 7-28 The ***Shader Basic Parameters*** *rollout with eight shaders displayed in the drop-down list*

Select the **Wire** check box in this rollout to render the material as wireframe, as shown in Figure 7-29. Select the **2-Sided** check box to apply the material to both sides of the selected faces. Select the **Face Map** check box to apply the maps or images to each face of the object, as shown in Figure 7-30. Select the **Faceted** check box to create a faceted object, as shown in Figure 7-31. In this case, each face of the surface will be rendered as flat face.

***Figure 7-29** The sphere geometry with the **Wire** check box selected*

***Figure 7-30** The sphere geometry with the **Face Map** check box selected*

***Figure 7-31** The sphere geometry with the **Faceted** check box selected*

Note

*1. To view the effect of the selection of the **Face Map** or **Faceted** check box on an object, you need to assign an image or a map to the object. You will learn more about assigning an image or a map to the object later in this chapter.*

*2. You can see the effect of the selection of the **Faceted** check box only after rendering.*

There are eight types of shaders in the drop-down list located on the top of this rollout, refer to Figure 7-28. These shaders provide different effects to the material after rendering. By default, the **Blinn** shader is selected in this drop-down list. Various shaders and their rollouts are discussed next.

Anisotropic Shader

The **Anisotropic** shader is used to create elliptical highlights, refer to Figure 7-32. This shader is suitable for creating glasses, brushed metals, and so on. To assign this shader to the material, select the **Anisotropic** option from the drop-down list in the **Shader Basic Parameters** rollout. On doing so, the **Anisotropic Basic Parameters** rollout will be displayed below the **Shader Basic Parameters** rollout, as shown in Figure 7-33. This rollout is discussed next.

Note

*To view the effects of shaders, you need to set the parameters in the **Basic Parameters** rollout of the corresponding shader.*

Anisotropic Basic Parameters Rollout: The options in the **Anisotropic Basic Parameters** rollout are used to set the colors, transparency, shine, and so on of the material.

The **Ambient**, **Diffuse**, and **Specular** color swatches are used to set the colors of the material. The **Ambient** color swatch is used to specify the color of an object in shadow. The **Diffuse** color swatch is used to specify the color of an object in direct light. It is the primary color of the material. The **Specular** color swatch is used to specify the color of the highlighted or the shiny part of the material, refer to Figure 7-34.

Figure 7-32 The sphere geometry with ***Anisotropic*** shader

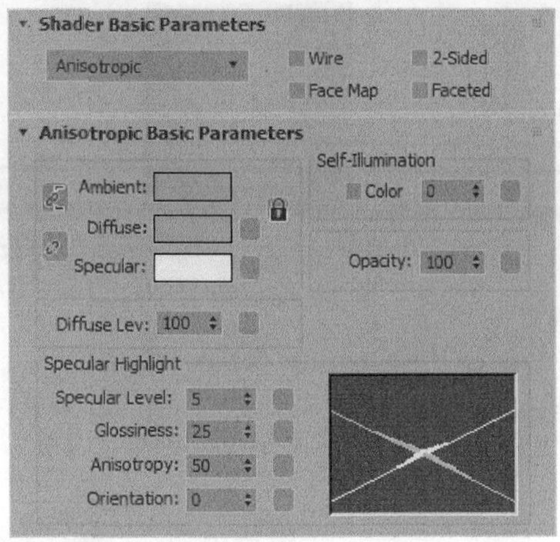

Figure 7-33 The ***Anisotropic Basic Parameters*** rollout

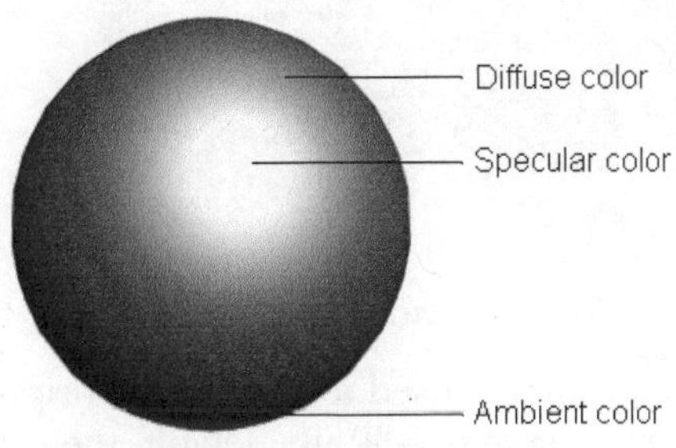

Figure 7-34 *The ambient, diffuse, and specular colors in a sphere*

To set the color of the material, select one of the color swatches; the **Color Selector** dialog box will be displayed along with the name of the color swatch that you have selected. Select a color and choose the **OK** button; the selected color will be displayed in the color swatch and the active sample slot.

Self-Illumination Area: The options in the **Self-Illumination** area are used to create incandescence effect by replacing shadows on the surface with color specified using the **Diffuse** color swatch. It creates an illusion of light being generated from the material. The value of the spinner in the **Self-Illumination** area specifies the percentage of shadow replaced with the color. To set the illumination of the object, select the **Color** check box in this area; the spinner on its right will be replaced by a color swatch.

You can change the intensity as well as the color for the self illumination using the color swatch. Choose the color swatch in the **Self-Illumination** area; the **Color Selector: Self-Illum Color** dialog box will be displayed. As you increase the value in the **Value** spinner, the intensity of the incandescence effect also increases, refer to Figures 7-35 and 7-36.

Figure 7-35 A sphere geometry without self-illumination

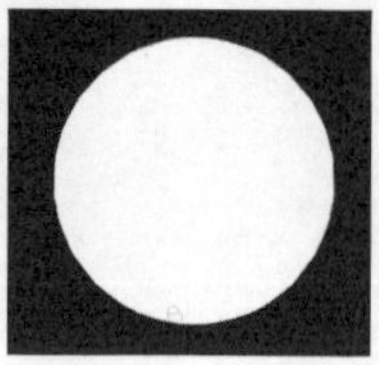

Figure 7-36 A sphere geometry with self-illumination

The value in the **Opacity** spinner is used to control the transparency of the material. By default, the value in the spinner is 100, which makes a material opaque. As you decrease the value, the transparency will increase, refer to Figure 7-37.

Figure 7-37 A teapot geometry within a transparent box

The value in the **Diffuse Lev** spinner is used to control the brightness of the diffuse color in the material, refer to Figures 7-38 and 7-39. By default, the value in this spinner is 100.

*Figure 7-38 The torus knot geometry with the default value in the **Diffuse Lev** spinner*

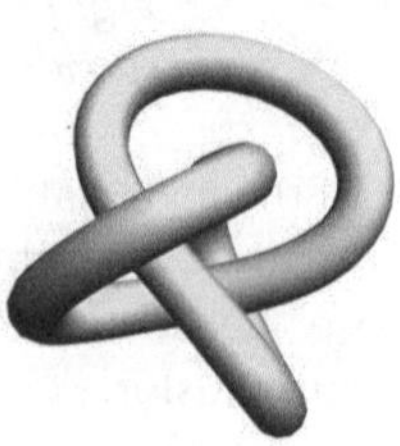

*Figure 7-39 The torus knot geometry with the value **150** in the **Diffuse Lev** spinner*

Specular Highlight Area: The options in the **Specular Highlight** area are used to set the shape, appearance, strength, and orientation of the specular highlight or the shiny part of the material.

The value in the **Specular Level** spinner is used to set the brightness or intensity of the specular highlight of the material. As you increase the value in the spinner, the brightness of the specular highlight will also increase, refer to Figures 7-40 and 7-41.

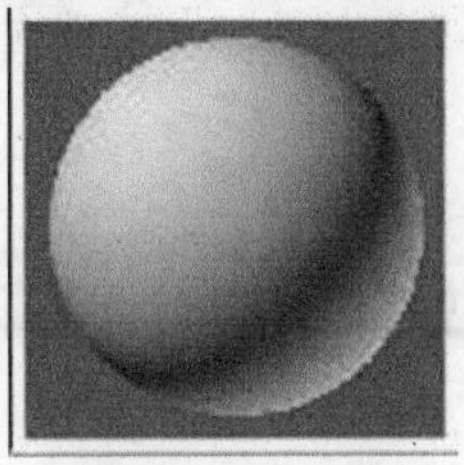

*Figure 7-40 The sphere geometry with the value **0** in the **Specular Level** spinner*

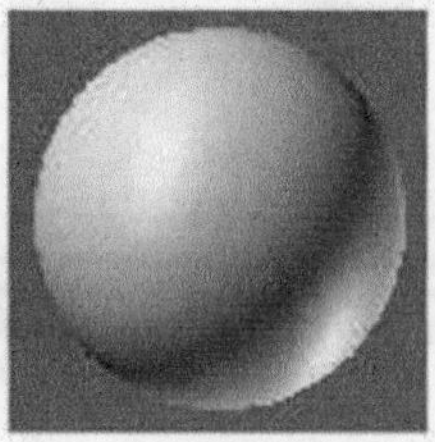

*Figure 7-41 The sphere geometry with the value **66** in the **Specular Level** spinner*

The value in the **Glossiness** spinner is used to set the size of the specular highlight of the material. However, if you increase the value in the **Glossiness** spinner, the size of the specular highlight will decrease, refer to Figures 7-42 and 7-43.

*Figure 7-42 The sphere geometry with less value in the **Glossiness** spinner*

*Figure 7-43 The sphere geometry with more value in the **Glossiness** spinner*

The value in the **Anisotropy** spinner is used to set the shape of the specular highlight of the material. As you increase the value in the **Anisotropy** spinner, the shape of the specular highlight will reduce, refer to Figures 7-44 and 7-45.

*Figure 7-44 The teapot geometry with less value in the **Anisotropy** spinner*

*Figure 7-45 The teapot geometry with more value in the **Anisotropy** spinner*

The value in the **Orientation** spinner is used to change the orientation of the specular highlight of the material in degrees. By default, its value is 0. By changing the value in the **Orientation** spinner, you can change the orientation of the specular highlight of the material, as shown in Figures 7-46 and 7-47.

Note

*In the **Specular Highlights** area, there is a graph on the right that graphically represents the changes in all spinners.*

*Figure 7-46 The teapot geometry with the value **0** in the **Orientation** spinner*

*Figure 7-47 The teapot geometry with the value **45** in the **Orientation** spinner*

Blinn Shader

The **Blinn** shader is used to create round and soft highlights, refer to Figure 7-48. To assign this shader to the material, select the **Blinn** option from the drop-down list available in the **Shader Basic Parameters** rollout; the **Blinn Basic Parameters** rollout will be displayed below the **Shader Basic Parameters** rollout. The **Ambient**, **Diffuse**, and **Specular** color swatches, the **Self-Illumination** area, and the **Opacity** spinner in this rollout are the same as those discussed in the **Anisotropic Basic Parameters** rollout.

In the **Specular Highlights** area, the **Specular Level** and **Glossiness** spinners are the same as those discussed in the **Anisotropic Shader**. The value in the **Soften** spinner is used to soften the effect of the specular highlight. By default, its value is 0.1.

*Figure 7-48 The sphere geometry with the **Blinn** shader*

Metal Shader

The **Metal** shader is used to give a metallic effect to objects, refer to Figure 7-49. To assign this shader to the material, select the **Metal** shader from the drop-down list available in the **Shader Basic Parameters** rollout; the **Metal Basic Parameters** rollout will be displayed below the **Shader Basic Parameters** rollout. The options in this rollout are the same as discussed in the **Anisotropic Basic Parameters** rollout.

*Figure 7-49 The teapot geometry with the **Metal** shader*

Multi-Layer Shader

The **Multi-Layer** shader is similar to the **Anisotropic** shader with the only difference that the **Multi-Layer** shader has two specular highlight controls. To assign this shader to the material, select the **Multi-Layer** shader from the drop-down list available in the **Shader Basic Parameters** rollout; the **Multi-Layer Basic Parameters** rollout will be displayed. In this rollout, the **Ambient** and **Diffuse** color swatches are same as those discussed in the **Anisotropic Basic Parameters** rollout. Also, the **Self-Illumination** area, the **Opacity** spinner, and the **Diffuse Level** spinner are same as those discussed in the **Anisotropic Basic Parameters** rollout.

The **Roughness** spinner is used to set the transition from diffuse color to the ambient color. By default, its value is 0 and it ranges from 0 to 100. When you increase the value in the **Roughness** spinner, the material becomes less shiny, refer to Figures 7-50 and 7-51.

*Figure 7-50 The teapot with less value in the **Roughness** spinner*

*Figure 7-51 The teapot with more value in the **Roughness** spinner*

In the **Multi-Layer Basic Parameters** rollout, there are two specular highlight areas, **First Specular Layer** and **Second Specular Layer**. You can use both highlights independently to produce complex and blend shadings in the material. The options in the **First Specular Layer** and the **Second Specular Layer** areas are same. However, you can use different settings to produce the blend shadings in the material, refer to Figure 7-52. These options are discussed next.

*Figure 7-52 The teapot with the **Multi-Layer** shader*

Choose the **Color** color swatch to change the specular color of the first and the second highlights in the respective areas. The **Level** spinner is used to set the brightness or the intensity of the specular highlight of the material. By default, its value is 0. As you increase the value in the spinner, the brightness of the specular highlight will also increase. The **Glossiness**, **Anisotropy**, and **Orientation** options are the same as those discussed in the **Anisotropic** shader.

Oren-Nayar-Blinn Shader

The **Oren-Nayar-Blinn** shader is a variant of the **Blinn** shader and is used to create dull or matte highlights, as shown in Figure 7-53. This shader can be used for rubber, clay, clothes, and so on. To assign this shader to the material, select the **Oren-Nayar-Blinn** shader from

*Figure 7-53 The teapot geometry with the **Oren-Nayer-Blinn** shader*

the drop-down list available in the **Shader Basic Parameters** rollout; the **Oren-Nayar-Blinn Basic Parameters** rollout will be displayed. The **Ambient**, **Diffuse**, and **Specular** color swatches, the **Self-Illumination** area, and the **Opacity** spinner in this rollout are the same as discussed in the **Anisotropic Basic Parameters** rollout. In the **Advanced Diffuse** area, the **Diffuse Level** and **Roughness** spinners are the same as discussed in the **Multi-Layer** shader.

In the **Specular Highlights** area, the **Specular Level**, **Glossiness**, and **Soften** spinners are the same as discussed in the **Blinn** shader.

Phong Shader

The **Phong** shader is very similar to the **Blinn** shader. The only difference is that the highlights produced by the **Phong** shader are stronger than those produced by the **Blinn** shader, refer to Figure 7-54. To assign this shader to the material, select the **Phong** shader from the drop-down list available in the **Shader Basic Parameters** rollout; the **Phong Basic Parameters** rollout will be displayed. The **Ambient**, **Diffuse**, and **Specular** color swatches, the **Self-Illumination** area, and the **Opacity** spinner in this rollout are the same as described in the **Anisotropic Basic Parameters** rollout. In the **Specular Highlights** area, the **Specular Level**, **Glossiness**, and **Soften** spinners are the same as those discussed in the **Blinn** shader.

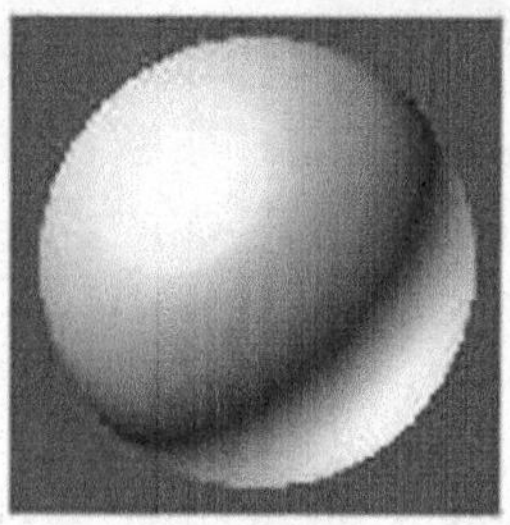

Figure 7-54 *The sphere geometry with the* ***Phong*** *shader*

Strauss Shader

The **Strauss** shader is used to create the metallic and non-metallic surfaces, refer to Figure 7-55. To assign this shader to the material, select the **Strauss** shader from the drop-down list; the **Strauss Basic Parameters** rollout will be displayed. This rollout is discussed next.

Figure 7-55 *The teapot geometry with the* ***Strauss*** *shader*

Strauss Basic Parameters Rollout: The **Strauss** shader does not have the **Ambient**, **Diffuse**, and **Specular** color swatches. Choose the **Color** swatch to change the color of the material. The value in the **Glossiness** spinner is used to set the size and the intensity of the specular highlight of the material. The value in the **Metalness** spinner is used to set the metallic effect in the material. The value in the **Opacity** spinner is used to set the transparency of the material.

Translucent Shader

The **Translucent** shader is used to create translucent materials. In such materials, the light gets scattered as it passes through them, refer to Figure 7-56. It is very similar to the **Blinn** shader. Additionally, it defines the translucency of the material. To assign this shader to the material, you need to select the **Translucent Shader** from the drop-down list in the **Shader Basic Parameters** rollout; the **Translucent Basic Parameters** rollout will be displayed. This rollout is discussed next.

*Figure 7-56 The sphere geometry with the **Translucent** shader*

Translucent Basic Parameters Rollout: Most of the options in this rollout are the same as discussed earlier. By default, the **Backside specular** check box is selected in this rollout. As a result, the specular highlight is displayed on both sides of the material.

Note

*Select the **Backside specular** check box in the **Specular Highlights** area in the **Translucent Basic Parameters** rollout to create materials such as plastic or smooth glass. Clear the **Backside specular** check box to create the frosted or rough material.*

In the **Translucency** area, the **Translucent Clr** swatch is used to define the color of the light that will be scattered inside the material. The **Filter Color** swatch is used to define the color of the light that will be transmitted by the material.

Architectural Material

The **Architectural** material is used to provide a highly realistic view of an object when rendered with photometric lights and radiosity, about which you will learn in the later chapters. To apply the **Architectural** material, choose the **Material Type** button on the right side of the **Material Name** drop-down list; the **Material/Map Browser** dialog box will be displayed. Choose the **Architectural** material from the **Material/Map Browser** dialog box; the **Architectural** label will be displayed on the **Material Type** button. Also, various rollouts such as **Physical Qualities**, **Special Effects**, and so on will be displayed below the **Architectural** button. You can use these rollouts to create new materials and modify the physical properties of those materials. The most commonly used rollouts are discussed next.

Templates Rollout

The drop-down list in the **Templates** rollout consists of a number of preset materials such as **Water**, **Glass-Clear**, **Metal**, **Paper**, and so on, as shown in Figure 7-57. On selecting one of the preset materials from the drop-down list, you will get a template in the selected sample slot for the type of material you have selected. After selecting the material, you can set the parameters in other rollouts to get a realistic view of the material, refer to Figure 7-58.

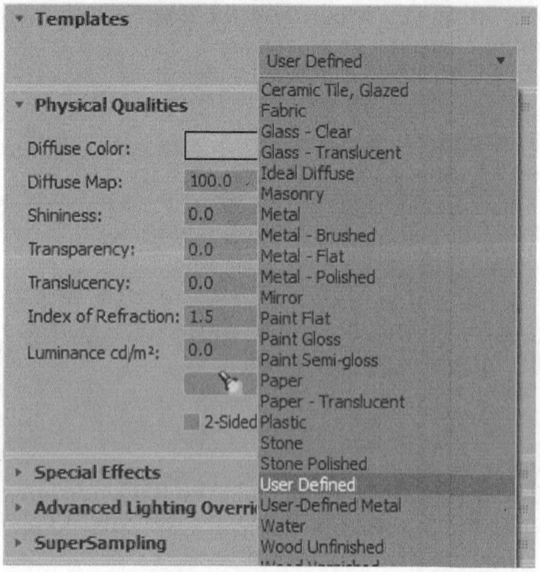

*Figure 7-57 The preset materials in the drop-down list in the **Templates** rollouts*

*Figure 7-58 The teapot geometry with the **Masonary** preset material applied*

Physical Qualities Rollout

The **Diffuse Color** swatch is used to specify the color of an object in direct light. It is the main color of the material. Choose the **Diffuse Color** swatch to define the color of the material. The **Diffuse Map** option is used to assign a map or an image to the material. To do so, choose the **Diffuse Map** button labeled as **None** on the right side of the **Diffuse Map** spinner; the **Material/Map Browser** dialog box will be displayed. Select one of the maps from the **Maps > General** rollout and double-click on it to assign it. The basic parameters rollouts of the selected map will be displayed. Set the parameters as per your requirement and then choose the **Go To Parent** button to go back to the previous level; the **None** label will be replaced by the name of the selected map. The spinner on the right side of the **Diffuse Map** option is used to set the amount of visibility of the map in the material in percentage. By default, its value is 100. On decreasing the value in this spinner, the visibility of the map in the material will be decreased. Note that by default, the check boxes located in between the spinners and the buttons in the **Physical Qualities** rollout are selected. As a result, the selected map will be displayed on the material.

The **Set color to texture average** button, available next to the **Diffuse Color** color swatch, will be activated only if you assign a diffuse map to the material using the **Diffuse Map** button. This button is used to set the diffuse color according to the map that you have assigned to the material using the **Diffuse Map** button. The **Shininess**, **Transparency**, and **Translucency** options in the **Physical Qualities** rollout are used to define the shine, transparency, and the translucency of the material. Also, you can assign a map or an image to these options as you did for the **Diffuse Map** option. The **Index of Refraction** spinner is used to set the amount of refraction of the light transmitted by the material. The **Luminance cd/m²** spinner is used to give the glow effect to the material. The luminance is measured in candelas per meter square. The **Set luminance from light** button uses the scene light to obtain the materials luminance. Select the **2-Sided** check box to assign the material on both sides of the selected faces.

Note
*The **Architectural** material gives a realistic result only with photometric lights.*

Raytrace Material

The **Raytrace** material creates highly refractive and reflective surfaces. When this material is assigned to an object in the scene, the materials/maps of other objects in the scene get reflected on it, as shown in Figure 7-59. It is an advance material and is used to provide realistic raytraced images. It also creates raytraced reflections and refractions, and takes a longer time to render. On selecting the **Raytrace** material, various rollouts will also be displayed below the **Material Type** button to create new materials and modify the properties of those materials. The **Raytrace Basic Parameters** rollout is the most commonly used rollout. This rollout is discussed next.

Raytrace Basic Parameters Rollout

The basic parameters in this rollout are similar to those used in the **Standard** material but the color swatches in this rollout act differently, refer to Figure 7-60. These color controls are discussed next.

*Figure 7-59 The teapot geometry with the **Raytrace** material applied*

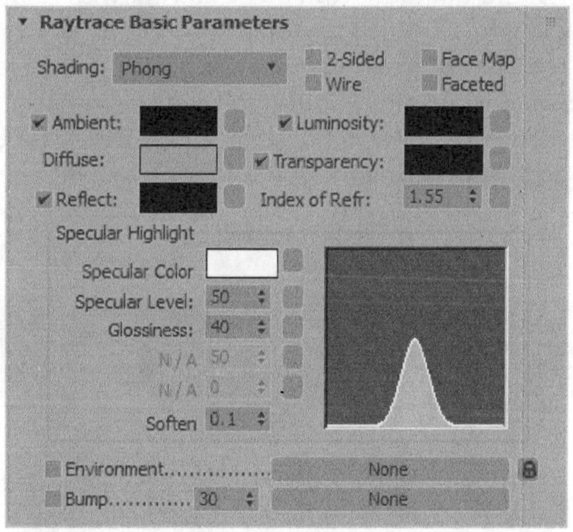

***Figure 7-60** The **Raytrace Basic Parameters** rollout*

By default, the check box on the left side of the **Ambient** color swatch is selected, which is used to specify the amount of absorption of the ambient light by the material. By default, the black color is selected in this color swatch and it specifies the maximum absorption of the ambient light by the material. On setting a lighter color in the **Ambient** color swatch, the ambient light will be reflected. If you clear the check box, the color swatch will be replaced by a spinner. The value in the spinner specifies the grayscale value.

The **Diffuse** color swatch specifies the color of the object without the specular highlight. The **Reflect** color swatch is used to specify the specular reflection color. By default, the color in this color swatch is black and the object does not reflect. If you change the color to white, then the object will reflect everything and will be visible. If you clear the check box, the color swatch will be replaced by a spinner. If you set the value in the **Reflect** spinner to 100, then the diffuse color will not be visible on the object. The value in the spinner specifies the grayscale value. If you select this check box again, the spinner will be replaced by the **Fresnel** option. This option adds the fresnel effect to the reflecting object resulting in a bit of extra reflection in the reflecting object.

The **Luminosity** color swatch is very similar to the **Self-Illumination** area in the **Standard** material. By default, the check box on the right of the **Luminosity** option is selected. If you clear the check box, the **Luminosity** label will be replaced by **Self-Illum** and the color swatch will be replaced by a spinner. The value in the spinner specifics the grayscale value.

The **Transparency** color swatch is used to define the transparency of the object. By default, the check box on the right of the **Transparency** option is selected. If you clear this check box, the **Transparency** color swatch is replaced by a spinner. The value in the spinner also defines the transparency of the object.

Blend Material

The **Blend** material is a compound material and is used to mix two different materials, as shown in Figure 7-61. You can assign this mixed or blend material as a single material. When you select the **Blend** material from the **Material/Map Browser** dialog box, the **Replace Material** message box will be displayed, as shown in Figure 7-62. Select the **Discard old material?** radio button to remove the current material of the selected sample slot. Select the **Keep old material as sub-material?** radio button to keep the material of the selected sample slot as a sub-material in the **Blend** material. Choose the **OK** button; the **Blend** material will be displayed in the **Material Type** button with a number of rollouts. The most commonly used rollout is discussed next.

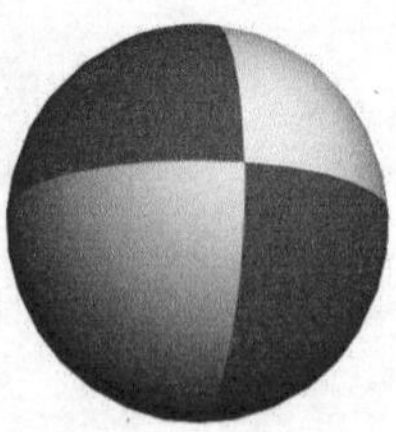

*Figure 7-61 The sphere geometry with the **Blend** material applied*

*Figure 7-62 The **Replace Material** message box*

Blend Basic Parameters Rollout

On the top of this rollout, there are two buttons, **Material 1** and **Material 2**, refer to Figure 7-63. These buttons are labeled with the name of the default materials and are used to select two different materials to blend. By default, the **Standard** material is displayed as the sub-material. Choose these buttons to assign desired materials. Next, choose the **Go To Parent** tool to go back to the **Blend** material.

The **Mask** button is used to insert an image or a map as a mask. The amount of blending of the two materials depends on the mask image. The lighter area of the mask image will show more of **Material 1** and the darker area of the mask image will show more of **Material 2**.

By default, the check boxes on the right side of the **Material 1**, **Material 2**, and **Mask** buttons are selected, which specify that the concerned material or the mask will be displayed on the object.

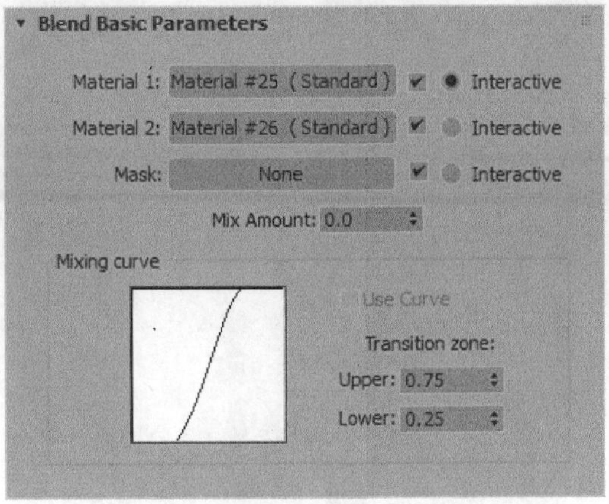

Figure 7-63 *The* ***Blend Basic Parameters*** *rollout*

If you clear any of the check boxes, the corresponding material or mask will not be displayed. Select the two **Interactive** radio buttons on the right side of the check boxes to specify the materials that will be displayed on the object in the shaded viewports. The value in the **Mix Amount** spinner is used to set the blending amount of the materials in percentage. When you insert a map using the **Mask** button, the **Mix Amount** spinner will become inactive.

The **Mixing curve** area is used to define the transition between two colors being blended. It affects the transition only when the mask map is applied to the **Mask** button. Select the **Use Curve** check box to apply the curve settings to the blending. This check box will be active only if you have assigned the mask map. In the **Transition zone** group, the values in the **Upper** and **Lower** spinners set the transition of the materials. The values in these spinners vary from 0 to 1.0.

Note
The blending of maps can be animated over time using the ***Mix Amount*** *spinner.*

Composite Material

The **Composite** material is similar to the **Blend** material and is used to mix ten different materials. You can assign this mixed material as a single material. On choosing the **Material Type** button, the **Material/Map Browser** dialog box will be displayed. Select the **Composite** material and choose the **OK** button; the **Replace Material** message box will be displayed. Select the **Discard old material?** radio button to remove the material of the selected sample slot. Else, select the **Keep old material as sub-material?** radio button to retain the material of the selected sample slot as a sub-material in the **Composite** material. Choose the **OK** button; the **Composite** material will be displayed in the **Material Type** button with a number of rollouts. The most commonly used rollout is **Composite Basic Parameters** rollout, which is discussed next.

Composite Basic Parameters Rollout

On the top of this rollout, there is the **Base Material** button which is labeled with the name of the material on it, refer to Figure 7-64. It is used to define the base material of the object. By default, the **Standard** material is displayed on it. Choose this button and set the parameters for the base material as required. Next, choose the **Go to Parent** tool to go back to the parent level.

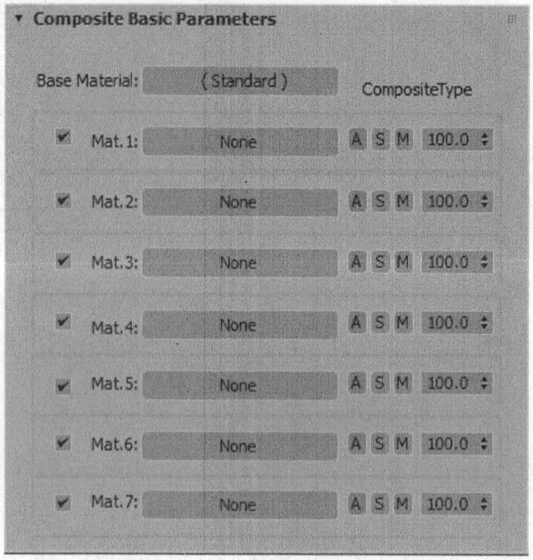

***Figure 7-64** The **Composite Basic Parameters** rollout*

There are nine buttons below the **Base Material** button, from **Mat.1** to **Mat.9**, labeled with **None**. These buttons are used to composite nine materials. Choose these buttons one by one to assign different materials; the **None** labels will be replaced by the names of the materials that will be assigned to them. The check boxes on the left side of these buttons are selected to display the corresponding materials in the objects. If you do not want to display any of the materials, then clear the respective check boxes.

The **A**, **S**, and **M** buttons are used to specify the composition of the materials. Choose the **A** button to use the additive color to compose the materials. It specifies that the color of the base material will be added to the color of the composed material. Choose the **S** button to use the subtractive color to compose. It specifies that the color of the composed material will be subtracted from the color of the base material. Choose the **M** button to blend the materials as discussed in the Blend Material section with the only difference that the option for masking is not available in this case. For each material, the spinner on the right of the **A**, **S**, and **M** buttons determines the amount of mixing of the respective material with the **Base Material**. When the **A** and **S** buttons are active, the value in the spinner ranges from 0 to 200. Whereas, when the **M** button is active, the value in the spinner ranges from 0 to 100.

Double Sided Material

The **Double Sided** material is used to assign two different materials to the front and back faces of an object, refer to Figures 7-65 and 7-66. Choose the **Double Sided** material from the **Material/ Map Browser** dialog box; the **Replace Material** message box will be displayed. Select the **Discard old material?** radio button from this dialog box to remove the material of the selected sample slot. Else, select the **Keep old material as sub-material?** radio button to retain the material of the selected sample slot as the sub-material in the **Double Sided** material. Choose the **OK** button;the **Double Sided** material will be displayed in the **Material Type** button with a number of rollouts. The **Double Sided Basic Parameters** rollout is discussed next.

*Figure 7-65 The object with the **Standard** material*

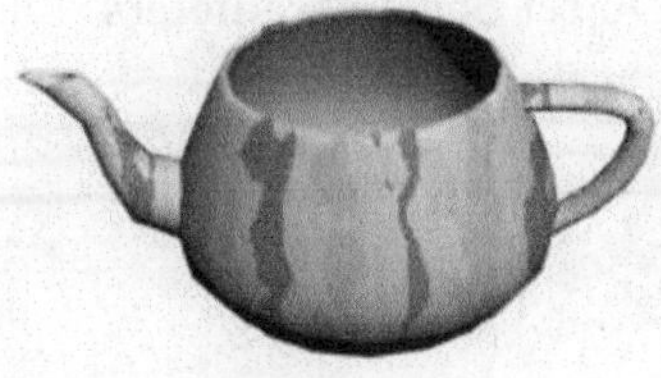

*Figure 7-66 The object with the **Double Sided** material*

Double Sided Basic Parameters Rollout

The **Translucency** spinner at the top of this rollout specifies the amount of blending of **Facing Material** and **Back Material**, refer to Figure 7-67. The value in this spinner varies from 0 to 100.0. If you set the value **100** in the **Translucency** spinner, the back material will completely cover the face material. Choose the buttons next to the **Facing Material** and **Back Material** options to select the material for the front and back sides of the object, respectively.

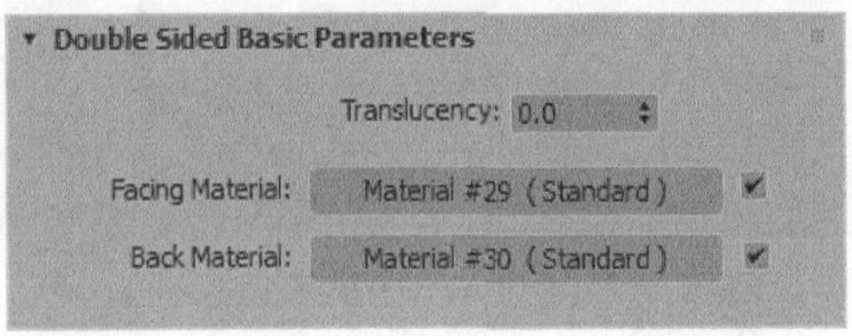

*Figure 7-67 The **Double Sided Basic Parameters** rollout*

Multi/Sub-Object Material

The **Multi/Sub-Object** material is used to assign different materials to an object at the sub-object level, as shown in Figure 7-68. Select the object to which the **Multi/Sub-Object** material is to be assigned. Convert the object to editable poly and then select the **Polygon** sub-object level. Next, select the group of polygons in the viewport, refer to Figure 7-69. Now, expand the **Polygon Material IDs** rollout and enter the value **1** in the **Set ID** spinner and press ENTER. Then, invert the selection and enter the value **2** in the **Set ID** spinner. Next, press ENTER; refer to Figure 7-70.

*Figure 7-68 The object with the **Multi/Sub-Object** material*

Figure 7-69 The object with group of polygons selected

Figure 7-70 The object with remaining polygons selected

Note that multiple numbers of IDs can be assigned to an object depending on the number of materials to be assigned to it. Once IDs are set to different parts of the object, choose the **Multi/Sub-Object** material from the **Material/Map Browser** dialog box; the **Replace Material** message box will be displayed. Select the **Discard old material?** radio button from it and choose the **OK** button; the **Multi/Sub-object** material will be displayed in the **Material Type** button. Also, the **Multi/Sub-Object Basic Parameters** rollout will be displayed, refer to Figure 7-71. This rollout is discussed next.

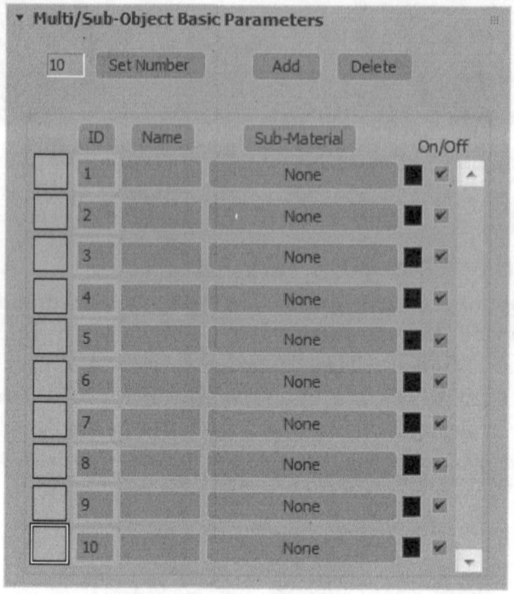

***Figure 7-71** The **Multi/Sub-Object** Basic Parameters rollout*

Multi/Sub-Object Basic Parameters Rollout

Choose the **Set Number** button in this rollout; the **Set Number of Materials** dialog box will be displayed. Enter **2** in the **Number of Materials** spinner and choose the **OK** button; the **Multi/Sub-Object Basic Parameters** rollout will display two entries instead of ten entries. Note that the value entered in the **Number of Materials** spinner should be equal to the number of IDs created for the object which in turn is equal to the entries in this rollout. Now, choose the **None** button for each of the IDs to assign the required sub-material. Also, you can enter the name of the sub-material in the **Name** text box. Next, assign the material to the object to see the effect of the **Multi-Sub-Object** material.

Note

*If you want to change only the color of the sub-material without assigning any map to it, then the color swatch next to it will be inactive. It will be activated only when you assign **Standard** material to it.*

Top/Bottom Material

The **Top/Bottom** material is used to assign two different materials on the top and bottom portions of the object, as shown in Figure 7-72. To do so, choose the **Top/Bottom** material from the **Material/Map Browser** dialog box; the **Replace Material** message box will be displayed. Select the **Discard old material?** radio button from this message box to remove the material of the selected sample slot. Else, select the **Keep old material as sub-material?** radio button to retain the material of the selected sample slot as the sub-material in the **Top/Bottom** material.

Choose the **OK** button; the **Top/Bottom** material will be displayed in the **Material Type** button with a number of rollouts. The **Top/Bottom Basic Parameters** rollout is discussed next.

Top/Bottom Basic Parameters Rollout

Choose the buttons next to **Top Material** and **Bottom** to select the material for the top and bottom portions of the object, respectively, refer to Figure 7-73. Choose the **Swap** button to exchange the material of the **Top Material** and **Bottom** buttons.

*Figure 7-72 The object with the **Top/Bottom** material applied*

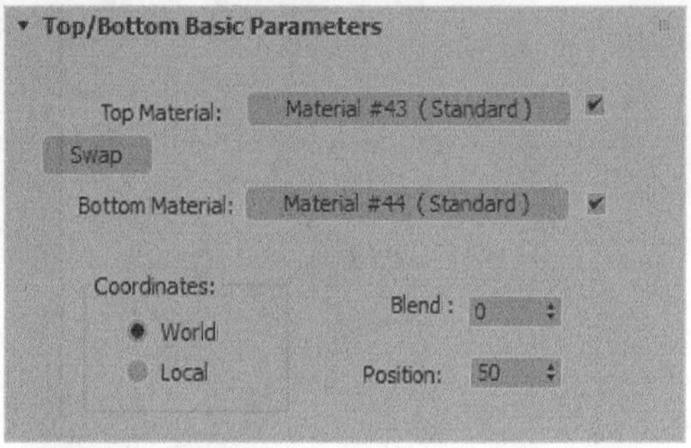

*Figure 7-73 The **Top/Bottom Basic Parameters** rollout*

The options in the **Coordinates** area are used to set the boundary between the top and bottom of the object. By default, the **World** radio button is selected and the faces will point up or down according to the world coordinates of the scene. In this case, if you transform the object, then the boundary remains constant at its place. If you select the **Local** radio button, then the faces will point up or down according to the local coordinates of the object. In this case, if you transform the object, the material will also get transformed. The **Blend** spinner is used to blend the edges of the top and bottom materials. The **Position** spinner is used to specify the position of the top and bottom materials on the object. By default, the value in both the spinners ranges from 0 to 100.0.

Physical Material

The **Physical Material** is a modern layered based material that is suitable for physically-based workflow. This material is compatible with both the mental ray and ART renderers. It also preserves the energy and ensures that the sum of various shading components does not exceed 100%. The light energy is only scattered or absorbed but not created. This material comes with many presets that you can access from the **Presets** rollout of the **Material Editor** dialog box, refer to Figure 7-74. Presets provide you the starting point to create various materials.

MAPS

In 3ds Max, maps are the default images assigned to a material. They are used to create texture for the objects to make them appear more realistic. In this section, you will learn about assigning the maps to the objects. When maps are assigned to the objects, the objects demonstrate best effects on applying lights.

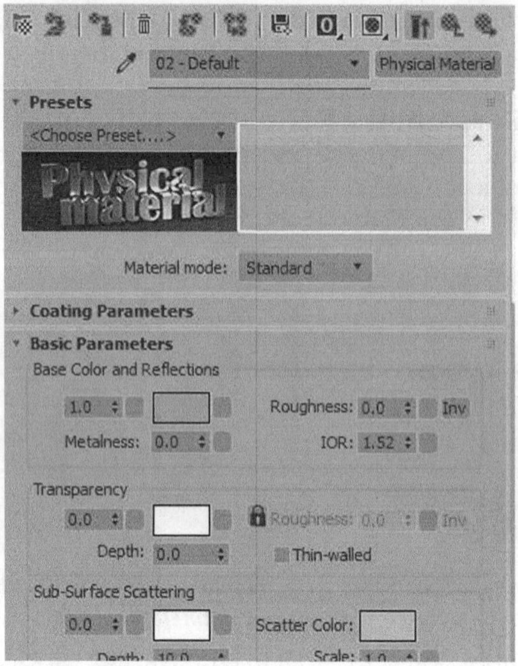

Figure 7-74 The **Presets** rollout

To assign a map to the material, choose **Modes > Compact Material Editor** from the material editor menu bar; the **Material Editor** dialog box will be displayed. Select one of the sample slots in the **Material Editor** dialog box to activate it. Now, in the basic parameters rollout of the selected material, choose the small square buttons on the right of the parameters available, refer to Figure 7-75; the **Material/Map Browser** dialog box will be displayed with a list of default maps available in 3ds Max. Next, select the required map from the **Maps > General** or **Maps > Scanline** rollouts and then choose the **OK** button; the name of the selected map will be displayed on the **Material Type** button and the rollouts related to that map will also be displayed. Set the parameters for the map in various rollouts displayed. Next, choose the **Go to Parent** tool to go back to the previous level; the small square button will be labeled as **M**. Also, when you move the cursor over the **M** button, it will display the name of the map that you have assigned to it.

Various types of maps available in the **Material/Map Browser** dialog box are discussed next.

Note

You can also assign maps using different options such as ***Ambient Color****,* ***Diffuse Color****,* ***Specular Color****, and so on to a material using the* ***Maps*** *rollout in the* ***Material Editor*** *dialog box. You need to choose the buttons on the right side of the options that are labeled as* ***None****, refer to Figure 7-75.*

Types of Map

In 3ds Max, the maps are categorized as bitmaps and procedural maps. The bitmaps are 2D images and they get pixelated when zoomed on them. The procedural maps are Noise, Tiles, Marble, Gradient, and so on and they do not get pixelated when zoomed on them. The maps can be categorized into 2D maps, 3D maps, Compositors, Color Mods, and so on. These maps are discussed next.

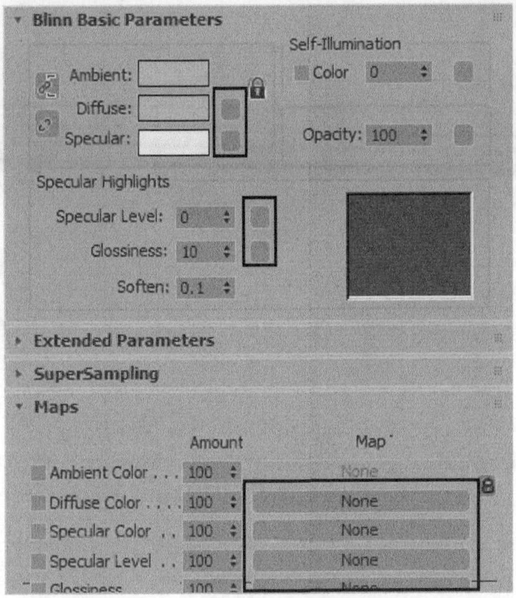

Figure 7-75 The square buttons highlighted for inserting maps

2D Maps

The 2D maps are two-dimensional images that can be assigned to geometric objects and are used to create an environment for the scene. The most commonly used two-dimensional maps such as **Bitmap**, **Checker**, **Combustion**, **Gradient**, **Gradient Ramp**, **Swirl**, and **Tiles** are discussed next.

Bitmap

The bitmaps are the simplest 2D images. To apply this map on an object, select the **Bitmap** map in the **Material/Map Browser** dialog box; the **Select Bitmap Image File** dialog box will be displayed. In this dialog box, navigate to a folder and select the image that you want to insert and choose the **Open** button; the image will be displayed in the selected sample slot. Also, various rollouts to modify the image map will be displayed in the **Material Editor** dialog box. Now, when the material is assigned to the object in the viewport, the object will be displayed with the assigned bitmap, as shown in Figure 7-76. You can select all the still or animated files that 3ds Max supports.

Checker

The **Checker** map is a combination of two colors, as shown in Figure 7-77. You can change or replace the colors with the images using the **Checker Parameters** rollout in the **Material Editor** dialog box.

Gradient

The **Gradient** map is used to create a ramp of three colors, as shown in Figure 7-78. You can modify or replace colors with images using the **Gradient Parameters** rollout of the **Material Editor** dialog box.

Figure 7-76 A sphere with the ***Bitmap*** *map applied*

Figure 7-77 A sphere with the ***Checker*** *map applied*

Figure 7-78 An object with the ***Gradient*** *map applied*

Gradient Ramp

The **Gradient Ramp** map is a 2D map similar to the **Gradient** map, as shown in Figure 7-79. However, in this map, you can use any numbers of colors and maps for creating the gradient. You can get the best effect using the **Gradient Ramp Parameters** rollout in the **Material Editor** dialog box.

Swirl

The **Swirl** map is a procedural map and is used to produce whirl effect in materials, as shown in Figure 7-80. You can modify the colors or replace the colors with the images using the **Swirl Parameters** rollout in the **Material Editor** dialog box.

Figure 7-79 A box with the ***Gradient Ramp*** *map applied*

Figure 7-80 A sphere with the ***Swirl*** *map applied*

Tiles

The **Tiles** map is a procedural map and is used to create bricks or tiles effect using different colors and maps, as shown in Figure 7-81. The better effect of this map can be acquired using different rollouts displayed in the **Material Editor** dialog box.

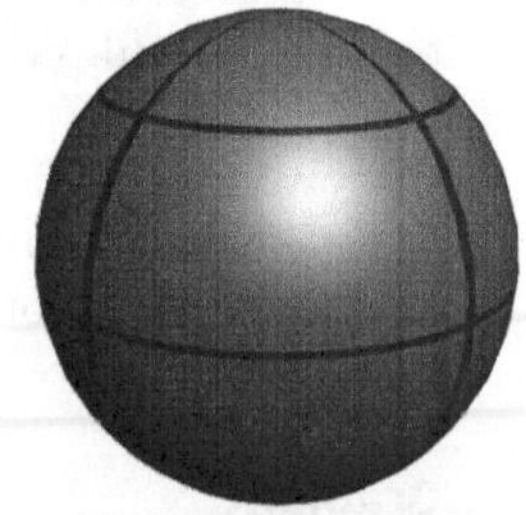

Figure 7-81 A sphere with the ***Tiles*** *map applied*

Substance Map and Map Output Selector Map

The **Substance** map is a collection of 2D textures. To use a texture from the **Substance** map, choose any of the desired map buttons from the **Material Editor** dialog box and select the **Map Output Selector** map from the **Maps** rollout in the **Material/Map Browser** dialog box. On doing so, the **Map Output Selector** map will be displayed in the **Material Type** button. Also, the **Parameters** rollout will be displayed, as shown in Figure 7-82. Next, choose the **None** button on the right of the **Source Map** parameter from the **Parameters** rollout and then select **Substance** from the **Material/Map Browser** dialog box; various rollouts such as **Global Substance Settings**, **Substance Package Browser**, **Coordinates**, and so on will be displayed in the **Material Editor** dialog box, as shown in Figure 7-83.

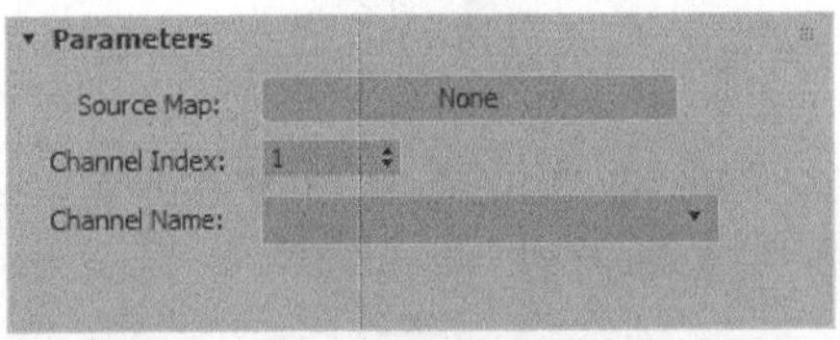

*Figure 7-82 The **Parameters** rollout of the **Map Output Selector** map*

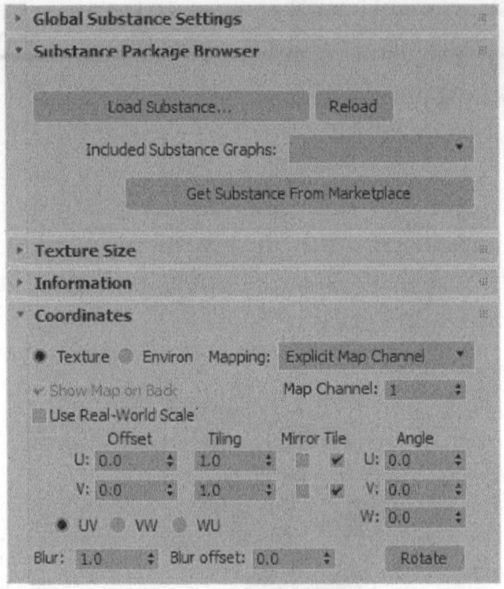

*Figure 7-83 The rollouts displayed on selecting the **Substance** map*

Now, choose the **Load Substance** button from the **Substance Package Browser** rollout; the **Browse from Substances** dialog box will be displayed. In this dialog box, select the desired texture and choose the **Open** button; the **Load Substance** button will be replaced by the texture you have selected. Also, the rollout for the respective texture parameters will be added at the bottom in the **Material Editor** dialog box. In this rollout, different parameters can be changed to get the desired result. Choose the **Get Substance From Marketplace** button to buy textures online. Next, choose the **Go to Parent** tool and select the desired channel name from the **Channel Name** drop-down list.

Vector Displacement Map

The **Vector Displacement** map is a procedural map and is used to displace the meshes in three dimensions. This map uses a range of colors to display its effect.

Vector Map

The **Vector Map** map is used to apply the vector-based graphics to objects. The image it generates is independent of display resolution. The **Vector Map** map supports a variety of industry-standard vector-graphic formats such as AutoCAD PAT Hatch, AI (Adobe Illustrator), SVG, PDF, and SVGZ.

Multi Tile Map

This map allows you to load multiple texture titles into the UV editor simultaneously. This map is useful for opening and displaying high resolution textures from the 3D painting applications such as ZBrush, Mudbox, and Mari.

Shape Map

You can use this map to create graphical textures in the in a 3ds Max scene that can be animated. It is useful in creating decals and logos directly in the scene without using an external image editor. All adjustments that you make to the shape are animatable.

To create a texture from the shape. Open the **Material Editor**, select a sample slot and then choose a material. Apply **Shape Map** to the **Diffuse** slot of the material. Apply the material to an object. 3ds Max displays the default shape logo in the viewport, as shown in Figure 7-84.

Now, create a shape such as circle, or line in the viewport. On the **Material Editor > Shape Parameters** rollout, choose the **None** button corresponding to the **Shape Object** parameter and then click on the shape you created in a viewport; the spline will be used as a texture, as shown in Figure 7-85.

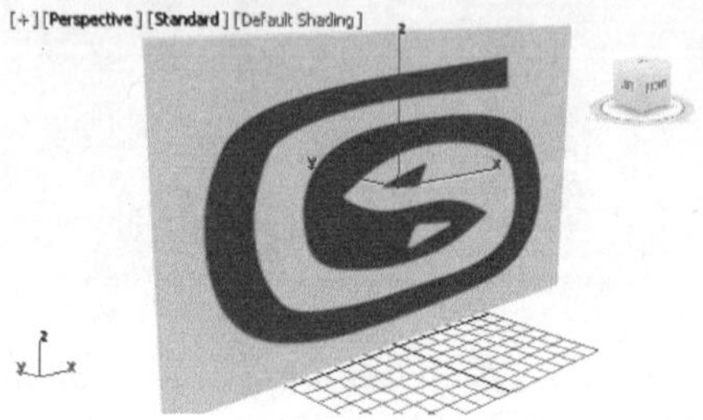

Figure 7-84 The default shape displayed in the viewport

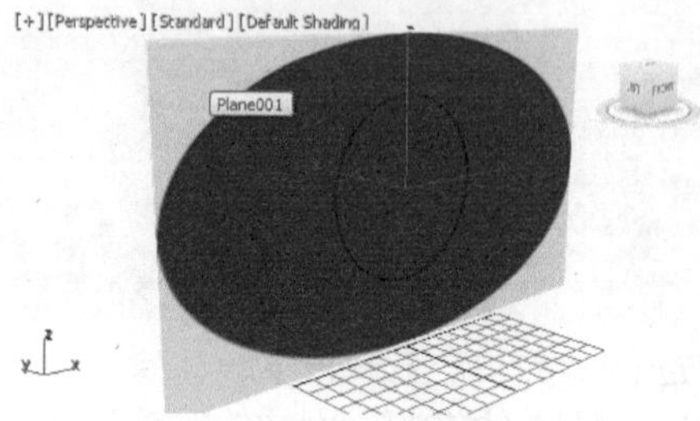

Figure 7-85 The spline texture shown in the viewport

To change the fill color and line color of the shape, use the **Fill Color** and **Line Color** swatches. You can also control the extent of the shape by using controls available in the **Map Boundary** area.

Text Map

This map is similar to the Shape Map with the difference that with this map a **TextPlus** object.

3D Maps

The 3D Maps are three-dimensional images that can be assigned to geometric objects. These are also known as procedural maps. The most commonly used three-dimensional maps such as **Cellular**, **Falloff**, **Noise**, and so on are discussed next.

Dent

The **Dent** map is used to produce material with 3D bumps on its surface. It is basically used as the **Bump** map available in the **Maps** rollout, refer to Figure 7-86. The effects of this map can be modified at an advanced level by using the **Dent Parameters** rollout in the **Material Editor** dialog box.

Cellular

The **Cellular** map is a 3D procedural map. It is used to produce materials such as sand, pebbled surfaces, and so on, as shown in Figure 7-87. The effects of this map can be modified at an advanced level using the **Cellular Parameters** rollout in the **Material Editor** dialog box.

Noise

The **Noise** map is used to create disturbance on the surface of an object by combining two colors or materials in different ways, as shown in Figure 7-88. The effects of this map can be modified at an advanced level using the **Noise Parameters** rollout in the **Material Editor** dialog box.

Figure 7-86 *A teapot with the **Dent** map applied*

Figure 7-87 *An object with the **Cellular** map applied*

Figure 7-88 *A sphere with the **Noise** map applied*

Smoke

The **Smoke** map is used to produce textures such as smoke from the fire, cloudy effect, or the beam of lights on the surface of an object, as shown in Figure 7-89. The effects of this map can be modified at an advanced level using the **Smoke Parameters** rollout of the **Material Editor** dialog box.

Speckle

The **Speckle** map is used to produce the texture of the patterned surfaces, as shown in Figure 7-90. The effects of this map can be modified at an advanced level using the **Speckle Parameters** rollout in the **Material Editor** dialog box.

Splat

The **Splat** map is used to produce texture such as splattered paint on the surface of an object, as shown in Figure 7-91. The effects of this map can be modified at an advanced level using the **Splat Parameters** rollout of the **Material Editor** dialog box.

Figure 7-89 *A sphere with the **Smoke** map applied*

Figure 7-90 *A box with the **Speckle** map applied*

Figure 7-91 *A box with the **Splat** map applied*

Stucco

The **Stucco** map is used to produce the textures such as plaster or cement on the surface of an object. You need to assign a **Bump** map using the **Maps** rollout to get its best effect, refer to Figure 7-92. The effects of this map can be modified at an advanced level using the **Stucco Parameters** rollout in the **Material Editor** dialog box.

Waves
The **Waves** map is used to create a wavy surface, as shown in Figure 7-93. The effects of this map can be modified at an advanced level using the **Waves Parameters** rollout in the **Material Editor** dialog box.

Wood
The **Wood** map is used to create the 3D wood texture on the surface of the object, refer to Figure 7-94. The effects of this map can be modified at an advanced level using the **Wood Parameters** rollout in the **Material Editor** dialog box.

*Figure 7-92 A wall with the **Stucco** map applied*

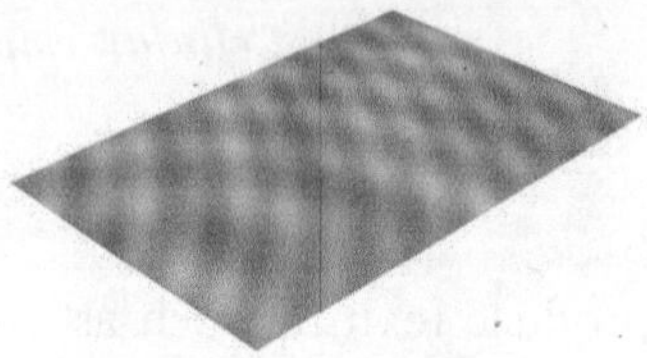

*Figure 7-93 A plane with the **Waves** map applied*

*Figure 7-94 A box with the **Wood** map applied*

Compositors Maps
The **Compositors** maps are used to combine the colors or the maps together. Various maps in this category are: **Composite**, **Mask**, **Mix**, and **RGB Multiply**.

Color Mods Maps
The **Color Mods** maps are used to modify or change the color of pixels in a material. Various maps in this category are: **Output**, **RGB Tint**, and **Vertex Color**.

Other Maps
There are some other types of maps such as **Raytrace**, **Flat Mirror**, and so on, which are used in a different way. These maps are discussed next.

Flat Mirror
The **Flat Mirror** map is used to create a material that generates reflection of other objects in the scene when assigned to the flat surfaces. You can get the best effect of this map using the **Flat Mirror Parameters** rollout in the **Material Editor** dialog box.

Raytrace
The **Raytrace** map is used to create the raytraced reflections and refractions on the surface of the objects. You can get the best effect of this map using the **Raytrace Parameters** rollout in the **Material Editor** dialog box.

Reflect/Refract

The **Reflect/Refract** map is used to produce the reflection and the refraction based on the objects in the scene. You can modify the effects using the **Reflect/Refract Parameters** rollout in the **Material Editor** dialog box.

Once you assign any of the above maps on the square button in the **Material Editor** dialog box, M will be displayed on it. If you right-click on this button, a shortcut menu will be displayed, as shown in Figure 7-95. Using the options in the shortcut menu, you can cut or copy the map and paste it at the desired place. You can also clear the unwanted map using the **Clear** option.

***Figure 7-95** The shortcut menu displayed on right-clicking on the **M** button*

TUTORIALS

Before starting the tutorials, you need to download the *c07_3dsmax_2017_tut.zip* file from *www.cadcim.com.* The path of the file is as follows: *Textbooks > Animation and Visual Effects > 3ds Max > Autodesk 3ds Max 2017: A Comprehensive Guide*

Extract the contents of the zip file and save them in the *Documents* folder.

Tutorial 1

In this tutorial, you will assign a map to the LCD monitor, as shown in Figure 7-96.

(Expected time: 15 min)

The following steps are required to complete this tutorial:

a. Create the project folder.
b. Open the file.
c. Assign the map to the LCD screen.
d. Assign material to support, back portion, speaker, and buttons.
e. Assign material to the front part.
f. Save and render the scene.

Creating the Project Folder

Create a new project folder with the name *c07_tut1* at *\Documents\3dsmax2017* and then save the file with the name *c07tut1*, as discussed in Tutorial 1 of Chapter 2.

***Figure 7-96** The model of LCD monitor*

Opening the File

In this section, you will open the file.

1. Choose **Open** from the **Application** menu; the **Open File** dialog box is displayed. In this dialog box, browse to the location *\Documents\c07_3dsmax_2017_tut* and select the *c07_tut1_start.max* file in it. Choose the **Open** button to open the file, refer to Figure 7-97.

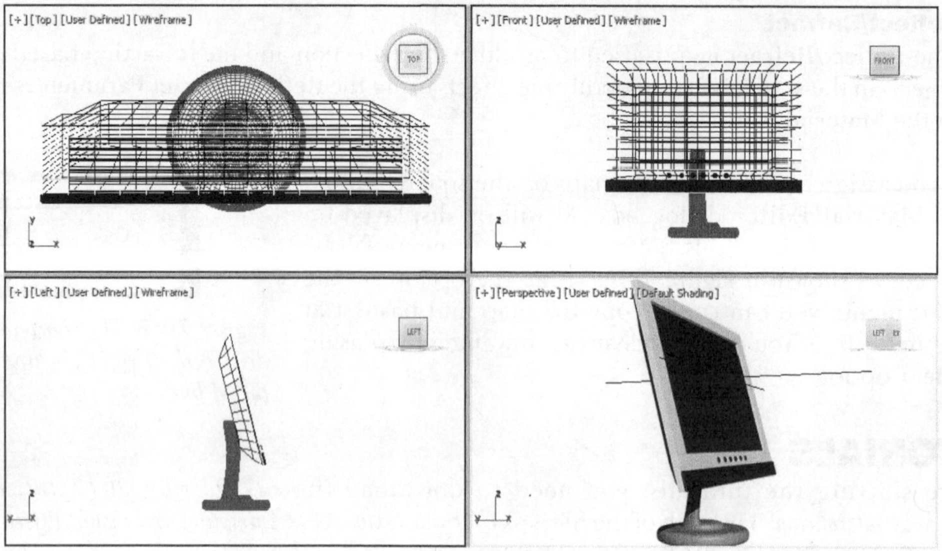

Figure 7-97 The LCD computer in viewports

2. Choose **Save As** from the **Application** menu; the **Save File As** dialog box is displayed. Browse to the location *\Documents\3dsmax2017\c07_tut1\scenes*. Save the file with the name *c07tut1.max* at this location.

Assigning the Map to the LCD Screen

In this section, you will apply an image to the LCD screen of the computer.

1. Display the image on your computer screen and press the PRT SCR keys. Next, open the **Paint** software and press the CTRL+V keys to paste the image. Now, save the file with the name *desktop_screen* in the *jpg* format at the following location: *\Documents\3dsmax2017\c07_tut1\sceneassets\images*.

2. Select *LCD monitor* from the Scene Explorer and then choose **Group > Open** from the menubar. Similarly, open the *monitor* group and then open the *front part* group. Select *screen* from the Scene Explorer and then choose the **Compact Material Editor** tool from the **Main Toolbar**; the **Material Editor** dialog box is displayed.

3. Select one of the sample slots from the **Material Editor** dialog box. In the **Material Name** drop-down list, enter **desktop background** and press the ENTER key. By default, the **Standard** material is displayed on the **Material Type** button. Make sure that the **Blinn** shader is selected in the **Shader Basic Parameters** rollout. You will use the same material for assigning the map.

   Next, you need to assign the *desktop_screen.jpg* image to the **Diffuse** map button.

4. In the **Blinn Basic Parameters** rollout, choose the **Diffuse** map button; the **Material/Map Browser** dialog box is displayed. Choose the **Bitmap** map from the **Maps > General** rollout and choose the **OK** button; the **Select Bitmap Image File** dialog box is displayed. As the project folder is already set, the *images* folder is displayed in the **Look in** drop-down list of

this dialog box. Select the file **desktop_screen.jpg** and then choose the **Open** button; the image is displayed in the selected sample slot.

5. Choose the **Go to Parent** tool.

6. In the **Specular Highlights** area, set the values as follows:

   Specular Level: **40** Glossiness: **16**

   Next, you need to apply the map to *screen*.

7. Make sure that *screen* is selected in the viewport and the *desktop background* material is selected in the **Material Editor** dialog box. Next, choose the **Assign Material to Selection** button; the *desktop background* material is assigned to *screen* of LCD computer in the viewport.

8. Now, choose the **Show Shaded Material in Viewport** button, if it is not already chosen; the *desktop background* material is displayed on *screen* in the Perspective viewport.

Assigning Material to Support, Back Portion, Speaker, and Buttons

In this section, you will assign material to *support, back portion,* and *speaker* by changing the parameters in the **Blinn Basic Parameters** rollout.

1. Select next unused sample slot from the **Material Editor** dialog box. In the **Material Name** drop-down list, enter **blackmat** and press the ENTER key. By default, the **Standard** material is displayed on the **Material Type** button. Make sure that the **Blinn** shader is selected in the **Shader Basic Parameters** rollout.

2. In the **Blinn Basic Parameters** rollout, choose the **Diffuse** color swatch to change the color of the material; the **Color Selector: Diffuse Color** dialog box is displayed. Set the values as follows:

   Red: **8** Green: **8** Blue: **8**

   Now, choose the **OK** button to close this dialog box.

3. Choose the **Specular** color swatch to change the color of specular highlights; the **Color Selector: Specular Color** dialog box is displayed. Set the values as follows:

   Red: **146** Green: **146** Blue: **146**

   Now, choose the **OK** button to close this dialog box.

4. In the **Specular Highlights** area, set the values as follows:

   Specular Level: **58** Glossiness: **54**

5. Select *support, back portion, speaker* and *buttons* from the Scene Explorer. Make sure *blackmat* material is selected in the Material Editor. Next, choose the **Assign Material to Selection** and **Show Shaded Material in Viewport** buttons; *blackmat* material is assigned to the selected objects.

Assigning Material to the Front Part

In this section, you will assign modified *blackmat* material to *front part*.

1. Make sure *blackmat* material is selected in the Material Editor. Next, drag it to next sample slot.

2. In the **Material Name** drop-down list, change the material name to **whitemat**.

3. In the **Blinn Basic Parameters** rollout, choose the **Diffuse** color swatch to change the color of the material; the **Color Selector: Diffuse Color** dialog box is displayed. Set the values as follows:

   Red: **254** Green: **249** Blue: **240**

   Now, choose the **OK** button to close this dialog box.

4. Assign the *whitemat* material to *front portion,* as discussed earlier.

Saving and Rendering the Scene

In this section, you will save the scene and then render it. You can also view the final rendered image of this model by downloading the file *c07_3dsmax_2017_rndr.zip* from *www.cadcim.com.* The path of the file is as follows: *Textbooks > Animation and Visual Effects > 3ds Max > Autodesk 3ds Max 2017: A Comprehensive Guide*

1. Change the background color of the scene to white, as discussed in Tutorial 1 of Chapter 2.

2. Choose **Save** from the **Application** menu.

3. Activate the Perspective viewport. Next, choose the **Render Production** tool from the **Main Toolbar**; the **Rendered Frame** window is displayed. This window shows the final output of the scene, refer to Figures 7-98 and 7-99.

Figure 7-98 The final output after rendering (view 1)

Figure 7-99 The final output after rendering (view 2)

Tutorial 2

In this tutorial, you will create and assign material to the objects in the scene, refer to Figure 7-100. **(Expected time: 30 min)**

Figure 7-100 The textured scene

The following steps are required to complete this tutorial:

a. Create the project folder.
b. Open the file.

c. Create material for bench.
d. Create material for street lamp.
e. Create material for dustbin.
f. Create material for pots and plants.
g. Save and render the scene.

Creating the Project Folder

Create a new project folder with the name *c07_tut2* at *\Documents\3dsmax2017* and save the file with the name *c07tut2*, as discussed in Tutorial 1 of Chapter 2.

Opening the File

In this section, you will open the file.

1. Open Windows Explorer and then browse to the *c07_3dsmax_2017_tut* folder and copy all jpeg files from this folder to *\Documents\3dsmax2017\c07_tut2\sceneassets\images.*

2. Choose the **Open** button from the **Application** menu; the **Open File** dialog box is displayed. In this dialog box, browse to *\Documents\c07_3dsmax_2017_tut* and then select the **c07_tut2_start.max** file from it. Choose the **Open** button to open the file, refer to Figure 7-101.

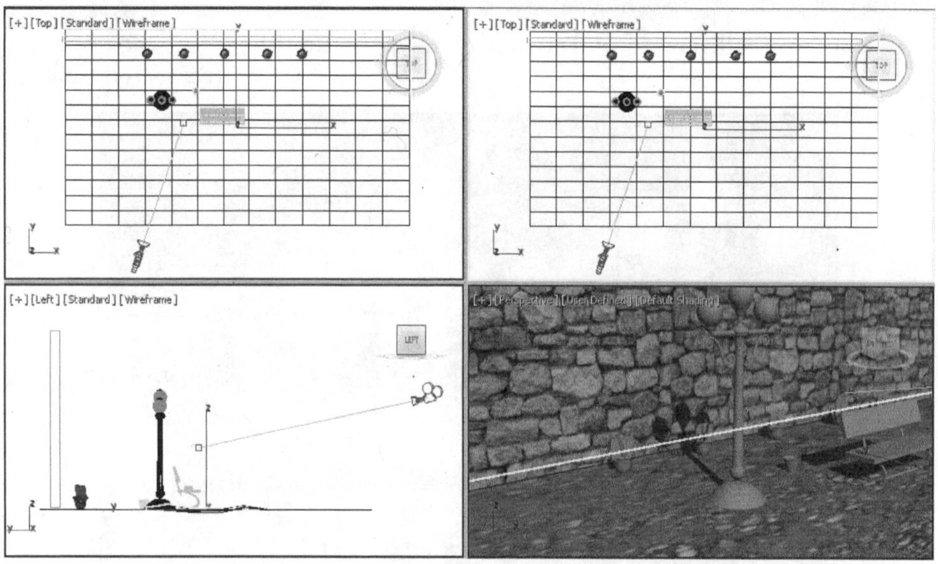

Figure 7-101 *The file displayed*

3. Choose the **Save As** button from the **Application** menu; the **Save File As** dialog box is displayed. Browse to the location *\Documents\3dsmax2017\c07_tut2\scenes*. Save the file with the name *c07tut2.max* at this location.

Creating Material for Bench

In this section, you will create material for bench using the **Standard** and **Architectural** materials.

1. Select *bench* from the Scene Explorer. Next, choose **Group > Open** from the menu bar; the *bench* group is opened.

2. Press the M key; the **Material Editor** dialog box is displayed. Select unused sample slot from the **Material Editor** dialog box. In the **Material Name** drop-down list, enter **wood**.

3. In the **Blinn Basic Parameters** rollout, choose the **Diffuse** map button located next to the **Diffuse** button; the **Material/Map Browser** dialog box is displayed. Choose the **Bitmap** map from **Maps > General** rollout and choose the **OK** button; the **Select Bitmap Image File** dialog box is displayed. As the project folder is already set, the *images* folder is displayed in the **Look in** drop-down list of this dialog box. Select the **wood.jpg** file and then choose the **Open** button; the image is displayed in the selected sample slot.

4. Select *back* from the *bench* group. Next, choose the **Assign Material to Selection** and **Show Shaded Material in Viewport** buttons from the **Material Editor** dialog box; the *wood* material is assigned to *back,* as shown in Figure 7-102.

   You will notice that the *wood* material is not displayed properly on *back*. To properly display this material, you need to follow the steps given next.

5. Make sure *back* is selected. Next, select the **UVW Map** modifier from the **Modifier List** drop-down list of the **Command Panel**; the modifier is displayed in the modifier stack and rollouts are displayed below the modifier stack.

6. In the **Parameters** rollout, select the **Box** radio button from the **Mapping** area. Next, select the **X** radio button and then choose the **Fit** button from the **Alignment** area; the texture is properly applied on *back,* as shown in Figure 7-103.

Figure 7-102 *The wood material assigned to back*

Figure 7-103 *The wood material displayed after using the* ***UVW Map*** *modifier*

7. Select *seat* from the Scene Explorer. In the **Material Editor** dialog box, make sure that *wood* material is selected. Next, choose the **Assign Material to Selection** button from the **Material Editor** dialog box; the material is assigned to *seat.*

8. Repeat the procedure in steps 5 and 6 to apply the **UVW Map** modifier to *seat.* Figure 7-104 shows the *wood* material assigned after using the **UVW Map** modifier.

9. Select all backsupports and supports of the *bench* group from the Scene Explorer. Next, select unused sample slot from the **Material Editor** dialog box. In the **Material Name** drop-down list, enter **black metal**.

10. Choose the **Standard** button on the right of the **Material Name** drop-down list; the **Material/ Map Browser** dialog box is displayed. Select the **Architectural** material from the **Materials > General** rollout and choose **OK**; the **Standard** material changes to **Architectural** material in the **Material Editor** dialog box.

11. In the **Material Editor** dialog box, select **Metal - Flat** from the drop-down list in the **Templates** rollout.

12. In the **Physical Qualities** rollout, choose the **Diffuse Color** color swatch; the **Color Selector: Diffuse** dialog box is displayed. In this dialog box, set the black color and choose **OK**.

13. Choose the **Assign Material to Selection** and **Show Shaded Material in Viewport** buttons from the **Material Editor** dialog box; the *black metal* material is assigned to all supports in the *bench* group.

14. Render the Perspective viewport; the rendered image is displayed, refer to Figure 7-105.

Figure 7-104 The wood material displayed after using the UVW Map modifier

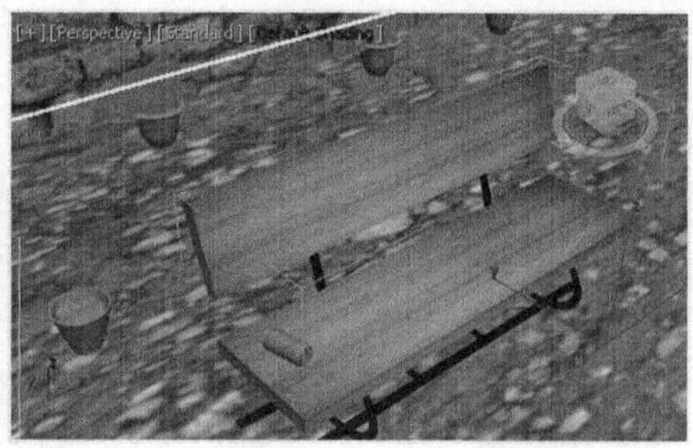

Figure 7-105 The rendered image

15. Select *bench* from the Scene Explorer. Next, choose **Group > Close** from the menu bar to close the *bench* group.

Creating Material for Street Lamp

In this section, you will create material for street lamp using the **Standard** and **Architectural** materials.

1. Select *street lamp* from the Scene Explorer. Next, choose **Group > Open** from the menu bar; the *street lamp* group is opened.

2. Select the *black metal* material from the **Material Editor** dialog box and drag it to unused sample slot. Next, change the name in the **Material Name** drop-down list to **green metal**.

3. In the **Physical Qualities** rollout, choose the **Diffuse Color** color swatch; the **Color Selector: Diffuse** dialog box is displayed. In this dialog box, set the values as follows and choose **OK**.

   Red: **16** Green: **28** Blue: **7**

4. Select all parts of *street lamp* except *dome01, dome02,* and *dome03.* Next, choose the **Assign Material to Selection** and **Show Shaded Material in Viewport** buttons from the **Material Editor** dialog box; the *green metal* material is assigned to selected parts of the *street lamp* group.

   Next, you will create material for domes.

5. Select next unused sample slot from the **Material Editor** dialog box. In the **Material Name** drop-down list, enter **dome**.

6. In the **Blinn Basic Parameters** rollout, select the check box in the **Self-Illumination** area; the **Color** spinner is changed to the **Color** color swatch. Choose the **Color** color swatch; the **Self-Illum Color** dialog box is displayed. Enter **198** in the **Red**, **Green**, and **Blue** spinners and choose **OK**.

7. Enter **75** in the **Opacity** spinner located below the **Self-Illumination** area.

8. Select *dome01, dome02,* and *dome03* from the Scene Explorer. Next, choose the **Assign Material to Selection** and **Show Shaded Material in Viewport** buttons from the **Material Editor** dialog box; the *dome* material is assigned to *dome01, dome02,* and *dome03.*

9. Render the Perspective viewport; the rendered image is displayed, refer to Figure 7-106.

Figure 7-106 *The rendered image*

10. Select *street lamp* from the Scene Explorer. Next, choose **Group > Close** from the menu bar to close the *street lamp* group.

Creating Material for Can

In this section, you will create material for *can* using the **Multi/Sub-Object** material. You will also change the default scanline renderer to mental ray renderer to use the material from the **Autodesk Material Library**.

1. Choose the **Render Setup** tool from the **Main Toolbar**; the **Render Setup: Scanline Renderer** dialog box is displayed.

2. In this dialog box, select **NVIDIA mental ray** from the **Renderer** drop-down list; the **Scanline Renderer** is changed to **NVIDIA mental ray** renderer.

3. Select next unused sample slot from the **Material Editor** dialog box. In the **Material Name** drop-down list, enter **canmat**.

4. Choose the **Standard** button on the right of the **Material Name** drop-down list; the **Material/Map Browser** dialog box is displayed. Select the **Multi/Sub-Object** material from the **Materials > General** rollout and choose **OK**; the **Replace Material** dialog box is displayed. In this dialog box, select the **Discard old material?** radio button and choose **OK**. The **Standard** material is replaced by the **Multi/Sub-Object** material in the **Material Editor** dialog box.

5. In the **Multi/Sub-Object Basic Parameters** rollout, choose the **Set Number** button; the **Set Number of Materials** dialog box is displayed. In this dialog box, enter **2** in the **Number of Materials** spinner and choose **OK**; sub-materials in the **Multi/Sub-Object Basic Parameters** rollout are reduced to 2.

6. Enter **body** in the **Name** text box of first sub-material and choose the **None** button at the right of this text box; the **Material/Map Browser** dialog box is displayed. In this dialog box, select the **Standard** material from the **Materials > Scanline** rollout and choose **OK**.

7. Select **Metal** from the drop-down list in the **Shader basic Parameters** rollout.

8. Choose the **Diffuse** map button from the **Metal Basic Parameters** rollout of the **Material Editor** dialog box; the **Material/Map Browser** dialog box is displayed. Choose the **Bitmap** map from the **Maps > General** rollout and choose the **OK** button; the **Select Bitmap Image File** dialog box is displayed. As the project folder is already set, the *images* folder is displayed in the **Look in** drop-down list of this dialog box. Select the **pepsi.jpg** file and then choose the **Open** button; the image is displayed in the selected sample slot.

9. Choose the **Go to Parent** tool. Next, enter **74** and **56** in the **Specular Level** and **Glossinesss** spinner of the **Specular Highlights** area, respectively. Next, choose the **Show Shaded Material in Viewport** button.

10. Choose the **Go to Parent** tool again. Next, enter **cap** in the **Name** text box of second sub-material and choose the **None** button at the right of this text box; the **Material/Map Browser** dialog box is displayed. In this dialog box, select **Aluminium - Polished** from the **Autodesk Material Library > Metal > Aluminium** rollout and choose **OK**; the **Autodesk Metal** material is displayed in the **Material Editor** dialog box.

11. In the **Material Editor** dialog box, select **Semi-polished** from the **Finish** drop-down list of the **Metal** rollout. Next, choose the **Go to Parent** tool to return to parent level. Next, choose the **Show Shaded Material in Viewport** button.

12. Select *can* from the **Scene Explorer** and choose the **Modify** tab from the **Command Panel**. Next, click on the arrow sign on the left of the **Editable Poly** in the modifier stack.

13. Select the **Polygon** sub-object level; it gets activated and turns yellow.

Note
*The **Editable Poly** objects and their sub-objects levels are discussed in detail in Chapter 8.*

14. Click on the cap of *can*; a polygon is selected, as shown in Figure 7-107. Next, enter **2** in the **Set ID** spinner of the **Polygon: Material IDs** area, if not already set.

15. Click on the cap of *can* again and then press CTRL+i; rest of the polygons of *can* are selected, as shown in Figure 7-108. Next, enter **1** in the **Set ID** spinner in the **Polygon: Material IDs** area, if not already set.

Figure 7-107 *Selected polygon of can*

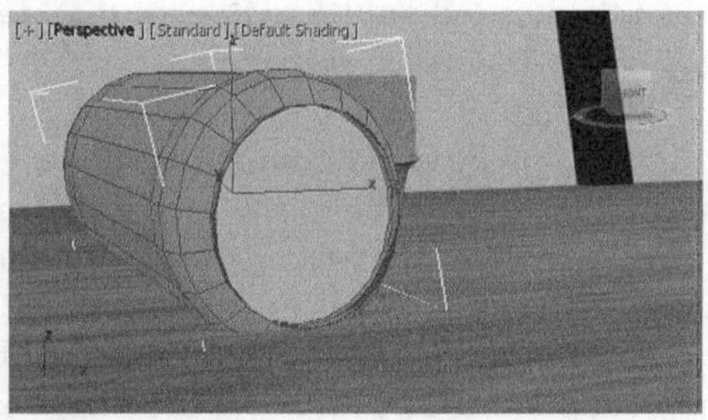

Figure 7-108 *Rest of the polygons selected*

16. In the modifier stack, select the **Polygon** sub-object level again to deactivate it.

17. Make sure *can* is selected. Next, choose the **Assign Material to Selection** button from the **Material Editor** dialog box; the *canmat* material is assigned to *can,* refer to Figure 7-109.

Creating Material for Dustbin

In this section, you will create material for *dustbin* using the **Standard** material.

1. Select unused sample slot from the **Material Editor** dialog box. In the **Material Name** drop-down list, enter **dustbinmat**.

2. In the **Blinn Basic Parameters** rollout, choose the **Diffuse** map button located next to the **Diffuse** color swatch; the **Material/Map Browser** dialog box is displayed. Choose the **Bitmap** map from the **Maps > General** rollout and choose the **OK** button; the **Select Bitmap Image File** dialog box is displayed. As the project folder is already set, the *images* folder is displayed in the **Look in** drop-down list of this dialog box. Select the **dustbin.jpg** file and then choose the **Open** button; the image is displayed in the selected sample slot.
3. Choose the **Go to Parent** tool. Next, enter **35** and **25** in the **Specular Level** and **Glossinesss**

spinners of the **Specular Highlights** area, respectively.

4. Select *dustbin* from the Scene Explorer. Next, assign the *dustbinmat* material to it, as discussed earlier, refer to Figure 7-110.

Figure 7-109 *The canmat material displayed*

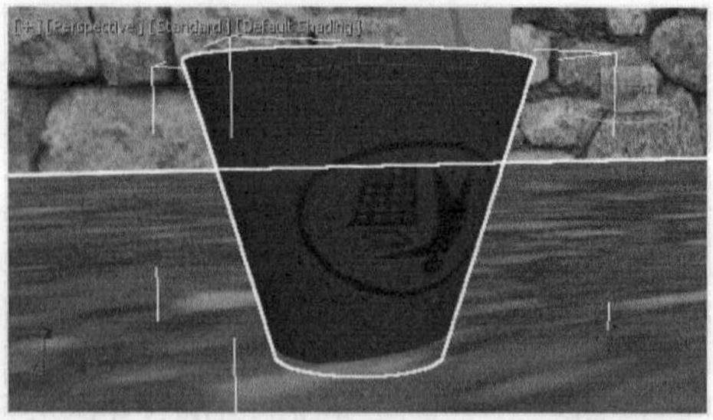

Figure 7-110 *The dustbinmat material displayed*

Next, you will create material for *garbage*.

5. Select the unused sample slot from the **Material Editor** dialog box. In the **Material Name** drop-down list, enter **garbagemat**.

6. In the **Blinn Basic Parameters** rollout, choose the **Diffuse** map button located next to the **Diffuse** color swatch; the **Material/Map Browser** dialog box is displayed. Choose the **Bitmap** map from the **Maps > General** rollout and choose the **OK** button; the **Select Bitmap Image File** dialog box is displayed. As the project folder is already set, the *images* folder is displayed in the **Look in** drop-down list of this dialog box. Select the **garbage.jpg** file and then choose the **Open** button; the image is displayed in the selected sample slot.

7. Assign the *garbagemat* material to *garbage*, as discussed earlier, refer to Figure 7-111.

Creating Material for Pots and Plants

In this section, you will assign material to pots and plants using the **Standard** material. You will use the **Opacity** map to assign texture to plants.

1. Select *pot_plants* from the Scene Explorer. Next, choose **Group > Open** from the menu bar; the *pot_plants* group is opened.

2. Select the unused sample slot from the **Material Editor** dialog box. In the **Material Name** drop-down list, enter **potmat**.

3. Choose the **Standard** button on the right of the **Material Name** drop-down list; the **Material/Map Browser** dialog box is displayed. In this dialog box, select **Plaster - Ventetian Rough** from the **Autodesk Material Library > Stucco** rollout and choose **OK**; the **Autodesk Generic** material is displayed in the **Material Editor** dialog box.

4. Choose the color swatch from the **Generic** rollout of the **Material Editor** dialog box; the **Color Selector: Generic_Color** dialog box is displayed. In this dialog box, set the values as follows:

   Red: **0.161** Green: **0.043** Blue: **0**

Choose **OK** to close the dialog box.

5. Make sure *pot* is selected. Next, select the **UVW Map** modifier from the **Modifier List** drop-down list of the **Command Panel**; the **UVW Map** modifier is displayed in the modifier stack and rollouts are displayed below the modifier stack.

6. In the **Parameters** rollout, select the **Cylindrical** radio button from the **Mapping** area. Next, select the **X** radio button and choose the **Fit** button from the **Alignment** area.

7. Make sure *pot* is selected. Next, assign the *potmat* material to it, as discussed earlier.

Next, you will create material for *plant1* and *plant2*.

8. Select the unused sample slot from the **Material Editor** dialog box. In the **Material Name** drop-down list, enter **plant**.

9. In the **Blinn Basic Parameters** rollout, choose the **Diffuse** map button located next to the **Diffuse** color swatch; the **Material/Map Browser** dialog box is displayed. Choose the **Bitmap** map from the **Maps > General** rollout and choose the **OK** button; the **Select Bitmap Image File** dialog box is displayed. As the project folder is already set, the *images* folder is displayed in the **Look in** drop-down list of this dialog box. Select the **plant_diff.jpg** file and then choose the **Open** button; the image is displayed in the selected sample slot.

10. Choose the **Go to Parent** tool. Next, choose the **Opacity** map button on the right of the **Opacity** spinner; the **Material/Map Browser** dialog box is displayed. Choose the **Bitmap** map from the **Maps > General** rollout and choose the **OK** button; the **Select Bitmap Image File** dialog box is displayed. As the project folder is already set, the *images* folder is displayed in the **Look in** drop-down list of this dialog box. Select the **plant_op.jpg** file and then choose the **Open** button; the image is displayed in the selected sample slot.

11. Choose the **Go to Parent** tool. Next, assign the *plant* material to *plant1* and *plant2,* as discussed earlier, refer to Figure 7-112.

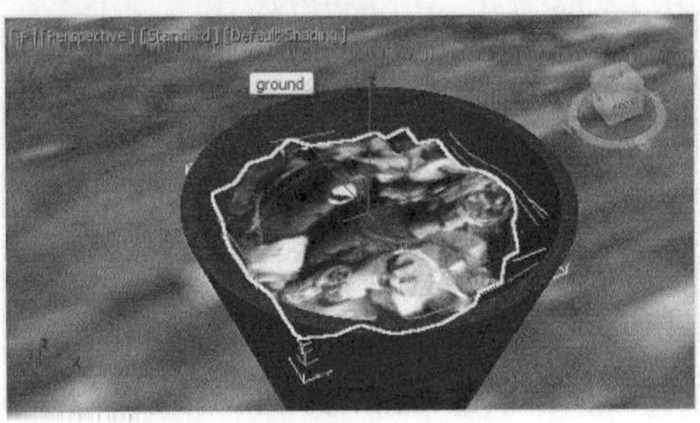

Figure 7-111 The garbagemat material applied

Figure 7-112 The plant material applied

Note

*You can also insert the **Diffuse** and **Opacity** maps using the **Maps** rollout.*

Next, you will apply material to *soil*.

12. Select the unused sample slot from the **Material Editor** dialog box. In the **Material Name** drop-down list, enter **clay**.

13. In the **Blinn Basic Parameters** rollout, choose the **Diffuse** map button located next to the **Diffuse** color swatch; the **Material/Map Browser** dialog box is displayed. Choose the **Bitmap** map from the **Maps > General** rollout and choose the **OK** button; the **Select Bitmap Image File** dialog box is displayed. As the project folder is already set, the *images* folder is displayed in the **Look in** drop-down list of this dialog box. Select the **clay.jpg** file and then choose the **Open** button; the image is displayed in the selected sample slot.

14. Choose the **Go to Parent** tool. Next, assign the *clay* material to *soil,* as discussed earlier, refer to Figure 7-113.

*Figure 7-113 The **clay** material applied to soil*

15. Select *pot_plants* from the Scene Explorer. Next, choose **Group > Close** from the menu bar to close the *pot_plants* group.

16. Similarly, open groups *pot_plants001, pot_plants002, pot_plants003,* and *pot_plants004.* Next, apply the **UVW Map** modifier to *pot001, pot002, pot003,* and *pot004.*

17. Assign *pot, plant,* and *clay* material to corresponding objects in these groups and then close the groups.

18. Close the **Material Editor** dialog box.

Saving and Rendering the Scene

In this section, you will save the scene and then render it. You can also view the final rendered image of this model by downloading the *c07_3dsmax_2017_rndr.zip* file from *www.cadcim.com.* The path of the file is as follows: *Textbooks > Animation and Visual Effects > 3ds Max > Autodesk 3ds Max 2017: A Comprehensive Guide*

1. Choose **Save** from the **Application** menu.
2. Activate the Perspective viewport. Next, choose the **Render Production** tool from the **Main**

Toolbar; the **Rendered Frame** window is displayed. This window shows the final output of the scene, refer to Figure 7-114.

Figure 7-114 *The final output of the scene*

Tutorial 3

In this tutorial, you will create brass material and assign it to a flower pot, as shown in Figure 7-115. **(Expected time: 15 min)**

The following steps are required to complete this tutorial:

a. Create the project folder.
b. Open the file.
c. Create brass material for the flower pot.
d. Save and render the scene.

Figure 7-115 *The model of a flower pot*

Creating the Project Folder

Create a new project folder with the name *c07_tut3* at *\Documents\3dsmax2017* and then save the file with the name *c07tut3*, as discussed in Tutorial 1 of Chapter 2.

Opening the File

In this section, you will open the file.

1. Open the Windows Explorer and then browse to the *c07_3dsmax_2017_tut* folder and copy the

Lakerem2.jpg file from this folder to the location *\Documents\3dsmax2017\c07_tut3\sceneassets\images*.

2. Choose **Open** from the **Application** menu; the **Open File** dialog box is displayed. In this dialog box, browse to the location *\Documents\c07_3dsmax_2017_tut* and select the *c07_tut3_start.max* file in it. Choose the **Open** button to open the file, refer to Figure 7-116.

Figure 7-116 *The flower pot geometry with a plant*

3. Choose **Save As** from the **Application menu**; the **Save File As** dialog box is displayed. Browse to the location *\Documents\3dsmax2017\c07_tut3\scenes*. Save the file with the name *c07tut3.max* at this location.

Creating Brass Material for the Flower Pot

In this section, you will create the brass material for the flower pot by using the **Compact Material Editor** tool.

1. Select *flower pot* in a viewport and choose the **Material Editor** tool from the **Main Toolbar**; the **Material Editor** dialog box is displayed.

2. Select one of the empty sample slots in the **Material Editor** dialog box. In the **Material Name** drop-down list of this dialog box, enter **brass**.

3. By default, the **Standard** material is displayed on the **Material Type** button and you need to use the same for creating the *brass* material.

   Next, you need to set parameters for the **Standard** material.

4. In the **Shader Basic Parameters** rollout, select the **Metal** shader option from the drop-down list; the **Metal Basic Parameters** rollout is displayed. Select the **2-Sided** check box.
5. In the **Metal Basic Parameters** rollout, choose the **Diffuse** color swatch to change the color

of the material; the **Color Selector** dialog box is displayed. Set the values as follows:

Red: **253** Green: **159** Blue: **37**

Now, choose the **OK** button to close this dialog box.

6. In the **Specular Highlights** area, set the values as follows:

   Specular Level: **80** Glossiness: **75**

   Next, you need to assign the **Reflection** map from the **Maps** rollout to get a realistic effect.

7. Expand the **Maps** rollout in the **Material Editor** dialog box; a list of maps is displayed.

8. Select the **Reflection** check box to make it active. Choose the **Reflection** map button that is labeled as **None** on the right of the **Reflection** spinner; the **Material/Map Browser** dialog box is displayed. Select the **Bitmap** map from the **Maps > General** rollout and choose the **OK** button; the **Select Bitmap Image File** dialog box is displayed.

   As the project folder is already set, the *images* folder is displayed in the **Look in** drop-down list of this dialog box.

9. Select the file *Lakerem2.jpg* from this dialog box and choose the **Open** button; the image is displayed in the selected sample slot, as shown in Figure 7-117.

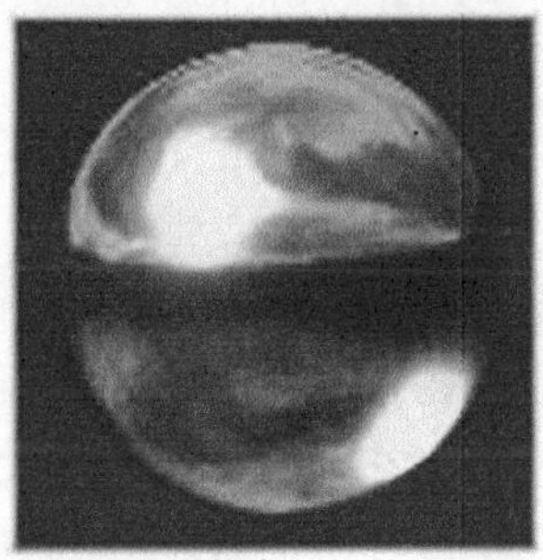

***Figure 7-117** The brass material displayed in the sample slot*

10. Choose the **Go to Parent** tool from the **Material Editor** dialog box. In the **Maps** rollout, set the value **50** in the **Reflection** spinner.

11. Make sure that *flower pot* is selected in the viewport and the *brass* material is selected in the **Material Editor** dialog box.

12. Choose the **Assign Material to Selection** button; the *brass* material is assigned to *flower pot*.

13. Choose the **Show Shaded Material in Viewport** button; the **brass** material is displayed on *flower pot* in the Perspective viewport.

Saving and Rendering the Scene

In this section, you will save the scene and then render it. You can also view the final rendered image of this model by downloading the *c07_3dsmax_2017_rndr.zip* file from *www.cadcim.com*. The path of the file is as follows: *Textbooks > Animation and Visual Effects > 3ds Max > Autodesk 3ds Max 2017: A Comprehensive Guide*

1. Choose **Save** from the **Application** menu.

2. Activate the Perspective viewport. Next, choose the **Render Production** tool from the **Main Toolbar**; the **Rendered Frame** window is displayed. This window shows the final output of the scene, refer to Figure 7-115.

Self-Evaluation Test

Answer the following questions and then compare them to those given at the end of this chapter:

1. Which of the following keys is used to invoke the **Material Editor** dialog box?

   (a) S (b) L
   (c) M (d) G

2. Which of the following buttons in the **Material Editor** dialog box is used to pick material from an object in the viewport to apply it to the active sample slot?

   (a) **Assign Material to Selection** (b) **Get Material**
   (c) **Pick Material from Object** (d) All of these

3. Which of the following materials is known as the **Compound** material?

   (a) **Blend** (b) **Composite**
   (c) **Double-Sided** (d) All of these

4. Which of the following materials has the **Templates** rollout to insert preset materials to the objects?

   (a) **Standard** (b) **Architectural**
   (c) **Raytrace** (d) **Composite**

5. Which of the following shaders in the **Standard** material is used to create elliptical highlights?

   (a) **Anisotropic** (b) **Blinn**
   (c) **Metal** (d) **Phong**

6. The _________ color swatch in the **Basic Parameters** rollout of shaders is used to specify the color of the objects in direct light.

7. The _________ shader in the **Standard** material is used to create matte highlights.

8. The _________ material is used to provide highly realistic raytraced images.

9. The **Material Editor** dialog box is used to create new materials and maps for objects to make them look more realistic. (T/F)

10. The **Get Material** tool is used to select materials or maps for the selected sample slot. (T/F)

11. The **Phong** shader is very similar to the **Oren-Nayar-Blinn** shader. (T/F)

Review Questions

Answer the following questions:

1. Which of the following maps in the **Material/Map Browser** dialog box is a 2D map?

   (a) **Checker** (b) **Bitmap**
   (c) Both (a) and (b) (d) **Wood**

2. Which of the following **Standard** maps is used to select the **Bitmap** image file to make the objects realistic?

   (a) **Checker** (b) **Dent**
   (c) **Bitmap** (d) All of these

3. Which of the following maps is used to produce textures such as plaster and cement?

   (a) **Stucco** (b) **Speckle**
   (c) **Splat** (d) **Smoke**

4. The __________ spinner in the **Basic Parameters** rollout of the **Standard** material is used to control the transparency of material.

5. The __________ material is used to create the preset materials such as **Glass**, **Water**, **Paper**, and so on.

6. The **Ambient** color swatch in the __________ material is used to specify the amount of absorption of the ambient light by the material.

7. The **Composite** maps are used to modify or change the color of pixels in a material. (T/F)

8. You can apply maps to different materials using the **Maps** rollout. (T/F)

9. The **Flat Mirror** map is used to generate reflections and refractions based on the objects in the scene. (T/F)

10. The **Anisotropic** shader in the **Standard** material has two specular highlight controls. (T/F)

EXERCISES

The rendered output of the models used in the following exercises can be accessed by downloading the *c07_3dsmax_2017_exr.zip* from *www.cadcim.com*. The path of the file is as follows: *Textbooks > Animation and Visual Effects > 3ds Max > Autodesk 3ds Max 2017: A Comprehensive Guide*

Exercise 1

Create the model of cups and glasses shown in Figure 7-118 using the **Line** tool and the **Lathe** modifier. To create the steel material, you need to use the **Oren-Nayar-Blinn** shader in the **Standard** material and the **Reflection** map in the **Maps** rollout. **(Expected time: 15 min)**

Exercise 2

Download the file *c07_3dsmax_2017_exr.zip* from *www.cadcim.com*. Extract the contents of the zipped file and open *c07_exr2_start* from it. Next, assign different maps and materials to give it a realistic view, as shown in Figure 7-119. **(Expected time: 15 min)**

Exercise 3

Create the model of a tea cup in the viewport, as shown in Figure 7-120. Next, create copper material using the **Phong** shader from the **Standard** material and assign it to the object. **(Expected time: 15 min)**

Figure 7-118 *The model of cups and glasses*

Figure 7-119 *The model of a room*

Figure 7-120 *The model of a tea cup*

Answers to Self-Evaluation Test

1. c, **2.** c, **3.** d, **4.** b, **5.** a, **6. Diffuse**, **7. Oren-Nayar-Blinn**, **8. Raytrace**, **9.** T, **10.** T, **11.** F

8

Modifying 3D Mesh Objects

Learning Objectives

After completing this chapter, you will be able to:

- *Convert objects into editable mesh*
- *Use sub-object levels*
- *Convert objects into editable poly*
- *Modify editable mesh and editable poly objects*

INTRODUCTION

In the previous chapters, you have learned to create different 3D objects and shapes using the tools in the **Create** tab of the **Command Panel**. In this chapter, you will learn to modify the 3D mesh objects at an advanced level.

MODIFYING 3D OBJECTS

To modify 3D objects, select the object and choose the **Modify** tab in the **Command Panel**; the Modify panel will be displayed with various rollouts. In the Modify panel, the default name and color of the object will be displayed at the top. The modifier stack displays the name of the tools that you have used for creating the object, as shown in Figure 8-1.

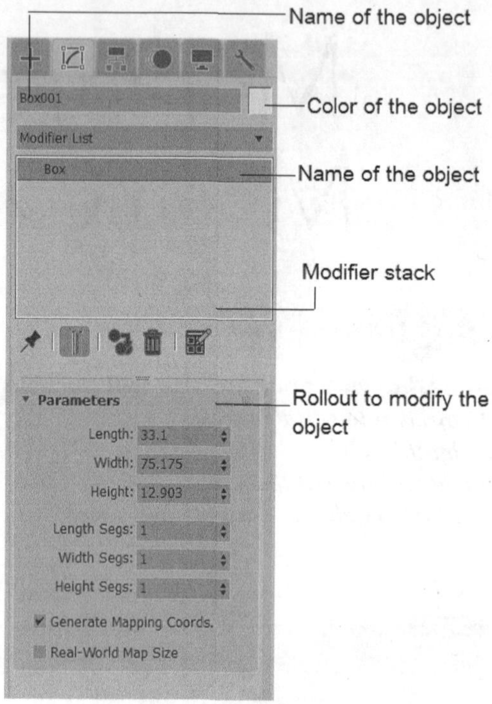

Figure 8-1 *The Modify panel*

Note

The rollouts at the bottom of the Modify panel are displayed based on the type of the object selected.

You can modify the selected object using one of the following methods:

1. By entering new parameters in the rollouts displayed in the Modify panel. (This has been discussed in the previous chapters).

2. By applying a modifier from the **Modifier List** drop-down list. (You will learn about applying modifiers in the later chapters).

3. By converting the object into editable mesh or editable poly.(These methods are discussed next).

Converting Objects into Editable Mesh

Most of the objects can be modified at advanced level by converting into editable mesh. When open splines such as line and arc are converted into editable mesh, only vertices are available because open splines have no face or edge. When an object is converted into an editable mesh, you get access to its sub-object levels. These sub-object levels help you to select the sub-objects of the object in the viewport. You need to move, rotate, and scale these sub-objects to modify the shape of the object.

You can convert an object into editable mesh using one of the following methods:

1. Create an object and select it in the viewport. Next, right-click on the object; a quad menu will be displayed. Choose the **Convert To:** option; a cascading menu will be displayed, as shown in Figure 8-2. Choose **Convert to Editable Mesh** from the cascading menu; the object will be converted into an editable mesh.

2. Create an object and select it in the viewport. Choose the **Modify** tab in the **Command Panel**; the modifier stack will be displayed in the Modify panel. In the modifier stack, right-click on the name of the tool which has been used to create the object; a shortcut menu will be displayed, as shown in Figure 8-3. Choose the **Editable Mesh** option from the shortcut menu; the object will be converted into an editable mesh.

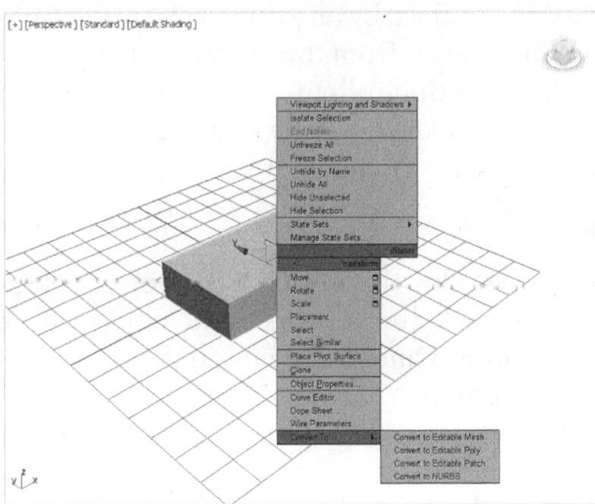

*Figure 8-2 The cascading menu displayed on choosing the **Convert To** option*

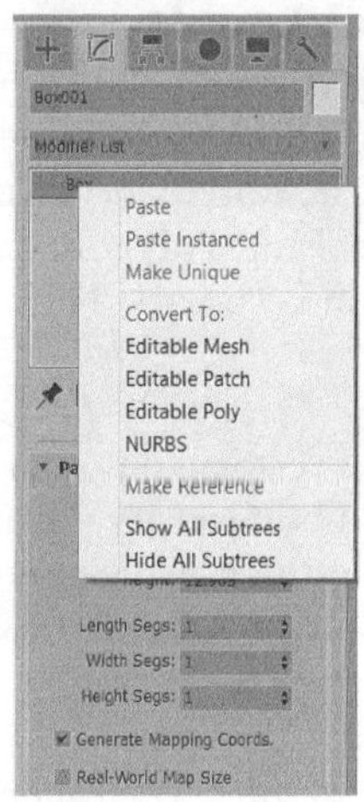

Figure 8-3 The shortcut menu displayed

3. Create an object and select it in the viewport. Choose the **Utilities** tab in the **Command Panel**; the **Utilities** rollout will be displayed, as shown in Figure 8-4. Choose the **Collapse** button in this rollout; the **Collapse** rollout will be displayed. Choose the **Collapse Selected** button in this rollout; the object will be converted into an editable mesh.

Note

After an object is converted into editable mesh using any of the above method, it cannot be modified using the creation parameters rollouts such as the ***Parameters*** *rollout. So, it is recommended to set the parameters of an object before converting it into an editable mesh.*

You need to use the following method to set the parameters of an object even after converting it into an editable mesh.

4. Create an object and select it in the modifier stack. Next, click on the **Modifier List** drop-down list and select **Edit Mesh** from it; the **Edit Mesh** modifier is applied to the object.

Sub-object Levels in Editable Mesh

When you convert an object into an editable mesh using any of the first three methods mentioned above, the label of the tool in the modifier stack will be replaced by **Editable Mesh**, which is known as object level. By clicking on the arrow sign on the left side of the **Editable Mesh**, you can view the sub-object levels such as **Vertex**, **Edge**, **Face**, **Polygon**, and **Element**, as shown in Figure 8-5. Various rollouts will also be displayed at the bottom of the modifier stack such as **Selection**, **Soft Selection**, **Edit Geometry**, and **Surface Properties**. These sub-object levels and rollouts are discussed next.

Sub-object Levels

The sub-object levels are used to modify the object by moving, rotating, and scaling the sub-objects. To do so, select one of the sub-object levels from the modifier stack; the selected sub object will be activated and turn yellow in the **Selection** rollout. Alternatively, you can select the **Vertex**, **Edge**, **Face**, **Polygon**, or **Element** sub-object levels by pressing 1, 2, 3, 4, or 5 respectively from the main keyboard. These sub-objects level are discussed next.

Vertex

A vertex is a point on an object. To modify the vertex of the object, select the **Vertex** sub-object level from the modifier stack; the vertices of the object will be displayed in the viewport, as shown in Figures 8-6 and 8-7. The number of vertices depends on the number of segments in the object.

Note

1. You need to set the number of segments in the object before converting the object into an editable mesh.

2. The sub-object components such as ***Vertex, Edge, Face, Polygon,*** *and* ***Element*** *are not visible on rendering.*

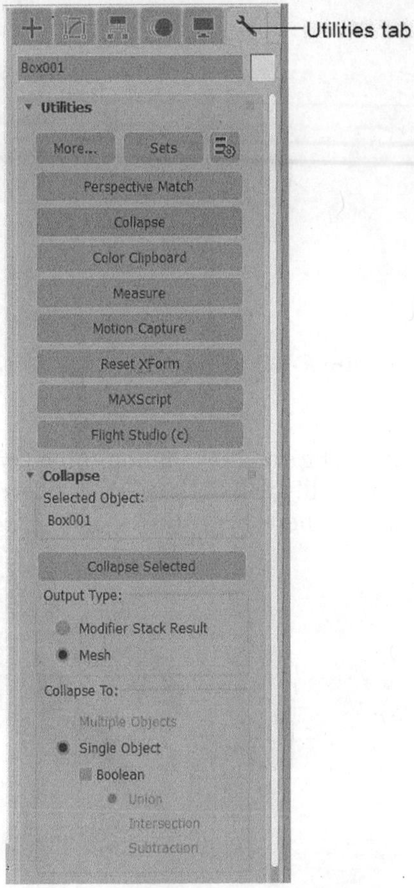

*Figure 8-4 The **Utilities** rollout displayed after choosing the **Utilities** tab*

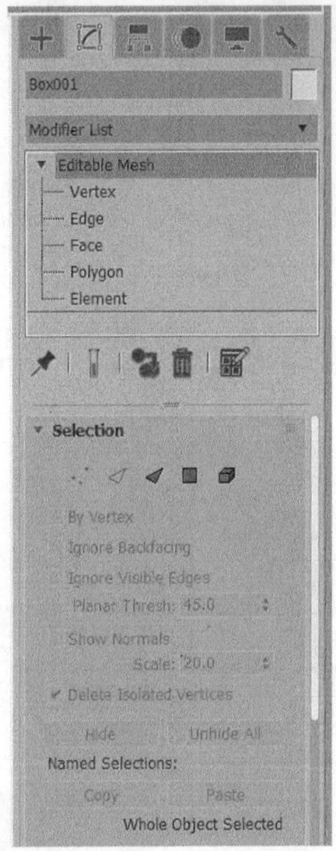

Figure 8-5 The sub-object levels of an object displayed

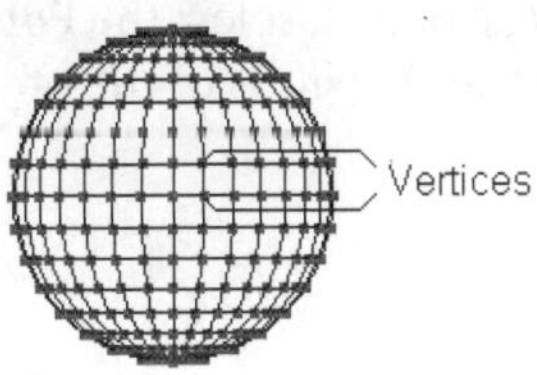

Figure 8-6 Displaying the vertices of the sphere

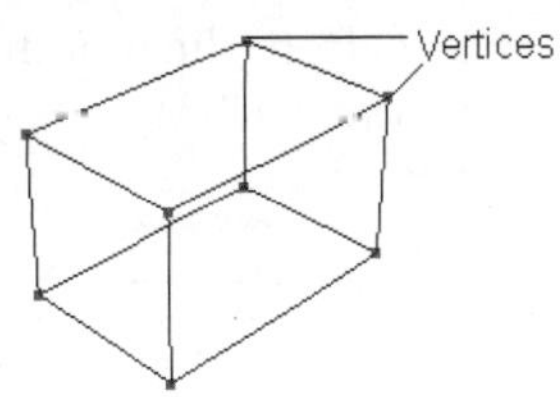

Figure 8-7 Displaying the vertices of the box

Edge

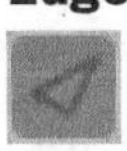

An edge is a line joining two vertices. To modify an edge of the object, select the **Edge** sub-object level from the modifier stack and then select the edge(s) of the object, refer to Figures 8-8 and 8-9.

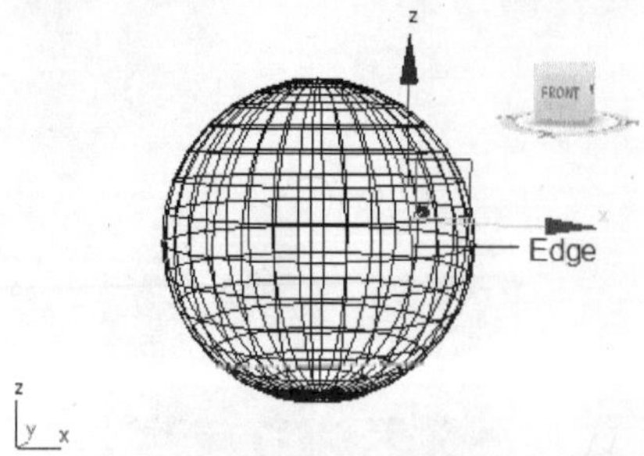

Figure 8-8 *Selecting the edges of the sphere*

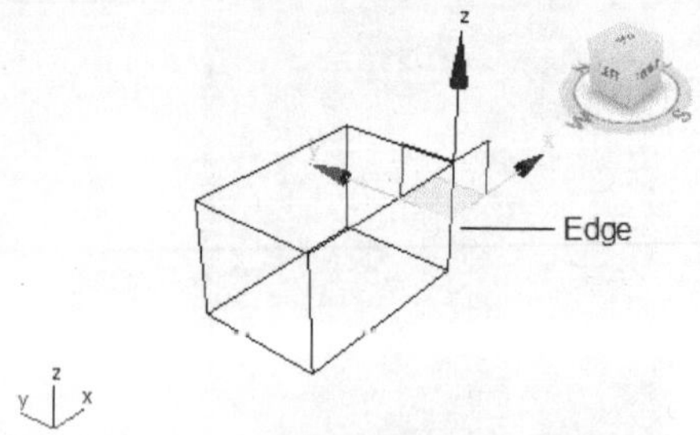

Figure 8-9 *Selecting the edge of the box*

Face

A face is a triangular shaped sub-object level formed by joining three vertices and three edges, as shown in Figure 8-10. To modify faces of an object, select the **Face** sub-object level from the modifier stack and then select the triangular faces of the object, as shown in Figure 8-11.

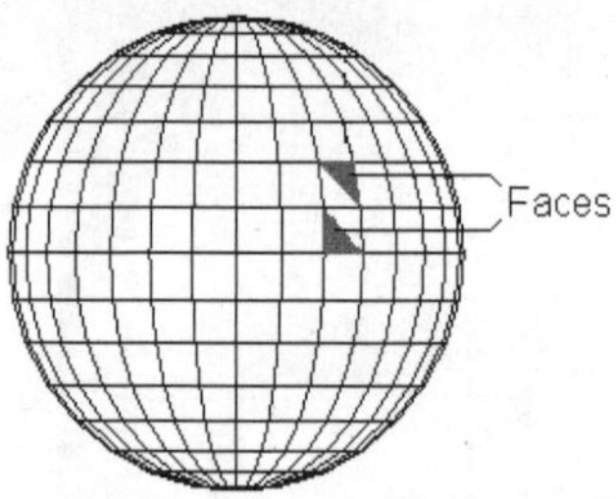

Figure 8-10 *The **Face** sub-object level*

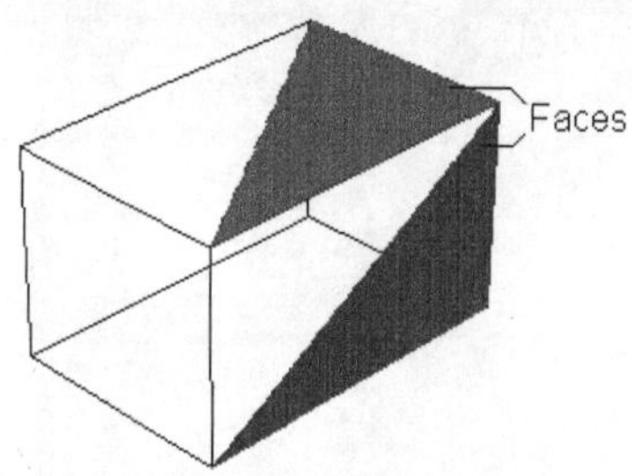

Figure 8-11 *A box with the faces selected*

Polygon

A polygon is a closed sequence of three or more edges connected by a surface, as shown in Figure 8-12. To modify polygons of the object, select the **Polygon** sub-object level from the modifier stack and then select the polygons of the object, as shown in Figure 8-13.

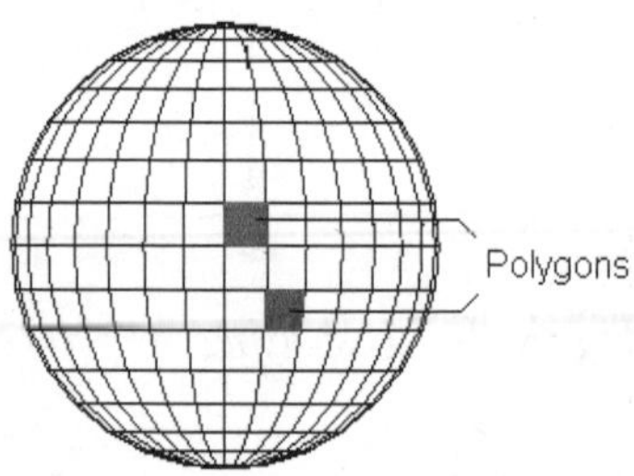

Figure 8-12 *The **Polygon** sub-object level*

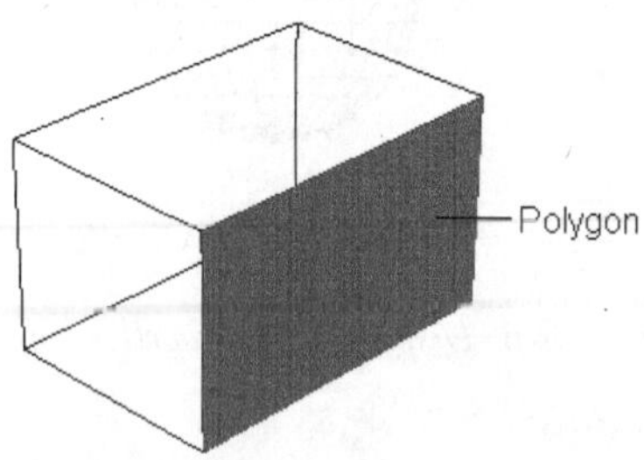

Figure 8-13 *The polygon of a box selected*

Element

An element is a group of two or more objects, as shown in Figure 8-14. To modify the elements of an object, select the **Element** sub-object level from the modifier stack and then select element of the object in the viewport, refer to Figures 8-14 and 8-15.

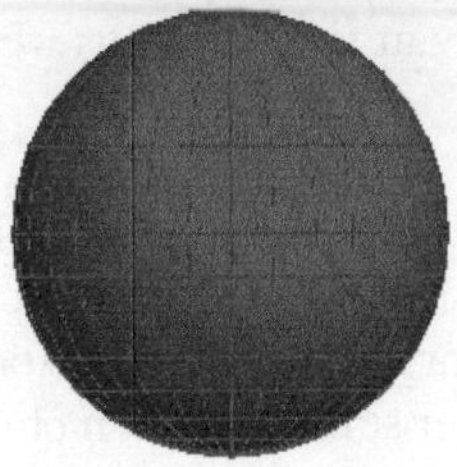

Figure 8-14 The element sub-object level

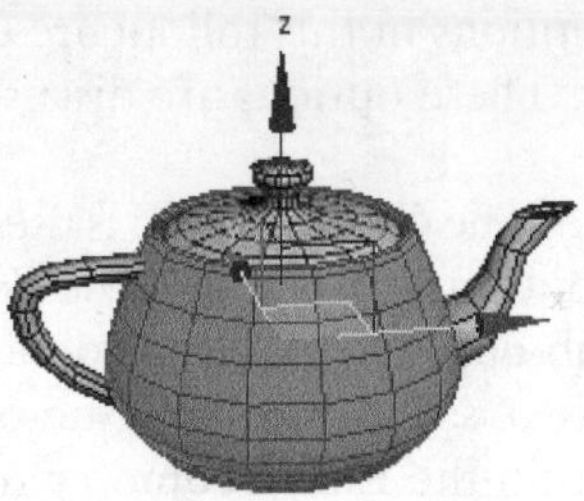

Figure 8-15 The element of the box selected

Rollouts

When you convert an object into editable mesh, various rollouts will be displayed at the bottom of the modifier stack in the Modify panel. These rollouts are discussed next.

Selection Rollout

The **Selection** rollout is used to toggle between various sub-object levels. In the **Selection** rollout, there are five buttons such as **Vertex**, **Edge**, **Face**, **Polygon**, and **Element**. These buttons are used to select the sub-objects levels of the object in the viewport and are discussed earlier in this chapter. Choose any of the buttons to activate the sub-object level of the object. The **By Vertex** check box will be activated on selecting the **Edge**, **Face**, **Polygon**, or **Element** sub-object level from the **Selection** rollout. The **By Vertex** check box is used to select all the sub-objects that are connected to the selected vertex of the object. For example, if you select the **Polygon** sub-object level and then select the **By Vertex** check box. On clicking on a vertex of the object in the viewport, all the polygons that are connected to the selected vertex will be selected. Select the **Ignore Backfacing** check box to select the sub-objects that are facing toward you in the viewports. Note that you cannot select backfacing sub-objects on selecting this check box.

Note

*When you select the **By vertex** check box and click on a vertex, sub-objects which use that vertex will be selected. You can also select the sub-objects by dragging a selection box around them.*

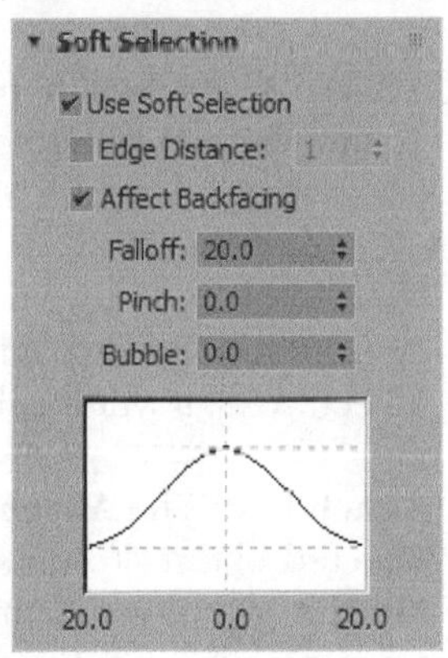

*Figure 8-16 The **Soft Selection** rollout*

Soft Selection Rollout

This rollout enables you to display a soft selection on an object. The options in this rollout are used to affect the action of movement, rotation, and scaling at sub-object level of the editable mesh object. To activate this rollout, you need to select a sub-object level. Next, to activate the other options of this rollout, select the **Use Soft Selection** check box, as shown in Figure 8-16. When you select the sub-objects of an object in the viewport, it shows the falloff in different color combinations. The influence of the colored zone is determined by the value set in the **Falloff** spinner. The shape of the falloff is controlled by the value in the **Pinch** and **Bubble** spinners, refer to Figure 8-16.

Edit Geometry Rollout

The options in this rollout are used to edit the geometry at the object as well as sub-object levels. These options are discussed next.

Create: The **Create** button is used to add the sub-objects to the selected object in the viewport. This button is available at the **Vertex**, **Face**, **Polygon**, and **Element** sub-object levels. To add the sub-objects, select the editable mesh object in the viewport and then choose the **Modify** tab. Next, select one of the sub-object levels in the modifier stack and then choose the **Create** button in the **Edit Geometry** rollout. Now, click anywhere in the viewport to add vertices to the selected object (if the **Vertex** sub-object level is selected), as shown in Figure 8-17. If you have selected the **Face** sub-object level, then click on the three vertices one by one to add a new face, as shown in Figure 8-18.

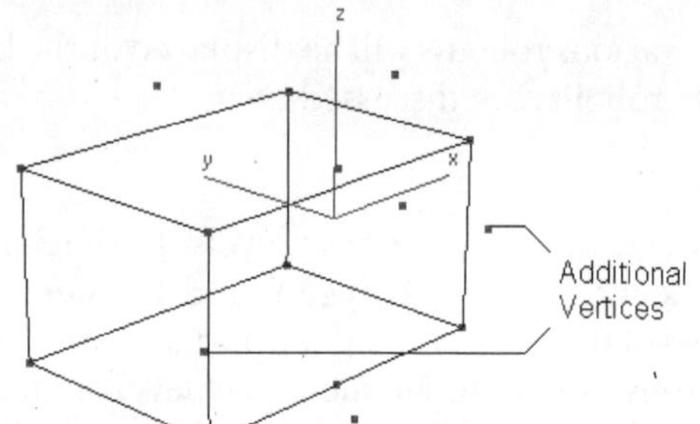

*Figure 8-17 Additional vertices created in a box using the **Create** button*

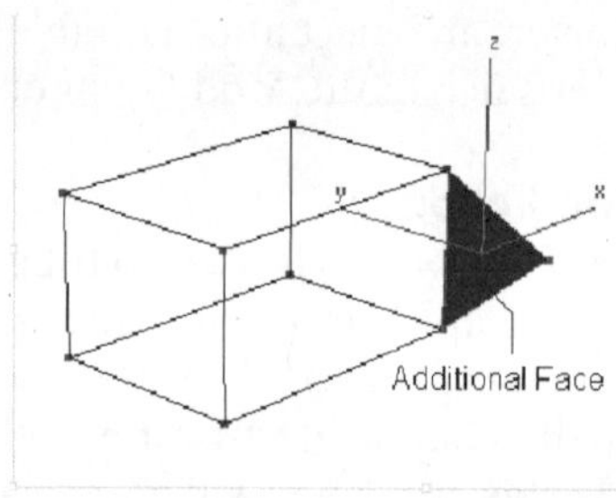

*Figure 8-18 A new face added to a box using the **Create** button*

Delete: The **Delete** button is used to delete the sub-objects in the selected object. To delete a sub-object, select the editable mesh object in the viewport and choose the **Modify** tab. Next, select one of the sub-objects levels in the modifier stack. Now, select the sub-object in the viewport that you want to delete and choose the **Delete** button; the selected sub-object will be deleted.

Attach: The **Attach** button is used to attach an object to the selected object in the viewport. To attach an object, select the editable mesh object in the viewport and choose the **Modify** tab. Next, choose the **Attach** button in the **Edit Geometry** rollout.

Now, when you move the cursor over another object in the viewport, the attach cursor will be displayed, as shown in Figure 8-19. Click on the object; it will be attached to the selected object. Also, it will display the same color and properties as those of the selected object.

Attach List: The **Attach List** button is used to attach a number of objects simultaneously to selected object. To do so, select the editable mesh object in the viewport and choose the **Modify** tab in the **Command Panel**. Now, choose the **Attach List** button from the **Edit Geometry** rollout; the **Attach List** dialog box will be displayed, as shown in Figure 8-20.

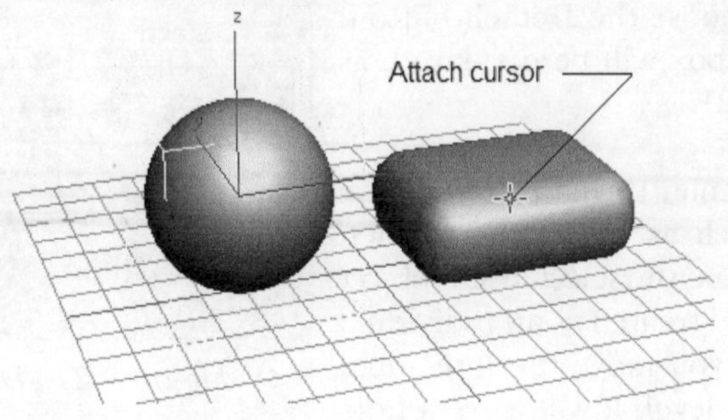

Figure 8-19 *The attach cursor after choosing the **Attach** button*

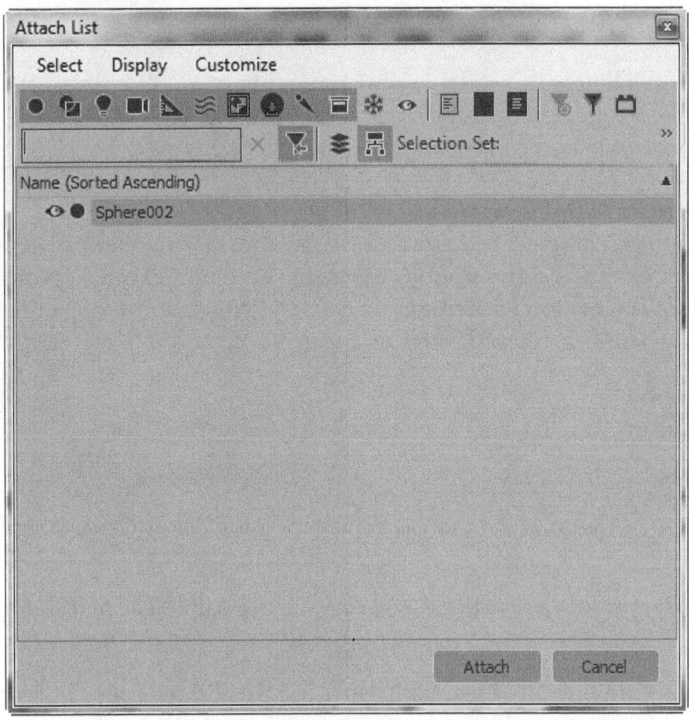

Figure 8-20 *The **Attach List** dialog box*

The **Attach List** dialog box displays a list of all the objects in the viewport. From this list, select the name of the objects that you want to attach by holding the CTRL or SHIFT key, and then choose the **Attach** button; the selected objects in the list will be attached to the object selected in the viewport. Note that these attached objects will display the same color and properties as that of the selected object.

Detach: The **Detach** button is used to detach the sub-objects from the selected object to make them individual objects. This button is available for the **Vertex**, **Face**, **Polygon**, and **Element** sub-object levels. To detach a sub-object, select the editable mesh object in the viewport, choose the **Modify** tab, and then select one of the sub-object levels in the modifier stack. Next, select the sub-object in the viewport that you want to detach as an individual object, and then choose the **Detach** button; the **Detach** dialog box will be displayed, as shown in Figure 8-21.

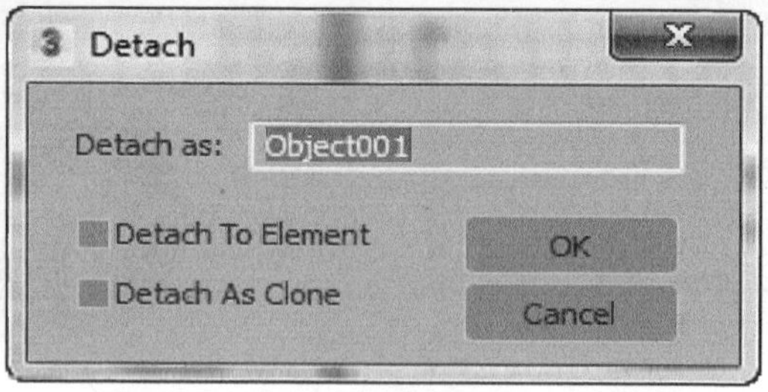

*Figure 8-21 The **Detach** dialog box*

In this dialog box, enter the name of the new object in the **Detach as** text box and then choose the **OK** button; the selected sub-object will be detached and treated as an individual object. Now, when you move the individual object at the object level, it will leave a hole in the original object. In the **Detach** dialog box, select the **Detach As Clone** check box, the selected sub-object will be copied and treated as individual object. Also, the original object will not get modified.

Break: The **Break** button is available only for the **Vertex** sub-object level. It creates a new vertex for each face attached to the selected vertices. If a vertex is used only by one face, then it will remain unaffected.

Turn: The **Turn** button is activated only for the **Edge** sub-object level. It is used to rotate the edges of an object. Select the editable mesh object in the viewport, choose the **Modify** tab, and then select the **Edge** sub-object level in the modifier stack. Now, choose the **Turn** button in the **Edit Geometry** rollout and select the edges of the object in the viewport one by one; the edges will be rotated, refer to Figures 8-22 and 8-23.

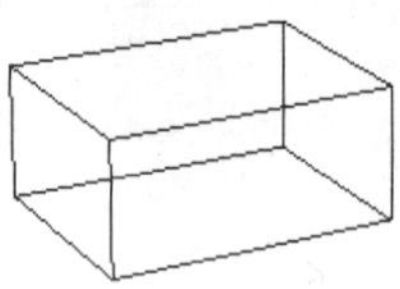

*Figure 8-22 The box before choosing the **Turn** button*

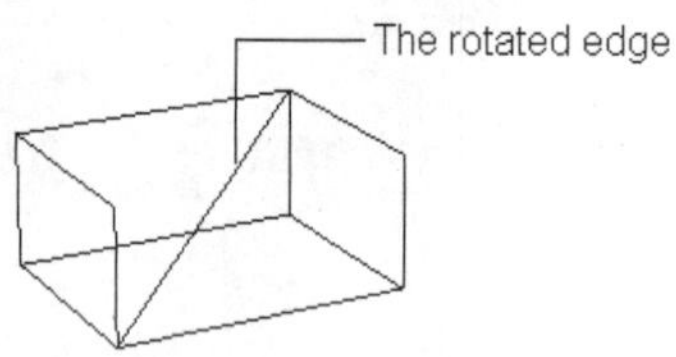

*Figure 8-23 The rotated edge of the box after choosing the **Turn** button*

Divide: The **Divide** button is available only for the **Edge**, **Face**, **Polygon**, and **Element** sub-object levels. It divides a face into three smaller faces. To do so, select the editable mesh object in the viewport, choose the **Modify** tab, and then select one of the sub-object levels in the modifier stack except **Vertex**. Next, choose the **Divide** button in the **Edit Geometry** rollout, and click on the sub-object in the viewport; the sub-object will be divided into three faces, refer to Figures 8-24 and 8-25.

Extrude: The **Extrude** button is available for the **Edge**, **Face**, **Polygon**, and **Element** sub-object levels. It is used to extrude the sub-objects either by dragging the cursor or by entering the value in the spinner. To do so, select the editable mesh object in the viewport, choose the **Modify** tab, and then select one of the sub-object levels in the modifier stack, except **Vertex**. Next, select the sub-object in the viewport and choose the **Extrude** button to activate it. Now, move the cursor over the selected sub-object; the extrude cursor will be displayed, as shown in Figure 8-26. Next, press and hold the left mouse button and move the cursor up or down for the extrusion; the value for the extrusion will be displayed in the spinner on the right of the **Extrude** button. You can enter the value directly in this spinner to extrude the selected sub-object, refer to Figure 8-27.

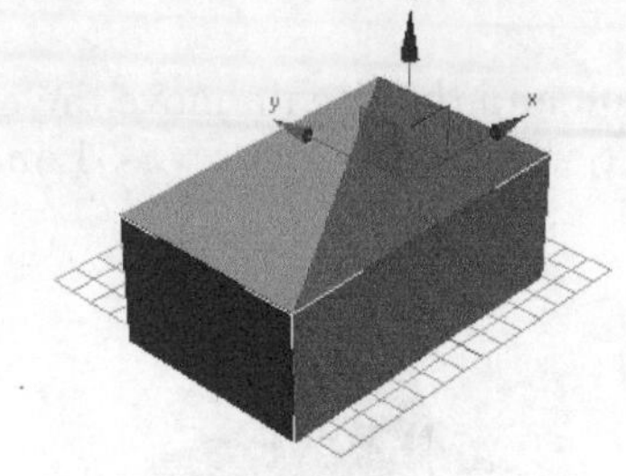

Figure 8-24 *The face before choosing the **Divide** button*

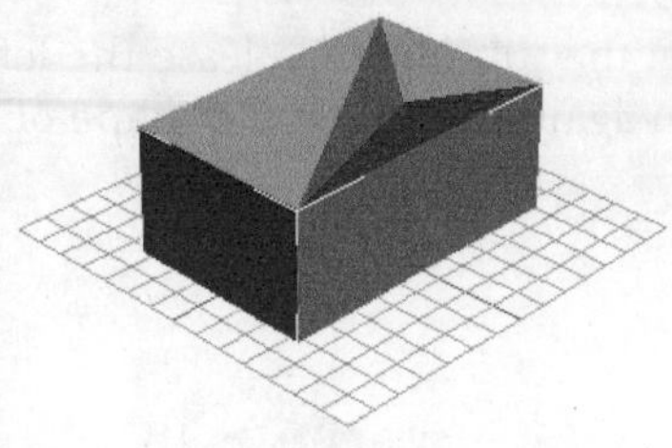

Figure 8-25 *The face divided after using the **Divide** button*

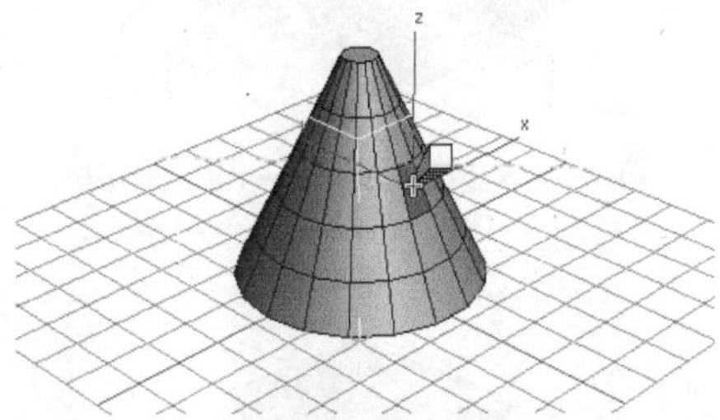

Figure 8-26 *The extrude cursor displayed over the selected polygon*

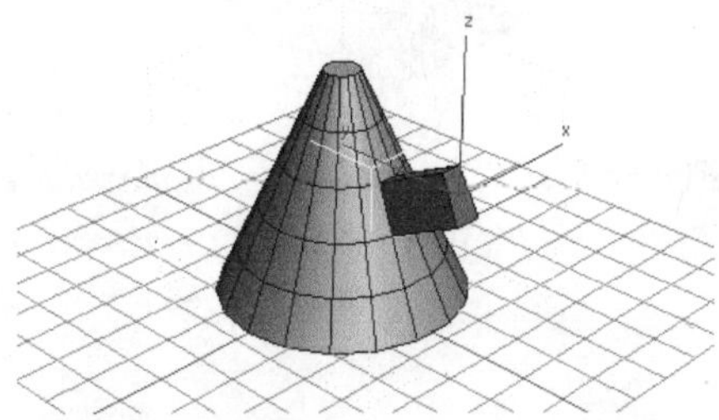

Figure 8-27 *The selected polygon sub-object after extrusion*

Note

*To extrude multiple sub-objects simultaneously, select sub-objects by holding the CTRL key, and then execute the **Extrude** command. You can also enter a negative value in the **Extrude** spinner for negative extrusion, refer to Figure 8-28.*

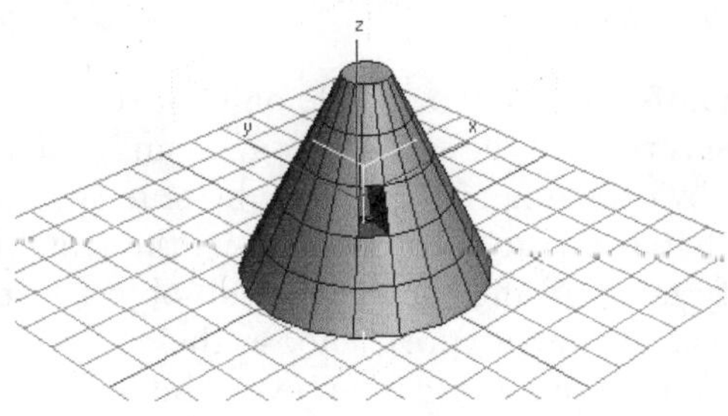

Figure 8-28 *The selected polygon after negative extrusion*

Bevel: The **Bevel** button is available only for the **Face**, **Polygon**, and **Element** sub-object levels. It is used to extrude and bevel an object. This button can perform the extrude and bevel functions at the same time.

You can bevel the sub-objects either by dragging the cursor or by entering the value in the spinner on the right side of the **Bevel** button. To do so, select the editable mesh object in the viewport. Choose the **Modify** tab, and then select one of the sub-object levels in the modifier stack, except **Vertex** and **Edge**. Next, select the sub-object in the viewport and then choose the **Bevel** button. Next, move the cursor over the selected sub-object; the bevel cursor will be displayed, as shown in Figure 8-29. Now, press and hold the left mouse button and move the cursor up or down to extrude the sub-object, as shown in Figure 8-30.

To bevel the sub-object, release the left mouse button and then again move the cursor up or down again to change the shape of the sub-object, as shown in Figures 8-31 and 8-32.

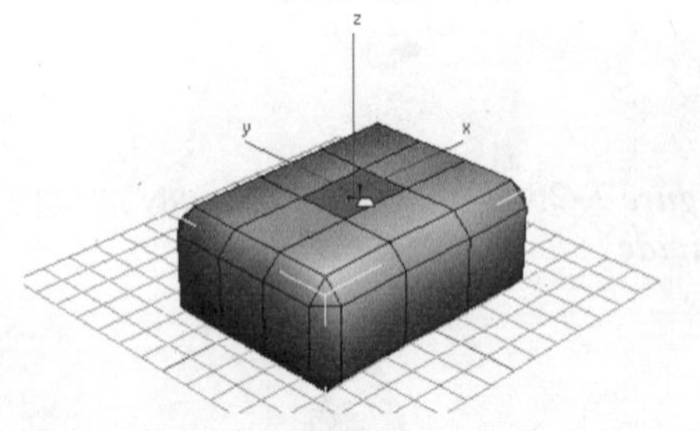

Figure 8-29 The bevel cursor displayed over the selected polygon

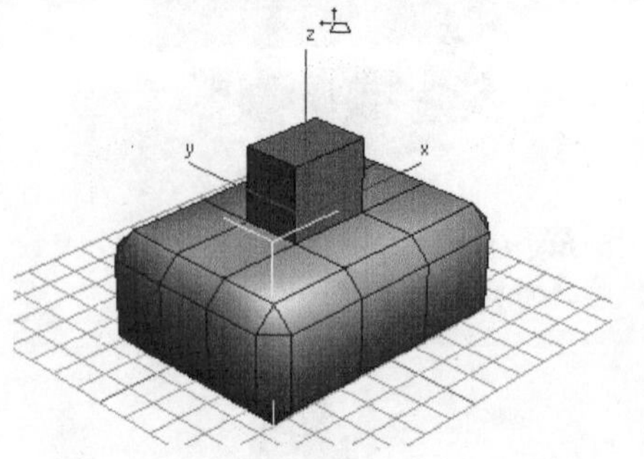

Figure 8-30 The polygon extruded

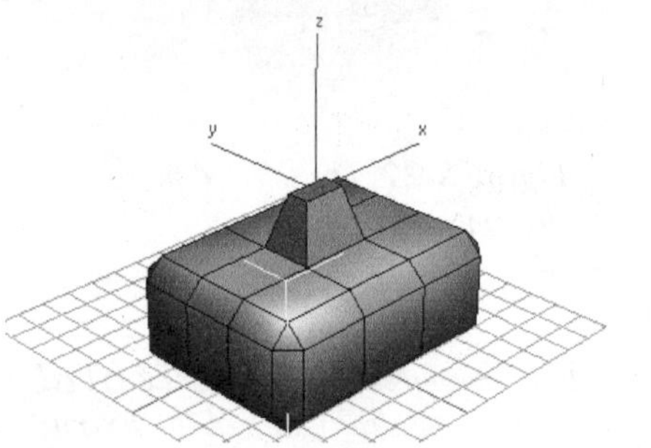

*Figure 8-31 The size of the extruded polygon reduced using the **Bevel** button*

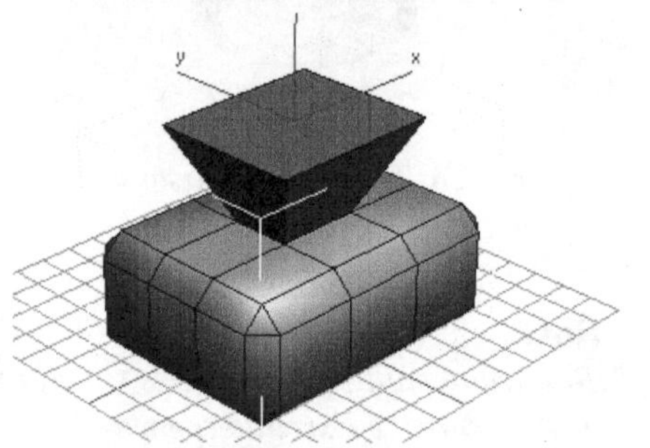

*Figure 8-32 The size of the extruded polygon increased using the **Bevel** button*

Chamfer: The **Chamfer** button is available only for the **Vertex** and **Edge** sub-object levels. It is used to cut the corners of the sub-object at an angle of 45-degree. You can chamfer the sub-objects either by dragging the cursor or by entering the value in the spinner on the right side of the **Chamfer** button. To do so, select the editable mesh object in the viewport, choose the **Modify** tab, and then select the sub-object level in the modifier stack. Next, select the sub-object in the viewport, choose the **Chamfer** button, and move the cursor over the selected sub-object; the chamfer cursor will be displayed, as shown in Figure 8-33. Next, press and hold the left mouse button, move the cursor up to the chamfer, and release the left mouse button; the sub-object will be chamfered at an angle of 45-degree, refer to Figures 8-34 and 8-35. As you move the cursor, the chamfer value will be displayed in the spinner on the right side of the **Chamfer** button. You can also enter the value directly in this spinner to chamfer the selected sub-object.

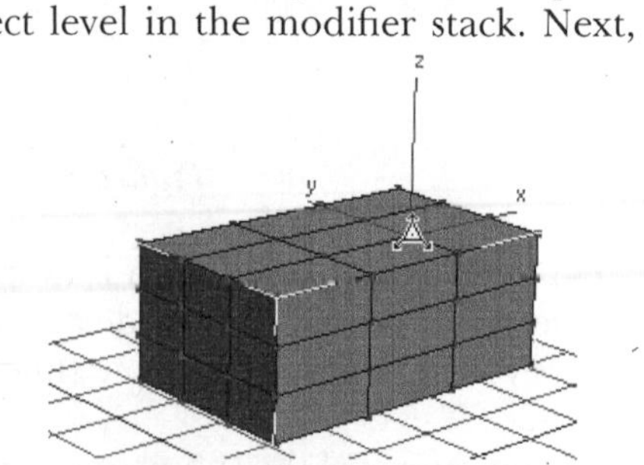

Figure 8-33 The chamfer cursor displayed over the selected vertex

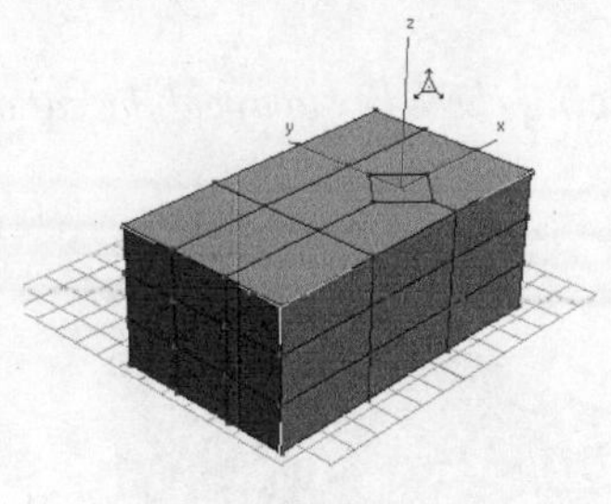

*Figure 8-34 The vertex sub-object chamfered using the **Chamfer** button*

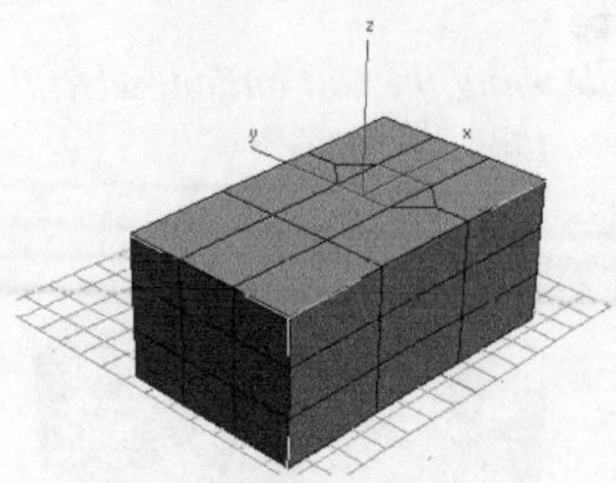

*Figure 8-35 The edge sub-object chamfered using the **Chamfer** button*

Slice Plane and **Slice**: The **Slice Plane** and **Slice** buttons are used to slice the sub-objects to create new vertices, faces, edges, polygons, and elements. To do so, select the editable mesh object in the viewport, choose the **Modify** tab and then select the sub-object level in the modifier stack. Next, select one or more sub-objects in the viewport and then choose the **Slice Plane** button; a yellow colored slice plane gizmo will be displayed in the viewport, as shown in Figure 8-36. Set the position of the slice plane gizmo over the selected sub-objects by moving or rotating it at the position where you want to slice them. Then, choose the **Slice** button; the selected sub-objects will be divided to create new sub-objects, as shown in Figure 8-37.

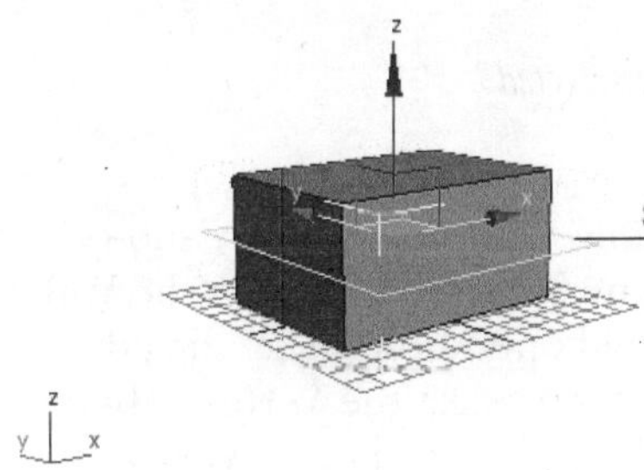

Figure 8-36 The slice plane gizmo displayed in the selected object

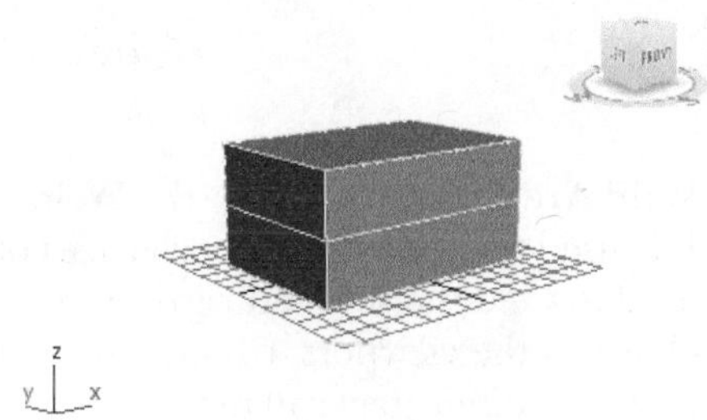

*Figure 8-37 The selected object sliced after choosing the **Slice** button*

Cut: The **Cut** button is available only for the **Edge**, **Face**, **Polygon**, and **Element** sub-object levels. It is used to cut the edge, face, polygon, or element of an object to create new vertices, edges, and faces. To do so, select the editable mesh object in the viewport. Choose the **Modify** tab, and then select any sub-object level in the modifier stack, except **Vertex**.

Next, choose the **Cut** button and move the cursor over the object; the cursor will change when it comes over any sub-object. Next, click on the sub-object to specify the first cut point and drag the mouse to specify the endpoint of the cut; a dotted line will be displayed, as shown in Figure 8-38. Now, click again to cut the sub-object and right-click to end the cut command; the object will be cut, refer to Figure 8-39.

You can also select the sub-object to be cut at a particular area, as shown in Figure 8-40.

Note

*While using the **Cut** button, select the **Ignore Backfacing** check box to avoid the cut on the back face of the sub-object.*

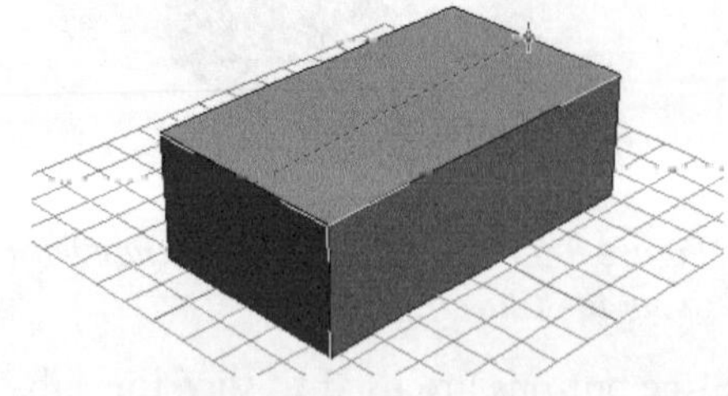

Figure 8-38 *The dotted lines*

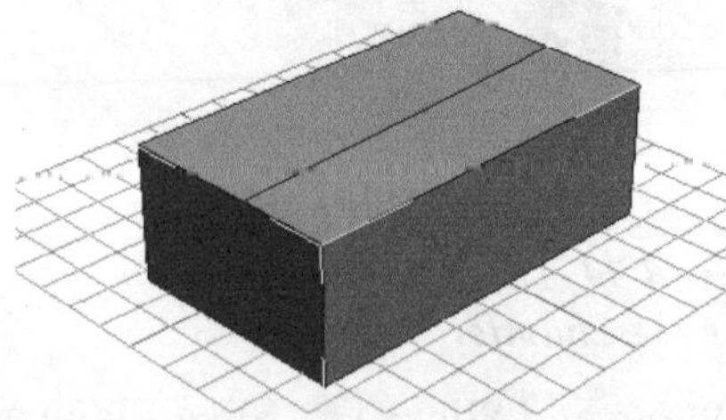

Figure 8-39 *The cut on the object after using the **Cut** button*

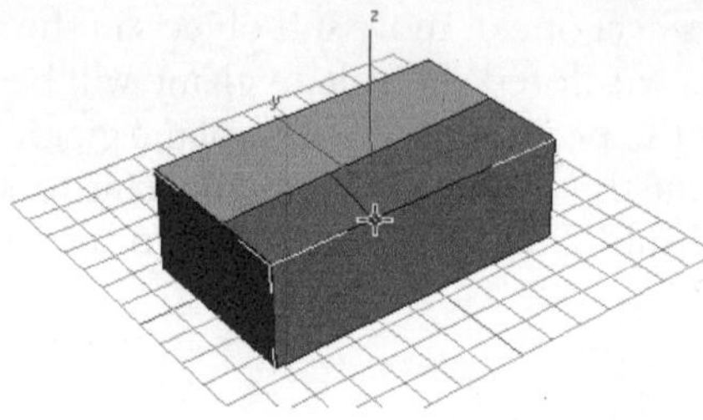

Figure 8-40 *The cut on the selected polygon*

Weld Area: The options in the **Weld** area are available only at the **Vertex** sub-object level. It is used to weld or join the vertices of the object. The **Selected** button in the **Weld** area is used to weld the selected vertices. To perform the weld operation, select the editable mesh object in the viewport. Choose the **Modify** tab, and then select the **Vertex** sub-object level in the modifier stack; all the vertices of the object will be displayed in the viewport. By using the rectangular marquee selection, select the vertices of the object which you need to weld together, refer to Figure 8-41. Now, set the value in the spinner located on the right side of the **Selected** button to define the weld threshold area. All the vertices that you want to weld together must be inside this area. Choose the **Selected** button; the vertices will be welded together, refer to Figure 8-42.

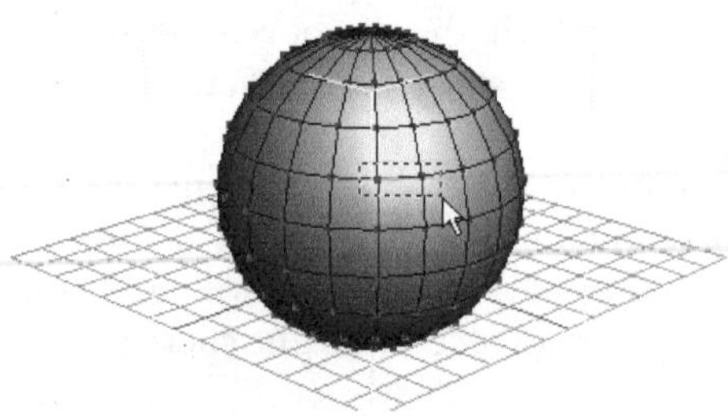

Figure 8-41 *The selection box around the vertices to be welded*

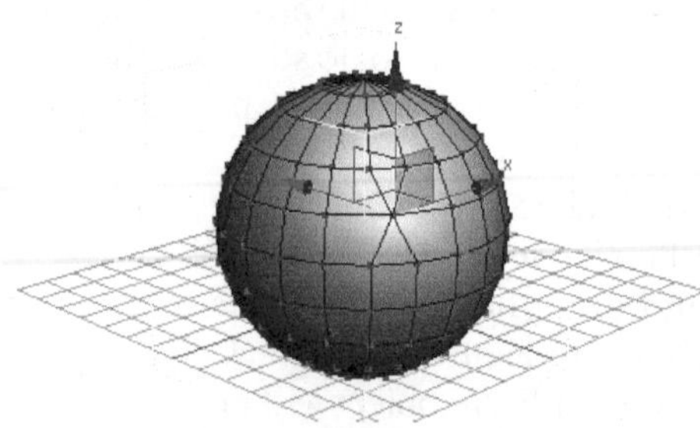

Figure 8-42 *The vertices welded together*

If the vertices are not within the weld threshold area whose value you have defined in the spinner, the **Weld** message box will be displayed, as shown in Figure 8-43, warning you that there is no vertex in the weld threshold area. Therefore, you need to increase the threshold area by modifying the value in the spinner, and then choose the **Selected** button again to weld the vertices.

The **Target** button in the **Weld** area is used to weld the selected vertices to the unselected target vertex. To do so, select the editable mesh object in the viewport and choose the **Modify** tab. Now, select the **Vertex** sub-object level in the modifier stack; all vertices of the object will be displayed in the viewport. Next, select the vertices of the object in the viewport by dragging a selection box around them, refer to Figure 8-44. Then, choose the **Target** button and move the vertices toward the unselected target vertex to which you want to weld the selected vertices. As you bring the selected vertices over the unselected target vertex, the cursor will convert into a arrow sign. Release the mouse button; the vertices will be welded to the target vertex, as shown in Figure 8-45.

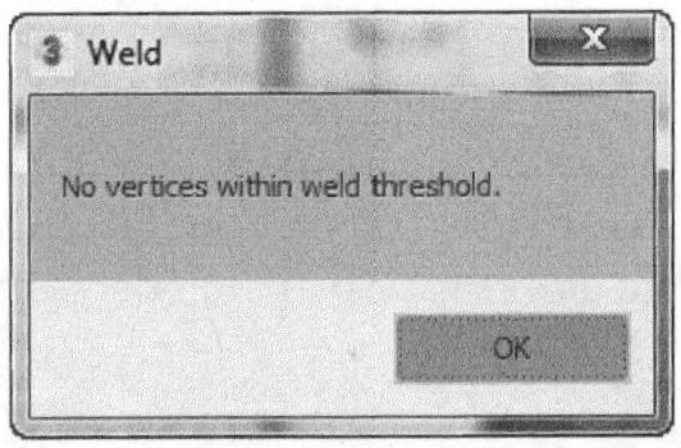

*Figure 8-43 The **Weld** message box*

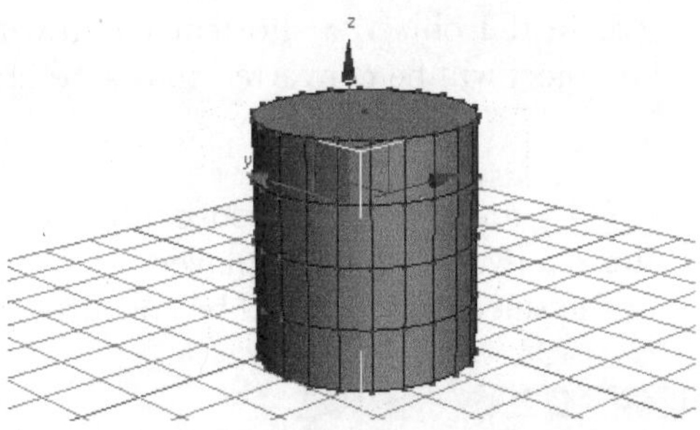

Figure 8-44 The vertices selected for welding

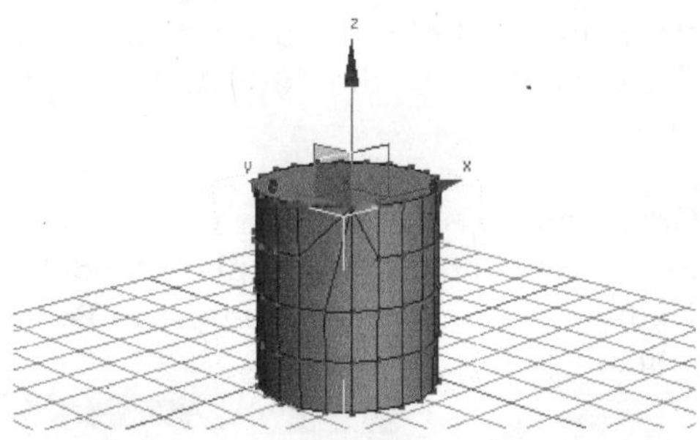

Figure 8-45 The selected vertices welded to the target vertex

Modifying Editable Mesh Objects Using Sub-object Levels

To get the advance level modeling of the objects, you need to convert the object into editable mesh object, which provides you the sub-object levels of an object as discussed earlier in this chapter. To view the sub-object levels, you need to click on the arrow sign on the left side of the **Editable Mesh** in the modifier stack. By using these sub-object levels, you can select the sub-objects in the viewport and modify the object in different ways.

On selecting one of the sub-object levels in the modifier stack, it will be activated and turn yellow. You can select a sub-object by clicking on it in the viewport. To select more than one sub-object simultaneously, hold the CTRL key, and select them one by one. Alternatively, you can drag a selection box around the sub-objects to select them simultaneously; they will turn red. After selecting the sub-objects, you can modify them using the following options:

1. You can move, rotate, and scale the selected sub-objects using the **Select and Move**, **Select and Rotate**, and **Select and Uniform Scale** tools, respectively from the **Main Toolbar**.

2. You can use different options in the **Edit Geometry** rollout, as described earlier in this chapter.

3. You can use different modifiers from the **Modifier List** drop-down list.

Converting Objects into Editable Poly

To modify an object with editable poly is same as modifying an object with the editable mesh. The only difference is that the editable poly works with the advance tools meant for polygonal mesh editing. To work with editable poly, convert the object into editable poly. To do so, you need to use one of the following methods:

1. Create an object and select it in the viewport. Next, right-click on the object; a quad menu will be displayed. Choose the **Convert To:** option; a cascading menu will be displayed. Choose the **Convert to Editable Poly** option from the cascading menu; the object will be converted into editable poly.

2. Create an object and select it in the viewport. Choose the **Modify** tab in the **Command Panel**; the modifier stack will be displayed in the Modify panel. In the modifier stack, right-click on the name of the tool which you have used to create the object; a shortcut menu will be displayed. Choose the **Editable Poly** option; the object will be converted into an editable poly.

3. Create an object and select it in the viewport. Next, move the cursor over the **Polygon Modeling** panel in the **Graphite Modeling Ribbon**; a flyout will be displayed, as shown in Figure 8-46. Choose the **Convert to Poly** option; the selected object will be converted into editable poly.

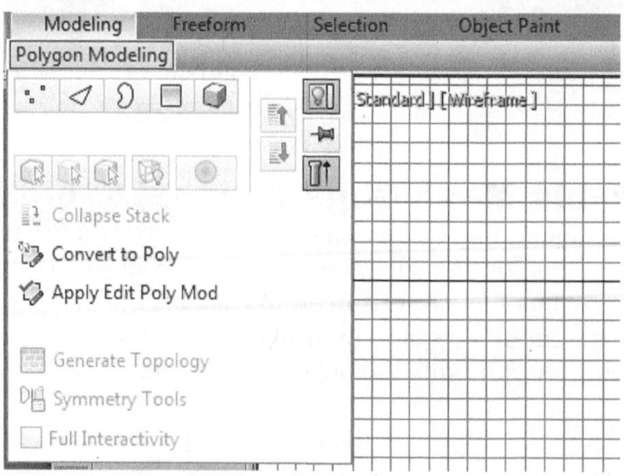

***Figure 8-46** Flyout displayed after moving the cursor over the **Polygon Modeling** panel*

> **Note**
>
> *When you convert an object into an editable poly, various panels will be displayed in the* ***Graphite Modeling Tools*** *tab such as* ***Edit, Geometry (All), Subdivision****, and so on. You will learn about these panels in the later chapters.*

> **Note**
>
> *After an object is converted into an editable poly using any of the above method, it cannot be modified using the creation parameters rollouts such as the* ***Parameters*** *rollout. So, it is recommended to set the parameters of an object before converting it into an editable poly.*

You need to use the following method to set the parameters of an object even after converting it into an editable poly.

4. Create an object and select it in the modifier stack. Next, click on the **Modifier List** drop-down list and select **Edit Poly** from it; the **Edit Poly** modifier is applied to the object.

> **Note**
>
> *When you convert an object into an editable poly using the fourth method, some of the rollouts and/or options are not available.*

Modifying Editable Poly Objects Using Sub-object Levels

On converting an object into an editable poly, the name of the tool in the modifier stack will be replaced by **Editable Poly**, which is known as the object level. Click on the arrow sign on the left side of **Editable Poly** to view the sub-object levels such as **Vertex**, **Edge**, **Border**, **Polygon**, and **Element**, refer to Figure 8-47. Various rollouts will also be displayed below the modifier stack such as **Selection**, **Soft Selection**, **Edit Geometry**, **Subdivision Surface**, **Subdivision Displacement**, and **Paint Deformation**, as shown in Figure 8-47. Other rollouts such as **Edit Vertices**, **Vertex Properties**, **Edit Edges**, **Edit Borders**, **Edit Polygons**, **Polygon: Material IDs**, **Polygon: Smoothing groups**, **Polygon: Vertex Colors**, and **Edit Elements** will also be displayed, depending on the selection of the sub-object level.

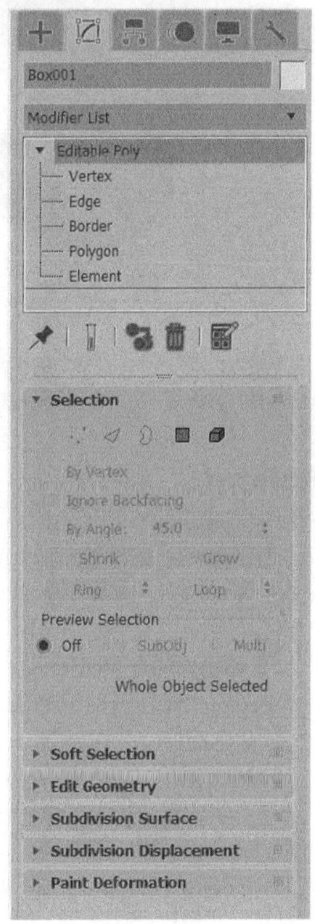

Figure 8-47 *Various rollouts displayed*

To modify the object using the sub-object levels, select one of the sub-object levels in the modifier stack; it activated and turns yellow. Now, select the sub-object by clicking on it in the viewport. To select more than one sub-object at a time, hold the CTRL key and select them one by one. Alternatively, you can drag a selection box around the sub-objects to select them simultaneously; they will turn red. After selecting the sub-objects, you can modify them using the following methods:

1. You can move, rotate, and scale the selected sub-objects using the **Select and Move**, **Select and Rotate**, and **Select and Uniform Scale** tools, respectively in the **Main Toolbar**.

2. You can use different modifiers from the **Modifier List** drop-down list, about which you will learn in the later chapters.

3. You can use various options available in different rollouts of the Modify panel for a particular sub-object level.

4. You can use different tools available in the **Graphite Modeling Ribbon**, about which you will learn in later chapters.

The sub-object levels and various rollouts in an editable poly object are discussed next.

Sub-object Levels

The editable poly objects consist of sub-objects levels. They are the **Vertex**, **Edge**, **Border**, **Polygon**, and **Element**. They do not have the **Face** sub-object level like the editable mesh. Therefore, you cannot select the triangular faces in the editable poly object. Additionally, the editable poly has the **Border** sub-object level. The **Vertex**, **Edge**, **Polygon**, and **Element** sub-objects are same as discussed in the editable mesh object. The **Border** sub-object is discussed next.

Border

The border is a series of edges that forms a ring around a hole in an object, as shown in Figures 8-48 and 8-49.

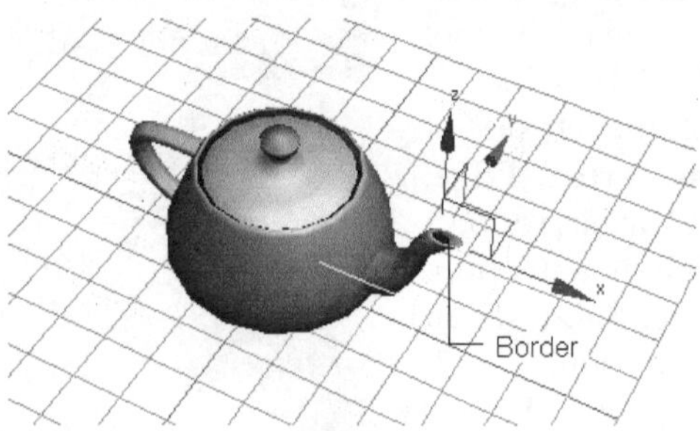

Figure 8-48 The border selected around the hole of the spout of a teapot

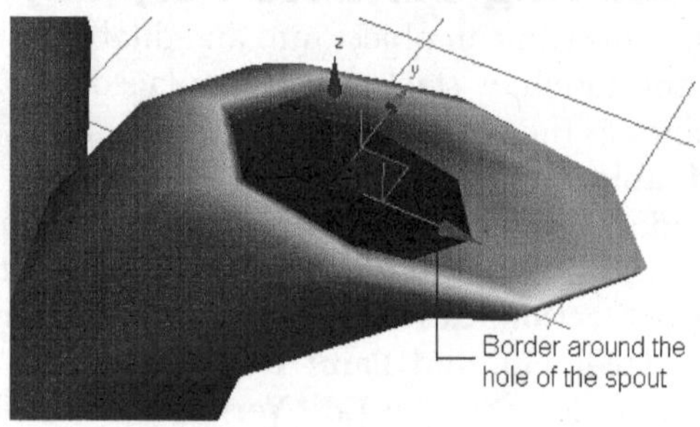

Figure 8-49 The maximized view of the border selected around the hole of the spout of a teapot

Rollouts

When you convert an object into editable poly, various rollouts will be displayed below the modifier stack. The number and name of the rollouts depend on the selection of the sub-object level. These rollouts are used to modify the objects at the sub-object levels and are discussed next.

Selection Rollout

In the **Selection** rollout, there are five buttons, **Vertex**, **Edge**, **Border**, **Polygon**, and **Element**, as shown in Figure 8-50. These buttons are used to select the sub-objects of an object in the viewport and are the same as described earlier. Choose any button to activate it. It is similar to selecting the sub-object level in the modifier stack. The other options in this rollout are discussed next.

Shrink/Grow: The **Shrink** and **Grow** buttons are available for all the sub-object levels in

Note

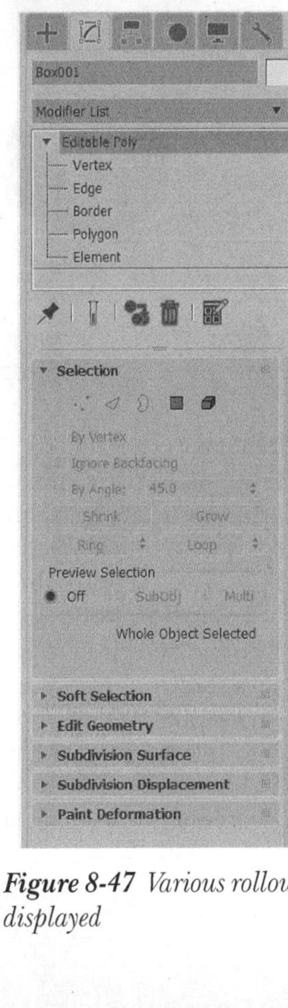

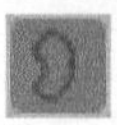

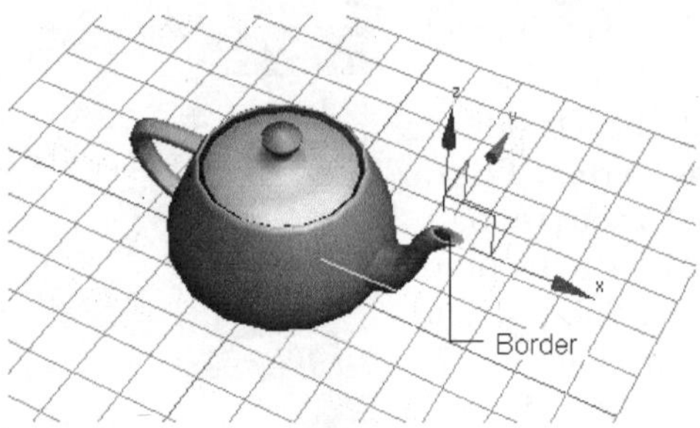

this rollout. The **Shrink** button is used to reduce the selection area of the sub-objects in the viewport. The **Grow** button is used to increase the selection area of the sub-objects in the viewport. To use these buttons, select the editable poly object in the viewport, choose the **Modify** tab, and then select one of the sub-object levels in the modifier stack. Next, select the sub-objects in the viewport. Choose the **Shrink** or **Grow** button in the **Selection** rollout; the selection area will decrease or increase in the viewport, refer to Figures 8-51, 8-52, and 8-53.

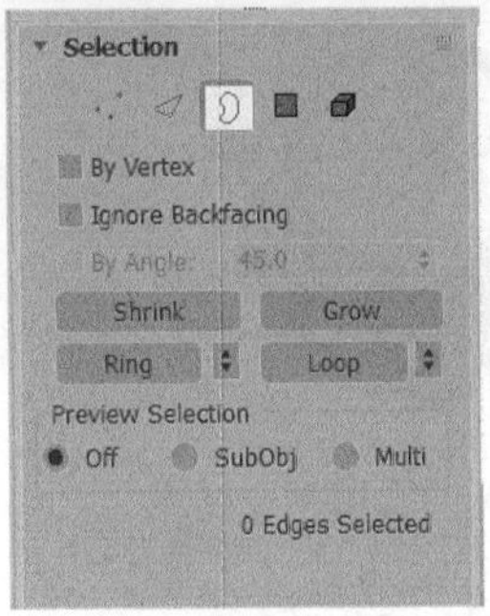

Figure 8-50 *The* ***Selection*** *rollout with the* ***Border*** *sub-object level selected*

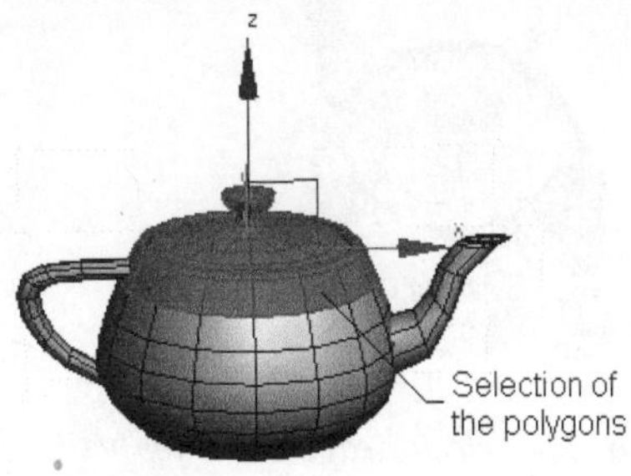

Figure 8-51 *The selection area in the teapot*

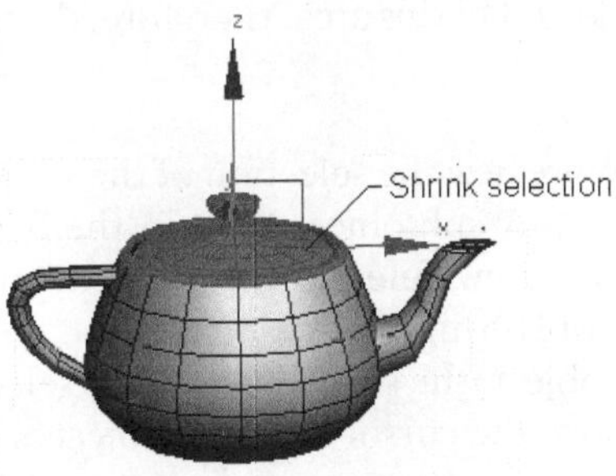

Figure 8-52 *The selection area in the teapot decreases after choosing the* ***Shrink*** *button*

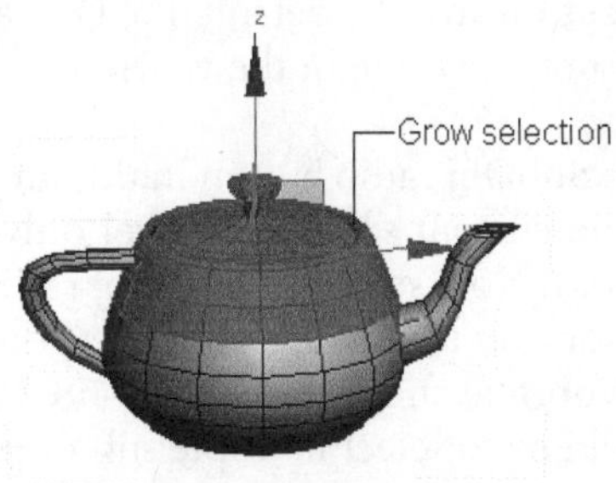

Figure 8-53 *The selection area in the teapot increases after choosing the* ***Grow*** *button*

Ring: The **Ring** button is available only for the **Edge** and **Border** sub-object levels. It is used to select all edges and borders of the object that are parallel to the selected edge. To do so, select an edge of the object in the viewport, as shown in Figure 8-54, and choose the **Ring** button; all the edges parallel to the selected edge will be selected, as shown in Figure 8-55.

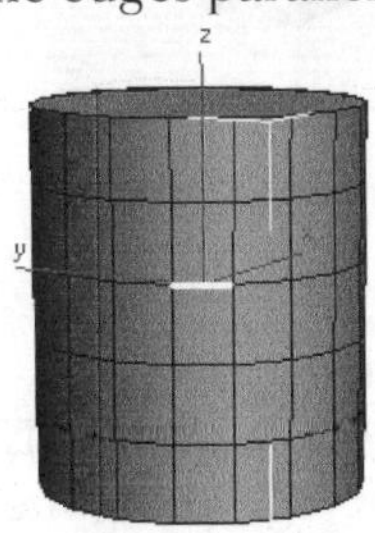

Figure 8-54 *An edge selected in a cylinder*

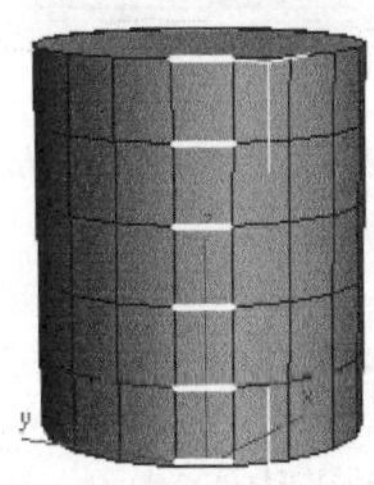

Figure 8-55 *The parallel edges selected after choosing the* ***Ring*** *button*

Loop: The **Loop** button is available only for the **Edge** and **Border** sub-object levels. It is used to select all the edges or borders of the object that are aligned with the selected edge or border. To use this button, select an edge or a border of the object in the viewport, as shown in Figure 8-56, and then choose the **Loop** button; all edges or borders that are aligned with the selected edge will be selected, as shown in Figure 8-57.

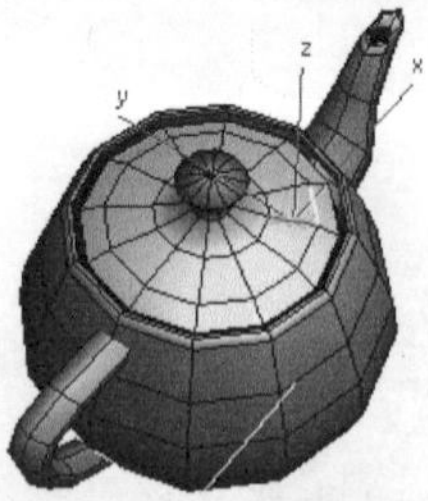

Figure 8-56 The selected edge of the teapot

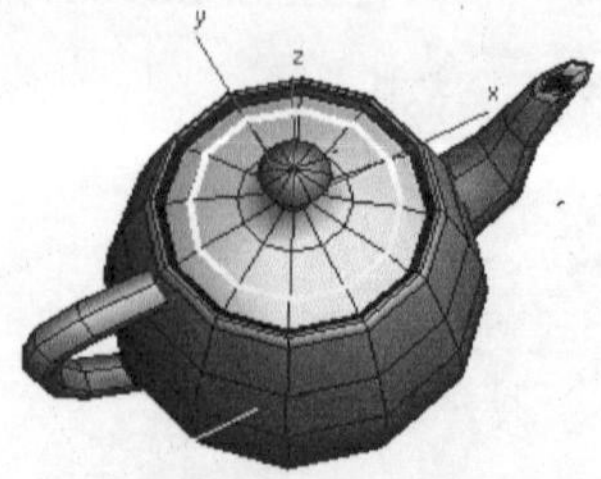

*Figure 8-57 The edges selected after choosing the **Loop** button*

Preview Selection Area: This area is used to preview the selection of sub-objects in the viewport before actually selecting them. To do so, you need to use the options in the **Preview Selection** area. By default, the **Off** radio button is selected in this area, therefore, the preview will not be visible in the viewport.

The **SubObj** radio button in this area enables you to preview the selection of the sub-objects at the current sub-object level only. To do so, select any sub-object level in the **Selection** rollout. Now, select the **SubObj** radio button in the **Preview Selection** area. Next, move the cursor over the object; the corresponding sub-object will be highlighted in yellow color in the viewport, as shown in Figure 8-58. Click on this sub-object; the sub-object will be selected. If you need to select multiple sub-objects at a time, move the cursor over the object and hold the CTRL key. Now, move the mouse over the sub-objects that you need to select; they will be highlighted, refer to Figure 8-59.

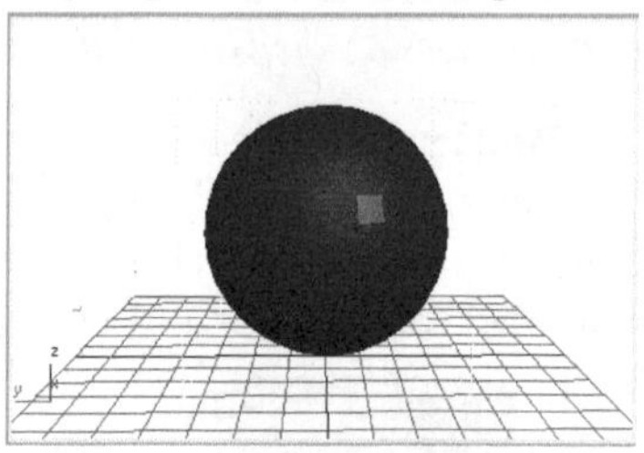

Figure 8-58 The selected sub-object level highlighted

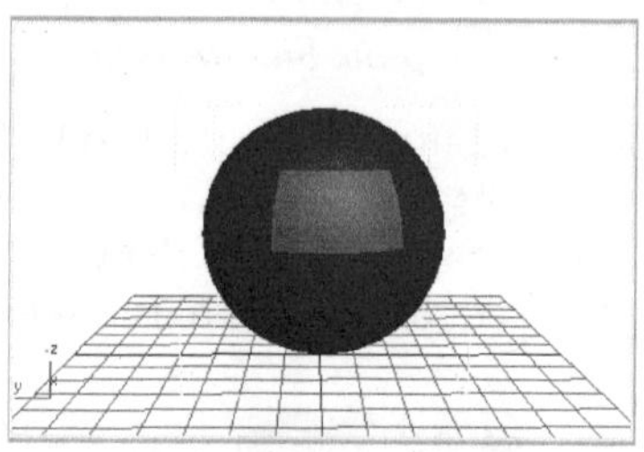

Figure 8-59 More than one polygon highlighted

Click on them and release the CTRL key; the highlighted sub-objects will be selected. Similarly, to deselect a sub-object from the current selection, hold the ALT key, and move the cursor over the sub-object that you want to deselect; it will be highlighted. Now, click on it; the highlighted sub-object will be deselected. To deselect more than one sub-object, you need to hold the ALT+CTRL keys.

The **Multi** radio button in the **Preview Selection** area works similar to the **SubObj** radio button. Additionally, the **Multi** radio button enables you to switch among the sub-object levels in the Modify panel while selecting the sub-object in the viewport. For example, if you move the cursor over the **Polygon** sub-object in the viewport, then the polygon of the object will be highlighted. Click on it; the highlighted polygon will be selected. Also, the **Polygon** sub-object level will be activated in the Modify panel. Similarly, if you select an edge, vertex, or element in the viewport, then the corresponding sub-object level will be activated in the Modify panel. Therefore, you do not need to manually switch among the sub-object levels.

Just below the **Preview Selection** area, a text line is displayed which provides the information about the current selection. Also, when you move the cursor over the object to highlight the sub-objects in the viewport, another text line will be displayed that will provide the information about the number and name of the highlighted sub-objects.

Soft Selection Rollout

The options in this rollout are the same as discussed in the editable mesh.

Edit Geometry Rollout

The options in this rollout are used to edit the geometry of an object. Some of the options in this rollout are discussed next.

Repeat Last: The **Repeat Last** button is used to repeat the recently used command. For example, if you have applied a command to a polygon of an object, and need to apply the same command upto the same level to other polygons, then select the other polygons in the viewport and choose the **Repeat Last** button; the same command will be applied to the selected polygons, refer to Figures 8-60 and 8-61.

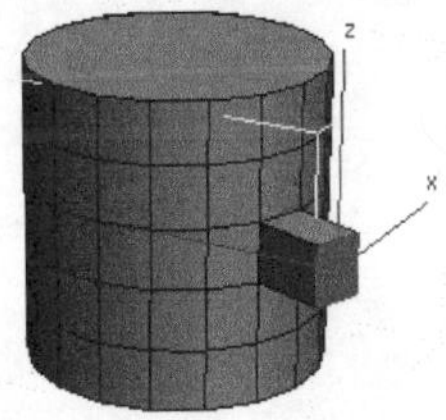

Figure 8-60 *The extruded polygon in a cylinder*

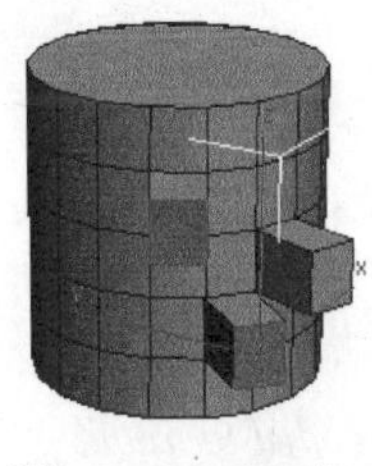

Figure 8-61 *The same extrusion on other polygons after choosing the **Repeat Last** button*

Constraints: The options in the **Constraints** area are used to define the existing geometry to constrain sub-object transformation. There are four radio buttons in this area. They are: **None**, **Edge**, **Face**, and **Normal**. By default, the **None** radio button is selected. As a result, no constraints will be applied to the existing geometry. The **Edge** radio button is used to constrain the sub-object transformation to edge boundaries. The **Face** radio button is used to constrain the sub-object transformations to the individual face. The **Normal** radio button is used to constrain each sub-object transformations to its normal.

Attach: The **Attach** button is the same as discussed in the editable mesh object. Choose the **Attach List** button on the right side of the **Attach** button to display the **Attach List** dialog box. The options in this dialog box are the same as discussed in the editable mesh object.

The **Create**, **Detach**, **Slice Plane**, **Slice**, and **Cut** buttons are the same as discussed in the editable mesh object.

Reset Plane: The **Reset Plane** button is used to reset the default position of the slice plane. When you choose the **Slice Plane** button, the **Reset Plane** and **Slice** buttons get activated.

QuickSlice: The **QuickSlice** button is used to slice an object or sub-objects very quickly and easily. To slice an object quickly, choose the **QuickSlice** button; a quick slice cursor will be displayed, as shown in Figure 8-62. Click in the viewport to define the first point of the slice plane; a slice plane will be displayed, refer to Figure 8-62. Move the cursor to define an angle for the slice and click again to specify the endpoint of the slice; the object will be sliced according to the slice plane, as shown in Figure 8-63. It affects the slice operation on the entire object. If you need to slice particular sub-objects, then you need to select them. Next, right-click to end the **QuickSlice** command.

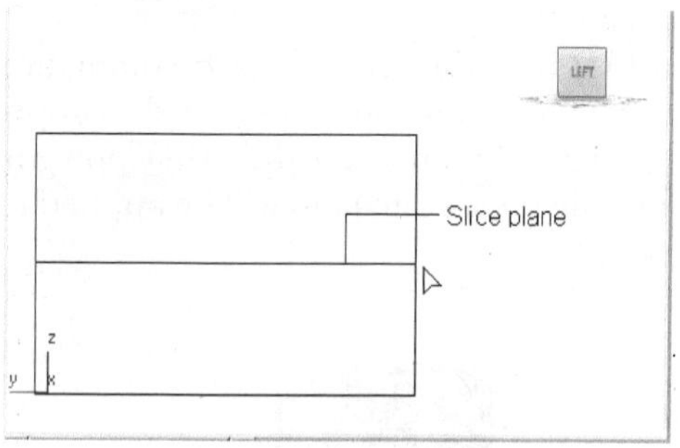

Figure 8-62 The quick slice cursor and slice plane displayed

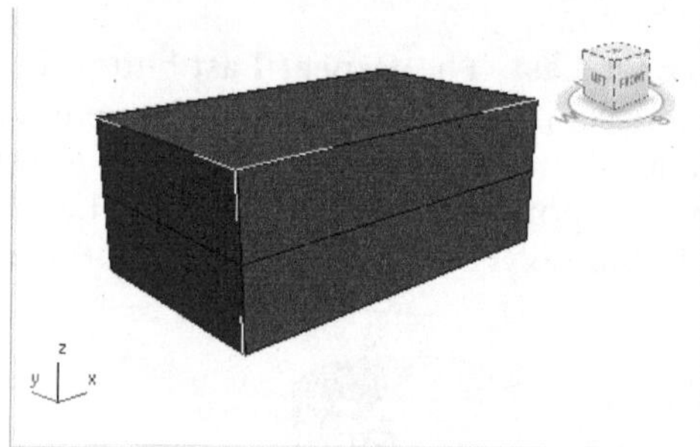

Figure 8-63 The box sliced in the Perspective viewport

> **Note**
> *It is recommended to avoid performing the slice operation in the Perspective viewport.*

MSmooth

The **MSmooth** button is used to smoothen the object or sub-objects. To smoothen the object, select it in the viewport, as shown in Figure 8-64, and then choose the **MSmooth** button in the **Edit Geometry** rollout; the object will be smoothened, as shown in Figure 8-65. Choose the **Settings** button on the right of the **MSmooth** button; the **MeshSmooth** caddy control will be displayed in the viewport, as shown in Figure 8-66. Set the value in the **Smoothness** spinner to define the smoothness of the object. The value in this spinner varies from 0.0 to 1.0.

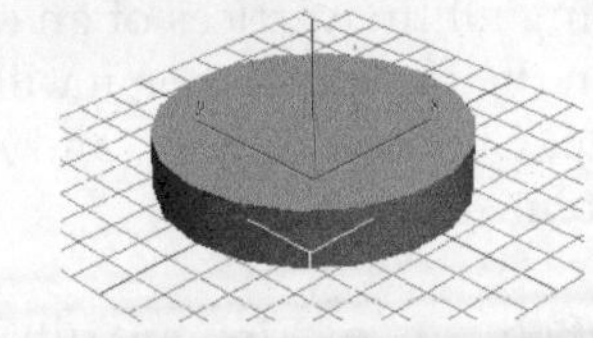

Figure 8-64 Selecting the cylinder in the viewport

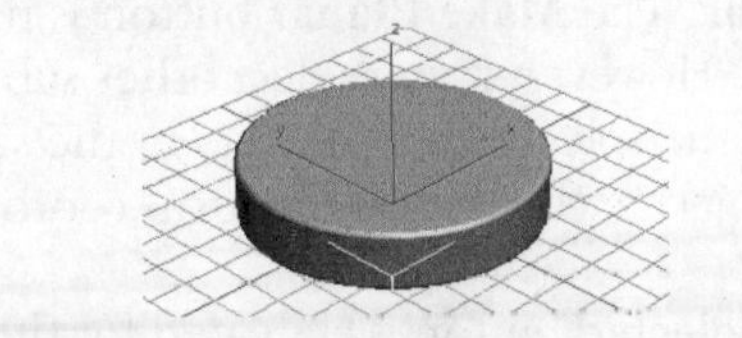

*Figure 8-65 The cylinder smoothened after choosing the **MSmooth** button*

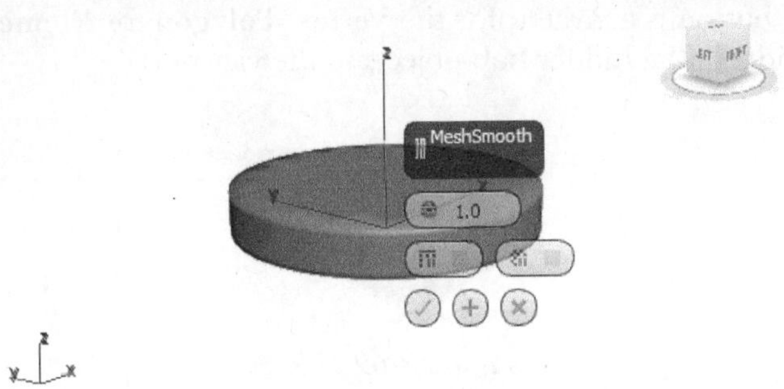

*Figure 8-66 The **MeshSmooth Selection** caddy control*

> **Note**
> *To view the spinner names in the caddy control, you need to move the cursor over the buttons in it; the corresponding name will be displayed the place of the name of the caddy control.*

Tessellate: The **Tessellate** button is used to increase the number of edges or faces in an object and smoothens the object. By default, when you choose the **Tessellate** button, the number of edges of the object will increase. To change the settings, choose the **Settings** button on the right side of the **Tessellate** button; the **Tessellate** caddy control will be displayed in the viewport, as shown in Figure 8-67. Next, click on the arrow placed on the **Edge** button; a drop-down list will be displayed to select the tessellation method, as shown in Figure 8-68. Select the **Edge** or the **Face** option and then choose the **Apply and Continue** button; the number of edges or faces will be increased in the object, refer to Figures 8-69, 8-70, and 8-71. If you need to apply the same settings again, then choose the **Apply and Continue** button again. To end the command and close the caddy control, choose the **OK** button. In case you need to close the caddy control without applying the settings to the selection, choose the **Cancel** button.

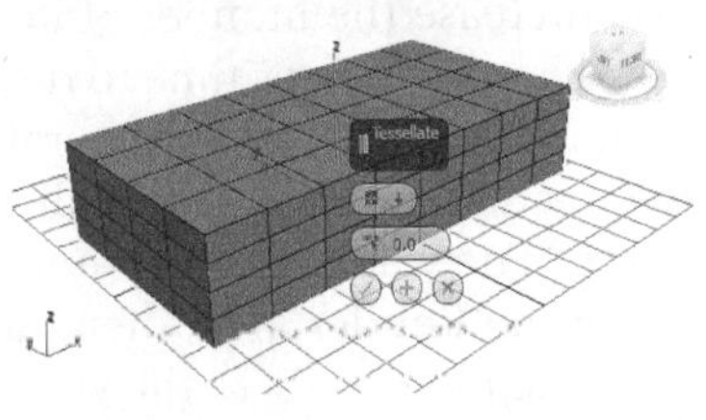

*Figure 8-67 The **Tessellate Selection** caddy control*

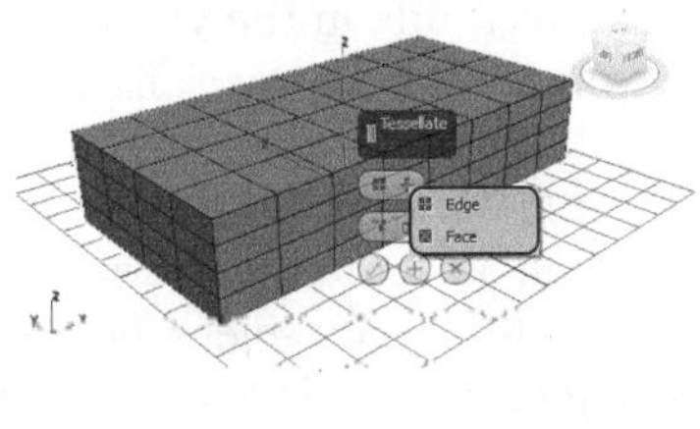

Figure 8-68 The drop-down list displayed after clicking on the arrow

Make Planar: The **Make Planar** button is used to bring all the vertices of an object in the same plane. However, if you select other sub-objects in the viewport, then it will enable you to bring all the selected sub-objects in the same plane. Choose the **X**, **Y**, and **Z** buttons to align the object according to the local coordinate system.

The **Hide Selected** button is activated for the **Vertex**, **Polygon**, or **Element** sub-object level. It is used to hide the selected sub-objects in the viewport.

The **Unhide All** button is activated for the **Vertex**, **Polygon**, or **Element** sub-object level. It is used to unhide all the hidden sub-objects in the viewport.

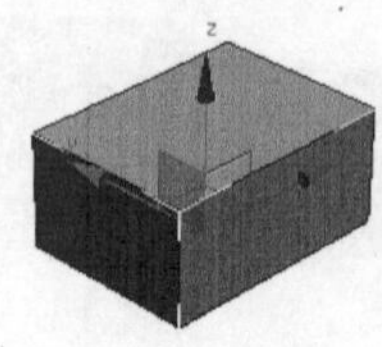

Figure 8-69 A box

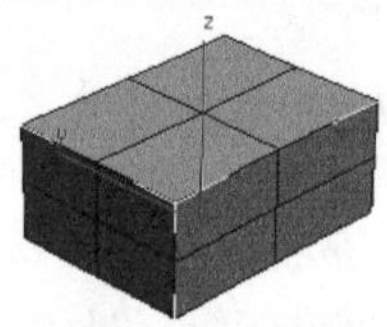

*Figure 8-70 The box after selecting the **Edge** radio button*

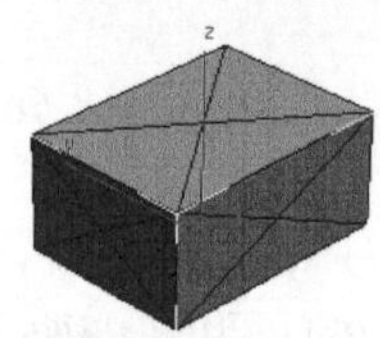

*Figure 8-71 The box after selecting the **Face** radio button*

The **Hide Unselected** button is activated for the **Vertex**, **Polygon**, or **Element** sub-object level. It is used to hide the unselected sub-objects in the viewport.

Subdivision Surface Rollout

The options in this rollout are used to apply the subdivision to the object to make it smooth. The different areas in this rollout are discussed next.

Display and **Render Areas**: The value in the **Iterations** spinner is used to specify the number of times the smooth algorithm will be applied to an object. If you select the **Iterations** check box in the **Render** area, then the value in the **Iterations** spinner of the **Display** area will show its effect only in the viewport. Note that when you increase the number of iterations in the spinner, the number of segments also increases and it takes longer time to display its effect in the viewport as well as on rendering. Therefore, increase the number of iterations as per your requirement. The **Smoothness** spinner is used to add new polygons to all vertices to smoothen object in the viewport as well as on rendering. The value in this spinner varies from 0.0 to 1.0. If you select the **Smoothness** check box in the **Render** area, then the value in the **Smoothness** spinner of the **Display** area will show the effect only in the viewport.

The **Iterations** and **Smoothness** spinners in the **Render** area are used to smoothen the polygon objects on rendering. To activate them, select the check boxes on the left side of the spinners.

Separate By Area: Select the **Smoothing Groups** check box in this area to stop the creation of new polygons at edges between faces that are not under the smoothing group. Select the **Materials** check box to stop the creation of new polygons at edges between the faces that do not share the material IDs.

Update Options Area: Select the **Always** radio button in this area to automatically view the output of the smoothness settings in the viewport as well as on rendering. Select the **When Rendering** radio button to view the output of the smoothness settings only at the time of rendering. Select the **Manually** radio button to view the output of the smoothness settings only when you choose the **Update** button below the **Manually** radio button. In this case, if you change the settings as per your requirement, then to update the settings you need to choose the **Update** button.

Paint Deformation Rollout

The options in this rollout are used to deform the surface of an object, refer to Figure 8-72. At the object level, it affects the vertices of the entire object, while at the sub-object level, it affects only the selected vertices of the object. This rollout has three buttons. The **Push/Pull** button is used to push or pull the vertices of the object. Choose the **Push/Pull** button to activate it and move the cursor over the object in the viewport; a light blue colored brush along with the cursor will be displayed in the viewport, as shown in Figure 8-73. Press the left mouse button; the brush will turn red. Drag the cursor to deform the surface of the object, as shown in Figure 8-74, and release the left mouse button; the object will be deformed. At the sub-object level, choose the **Push/Pull** button to activate it and move the cursor over the selected sub-objects; a light blue colored brush will be displayed in the viewport. Now, click on it to deform the surface and right-click to exit the command. While performing the push/pull command, the object will be pushed or pulled, depending on the value that you have entered in the **Push/Pull Value** spinner.

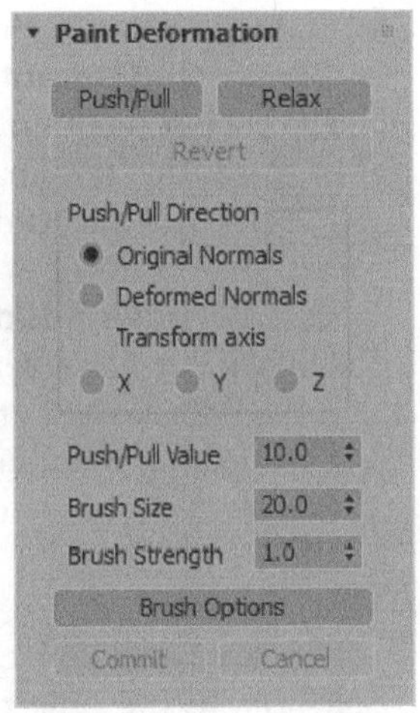

*Figure 8-72 The **Paint Deformation** rollout*

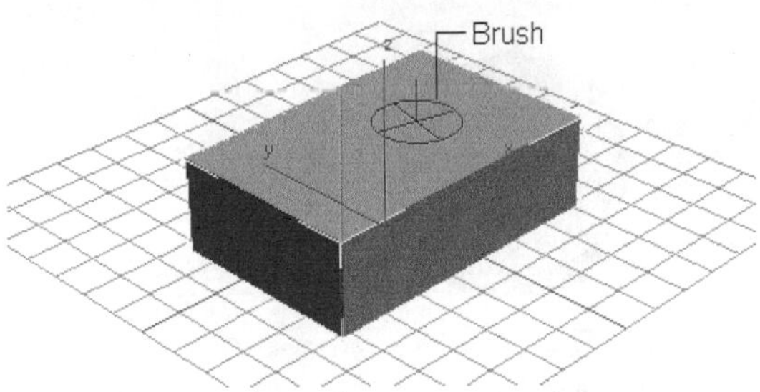

*Figure 8-73 The brush displayed on choosing the **Push/Pull** button*

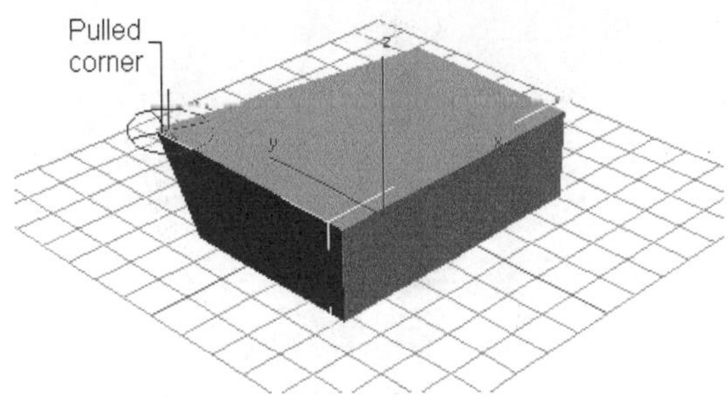

Figure 8-74 The object deformed at the corner vertex

The **Relax** button is used to maintain the distance between the vertices of an object. The **Revert** button is used to erase the effect of the **Push/Pull** button by clicking on the same vertices or object. To reverse the effect of the **Push/Pull** button simultaneously while using it, you need to hold the CTRL key and click on the same vertex.

Push/Pull Direction Area: The radio buttons in this area are used to specify the direction of the push or pull over the object. If you select the **Original Normals** radio button, then after pushing or pulling, the vertices of the object will move in the direction of its normal before deformation. If you select the **Deformed Normals Transform axis** radio button, then after pushing or pulling, the vertices of the object will move in the direction of its normal after deformation. Select the **X**, **Y**, or **Z** radio button to move the vertices along the direction of the selected radio button.

As mentioned earlier, the value in the **Push/Pull Value** spinner is used to specify the extent of pushing or pulling the vertices of an object. The positive value enables you to pull the vertices, and the negative value enables you to push the vertices. The **Brush Size** spinner is used to specify the size of the brush cursor in the viewport. The value in the **Brush Strength** spinner is used to specify the strength of the brush by which it applies the push or pull effect. It varies from 0.0 to 1.0. Choose the **Brush Options** button; the **Painter Options** dialog box will be displayed. You can set various parameters of the brush in this dialog box. Choose the **Commit** button to deform the object permanently. Note that you cannot use the **Revert** button after choosing the **Commit** button. Choose the **Cancel** button to erase all the changes that you made to deform the object. However, if you have already committed the effects, then you cannot use the **Cancel** button to erase the effects.

Edit Vertices Rollout

On selecting the **Vertex** sub-object level, the **Edit Vertices** rollout will be displayed in the Modify panel, as shown in Figure 8-75. The options in this rollout are used to edit the vertices of an object. To delete the vertices of an object, select them in the viewport and choose the **Remove** button; the vertices will be deleted.

Figure 8-75 *The* ***Edit Vertices*** *rollout*

Alternatively, you can press the DELETE key, but it will create a hole in the object. The **Connect** button is used to connect the two selected vertices by creating an edge between them, refer to Figures 8-76 and 8-77.

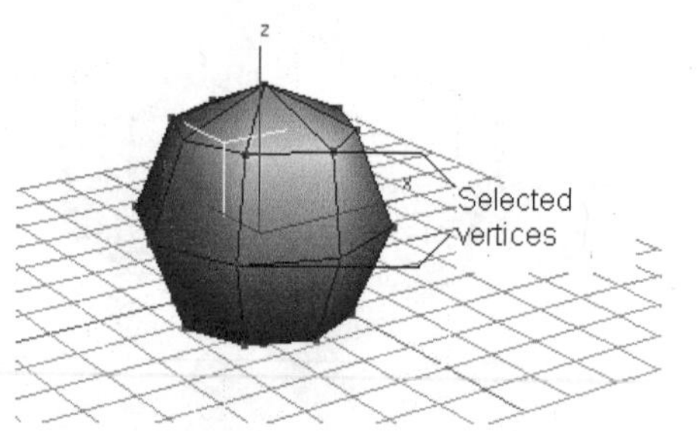

Figure 8-76 *The vertices selected in the object*

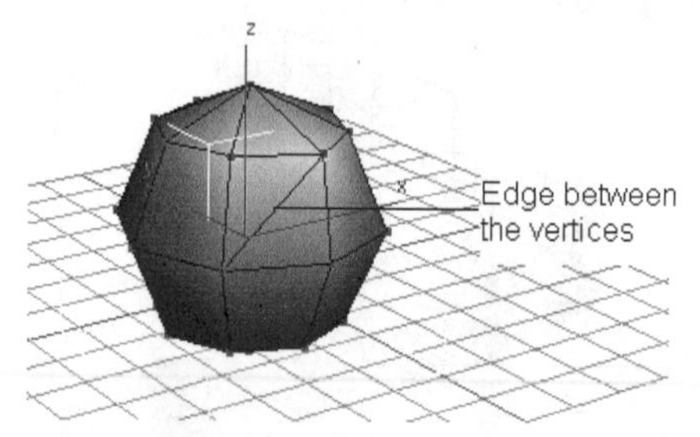

Figure 8-77 *The edge created between the vertices selected*

Choose the **Remove Isolated Vertices** button to remove the vertices that are not attached to any polygon in the object. Choose the **Remove Unused Map Verts** button to remove the vertices that cannot be used for mapping. The **Weight** spinner is used to set the weight of the vertex that specifies the smoothness towards the vertex in the output.

The **Break**, **Extrude**, **Weld**, **Chamfer**, and **Target Weld** buttons are the same as discussed in the editable mesh. Also note that the **Extrude**, **Weld**, and **Chamfer** buttons have the **Settings** button on the right side to apply the selected command more accurately.

Edit Edges Rollout

On selecting the **Edge** sub-object level, the **Edit Edges** rollout will be displayed, as shown in Figure 8-78. The options in this rollout are used to edit the edges of an object. The **Insert Vertex** button is used to add a vertex to the edge. To do so, choose the **Insert Vertex** button; the vertices of the object will be displayed in the viewport. Now, click on an edge of the object; a new vertex will be created. Right-click to exit the command. To delete an edge of the object, select the edge in the viewport, and choose the **Remove** button; the selected edge will be deleted. Alternatively, you can press the DELETE key, but it will create a hole in the object.

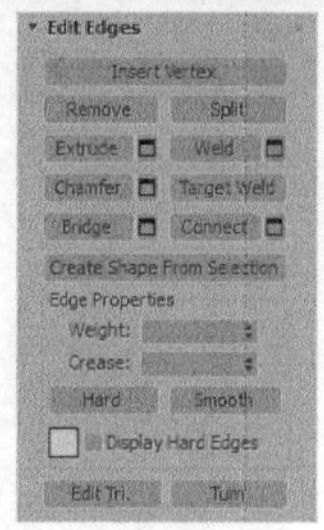

*Figure 8-78 The **Edit Edges** rollout*

The **Connect** button is used to connect the two selected edges by creating a new edge between them. Choose the **Settings** button on the right side of the **Connect** button; the **Connect Edges** caddy control will be displayed in the viewport, as shown in Figure 8-79. It is used to set the parameters of the additional edge created using the **Connect** button.

The value in the **Segments** spinner in this caddy control is used to specify the number of new edges to be created in between the selected edges. The value in the **Pinch** spinner is used to set the distance between the new edges. The value in the **Slide** spinner specifies the position of the new edges. By default, the new edges are created at the center.

To set the number of segments per chamfer, select an edge of the object in the viewport. Now, choose the **Settings** button on the right of the **Chamfer** button; the **Chamfer** caddy control will be displayed in the viewport, as shown in Figure 8-80.

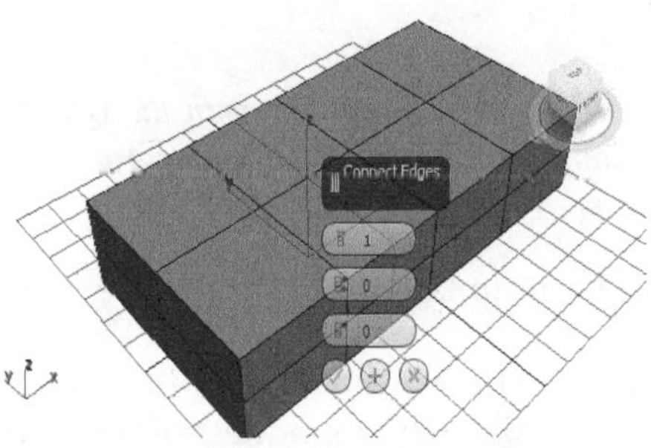

*Figure 8-79 The **Connect Edges** caddy control in the viewport*

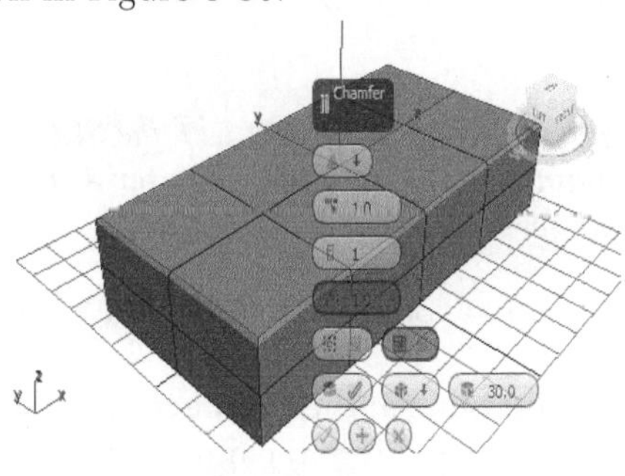

*Figure 8-80 The **Chamfer** caddy control in the viewport*

In this caddy control, click on the down arrow of the **Chamfer Type** button; a flyout will be displayed with two options, **Standard Chamfer** and **Quad Chamfer**, refer to Figure 8-81.

The caddy control displayed on choosing **Standard Chamfer** from the **Chamfer Type** flyout is shown in Figure 8-80. The caddy control displayed on choosing **Quad Chamfer** from the **Chamfer Type** flyout is shown in Figure 8-82.

Set the value in the **Edge Chamfer Amount** spinner to specify the amount of chamfering for the selected edge. Figures 8-83 and 8-84 display the selected edges chamfered with the **Standard Chamfer** type and **Quad Chamfer** type, respectively.

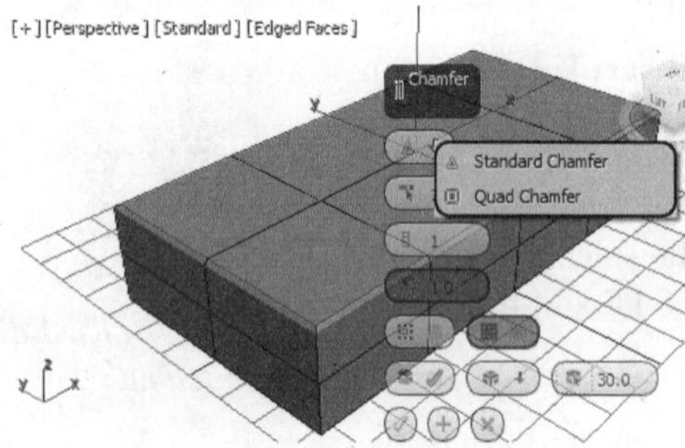

*Figure 8-81 The **Chamfer Type** flyout*

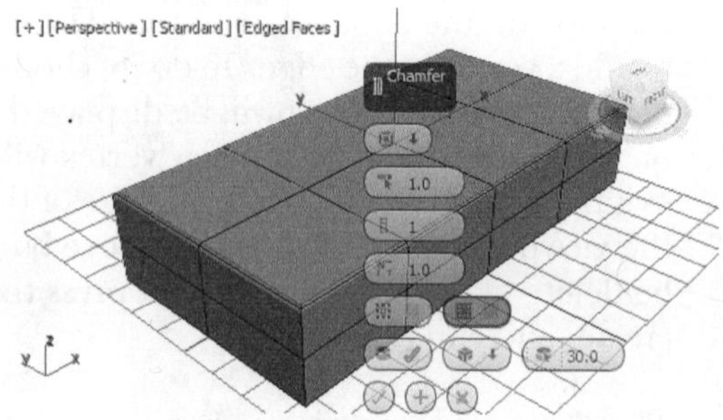

*Figure 8-82 The **Chamfer** caddy control on choosing **Quad Chamfer** from the flyout*

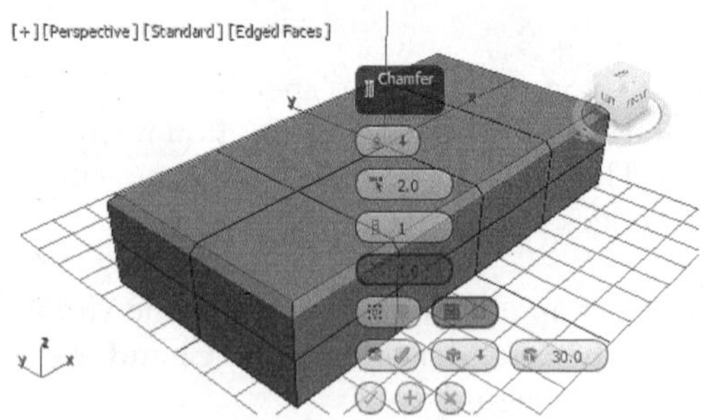

*Figure 8-83 Chamfering with the **Standard Chamfer** type and **Edge Chamfer Amount** spinner = 2*

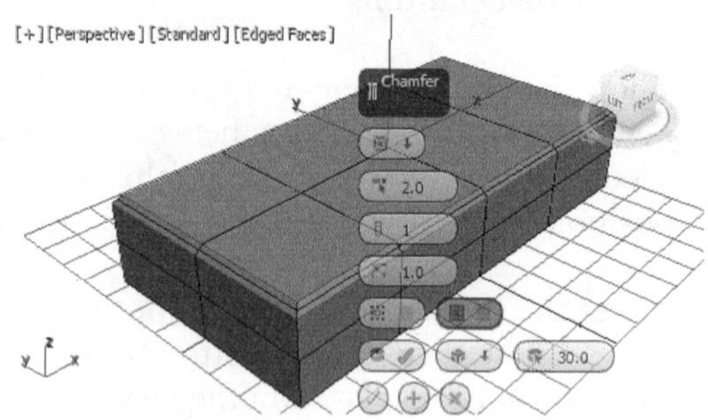

*Figure 8-84 Chamfering with the **Quad Chamfer** type and **Edge Chamfer Amount** spinner = 2*

Note that you need to move the cursor over the buttons to know their respective names.

Set the value in the **Connect Edge Segments** spinner to define the number of segments in the chamfer. More the number of the segments, more will be the roundness of the chamfer. Figures 8-85 and 8-86 display the selected edges chamfered with the **Standard Chamfer** type and **Quad Chamfer** type, respectively. You will notice that in the **Standard Chamfer** type, the no of polygons created are equal to the value in the **Connect Edge Segments** spinner for each chamfered edge. However, in the **Quad Chamfer** type, the no of polygons created are double the value in the **Connect Edge Segments** spinner for each chamfered edge.

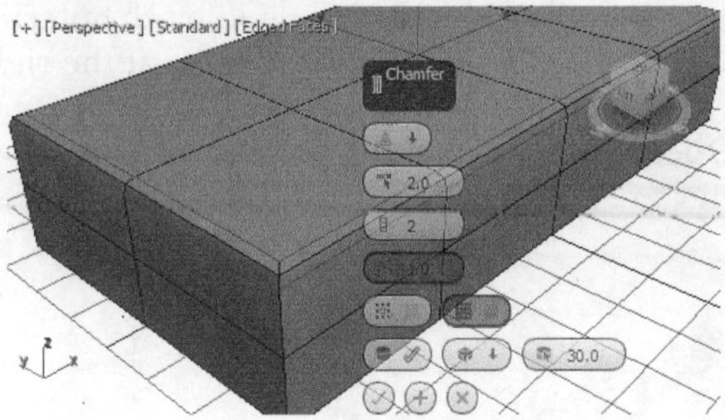

*Figure 8-85 Chamfering with the **Standard Chamfer** type and the **Connect Edge Segments** spinner = 2*

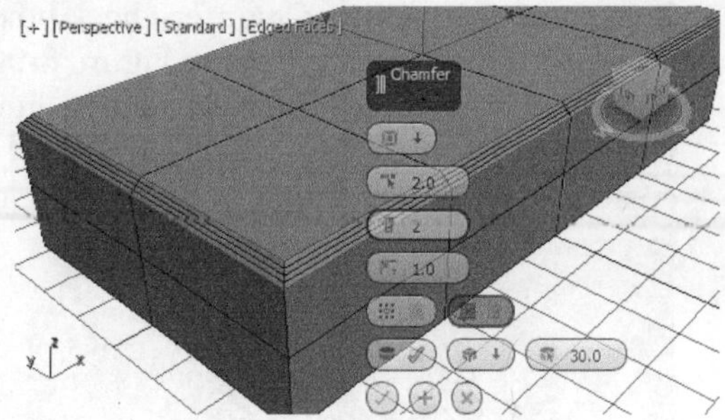

*Figure 8-86 Chamfering with the **Quad Chamfer** type and the **Connect Edge Segments** spinner = 2*

The **Edge Tension** spinner is activated only for the **Quad Chamfer** type. It determines the angle between the new polygons generated by chamfering edges between non-coplanar polygons. Figures 8-87 through 8-89 display the chamfered edges with the value **1**, **0.5**, and **0**, respectively, in the **Edge tension** spinner. The lower the value of the **Edge Tension** spinner, higher will be the angle between the new polygons generated by chamfering edges between non-coplanar polygons.

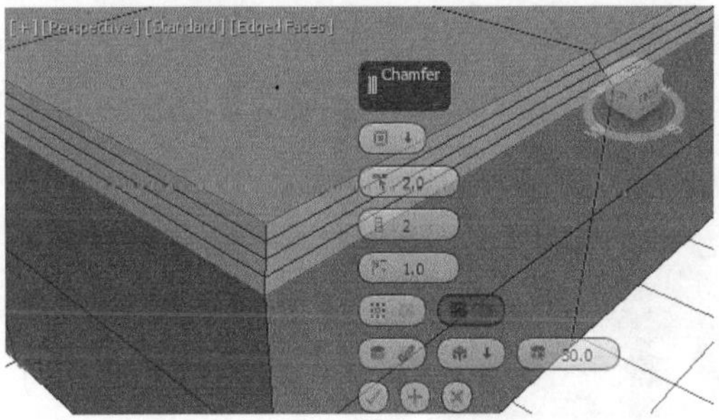

*Figure 8-87 Chamfering with the **Edge Tension** spinner = 1*

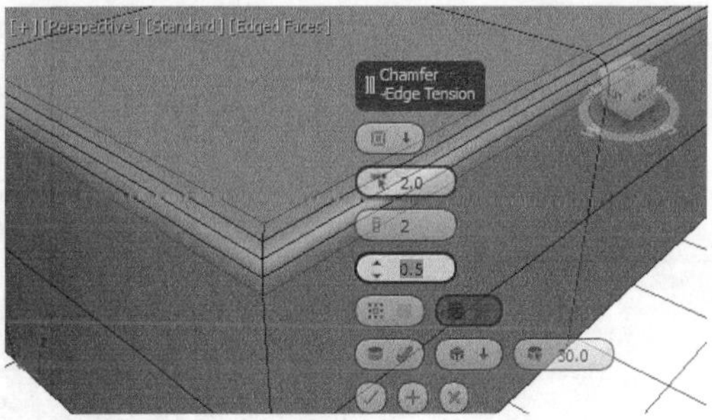

*Figure 8-88 Chamfering with the **Edge Tension** spinner = 0.5*

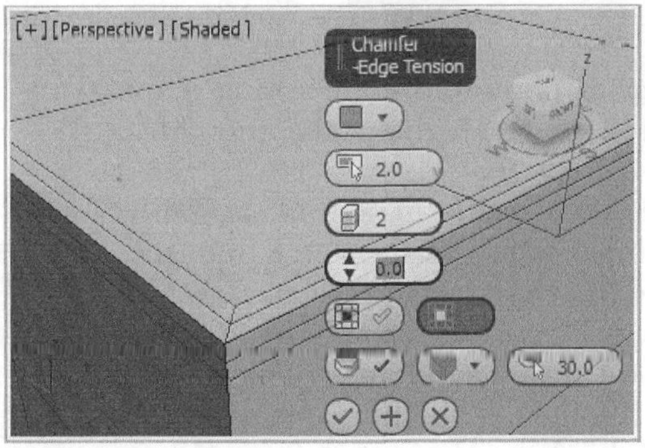

*Figure 8-89 Chamfering with the **Edge Tension** spinner = 0*

If you select the **Open Chamfer** check box, the polygons which are created by chamfering process will be deleted, refer to Figure 8-90. The **Invert Open** spinner located at the right of the **Open** spinner is activated only when the **Open** check box is selected and the **Quad Chamfer** type is chosen. Select the **Invert Open** check box; all the polygons except those created while chamfering will be deleted, refer to Figure 8-91.

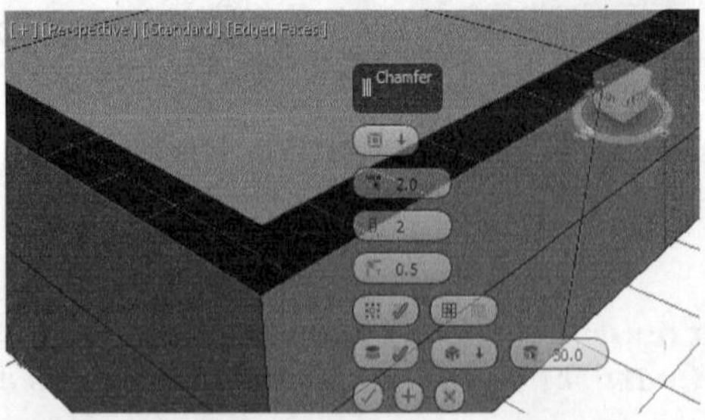

Figure 8-90 The deleted polygons

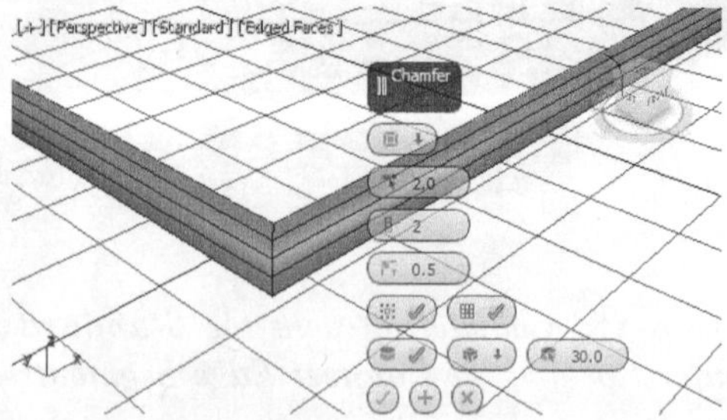

***Figure 8-91** The remaining polygons after selecting the **Invert Open** check box*

Click on the down arrow of the **Smooth Type** button; a flyout will be displayed, as shown in Figure 8-92. Choose the desired option from the flyout and then select the **Smooth** check box at the left of the **Smooth Type** button to smoothen the portion as per the option chosen from the flyout.

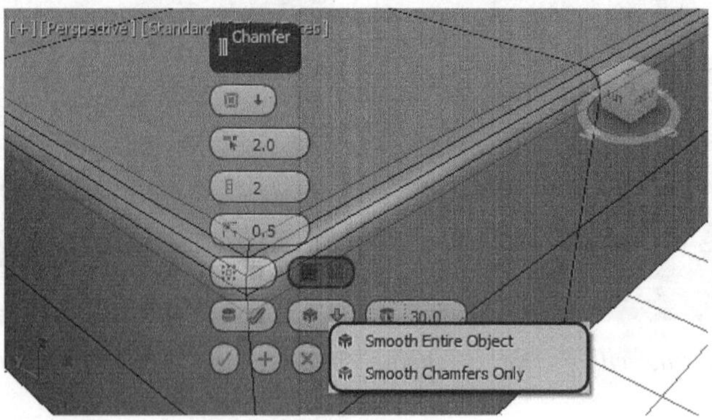

***Figure 8-92** The flyout displayed*

The value of the **Smooth Threshold** spinner ranges from 0 to 180. The more the value of the **Smooth Threshold** spinner, higher is the smoothness.

The **Create Shape From Selection** button in the **Edit Edges** rollout is used to create a spline shape from the selected edges. To do so, select the edges of an object in the viewport and then choose the **Create Shape From Selection** button; the **Create Shape** dialog box will be displayed, as shown in Figure 8-93. Enter a name in the **Curve Name** text box for the newly created shape. Select the **Smooth** or **Linear** radio button to create a smooth or a linear curve, respectively. Next, choose the **OK** button; a spline will be created along with the selected edges, as shown in Figures 8-94 and 8-95.

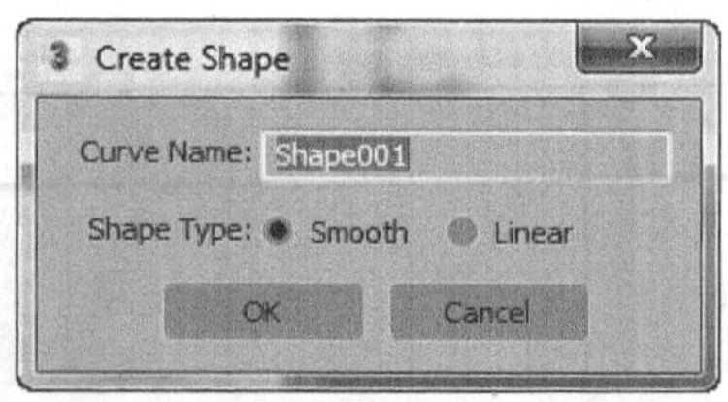

***Figure 8-93** The **Create Shape** dialog box*

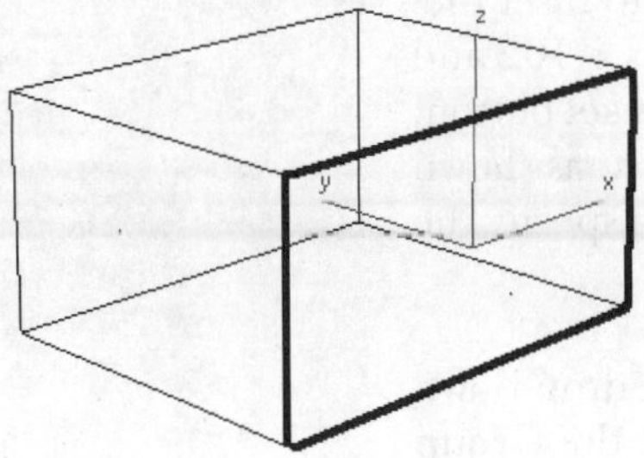

Figure 8-94 The edges selected in the box

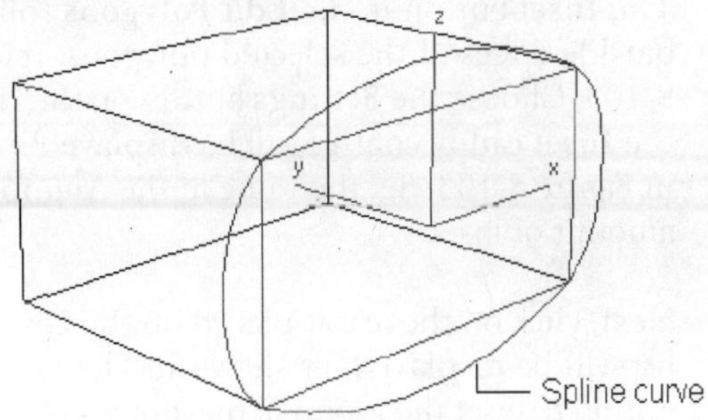

Figure 8-95 The spline created after using the ***Create Shape From Selection*** *button*

Edit Borders Rollout

On selecting the **Border** sub-object level, the **Edit Borders** rollout will be displayed, as shown in Figure 8-96. The options in this rollout are used to edit the border of an object. The **Cap** button is used to create a polygon to cap the selected border of the object.

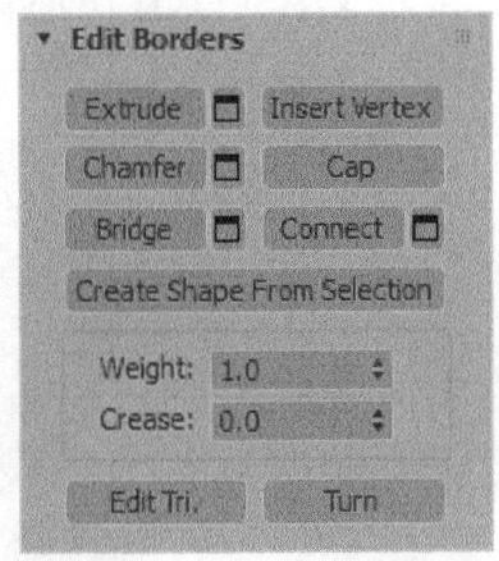

Figure 8-96 The ***Edit Borders*** *rollout*

To do so, select the border of the object in the viewport and then choose the **Cap** button; a polygon will be displayed to cap the border, as shown in Figures 8-97 and 8-98. The other options in this rollout are the same as described earlier in this chapter.

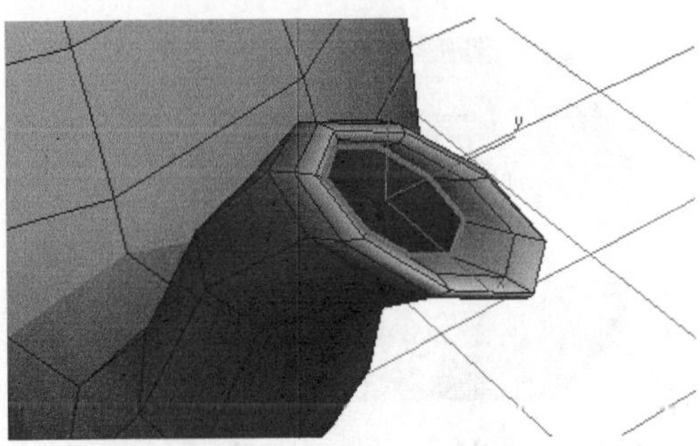

Figure 8-97 The selected border of the spout of a teapot

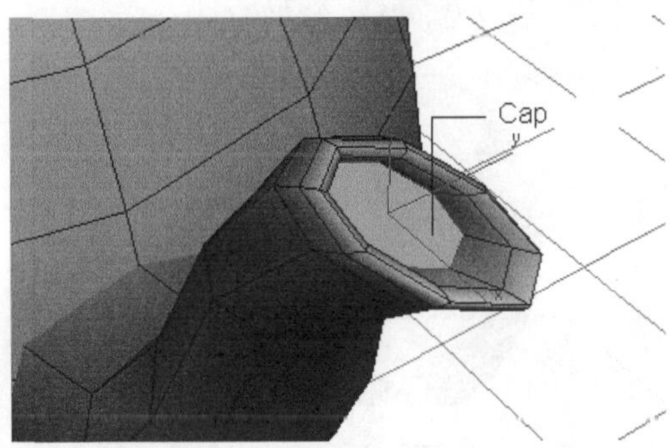

Figure 8-98 The cap after choosing the ***Cap*** *button*

Edit Polygons Rollout

When you select the **Polygon** sub-object level, the **Edit Polygons** rollout will be displayed, as shown in Figure 8-99. The options in this rollout are used to edit the polygons of the object. The **Outline** button is used to increase or decrease the outside edges of the selected polygons, refer to Figures 8-100 and 8-101. Choose the **Settings** button on the right of the **Outline** button; the **Outline** caddy control will be displayed in the viewport, refer to Figure 8-101. Set the value in the **Amount** spinner to specify the increment or decrement of the outside edge of the selected polygon. Choose the **OK** button to apply the function and exit the **Outline** dialog box.

The **Inset** button in the **Edit Polygons** rollout is used to inset the outside edges of the selected polygons, refer to Figures 8-102 and 8-103. Choose the **Settings** button on the right of the **Inset** button; the **Inset** caddy control will be displayed in the viewport, as shown in Figure 8-103. Set the value in the **Amount** spinner to specify the amount of inset.

Next, click on the arrow placed on the **Group** button; a drop-down list will be displayed, as shown in Figure 8-104. Select the **Group** option to inset the group of polygons. Select the **By Polygon** option to inset the polygons in the group individually. Choose the **OK** button to apply the function and exit the caddy control. The **Flip** button in the **Edit Polygons** rollout is used to flip the direction of the selected polygons.

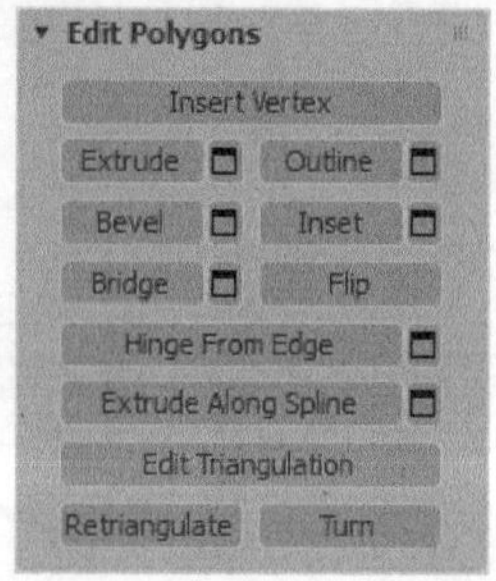

*Figure 8-99 The **Edit Polygons** rollout*

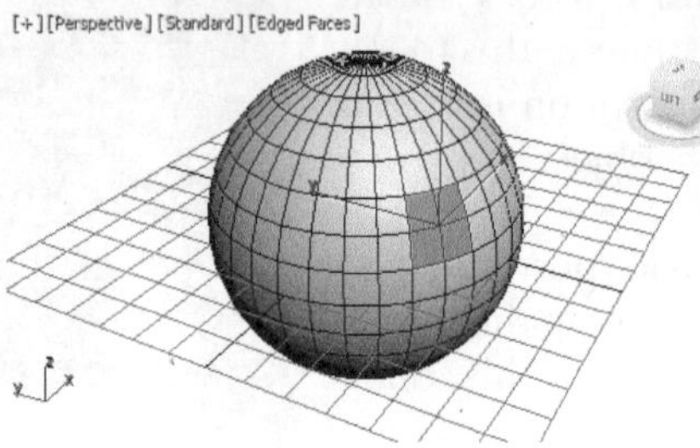

Figure 8-100 *The selected polygons in a sphere*

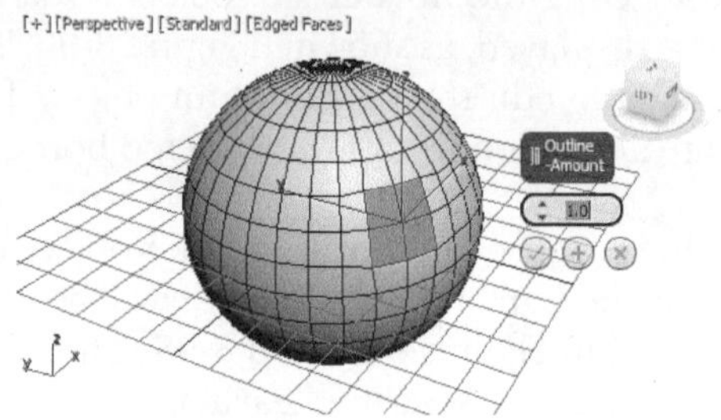

Figure 8-101 *The selected polygons after choosing the **Outline** button*

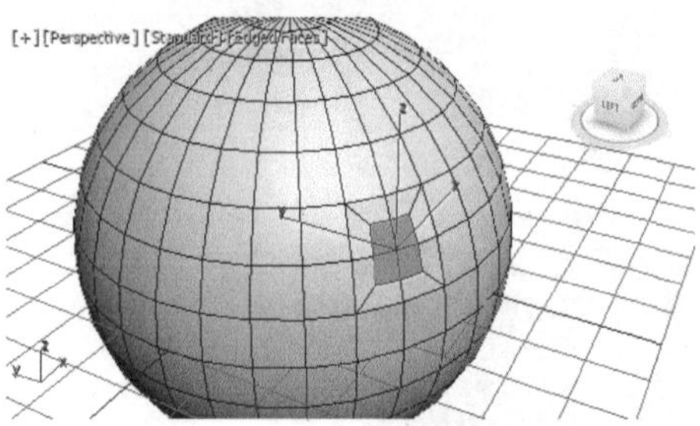

Figure 8-102 *The group of polygons inset on selecting the **Group** option*

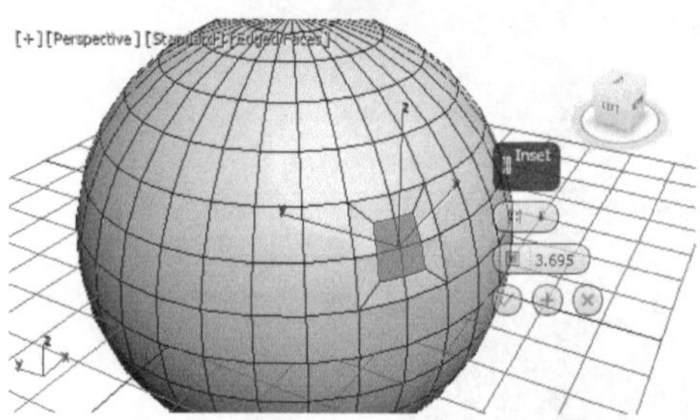

Figure 8-103 *The **Inset** caddy control displayed*

The **Hinge From Edge** button is used to create a hinge on the selected polygon along the edge. To do so, select a polygon of the object in the viewport and choose the **Hinge From Edge** button.

Now, move the cursor on an edge of the selected polygon, as shown in Figure 8-105, and drag the cursor in the vertical direction; the hinge will be created, as shown in Figure 8-106.

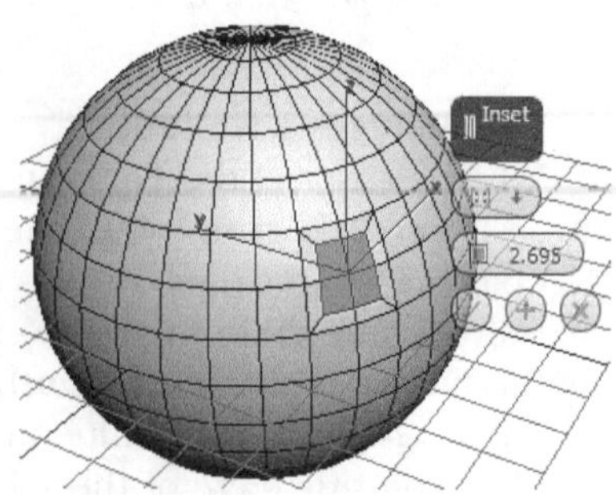

Figure 8-104 *The drop-down list displayed in the **Inset** caddy control*

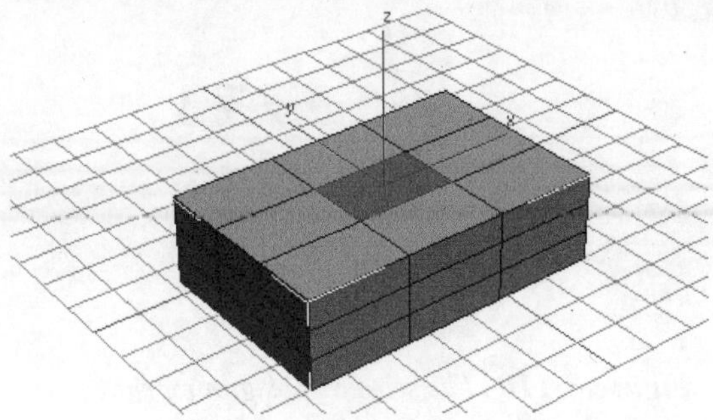

Figure 8-105 The polygon selected in the box

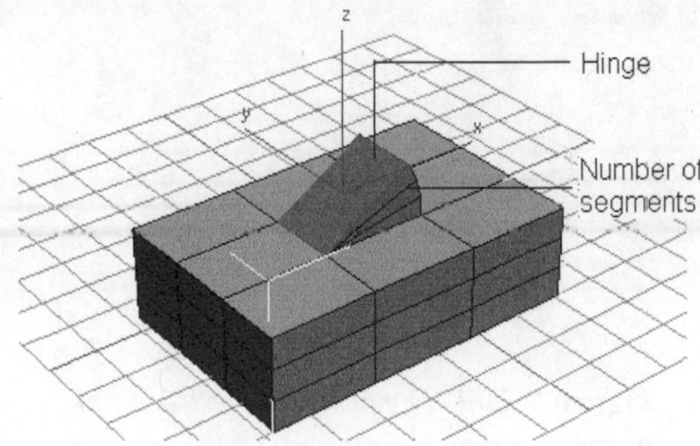

*Figure 8-106 The hinge created on choosing the **Hinge From Edge** button*

You can also create a hinge on the polygon using the **Settings** button on the right side of the **Hinge From Edge** button. To do so, select a polygon of the object in the viewport and choose the **Settings** button; the **Hinge From Edge** caddy control will be displayed in the viewport, as shown in Figure 8-107. The value in the **Angle** spinner is used to specify the angle of rotation. You can set a positive or a negative value in this spinner.

The **Segments** spinner is used to specify the number of segments in the selected polygon. Choose the **Pick Hinge** button to activate it and click on an edge of the selected polygon in the viewport; the hinge will be created. Choose the **OK** button to close the caddy control.

The **Extrude Along Spline** button in the **Edit Polygons** rollout is used to extrude the polygons of an object along the spline in the viewport. To do so, select a polygon of the editable poly object in the viewport. Now, choose the **Settings** button on the right side of the **Extrude Along Spline** button; the **Extrude Along Spline** caddy control will be displayed in the viewport, as shown in Figure 8-108.

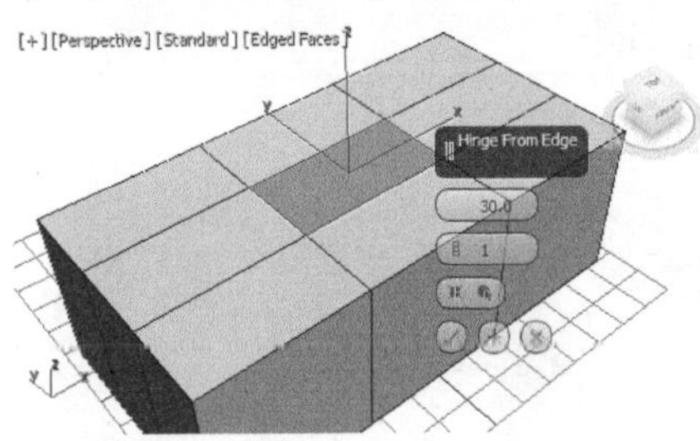

*Figure 8-107 The **Hinge From Edge** caddy control*

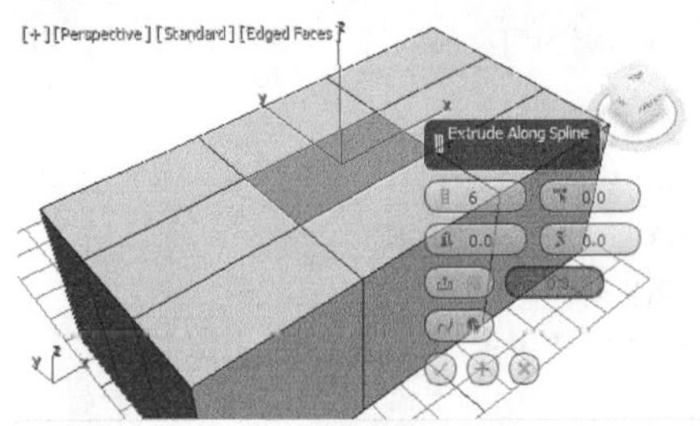

*Figure 8-108 The **Extrude Along Spline** caddy control*

Choose the **Pick Spline** button in the caddy control to activate it and then select the spline in the viewport, as shown in Figure 8-109; the selected polygon will be extruded along the spline, as shown in Figure 8-110. Set the parameters of the extruded spline using the options in the **Extrude Polygons Along Spline** caddy control.

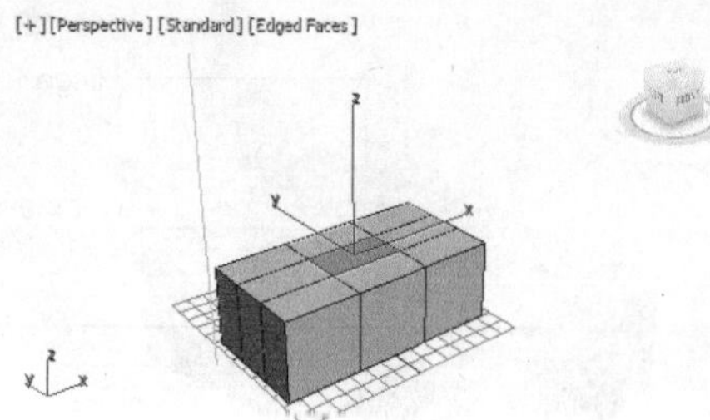

Figure 8-109 *The polygon selected in the plane and the spline*

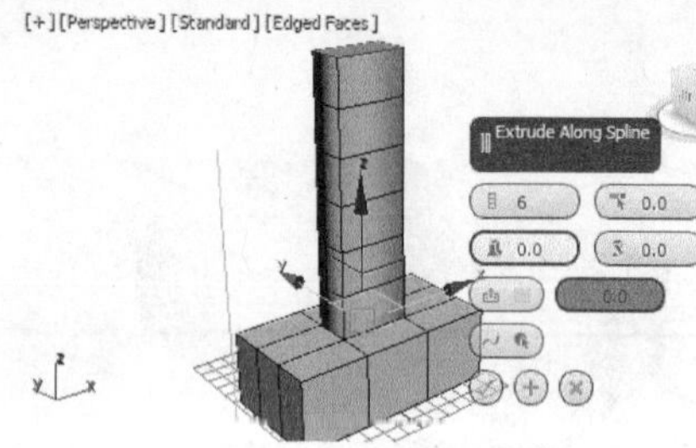

Figure 8-110 *The selected polygon extruded along the spline*

TUTORIALS

Tutorial 1

In this tutorial, you will create a golf ball, as shown in Figure 8-111, by modifying the standard primitives at advanced level. **(Expected time: 20 min)**

Figure 8-111 *A golf ball model*

The following steps are required to complete this tutorial:

a. Create the project folder.
b. Create a golf ball.
c. Convert the golf ball.
d. Modify the golf ball.
e. Save and render the scene.

Creating the Project Folder

Create a new project folder with the name *c08_tut1* at *\Documents\3dsmax2017* and then save the file with the name *c08tut1*, as discussed in Tutorial 1 of Chapter 2.

Creating a Golf Ball

In this section, you will create a golf ball by using the **Geosphere** tool.

1. Activate the Top viewport and choose **Create > Geometry** in the **Command Panel**; the **Standard Primitives** option is displayed by default in the drop-down list below the **Geometry** button. Now, choose the **GeoSphere** tool from the **Object Type** rollout.

2. Expand the **Keyboard Entry** rollout and set the value **130.0** in the **Radius** spinner. Next, choose the **Create** button; a geosphere is created in the viewports.

3. In the **Parameters** rollout, set the value **8** in the **Segments** spinner.

4. Choose the **Zoom Extents All** tool to display the geosphere in viewports, as shown in Figure 8-112.

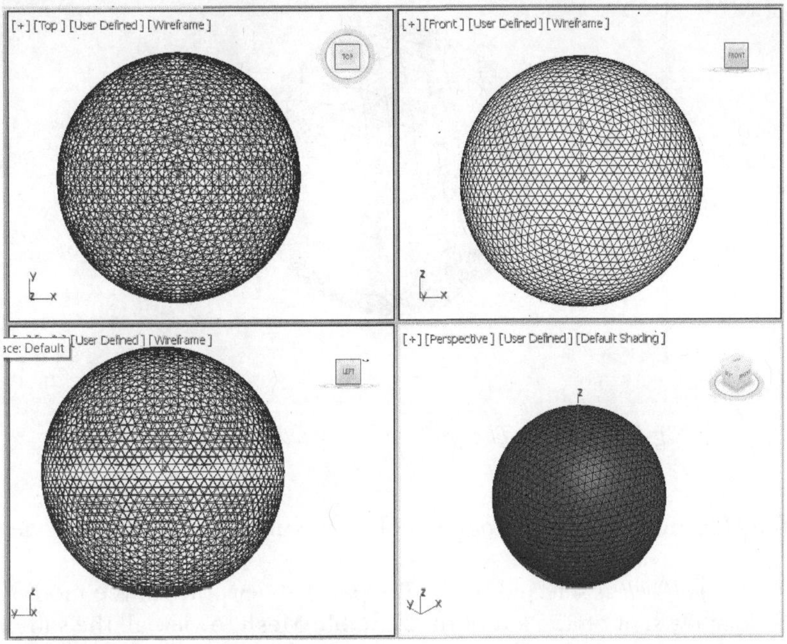

Figure 8-112 *The geosphere displayed in viewports*

5. In the **Name and Color** rollout, enter **golf ball**; the geosphere is named as *golf ball.*

6. Use the color swatch to change the color of *golf ball* to white.

   Next, you need to convert *golf ball* into an editable mesh and modify it using the sub-object levels.

Converting the Golf Ball into an Editable Mesh

In this section, you will convert *golf ball* into an editable mesh.

1. Select *golf ball* in any viewport and right-click on it; a quad menu is displayed. Choose **Convert To > Convert to Editable Mesh**; the *golf ball* is converted into an editable mesh.

Note

When you convert the golf ball into an editable mesh, the ***GeoSphere*** *label in the modifier stack gets replaced by the* ***Editable Mesh****.*

Modifying the Golf Ball Using the Sub-object Levels

In this section, you will modify *golf ball* to give it a perfect shape.

1. Activate the Perspective viewport. Choose the **Zoom** tool and zoom in the Perspective viewport to view *golf ball*, as shown in Figure 8-113.

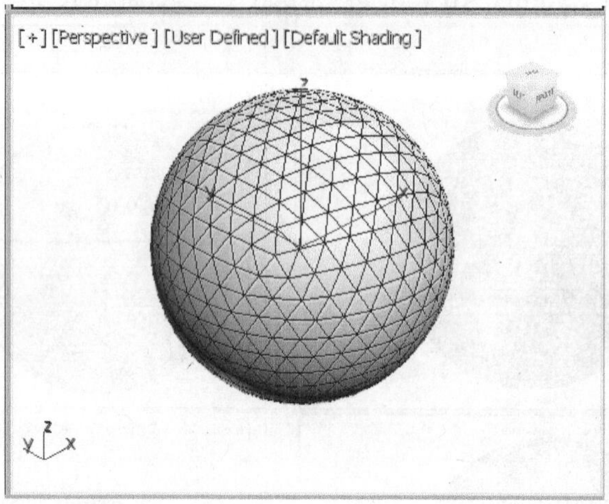

Figure 8-113 The golf ball geometry zoomed in the Perspective viewport

2. Choose the **Maximize Viewport Toggle** tool to maximize the Perspective viewport.

3. Make sure that *golf ball* is selected in the Perspective viewport. In the modifier stack, click on the black arrow sign on the left of the **Editable Mesh** to view all the sub-object levels.

4. Select the **Polygon** sub-object level; it turns yellow and gets activated.

5. Press the CTRL+A keys to select all the polygons of *golf ball*, as shown in Figure 8-114.

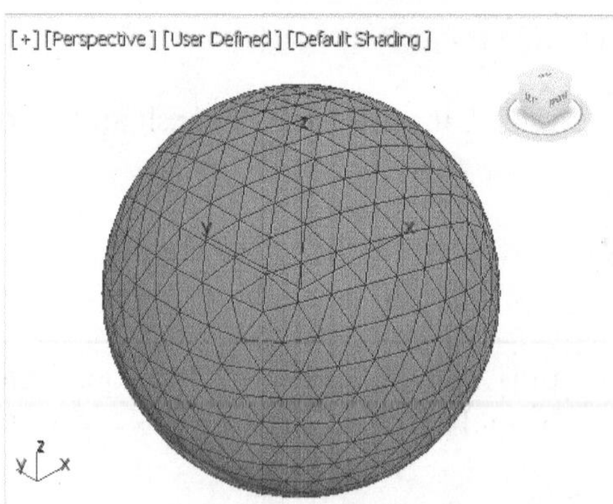

Figure 8-114 All polygons in the golf ball selected

6. Select the **Edge** sub-object level in the modifier stack.

7. Press the CTRL+A keys to select all the edges of *golf ball*, as shown in Figure 8-115.

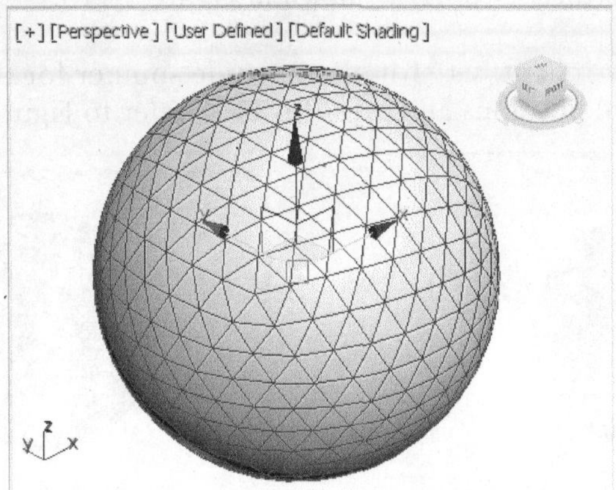

Figure 8-115 *All edges of golf ball selected*

Now, if you select the **Polygon** sub-object level in the modifier stack, all the polygons of golf ball will be selected in the viewport. And, if you select the **Edge** sub-object level, then all the edges of golf ball will be selected in the viewport.

8. In the **Edit Geometry** rollout, set the value of the **Chamfer** spinner to **5** and press ENTER; all the selected edges of *golf ball* are chamfered and hexagonal polygons are created, as shown in Figure 8-116.

Note

After entering a value in the ***Chamfer*** *spinner and pressing the ENTER key, the value in the spinner automatically changes to 0.*

9. Now, in the modifier stack, select the **Polygon** sub-object level; all the polygons of *golf ball* get selected except the new hexagonal polygons, as shown in Figure 8-117.

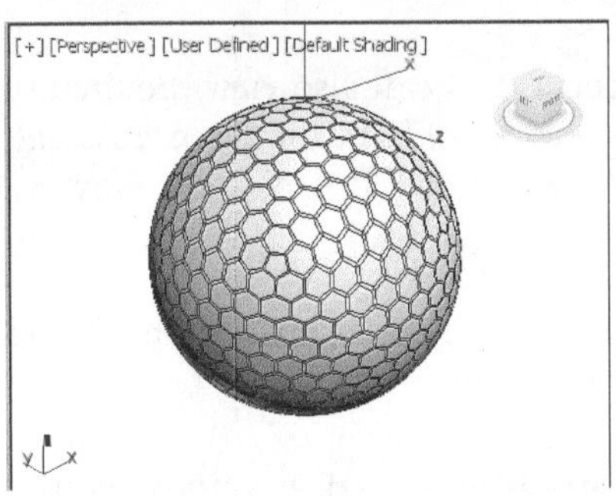

Figure 8-116 *All edges of golf ball chamfered*

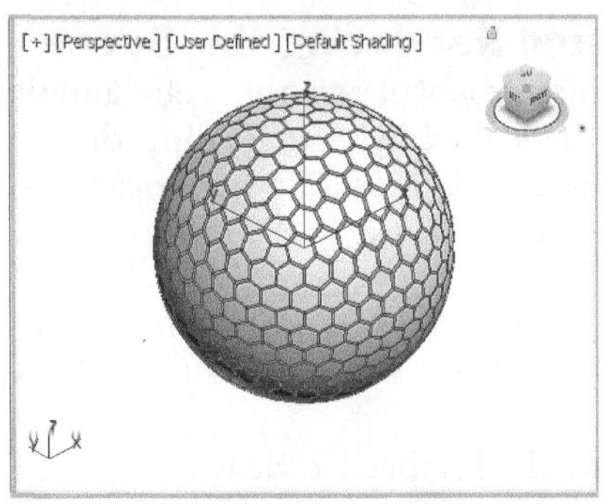

Figure 8-117 *All polygons in golf ball, except new hexagonal polygons selected*

Next, you need to select all new hexagonal polygons of *golf ball*.

10. Choose the **Select Invert** option from the **Edit** menu; all the new hexagonal polygons of *golf ball* are selected in the viewport, as shown in Figure 8-118.

11. In the **Edit Geometry** rollout, set **-1** in the **Extrude** spinner for the negative extrusion of the selected hexagonal polygons and press ENTER, refer to Figure 8-119.

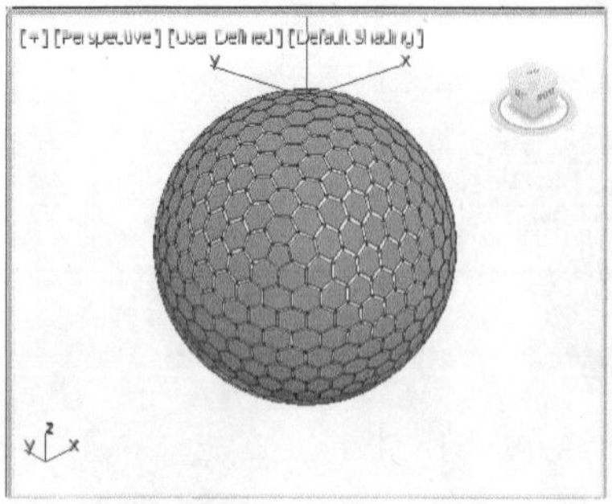

Figure 8-118 *All hexagonal polygons of golf ball selected in the viewport*

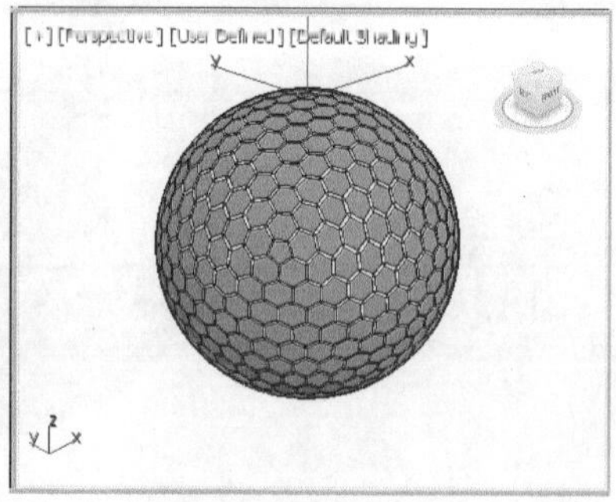

Figure 8-119 *Hexagonal polygons displayed after negative extrusion*

12. Enter **-4** in the **Bevel** spinner of the **Edit Geometry** rollout to bevel the selected hexagonal polygons and then press ENTER.

Now, you need to smoothen the selected polygons of *golf ball*.

13. Select the **MeshSmooth** modifier from the **Modifier List** drop-down list at the top of the modifier stack in the Modify panel. Use the default settings for the **MeshSmooth** modifier; the *golf ball* is smoothened, refer to Figure 8-120.

14. Click anywhere in the viewport to deselect the sub-objects; *golf ball* is displayed in the viewport.

15. Choose the **Maximize Viewport Toggle** tool to view *golf ball* in viewports.

Saving and Rendering the Scene

In this section, you will save the scene and then render it. You can also view the final rendered image of this model by downloading the *c08_3dsmax_2017_rndr.zip* file from *www.cadcim.com*. The path of the file is as follows: *Textbooks > Animation and Visual Effects > 3ds Max > Autodesk 3ds Max 2017: A Comprehensive Guide*

1. Change the background color of the scene to white, as discussed in Tutorial 1 of Chapter 2. Next, choose **Save** from the **Application** menu.

2. Activate the Perspective viewport. Next, choose **Save** from the **Application** menu.

3. Choose the **Render Production** tool from the **Main Toolbar**; the **Rendered Frame** window is displayed. This window shows the final output of *golf ball*, as shown in Figure 8-121.

4. Close this window.

Figure 8-120 The golf ball geometry after applying the Mesh Smooth modifier

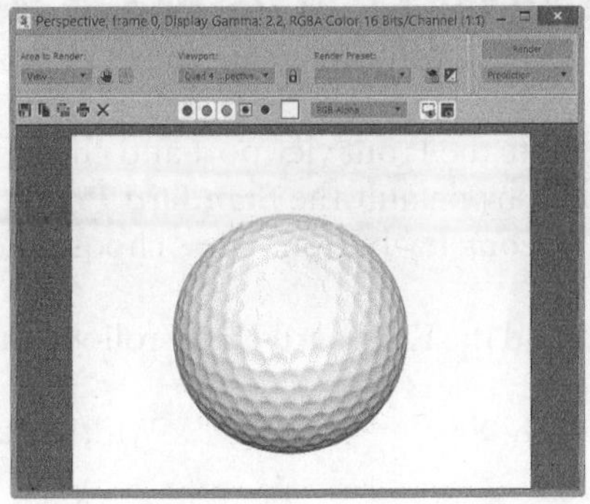

Figure 8-121 The final output after rendering

Tutorial 2

In this tutorial, you will create the model of an LCD monitor, as shown in Figures 8-122 and 8-123, by modifying 3D mesh objects at advanced level. **(Expected time: 30 min)**

Figure 8-122 The model of an LCD monitor (view 1)

Figure 8-123 The model of an LCD monitor (view 2)

The following steps are required to complete this tutorial:

a. Create the project folder.
b. Create the front portion of monitor.
c. Create the back portion of monitor.
d. Create speakers.
e. Create buttons.
f. Create the support of monitor.
g. Save and render the scene.

Creating the Project Folder

Create a new project folder with the name *c08_tut2* at *\Documents\3dsmax2017* and then save the file with the name *c08tut2*, as discussed in Tutorial 1 of Chapter 2.

Creating the Front Portion of Monitor

In this section, you will create the front portion of the LCD monitor.

1. Activate the Front viewport and choose **Create > Geometry** in the **Command Panel**. In this panel, by default the **Standard Primitives** option is displayed in the drop-down list below the **Geometry** button. Now, choose the **Box** tool from the **Object Type** rollout.

2. Expand the **Keyboard Entry** rollout and set the following values in their respective spinners:

   Length: **86** Width: **128** Height: **3.0**

3. Choose the **Create** button; a box is displayed in the viewports.

4. In the **Parameters** rollout, set the values as follows:

   Length Segs: **12** Width Segs: **15** Height Segs: **1**

5. Choose the **Zoom Extents All** tool; a box is displayed in all the viewports, as shown in Figure 8-124.

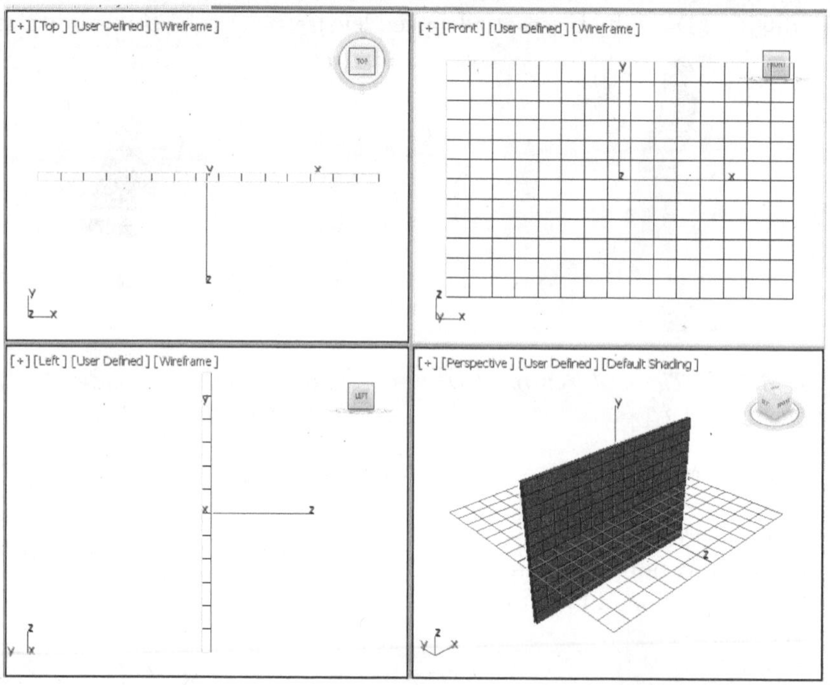

Figure 8-124 *The box for the front portion of the monitor displayed in viewports*

6. In the **Name and Color** rollout, enter **front portion**; the box is named as *front portion*. Also, change the color of *front portion* to white.

   Next, you need to convert *front portion* into an editable poly to modify it using sub-object levels.

7. Select *front portion* in any viewport and right-click on it; a quad menu is displayed. Choose the **Convert To:** option; a cascading menu is displayed. Choose **Convert to Editable Poly**; *front portion* is converted into an editable poly.

   When you convert *front portion* into an editable poly, the name of the **Box** tool in the modifier stack gets replaced with **Editable Poly**. Next, you need to modify *front portion* using sub-object levels in the modifier stack to give it a shape similar to the front portion of the monitor.

8. Activate the Front viewport and choose the **Maximize Viewport Toggle** tool to maximize the viewport.

9. Make sure that *front portion* is selected in the viewport. In the modifier stack, click on the arrow sign on the left of the **Editable Poly** to view all the sub-object levels.

10. Select the **Polygon** sub-object; it turns yellow and gets activated.

11. In the **Selection** rollout, select the **Ignore Backfacing** check box, refer to Figure 8-125.

12. In the Front viewport, hold the CTRL key and select all polygons of *front portion*, except the outer rows, refer to Figure 8-126.

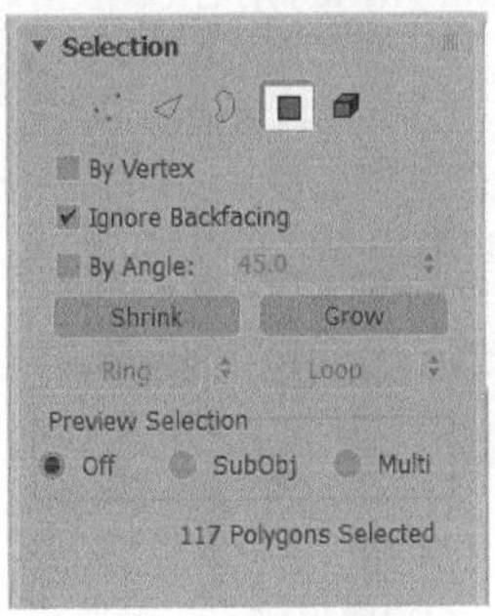

*Figure 8-125 The **Ignore Backfacing** check box selected*

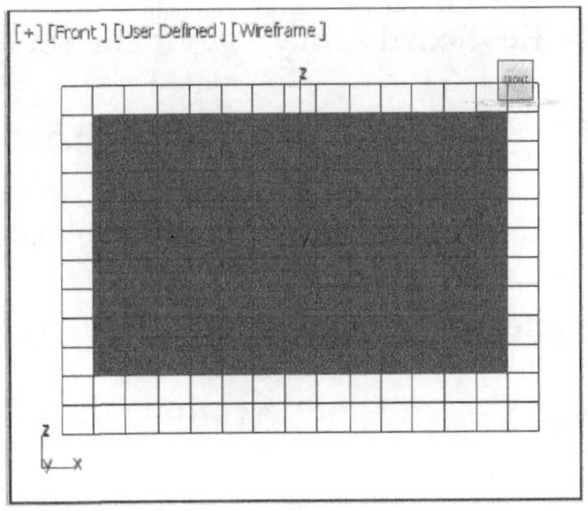

Figure 8-126 All polygons selected in the Front viewport

Note

*You can also use the **Grow** button in the **Selection** rollout to increase the selection area of polygons in the viewport.*

13. In the **Edit Polygons** rollout, choose the **Settings** button on the right side of the **Extrude** button to extrude the selected polygons; the **Extrude Polygons** caddy control is displayed in the viewport, as shown in Figure 8-127. In the **Height** spinner, set the value **-3** for negative extrusion and choose **OK** twice to close the caddy control.

14. Click on the **Polygon** sub-object level in the modifier stack to deactivate it. Next, click anywhere in the viewport to deselect *front portion*.

15. Choose the **Maximize Viewport Toggle** tool to view all the four viewports simultaneously. The extrusion effect is displayed in the Perspective viewport, as shown in Figure 8-128.

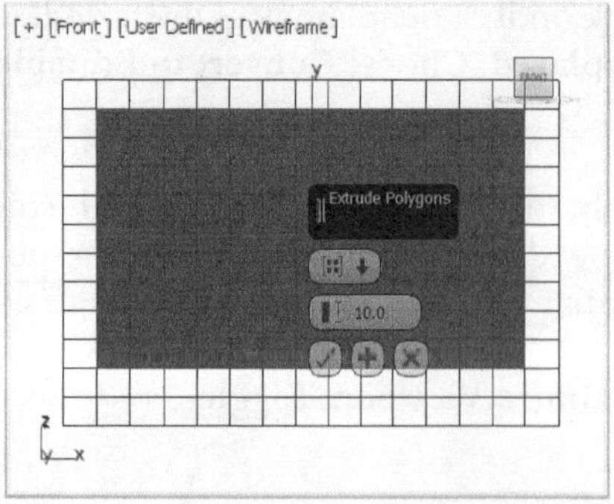

*Figure 8-127 The **Extrude Polygons** caddy control*

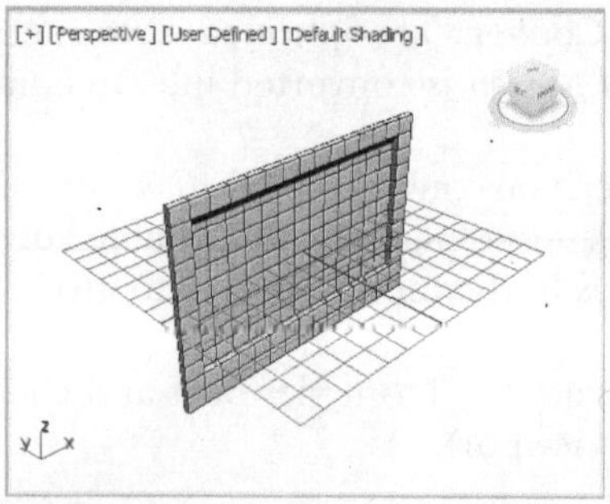

Figure 8-128 The extrusion effect displayed in the Perspective viewport

Now, you need to create a box for the screen of *front portion*.

16. Activate the Front viewport, choose **Create > Geometry** from the **Command Panel**. In this panel, the **Standard Primitives** option is displayed by default in the drop-down list below the **Geometry** button. Now, choose the **Box** tool from the **Object Type** rollout.

17. Expand the **Keyboard Entry** rollout and set the following values in their respective spinners:

    Length: **72** Width: **110.5** Height: **0.5**

18. Choose the **Create** button; a box is displayed in the viewports.

19. In the **Parameters** rollout, set the values as follows:

    Length Segs: **5** Width Segs: **5** Height Segs: **5**

20. In the **Name and Color** rollout, enter **screen**; the box is named as *screen*. Change the color of *screen* to black. Figure 8-129 shows *screen* in the viewports.

21. Group *screen* and *front portion* as discussed earlier and name it as *front part*.

Creating the Back Portion of Monitor

In this section, you will create the back portion of the monitor.

1. Activate the Front viewport, choose **Create > Geometry** from the **Command Panel**. Now, choose the **Box** tool from the **Object Type** rollout.

2. Expand the **Keyboard Entry** rollout and set the following values in their respective spinners:

    Length: **86** Width: **128** Height: **5.0**

3. Choose the **Create** button; a box is displayed in viewports.

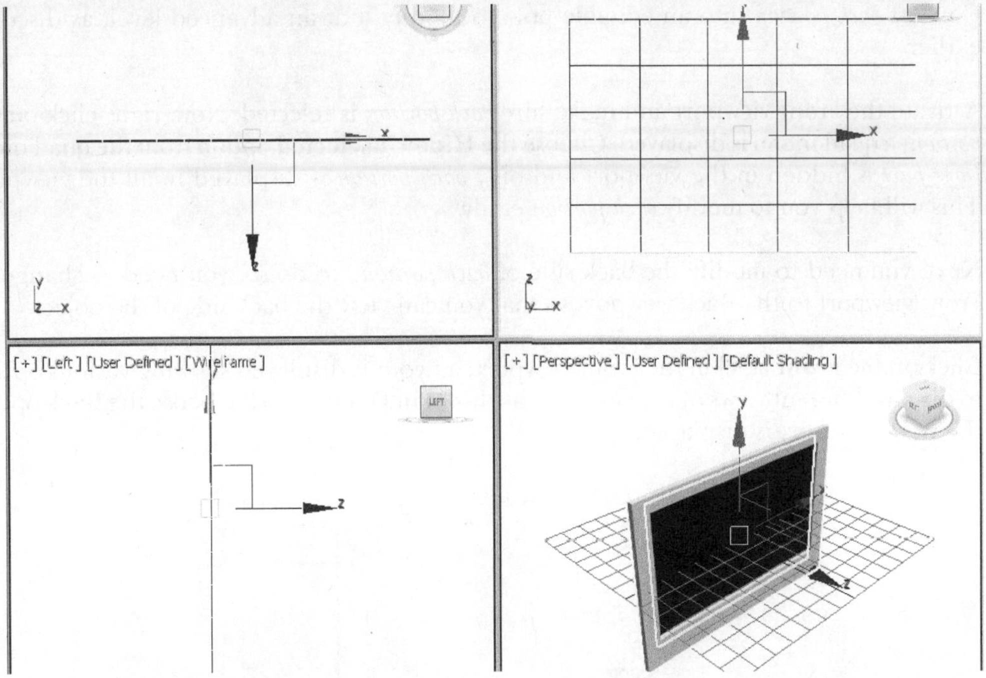

Figure 8-129 The screen geometry in the viewports

4. In the **Parameters** rollout, set the values as follows:

   Length Segs: **12** Width Segs: **15** Height Segs: **1**

5. In the **Name and Color** rollout, enter **back portion** and press ENTER; the box is named as *back portion*. Now, change the color of *back portion* to black.

6. Activate the Left viewport and align *back portion* with the back of *front part*, as shown in Figure 8-130.

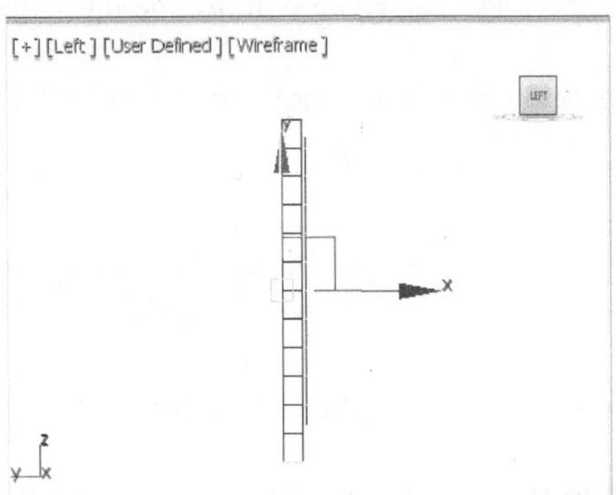

Figure 8-130 Alignment of the back portion with the front part in the Left viewport

7. Convert *back portion* into an editable poly to modify it at an advanced level, as discussed earlier.

8. Activate the Front viewport and make sure *back portion* is selected. Now, right-click on *back portion*; a quad menu is displayed. Choose the **Hide Unselected** option from the quad menu; *front part* is hidden in the viewport and only *back portion* is displayed in all the viewports. This will help you to modify *back portion* easily.

   Next, you need to modify the back side of *back portion*. To do so, you need to change the Front viewport to the Back viewport so that you can view the back side of the object.

9. Click on the **Front** label in the Front viewport; a flyout is displayed showing various options to display different views of the viewport, as shown in Figure 8-131. Choose the **Back** option; the Back viewport is displayed.

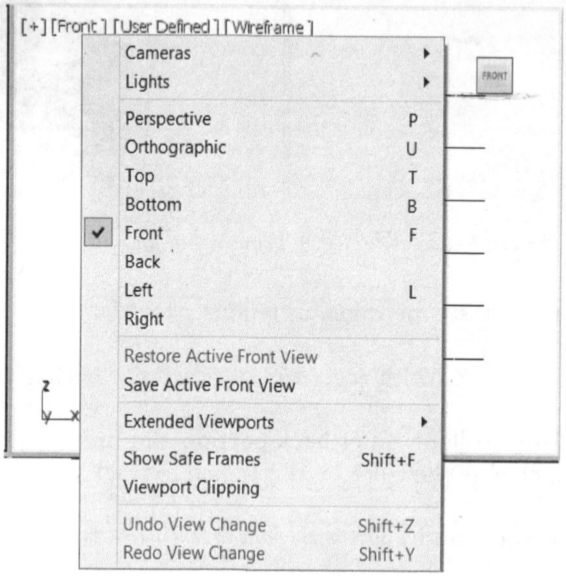

Figure 8-131 *A flyout showing various options to display views*

10. In the modifier stack, click on the arrow sign on the left of **Editable Poly** to view all the sub-object levels.

Tip
To perform precise modeling at an advanced level, you can invoke the ***Maximize Viewport Toggle*** *tool.*

11. Select the **Polygon** sub-object level; it turns yellow and gets activated.

12. In the Back viewport, hold the CTRL key and select the outer polygons of *back portion*, as shown in Figure 8-132.

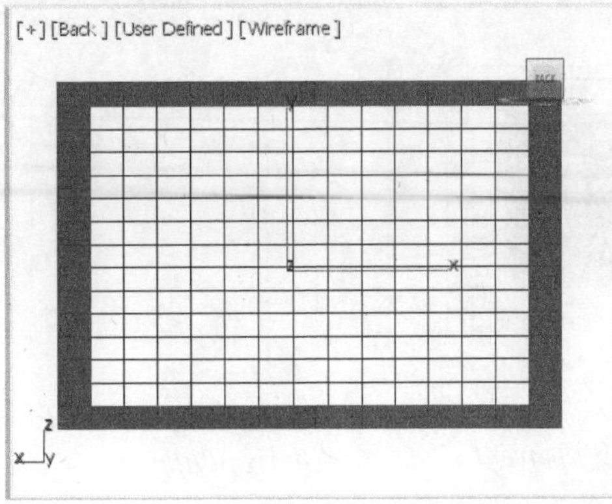

Figure 8-132 The outer polygons selected in back portion

13. Right-click on the **Select and Uniform Scale** tool from the **Main Toolbar**; the **Scale Transform Type-In** dialog box is displayed. In the **Offset: Screen** area, set the value **90** in the **%** spinner and press ENTER; the selected polygons are uniformly scaled to 90 percent, as shown in Figure 8-133. Next, close this dialog box.

14. Click anywhere in the viewport to deselect polygons.

15. In the **Selection** rollout, select the **Ignore Backfacing** check box. Next, choose the **Select Object** tool and select the inner polygons by using the rectangular cross selection, as shown in Figure 8-134.

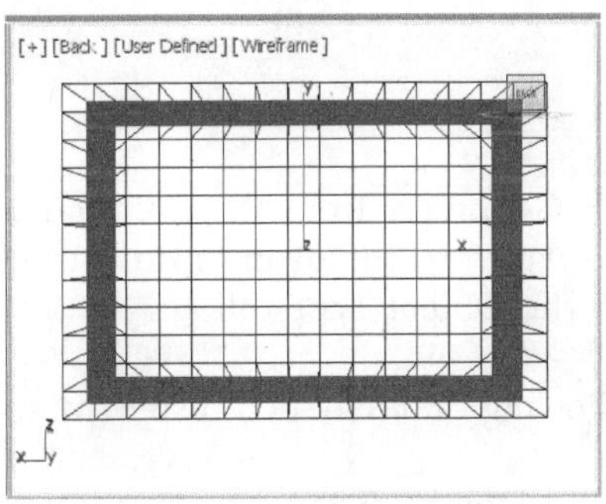

Figure 8-133 The selected polygons uniformly scaled in back portion

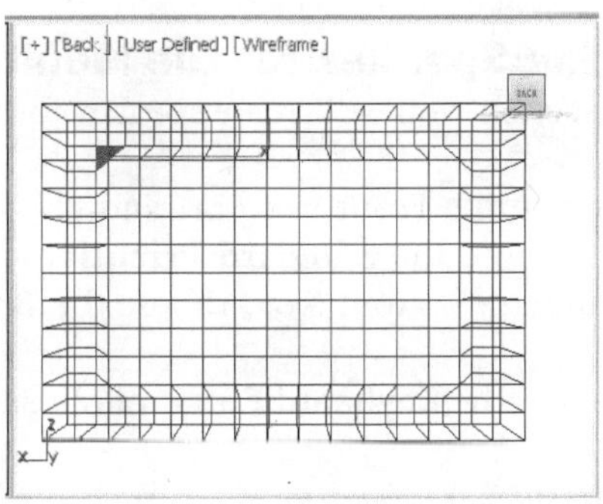

Figure 8-134 Selecting the inner polygons in back portion

16. Right-click on the **Select and Uniform Scale** tool from the **Main Toolbar**; the **Scale Transform Type-In** dialog box is displayed. In the **Offset: Screen** area, set the value **90** in the **%** spinner and press ENTER; the selected polygons are uniformly scaled to 90 percent, as shown in Figure 8-135. Next, close this dialog box.

17. Activate the Left viewport and make sure that the polygons are still selected. Right-click on the **Select and Move** tool; the **Move Transform Type-In** dialog box is displayed. In the **Offset: Screen** area, enter **-7** in the **X** spinner and press ENTER; the selected polygons move in the horizontal direction, as shown in Figure 8-136. Next, close this dialog box.

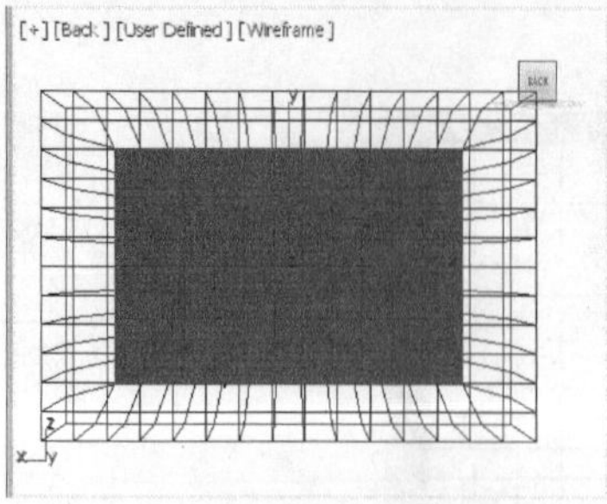

Figure 8-135 The selected polygons uniformly scaled to 90 percent

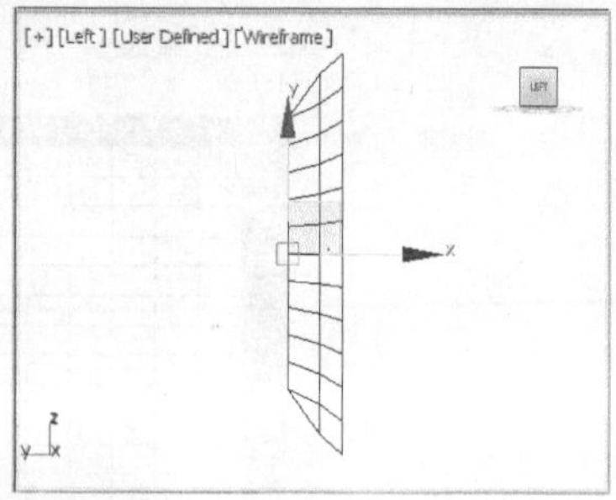

Figure 8-136 Selected polygons dragged horizontally

18. Select the **Polygon** sub-object level in the modifier stack to deactivate it. Next, click anywhere in the viewport to deselect the object in the viewport.

Note
While working in the Back or Left viewport, you can view the output of the modification in the Perspective viewport using the Orbit tool.

19. Change the Back viewport to Front viewport as described earlier. Now, right-click in the viewport; a quad menu is displayed. Choose the **Unhide All** option; all objects are displayed in the viewports.

20. Select *back portion* and *front part* in any viewport and group them as *monitor*.

Creating Speaker for the Monitor

In this section, you will create speaker for the monitor.

1. Activate the Front viewport and choose **Create > Geometry** from the **Command Panel**. By default, the **Standard Primitives** option is displayed in the drop-down list below the **Geometry** button. Now, choose the **Box** tool from the **Object Type** rollout.

2. Expand the **Keyboard Entry** rollout and set the following values in their respective spinners:

   Length: **7.0** Width: **128** Height: **0.2**

3. Choose the **Create** button; a box is displayed in the viewports.

4. In the **Parameters** rollout, make sure the value in the **Length Segs** and **Width Segs** spinners is **15** and in the **Height Segs** spinner is **1**.

5. In the **Name and Color** rollout, enter **speaker**; the box is named as *speaker*. Also, change the color of *speaker* to black.

6. Align *speaker* in viewports with *monitor*, as shown in Figure 8-137.

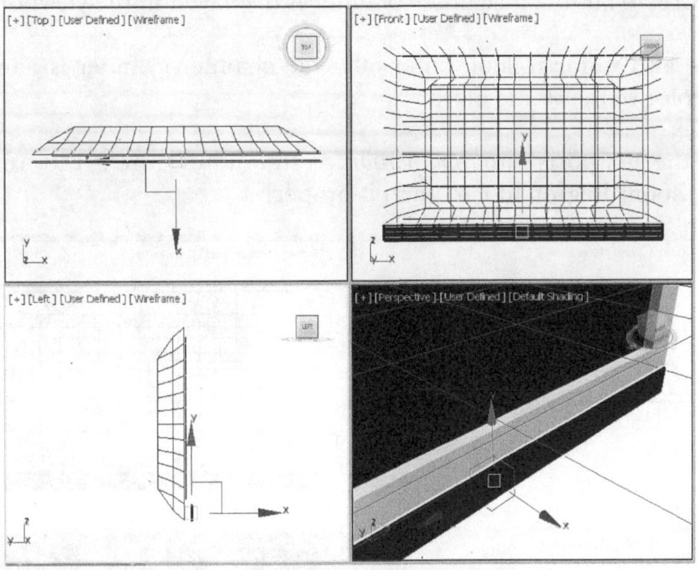

Figure 8-137 Alignment of the speaker with the monitor in viewports

You need to apply the **Lattice** modifier to *speaker* from the **Modifier List** drop-down list located at the top of modifier stack.

7. Make sure that *speaker* is selected in the viewport. Next, choose the **Modify** tab in the **Command Panel** and then select the **Lattice** modifier from the **Modifier List** drop-down list; the **Lattice** modifier is displayed in the modifier stack.

8. In the **Parameters** rollout of the **Lattice** modifier, select the **Struts Only from Edges** radio button. In the **Struts** area, set the value **0.5** in the **Radius** spinner. Also, select the **Smooth** check box.

9. Click anywhere in the viewport to deselect *speaker* and choose the **Zoom Extents All** tool to view all objects in all the viewports.

Creating Buttons

In this section, you will create buttons for the monitor by using the **ChamferCyl** tool.

1. Activate the Front viewport and choose **Create > Geometry** in the **Command Panel**. Now, select **Extended Primitives** from the drop-down list below the **Geometry** button and choose the **ChamferCyl** tool from the **Object Type** rollout.

2. Expand the **Keyboard Entry** rollout and set the values as follows;

   Radius: **1.5** Height: **1.0** Fillet: **0.5**

3. Choose the **Create** button; a chamfer cylinder is displayed in the viewports.

4. In the **Name and Color** rollout, enter **b01**; the chamfer cylinder is named as *b01*. Also, change the color of the *b01* to black.

5. Align *b01* in the viewports with *front portion*, as shown in Figure 8-138. You need to choose the **Zoom** or **Zoom Region** tool to align it properly.

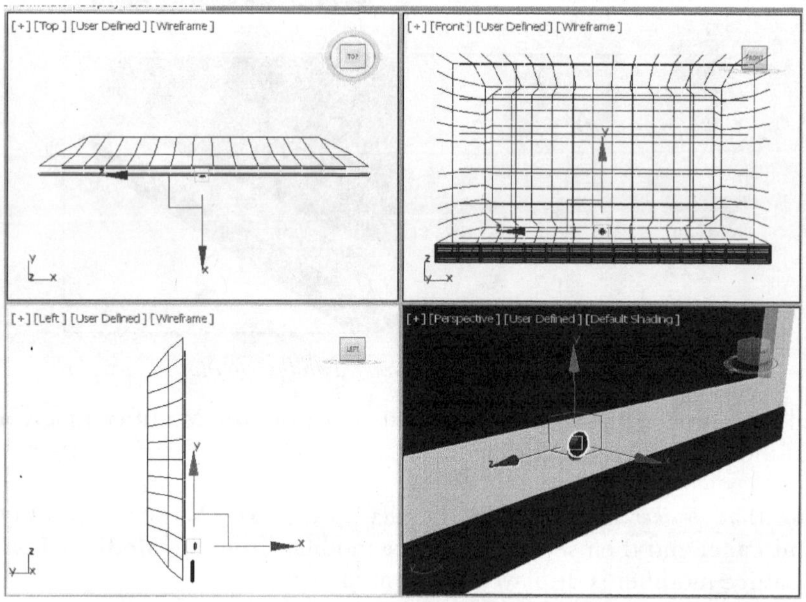

Figure 8-138 *Alignment of b01 with front portion in viewports*

6. In the Front viewport, create five copies of *b01*. They are automatically named as *b002, b003, b004, b005*, and *b006*. Next, align them in the viewports, as shown in Figure 8-139.

7. Select all the objects in the viewport and group them as *LCD Monitor*.

8. Activate the Left viewport and select *LCD Monitor*. Now, right-click on the **Select and Rotate** tool from the **Main Toolbar**; the **Rotate Transform Type-In** dialog box is displayed. In the **Offset: Screen** area, set the value **15** in the **Z** spinner and press the ENTER key.

   Next, close this dialog box; *LCD Monitor* is displayed in the viewports, as shown in Figures 8-140 and 8-141.

Creating the Support for the Monitor

In this section, you will create support for the monitor by using the **ChamferCyl** tool

1. Activate the Top viewport and choose **Create > Geometry** in the **Command Panel**. Next, select **Extended Primitives** from the drop-down list below the **Geometry** button, and then choose the **ChamferCyl** tool from the **Object Type** rollout.

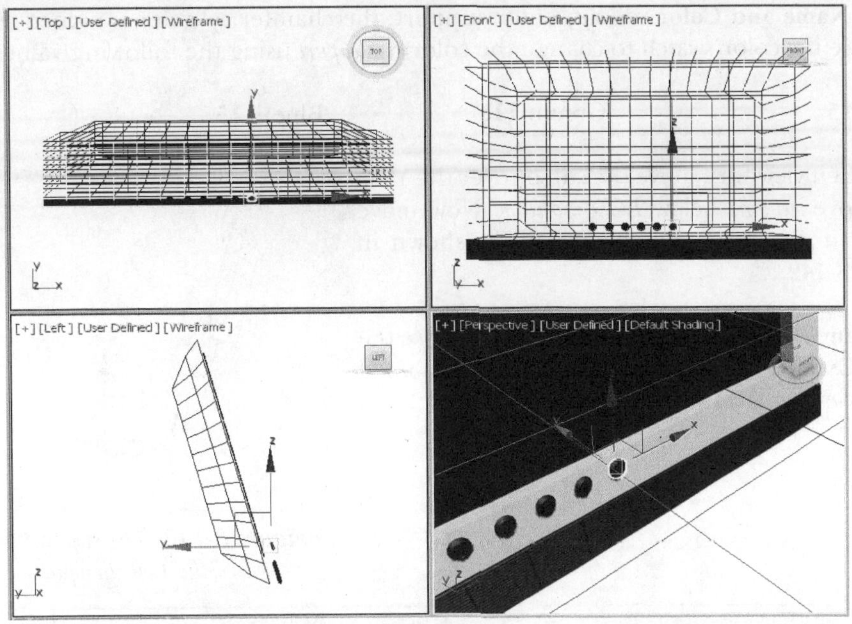

Figure 8-139 *Alignment of b002, b003, b004, b005, and b006 in viewports*

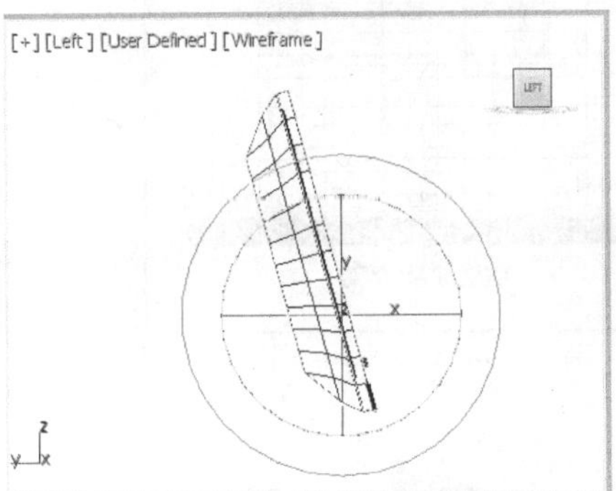

Figure 8-140 *The LCD monitor group displayed after being rotated it in the Left viewport*

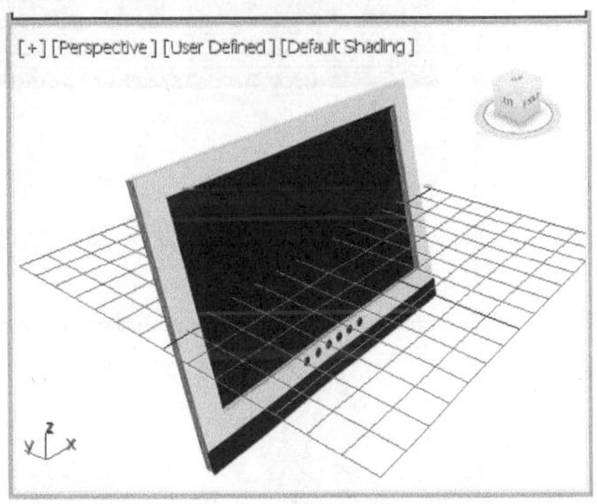

Figure 8-141 *The LCD monitor group displayed in the Perspective viewport*

2. Expand the **Keyboard Entry** rollout and set the following values in their respective spinners:

   Radius: **23.698**   Height: **6.091**   Fillet: **2.284**

3. Choose the **Create** button from the **Command Panel**; a chamfer cylinder is displayed in viewports.

4. In the **Parameters** rollout, set the values as follows:

   Fillet Segs: **5**   Sides: **18**   Cap Segs: **4**

5. In the **Name and Color** rollout, enter **support**; the chamfer cylinder is named as *support*. Also, use the color swatch to change the color of *support* using the following values:

   Red: **115** Green: **115** Blue: **115**

6. In the Left viewport, move the cursor over the Y axis and move *support* below *LCD monitor*. Now move *support* in the horizontal direction, as shown in Figure 8-142.

7. Make sure that *support* is selected. Next, choose the **Zoom Extents All Selected** tool; *support* is zoomed in the viewports, as shown in Figure 8-143.

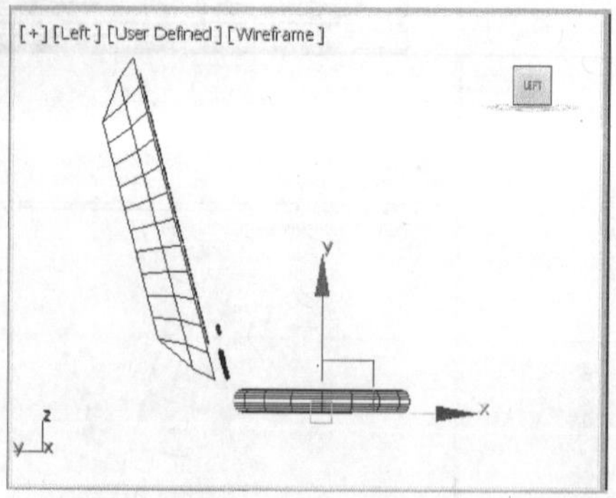

***Figure 8-142** The support geometry moved in the Left viewport*

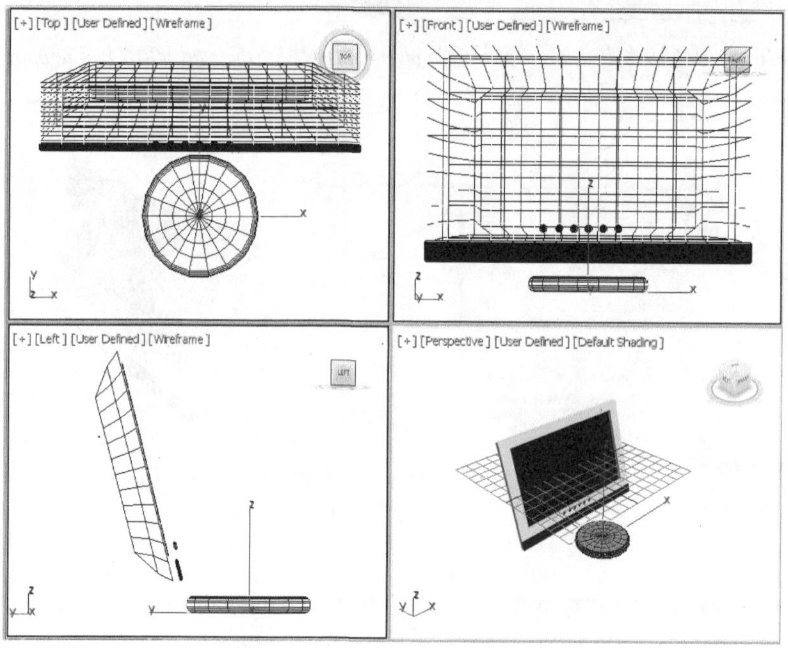

***Figure 8-143** The support geometry zoomed in viewports*

8. Convert *support* into an editable poly to modify it to an advanced level.

9. In the modifier stack, click on the plus sign on the left of **Editable Poly** to view all the sub-object levels.

10. Select the **Polygon** sub-object level; it turns yellow and gets activated.

11. Press and hold the CTRL key and select the inner polygons of *support* in the Top viewport, as shown in Figure 8-144.

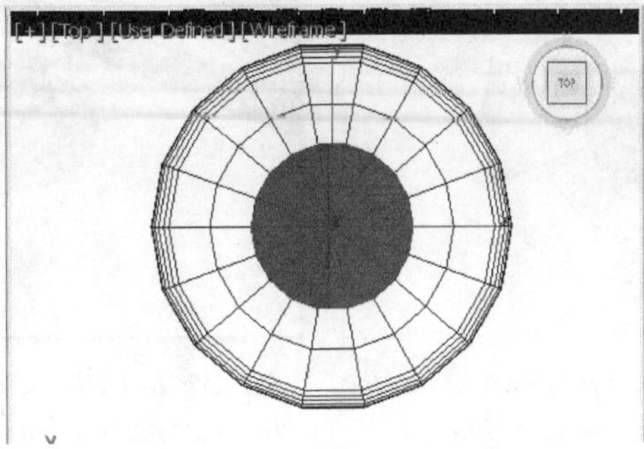

Figure 8-144 *The inner polygons of support selected*

12. In the **Edit Polygons** rollout, choose the **Settings** button on the right of the **Extrude** button; the **Extrude Polygons** caddy control is displayed in the viewport. Set the value **2.0** in the **Height** spinner, refer to Figure 8-145, and choose the **OK** button twice to close this caddy control.

13. Choose the **Settings** button on the right of the **Bevel** button; the **Bevel** caddy control is displayed in the viewport. Set the value **1.0** in the **Height** spinner, refer to Figure 8-146, press ENTER, and choose **OK** twice to close the caddy control; the support is displayed in viewport. Figures 8-147 and 8-148 shows the support displayed in the Top and Perspective viewports, respectively.

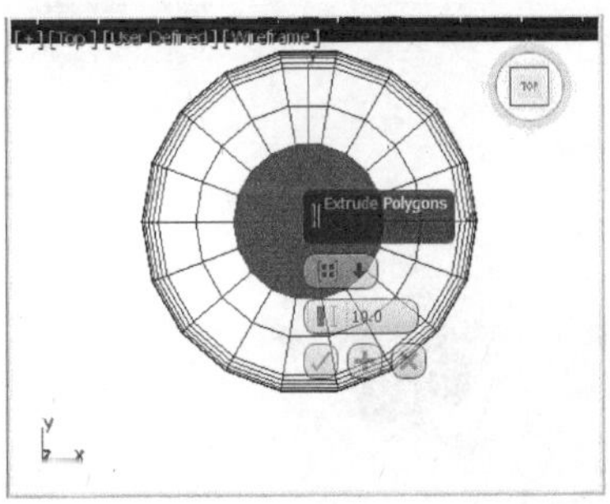

Figure 8-145 *The **Extrude Polygons** caddy control*

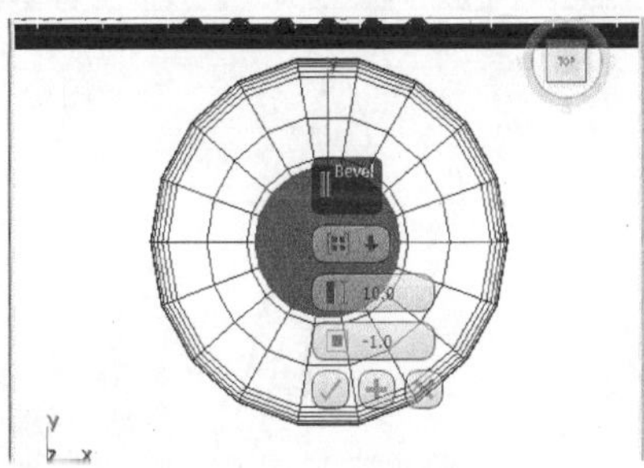

Figure 8-146 *The value set in the **Height** spinner of the **Bevel** caddy control*

14. Select the **Polygon** sub-object level in the modifier stack to deselect it and then click anywhere in the viewport to deselect the object.

15. Choose the **Zoom Extents All** tool and align *support* in the viewports, as shown in Figure 8-149.

16. Select *support* and choose the **Zoom Extents All Selected** tool. Now, select the **Polygon** sub-object level in the modifier stack; all the selected polygons are displayed.

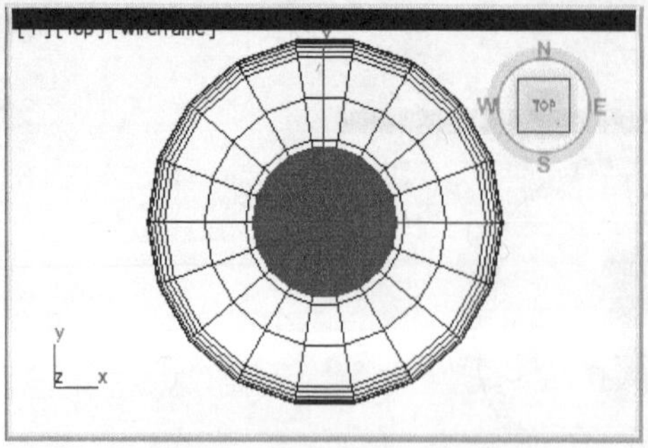

Figure 8-147 *The selected polygons in the Top viewport after extruding and beveling*

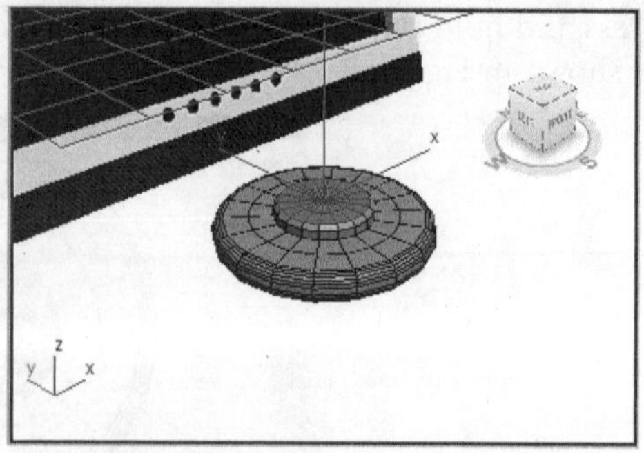

Figure 8-148 *The selected polygons in the Perspective viewport after extruding and beveling*

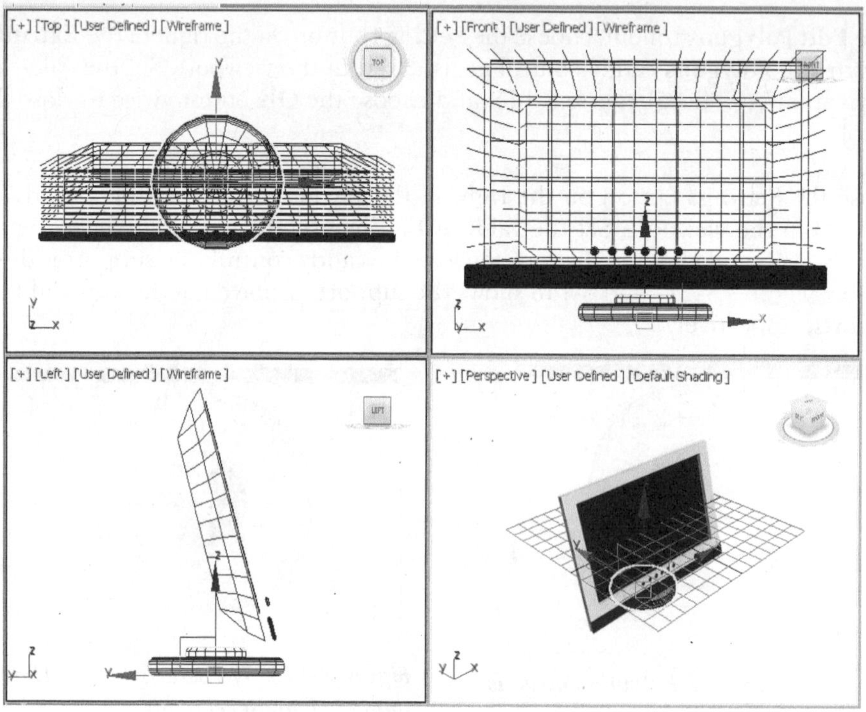

Figure 8-149 *Alignment of support in viewports*

17. Activate the Perspective viewport and set the view using the **Zoom**, **Select and Move** and **Orbit** tools, as shown in Figure 8-150. Next by holding the ALT key, deselect the polygons except the five polygons on the back, refer to Figure 8-151.

18. Select the **Polygon** sub-object level in the modifier stack to deactivate it and then click anywhere in the viewport to deselect the object.

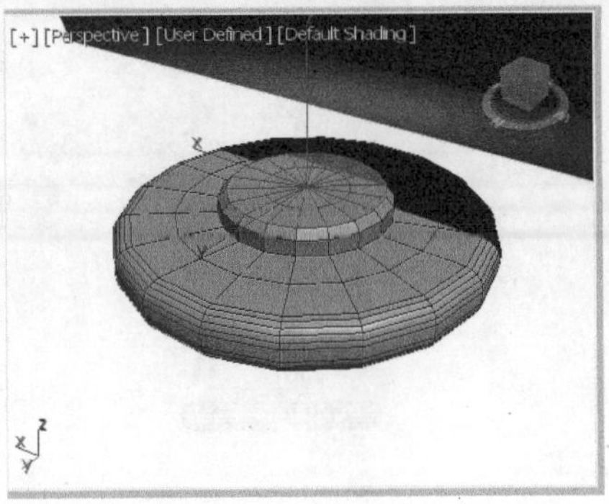

*Figure 8-150 The view of the Perspective viewport after using the **Zoom** and **Orbit** tools*

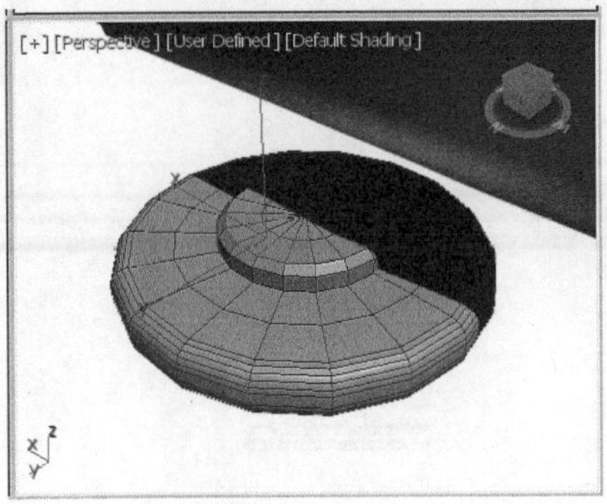

Figure 8-151 The polygons selected in the Perspective viewport

19. Choose the **Zoom Extents All** tool and set the view of the Perspective viewport to view the back side of *LCD monitor*, as shown in Figure 8-152.

20. Activate the Left viewport and select *support* from it. Next, select the **Polygon** sub-object level; all the selected polygons are highlighted.

21. In the **Edit Polygons** rollout, choose the **Settings** button on the right of the **Extrude** button; the **Extrude Polygons** caddy control is displayed. Set the value **29** in the **Height** spinner, press ENTER and choose **OK** twice to close this caddy control; the selected polygons are extruded and displayed in the Left viewport, as shown in Figure 8-153.

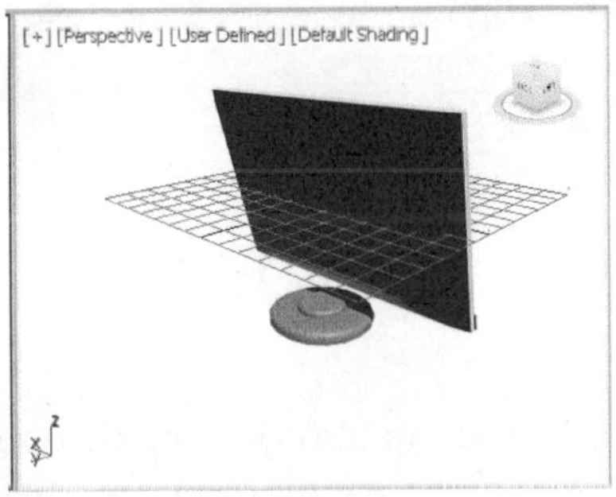

Figure 8-152 The back side geometry of LCD monitor in the Perspective viewport

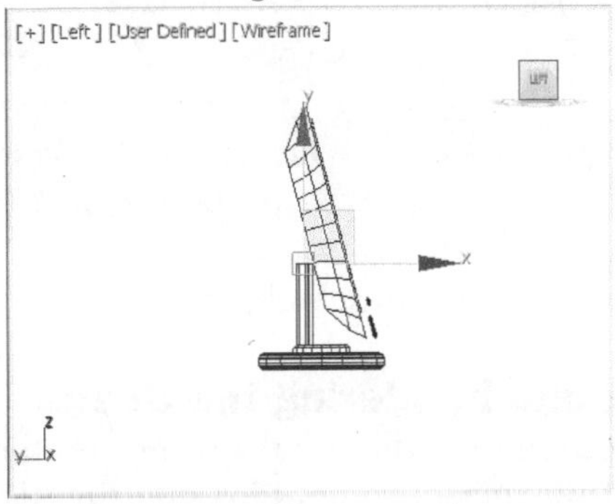

Figure 8-153 The selected polygons extruded in the Left viewport

22. In the Left viewport, move the cursor over the horizontal axis and drag the selected polygons horizontally toward the right side until they touch *LCD monitor*, as shown in Figure 8-154.

23. In the **Edit Polygons** rollout, again choose the **Settings** button on the right of the **Extrude** button; the **Extrude Polygons** caddy control is displayed. Set the value **19** in the **Height** spinner and press ENTER. Next, choose **OK** twice to close this caddy control. The *support* is extruded in the Left viewport, as shown in Figure 8-155.

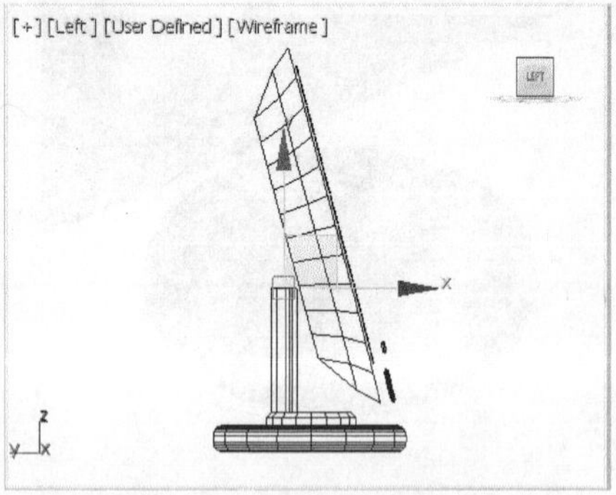

Figure 8-154 *The support geometry in the Left viewport after moving it horizontally*

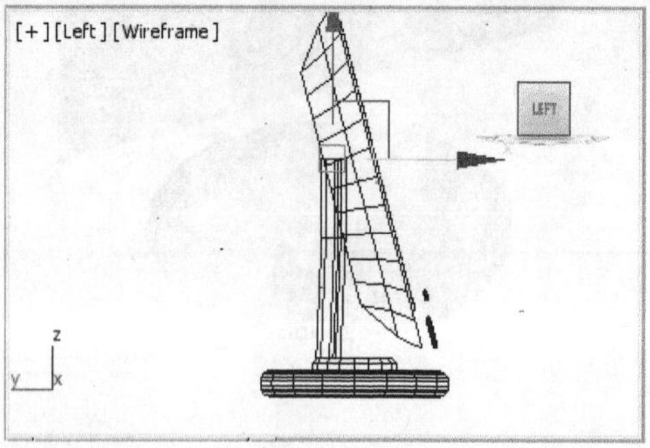

Figure 8-155 *The support geometry in the Left viewport after extrusion*

24. In the Left viewport, move the cursor over the horizontal axis, and drag the selected polygons horizontally toward the left to align them with *LCD monitor*, as shown in Figure 8-156.

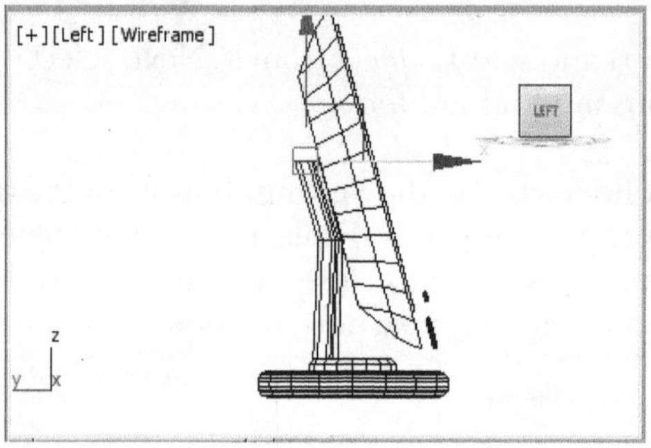

Figure 8-156 *The selected polygons of support in the Left viewport*

25. Select the **Polygon** sub-object level in the modifier stack to deselect it.

Saving and Rendering the Scene

In this section, you will save the scene and then render it. You can also view the final rendered image of this model by downloading the file *c08_3dsmax_2017_rndr.zip* from *www.cadcim.com.* The path of the file is as follows: *Textbooks > Animation and Visual Effects > 3ds Max > Autodesk 3ds Max 2017: A Comprehensive Guide.*

1. Choose **Save** from the **Application** menu.

2. Activate the Perspective viewport. Next, choose the **Render Production** tool from the **Main Toolbar**; the **Rendered Frame** window is displayed. This window shows the final output of the scene, refer to Figures 8-122 and 8-123.

Self-Evaluation Test

Answer the following questions and then compare them to those given at the end of this chapter:

1. Which of the following options is used to modify the 3D mesh object by using sub-object levels?

   (a) **Convert to Editable Mesh** (b) **Convert to Editable Poly**
   (c) both (a) and (b) (d) None of these

2. Which of the following sub-objects is not a part of the editable poly objects?

   (a) **Border** (b) **Face**
   (c) **Polygon** (d) **Element**

3. Which of the following rollouts does not belong to editable mesh objects?

   (a) **Subdivision Surface** (b) **Subdivision Displacement**
   (c) **Paint Deformation** (d) All of these

4. Which of the following buttons in the **Edit Geometry** rollout of editable mesh object is used to rotate the edge within its boundary?

   (a) **Extrude** (b) **Chamfer**
   (c) **Turn** (d) **Divide**

5. The __________ check box in the **Selection** rollout is used to avoid selecting backfacing sub-objects.

6. You can set the number of segments per chamfer using the **Settings** button on the right of the **Chamfer** button in the **Edit Edges** rollout. (T/F)

7. You can view sub-objects such as vertex, polygons, and so on in the rendered output. (T/F)

8. The **Border** sub-object in the editable poly objects is a series of edges that forms a ring around a hole in the a object. (T/F)

Review Questions

Answer the following questions:

1. Which of the following buttons in editable poly objects is used to define the selection area of sub-objects?

   (a) **Shrink** (b) **Grow**
   (c) **Ring** (d) All of these

2. Which of the following buttons in editable poly objects is used to repeat the recently used command?

   (a) **Collapse** (b) **Quick Slice**
   (c) **Repeat Last** (d) **Make Planar**

3. You can attach a number of objects to the selected object simultaneously by choosing the **Attach** button in the Modify panel. (T/F)

4. The **Break** button is available only for the __________ sub-object level.

5. The __________ button is used to divide a face into __________ smaller faces.

6. The __________ button is used to extrude sub-objects.

EXERCISE

The rendered output of the model used in the following exercise can be accessed by downloading the *c08_3dsmax_2017_exr.zip* from *www.cadcim.com*. The path of the file is as follows: *Textbooks > Animation and Visual Effects > 3ds Max > Autodesk 3ds Max 2017: A Comprehensive Guide*

Exercise 1

Create the model of a bed shown in Figure 8-157 using dimensions of your choice.

(Expected time: 30 min)

Figure 8-157 The model of a bed

Answers to Self-Evaluation Test

1. c, **2.** b, **3.** d, **4.** c, **5. Ignore Backfacing**, **6.** T, **7.** F, 8. T

9

Graphite Modeling Technique

Learning Objectives

After completing this chapter, you will be able to:

- *Customize the graphite modeling toolset interface*
- *Work with panels in the graphite modeling toolset*

INTRODUCTION

The graphite modeling is a technique in 3ds Max which is used to simplify the modeling process. The tools in the graphite modeling toolset are used for editing mesh and polygonal objects. These tools and their usage are discussed in this chapter.

GRAPHITE MODELING TOOLSET

The graphite modeling toolset is available in the ribbon below the **Main Toolbar**, as shown in Figure 9-1 and is used for polygonal modeling.

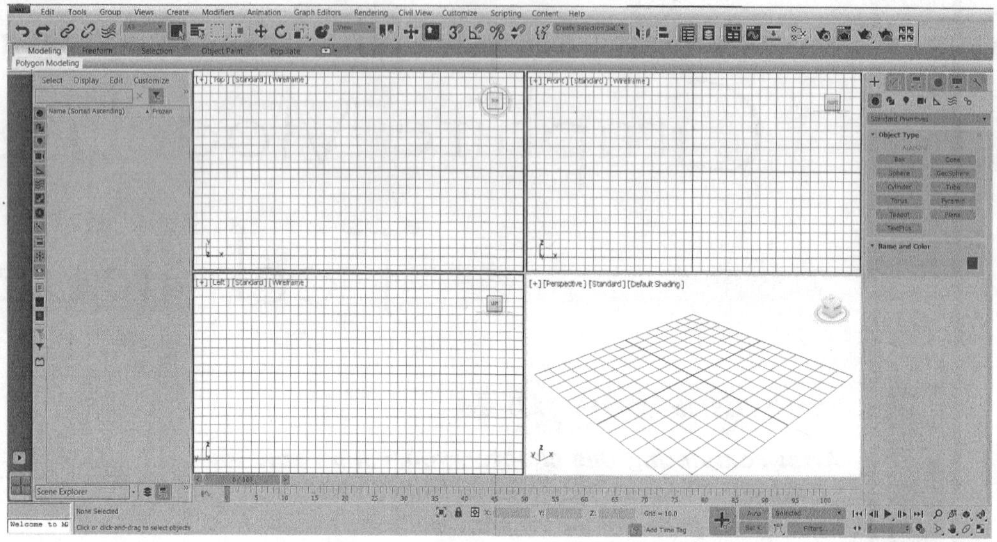

Figure 9-1 *The graphite modeling toolset*

If this toolset is not displayed, right click on the **Main Toolbar**; a shortcut menu will be displayed, as shown in Figure 9-2. Select the **Ribbon** option from the shortcut menu; the graphite modeling toolset will be displayed below the **Main Toolbar**.

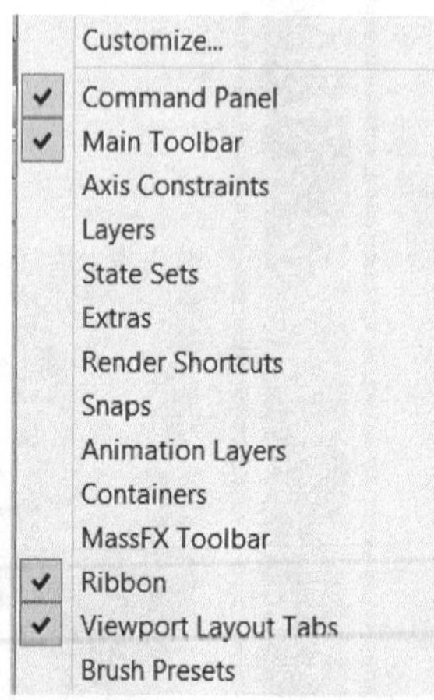

Figure 9-2 *The shortcut menu displayed on right-clicking the* ***Main Toolbar***

Modeling Tab

The **Modeling** tab contains a number of tools that are required for polygon modeling. These tools are organized into various panels. These panels are discussed next.

Polygon Modeling Panel

The tools in the **Polygon Modeling** panel are used to switch between different sub-object levels, convert objects into an editable poly or edit poly objects, and so on. To convert an object into an editable poly, select the object in the viewport and double-click on the **Modeling** tab from the ribbon; the **Polygon Modeling** panel will be displayed, as shown in Figure 9-3. Next, expand the **Polygon Modeling** panel, refer to Figure 9-4. Now, choose the **Convert to Poly** tool from the expanded panel; the selected object will be converted into an editable poly. Also, various panels will be displayed in the **Modeling** tab such as **Edit**, **Geometry (All)**, **Subdivision**, and so on. The tools in the expanded panel are discussed next.

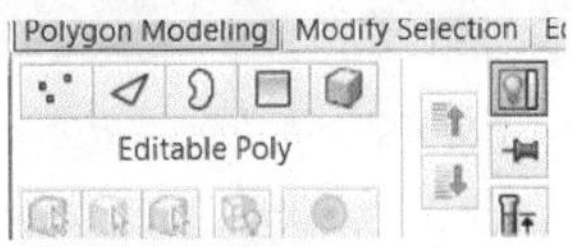

Figure 9-3 The ***Polygon Modeling*** *panel*

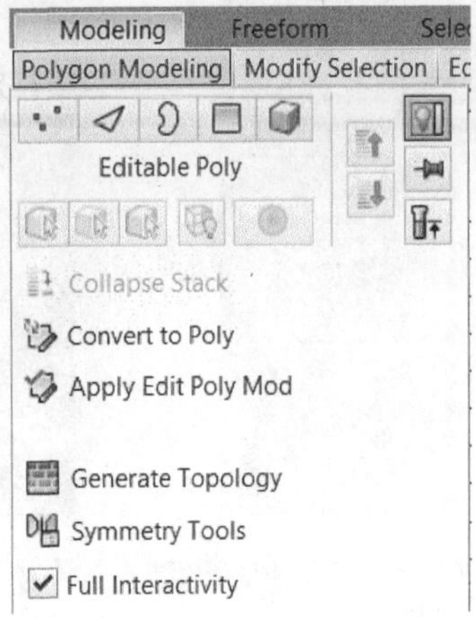

Figure 9-4 The ***Polygon Modeling*** *panel expanded*

Collapse Stack

The **Collapse Stack** tool is used to collapse all the modifiers in the modifier stack to an editable poly object. This editable poly object will preserve all the effects that were created on the object.

Note

The modifiers in the modifier stack will collapse only if they are applied to an editable poly object.

Convert to Poly

The **Convert to Poly** tool is used to convert the selected object into an editable poly object. Note you can use the tools from the graphite modeling toolset on an object only if the object is converted into an editable poly.

Most of the tools in the **Polygon Modeling** panel have been explained in the previous chapters. The remaining tools are discussed next.

Generate Topology

The **Generate Topology** tool is used to convert a mesh into a procedurally generated pattern. To do so, select an editable poly object in the viewport and choose the **Generate Topology** tool from the **Polygon Modeling** panel; the **Topology** dialog box will be displayed, as shown in Figure 9-5.

Choose a procedural pattern from the **Topology** dialog box; the corresponding topology pattern will be applied to the selected editable poly object, refer to Figures 9-6 and 9-7.

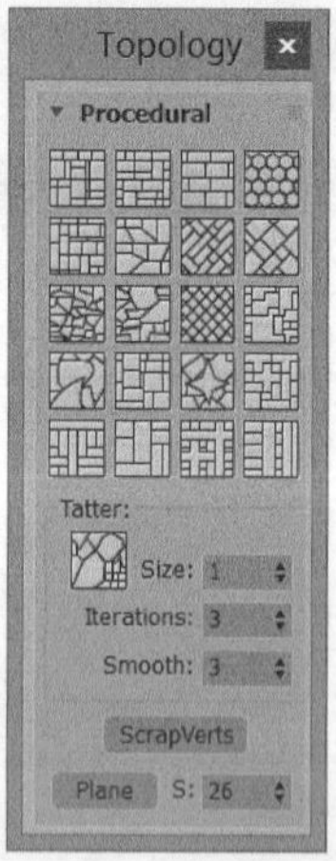

*Figure 9-5 The **Topology** dialog box*

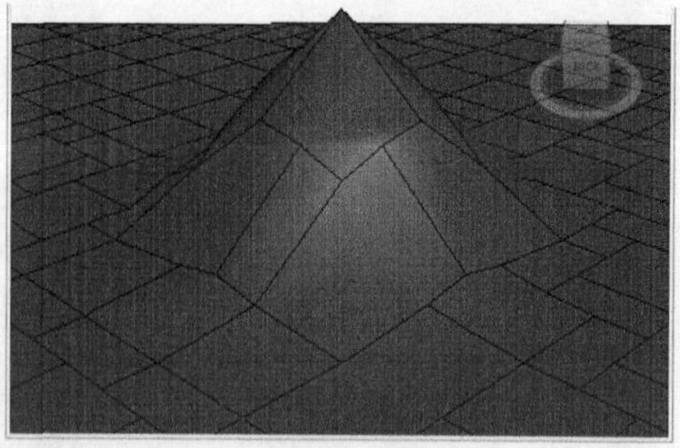

*Figure 9-6 The **Floor2** topology pattern displayed on the polygonal object*

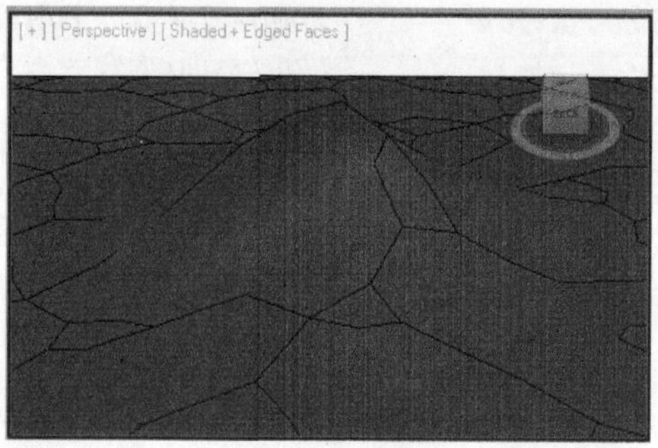

*Figure 9-7 The **Smoothstar** topology pattern*

Toggle Command Panel

The **Toggle Command Panel** tool is used to toggle the visibility of the **Command Panel**.

Pin Stack

The **Pin Stack** tool is used to lock the modifier stack and the modeling ribbon controls.

Next Modifier

The **Next Modifier** tool is used to move the selected modifier one step up in the modifier stack.

Previous Modifier

The **Previous Modifier** tool is used to move the selected modifier, one step down in the modifier stack.

Show End Result

The **Show End Result** tool is used to display the final state of object with all modifiers applied.

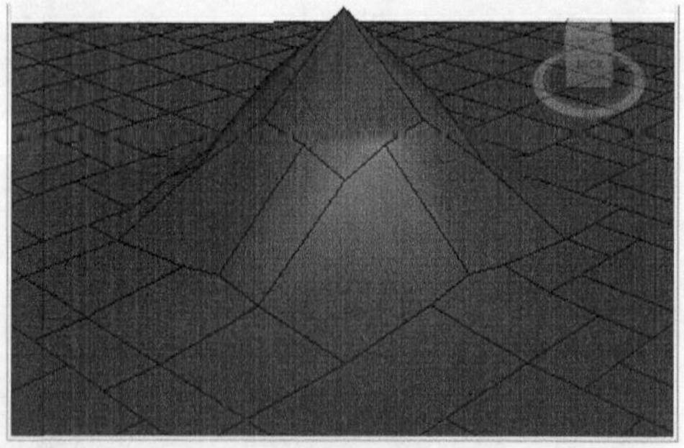

Use Soft Selection

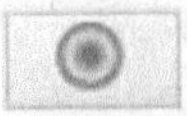

The **Use Soft Selection** tool is available only at the sub-object levels. It is used to deform an object in such a way that the deformation is maximum at the center and gradually decreases toward the end of the selection. If you select one of the sub-objects of an object and transform it without choosing the **Use Soft Selection** tool, then only the selected sub-object will be affected, refer to Figure 9-8. Now, choose the **Use Soft Selection** tool and then select the sub-objects in the viewport to transform. You will notice that partial sub-objects will also get selected near the selected sub-objects and will be viewed in color gradient. Also, on performing the transforms on the selected sub-objects, the transforms will be maximum at the center and will decrease toward the end, refer to Figure 9-9.

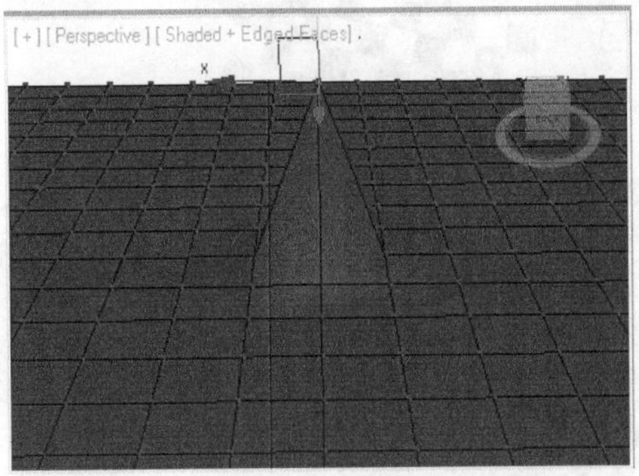

*Figure 9-8 Vertex moved without choosing the **Use Soft Selection** tool*

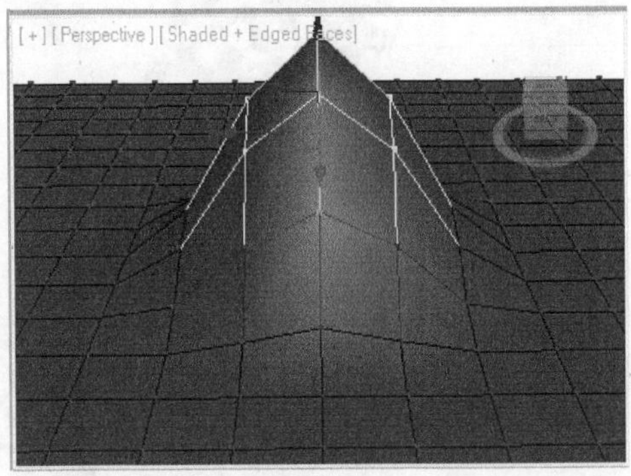

*Figure 9-9 Vertex moved after choosing the **Use Soft Selection** tool*

Edit Panel

The tools in the **Edit** panel are used to modify a mesh object, refer to Figure 9-10. These tools are discussed next.

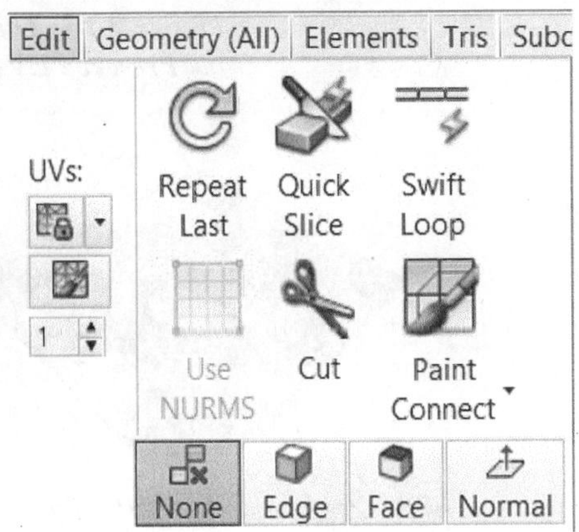

*Figure 9-10 The **Edit** panel*

Preserve UVs

The **Preserve UVs** tool is used to edit sub-objects without affecting the original UV mapping of the object. To edir sub-objects without affecting original UV mapping, convert the given object into an editable poly object. Now, apply a checker map to it, as shown in Figure 9-11. Next, select the **Vertex** sub-object level of the selected object and modify the vertices, refer to Figure 9-12; the UV mapping of the object will be distorted as the vertices are moved. Now, choose the **Preserve UVs** tool from the **Edit** panel and move the vertices again. On doing so, you will observe that the UV mapping is not distorted, refer to Figure 9-13.

Tweak

The **Tweak** tool is used to adjust the UVW mapping of an object directly in the viewport without applying any modifier to it. To adjust the UVW mapping of an object directly in the viewport, convert the object into an editable poly object and apply a checker map to it, as shown in Figure 9-14. Select the **Vertex** sub-object level, choose the **Tweak** tool from the **Edit** panel, and then move the cursor over the vertices to drag the texture, as shown in Figure 9-15.

Figure 9-11 Checker map applied to an object

*Figure 9-12 Checker map distorted before choosing the **Preserve UVs** tool*

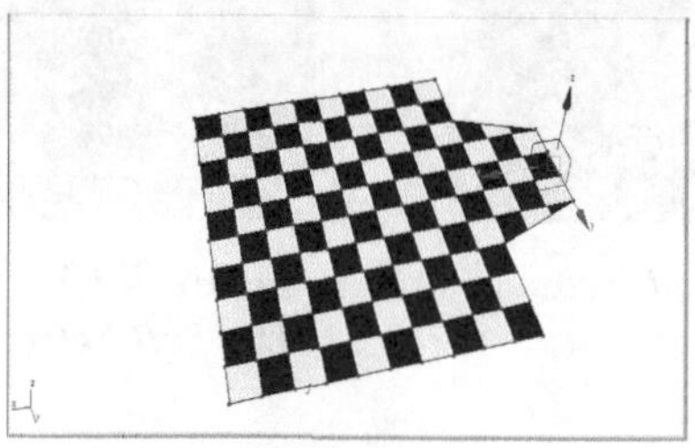

*Figure 9-13 The checker map after choosing the **Preserve UVs** tool*

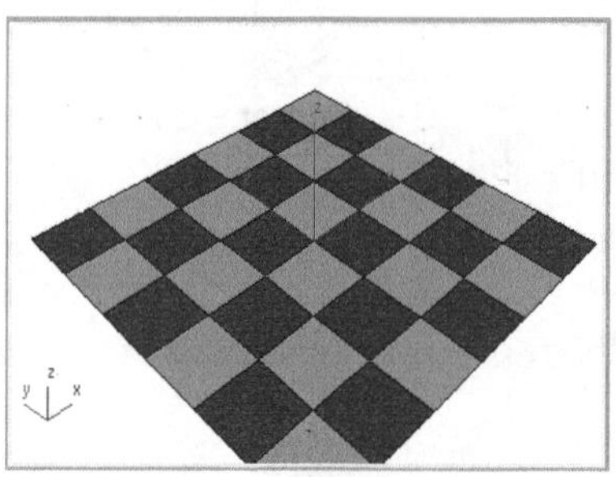

Figure 9-14 Checker map applied to an object

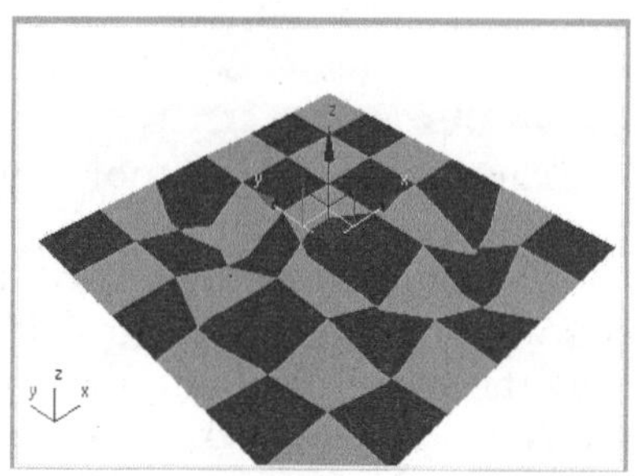

*Figure 9-15 Checker map tweaked using the **Tweak** tool*

SwiftLoop

The **SwiftLoop** tool is used to add edge loops to the selected object. To add edge loops to a selected object, convert the object into an editable poly object and then choose the **SwiftLoop** tool from the **Edit** panel and move the cursor over the created object in the viewport; a green colored gizmo will be displayed along with the cursor to show where the edge loops will be created, as shown in Figure 9-16. Next, click on the object; an edge loop will be created, as shown in Figure 9-17. Right-click to exit the command.

Paint Connect

The **Paint Connect** tool is used to add segments between edges and vertices. To add segments, convert the object into an editable poly object in the viewport and choose the **Paint Connect** tool from the **Edit** panel. Next, press and hold the left mouse button on a vertex or on an edge of the object and then drag it to another edge or vertex. Now, release the left mouse button; a new segment will be created, refer to Figure 9-18.

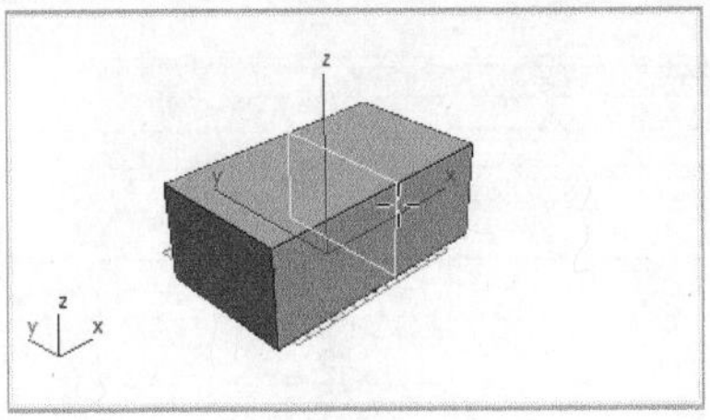

Figure 9-16 A green colored gizmo displayed on the object

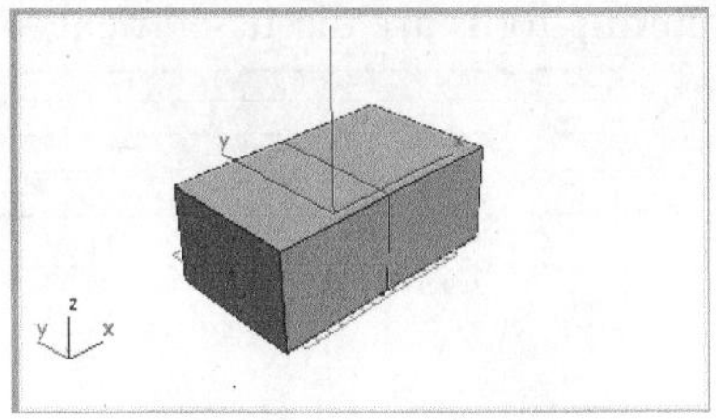

Figure 9-17 A new edge loop created using the ***SwiftLoop*** *tool*

Geometry (All) Panel

The **Geometry (All)** panel in the modeling tab consists of the subsets of modeling tools from the **Edit Geometry** rollout, refer to Figure 9-19. Most of the tools in this panel have already been discussed in the previous chapters. The remaining tools are discussed next.

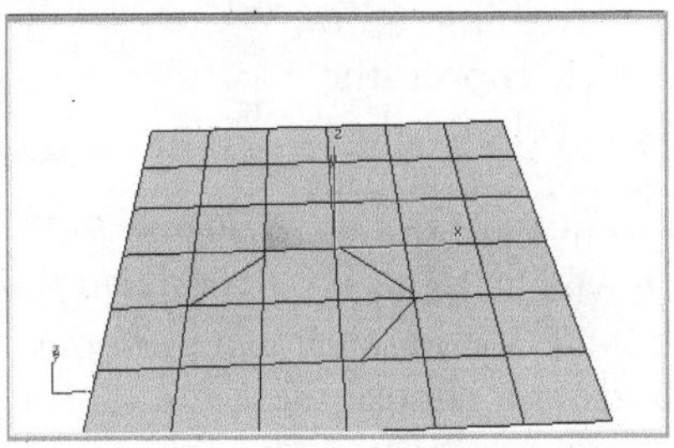

Figure 9-18 New segments created on an object using the ***Paint Connect*** *tool*

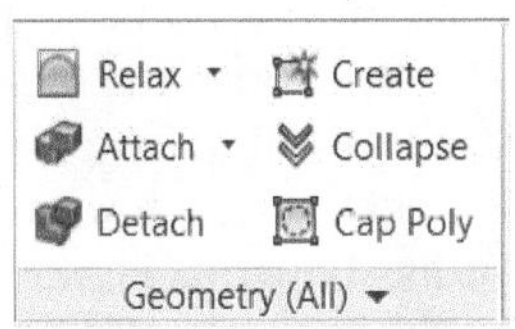

Figure 9-19 The ***Geometry (All)*** *panel*

Note

The tools displayed in the panels depend on the sub-object level selected in the modifier stack.

Cap Poly

The **Cap Poly** tool is available at all sub-object levels except **Polygon** and **Element**. It is used to create a new polygon from the edge or vertex selection. To create a new polygon from an edge, convert the object into an editable poly and create a hole in it, refer to Figure 9-20. Next, select the **Edge** sub-object level and then select the edge that covers the hole. Now, choose the **Cap Poly** button from the **Geometry (All)** panel; the hole will be covered by a polygon, refer to Figure 9-21.

Modify Selection Panel

The **Modify Selection** panel is used to modify the sub-objects of an object using various tools. Using this panel, you can grow or shrink your selection uniformly in all directions in a loop or in rings. By default, the **Modify Selection** panel is not visible in the **Modeling** tab. To view the **Modify Selection** panel, first convert the given object into editable poly and then select the sub-object level of that object; the **Modify Selection** panel will be displayed, as shown in Figure 9-22. Most of the tools in this panel are similar to those discussed in Chapter 8. The remaining tools are discussed next.

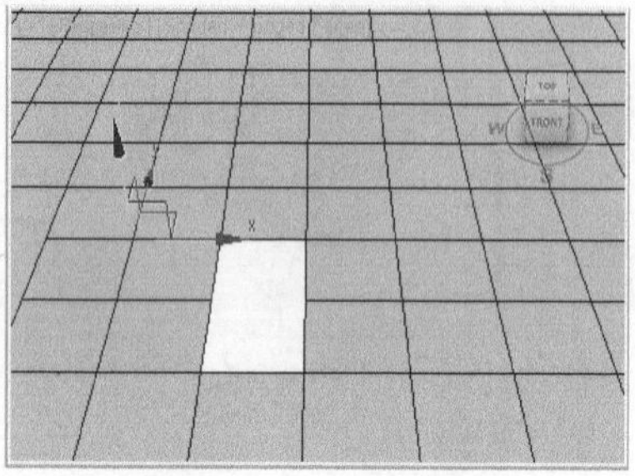

Figure 9-20 *An object with a hole*

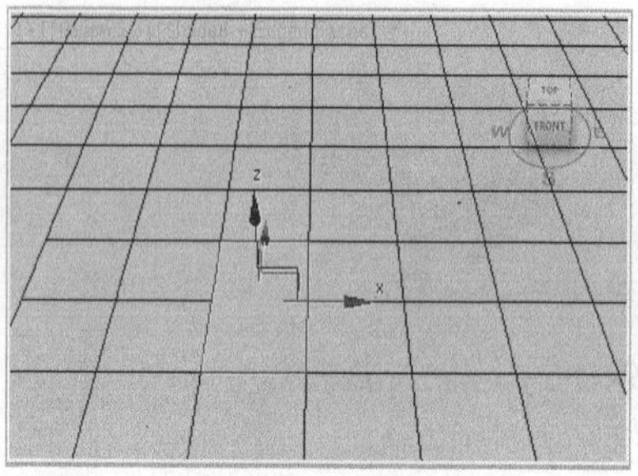

Figure 9-21 *The hole covered after choosing the **Cap Poly** tool*

Loop

The **Loop** tool is used to loop the selected sub-object level in an editable poly object. For example, to loop the polygons of an editable poly object, choose the **Polygon** tool from the **Polygon Modeling** panel and then select a polygon in the editable poly object, as shown in Figure 9-23. Next, choose the **Loop** tool from the **Modify Selection** panel; all the polygons through which the loop passes will be selected, as shown in Figure 9-24. If you select two polygons on an object in one direction, as shown in Figure 9-25, and then choose the **Loop** tool; the loop will be created, as shown in Figure 9-26. Similarly, you can create loops for other sub-objects.

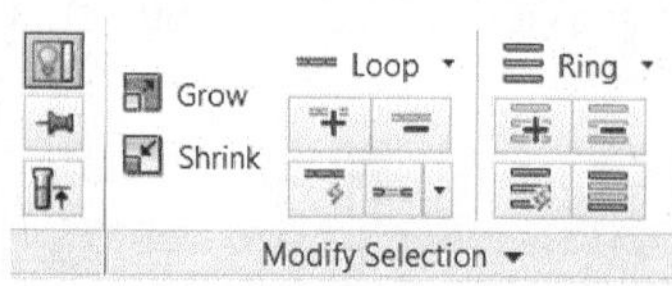

Figure 9-22 *The **Modify Selection** panel*

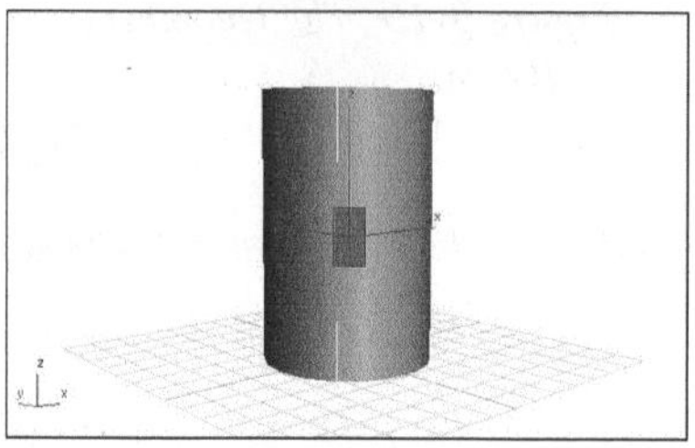

Figure 9-23 *A polygon selected to create a loop selection*

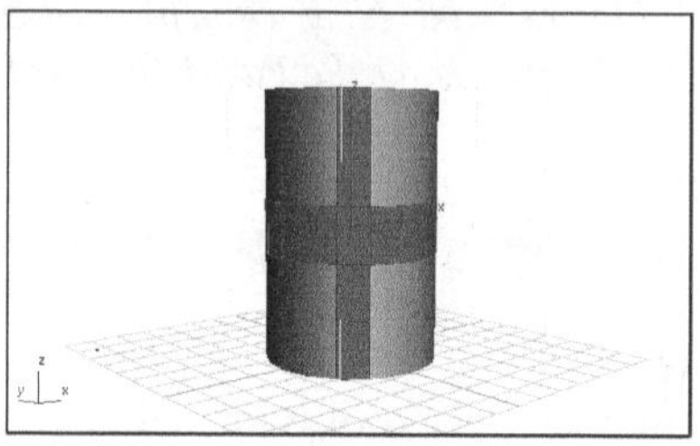

Figure 9-24 *The polygons selected after choosing the **Loop** tool*

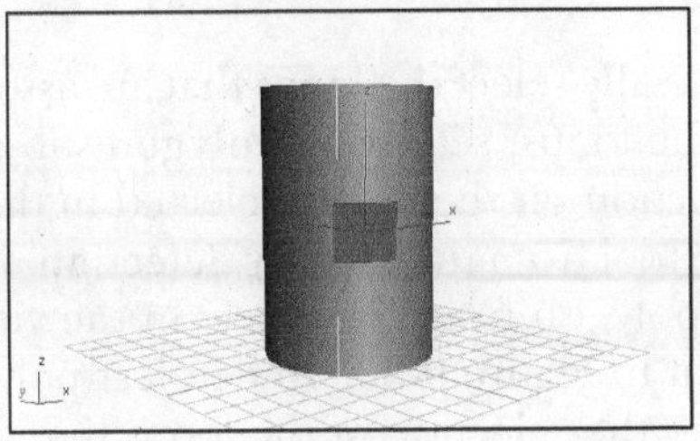

Figure 9-25 Two polygons selected to create a loop

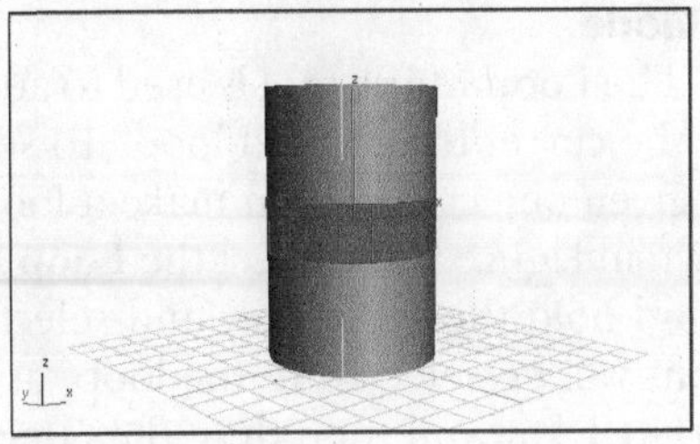

*Figure 9-26 The loop created after choosing the **Loop** tool*

Note

*The **Loop** tool in the graphite modeling tab is different from the one shown in the **Selection** rollout in the **Command Panel**. It helps you create a loop for all sub-objects whereas the **Loop** tool in the **Selection** rollout is used to create a loop for the **Edge** sub-objects only.*

Loop Cylinder Ends

The **Loop Cylinder Ends** tool is used to select the vertex and edge loops. It is available only at the **Vertex** and **Edge** sub-object levels. When a vertex or an edge is selected, a drop-down is displayed. On clicking this drop-down, the **Loop Cylinder Ends** tool is displayed. The process of creating the selection loop is similar to that explained for the **Loop** tool.

Grow Loop

The **Grow Loop** tool is used to grow the selection loop based on the current sub-object selection. To grow the selection loop, select the **Polygon** sub-object level of the given object and select a polygon, refer to Figure 9-27. Next, choose the **Grow Loop** tool from the **Modify Selection** panel; the sub-objects at the ends of the loop will be selected, refer to Figures 9-28.

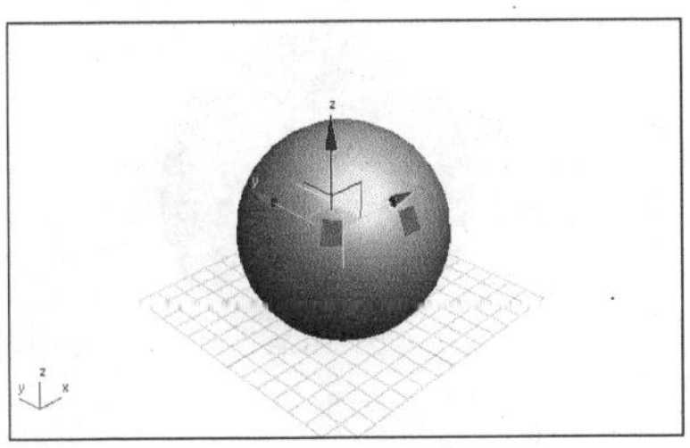

Figure 9-27 The polygons selected on a sphere

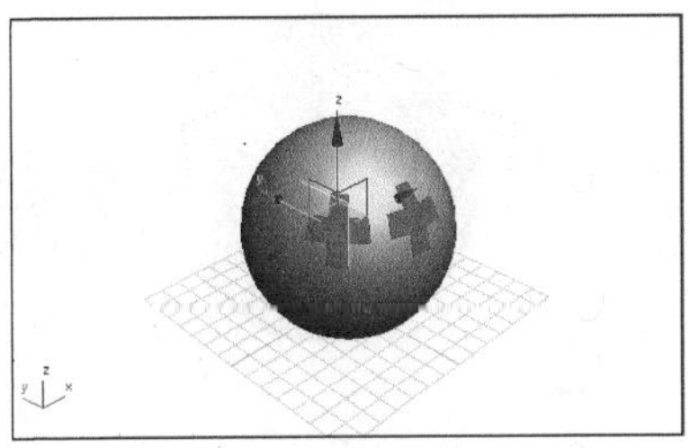

*Figure 9-28 The polygons selected after choosing the **Grow Loop** tool*

Shrink Loop

The **Shrink Loop** tool is used to reduce the selection loop based on the current sub-object selection.

Note

*The **Shrink Loop** tool cannot be used for circular loops. To use this tool, you need to select one or more than one non-circular loop.*

Loop Mode

The **Loop Mode** tool is used to automatically select the loops that are associated with the currently selected loop. To select the loops, select the **Polygon** sub-object level of the given object and then make a loop selection on the object selected in the viewport, as shown in Figure 9-29. select the **Loop Mode** tool from the **Modify Selection** panel. Next, press and hold the CTRL key and select any polygon from the object in the viewport; the polygons will be selected in the loop, as shown in Figure 9-30. To deselect polygon loops, use the ALT key and then drag the cursor over the selection of the loops that you want to deselect.

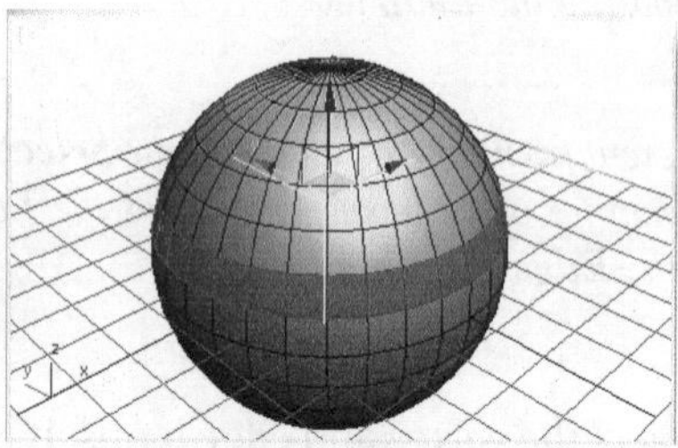

Figure 9-29 *The loop selection*

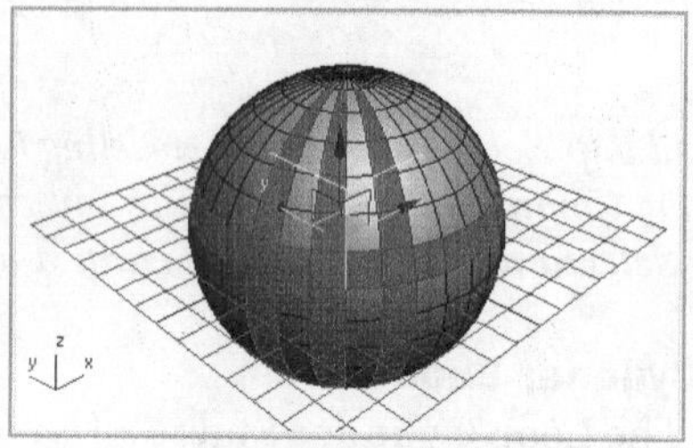

Figure 9-30 *The selected polygons after choosing the **Loop Mode** tool*

Dot Loop

The **Dot Loop** tool available in the **Dot Loop** drop-down is used to select alternate polygons (or other sub-objects) of an object. To dot loop the polygons of an editable poly object, select the **Polygon** sub-object level of the given object and select two adjacent polygons of that object, as shown in Figure 9-31. Next, choose the **Dot Loop** tool from the **Modify Selection** panel; the alternate polygons will be selected in the form of a loop, as shown in Figure 9-32.

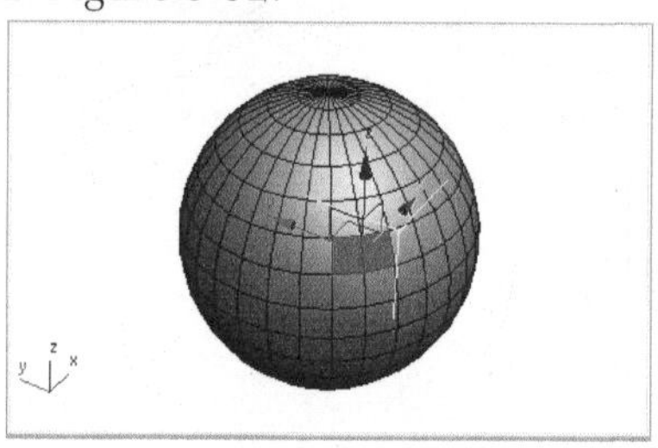

Figure 9-31 *Two adjacent polygons selected*

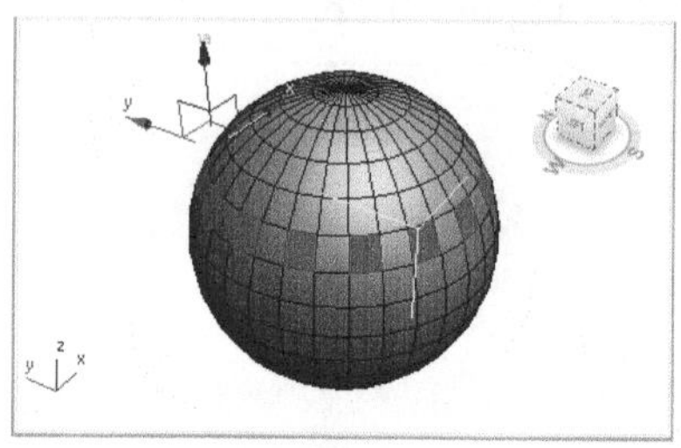

Figure 9-32 *The selection loop on choosing the **Dot Loop** tool*

Note

*The **Dot Loop** drop-down has two other tools: **Dot Loop Opposite** and **Dot Loop Cylinder**. The function of these tools is similar to the function of the **Dot Loop** tool.*

Ring

The **Ring** tool is used to select the sub-objects of the selected object in the form of ring. To do so, select the **Polygon** sub-object level of the selected object and select two adjacent polygons of the object, as shown in Figure 9-33. Next, choose the **Ring** tool from the **Modify Selection** panel; the selection will be made in the form of a ring, as shown in Figure 9-34.

Note

The function of the ***Grow Ring****,* ***Shrink Ring****,* ***Ring Mode****, and* ***Dot Ring*** *tools is similar to the function of the* ***Grow Loop****,* ***Shrink Loop****,* ***Loop Mode****, and* ***Dot Loop*** *tools, respectively.*

Outline

The **Outline** tool is used to create an outline around the selected sub-object level. This tool mainly works with the **Edge** sub-object level. To create an outline, select an edge of the selected object in the viewport, refer to Figure 9-35. Next, expand the **Modify Selection** panel, refer to Figure 9-36 and then choose the **Outline** tool from it; an outline will be created around the selected edge, as shown in Figure 9-37.

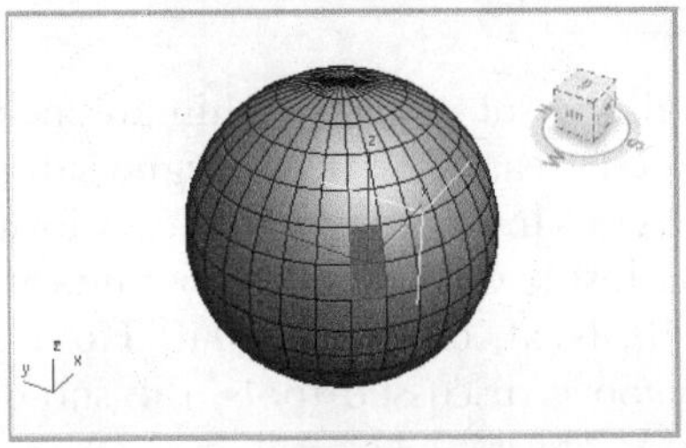

Figure 9-33 *Two adjacent polygons selected*

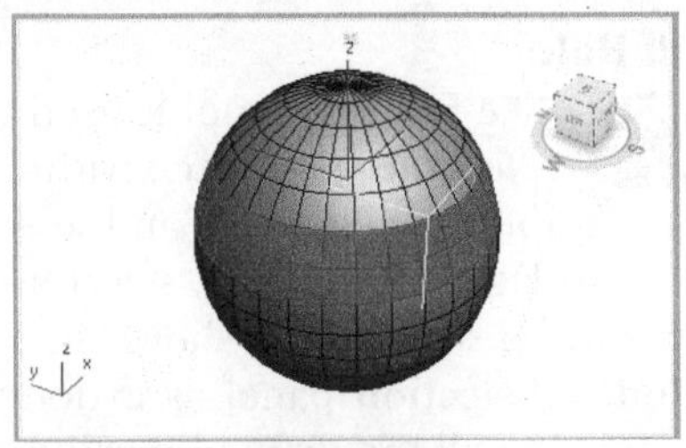

Figure 9-34 *The sub-objects selected in the form of a ring*

Figure 9-35 *The edges selected*

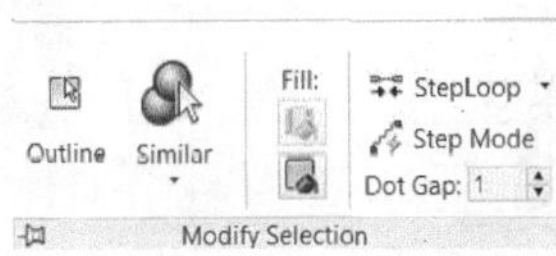

Figure 9-36 *The* ***Modify Selection*** *panel expanded*

Figure 9-37 *An outline created around the selected edges*

Similar

The **Similar** tool is used to select the sub-objects that are similar to the preselected sub-objects. To select a sub-object similar to the preselected sub-object, select a sub-object of the editable poly object in the viewport. Next, expand the **Modify Selection** panel and choose the **Similar** tool from it; the sub-objects that are similar to the preselected sub-object will be selected. When you click on the down arrow below the **Similar** tool; various radio buttons will be displayed. These radio buttons are **Edge Count**, **Face Areas**, **Topology**, and **Normal Direction**.

Fill

The **Fill** tool is used to select all the sub-objects between two selected sub-objects. To do so, select the **Polygon** sub-object level of an object and select two polygons, as shown in Figure 9-38. Now, choose the **Fill** tool from the **Modify Selection** panel; all the sub-objects between the selected sub-objects will be selected, as shown in Figure 9-39.

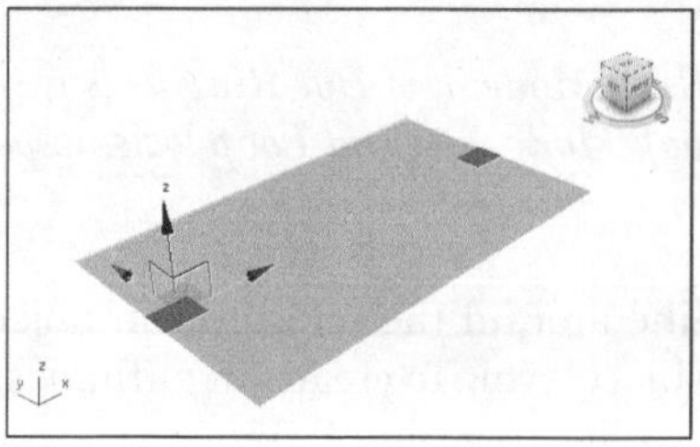

Figure 9-38 Two polygons selected

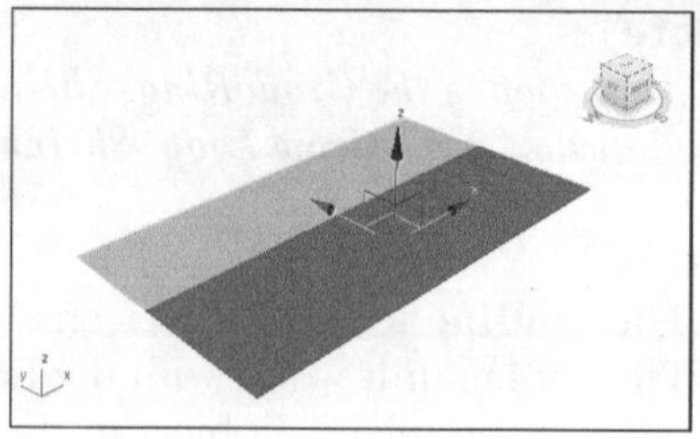

Figure 9-39 All sub-objects selected between the two selected polygons

Fill Hole

The **Fill Hole** tool is used to select all the sub-objects within an enclosed area. To select the sub-objects within an enclosed area, select the **Polygon** sub-object level of the selected object and select the polygons in such a way that they form a boundary, refer to Figure 9-40. Now, select a sub-object inside or outside the boundary to define the area to be selected, as shown in Figure 9-40. Next, choose the **Fill Hole** tool from the **Modify Selection** panel as is done for the above discussed tools; the sub-objects will be selected to fill the defined portion, as shown in Figure 9-41.

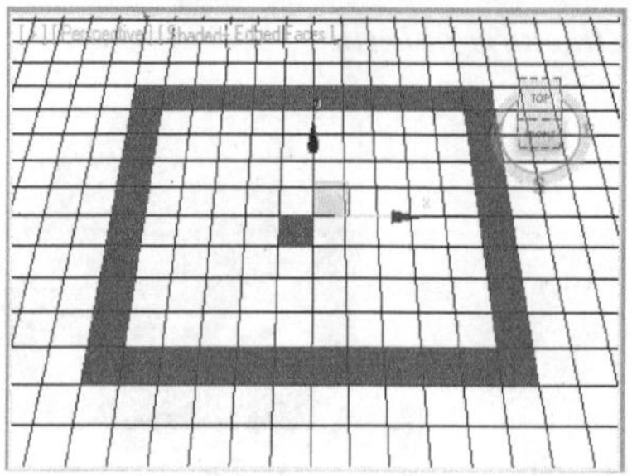

Figure 9-40 The sub-objects selected to create a boundary

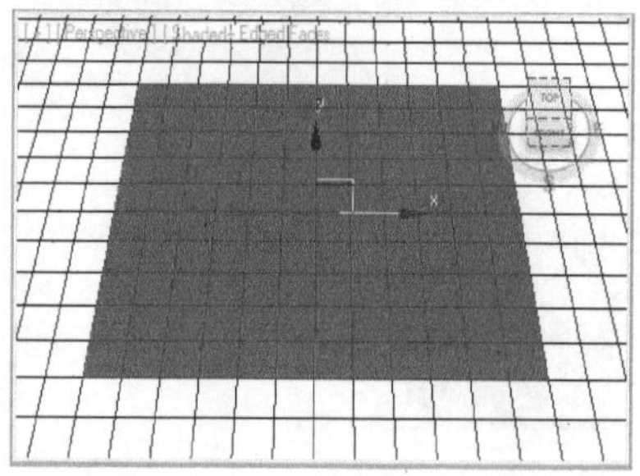

Figure 9-41 All sub-objects selected to fill the defined boundary

Loops Panel

The tools in the **Loops** panel are used to create edge loops on the selected object. By default, the **Loops** panel will not be visible in the **Graphite Modeling Tools** tab. To view this panel, you need to select **Vertex**, **Edge**, or **Polygon** sub-object level of the editable poly object. Most of the tools in this panel are available at the **Edge** sub-object level and the remaining tools are available at the **Vertex** or **Polygon** sub-object level of an object. The most commonly used tools in this panel are discussed next.

Connect

The **Connect** tool is available for the **Vertex** and **Edge** sub-object levels of an object. It is used to connect two selected vertices or edges by creating a new edge between them. To connect two vertices using the **Connect** tool, select the **Vertex** sub-object level of the selected object and select two vertices, as shown in Figure 9-42. Now, choose the **Connect** tool from the **Loops** panel; a new edge connecting the selected vertices will be created, as shown in Figure 9-43. You can also select multiple vertices and connect them, as shown in Figure 9-44.

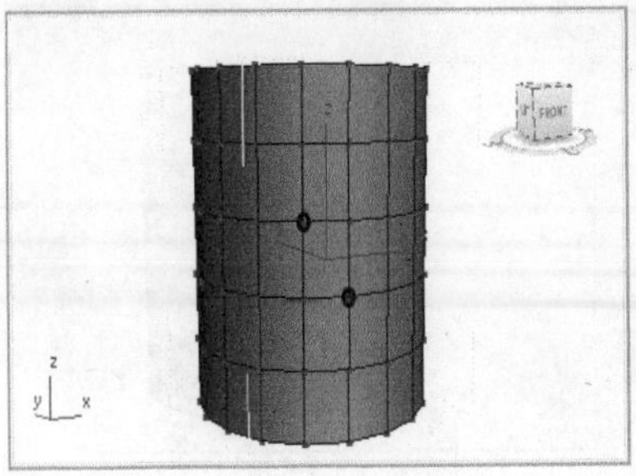

Figure 9-42 *The two vertices selected*

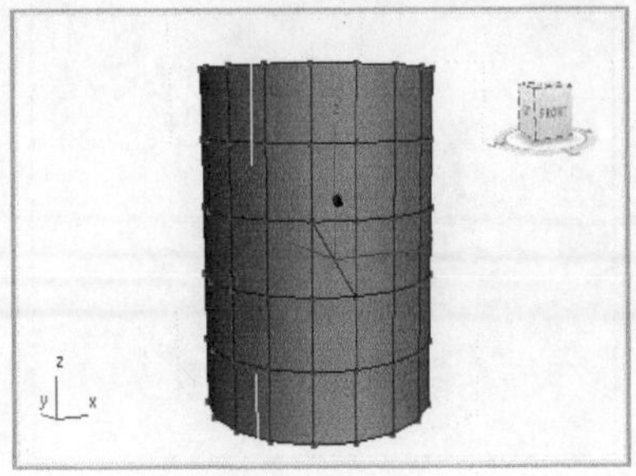

Figure 9-43 *A new edge created between the two selected vertices*

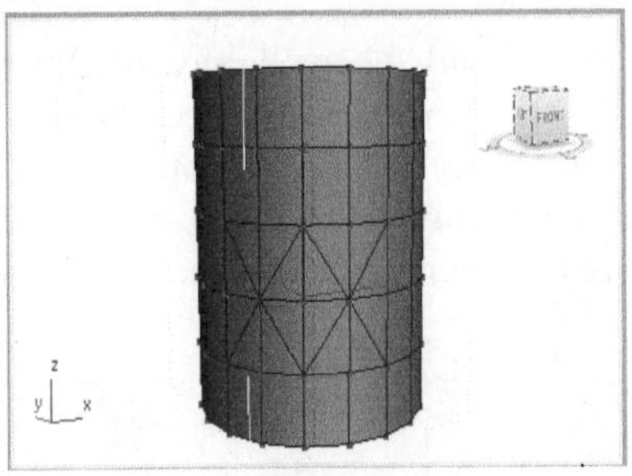

Figure 9-44 *Multiple vertices connected on choosing the* ***Connect*** *tool*

Note

If you select four vertices of a four-sided polygon and choose the ***Connect*** *tool, then only two vertices will be connected by an edge. To create a connection between all the four vertices, you need to choose the* ***Cut*** *tool from the* ***Edit*** *panel.*

To connect edges using the **Connect** tool, select the **Edge** sub-object level of the selected object, and select the edges, as shown in Figure 9-45. Now, choose the **Connect** tool from the **Loops** panel; the selected edges will be connected by the new edges, as shown in Figure 9-46. You can also create multiple edges. To do so, expand the drop-down list next to the **Connect** tool and select the **Connect Settings** tool from the drop-down list; the **Connect Edges** caddy control will be displayed in the viewport, as shown in Figure 9-47. Enter the required number of segments in the **Segments** spinner and choose the **OK** button; multiple edges will be created, as shown in Figure 9-48.

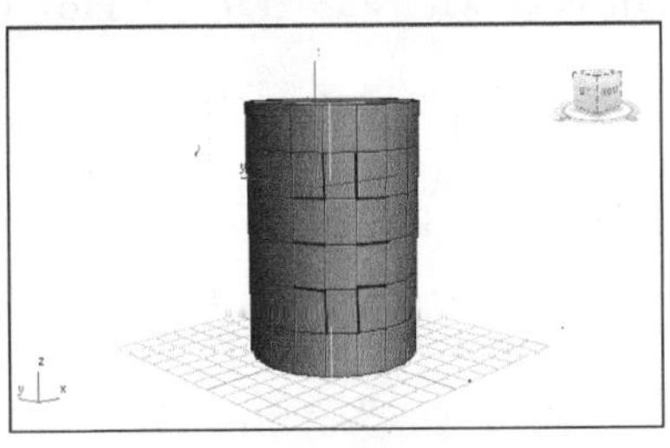

Figure 9-45 *The edges selected*

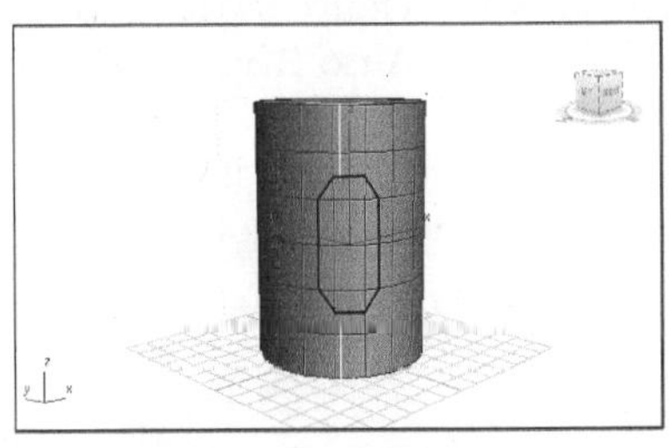

Figure 9-46 *The selected edges connected by new edges*

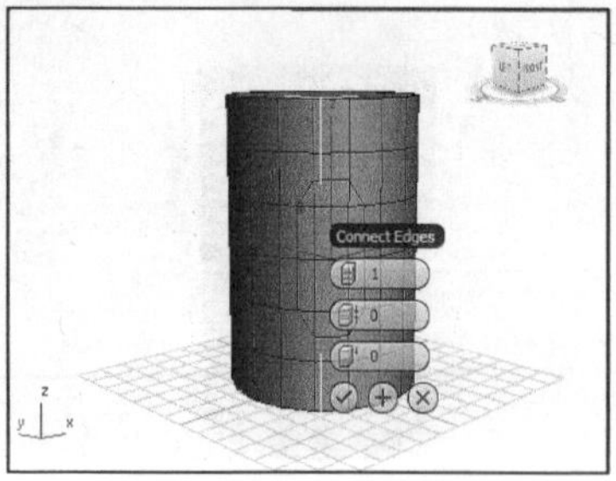

*Figure 9-47 The **Connect Edges** caddy control*

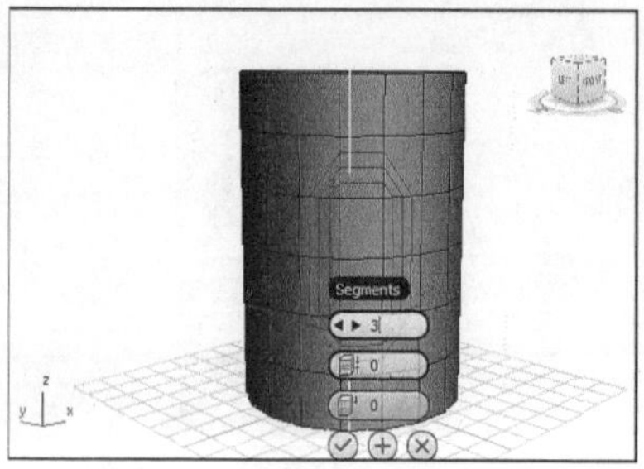

Figure 9-48 Multiple edges created between the selected edges

Dist Connect

The **Dist Connect** tool will only be available only for the **Vertex** and **Edge** sub-object levels of an object. In the **Vertex** sub-object mode, this tool helps to connect two vertices that are at a distance from each other in an intervening mesh. To do so, select the vertices, as shown in Figure 9-49. Next, choose the **Dist Connect** tool from the **Loops** panel; a connection between the selected vertices will be created, as shown in Figure 9-50.

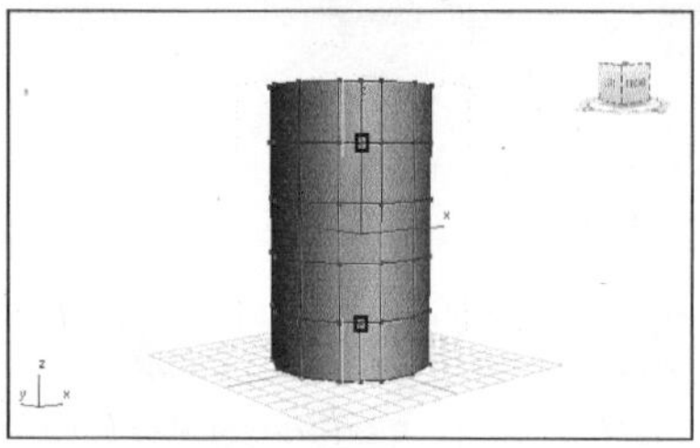

Figure 9-49 Two vertices selected

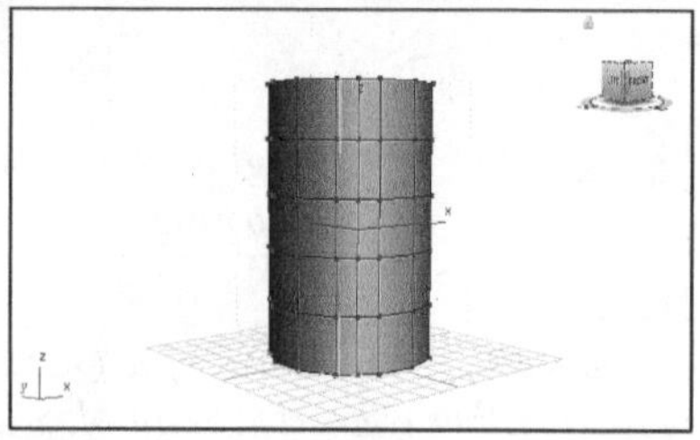

Figure 9-50 Connection created between the selected vertices

Similarly, you can create a connection between two distant edges of an object by using the **Dist Connect** tool.

Flow Connect

The **Flow Connect** tool will only be available for the **Edge** sub-object level of an object. This button enables you to connect the selected edge across one or more edge rings. To do so, select the **Edge** sub-object level of an object and select one of its edges, as shown in Figure 9-51. Next, expand the drop-down list next to the **Flow Connect** tool and select the **Auto Ring** check box.

The **Auto Ring** check box is used to automatically create a full edge loop. Next, choose the **Flow Connect** tool to connect the complete edge loop of the selected edge, as shown in Figure 9-52.

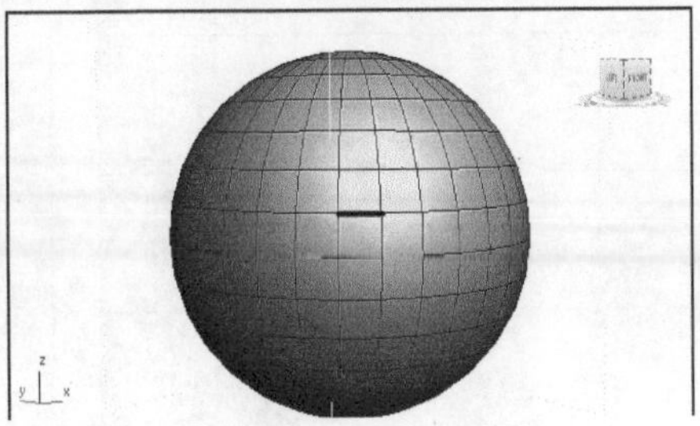

Figure 9-51 An edge selected on the sphere

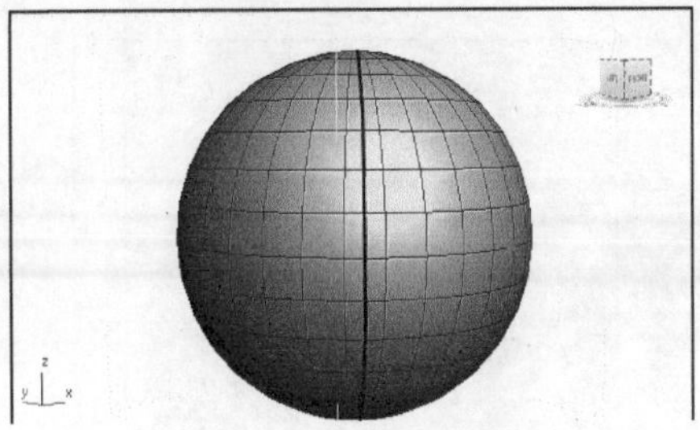

Figure 9-52 The complete edge loop of the selected edge

Insert Loop

The **Insert Loop** tool will only be available for the **Edge**, **Vertex**, and **Polygon** sub-object levels of an object. It is used to insert edges by creating a loop around the selected sub-objects. To insert a loop along the polygon sub-objects, select one or more pairs of adjacent polygons of the object, as shown in Figure 9-53. Next, choose the **Insert Loop** tool from the **Loops** panel; an edge loop will be created, as shown in Figure 9-54. Similarly, you can create loop vertically if you select one or more pairs of the adjacent polygons vertically in the object.

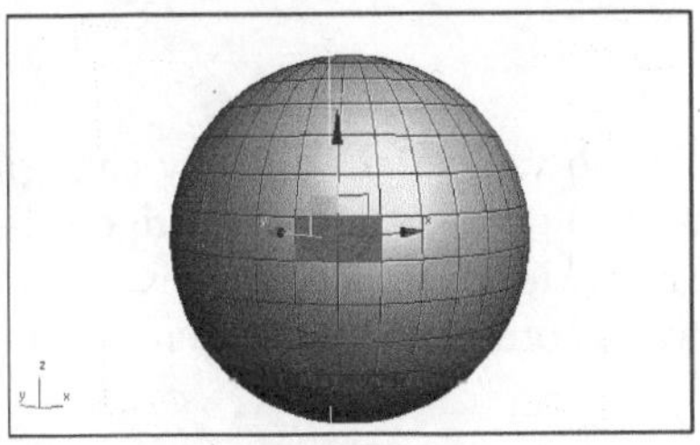

Figure 9-53 The polygons selected on an object

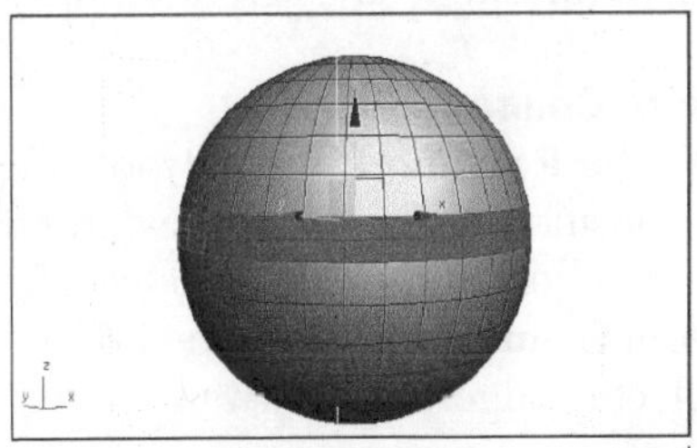

*Figure 9-54 An edge loop created along the selected polygons using the **Insert Loop** tool*

Remove Loop

The **Remove Loop** tool is used to remove the selected loops at the current sub-object level. In the **Vertex** sub-object level, you need to select one or more pair of vertices whereas in the **Edge** and **Polygon** sub-object levels, you need to select one or more edges and one or more polygons, respectively, to remove the loop.

Build End

The **Build End** tool is used to build a quad at the end of any two parallel loops. To do so, select two vertices that are at the end of two parallel loops, as shown in Figure 9-55, and then choose the **Build End** tool; a quad will be built, as shown in Figure 9-56. Similarly, you can use the **Edge** sub-object level to build a quad at the end of the two parallel loops.

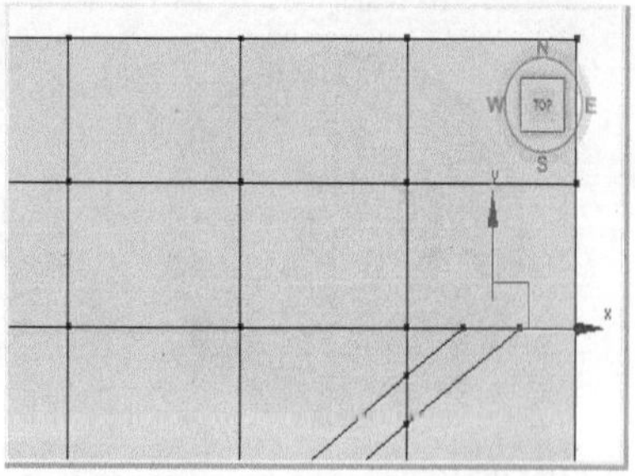

Figure 9-55 The two vertices selected

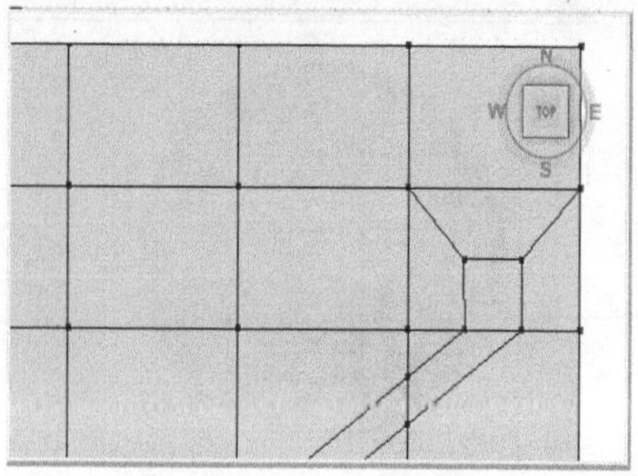

Figure 9-56 A quad built at the ends of the two selected vertices

Build Corner

The **Build Corner** tool will only be available for the **Vertex** and **Edge** sub-object levels. This button is mainly used to add a corner edge to an object by forming an edge-loop turn. To add corner edge, select the two end vertices that terminate two loops. Note that these loops should be at right angles and should end at adjacent sides of the same quad polygon. Next, choose the **Build Corner** button from the **Loops** panel; a quad corner will be created. Similarly, you can use the **Edge** sub-object level to add a quad corner to the end of the selected edges.

Random Connect

The **Random Connect** tool is used to connect the selected edges by changing the position of the newly created edges randomly. To do so, select the **Edge** sub-object level of an object and select the edges, as shown in Figure 9-57. Next, choose the **Random Connect** tool from the **Loops** panel; a random connection will be created between the selected edges, as shown in Figure 9-58.

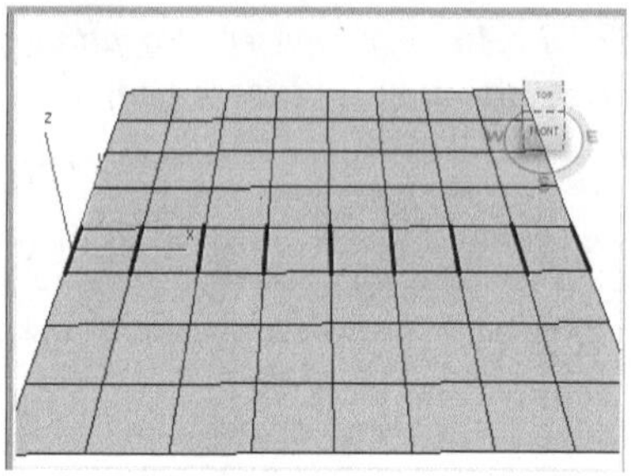

Figure 9-57 The edges selected

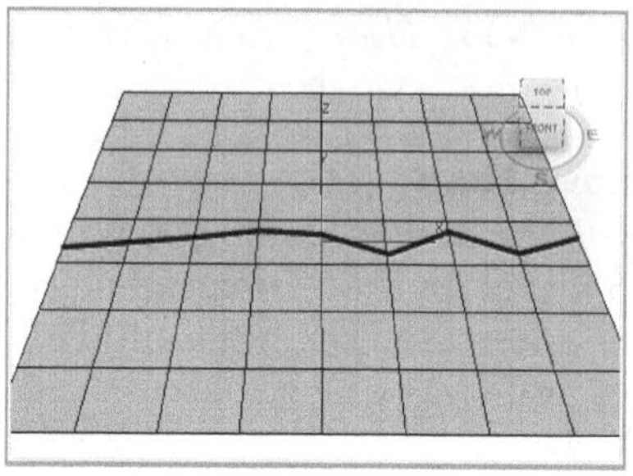

Figure 9-58 Randomly connected edges

TUTORIAL

Tutorial 1

In this tutorial, you will create the model of computer table, as shown in Figure 9-59, using the graphite modeling toolset. **(Expected time: 30 min)**

Figure 9-59 The model of a computer table

The following steps are required to complete this tutorial:

a. Create the project folder.
b. Create the tabletop and supports.
c. Create the CPU base.
d. Create top and bottom shelves.
e. Create the keyboard support.
f. Save and render the scene.

Creating the Project Folder

Create a new project folder with the name *c09_tut1* at *\Documents\3dsmax2017* and then save the file with the name *c09tut1*, as discussed in Tutorial 1 of Chapter 2.

Creating the Tabletop and Supports

In this section, you will create the tabletop and supports using the **Box** tool.

1. Activate the Top viewport and choose **Create > geometry** from the **Command Panel**. Now, choose the **Box** tool from the **Object Type** rollout. Next, create a box in the Top viewport.

2. Choose the **Modify** tab from the **Command Panel**. Next, in the **Parameters** rollout, set the parameters as given next:

   Length: **121** Width: **234** Height: **9**

   Length Segs: **10** Width Segs: **24**

3. Rename *box001* as *computer table*. Next, choose the **Zoom Extents All** tool. The *computer table* is displayed in the viewports, as shown in Figure 9-60.

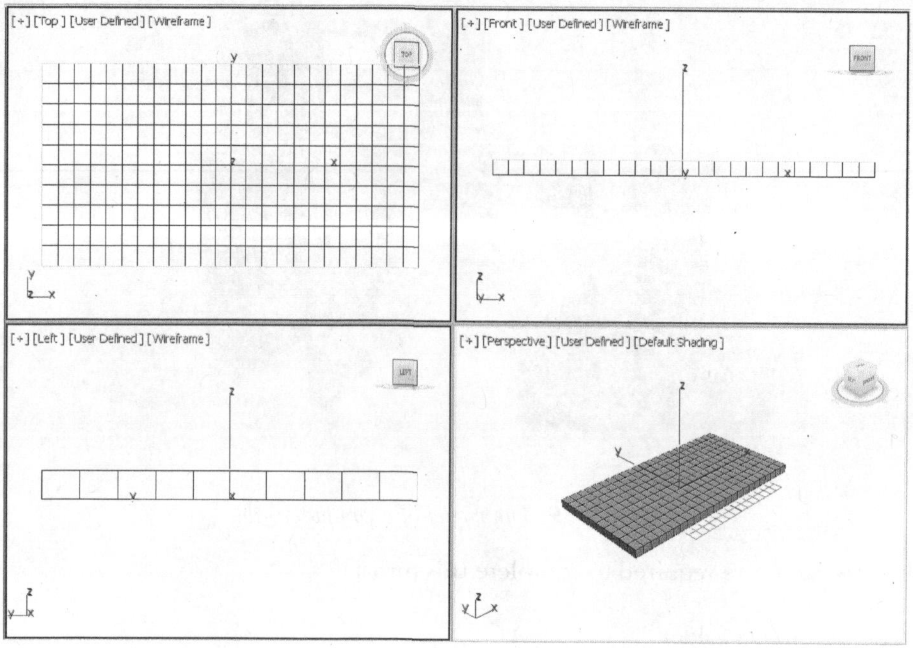

Figure 9-60 *The computer table geometry displayed in the viewports*

4. Choose the **Modeling** tab below the **Main Toolbar**. Next, expand the **Polygon Modeling** panel and then choose the **Convert to Poly** tool from it; *computer table* is converted into an editable poly.

5. Switch from the Top viewport to the Bottom viewport and select the **Polygon** sub-object level. Next, select the polygons of *computer table*, as shown in Figure 9-61.

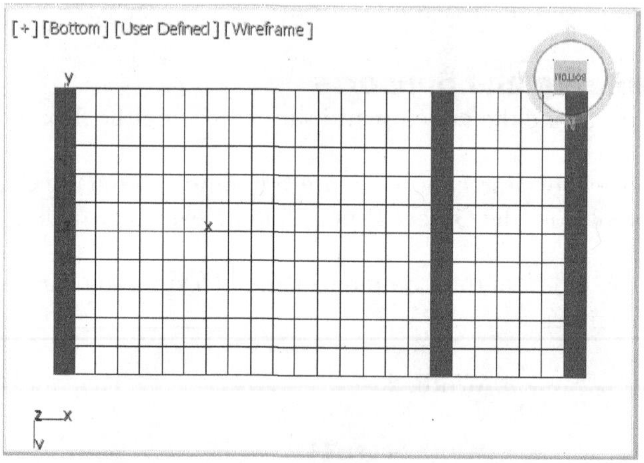

Figure 9-61 *Selected polygons of computer table*

6. Choose the **Extrude Settings** button from the **Extrude** drop-down in the **Polygons** panel, as shown in Figure 9-62; the **Extrude** caddy control is displayed in the viewport, refer to Figure 9-63.

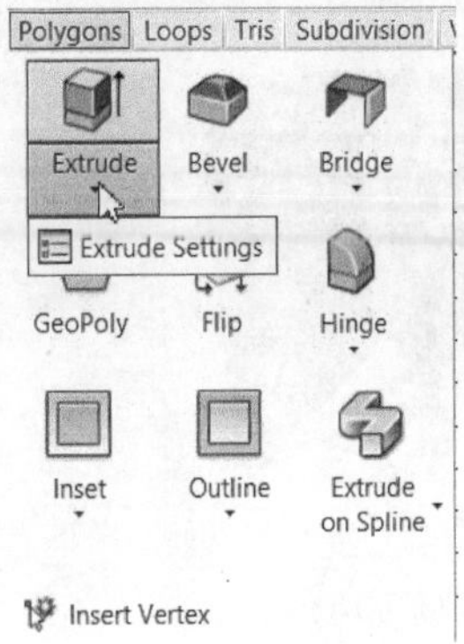

Figure 9-62 *Choosing* ***Extrude Settings*** *from the* ***Extrude*** *drop-down*

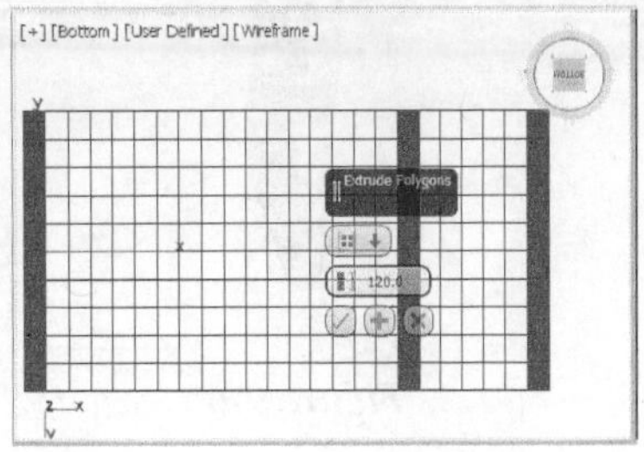

Figure 9-63 *The* ***Extrude*** *caddy control*

7. Set the value **110** in the **Height** spinner and choose the **OK** button; the selected polygons are extruded, as shown in Figure 9-64.

Creating the CPU Base

In this section, you will create the CPU base by extruding the polygons of *computer table.*

1. Switch from the Bottom viewport to the Top viewport. Next, select the **Edge** sub-object level. Activate the Perspective viewport and then select an edge from each extruded part, as shown in Figure 9-65.

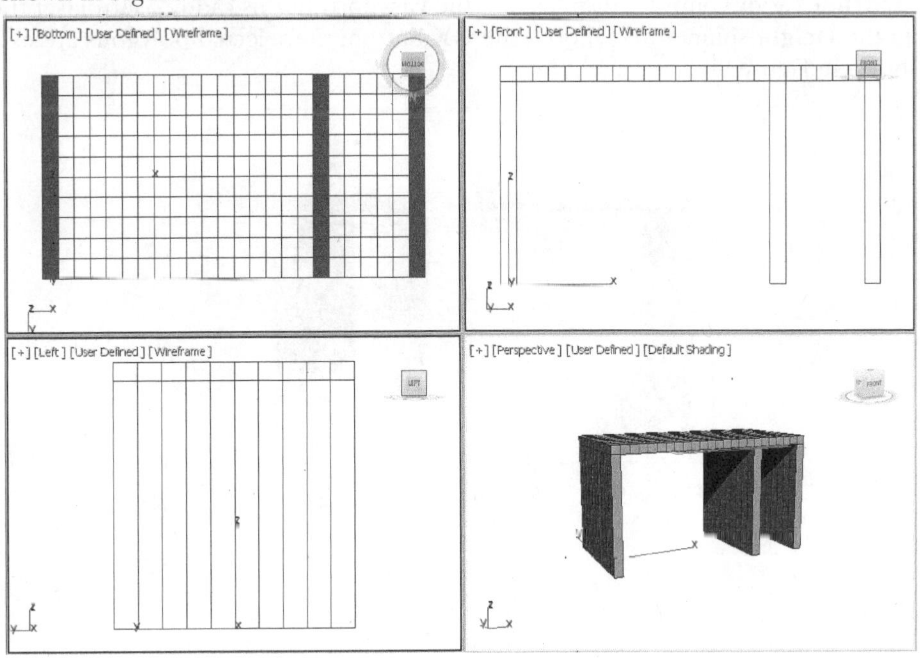

Figure 9-64 *The selected polygons extruded*

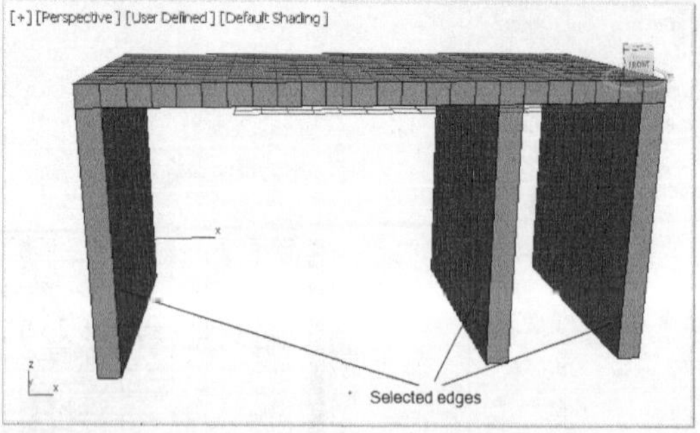

Figure 9-65 Selected edges of computer table

2. Choose the **Ring** tool from the **Modify Selection** panel; rings of all the selected edges are selected.

3. Choose the **Connect Settings** button from the **Connect** drop-down in the **Loops** panel; the **Connect** caddy control is displayed in the viewport.

4. In the **Connect** caddy control, set the value **12** in the **Segments** spinner and choose the **OK** button; the edges are added as shown in Figure 9-66.

5. Select the **Polygon** sub-object level. Next, select the polygons, as shown in Figure 9-67.

6. Choose the **Extrude Settings** button from the **Extrude** drop-down in the **Polygons** panel; the **Extrude** caddy control is displayed in the viewport. In this caddy control, set the value **55** in the **Height** spinner and choose the **OK** button; the selected polygons are extruded, as shown in Figure 9-68.

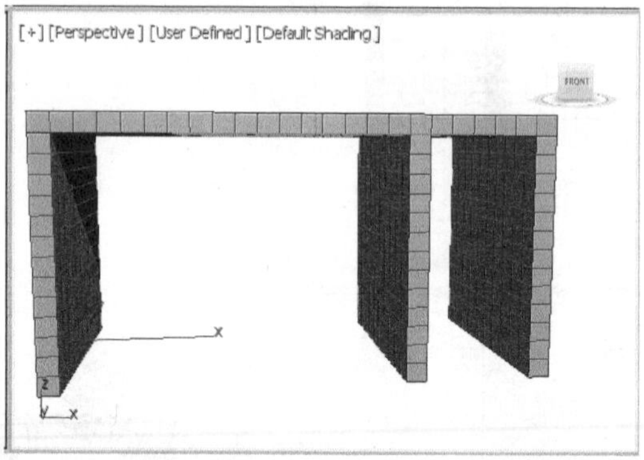

Figure 9-66 Edges added to the computer table

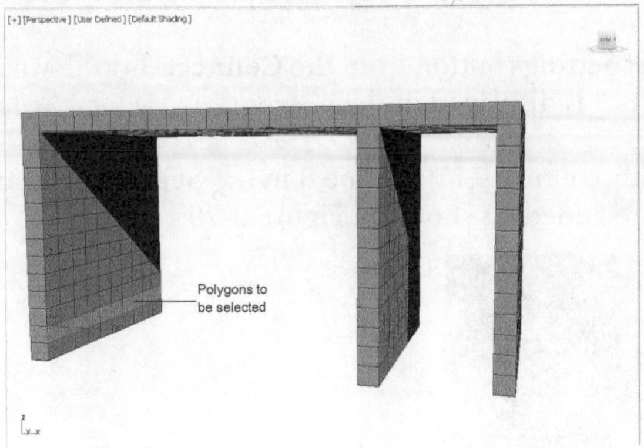

Figure 9-67 The selected polygons of computer table

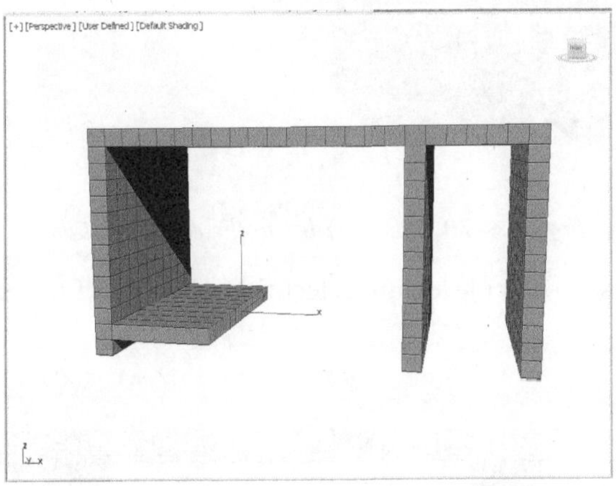

Figure 9-68 The extruded polygons of computer table

7. Select the **Edge** sub-object level and then select an edge from the extruded part, as shown in Figure 9-69.

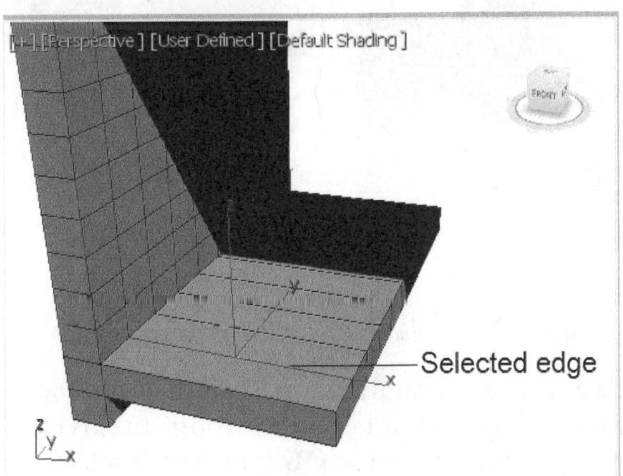

Figure 9-69 The selected edge of computer table

8. Choose the **Ring** tool from the **Modify Selection** panel; ring of the selected edge is selected.

9. Choose the **Connect Settings** button from the **Connect** drop-down in the **Loops** panel; the **Connect** caddy control is displayed in the viewport.

10. In the **Connect** caddy control, set the value **8** in the **Segments** spinner and choose the **OK** button; the edges are added, as shown in Figure 9-70.

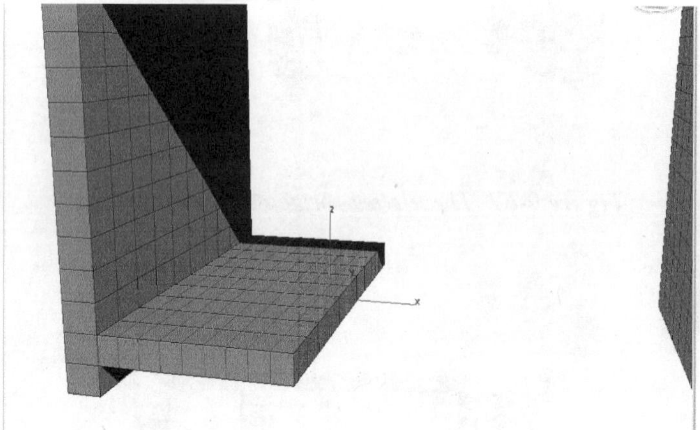

Figure 9-70 *Edges added to the computer table*

11. Select the **Polygon** sub-object level and select the polygons of the extruded part, as shown in Figure 9-71.

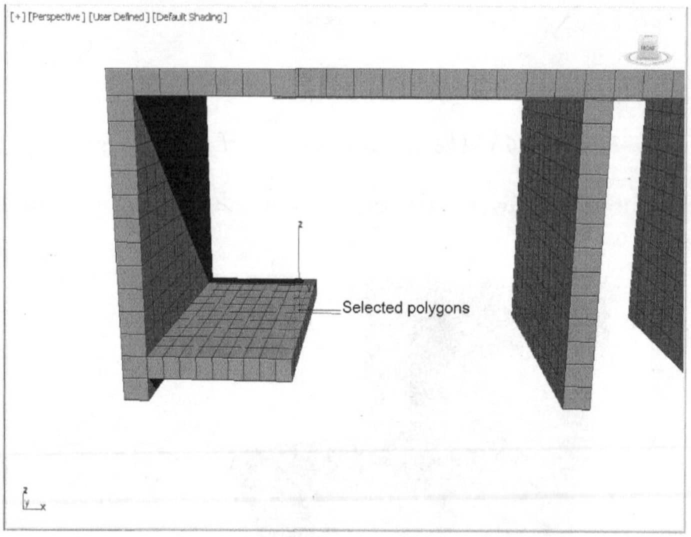

Figure 9-71 *Selected polygons of computer table*

12. Choose the **Extrude Settings** button from the **Extrude** drop-down in the **Polygons** panel; the **Extrude** caddy control is displayed in the viewport. In this caddy control, set the value **30** in the **Height** spinner and choose the **OK** button; the selected polygons are extruded, as shown in Figure 9-72.

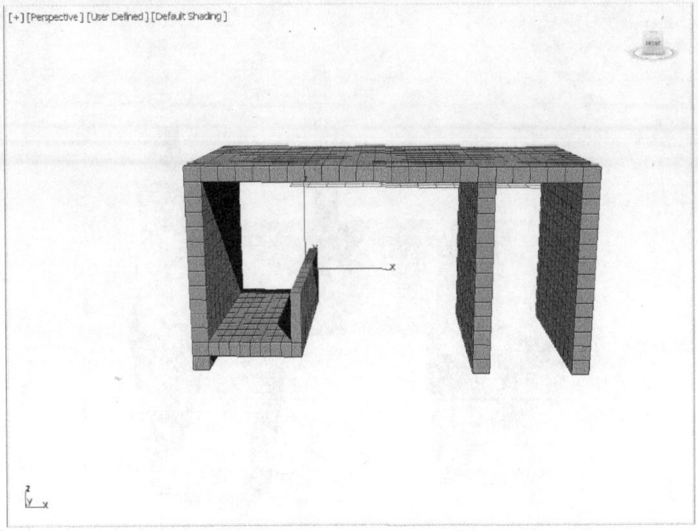

Figure 9-72 Extruded polygons of computer table

Creating Top and Bottom Shelves

In this section, you will create top and bottom shelves of *computer table* by using the **Bridge** and **Extrude** tools.

1. Select the polygons from the top of *computer table*, as shown in Figure 9-73.

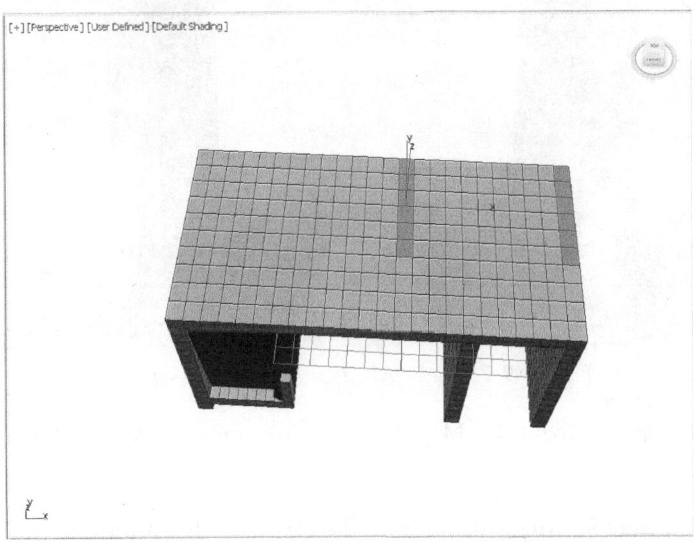

Figure 9-73 Selected polygons of computer table

2. Choose the **Extrude Settings** button from the **Extrude** drop-down in the **Polygons** panel; the **Extrude** caddy control is displayed in the viewport. In this caddy control, set the value **60** in the **Height** spinner and choose the **OK** button; the selected polygons are extruded, as shown in Figure 9-74.

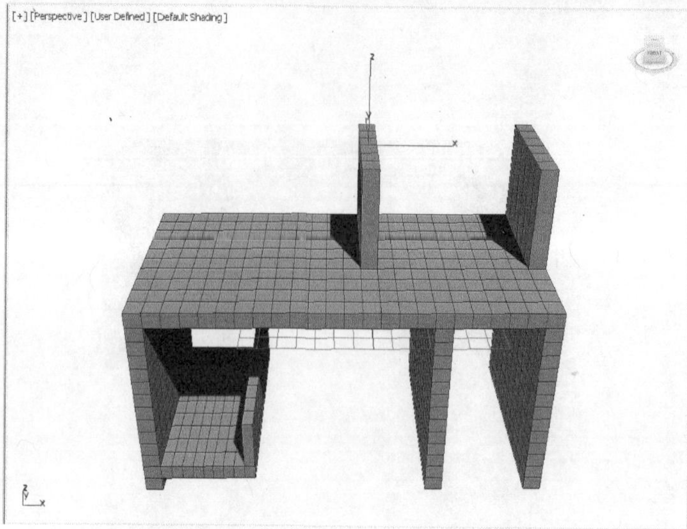

***Figure 9-74** Extruded polygons of computer table*

3. Select the **Edge** sub-object level and then select two edges from the extruded part, as shown in Figure 9-75.

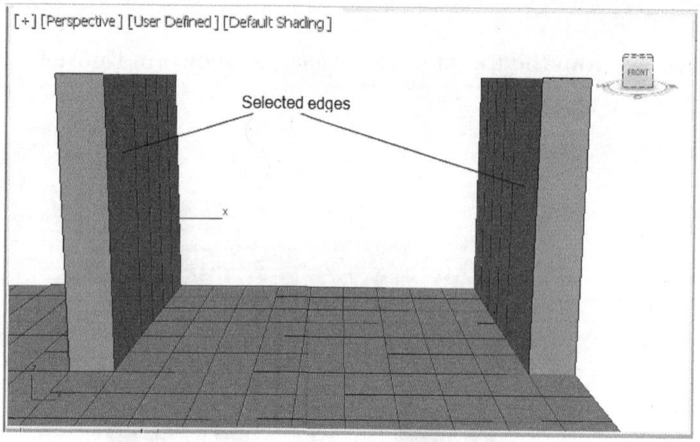

***Figure 9-75** Selected edges of the extruded part*

4. Choose the **Ring** tool from the **Modify Selection** panel; rings of the selected edges are selected.

5. Choose the **Connect Settings** button from the **Connect** drop-down in the **Loops** panel; the **Connect** caddy control is displayed in the viewport.

6. In the **Connect** caddy control, set the value **2** in the **Segments** spinner and **-64** in the **Pinch** spinner, refer to Figure 9-76 and choose the **OK** button; two edges are added at the center of the extruded part, as shown in Figure 9-76.

7. Select two edges from the upper part of the extruded portion, as shown in Figure 9-77.

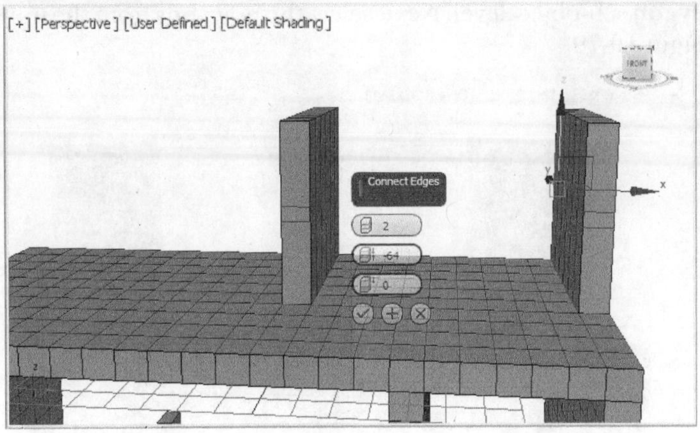

Figure 9-76 *Added edges at the center of the extruded part*

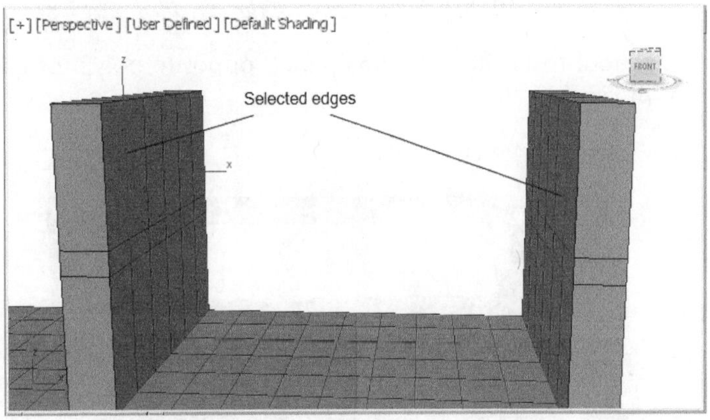

Figure 9-77 *Selected edges from the upper portion of extruded part*

8 Choose the **Insert Loop** tool from the **Loops** panel; two edge loops are added. Choose the **Select and Move** tool and align the edge loops, as shown in Figure 9-78.

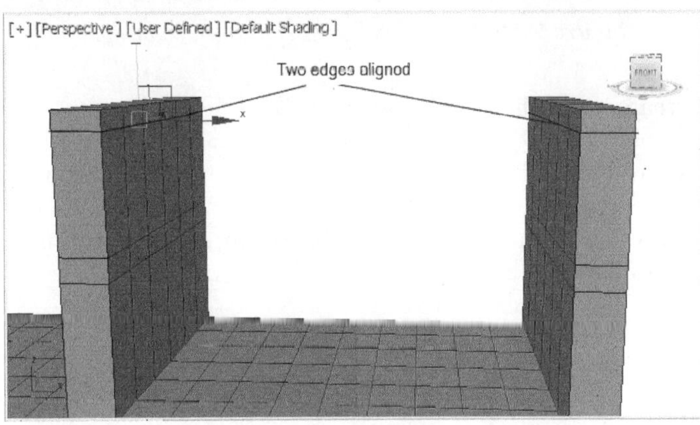

Figure 9-78 *Two edges aligned*

9. Select the **Polygon** sub-object level. Next, select the polygons from the upper extruded part, as shown in Figure 9-79.

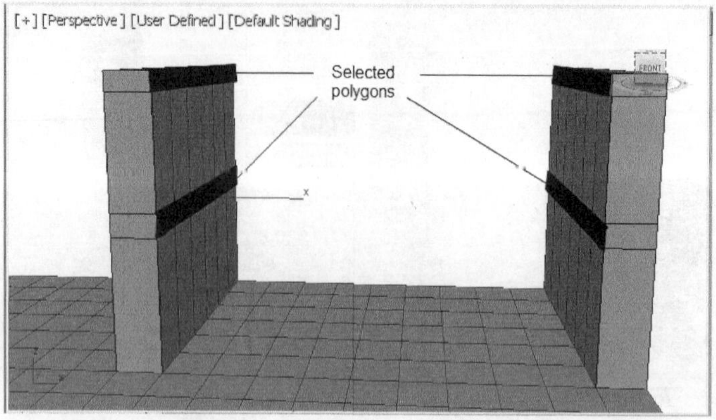

Figure 9-79 *Selected polygons of the extruded part*

10. Choose the **Bridge** tool from the **Polygons** panel; opposite polygons get connected by a bridge, as shown in Figure 9-80.

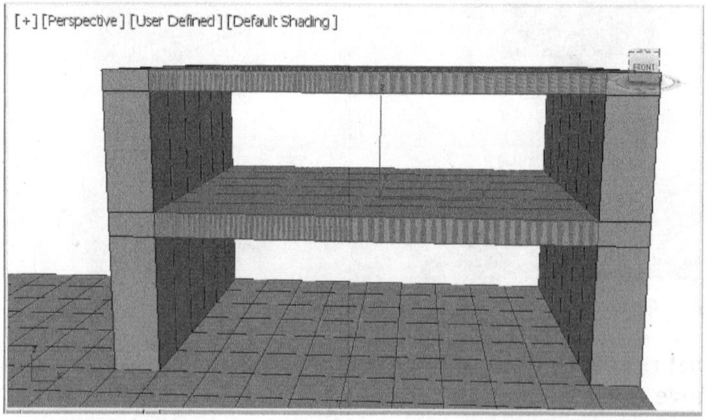

Figure 9-80 *Selected polygons connected by bridges*

Next, you will create lower shelves of *computer table.*

11. Select the polygons from the lower part of computer table, as shown in Figure 9-81.

12. Choose the **Bridge** tool from the **Polygons** panel; opposite polygons get connected by a bridge, as shown in Figure 9-82.

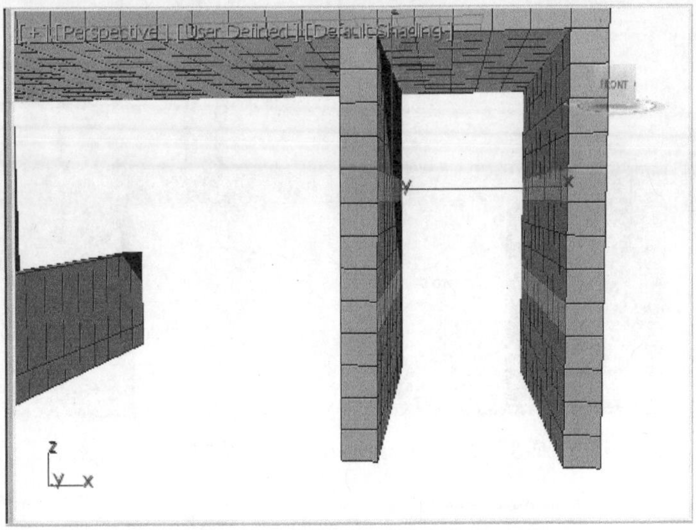

Figure 9-81 Selected polygons of the lower parts

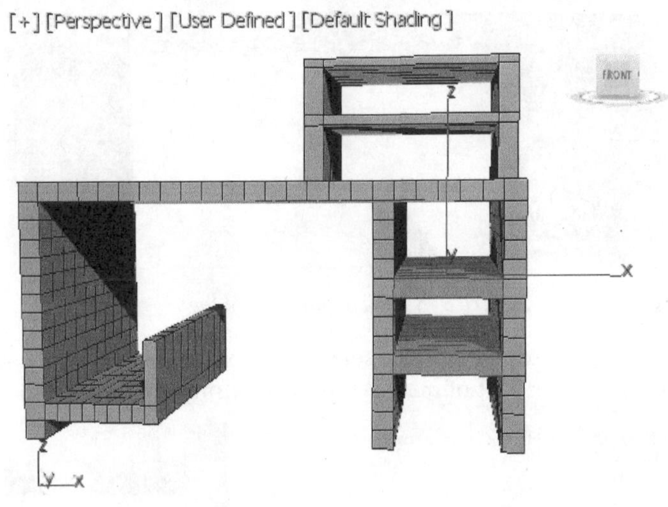

Figure 9-82 Selected polygons connected by bridge

Creating the Keyboard Support

In this section, you need to create the keyboard support by chamfering edges and extruding polygons.

1. Select the **Edge** sub-object level and then select two edges from the lower left part of *computer table*, as shown in Figure 9-83.

2. Choose the **Inset Loop** tool from the **Loops** panel; two edge loops are added, as shown in Figure 9-84.

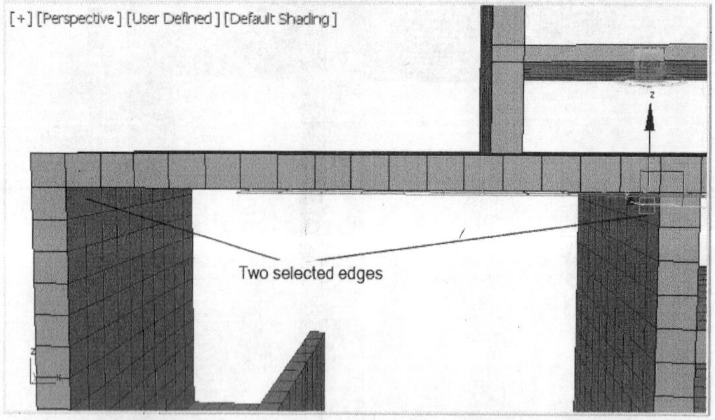

Figure 9-83 *Two edges selected from the lower left part*

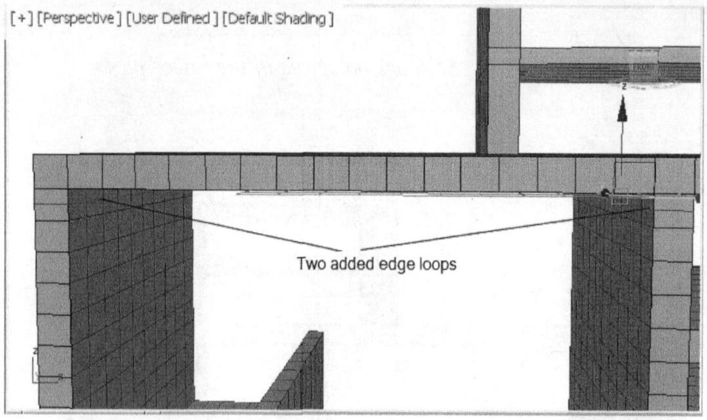

Figure 9-84 *Two added edge loops*

3. Make sure that the added edge loops are selected. Next, press the CTRL key and select two more edges from the lower part of *computer table*, as shown in Figure 9-85.

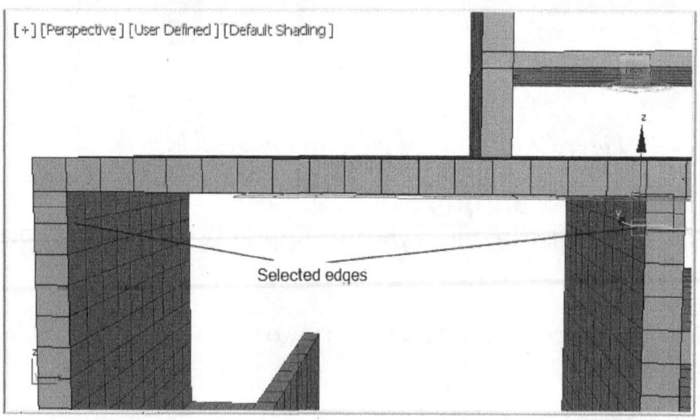

Figure 9-85 *Two edges selected*

4. Choose the **Loop** tool from the **Modify Selection** panel; two edge loops get added to the selection, as shown in Figure 9-86.

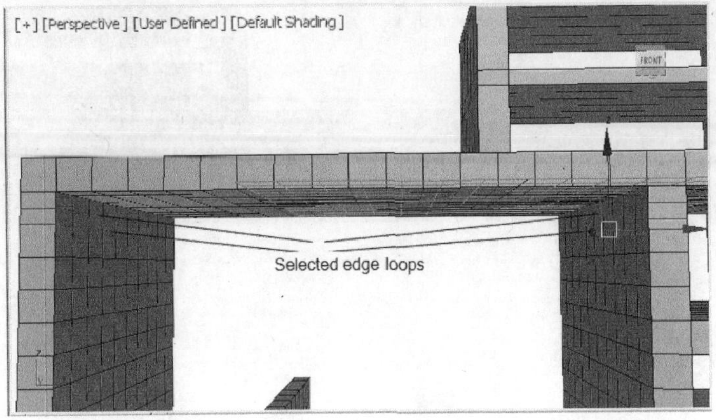

Figure 9-86 *Selected edge loops*

5. Choose the **Chamfer Settings** button from the **Chamfer** drop-down in the **Edges** panel; the **Chamfer** caddy control is displayed in the viewport. In this caddy control, set the value **0.5** in the **Edge Chamfer Amount** spinner and choose the **OK** button; the selected edge loops are chamfered, as shown in Figure 9-87.

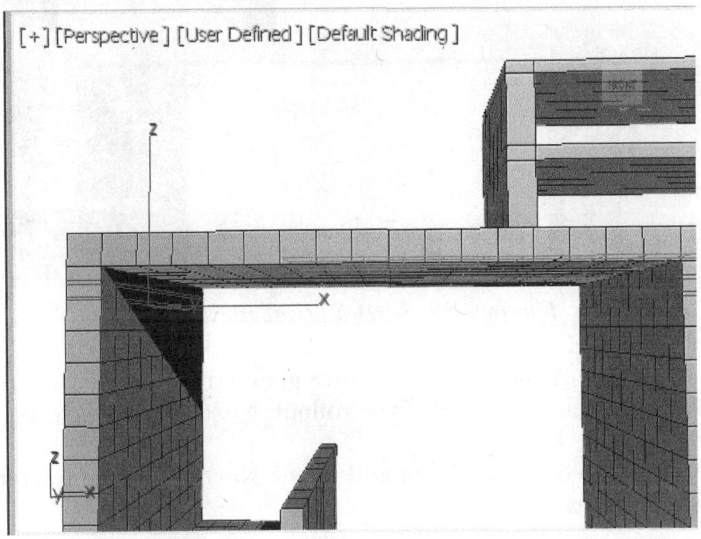

Figure 9-87 *Two edge loops chamfered*

6. Select the **Polygon** sub-object level and then select the polygons between the chamfered edge loops, as shown in Figure 9-88.

7. Choose the **Extrude Settings** button from the **Extrude** drop-down in the **Polygons** panel; the **Extrude** caddy control is displayed in the viewport. In this caddy control, set the value **5.5** in the **Height** spinner and choose the **OK** button; the selected polygons are extruded, as shown in Figure 9-89.

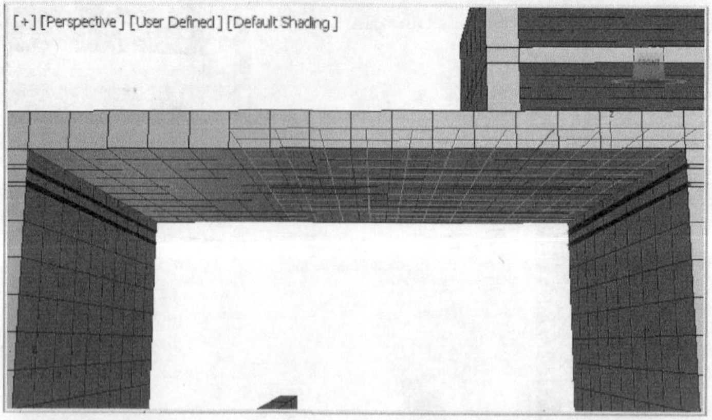

Figure 9-88 Selected polygons between the chamfered edges

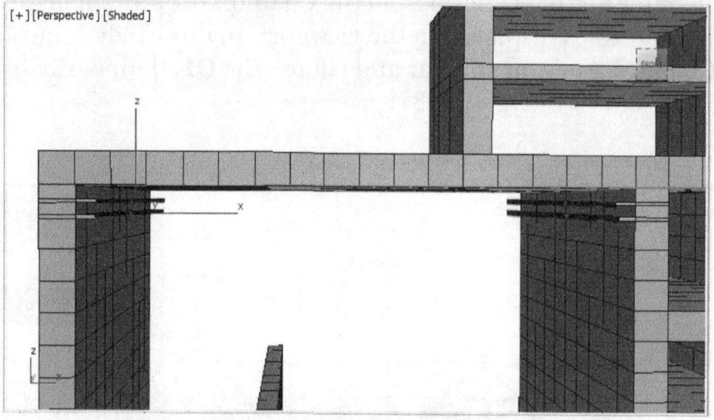

Figure 9-89 Selected polygons extruded

8. Activate the Top viewport and choose **Create > geometry** from the **Command Panel**. Now, choose the **Box** tool from the **Object Type** rollout. Next, create a box in the Top viewport.

9. Choose the **Modify** tab from the **Command Panel**. Next, in the **Parameters** rollout, set the parameters as given next:

   Length:**109.45**   Width: **160**   Height: **2.8**

10. Modify the name of the box as *Keyboard support*. Next, align it in the viewports, as shown in Figure 9-90.

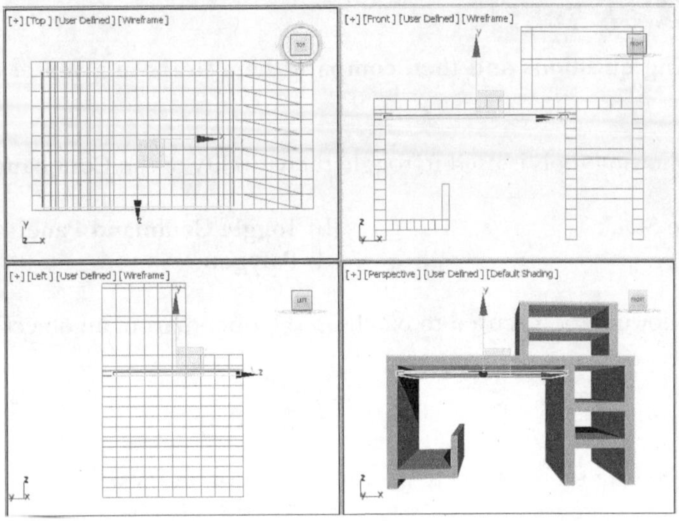

Figure 9-90 The Keyboard support geometry aligned in the viewports

11. Now, you need to apply texture to the model. You can download the *c09_3dsmax_2017_tut.zip* file from *www.cadcim.com* and extract the contents of the zip file. Next, save *wood.jpg* at the location *\Documents\3dsmax2017\c09_tut1\sceneassets\images* and apply texture to the model, as discussed in the earlier chapters.

Saving and Rendering the Scene

In this section, you will save the scene and then render it. You can view the final rendered image of this model by downloading the *c09_3dsmax_2017_rndr.zip* file from *www.cadcim.com*. The path of the file is as follows: *Textbooks > Animation and Visual Effects > 3ds Max > Autodesk 3ds Max 2017: A Comprehensive Guide*

1. Change the background color of the scene to white, as discussed in Tutorial 1 of Chapter 2. Choose **Save** from the **Application** menu.

2. Activate the Perspective viewport. Next, choose the **Render Production** tool from the **Main Toolbar**; the **Rendered Frame** window is displayed. This window shows the final output of the scene, refer to Figure 9-91.

Figure 9-91 The rendered model of computer table

Self-Evaluation Test

Answer the following questions and then compare them to those given at the end of this chapter:

1. Which of the following tools is used to toggle the visibility of the **Command Panel**?

   (a) **Collapse Stack** (b) **Toggle Command Panel**
   (c) **Edit** (d) **Polygon**

2. Which of the following tools is used to patch up the open part of an object?

   (a) **Outline** (b) **Fill**
   (c) **Patch Poly** (d) **Cap Poly**

3. Which of the following tools is used to prevent distortion in UVs?

   (a) **Preserve UVs** (b) **Distort UVs**
   (c) **Tweak (UVs)** (d) All of these

4. The __________ check box is used to automatically create a full edge loop.

5. The __________ tool is used to edit the sub-objects without affecting the original UV mapping of the object.

6. The __________ tool is used to show the final effect of all the modifiers applied to an object.

7. The **Grow Loop** tool is used to shrink the selection loop. (T/F)

8. The **Generate Topology** is used to collapse all the modifiers together in the modifier stack. (T/F)

Review Questions

Answer the following questions:

1. Which of the following tools is used to add segments between the edges and vertices?

   (a) **SwiftLoop** (b) **Connect**
   (c) **Paint Connect** (d) **Inset Loop**

2. Which of the following tools is used to connect two distant vertices in an intervening mesh?

   (a) **Distance Connect** (b) **Connect**
   (c) **Flow Connect** (d) **Random Connect**

3. Which of the following tools is used to create a quad at the end of two parallel loops?

(a) **Build Corner** (b) **Build End**
(c) **Build Quad** (d) None of them

4. The __________ tool is used to deform an object.

5. The __________ panel is used to modify the mesh object.

6. The **SwiftLoop** tool is used to add edge loops to the selected object. (T/F)

7. The **Remove Loop** tool works exactly similar to the **Insert Loop** tool. (T/F)

EXERCISE

The rendered output of the scene used in the Exercise 1 can be accessed by downloading the *c09_3dsmax_2017_exr.zip* file from *www.cadcim.com*. The path of the file is as follows: *Textbooks > Animation and Visual Effects > 3ds Max > Autodesk 3ds Max 2017: A Comprehensive Guide*

Exercise 1

Create a model of an acoustic guitar and apply texture to it, refer to Figure 9-92.
(Expected time: 50 min)

Figure 9-92 *The model of the guitar*

Answers to Self-Evaluation Test

1. b, **2.** d, **3.** a, **4. Auto Ring**, **5. Preserve UVs**, **6. Show end result**, **7.** F, **8.** F

10

NURBS Modeling

Learning Objectives

After completing this chapter, you will be able to:

- *Create NURBS curves*
- *Create NURBS surfaces*
- *Convert splines into NURBS curves*
- *Convert splines and extended splines into NURBS surfaces*
- *Convert primitives into NURBS surfaces*
- *Create NURBS models*
- *Understand NURBS sub-objects*

INTRODUCTION

The NURBS (Non-Uniform Rational Basis Splines) curves and surfaces are used to create complex 3D models. The NURBS objects use the mathematical calculations to create accurate complex 3D objects from 2D splines. In this chapter, you will learn to create smooth editable 3D models by using the NURBS curves and surfaces.

NURBS CURVES

The NURBS curves are similar to the splines and are used to create complex surfaces for creating 3D models. You can use the NURBS curves to create the 3D surfaces using the **Lathe** and **Extrude** modifiers. Also, you can loft the NURBS curves to create the loft objects. In 3ds Max, there are two types of NURBS curves, point curve and CV curve. These curves are discussed next.

Point Curve

Menu bar:	Create > NURBS > Point Curve
Command Panel:	Create > Shapes > NURBS Curves > Object Type rollout > Point Curve

The point curves are the NURBS curves. These curves consist of points that are constrained to lie on them, refer to Figure 10-1. To create a point curve, choose **Create > Shapes** in the **Command Panel**; a drop-down list will be displayed below the **Shapes** button. Select the **NURBS Curves** option from the drop-down list; the tools to create the point curve and the CV curve will be displayed in the **Object Type** rollout, as shown in Figure 10-2. Activate the viewport in which you want to create the point curve. Now, choose the **Point Curve** tool from the **Object Type** rollout; the **Name and Color**, **Rendering**, **Keyboard Entry**, and **Create Point Curve** rollouts will be displayed. Next, click in the viewport to create the first point and then click again to create the second point; the first segment is created. Then, continue clicking in the viewport to add more points to the curve. Now, right-click to end the creation; a point curve will be created in the viewport, refer to Figure 10-1. The **Create Point Curve** rollout is discussed next.

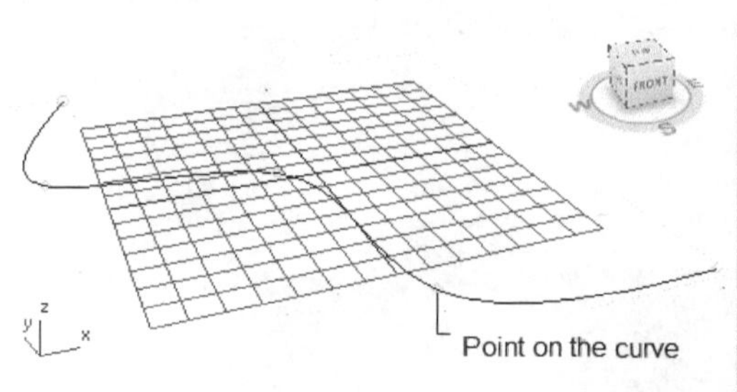

Figure 10-1 *A point curve*

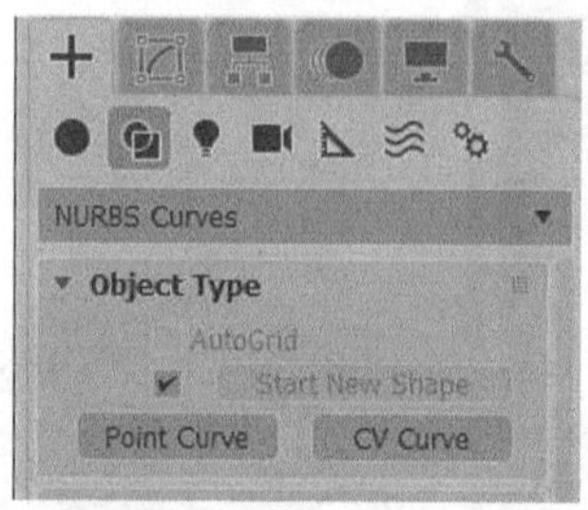

Figure 10-2 *The tools for creating NURBS curves*

Tip
While creating a point curve, if you want to remove the last point that you have created, press the BACKSPACE key.

Note

*The options in the **Rendering** and **Keyboard Entry** rollouts are the same as discussed in Chapter 5.*

Create Point Curve Rollout

The options in the **Interpolation** area of this rollout are the same as those discussed in Chapter 5. The **Draw In All Viewports** check box is selected by default in this rollout, as shown in Figure 10-3. It is used to display a 3D curve in all the viewports simultaneously. For example, you can start by creating the first point in the Top viewport, continue creating the additional points in the Left viewport, and finish the creation of the point curve in the Front viewport.

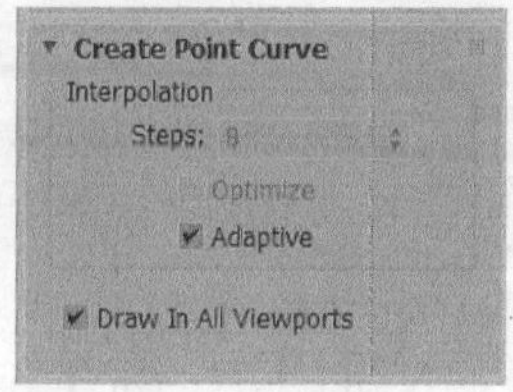

***Figure 10-3** The **Create Point Curve** rollout*

CV Curve

Menu bar:	Create > NURBS > CV Curve
Command Panel:	Create > Shapes > NURBS Curves > Object Type rollout > CV Curve

The CV curves are the NURBS curves that are controlled by the control vertices (CVs). The CVs are the points that lie outside the curve and control the shape of the CV curve. The CVs of a NURBS curve are connected with a lattice known as control lattice, which encloses the curve, refer to Figure 10-4. When you move the CVs in a CV curve, the control lattice gets changed, therefore, the shape of the CV curve also gets changed.

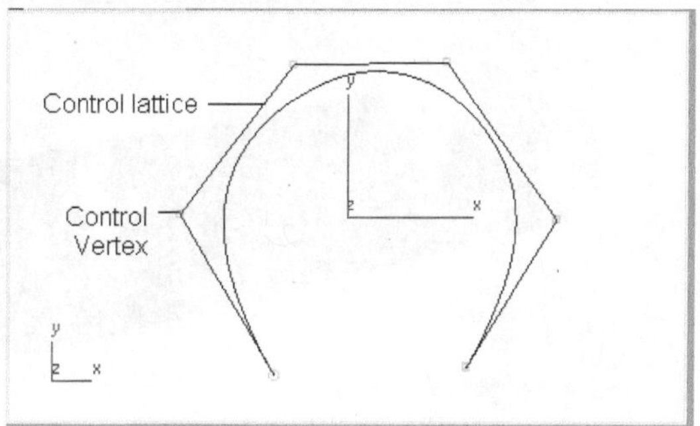

***Figure 10-4** A CV curve*

To create a CV curve, choose **Create > Shapes** in the **Command Panel**; a drop-down list will be displayed. Select the **NURBS Curves** option from this drop-down list and activate the viewport in which you want to create the CV curve. Now, choose the **CV Curve** tool from the **Object Type** rollout; the **Name and Color**, **Rendering**, **Keyboard Entry**, and **Create CV Curve** rollouts will be displayed. Next, click and drag the cursor in the viewport to create the first point and the first segment and then continue clicking in the viewport to add more points in the curve; a CV curve will be created, as shown in Figure 10-4. Next, right-click in the viewport to end the creation.

Note

*The rollouts that are displayed on invoking the **CV Curve** tool are the same as those discussed in the point curve.*

NURBS SURFACES

The NURBS surfaces are the base of the NURBS model. The NURBS models can be created by modifying the NURBS surfaces at an advanced level. In 3ds Max, there are two types of NURBS surfaces, point surface and CV surface. These surfaces are discussed next.

Point Surface

Menu bar:	Create > NURBS > Point Surface
Command Panel:	Create > Geometry > NURBS Surfaces > Object Type rollout > Point Surf

The point surfaces are the NURBS surfaces in which the points are constrained to lie on the surface, refer to Figure 10-5. To create a point surface, choose **Create > Geometry** in the **Command Panel**; a drop-down list will be displayed below the **Geometry** button. Select the **NURBS Surfaces** option from this drop-down list; the tools to create the NURBS surfaces will be displayed in the **Object Type** rollout, as shown in Figure 10-6. Activate the viewport in which you want to create the point surface. Now, choose the **Point Surf** tool from the **Object Type** rollout; the **Name and Color**, **Keyboard Entry**, and **Create Parameters** rollouts will be displayed. Next, press and hold the left mouse button on the upper left corner of the viewport and drag the cursor toward the lower right corner of the viewport to specify the length and width of the point surface. Release the left mouse button; a point surface will be created in the viewport, refer to Figure 10-5. The rollouts that are displayed on choosing the **Point Surf** tool are discussed next.

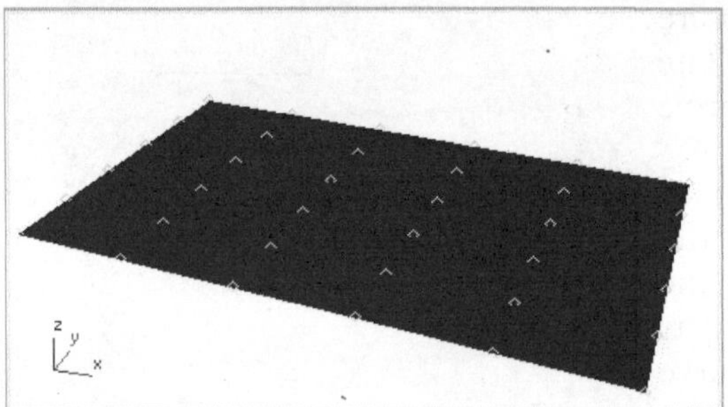

Figure 10-5 *A point surface*

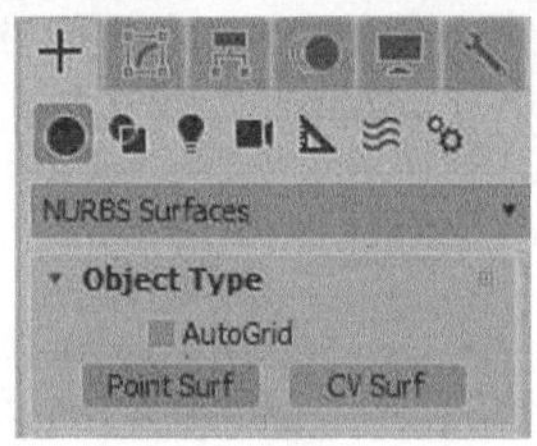

Figure 10-6 *The tools displayed to create NURBS surfaces*

Keyboard Entry Rollout

This rollout is used to create the point surface by entering the parameters using the keyboard. Set the values in the **Length** and **Width** spinners to specify the length and width of the point surface. Now, set the values in the **Length Points** and **Width Points** spinners to specify the number of points along the length and width of the point surface. Next, choose the **Create** button; a point surface will be created in the viewports.

Create Parameters Rollout

The parameters in this rollout are used to modify the dimensions of the point surface, refer to Figure 10-7. Set the values in the **Length** and **Width** spinners to specify the length and width of the point surface. Set the values in the **Length Points** and **Width Points** spinners to specify the points along the length and width of the point surface. You can modify the geometry of the point surface by moving the points on it, as shown in Figure 10-8. To do so, select the point surface in the viewport and choose the **Modify** tab in the **Command Panel**. In the modifier stack, click on the plus sign on the left side of the **NURBS Surface**; the **Surface** and **Point** sub-object levels will be displayed. Select the **Point** sub-object level and then select the points in the viewport to modify them.

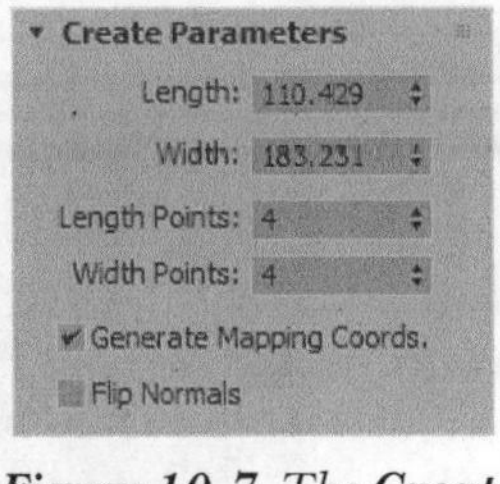

Figure 10-7 *The* ***Create Parameters*** *rollout*

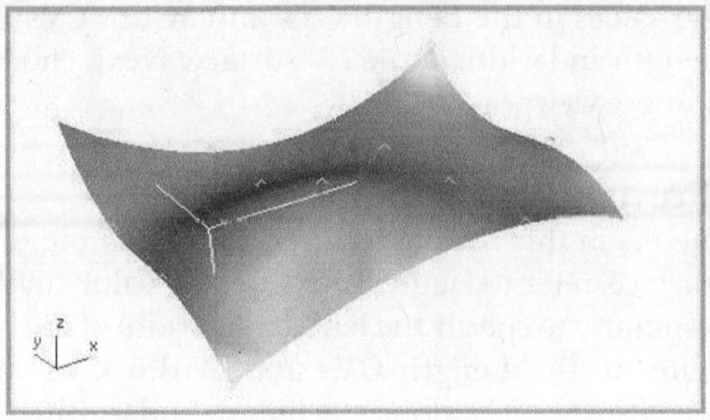

Figure 10-8 *The points in the point surface moved*

CV Surface

Menu bar:	Create > NURBS > CV Surface
Command Panel:	Create > Geometry > NURBS Surfaces > Object Type rollout > CV Surf

The CV surfaces are the NURBS surfaces that are controlled by control vertices (CVs). The CVs are the points that lie outside the surface and control the shape of the CV surface. The CVs of a NURBS surface are connected with a lattice known as control lattice that encloses the surface, refer to Figure 10-9. To create a CV surface, choose **Create > Geometry** in the **Command Panel**; a drop-down list will be displayed. Select the **NURBS Surfaces** option from the drop-down list; the tools to create NURBS surfaces will be displayed in the **Object Type** rollout. Activate the viewport in which you want to create the CV surface. Now, choose the **CV Surf** tool from the **Object Type** rollout; the **Name and Color**, **Keyboard Entry**, and **Create Parameters** rollouts will be displayed. Next, click on the upper left corner of the viewport and move the cursor toward the lower right corner of the viewport to specify the length and width of the CV surface. Click again on the screen; a CV surface will be created in the viewport, as shown in Figure 10-9. The rollouts that are displayed on invoking the **CV Surf** tool are discussed next.

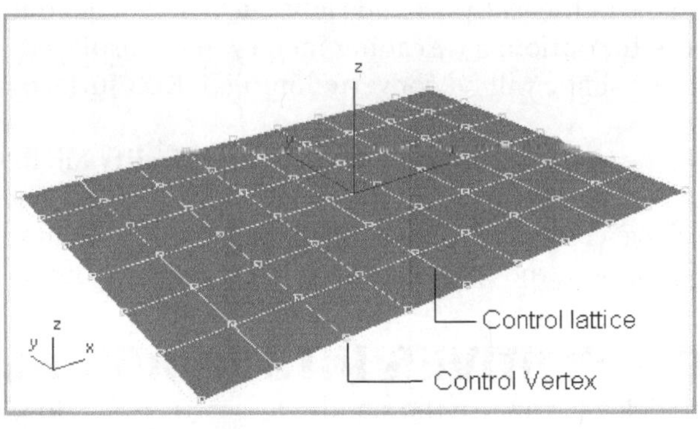

Figure 10-9 *A CV surface*

Keyboard Entry Rollout

You can also create a CV surface by entering the values in the spinners in this rollout. Set the values in the **Length** and **Width** spinners to specify the length and width of the CV surface.

Now, set the values in the **Length CVs** and **Width CVs** spinners to specify the control vertices along the length and width of the CV surface. Next, choose the **Create** button; a CV surface will be created in the viewports.

Create Parameters Rollout

The parameters in this rollout are used to modify the dimensions of the CV surface, refer to Figure 10-10. Set the values in the **Length** and **Width** spinners to specify the length and width of the CV surface. Set the values in the **Length CVs** and **Width CVs** spinners to specify the control vertices along the length and width, respectively of the CV surface. The **Automatic Reparam.** area has three radio buttons, namely **None**, **Chord length**, and **Uniform**. These radio buttons are used to edit parameters.

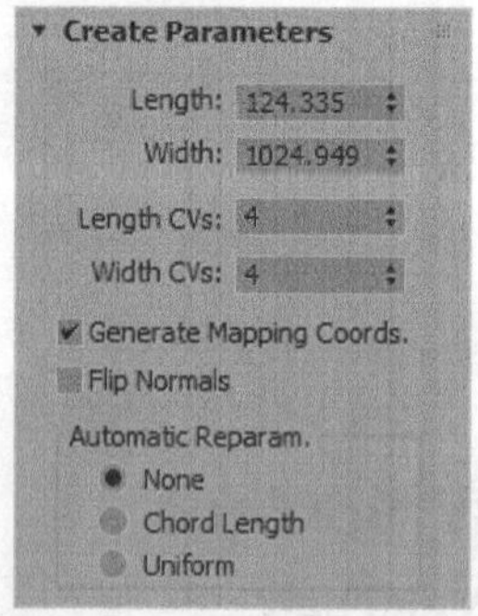

***Figure 10-10** The **Create Parameters** rollout*

> **Note**
> *If you deselect the NURBS surface objects in the viewport, then the **Create Parameters** rollout will not be displayed again. So, it is recommended to make all the changes before deselecting it.*

CONVERTING SPLINES AND EXTENDED SPLINES INTO NURBS SURFACES

To create a NURBS model, you can also use the splines or the extended splines shapes instead of using the point curve or the CV curve. To do so, you need to convert them into NURBS surfaces.

First, choose **Create > Shapes** in the **Command Panel**; a drop-down list will be displayed with the **Splines** option selected by default. Next, choose one of the tools in the **Object Type** rollout and create a spline shape in the viewport. Now, you can convert the spline shape into NURBS surfaces using one of the following methods:

1. Select the spline shape in the viewport and right-click on it; a quad menu will be displayed. Choose the **Convert To:** option; a cascading menu will be displayed. Now, choose **Convert to NURBS**; the spline shape will be converted into NURBS surface.

2. Select the spline shape in the viewport and choose the **Modify** tab in the **Command Panel**; the modifier stack will be displayed. In the modifier stack, right-click on the name of the tool by which you have created the spline shape; a shortcut menu will be displayed. Now, choose the **NURBS** option; the spline shape will be converted into a NURBS surface.

CONVERTING PRIMITIVES INTO NURBS SURFACES

To create a NURBS model, you can use the standard primitives. To do so, you need to convert them into NURBS surfaces. First, create an object that you want to convert into NURBS surface. Next, select it in the viewport and follow one of the methods that has been discussed for converting a spline into NURBS surfaces.

MODIFYING NURBS OBJECTS

You can modify a NURBS object using the options available in the Modify panel. To do so, select the NURBS object in the viewport and then choose the **Modify** tab in the **Command Panel**; various rollouts will be displayed in the Modify panel. The options in these rollouts are used to modify the NURBS objects. These rollouts are discussed next.

Note

1. Most of the rollouts are same for the NURBS curves and surfaces.

*2. The options in the **Rendering** rollout are same as discussed earlier.*

General Rollout

This rollout will be available for all NURBS objects. The buttons on the top in the **General** rollout are used to add more objects to the selected NURBS object. The **Display** area is used to define the way in which the NURBS object will be displayed in the viewports, refer to Figure 10-11.

The **Attach** button is used to add other objects to the selected NURBS object in the viewport. Once the objects in the viewport are added to the selected NURBS object, they will be converted into NURBS objects, and will become the sub-object of the NURBS object.

Also, the original parameters of the additional objects will be lost. Choose the **Attach Multiple** button to add more than one object to the selected NURBS object at the same time. The **Reorient** check box is used to orient the attached object to the NURBS object.

The **Import** and **Import Multiple** buttons are also used to perform the same function as the **Attach** and **Attach Multiple** buttons. The only difference is that while using the **Import** and **Import Multiple** buttons, the original parameters of the objects are not lost.

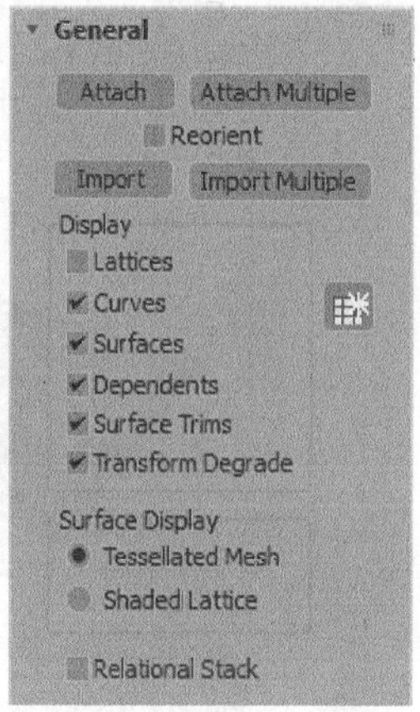

***Figure 10-11** The **General** rollout*

Display Area

The check boxes in the **Display** area are used to define the way in which the NURBS object will be displayed in the viewports. In the NURBS curves objects, the **Lattices**, **Curves**, and **Dependents** check boxes are displayed in the **Display** area. But in the NURBS surfaces objects, three additional check boxes are displayed. These are **Surfaces**, **Surface Trims**, and **Transform Degrade**. You need to select the required check box to make the corresponding option available in the viewport.

Surface Display Area

This area is available only for the NURBS surface objects. By default, the **Tessellated Mesh** radio button is selected in this area. As a result, the selected NURBS object will be displayed as iso lines, mesh, or as both isolines and mesh in the viewport depending on the settings made in the **Display Line Parameters** rollout, refer to Figures 10-12 and 10-13.

Select the **Shaded Lattice** radio button to display the NURBS surface object as shaded lattices in the shaded viewports, as shown in Figure 10-14.

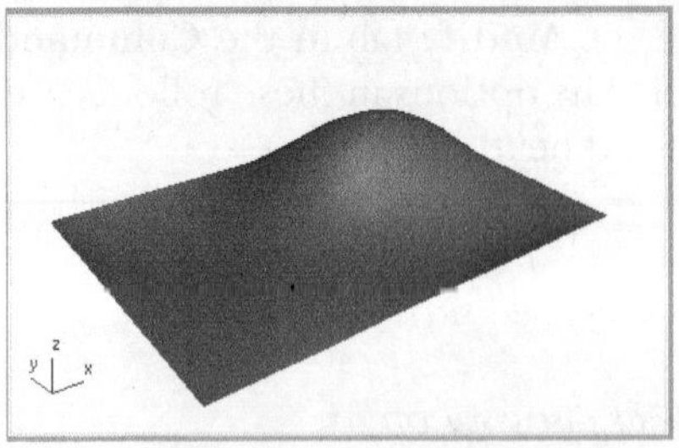

Figure 10-12 The NURBS surface object displayed as a mesh object

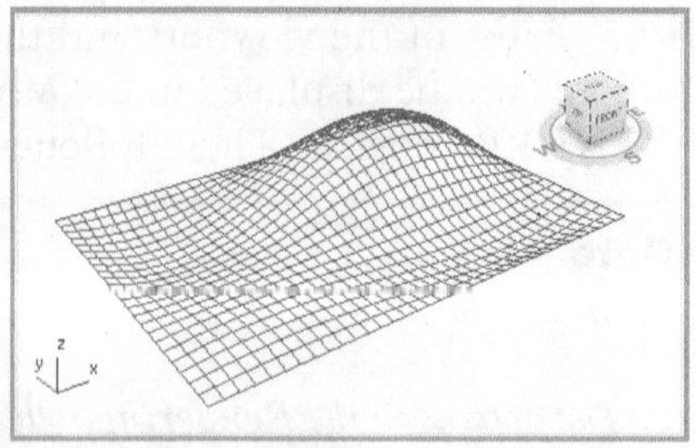

Figure 10-13 The NURBS surface object displayed as iso lines

NURBS Creation Toolbox

This button is displayed on the right side of the **Display** area. When you choose this button, the **NURBS** toolbox will be displayed, as shown in Figure 10-15. In this toolbox, buttons available in the **Create Points**, **Create Curves**, and **Create Surfaces** rollouts are available as icons. These buttons are discussed later in this chapter.

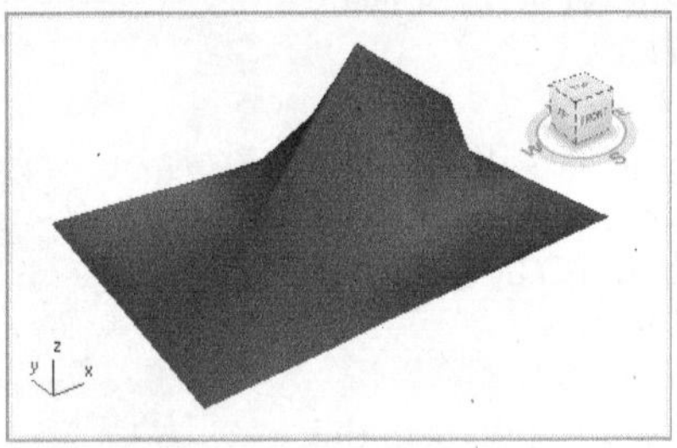

Figure 10-14 The NURBS surface object displayed as shaded lattices

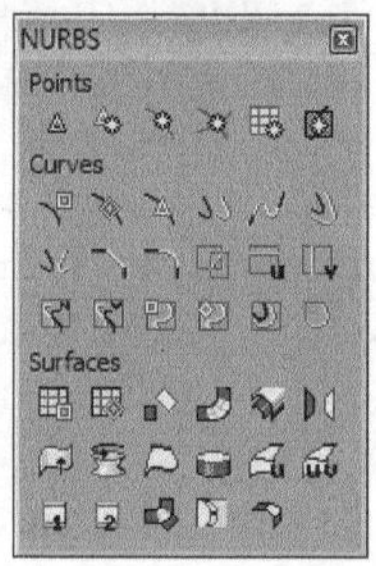

Figure 10-15 The ***NURBS*** *toolbox*

Display Line Parameters Rollout

This rollout is available only for the NURBS surface objects, refer to Figure 10-16. The values in the **U Lines** and **V Lines** spinners define the number of iso lines that are used to create the wireframe of the NURBS surface object in the viewport. Select the **Iso Only** radio button to display only the iso lines of the NURBS surface object in all viewports. The **Iso And Mesh** radio button is selected by default. It is used to display the iso lines of the NURBS object in those viewports that are set to display the wireframes. Also, the shaded viewports display the shaded surface of the NURBS object. Select the **Mesh Only** radio button to display the NURBS object as a wire mesh in those viewports that are set to display the wireframes. Also, the shaded viewports display the shaded surface of the NURBS object.

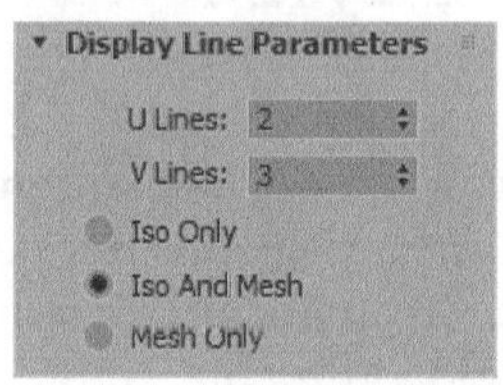

Figure 10-16 The ***Display Line Parameters*** *rollout*

Note

In the NURBS modeling, an iso line, similar to a contour line is known as a line of constant parameter value.

Tip

*To set the viewport to display the wireframes, click on the Shaded viewport label; a quad menu will be displayed. Now, choose the **Wireframe** option in it. Alternatively, you can press the F3 key.*

Before working with the other rollouts, you need to learn about the NURBS sub-objects. The buttons in the **Create Points**, **Create Curves**, and **Create Surfaces** rollouts are used to add the sub-objects to the NURBS curve and surface objects. These sub-objects can be dependent or independent. In other words, they can be child or parent sub-objects. For example, in the loft object shown in Figure 10-17, the surfaces are the dependent sub-objects as they are created from the curves. If you make any change in the curve, then the surface of the loft object will also be affected. But, the curves are the independent sub-objects because they are not created from any other object.

Create Points Rollout

The buttons in this rollout are used to add the point sub-objects to a NURBS object, refer to Figure 10-18. You can add the point sub-objects on the curve or surface as well as outside the curve or surface. These additional points help you to fit the curves or to trim the curves. To create different types of points, select the NURBS object in the viewport, choose the **Modify** tab, and then choose the corresponding button from the **Create Points** rollout. Alternatively, choose the **Nurbs Creation Toolbox** button from the **General** rollout; the **NURBS** toolbox will be displayed. The buttons in the **Create Points** rollout are discussed next.

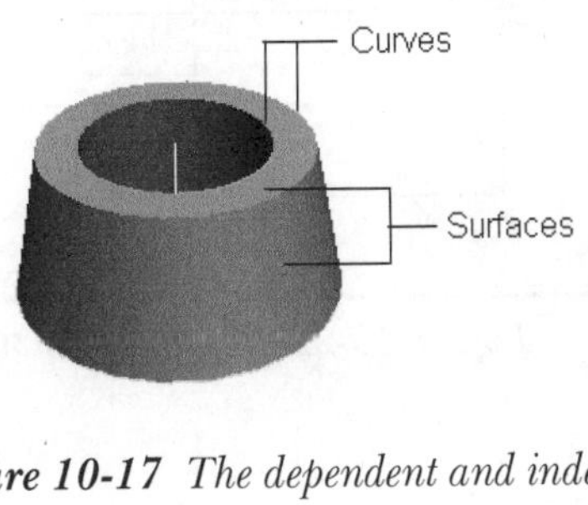

***Figure 10-17** The dependent and independent sub-objects in a loft object*

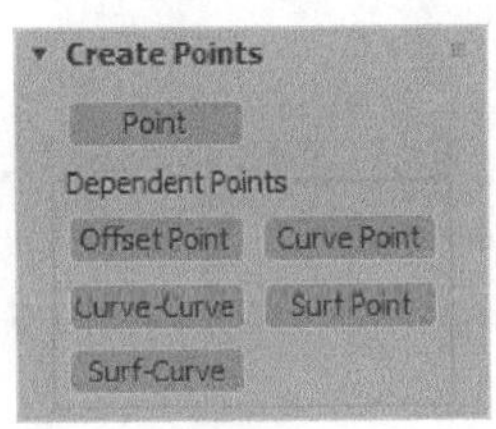

***Figure 10-18** The **Create Points** rollout*

Point

If you want to add an independent point, then select the NURBS object in the viewport. Next, choose the **Point** button in the **Create Points** rollout. Now, when you move the cursor in the viewport, the shape of cursor will change, as shown in Figure 10-19. Now, click in the viewport to create a point and continue clicking to add more points. Next, right-click to exit the command. These points will be displayed as triangles in the viewport, as shown in Figure 10-20.

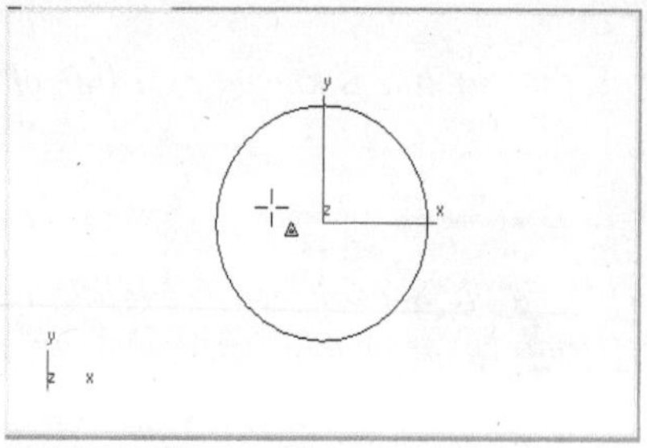

Figure 10-19 *The cursor displayed to create independent points*

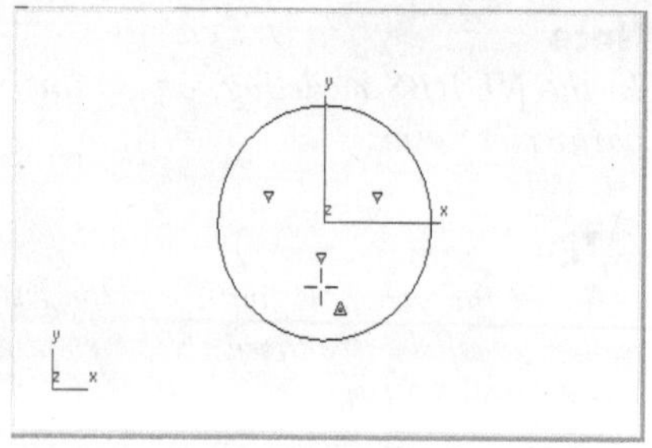

Figure 10-20 *The independent points created in the viewport*

Offset Point

An offset point is a dependent sub-object and lies at a specified distance from the parent point. To create an offset point, select the NURBS object in the viewport. Next, choose the **Offset Point** button in the **Dependent Points** area of the **Create Points** rollout; the **Offset Point** rollout will be displayed at the bottom in the Modify panel, as shown in Figure 10-21. Now, move the cursor over the existing point to be used as parent point in the viewport; the shape of cursor will change. Click on the existing point; a dependent offset point will be created as green asterisk in the viewport, as shown in Figure 10-22. Next, in the Modify panel, expand the **Offset Point** rollout and set the values in the **X, Y,** and **Z** spinners to offset the new point from the original position. As you set the values in these spinners, the distance between the offset point and its parent will be displayed as red line, as shown in Figure 10-23. If you do not want to change the position of the offset point, then select the **At Point** radio button in the **Offset Point** rollout.

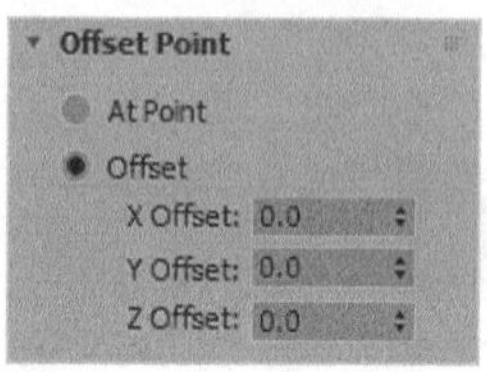

Figure 10-21 *The* ***Offset Point*** *rollout*

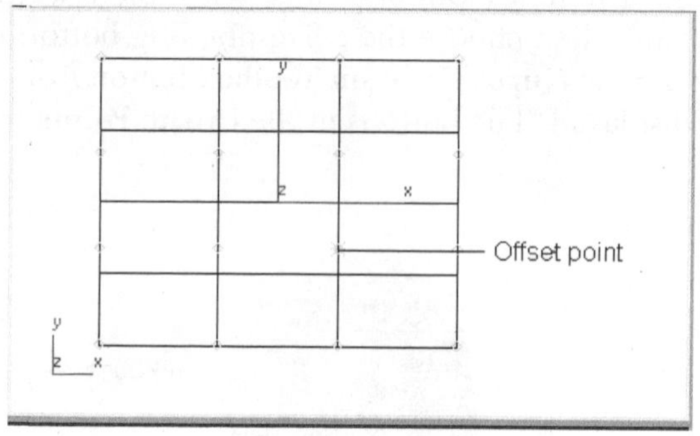

Figure 10-22 *The offset point displayed*

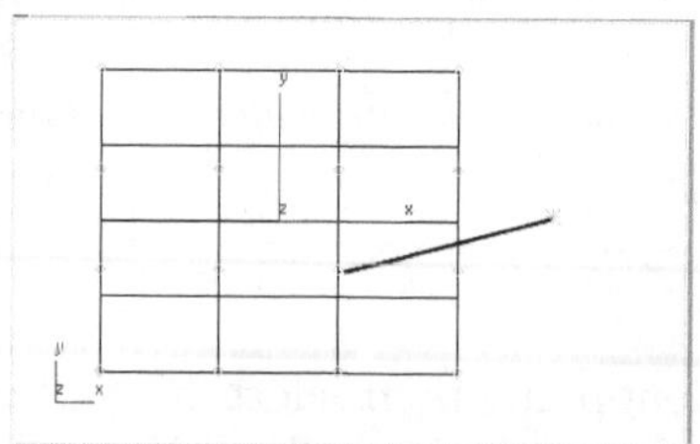

Figure 10-23 *The red line displayed between the parent point and the offset point*

Note

The independent point sub-objects will be displayed as black triangles in the viewports. And, the dependent point sub-objects will be displayed as green asterisks in the viewports.

Curve Point

A curve point is also a dependent sub-object and lies on a NURBS curve. To create a curve point, select the NURBS curve object in the viewport. Next, choose the **Curve Point** button in the **Dependent Points** area of the **Create Points** rollout; the **Curve Point** rollout will be displayed in the Modify panel, as shown in Figure 10-24. Now, move the cursor over the curve; the curve will turn blue. Also, a blue box along with the cursor will be displayed on the curve, as shown in Figure 10-25. Now, position the blue box on the curve at the location where you want to add a point and then click to add it. Next, you need to modify the parameters in the **Curve Point** rollout, which is discussed next.

Curve Point Rollout

Set the value in the **U Position** spinner to define the position of the point on the curve. The **On Curve** radio button is selected by default and is used to position the point on the curve. Select the **Offset** radio button to offset the points from the curve. Set the values in the **X**, **Y**, and **Z** spinners to define the location of the point in space.

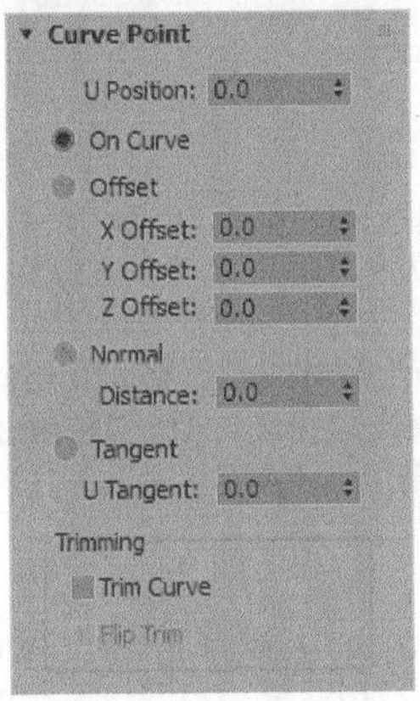

Figure 10-24 The ***Curve Point*** *rollout*

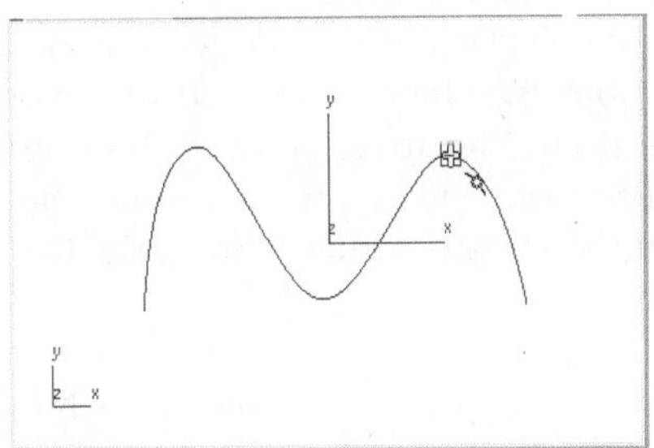

Figure 10-25 *A blue box displayed along with the cursor*

Select the **Normal** radio button to offset the point along the curve's normal at the U position. Set the value in the **Distance** spinner to specify the distance of the point from the curve's normal. Select the **Tangent** radio button to offset the point along the tangent at the U position. Set the value in the **U Tangent** spinner to specify the distance of the point from the curve along the tangent.

The options in the **Trimming** area are used to trim the curve. Select the **Trim Curve** check box to trim the curve according to the position of the curve point, refer to Figures 10-26 and 10-27. Select the **Flip Trim** check box to trim the curve in the opposite direction, refer to Figure 10-28.

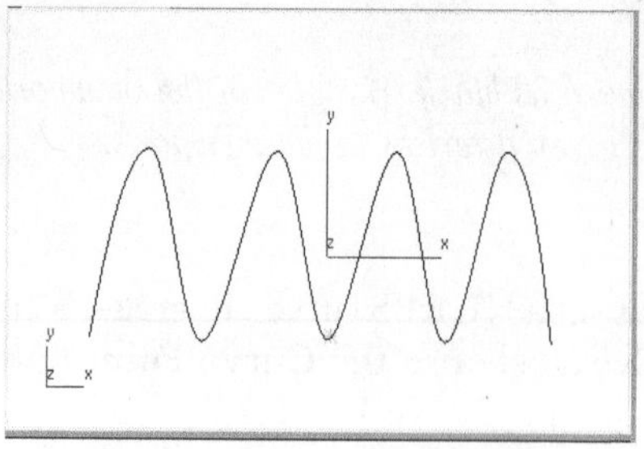

Figure 10-26 *A curve point placed on the curve*

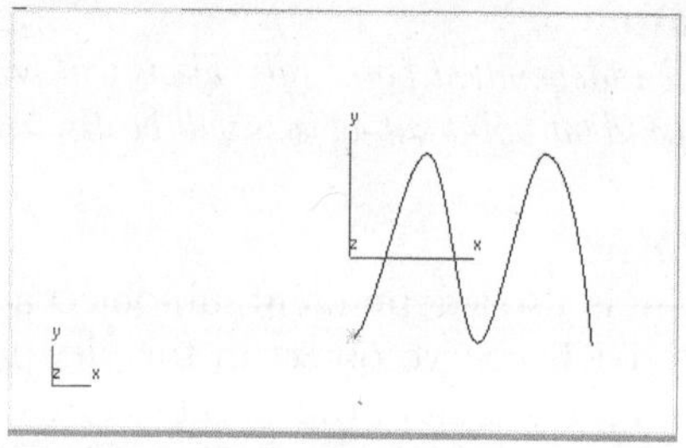

Figure 10-27 *The curve after selecting the* ***Trim Curve*** *check box*

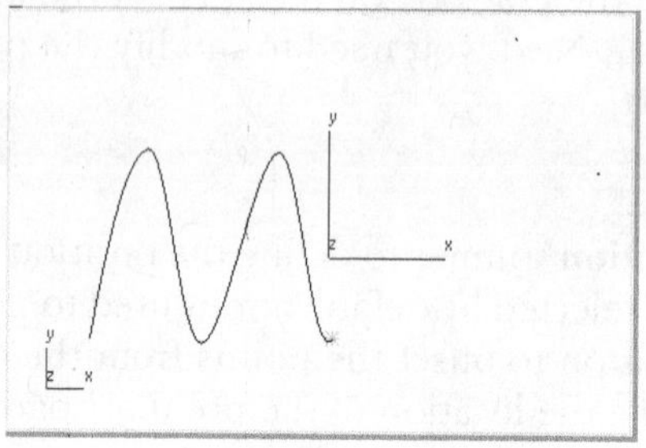

Figure 10-28 *The curve after selecting the* ***Flip Trim*** *check box*

Curve-Curve Point

The curve-curve point is a dependent point sub-object created at the intersection of two NURBS curve objects, refer to Figure 10-29. Note that to create a curve-curve point, the two NURBS curves should be attached to each other and there should be an intersection between the two NURBS curves. To create this point, choose the **Curve-Curve** button in the **Dependent Points** area of the **Create Points** rollout; the **Curve-Curve Intersection** rollout will be displayed in the Modify panel.

Now, move the cursor over one of the NURBS curves; a blue box will be displayed along with the cursor and click on it. Next, drag the cursor from first curve to the second curve and click on it; an intersection point will be created at the nearest intersection between the two curves, refer to Figure 10-29. You can modify the curve-curve point by specifying the parameters in this rollout.

Surf Point

A surface point is also a dependent sub-object and lies on a NURBS surface. To create a surface point, select the NURBS surface object in the viewport. Now, choose the **Surf Point** button in the **Dependent Points** area of the **Create Points** rollout; the **Surface Point** rollout will be displayed in the Modify panel. Now, move the cursor over the NURBS surface; a pair of intersecting blue lines will be displayed along with the cursor, as shown in Figure 10-30.

Click on the surface where you want to add a point and then modify its parameters in the **Surface Point** rollout in the Modify panel. Next, right-click to exit the command. The options in the **Surface Point** rollout are the same as those discussed earlier in the **Curve Point** rollout.

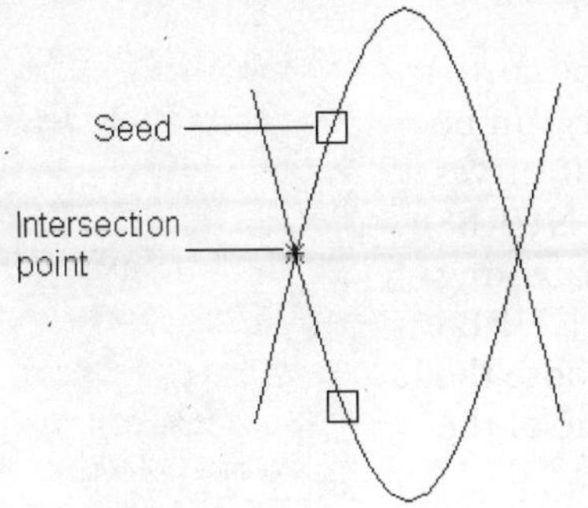

Figure 10-29 The intersection point created

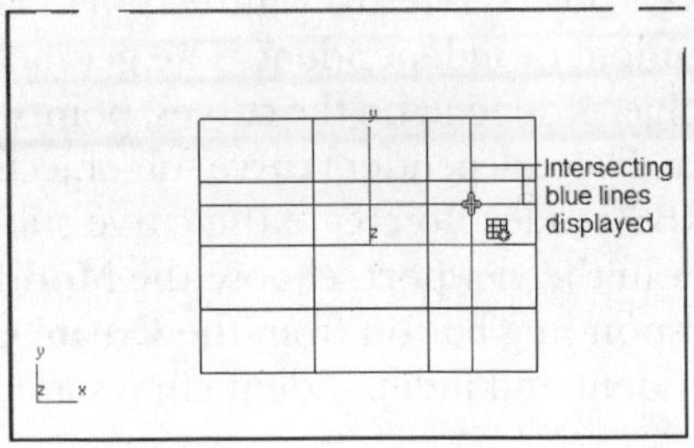

Figure 10-30 The blue lines displayed

Surf-Curve Point

The surface-curve point is a dependent point sub-object created at the intersection of a NURBS curve and a NURBS surface object, refer to Figure 10-31. Note that to create a surface-curve point, the NURBS curve and the NURBS surface should be attached to each other. To create this point, select the NURBS surface and then choose the **Surf-Curve** button in the **Dependent Points** area of the **Create Points** rollout; the **Surface-Curve Intersection Point** rollout will be displayed in the Modify panel. Now, move the cursor over the NURBS curve; a blue box will be displayed along with the cursor. Click on the curve to place the first seed. Next, move the cursor over the NURBS surface object and click on it to place the second seed; an intersection point will be created at the nearest intersection between the curve and the surface that is nearest to the seed point, refer to Figures 10-31, 10-32, and 10-33. You can modify the surface-curve point by specifying the parameters in the **Surface-Curve Intersection Point** rollout.

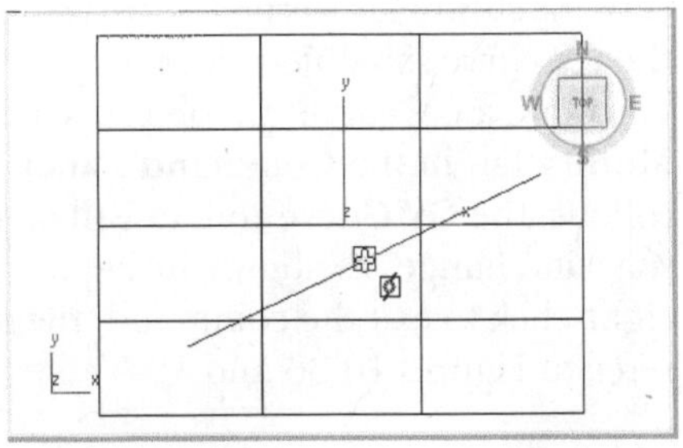

Figure 10-31 A seed created on the NURBS curve

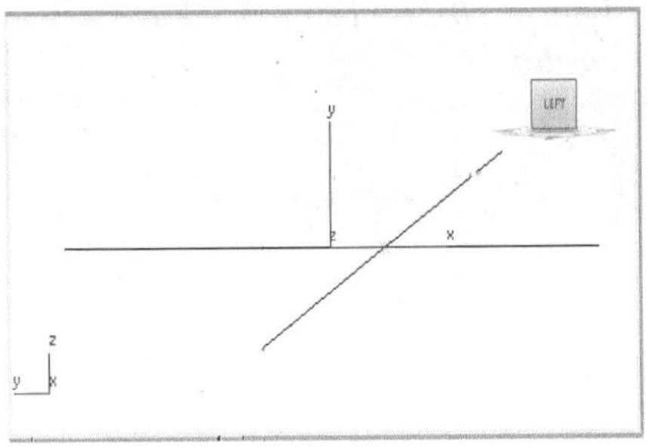

Figure 10-32 A surface curve intersection point created in the Left viewport

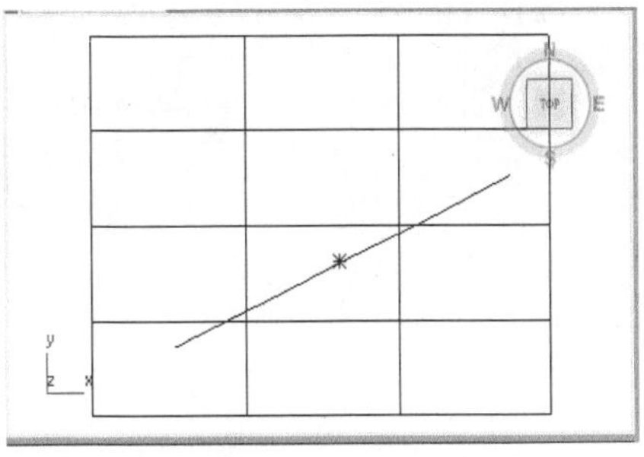

Figure 10-33 A surface curve intersection point created in the Top viewport

Note

The buttons (tools) in the ***Create Points*** *rollout are also available in the* ***NURBS*** *toolbox in the* ***General*** *rollout.*

Create Curves Rollout

The buttons in this rollout are used to add the curve sub-objects to a NURBS object, refer to Figure 10-34. The curve sub-objects can be dependent or independent. The geometry of the dependent curves sub-objects depend on the curves, points, and surfaces of the NURBS object. The independent curve sub-objects can be added to an existing NURBS model. To create the curve sub-objects, select the NURBS object in the viewport, choose the **Modify** tab, and then choose the corresponding button from the **Create Curves** rollout. Some of the dependent and independent curves are discussed next.

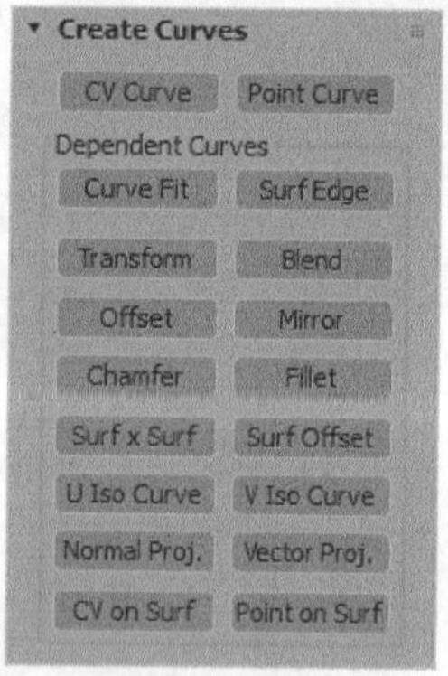

***Figure 10-34** The **Create Curves** rollout*

CV Curve

The CV curve sub-object is an independent curve sub-object. It is very much similar to the CV curve object. The only difference is that the CV curve sub-object does not provide the thickness on rendering. To create a CV curve sub-object, select the NURBS object in the viewport and then choose the **Modify** tab in the **Command Panel**. Now, choose the **CV Curve** button in the **Create Curves** rollout; the **CV Curve** rollout will be displayed in the Modify panel. Also, the shape of the cursor will change, as shown in Figure 10-35. Now, create a CV curve in the viewport and then right-click to exit the command; the new CV curve will be added to the existing NURBS object, refer to Figures 10-36 and 10-37.

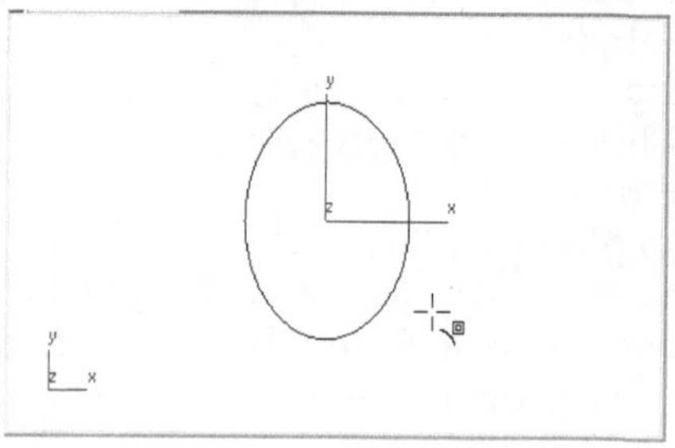

***Figure 10-35** The changed shape of the cursor*

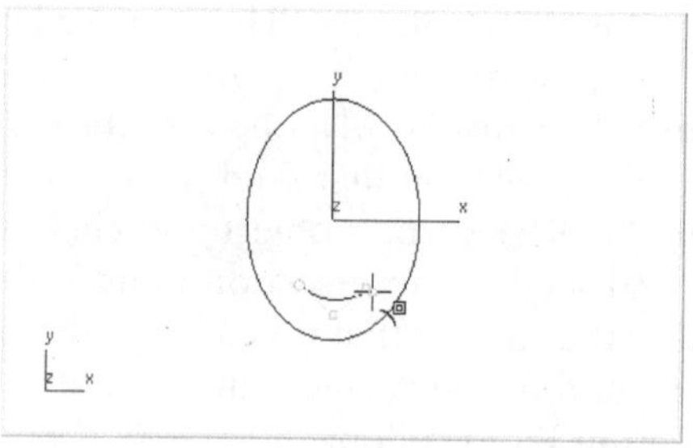

***Figure 10-36** The new CV curve created*

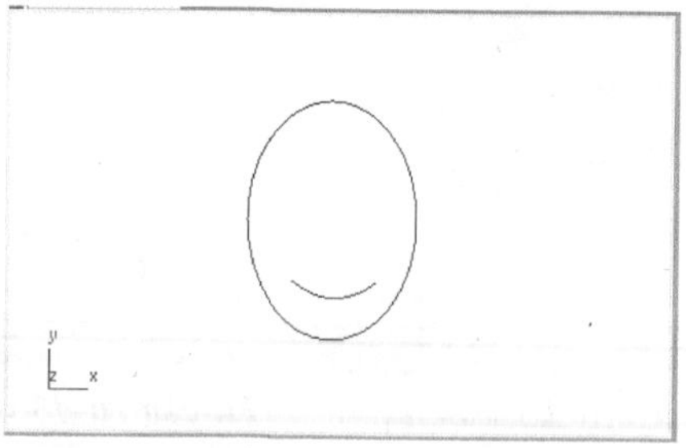

***Figure 10-37** The new CV curve attached to the NURBS object*

Point Curve

The point curve sub-object is also an independent curve sub-object and is very similar to the point curve object. The only difference is that the point curve sub-object does not provide the thickness on rendering. To create a point curve sub-object, select the NURBS object in the viewport. Now, choose the **Point Curve** button from the **Create Curves** rollout; the **Point Curve** rollout will be displayed in the Modify panel. Now, create a point curve in the viewport and right-click to exit the command; the new point curve will be added to the existing NURBS object.

Curve Fit

The fit curve is a dependent curve sub-object and is created between the existing points in a NURBS object. A fit curve can be created using any type of points such as curve points, surface points, independent points, and so on. To create a fit curve, select the NURBS object in the viewport and choose the **Modify** tab in the **Command Panel**. Next, choose the **Curve Fit** button in the **Dependent Points** area of the **Create Curves** rollout; the cursor will get changed. Also, the **Point Curve** rollout will be displayed in the Modify panel. Notice that there are no parameters in this rollout. Next, move the cursor over a point in the viewport and click to create the starting point of the curve fit. Now, drag the cursor to another point and click on it to continue the creation of the curve fit, refer to Figures 10-38 and 10-39. Next, right-click to exit the command.

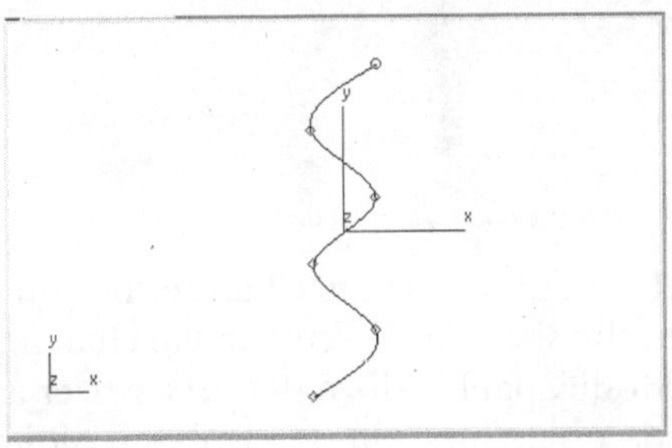

Figure 10-38 *A NURBS curve object*

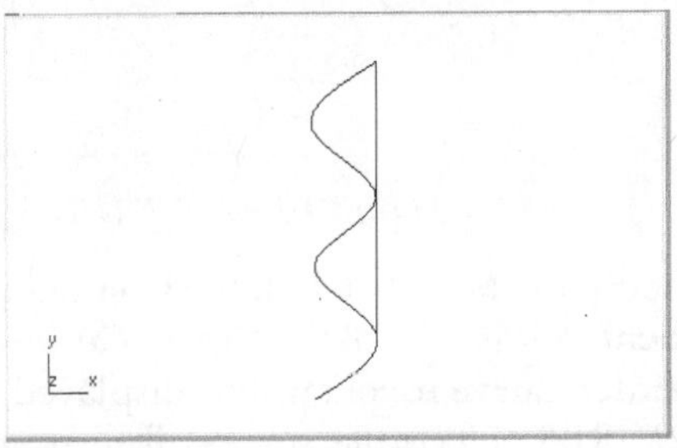

Figure 10-39 *A fit curve created between the points in a NURBS curve object*

Transform

The transform curve is a dependent curve sub-object. It is a duplicate of the original curve and can be modified to a different position, rotation, or scale. To create a transform curve, select the NURBS curve in the viewport and choose the **Modify** tab in the **Command Panel**. Next, choose the **Transform** button in the **Dependent Points** area of the **Create Curves** rollout; the cursor will get changed. Then, move the cursor over the NURBS curve; it will turn blue. Now, press and hold the left mouse button on the curve, drag the cursor to create the duplicate of the selected curve, and then release the left mouse button; a transform curve will be created, refer to Figures 10-40 and 10-41.

To rotate or scale the duplicate curve, select the **Curve** sub-object level in the modifier stack, and then select the duplicate curve in the viewport. Next, rotate or scale the duplicate curve without affecting the original curve.

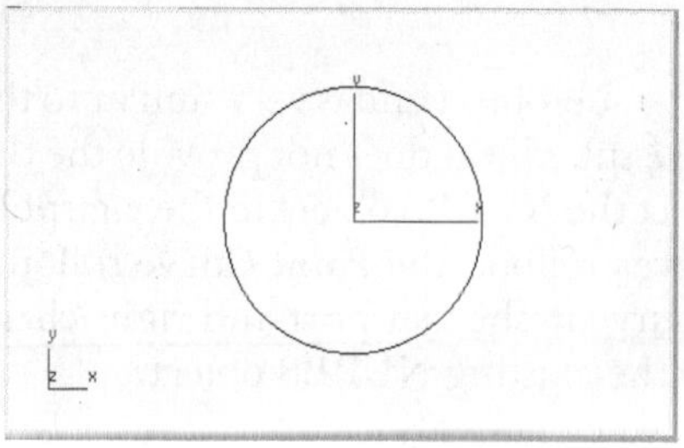

Figure 10-40 A NURBS curve object

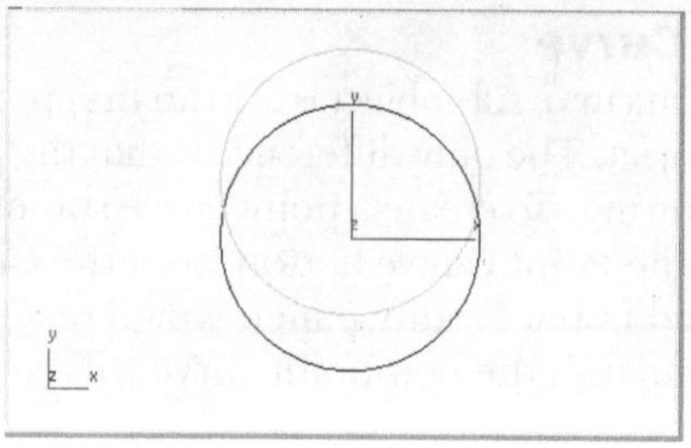

Figure 10-41 A transform curve created

Chamfer

The chamfer curve is a dependent curve sub-object. It is a straight line between two intersecting parent curve sub-objects. To create a chamfer curve, select the NURBS object that has the intersecting and attached curve sub-objects, as shown in Figure 10-42.

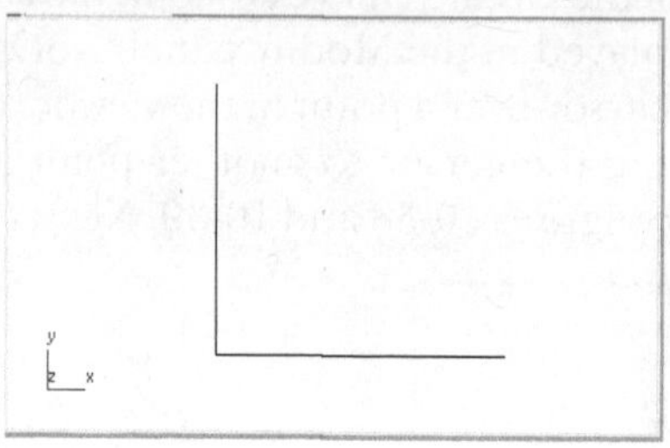

Figure 10-42 A NURBS curve to create a chamfer curve

Now, choose the **Modify** tab in the **Command Panel**. Then, choose the **Chamfer** button in the **Dependent Points** area of the **Create Curves** rollout; the shape of the cursor will change. Also, the **Chamfer Curve** rollout will be displayed in the Modify panel. Move the cursor over a curve in the NURBS object; the curve will turn blue. Also, a blue box will be displayed along with the cursor. Click on the curve to place the first seed to define the intersection to be chamfered. Then, move the cursor over another curve in the NURBS object and click to place another seed; a chamfer curve will be created, refer to Figures 10-43 and 10-44. You can modify the chamfer curve using the parameters in the **Chamfer Curve** rollout in the Modify panel and then right-click to exit the command.

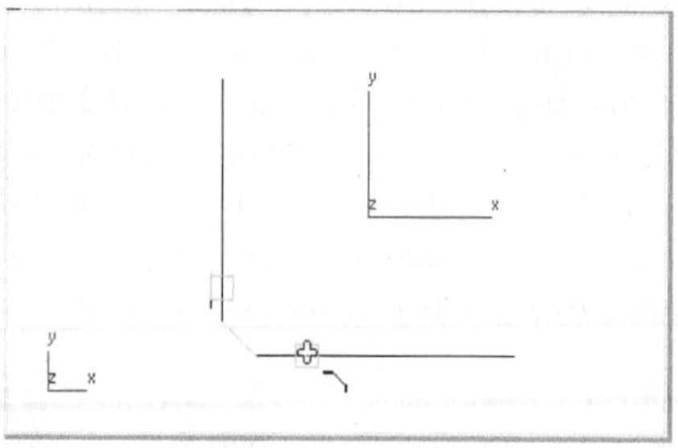

Figure 10-43 The seeds placed on the curves

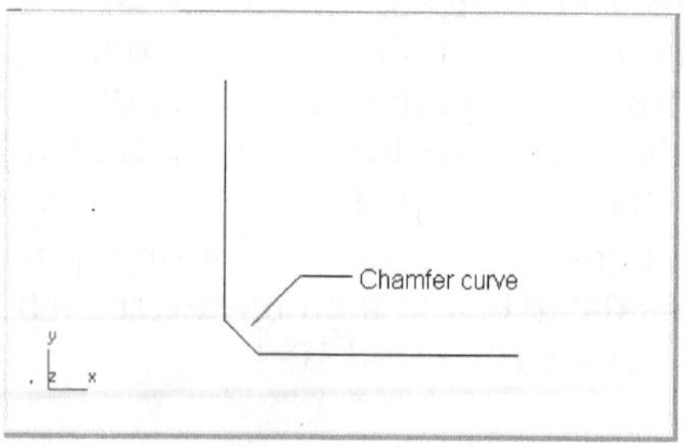

Figure 10-44 A chamfer curve created

Note

While creating a chamfer curve, one or both the curves of the NURBS object get trimmed. To avoid the trimming of the curves, you can modify their parameters in the ***Chamfer Curve*** *rollout.*

Surf Edge

The surf edge curve is also a dependent curve and it lies on the boundary of the surface. The edge can be an outside edge or a trim edge. To create a surf edge curve, select the NURBS surface. Next, choose the **Modify** tab in the **Command Panel**. Choose the **Surf Edge** button in the **Dependent Points** area of the **Create Curves** rollout; the cursor will change. Also, the **Surface Edge Curve** rollout will be displayed in the Modify panel. Move the cursor over an edge in the NURBS object; the edge will be highlighted. Now, click on the edge; the surface edge will be created. Also, a seed will be displayed on the edge, as shown in Figure 10-45.

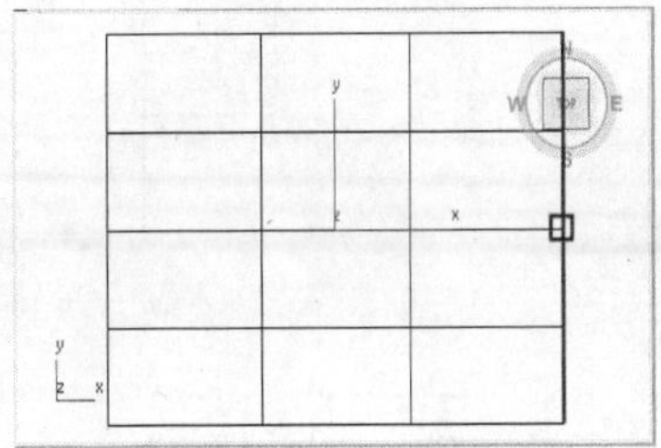

***Figure 10-45** A surface edge curve created*

Note

*The buttons (tools) in the **Create Curves** rollout are also available in the **NURBS** toolbox in the **General** rollout.*

Create Surfaces Rollout

The buttons in the **Create Surfaces** rollout are used to add surface sub-objects to a NURBS object, as shown in Figure 10-46. The surface sub-objects can be dependent or independent. The geometry of the dependent surface sub-object depends on the curves and surfaces of another NURBS object. To create the surface sub-objects, select the NURBS object in the viewport, choose the **Modify** tab in the **Command Panel**, and then choose the corresponding button from the **Create Surfaces** rollout. Some of the dependent and independent surfaces are discussed next.

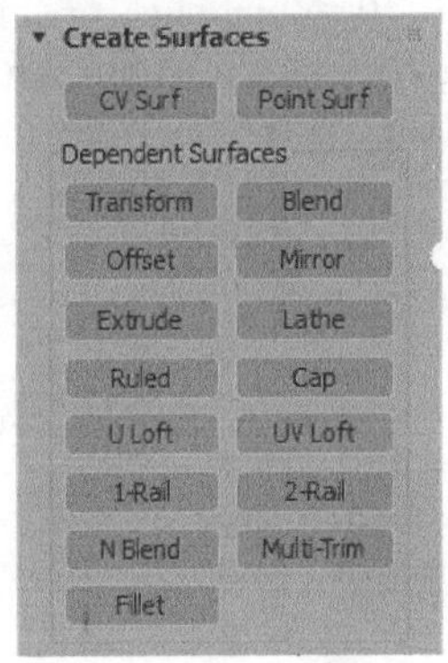

***Figure 10-46** The **Create Surfaces** rollout*

Note

*The CV surface and point surface sub-objects are independent sub-objects. They can be added to the existing NURBS object using the **CV Surf** and **Point Surf** buttons in the **Create Surfaces** rollout.*

Blend

A blend surface is a dependent surface sub-object that is used to connect two surfaces, two curves, or a curve to a surface. To create a blend surface, select the NURBS object in the viewport that contains two or more attached curves or surface sub-objects. Next, choose the **Modify** tab in the **Command Panel** and then choose the **Blend** button in the **Dependent Points** area of the **Create Surfaces** rollout; the **Blend Surface** rollout will be displayed. Next, move the cursor over the edge that you want to connect; the edge will turn blue. Click on the edge and move the cursor over the edge of another NURBS object, as shown in Figure 10-47. Now, click on the edge of another NURBS object; a blend surface will be created between the two NURBS objects, as shown in Figure 10-48. You can modify the blend surface using the parameters in the **Blend Surface** rollout in the Modify panel. Next, right-click to exit the command.

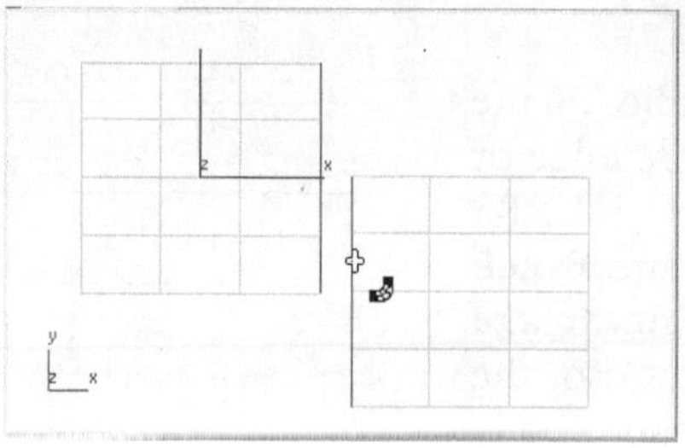

Figure 10-47 *The cursor placed over another edge*

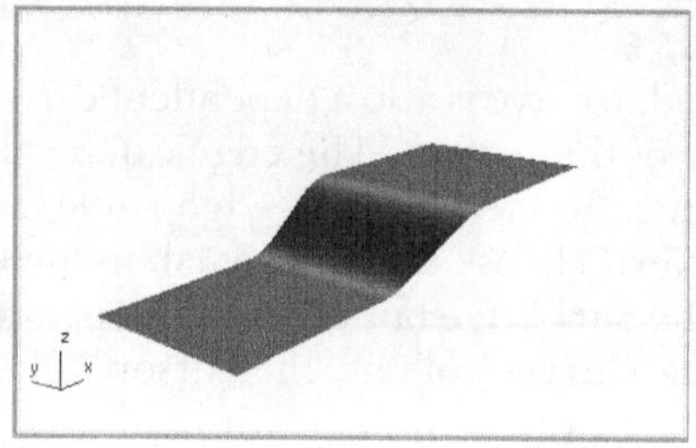

Figure 10-48 *A blend surface created*

Ruled

A ruled surface is a dependent sub-object. It can be created between two curve sub-objects. To create a ruled surface, select the NURBS object in the viewport that contains two or more curves. Next, choose the **Modify** tab in the **Command Panel** and then choose the **Ruled** button in the **Dependent Points** area of the **Create Surfaces** rollout; the **Ruled Surf** rollout will be displayed. Next, move the cursor over the curve that you want to use to create the ruled surface; the curve will turn blue. Now, click on the curve and move the cursor over another curve, refer to Figure 10-49. Now, click on another curve; a ruled surface will be created between the two NURBS curves, as shown in Figure 10-50. You can modify the ruled surface using the parameters in the **Ruled Surf** rollout in the Modify panel. Then, right-click to exit the command.

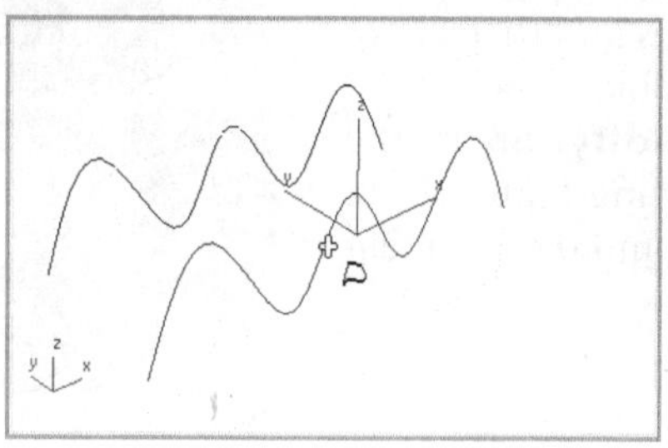

Figure 10-49 *The cursor displayed to create the ruled surface*

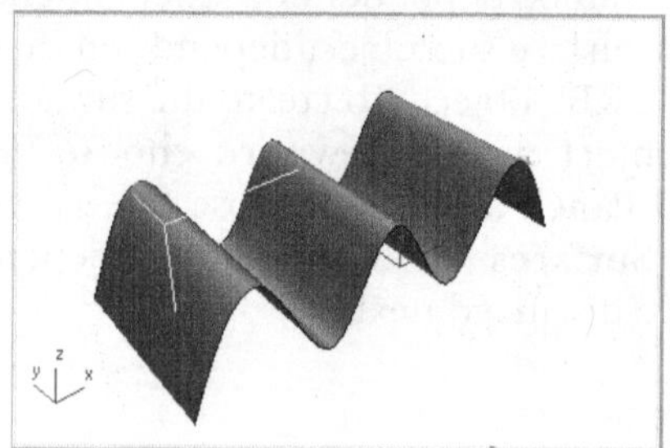

Figure 10-50 *A ruled surface created*

U Loft

A U loft surface is a dependent surface sub-object and it is created across multiple curve sub-objects. To get the best effect, the curves that are to be used for U lofting should have same number of CVs. To create a U loft surface, select one of the NURBS curves in the viewport. Choose the **Modify** tab in the **Command Panel** and then choose the **U Loft** button in the **Dependent Points** area of the **Create Surfaces** rollout; the **U Loft Surface** rollout will be displayed. Next, move the cursor over the first curve that you want to use for creating the U loft surface; it will turn blue. Now, click on it and then click on all curves one-by-one to add them into the U loft surface. When you click on the curves, their names will be displayed in the **U Curves** area of the **U Loft Surface** rollout. Also, while adding the curves to the U loft surface, green colored iso lines of the U loft surface will be displayed in the viewport, as shown in Figure 10-51. Next, right-click to end the command; a U loft surface will be created, as shown in Figure 10-52. Now, you can modify the U loft surface using the parameters in the **U Loft Surface** rollout. Next, right-click to exit the U loft command.

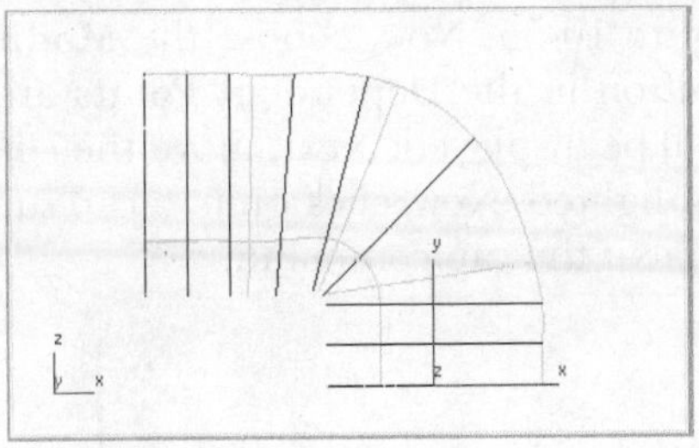

Figure 10-51 *The green iso lines of the U loft surface displayed*

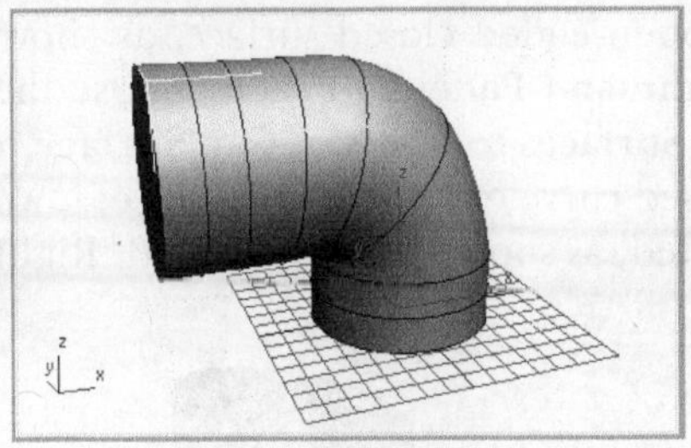

Figure 10-52 *A U loft surface created*

1-Rail

The 1-rail sweep surface is a dependent sub-object. To create a 1-rail sweep surface, minimum two curves are required in the viewport. One curve is used to define the cross-section of the surface and another curve is used to define the edge of the surface, which is known as rail. Before creating a sweep surface, you need to make sure that the cross-section curve is intersecting the rail curve. If two cross section curves are used, the first cross-section curve should intersect the starting point of the rail and the last cross-section curve should intersect at the end point of the rail. Also, the curves that you are using to create the cross-section of the surface should have the same direction.

Create the rail and cross-section curves, as shown in Figure 10-53. Select the rail curve and choose the **Modify** tab in the **Command Panel**.Next, choose the **1-Rail** button in the **Dependent Points** area of the **Create Surfaces** rollout; the **1-Rail Sweep Surface** rollout will be displayed. Next, move the cursor over the rail curve; the rail curve will turn blue. Click on it; the name of the rail curve will be displayed in the **Rail Curve** text box of the **1-Rail Sweep Surface** rollout. Select the cross-section curve. When you click on the cross-section curve, its name will be displayed in the **Section Curves** area of the **1-Rail Sweep Surface** rollout. Next, right-click to end the command; a 1-rail surface will be created, as shown in Figure 10-54. You can modify the 1-rail surface using the parameters in the **1-Rail Sweep Surface** rollout. Now, right-click to exit the 1-rail command.

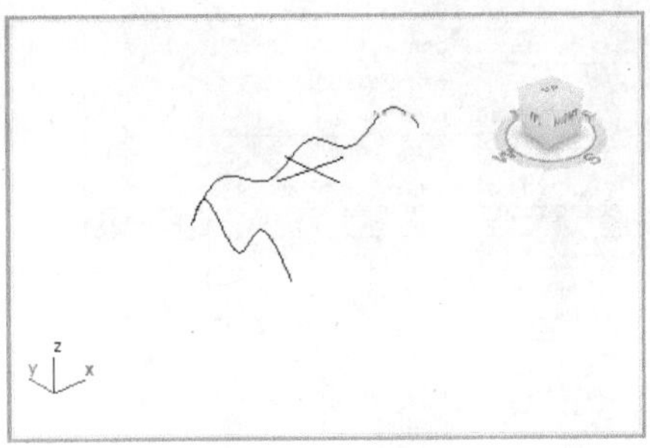

Figure 10-53 *The curves to create 1-rail surface*

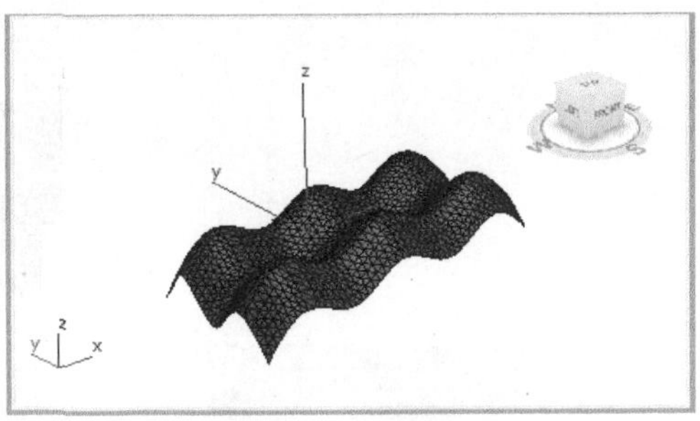

Figure 10-54 *The 1-rail surface created*

Cap

The cap surface is a dependent sub-object and is created to cap a closed curve or an edge of a closed surface. To create a cap surface, select the NURBS object that has either a closed curve or an open-ended closed surface, as shown in Figure 10-55. Now, choose the **Modify** tab in the **Command Panel** and then choose the **Cap** button in the **Dependent Points** area of the **Create Surfaces** rollout; the **Cap Surface** rollout will be displayed. Next, move the cursor over the closed curve or the closed surface; it will be highlighted. Now, click on it; a cap surface will be created, as shown in Figure 10-56. Right-click to exit the cap command.

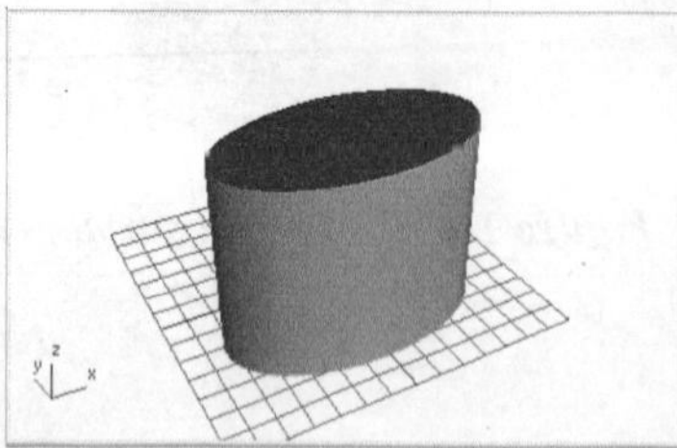

Figure 10-55 *An open ended closed surface*

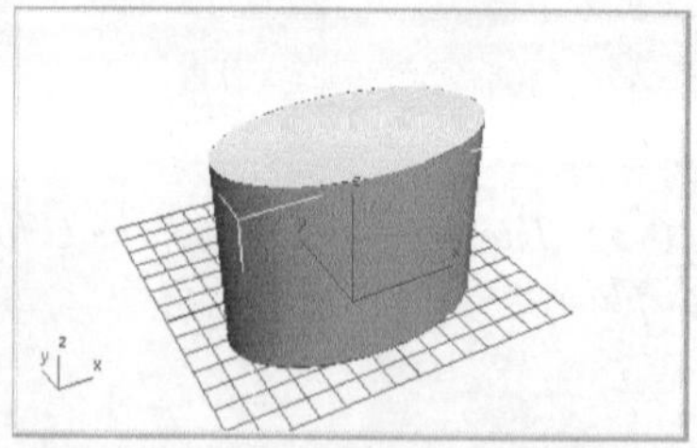

Figure 10-56 *A cap created to cap the open end of the closed surface*

EDITING NURBS SUB-OBJECTS

After creating a NURBS model or an object, you can edit it at the sub-object level. To do so, select the NURBS object in the viewport and choose the **Modify** tab in the **Command Panel**; the rollouts will be displayed in the Modify panel to modify the NURBS object. You have already learned about modifying NURBS objects in the previous section. Now, to modify the NURBS object at the sub-object level, select the sub-object levels in the modifier stack. First, click on the arrow sign on the left side of **NURBS Surface** to display all the sub-object levels in the selected NURBS object, refer to Figure 10-57. Now, select a sub-object level in the modifier stack; it will turn yellow and gets activated. Also, various rollouts related to the selected sub-object level will be displayed below the modifier stack. Alternatively, right-click in the viewport; a quad menu will be displayed, as shown in Figure 10-58.

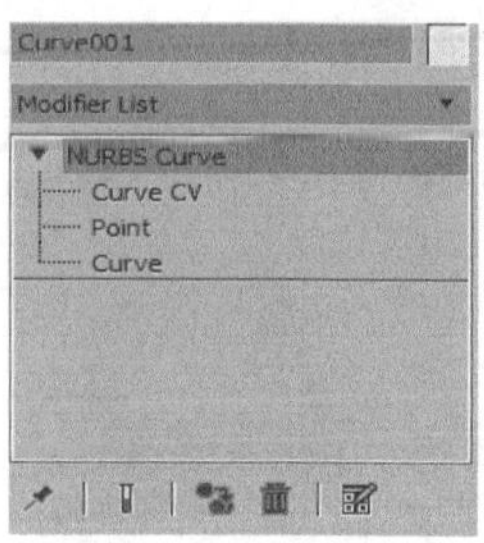

Figure 10-57 *The sub-object levels displayed in the modifier stack*

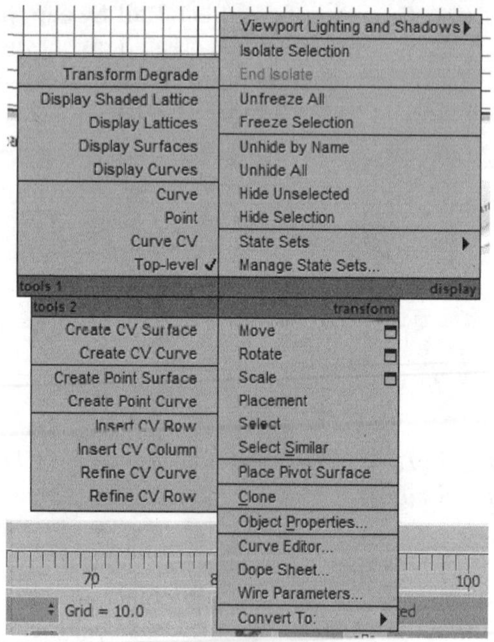

Figure 10-58 *The quad menu displayed*

Now, choose the sub-object level that you want to modify; it will also be activated in the modifier stack. Select the sub-object in the viewport and then modify it using the transforms or the rollouts displayed in the Modify panel.

TUTORIALS

Before starting the tutorials, you need to download the *c10_3dsmax_2017_tut.zip* file from *www.cadcim.com*. The path of the file is as follows: *Textbooks > Animation and Visual Effects > 3ds Max > Autodesk 3ds Max 2017: A Comprehensive Guide*

Extract the contents of the zipped file and save them in the *Documents* folder.

Tutorial 1

In this tutorial, you will create a washbasin, as shown in Figure 10-59, using the NURBS tools.

(Expected time: 60 min)

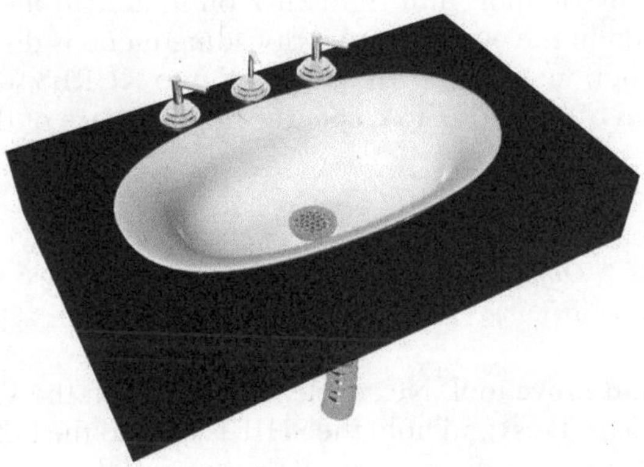

Figure 10-59 *The model of a washbasin*

The following steps are required to complete this tutorial:

a. Create the project folder.
b. Create the profile curve for washbasin.
c. Create the washbasin surface.
d. Create sieve and duct.
e. Create the slab.
f. Create washbasin taps.
g. Assign NVIDIA mental ray renderer and materials.
h. Save and render the scene.

Creating the Project Folder

Create a new project folder with the name *c10_tut1* at *\Documents\3dsmax2017* and then save the file with the name *c10tut1*, as discussed in Tutorial 1 of Chapter 2.

Creating the Profile Curve for Washbasin

In this section, you will create the profile curve for washbasin using the **Ellipse** tool.

1. Activate the Top viewport. Next, choose **Create > Shapes** in the **Command Panel** and then choose the **Ellipse** tool from the **Object Type** rollout.

2. Expand the **Keyboard Entry** rollout and set the parameters as follows:

   Length: **111.739** Width: **202.96**

   Choose the **Create** button; an ellipse is created with the name *Ellipse001*.

3. Choose the **Zoom Extents All** tool.

   Next, you need to convert *Ellipse001* to NURBS surface.

4. Select *Ellipse001* in any viewport and right-click on it; a quad menu is displayed. Choose the **Convert To** option in the quad menu; a cascading menu is displayed. Now, choose the **Convert to NURBS** option; *Ellipse001* is converted into NURBS surface. Next, you need to create multiple copies of *Ellipse001* to create the outer surface of the washbasin.

> **Tip**
> *You can also create an elliptical curve using the* ***CV Curve*** *tool from* ***Create > Shapes > NURBS Curves > Object Type*** *rollout in the* ***Command Panel****. In this case, you need not convert curve to NURBS curve.*

5. Choose the **Select and Move** tool. Next, select *Ellipse001* in the Front viewport and move the cursor over its Y axis. Press and hold the SHIFT key and the left mouse button and then move *Ellipse001* to the upward direction until the value of the **Y** spinner in the coordinates display becomes about 16. Now, release the left mouse button and the SHIFT key; the **Clone Options** dialog box is displayed. Set the value **3** in the **Number of Copies** spinner and choose the **OK** button; *Ellipse001, Ellipse002, Ellipse003*, and *Ellipse004* are displayed in viewports, as shown in Figure 10-60.

   Next, you need to create the ellipses for the inner surface of the washbasin.

6. Make sure *Ellipse004* (top ellipse) is selected in the Front viewport. Now, move the cursor over the vertical axis of *Ellipse004*. Press and hold the SHIFT key and the left mouse button and then move *Ellipse004* in the downward direction until the value in the **Y** spinner in the coordinates display becomes about -8. Now, release the left mouse button and the SHIFT key; the **Clone Options** dialog box is displayed. Make sure the value **1** is displayed in the **Number of Copies** spinner and choose the **OK** button; *Ellipse005* is displayed in viewports.

7. Modify the color of *Ellipse005* in such a way that you can differentiate between the curves for the inner and the outer surfaces.

8. Make sure *Ellipse005* is selected in the Front viewport and move the cursor over its vertical axis. Press and hold the SHIFT key and the left mouse button, and move *Ellipse005* in the downward direction until the value in the **Y** spinner in the coordinates display becomes about

-16. Now, release the left mouse button and the SHIFT key; the **Clone Options** dialog box is displayed. Set the value **3** in the **Number of Copies** spinner and choose the **OK** button; *Ellipse006, Ellipse007*, and *Ellipse008* are created in all viewports. Now, there are total eight NURBS curves in the viewports.

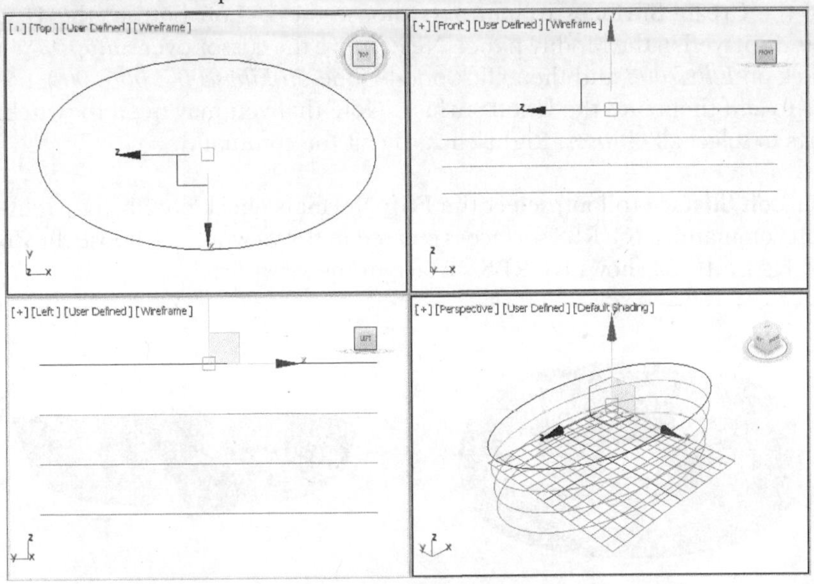

Figure 10-60 All ellipses displayed in viewports

Next, you need to scale ellipses in the Front viewport.

9. Choose the **Select and Uniform Scale** tool from the **Main Toolbar** and scale the NURBS curves uniformly in the Front viewport, as shown in Figure 10-61.

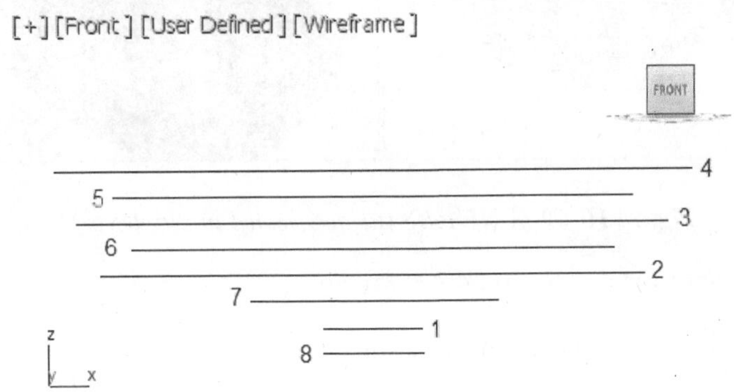

Figure 10-61 All NURBS curves scaled in the Front viewport

Creating the Washbasin Surface

In this section, you will create a surface between the NURBS curves to give it the desired shape by using the **U Loft** button.

1. Select *Ellipse008* in the Front viewport and choose the **Modify** tab, if it is not already chosen. The **NURBS Surface** is displayed in the modifier stack and all rollouts required to modify the NURBS object are displayed below the modifier stack.

2. Expand the **Create Surfaces** rollout and choose the **U Loft** button; the **U Loft Surface** rollout is displayed in the Modify panel. Next, move the cursor over *Ellipse008*; it turns blue. Now, click on *Ellipse008* and then click one-by-one on *Ellipse007, 006, 005, 004, 003, 002,* and *001* to add them into the U loft surface. Note that you may need to switch to different viewports to select all ellipses. Right-click to exit the command.

3. In the **U Loft Surface** rollout, select the **Flip Normals** check box. Next, right-click to exit the U loft command; a NURBS surface is created in the viewports. Choose the **Zoom Extents All** tool. Figure 10-62 shows NURBS surface in the viewports.

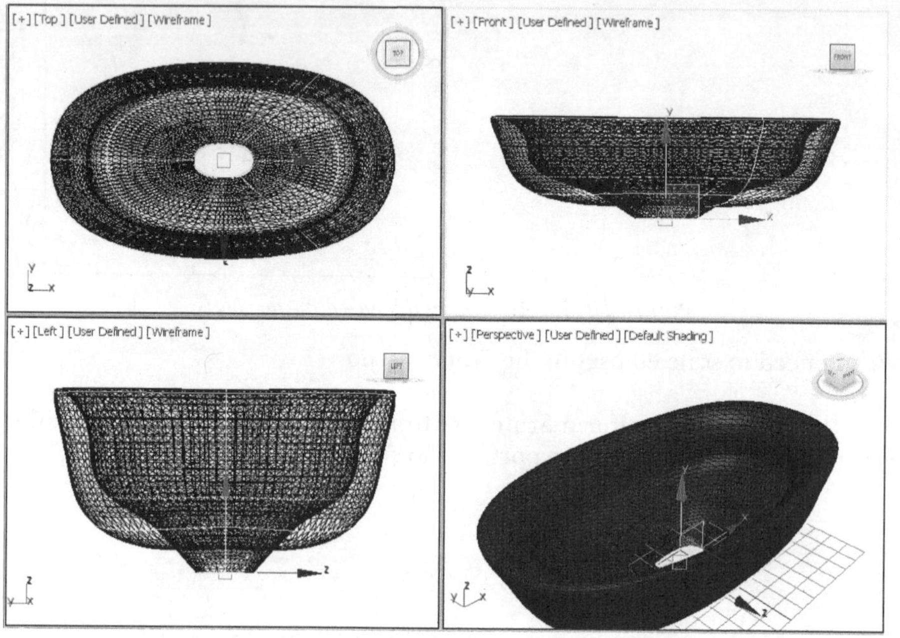

***Figure 10-62** A NURBS surface created in viewports*

4. Modify the name of the surface to *washbasin*.

   Next, you need to modify the shape of washbasin.

5. Select *washbasin* in Front viewport and click on the arrow sign on the left side of the **NURBS Surface** in the modifier stack; all the sub-object levels are displayed.

6. Select the **Curve** sub-object level and modify the shapes using the **Select and Move** and **Select and Uniform Scale** tools till you will get a perfect shape of washbasin, refer to Figure 10-63. Note that you need to scale *Ellipse008* to a circular shape to fit the sieve in it.

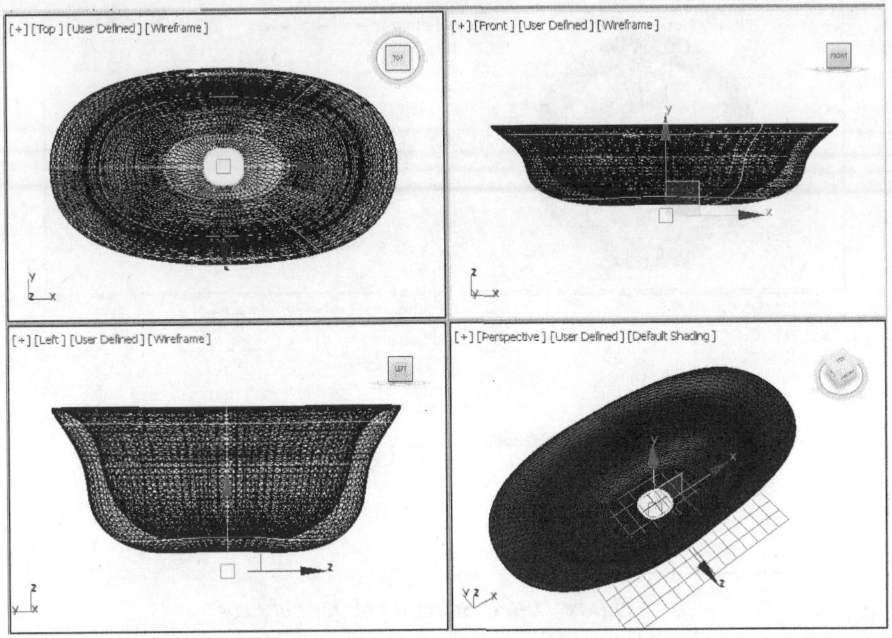

***Figure 10-63** The washbasin modified at the **Curve** sub-object level*

7. Again, select the **Curve** sub-object level in the modifier stack to exit the **Curve** sub-object level.

Creating Sieve and Duct

In this section, you will create a washbasin sieve and duct by using the **Cylinder** tool.

1. Choose the **Cylinder** tool from **Create > Geometry > Standard Primitives** in the **Command Panel**. Now, create a cylinder in the Top viewport at the center of *washbasin*.

2. Change the name of the cylinder to *sieve*. Next, in the **Parameters** rollout, modify the radius of *sieve* to the same value as that of *Ellipse008* by using the **Select and Uniform Scale** tool. Also, change the values of the following parameters:

   Height: **1.0** Height Segments: **20** Sides: **30**
   Cap Segments: **4**

3. Hide *washbasin* to get more space to perform the boolean command and choose the **Zoom Extents All** tool.

4. Convert *sieve* into editable poly. Next, select the **Polygon** sub-object level and select outer polygons from all the viewports, as shown in Figure 10-64.

5. Choose the **Select and Move** tool and move the selected polygons upward and then scale them, as shown in Figure 10-65.

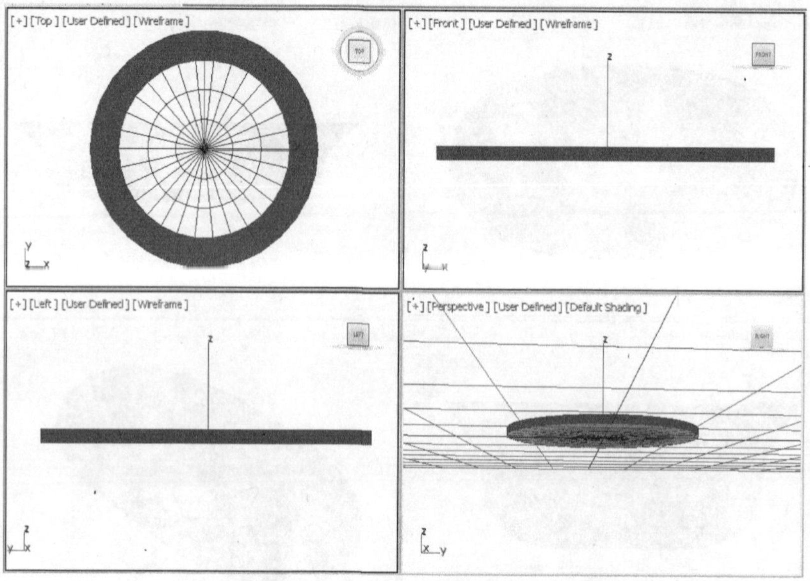

Figure 10-64 Selected polygons of sieve

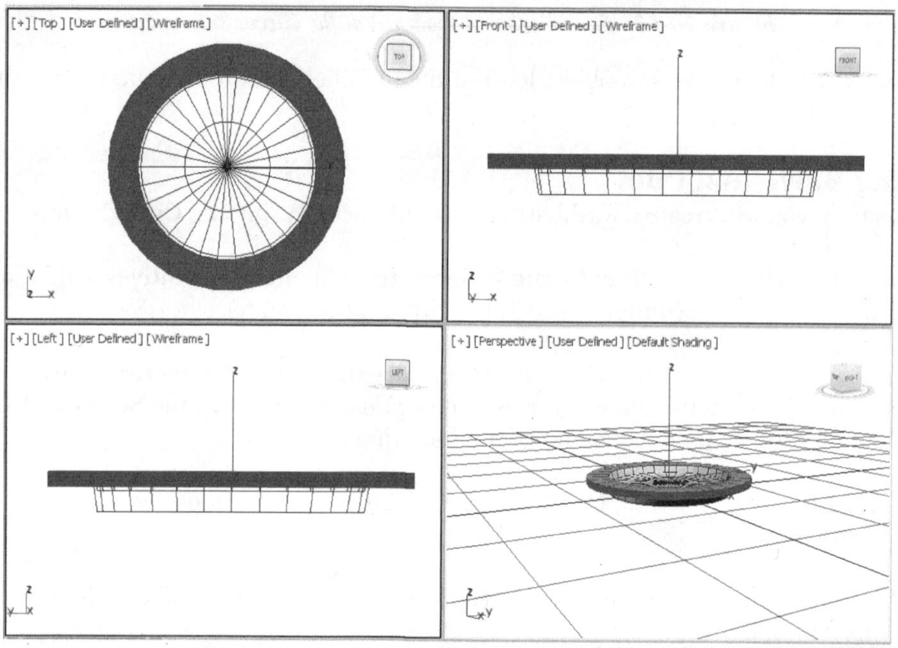

Figure 10-65 The selected polygons moved and scaled

6. Select the **Polygon** sub-object level again to deactivate it. Next, choose the **Cylinder** tool from **Create > Geometry > Standard Primitives** in the **Command Panel**.

7. Create a cylinder in the Top viewport at the center of *sieve* and set its radius to **0.8** and height to **10.0**.

8. Create copies of the cylinder according to the radius of *sieve* and arrange them, as shown in Figure 10-66.

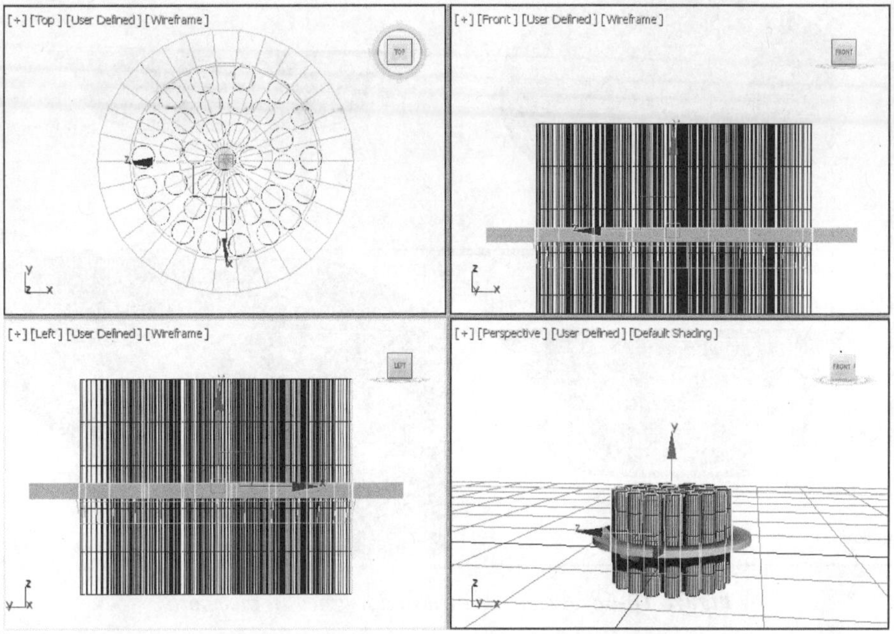

Figure 10-66 *Cylinders created and aligned*

9. Select *sieve* in the Top viewport and choose the **ProBoolean** tool from **Create > Geometry > Compound Objects** in the **Command Panel**. In the **Pick Boolean** rollout, choose the **Start Picking** button and click on the cylinders in any viewport one-by-one. Next, right-click to exit the command; a *sieve* is created, as shown in Figure 10-67.

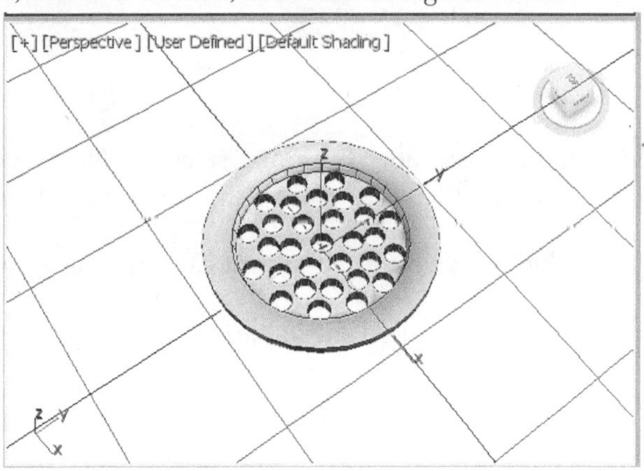

Figure 10-67 *A sieve created in the Perspective viewport*

10. Modify the color of sieve to light grey and then unhide *washbasin* in the viewports. Next, align *sieve* in the viewports, as shown in Figure 10-68.

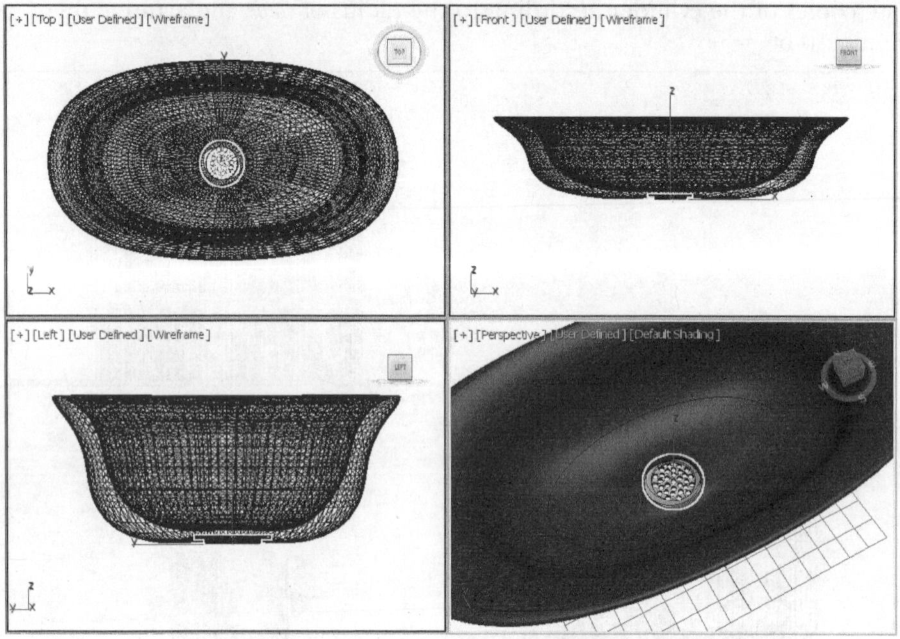

Figure 10-68 *A sieve created and aligned in viewports*

To create a duct, you need to choose the **Hose** tool from the **Extended Primitives**.

11. Create a hose in the Top viewport and set its height in the **Height** spinner in the **Free Hose Parameters** area according to *washbasin* size. Also, set the parameters in the **Common Hose Parameters** rollout as follows:

    Segments: **80** Cycles: **15**

    Hose Shape Area

    Make sure that the **Round Hose** radio button is selected. Next, set the diameter in the **Diameter** spinner and sides in the **Sides** spinner according to the radius of the sieve.

12. Modify the name of the hose to *duct* and align it in viewports, as shown in Figure 10-69.

13. Apply the **Bend** modifier to *duct* and set the values in the **Parameters** rollout as follows:

    Bend Area
    Angle: **40**

    Bend Axis Area
    Make sure that the **Z** radio button is selected.

14. Rotate *duct* in the Top viewport and align it in viewports, as shown in Figure 10-70.

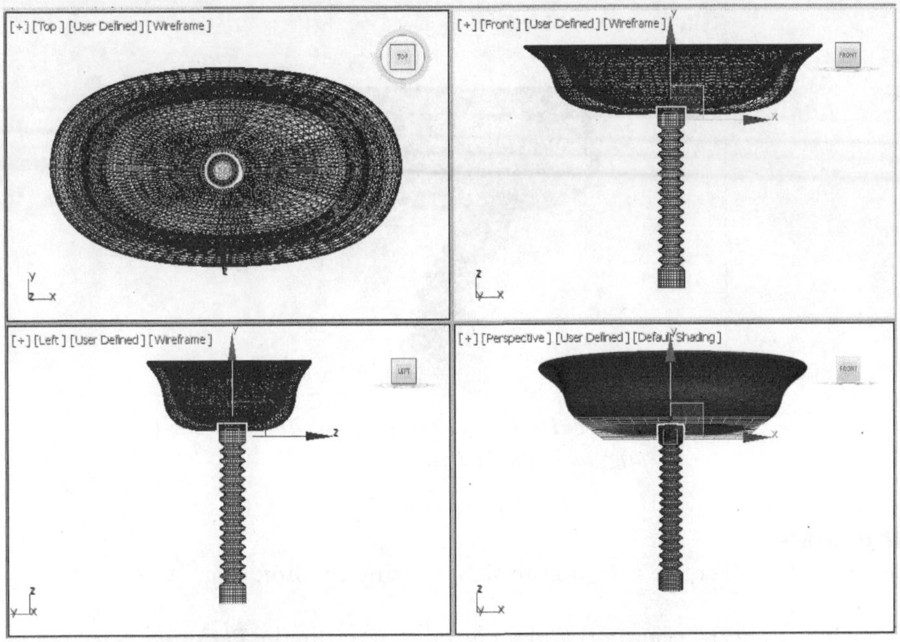

Figure 10-69 A duct created and aligned in viewports

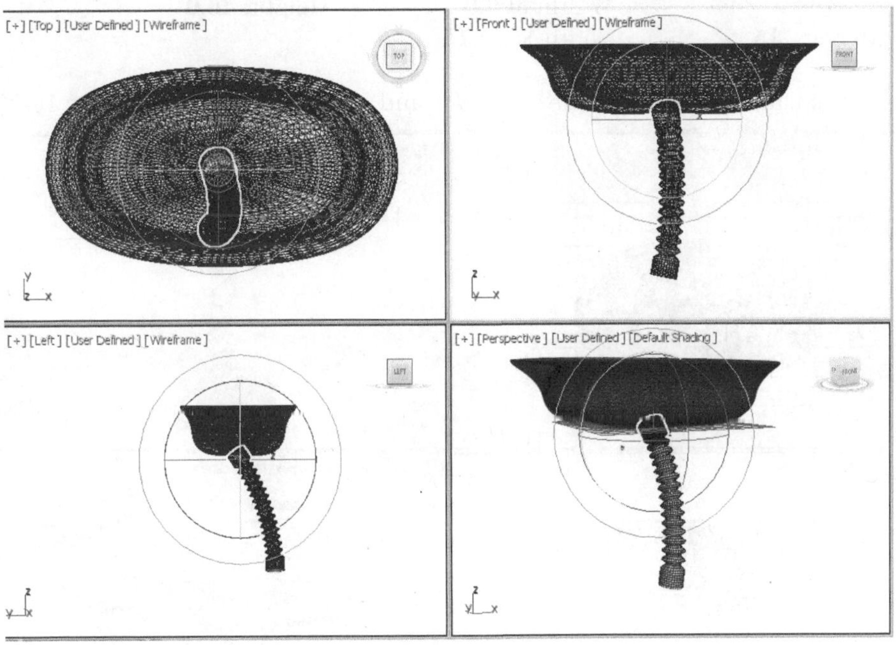

Figure 10-70 The duct geometry rotated and aligned in viewports

15. Convert *duct* into editable poly and select the **Vertex** sub-object level. Next, move and rotate its vertices to align with *washbasin* in the Left viewport, as shown in Figure 10-71.

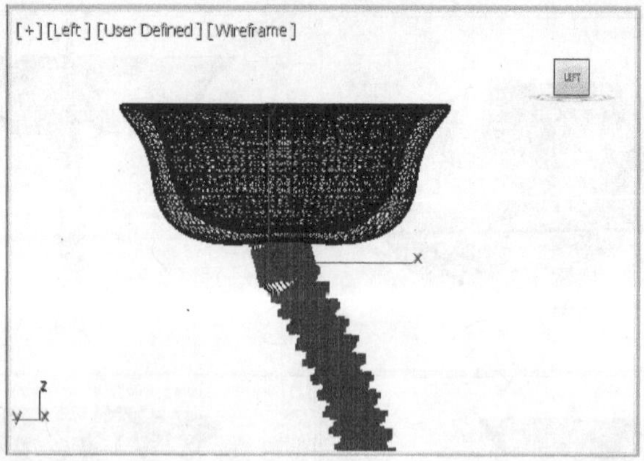

Figure 10-71 *The vertices of duct aligned in the Left viewport*

Creating Slab

In this section, you will create a washbasin slab by using the **Box** tool.

1. Create a box in the Top viewport and set its parameters in the **Parameters** rollout as follows:

   Length: **190.0** Width: **300.0** Height: **46.0**
   Length Segs: **15** Width Segs: **15**

2. Modify the name of the box to *washbasin slab* and align it, as shown in Figure 10-72.

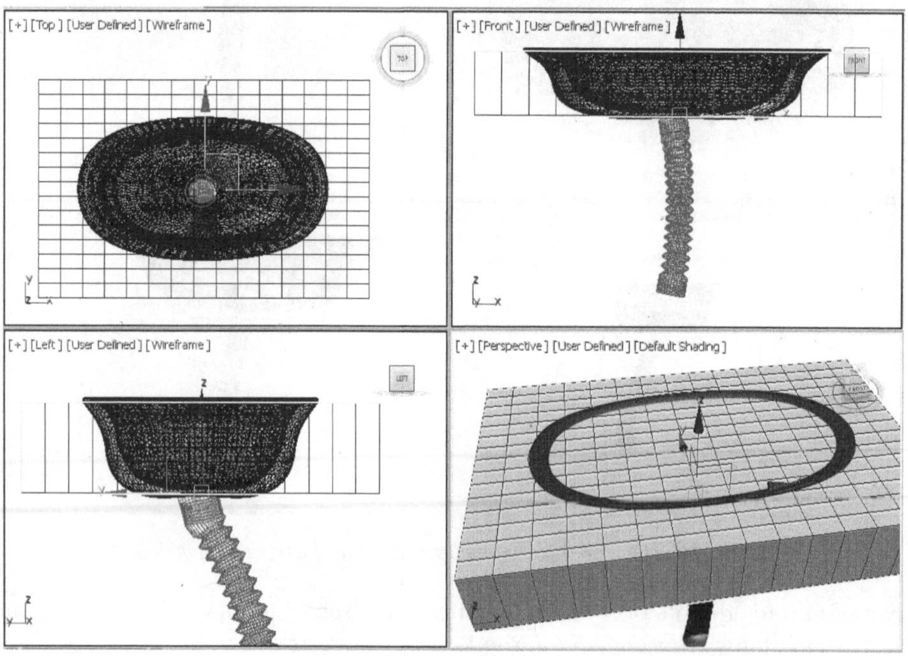

Figure 10-72 *The washbasin slab created and aligned in viewports*

3. Convert *washbasin slab* into editable poly and select the **Polygon** sub-object level.

4. Now, select the inner polygons of *washbasin slab,* as shown in Figure 10-73. Next, delete them, refer to Figure 10-74.

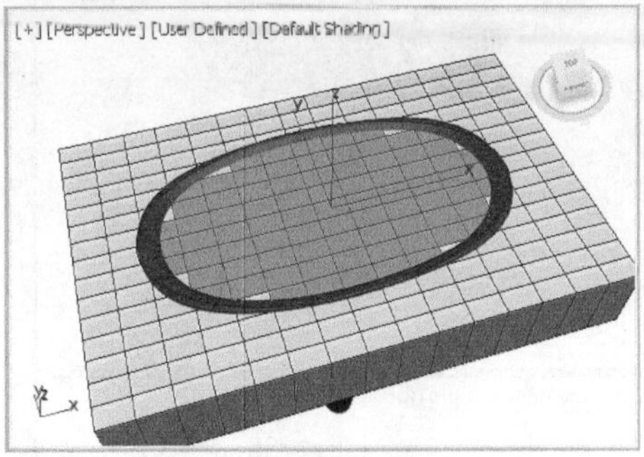

Figure 10-73 The inner polygons selected to be deleted

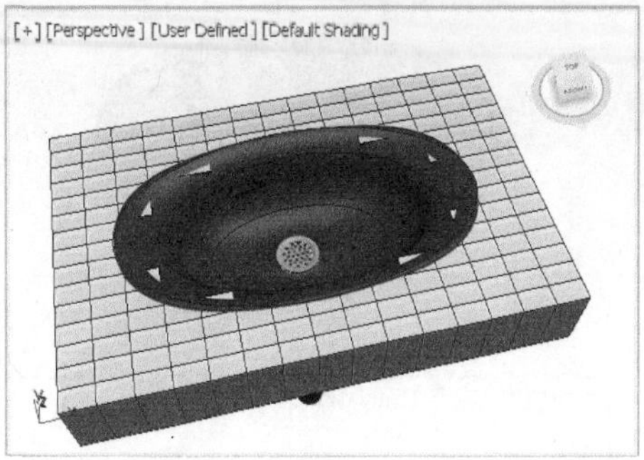

Figure 10-74 The washbasin slab after deleting the polygons

5. Select the **Vertex** sub-object level and modify the vertices of *washbasin slab* to view the inner portion of *washbasin* properly, as shown in Figure 10-75.

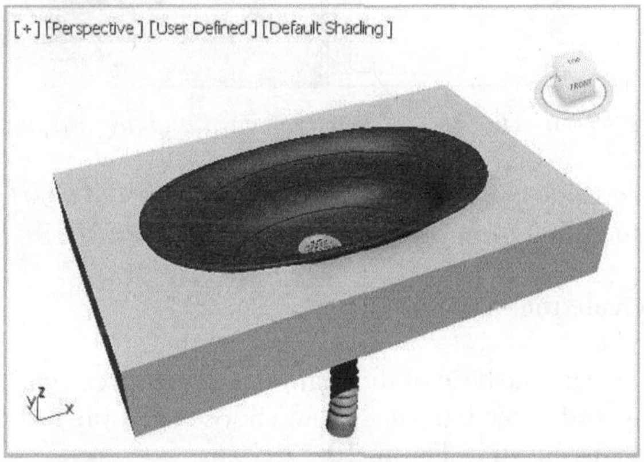

Figure 10-75 The vertices moved to view the inner portion of washbasin

Creating Washbasin Taps

In this section, you will create washbasin taps by using the **Cylinder** tool.

1. Create a cylinder in the Top viewport and set its parameters in the **Parameters** rollout as follows:

   Radius: **12.0** Height: **3.0**

2. In the Front viewport, create four copies of the cylinder vertically in the downward direction. Now, set the radius of all four cylinders as **2.0**, **3.0**, **8.0**, and **10.0** from top to bottom. Now, select the cylinders having radius **2.0** and **3.0**, and set their height to **20.0**.

3. Align the cylinders using the **Select and Move** and **Select and Rotate** tools, as shown in Figure 10-76. Also, group all of them and name the group as *tap01*.

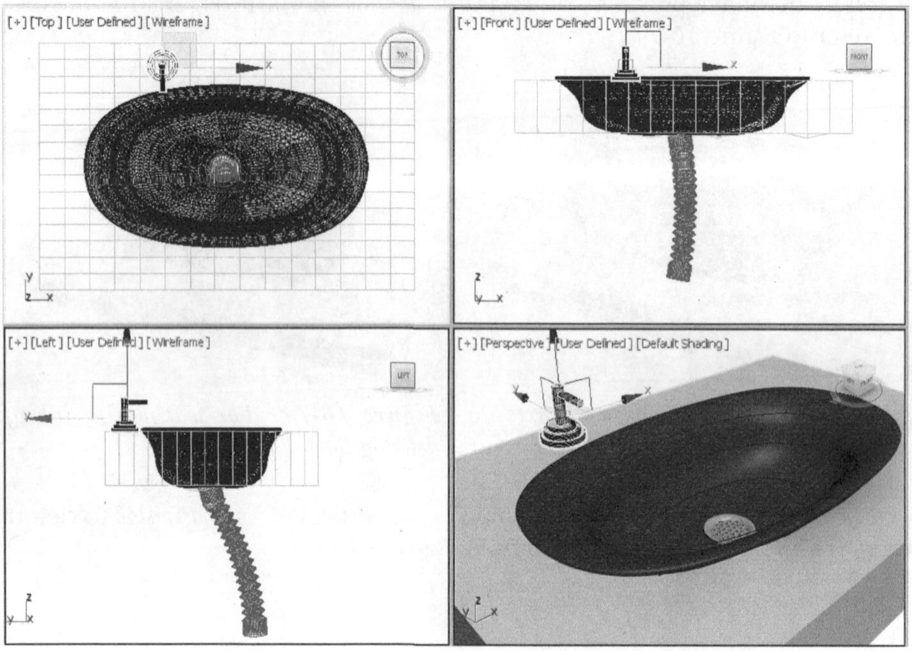

Figure 10-76 *The tap01 geometry created and aligned in viewports*

4. Align *tap01* on the left side of *washbasin*. Also, create a copy of *tap01*, which is automatically named as *tap002*, and align it on the right side of *washbasin*.

   Now, you need to create the main tap.

5. As discussed above, create the base of the main tap using three cylinders of radius **8.0**, **10.0**, and **12.0**, and group and name it as *base*. Now, choose the **Line** tool and create a line spline in the Left viewport, as shown in Figure 10-77.

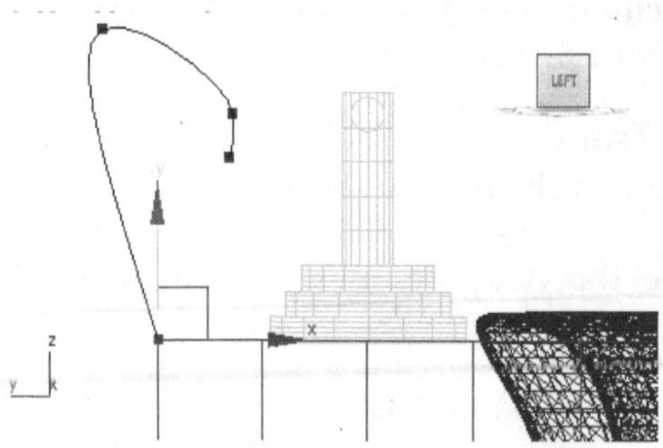

Figure 10-77 *The line spline created in the Left viewport*

6. Now, create a cylinder in the Top viewport and set its parameters in the **Parameters** rollout as follows:

   Radius: **3.0** Height: **20.0** Height Segments: **30**

7. Make sure that the cylinder is selected in the viewport and apply the **PathDeform** modifier to it; the **Parameters** rollout is displayed in the Modify panel.

8. In the **Parameters** rollout of the **PathDeform** modifier, choose the **Pick Path** button and then select the line spline in the viewport; a line is created at the center of the cylinder. Now, set the value in the **Stretch** spinner to get a shape similar to the tap.

Note
*The number of segments in the object should be high to get the smoothness on applying the **Path-Deform** modifier.*

9. Group the line spline and the cylinder as *upper tap* and then align it with *base* in viewports using the **Select and Move** and **Select and Rotate** tools, as shown in Figure 10-78.

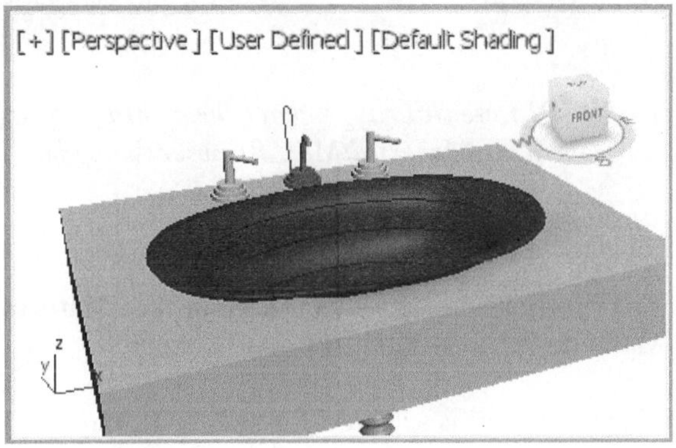

Figure 10-78 *Alignment of upper tap and base*

10. Group *base* and *upper tap* as *main tap* and then align it, as shown in Figure 10-79.

Assigning the NVIDIA mental ray Renderer and Materials

In this section, you will apply the NVIDIA mental ray renderer by using the **Render Setup** tool.

1. To assign the NVIDIA mental ray renderer to the scene, choose the **Render Setup** tool; the **Render Setup** dialog box is displayed.

2. In this dialog box, select **NVIDIA mental ray** option from the **Renderer** drop-down list and then choose the **OK** button.

3. Close the **Render Setup** dialog box.

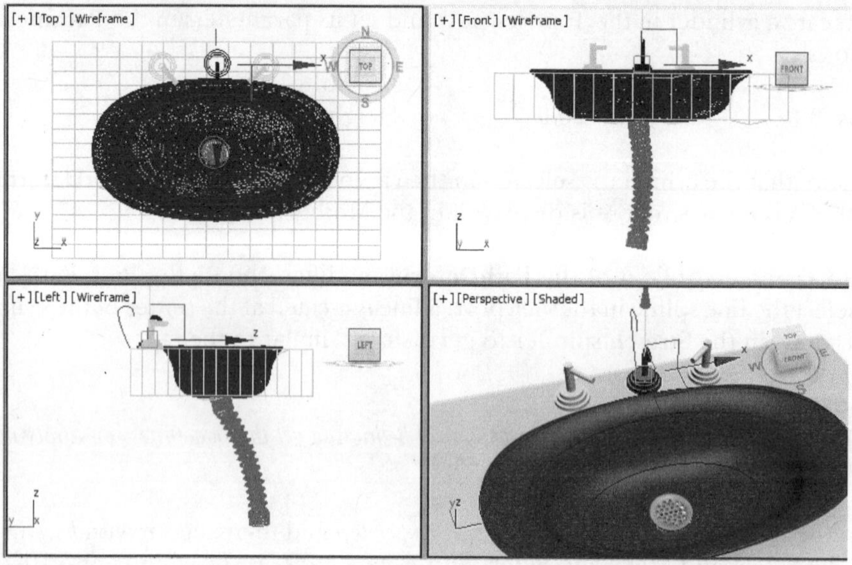

Figure 10-79 Alignment of the main tap in viewports

Note

*When you assign the **NVIDIA mental ray** renderer, the **mental ray** rollout will be displayed with some additional materials in the **Material/Map Browser** dialog box.*

Next, you need to assign materials to the objects.

4. Select *washbasin* in the viewport and choose the **Compact Material Editor** tool from the **Main Toolbar**; the **Material Editor** dialog box is displayed.

   By default, the **Standard** material is selected for the **01-Default** sample slot.

5. Select the **01-Default** sample slot and modify its name in the **Material Name** text box to *washbasin*.

6. Choose the **Material Type** button that is labeled as **Standard** in the **Material Editor** dialog box; the **Material/Map Browser** dialog box is displayed. Select the **Architectural** material from the **Materials > Standard** rollouts and then choose the **OK** button. Notice that the **Material Type** button is labeled as **Architectural** now.

7. In the **Templates** rollout, select the **Ceramic Tile, Glazed** option from the drop-down list. Also, in the **Physical Qualities** rollout, choose the **Diffuse Color** color swatch and set the values in the **Color Selector: Diffuse** dialog box as follows:

   Red: **199** Green: **247** Blue: **251**

8. Make sure that *washbasin* is selected in the viewport and choose the **Assign Material to Selection** button; the *washbasin* material is assigned to *washbasin* in the viewport.
   Next, you need to assign the material to *washbasin slab*.

9. Select the **02-Default** sample slot and modify its name in the **Material Name** text box to *washbasin slab*.

10. Assign the **Ceramic Tile, Glazed** architectural material to the selected sample slot as discussed above. In the **Physical Qualities** rollout, choose the **Diffuse Color** color swatch and assign black color to it. Also, assign the *washbasin slab* material to *washbasin slab* in the viewport.

    Next, you need to assign the material to the taps.

11. Select the **03-Default** sample slot and modify its name in the **Material Name** text box to *tap*.

12. Choose the **Material Type** button that is labeled as **Standard** from the **Material Editor** dialog box; the **Material/Map Browser** dialog box is displayed. Select the **Arch & Design** material from the **Materials > mental ray** rollouts and then choose the **OK** button. Notice that the **Material Type** button is labeled as **Arch & Design** now.

13. In the **Templates** rollout, select the **Chrome** material in the drop-down list.

14 Select *main tap*, *tap01*, and *tap002* from the Scene Explorer and then assign the **tap** material to them.

    Next, you need to assign the material to the duct and sieve.

15. Select the **04-Default** sample slot and modify its name in the **Material Name** text box to *duct and sieve*.

16. Select the **Chrome** material as discussed above. Then, in the **Main material parameters** rollout, choose the color swatch in the **Reflection** area and select the light gray color in it.

17. Select *duct* and *sieve* in the viewport and then assign the **duct and sieve** material to them. Close the **Material Editor** dialog box.

Saving and Rendering the Scene

In this section, you will save the scene and then render it. You can also view the final rendered image of this model by downloading the *c10_3dsmax_2017_rndr.zip* file from *www.cadcim.com*. The path of the file is as follows: *Textbooks > Animation and Visual Effects > 3ds Max > Autodesk 3ds Max 2017: A Comprehensive Guide*

1. Change the background color of the scene to white, as discussed in Tutorial 1 of Chapter 2.

2. Activate the Perspective viewport. Next, choose **Save** from the **Application** menu.

3. Choose the **Render Production** tool from the **Main Toolbar**; the **Rendered Frame** window is displayed, which shows the final output of the scene, refer to Figure 10-80.

4. Close the **Rendered Frame** window.

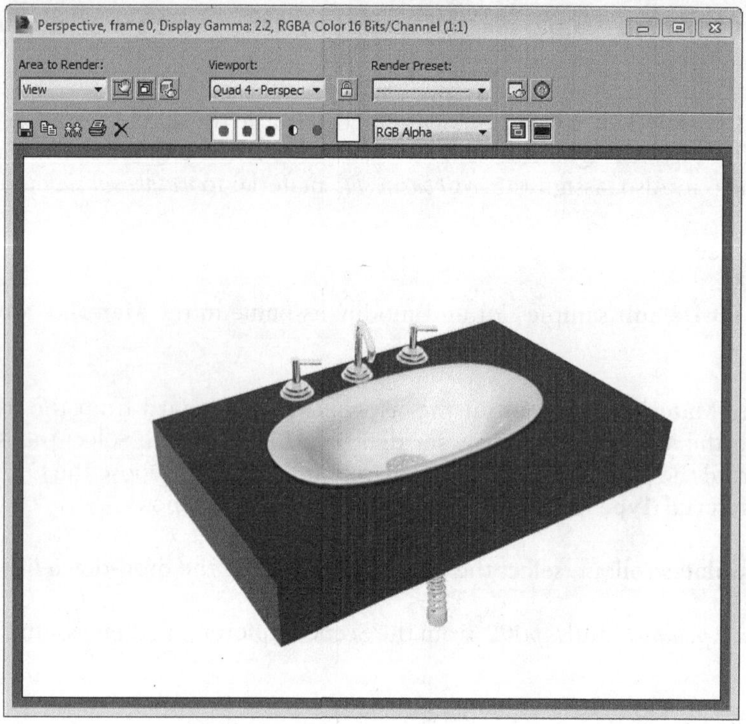

Figure 10-80 The final output at rendering

Tutorial 2

In this tutorial, you will create a hat, as shown in Figures 10-81 and 10-82, using the NURBS curves. **(Expected time: 30 min)**

Figure 10-81 The model of cap (view 1)

Figure 10-82 The model of cap (view 2)

The following steps are required to complete this tutorial:

a. Create the project folder.
b. Create NURBS curves using splines.
c. Create and modify the hat.

d. Assign the material.
e. Save and render the scene.

Creating the Project Folder

1. Create a new project folder with the name *c10_tut2* at *\Documents\3dsmax2017* and then save the file with the name *c10tut2*, as discussed in Tutorial 1 of Chapter 2.

2. Open the Windows Explorer and then browse to the *c10_3dsmax_2017_tut* folder and copy the *cloth.jpg* file from this folder to *\Documents\3dsmax2017\c10_tut2\sceneassets\images*.

Creating NURBS Curves Using Splines

In this section, you will create the circular NURBS curves for the hat.

1. Choose **Create > Shapes** in the **Command Panel** and then choose the **Circle** tool from the **Object Type** rollout.

2. Create a circle in the Top viewport; it is automatically named as *Circle001*. Next, set its radius to **45** in the **Radius** spinner of the **Parameters** rollout.

3. Make sure that *Circle001* is selected in the Top viewport. Right-click on the **Select and Uniform Scale** tool from the **Main Toolbar**; the **Scale Transform Type-In** dialog box is displayed, as shown in Figure 10-83. Now, in the **Absolute:Local** area, set the value **111.0** in the **X** spinner; *Circle001* is scaled along the X-axis, as shown in Figure 10-84. Now, close this dialog box.

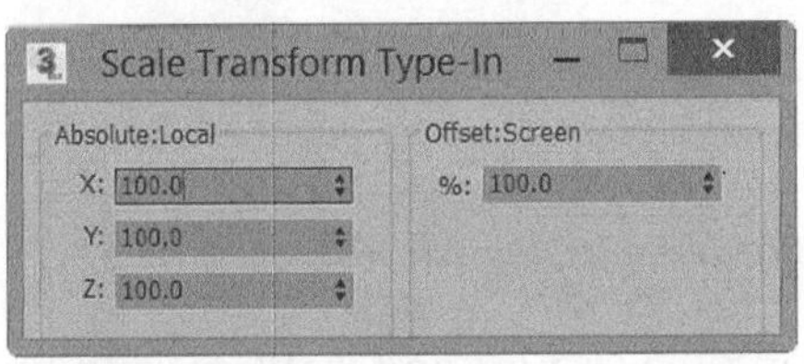

*Figure 10-83 The **Scale Transform Type-In** dialog box*

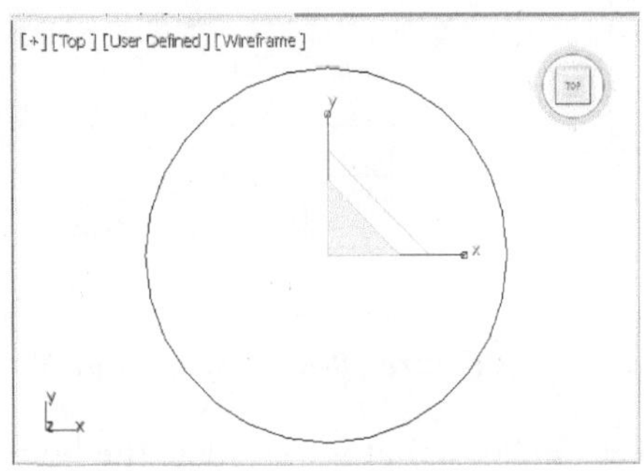

Figure 10-84 The Circle001 spline scaled along the X-axis

4. Convert *Circle001* into NURBS surface and choose the **Zoom Extents All** tool.

5. Click on the black arrow on the left of **NURBS Surface** in the modifier stack; all the sub-object levels are displayed.

6. Select the **Curve** sub-object level. Next, select the curve in the viewport. Now, choose the **Rebuilt** button in the **CV Curve** rollout; the **Rebuilt CV Curve** dialog box is displayed. Now, set **20** in the spinner next to the **Number** radio button, refer to Figure 10-85. Next, choose the **OK** button. Click on the **Curve** sub-object level to deactivate it.

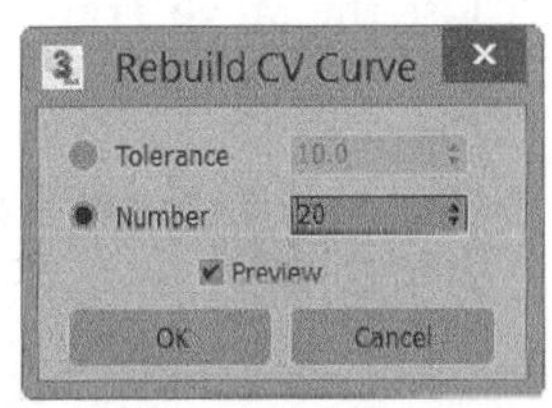

*Figure 10-85 The **Rebuild CV Curve** dialog box*

Next, you need to create multiple copies of *Circle001* to create the surface.

7. Choose the **Select and Move** tool and select *Circle001* in the Front viewport and move the cursor over its vertical axis. Press and hold the SHIFT key and the left mouse button, and then move *Circle001* in the upward direction until the value in the **Y** spinner in the coordinates display becomes about **17**. Now, release the left mouse button and the SHIFT key; the **Clone Options** dialog box is displayed. Set the value **4** in the **Number of Copies** spinner and choose the **OK** button, *Circle002, Circle003, Circle004*, and *Circle005* are created in viewports.

8. Choose the **Zoom Extents All** tool; the circular NURBS curves are displayed in the viewports, as shown in Figure 10-86.

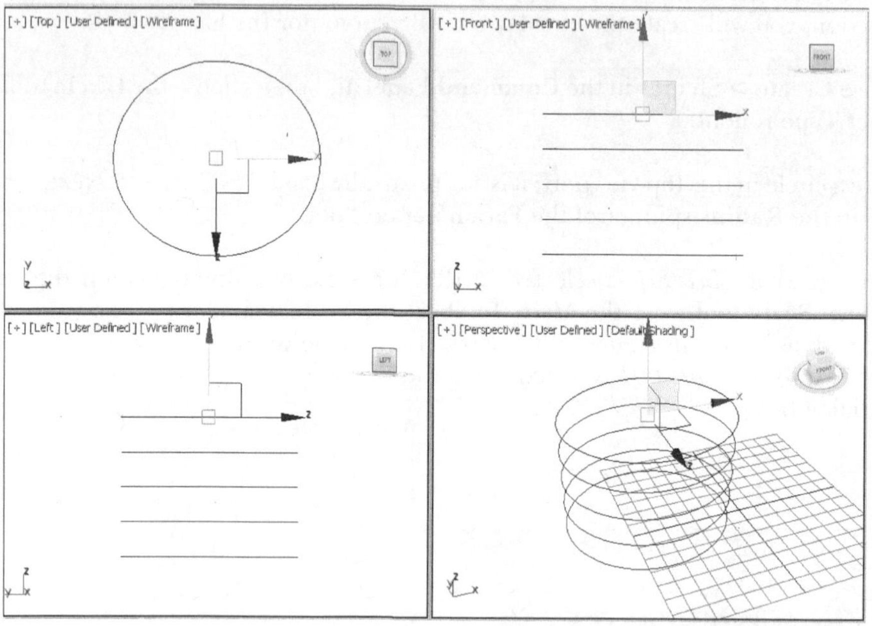

Figure 10-86 *The circular NURBS curves displayed in viewports*

9. Select *Circle001* that is placed at the bottom in the viewport and right-click on the **Select and Move** tool; the **Move Transform Type-In** dialog box is displayed. In the **Offset:Screen** area, set the value **13** in the **Y** spinner and press the ENTER key; *Circle001* moves in the vertical direction, as shown in Figure 10-87.

10. Close the **Move Transform Type-In** dialog box.

11. Select *Circle001* and then by pressing CTRL key, select *Circle002*. Next, right-click on the **Select and Uniform Scale** tool; the **Scale Transform Type-In** dialog box is displayed. In the **Offset:Screen** area, set the value **119** in the **%** spinner and press the ENTER key; *Circle001* and *Circle002* are scaled, as shown in Figure 10-88.

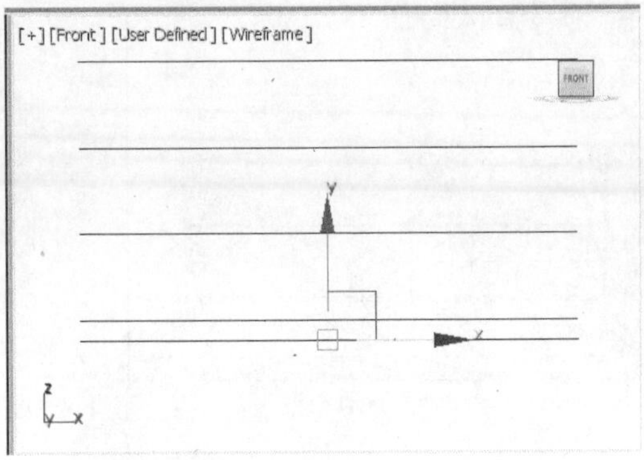

Figure 10-87 *The Circle001 spline moved vertically*

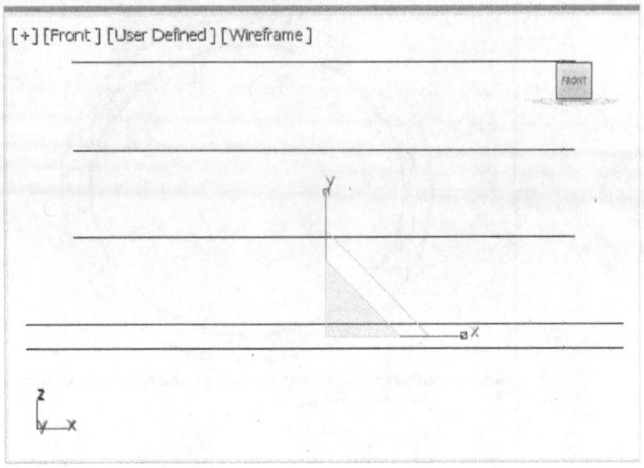

Figure 10-88 *The Circle001 and Circle002 splines scaled vertically*

12. Close the **Scale Transform Type-In** dialog box and choose the **Zoom Extents All** tool.

Creating and Modifying Hat

In this section, you will create a surface between the NURBS curves in the viewport to give it a shape by using the **U Loft** button.

1. Select *Circle001* placed at the bottom in the Front viewport.

2. Choose the **Modify** tab, if it is not already chosen; the **NURBS Surface** is displayed in the modifier stack. All rollouts to modify the NURBS object are also displayed below the modifier stack.

3. Make sure the **General** rollout is expanded and choose the **NURBS Creation Toolbox** button; the **NURBS** toolbox is displayed. Now, choose the **Create U Loft Surface** button from the **Surfaces** section; the **U Loft Surface** rollout is displayed in the Modify panel. Next, move the cursor over *Circle001*; it turns blue. Now, click on it and then one-by-one click on *Circle002, 003, 004,* and *005* to add them into the U loft surface. Now, right-click to end the command. In the **U Loft Surface** rollout, select the **Flip Normals** check box. Next, right-click to exit the **U loft** command; a NURBS surface is created in the viewports, as shown in Figure 10-89.

4. Now, choose the **Create Cap Surface** button from the **Surfaces** section in the **NURBS** toolbox; the **Cap Surface** rollout is displayed in the Modify panel. Now, move the cursor over *Circle005*, which is placed at the top in the Front viewport, and then click on it. Also, in the **Cap Surface** rollout, select the **Flip Normals** check box. The open surface is now capped at one end, as shown in Figure 10-90. Next, right-click to exit the **Create Cap Surface** command.

5. Modify the name of the surface to *hat* in the **Name and Color** rollout.

   Next, you need to modify *hat* to give it a shape that is exactly similar to a hat.

6. Select *hat* in any viewport and click on the plus sign on the left side of **NURBS Surface** in the modifier stack; all the sub-object levels are displayed.

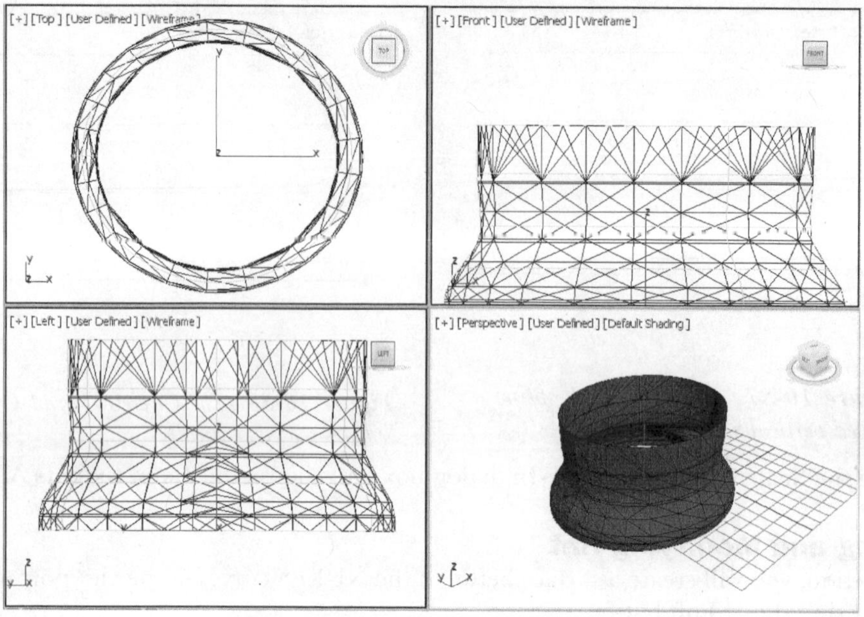

Figure 10-89 *A NURBS surface created*

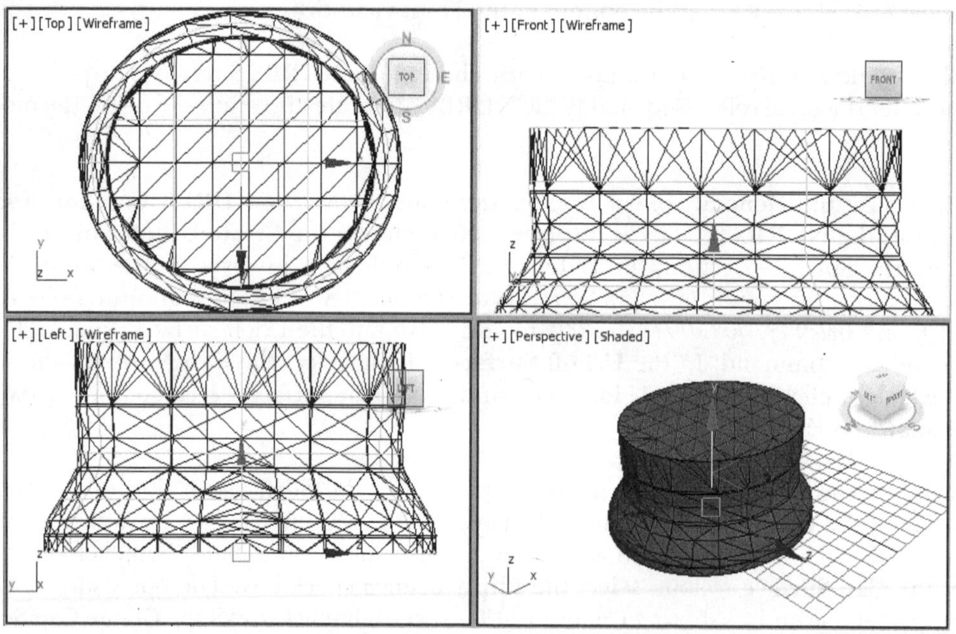

Figure 10-90 *The NURBS surface capped at one end*

7. Select the **Curve** sub-object level. In the Front viewport, modify the NURBS curves using the **Select and Move** and **Select and Uniform Scale** tools, as shown in Figure 10-91.

8. Again, select the **Curve** sub-object level in the modifier stack to exit the command.

9. Select the **Curve CV** sub-object level; all control vertices are displayed in the viewport. Now, select the outer control vertices of the bottom curves, refer to Figure 10-90. Next, move them until the value in the **Y** spinner in the coordinate display becomes about **15**, as shown in Figure 10-92.

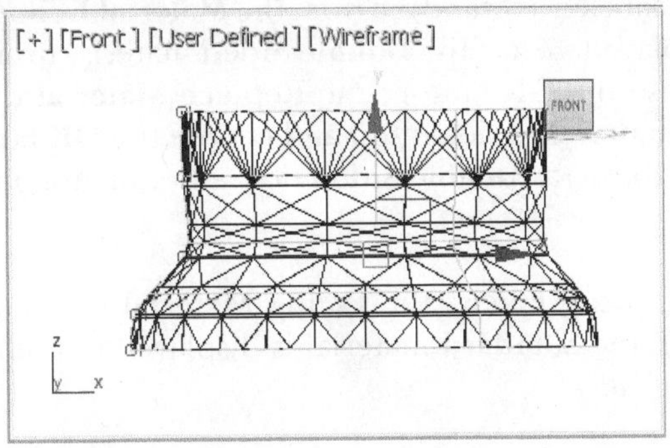

Figure 10-91 *The NURBS curves modified in the Front viewpor t*

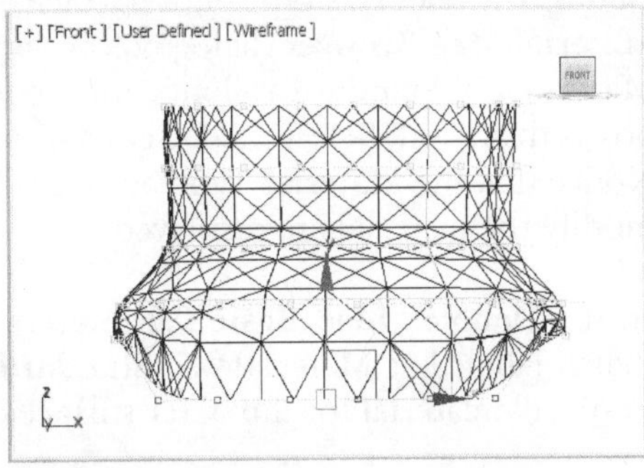

Figure 10-92 *The outer control vertices moved vertically*

10. Now, modify the surface using the control vertices and curves to get the required shape, as shown in Figure 10-93.

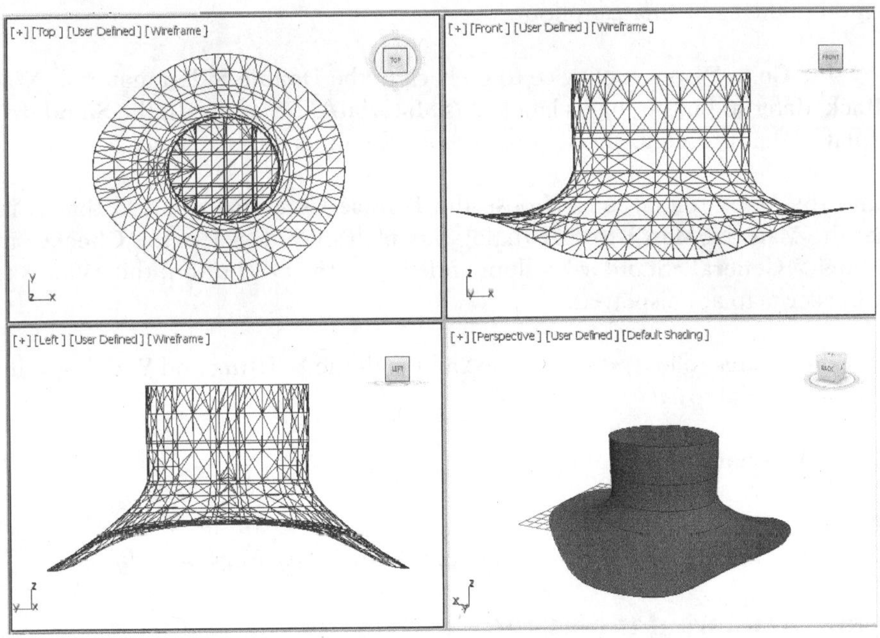

Figure 10-93 *The surface modified at the sub-object level*

Assigning the Material

In this section, you will assign the material to the hat by using the **Material Editor** dialog box.

1. Select *hat* in the viewport and choose the **Material Editor** tool from the **Main Toolbar**; the **Material Editor** dialog box is displayed.

2. By default, the **Standard** material is selected in the **Material Editor** dialog box. Select the **01-Default** sample slot and modify its name to *hat* in the **Material Name** text box.

3. Choose the **Material Type** button which is labeled as **Standard** from the **Material Editor**; the **Material/Map Browser** dialog box is displayed. Select the **Double Sided** material from the **Materials > Standard** rollouts and choose the **OK** button; the **Replace Material** dialog box is displayed. Select the **Discard old material** radio button and choose the **OK** button. Notice that the **Material Type** button is labeled as **Double Sided** now. Also, the rollouts to modify the material are displayed.

4. In the **Double Sided Basic Parameters** rollout, choose the **Facing Material** map button that is labeled as **Material#X (Standard)**; the **Standard** material is displayed that is used to specify material for the outer surface of *hat*.

5. Now, expand the **Maps** rollout, and choose the **Diffuse Color** map button that is labeled as **None**; the **Material/Map Browser** dialog box is displayed. Select the **Bitmap** map from the **Maps > General** rollout and choose the **OK** button; the **Select Bitmap Image File** dialog box is displayed. Now, select the file *cloth.jpg* and choose the **Open** button; the selected image is displayed in the sample slot. Make sure that the **Use Real-World Scale** check box is cleared in the **Coordinates** rollout.

6. Choose the **Go to Parent** tool twice to go back to the **Double Sided** material. Now, choose the **Back Material** button that is labeled as **Material#X (Standard)**; the **Standard** material is displayed that is used to specify material for the inner surface of *hat*.

7. Expand the **Maps** rollout, and choose the **Diffuse Color** map button that is labeled as **None**; the **Material/Map Browser** dialog box is displayed. Select the **Checker** map from the **Maps > General>Standard** rollout and choose the **OK** button; the rollouts to modify the **Checker** map are displayed.

8. In the **Coordinates** rollout, set the value **25** in both the **U Tiling** and **V Tiling** spinners and assign *hat* material to *hat*.

9. Close the **Material Editor** dialog box.

Note

If you want to swap the materials on the geometry assign the ***Normal*** *modifier.*

Saving and Rendering the Scene

In this section, you will save the scene and then render it. You can also view the final rendered image of this model by downloading the file *c10_3dsmax_2017_rndr.zip* from *www.cadcim.com.*

The path of the file is as follows: *Textbooks > Animation and Visual Effects > 3ds Max > Autodesk 3ds Max 2017: A Comprehensive Guide.*

1. Change the background color of the scene to white, as discussed in Tutorial 1 of Chapter 2.

2. Choose **Save** from the **Application** menu.

3. Activate the Perspective viewport and set the view using the **Orbit** tool to see the inner and outer surfaces of *hat*.

4. Choose the **Render Production** tool in the **Main Toolbar**; the **Rendered Frame** window is displayed with the final output of the scene, refer to Figure 10-94.

5. Close this window.

***Figure 10-94** The final output after rendering*

Self-Evaluation Test

Answer the following questions and then compare them to those given at the end of this chapter:

1. In which of the following NURBS surfaces, the points are constrained to lie on the surface?

   (a) **Point Surface** (b) **CV Curve**
   (c) **Point Curve** (d) **CV Surface**

2. Which of the following buttons in the **Create Points** rollout is used to add the independent point sub-object to a NURBS object?

   (a) **Point** (b) **Surf-Curve**
   (c) **Curve-Curve** (d) **Surf-Point**

3. Which of the following buttons in the **Create Surfaces** rollout is used to add the dependent surface sub-object to a NURBS object?

   (a) **Transform** (b) **Extrude**
   (c) **U Loft** (d) All of these

4. Which of the following buttons in the **Create Points** rollout is used to add the dependent point sub-object to a NURBS object?

   (a) **Offset Point** (b) **Curve Point**
   (c) **Curve-Curve** (d) All of these

5. The NURBS curves are the shape objects and are used to create complex surfaces to create the 3D models. (T/F)

6. The point curves are the NURBS curves in which the points lie outside the curve. (T/F)

7. In the NURBS modeling, an iso line is known as a line of constant parameter value similar to a contour line. (T/F)

8. The CV curves are the NURBS curves that are controlled by __________.

9. The CVs are the points that lie __________ the surface and control the __________ of the CV surface.

10. While creating a point curve, if you want to remove the last point that you have created, then press the __________ key.

Review Questions

Answer the following questions:

1. Which of the following buttons in the **Create Curves** rollout is used to add the dependent curve sub-object to a NURBS object?

   (a) **Transform** (b) **Blend**
   (c) **Chamfer** (d) All of these

2. Which of the following buttons in the **Create Surfaces** rollout is used to add the surface sub-object to a NURBS object?

   (a) **1-Rail** (b) **2-Rail**
   (c) **Offset** (d) All of these

3. Which of the following buttons in the **Create Curves** rollout is used to add the curve sub-object to a NURBS object?

   (a) **1-Rail** (b) **U Loft**
   (c) **Cap** (d) None of these

4. You cannot convert the torus knot and prism from extended primitives into NURBS surface. (T/F)

5. To create a NURBS model, you can also use the splines or extended splines shapes instead of using the point curve or the CV curve. (T/F)

6. The buttons in the **NURBS** toolbox perform the same functions as the buttons in the **Create Points**, **Create Curves**, and **Create Surfaces** rollouts. (T/F)

7. The __________ check box is used to create a 3D curve in all viewports simultaneously.

8. In the viewports, the dependent point sub-objects will be displayed as __________ and the independent point sub-objects will be displayed as __________.

9. The __________ button in the **Create Surfaces** rollout is used to create a surface sub-object between two curve sub-objects.

EXERCISE

The rendered output of the model used in the following exercise can be accessed by downloading the *c10_3dsmax_2017_exr.zip* file from *www.cadcim.com*. The path of the file is as follows: *Textbooks > Animation and Visual Effects > 3ds Max > Autodesk 3ds Max 2017: A Comprehensive Guide*

Exercise 1

Start Autodesk 3ds Max 2017 and then perform the following operations:

1. Choose **Create > Shapes** in the **Command Panel**; a drop-down list will be displayed. Select the **NURBS Curves** option from the drop-down list. Now, activate the Top viewport and choose the **Point Curve** tool from the **Object Type** rollout. Next, create two or more point curves in the viewport. Finally, choose the **Modify** tab in the **Command Panel** and attach the NURBS curves in the viewport using the **Attach Multiple** tool.

2. Create a spline or a curve in the viewport from **Create > Shapes > Splines** in the **Command Panel**. Now, convert it into NURBS curve using the methods discussed in the chapter.

3. Create a NURBS object in the viewport that contains two or more curves or surface sub-objects. Choose the **Modify** tab in the **Command Panel** and then choose the **Blend** button from the **Create Surfaces** rollout. Next, move the cursor over the edge; it turns blue. Now, click on the edge and move the cursor over the edge of another NURBS object, and click on it; a blend surface will be created between the two NURBS objects. Next, modify the blend surface using the parameters in the **Blend Surface** rollout in the modify panel and right-click to exit the command.

4. Create a NURBS curve in the viewport, as shown in Figure 10-95. Next, create a NURBS model, as shown in Figure 10-96 using the **U Loft** tool. Also, apply a material to it.

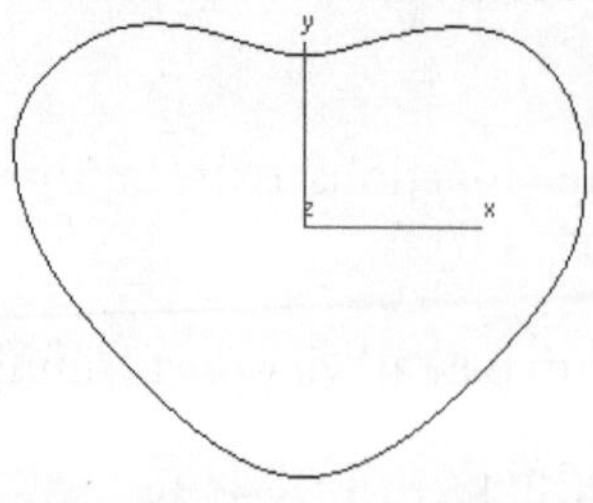

Figure 10-95 The NURBS curve to create the model of heart

Figure 10-96 The model of heart

Answers to Self-Evaluation Test

1. a, **2.** a, **3.** d, **4.** d, **5.** T, **6.** F, **7.** T, **8.** control vertices (CVs), **9.** outside; shape, **10.** BACKSPACE

11

Compound Objects

Learning Objectives

After completing this chapter, you will be able to:

- *Create compound objects*
- *Modify compound objects*

INTRODUCTION

In this chapter, you will create complex models by combining two or more existing objects into a single object. The different techniques explained in this chapter will help you to combine different 2D and 3D shapes that would otherwise be difficult or impossible to do.

COMPOUND OBJECTS

In 3ds Max, the compound objects are created by combining two or more objects. There are twelve tools to create various compound objects. To create these compound objects, you need to choose the respective tools. To create a compound object, choose **Create > Geometry** in the **Command Panel**; a drop-down list will be displayed below the **Geometry** button. Select the **Compound Objects** option from the drop-down list; the **Object Type** rollout will be displayed with all the tools to create compound objects, refer to Figure 11-1. The most commonly used tools to create compound objects are discussed next.

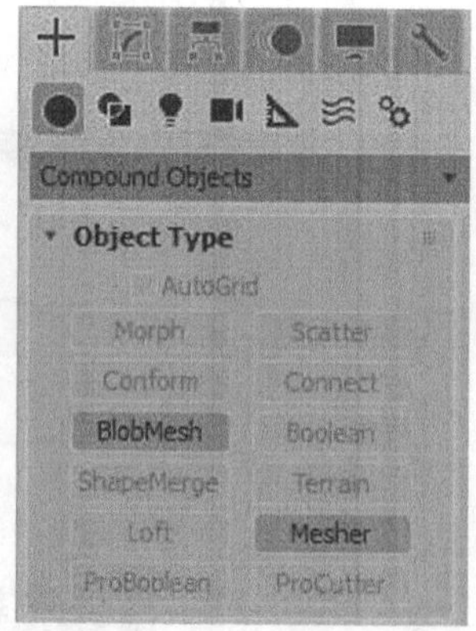

Figure 11-1 The tools for creating compound objects displayed in the rollout

Boolean

Enhanced

Menu bar: Create > Compound > Boolean
Toolbar: Create > Geometry > Compound Objects > Object Type rollout > Boolean

The **Boolean** tool is used to trim or combine objects in an operation. To carry out boolean operation, you need two objects. The objects to be operated upon are known as operands. To create a boolean object, first create two overlapping objects in the viewport, refer to Figure 11-2. Select one of the objects in the viewport. Choose **Create > Geometry** in the **Command Panel**; a drop-down list will be displayed. Select the **Compound Objects** option from the drop-down list and choose the **Boolean** tool from the **Object Type** rollout; the **Name and Color**, **Boolean Parameters**, and **Operand Parameters** rollouts will be displayed, refer to Figure 11-3.

The name of the selected object will appear in the **Operand** list of the **Boolean Parameters** rollout in the Modify panel, refer to Figure 11-4. Now, choose the **Add Operands** button from the **Boolean Parameters** rollout and click on the other objects in the viewport; the name of the selected object will appear in the **Operand** list of the **Boolean Parameters** rollout.

In the **Operand Parameters** rollout, you can select the boolean operations such as **Subtract**, **Merge**, **Intersect**. By default, the **Union** option is selected in this rollout. As a result, the volume of the objects is combined, refer to Figure 11-5 and their name appears in the **Operand** list. Figure 11-6 shows the result of the **Subtract** boolean operation.

The **Imprint** check box in this rollout imprints the intersection edges between the operands and the original mesh without removing or adding faces, as shown in Figure 11-7. The **Cookie** check box enables the Cookie Cutter feature that restricts you from adding faces from the operands into the original mesh, refer to Figure 11-8.

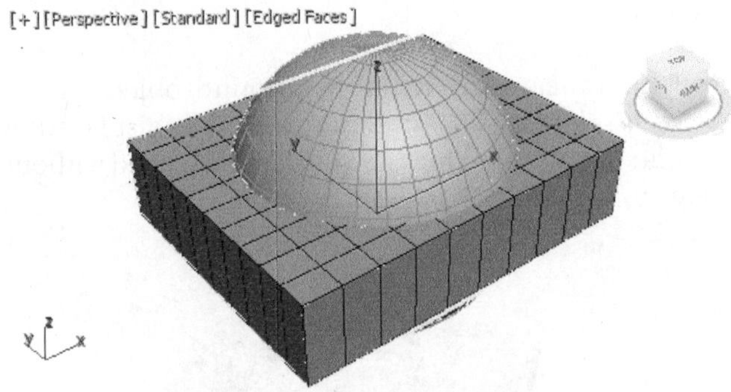

Figure 11-2 Two overlapping objects created in the viewport

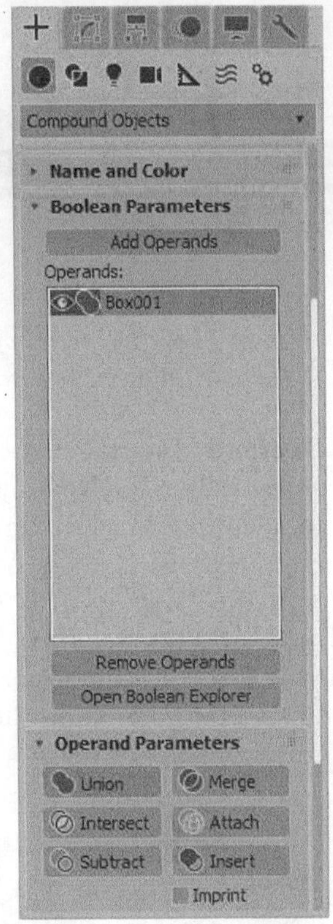

Figure 11-3 Partial view of the rollouts displayed on choosing the **Boolean** tool

Figure 11-4 The **Operand** list

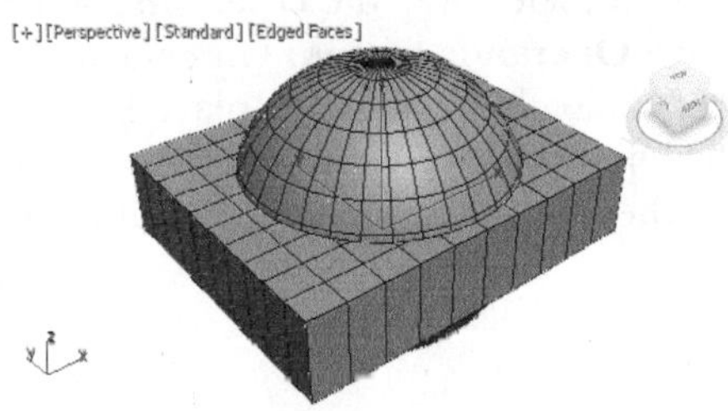

Figure 11-5 The result of the **Union** operation

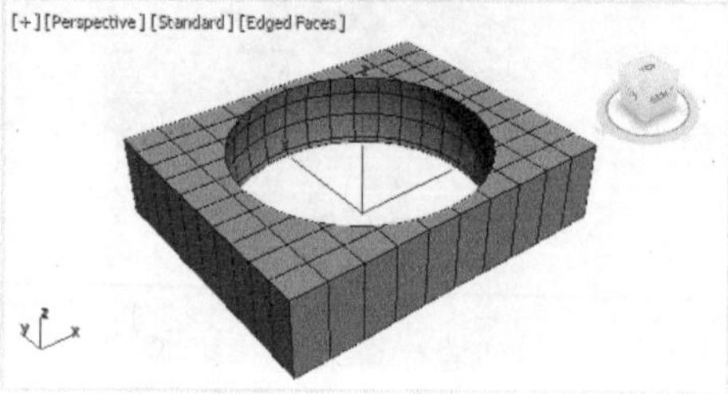

Figure 11-6 *The result of the* ***Subtraction*** *operation*

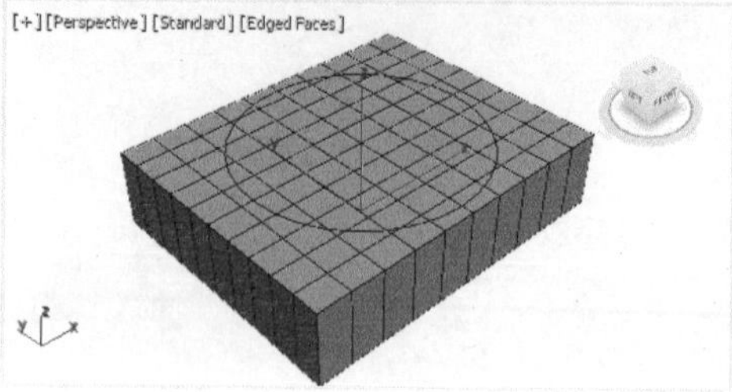

Figure 11-7 *The result after selecting the* ***Imprint*** *check box*

The **Apply Operand Material** check box applies the material of the added operand to the entire compound object. When the **Retain Original Material** check box is selected, 3ds Max keeps the existing material applied to the compound object.

The options in the **Display** area control the appearance of the compound object in the viewports. By default, the **Result** radio button is selected. As a result, final result is displayed in the viewports. If you select the **Operands** radio button, the operands will be displayed without boolean operation performed on them, refer to Figure 11-9.

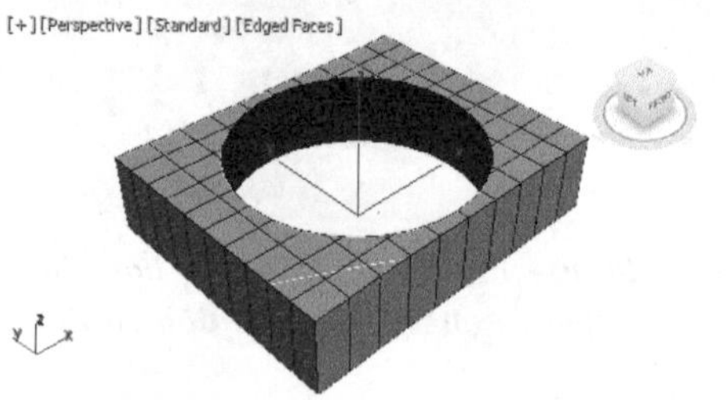

Figure 11-8 *The result after selecting the* ***Cookie*** *check box*

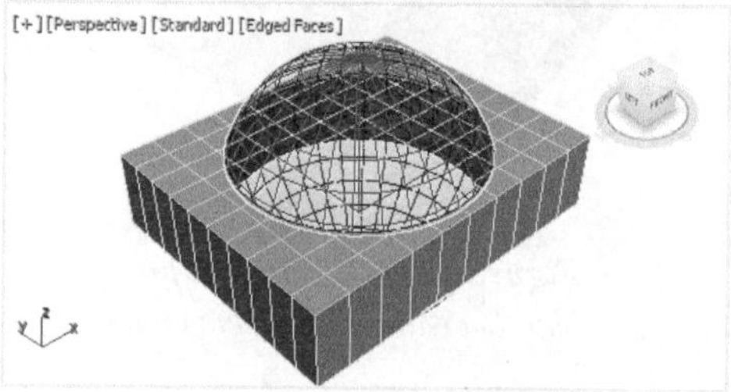

Figure 11-9 *The result after selecting the* ***Operands*** *radio button*

The **Selected Operands** radio button is used for displaying the selected operands. When this radio button is selected, the current boolean operation gets highlighted in the viewport. Select the **Display as Shaded** radio button to display the operands in the shaded mode.

To remove an operand, select it in the **Operand** list of the **Boolean Parameters** rollout and then choose the **Remove Operands** button. On choosing the **Open Boolean Explorer** button, the **Boolean Explorer** dialog box will be displayed, as shown in Figure 11-10. Whenever you add an operand to the **Operand** list, it automatically appears in the **Boolean Explorer**. You can also drag objects from the **Scene Explorer** to the **Boolean Explorer** to add them as new operands.

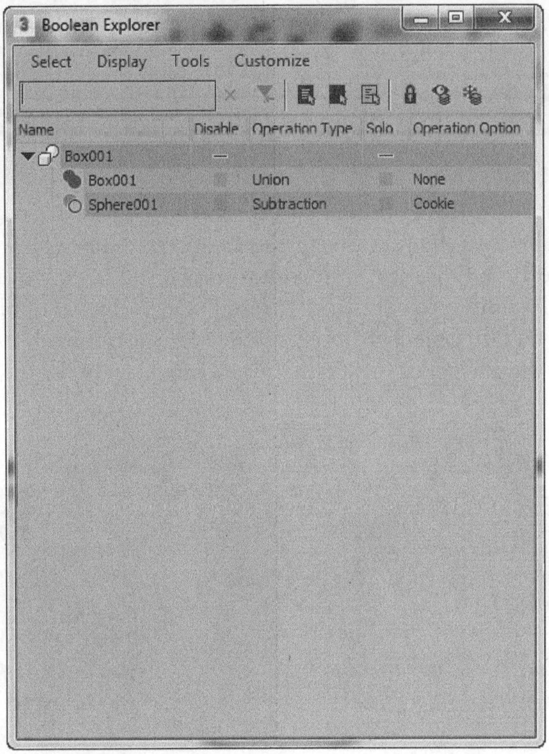

*Figure 11-10 The **Boolean Explorer** dialog box*

Terrain

Menu bar:	Create > Compound > Terrain
Toolbar:	Create > Geometry > Compound Objects > Object Type rollout > Terrain

The terrain compound objects are created from splines. In this case, the splines represent the contour lines. The contour lines are the lines drawn on a map, which connect the points of equal height. Usually, the terrain objects are used to add buildings and roads to them to create virtual cities. To create a terrain object, first create the contour lines in the Top viewport using the **Line** tool, as shown in Figure 11-11. Align these lines in the Front viewport, as shown in Figure 11-12.

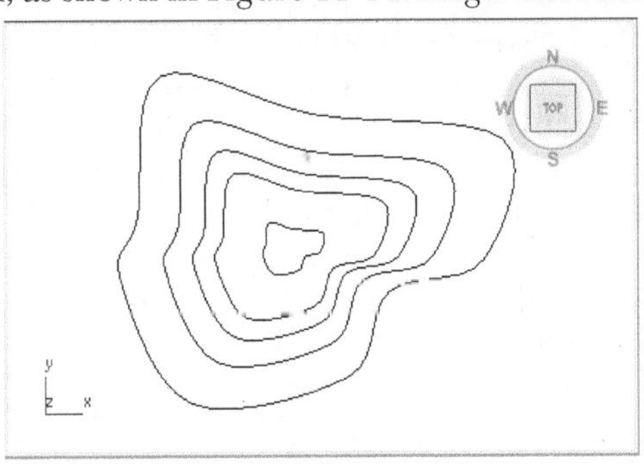

Figure 11-11 The contour lines created for the terrain object in the Top viewport

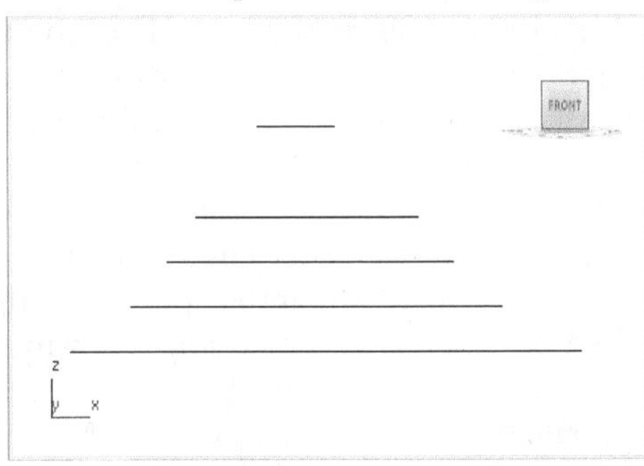

Figure 11-12 The contour lines aligned for the terrain object in the Front viewport

You can also import an AutoCAD drawing file to use as contour data. Next, select all the contour lines and choose the **Terrain** tool from the **Object Type** rollout of the **Compound Objects**; a 3D terrain object will be created, as shown in Figure 11-13. The **Name and Color**, **Pick Operand**, **Parameters**, **Simplification**, and **Color by Elevation** rollouts will also be displayed to modify the terrain object. The most commonly used rollouts related to this tool are discussed next.

Pick Operand Rollout

The **Pick Operand** button in this rollout is used to add splines to the terrain object, refer to Figure 11-14. To add splines to the terrain object, first create new splines and select the terrain object. Next, choose the **Pick Operand** button and move the cursor over the new spline in the viewport; the cursor will change to selection cursor. Next, select the additional splines one by one to add them to the terrain object. In this rollout, the four radio buttons, **Reference**, **Copy**, **Move**, and **Instance** are used to specify the type of new contours to be added to the terrain object.

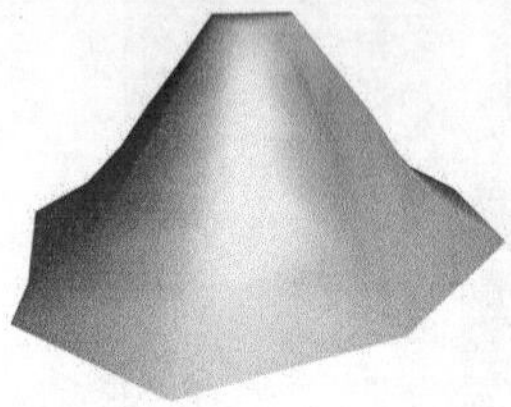

Figure 11-13 *The terrain object created from the contour lines*

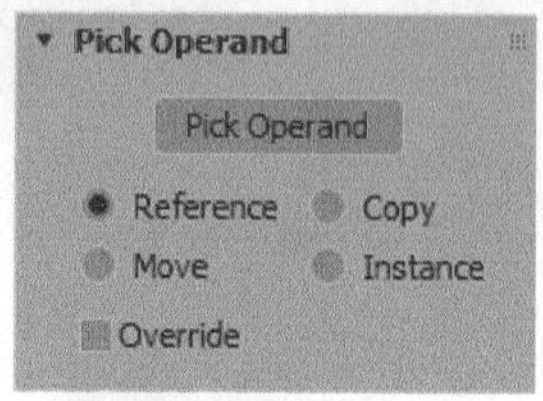

Figure 11-14 *The* ***Pick Operand*** *rollout*

Parameters Rollout

The areas in this rollout are discussed next.

Operands Area

The list box on the top of the **Operands** area displays the list of the current operands in the viewport, refer to Figure 11-15. The **Delete Operand** button is used to delete the selected operand or contour lines from the terrain object. To delete a selected operand, select the name of the operand that you want to delete from the list box and choose the **Delete Operand** button.

Form Area

The radio buttons in this area are used to specify the type of terrain object to be created. By default, the **Graded Surface** radio button is selected. As a result, an empty surface is created for the open bottom of the terrain object. Select the **Graded Solid** radio button to create cover at the open bottom of the terrain. Select the **Layered Solid** radio button to create the layered terrain objects such as cardboard architectural model, as shown in Figure 11-16. Select the **Stitch Border** check box to prevent the creation of new triangles at the edges of the terrain object when the splines are open. Select the **Retriangulate** check box to create more precise terrain objects by following the contour lines more closely.

Note

You can select the different radio buttons and check boxes in the ***Form*** *area to view their effect on the terrain object in the viewport.*

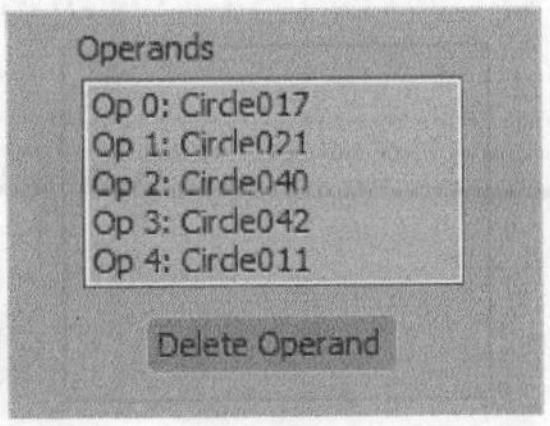

*Figure 11-15 Different areas in the **Parameters** rollout*

*Figure 11-16 The terrain object with the **Layered Solid** radio button selected*

Display Area

The options in the **Display** area are used to specify the terrain object that will be displayed in the viewports. By default, the **Terrain** radio button is selected. As a result, the terrain object is displayed over the contour lines.

The **Contours** radio button is used to display only the contour lines of the terrain object in the viewport. The **Both** radio button is used to display the terrain as well as the contour lines in the viewport. The options in the **Update** area are the same as those discussed in the previous chapters.

Simplification Rollout

The options in this rollout are used to simplify the mesh of the terrain object, refer to Figure 11-17. The areas in this rollout are discussed next.

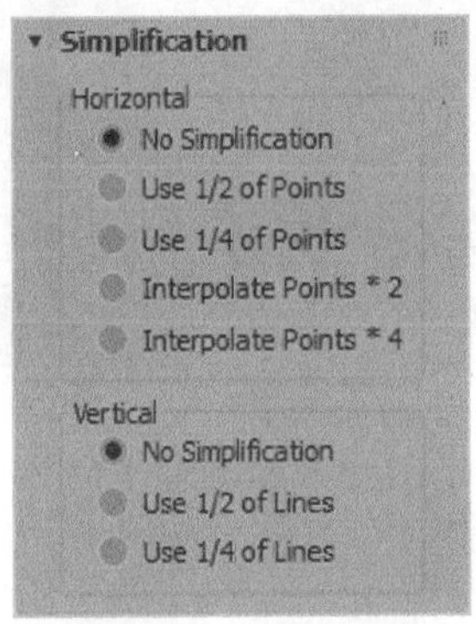

*Figure 11-17 Different areas in the **Simplification** rollout*

Horizontal Area

The options in this area are used to set the number of vertices used in the terrain object. By default, the **No Simplification** radio button is selected and is used to include all vertices on the contour splines. Select the **Use 1/2 of Points** radio button to use half of the vertices of every contour line in the terrain object. Select the **Use 1/4 of Points** radio button to use one/fourth of the vertices of every contour line in the terrain object. Select the **Interpolate Points * 2** radio button to double the vertices of every contour line in the terrain object. Select the **Interpolate Points * 4** radio button to multiply the vertices of every contour line four times in the terrain object.

Vertical Area

The options in this area are used to set the number of contour lines used in the terrain object. By default, the **No Simplification** radio button is selected and is used to include all the selected contour lines in the terrain object. Select the **Use 1/2 of Lines** radio button to use half of the lines in the terrain object. Select the **Use 1/4 of Lines** radio button to use one-fourth of the contour lines in the terrain object.

Color by Elevation Rollout

The options in this rollout are used to set the color of the terrain object on the basis of the elevation of the terrain object.

Scatter

Menu bar:	Create > Compound > Scatter
Toolbar:	Create > Geometry > Compound Objects > Object Type rollout > Scatter

The **Scatter** tool is used to randomly distribute the source object as an array or over the surface of the distribution object. To create a scatter object, first create an object to be used as the source object and create another object to be used as the distribution object. Next, select the source object and choose the **Scatter** tool from the **Object Type** rollout of the **Compound Objects**; the **Pick Distribution Object**, **Scatter Objects**, **Transforms**, **Display**, and **Load/Save Presets** rollouts will be displayed. Now, choose the **Pick Distribution Object** button in the **Pick Distribution Object** rollout and move the cursor over the distribution object; the shape of the cursor will change into a selection cursor. Select the distribution object in the viewport. Next, expand the **Scatter Objects** rollout. In the **Source Object Parameters** area, set the required value in the **Duplicates** spinner to create a number of duplicates of the source object, refer to Figures 11-18 and 11-19. The most commonly used rollouts of this tool are discussed next.

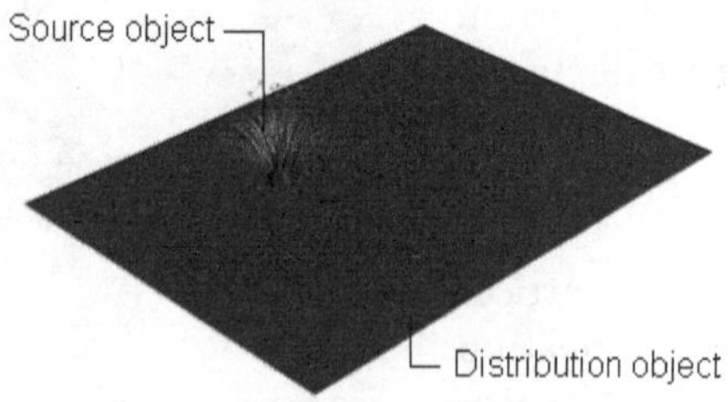

Figure 11-18 The distribution and source objects

Figure 11-19 The duplicates of the source object distributed over the distribution object

Pick Distribution Object Rollout

The **Pick Distribution Object** button in this rollout is used to select the distribution object in the viewport as discussed above. When you select the distribution object, the name of the selected object will be displayed next to the **Object** option at the top of the **Pick Distribution Object** rollout, refer to Figure 11-20. The four radio buttons, **Reference**, **Copy**, **Move**, and **Instance** in this rollout are used to specify the type of distribution object to be added to the scatter object.

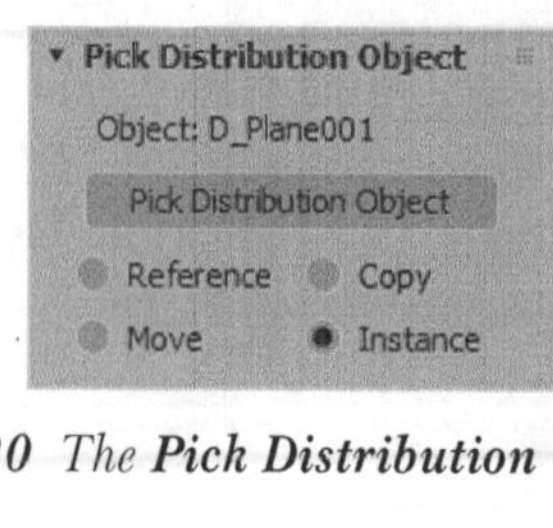

*Figure 11-20 The **Pick Distribution Object** rollout*

Scatter Objects Rollout

The areas in this rollout are discussed next.

Distribution Area

The two radio buttons in this area are used to specify the method of distribution of the source object. By default, the **Use Distribution Object** radio button is selected, which is used to scatter the source object according to the geometry of the distribution object. If you select the **Use Transforms Only** radio button to distribute the source object, then the distribution object is not needed. Instead, you need to use the **Transforms** rollout to position the duplicates of the source object.

To position the duplicates of the source object, select the source object and choose the **Scatter** tool from the **Object Type** rollout in the **Compound Objects**. Make sure that the **Use Transforms Only** radio button is selected in the **Scatter Objects** rollout. Set the number of copies that you want to scatter in the **Duplicates** spinner. Next, expand the **Transforms** rollout and set the transform parameters using various options in it.

Objects Area

The list box in this area displays a list of source objects and the distribution objects, refer to Figure 11-21. Select the objects in the list; their names will be displayed in the modifier stack. On selecting the name of an object in the modifier stack, the corresponding **Parameters** rollout will be displayed in the Modify panel. You can modify the object using this rollout. The **Source Name** and **Distribution Name** text boxes display the names of the source object and the distribution object, respectively. You can also modify their names by entering new names in the text box. The **Extract Operand** button is used to create an instance or a copy of the selected object in the viewport depending on the selection of the radio button below it.

Source Object Parameters Area

The **Duplicates** spinner in this area is used to specify the number of source objects to be copied. Set the value in the **Base Scale** spinner to reduce the size of the source object, refer to Figure 11-22. The value in the **Vertex Chaos** spinner is used to create a disturbance in the source object. The value in the **Animation Offset** spinner is used to create a wavy animation.

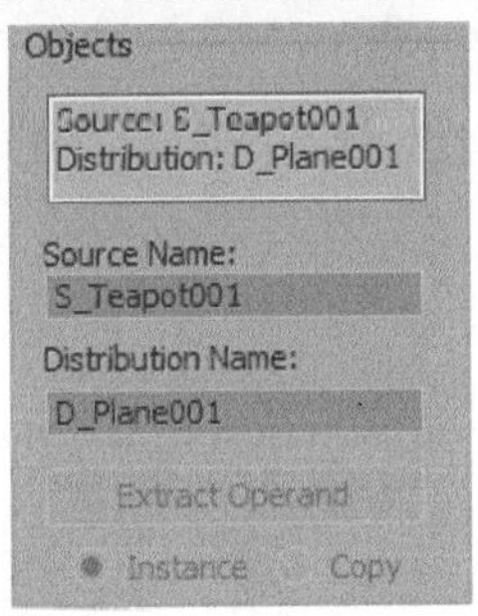

*Figure 11-21 The **Objects** area*

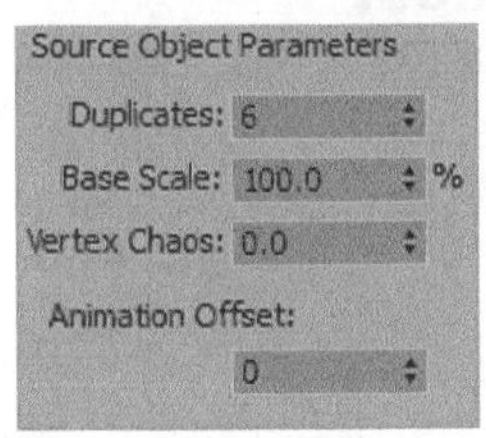

*Figure 11-22 The **Source Object Parameters** area*

Distribution Object Parameter Area

The options in this area are used to arrange the copied source object over the distribution object.

Display Area

The radio buttons in the **Display** area are used to display the output before and after scattering. In this area, the **Result** radio button is selected by default. As a result, the final output is displayed after scattering. You can select the **Operands** radio button to display the objects before scattering.

Transforms Rollout

Set the values in various spinners of this rollout to specify the random transform offsets for each copied source object.

Connect

Menu bar:	Create > Compound > Connect
Toolbar:	Create > Geometry > Compound Objects > Object Type rollout > Connect

The **Connect** tool is used to connect two or more objects at the holes on their surfaces. To connect the objects, create two objects and then convert them into editable objects. Next, select the **Polygon** or **Face** sub-object level in the modifier stack. Now, select the sub-objects of the editable objects in the viewport and then press the DELETE key to delete the selected face or polygon sub-objects, refer to Figure 11-23. Note that you need to position the objects in such a way that the holes should face each other, as shown in Figure 11-24. Next, select one of the objects and choose the **Connect** tool from the **Object Type** rollout in the **Compound Objects**. Choose the **Pick Operand** button in the **Pick Operand** rollout and move the cursor over the second object in the viewport; the shape of the cursor will change into a selection cursor. Select another object; new faces will be created to connect the holes of the objects, as shown in Figure 11-24. Next, right-click to exit the command.

When you choose the **Connect** tool, the **Name and Color**, **Pick Operand**, **Parameters**, and **Display/Update** rollouts will be displayed, refer to Figure 11-25. The most commonly used rollouts are discussed next.

Pick Operand Rollout

As mentioned earlier, the **Pick Operand** rollout is used to select another object in the viewport. The **Pick Operand** button in this rollout has been discussed in the previous section.

Parameters Rollout

The areas in this rollout are discussed next.

Operands Area

The options in this area are the same as those discussed in the boolean compound objects.

Interpolation Area

The **Segments** spinner in this area is used to increase the number of segments in new faces connecting the holes of the two objects. The **Tension** spinner is used to create a curve between the connecting faces. To create a curve, the value in the **Segments** spinner should be high.

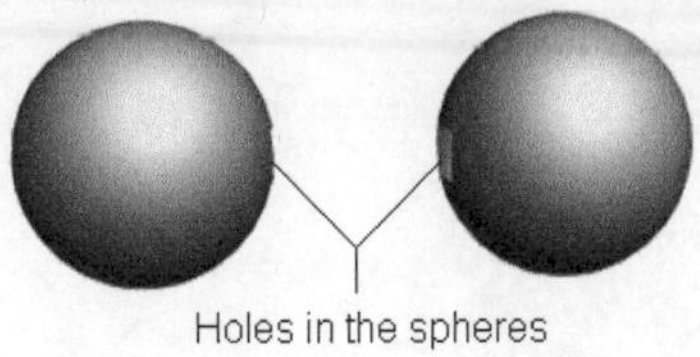

Figure 11-23 Two spheres with holes on their surfaces

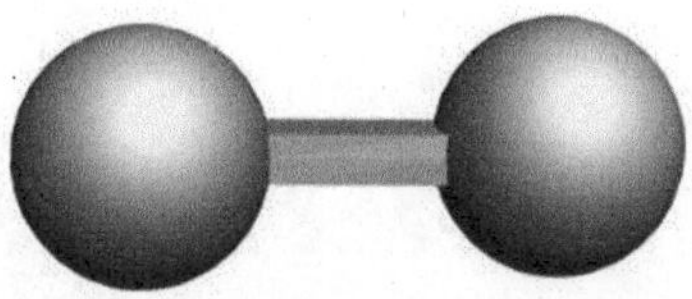

*Figure 11-24 The spheres after performing the **Connect** operation*

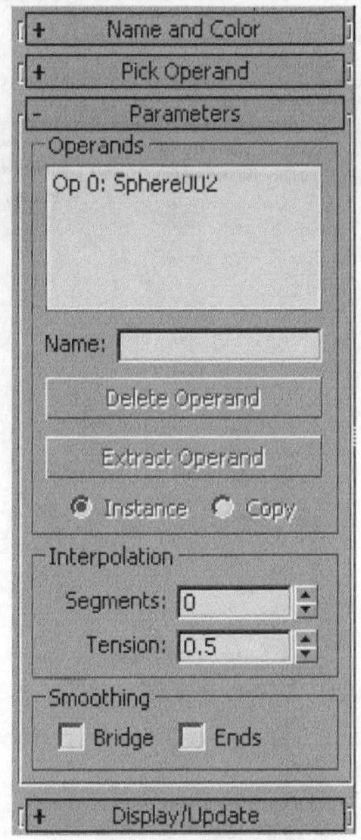

*Figure 11-25 The rollouts displayed after choosing the **Connect** tool*

Smoothing Area

The **Bridge** check box in this area is used to apply smoothness to the connecting faces of the object. The **Ends** check box is used to apply smoothness to the faces that are at the border of the old and new surfaces of the object.

Display/Update Area

The options in the **Display/Update** area are the same as those discussed in the **Boolean** tool.

Loft

Menu bar:	Create > Compound > Loft
Toolbar:	Create > Geometry > Compound Objects > Object Type rollout > Loft

The **Loft** tool is used to create 3D geometry or loft objects from 2D shapes. For creating a loft object, you need to create a path and shape spline in the viewport.

To create a loft object, choose **Create > Shapes > Splines** in the **Command Panel**. Next, create a spline that you need to loft and create another spline to be used as a path, refer to Figure 11-26. Select the spline in the viewport that you want to loft along the path. Choose the **Loft** tool from the **Object Type** rollout in the **Compound Objects**; the **Name and Color**, **Creation Method**, **Surface Parameters**, **Path Parameters**, and **Skin Parameters** rollouts will be displayed, as shown in Figure 11-27. Now, choose the **Get**

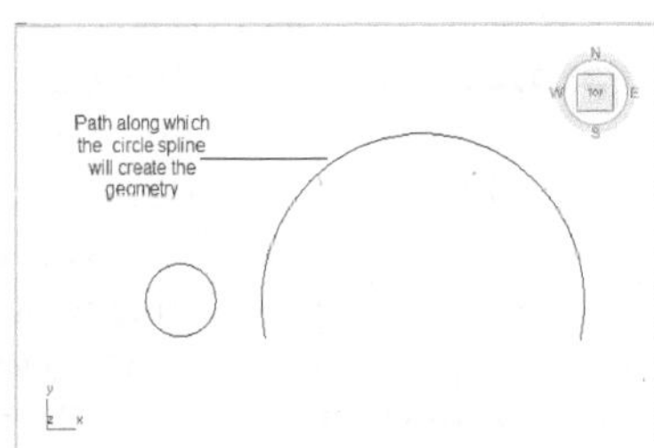

Figure 11-26 Two splines to create a loft object

Path button in the **Creation Method** rollout and move the cursor over the path spline in the viewport; the shape of the cursor will change into a selection cursor. Select the path spline; the loft object will be created along the shape of the path spline, refer to Figure 11-28.

Figure 11-27 *Partial view of the rollouts displayed after invoking the* ***Loft*** *tool*

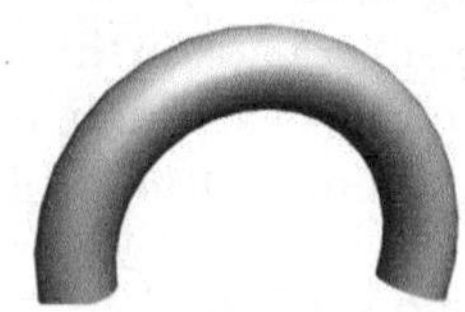

Figure 11-28 *The loft object created*

You can also create a loft object using the **Get Shape** button in the **Creation Method** rollout. To do so, first you need to select the path spline, and then choose the **Loft** tool from the **Object Type** rollout in the **Compound Objects**. Choose the **Get Shape** button in the **Creation Method** rollout; a selection cursor will be displayed in the viewport, which will prompt you to select the shape spline. Select the shape spline; the loft object will be created along the path. The most commonly used rollouts to modify the loft objects are discussed next.

Creation Method Rollout

The options in the **Creation Method** rollout are used to select the path spline or the shape spline in the viewports to create a loft object. If you first select the shape spline in the viewport, then you need to choose the **Get Path** button in the **Creation Method** rollout to select the path spline in the viewport, along which the shape will be extruded to create a loft object. If you first select the path spline in the viewport, then you need to choose the **Get Shape** button in the **Creation Method** rollout to select the shape spline in the viewport to create a loft object along the path. Select the **Copy**, **Instance**, or **Move** radio button to specify the type of path or shape added to the loft object.

Surface Parameters Rollout

The options in the **Surface Parameters** rollout are used to specify the smoothness and the mapping coordinates of the lofting surface. The areas in this rollout are discussed next.

Smoothing Area

In this area, the **Smooth Length** and **Smooth Width** check boxes are selected by default. The **Smooth Length** check box is used to create the smoothness along the length of the path. The **Smooth Width** check box is used to create smoothness around the circumference of the path.

Mapping Area

The **Apply Mapping** check box in this area is used to apply the mapping coordinates to the loft object. On selecting this check box, the other options in this rollout will be activated. Set the value in the **Length Repeat** spinner to specify the number of times the map will be repeated along the length of the path. Set the value in the **Width Repeat** spinner to specify the number of times the map will be repeated around the circumference of the path.

Materials Area

In this area, the **Generate Material IDs** and **Use Shape IDs** check boxes are selected by default. The **Generate Material IDs** check box is used to create the material IDs for the loft object. The **Use Shape IDs** check box is used to create the material IDs from the spline material IDs. The material ID is the identification number that determines the sub-material in the **Multi/Sub-Object** material.

Output Area

The options in the **Output** area are used to define the type of the loft object to be displayed. By default, the **Mesh** radio button is selected and it is used to produce a mesh object. The **Patch** radio button is used to produce a patch object.

Path Parameters Rollout

If you use more than one shape to create a complex loft object, then the options in this rollout will be used to specify the position of multiple shapes along the path of the loft object. Set the value in the **Path** spinner to define the distance between the multiple shapes along the path. Select the **On** check box; the **Snap** spinner will be activated. Set the value in the **Snap** spinner to define the snap increments while setting the value in the **Path** spinner. For example, if you set the value 10.0 in the **Snap** spinner, then on setting the value in the **Path** spinner, it will be increased in the multiples of 10.0. By default, the **Percentage** radio button is selected. Therefore, the values in the **Path** and **Snap** spinners are defined as the percentage of the total path length. Select the **Distance** radio button to define the values in the **Path** and **Snap** spinners as the distance from the first vertex of the path. To place the shapes on the path steps and vertices, select the **Path Steps** radio button.

Skin Parameters Rollout

The options in this rollout are used to simplify the mesh or patch object.

Deformations Rollout

This rollout will be available only when you choose the **Modify** tab in the **Command Panel**. The options in this rollout are used to modify the loft objects to get different shapes, refer to Figure 11-29. You can scale, twist, teeter, bevel, and fit the loft objects using the tools in this rollout. To modify a loft object, first select it in the viewport and then choose the **Modify** tab in the **Command Panel**. Now, expand the **Deformations** rollout and choose one of the tools in this rollout to modify the selected loft object; the respective **Deformation** dialog box will be displayed.

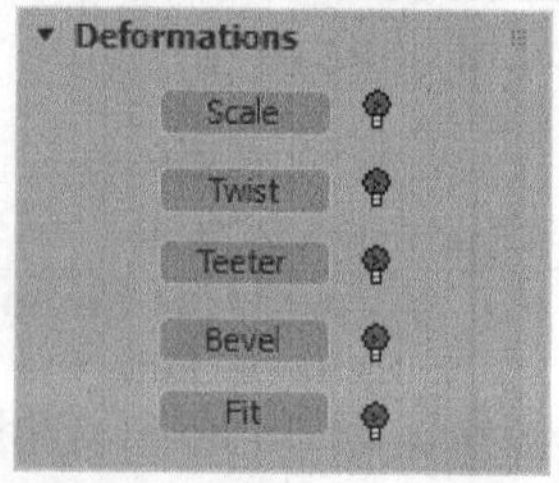

*Figure 11-29 The **Deformations** rollout*

The **Scale Deformation(X)** dialog box is shown in Figure 11-30. By default, a horizontal red line is displayed in this dialog box that represents the path steps along the X-axis of the loft object. The left point on the line represents the first vertex of the path.

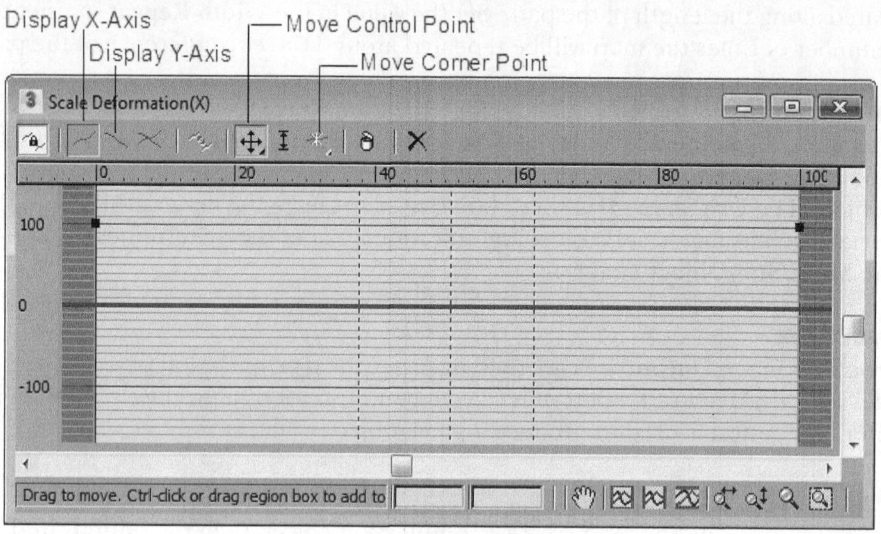

***Figure 11-30** The **Scale Deformation(X)** dialog box*

The right point on the line represents the last vertex of the path. To modify the loft object along its X-axis, choose the **Move Control Point** button at the top in the dialog box, refer to Figure 11-30. Now, move the cursor over the first or the last vertex; the shape of the cursor will change.

Press and hold the left mouse button on the vertex and move the cursor vertically to scale the shape of the loft object. You can also insert more vertices in between these two vertices. To do so, choose the **Insert Corner Point** button on the top of the dialog box and click on the path where you want to insert the vertices. To modify the loft object along the Y-axis, choose the **Display Y-Axis** button at the top in the dialog box; the path for the Y-axis will be displayed in green color. Figures 11-31 through 11-35 show the loft objects modified using the **Scale**, **Twist**, **Fit**, **Bevel**, and **Teeter** tools.

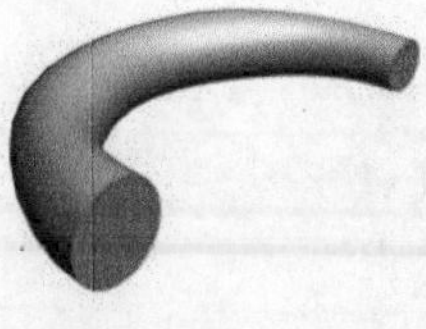

*Figure 11-31 The loft object modified using the **Scale** tool*

*Figure 11-32 The loft object modified using the **Twist** tool*

*Figure 11-33 The loft object modified using the **Fit** tool*

*Figure 11-34 The loft object modified using the **Bevel** tool*

*Figure 11-35 The loft object modified using the **Teeter** tool*

ShapeMerge

Menu bar:	Create > Compound > ShapeMerge
Toolbar:	Create > Geometry > Compound Objects > Object Type rollout > ShapeMerge

In a shape merge object, the shape is either embedded in the mesh object or subtracted from it. To create a shape merge object, first you need to create a mesh object and a shape, and then align them, as shown in Figure 11-36. Next, select the mesh object and choose the **ShapeMerge** tool from the **Object Type** rollout of the **Compound Objects**. Next, choose the **Pick Shape** button in the **Pick Operand** rollout; a selection cursor will be displayed that will prompt you to select the shape spline. Select the shape spline and right-click to exit the shape merge command.

To view the shape merge object with the embedded shape in it, select the shape merge object. Choose the **Modify** tab in the **Command Panel** and select the **Face Extrude** modifier from the **Modifier List** drop-down list. In the **Parameters** rollout of the **Face Extrude** modifier, set the value in the **Amount** spinner; the shape will be embedded in the mesh object, as shown in Figure 11-37.

To view the subtracted shape in the shape merge object, select the **ShapeMerge** object level in the modifier stack; various rollouts will be displayed. In the **Parameters** rollout, select the **Cookie Cutter** radio button in the **Operation** area; the shape will be subtracted from the mesh object, as shown in Figure 11-38. When you choose the **ShapeMerge** tool, the **Name and Color**, **Pick Operand**, **Parameters**, and **Display/Update** rollouts will be displayed, as shown in Figure 11-39. These rollouts are discussed next.

***Figure 11-36** Alignment of the shape with the mesh object*

***Figure 11-37** The shape embedded in the mesh object*

***Figure 11-38** The shape subtracted from the mesh object*

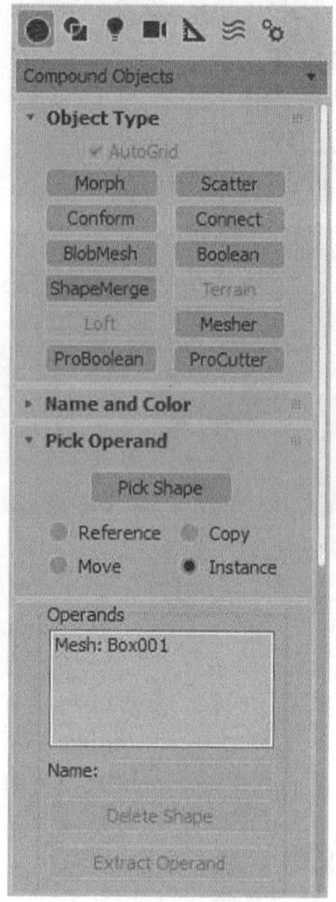

***Figure 11-39** Partial view of the rollouts displayed after invoking the **ShapeMerge** tool*

Pick Operand Rollout

The **Pick Shape** button in the **Pick Operand** rollout is used to select the shape in the viewport and to merge it in the mesh object. The other options are same as discussed earlier.

Parameters Rollout

The areas in this rollout are discussed next.

Operands Area

The options in this area are the same as discussed earlier.

Operation Area

By default, the **Merge** radio button is selected. This radio button is used to create an embedded shape merge object. Select the **Cookie Cutter** radio button to create the subtracted shape merge object. Select the **Invert** check box to invert the effects of the **Merge** or the **Cookie Cutter** radio button.

Display/Update Rollout

The options in this rollout are the same as discussed earlier.

Conform

Menu bar: Create > Compound > Conform
Toolbar: Create > Geometry > Compound Objects > Object Type rollout > Conform

The **Conform** tool is used to adjust the position of an object over another object such that the object completely fits on another object according to its shape, refer to Figure 11-40. The object that is to be positioned over another object is known as the Wrapper object, whereas the object on which the Wrapper object will be positioned is known as the Wrap-To object.

To create a conform object, you need two objects. One of these objects will be used as the Wrapper object and another as the Wrap-To object. Position both the objects, refer to Figure 11-40. Select the Wrapper object and then choose the **Conform** tool from the **Object Type** rollout in the **Compound Objects**. Choose the **Pick Wrap-To Object** button in the **Pick Wrap-To Object** rollout; a selection cursor will be displayed which will prompt you to select the Wrap-To object. Select the Wrap-To object; the Wrapper object will be positioned over the Wrap-To object in such a way that it fits according to the shape of the Wrap-To object, as shown in Figure 11-41. Next, you need to set the other parameters in the various rollouts displayed on invoking the **Conform** tool. These rollouts are discussed next.

*Figure 11-40 The road (Wrapper object) fitted over a hilly area (Wrap-To object) before using the **Conform** tool*

*Figure 11-41 The road (Wrapper object) fitted over a hilly area (Wrap-To object) after using the **Conform** tool*

Pick Wrap-To Object Rollout

The **Pick Wrap-To** button in this rollout is used to select the Wrap-To object in the viewport. The other options are the same as discussed earlier in this chapter.

Parameters Rollout

The areas in this rollout are discussed next.

Objects Area

The options in this area are the same as discussed earlier in this chapter.

Vertex Projection Direction Area

The **Vertex Projection Direction** area consists of different radio buttons that are used to specify the projection of the vertices in the conform object.

Wrapper Parameters Area

Set the value in the **Default Projection Distance** spinner to adjust the distance of a vertex in the Wrapper object from its default position so that it intersects the Wrap-To object. Set the value in the **Standoff Distance** spinner to adjust the distance between a vertex of the Wrapper object and the surface of the Wrap-To object.

The **Update** and **Display** areas are the same as discussed earlier.

ProBoolean

Menu bar:	Create > Compound > ProBoolean
Toolbar:	Create > Geometry > Compound Objects > Object Type rollout > ProBoolean

The **ProBoolean** tool is used to perform some advanced functions in a boolean operation. In this process, you can select multiple objects to boolean at a time, change the boolean operations, and reorder the operands. The objects that are used to create the proboolean object are called as operands. You need to perform the boolean operations on these operands using the **ProBoolean** tool.

To create a proboolean object, create two or more objects in the viewport and arrange them such that they should intersect each other, refer to Figure 11-42. Now, select the object on which you want to perform the boolean operation. Next, choose the **ProBoolean** tool from the **Object Type** rollout in the **Compound Objects**; the **Name and Color**, **Pick Boolean**, **Parameters**, and **Advanced Options** rollouts will be displayed. Next, choose the operation that you want to perform in the **Operations** area of the **Parameters** rollout. Now, choose the **Start Picking** button in the **Pick Boolean** rollout and move the cursor over another object; the boolean cursor will be displayed. Now, click on the object to perform the boolean operation. Note that the **Start Picking** button remains active and you can select one or more objects to perform the boolean operation. Select other objects in the viewport one by one to perform the boolean operation. Then, choose the **Start Picking** button again to deactivate it, refer to Figures 11-43, 11-44, and 11-45.

Note

When you select the objects to perform a boolean operation in the viewport, they will be displayed as operands in the text field of the ***Sub-objects Operations*** *area in the* ***Parameters*** *rollout.*

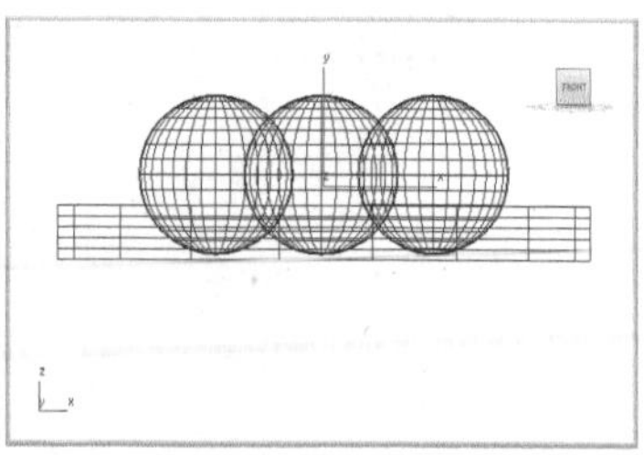

Figure 11-42 The objects to perform the proboolean operation in the Front viewport

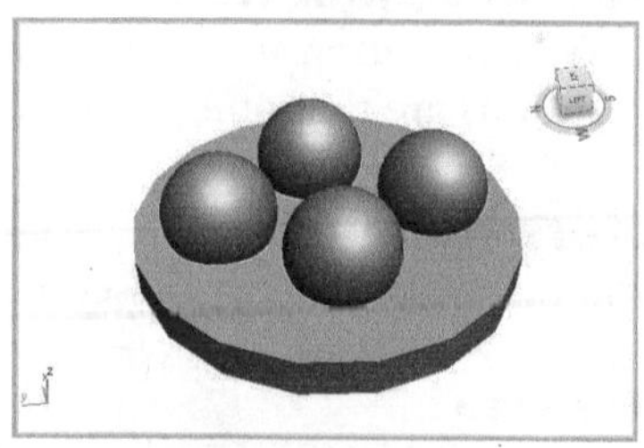

Figure 11-43 The objects to perform the proboolean operation in the Perspective viewport

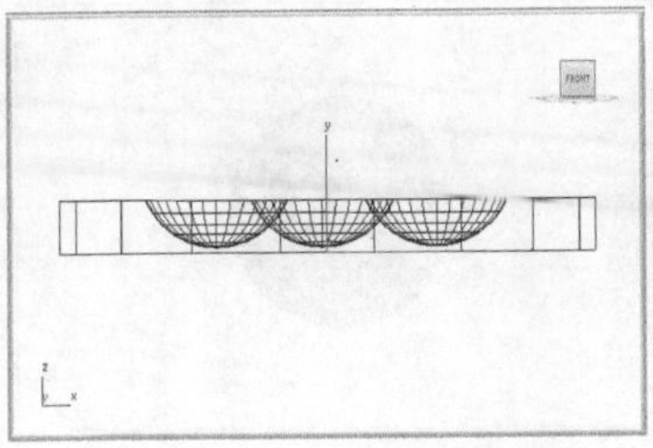

Figure 11-44 The objects after performing the proboolean operation in the Front viewport

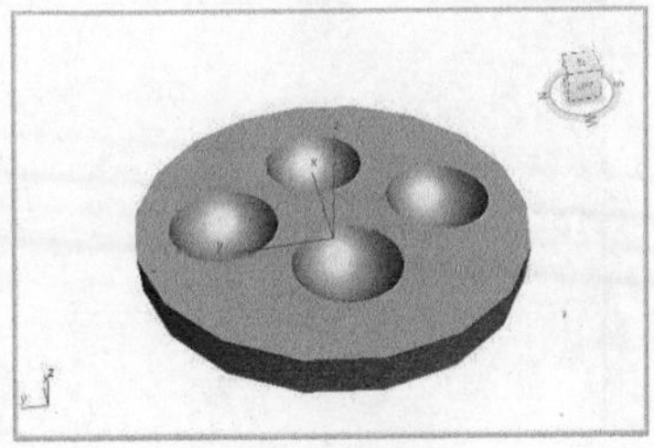

Figure 11-45 The objects after performing the proboolean operation in the Perspective viewport

The most commonly used rollouts are discussed next.

Pick Boolean Rollout

The **Start Picking** button in this rollout is used to select the operands in the viewport to perform the proboolean operation. The other options in this rollout are the same as discussed earlier in this chapter.

Parameters Rollout

The **Parameters** rollout is used to define the type of the proboolean operation. The areas in this rollout are discussed next.

Operation Area

The options in the **Operation** area are used to specify the type of proboolean operations to be performed on the operands. You need to select one of the radio buttons in this area before choosing the **Start Picking** button in the **Pick Boolean** rollout to perform different boolean operations.

The **Union**, **Intersection**, and **Subtraction** radio buttons are the same as discussed earlier in this chapter. The **Merge** radio button is used to join the objects into a single object. You can also select one of the check boxes in this area to create more effects.

Select the **Imprint** check box to print the outline of the intersecting edges of the object, refer to Figures 11-46, 11-47, and 11-48. Select the **Cookie** check box to delete the faces of the original object, as shown in Figure 11-49.

The options in the **Display** area are the same as discussed earlier.

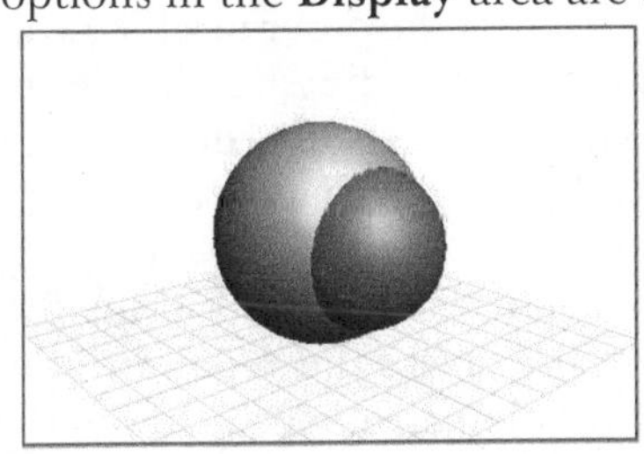

Figure 11-46 The two spheres intersecting each other to perform the boolean operation

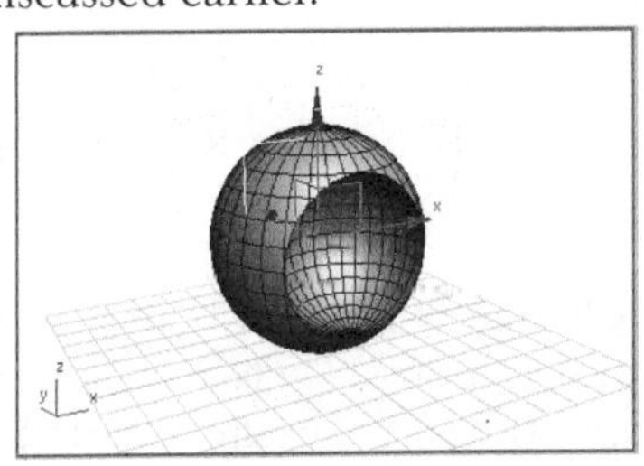

Figure 11-47 The proboolean object after performing the boolean operation

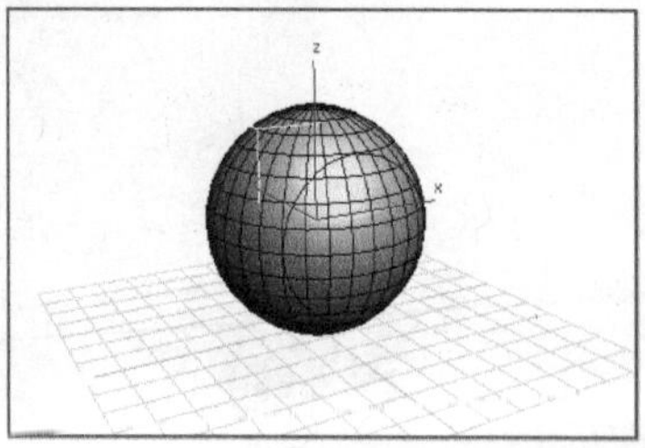

*Figure 11-48 The proboolean object after selecting the **Imprint** check box*

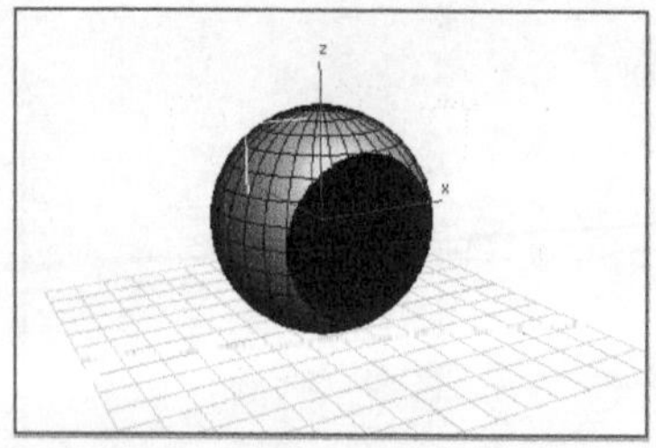

*Figure 11-49 The proboolean object after selecting the **Cookie** check box*

Apply Material Area

Select the **Apply Operand Material** radio button in this area to apply the material of the operand to the new faces created by the proboolean operation. Select the **Retain Original Material** radio button to apply the material of the original object to the new faces created by using the proboolean operation, refer to Figures 11-50, 11-51, and 11-52.

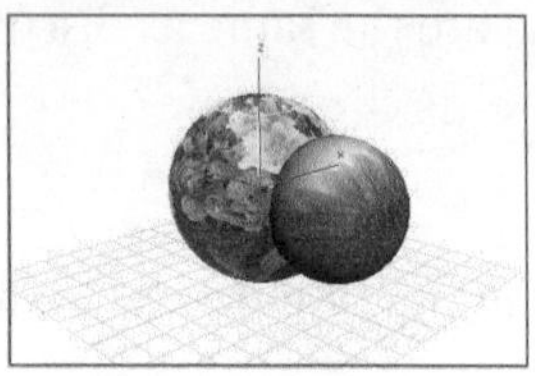

Figure 11-50 The two spheres with materials applied on them

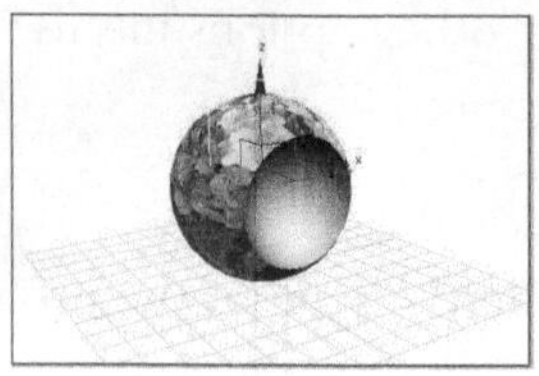

*Figure 11-51 The proboolean object after selecting the **Apply Operand Material** radio button*

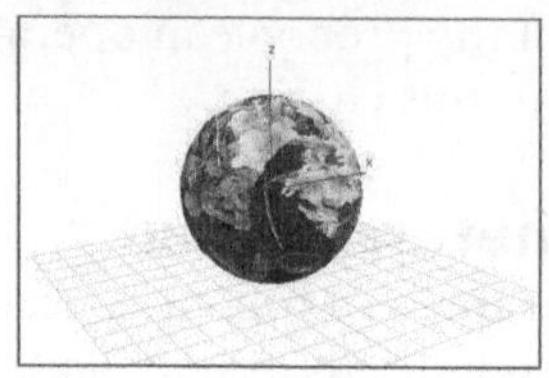

*Figure 11-52 The proboolean object after selecting the **Retain Original Material** radio button*

Sub-object Operations Area

The options in this area are used on the operands created in the viewport. These operands are also highlighted in the list given at the bottom of the **Sub-object Operations** area. The **Extract Selected** button is used to extract a copy or an instance of the selected operand of the boolean object from the list. To do so, select the boolean object in the viewport, choose the **Modify** tab in the **Command Panel**, and then select the operand that you want to extract from the list in the **Parameters** rollout. Next, select the **Copy** radio button to create a copy of the selected operand. Select the **Remove** radio button to remove the selected operand from the list or select the **Inst** radio button to create an instance of the selected operand. Next, choose the **Extract Selected** button to extract the selected operand.

The **Reorder Ops** button is used to change the order of the boolean operations in the viewport. To do so, select an operand in the list and then set the order in which you want the boolean operation to be performed by entering the corresponding number in the spinner on the right side of the **Reorder Ops** button. Next, choose the **Reorder Ops** button; the order of the boolean operations will be changed in the list as well as in the viewport.

The **Change Operation** button is used to change the type of operation for the selected operand. To do so, select the operand in the list and select the required operation by selecting the corresponding radio button in the **Operation** area. Next, choose the **Change Operation** button; the operand will show the changed boolean operation.

ProCutter

Menu bar:	Create > Compound > ProCutter
Toolbar:	Create > Geometry > Compound Objects > Object Type rollout > ProCutter

The **ProCutter** tool is used to break an object into separate objects with the help of the mesh objects. The mesh objects that are used to break the object are known as cutters and the object that is divided by cutters is known as the stock object.

To create a procutter object, first create an object to be broken into separate objects. Create one or more mesh objects to be used as cutters. Align both the objects, as shown in Figures 11-53 and 11-54.

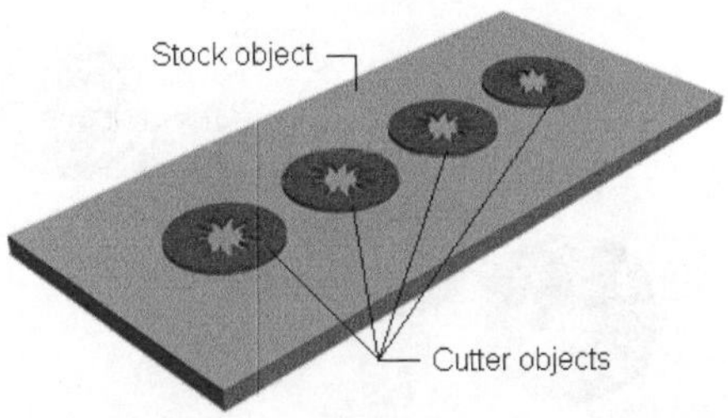

Figure 11-53 The cutter and stock objects aligned for the procutter operation

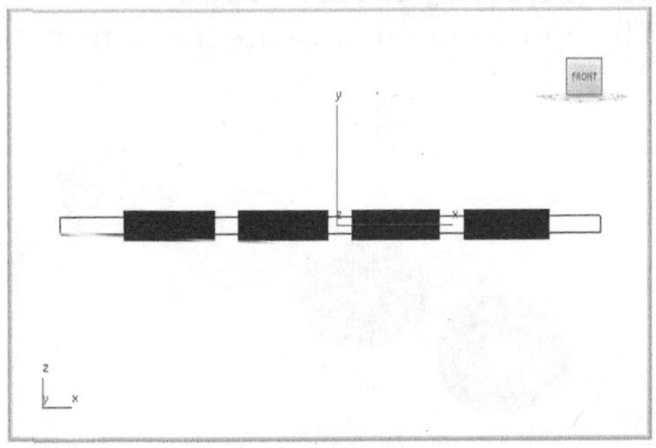

Figure 11-54 The cutter and stock objects before performing the procutter operation in the Front viewport

Select one of the cutter objects and then choose the **ProCutter** tool from the **Object Type** rollout in the **Compound Objects**; the **Name and Color**, **Cutter Picking Parameters**, **Cutter Parameters**, and **Advanced Options** rollouts will be displayed. In the **Cutter Picking Parameters** rollout, choose the **Pick Cutter Objects** button and select the additional cutters in the viewport. Next, choose the **Pick Stock Objects** button and select the object that you want to cut in the viewport; the object will be cut, as shown in Figure 11-55. Right-click to exit the command. The most commonly used rollouts are discussed next.

Cutter Picking Parameters Rollout

The **Pick Cutter Objects** button in this rollout is used to select the objects or cutters in the viewport that are used to divide the object. The **Pick Stock Objects** button is used to select the object that will be separated by the cutters. The other options in this rollout are the same as discussed earlier.

Figure 11-55 The cutter and stock objects after performing the procutter operation

Cutter Parameters Rollout

The **Cutter Parameters** rollout is used to define the type of procutter operations. The areas in this rollout are discussed next.

Cutting Options Area

The check boxes in this area are used to define the final output of the procutter operation. The **Stock Outside Cutter** check box is used to get the parts of the stock object that are outside the cutters, refer to Figure 11-55. Select the **Stock Inside Cutter** check box to get the parts of the stock object that are inside the cutters, refer to Figure 11-56. Select the **Cutter Outside Stock** check box to get the parts of the cutters that are outside the stock object, as shown in Figure 11-57.

The options in the **Display** and **Apply Material** areas are same as discussed earlier.

Sub-object Operations Area

The options in this area are the same as discussed in the **ProBoolean** compound object.

***Figure 11-56** The cutter and stock objects after selecting the **Stock Inside Cutter** check box*

***Figure 11-57** The cutter and stock objects after selecting the **Cutter Outside Stock** check box*

TUTORIALS

Before starting the tutorials, you need to download the *c11_3dsmax_2017_tut.zip* file from *www.cadcim.com*. The path of the file is as follows: *Textbooks > Animation and Visual Effects > 3ds Max > Autodesk 3ds Max 2017: A Comprehensive Guide*

Extract the contents of the zipped file and save them in the *Documents* folder.

Tutorial 1

In this tutorial, you will create a toothpaste tube using the **Loft** and **Boolean** tools, as shown in Figure 11-58. **(Expected time: 30 min)**

***Figure 11-58** The model of a toothpaste tube*

The following steps are required to complete this tutorial:

a. Create the project folder.
b. Create the body of toothpaste tube.
c. Create the cap of toothpaste tube.
d. Assign materials and maps to the tube.
e. Save and render the scene.

Creating the Project Folder

1. Create a new project folder with the name *c11_tut1* at *\Documents\3dsmax2017* and then save the file with the name *c11tut1*, as discussed in Tutorial 1 of Chapter 2.

2. Open the Windows Explorer and then browse to the *c11_3dsmax_2017_tut* folder and copy the *toothpaste_tube.jpg* file from this folder to *\Documents\3dsmax2017\c11_tut1\sceneassets\images*.

Creating the Body of Toothpaste Tube

In this section, you will create the body of toothpaste tube by using the **Loft** tool.

1. Activate the Front viewport. Choose **Create > Shapes** from the **Command Panel**; the **Splines** option is displayed in the drop-down list in the **Command Panel**. Next, choose the **Circle** tool from the **Object Type** rollout.

2. Create a circle in the viewport to use it as a shape spline. It is automatically named as *Circle001*.

3. In the **Parameters** rollout, set the value **4.0** in the **Radius** spinner.

4. Create another circle in the Front viewport, refer to Figure 11-60, to use as a shape spline and set the value **16.0** in the **Radius** spinner. It is automatically named as *Circle002*.

5. Choose the **Line** tool from **Create > Shapes > Splines > Object Type** rollout in the **Command Panel**.

6. Create a line in the Top viewport to use as a path spline. You can assume your own dimensions for the length of the line, refer to Figure 11-59. The line is automatically named as *Line001*.

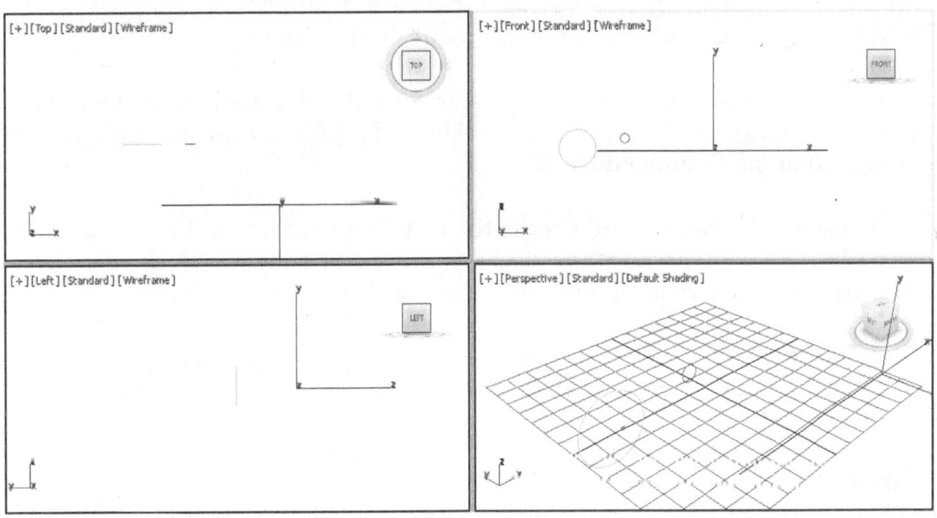

Figure 11-59 *The Circle001, Circle002, and Line001 splines in viewports*

7. Activate the Front viewport and choose the **Rectangle** tool from **Create > Shapes > Splines > Object Type** rollout in the **Command Panel**. Create a rectangle to use as a shape spline. The rectangle is automatically named as *Rectangle001*.

8. In the **Parameters** rollout of *Rectangle001*, set the following parameters:

   Width: **55.033** Length: **5.76** Corner Radius: **1.0**

   The *Rectangle001* spline is displayed in the viewports, as shown in Figure 11-60.

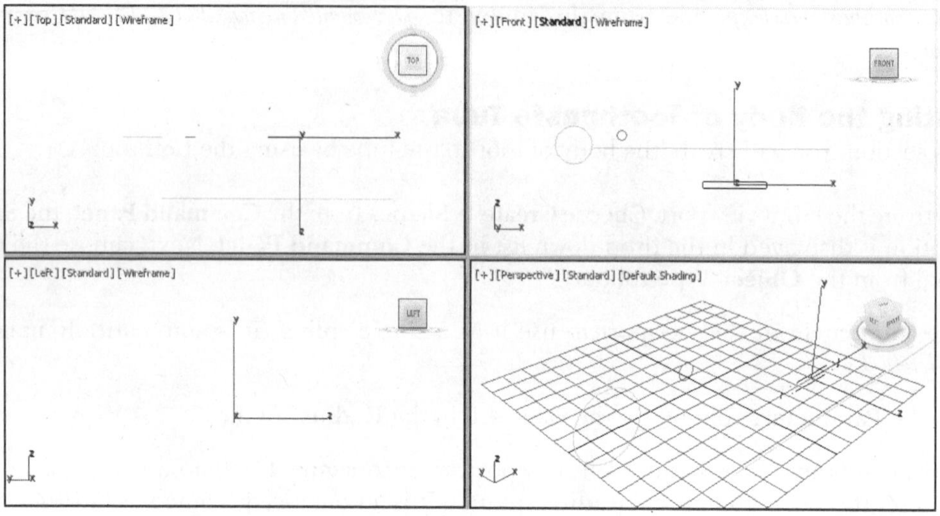

Figure 11-60 *The Rectangle001 displayed in viewports*

Next, you will create a loft object using the shape splines, path spline, and the **Loft** tool. You will use *Circle001*, *Circle002*, and *Rectangle001* as the shape splines and *Line001* as the path spline.

9. Activate the Front viewport, select *Line001* spline in the viewport.

10. Choose **Create > Geometry** from the **Command Panel**. Select **Compound Objects** from the drop-down list and then choose the **Loft** tool from the **Object Type** rollout; various rollouts are displayed in the **Command Panel**.

11. In the **Creation Method** rollout, choose the **Get Shape** button and move the cursor over *Circle001* in the Front viewport; the shape of the cursor changes. Now, select *Circle001*; a shape is created, as shown in Figure 11-61. The new shape is automatically named as *Loft001*.

12. Make sure that *Loft001* is selected in the viewport. In the **Path Parameters** rollout, set the value **8.0** in the **Path** spinner to define the distance between *Circle001* and *Circle002* along *Line001*.

Note

*The value in the **Path** spinner is set according to the length of the line spline.*

13. In the **Creation Method** rollout, choose the **Get Shape** button and move the cursor over *Circle002* in the Front viewport; the shape of the cursor changes. Select *Circle002*; the shape of the tube is created, refer to Figure 11-62. Again, choose the **Get Shape** button to exit the command.

Next, you need to create the shape of the lower portion of the tube. To do so, activate the Top viewport.

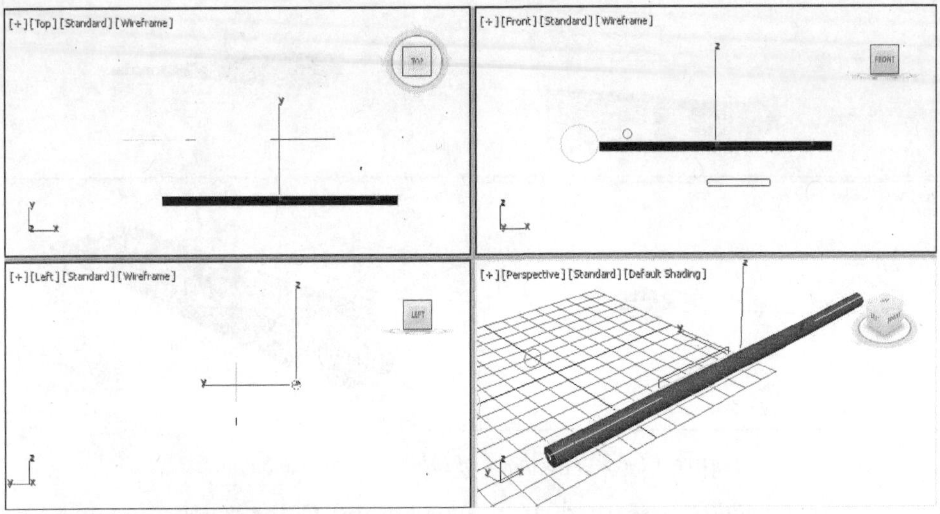

Figure 11-61 *A shape created along the path spline (Line001)*

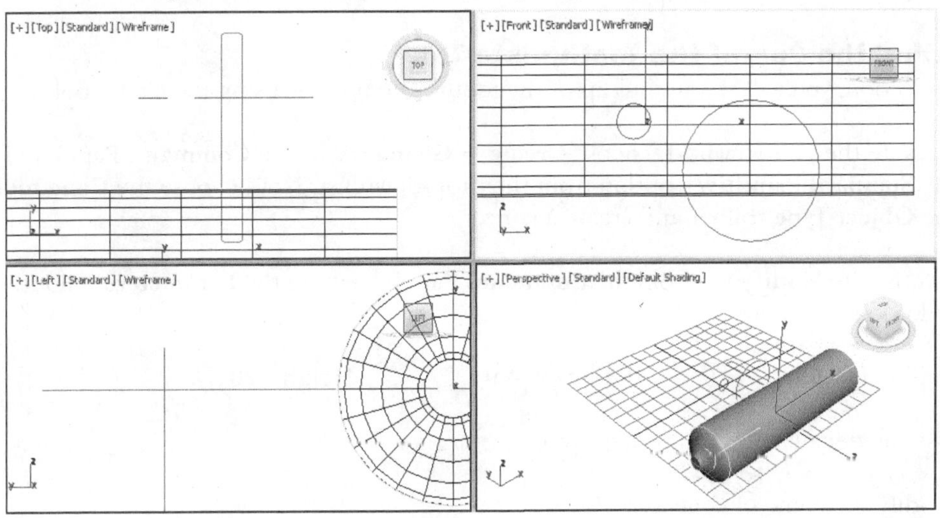

Figure 11-62 *The shape of the tube created along the path spline*

14. Make sure that *Loft001* is selected in the viewport. In the **Path Parameters** rollout, set the value **98.0** in the **Path** spinner.

15. In the **Creation Method** rollout, choose the **Get Shape** button and move the cursor over *Rectangle001* in the Front viewport; the shape of the cursor changes. Select *Rectangle001*; the shape of tube is created, refer to Figure 11-63. Next, right-click in the viewport to exit the loft command.

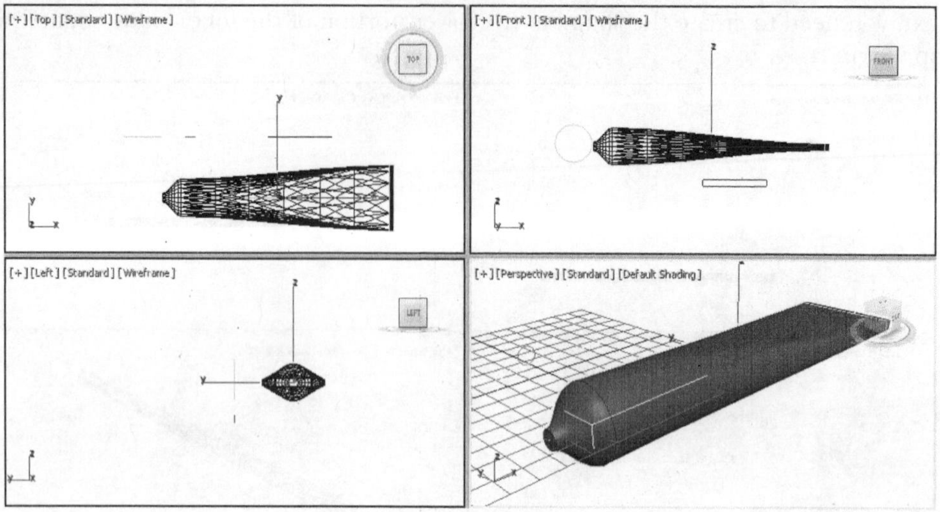

Figure 11-63 The shape of tube created in viewports

16. Make sure that *Loft001* is selected. In the **Name and Color** rollout, rename *Loft001* to *toothpaste tube*.

Creating the Cap of the Toothpaste Tube

In this section, you will create the cap of the toothpaste tube by using the **Cone** tool.

1. Activate the Left viewport, choose **Create > Geometry** in the **Command Panel** and select the **Standard Primitives** option from the drop-down list. Now, choose the **Cone** tool from the **Object Type** rollout and create a cone.

2. Choose the **Modify** tab from the **Command Panel**. Next, in the **Parameters** rollout, set the following parameters:

   Radius 1: **9.0** Radius 2: **4.0** Height: **20**

   Use the default values for other options.

3. Modify the name of cone as *cap01*.

4. Make sure that *cap01* is selected. Next, right-click on it; a quad menu is displayed. Choose the **Hide Unselected** option to temporarily hide other objects in the viewport.

5. Choose the **Zoom Extents All Selected** tool; *cap01* is zoomed in the viewports, as shown in Figure 11-64.

   Next, you need to create a hole in *cap01* to create the space for inserting the top portion of *toothpaste tube*. To do so, you need to use the **Boolean** tool in **Compound Objects**.

6. Activate the Top viewport and select *cap01*.

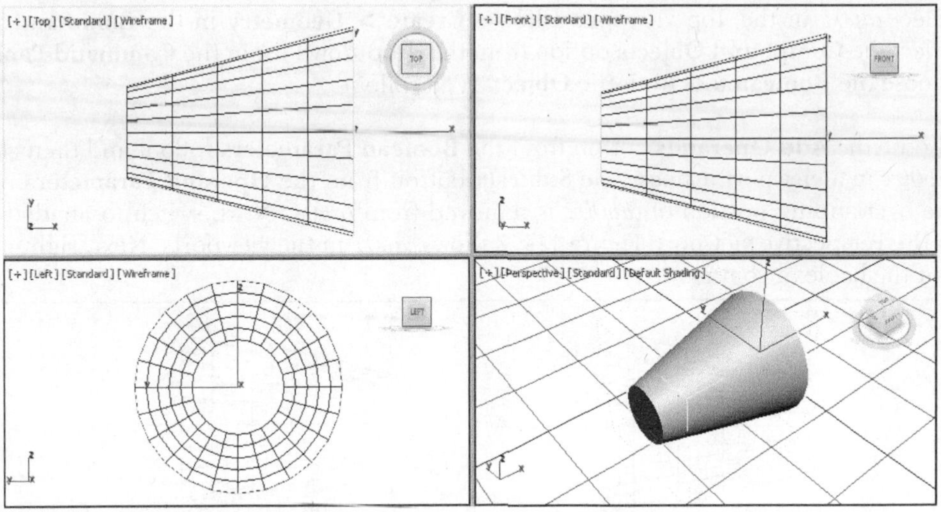

Figure 11-64 The cap01 geometry zoomed in viewports

7. Choose the **Use Selection Center** tool from the Use Pivot Center flyout in the **Main Toolbar**; the coordinate gizmo moves to the center of *cap01*. Also, choose the **Select and Uniform Scale** tool.

Note

*The tools available in the **Use Center** flyout determine the geometric center for the scale and rotate operations.*

8. Activate the Perspective viewport and make sure the cap is selected. Press and hold the SHIFT key and the left mouse button and move the cursor down until the value in the X, Y, and Z coordinates in the coordinate display becomes **90** and then release the left mouse button and the SHIFT key; the **Clone Options** dialog box is displayed. Make sure that the **Copy** radio button is selected and **1** is set in the **Number of Copies** spinner and then choose the **OK** button; *cap002* is displayed, as shown in Figure 11-65. You need to switch to wireframe mode in the Perspective viewport to view *cap002*, refer to Figure 11-65.

9. Activate the Front viewport and then choose the **Select and Move** tool and align *cap002* with *cap01*, as shown in Figure 11-66.

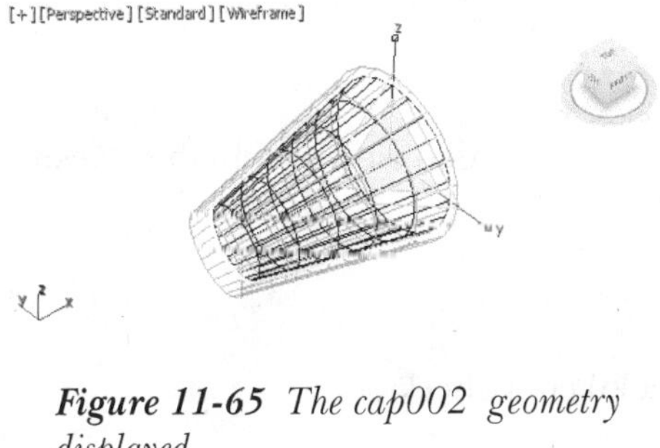

Figure 11-65 The cap002 geometry displayed

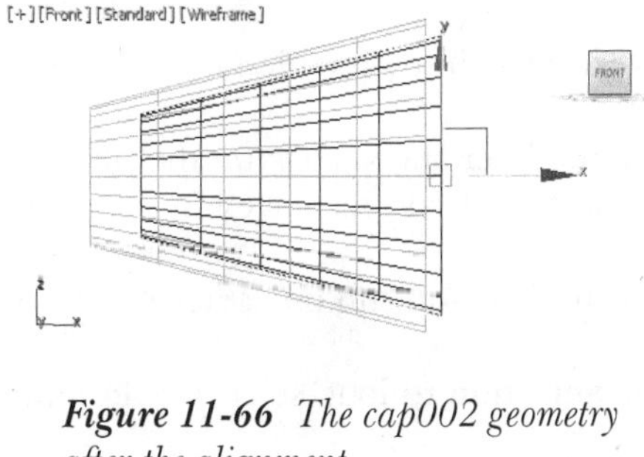

Figure 11-66 The cap002 geometry after the alignment

10. Select *cap01* in the Top viewport. Choose **Create > Geometry** in the **Command Panel**. Select the **Compound Objects** option from the drop-down list in the **Command Panel** and choose the **Boolean** tool from the **Object Type** rollout.

11. Choose the **Add Operands** button from the **Boolean Parameters** rollout and then click on *cap002* in a viewport. Choose the **Subtract** button from the **Operand Parameters** rollout; the overlapping portion of *cap002* is removed from *cap01*. Next, switch to Shaded mode in the Perspective viewport. Figure 11-67 shows *cap01* in the viewports. Next, right-click to exit the boolean command.

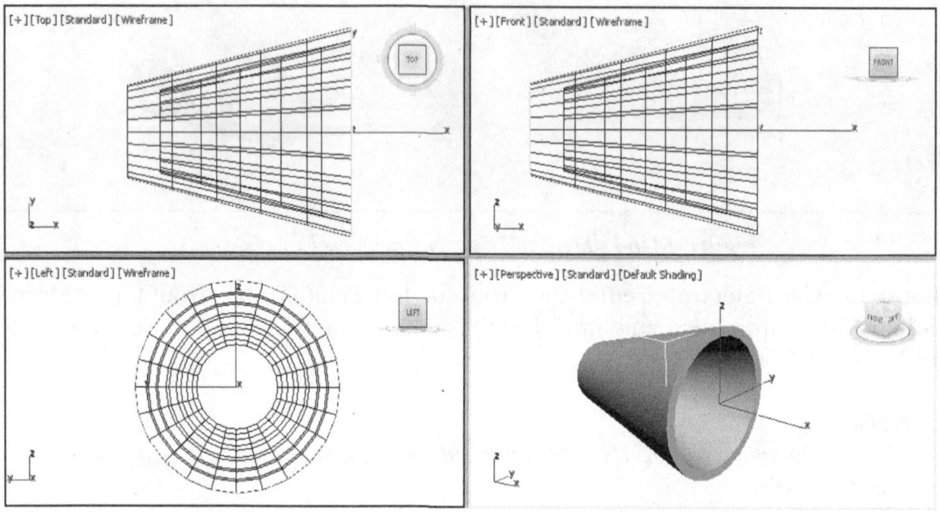

Figure 11-67 *The cap01 after performing the Subtraction(A-B) boolean operation in viewports*

12. In the **Pick Boolean** rollout, select the **Move** radio button, if it is not already selected. Choose the **Pick Operand B** button and move the cursor over *cap002*; the shape of the cursor changes. Select *cap002*; the overlapping portion of *cap002* is removed from *cap01*.

Note

To view the effect of the boolean operation in the Perspective viewport, you need to use the ***Orbit*** *tool.*

Next, you need to modify the cap using its sub-objects to make it look realistic.

13. Convert *cap01* into editable mesh object.

14. In the modifier stack, click on the plus (+) sign on the left side of **Editable Mesh**; all the sub-object levels are displayed.

15. Select the **Polygon** sub-object level to activate it.

16. In the **Selection** rollout, select the **Ignore Backfacing** check box.

17. In the Left viewport, select the alternative row of polygons of *cap01* by holding the CTRL key, as shown in Figure 11-68.

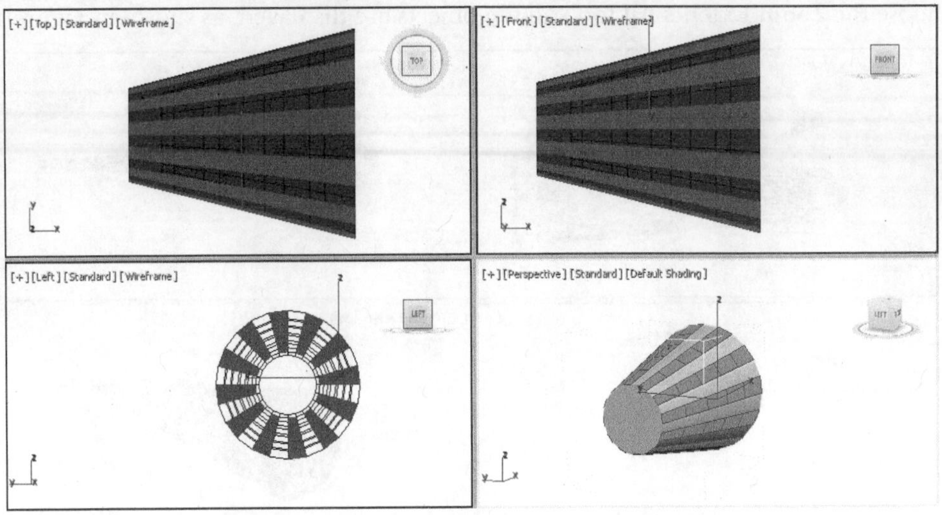

Figure 11-68 The selected polygons of cap01

18. Create a selection set of the selected polygons.

> **Note**
> *You can use the selection set of the selected objects or sub-objects, if needed. To create a selection set, enter **selected polygons** in the **Named Selection Sets** drop-down list in the **Main Toolbar** and press ENTER, refer to Figure 11-69.*

19. In the **Edit Geometry** rollout, set the value **0.1** in the **Extrude** spinner, and then press the ENTER key; the selected polygons are extruded.

20. The extruded polygons are displayed, as shown in Figure 11-70. In the modifier stack, select the **Polygon** sub-object level again to deactivate it.

***Figure 11-69** The **Named Selection Sets** drop-down list*

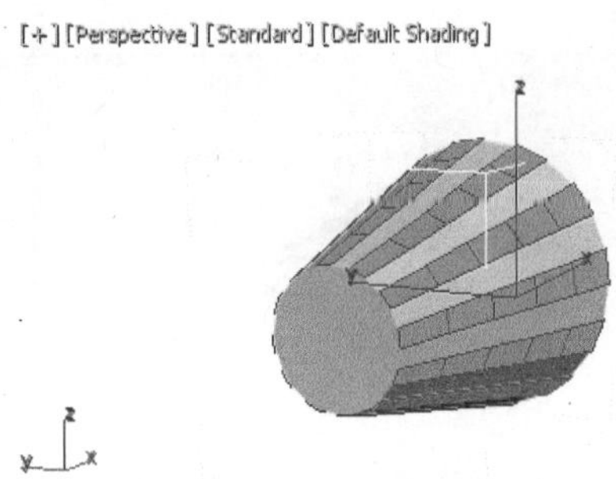

***Figure 11-70** The extruded polygons in the Perspective viewport*

21. Right-click in any of the viewports; a quad menu is displayed. Choose the **Unhide All** option; all the objects and shapes are displayed in the viewport.

22. Choose the **Zoom Extents All** tool; all the objects are displayed, as shown in Figure 11-71.

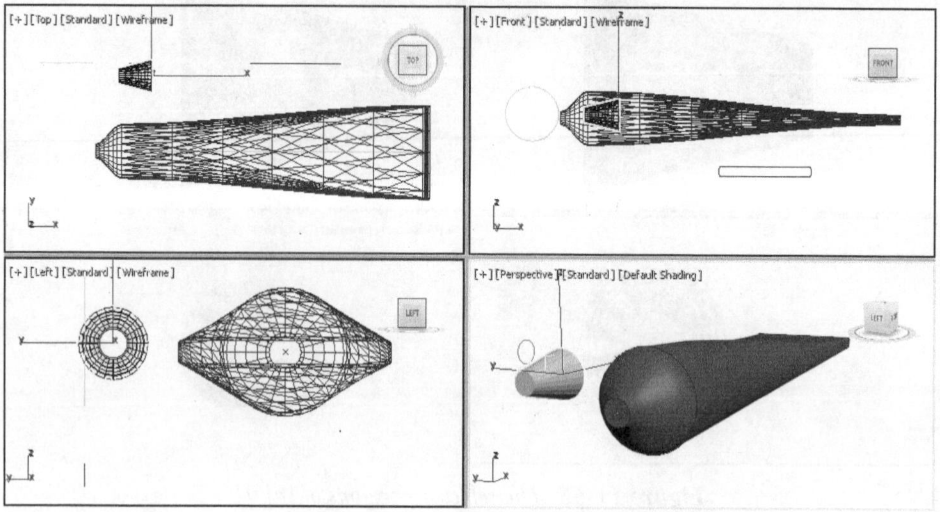

***Figure 11-71** The objects in the viewports*

23. Make sure *cap01* is selected and then choose the **Use Pivot Point Center** tool from the **Main Toolbar**. Now, align *cap01* with *toothpaste tube* using the **Select and Move** tool in viewports, as shown in Figure 11-72.

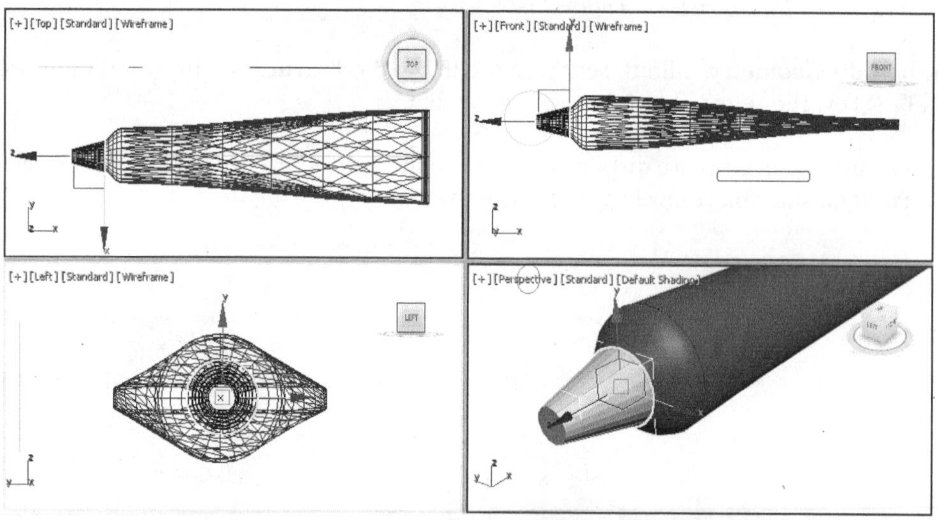

***Figure 11-72** The cap01 geometry in the viewports after being aligned with toothpaste tube*

24. Select *Circle001*, *Circle002*, *Line001*, and *Rectangle001* shapes from the Scene Explorer using the CTRL key. Next, press the DELETE key to delete all the shapes from the scene.

Assigning Materials and Maps to the Tube

In this section, you will assign the materials and maps to *toothpaste tube*.

1. Select *toothpaste tube* in any of the viewports. Next, choose **Rendering > Material Editor > Compact Material Editor** from the menu bar; the **Material Editor** dialog box is displayed. Make sure the first sample slot is selected in the **Material Editor** dialog box. By default, the **Standard** material is selected in it and you need to use the same for *toothpaste tube*.

2. Make sure that the **Blinn** shader is selected in the **Shader Basic Parameters** rollout. In the **Blinn Basic Parameters** rollout, choose the **Diffuse** map button on the right side of the **Diffuse** color swatch; the **Material/Map Browser** dialog box is displayed. Expand the **Maps > General** rollout and select the **Bitmap** map. Next, choose the **OK** button; the **Select Bitmap Image File** dialog box is displayed. As the project folder is already set, the *images* folder is displayed in the **Look in** drop-down list of this dialog box.

3. Select the file *toothpaste_tube.jpg* and choose the **Open** button; the image is displayed in the selected sample slot. Also, the rollouts to modify the bitmap are displayed in the **Material Editor** dialog box. Now, choose the **Go to Parent** tool to go back to the parent level.

4. In the **Specular Highlights** area, set the following parameters:

   Specular Level: **56** Glossiness: **40**

5. Make sure that *toothpaste tube* is selected in the viewport. Next, choose the **Assign Material to Selection** tool in the **Material Editor** dialog box. Also, choose the **Show Shaded Material in Viewport** tool to display the map in the viewport.

6. You will notice that the map in *toothpaste tube* is not showing properly, refer to Figure 11-73. To align the map properly, you need to apply the **UVW Map** modifier.

7. Choose the **Modify** tab in the **Command Panel**. Select the **UVW Map** modifier from the **Modifier List** drop-down list; the **UVW Map** modifier is displayed in the modifier stack. Also, the **Parameters** rollout is displayed in the Modify panel.

8. In the **Parameters** rollout, select the **Box** radio button.

9. In the **Alignment** area of the **Parameters** rollout, select the **Z** radio button and set the value **0.5** in the **Height** spinner. You can set values in the **Length** and **Width** spinners and align the gizmo as per the length and width of the tube to align the map properly, refer to Figure 11-74.

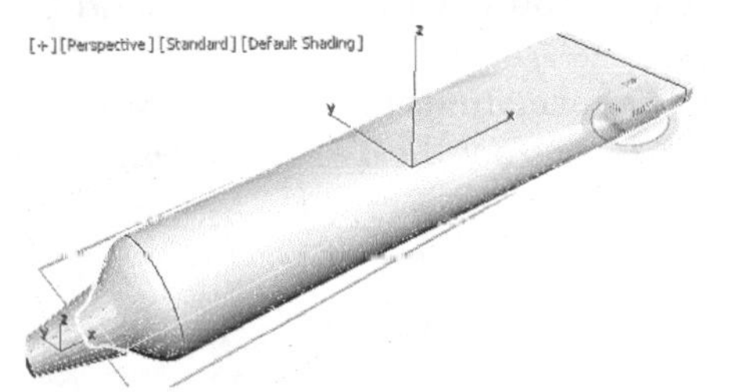

Figure 11-73 *The map on the toothpaste tube*

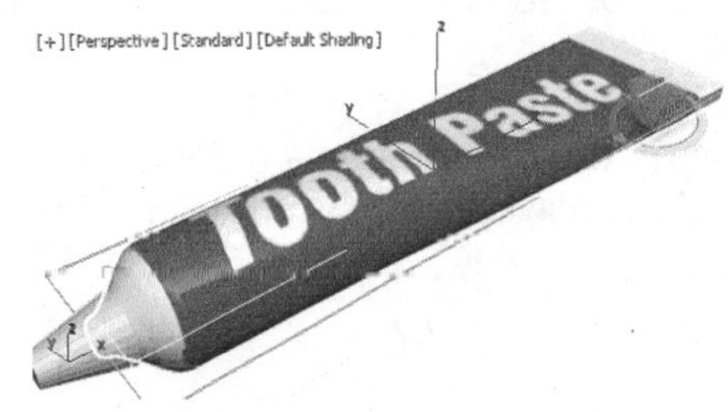

Figure 11-74 *The map on the toothpaste tube after applying the* ***UVW Map*** *modifier*

Next, you will create the material for *cap01*.

10. Select *cap01* in the viewport and select another sample slot in the **Material Editor** dialog box.

11. By default, the **Standard** material is selected in the **Material Editor** dialog box and you will use the same for *cap01*. Make sure that the **Blinn** shader is selected in the **Shader Basic Parameters** rollout. In the **Blinn Basic Parameters** rollout, choose the **Diffuse** color swatch; the **Color Selector: Diffuse Color** dialog box is displayed. Select the white color and choose the **OK** button to close the dialog box.

12. In the **Specular Highlights** area, set the following parameters:

    Specular Level: **44** Glossiness: **16**

13. Make sure that *cap01* is selected in the viewport. Next, choose the **Assign Material to Selection** tool in the **Material Editor** dialog box. Also, choose the **Show Shaded Material in Viewport** tool to display the map in the viewport. The toothpaste tube is displayed, refer to Figure 11-75. Close the **Material Editor** dialog box.

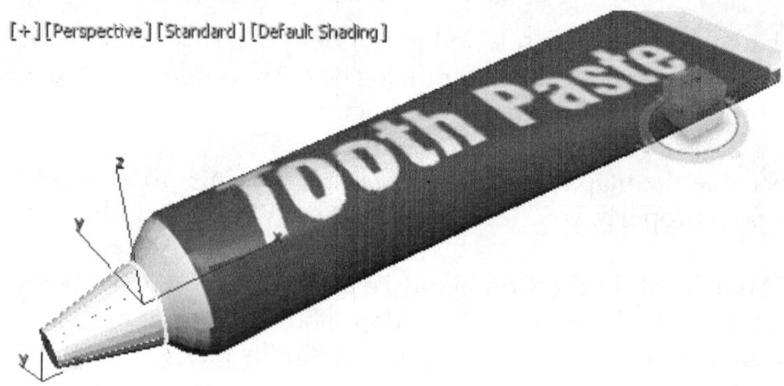

***Figure 11-75** The toothpaste tube after the map assigned*

Next, you need to apply the twist deformation.

14. Select *toothpaste tube* in the viewport and choose the **Modify** tab in the **Command Panel**.

15. In the modifier stack, select **Loft** and expand the **Deformations** rollout in the Modify panel. Now, in the **Deformations** rollout, choose the **Twist** button; the **Twist Deformation** dialog box is displayed, as shown in Figure 11-76.

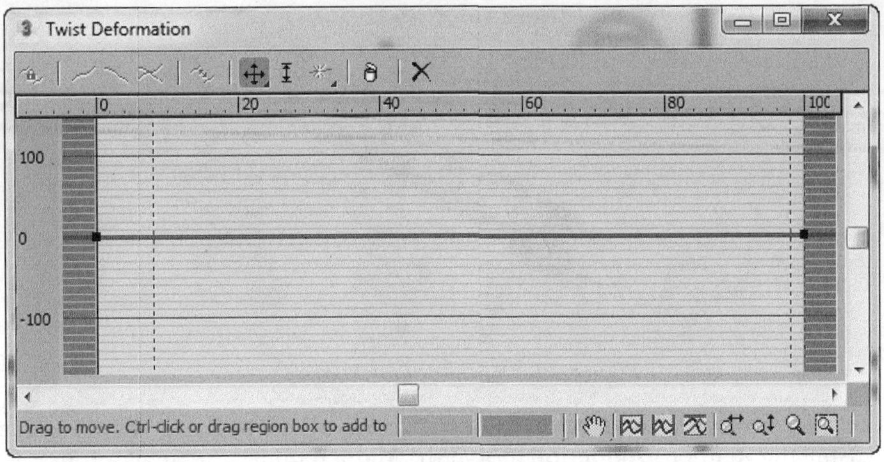

Figure 11-76 *The **Twist Deformation** dialog box*

16. In the **Twist Deformation** dialog box, choose the **Move Control Point** tool. Next, move the first vertex point (placed on the left side) vertically downward to **-65.0**. Alternatively, you can set the exact value in the edit box given at the bottom of this dialog box, refer to Figure 11-77; the toothpaste tube geometry gets twisted, as shown in Figure 11-78. Close the **Twist Deformation** dialog box.

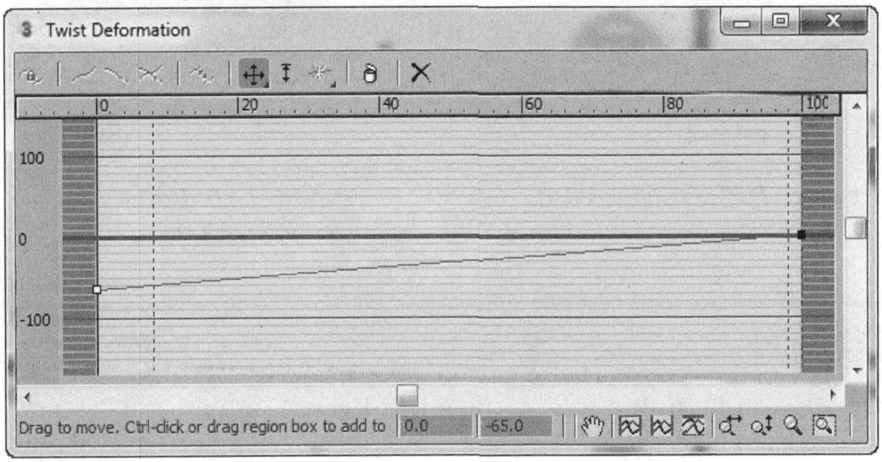

Figure 11-77 *The first vertex point moved in the **Twist Deformation** dialog box*

Saving and Rendering the Scene

In this section, you will save the scene and then render it. You can also view the final rendered image of this model by downloading the file *c11_3dsmax_2017_rndr.zip* from *www.cadcim.com*. The path of the file is as follows: *Textbooks > Animation and Visual Effects > 3ds Max > Autodesk 3ds Max 2017: A Comprehensive Guide*

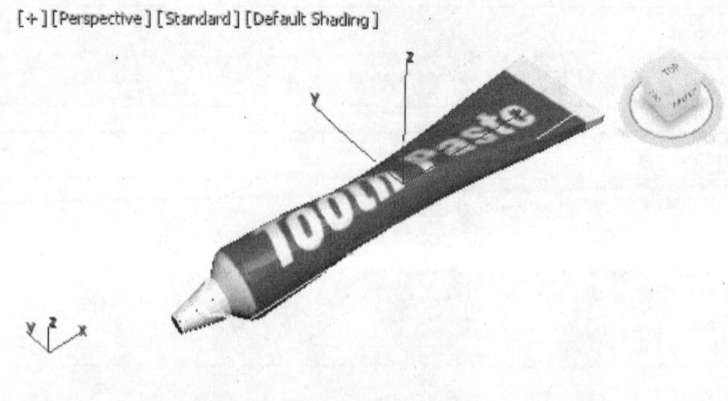

Figure 11-78 *Twisted toothpaste tube*

1. Choose **Save** from the **Application** menu. Activate the Perspective viewport. Render the scene using the **Render Production** tool in the **Main Toolbar**; the final output is displayed, refer to Figures 11-79 and 11-80.

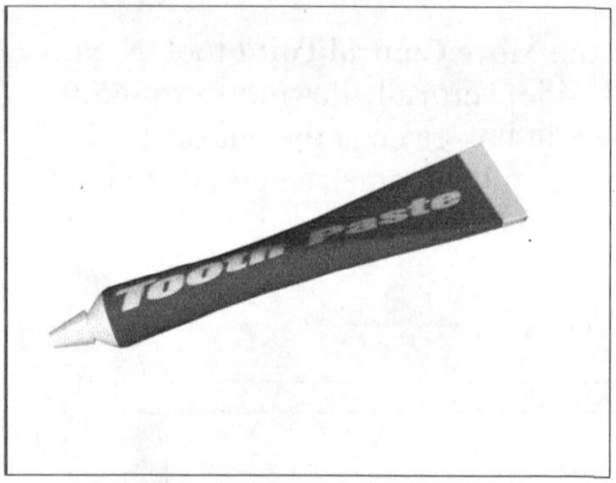

Figure 11-79 *The final output after rendering (view 1)*

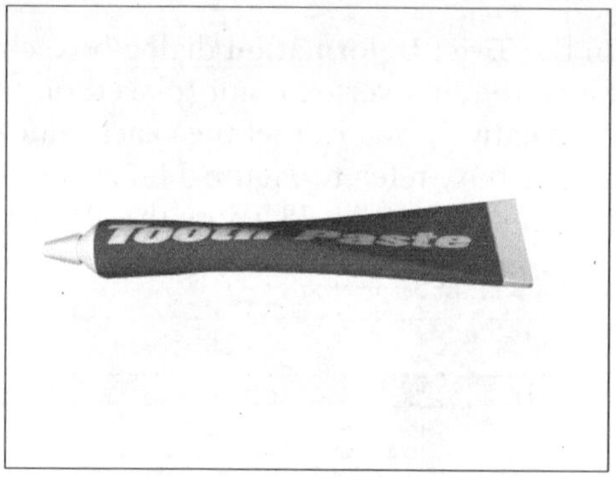

Figure 11-80 *The final output after rendering (view 2)*

Tutorial 2

In this tutorial, you will create a scene, as shown in Figure 11-81, using different compound objects. **(Expected time: 60 min)**

The following steps are required to complete this tutorial:

a. Create the project folder.
b. Create the ground.
c. Create hills.
d. Create plants.
e. Create road over ground.
f. Create background for the final output.
g. Save and render the scene.

Figure 11-81 Scene for Tutorial 2

Creating the Project Folder

1. Create a new project folder with the name *c11_tut2* at *\Documents\3dsmax2017* and then save the file with the name *c11tut2*, as discussed in Tutorial 1 of Chapter 2.

2. Open the Windows Explorer and then browse to the *c11_3dsmax_2017_tut* folder and copy the *Grass.jpg, SANDSHORE.jpg*, and *Road.jpg* files from this folder to *\Documents\3dsmax2017\c11_tut2\sceneassets\images.*

Creating the Ground

In this section, you will create a ground by using the **Plane** tool.

1. Activate the Top viewport. Choose **Create > Geometry** in the **Command Panel**; the **Standard Primitives** option is displayed by default in the drop-down list. Choose the **Plane** tool and create a plane.

2. In the **Parameters** rollout, set the following parameters:

Length: **383.432**	Width: **395.936**
Length Segs: **20**	Width Segs: **20**

   Next, you need to edit the plane using its sub-objects to make it look like a hilly surface.

3. Make sure that the plane is selected in the Top viewport and then convert it into an editable poly object. Choose the **Zoom Extents All** tool.

4. In the modifier stack, expand **Editable Poly** by clicking on the plus sign on its left side. Select the **Vertex** sub-object level; all the vertices of the plane are displayed in the viewports, as shown in Figure 11-82.

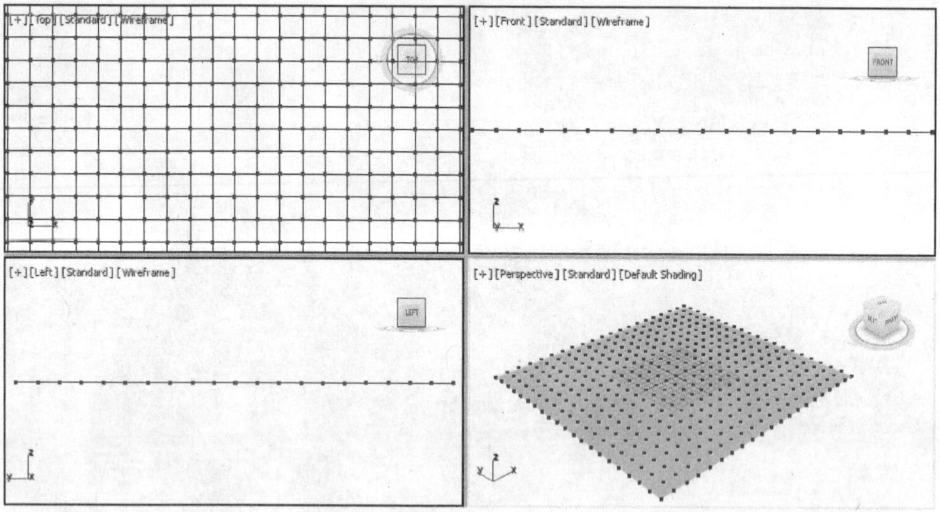

Figure 11-82 All vertices displayed in viewports

5. In the Top viewport, select a vertex, as shown in Figure 11-83. Now, in the **Selection** rollout, choose the **Grow** button twice to select the vertices, as shown in Figure 11-84.

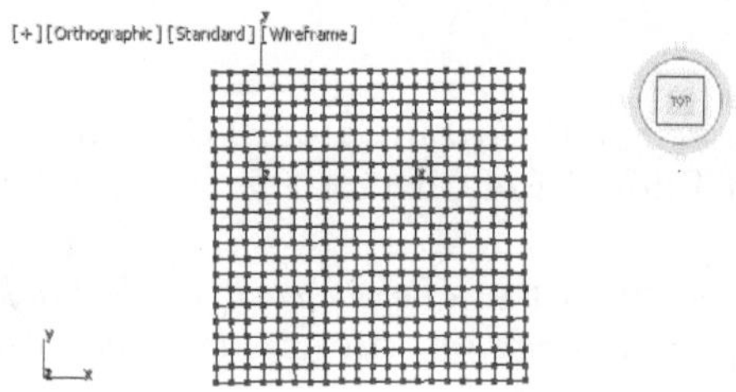

Figure 11-83 *A vertex selected in the Top viewport*

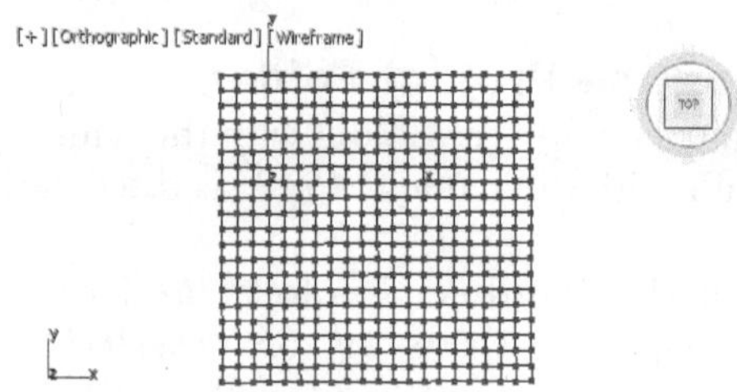

Figure 11-84 *The vertices selected after choosing the **Grow** button*

6. Activate the Front viewport. Move the cursor over the vertical axis and drag the selected vertices up by one grid point, refer to Figures 11-85 and 11-86.

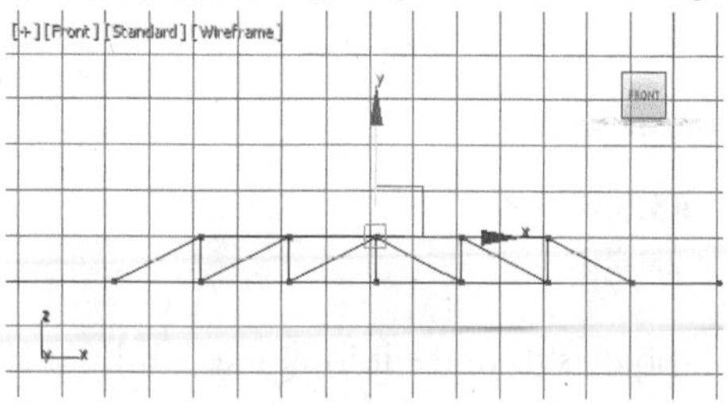

Figure 11-85 *The selected vertices dragged up in the Front viewport*

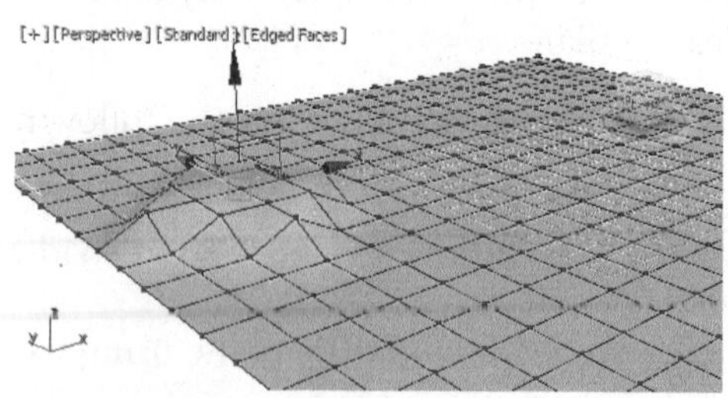

Figure 11-86 *The selected vertices dragged up in the Perspective viewport*

7. Zoom in the Perspective viewport and create the hilly surface by selecting vertices at different places on the plane using the same method as discussed in steps 5 and 6, as shown in Figure 11-87.

8. Deselect the **Vertex** sub-object level in the modifier stack. Then, apply the **MeshSmooth** modifier from the **Modifier List** drop-down list, as discussed earlier, to make the surface smooth, as shown in Figure 11-88.

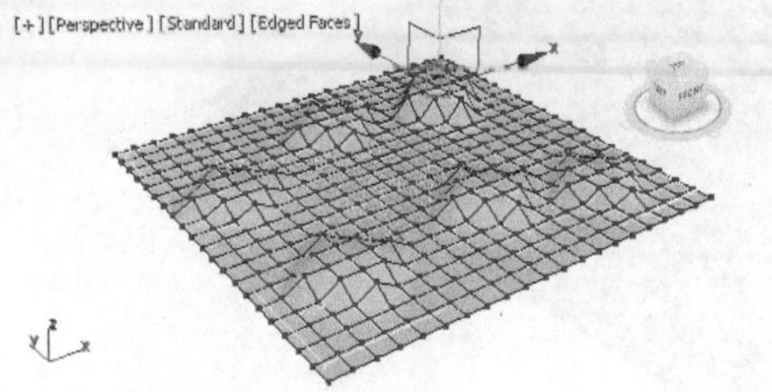

Figure 11-87 The hilly surface created using the vertices of the plane

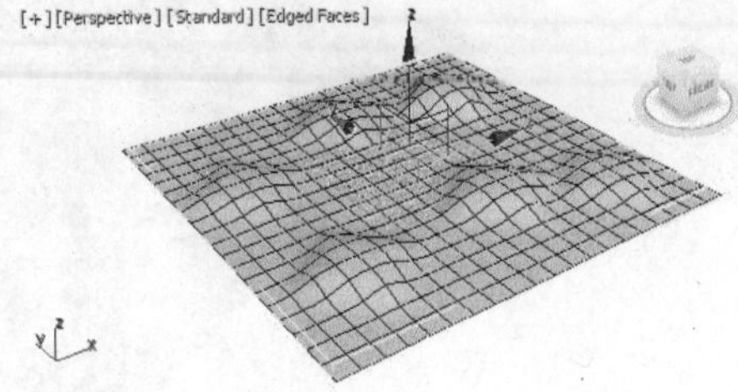

*Figure 11-88 The hilly surface after applying the **MeshSmooth** modifier*

Next, you need to assign a map to the plane to give it a realistic look.

9. Make sure that the plane is selected in the viewport. Next, choose **Rendering> Material Editor > Compact Material Editor** from the menu bar; the **Material Editor** dialog box is displayed.

10. Select the **01-Default** sample slot in the **Material Editor** dialog box. Choose the **Diffuse** map button on the right side of the **Diffuse** color swatch; the **Material/Map Browser** dialog box is displayed. Select the **Bitmap** map from the **Maps > General** rollout and choose the **OK** button; the **Select Bitmap Image File** dialog box is displayed. As the project folder is already set, the *images* folder is displayed in the **Look in** drop-down list of this dialog box. Select the file *Grass.jpg* from this dialog box and then choose the **Open** button; the selected image is displayed in the selected sample slot.

11. In the **Coordinates** rollout of the **Material Editor** dialog box, set the values as given next.

    U-Tiling: **5** V-Tiling: **5**

12. Make sure that the plane is selected in the viewport. Next, choose the **Assign Material to Selection** tool from the **Material Editor** dialog box. Now, choose the **Show Shaded Material in Viewport** tool to display the map in the viewports. The map is assigned to the plane and displayed in the Perspective viewport, as shown in Figure 11-89. Now, close the **Material Editor** dialog box.

13. Set the view of the plane in the Perspective viewport using the viewport navigation tools such as **Zoom**, **Orbit**, as shown in Figure 11-90.

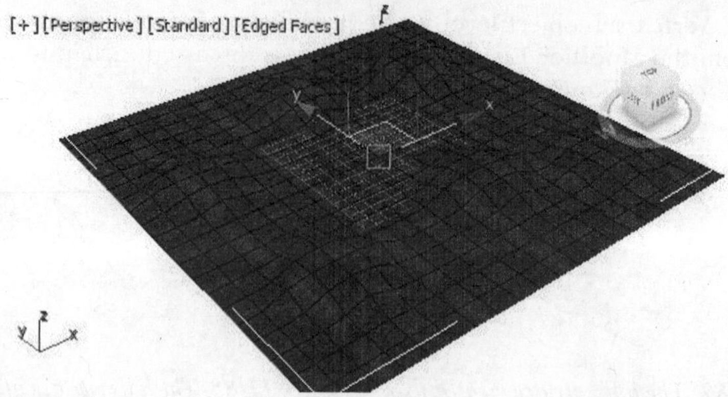

Figure 11-89 The plane with the map assigned in the perspective viewport

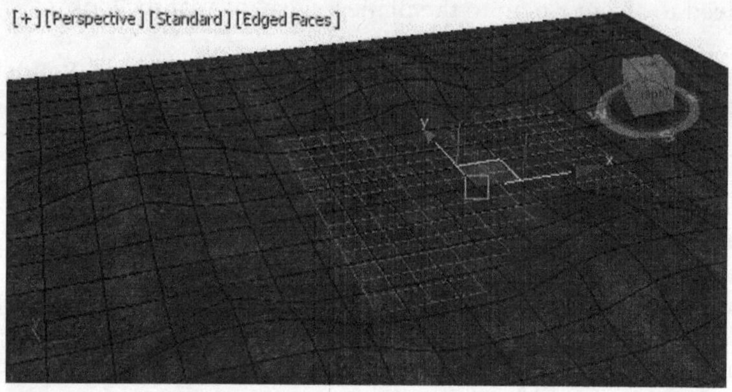

Figure 11-90 The plane after using the viewport navigation tools

14. Name the plane as *ground* in the **Name and Color** rollout.

Creating Hills

In this section, you will create hills by using the **Terrain** tool in **Compound Objects**.

1. Activate the Top viewport, Next, choose **Create > Shapes** in the **Command Panel**. Also, choose the **Line** tool from the **Object Type** rollout.

2. In the **Creation Method** rollout, select the **Corner** radio button in the **Initial Type** area and select the **Smooth** radio button in the **Drag Type** area.

3. Create a close line spline, as shown in Figure 11-91.

4. Hide *ground* temporarily, as discussed earlier, to get more room to create hills.

5. Activate the Front viewport and create four copies of the line spline, refer to Figure 11-92.

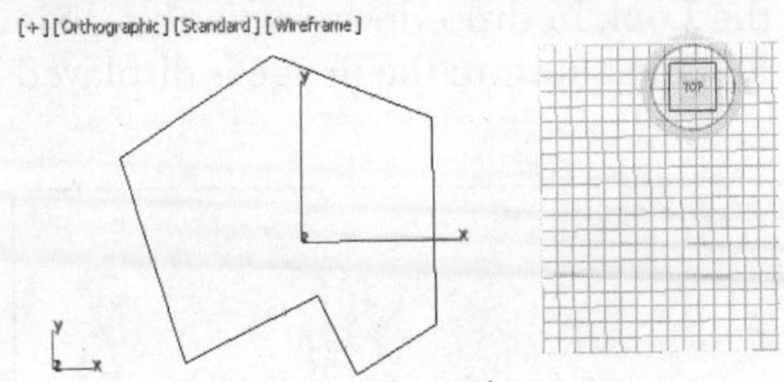

Figure 11-91 A close line spline created in the Top viewport

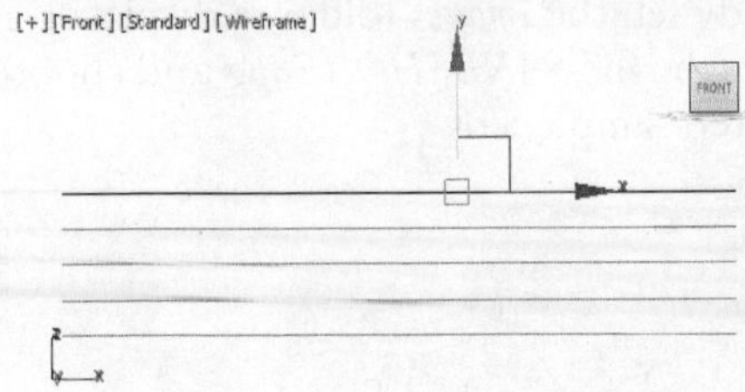

Figure 11-92 Four copies of the line spline created in the Front viewport

6. Choose the **Select and Uniform Scale** tool and scale the lines in the Front viewport, as shown in Figure 11-93.

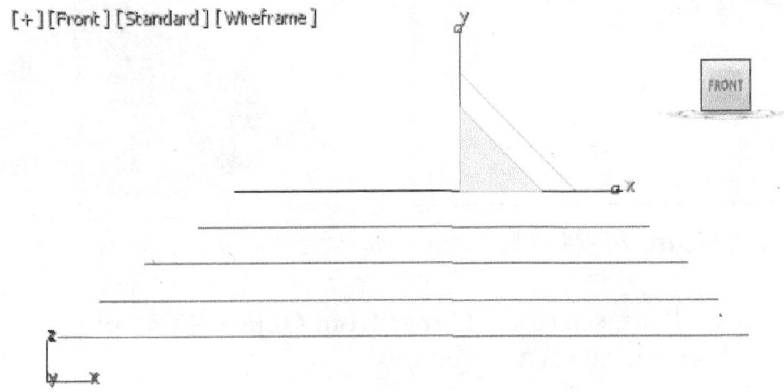

Figure 11-93 The scaled lines after using the ***Select and Uniform Scale*** *tool*

7. Choose the **Select Object** tool and select all the lines by dragging a selection box around them.

8. Choose **Create > Geometry** in the **Command Panel** and select **Compound Objects** from the drop-down list displayed below the **Geometry** button. Choose the **Terrain** tool from the **Object Type** rollout; the terrain object is created, as shown in Figure 11-94. Right-click to exit the command.

9. Click on the terrain object again and then modify the name of the terrain object as *hill01*.

   Next, you need to assign a map to *hill01*.

10. Make sure that *hill01* is selected in the viewport. Press the M key to open the **Material Editor** dialog box.

11. Select the **02-Default** sample slot in the **Material Editor** dialog box. Select the **Diffuse** map button on the right of the **Diffuse** color swatch; the **Material/Map Browser** dialog box is displayed. Select the **Bitmap** map from the **Maps > General** rollout and choose the **OK** button; the **Select Bitmap Image File** dialog box is displayed. As the project folder is

already set, the *images* folder is displayed in the **Look in** drop-down list of this dialog box. Select the file *SANDSHORE.jpg* and choose the **Open** button; the image is displayed in the selected sample slot.

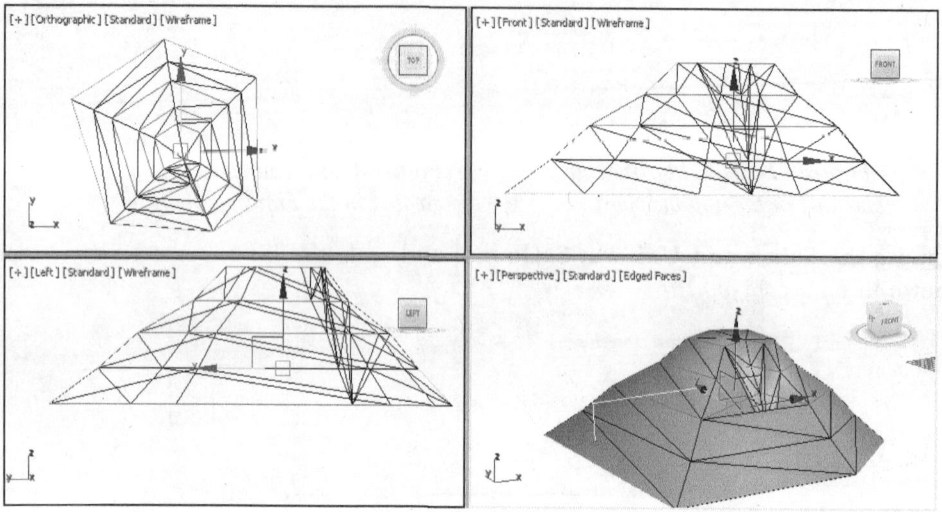

Figure 11-94 *The terrain object created in viewports*

12. In the **Coordinates** rollout, select the **Planar from Object XYZ** option from the **Mapping** drop-down list and set the values as given next.

    X-Tiling: **3** Y-Tiling: **3**

13. Make sure that *hill01* is selected in the viewport. Next, choose the **Assign Material to Selection** tool in the **Material Editor** dialog box. Then, choose the **Show Shaded Material in Viewport** tool to display the map in the viewport. The map is assigned to *hill01*, as shown in Figure 11-95. Now, close the **Material Editor** dialog box.

14. Unhide *ground*. Next, scale and align *hill01* with *ground*, and delete all the lines, refer to Figure 11-96.

15. Create multiple copies of *hill01* as required. Now, scale, rotate, and align them, as shown in Figure 11-97.

16. Apply the **MeshSmooth** modifier to hills as discussed earlier.

Creating Plants

In this section, you will create plants by using the **Foliage** tool.

1. Activate the Top viewport. Choose **Create > Geometry** from the **Command Panel** and select **AEC Extended** from the drop-down list. Now, choose the **Foliage** tool from the **Object Type** rollout; various rollouts are displayed in the Modify panel.

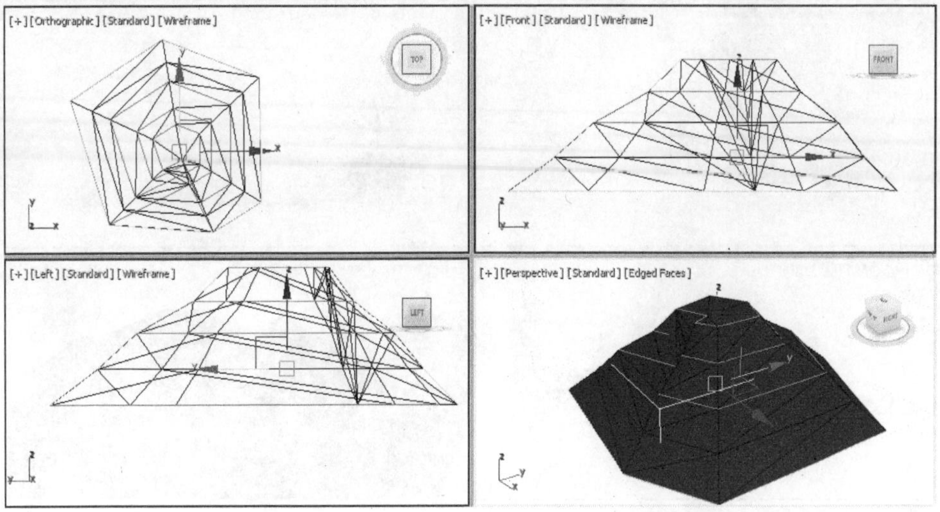

***Figure 11-95** The map assigned to hill01*

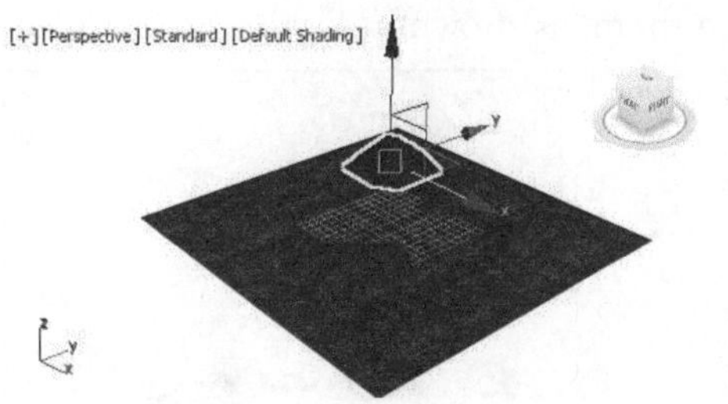

***Figure 11-96** The hill01 after scaling and aligning with the ground*

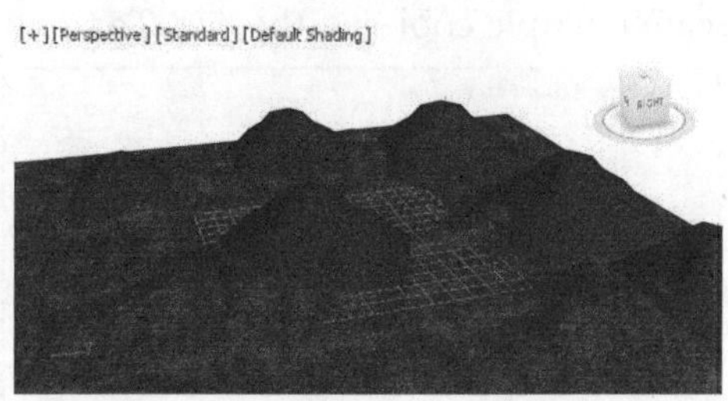

***Figure 11-97** The hills displayed after scaling and alignment*

2. In the **Favorite Plants** rollout, double-click on the **Banyan tree** option; the tree is displayed in the viewports.

3. Name the plant as *tree01* in the **Name and Color** rollout.

4. Make sure that *tree01* is still selected. Choose the **Modify** tab in the **Command Panel**; the **Parameters** rollout is displayed.

5. In the **Parameters** rollout, set the value **25.0** in the **Height** spinner. Use default values for the other options.

6. Choose the **Select and Move** tool and align *tree01* in the viewports, as shown in Figure 11-98.

7. Activate the Top viewport. In the **Favorite Plants** rollout, double-click on the **Society Garlic** option; the tree is displayed in the viewports. In the **Parameters** rollout, make sure the value **18.0** is set in the **Height** spinner. Use default values for other options.

8. Modify the name of the plant as *tree02* in the **Name and Color** rollout.

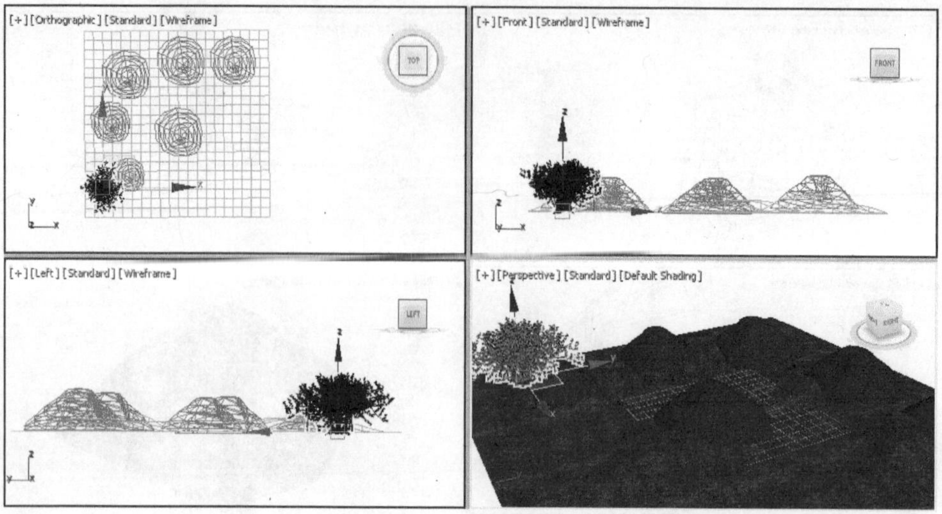

Figure 11-98 *Alignment of the tree01 in viewports*

9. Create multiple copies of the *tree02* and align them, as shown in Figure 11-99.

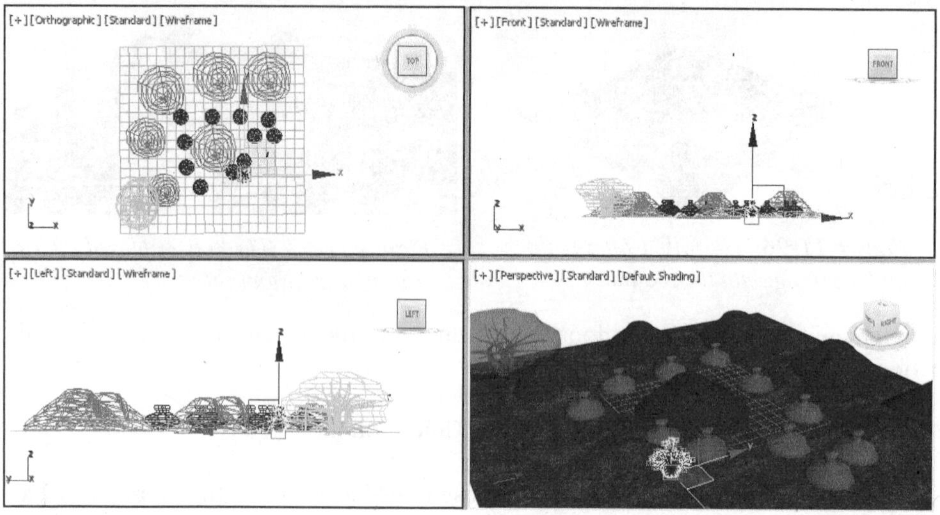

Figure 11-99 *Alignment of trees in viewports*

Creating Road over Ground

First, you need to use the **Loft** tool for creating the road and then use the **Conform** tool to adjust road according to *ground*. To create the loft object, you need to create a path spline and a shape spline in the viewport.

1. Activate the Top viewport and choose **Create > Shapes** in the **Command Panel**; the **Splines** option is displayed in the drop-down list. Choose the **Line** tool from the **Object Type** rollout and create a line, as shown in Figure 11-100, which will be used as a path spline.

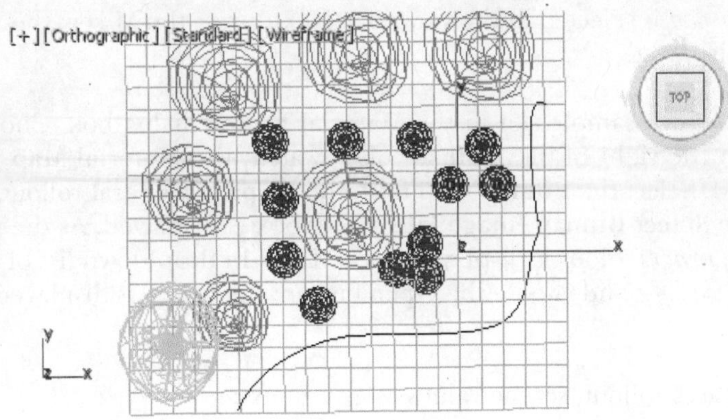

Figure 11-100 The line created in the Top viewport

2. Activate the Front viewport and create a rectangular spline using the **Rectangle** tool. It will be used as a shape spline. Set its parameters as follows:

   Length: **4.0** Width: **30.702**

3. Make sure that the line is selected in the viewport. Choose **Create > Geometry** in the **Command Panel**. Now, select the **Compound Objects** option from the drop-down list. Choose the **Loft** tool from the **Object Type** rollout. Choose the **Get Shape** button in the **Creation Method** rollout and move the cursor over the rectangle in the Top viewport; the shape of the cursor changes. Select the rectangle; a shape is created.

4. The new shape is automatically named as *Loft001*. Rename it as *road*.

5. Align *road* in the viewports, as shown in Figure 11-101.

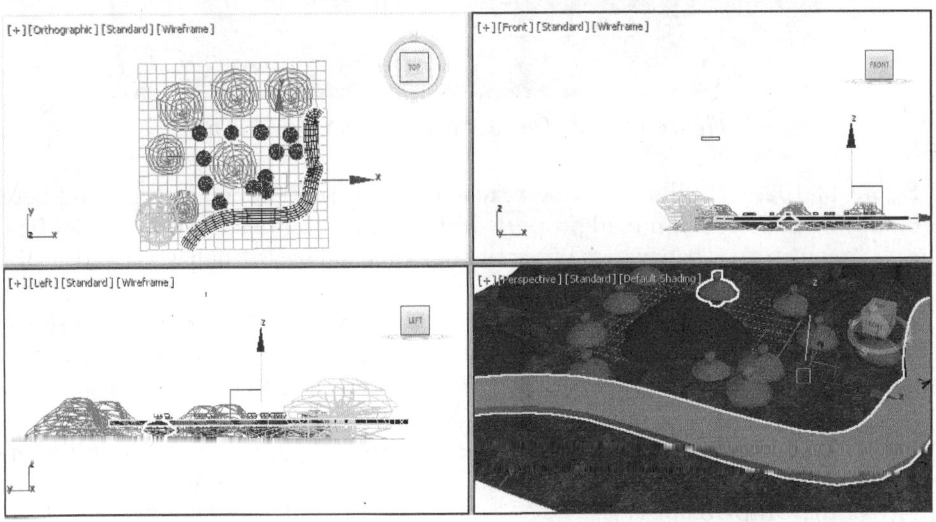

Figure 11-101 The road geometry aligned with ground

Now, assign a map to *road*.

6. Make sure that *road* is selected in the viewport. Next, press the M key; the **Material Editor** dialog box is displayed.

7. Select the **03-Default** sample slot in the **Material Editor** dialog box. Choose the **Diffuse** map button on the right of the **Diffuse** color swatch; the **Material/Map Browser** dialog box is displayed. Select the **Bitmap** map from the **Maps > General** rollout and choose the **OK** button; the **Select Bitmap Image File** dialog box is displayed. As the project folder is already set, the *images* folder is displayed in the **Look in** drop-down list of this dialog box. Select the file *Road.jpg* and choose the **Open** button; the image is displayed in the selected sample slot.

8. In the **Coordinates** rollout, set the values as given next:

   U-Tiling: **5** V-Tiling: **5**

9. Make sure that *road* is selected in the viewport. Next, choose the **Assign Material to Selection** tool from the **Material Editor** dialog box. Then, choose the **Show Shaded Material in Viewport** tool to display the map in the viewport, as shown in Figure 11-102. Close the **Material Editor** dialog box.

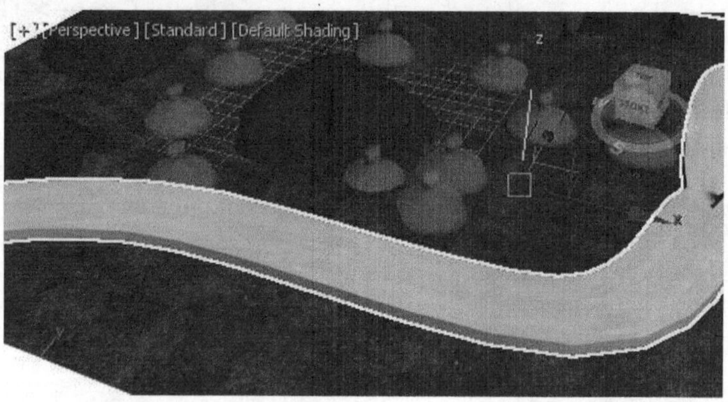

***Figure 11-102** The road after assigning map to it*

In Figure 11-102, you will notice that road is not properly aligned with ground because of its bumpy surface. To align road properly with ground, you need to use the **Conform** tool. The *road* geometry will behave as a Wrapper object and *ground* will behave as a Wrap-To object.

10. Select *road* and choose the **Conform** tool from **Compound Objects**. Choose the **Pick Wrap-To Object** button and move the cursor over *ground*; the selection cursor is displayed. Select *ground*; *road* is positioned over *ground* to fit according to the shape of *ground*.

11. In the **Wrapper Parameters** area of the **Parameters** rollout, set the value in the **Standoff Distance** spinner to adjust the distance between the vertex of the Wrapper object and the surface of the Wrap-To object.

12. In the **Update** area of the **Parameters** rollout, select the **Hide Wrap-To Object** check box; the scene is displayed, as shown in Figure 11-103. Also, apply the **MeshSmooth** modifier to the conform object.

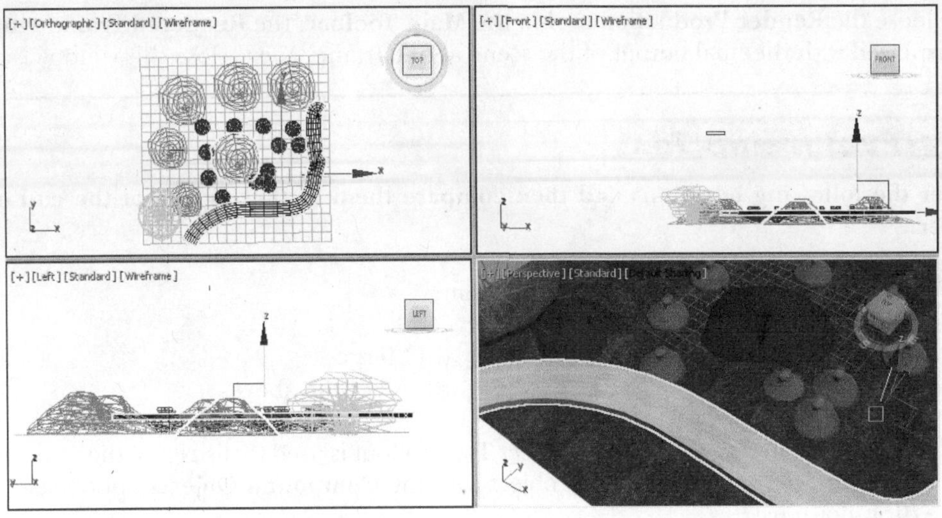

*Figure 11-103 The scene after using the **Conform** tool*

Creating Background for the Final Output

In this section, you will assign a map to the background to make the scene more realistic.

1. Choose **Rendering > Environment** from the menu bar; the **Environment and Effects** dialog box is displayed.

2. In the **Common Parameters** rollout, choose the **Environment Map** button that is labeled as **None**; the **Material/Map Browser** dialog box is displayed. Select the **Noise** map from the **Maps > General** rollout and choose the **OK** button; the **Map X Noise** name is displayed in the **Environment Map** button.

3. Now, choose the **Material Editor** tool from the **Main Toolbar**, the **Material Editor** dialog box is displayed. Press and hold the left mouse button on the **Map X Noise** label from the **Environment Map** button and drag the cursor to the **04-Default** sample slot; the **Instance (Copy) map** dialog box is displayed.

4. Make sure the **Instance** radio button is selected in this dialog box and then choose **OK**; the **Map X Noise** will be added to the default 04-sample slot. In the **Noise Parameters** rollout, select the **Turbulence** radio button. Next, set the value **8.8** in the **Levels** spinner and **200** in the **Size** spinner. Next, select the blue color in the **Color #1** swatch and make sure white color is selected in the **Color #2** swatch.

Saving and Rendering the Scene

In this section, you will save the scene and then render it. You can also view the final rendered image of this model by downloading the file *c11_3dsmax_2017_rndr.zip* from *www.cadcim.com*. The path of the file is as follows: *Textbooks > Animation and Visual Effects > 3ds Max > Autodesk 3ds Max 2017: A Comprehensive Guide*

1. Activate the Perspective viewport. Next, choose **Save** from the **Application** menu.

2. Choose the **Render Production** tool in the **Main Toolbar**; the **Rendered Frame** window is displayed with the final output of the scene at one frame. Next, close this window.

Self-Evaluation Test

Answer the following questions and then compare them to those given at the end of this chapter:

1. Which of the following is a boolean operation?

   (a) **Union** (b) **Merge**
   (c) **Intersect** (d) All of the above

2. Which of the following tools in the **Object Type** rollout is used to distribute the source object over the surface of the distribution object with the **Compound Objects** option selected in the drop-down list?

   (a) **Scatter** (b) **Loft**
   (c) **Conform** (d) **Terrain**

3. Which of the following tools is used to connect two or more objects at the holes on their surfaces?

   (a) **ShapeMerge** (b) **Conform**
   (c) **Connect** (d) None of these

4. Which of the following tools is used to create 3D objects using the 2D shapes by lofting them along a spline path?

   (a) **ProBoolean** (b) **ProCutter**
   (c) **Connect** (d) **Loft**

5. Which of the following tools is used to adjust the position of an object exactly on a hilly surface?

   (a) **Loft** (b) **Connect**
   (c) **Boolean** (d) **Conform**

6. In a terrain object, select the __________ radio button in the **Form** area of the **Parameters** rollout to create layered objects such as the cardboard architectural models.

7. The __________ area in the **Surface Parameters** rollout of a loft object is used to smoothen the length and circumference of the path.

8. The __________ tool is used to select multiple objects at a time to perform boolean operation.

9. The terrain objects are created from the mesh objects. (T/F)

10. The **Reorder Ops** button in the **Parameters** rollout of a proboolean object is used to change the order of boolean operations in the viewport. (T/F)

Review Questions

Answer the following questions:

1. Which of the following boolean operations is used to remove the non-overlapping portions of two objects?

   (a) **Intersect** (b) **Merge**
   (c) **Insert** (d) None of these

2. Which of the following tools is used to break an object into separate objects using the mesh objects as cutter?

   (a) **ProBoolean** (b) **Conform**
   (c) **Scatter** (d) **ProCutter**

3. Which of the following tools is used to create terrain objects?

   (a) **Scatter** (b) **Conform**
   (c) **ProBoolean** (d) **Terrain**

4. The __________ check box in the **Cutter Parameters** rollout of the **ProCutter** tool is used to get the parts of the stock object that are outside the cutters.

5. The options in the __________ rollout of the **Terrain** tool are used to set the complexity of the terrain object.

6. The __________ area in the **Scatters Object** rollout of the **Scatter** tool is used to arrange the copied source object over the distribution object.

7. The **Change Operation** button in the **Parameters** rollout of the **ProBoolean** tool is used to change the type of boolean operation for the selected operand. (T/F)

8. The options in the **Color by Elevation** rollout of the **Terrain** tool are used to set the color of terrain object on the basis of its elevation. (T/F)

9. The **Imprint** check box in the **Parameters** rollout of the **ProBoolean** tool is used to delete the faces of the original object. (T/F)

10. The two objects that are used to create boolean objects are known as Operands. (T/F)

EXERCISES

The rendered output of the models used in the following exercises can be accessed by downloading the *c11_3dsmax_2017_exr.zip* file from *www.cadcim.com*. The path of the file is as follows: *Textbooks > Animation and Visual Effects > 3ds Max > Autodesk 3ds Max 2017: A Comprehensive Guide*

Exercise 1

Create the model shown in Figure 11-104 using the **ShapeMerge** tool in the **Compound Objects**. **(Expected time: 15 min)**

Exercise 2

Create the model shown in Figure 11-105 using the **Loft** tool in the **Compound Objects**. **(Expected time: 20 min)**

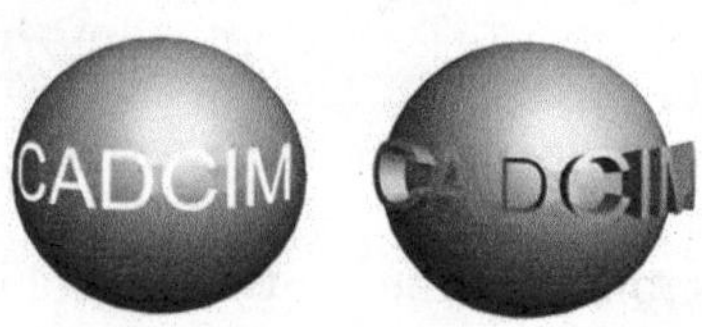

Figure 11-104 *Model to be created in Exercise 1*

Figure 11-105 *Model to be created in Exercise 2*

Answers to Self-Evaluation Test

1. d, **2.** a, **3.** c, **4.** d, **5.** d, **6. Layered Solid**, **7. Smoothing**, **8. ProBoolean**, **9.** F, **10.** T

12

Modifiers

Learning Objectives

After completing this chapter, you will be able to:

- *Use modifiers*
- *Understand the types of modifiers*
- *Create complex objects using modifiers*

INTRODUCTION

In this chapter, you will learn about modifiers. As the name indicates, modifiers are used to modify an object. They enable you to create models that would otherwise be quite difficult to create.

MODIFIERS AND MODIFIER STACK

In 3ds Max, the modifiers are used to modify an object. You can apply more than one modifier to an object. The modifiers can also be used to modify the object at sub-object levels.

To apply a modifier to an object, select the object in the viewport and then choose the **Modify** tab in the **Command Panel**; the **Modifier List** drop-down list will be displayed, as shown in Figure 12-1. To view the options in the drop-down list, click on the arrow on the right of **Modifier List**, as shown in Figure 12-2. There are different types of modifiers in this list. Select the modifier that you want to apply to the object; the selected modifier will be displayed in the modifier stack along with various rollouts in the Modify panel to modify the object, refer to Figure 12-3.

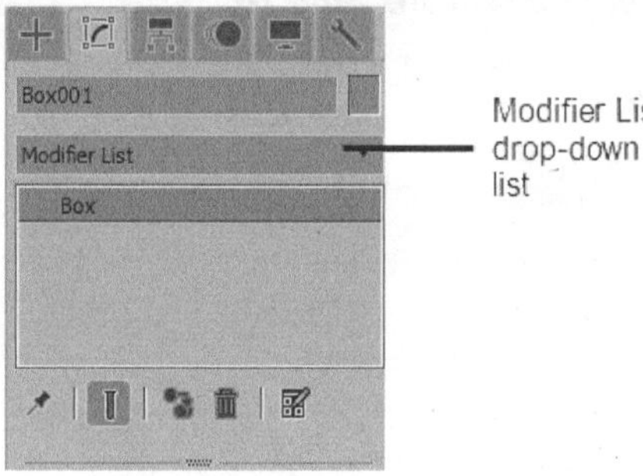

*Figure 12-1 The **Modifier List** drop-down list*

*Figure 12-2 Partial view of the **Modifier List** drop-down list*

Note

*The modifiers are displayed in the **Modifier List** drop-down list based on the selection of the object in the viewport.*

In the modifier stack, there is an eye icon, refer to Figure 12-3. It is used to show or hide the effects of the modifier in the viewport. By default, this icon is active. Click on this icon to make it inactive; the button will become dark and the effect of the modifier will not be displayed in the viewport. The buttons at the bottom of the modifier stack are used to manage the modifier stack. These buttons are discussed next.

The **Pin Stack** button is used to lock the modifier stack for the selected object in the viewport. If you choose the **Pin Stack** button for the selected object in the viewport, and then select another object in the viewport, the **Modify** tab will display the modifier stack and the rollouts for the pinned object only.

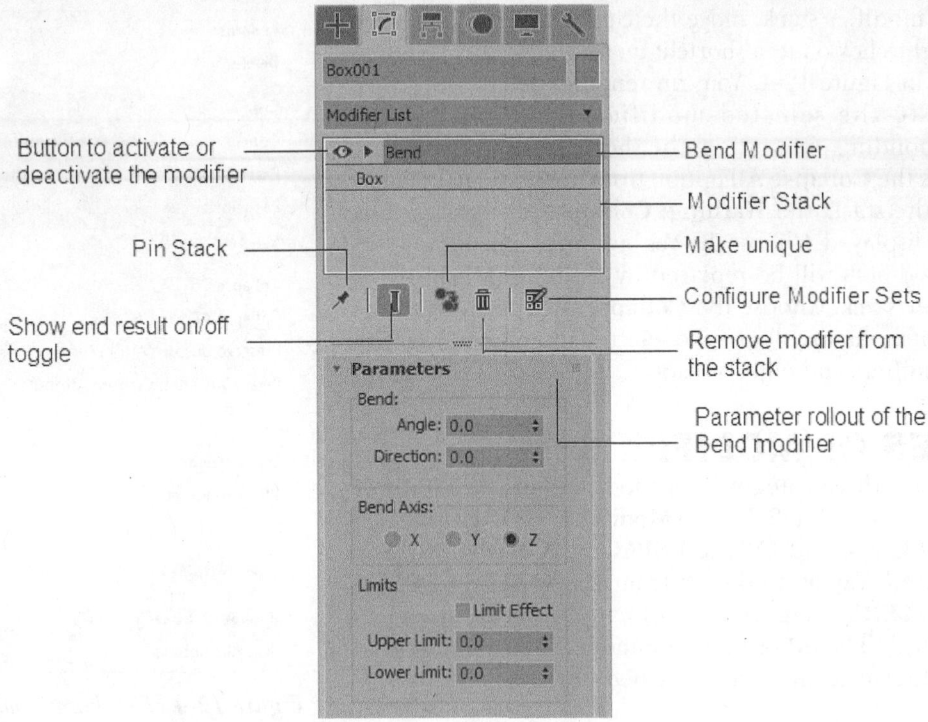

***Figure 12-3** The modifier stack*

The **Show end result on/off toggle** button is used to toggle the effect of all the modifiers in the modifier stack on the selected object in the viewport. If this button is deactivated, then the selected object in the viewport will display only the effect of the selected modifier in the modifier stack.

The **Make unique** button is used to convert an instanced object into a unique copy. On making the instanced objects unique, they become independent and you can modify them independently without affecting the other objects in the viewport. By default, this button is inactive. When you create the instance of an object, this button will be activated. Select the instanced object in the viewport and choose the **Make unique** button in the modifier stack to make it unique.

The **Remove modifier from the stack** button is used to remove the selected modifier from the modifier stack.

The **Configure Modifier Sets** button is used to control the display of the modifiers in the modifier stack.

Note

1. If you change the order of the modifiers applied to an object in the modifier stack, the object will display different effects.

2. The object should have more number of segments to get the best effect of the applied modifier.

In the modifier stack, move the cursor over the modifier and right-click on it; a shortcut menu will be displayed, as shown in Figure 12-4. You can rename, delete, cut, copy, or paste the selected modifiers by choosing the corresponding option from the shortcut menu displayed. Choose the **Collapse All** option from the menu to collapse the entire stack; the **Warning: Collapse All** message box will be displayed. Choose the **Yes** button; all the parameters and modifiers will be replaced by **Editable Mesh** in the modifier stack. Choose the **Collapse To** option from the shortcut menu to collapse the selected modifier along with the modifiers and objects below it.

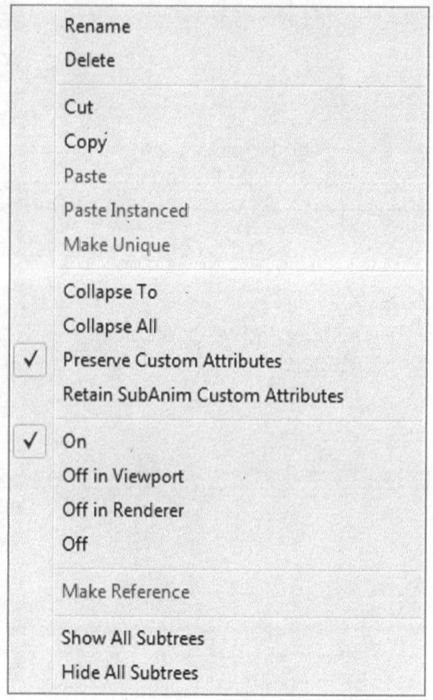

***Figure 12-4** The shortcut menu displayed on right-clicking on the modifier in the modifier stack*

TYPES OF MODIFIERS

There are three categories of modifiers in the **Modifier List** drop-down list: **Selection Modifiers**, **WORLD-SPACE MODIFIERS**, and **OBJECT-SPACE MODIFIERS**. The **Bend** and **Taper** modifiers from the **OBJECT-SPACE MODIFIERS** category have already been discussed in Chapter 3. The other most commonly used modifiers in these three categories are discussed next.

Mesh Select Modifier

The **Mesh Select** modifier is used to access the sub-object levels without converting the object into an editable mesh. To work with this modifier, select the object in the viewport and choose the **Modify** tab in the **Command Panel**. In the modifier stack, click on the arrow on the right side of the **Modifier List** drop-down list and select the **Mesh Select** modifier from the **Selection Modifiers** category. Alternatively, choose **Modifiers > Selection Modifiers > Mesh Select** from the menu bar; the **Mesh Select** modifier will be displayed in the modifier stack with various rollouts in the Modify panel, refer to Figure 12-5. Click on the arrow sign on the left of the **Mesh Select** modifier in the modifier stack; the sub-object levels will be displayed. Now, select any of the sub-object levels and then select the corresponding sub-objects of the object in the viewport. Next, apply another modifier; it will affect only the selected sub-objects in the viewport. The most commonly used rollout is discussed next.

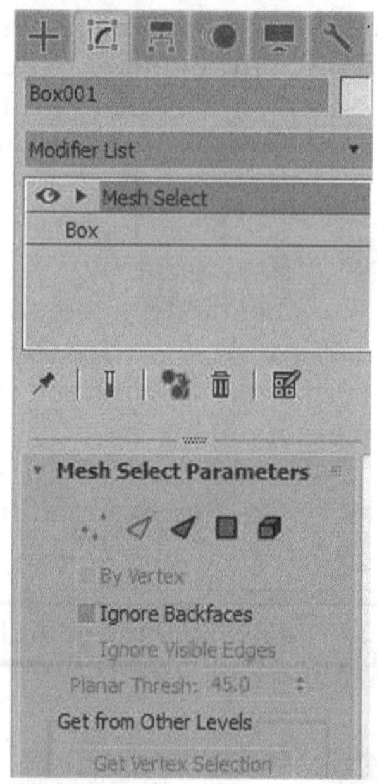

***Figure 12-5** Partial view of the rollouts displayed on selecting the **Mesh Select** modifier*

Mesh Select Parameters Rollout

In the **Mesh Select Parameters** rollout, there are five buttons **Vertex**, **Edge**, **Face**, **Polygon**, and **Element**. These buttons are used to select the sub-objects of the object and are same as described in Chapter 8. Choose any button to activate the sub-object and is same as selecting the sub-object level in the modifier stack. When you choose any of the buttons, the transform tools such as **Select and Rotate**, **Select and Move**, and so on will be disabled in the **Main Toolbar**.

The options in the **Get from Other Levels** area are used to apply the selection of the sub-objects from one sub-object level to another. The **Get Vertex Selection** button is available for the **Face**, **Edge**, **Polygon**, and **Element** sub-object levels. Choose this button to select the faces of the object based on the last selection of the vertices. The **Get Face Selection** button is available only for the **Vertex** and **Edge** sub-object levels. Choose this button to select the vertices of the object based on the last selection of the faces, polygons, and elements. The **Get Edge Selection** button is available for the **Vertex**, **Face**, **Polygon**, and **Element** sub-object levels. Choose this button to select the faces based on the last selection of the edges.

Displace Modifier

The **Displace** modifier is used to deform the shape of an object. You can distort the object either by using the gizmo of the modifier or by using the bitmap image. To apply the **Displace** modifier, select the object in the viewport and choose the **Modify** tab in the **Command Panel**. Now, click on the **Modifier List** drop-down list and select the **Displace** modifier from the **OBJECT-SPACE MODIFIERS** category. Alternatively, choose **Modifiers > Parametric Deformers > Displace** from the menu bar; the **Displace** modifier will be displayed in the modifier stack and the **Parameters** rollout will be displayed in the Modify panel. You need to use the options in this rollout to distort the surface of the object. These options are discussed next.

Parameters Rollout

The most commonly used areas in this rollout are discussed next.

Displacement Area

The options in this area are used to specify the amount of displacement of an object from the position of its gizmo, refer to Figure 12-6. By default, the value in the **Strength** and **Decay** spinners is 0 which indicates that there will be no displacement. Set the value more than 0 in the **Strength** spinner to displace the object away from the gizmo. Set the value less than 0 in the **Strength** spinner to displace the object toward the gizmo. Set the value in the **Decay** spinner to decrease the strength of the displacement based on the distance of the object from the gizmo.

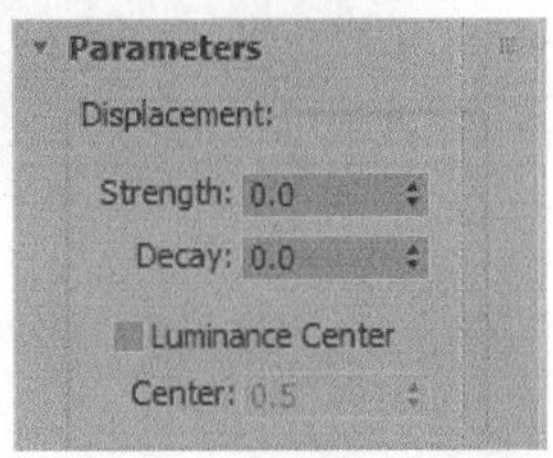

*Figure 12-6 The **Displacement** area in the **Parameters** rollout*

Image Area

The options in this area are used to choose a bitmap or map as the source for the displacement. The button labeled as **None** at the top of the **Bitmap** group is used to assign a bitmap image to the object for displacement. To do so, create a plane with heavy segments and then apply the **Displace** modifier. Next, choose the **None** button from the **Bitmap** group; the **Select Displacement Image** dialog box will be displayed. Select the image of your choice and choose the **Open** button; the name of the image will be displayed on the button. Next, set the values in the **Strength** and **Decay** spinners in the **Displacement** area to view the displacement, refer to Figures 12-7 and 12-8. Choose the **Remove Bitmap** button to remove the assigned bitmap image.

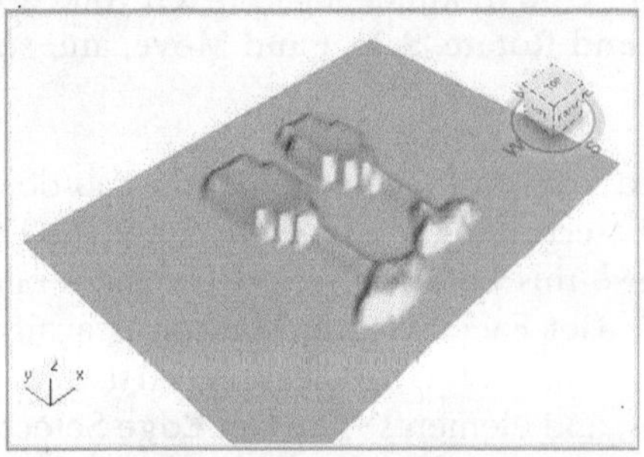

*Figure 12-7 The plane after using the bitmap image in the **Displace** modifier*

Figure 12-8 The bitmap image that has been used for displacement in Figure 12-7

The button, labeled as **None** at the top of the **Map** group, is used to assign a map to the object for displacement. To do so, choose the button; the **Material/Map Browser** dialog box will be displayed. Select the map of your choice from the **Maps > General** rollout and choose the **OK** button; the name of the map will be displayed on the button. Next, set the values in the **Strength** and **Decay** spinners in the **Displacement** area to view the displacement, refer to Figures 12-9 and 12-10. Choose the **Remove Map** button to remove the assigned map. Set the value in the **Blur** spinner to soften the edges of the map or bitmap.

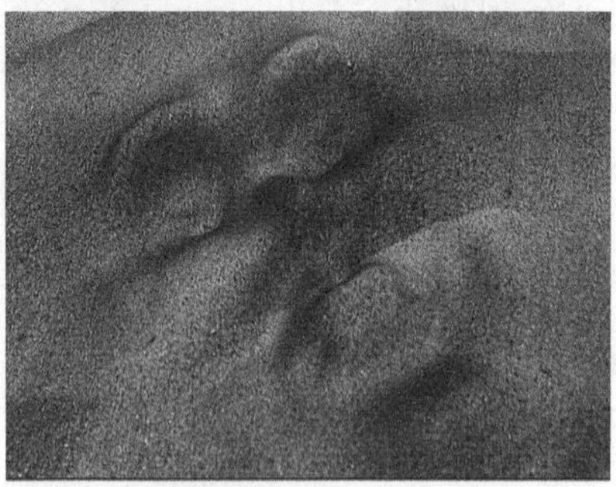

*Figure 12-9 The plane after using the map image in the **Displace** modifier*

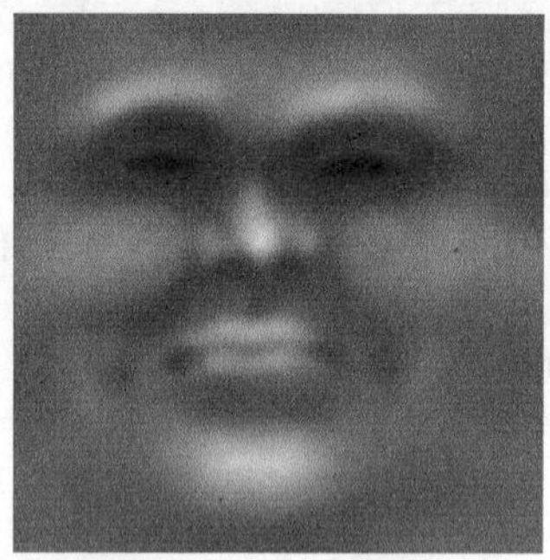

Figure 12-10 The map image that has been used for displacement in Figure 12-9

Note
You can apply the map and bitmap images simultaneously.

Set the parameters in the **Map**, **Channel**, and **Alignment** areas to define the placement or alignment of the map on the object.

Extrude Modifier

The **Extrude** modifier is used to convert a 2D spline into a 3D object. It provides thickness and depth to a spline. To apply the **Extrude** modifier, select the spline in the viewport and choose the **Modify** tab in the **Command Panel**. Now, select the **Extrude** modifier from the **OBJECT-SPACE MODIFIERS** category in the **Modifier List** drop-down list. Alternatively, choose **Modifiers > Mesh Editing > Extrude** from the menu bar; the modifier will be displayed in the modifier stack and the **Parameters** rollout will be displayed below the modifier stack in the Modify panel, as shown in Figure 12-11. Next, you need to use the options in the **Parameters** rollout to view the effects of the **Extrude** modifier. These options are discussed next.

Parameters Rollout

The **Amount** spinner in this rollout is used to specify the amount of extrusion of the spline, refer to Figures 12-12 and 12-13. Set the value in the **Segments** spinner to specify the number of segments in the extruded object. The areas in this rollout are discussed next.

Capping Area

By default, the **Cap Start** and **Cap End** check boxes are selected in the **Capping** area. They are used to place a plane surface at the start and end of the extruded object. Clear the **Cap Start** check box to remove the surface at the start of the extruded object. Similarly, clear the **Cap End** check box to remove the surface at the end of the extruded object.

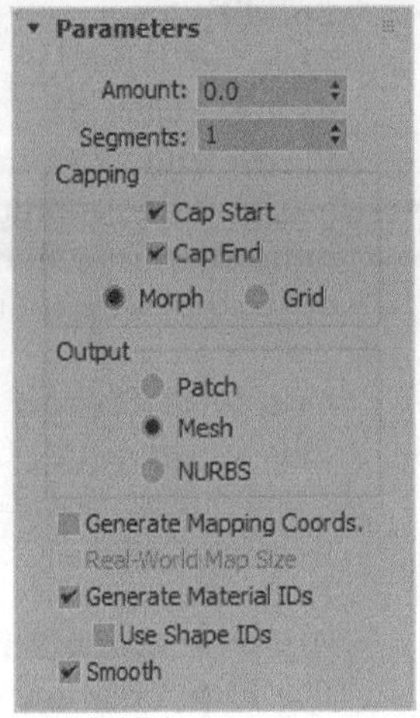

*Figure 12-11 The **Parameters** rollout*

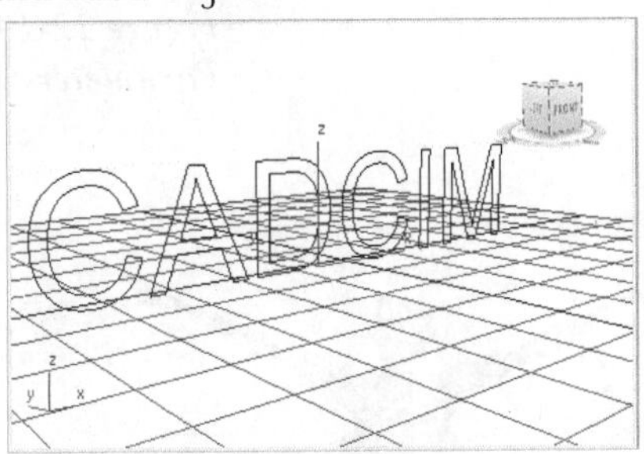

*Figure 12-12 The text spline before applying the **Extrude** modifier*

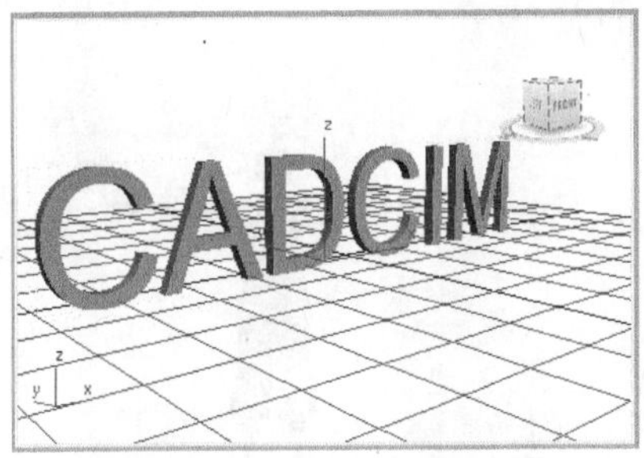

*Figure 12-13 The text spline after applying the **Extrude** modifier*

Output Area

The options in this area are used to specify the type of the object to be created by the **Extrude** modifier. By default, the **Mesh** radio button is selected that produces a mesh object. Select the **Patch** or **NURBS** radio button to produce the patch object or the nurbs object.

Melt Modifier

The **Melt** modifier is used to apply a realistic melting effect to all types of objects. To apply the **Melt** modifier, select the editable object in the viewport and choose the **Modify** tab in the **Command Panel**. Now, select the **Melt** modifier from the **OBJECT-SPACE MODIFIERS** category in the **Modifier List** drop-down list. Alternatively, choose **Modifiers > Animation > Melt** from the menu bar; the modifier will be displayed in the modifier stack and the **Parameters** rollout will be displayed below the modifier stack in the Modify panel, as shown in Figure 12-14. You can use the options in the **Parameters** rollout to view the effects of the **Melt** modifier. These options are discussed next.

Parameters Rollout

Set a value in the **Amount** spinner of the **Melt** area to specify melting amount for the editable poly, refer to Figure 12-15 and 12-16. Set the value in the **% of Melt** spinner in the **Spread** area to specify melting percentage.

Solidity Area

This area is used to define the relative height of the center of the melted object. This area has five radio buttons: **Ice**, **Glass**, **Jelly**, **Plastic** and **Custom.** These radio buttons determine the relative height of the center of ice, glass, jelly, and plastic. Select the **Custom** radio button to define the custom solidity of the object and its melting process that varies between 0.2 to 30.0.

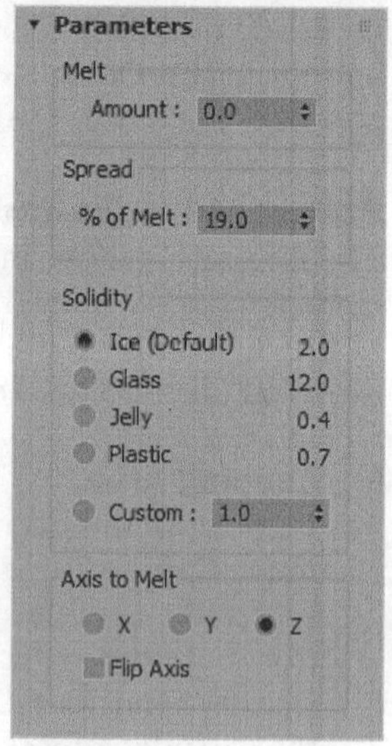

Figure 12-14 The ***Parameters*** *rollout*

Axis to Melt Area

This area is used to define the axis on which the object will melt. By default, the melting axis is set to Z. You can change it to X and Y, as required.

Flip Axis Radio Button

The **Flip Axis** radio button is used to reverse the direction of the selected axis of melting which normally occurs from the positive direction to the negative direction.

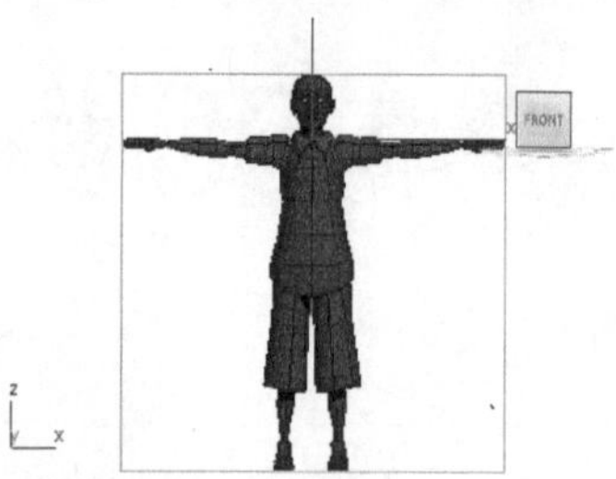

Figure 12-15 The object before applying the ***Melt*** *modifier*

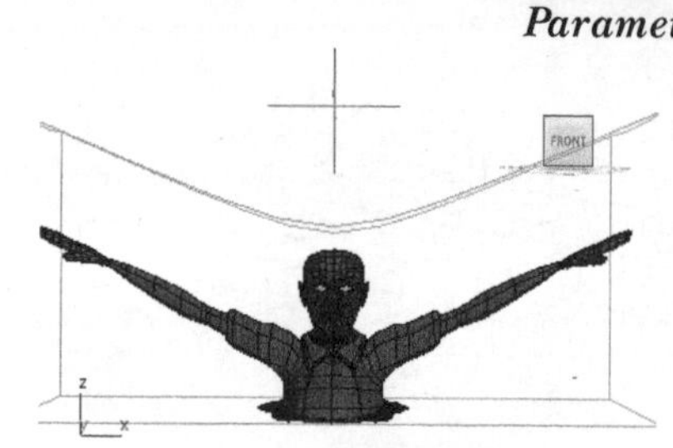

Figure 12-16 The object after applying the ***Melt*** *modifier*

ProOptimizer Modifier

This modifier is used to reduce the number of vertices in an object while preserving the object's appearance. It helps in reducing a scene's memory requirements, simplifying the modeling, and improving the speed of viewport display and render. To apply the **ProOptimizer** modifier, select the editable poly object in the viewport and choose the **Modify** tab in the **Command Panel**. Now, select the **ProOptimizer** modifier from the **OBJECT-SPACE MODIFIERS** category in the **Modifier List** drop-down list. Alternatively, choose **Modifiers > Mesh Editing > ProOptimizer** from the menu bar; the modifier will be displayed in the modifier stack and the **Optimization Level** rollout will be displayed below the modifier stack in the Modify Panel, as shown in Figure 12-17. Next, you need to use the options in the **Optimization Level** rollout to view the effects of the **ProOptimizer** modifier. This rollout is discussed next.

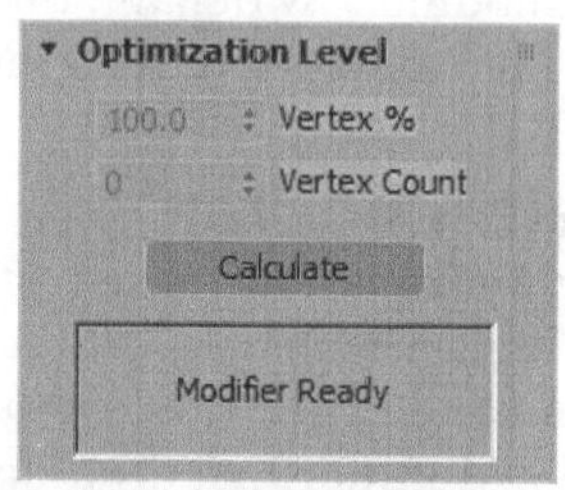

Figure 12-17 The ***Optimization Level*** *rollout*

Opitimization Level Rollout

The **Calculate** button in the **Optimization Level** rollout is used to calculate the total number of vertices and faces. Set the value in the **Vertex %** spinner of the **Optimization Level** area to specify the percentage of the vertices that should be reduced, refer to Figures 12-18 and 12-19.

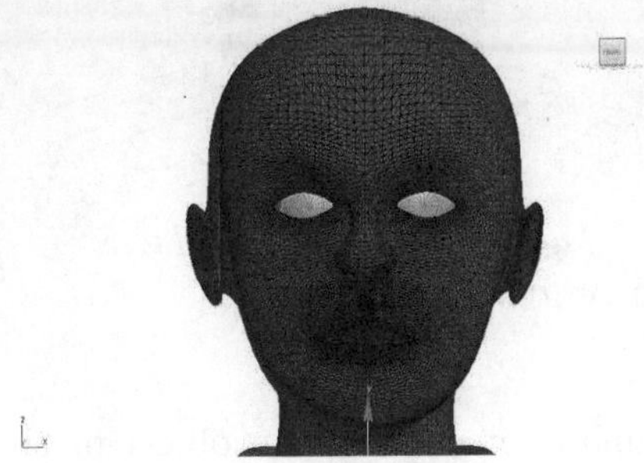

***Figure 12-18** The object before applying the **ProOptimizer** modifier*

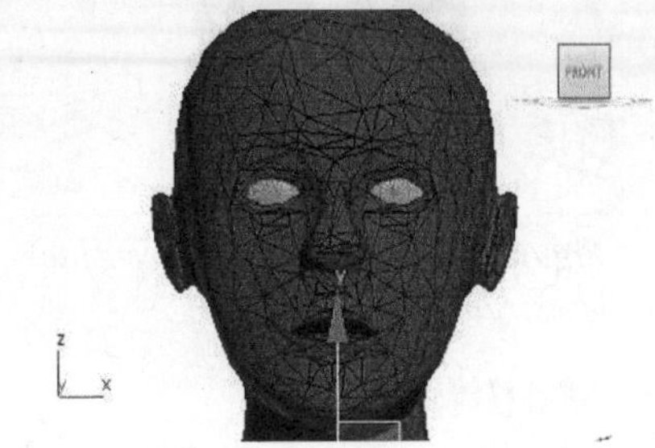

***Figure 12-19** The object after applying the **ProOptimizer** modifier*

Set the value in the **Vertex Count** spinner of the **Optimization Level** rollout to specify the amount of vertices in the object. The **Status** window available below the **Calculate** button is used to display the status of the **ProOptimizer** modifier. Before the **Calculate** button is chosen, the **Status** window will display the text, **Modifier Ready**. However, after choosing the **Calculate** button, it will display the statistics that describes the before and after effects on the vertex and face count of an object.

Face Extrude Modifier

This modifier is used to extrude the selected faces along their normals. A normal is an invisible line coming straight out of a face in a particular direction. To apply the **Face Extrude** modifier, first convert the object into an editable poly object. Next, select the **Face** sub-object level and then select the faces of the object in the viewport. Now, select the **Face Extrude** modifier from the **OBJECT-SPACE MODIFIERS** category in the **Modifier List** drop-down list.

Alternatively, choose **Modifiers > Mesh Editing > Face Extrude** from the menu bar; the **Face Extrude** modifier will be displayed in the modifier stack and also the **Parameters** rollout will be displayed below the modifier stack in the Modify Panel, as shown in Figure 12-20. Now, you need to use the options in the **Parameters** rollout to view the effect of the **Face Extrude** modifier on the selected faces, refer to Figure 12-20. These options are discussed next.

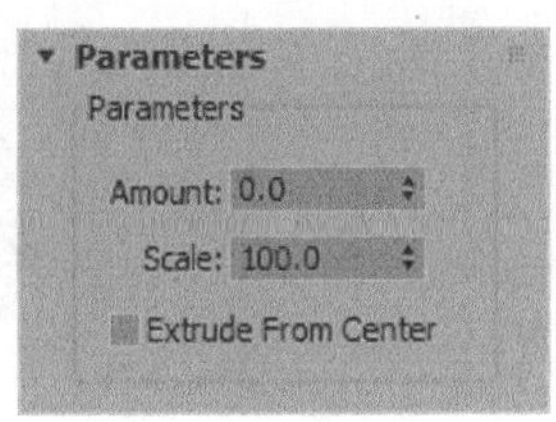

***Figure 12-20** The **Parameters** rollout*

Parameters Rollout

The **Amount** spinner of the **Parameters** area in this rollout is used to specify the amount of extrusion of the selected faces, refer to Figures 12-21 and 12-22. Set the value in the **Scale** spinner to specify the percentage of the original face size used for the extruded face.

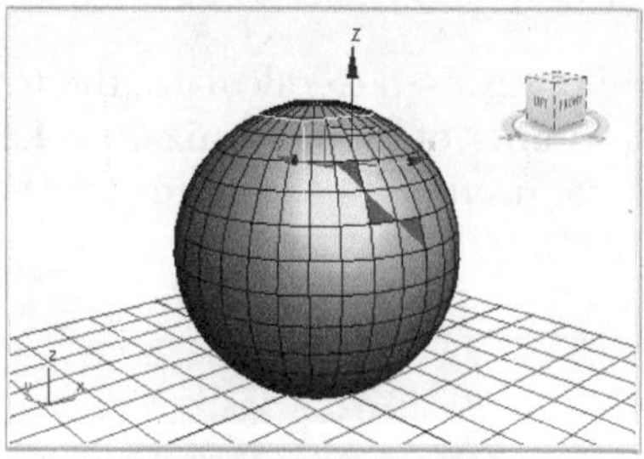

Figure 12-21 The faces selected to be extruded in a sphere

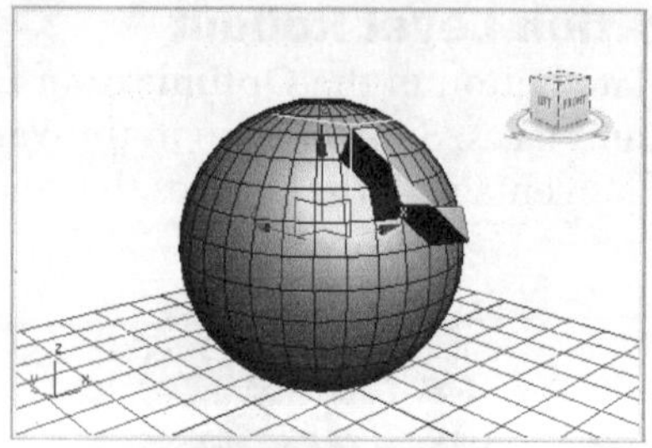

Figure 12-22 The selected faces extruded

Lattice Modifier

The **Lattice** modifier is used to convert the segments or edges of an object or shape into wireframes or cylindrical struts. To apply the **Lattice** modifier, select the object or shape in the viewport and choose the **Modify** tab in the **Command Panel**. Now, select the **Lattice** modifier from the **OBJECT-SPACE MODIFIERS** category in the **Modifier List** drop-down list. Alternatively, choose **Modifiers > Parametric Deformers > Lattice** from the menu bar; the modifier will be displayed in the modifier stack and its effect will be displayed on the object, as shown in Figure 12-23. The **Parameters** rollout will also be displayed below the modifier stack, as shown in Figure 12-24. Now, you need to use the options in the **Parameters** rollout to modify the effects of the **Lattice** modifier. These options are discussed next.

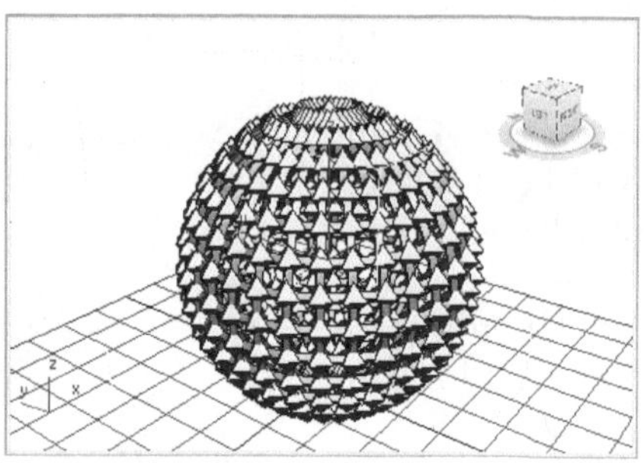

*Figure 12-23 The sphere after applying the **Lattice** modifier*

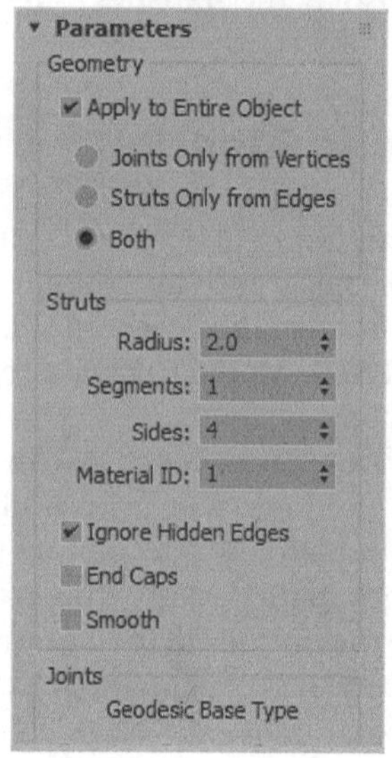

*Figure 12-24 Partial view of the **Parameters** rollout*

Parameters Rollout

The options in this rollout are used to specify whether wireframes will be displayed on joints, struts, or on both of them. The areas in this rollout are discussed next.

Geometry Area

In this area, the **Apply to Entire Object** check box is selected by default. As a result, wireframe is applied to all the segments or edges of the object. If you clear this check box, then the wireframes will be applied only to the selected segments or edges of the object.

By default, the **Both** radio button is selected to apply wireframes on both struts and joints, refer to Figure 12-24. Select the **Joints Only from Vertices** radio button to display the wireframes only on the joints generated from the vertices of the object, as shown in Figure 12-25. Select the **Struts Only from Edges** radio button to display the wireframes only on the struts generated from the edges of the object, as shown in Figure 12-26.

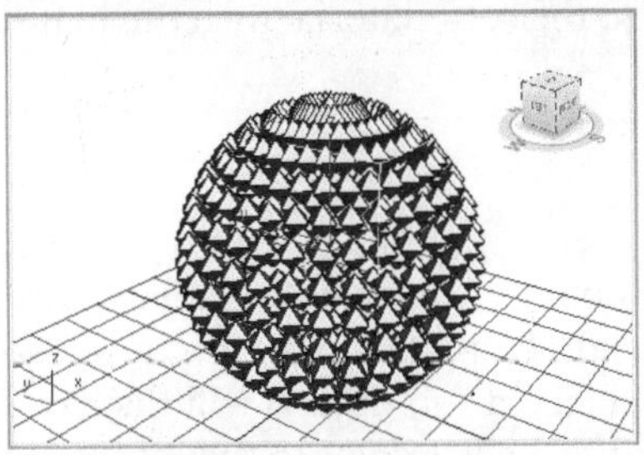

*Figure 12-25 The sphere after selecting the **Joints Only from Vertices** radio button*

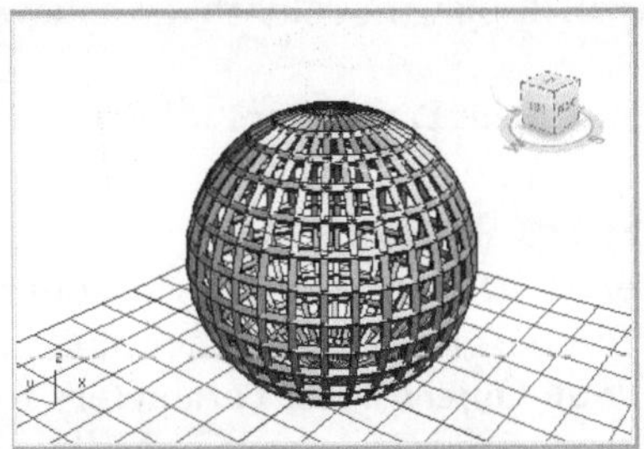

*Figure 12-26 The sphere after selecting the **Struts Only from Edges** radio button*

Struts Area

The options in this area are activated only if the **Struts Only from Edges** or **Both** radio button is selected in the **Geometry** area. Set the value in the **Radius** spinner to define the radius of the struts. Set the value in the **Segments** spinner to specify the number of segments along the struts. Set the value in the **Sides** spinner to specify the number of sides around the circumference of the struts. Set the value in the **Material ID** spinner to specify the material id for the struts to apply the material.

Joints Area

The options in this area are activated only if the **Joints Only from Vertices** or **Both** radio button is selected in the **Geometry** area. There are three radio buttons in the **Geodesic Base Type** group that specify the type of polyhedron to be used for the joints. By default, the **Octa** radio button is selected and is used to create the octahedron joints. Select the **Tetra** or the **Icosa** radio button to create the tetrahedron or icosahedron joints, respectively. The other options are the same as discussed in the **Struts** area.

Material Modifier

The **Material** modifier is used to assign material ID to an object or sub-objects. The material ID of an object is the value given to specify the sub-material that is applied to it from the **Multi/Sub-Object** material. You can apply different materials to the selected sub-objects by assigning different material IDs to them. To do so, create an object in the Top viewport. Choose the **Material Editor** tool from the **Main Toolbar** and apply the **Multi/Sub-Object** material to the object, as described earlier in Chapter 7; the **Multi/Sub-Object Basic Parameters** rollout will be displayed in the **Material Editor** dialog box, as shown in Figure 12-27. In this rollout, assign two different colors to the first two sub-materials using the color swatches on the right side. By default, the first two sub-materials have the material IDs, 1 and 2. Now, assign the **Multi/Sub-Object** material to the object in the viewport. Next, make sure that the object is selected and apply the **Mesh Select** modifier to it. Select the **Polygon** sub-object level and select the polygons of the object in the viewport. Now, make sure that the **Polygon** sub-object level is active and select the **Material** modifier from the **OBJECT-SPACE MODIFIERS** category in the **Modifier List** drop-down list. You can also choose **Modifiers > Surface > Material** from the menu bar; the **Material** modifier will be displayed in the modifier stack and the **Parameters** rollout will be displayed. Now in the **Material ID** spinner of the **Parameters** rollout, set the value **1**; the selected polygons will display the color that you have assigned to the sub-material with the material ID 1. Select another set of polygons and set the value **2** in the **Material ID** spinner; the selected polygons will display the color that you have assigned to the sub-material with the material ID 2.

The options in the **Parameters** rollout are discussed next.

Parameters Rollout

The **Material ID** spinner in this rollout is used to change the material ID of the selected sub-object in the viewport. Set the value in the **Material ID** spinner that you have assigned in the **Multi/Sub-Object Basic Parameters** rollout; the selected sub-objects will display the color of the same material ID. For example, if you have assigned yellow color to the material ID 1 and red color to the material ID 2 in the **Multi/Sub-Object Basic Parameters** then on entering the value **1** in the **Material ID** spinner, the selected sub-objects will appear yellow. If you enter the value **2** in the **Material ID** spinner, the selected sub-objects will appear red, refer to Figure 12-28.

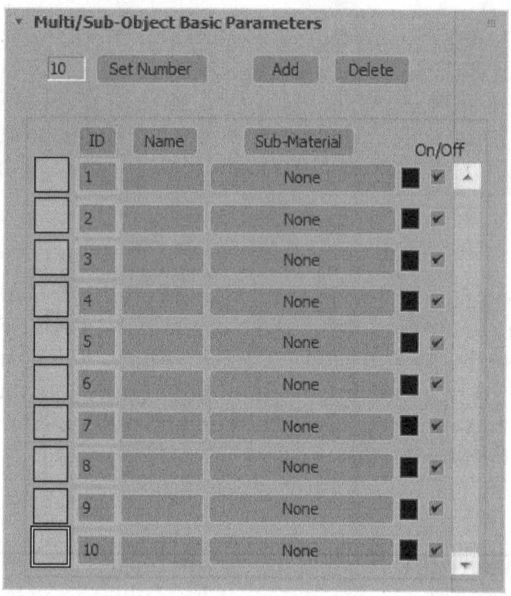

*Figure 12-27 Partial view of the **Multi/Sub-Object Basic Parameters** rollout in the **Material Editor** dialog box*

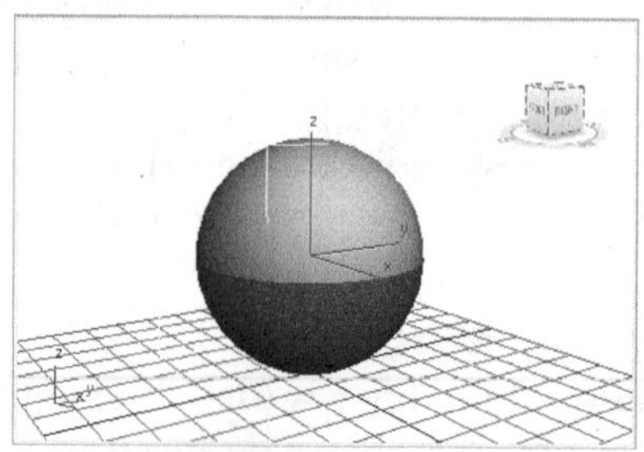

*Figure 12-28 The object displayed in two different colors after applying the **Material** modifier*

Noise Modifier

The **Noise** modifier is used to generate disturbances on the surface of an object to create irregular surfaces. It can also be used to animate water or wavy surfaces.

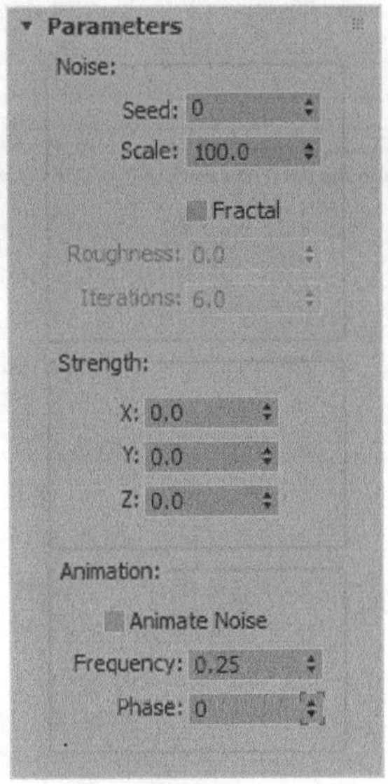

*Figure 12-29 The **Parameters** rollout*

To apply the **Noise** modifier, select the object in the viewport and choose the **Modify** tab in the **Command Panel**. Now, select the **Noise** modifier from the **OBJECT-SPACE MODIFIERS** category in the **Modifier List** drop-down list. You can also choose **Modifiers > Parametric Deformers > Noise** from the menu bar; the **Noise** modifier will be displayed in the modifier stack and the **Parameters** rollout will also be displayed in the Modify panel. Next, you need to use the options in the **Parameters** rollout, refer to Figure 12-29, to apply the effects of the **Noise** modifier on the selected object. These options are discussed next.

Parameters Rollout

The options in this rollout are used to generate noise effects in an object, as shown in Figure 12-30. The areas in this rollout are discussed next.

Noise Area

The options in this area are used to define the appearance of the surface of the object on applying the **Noise** modifier. Set the value in the **Seed** spinner to specify the starting point for generating the noise randomly in the object. Set the value in the **Scale** spinner to specify the size of noise effects. By default, the value in the **Scale** spinner is 100. A higher value in this spinner produces smoother noise effects and a lower value produces scraggy noise effects. By default, the **Fractal** check box is cleared. Select the **Fractal** check box to produce the fractal-based noise effects, refer to Figure 12-31. When you select the **Fractal** check box, the **Roughness** and **Iterations** spinners get activated that are used to set the fractal effects in the noise. Set the lower value in the **Roughness** spinner to produce smooth fractal effects in noise. Set the higher value in the **Roughness** spinner to produce rough fractal effects in noise. The value in the **Roughness** spinner varies from 0 to 1.0. Set the value in the **Iterations** spinner to apply the fractal effects multiple times. By default, the value in the **Iterations** spinner is 1.0. It varies from 1.0 to 10.0.

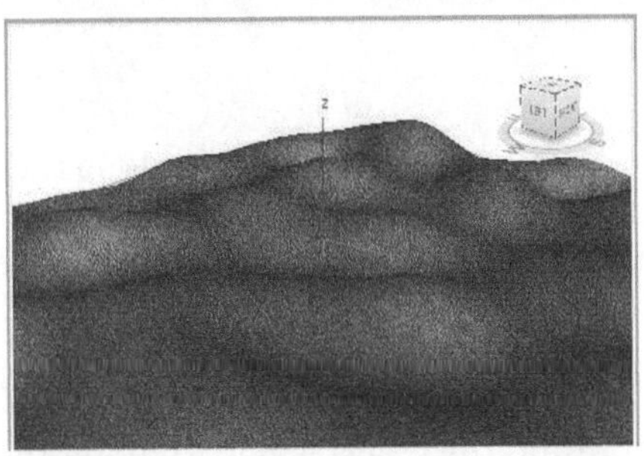

*Figure 12-30 The plane with the **Noise** modifier applied*

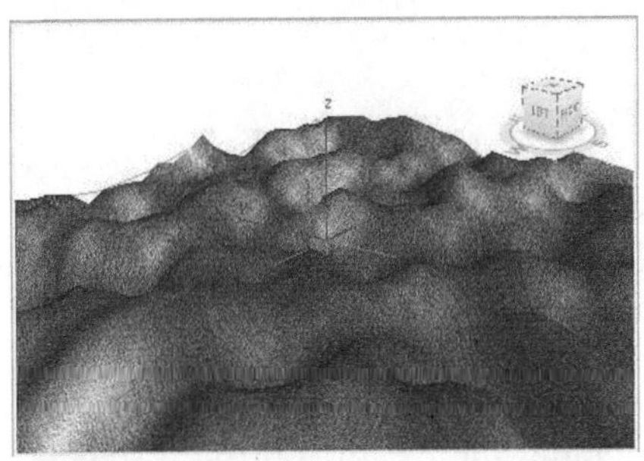

*Figure 12-31 The plane with the **Fractal** checkbox selected*

Note

1. The number of segments in an object should be more for generating better effct by the ***Noise*** *modifier.*

2. You can also create the terrain objects using this modifier.

Strength Area

The options in this area are used to specify the strength of the noise effects. By default, the value in the **X**, **Y**, and **Z** spinners is 0 that produces no noise effects in the object. Set the value in these spinners to generate the strength of the noise effects.

Animation Area

The options in this area are used to animate the noise effects of the object. To view the animation effects, you need to select the **Animate Noise** check box. Set the value in the **Frequency** spinner to specify the speed of the animation of noise waves. The lower value produces a slow animation and the higher value produces a fast animation. Set the value in the **Phase** spinner to set the start point and the end point of the wave animation along with the frames in the time slider.

Twist Modifier

The **Twist** modifier is used to produce the swirling effect on an object. To apply the **Twist** modifier, select an object in the viewport. Select the **Twist** modifier from the **OBJECT-SPACE MODIFIERS** category in the **Modifier List** drop-down list. Alternatively, choose the **Modifiers > Parametric Deformers > Twist** from the menu bar; the **Twist** modifier will be displayed in the modifier stack and the **Parameters** rollout will also be displayed in the Modify panel. Next, you need to use the options in the **Parameters** rollout, refer to Figure 12-32, to apply the effects of the **Twist** modifier to the object. The **Parameters** rollout is discussed next.

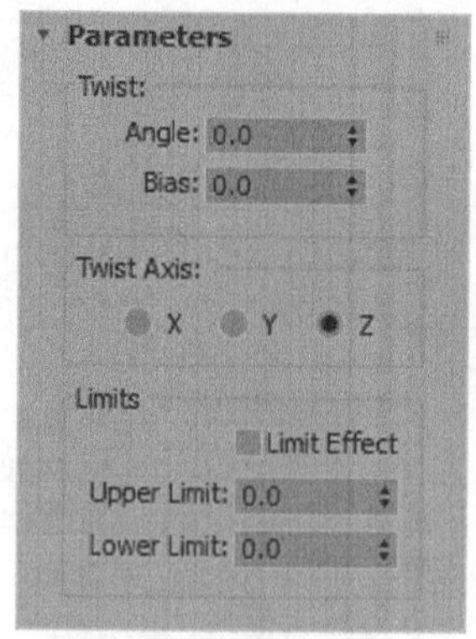

***Figure 12-32** The **Parameters** rollout*

Parameters Rollout

This rollout is used to set the parameters to generate swirling effects on an object, refer to Figure 12-33. The areas in this rollout are discussed next.

Twist Area

Set the value in the **Angle** spinner to specify the amount of twist in degrees along the selected axis in the **Twist Axis** area. Set the value in the **Bias** spinner to shift the twist at one of the ends of the object. By default, the value in this spinner is 0, which specifies that the twist is uniform along the length of the object. It varies from 100 to -100.

Twist Axis Area

By default, the **Z** radio button is selected. As a result, the object will twist along the Z-axis. Select the **X** or the **Y** radio button to twist the object along the X-axis or the Y-axis, respectively.

Limits Area

The options in this area are used to define the portion of an object to which the twist effects will be applied, refer to Figure 12-34. Select the **Limit Effect** check box to apply the limits to the twist effects of the object. Set the value in the **Upper Limit** spinner to specify the upper limit for the twist effect. Set the value in the **Lower Limit** spinner to specify the lower limit for the twist effect.

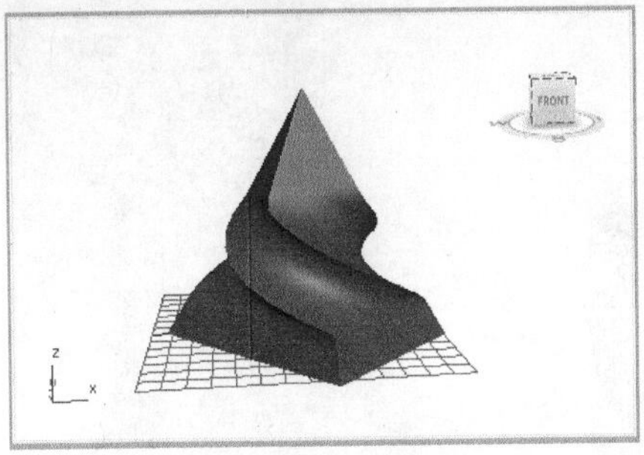

***Figure 12-33** The **Twist** modifier applied to the pyramid object*

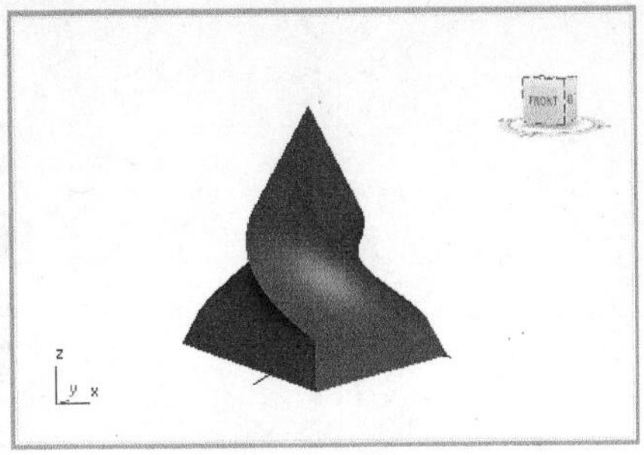

***Figure 12-34** The **Twist** modifier applied to a portion of the pyramid object using the options in the **Limits** area*

Lathe Modifier

The **Lathe** modifier is a shape modifier that is used to create a 3D object by rotating a shape about an axis. The direction of the axis of revolution depends on the pivot point of the shape. To apply the **Lathe** modifier on an object, create a shape with the spline in the Front viewport and choose the **Modify** tab in the **Command Panel**. Now, select the **Lathe** modifier from the **OBJECT-SPACE MODIFIERS** category in the **Modifier List** drop-down list. Alternatively, choose **Modifiers > Patch/Spline Editing > Lathe** from the menu bar; the 2D shape will be converted into a 3D object, as shown in Figures 12-35 and 12-36. And, the modifier will be displayed in the modifier stack. The **Parameters** rollout will also be displayed below the modifier stack, refer to Figure 12-37. This rollout is discussed next.

Parameters Rollout

Set the value in the **Degrees** spinner to specify the amount of rotation of the object in degrees around the axis specified in the **Direction** area. The **Weld Core** check box is used to weld the vertices which are on the axis of revolution. The **Flip Normals** check box is used to flip the normals of the lathed object. Set the value in the **Segments** spinner to specify the desired number of segments around the axis of revolution. The areas in this rollout are discussed next.

Capping Area

The options in this area are the same as described in the **Extrude** modifier.

Direction Area

Choose the **X**, **Y**, or **Z** button to specify the axis around which the objects will rotate while applying the **Lathe** modifier.

Align Area

Choose the **Min**, **Center**, or **Max** button to align the spline with the axis of revolution.

Figure 12-35 *The* ***Line*** *spline*

Figure 12-36 *The* ***Line*** *spline after applying the* ***Lathe*** *modifier*

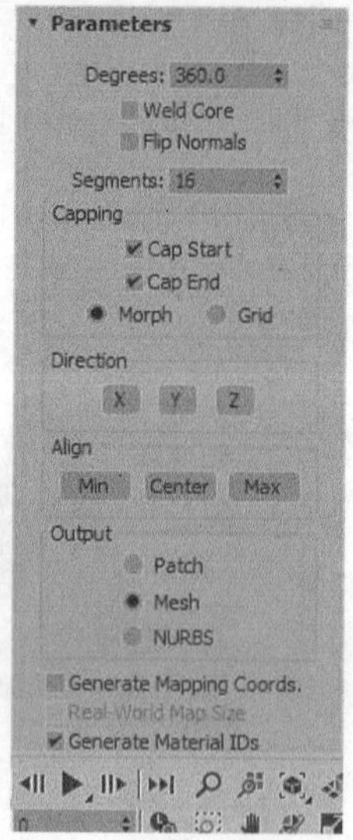

Figure 12-37 *Partial view of the* ***Parameters*** *rollout*

MeshSmooth Modifier

The **MeshSmooth** modifier is used to produce smoothness in 3D mesh objects. To apply the **MeshSmooth** modifier, select an object in the viewport. Select the **MeshSmooth** modifier from the **OBJECT-SPACE MODIFIERS** category in the **Modifier List** drop-down list; the edges of the object will become smoother, as shown in Figures 12-38 and 12-39. Alternatively, you can choose **Modifiers > Subdivision Surfaces > MeshSmooth** from the menu bar; the **MeshSmooth** modifier will be displayed in the modifier stack and various rollouts will also be displayed below the modifier stack. The most commonly used rollout is discussed next.

Figure 12-38 *The surface before applying the* ***MeshSmooth*** *modifier*

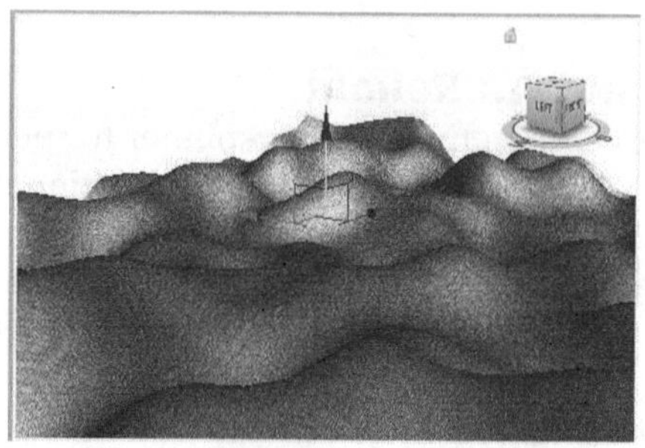

Figure 12-39 *The surface after applying the* ***MeshSmooth*** *modifier*

Subdivision Amount Rollout

Set the value in the **Iterations** spinner to specify the number of times you want to apply the **MeshSmooth** modifier, refer to Figure 12-40. Set the value in the **Smoothness** spinner to smoothen the edges of the object. The **Iterations** and **Smoothness** spinners in the **Render Values** area determine the effects of the **MeshSmooth** modifier at rendering. To activate these spinners, you need to select the check boxes on their left.

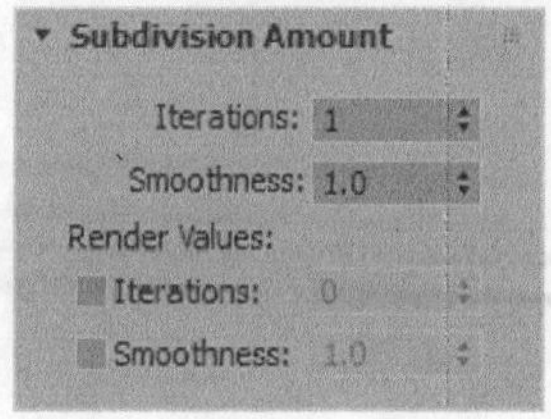

Figure 12-40 The ***Subdivision Amount*** *rollout*

Tessellate Modifier

The **Tessellate** modifier is used to subdivide the faces of an object. It provides smoothness to curved surfaces for rendering. To apply the **Tessellate** modifier on an object, create an object in the viewport and convert it into an editable mesh object. Select the sub-objects of the object in the viewport and select the **Tessellate** modifier from the **OBJECT-SPACE MODIFIERS** category in the **Modifier List** drop-down list. Alternatively, choose **Modifiers > Mesh Editing > Tessellate** from the menu bar; the selected sub-objects will be subdivided into faces, as shown in Figures 12-41 and 12-42. When you apply the **Tessellate** modifier on an object, the entire object is tessellated. The **Parameters** rollout of the **Tessellate** modifier is shown in Figure 12-43. This rollout is discussed next.

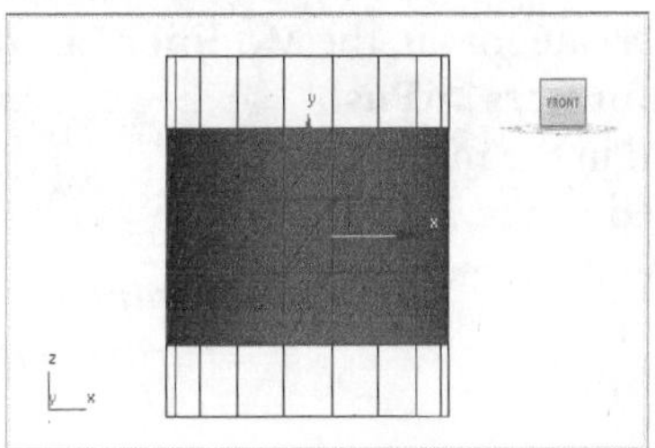

Figure 12-41 *The sub-objects selected in an object to apply the* ***Tessellate*** *modifier*

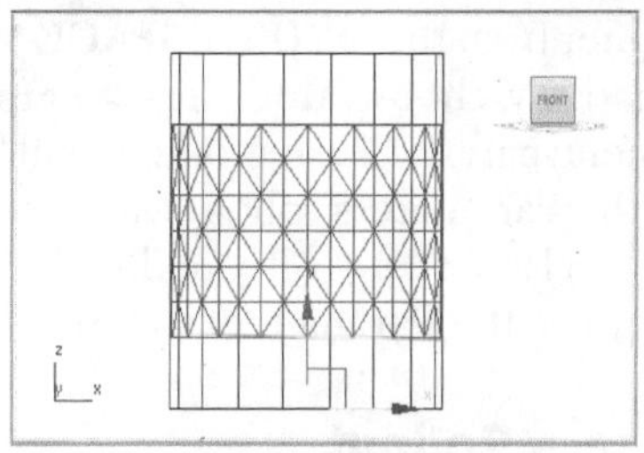

Figure 12-42 *The selected sub-objects converted into triangular faces after applying the* ***Tessellate*** *modifier*

Parameters Rollout

In the **Operate On** group, there are two buttons: **Faces** and **Polygons**. These buttons are used to define whether the modifier will be applied to the faces or the polygons of the object. The **Faces** button is chosen by default and it displays the selected sub-objects as triangular faces, refer to Figure 12-42. Choose the **Polygons** button to display the sub-objects as polygonal faces, as shown in Figure 12-44.

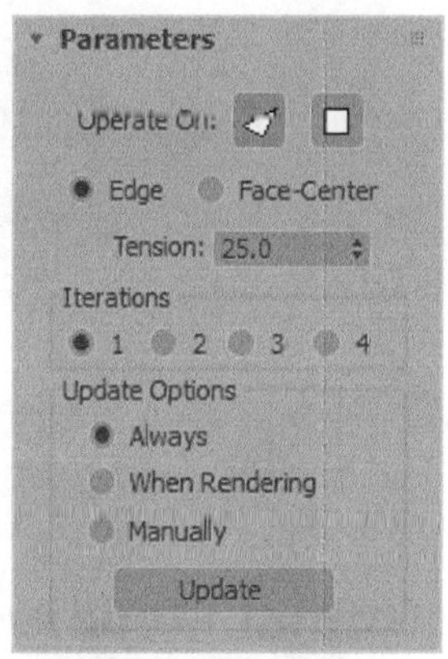

Figure 12-43 *The* ***Parameters*** *rollout*

By default, the **Edge** radio button is selected and is used to subdivide the selection from the middle of each edge. Select the **Face-Center** radio button to subdivide the faces of the selection from the center to the vertex corners, as shown in Figure 12-45. The **Tension** spinner will be activated only if the **Edge** radio button is selected. The 0 value in the **Tension** spinner specifies that the new faces are flat. The positive value in this spinner specifies that the new faces are convex. The negative value in this spinner specifies that the new faces are concave.

By default, the **1** radio button is selected in the **Iterations** area. Select the **2**, **3**, or **4** radio button to specify the number of times the modifier will be applied to the selection.

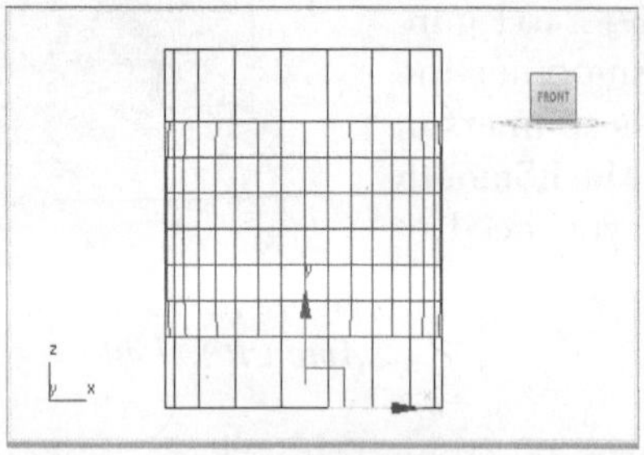

*Figure 12-44 The selected sub-objects converted into polygonal faces after choosing the **Polygons** button*

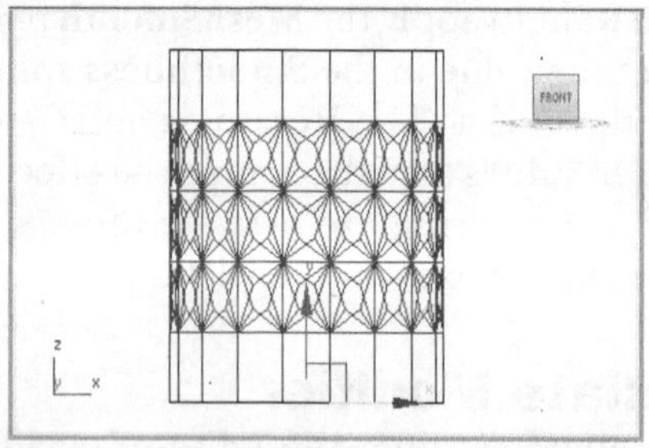

*Figure 12-45 The selected sub-objects converted into triangular faces after choosing the **Face-Center** radio button*

Push Modifier

The **Push** modifier is used to push an object inward or outward along the normals of its faces. A normal is an invisible line coming straight out of a face in a particular direction. To apply the **Push** modifier to an object, select the object or the sub-objects in the viewport and select the **Push** modifier from the **OBJECT-SPACE MODIFIERS** category in the **Modifier List** drop-down list. Alternatively, choose **Modifiers >Parametric Deformers > Push** from the menu bar; the **Push** modifier will be displayed in the modifier stack and the **Parameters** rollout will also be displayed in the Modify panel, refer to Figure 12-46. To modify the effects of the **Push** modifier, you need to use the **Parameters** rollout, which is discussed next.

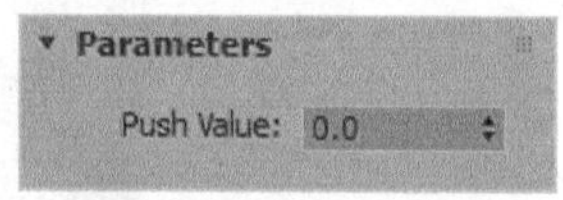

*Figure 12-46 The **Parameters** rollout*

Parameters Rollout

Set the value in the **Push Value** spinner to view the effects of the **Push** modifier, refer to Figures 12-47 and 12-48.

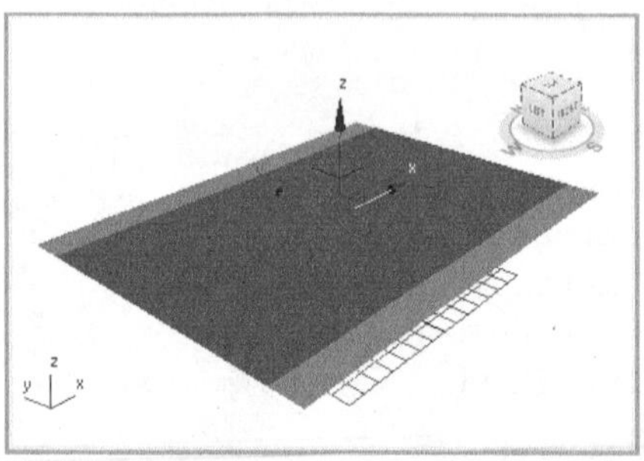

*Figure 12-47 The selected sub-objects of a plane before applying the **Push** modifier*

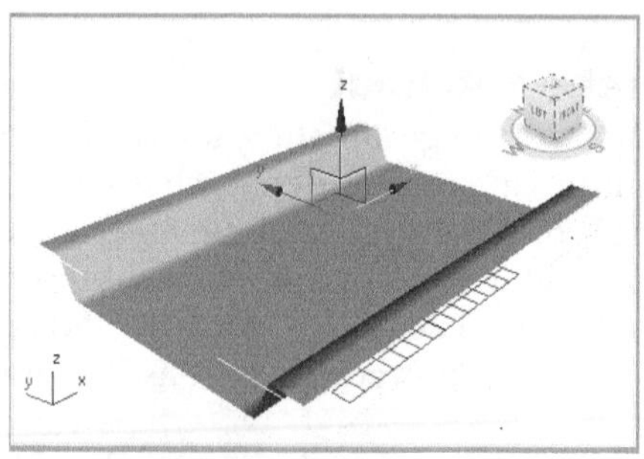

*Figure 12-48 The plane after applying the **Push** modifier*

Normal Modifier

The **Normal** modifier is used to flip the normals of an object without converting it into the editable mesh. To apply the **Normal** modifier to an object, select the object in the viewport and then select the **Normal** modifier from the **OBJECT-SPACE MODIFIERS** category in the

Modifier List drop-down list. Alternatively, you can choose **Modifiers > Mesh Editing > Normal Modifier** from the menu bar; the normals of the object will be reversed, refer to Figures 12-49 and 12-50. Also, the **Parameters** rollout will be displayed in the Modify panel, as shown in Figure 12-51. The **Parameters** rollout is discussed next.

Figure 12-49 The object with two different materials on the inner and outer sides

*Figure 12-50 The inner and outer materials interchanged after applying the **Normal** modifier*

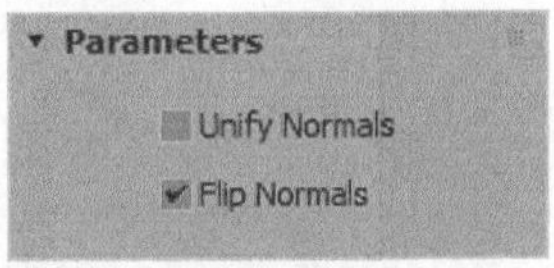

*Figure 12-51 The **Parameters** rollout*

Parameters Rollout

By default, the **Flip Normals** check box is selected. It is used to reverse the direction of the normals of all faces of the selected object. Select the **Unify Normals** check box to make all the normals of the object point in the same direction.

Edit Mesh Modifier

The **Edit Mesh** modifier is used to convert the object into editable mesh. The procedure to do so has already been discussed in Chapter 8. The **Edit Mesh** modifier and the editable mesh object provide the same sub-object levels to modify the object at an advanced level. The main difference is that you can retain the object creation parameters and then use them to edit the object even after applying the **Edit Mesh** modifier. Note that you cannot animate the sub-objects of an object after applying the **Edit Mesh** modifier.

To apply the **Edit Mesh** modifier to an object, select the object in the viewport and choose the **Modify** tab in the **Command Panel**. Now, select the **Edit Mesh** modifier from the **OBJECT-SPACE MODIFIERS** category in the **Modifier List** drop-down list. Alternatively, choose **Modifiers > Mesh Editing > Edit Mesh** from the menu bar; the modifier will be displayed in the modifier stack and the rollouts will also be displayed below the modifier stack in the Modify panel. Next, modify the object at sub-object levels as discussed in the previous chapters.

Similarly, the **Edit Patch** and **Edit Poly** modifiers are used to convert the object into an editable patch and editable poly respectively. The only difference is that the **Edit Patch** and **Edit Poly** modifiers retain the object creation parameters.

UVW Map Modifier

The **UVW Map** modifier is used to adjust the mapping coordinates on an object. Sometimes when you apply maps to objects, they are not displayed properly on its surface. To apply the map properly, you need to adjust the mapping coordinates on the object. The UVW coordinate system is the same as the XYZ coordinate system. The U, V, and W axes of a map correspond to the X, Y, and Z axes, respectively.

To apply the **UVW Map** modifier, select the object in the viewport and then select the **UVW Map** modifier from the **OBJECT-SPACE MODIFIERS** category in the **Modifier List** drop-down list. Alternatively, choose **Modifiers > UV Coordinates > UVW Map** from the menu bar; the **UVW Mapping** will be displayed in the modifier stack and the **Parameters** rollout will also be displayed below the modifier stack. The **Parameters** rollout is discussed next.

Parameters Rollout

The options in this rollout are used to set the mapping coordinates on an object, refer to Figure 12-52. These options are discussed next.

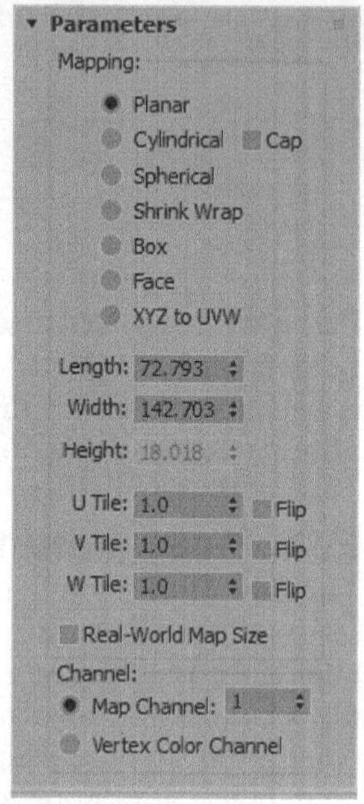

***Figure 12-52** Partial view of the **Parameters** rollout*

Mapping Area

The options in this area are used to adjust the type of mapping coordinates and the tiling used on an object. There are seven types of mapping coordinates such as Planar, Cylindrical, Spherical, and so on. The radio buttons available for these mapping coordinates are discussed next.

By default, the **Planar** radio button is selected. As a result, the map is projected from a single flat plane to an object, as shown in Figure 12-53.

Select the **Cylindrical** radio button to project the map onto a cylinder, as shown in Figure 12-54. On selecting the **Cylindrical** radio button, the **Cap** check box will be activated. Select the **Cap** check box to apply mapping coordinates to the cap of the object, as shown in Figure 12-55.

Select the **Spherical** radio button to project the map onto a sphere, refer to Figure 12-56. On selecting the **Shrink Wrap** radio button, the map will be projected onto a sphere. But in this case, the corners of the map will be truncated and they will join at a single pole, refer to Figure 12-57. Select the **Box** radio button to project six planar maps from the six sides of a box, refer to Figure 12-58. Select the **Face** radio button to project a copy of the map to every face of the object, refer to Figure 12-59.

Select the **XYZ to UVW** radio button to translate the XYZ coordinates of the procedural map into the UVW mapping coordinates. If you modify the object by changing its shape, the coordinates will adjust to match the new shape, as shown in Figure 12-60.

Figure 12-53 A box with the Planar mapping coordinate

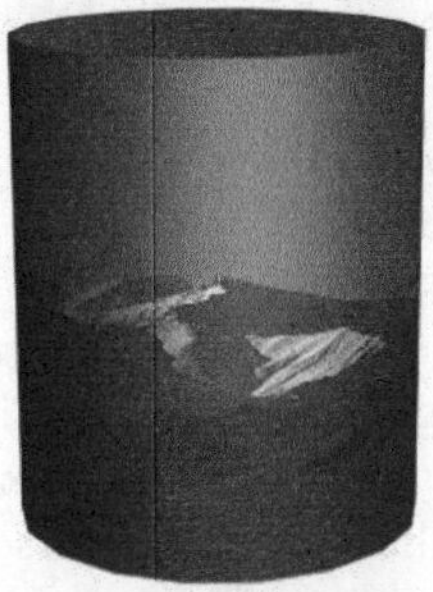

Figure 12-54 A cylinder with the Cylindrical mapping coordinates

Figure 12-55 The Cylindrical mapping coordinates applied to a cylinder and its cap

Figure 12-56 The Spherical mapping coordinates applied to a sphere

Figure 12-57 The Shrink Wrap mapping coordinates applied to a sphere

Figure 12-58 The Box mapping coordinates applied to a box

Figure 12-59 The Face mapping coordinates applied to a sphere

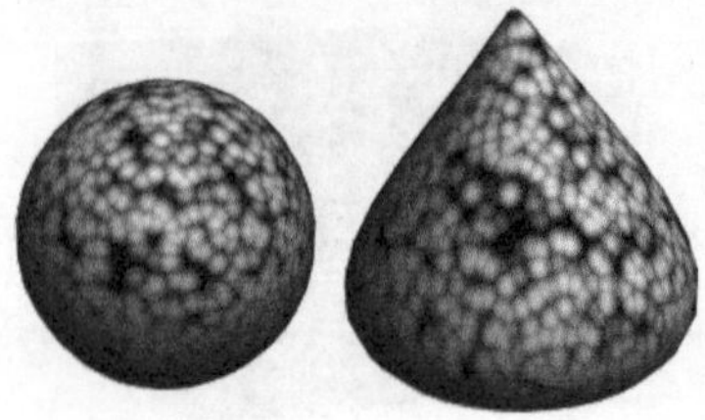

Figure 12-60 Coordinates of the object adjusted to match the new shape

Note

The 3D maps such as **Cellular**, **Falloff**, *and* **Noise** *are known as procedural maps. These maps have already been discussed in Chapter 7.*

Set the value in the **Length**, **Width**, and **Height** spinners to define the length, width, and height of the modifier gizmo. Set the value in the **U Tile**, **V Tile**, and **W Tile** spinners to define the tiling for the map in the X, Y, and Z axes. The value 1 in these spinners indicates that the map has been applied only once. Select the **Flip** check box to reverse the direction of the map.

The **Real-World Map Size** check box is used to control the scaling of the textured mapped materials applied to the object. You can set these values using the **Use Real-World Scale** check box in the **Coordinates** rollout of the applied material in the **Material Editor** dialog box.

Channel Area

By default, the **Map Channel** radio button is selected. The value 1 in the **Map Channel** spinner is used to define that the object has 1 UVW mapping coordinate. Set the value in this spinner to assign more than one UVW mapping coordinates. An object can have up to 99 UVW mapping coordinates.

Alignment Area

The options in this area are used to define the alignment of the gizmo of the modifier with the object.

FFD (Free-Form Deformation) Modifiers

In Autodesk 3ds Max, the FFD modifiers are used to deform objects by creating a box around them. This box is made up of lattice and control points. You can deform an object using these control points and lattice. There are five different types of FFD modifiers: **FFD 2x2x2**, **FFD 3x3x3**, **FFD 4x4x4**, **FFD(box)**, and **FFD(cyl)**, refer to Figures 12-61 through 12 65.

The different types of FFD modifiers are based on the number of control points. The **FFD 2x2x2** modifier provides a lattice box with two control points on all the edges of an object. Similarly, the **FFD 3x3x3** and **FFD 4x4x4** modifiers provide the lattice boxes with three and four control points, respectively on all the edges.

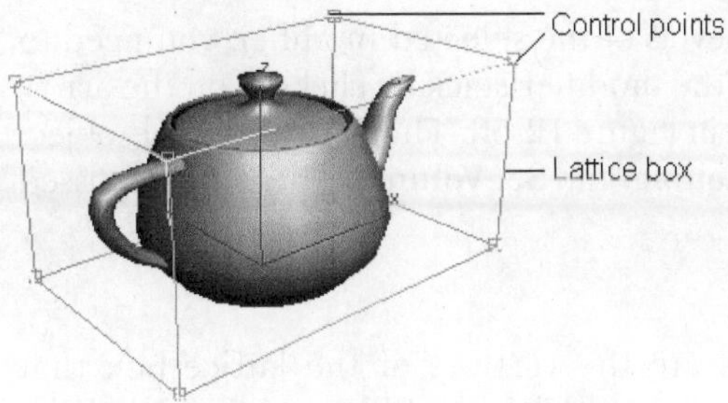

***Figure 12-61** The **FFD 2x2x2** modifier applied to an object*

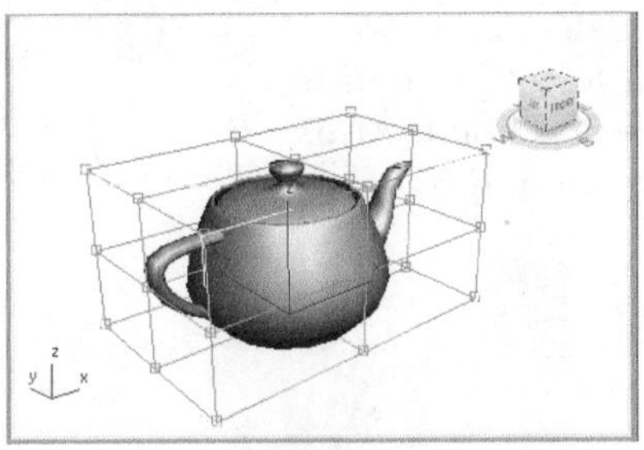

***Figure 12-62** The **FFD 3x3x3** modifier applied to an object*

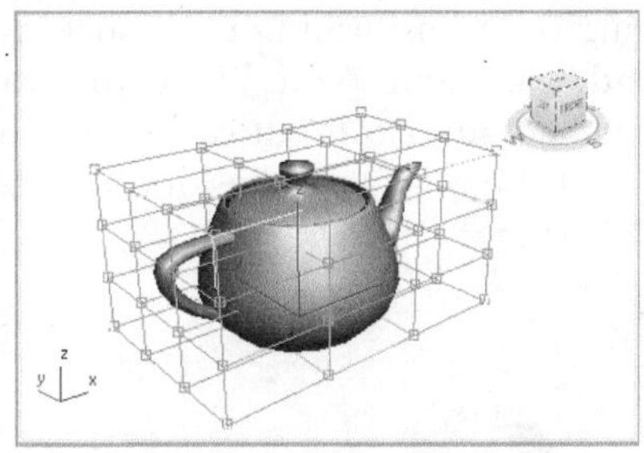

***Figure 12-63** The **FFD 4x4x4** modifier applied to an object*

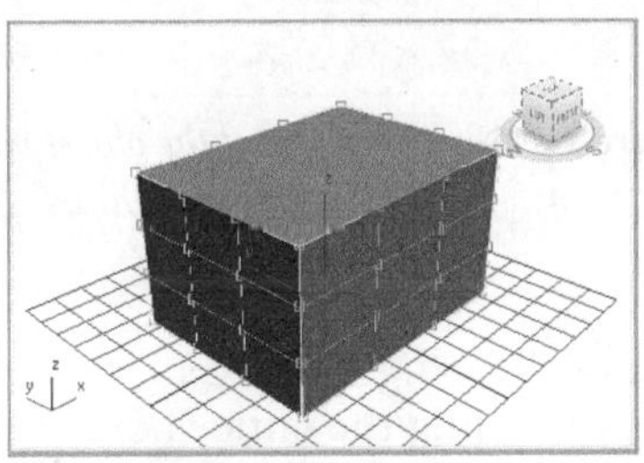

***Figure 12-64** A box object with the **FFD(box)** modifier applied*

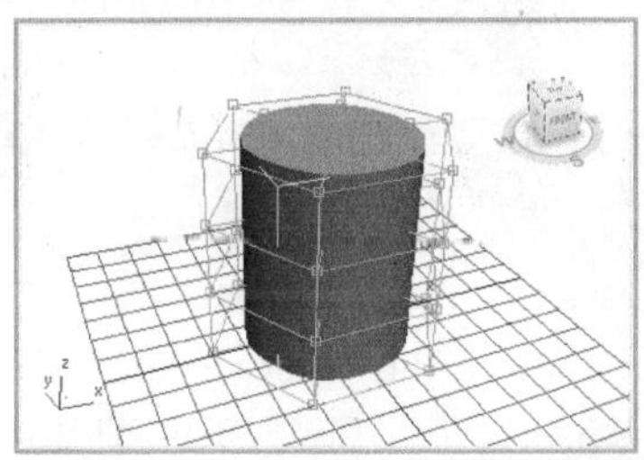

***Figure 12-65** A cylindrical object with the **FFD(cyl)** modifier applied*

The **FFD(box)** and **FFD(cyl)** modifiers are used with the box-shaped and cylinder-shaped objects. In these modifiers, you can adjust the number of control points in the lattice box in the **Parameters** rollout.

To apply the FFD modifiers, select an object in the viewport and then select one of the **FFD** modifiers from the **OBJECT-SPACE MODIFIERS** category in the **Modifier List** drop-down list. Alternatively, choose **Modifiers > Free Form Deformers** from the menu bar to select the FFD modifiers; the lattice box with the control points will be displayed around the selected object in the viewport. The selected FFD modifier will be displayed in the modifier stack. Also, the **FFD Parameters** rollout will be displayed below the modifier stack in the Modify panel. To deform the object using the FFD modifiers, you need to use the sub-objects levels of the modifier in the modifier stack. The sub-object levels and **FFD Parameters** rollout are discussed next.

Sub-Object Levels

To view the sub-object levels of the selected modifier, you need to expand the modifier in the modifier stack by clicking on the arrow sign on its left, as shown in Figure 12-66. There are three sub-object levels, **Control Points**, **Lattice**, and **Set Volume**. These are discussed next.

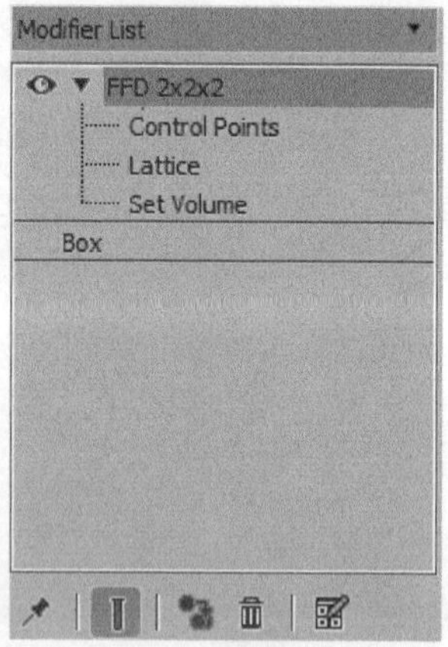

Figure 12-66 *The sub-object levels in the modifier stack*

Control Points

The control points are the vertices of the lattice box that surround the object after applying the FFD modifier. Select the **Control Points** sub-objects level; the level will be activated and now you will be able to select the control points of the lattice in the viewport. Next, select the control points and manipulate them using the transforming tools such as **Select and Move**, **Select and Scale**, and so on. When you transform the control points, the shape of the lattice box will be modified. Also, the shape of the object will be modified accordingly, refer to Figures 12-67 and 12-68.

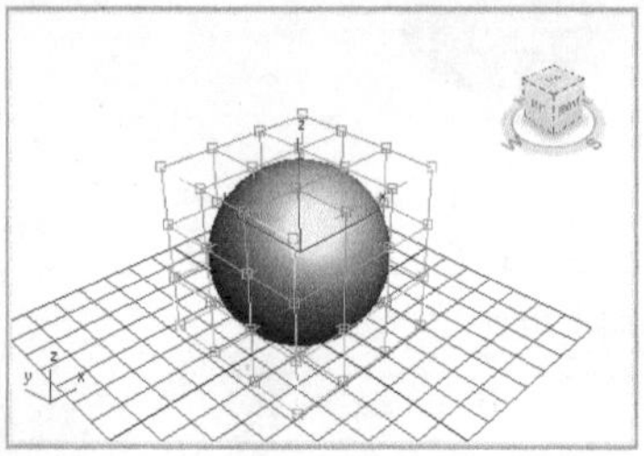

Figure 12-67 *The FFD modifier applied to the objects*

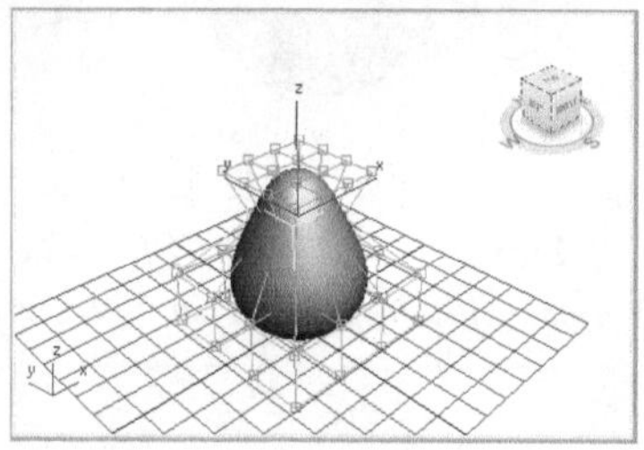

Figure 12-68 *The shape of the object modified after transforming the control points*

Lattice

Select the **Lattice** sub-object level; the lattice box will be highlighted in the viewport. Next, you can reshape the object by moving, rotating, or scaling the lattice box.

Set Volume

If you select this sub-object level, then the control points of the lattice box will turn green in color. You can select these green control points and move them to fit according to the shape of the object without affecting the object.

FFD Parameters Rollout

This rollout is displayed in the Modify panel, as shown in Figure 12-69. The most commonly used areas in this rollout are discussed next.

Display Area

By default, the **Lattice** check box is selected. It is used to display the lines connecting the control points of the lattice box. On clearing the check box, only the control points of the lattice will be displayed in the viewport. Select the **Source Volume** check box to display the original shape of the lattice box. If you clear the check box, then the modified shape of the lattice box will be displayed in the viewport.

Deform Area

By default, the **Only In Volume** radio button is selected. It is used to deform the part of the object that is inside the lattice box. On selecting the **All Vertices** radio button, the entire object whether it is inside or outside the lattice box can be deformed.

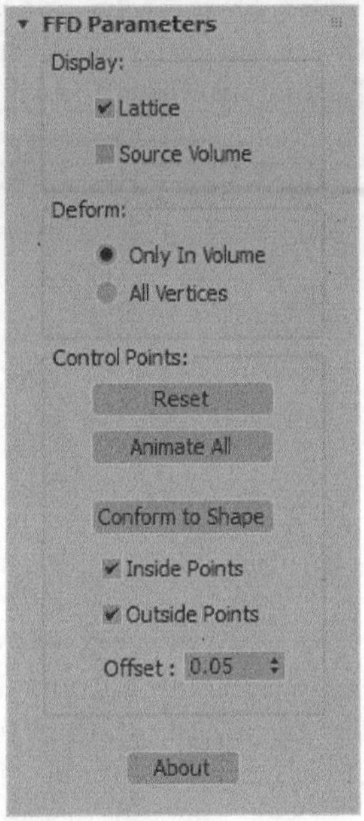

*Figure 12-69 Partial view of the **FFD Parameters** rollout*

Control Points Area

This area is used to modify the control points of the lattice box. Choose the **Reset** button to bring all control points to their original position. If you animate the control points, then a controller will be assigned to each control point. Choose the **Animate All** button to place the controllers in the track view for each control point. In the track view, you can view, edit, copy, or adjust the number of animation keys at the same time. You will learn more about adjusting the animation keys in the later chapters.

Choose the **Conform to Shape** button to bring the FFD control points to the intersection of the object with a straight line from the object's center to the original location of control points. The **Inside Points** and **Outside Points** check boxes are selected by default. If you clear the **Inside Points** check box, then the control points that are inside the lattice box will not be affected. If you clear the **Outside Points** check box; the control points that are outside the lattice box will not be affected. Set the value in the **Offset** spinner to specify the distance of the control points from the surface of the object.

Dimensions Area

This area is available only for the **FFD(box)** and **FFD(cyl)** modifiers and is used to define the number of control points in the lattice box. Choose the **Set Number of Points** button; the **Set FFD Dimensions** dialog box will be displayed, refer to Figure 12-70. Set the value in the **Length**, **Width**, and **Height** spinners to specify the number of control points on each axis of the lattice box. Note that for the **FFD(cyl)** modifiers, the spinners displayed would be the **Side**, **Radial** and **Height**.

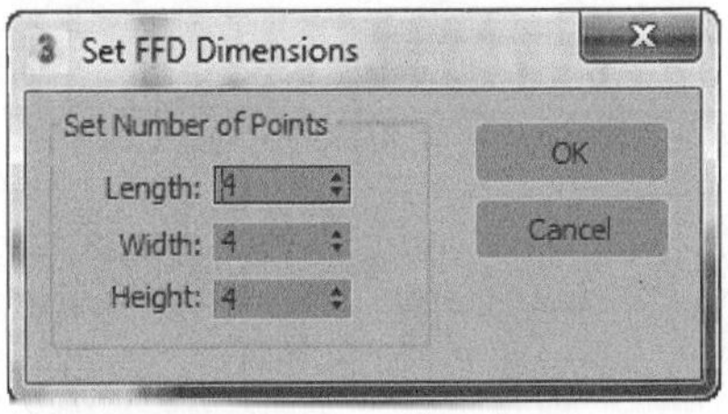

*Figure 12-70 The **Set FFD Dimensions** dialog box*

TUTORIALS

Before starting the tutorials, you need to download the *c12_3dsmax_2017_tut.zip* file from *www.cadcim.com*. The path of the file is as follows: *Textbooks > Animation and Visual Effects > 3ds Max > Autodesk 3ds Max 2017: A Comprehensive Guide*

Extract the contents of the zip file and save them in the *Documents* folder.

Tutorial 1

In this tutorial, you will create the 3D model of a tennis racket, as shown in Figure 12-71, using the **Lattice** modifier and shape splines. **(Expected time: 30 min)**

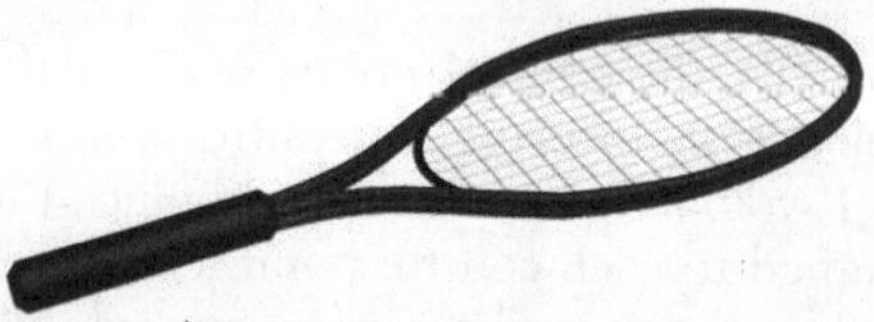

Figure 12-71 A tennis racket model

The following steps are required to complete this tutorial:

a. Create the project folder.
b. Create the head of the racket.
c. Create the shaft of the racket.
d. Create the handle of the racket.
e. Save and render the scene.

Creating the Project Folder

Create a new project folder with the name *c12_tut1* at *\Documents\3dsmax2017* and then save the file with the name *c12tut1*, as discussed in Tutorial 1 of Chapter 2.

Creating the Head of the Racket

In this section, you will create the head of the racket by using the **Ellipse** tool.

1. Choose **Create > Shapes** in the **Command Panel**; the **Splines** option is displayed in the drop-down list. Choose the **Ellipse** tool from the **Object Type** rollout.

2. Activate the Top viewport and create an ellipse. Choose the **Modify** tab in the **Command Panel**. Expand the **Rendering** rollout and select the **Enable In Renderer** and **Enable In Viewport** check boxes.

   Select the **Rectangular** radio button and enter the values given next:

   Length: **1.0** Width: **3.0**

   Make sure that the **Auto Smooth** check box is selected.

3. In the **Parameters** rollout, set the parameters as follows:

   Length: **145.894** Width: **93.72**

4. Modify the name of the ellipse to *head* and change its color to black.

   Next, you need to create the stringed area inside *head*.

5. Choose **Create > Geometry** in the **Command Panel**. Next, choose the **Plane** tool from **Standard Primitives** and create a plane in the Top viewport. In the **Parameters** rollout, set the following parameters:

   Length: **148.314** Width: **131.401**
   Length Segs: **12** Width Segs: **12**

6. Modify the name of the plane to *stringed area* and change its color to black. Now, align *stringed area* at the center of *head*, refer to Figure 12-72.

   Next, you need to modify *stringed area*.

7. Choose the **Maximize Viewport Toggle** tool to maximize the Top viewport.

8. Select *stringed area* in the viewport and choose the **Modify** tab in the **Command Panel**. Next, select the **Edit Mesh** modifier from the **OBJECT-SPACE MODIFIERS** category in the **Modifier List** drop-down list; the **Edit Mesh** modifier is displayed in the modifier stack and different rollouts are also displayed below the modifier stack.

Note

*By applying the **Edit Mesh** modifier, the name of the **Plane** tool will be displayed in the modifier stack. To modify creation parameters of the plane, you can select it from the modifier stack and set new values in the rollouts displayed in the Modify panel.*

9. In the **Selection** rollout, choose the **Vertex** button; all the vertices of *stringed area* are displayed in the viewport, as shown in Figure 12-73.

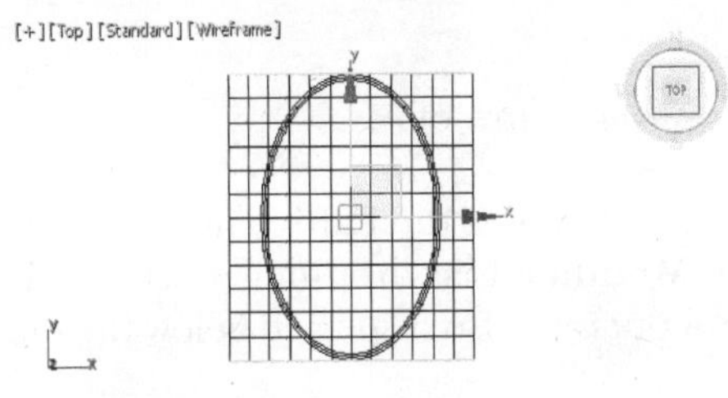

Figure 12-72 *The plane created in the Top viewport*

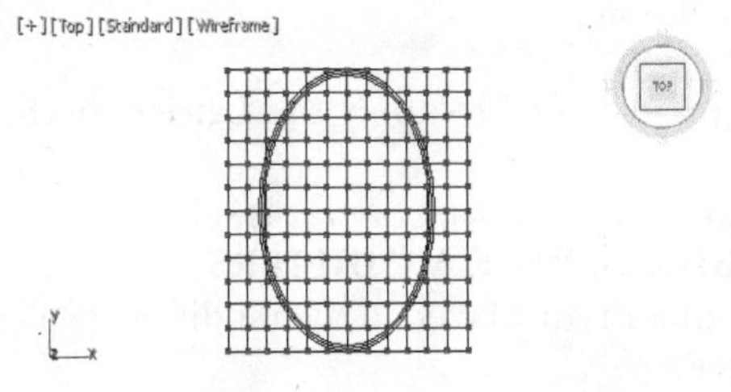

Figure 12-73 *The vertices of the stringed area displayed in the Top viewport*

   Next, you need to select and move the vertices of *stringed area* one by one and then arrange them to form the shape of the head.

10. Move the vertices to the exact location by choosing the **Zoom Region** tool and drag a selection box around the vertices of the upper left portion of *stringed area* to zoom in on them, refer to Figures 12-74 and 12-75.

11. Choose the **Select and Move** tool to select the vertices one by one and arrange them to form the shape of *head*, as shown in Figure 12-76.

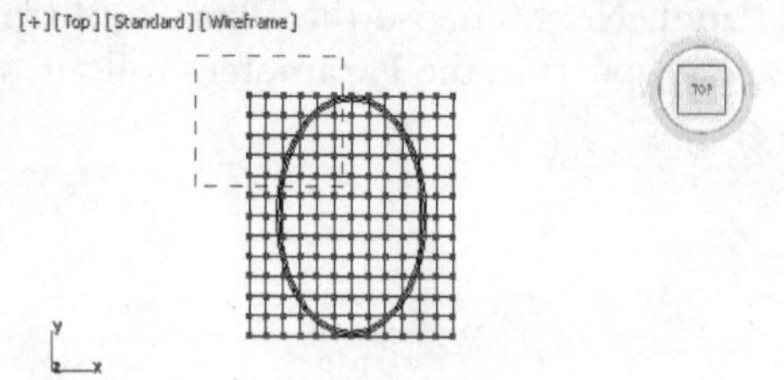

Figure 12-74 A selection box dragged around the vertices using the ***Zoom Region*** *tool*

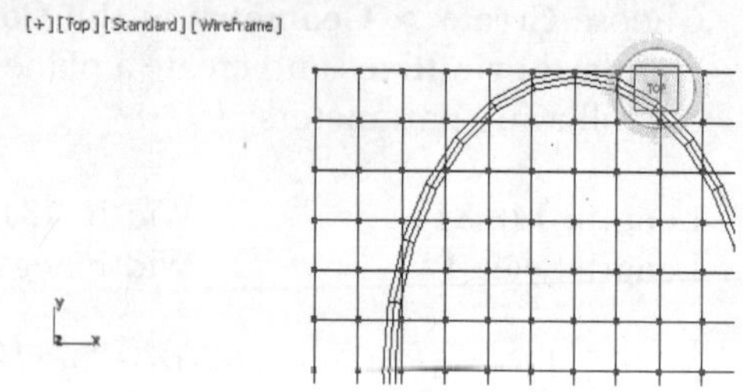

Figure 12-75 The selected area zoomed in

12. Choose the **Zoom Extents** tool; *head* and *stringed area* are displayed in the active viewport, refer to Figure 12-77.

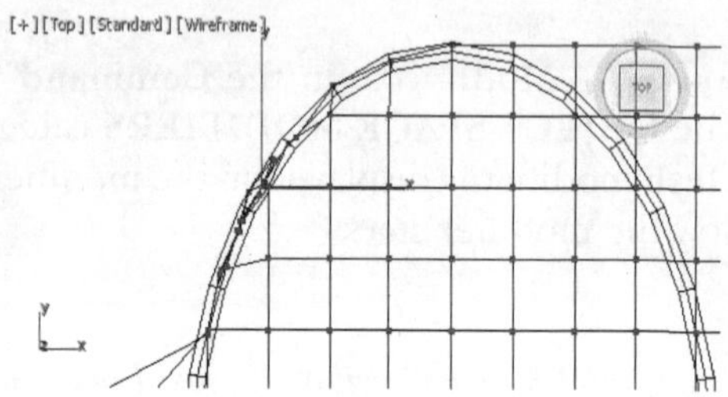

Figure 12-76 The vertices arranged to form the shape of the head

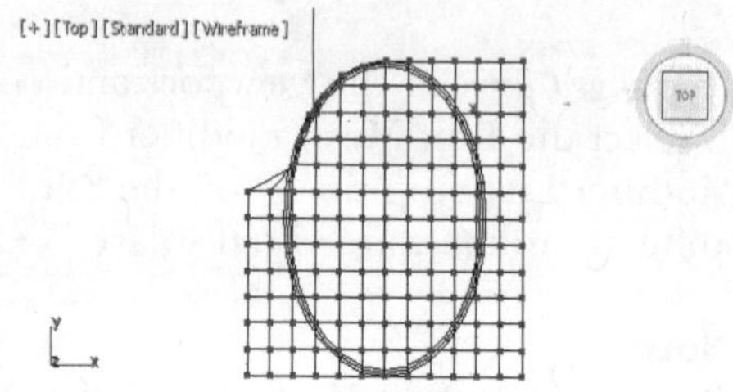

Figure 12-77 The objects after invoking the ***Zoom Extents*** *tool*

13. Follow the procedure discussed in steps 10 and 11 for the outer vertices and arrange them, as shown in Figure 12-78. Choose the **Vertex** button again in the **Selection** rollout to exit the sub-object level.

    Next, you need to apply the **Lattice** modifier to *stringed area* of *head*.

14. Make sure that *stringed area* is selected in the viewport. Select the **Lattice** modifier from the **OBJECT-SPACE MODIFIERS** category in the **Modifier List** drop-down list; the **Lattice** modifier is displayed in the modifier stack and rollouts are also displayed below the modifier stack.

15. In the **Parameters** rollout, set the following parameters:

    Select the **Struts Only from Edges** radio button.

    Struts area
    Radius: **0.2**

    Stringed area is displayed, as shown in Figure 12-79.

16. Group *stringed area* and *head* as *racket head*.

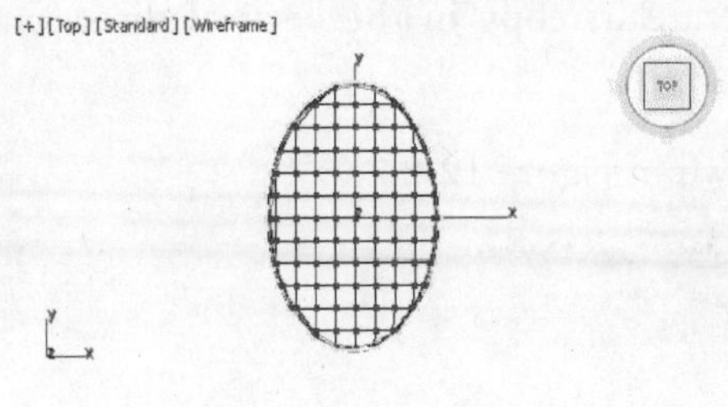

Figure 12-78 All outer vertices arranged to form the shape of the head

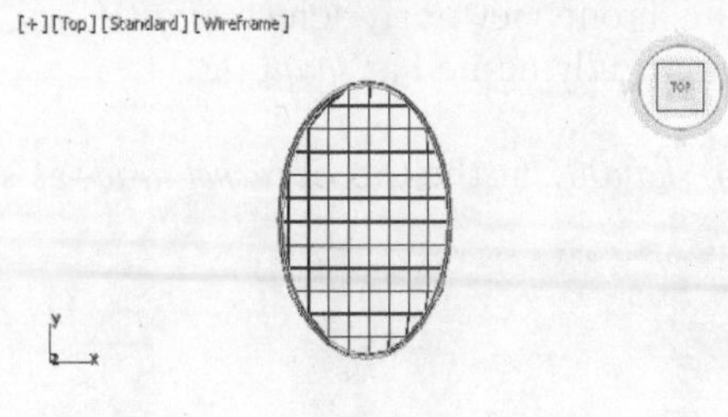

*Figure 12-79 The stringed area after applying the **Lattice** modifier*

Creating the Shaft of the Racket

In this section, you will create the shaft of the racket using the **Line** tool.

1. Choose the **Zoom** tool and zoom in the Top viewport to get sufficient room for creating the shaft of the racket, as shown in Figure 12-80.

2. Choose **Create > Shapes** in the **Command Panel**; the **Splines** option is displayed in the drop-down list. Choose the **Line** tool from the **Object Type** rollout.

3. In the **Creation Method** rollout, select the **Smooth** radio button in the **Initial Type** area and then select the **Smooth** radio button in the **Drag Type** area.

4. In the Top viewport, click and drag the cursor to create a line around *racket head*, as shown in Figure 12-81.

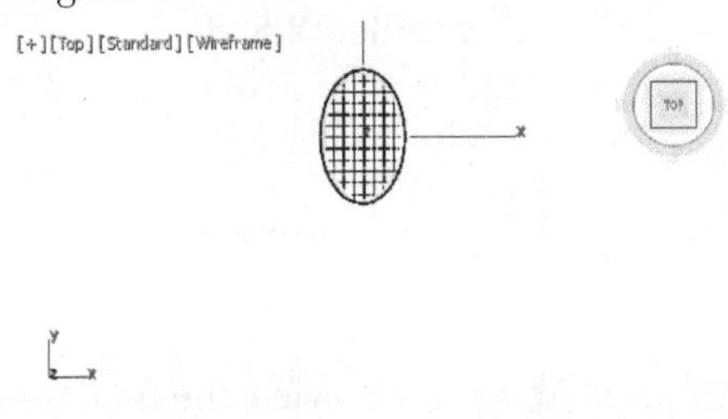

Figure 12-80 The racket head in the Top viewport

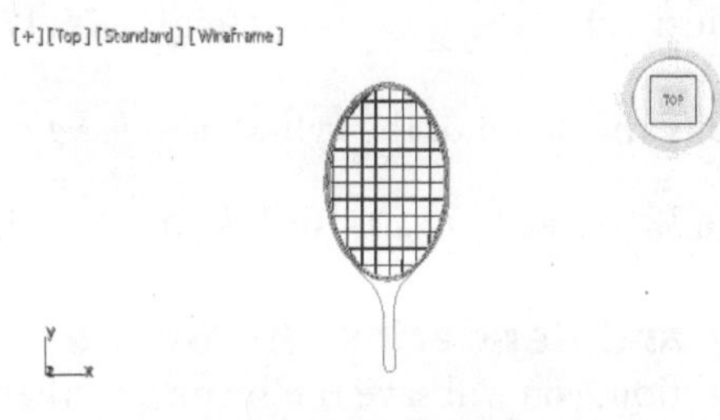

Figure 12-81 A line created around the racket head

5. In the **Rendering** rollout, make sure the **Enable In Renderer** and **Enable In Viewport** check boxes are selected. Also, select the **Radial** radio button and then enter the value **3** in the **Thickness** spinner.

6. Modify the name of the line to *shaft01* and then modify its color by setting the following parameters:

   Red: **8** Green: **8** Blue: **136**

7. Choose the **Maximize Viewport Toggle** tool and activate the Front viewport. Now, align *shaft01* at the bottom of *racket head*, refer to Figure 12-82.

8. In the Front viewport, select *shaft01* and create its copy in the vertical direction. It is automatically named as *shaft002*.

9. Align *shaft002* at the top of *racket head*, as shown in Figure 12-83.

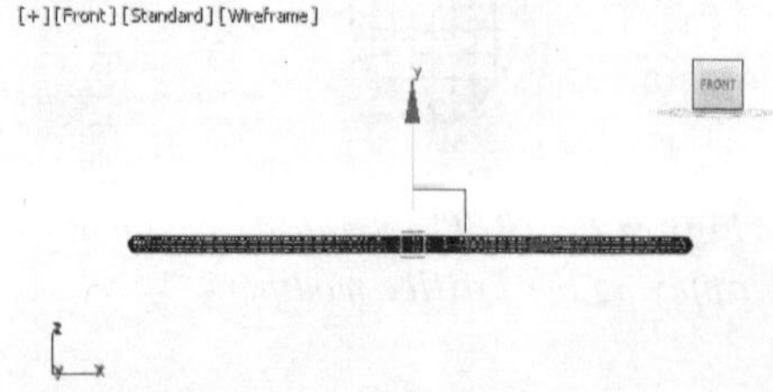

Figure 12-82 Alignment of the shaft01 at the bottom of the racket head

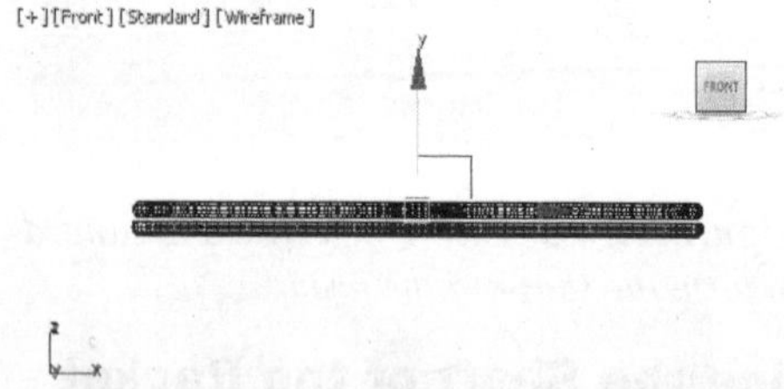

Figure 12-83 Alignment of the shaft002 at the top of the racket head

Creating the Handle of the Racket

In this section, you will create the handle of the racket by using the **ChamferCyl** tool from **Extended Primitives**.

1. Choose the **ChamferCyl** tool from **Extended Primitives** in the **Command Panel** and create a chamfer cylinder in the Front viewport.

2. In the **Parameters** rollout, set the following parameters:

   Radius: **7.0** Height: **74.477** Fillet: **2.816**

3. Modify the name of the cylinder to *handle* and change its color to black.

4. Align *handle* with *shaft01* and *shaft002* in viewports, as shown in Figure 12-84.

Saving and Rendering the Scene

In this section, you will save the scene and then render it. You can also view the final rendered image of this model by downloading the file *c12_3dsmax_2017_rndr.zip* from *www.cadcim.com*. The path of the file is as follows: *Textbooks > Animation and Visual Effects > 3ds Max > Autodesk 3ds Max 2017: A Comprehensive Guide*

1. Change the background color of the scene to white as described in the previous chapters.

2. Choose **Save** from the **Application** menu. Next, activate the Perspective viewport.

3. Choose the **Render Production** tool from the **Main Toolbar**; the **Rendered Frame** window is displayed with the final output of the tennis racket, as shown in Figure 12-85. Next, close this window.

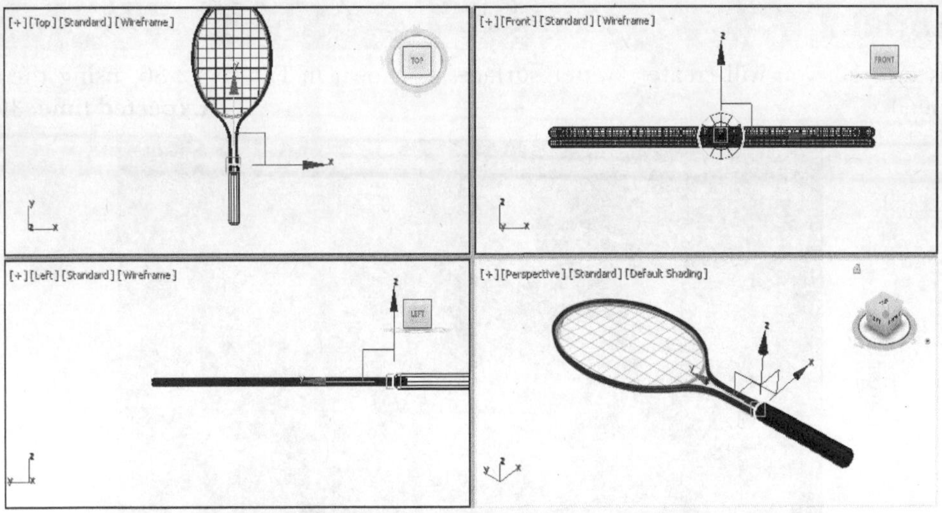

Figure 12-84 *Alignment of handle in viewports*

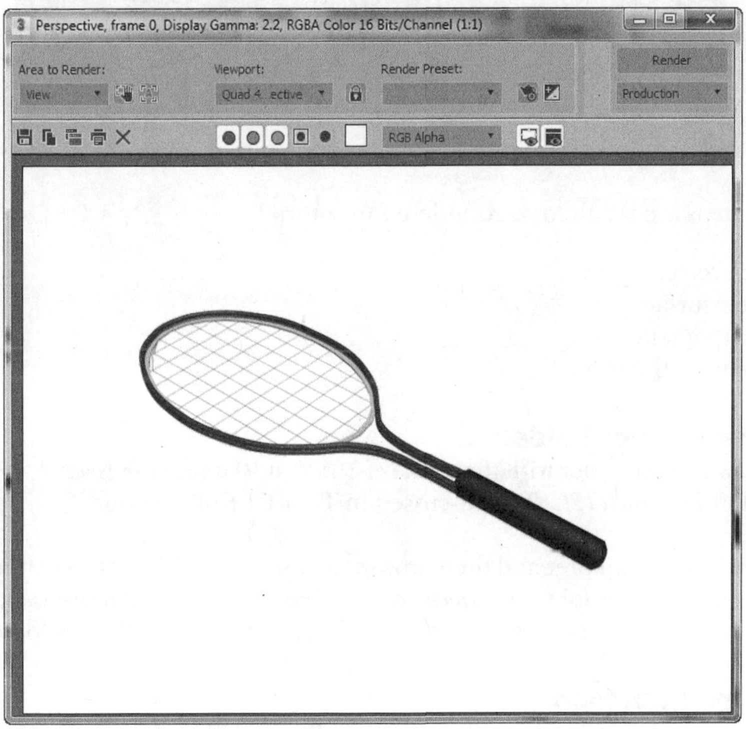

Figure 12-85 *The final output*

Tutorial 2

In this tutorial, you will create a water surface, as shown in Figure 12-86, using the **Noise** modifier. **(Expected time: 30 min)**

Figure 12-86 *The water surface*

The following steps are required to complete this tutorial:

a. Create the project folder.
b. Create water surface.
c. Create environment.
d. Save and render the scene.

Creating the Project Folder

1. Create a new project folder with the name *c12_tut2* at *\Documents\3dsmax2017* and then save the file with the name *c12tut2*, as discussed in Tutorial 1 of Chapter 2.

2. Open the Windows Explorer and then browse to the *c12_3dsmax_2017_tut* folder. Next, copy the *sky.jpg* file from this folder to *\Documents\3dsmax2017\c12_tut2\sceneassets\images* and the *water_surface.mat* in the *\Documents\3dsmax2017\c12_tut2\materiallibraries* folder.

Creating Water Surface

In this section, you will create a plane by using the **Plane** tool and then you need to apply the **Noise** modifier to give it the wavy effect.

1. Choose **Create > Geometry** in the **Command Panel**; the **Standard Primitives** option is displayed in the drop-down list. Choose the **Plane** tool from the **Object Type** rollout.

2. Activate the Top viewport and create a plane. In the **Parameters** rollout, set the following values:

   Length: **669.234** Width: **788.627**
   Length Segs: **10** Width Segs: **10**

3. Choose the **Zoom Extents All** tool to display the objects to their extent in the viewports.

4. Modify the name of the plane to *water surface*.

5. Activate the Perspective viewport and set its view using the **Orbit** and **Zoom** tools, as shown in Figure 12-87.

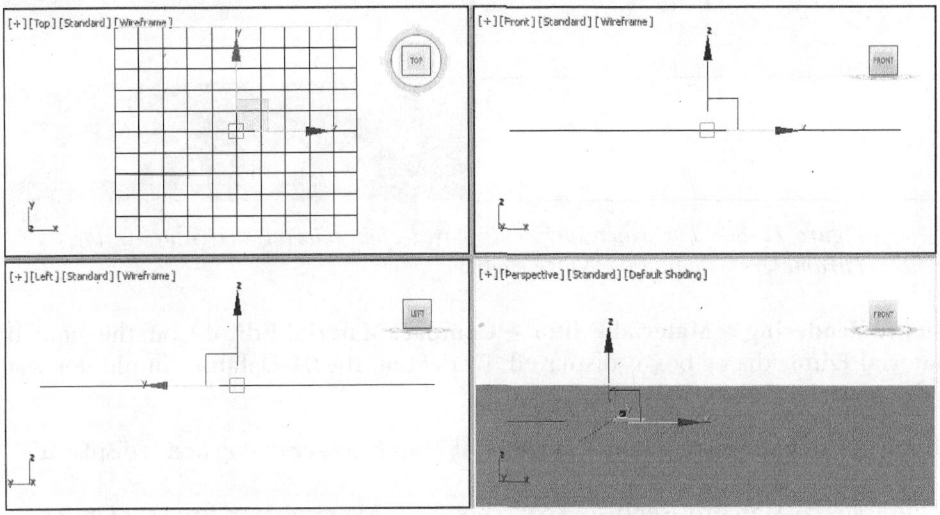

Figure 12-87 *The water surface in viewports*

Next, you need to apply the **Noise** modifier to *water surface*.

6. Make sure that *water surface* is selected in the viewport. Choose the **Modify** tab in the **Command Panel**; the **Modifier List** drop-down list is displayed. Select the **Noise** modifier from the **OBJECT-SPACE MODIFIERS** category in the **Modifier List** drop-down list; the **Noise** modifier is displayed in the modifier stack and the **Parameters** rollout is displayed in the Modify panel.

7. In the **Parameters** rollout, set the following parameters:

   Noise area
   Select the **Fractal** check box.
   Roughness: **0.5** Iterations: **6.0**

   Strength area
   X: **120.0** Y: **150.0** Z: **5.0**

After setting the values, *water surface* is displayed, as shown in Figure 12-88. Next, you need to assign the material to *water surface* to make it look realistic.

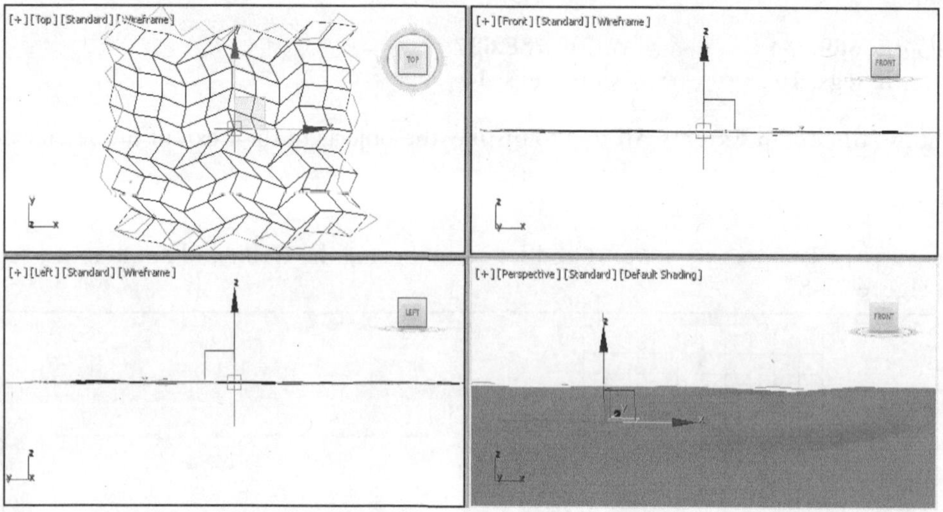

***Figure 12-88** The water surface displayed after entering the values in the **Parameters** rollout of the **Noise** modifier*

8. Choose **Rendering > Material Editor > Compact Material Editor** from the menu bar; the **Material Editor** dialog box is displayed. By default, the **01-Default** sample slot is selected in the **Material Editor** dialog box.

9. Choose the **Get Material** button; the **Material/Map Browser** dialog box is displayed.

10. In the **Material/Map Browser** dialog box, choose the **Material/Map Browser Options** button; a flyout is displayed. Choose the **Open Material Library** option from the flyout, as shown in Figure 12-89; the **Import Material Library** dialog box is displayed.

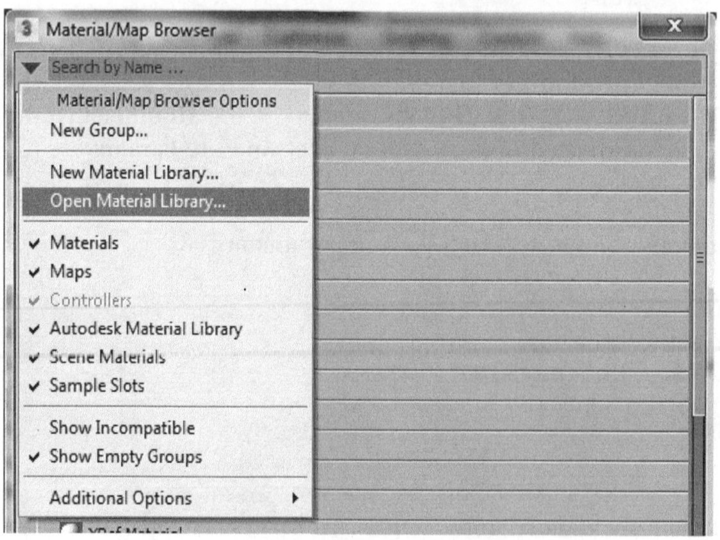

***Figure 12-89** Choosing the **Open Material Library** option from the flyout*

11. As the Project folder is already set, the path *\Documents\3dsmax2017\c12_tut2\materiallibraries* is displayed in the **Look in** drop-down list of this dialog box. Select the **water_surface.mat** file from the dialog box and choose the **Open** button; the *water_surface.mat* material library is added to the **Material/Map Browser** dialog box.

12. Expand *water_surface.mat,* if it is not already expanded. Next, double-click on the **water surface** material; the **water surface** material is displayed in the sample slot. Also, the name of the sample slot is replaced with the **water surface** in the **Material Name** drop-down list.

13. Close the **Material/Map Browser** dialog box.

14. In the **Material Editor** dialog box, choose the **Diffuse** color swatch from the **Raytrace Basic Parameters** rollout; the **Color Selector: Diffuse Color** dialog box is displayed. Set the values in the dialog box as follows:

    Red: **164** Green: **214** Blue: **249**

15. Choose the **OK** button to close the **Color Selector: Diffuse Color** dialog box.

16. In the **Material Editor** dialog box, make sure that *water surface* material is selected. Also, select *water surface* in the viewport. Next, choose the **Assign Material to Selection** button; the *water surface* material is assigned to *water surface.*

17. Choose the **Show Shaded Material in Viewport** button to view the material in the viewport. Close the **Material Editor** dialog box.

Note

You need to render the scene in the Perspective viewport to view the realistic effect of the ***Noise*** *modifier and the material.*

Creating Environment

In this section, you will apply the map to the environment to make the scene realistic.

1. Choose **Rendering > Environment** from the menu bar; the **Environment and Effects** dialog box is displayed.

2. By default, the **Environment** tab is chosen. You need to set the parameters in the **Common Parameters** rollout in this tab. In the **Background** area, choose the **Environment Map** button labeled as **None**; the **Material/Map Browser** dialog box is displayed.

3. In the **Material/Map Browser** dialog box, type **bitmap** in the **Search by Name** area; the **Bitmap** map is displayed in the drop-down list. Select the **Bitmap** map and choose the **OK** button; the **Select Bitmap Image File** dialog box is displayed. Select a sky image of your choice from the desired location. Next, choose the **Open** button; the name of the map is displayed on the **Environment Map** button.

4. Now, choose the **Material Editor** tool from the **Main Toolbar**, the **Material Editor** dialog box is displayed.

5. Press and hold the left mouse button on the **Map # X(Sky.jpg)** name from the **Environment Map** button of the **Environment and Effects** dialog box and drag the cursor to the **02-Default** sample slot of the **Material Editor** dialog box; the **Instance (Copy)map** dialog box is displayed.

6. Select the **Instance** radio button from this dialog box and choose **OK**; the sky image will be added to the **02-Default** sample slot. In the **Coordinates** rollout, enter the value **2** in the **U** and **V Tiling** spinners. In the **Cropping/Placement** area, select the **Place** radio button. Next, enter **0.333** value in the **U** spinner and **0.479** in the **V** spinner. Similarly, make sure **0.667** is set in the **W** spinner and **0.521** in the **H** spinner. Next, close the **Material Editor** dialog box and the **Environment and Effects** dialog box.

Note
To view the environment map in the scene, you need to render the Perspective viewport.

Saving and Rendering the Scene

In this section, you will save the scene and then render it. You can also view the final rendered image of this model by downloading the file *c12_3dsmax_2017_rndr.zip* from *www.cadcim.com.* The path of the file is as follows: *Textbooks > Animation and Visual Effects > 3ds Max > Autodesk 3ds Max 2017: A Comprehensive Guide.*

1. Choose **Save** from the **Application** menu.

2. Choose the **Render Production** tool from the **MainToolbar**; the rendered image is displayed. The final output of the scene at one frame is shown in Figure 12-90.

3. Close this window.

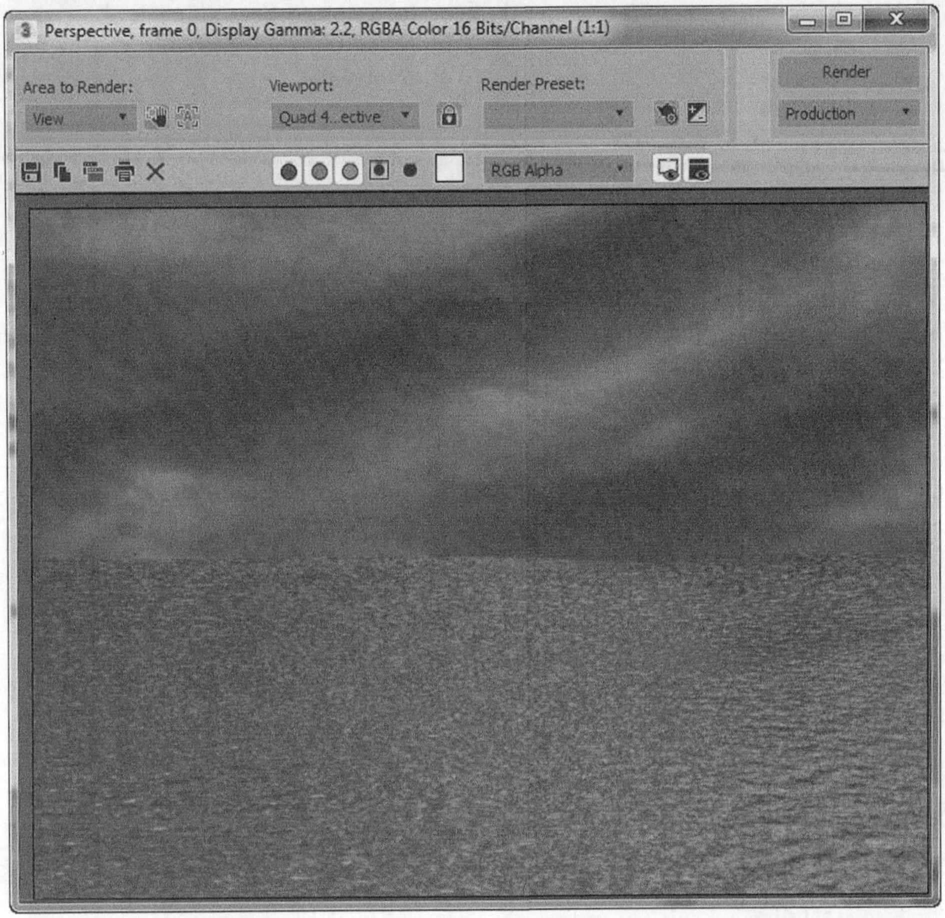

Figure 12-90 The final output of the scene after rendering

Self-Evaluation Test

Answer the following questions and then compare them to those given at the end of this chapter:

1. Which one of the following tabs in the **Command Panel** is used to apply a modifier to an object?

   (a) **Create** (b) **Modify**
   (c) **Motion** (d) **Utilities**

2. Which of the following modifiers is used to deform the shape of an object using bitmap images?

   (a) **Mesh Select** (b) **Displace**
   (c) **Material** (d) **Edit Mesh**

3. Which of the following modifiers is used to produce smoothness in mesh objects?

(a) **MeshSmooth** (b) **Normal**
(c) **Edit Mesh** (d) **Lathe**

4. Which of the following modifiers is used to deform objects by creating a box around them?

(a) **FFD 2x2x2** (b) **FFD 3x3x3**
(c) **FFD 4x4x4** (d) All of these

5. The __________ modifier is used to sub-divide the faces of an object which results in smoothness of the curved surfaces of the object.

6. The __________ modifier is used to adjust the mapping coordinates on an object.

7. An object can have up to __________ UVW mapping coordinates.

8. The **Face Extrude** modifier is used to convert a 2D spline into a 3D object. (T/F)

9. You can apply different materials to the selected sub-objects using the **Material** modifier. (T/F)

10. On selecting the **Flip Normals** check box in the **Parameters** rollout of the **Normal** modifier, the direction of normals of all the faces of the selected object is reversed. (T/F)

Review Questions

Answer the following questions:

1. Which of the following sub-object levels is a part of the FFD modifiers?

(a) **Lattice** (b) **Control points**
(c) **Set Volume** (d) All of these

2. Which of the following areas in the **Parameters** rollout of the **UVW Map** modifier is used to adjust the type of mapping coordinates?

(a) **Channel** (b) **Alignment**
(c) **Mapping** (d) None of these

3. Which of the following modifiers is used to push an object inward or outward along the normals of the faces?

(a) **Twist** (b) **Normal**
(c) **Push** (d) **Lattice**

4. The __________ modifier is used to create disturbances on the surface of an object to produce irregular surface.

5. The __________ modifier is used to extrude the selected faces along their normals.

6. The __________ modifier is a shape modifier and is used to create a 3D object by rotating a shape about an axis.

7. When you apply FFD modifiers to an object, a box made up of lattice and control points is created around the object. (T/F)

8. The **Edit Mesh** modifier and the editable mesh object provide different sub-object levels to modify objects. (T/F)

9. The normal of a face is a line perpendicular to it. (T/F)

10. The **Iterations** area in the **Parameters** rollout of the **Tessellate** modifier is used to apply smoothness to the selected object. (T/F)

EXERCISES

The rendered output of the models used in the following exercises can be accessed by downloading the *c12_3dsmax_2017_exr.zip* file from *www.cadcim.com*. The path of the file is as follows: *Textbooks > Animation and Visual Effects > 3ds Max > Autodesk 3ds Max 2017: A Comprehensive Guide*

Exercise 1

Create the model of a basket, as shown in Figure 12-91, using the **Lattice** modifier.

(Expected time: 15 min)

Figure 12-91 *The model of a basket*

Exercise 2

Create the model of a chair, as shown in Figure 12-92, using the **Bend** and **Taper** modifiers.
(Expected time: 15 min)

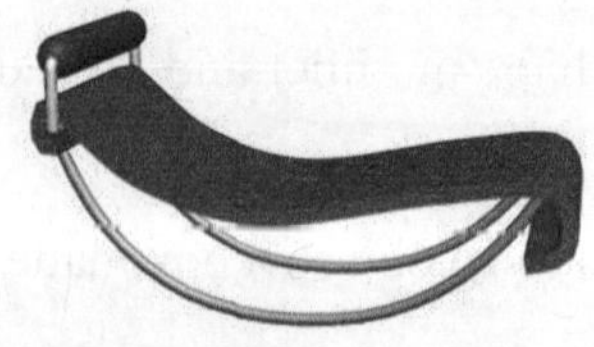

Figure 12-92 *The model of a chair*

Exercise 3

Create the model of a bowl, as shown in Figure 12-93, using the **Lathe** and **MeshSmooth** modifiers.
(Expected time: 15 min)

Figure 12-93 *The model of a bowl*

Answers to Self-Evaluation Test

1. b, **2**. b, **3**. a, **4**. d, **5**. **Tessellate**, **6**. **UVW**, **7**. 99, **8**. F, **9**. T, **10**. T

13

Lights and Cameras

Learning Objectives

After completing this chapter, you will be able to:

- *Work with standard lights*
- *Work with photometric lights*
- *Use the Place Highlight tool*
- *Work with Camera tools*
- *Understand camera viewport controls*
- *Work with the Align Camera tool*

INTRODUCTION

In 3ds Max, lights are used to illuminate a scene to make it realistic. They are also used to create the sources of illumination such as street lights, flashlights, and so on. The two main categories of lights available in 3ds max are: **Standard** and **Photometric**. In these categories, different types of lights are available. You need to select one or more lights based on the requirement of a scene. The Photometric lights provide more realistic lighting effects but they are more complex than the Standard lights.

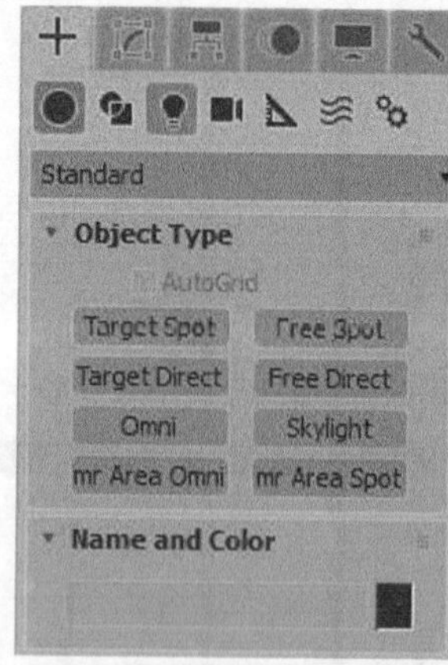

***Figure 13-1** The tools to create standard lights in the **Object Type** rollout*

STANDARD LIGHTS

In 3ds Max, the Standard lights are objects that simulate lights. You can create eight types of Standard lights in 3ds Max. To create a light in a scene, choose **Create > Lights** in the **Command Panel**. By default, the **Photometric** option will be displayed in the drop-down list below the **Lights** button. Select the **Standard** option from the drop-down list. You can choose one of the tools available in the **Object Type** rollout to create different types of lights in the viewport, refer to Figure 13-1. When you choose a tool from the **Object Type** rollout, various rollouts will be displayed. These rollouts are used to modify the parameters of lights. The tools in the **Object Type** rollout are discussed next.

Omni

Menu bar:	Create > Lights > Standard Lights > Omni
Command Panel:	Create > Lights > Standard > Object Type rollout > Omni

The **Omni** tool is used to create an omni light in the viewport. An omni light is a single point in space that projects the rays uniformly in all directions. To create an omni light, choose the **Omni** tool; the **Name and Color**, **General Parameters**, **Intensity/Color/Attenuation**, **Advanced Effects**, **Shadow Parameters**, and **Shadow Map Params** rollouts will be displayed in the Modify panel. Move the cursor in the viewport; the shape of the cursor will change. Click in the viewport to place the light. You can continue clicking in the viewport to add more than one light. Next, right-click in the viewport to exit the command. To modify the parameters of a light, select the light and choose the **Modify** tab in the **Command Panel**; various rollouts will be displayed. These rollouts are used to modify the parameters of the selected light. The most commonly used rollouts are discussed next.

Name and Color Rollout

This rollout is used to modify the name of the selected light by entering the new name in the text box. You can also modify the color of the selected light using the color swatch. But, this will only change the color of the icon of the light in the viewport and will not affect the color of the light being emitted.

General Parameters Rollout

The options in this rollout are used to set the parameters of the selected light, refer to Figure 13-2. In the **Light Type** area of this rollout, the **On** check box is selected by default. As a result, the light will illuminate the scene, refer to Figures 13-3 and 13-4. If you clear the **On** check box, then the light will not illuminate the scene. The drop-down list on the right side of the **On** check box is used to define the type of light. By default, the **Omni** option is selected in this drop-down list. You can also select the **Directional** or the **Spot** option to convert the omni light into directional or spot light.

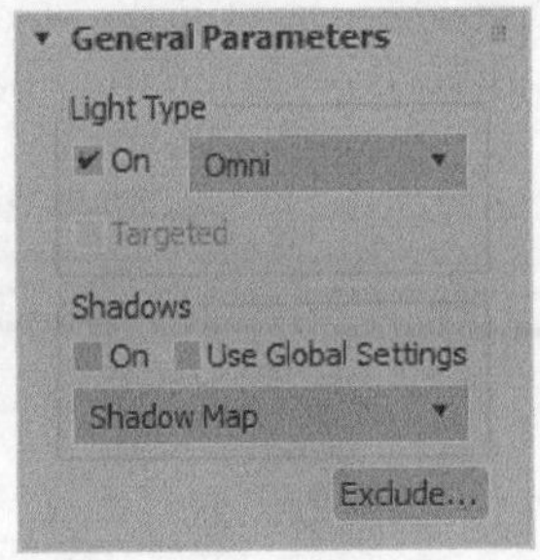

***Figure 13-2** The **General Parameters** rollout*

The **Targeted** check box is activated only if the **Directional** or **Spot Light** option is selected from the drop-down list. On selecting any of these options, a spinner will be displayed next to the **Targeted** check box. The value in the spinner is used to specify the distance of the target from the light. You will learn about the spot and directional lights later in this chapter.

***Figure 13-3** The scene without any light*

***Figure 13-4** The scene with the omni lights applied*

Note

*1. By default, the **Standard** shading mode is selected in the viewport, refer to the Figure 13-5. Click on the **Standard** label, a flyout will be displayed. Next, choose **Lights and Shadows > Shadows** from the flyout to display the shadows in the viewport, refer to Figure 13-6.*

*2. If you want to see high quality lights and shadows in the viewport, select the **High Quality** shading mode. Alternatively, you can press Shift+F3.*

In the **Shadows** area, select the **On** check box. As a result, the light will cast shadows of the object on rendering. Alternatively, when you place a light in the viewport, select it and right-click on it; a quad menu will be displayed, as shown in Figure 13-7. Choose the **Cast Shadows** option; the shadows of the object will be displayed on rendering.

If a scene consists of more than one light, you can use the **Light Lister** tool to display and change the settings of lights in a single window. To do so, choose **Tools > Light Lister** from the menu bar; the **Light Lister** window will be displayed, as shown in Figure 13-8. This window will display the information of all lights used in the scene. Now, select the check box(es) in the **Shadows** column; the shadows of the light corresponding to the selected check box(es) will be displayed on rendering.

The drop-down list next to the **Shadows** check box in the **Light Lister** window is used to select the types of shadow that the light will cast.

The **Use Global Settings** check box is located next to the **On** check box. This check box is used to cast shadows of the light as per the global settings. The drop-down list below the check boxes is used to specify the shadow map that the renderer will use while generating the shadows of the light. By default, the **Shadow Map** is selected in this drop-down list. It specifies the map which the renderer will use, while generating the shadows of the light.

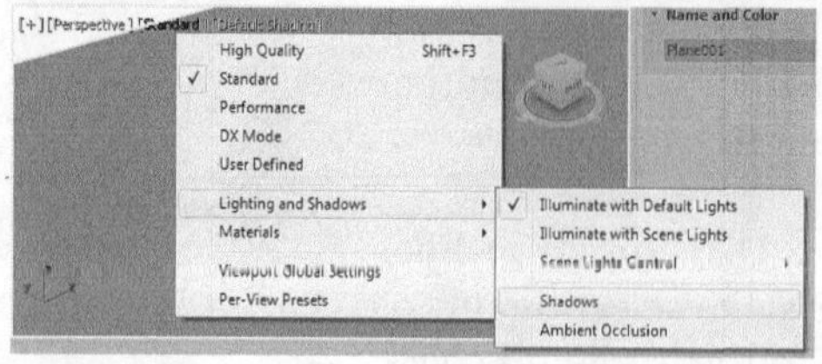

Figure 13-5 The cascading menu displayed in the viewport

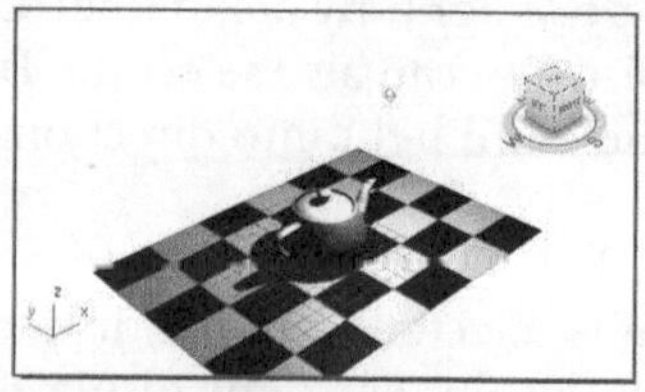

Figure 13-6 The shadows displayed in the viewport

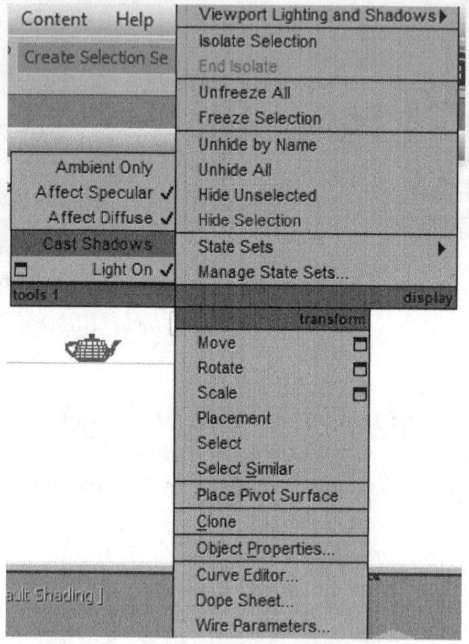

Figure 13-7 The quad menu displayed in the viewport

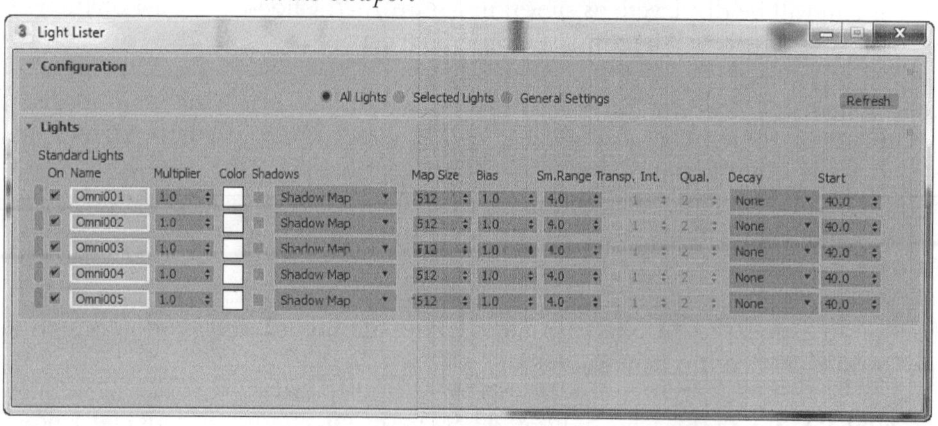

*Figure 13-8 The **Light Lister** window*

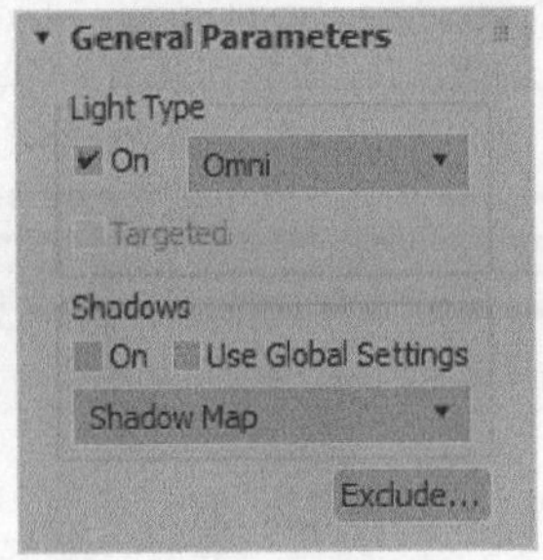

The **Exclude** button is used to select the objects in the scene that you do not want to get affected by the light at rendering. By default, the light affects all objects in the scene. To exclude or include an object from the effect of the light, choose the **Exclude** button; the **Exclude/Include** dialog box will be displayed, as shown in Figure 13-9.

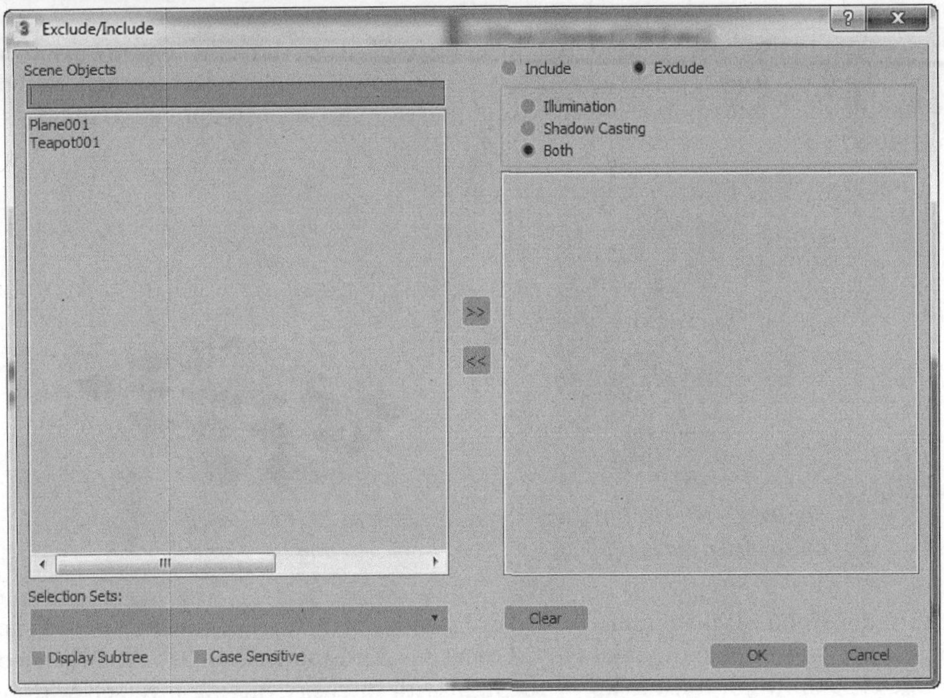

***Figure 13-9** The **Exclude/Include** dialog box*

The **Scene Objects** area on the left side of this dialog box displays the list of all objects in the current scene. On the top right of this dialog box, there are two radio buttons namely, **Include** and **Exclude**. By default, the **Exclude** radio button is selected. As a result, the objects will be excluded from the effect of light. To do so, select the objects that you want to exclude from the list displayed in the **Scene Objects** area. Then, choose the right arrow button; the selected objects will be excluded from the selected light. Also, they will be displayed in the area on the right side of this dialog box. Similarly, to include the excluded objects again, select the excluded objects from the area on the right side, and choose the left arrow button; the selected objects will be included. Next, choose the **OK** button.

Intensity/Color/Attenuation Rollout

The options in this rollout are used to set the color, intensity, and attenuation of the light, refer to Figure 13-10. The decrease in the intensity of light with distance is called attenuation. The **Multiplier** spinner in this rollout is used to set the intensity of the light. By default, the value in this spinner is 1.0. You can increase or decrease the value to increase or decrease the brightness of the light. Choose the color swatch on the right side of the **Multiplier** spinner; the **Color Selector: Light Color** dialog box will be displayed. Select the color of the light and choose the **OK** button to assign a new color to the light. The areas in the **Intensity/Color/Attenuation** rollout are discussed next.

Note

*If you increase the value in the **Multiplier** spinner to a very high extent, the scene will burned out. So, it is recommended that you increase the value gradually as required for the scene.*

Decay Area

The options in this area are used to reduce the intensity of the light over the distance. The **Type** drop-down list is used to define the type of decay that will be used for the selected light. By default, the **None** option is selected and therefore no decay is applied to the light, refer to Figure 13-11.

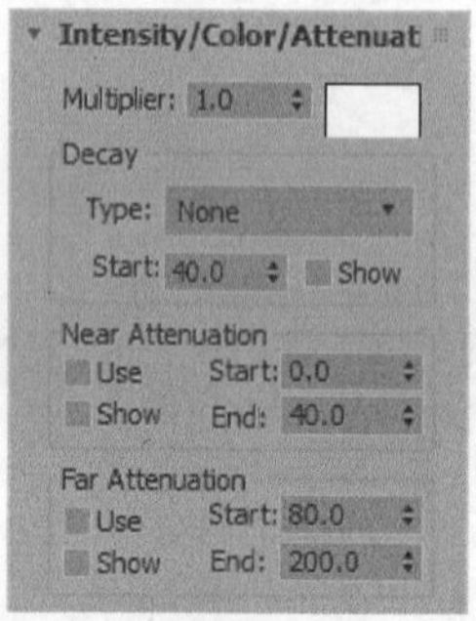

*Figure 13-10 The **Intensity/ Color/Attenuation** rollout*

*Figure 13-11 The effect of light on selecting the **None** option*

In this case, if you use the options in the **Far Attenuation** area, then the decay will be applied to the light according to the values in the **Start** and **End** spinners. Select the **Inverse** option in the **Type** drop-down list to apply the light with intensity varying inversely with respect to distance, as shown in Figure 13-12. Select the **Inverse Square** option to apply the light intensity that varies with square inverse proportion with respect to distance, as shown in Figure 13-13.

*Figure 13-12 The effect of light on selecting the **Inverse** option*

*Figure 13-13 The effect of light on selecting the **Inverse Square** option*

The **Inverse** and **Inverse Square** options use some mathematical equations to apply the decay effect on the light. When you select the **Inverse** or the **Inverse Square** option, the gizmo will be displayed in the viewport for the selected light to define the distance from where the decay starts. Set the value in the **Start** spinner of the **Decay** area to specify the distance from where the decay starts. On selecting the **Show** check box, a gizmo will be displayed even if the light is not selected.

Near Attenuation Area

The **Near Attenuation** area is used to set the distance at which the light begins to fade in. Select the **Use** check box to enable the near attenuation for the selected light; a gizmo will be displayed in the viewport to define the near attenuation. Select the **Show** check box to display the gizmo in the viewport even if the light is not selected. Set the value in the **Start** spinner to define the distance at which the light begins to fade in. Set the value in the **End** spinner to define the distance at which the light reaches its maximum value that is 100%.

Far Attenuation Area

The **Far Attenuation** area is used to set the distance at which the light begins to fade out. Select the **Use** check box to enable the far attenuation for the selected light; a gizmo will be displayed in the viewport to define the far attenuation. Select the **Show** check box to display the gizmo in the viewport even if the light is not selected. Set the value in the **Start** spinner to define the distance at which the light begins to fade out. Set the value in the **End** spinner to define the distance at which the light reaches its minimum value that is zero.

Advanced Effects Rollout

The options in this rollout are used to set the effects of light on surfaces, refer to Figure 13-14. This rollout is also used to provide settings for the projector lights. The areas in this rollout are discussed next.

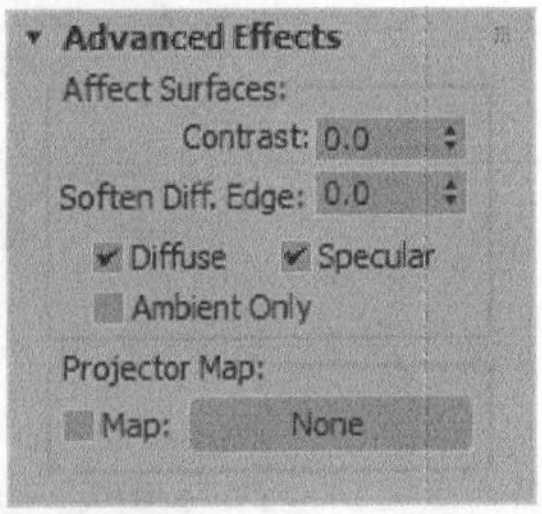

***Figure 13-14** The **Advanced Effects** rollout*

Affect Surfaces Area

The **Contrast** spinner in this area is used to adjust the contrast between different areas of the object that are affected by the diffuse and ambient lights. By default, the value in this spinner is 0, which provides the normal contrast. Set the value in the **Soften Diff. Edge** spinner to soften the transition between the ambient and the diffuse areas. The **Diffuse** and **Specular** check boxes are selected by default and are used to affect the diffuse and specular light areas, respectively. If you clear the **Diffuse** or **Specular** check box, the light will not affect the diffuse or specular property of the surface. On selecting the **Ambient Only** check box, the light will affect only the ambient area of the illumination.

Projector Map Area

This area is used to make a light act as a projector. To do so, select the light in the viewport and choose the **Modify** tab in the **Command Panel**. Now, in the **Projector Map** area of the **Advanced Effects** rollout, select the **Map** check box to enable the projector effect. Next, choose the **None** button; the **Material/Map Browser** dialog box will be displayed. Choose the map type from the **Material/Map Browser** dialog box; the name of the material will be displayed on the **None** button and the selected map will be projected in the scene at rendering.

Note

*You can adjust the settings of the projector map in the **Material Editor** dialog box.*

Shadow Parameters Rollout

The options in this rollout are used to control the properties of the shadow, refer to Figure 13-15. Choose the color swatch from the **Object Shadows** area to modify the color of the shadow. The **Dens.** spinner is used to adjust the density of the shadow. By default, the value in this spinner is 1.0. On increasing the value, the shadow will become denser or darker. Select the **Map** check box to assign a map to the shadow. To do so, choose the map button labeled as **None** and assign a map as discussed earlier; the selected map will be displayed in the shadow, as shown in Figure 13-16. Select the **Light Affects Shadow Color** check box to blend the color of the light with the shadow.

The **Atmosphere Shadows** area in the **Shadow Parameters** rollout is used to enable the different atmospheric effects, such as volume fog, to cast shadows in a scene. The **On** check box is used to cast the shadow by using the atmospheric effect, when the light passes through them. The **Opacity** spinner is used to control the opacity of the shadows cast by the atmospheric effect. The **Color Amount** spinner is used to adjust the blending of the atmosphere's color and the shadow color.

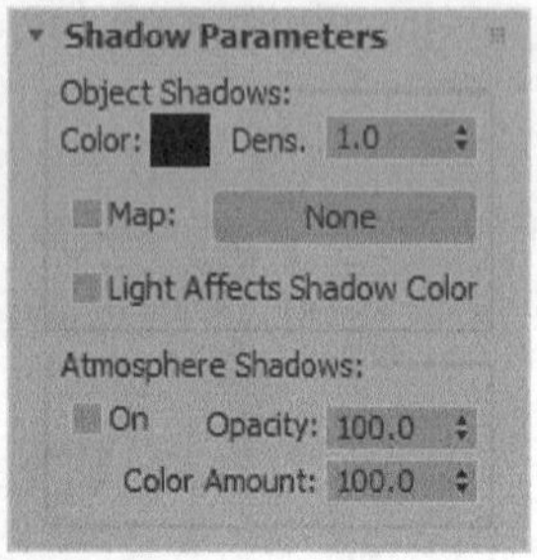

Figure 13-15 The ***Shadow Parameters*** *rollout*

Figure 13-16 A dent map used as a shadow map

Atmospheres & Effects Rollout

The options in this rollout are used to assign special effects such as fog, lighting effects, and so on to the environment on rendering, refer to Figures 13-17 and 13-18. To assign a special effect to the scene, select the light in the viewport and expand the **Atmospheres & Effects** rollout. Now, choose the **Add** button; the **Add Atmosphere or Effect** dialog box will be displayed, as shown in Figure 13-19. Select the effect from this dialog box to add it to the light selected in the viewport and choose the **OK** button; the selected effect will be displayed in the **Atmospheres & Effects** rollout. Next, select the effect from the **Atmospheres & Effects** rollout and choose the **Setup** button; the **Environment and Effects** dialog box will be displayed, refer to Figure 13-20. You can set the parameters of the selected effect using the corresponding rollout in this dialog box. If you want to delete an effect from the scene, select the effect in the **Atmospheres & Effects** rollout and choose the **Delete** button.

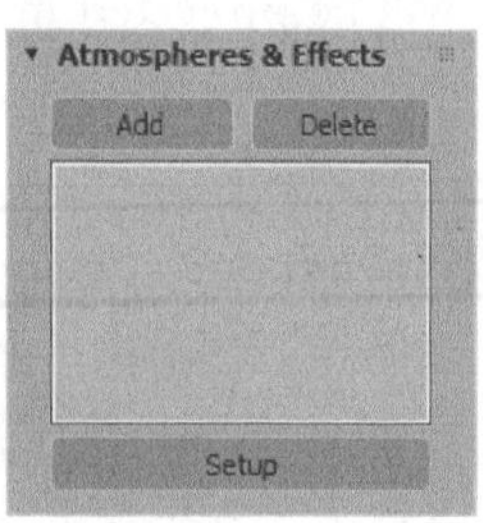

Figure 13-17 The ***Atmospheres & Effects*** *rollout*

Figure 13-18 The lens effect applied to the omni light

Note

To view the hidden rollouts of the selected effect in the ***Environment and Effects*** *dialog box, hover the cursor over the dialog box until the shape of the cursor changes to the hand icon. Next, drag the cursor up or down to see the hidden rollouts.*

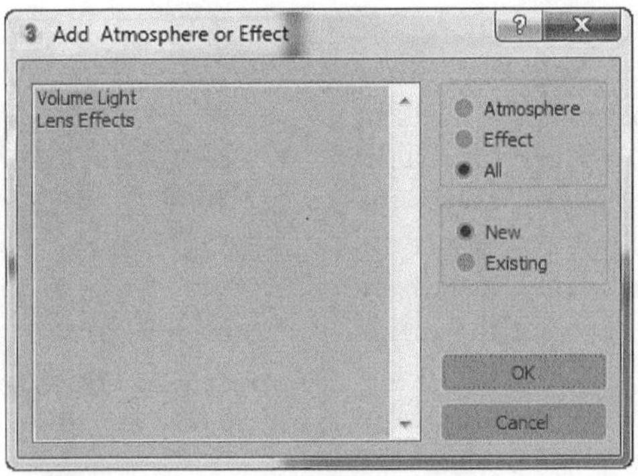

Figure 13-19 The ***Add Atmosphere or Effect*** *dialog box*

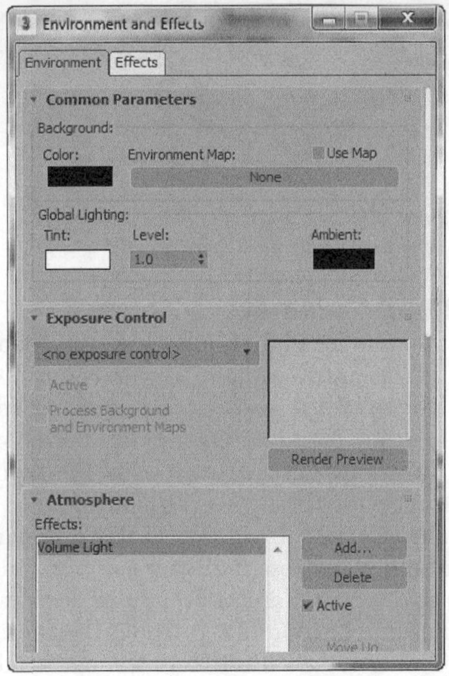

Figure 13-20 The ***Environment and Effects*** *dialog box*

Target Spot

Menu bar:	Create > Lights > Standard Lights > Target Spotlight
Command Panel:	Create > Lights > Standard > Object Type rollout > Target Spot

The **Target Spot** tool is used to create the spot lights. A spot light projects the rays in a particular direction from a source, refer to Figure 13-21. The target spot light also has a target spot to locate the target, refer to Figure 13-22. To create a target spot light, choose the **Target Spot** tool; the **Name and Color**, **General Parameters**, **Intensity/Color/Attenuation**, **Spotlight Parameters**, **Advanced Effects**, **Shadow Parameters**, and **Shadow Map Params** rollouts will be displayed. Now, move the cursor over the viewport; the shape of the cursor will change. Press and hold the left mouse button to specify the starting point of the light and drag the cursor to locate the target of the light. Release the left mouse button; a target spot light will be created. Next, you can modify the parameters of the light using various rollouts displayed in the **Command Panel**. To exit the light command, right-click in the viewport.

Note

The ***Name and Color****,* ***General Parameters****,* ***Intensity/Color/Attenuation****,* ***Advanced Effects****,* ***Shadow Parameters****, and* ***Atmospheric Effects*** *rollouts are same for all types of lights as discussed in the omni light.*

*Figure 13-21 The effect of the target spot light with the **Volume Light** effect*

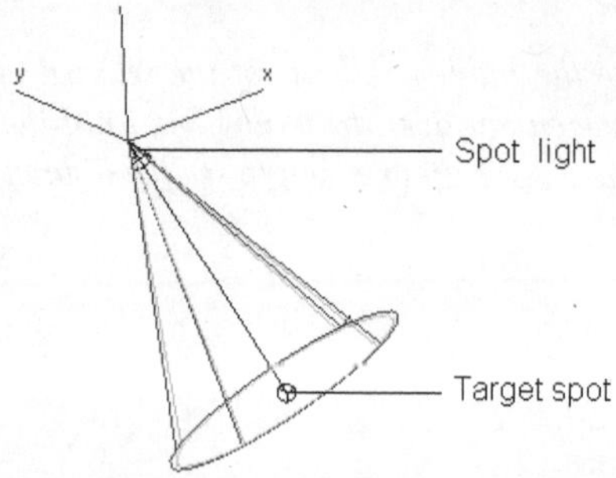

Figure 13-22 The target spot light

Spotlight Parameters Rollout

The options in the **Light Cone** area of this rollout are used to set the effects of the target spotlight, refer to Figure 13-23. Select the **Show Cone** check box to view the cone in the viewport even if the light is not selected. Select the **Overshoot** check box to project the light in all directions, but the shadows of the light will fall within the distance specified in the **Falloff/Field** spinner. When you select the **Overshoot** check box, the **Hotspot/Beam** spinner will be deactivated. The **Hotspot/Beam** spinner is used to set the angle of the cone of the target spot light in degrees. The hotspot is the part of the light cone that provides the most acute illumination. Set the value in the **Falloff/Field** spinner to adjust the angle of the falloff of the light. The falloff is the area at which the light intensity falls to zero.

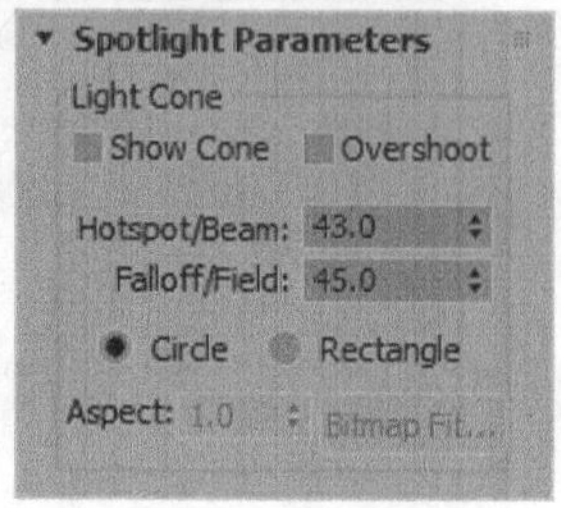

*Figure 13-23 The **Spotlight Parameters** rollout*

By default, the **Circle** radio button is selected. It provides a circular shape to the hotspot and falloff areas. Select the **Rectangle** radio button to provide a rectangular shape to the hotspot and falloff areas. On selecting the **Rectangle** radio button, the **Aspect** spinner and **Bitmap Fit** button get activated. Set the value in the **Aspect** spinner to adjust the aspect ratio. The aspect ratio is the ratio of the width to the height. You need to set the aspect ratio to match a particular bitmap. Choose the **Bitmap Fit** button; the **Select Image File to Fit** dialog box will be displayed. Select the bitmap image and choose the **Open** button; 3ds Max will adjust the aspect ratio in the **Aspect** spinner according to the image selected in the **Select Image File to Fit** dialog box.

Free Spot

Menu bar:	Create > Lights > Standard Lights > Free Spotlight
Command Panel:	Create > Lights > Standard > Object Type rollout > Free Spot

The **Free Spot** tool is similar to the **Target Spot** tool but a free spot light does not have any target, refer to Figure 13-24. All the rollouts used to adjust the free spot light are the same as those discussed in the target spot light.

Note

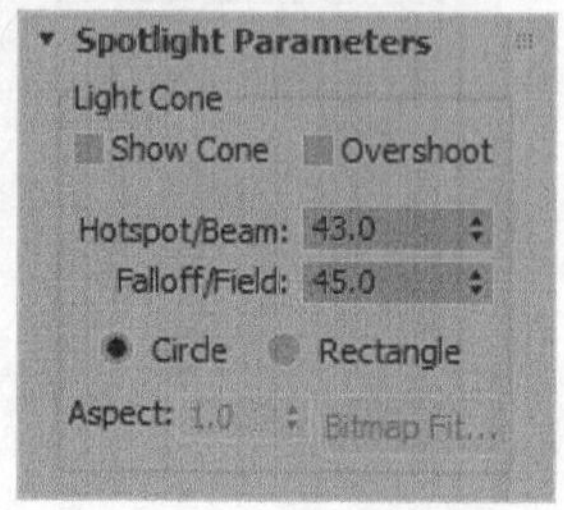

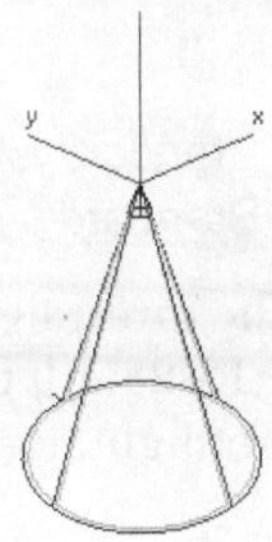

Figure 13-24 The free spot light

Target Direct

Menu bar:	Create > Lights > Standard Lights > Target Direct
Command Panel:	Create > Lights > Standard > Object Type rollout > Target Direct

The **Target Direct** tool is used to create direct lights. A direct light projects the rays in a particular direction from a source. But it projects the parallel rays instead of a cone, refer to Figures 13-25 and 13-26. The target direct light simulates the sunlight.

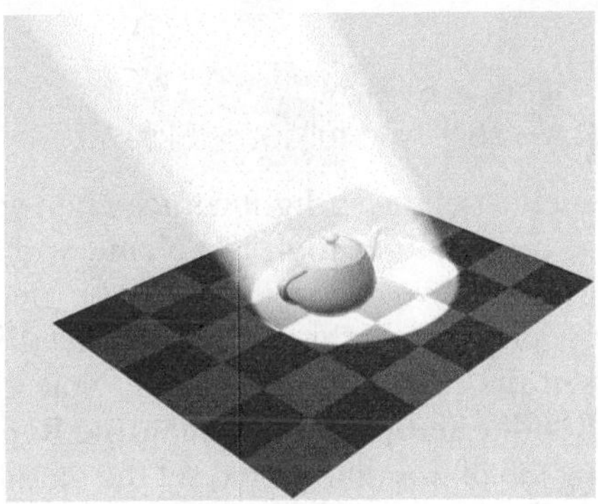

Figure 13-25 The effect of the target direct light

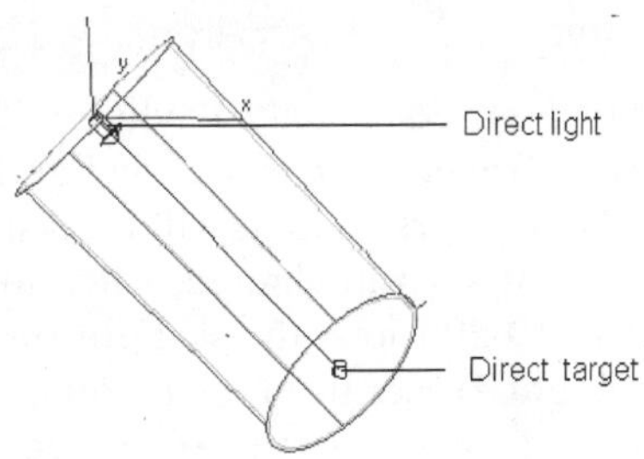

Figure 13-26 The target direct light

To create a target direct light, choose the **Target Direct** tool; the **Name and Color**, **General Parameters**, **Intensity/Color/Attenuation**, **Directional Parameters**, **Advanced Effects**, **Shadow Parameters**, and **Shadow Map Params** rollouts will be displayed. Move the cursor over the viewport; the shape of the cursor will change. Next, press and hold the left mouse button to specify the starting point of the light and drag the mouse to specify the target of the light. Release the left mouse button; the target direct light will be displayed in viewports. Next, you can modify the parameters of the light using various rollouts in the **Command Panel**. Most of the rollouts are same as discussed earlier in this chapter, except the **Directional Parameters** rollout. The options in the **Directional Parameters** rollout are same as those discussed in the **Spotlight** Parameters rollout of the target spot light, refer to Figure 13-27.

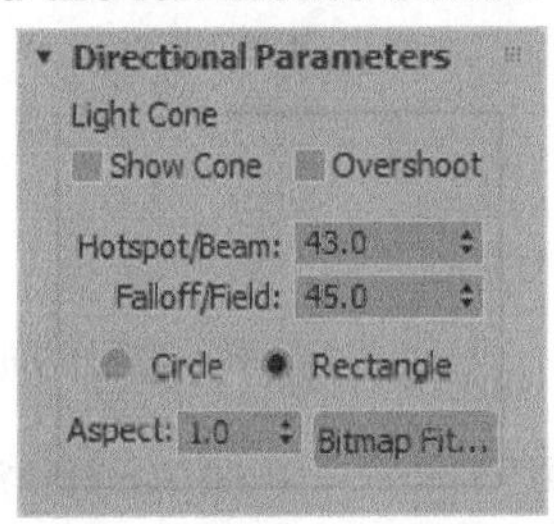

*Figure 13-27 The **Directional Parameters** rollout*

Free Direct

Menu bar:	Create > Lights > Standard Lights > Free Direct
Command Panel:	Create > Lights > Standard > Object Type rollout > Free Direct

The **Free Direct** tool is also used to create the direct light but unlike the target direct light, this light does not have a target, refer to Figure 13-28. All the rollouts to adjust the free direct light are same as those discussed in the target spot light.

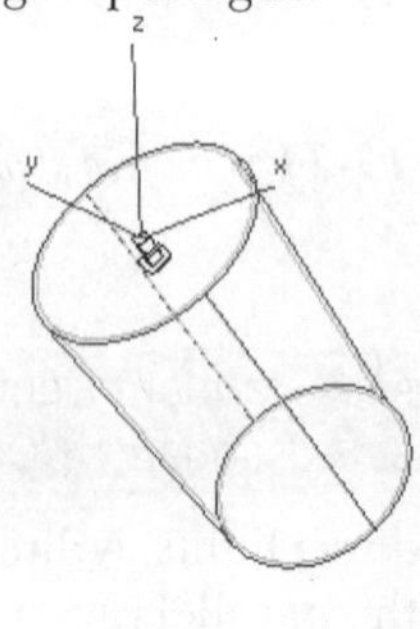

Figure 13-28 *The free direct light*

Skylight

Menu bar:	Create > Lights > Standard Lights > Skylight
Command Panel:	Create > Lights > Standard > Object Type rollout > Skylight

The **Skylight** tool is used to create daylights. The best effect of the skylight comes when you use it with the **Light Tracer**. To create a skylight, choose the **Skylight** tool; the **Name and Color** and **Skylight Parameters** rollouts will be displayed. Now, move the cursor over the viewport; the shape of the cursor will change. Click in the viewport; the light will be displayed in the viewport. Figure 13-29 shows the skylight displayed in the Perspective viewport. Now, choose **Rendering > Light Tracer** from the menu bar; the **Render Setup: Default Scanline Renderer** dialog box will be displayed. In the **Advanced Lighting** tab of this dialog box, set the parameters as required and then choose the **Render** button; the effect of the light will be displayed, refer to Figure 13-30. The **Name and Color** rollout is similar to other tools, as discussed earlier. The **Skylight Parameters** rollout is discussed next.

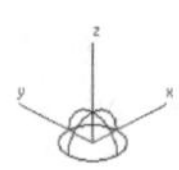

Figure 13-29 *The skylight*

Figure 13-30 *The effect of the skylight*

Skylight Parameters Rollout

The **On** check box is selected by default in this rollout, which enables the skylight to be used in the scene, refer to Figure 13-31. Set the value in the **Multiplier** spinner to define the intensity of the light. The areas in this rollout are discussed next.

Sky Color Area

By default, the **Sky Color** radio button is selected. Choose the color swatch on the right side of the **Sky Color** radio button to select the color for the skylight. The **Map** check box is selected by default. It is used to insert a map along with the light that affects the skylight. By default, the value in the spinner on the right side of the **Map** check box is 100.0. If you decrease the value, the color of the map will be mixed with the sky color. Choose the **Map** button labeled as **None**; the **Material/Map Browser** dialog box will be displayed. Select the desired map and choose the **OK** button to display the map along with the light.

Figure 13-31 The ***Skylight Parameters*** *rollout*

Select the **Use Scene Environment** radio button to use the color that you have set in the **Environment and Effects** dialog box for the skylight.

Render Area

The parameters in this area are deactivated if the **Light Tracer** or **Radiosity** plugin is used. Select the **Cast Shadows** check box to project a shadow with the light. Set the value in the **Rays per Sample** spinner to define the number of rays in the skylight projecting in the scene. Set the value in the **Ray Bias** spinner to define the closest distance at which an object can project the shadows in the scene.

mr Area Omni

Menu bar:	Create > Lights > mental ray > mr Area Omni
Command Panel:	Create > Lights > Standard > Object Type rollout > mr Area Omni

The **mr Area Omni** tool is used with the mental ray renderer. It is used to create an area omni light, refer to Figure 13-32. If you use the area omni light and render the scene using the default scanline renderer, then its effects will be similar to the standard omni light. To view the best effect of the mr area omni light, you need to change the renderer.

Figure 13-32 The effect of the area omni light

To render the scene with the **NVIDIA mental ray** renderer, choose the **Render Setup** tool from the **Main Toolbar**; the **Render Setup: Default Scanline Renderer** dialog box will be displayed. Next, select the **NVIDIA mental ray** option from the **Renderer**

drop-down list and choose the **Render** button. Now, the scene will be rendered using the mental ray renderer. Alternatively, expand the **Assign Renderer** rollout in the **Common** tab. Next, choose the **Choose Renderer** button on the right side of the **Production** label, as shown in Figure 13-33; the **Choose Renderer** dialog box will be displayed, refer to Figure 13-34. Select the **NVIDIA mental ray** option and choose the **OK** button; the **Default Scanline Renderer** text will be replaced with the **NVIDIA mental ray** text in the **Production** text box and close the **Render Setup** dialog box.

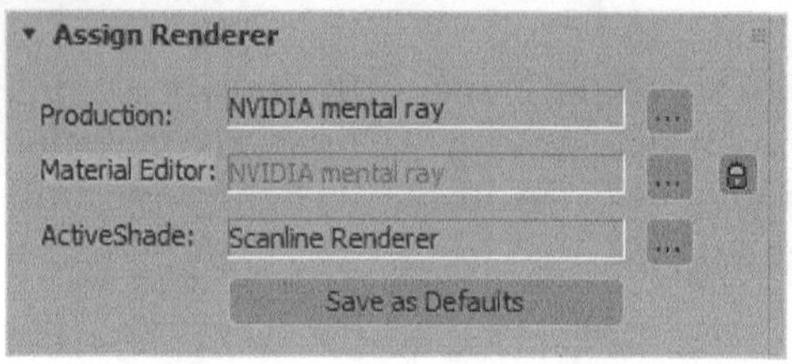

*Figure 13-33 The **Choose Renderer** button highlighted in the **Assign Renderer** rollout*

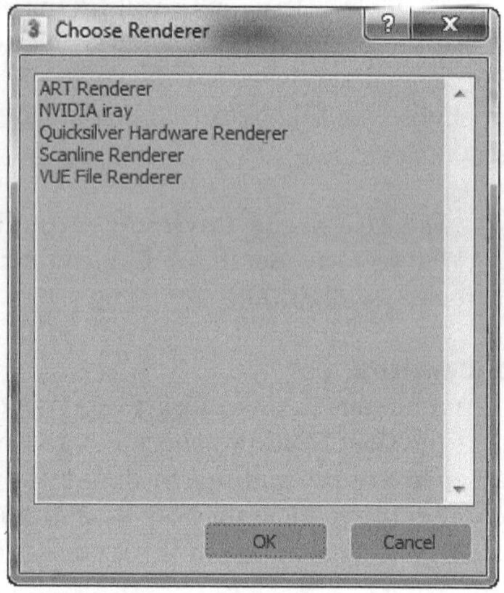

*Figure 13-34 The **Choose Renderer** dialog box*

To create a mental ray area omni light, choose the **mr Area Omni** tool; the **Name and Color**, **General Parameters**, **Intensity/Color/Attenuation**, **Advanced Effects**, **Shadow Parameters**, **Ray Traced Shadow Params**, and **Area Light Parameters** rollouts will be displayed in the **Command Panel**. Now, move the cursor over the viewport; the shape of the cursor will change. Click in the viewport; the light will be displayed in the viewport. Next, you can modify the parameters of the light using various rollouts in the **Command Panel**. Most of the rollouts are same as discussed earlier in the omni light. The **Area Light Parameters** rollout is discussed next.

Area Light Parameters Rollout

In this rollout, the **On** check box is selected by default, refer to Figure 13-35. As a result, the light illuminates all objects in the scene. Select the **Show Icon in Renderer** check box to display a shape at the location of the area light on rendering. To view the shape on rendering, you need to render the scene using the **NVIDIA mental ray** renderer. The **Type** drop-down list is used to select the type of shape for the area light. By default, the **Sphere** option is selected. Select the **Cylinder** option to display a cylindrical shape. Set the value in the **Radius** spinner to set the radius of the shape displayed. Note that when you select **Cylinder** from the **Type** drop-down list, the **Height** spinner is also activated. Set the value in this spinner to define the height of the cylindrical shape displayed. The **Samples** area in this rollout is discussed next.

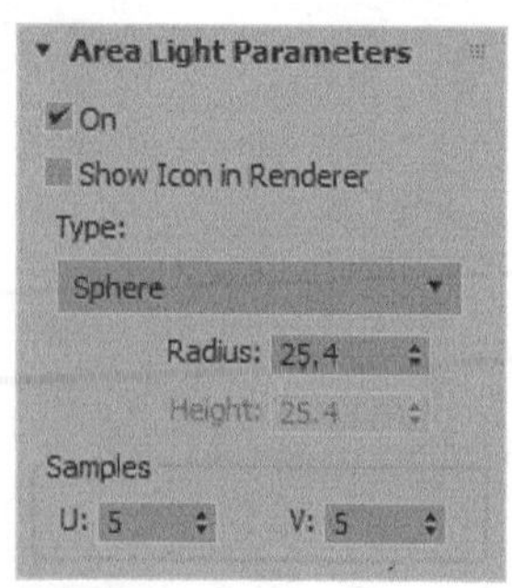

*Figure 13-35 The **Area Light Parameters** rollout*

Samples Area

The options in this area are used to set the quality of the shadow projected by the area omni light. Set the value in the **U** spinner to specify the number of subdivisions along the radius, or the height of the sphere or cylinder. Set the value in the **V** spinner to specify the number of angular subdivisions in the shape.

mr Area Spot

Menu bar:	Create > Lights > mental ray > mr Area Spot
Command Panel:	Create > Lights > Standard > Object Type rollout > mr Area Spot

The mental ray area spot light emits light from a rectangular or disc shaped area rather than from a fixed point, refer to Figure 13-36. To create mental ray area spot light, choose the **mr Area Spot** tool; the **Name and Color**, **General Parameters**, **Intensity/Color/Attenuation**, **Spotlight Parameters**, **Advanced Effects**, **Shadow Parameters**, **Ray Traced Shadow Params**, and **Area Light Parameters** rollouts will be displayed. Move the cursor over the viewport; the shape of the cursor will change. Now, press and hold the left mouse button to specify the location of the light, drag the cursor to locate the target of the light, and release the left mouse button; the light will be displayed in the viewports. You can modify the parameters of the light using various rollouts displayed in the **Command Panel**. Most of the rollouts have already been discussed. The **Area Light Parameters** rollout for the area spot light is discussed next.

Area Light Parameters Rollout

The options in this rollout are same as discussed for the **mr Area Omni** tool, refer to Figure 13-37. In the **Type** drop-down list, the **Rectangle** shape is selected by default. It is used to display the area spot light in a rectangular shape. Specify the height and width in the **Height** and **Width** spinners, respectively. Select the **Disc** shape in the **Type** drop-down list to display the light in circular shape; the **Radius** spinner will get activated. Set the value in this spinner to specify the radius of the shape.

Figure 13-36 The effect of the area spot light

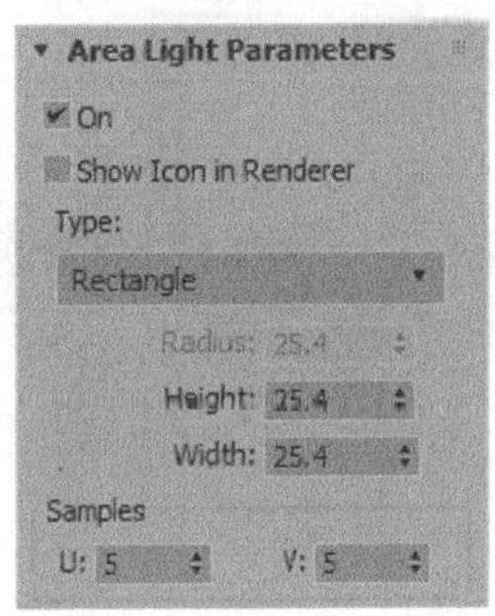

***Figure 13-37** The **Area Light Parameters** rollout*

PHOTOMETRIC LIGHTS

The photometric lights are used to add realistic light effects to the scenes. The photometric lights use the light energy values to calculate the lights accurately as they are in the real world.

To create a photometric light in a scene, choose **Create > Lights** in the **Command Panel**; the **Photometric** light will be displayed by default in the drop-down list below the **Lights** button. Also, various tools to create photometric lights will be displayed in the **Object Type** rollout. These tools are **Target Light**, **Free Light**, **mr Sky Portal**, and **Sun Positioner**, refer to Figure 13-38. Choose one of these tools and create the light in the viewport. If you choose the **Target Light** or **Free Light** tool and if you are using the **Default Scanline Renderer**, the **Photometric Light Creation** message box will be displayed, asking if you want to use the Logarithmic Exposure Control, refer to Figure 13-39. Choose the **Yes** button in this message box. When you choose a tool from the **Object Type** rollout, various rollouts will be displayed to modify the parameters of the corresponding light. Note that if you choose the **Target Light** tool or **Free Light** tool and are using the **NVIDIA mental ray Renderer**, the **Photometric Light Creation** message box will be displayed, asking if you want to use the mr Photographic Exposure Control, refer to Figure 13-40.

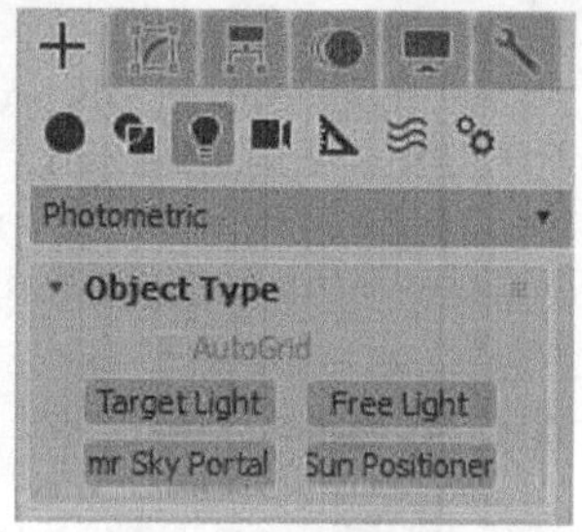

Figure 13-38 *Various tools to create* ***Photometric*** *lights*

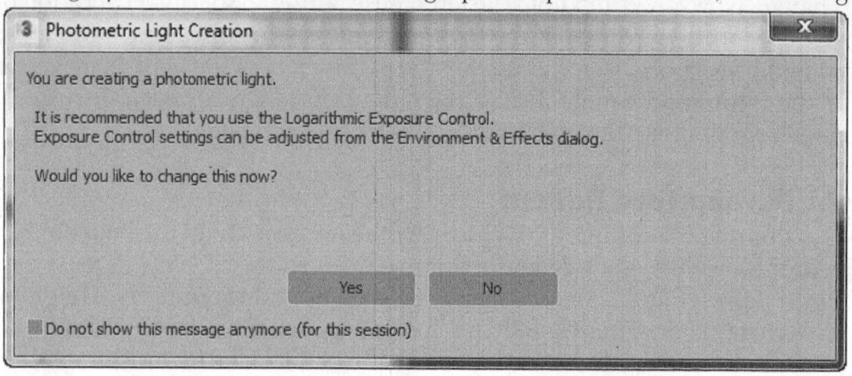

Figure 13-39 *The* ***Photometric Light Creation*** *message box*

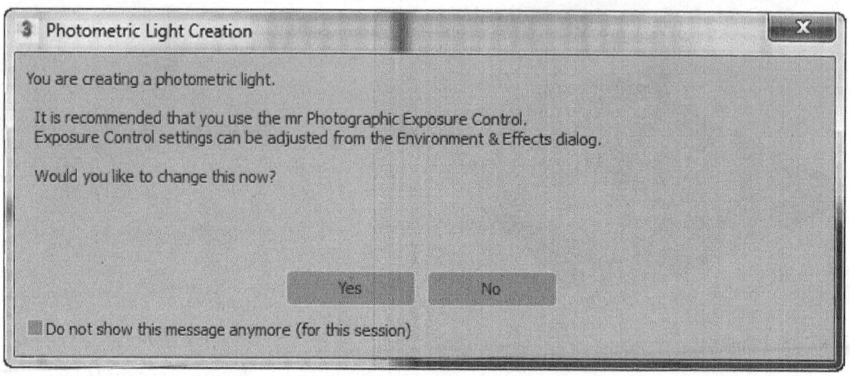

Figure 13-40 *The* ***Photometric Light Creation*** *message box*

The **Name and Color**, **General Parameters**, **Shadow Parameters**, **Advanced Effects**, and **Atmospheres & Effects** rollouts for photometric lights are same as discussed in the standard lights. The **Intensity/Color/Attenuation**, **Templates**, and **Shape/Area Shadows** rollouts for the target light and the free light are discussed next.

Templates Rollout

The options in this rollout are used to specify preset light types such as 40W bulb, Street 400W lamp, and so on, refer to Figure 13-41. To do so, select a light in the viewport and click on the down arrow at the bottom of the **Templates** rollout; a drop-down list will be displayed, as shown in Figure 13-41. Select the required light type from the drop-down list. You will notice a change in the light effect in the viewport. Also, the description of the selected light will be displayed in the text area just above the drop-down list.

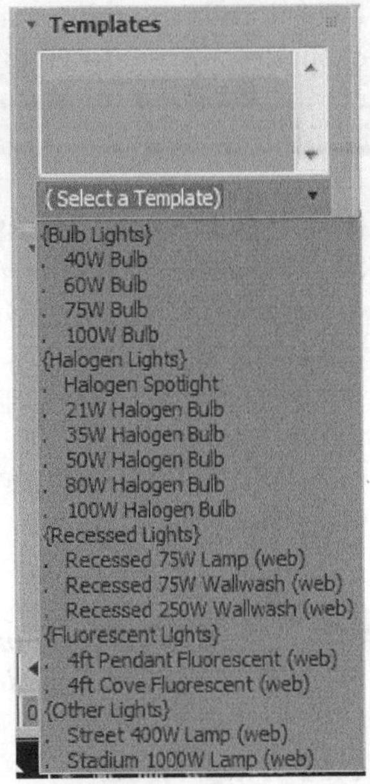

*Figure 13-41 The **Templates** rollout and the drop-down list displayed to select the type of light*

Intensity/Color/Attenuation Rollout

The options in this rollout are used to set the intensity, color, dimness, and attenuation of the light, refer to Figure 13-42. The areas in this rollout are discussed next.

Color Area

The drop-down list on the top of this area displays different common lamp specifications. By default, the **D65 Illuminant (Reference White)** option is selected in the drop-down list. Select the other options; the color in the color swatch on the right side of the **Kelvin** radio button will change according to the selection in this drop-down list. Select the **Kelvin** radio button to specify the color of the light by setting the color temperature in the spinner on the right of this radio button. The value in this spinner is in kelvin unit. As you change the value (temperature) of this spinner, the color in the color swatch will change accordingly. Choose the **Filter Color** color swatch to specify the color of the color filter.

Intensity Area

The options in this area specify the intensity of the light. By default, the **cd** radio button is selected that measures the intensity of the light in candela unit. Select the **lm** radio button to measure the intensity of the light in lumen unit. Select the **lx at** radio button to measure the intensity in lux unit. Set the values in the spinners below these radio buttons to specify the intensity of the light.

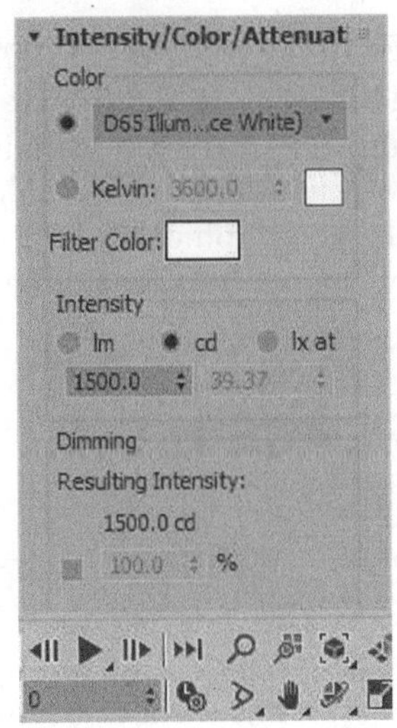

*Figure 13-42 The **Intensity/Color/Attenuation** rollout*

Dimming Area

The options in this area are used to set the intensity by dimming the light. The resulting intensity is set by the value specified in the **Resulting Intensity** spinner. By default, this spinner is not active. Select the **Resulting Intensity** check box. Next, enter a value in the spinner. A value of 100 indicates that the light will be displayed with its full intensity. Select the **Incandescent lamp color shift when dimming** check box to simulate an incandescent light as the light gets dimmed.

Shape/Area Shadows Rollout

The options in this rollout are used to specify a light shape that generates the shadows, refer to Figure 13-43. The controls in this rollout work with the **NVIDIA mental ray** renderer. The areas in this rollout are discussed next.

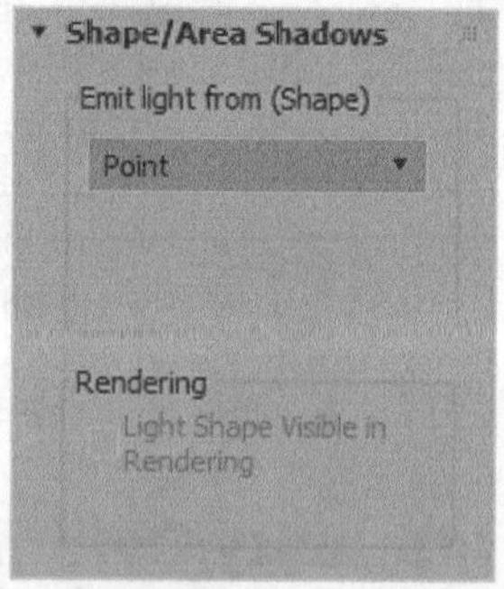

*Figure 13-43 The **Shape/Area Shadows** rollout*

Emit light from (Shape) Area

The drop-down list on the top in this area is used to select the shape for generating the shadows. On selecting an option from the drop-down list (except the **Point** option), the dimension controls related to the selected option will be displayed at the bottom of this area. You can set the dimensions in the respective spinners to modify the shape. Also, the **Shadows Samples** drop-down list will be displayed in the **Rendering** area.

Note

*If you choose the **Point** shape from the drop-down list in the **Emit Light from (Shape)** area, then the **Shadows Samples** drop-down list will not be available in the **Rendering** area.*

Rendering Area

Select the **Light Shape Visible in Rendering** check box to view the light shape at rendering. The different options in the **Shadows Samples** drop-down list are used to set the quality of the shadows of the light.

Sunlight Positioner

New

The Sunlight Positioner is the alternative to the Daylight System. The new Sun Positioner and Physical Sky system in 3ds Max is used with the modern renderer for physically-accurate workflow. Like other Sunlight and Daylight systems in 3ds Max, Sunlight Positioner also follows the geographically correct angle and movement of the sun over a given location on earth. Most of the controls for Sunlight Positioner are similar to that of the Daylight system discussed in Chapter 15.

PLACE HIGHLIGHT TOOL

Menu bar:	Tools > Align > Place Highlight
Main Toolbar:	Align flyout > Place Highlight
Keyboard:	CTRL + H

The **Place Highlight** tool is used to align a light with an object to position its highlight accurately. Before performing the alignment, make sure that the object with highlight is visible in the viewport. Now, select the light in the viewport and choose the **Place Highlight** tool; the shape of the cursor will change. Next, move the cursor over the object on which you want to place the highlight; a selection cursor will be displayed, as shown in Figure 13-44. Click on it; the light will be aligned accordingly and the highlight will be repositioned, refer to Figure 13-45.

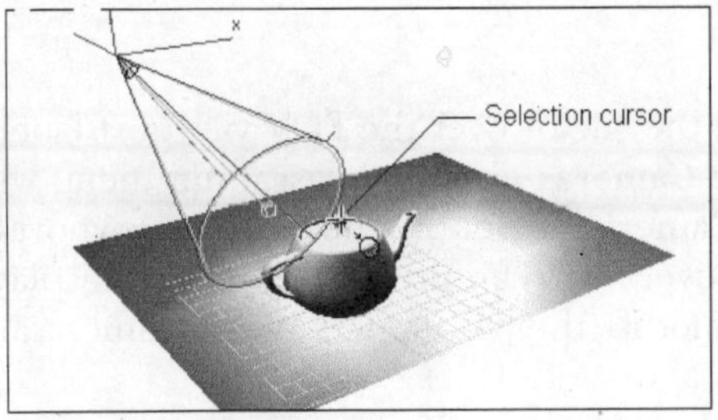

Figure 13-44 The selection cursor displayed after invoking the ***Place Highlight*** *tool*

Figure 13-45 The light aligned as per the selection of the face of the object

CAMERAS

In 3ds Max, the cameras are used to adjust a particular view in a scene. These cameras act as the still image or video cameras in the real world. There are three types of cameras in 3ds Max 2017, namely Target, Free and Physical. The target camera has two parts, the target camera and a target object, as shown in Figure 13-46. It displays the view according to the position of the target object. You can move the target object and the target camera independently. The free camera does not have any target object, as shown in Figure 13-47. It displays the view in the direction of the camera. You can use the free camera to perform the walkthrough animation. The physical camera uses exposure control and produces photorealistic renderings.

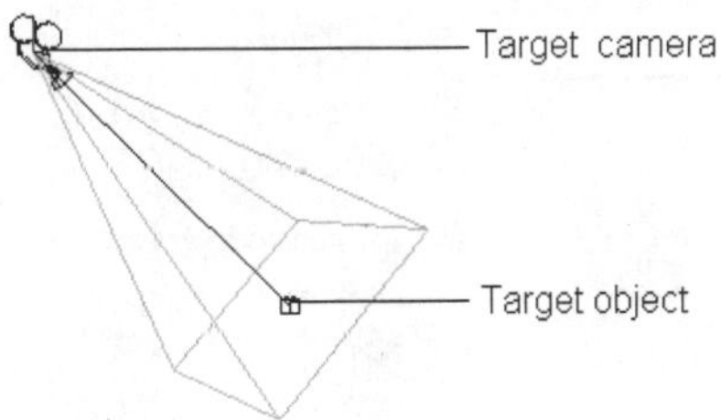

Figure 13-46 The target camera

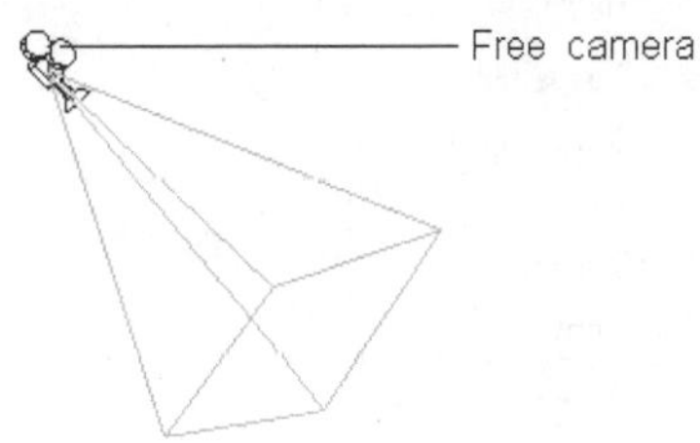

Figure 13-47 The free camera

Creating a Target Camera

Menu bar:	Create > Cameras > Target Camera
Command Panel:	Create > Cameras > Standard > Object Type rollout > Target

To create a target camera, choose **Create > Cameras** in the **Command Panel**; the **Standard** option will be displayed in the drop-down list below the **Cameras** button. You can use the tools in the **Object Type** rollout to create cameras, refer to Figure 13-48. Choose the **Target** tool; the **Name and Color**, **Parameters**, and **Depth of Field Parameters** rollouts will be displayed in the **Command Panel**. Next, move the cursor over the viewport; the shape of cursor will change. Press and hold the left mouse button to specify the location of the camera, drag the cursor to specify the target of the camera, and release the left mouse button; the target camera will be displayed in the viewports. You can modify the parameters of the camera using

Figure 13-48 The Object Type rollout with tools to create cameras

the rollouts displayed in the **Command Panel**. Next, right-click in the viewport to exit the command.

To display the camera view in the viewport, move the cursor over the POV viewport label and click on it; a flyout will be displayed. Choose the **Cameras** option; a cascading menu will be displayed, as shown in Figure 13-49. Choose the **Camera001** option; the current viewport label will be replaced by the Camera001 label. Alternatively, you can press the C key to display the camera view. The **Parameters** rollout is used to modify the parameters of the camera and is discussed next.

Parameters Rollout

To modify the parameters of the camera, make sure that the camera is selected in the viewport. Next, choose the **Modify** tab in the **Command Panel**; the **Parameters** rollout will be displayed, as shown in Figure 13-50.

The **Lens** spinner in this rollout is used to specify the focal length of the camera in millimeters. The focal length is the distance between the camera lens and its focus. Set the value in the **FOV** spinner to specify the field of view of the camera in degrees. The field of view (FOV) determines the area that the camera can view in the viewport. The **Stock Lenses** area in this rollout is discussed next.

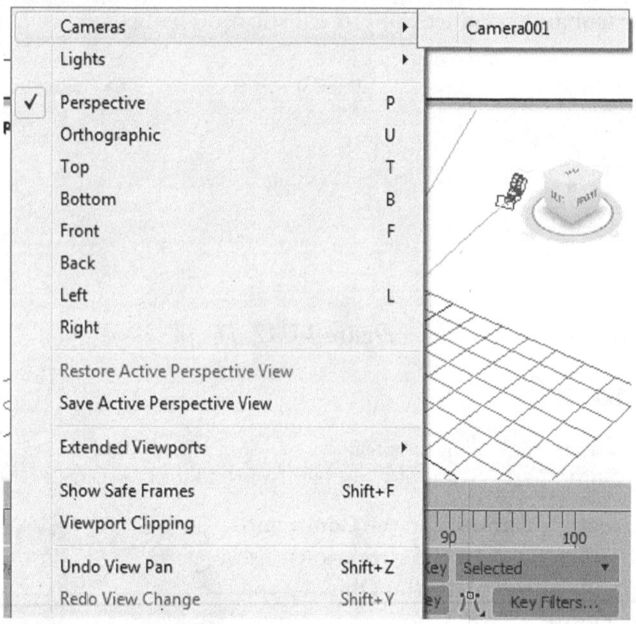

*Figure 13-49 The cascading menu displayed on choosing the **Cameras** option*

*Figure 13-50 Partial view of the **Parameters** rollout*

Stock Lenses Area

Choose one of the buttons in this area to set the focal length of the camera in millimeters. On choosing a button in this area, the value in the **Lens** and **FOV** spinners will also change automatically.

The **Type** drop-down list is used to set the type of camera in the viewport. The **Target Camera** is selected by default in this drop-down list. Select the **Free Camera** option to use the free camera. Select the **Show Cone** check box to view the FOV cone in all viewports, even if the camera is not selected. Select the **Show Horizon** check box to view the horizon line displayed in dark gray color in the Camera viewport.

Creating a Free Camera

Menu bar:	Create > Cameras > Free Camera
Command Panel:	Create > Cameras > Standard > Object Type rollout > Free

To create a free camera, choose **Create > Cameras** in the **Command Panel**; the **Standard** option will be displayed in the drop-down list. Choose the **Free** tool from the **Object Type** rollout; the **Name and Color**, **Parameters**, and **Depth of Field Parameters** rollouts will be displayed. Move the cursor over the viewport; the shape of the cursor will change. Now, click in the viewport; the camera will be displayed in the viewports. You can modify the parameters of the camera using the rollouts displayed in the **Command Panel**. The options in these rollouts are the same as those discussed in the target camera.

Creating a Physical Camera

Menu bar:	Create > Cameras > Create Physical Camera From View
Command Panel:	Create > Cameras > Standard > Object Type rollout > Physical

This camera is used to create photorealistic, physically based renderings. To create a physical camera, choose **Create > Cameras** in the **Command Panel**; the **Standard** option will be displayed in the drop-down list below the **Cameras** button. Choose the **Physical** tool; the **Name and Color**, **Basic**, **Physical Camera**, **Exposure**, **Bokeh(Depth of Field)**, **Perspective Control**, **Lens Distortion**, and **Miscellaneous** rollouts will be displayed in the **Command Panel**, refer to Figure 13-51. Next, move the cursor over the viewport; the shape of cursor will change. Press and hold the left mouse button to specify the placement of the camera, drag the cursor to specify the target of the camera, and release the left mouse button; the physical camera will be displayed in the viewports. You can modify the parameters of the camera using the rollouts displayed in the **Command Panel**. Next, right-click in the viewport to exit the command.

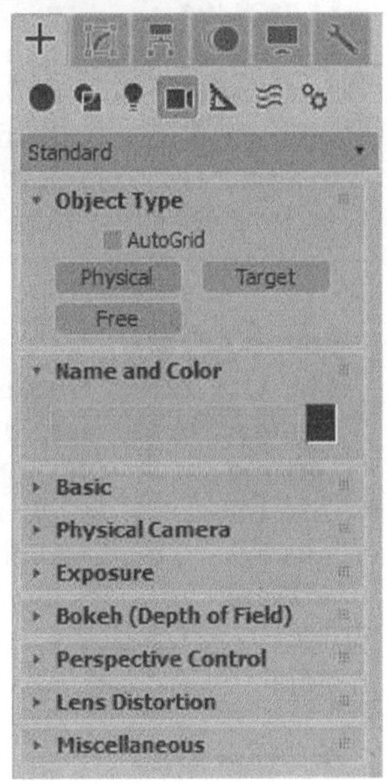

***Figure 13-51** Various rollouts to create a physical camera*

To display the camera view in the viewport, move the cursor over the POV viewport label and click on it; a flyout will be displayed. Choose the **Cameras** option; a cascading menu will be displayed. Choose the **PhysCamera001** option; the current viewport label will be replaced by the PhysCamera001 label. Alternatively, you can press the C key to display the camera view. The commonly used rollouts are discussed next.

Basic Rollout

The options in the **Basic** rollout are discussed next.

Targeted

The **Targeted** check box is selected by default. It is used to specify that the camera has a target.

Target Distance

The **Target Distance** spinner is used to specify the distance of a target with focal plane.

Viewport Display Area

The options in the **Show Cone** drop-down list of this area are used to specify whether the camera cone will be displayed always, never, or on selection. The **Show Horizon Line** check box is used to display the horizontal line in the Camera viewport.

Physical Camera Rollout

The options in the **Physical Camera** rollout are discussed next.

Film/Sensor Area

The options in the **Preset** drop-down list are used to specify the film sensor of a physical camera. The **Width** spinner allows you to specify a custom film sensor width. If you enter a custom width in this spinner, the **preset** drop-down list will change to **Custom**.

Lens Area

The **Focal Length** spinner is used to specify the focal length of lens. If you select the check box located below it, the **Specify FOV** spinner will be activated. You can set the value in this spinner to specify the field of view in degrees. Similarly, set the value in the **Zoom** spinner to adjust the zoom level of camera. The **Aperture** spinner allows you to set the aperture as an f-number or f-step. This spinner allows you to zoom the camera without changing its position.

Focus Area

The **Use Target Distance** radio button is used to set the focal distance same as the target distance. If you want the focal distance to be different than the target distance, select the **Custom** radio button; the **Focus Distance** spinner will be activated. Next, set the value in this spinner to change the focal distance. The **Lens Breathing** spinner is used to move the lens toward the focal distance or away from it to adjust the field of view. The **Enable Depth of Field** check box is clear by default. If selected, the camera generates the depth of field (blur offset) based on the aperture settings. The blurring occurs at a distance which is not equal to the focal distance.

Shutter Area

The options in the **Type** drop-down list are used to specify the unit of shutter speed. The **Duration** spinner is used to set the shutter speed. Note that the shutter speed depends on the type of unit specified in the **Type** drop-down list. Select the check box below the **Duration** spinner; the **Offset** spinner will be activated. The **Offset** spinner allows you to control the timing of the opening of the shutter related to the start of each frame. The timing is dependent on the option that you select from the **Type** drop-down list.

The **Enable Motion Blur** spinner is used to generate the motion blur.

Exposure Rollout

The options in the **Exposure** rollout are discussed next.

Exposure Control Installed

If the exposure control is already activated for the physical camera, the **Exposure Control Installed** button in this rollout is deactivated and the label of the button reads "**Exposure Control Installed**". Also, the **Physical Camera Exposure Control** option selected in the drop-down list of the **Exposure Control** rollout in the **Environment and Effects** dialog box changes to **Physical Camera Exposure Control**. If you select the option other than the **Physical Camera Exposure Control** option in this drop-down list, the **Exposure Control Installed** button changes to the **Install Exposure Control** button and the other parameters in the **Exposure** rollout are deactivated. Choose the **Install Exposure Control** button; the **Physical Camera Exposure Control** message box will be displayed. Choose the **OK** button in this message box; the **Install Exposure Control** button will be replaced by the **Exposure Control Installed** button and the **Physical Camera Exposure Control** option will be selected in the drop-down list of the **Exposure Control** rollout in the **Environment and Effects** dialog box.

Exposure Gain Area

When you select the **Manual** radio button, the spinner next to it will be activated. You can use the value in this spinner to set exposure gain via an ISO value. Exposure value is directly proportional to the value in this spinner. The **Target** radio button is selected by default. The more the value in the spinner, the lesser will be the exposure value.

White Balance Area

The **Illuminant** radio button is selected by default. As a result, the drop-down list below it will be activated. The options in this drop-down list consist of various standard light sources. The color swatch next to it changes based on the option selected in the drop-down list and sets the color balance. If you select the **Temperature** radio button, the spinner below it will be activated. The color swatch next to it changes depending on the value set in the spinner and is used to set the color balance. If you select the **Custom** radio button, the color swatch below it will be activated. You can set the color in this color swatch to set the color balance.

Enable Vignetting

If you select the **Enable Vignetting** check box, the **Amount** spinner will be activated. More the value in the **Amount** spinner, more will be the vignetting effect. This effect results in darkness at the edges of the film plane at rendering.

Bokeh (Depth of Field) Rollout

When the **Enable Depth of Field** check box is selected in the **Physical Camera** rollout, a pattern is created in the areas of the image that are out of focus. This is known as Bokeh effect. The options in the **Bokeh (Depth of Field)** rollout are discussed next.

Aperture Shape Area

This area defines the pattern shape. By default, the **Circular** radio button is selected. As a result, circular shaped pattern is created. If you select the **Bladed** radio button, the sharp edge shaped pattern is created in which the number of edges in the shape depend on the value in the **Blades** spinner. The **Rotation** spinner is used to specify the angle of rotation for all shapes in the pattern. If you select the **Custom Texture** radio button, the **None** radio button is activated. Choose the **None** button to select a map. This map replaces the shape in a pattern.

Center Bias (Ring Effect) Area

If you move the slider toward right or enter a positive value in the spinner next to it, the amount of blurriness is more in the out of focus parts of the image and vice-versa.

Optical Vignetting (Cat Eye) Area

This option vignettes the rendered frame for simulating the cat's eye effect. The highlights appear to be elliptical instead of round.

Anisotropy (Anamorphic Lens) Area

This slider lets you stretch the aperture vertically (negative value) or horizontally (positive value). This stretching simulates anamorphic lens effect.

Perspective Control Rollout

The options in the **Perspective Control** rollout are discussed next.

Lens Shift Area

The spinners in this area are used to move the camera view horizontally or vertically without changing its position or orientation.

Tilt Correction Area

The spinners in this area are used to tilt the camera horizontally or vertically and to correct the perspective. The **Auto Vertical Tilt Correction** check box is used to auto correct the tilt correction along the Z axis.

Lens Distortion Rollout

The options in the **Lens Distortion** rollout are discussed next.

Distortion Type Area

The **None** radio button is selected by default. As a result, there is no distortion applied. Select the **Cubic** radio button; the **Amount** spinner will be activated. The positive value in this spinner results in pincushion distortion whereas negative value in this spinner results in barrel distortion. If you select the **Texture** radio button, the **None** button will be activated. Choose the **None** button to select a map. The distortion of the image depends on the colors in the image.

Miscellaneous Rollout

The options in the **Miscellaneous** rollout are discussed next.

Clipping Planes Area

Select the **Enable** check box to add near and far clipping planes. Specify the distance of the near clipping plane from the camera in the **Near** spinner and the distance of the far clipping plane from the camera in the **Far** spinner. Note that the objects in between the camera and the near clipping plane and the objects which are outside the far clipping plane will not be visible in renderings.

Environment Ranges Area

The values in the **Near Range** and **Far Range** spinners specify the near and far range limits, respectively for the atmospheric effects added in the scene.

ALIGN CAMERA TOOL

Menu bar:	Tools > Align > Align Camera
Main Toolbar:	Align flyout > Align Camera

The **Align Camera** tool is used to align a camera normal to a selected surface. To align a camera, select it in the viewport and then choose the **Align Camera** tool; the shape of the cursor will change. Next, move the cursor over the surface of the object; a selection cursor will be displayed, as shown in Figure 13-52. Select the face; the camera will be aligned accordingly, refer to Figures 13-53, 13-54, and 13-55.

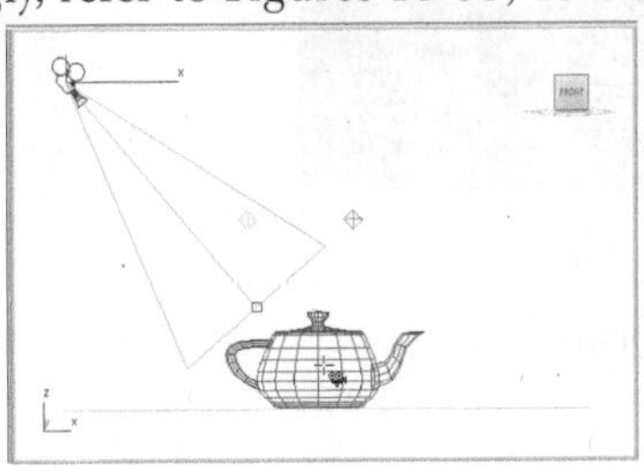

Figure 13-52 *The cursor displayed on the object to get the proper alignment*

Figure 13-53 *The Camera viewport before alignment*

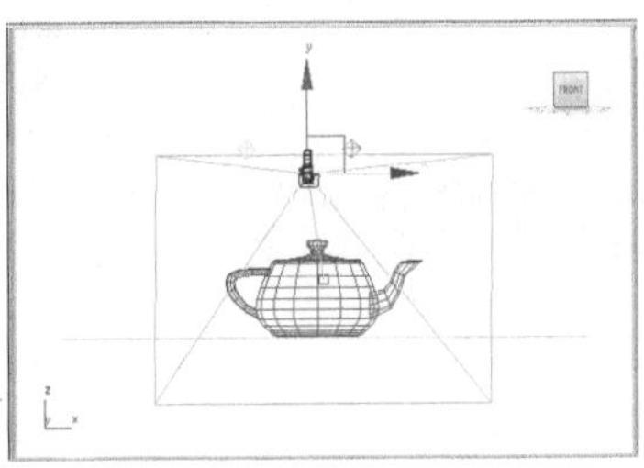

Figure 13-54 *The new position of the camera after using the **Align Camera** tool*

Figure 13-55 *The Camera viewport after using the **Align Camera** tool*

TUTORIALS

Before starting the tutorials, you need to download the *c13_3dsmax_2017_tut.zip* file from *www.cadcim.com*. The path of the file is as follows: *Textbooks > Animation and Visual Effects > 3ds Max > Autodesk 3ds Max 2017: A comprehensive Guide*

Extract the contents of the zipped file and save them in the *Documents* folder.

Tutorial 1

In this tutorial, you will create a scene, as shown in Figure 13-56, by using the lights, materials and maps. **(Expected time: 30 min)**

Figure 13-56 *The scene to be created*

The following steps are required to complete this tutorial:

a. Create the project folder.
b. Open the file.
c. Create lights.
d. Save and render the scene.

Creating the Project Folder

1. Create a new project folder with the name *c13_tut1* at *\Documents\3dsmax2017* and then save the file with the name *c13tut1*, as discussed in Tutorial 1 of Chapter 2.

2. Open the Windows Explorer and then browse to the *c13_3dsmax_2017_tut* folder and copy the *sky_1.jpg* file from this folder to *\Documents\3dsmax2017\c13_tut1\sceneassets\images*.

Opening the File

1. Choose **Open** from the **Application** menu; the **Open File** dialog box is displayed. In this dialog box, browse to the location *\Documents\c13_3dsmax_2017_tut* and select the **c13_tut1_start.max** file from it. Choose the **Open** button to open the file, refer to Figure 13-57.

2. Choose **Save As** from the **Application** menu; the **Save File As** dialog box is displayed. Browse to the location *\Documents\3dsmax2017\c13_tut1\scenes*. Save the file with the name *c13tut1.max* at this location.

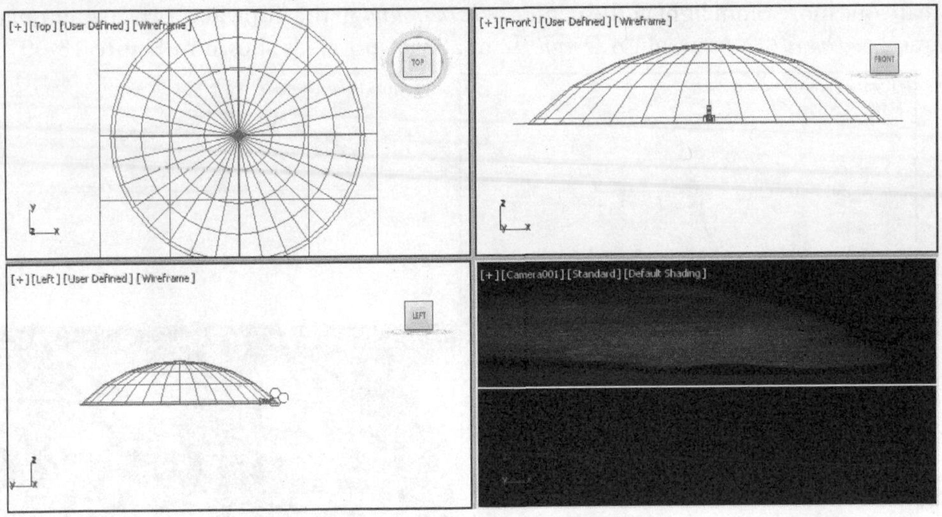

Figure 13-57 The c13_tut1_start.max file

Creating Lights

In this section, you will create lights by using the **Omni** tool.

1. Activate the Top viewport. Choose **Create > Lights** in the **Command Panel**; the **Photometric** option is displayed in the drop-down list below the **Lights** button. Choose the **Standard** option from the drop-down list.

2. Choose the **Omni** tool from the **Object Type** rollout in the **Command Panel** and click in the Top viewport; the omni light is displayed in the viewports. It is automatically named as *Omni001*.

3. Choose the **Select and Move** tool and align *Omni001* in the viewports, as shown in Figure 13-58.

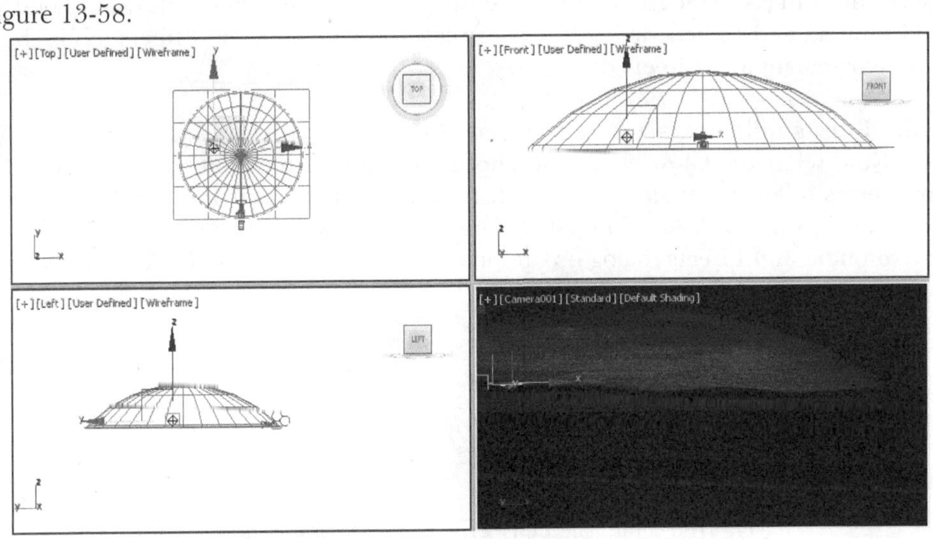

Figure 13-58 Alignment of Omni001 in the viewports

4. Create one more omni light at the center of *background* in the Top viewport. It is automatically named as *Omni002*. Now, align *Omni002* in all viewports, as shown in Figure 13-59.

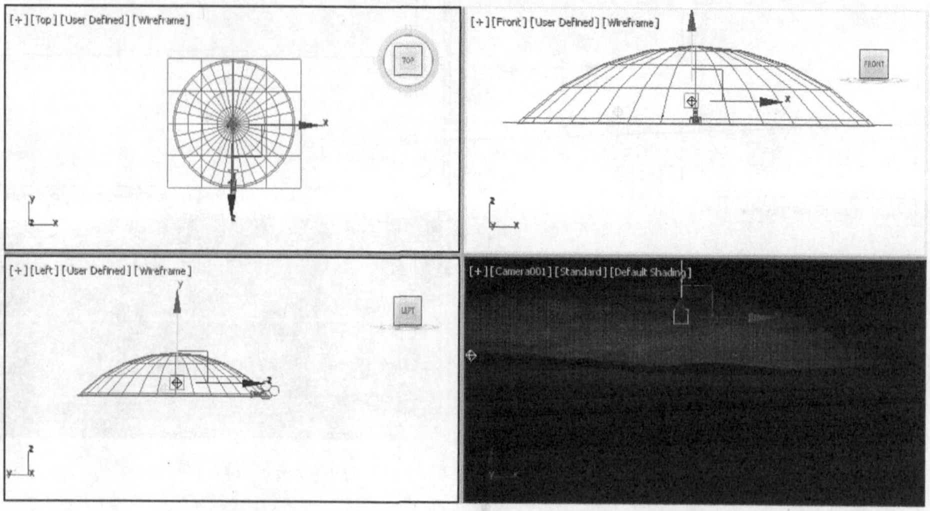

Figure 13-59 *Alignment of Omni002 in the viewports*

Next, you need to modify *Omni002* light to create the sun effect.

5. Make sure that *Omni002* light is selected and then choose the **Modify** tab in the **Command Panel**; the rollouts to modify the light are displayed in the modify panel.

6. Expand the **Atmospheres & Effects** rollout and choose the **Add** button; the **Add Atmosphere or Effect** dialog box is displayed. Select the **Lens Effects** option and then choose the **OK** button; the **Lens Effects** option is displayed in the text area of the **Atmospheres & Effects** rollout. Next, you need to modify the parameters of **Lens Effects**.

7. Select **Lens Effects** in the **Atmospheres & Effects** rollout and choose the **Setup** button; the **Environment and Effects** dialog box is displayed. By default, the **Effects** tab is chosen in the **Environment and Effects** dialog box.

8. In the **Effects** rollout, make sure the **Lens Effects** option is selected under the **Effects** area. Now, select the **Glow** effect and choose the right arrow button in the **Lens Effects Parameters** rollout; the **Glow** effect is displayed in the list available on the right side, as shown in Figure 13-60. Also, the **Glow Element** rollout is displayed at the bottom of the **Environment and Effects** dialog box to modify the parameters of the **Glow** effect.

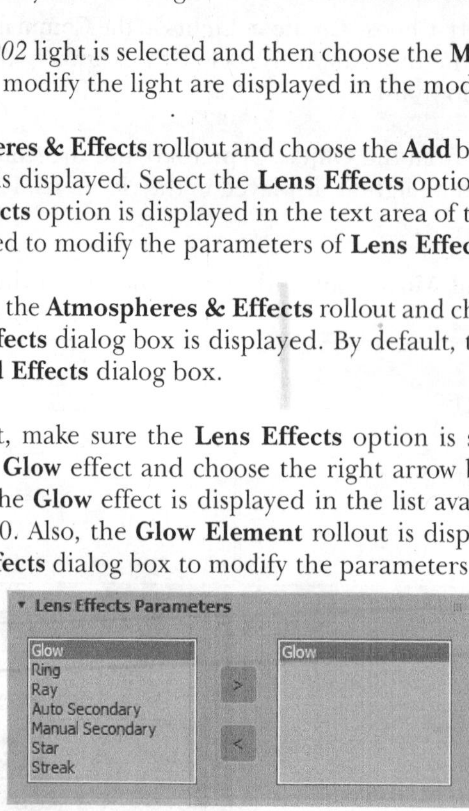

Figure 13-60 *The* ***Lens Effects Parameters*** *rollout*

Note

1. To view all rollouts, you need to scroll inside the dialog box.

2. You can view the effects of the ***Lens Effects*** *option only after rendering.*

9. In the **Glow Element** rollout, set the value **20.0** in the **Size** spinner. Use the default values for other options. In the **Lens Effects Parameters** rollout, select the **Ray** effect and choose the right arrow button; the **Ray** effect is displayed in the text area available on the right side. Also, the **Ray Element** rollout is displayed at the bottom of the **Environment and Effects** dialog box to modify the parameters of the **Ray** effect.

10. In the **Ray Element** rollout, set the values in the spinners as follows and close the **Environment and Effects** dialog box.

    Size: **50.0** Num: **20**

Saving and Rendering the Scene

In this section, you will save the scene and then render it. You can also view the final rendered image of this model by downloading the file *c13_3dsmax_2017_rndr.zip* from *www.cadcim.com.* The path of the file is as follows: *Textbooks > Animation and Visual Effects > 3ds Max > Autodesk 3ds Max 2017: A Comprehensive Guide*

1. Choose **Save** from the **Application** menu. Next, activate the Camera001 viewport.

2. Choose the **Render Production** tool; the **Rendered Frame** window is displayed showing the final output of the scene at one frame, as shown in Figure 13-61.

***Figure 13-61** The final output of the scene*

3. Close the **Rendered Frame** window.

Tutorial 2

In this tutorial, you will illuminate a room by using the **Omni** and **Target Direct** tools, as shown in Figure 13-62. **(Expected time: 30 min)**

Figure 13-62 The illuminated room

The following steps are required to complete this tutorial:

a. Create the project folder.
b. Open the file.
c. Create lights.
d. Create the background.
e. Save and render the scene.

Creating the Project Folder

Create a new project folder with the name *c13_tut2* at *\Documents\3dsmax2017* and then save the file with the name *c13tut2*, as discussed in Tutorial 1 of Chapter 2. Now, copy *Finishes.Masonry Flooring.Marble.Beige-Grid.jpg* and *CLOUDS4.jpeg* files to *\Documents\3dsmax2017\c13_tut2\sceneassets\images*.

Opening the File

1. Choose **Open** from the **Application** menu; the **Open File** dialog box is displayed. In this dialog box, browse to the location *\Documents\c13_3dsmax_2017_tut* and select the **c13_tut2_start.max** file from it. Choose the **Open** button to open the file, refer to Figure 13-63.

2. Choose **Save As** from the **Application** menu; the **Save File As** dialog box is displayed. Browse to the location *\Documents\3dsmax2017\c13_tut2\scenes*. Save the file with the name *c13tut2.max* at this location.

Creating Lights

In this section, you will create lights by using the **Omni** and **Target Direct** tools.

1. Activate the Top viewport. Choose **Create > Lights** in the **Command Panel** and select the **Standard** option from the drop-down list. Next, choose the **Omni** tool from the **Object Type**

rollout. Next, click in the Top viewport; the omni light is displayed in the viewport and it is automatically named as *Omni001*.

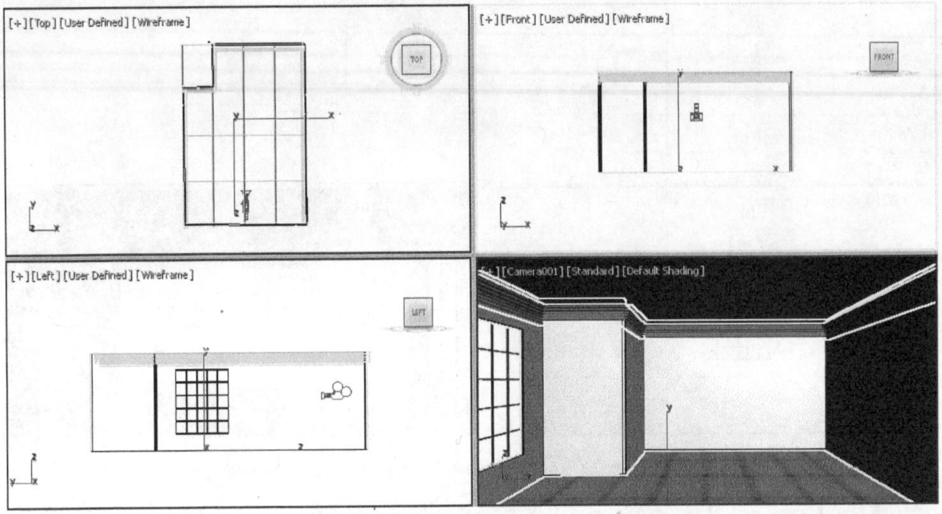

Figure 13-63 The c13_tut2_start.max file

2. In the **Modify** tab, set the following parameters:

   General Parameters rollout
   Select the **On** check box in the **Shadows** area

   Intensity/Color/Attenuation rollout
   Set the value **0.6** in the **Multiplier** spinner

3. Select the **Multiplier** color swatch and modify the colors by setting the following parameters:

   Red: **255** Green: **219** Red: **181**

4. Align *Omni001* in viewports, as shown in Figure 13-64.

   Next, you need to create the target direct light in the scene to give the shadow effect.

5. Activate the Front viewport, choose the **Zoom** tool, and zoom out until the objects are displayed about half of their original size.

6. Choose the **Target Direct** tool from **Create > Lights > Standard > Object Type** rollout in the **Command Panel**. Move the cursor on the left side of the Front viewport; the shape of the cursor changes. Next, press and hold the left mouse button to specify the location of the light and drag the cursor near the front portion of *wall001* to specify the target of the light. Release the left mouse button; the light is displayed in all viewports and it is automatically named as *Direct001*.

7. Choose the **Modify** tab in the **Command Panel**; various rollouts are displayed to modify the target direct light.

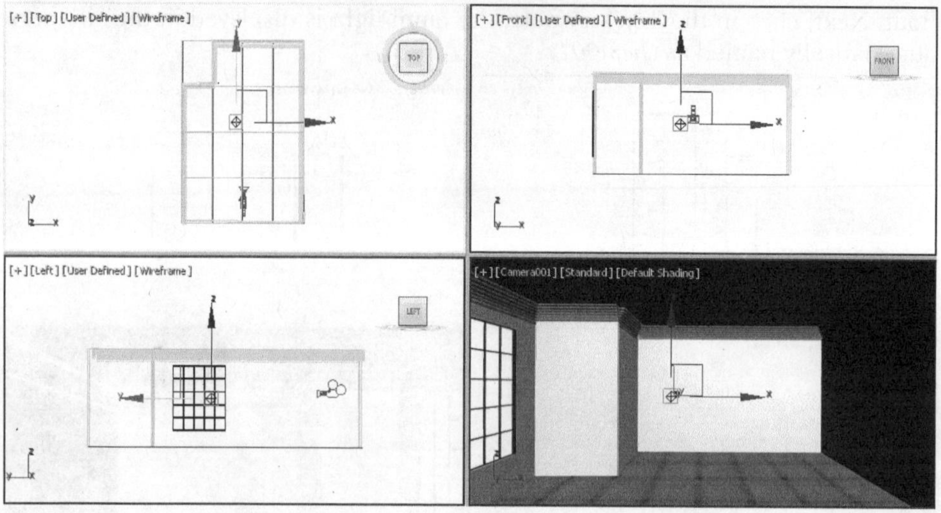

Figure 13-64 The Omni001 light in viewports

8. Expand the **General Parameters** rollout and select the **On** check box in the **Shadows** area.

9. In the **Directional Parameters** rollout, select the **Rectangle** radio button and set the values in the respective spinners as given below.

   Hotspot/Beam: **84.0** Falloff/Field: **86.0**

10. Expand the **Atmospheres & Effects** rollout and choose the **Add** button; the **Add Atmosphere or Effect** dialog box is displayed. Select the **Volume Light** option and choose the **OK** button; the **Volume Light** option is displayed in the text area of the **Atmospheres & Effects** rollout.

    Next, you need to modify the parameters of the **Volume Light**.

11. Select the **Volume Light** option in the **Atmospheres & Effects** rollout and choose the **Setup** button; the **Environment and Effects** dialog box is displayed. The **Environment** tab is chosen by default in the **Environment and Effects** dialog box.

12. In the **Atmosphere** rollout, make sure the **Volume Light** option is selected in the **Effects** area. Set the value **1.5** in the **Density** spinner of the **Volume** area in the **Volume Light Parameters** rollout. Use the default values for other options and close the **Environment and Effects** dialog box.

Note
*You can also use different settings in the **Volume Light Parameters** rollout to give different effects in the scene.*

13. Align *Direct001* light in the viewports to cover window, as shown in Figure 13-65.

Note
You can adjust the position of the Camera001 to view the scene with desired light effects.

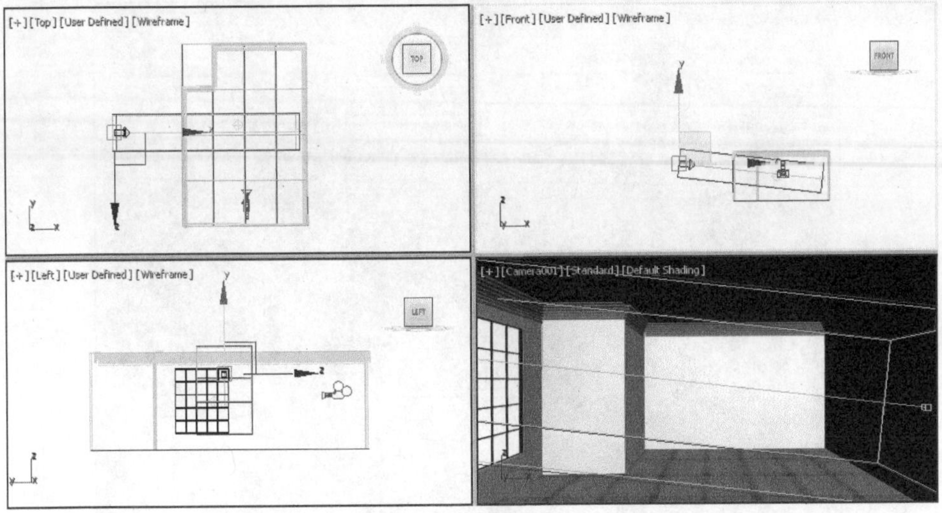

Figure 13-65 Alignment of the Direct001 light in viewports

Creating Background

In this section, you will create a background for the scene across the window.

1. Choose **Rendering > Environment** from the menu bar; the **Environment and Effects** dialog box is displayed.

2. The **Environment** tab is chosen by default in the **Environment and Effects** dialog box. In the **Background** area of the **Common Parameters** rollout, choose the **Environment Map** button that is currently labeled as **None**; the **Material/Map Browser** dialog box is displayed.

3. Select the **Bitmap** map and choose the **OK** button; the **Select Bitmap Image File** dialog box is displayed. As the project folder is already set, the *images* folder is displayed in the **Look in** drop-down list of this dialog box. Select the **CLOUDS4.jpg** file and choose the **Open** button; the selected image is displayed in the background after rendering. Close the **Environment and Effects** dialog box.

Saving and Rendering the Scene

In this section, you will save the scene and then render it. You can also view the final rendered image of this model by downloading the file *c13_3dsmax_2017_rndr.zip* from *www.cadcim.com*. The path of the file is as follows: *Textbooks > Animation and Visual Effects > 3ds Max > Autodesk 3ds Max 2017: A Comprehensive Guide*

1. Choose **Save** from the **Application** menu. Activate the Camera001 viewport.

2. Choose the **Render Production** tool in the **Main Toolbar**; the **Rendered Frame** window is displayed, showing the final output of the scene, as shown in Figure 13-66.

Figure 13-66 The final output after rendering

3. Close this window.

Tutorial 3

In this tutorial, you will illuminate a night scene of a room using photometric lights, refer to Figure 13-67. **(Expected time: 30 min)**

The following steps are required to complete this tutorial:

a. Create the project folder.
b. Open the file.
c. Create the roof light.
d. Create wall lights.
e. Save and render the scene.

Creating the Project Folder

1. Create a project folder with the name *c13_tut3* in the *3dsmax2017* folder, as discussed in Tutorial 1 of Chapter 2.

2. Open Windows Explorer and then browse to *\Documents\c13_3dsmax_2017_tut*. Next, copy all jpeg files to *\Documents\3dsmax2017\c13_tut3\sceneassets\images*. Also, copy *1.IES* file to *\Documents\3dsmax2017\c13_tut3\sceneassets\photometric*.

Figure 13-67 The illuminated night scene of a room

Opening the File

1. Choose **Open** from the **Application** menu; the **Open File** dialog box is displayed. In this dialog box, browse to the location *\Documents\c13_3dsmax_2017_tut* and select the **c13_tut3_start.max** file from it. Choose the **Open** button to open the file, refer to Figure 13-68.

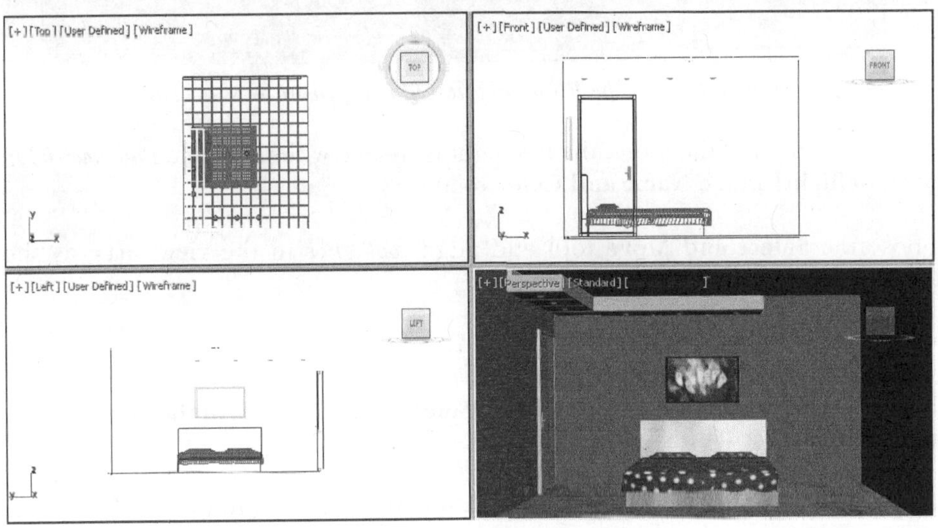

Figure 13-68 The c13_tut3_start.max file

2. Choose **Save As** from the **Application** menu; the **Save File As** dialog box is displayed. Browse to the location *\Documents\3dsmax2017\c13_tut3\scenes*. Save the file with the name *c13tut3.max* at this location.

Creating the Roof Light

In this section, you will create the roof light by using the **Free Light** tool. You will also change the renderer from scanline renderer to mental ray renderer.

1. Choose the **Render Setup** tool from the **Main Toolbar**; the **Render Setup: Default Scanline Renderer** dialog box is displayed.

2. In this dialog box, click on the **Renderer** drop-down list and select **NVIDIA mental ray**; the **Default Scanline Renderer** is changed to **NVIDIA mental ray** renderer.

3. Choose the **Maximize Viewport Toggle** tool to view all the viewports and activate the Top viewport. Choose **Create > Lights** from the **Command Panel**. By default, the **Photometric** option is displayed in the drop-down list below the **Lights** button.

4. Choose the **Free Light** tool from the **Object Type** rollout; the **Photometric Light Creation** message box is displayed, refer to Figure 13-69. Next, choose **Yes** from this message box. Also, various rollouts are displayed in the **Command Panel**.

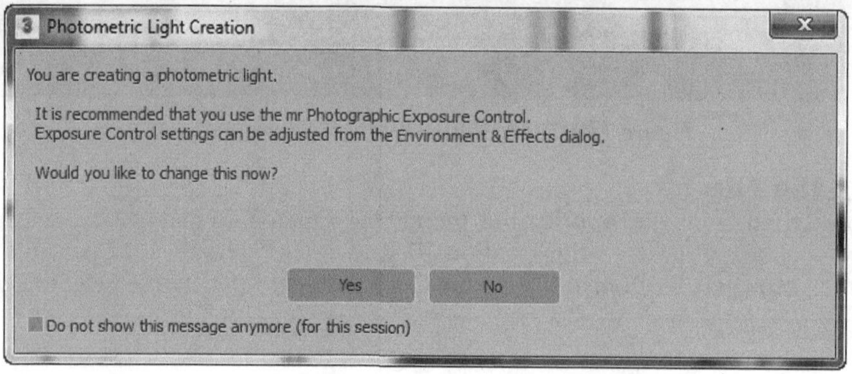

Figure 13-69 *The* ***Photometric Light Creation*** *message box*

5. Click at the center of the room; the free light is created with the name *PhotometricLight001*. Enter **rooflight1** in the **Name and Color** rollout.

6. Choose the **Select and Move** tool and align *rooflight1* in the viewports, as shown in Figure 13-70.

   Next, you will modify the shape of *rooflight1*.

7. Choose the **Modify** tab in the **Command Panel.** Next, in the **Templates** area, select **40W Bulb** from the drop-down list.

8. In the **Emit light from (Shape)** area of the **Shape/Area Shadows** rollout, make sure the **Point** option is selected in the drop-down list.

   Next, you will modify the parameters of *rooflight1* to lit the room with proper intensity, colors, and shadows.

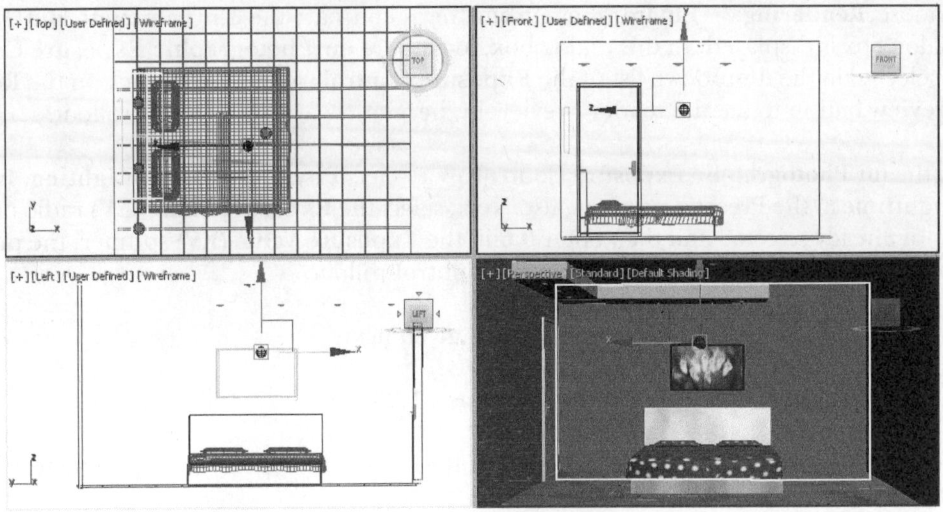

Figure 13-70 The rooflight1 aligned in the viewports

9. In the **General Parameters** rollout, make sure the **On** check box is selected in the **Shadows** area. Next, select **Ray Traced Shadows** in the drop-down list below this check box.

10. In the **Shadow Parameters** rollout, enter **0.7** in the **Dens.** spinner. Next, choose the **Color** color swatch; the **Color Selector: Shadow Color** dialog box is displayed. In this dialog box, enter **15** in the **Red**, **Green**, and **Blue** spinners and then choose the **OK** button to close the dialog box.

11. Make sure the **Uniform Spherical** option is selected in the drop-down list located in the **Light Distribution (Type)** area.
The **Uniform Spherical** option is used to spread light in all directions.

12. Make sure the **Kelvin** radio button is selected.

13. Set the value **6500** in the **Kelvin** spinner; the color swatch located next to the **Kelvin** spinner is changed to white. Next, choose the **Filter Color** color swatch located below it; the **Color Selector: Filter Color** dialog box is displayed. In this dialog box, make sure the value in the **Red**, **Green**, and **Blue** spinners is set to **255** and then choose the **OK** button to close the dialog box.

Note

*The value in the **Kelvin** spinner and the color in the **Filter Color** color swatch together define the color shade of the light being created. You can use different combinations of the spinner value and color shade in the color swatch to achieve a variety of light color shades.*

Next, you will set the intensity of *rooflight1*.

14. In the **Intensity** area of the **Intensity/Color/Attenuation** rollout, select the **lm** radio button; the value in the first spinner located below the **lm** radio button changes and displays the intensity of the light in Lumen. Next, set the value **40** in this spinner; the intensity of the light is changed.

15. Choose **Rendering > Environment** from the menu bar; the **Environment and Effects** dialog box is displayed. In this dialog box, Make sure **mr Photographic Exposure Control** is selected in the drop-down list of the **Exposure Control** rollout. Next, click on the **Render Preview** button to see the render preview in the window available in this rollout.

16. In the **mr Photographic Exposure Control** area, select **Physically Based Lighting, Indoor Nighttime** in the **Preset** drop-down list. Next, select the **Exposure Value (EV)** radio button, if not already selected and then enter **0.6** in the **Exposure Value (EV)** spinner; the preview of the render is updated in the **Exposure Control** rollout.

17. In the **Image Control** area, set the values as given next:

    Highlights (Burn): **0.5** Midtones: **1.25** Shadows: **0.1**

    Now, you will render the scene to view the effect of modifying *rooflight1* parameters in the scene.

18. Activate the perspective viewport. Next, choose the **Render Production** tool from the **Main Toolbar**; the rendered image is displayed, refer to Figure 13-71.

Figure 13-71 The rendered image

Creating Wall Lights

In this section, you will create wall lights by using the **Target Light** tool. You will also use IES file to achieve a specific light pattern.

1. Switch from the Left viewport to the Right viewport. Now, activate the Front viewport. Choose **Create > Lights** from the **Command Panel**. Next, choose the **Target Light** tool from the **Object Type** rollout; various rollouts are displayed in the **Command Panel**.

2. Click at a point and drag the cursor downward. Next, release the left mouse button; a target light is created. In the **Name and Color** rollout, enter **spot light1**. Next, choose the **Select and Move** tool and then select *spot light1* and *spot light1.Target*. Now, align them in the viewports, as shown in Figure 13-72.

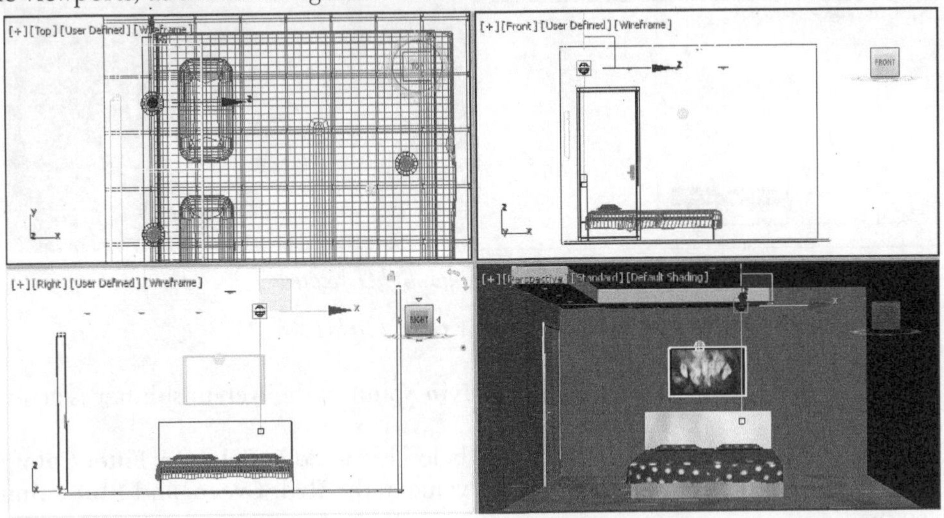

Figure 13-72 *The spot light1 and spot light1.Target aligned in the viewports*

Next, you need to modify the parameters of *spot light1*.

3. Select *spot light1* and then choose the **Modify** tab in the **Command Panel**. In the **General Parameters** rollout, select the **Photometric Web** option in the drop-down list from the **Light Distribution (Type)** area; a **Distribution (Photometric Web)** rollout is displayed in the **Command Panel**.

   Now, you will use a standard photometric IES file to create a specific lighting pattern.

   These IES files are standard files provided by light manufacturers and are available on the internet for free download.

4. In the **Emit light from (Shape)** area of the **Shape/Area Shadows** rollout, make sure the **Point** option is selected in the drop-down list.

5. Choose the **< Choose Photometric File >** button from the **Distribution (Photometric Web)** rollout; the **Open a Photometric Web File** dialog box is displayed. As the project folder is already set, the *photometric* folder of this project is displayed in the **Look in** drop-down list. Next, select the **1.ies** file from this dialog box and then choose the **Open** button; the label of the button is replaced by the name of the selected file. Also, the lighting pattern is displayed in the window located above this button. Next, set the value in the **Y Rotation** spinner to rotate *spot light1*, as shown in Figure 13-73.

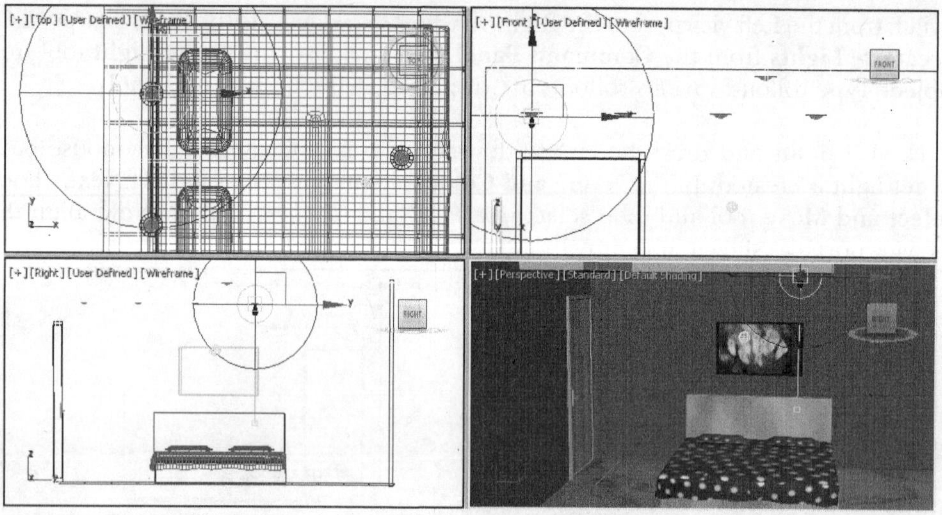

Figure 13-73 *The spot light1 rotated*

Next, you need to set the intensity and color of *spot light1*.

6. Select the radio button located near the **Kelvin** Spinner; the **Kelvin** spinner is activated.

7. Choose the **Filter Color** color swatch located below it; the **Color Selector: Filter Color** dialog box is displayed. In this dialog box, set the value in the **Red**, **Green**, and **Blue** spinners as given next:

   Red: **164** Green: **165** Blue: **112**

   Choose the **OK** button to close the dialog box; the color in the **Filter Color** color swatch is changed.

8. In the **Intensity** area of the **Intensity/Color/Attenuation** rollout, select the **lm** radio button; the value in the first spinner located below this radio button changes and displays the intensity of the light in Lumen. Next, set the value **4** in this spinner.

9. In the **Far Attenuation** area of the **Intensity/Color/Attenuation** rollout, select the **Use** and **Show** check boxes. Next, set **10** and **34** in the **Start** and **End** spinners, respectively.

10. Activate the Perspective viewport. Next, choose the **Render Production** tool from the **Main Toolbar** to view the render.

    Next, you will add glow to the source of *spot light1*.

11. Choose **Rendering > Material Editor > Compact Material Editor** from the menu bar; the **Material Editor** dialog box is displayed. In this dialog box, choose **Utilities > Reset Material Editor Slots** from the Material Editor menu bar; all slots in the **Material Editor** dialog box are empty. Now, select any empty slot in it and modify its name in the **Material Name** text box to *lamp dome material*.

12. Select the **Color** check box in the **Self-Illumination** area of the **Blinn Basic Parameters** rollout. Next, choose the **Color** color swatch and change its color to white.

13. Choose the **Diffuse** and **Specular** color swatches from the **Blinn Basic Parameters** rollout and change its color to white.

14. Set the value **81** in the **Specular Level** spinner and **51** in the **Glossiness** spinner of the **Blinn Basic Parameters** rollout.

15. Select *lamp holder dome* from the Scene Explorer. Next, choose the **Assign Material to Selection** button from the **Material Editor** dialog box; the self illuminating material is applied to *lamp holder dome*.

16. Choose the **Render Production** tool from the **Main Toolbar**; the rendered image is displayed, as shown in Figure 13-74. You will notice glow at the source of *spot light1*.

Figure 13-74 *The rendered image*

17. Activate the Right viewport and select *spot light1* and *spot light1.Target*. Next, press and hold the SHIFT key and drag the cursor to the adjacent lamp holder located at the left of *spot light1*. Release the left mouse button; the **Clone Options** dialog box is displayed. In this dialog box, select the **Copy** radio button. Set the value **2** in the **Number of Copies** spinner and choose the **OK** button; two copies of *spot light1* and *spot light1.Target* are created in the viewports. Next, choose the **Select and Move** tool and align these lights in the viewports, as shown in Figure 13-75.

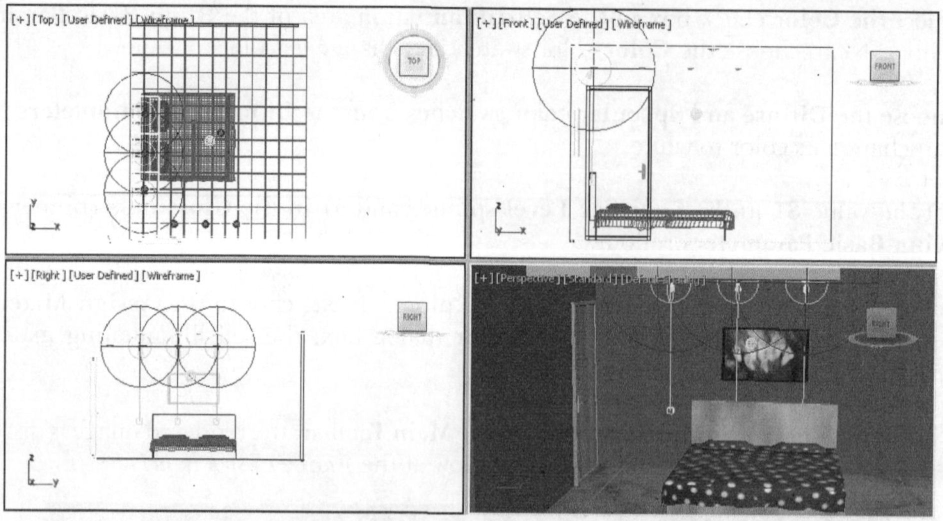

Figure 13-75 Copies of spot light1 and spot light1.Target aligned in the viewports

18. Assign the *lamp dome material* to *lamp holder dome 001, lamp holder dome 002* and *lamp holder dome 006* to add glow at the source of lights in the scene.

Note
You can create copies of spot light1 and spot light1.Target and place them at the remaining spot lights of the false ceiling. You need to assign the lamp dome material to remaining lamp holder domes.

Saving and Rendering the Scene

In this section, you will save the scene and then render it. You can also view the final rendered image of this model by downloading the file *c13_3dsmax_2017_rndr.zip* from *www.cadcim.com.* The path of the file is as follows: *Textbooks > Animation and Visual Effects > 3ds Max > Autodesk 3ds Max 2017: A Comprehensive Guide*

1. Choose **Save** from the **Application** menu.

2. Activate the Perspective viewport. Next, choose the **Render Production** tool from the **Main Toolbar**; the rendered image is displayed, refer to Figure 13-76.

   You can improve the rendered output further by performing the following steps:

3. Drag the rendered frame window upward to see the parameters available below it. Next, move the slider below the **Final Gather Precision** text box toward right so that **Low** is displayed in that text box.

4. In the **Trace/Bounces Limits** area, enter **2** in the **FG Bounces** spinner. Next, render the output. You will notice the change in the rendered output.

Figure 13-76 The rendered image

Tutorial 4

In this tutorial, you will set up a daylight exterior scene, refer to Figures 13-77.

(Expected time: 30 min)

The following steps are required to complete this tutorial:

a. Create the project folder.
b. Open the file.
c. Set up physical camera settings.
d. Set up the skylight.
e. Set up the daylight system.
f. Save and render the scene.

Creating the Project Folder

1. Create a project folder with the name *c13_tut4* in the *3dsmax2017* folder, as discussed in Tutorial 1 of Chapter 2.

2. Open Windows Explorer and then browse to *\Documents\c13_3dsmax_2017_tut*. Next, copy all jpeg files to *\Documents\3dsmax2017\c13_tut4\sceneassets\images*.

Figure 13-77 The daylight exterior scene

Opening the File

1. Choose **Open** from the **Application** menu; the **Open File** dialog box is displayed. In this dialog box, browse to the location *\Documents\c13_3dsmax_2017_tut* and select the **c13_tut4_start.max** file from it. Choose the **Open** button to open the file, refer to Figure 13-78.

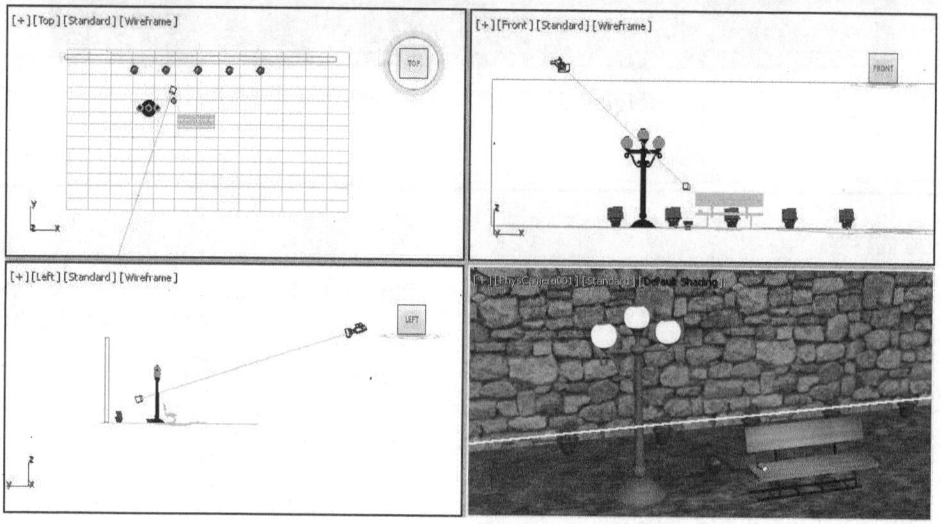

Figure 13-78 The c13_tut4_start.max file

2. Choose **Save As** from the **Application** menu; the **Save File As** dialog box is displayed. Browse to the location *\Documents\3dsmax2017\c13_tut4\scenes*. Save the file with the name *c13tut4.max* at this location.

Setting Up Physical Camera Settings

1. Choose **Rendering > Environment** from menu bar; the **Environment and Effects** dialog box is displayed.

2. Select **Physical Camera Exposure Control** from the drop-down list in the **Exposure Control** rollout, if not already selected; the **Physical Camera Exposure Control** rollout is added in the **Environment and Effects** dialog box.

3. In this rollout, enter **8** in the **Exposure Value** spinner of the **Global Exposure** area.

4. Choose the **Render Preview** button from the **Exposure Control** rollout; the render preview is displayed in the window of this rollout, as shown in Figure 13-79. Minimize the **Environment and Effects** dialog box.

5. Render the PhysCamera001 viewport; the rendered image is displayed, as shown in Figure 13-80.

Figure 13-79 *The render preview displayed*

Figure 13-80 *The rendered image*

Setting up the Skylight

1. Activate the Top viewport. Choose **Create > Lights** in the **Command Panel** and select the **Standard** option from the drop-down list. Next, choose the **skylight** tool from the **Object Type** rollout. Next, click in the Top viewport; the skylight is displayed in the viewport and it is automatically named as *Sky001*.

2. Choose the **Modify** tab from the **Command Panel**. In the **Skylight Parameters** area, enter **0.3** in the **Multiplier** spinner. Next, choose the color swatch located next to the **Sky Color** radio button; the **Color Selector: Color** dialog box is displayed. Enter the following values in this dialog box.

   Red: **236** Green: **223** Blue:**173**

   Choose the **OK** button to close the **Color Selector: Color** dialog box.

3. Select the **Cast Shadows** check box from the **Render** area. Also, enter **5** in the **Rays per Sample** spinner.

4. Render the PhysCamera001 viewport; the rendered image is displayed, refer to Figure 13-81.

Figure 13-81 The rendered image

Setting Up the Daylight System

1. Activate the Top viewport. Choose **Create > Systems** from the **Command Panel** and make sure the **Standard** option is selected in the drop-down list. Next, choose the **Daylight** tool from the **Object Type** rollout.

Note

You will learn the Daylight System in detail in Chapter 15.

2. Click at a point in the Top viewport. Next, drag the cursor to create a compass and then release the left mouse button. Now, drag the cursor to specify the height and click again; the daylight system is added in the scene and automatically named as *Daylight001*.

3. Choose the **Modify** tab from the **Command Panel**. You will notice that **Skylight** is selected in the **Skylight** drop-down list.

4. Select the **Show Cone** check box in the **Directional Parameters** rollout to see the cone in the viewport. Also, make sure that the **Circle** radio button is selected in this rollout.

5. Adjust the value in the **Falloff/Field** spinner so that the scene is covered inside the cone, refer to Figure 13-82.

6. In the **Shadows** area of the **General Parameters** rollout, select **Area Shadows** from the drop-down list.

7. In the **Shadow Parameters** rollout, enter **0.7** in the **Dens.** spinner.

8. Choose the **Setup** button from the **Position** area of the **Daylight Parameters** rollout; the **Assign Controller** and **Control Parameters** rollouts are displayed in the **Command Panel**.

9. In the **Time** area of the **Control Parameters** rollout, enter **9** in the **Hours** spinner.

10. In the **Location** area of the **Control Parameters** rollout, enter **96** in the **North Direction** spinner.

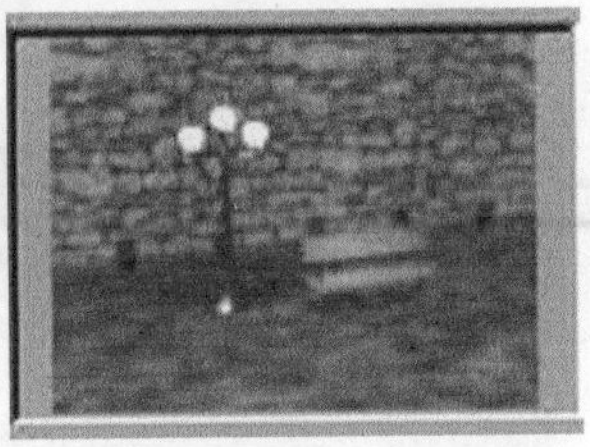

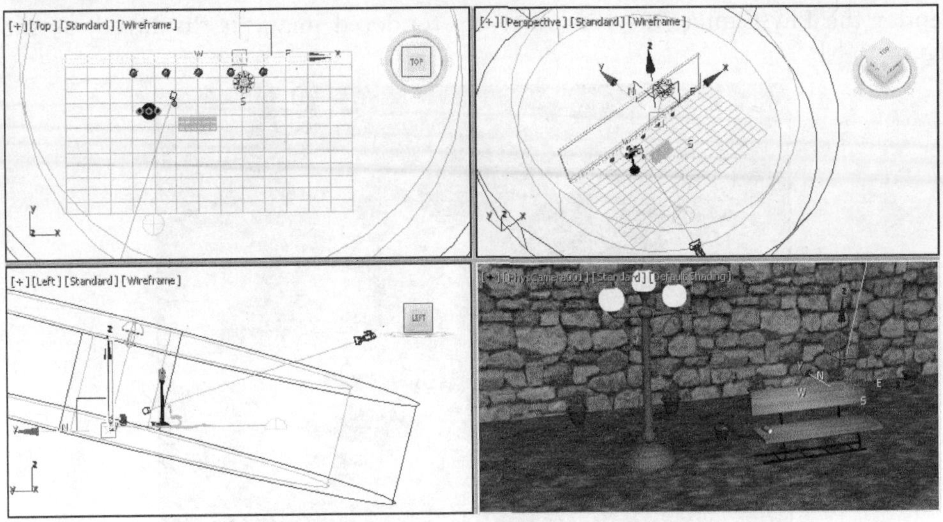

Figure 13-82 The Daylight cone adjusted

11. In the **Site** area of the **Control Parameters** rollout, enter **614** in the **Orbit Scale** spinner. Figure 13-83 shows the position of *Daylight001* in the viewports.

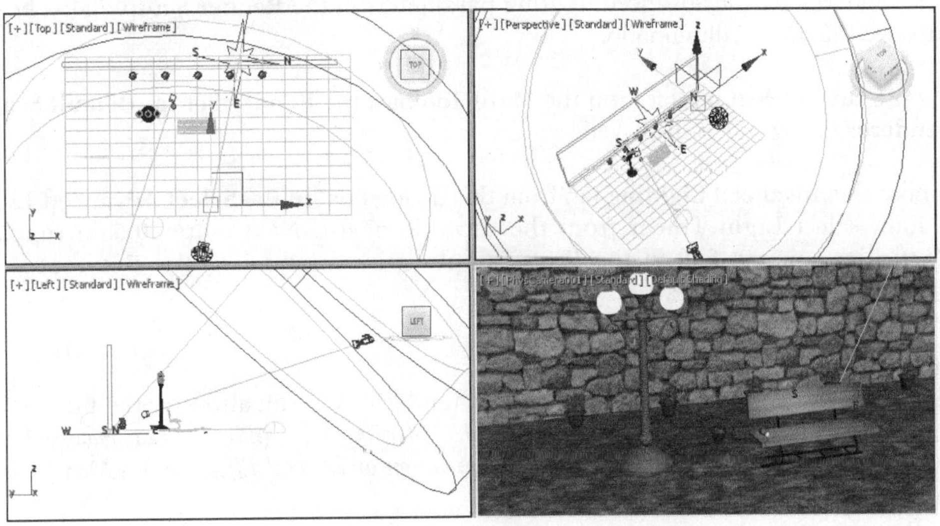

Figure 13-83 The Daylight cone adjusted

Next, you will see the render preview in the **Environment and Effects** dialog box.

12. Choose the **Render Preview** button from the **Exposure Control** rollout of the **Environment and Effects** dialog box. You will notice that the scene appears burned in the preview displayed in the window of this rollout.

13. Enter **13** in the **Exposure for all Cameras/Views** spinner; the preview in the window is changed. Close the **Environment and Effects** dialog box.

14. Render the PhysCamera001 viewport; the rendered image is displayed, as shown in Figure 13-84.

Figure 13-84 The rendered image

Next, you will use the advanced lighting parameters in the **Render Setup** dialog box to improve the overall illumination.

15. Choose **Render Setup** tool from the **Main Toolbar**; the **Render Setup: Default Scanline Renderer** dialog box is displayed.

16. Choose the **Advanced Lighting** tab from this dialog box. In the **Select Advanced Lighting** rollout, select **Light Tracer** from the drop-down list. Next, enter **0.5** in the **Global Multiplier** spinner, **350** in the **Rays/Sample** spinner, and **1** in the **Bounces** spinner. Next, close the dialog box.

Saving and Rendering the Scene

In this section, you will save the scene and then render it. You can also view the final rendered image of this scene by downloading the file *c13_3dsmax_2017_rndr.zip* from *www.cadcim.com*. The path of the file is as follows: *Textbooks > Animation and Visual Effects > 3ds Max > Autodesk 3ds Max 2017: A Comprehensive Guide*

1. Choose **Save** from the **Application** menu.

2. Activate the PhysCamera viewport. Next, choose the **Render Production** tool from the **Main Toolbar**; the rendered image is displayed, refer to Figure 13-85.

Figure 13-85 The final output

Self-Evaluation Test

Answer the following questions and then compare them to those given at the end of this chapter:

1. Which of the following tools is used to create the photometric lights?

   (a) **Target Light** (b) **Free Light**
   (c) **mr Sky Portal** (d) All of these

2. Which of the following spinners is used to define the intensity of the light in the **Intensity/Color/Attenuation** rollout?

   (a) **Color Amount** (b) **Start**
   (c) **Multiplier** (d) None of these

3. Which of the following tools is used to create the area omni light?

   (a) **Target spot** (b) **mr Area Omni**
   (c) **Free Direct** (d) None of these

4. To assign special effects to the environment such as fog and glow, you need to use the __________ rollout in the **Modify** tab of the **Command Panel**.

5. To view the shadow of an object, you need to select the __________ check box in the __________ area of the **General Parameters** rollout.

6. The options in the _________ rollout are used to control the properties of the shadow.

7. The **Target Spot** tool is the only tool used to create a spot light. (T/F)

8. The standard lights use the light energy values to create realistic scenes. (T/F)

9. The **Exclude** button is used to define the number of objects in a scene that will be affected by the light on rendering. (T/F)

10. The decrease in the intensity of light with distance is called attenuation. (T/F)

Review Questions

Answer the following questions:

1. Which of the following tools is used to align light with an object for positioning its highlight accurately?

   (a) **Place Highlight** (b) **Align**
   (c) **Align Camera** (d) None of these

2. Which of the following rollouts is not used with the photometric lights?

   (a) **Intensity/Color/Attenuation** (b) **Atmospheres & Effects**
   (c) **Shadow Parameters** (d) All of these

3. Which of the following is a type of camera used in Autodesk 3ds Max?

   (a) Target camera (b) Free camera
   (c) Physical (d) All of the above

4. In the **Parameters** rollout of the target camera, set the value in the _________ spinner to specify the field of view for the camera in degrees.

5. To display the camera view in the viewport, you need to press the _________ key.

6. The _________ tool in the **Main Toolbar** is used to align a camera with a selected face normal of an object.

7. In the **Name and Color** rollout of the lights, you can use the color swatch to modify the color of the light. (T/F)

8. The distance between the camera lens and its focus is called the focal length of the lens. (T/F)

EXERCISES

The rendered output of the models used in the following exercises can be accessed by downloading the *c13_3dsmax_2017_exr.zip* file from *www.cadcim.com*. The path of the file is as follows: *Textbooks > Animation and Visual Effects > 3ds Max > Autodesk 3ds Max 2017: A Comprehensive Guide*

Exercise 1

Create a scene using the standard primitives and target spot lights, as shown in Figure 13-86.

(Expected time: 15 min)

Figure 13-86 *The target spot lights illuminating the wall*

Exercise 2

Create a scene using the standard primitives and target spot lights, as shown in Figure 13-87.

(Expected time: 30 min)

Figure 13-87 *Various lights illuminating the room*

Hints:

1. Create the hollow effect on the roof using the **ProBoolean** compound object and use the **Free Point** photometric light.

2. Create a **Target Spot** standard light for highlighting the object. You need to add the **Volume** effect using the **Atmospheres & Effects** rollout for the projector effect. Also, apply the projector map using the **Advanced Effects** rollout to get a realistic effect.

Exercise 3

Create a scene using the standard primitives and target spot lights, as shown in Figure 13-88. **(Expected time: 15 min)**

Figure 13-88 *The scene illuminated by the spot lights*

Hint:

1. Create three target spot lights and adjust their positions in all viewports. Choose separate colors for all three lights using the color swatch in the **Intensity/Color/Attenuation** rollout.

Answers to Self-Evaluation Test

1. d, **2.** c, **3.** b, **4. Atmospheres & Effects**, **5. On, Shadows**, **6. Shadow Parameters**, **7.** F, **8.** F, **9.** T, **10.** T

14

Animation Basics

Learning Objectives

After completing this chapter, you will be able to:

- *Work with the time slider*
- *Use animation playback controls*
- *Use animation and time controls*
- *Morph compound object*
- *Render and preview an animation*
- *Apply various rendering effects to a scene*

INTRODUCTION

The basic concept of computer animation is to define different positions, rotations, and scaling of an object at different key points in a sequence in the time slider. These defined points are known as keyframes. The interpolation between the keyframes consists of the information of the actions performed between those keyframes. When you play the animation, the computer plays a series of frames quickly and the object seems to be moving.

In 3ds Max, the standard frame rate is 30 frames per second. It means, if you want to create an animation for one minute, then you need to adjust about 1,800 frames. Therefore, before starting an animation, you need to calculate the frames according to the time limit. Using this software, you can create character animation and animation based on different types of motions that you see in real life. You can also create special lighting effects in the scene by animating lights and cameras. In this chapter, you will learn basics of animation.

TIME SLIDER AND ANIMATION PLAYBACK CONTROLS

3ds Max provides various options to animate objects that you create in it. To do so, you need to be familiar with the animation playback controls and time slider. These controls enable you to play, pause, and stop an animation. They are available at the lower right corner of the 3ds Max interface and are discussed here briefly.

Time Slider

The time slider displays the current frame and the total number of frames in the current time segment, refer to Figure 14-1. You can view the animation at each frame by dragging the time slider.

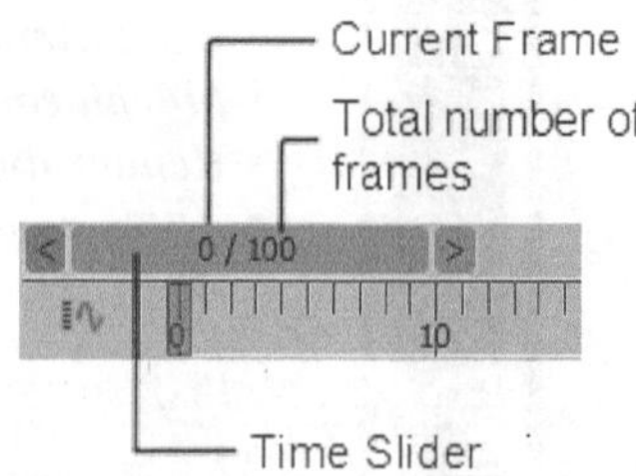

Figure 14-1 *The time slider*

Note

The time segment is the total range of frames that you can access using the time slider. By default, it ranges from 0 to 100. You can set the range using the ***Time Configuration*** *dialog box. You will learn about this dialog box in the later section.*

Animation Playback Controls

The animation playback controls are used to play and stop the animation in the active viewport. These controls are discussed next.

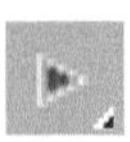

The **Play Animation** button is used to play or start the animation in the active viewport. When you click on the **Play Animation** button, it turns into a stop button.

The **Stop Animation** button is used to stop the animation. This button is displayed when you play the animation.

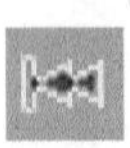

The **Go to Start** button is used to set the time slider at the first frame of the active time segment.

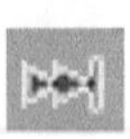

The **Go to End** button is used to set the time slider at the last frame of the active time segment.

The **Previous Frame** button is used to move the time slider one frame at a time in the reverse direction. You can view the current frame on the time slider when it moves from one frame to another.

The **Next Frame** button is used to move the time slider one frame at a time in the forward direction.

UNDERSTANDING ANIMATION AND TIME CONTROLS

In 3ds Max, different types of tools are available at the bottom of the screen to control animation and its time settings, refer to Figure 14-2. You have already learned about the time slider and the animation playback controls in the previous section. The other controls are discussed next.

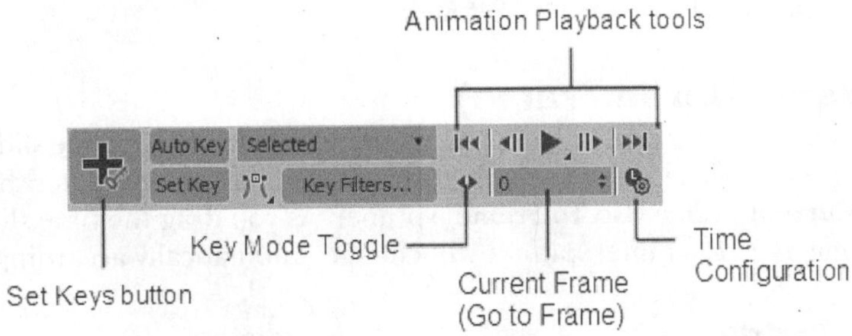

Figure 14-2 The time control tools

Toggle Auto Key Mode

The **Toggle Auto Key Mode** button, which is labeled as **Auto Key**, is used to turn on the auto key animation mode. When you choose the **Toggle Auto Key Mode** button, it turns red. Also, the background of the time slider and the border of the active viewport turns red, indicating that you are in the animation mode. Now, if you make any changes in the object, the changes will be keyframed in the time slider.

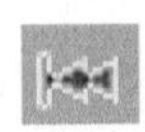

To perform an animation using the **Toggle Auto Key Mode** button, first you need to make sure that the object that you want to animate is selected in the viewport. Choose the **Go to Start** button to set the time slider to the first frame. Next, choose the **Toggle Auto Key Mode** button to turn on the auto key animation mode; it will turn red. Now, drag the time slider to a frame other than 0 and animate the selected object by modifying its parameters or by transforming the object; a keyframe will be created on that frame and at frame 0 on the track bar below the time slider. Again, move the time slider to another frame and change the parameters. You can continue this process until you get all the keyframes in a sequential order for your animation. Next, choose the **Toggle Auto Key Mode** button again to turn it off. Choose the **Play Animation** button to view the animation of the selected object in the current viewport.

Toggle Set Key Mode

The **Toggle Set Key Mode** button that is labeled as **Set Key** is used to turn on the set key animation mode. In this mode, you need to set keys for the animation of the selected object by choosing the **Set Keys** button on the left side of the **Toggle Set Key Mode** button.

To perform an animation using the **Toggle Set Key Mode** button, select the object in the viewport that you want to animate. Choose the **Go to Start** button to set the time slider to the first frame. Next, choose the **Toggle Set Key Mode** button to turn on the set key animation mode; the button will turn red. Choose the **Set Keys** button; it will flash in red color and a keyframe will be set for the current position of the selected object. Now, drag the time slider to set a frame other than 0 and animate the selected object. Again, choose the **Set Keys** button; it will flash in red color and another keyframe will be set on the track bar for the changed position. You can continue this process until you get all the keyframes in a sequential order for your animation. Then, choose the **Toggle Set Key Mode** button to turn it off. Also, choose the **Play Animation** button to view the animation of the selected object in the current viewport.

Note
*If you transform an object when the **Toggle Set Key Mode** button is chosen, then the keyframe will be set only when you choose the **Set Keys** button.*

Current Frame (Go To Frame)

The value in this spinner shows the current frame number at which the time slider is positioned. While animating your scene, if you want to go to another frame, you can enter the frame number directly in the **Current Frame (Go To Frame)** spinner. As you drag the time slider, the value in the Current Frame (Go To Frame) spinner will change automatically according to its position.

Key Mode Toggle

By default, the **Key Mode Toggle** button is not activated. If activated, it allows you to jump between the keyframes directly. To understand the function of this button, you need to select the animated object in the viewport. Next, choose the **Key Mode Toggle** button; the **Previous Frame** and **Next Frame** buttons in the animation playback controls will be replaced with the **Previous Key** and **Next Key** buttons, refer to Figures 14-3 and 14-4. Choose the **Previous Key** or **Next Key** button to move the time slider from one keyframe to the other.

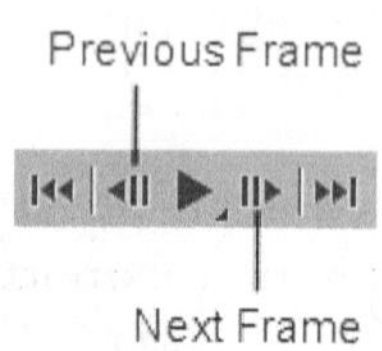

***Figure 14-3** Animation playback controls before choosing the **Key Mode Toggle** button*

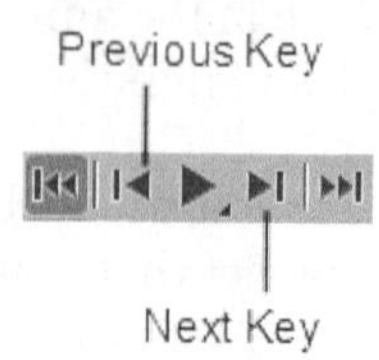

***Figure 14-4** Animation playback controls after choosing the **Key Mode Toggle** button*

Time Configuration

The **Time Configuration** button is used to set the length of an animation by defining the number of frames in the track bar. It is also used to set the frame rate, time display, and so on.

To set these parameters, choose the **Time Configuration** button; the **Time Configuration** dialog box will be displayed, as shown in Figure 14-5. You need to use the options in this dialog box to set the animation length, frame rate, and time display. The options in this dialog box are discussed next.

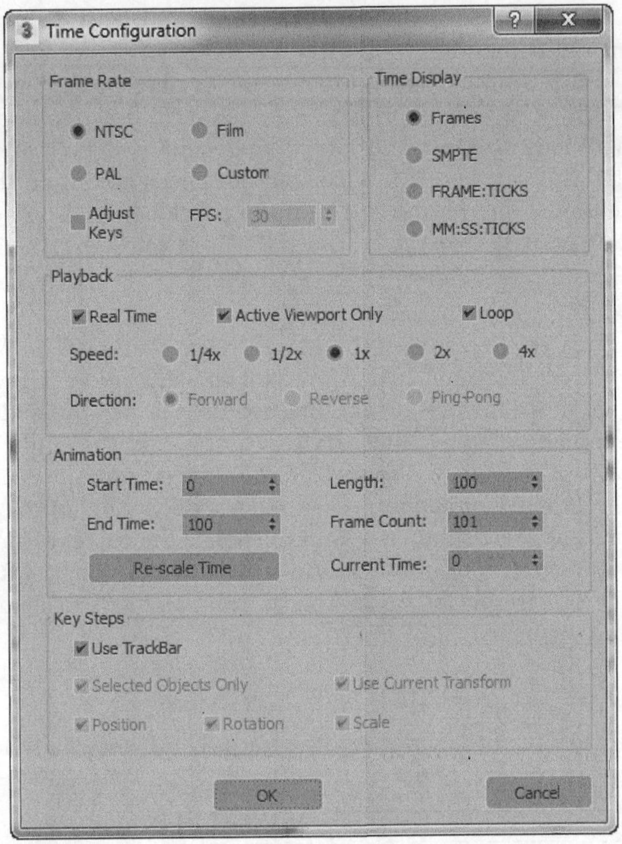

*Figure 14-5 The **Time Configuration** dialog box*

Frame Rate Area

There are four radio buttons in this area, namely **NTSC**, **Film**, **PAL**, and **Custom**. These radio buttons are used to define a particular frame rate for the animation in frames per second. By default, the **NTSC** radio button is selected. On selecting the **Custom** radio button, the **FPS** spinner is activated wherein you can specify the frame rate in seconds for the animation. If you select the **Adjust Keys** check box, 3ds Max scales the keys to whole frame when you rescale the animation length.

Time Display Area

The radio buttons in this area are used to define the method of time displayed in the time slider. The radio buttons in this area are **Frames**, **SMPTE**, **FRAME: TICKS**, and **MM:SS: TICKS**. By default, the **Frames** radio button is selected.

Playback Area

This area is used to specify the playback speed and the viewport in which the animation will be played. By default, the **Real Time** check box in this area is selected. As a result, animation is played at the selected playback speed and frames are skipped so that the animation synchronizes with the current frame rate settings. You can select one of the radio buttons such as **1/4x**, **1/2x**, and so on in the **Speed** group to define the speed of the animation. If you clear the **Real Time** check box, then the **Speed** group will be deactivated and the **Direction** group will be activated. The radio buttons in the **Direction** group are used to define the direction of the animation. The direction of the animation can be forward, reverse, or ping-pong. The ping-pong direction means that first the animation will be played in the forward direction and then in the reverse direction. The **Active Viewport Only** check box is selected by default and is used to play the animation only in the active viewport. If you clear this check box, then the animation will be simultaneously played in all the viewports. The **Loop** check box is also selected by default and is used to play the animation repeatedly.

Animation Area

The options in this area are used to set the length of animation. The default values in the spinners of this area specify the number of frames for the animation. The **Start Time** and **End Time** spinners are used to specify the current time segment in the time slider. The current time segment is the total range of frames that you can access using the time slider. The **Length** spinner is used to specify the total number of frames in the current time segment or the length of the animation. The **Frame Count** spinner is used to specify the number of frames that will be rendered. The **Current Time** spinner is used to specify the current frame number at which the time slider is positioned. If you choose the **Re-scale Time** button, the **Re-scale Time** dialog box will be displayed. You can specify the options in this dialog box to change the existing time segment to a new time segment.

Track Bar

The track bar lies between the time slider and the status bar. It shows a timeline with the frame numbers in it, as shown in Figure 14-6.

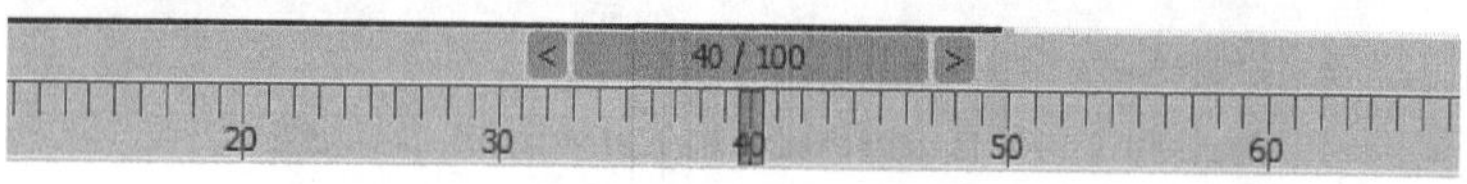

Figure 14-6 Partial view of the track bar

Track View

Menu bar:	Graph Editors > Track View - Curve Editor
	Graph Editors > Track View - Dope Sheet
Main Toolbar:	Curve Editor (Open)

The track view is used to control the animation keys in the animation created by you. You can also insert sound in the scene and create its notes. The track view uses two different modes, **Curve Editor** and **Dope Sheet**. In the **Curve Editor** mode, the animation is displayed as the function curve on a graph, refer to Figure 14-7. In the **Dope Sheet** mode, the animation is displayed as a spreadsheet of keys, refer to Figure 14-8.

To edit the animation of an object using **Curve Editor**, select the animated object and choose the **Curve Editor (Open)** tool from the **Main Toolbar**; the **Track View - Curve Editor** window will be displayed, refer to Figure 14-7. The pull-down menus on the top of this window are used to choose different options to edit the animation. The hierarchy on the left side of this window is used to display all the objects of the scene. To view the sub-options in this tree, you need to

click on the plus sign (+). The edit window on the right of the hierarchy tree is used to edit the animation of the objects using the tangent handles available on the keys found on the curves.

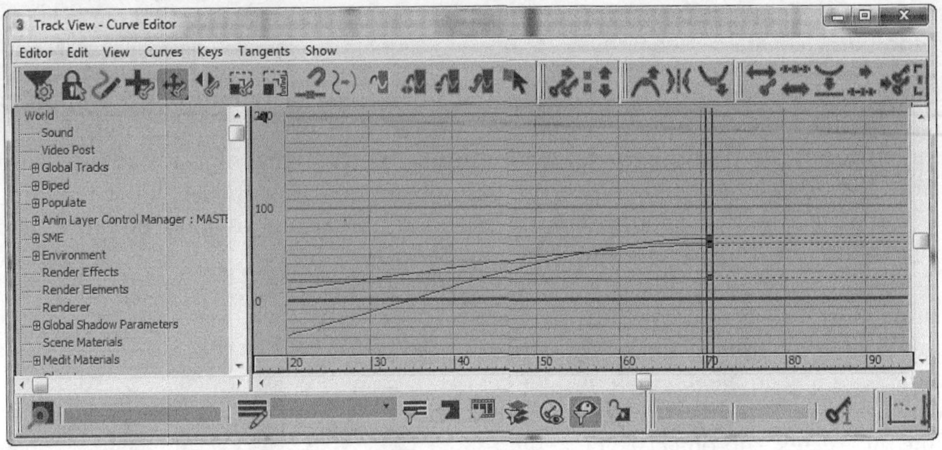

Figure 14-7 The ***Track View - Curve Editor*** *window*

To edit the animation of an object using **Dope Sheet**, select the animated object and choose **Graph Editors > Track View - Dope Sheet** from the menu bar; the **Track View - Dope Sheet** window will be displayed, refer to Figure 14-8.

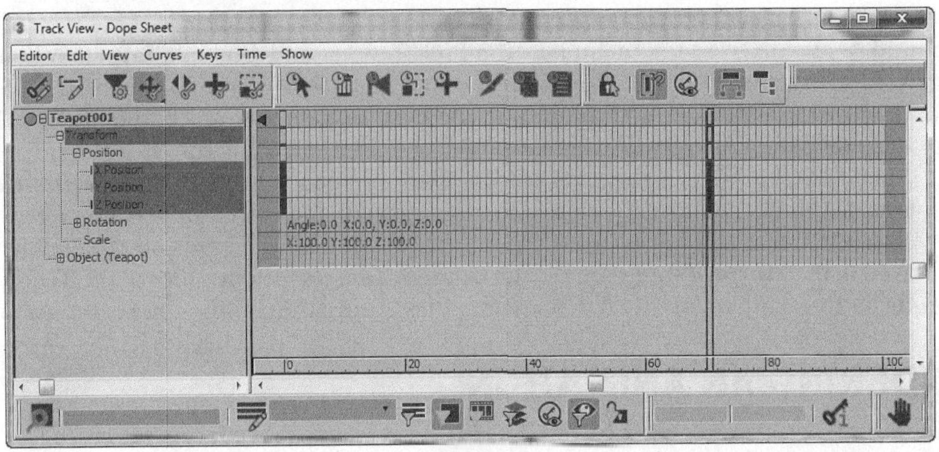

Figure 14-8 The ***Track View - Dope Sheet*** *window*

In this window, you can view all the keys in a spreadsheet format. You need to select the keys and edit them according to the animation.

Tip

You can also invoke ***Track View - Curve Editor*** *in place of the track bar. To do so, choose the* ***Open Mini Curve Editor*** *button on the left side of the track bar.*

MORPH COMPOUND OBJECT

Menu bar:	Create > Compound > Morph
Main Toolbar:	Create > Geometry > Compound Objects > Object Type rollout > Morph

The **Morph** tool is used to create morphing in the objects. The morphing is an animation technique in which the morph object combines two or more objects by matching their vertices in a sequential form to produce the animation result. The original object is known as the base object and the other object into which the base object gets morphed is known as the target object. Note that to perform morphing, the base and target objects must be mesh, patch, or poly objects and they should have the same number of vertices.

To create a morph object, first create an object and convert it into an editable object. This object will be the base object. Next, create two copies of the object and modify their shapes by selecting the **Vertex** sub-object level, refer to Figure 14-9. You can also give the shape of your choice to the objects. These objects will be the target objects. Now, choose the **Toggle Auto Key Mode** button to turn it on and choose the **Go to Start** button to move the time slider to frame 0. Select the base object and choose **Create > Compound > Morph** from the menu bar; the **Pick Targets** and **Current Targets** rollouts will be displayed in the modify panel. Next, set the value **35** in the **Current Frame (Go To Frame)** spinner to move the time slider to frame 35. In the **Pick Targets** rollout, choose the **Pick Target** button and move the cursor over the first target object; a selection cursor will be displayed. Select the first target object in the viewport. Similarly, set the value **70** in the **Current Frame (Go To Frame)** spinner to move the time slider to frame 70 and select the second target object. When you select the target objects in the viewport, the names of the base and target objects will be displayed in the **Morph Targets** area of the **Current Targets** rollout. Choose the **Toggle Auto Key Mode** button again to turn it off. Choose the **Play Animation** button to view the animation.

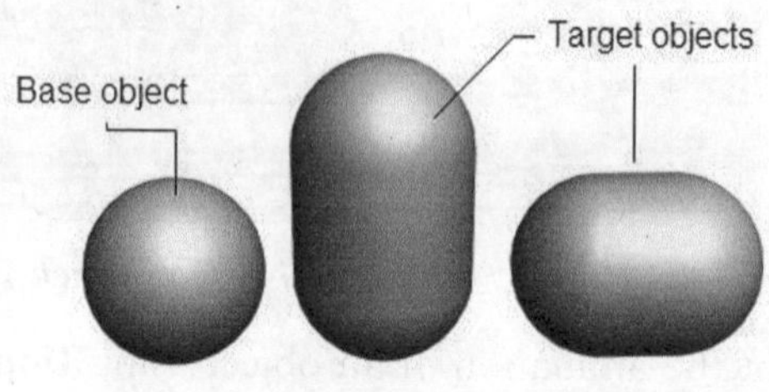

Figure 14-9 *The base and target objects for morphing*

RENDERING AN ANIMATION

Menu bar:	Rendering > Render Setup
Main Toolbar:	Render Setup
Keyboard:	F10

Rendering is a process of generating a 2-dimensional image from a 3-dimensional scene. It shows the lighting effects, materials applied, background, and other settings that you set for the scene. In earlier chapters, you have already learned about the basic rendering for still images. The advanced rendering used for the animated scene is discussed next.

To render the final animation, choose the **Render Setup** tool; the **Render Setup: Scanline Renderer** dialog box will be displayed, as shown in Figure 14-10. The **Common** tab is chosen by default in this dialog box. Set the parameters in different rollouts displayed in the **Common** tab. Also, in the **View to Render** drop-down list located at the top area of this dialog box, select the viewport that you want to render.

Next, choose the **Render** button; the **Perspective, frame 0, Display Gamma:2.2, RGBA Color 16 Bits/Channel (1:1)** dialog box and the **Rendering** dialog box will be invoked, displaying the rendering progress, refer to Figure 14-11. Various options and rollouts in the **Render Setup: Scanline Renderer** dialog box are discussed next.

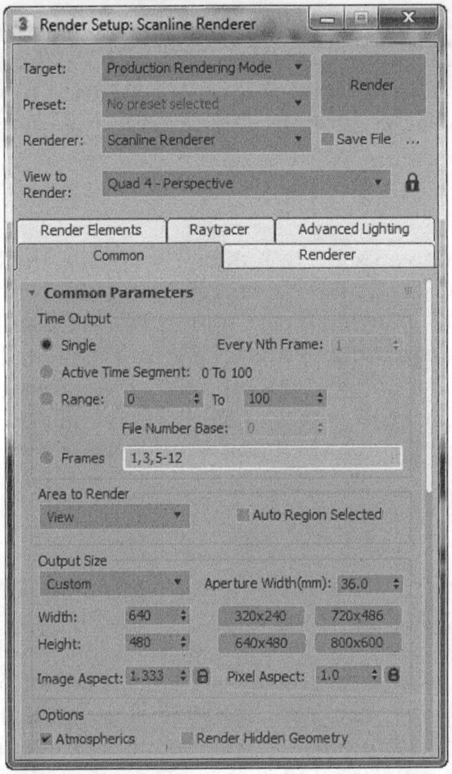

*Figure 14-10 The **Render Setup: Scanline Renderer** dialog box*

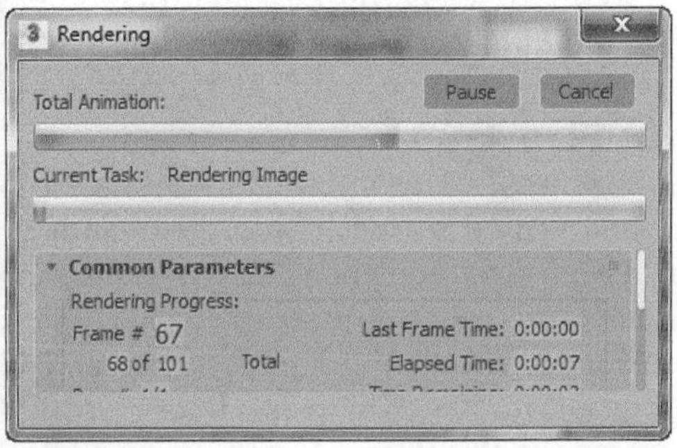

*Figure 14-11 The **Rendering** dialog box*

Target

This drop-down list is used for specifying rendering mode. Some of the rendering modes available in this drop-down list are **Production Rendering Mode**, **Iterative Rendering Mode**, **A360 Cloud Rendering Mode**.

Preset

This drop-down list is used for specifying presets. Some of the presets available in this drop-down list are **3dsmax.scanlight.radiosity.high**, and **lighting.analysis.assistant.preset**. You can also load and save a preset using the **Load Preset** and **Save Preset** options, respectively, from the drop-down list.

Renderer

This drop-down list is used for specifying renderer. By default, the **Scanline renderer** is selected.

View to Render

You can select a view to be rendered from this drop-down list. By default, **Quad 4 - Perspective** is selected in it.

Common Parameters Rollout

There are different types of renderers to render the scene in 3ds Max such as **NVIDIA mental ray** renderer, **VUE File Renderer**, and so on. The options in this rollout are used to set the parameters common for all types of renderers. The commonly used areas in this rollout are discussed next.

Time Output Area

This area is used to set the number of frames that you want to render. By default, the **Single** radio button is selected that enables you to render only a single frame. To render the animation, you need to select the **Active Time Segment** radio button. This radio button renders all the frames in the current time segment. Select the **Range** radio button to specify a range of frames for rendering by entering the start and end frame numbers in the spinners given on the right of this radio button. The **Frames** radio button allows you to render the frame numbers of your choice. To do so, select this radio button and enter the required frame number in the text box given on the right of this radio button.

Output Size Area

The options in this area are used to define the size of the rendered image. The drop-down list in this area is used to specify industry-standard film and video aspect ratios. You can choose one of the formats and then use the remaining group controls to set the output resolution. You can also set the aspect ratio and resolution of your choice by using the **Custom** option. Choose one of the default buttons, **320x240**, **640x480**, **720x486**, or **800x600** to define the size of the output window. When you choose any of these buttons, the corresponding values will be displayed in the **Width** and **Height** spinners. You can also set the values manually in the **Width** and **Height** spinners to define the size.

Options Area

The check boxes in this area are used to filter the options to render for the final output such as atmosphere, lighting effects, and so on.

Advanced Lighting Area

The check boxes in this area are used to select options for using advanced lighting and for computing it on per-frame basis when required.

Bitmap Performance and Memory Options Area

This area is used to decide whether 3ds Max will use the full resolutions maps or the proxies of the maps at rendering. To assign the settings, choose the **Setup** button in this area; the **Global Settings and Defaults for Bitmap Proxies** dialog box will be displayed. You can set the required parameters in this dialog box.

Render Output Area

This area is used to specify a file where the rendered animation can be saved. To do so, choose the **Files** button; the **Render Output File** dialog box will be displayed. Enter the name of the file in the **File name** text box and then select the type of file from the **Save as type** drop-down list. Next, choose the **Save** button. If you have selected the **AVI File (*.avi)** file type, the **AVI File Compression Setup** dialog box will be displayed. Use the default settings and choose the **OK** button; the **Save File** check box will get selected and the path of the file will be displayed just below the **Files** button in the **Render Output** area.

Assign Renderer Rollout

This rollout is used to set the renderer for the scene. The **Production** option is used to assign a renderer for the graphics. The **Material Editor** option is used to assign a renderer for the sample slots in the **Material Editor** dialog box. The **ActiveShade** option is used to assign a renderer for the lighting effects in the scene, refer to Figure 14-12.

To assign the renderer, choose the **Choose Renderer** button on the right of the options given in this rollout; the **Choose Renderer** dialog box will be displayed, as shown in Figure 14-13. Select the renderer and choose the **OK** button; the name of the selected renderer will be displayed in the text box on the right of the selected option. Choose the **Save as Defaults** button in the **Assign Renderer** rollout to save the settings as default settings for further use.

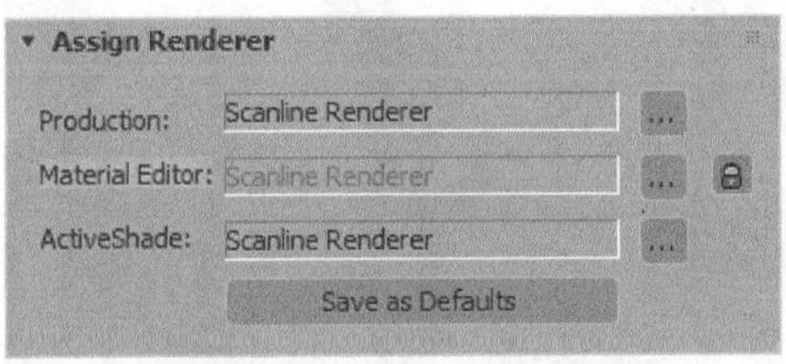

*Figure 14-12 The **Assign Renderer** rollout*

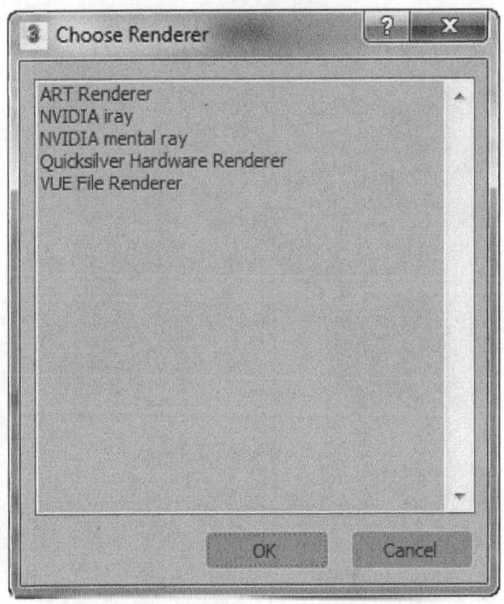

*Figure 14-13 The **Choose Renderer** dialog box*

Note

*If you install any additional renderer plug-ins in 3ds Max, the renderer types will be added to the **Choose Renderer** list.*

PREVIEWING AN ANIMATION

If a scene has a large number of objects, lights, and special effects, it may take a longer time to render the final animation and therefore, you will not be able to know how the final render would look like. However, in 3ds Max, you can preview its render. Note that the preview will be in low resolution and will display the diffuse color maps only. Therefore, it takes lesser time to render. You can have a look at your animation before the final rendering.

To create a preview animation, choose **Tools > Preview - Grab Viewport > Create Preview Animation** from the menu bar; the **Make Preview** dialog box will be displayed, as shown in Figure 14-14. Alternatively, choose **Create Preview > Create Preview Animation** from the General viewport label menu to invoke the **Make Preview** dialog box, refer to Figure 14-15. Set the parameters for different options in this dialog box and select the viewport that you want to render from the **Render Viewport** drop-down list which is located at the bottom of the dialog box. Next, choose the **Create** button; the **Video Compression** dialog box will be displayed. Use the default settings and choose the **OK** button; the rendering of the preview will start. Once the preview has been created, it will automatically start in the Windows Media Player.

To view the last preview animation, choose **Tools > Preview - Grab Viewport > Play Preview Animation** from the menu bar; the animation will start playing in the Windows Media Player. Alternatively, choose **Create Preview > Play Preview Animation** from the General viewport label menu, refer to Figure 14-15.

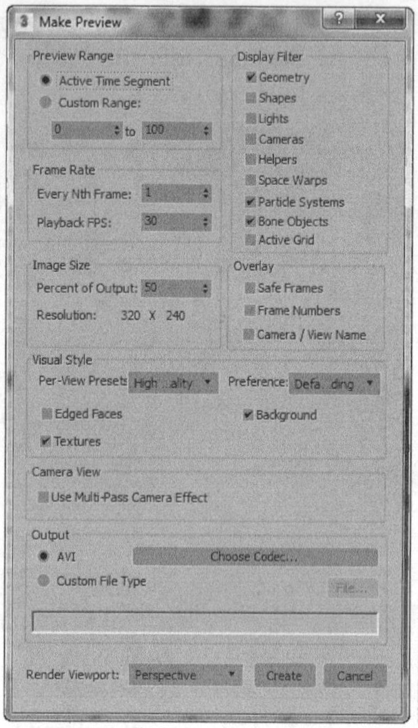

*Figure 14-14 The **Make Preview** dialog box*

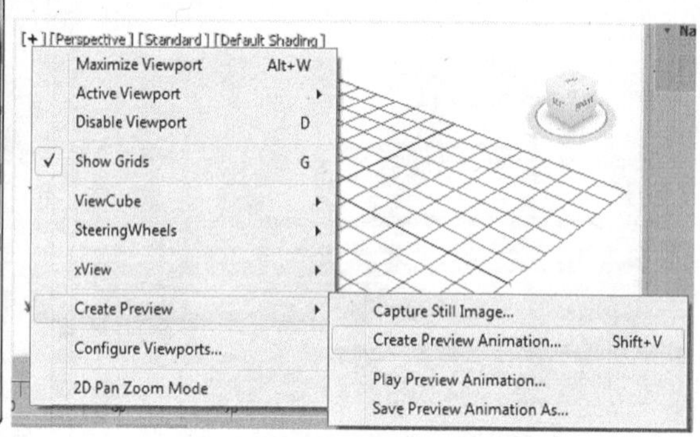

Figure 14-15 The flyout and the cascading menu of the General viewport label

RENDERING EFFECTS

The Rendering effects are the special effects assigned to a scene. These effects are visible only on rendering. To assign a rendering effect to a scene, choose **Rendering > Effects** from the menu bar; the **Environment and Effects** dialog box will be displayed, as shown in Figure 14-16. The **Effects** tab is chosen by default. In the **Effects** rollout of this tab, choose the **Add** button; the **Add Effect** dialog box will be displayed, as shown in Figure 14-17. Select the rendering effect from the list given in this dialog box and choose the **OK** button; the selected rendering effect will be displayed in the **Effects** text area of the **Effects** rollout. Also, the rollouts related to the selected effect will be displayed in the **Environment and Effects** dialog box. Next, set the parameters for

the selected rendering effect in these rollouts and close the dialog box. Now, render the final scene; the rendering effects will be displayed in the final rendered image.

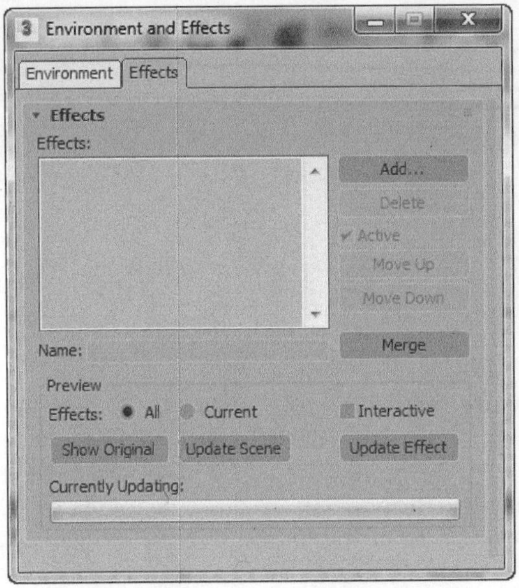

Figure 14-16 The ***Environment and Effects*** *dialog box*

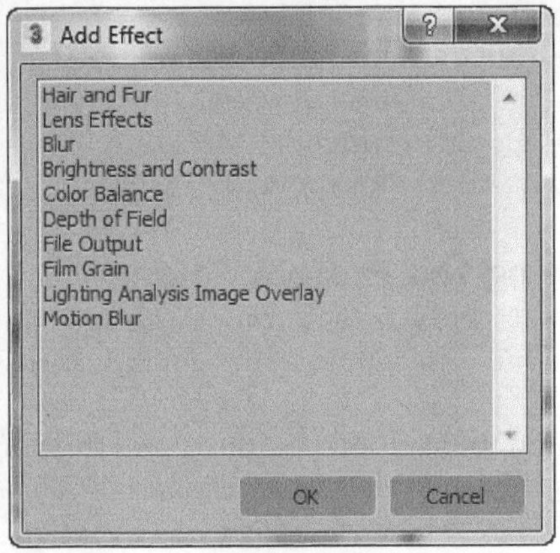

Figure 14-17 The ***Add Effect*** *dialog box*

TUTORIALS

Before starting the tutorials, you need to download the *c14_3dsmax_2017_tut.zip* file from *www.cadcim.com*. The path of the file is as follows: *Textbooks > Animation and Visual Effects > 3ds Max > Autodesk 3ds Max 2017: A Comprehensive Guide*

Extract the contents of the zipped file and save them in the *Documents* folder.

Tutorial 1

In this tutorial, you will create a walkthrough in a water tunnel, refer to Figures 14-18 and 14-19. **(Expected time: 60 min)**

Figure 14-18 Animated scene for tunnel at frame 600

Figure 14-19 Animated scene for tunnel at frame 920

The following steps are required to complete this tutorial:

a. Create the project folder.
b. Create a tunnel.
c. Create a camera.
d. Create water surface.
e. Create and assign materials to water surface.
f. Create walkthrough.
g. Rescale the active time segment.
h. Create animation in water.
i. Assign environment to the scene.
j. Save and render the scene.

Creating the Project Folder

1. Create a new project folder with the name *c14_tut1* at *\Documents\3dsmax2017* and then save the file with the name *c14tut1*, as discussed in Tutorial 1 of Chapter 2.

2. Open the Windows Explorer and then browse to the *c14_3dsmax_2017_tut* folder. Next, copy the files *tunnel_material.jpg* and *ice_environment.jpg* at the location *\Documents\3dsmax2017\c14_tut1\sceneassets\images*.

Creating a Tunnel

To create a tunnel, you need to use various splines and the **Loft** tool from **Compound Objects**.

1. Activate the Front viewport. Choose **Create > Shapes** in the **Command Panel**; the **Splines** option is displayed by default in the drop-down list below the **Shapes** button. Choose the **Donut** tool from the **Object Type** rollout.

2. Create a donut in the Front viewport. It is automatically named as *Donut001*. Now, set its parameters in the **Parameters** rollout as follows:

   Radius 1: **720.539** Radius 2: **848.293**

3. In the **Interpolation** rollout, set the value **20** in the **Steps** spinner.

4. Choose the **Zoom Extents All** tool to view *Donut001* in the viewports properly.

5. Activate the Top viewport. Choose the **Zoom** tool and zoom out the viewport so that *Donut001* is visible to half of its original size.

6. Choose the **Line** tool from **Create > Shapes > Splines > Object Type** rollout in the **Command Panel**. In the **Creation Method** rollout, select the **Corner** and **Smooth** radio buttons in the **Initial Type** and **Drag Type** areas, respectively.

7. Create a line in the Top viewport, as shown in Figure 14-20. It is automatically named as *Line001*.

Next, you need to create a loft compound object.

8. Make sure *Line001* is selected in the Top viewport. Choose **Create > Geometry** in the **Command Panel**; the **Standard Primitives** option is displayed by default in the drop-down list below the **Geometry** button. Select the **Compound Objects** option from the drop-down list and choose the **Loft** tool from the **Object Type** rollout.

9. In the **Creation Method** rollout of the **Loft** tool, choose the **Get Shape** button and move the cursor over *Donut001* in the Front viewport; the shape of the cursor changes, as shown in Figure 14-21. Click on *Donut001*; the shape of a tunnel is created in the viewports. Right-click to exit the command. Choose the **Zoom Extents All** tool to view the entire shape in the viewports, as shown in Figure 14-22.

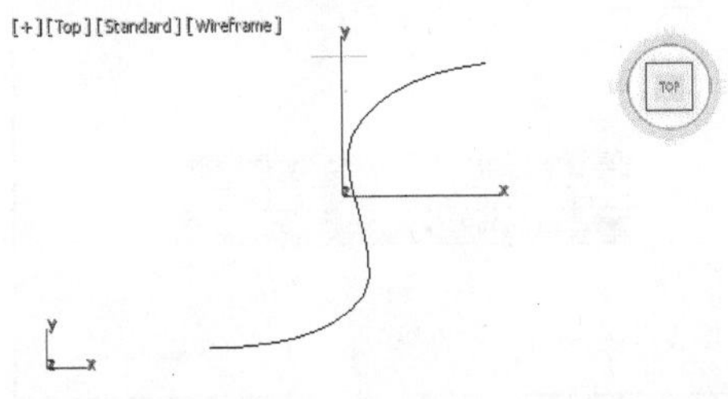

Figure 14-20 *A line created for the tunnel*

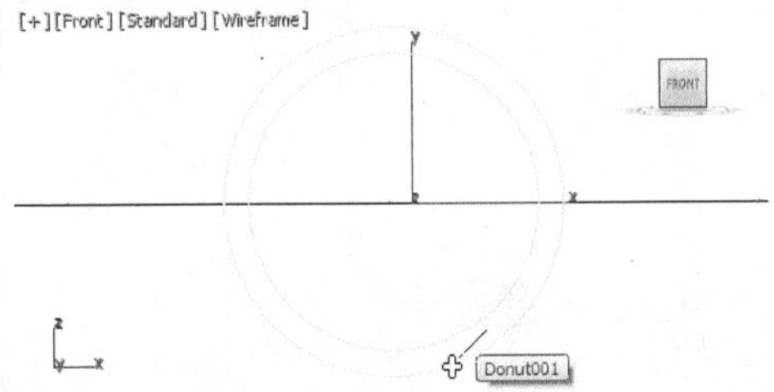

Figure 14-21 *The cursor displayed after moving it over Donut001*

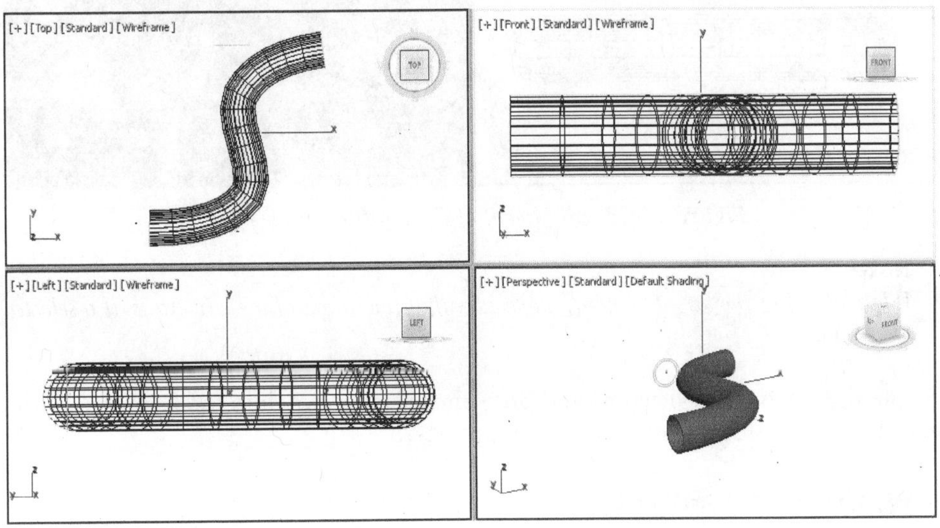

Figure 14-22 *The shape of the tunnel created in the viewports using the* ***Loft*** *tool*

Note

If the shape displayed after using the ***Loft*** *tool is not similar to the tunnel shown in Figure 14-22, you need to modify the placement of vertices of Line001 spline at the* ***Vertex*** *sub-object level.*

10. The lofted object is automatically named as *Loft001*. Modify its name to *water tunnel*.

Creating a Camera

In this section, you will create a walkthrough inside *water tunnel* by using the **Target** camera tool.

1. Activate the Front viewport. Choose **Create > Cameras** in the **Command Panel** and then choose the **Target** tool from the **Object Type** rollout.

2. In the Front viewport, create a target camera and align it in all the viewports using the **Select and Move** and **Select and Rotate** tools, refer to Figure 14-23. It is automatically named as *Camera001*.

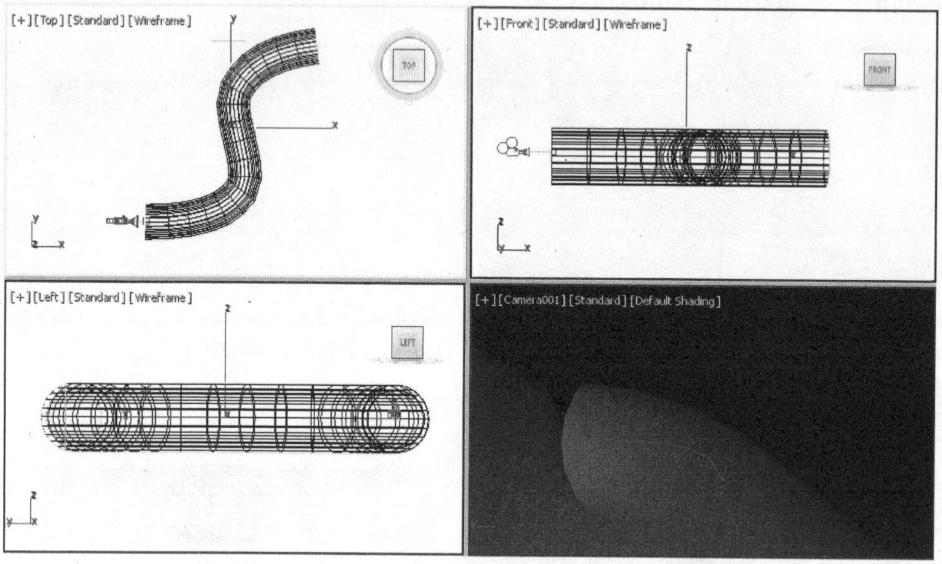

Figure 14-23 Alignment of Camera001 in viewports

Note

While aligning the target camera, make sure that the target of the camera is also selected along with Camera001.

3. Activate the Perspective viewport and press the C key to switch to the Camera001 viewport; the camera view is displayed, refer to Figure 14-23.

Creating the Water Surface

In this section, you will create water surface by using the **Plane** tool.

1. Choose the **Plane** tool from **Standard Primitives** in the **Command Panel**. Create a plane in the Top viewport.

2. In the **Parameters** rollout, set the values in the **Length** and **Width** spinners so that the plane covers the area around the tunnel, refer to Figure 14-24. Also, set the values in the **Length Segs** and **Width Segs** spinners to **30**.

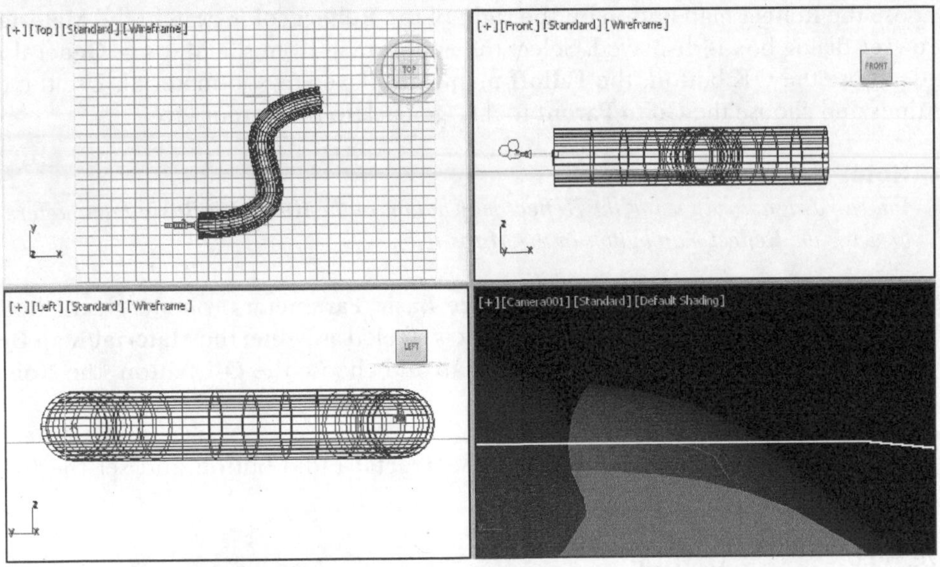

Figure 14-24 The water surface created and aligned in viewports

3. Name the plane in the **Name and Color** rollout as **water surface** and align it in the viewports, refer to Figure 14-24.

   Next, you need to create and assign materials to *water tunnel* and *water surface*.

Creating and Assigning Materials to Water Surface

In this section, you will create materials for *water surface*.

1. Make sure *water surface* is selected in any viewport and then choose **Rendering > Material Editor > Compact Material Editor** from the menu bar; the **Material Editor** dialog box is displayed.

2. Make sure the **01-Default** sample slot is selected and then modify the name of the material in the **Material Name** drop-down list to **water surface material**.

3. Choose the **Material Type** button that is currently labeled as **Standard**; the **Material/Map Browser** dialog box is displayed. Select the **Raytrace** material from **Materials > General** and choose the **OK** button; the **Standard** material is replaced by the **Raytrace** material.

   Make sure in the **Raytrace Basic Parameters** rollout, the **Phong** shader is selected in the **Shading** drop-down list.

4. Choose the **Diffuse** color swatch; the **Color Selector: Diffuse** dialog box is displayed. Set the following values and then choose the **OK** button.

   Red: **136** Green: **210** Blue: **213**

5. Choose the **Reflect** map button on the right of the **Reflect** color swatch; the **Material/Map Browser** dialog box is displayed. Select the **Falloff** map from the **Maps > General** rollout and choose the **OK** button; the **Falloff** map is displayed as sub-material. Use the default settings and choose the **Go to Parent** tool to go back to the parent level.

Note

*You can assign a map using the **Reflect** map button in the **Raytrace Basic Parameters** rollout or using the **Reflect** map button in the **Maps** rollout.*

6. Select the **Bump** check box in the **Raytrace Basic Parameters** rollout. Next, choose the button on the right of the **Bump** spinner that is labeled as **None**; the **Material/Map Browser** dialog box is displayed. Select the **Noise** map and choose the **OK** button; the **Noise** map is displayed as sub-material.

7. In the **Noise Parameters** rollout, select the **Fractal** radio button and set the following parameters:

   Size: **30.0** Low: **1.0**

8. Choose the **Go to Parent** tool to go back to the parent level. Alternatively, you can select the **water surface material** option from the **Material Name** drop-down list.

9. Make sure that *water surface* is selected in the viewport, and then choose the **Assign Material to Selection** tool; the *water surface material* is assigned to *water surface* in the viewport.

   Next, you need to create material for *water tunnel* to make it look more realistic.

10. Select the **02-Default** sample slot and modify its name in the **Material Name** drop-down list to **water tunnel material**.

11. In the **Shader Basic Parameters** rollout, make sure that the **Blinn** shader is selected in the drop-down list.

    Next, you need to assign a map to the selected sample slot.

12. In the **Blinn Basic Parameters** rollout, choose the **Diffuse** map button on the right of the **Diffuse** color swatch; the **Material/Map Browser** dialog box is displayed. Select the **Bitmap** map and choose the **OK** button; the **Select Bitmap Image File** dialog box is displayed. As the project folder is already set, the *images* folder is displayed in the **Look in** drop-down list of this dialog box. Select the file *tunnel_material.jpg* from this folder and choose the **Open** button; the selected image is displayed in the sample slot.

13. Choose the **Go to Parent** tool. Expand the **Maps** rollout and then select the **Bump** check box to make it available for material. Choose the **Bump** map button that is labeled as **None**; the **Material/Map Browser** dialog box is displayed. Select the **Bitmap** map and choose the **OK** button; the **Select Bitmap Image File** dialog box is displayed. Browse to the same image *(tunnel_material.jpg)* that you used for the **Diffuse** map and choose the **Open** button; various rollouts are displayed to modify the coordinates of the map.

14. In the **Coordinates** rollout, set the value to **4** in the **U Tiling** and **V Tiling** spinners. Next, choose the **Go to Parent** tool to go back to the parent level; the name of the selected image is displayed over the **Bump** map button.

15. In the **Bump** spinner, set the value to **40**.

16. Make sure that *water tunnel* is selected in the viewport, and then choose the **Assign Material to Selection** tool; the *water tunnel material* is assigned to *water tunnel* in the viewport.

17. Close the **Material Editor** dialog box.

18. Activate the Camera001 viewport and choose the **Render Production** tool to view the maps and materials assigned to the objects. The scene is displayed, as shown in Figure 14-25.

Figure 14-25 The scene after assigning the materials

Creating Walkthrough

In this section, you will create a walkthrough.

1. Activate the Top viewport and choose the **Maximize Viewport Toggle** tool to maximize it.

2. Create a line from the lower left side to the upper right side of the viewport according to the shape of the *water tunnel*, as shown in Figure 14-26. Alternatively, you can also use the *Line001* spline created earlier to loft the tunnel.

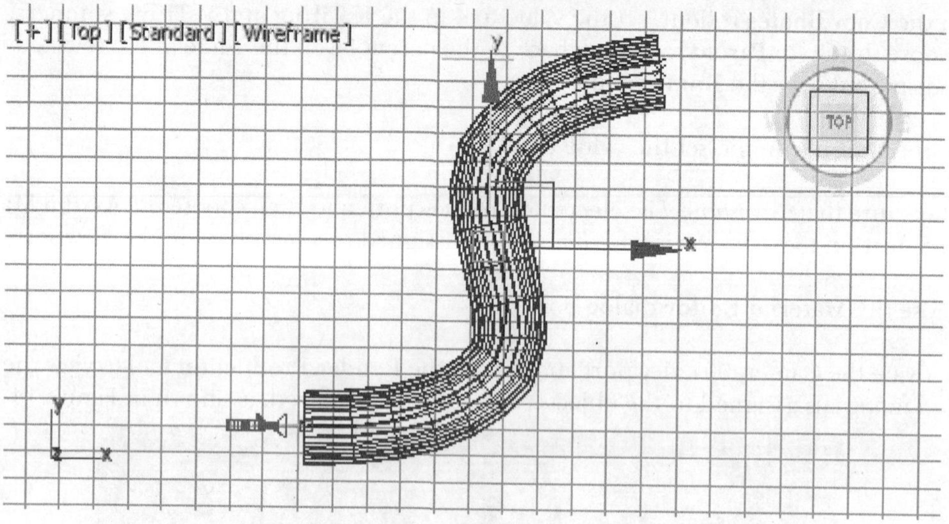

Figure 14-26 *A line created for the path*

3. Modify the name of the line as *path* and align it in the viewports, as shown in Figure 14-27. Next, choose the **Maximize Viewport Toggle** tool.

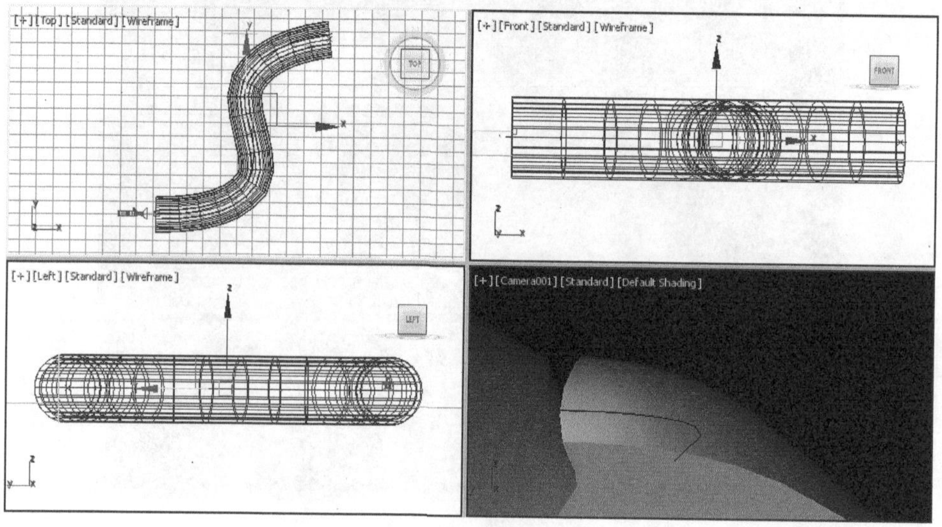

Figure 14-27 *The path aligned in viewports*

Next, you need to increase the number of frames in the track bar to create a smooth animation.

4. Choose the **Time Configuration** button at the bottom of the screen; the **Time Configuration** dialog box is displayed. In the **Animation** area of this dialog box, set the value **1000** in the **End Time** spinner and press the ENTER key; the number of frames increases in the track bar. Choose the **OK** button to exit the dialog box.

Next, you need to move *Camera001* along with *path*.

5. Select *Camera001* in any viewport and choose the **Motion** tab in the **Command Panel**. By default, the **Parameters** tab is chosen in this panel.

6. Expand the **Assign Controller** rollout in the **Parameters** tab and then choose the **Position : Position XYZ** option from it; the **Assign Controller** button is activated, as shown in Figure 14-28.

7. Choose the **Assign Controller** button; the **Assign Position Controller** dialog box is displayed. Choose the **Path Constraint** option and then choose the **OK** button to exit the dialog box; various rollouts are displayed below the **Assign Controller** rollout.

8. In the **Path Parameters** rollout, choose the **Add Path** button, refer to Figure 14-29. Next, select *path* from the Scene Explorer. Also, *Camera001* is moved along with *path* in the viewport. Right-click to exit the command.

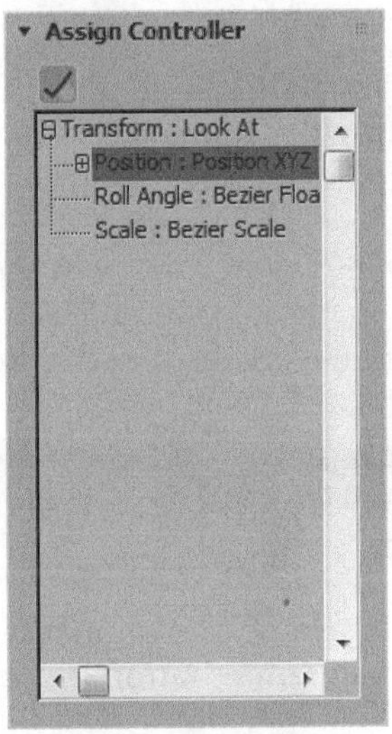

*Figure 14-28 The **Assign Controller** rollout*

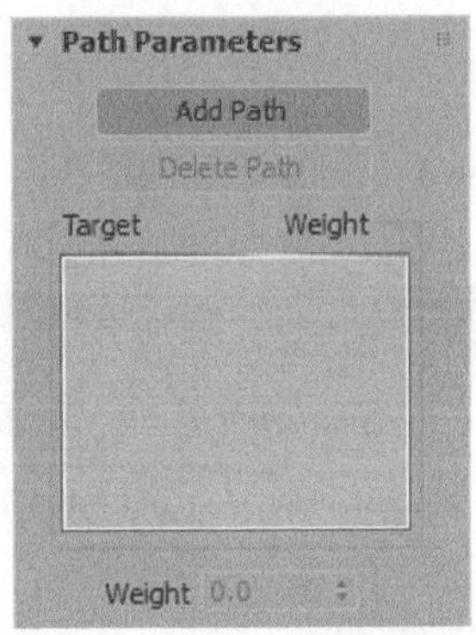

*Figure 14-29 Partial view of the **Path Parameters** rollout*

9. Activate the Top viewport and choose the **Play Animation** button from the time controls area; you will notice that *Camera001* moves along with *path* but the movement is not proper. To create a proper movement, you need to adjust the target of *Camera001* at different frames.

10. Choose the **Go to Start** button to drag the time slider to frame 0. Next, choose the **Toggle Auto Key Mode** button to turn on the animation mode.

11. Select *Camera001.Target* from the Scene Explorer.

12. In the Top viewport, position *Camera001.Target* using the **Select and Move** tool, as shown in Figure 14-30.

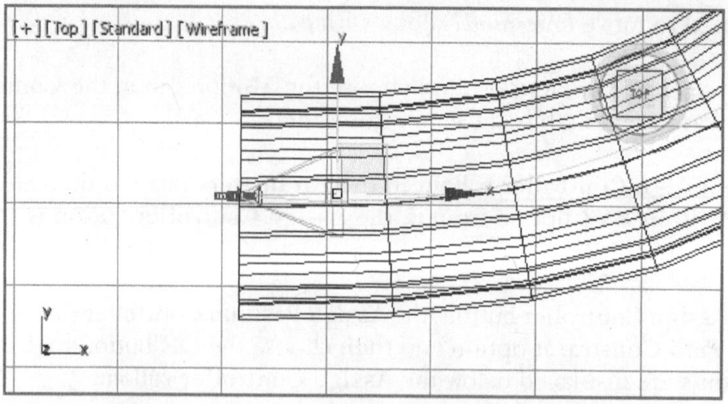

Figure 14-30 The camera and its target at frame 0

Note

While aligning the Camera001.Target, you need to view Camera001 viewport simultaneously to make sure that the animation is proper.

13. Drag the time slider to frame 153 and move *Camera001.Target* along the path, as shown in Figure 14-31. To move the time slider to a particular frame, you can also enter the frame number in the Current Frame (Go to frame) spinner.

14. Similarly, add keyframes at 300, 429, 581, 700, 801, 935, and 1000 frames.

After creating the frame-by-frame animation, the frames are displayed in the track bar, as shown in Figure 14-31.

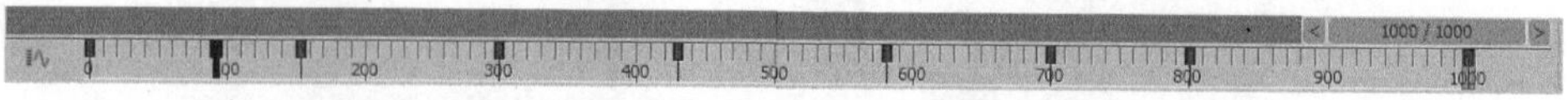

Figure 14-31 The track bar after creating the animation

15. Choose the **Toggle Auto Key Mode** button to turn off the animation mode and activate Camera001 viewport. Next, choose the **Play Animation** button; *Camera001* starts moving along *path* inside the tunnel.

Note

You can also use your own dimensions to align Camera001.Target at different frames.

Rescaling the Active Time Segment

While playing animation, if you feel that the pace of animation is very fast, you can increase the number of frames in the active time segment to make it slow and smooth.

1. Choose the **Time Configuration** button at the bottom of the 3ds Max screen; the **Time Configuration** dialog box is displayed. In the **Animation** area of this dialog box, choose the **Re-scale Time** button; the **Re-scale Time** dialog box is displayed.

2. In the **New** area, set a new value in the **End Time** spinner and choose the **OK** button to exit the dialog box; the active time segment and animation keys are adjusted accordingly. Choose the **OK** button in the **Time Configuration** dialog box to close it.

Creating Animation in Water

In this section, you will create animated waves on the water surface by using the **Compact Material Editor** tool.

1. Choose the **Compact Material Editor** tool from the **Main Toolbar**; the **Material Editor** dialog box is displayed.

2. Select the **water surface material** sample slot. Now, in the **Raytrace Basic Parameters** rollout, choose the **Bump** map button that is labeled as **Map# X (Noise)**; various rollouts are displayed for the **Noise** modifier.

   Next, you need to set the keys on the parameters of the **Noise** modifier to animate *water surface*.

3. Choose the **Go to Start** button to drag the time slider to frame 0. Next, choose the **Toggle Auto Key Mode** button to turn on the animation mode; the selected sample slot is surrounded by a red border, which indicates that the animation mode is active.

4. In the **Noise Parameters** rollout, make sure that the value in the **Phase** spinner is 0.0 at frame 0. Next, choose the **Go to End** button to move the time slider to the end frame, and then set the value **7.0** in the **Phase** spinner and then press ENTER; the color of the border of arrows of the spinner turns red.

5. Choose the **Toggle Auto Key Mode** button to turn off the animation mode and close the **Material Editor** dialog box.

Assigning Environment to the Scene

In this section, you will create environment to the scene.

1. Choose **Rendering > Environment** from the menu bar; the **Environment and Effects** dialog box is displayed.

2. The **Environment** tab is chosen by default. In the **Background** area of the **Common Parameters** rollout, choose the **Environment Map** button that is labeled as **None**; the **Material/Map Browser** dialog box is displayed.

3. Select the **Bitmap** map and choose the **OK** button; the **Select Bitmap Image File** dialog box is displayed. Select *ice_environment.jpg* image and choose the **Open** button; the selected image is displayed as background after rendering. Close the **Environment and Effects** dialog box.

   Note that when *Camera001* moves toward the end frames, then only the background of the scene is displayed in the animation.

Saving and Rendering the Scene

In this section, you will save the scene and then render it. You can also view the final rendered image sequence by downloading the file *c14_3dsmax_2017_rndr.zip* from *www.cadcim.com*. The path of the file is as follows: *Textbooks > Animation and Visual Effects > 3ds Max > Autodesk 3ds Max 2017: A Comprehensive Guide*

1. Choose the **Render Setup** tool from the **Main Toolbar**; the **Render Setup: Default Scanline Renderer** dialog box is displayed. In this dialog box, the **Common** tab is chosen by default. Also, various rollouts are displayed in the **Common** tab.

2. In the **Common Parameters** rollout, select the **Active Time Segment** radio button in the **Time Output** area.

3. In the **Output Size** area, choose the **640x480** button.

4. In the **Render Output** area, choose the **Files** button; the **Render Output File** dialog box is displayed. Enter a name for the file in the **File name** text box and then select the **AVI File (*.avi)** file type from the **Save as type** drop-down list and specify the desired location of the file in the **Save in** text box. Next, choose the **Save** button; the **AVI File Compression Setup** dialog box is displayed. Use the default settings and choose the **OK** button to exit the dialog box.

5. Choose **Save** from the **Application** menu.

6. Make sure the **Quad 4 - Camera001** option is selected in the **View to Render** drop-down list in the **Render Setup: Default Scanline Renderer** dialog box. Next, choose the **Render** button; both the **Camera001, frame#** window and the **Rendering** dialog box are displayed showing the rendering process.

   After the completion of the rendering process, the final output of the animation is saved at the specified location in the *.AVI format. You can view the final output of the animation by opening the corresponding *.AVI file.

Tutorial 2

In this tutorial, you will create an animated scene that contains light effects and animation of lights and objects, as shown in Figure 14-32. **(Expected time: 60 min)**

The following steps are required to complete this tutorial:

a. Create the project folder.
b. Create the wireframe earth sphere.
c. Create the text.
d. Add camera to the scene.
e. Create the animated space background.
f. Create and animate lights in the scene.
g. Animate the wireframe earth sphere and the text.
h. Save and render the scene.

Figure 14-32 The animated scene

Creating the Project Folder

1. Create a new project folder with the name *c14_tut2* at *\Documents\3dsmax2017* and then save the file with the name *c14tut2*, as discussed in Tutorial 1 of Chapter 2.

2. Open the Windows Explorer and then browse to the *c14_3dsmax_2017_tut* folder. Next, copy *EarthMap_colored.jpg* and *EarthMap_b&w.jpg* at the location *\Documents\3dsmax2017\c14_tut2\sceneassets\images*.

Creating the Wireframe Earth Sphere

In this section, you will create two spheres to create a wireframe earth sphere.

1. Choose the **Sphere** tool from **Standard Primitives** in the **Command Panel** and create a sphere in the Top viewport.

2. Modify the name of the sphere to *earth sphere*. Set the value of the **Radius** spinner to **58.42** in the **Parameters** rollout. Next, right-click to exit the tool.

3. Make sure that *earth sphere* is selected and then choose **Edit > Clone** from the menu bar; the **Clone Options** dialog box is displayed.

4. Select the **Copy** radio button in the **Object** area and enter *wireframe sphere* in the **Name** text box. Next, choose the **OK** button to close the dialog box. In the **Parameters** rollout, set the radius of *wireframe sphere* to **58.0** in the **Radius** spinner.

   Next, you need to apply maps and material to the *earth sphere* and the *wireframe sphere*.

5. Select *earth sphere* in any viewport and press the M key; the **Material Editor** dialog box is displayed.

6. Select the **01-Default** sample slot, if it is not already selected and then modify its name in the **Material Name** drop-down list to **earth map**.

7. In the **Shader Basic Parameters** rollout, make sure that the **Blinn** shader is selected in the drop-down list, and then select the **2-Sided** check box.

   Next, you need to assign a map to the shader.

8. In the **Blinn Basic Parameters** rollout, choose the **Diffuse** map button on the right of the **Diffuse** color swatch; the **Material/Map Browser** dialog box is displayed. Select the **Bitmap** map and choose the **OK** button; the **Select Bitmap Image File** dialog box is displayed. As the project folder is already set, the *images* folder is displayed in the **Look in** drop-down list of this dialog box. Select the file *EarthMap_colored.jpg* and choose the **Open** button; the selected image is displayed in the sample slot. Also, various rollouts are displayed to modify the coordinates of the map.

9. Choose the **Go to Parent** tool to go back to the parent level and then choose the **Opacity** map button in the **Blinn Basic Parameters** rollout; the **Material/Map Browser** dialog box is displayed. Select the **Bitmap** map and choose the **OK** button; the **Select Bitmap Image File** dialog box is displayed. Select the *EarthMap_b&w.jpg* image and choose the **Open** button; the selected image is displayed in the sample slot, as shown in Figure 14-33.

Figure 14-33 *The earth map in the sample slot*

10. Choose the **Go to Parent** tool again and make sure *earth sphere* is selected in the viewport. Next, choose the **Assign Material to Selection** tool; *earth map* is assigned to *earth sphere* in the viewport.

11. Choose the **Show Shaded Material in Viewport** tool to view the assigned map in the viewport.

12. Render the Perspective viewport to view the map applied using the **Render Production** tool, as shown in Figure 14-34.

    Next, you need to create material for *wireframe sphere*.

13. Select the **02-Default** sample slot and modify its name in the **Material Name** drop-down list to **wireframe map**.

14. In the **Shader Basic Parameters** rollout, make sure that the **Blinn** shader is selected in the drop-down list and then select the **Wire** check box; wireframes are displayed in the sample slot, as shown in Figure 14-35.

15. In the **Blinn Basic Parameters** rollout, choose the **Diffuse** color swatch; the **Color Selector: Diffuse Color** dialog box is displayed. Set the values in the **Red**, **Green**, and **Blue** spinners as given next and choose the **OK** button to exit the dialog box.

    Red: **239** Green: **106** Blue: **18**

Figure 14-34 The earth map applied to the earth sphere after rendering

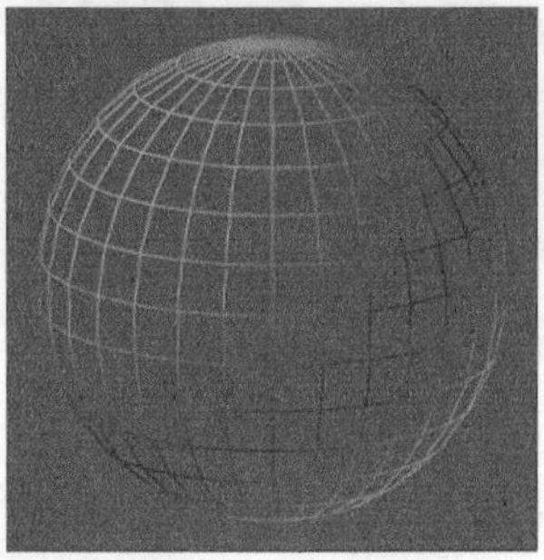

Figure 14-35 Wireframes displayed in the sample slot

16. In the **Specular Highlights** area, set the value **53** in the **Specular Level** spinner.

17. Select *wireframe sphere* in the viewport and then choose the **Assign Material to Selection** tool; the **wireframe map** is assigned to *wireframe sphere* in the viewport.

18. Choose the **Show Shaded Material in Viewport** button to view the assigned map in the viewport. Close the **Material Editor** dialog box.

19. Choose the **Zoom Extents All** tool to view both the spheres in the viewports.

    Next, you need to align *wireframe sphere* with *earth sphere.*

20. Select *wireframe sphere* in the viewport and choose the **Align** tool from the **Main Toolbar**; the shape of the cursor changes. Next, select *earth sphere* in the viewport; the **Align Selection (earth sphere)** dialog box is displayed.

21. In the **Align Position (earth sphere)** area, select the **X Position**, **Y Position**, and **Z Position** check boxes. Next, select the **Pivot Point** radio button both in the **Current Object** and **Target Object** areas. Next, choose the **OK** button to close the dialog box.

22. Choose the **Zoom Extents All** tool; *wireframe sphere* is aligned with *earth sphere* in the viewports, as shown in Figure 14-36.

23. Activate the Perspective viewport. Choose the **Render Production** tool from the **Main Toolbar**; the rendered sphere is displayed in the **Rendered Frame** window, as shown in Figure 14-37.

24. Select *wireframe sphere* and *earth sphere* in the viewport simultaneously and then group them as *wireframe earth sphere*.

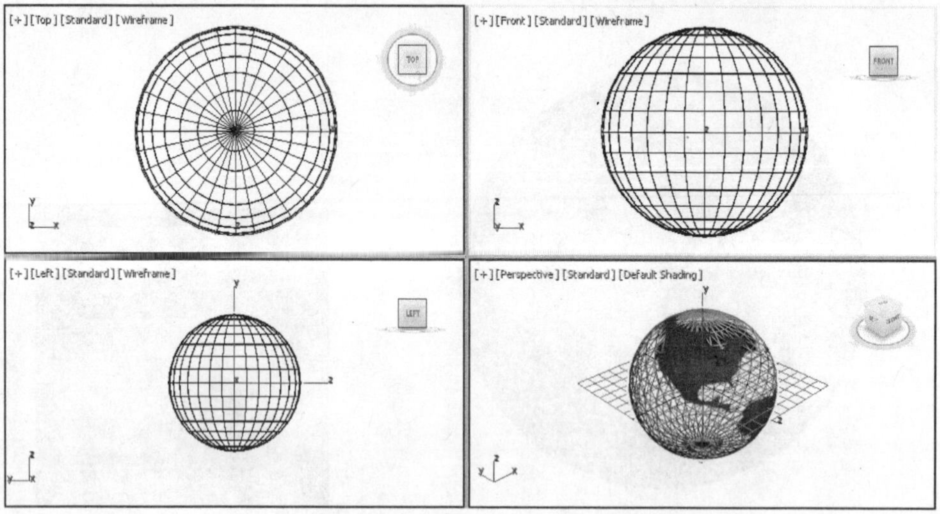

Figure 14-36 Alignment of the wireframe and the earth sphere in viewports

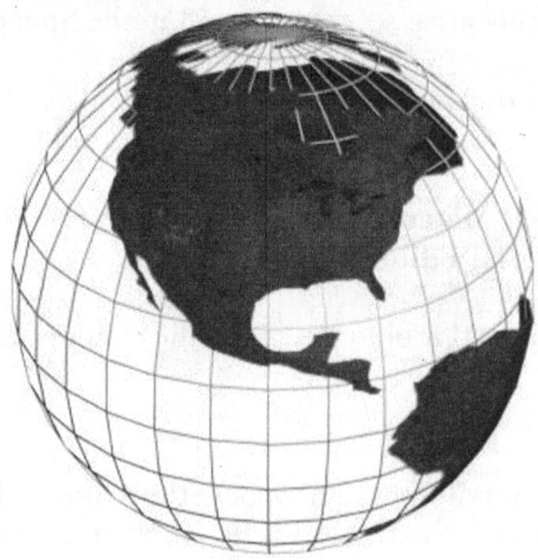

Figure 14-37 The sphere at rendering

Creating the Text

In this section, you will create the text around the *wireframe earth sphere* by using the **Text** tool.

1. Choose the **Text** tool from **Create > Shapes > Splines > Object Type** rollout in the **Command Panel**. In the **Parameters** rollout, set the values as follows:

   Select the **Arial Italic** font type from the drop-down list located on the top of the rollout.

   Make sure that the left alignment button is chosen.
   Size: **30.0**

Text area
Enter **CADCIM Technologies**.

2. Click in the center of Front viewport; the **CADCIM Technologies** text is displayed in viewports. It is automatically named as *Text001*.

3. Choose the **Zoom Extents All** tool and align *Text001* in the viewports, as shown in Figure 14-38.

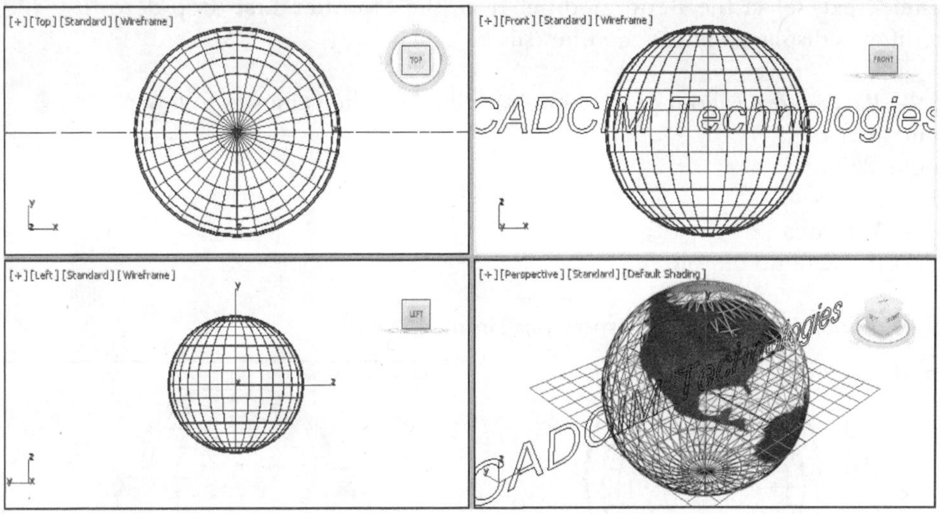

Figure 14-38 *Alignment of Text001 in viewports*

Now, you need to apply the **Extrude** modifier to add depth to the text.

4. Make sure that *Text001* is selected in the viewport. Choose the **Modify** tab in the **Command Panel**. Next, select the **Extrude** modifier from the **Modifier List** drop-down list; the **Extrude** modifier is displayed in the modifier stack.

5. In the **Parameters** rollout of the **Extrude** modifier, set the value **3.0** in the **Amount** spinner.

Next, you need to apply material to *Text001*.

6. Choose the **Material Editor** tool; the **Material Editor** dialog box is displayed. Select the **03-Default** sample slot and change its name to **text material** in the **Material Name** drop-down list.

7. In the **Blinn Basic Parameters** rollout, choose the **Diffuse** color swatch; the **Color Selector: Diffuse Color** dialog box is displayed. Set the following values in the **Red**, **Green**, and **Blue** spinners and then choose the **OK** button to exit the dialog box.

Red: **253** Green: **185** Blue: **2**

8. Make sure *Text001* is selected in the viewport and then choose the **Assign Material to Selection** tool; the **text material** is assigned to *Text001* in the viewport. Close the **Material Editor** dialog box.

   Next, you need to apply the **Bend** modifier to *Text001* such that it is set around *wireframe earth sphere*.

9. Make sure *Text001* is selected in the viewport and then choose the **Modify** tab in the **Command Panel**. Next, select the **Bend** modifier from the **Modifier List** drop-down list; the **Bend** modifier is displayed in the modifier stack.

10. In the **Parameters** rollout of the **Bend** modifier, set the values as follows:
    Bend area
    Angle: **237.5**

    Bend Axis area
    Select the **X** radio button.

11. Align *Text001* in viewports, as shown in Figure 14-39.

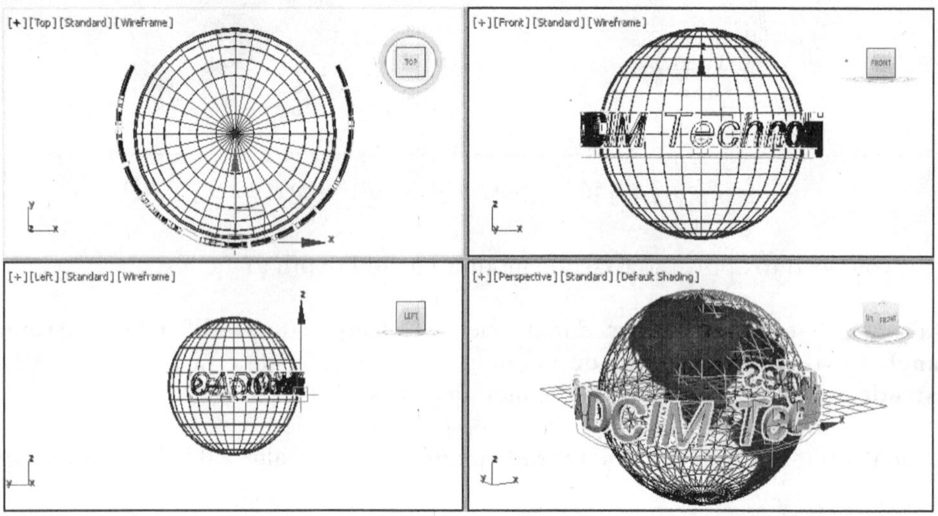

Figure 14-39 *The Text001 aligned in viewports after applying the* ***Extrude*** *and* ***Bend*** *modifiers*

Adding Camera to the Scene

In this section, you will add camera to the scene.

1. Choose the **Zoom All** tool and zoom out all viewports simultaneously to make a proper room around *wireframe earth sphere*.

2. Choose the **Free** tool from **Create > Cameras** in the **Command Panel** and click in the Front viewport; a free camera is displayed in all the viewports and is automatically named as *Camera001*.

3. Align *Camera001* in viewports to view the front side of the scene and then press the C key in the Perspective viewport to activate the Camera001 viewport, as shown in Figure 14-40.

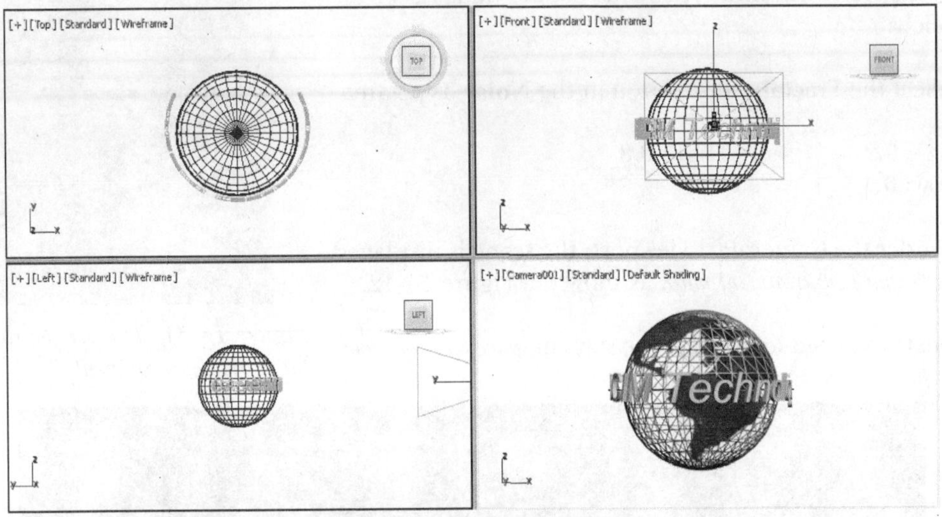

Figure 14-40 The Camera001 aligned in viewports

Creating Animated Space Background

In this section, you will create background for the scene.

1. Choose **Rendering > Environment** from the menu bar; the **Environment and Effects** dialog box is displayed with the **Environment** tab chosen by default. Also, various rollouts are displayed in the **Environment** tab.

2. In the **Common Parameters** rollout, choose the **Environment Map** button in the **Background** area; the **Material/Map Browser** dialog box is displayed. Select the **Noise** map from the **Maps > General** rollout and choose the **OK** button; the **Noise** map is displayed on the **Environment Map** button and applied as background.

   Next, you need to set the parameters of the **Noise** map.

3. Press the M key to invoke the **Material Editor** dialog box. Select the **04-Default** sample slot.

4. In the **Environment and Effects** dialog box, press and hold the cursor over the **Environment Map** button and drag it to the **04-Default** sample slot in the **Material Editor** dialog box. Next, release the left mouse button; the **Instance (Copy) Map** dialog box is displayed. Make sure the **Instance** radio button is selected and choose the **OK** button; the **04-Default** sample slot is displayed, as shown in Figure 14-41. Also, various rollouts to modify the **Noise** map are displayed.

5. Modify the name of the sample slot in the **Material Name** drop-down list to **space environment map**.

Next, you need to modify the parameters of the **Noise** map.

6. In the **Noise Parameters** rollout, set the values as given below:

   Select the **Fractal** radio button in the **Noise Type** area.

   Size: **0.2** High: **0.8**
   Low: **0.7**

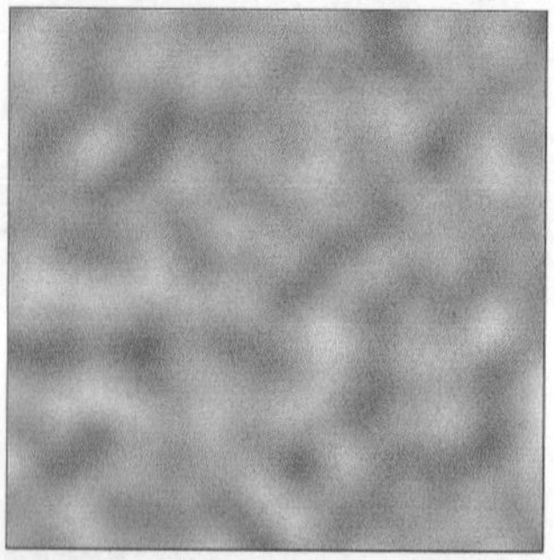

*Figure 14-41 The sample slot with the **Noise** environment*

7. Render the Camera001 viewport; the scene is displayed with *space environment map*, as shown in Figure 14-42.

   Next, you need to animate the stars in *space environment map*.

Figure 14-42 The scene with the space environment map

8. Choose the **Time Configuration** button; the **Time Configuration** dialog box is displayed. In the **Animation** area of this dialog box, set the value **1000** in the **End Time** spinner and press the ENTER key; the number of frames in the active time segment increases to 1000. Choose the **OK** button to exit the dialog box.

9. Choose the **Toggle Auto Key Mode** button to turn on the animation mode and then make sure the time slider is set to frame 0. In the **Noise Parameters** rollout of the **Material Editor** dialog box, make sure that the value in the **Phase** spinner is 0.0 at frame 0.

10. Choose the **Go to End** button to move the time slider to frame 1000. In the **Noise Parameters** rollout, set the value **7.0** in the **Phase** spinner. The stars in *space environment map* appear to be blinking in the final output at rendering.

11. Choose the **Toggle Auto Key Mode** button to turn off the animation mode and then close the **Material Editor** dialog box. Also, close the **Environment and Effects** dialog box.

Creating and Animating Lights in the Scene

To create light in the scene, you need to create omni and spot lights in the scene.

1. Choose the **Zoom** tool and zoom out the Top, Front, and Left viewports to create proper room around *wireframe earth sphere*, refer to Figure 14-43.

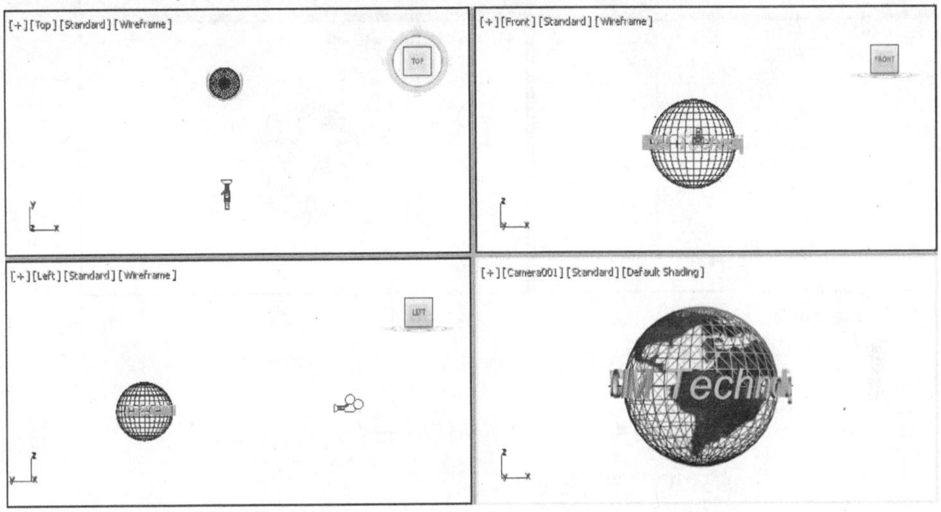

Figure 14-43 *The wireframe earth sphere zoomed out*

2. Activate the Top viewport and choose the **Omni** tool from **Create > Lights > Standard > Object Type** rollout in the **Command Panel**. In the Top viewport, click at the center of *wireframe earth sphere*; an omni light is displayed in all the viewports. It is automatically named as *Omni001*. Right-click to exit the command. Next, align *Omni001* light in all the viewports, refer to Figure 14-44.

3. Create four copies of *Omni001* light and align all lights, as shown in Figure 14-44.

Note

*If your scene has more lighting effects, then choose the **Modify** tab from the **Command Panel** and set the intensity of omni lights. To do so, you need to modify the value in the **Multiplier** spinner of the **Intensity/Color/Attenuation** rollout.*

Next, you need to add advance effects to omni lights.

4. In the Front viewport, select the omni light that is placed on the left side of *wireframe earth sphere*, as shown in Figure 14-45.

5. Choose the **Modify** tab in the **Command Panel** and expand the **Atmospheres & Effects** rollout. Choose the **Add** button; the **Add Atmosphere or Effect** dialog box is displayed. Select the **Lens Effects** option and choose the **OK** button to exit the dialog box; the **Lens Effects** option is displayed in the **Atmospheres & Effects** rollout.

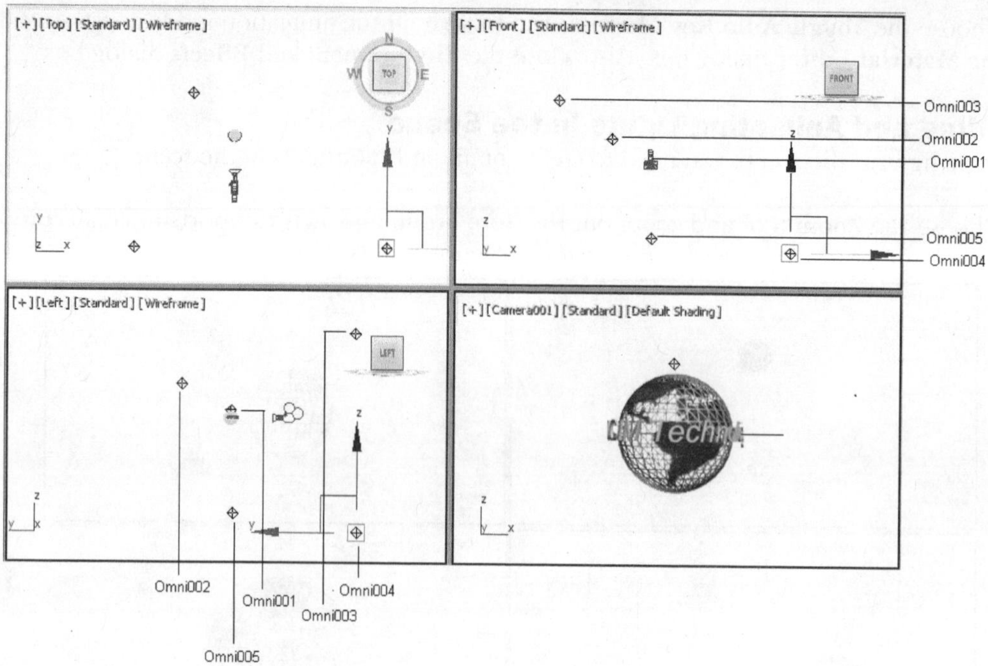

Figure 14-44 Omni lights aligned in viewports

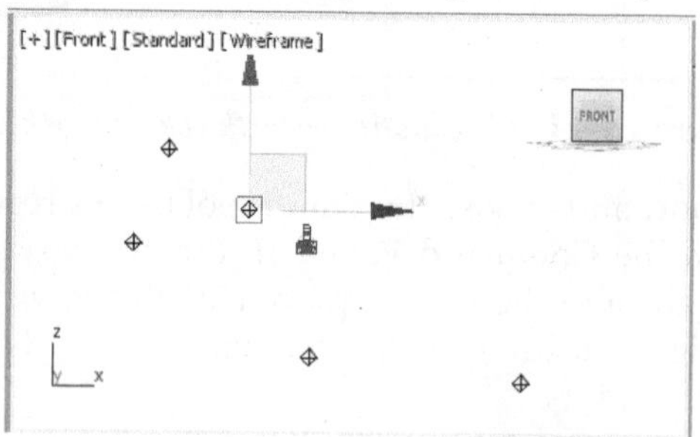

Figure 14-45 Omni light selected to add the advance effects

Next, you need to set the parameters for the **Lens Effects**.

6. Select the **Lens Effects** option in the **Atmospheres & Effects** rollout and choose the **Setup** button; the **Environment and Effects** dialog box is displayed with the **Effects** tab chosen. Also, various rollouts are displayed in this tab.

7. In the **Lens Effects Parameters** rollout, select the **Glow** option and choose the arrow that is pointing toward the right; the **Glow** effect is now available for the omni light at rendering. Also, the **Glow Element** rollout is displayed in the **Environment and Effects** dialog box to modify the parameters of the **Glow** effect.

8. In the **Glow Element** rollout, set the values as follows:

   Size: **6**   Intensity: **150.0**

9. In the **Lens Effects Parameters** rollout, select **Ray** and then choose the arrow that is pointing toward right; the **Ray** effect is now available for the omni light at rendering. Also, the **Ray Element** rollout is displayed in the **Environment and Effects** dialog box to modify the parameters of the **Ray** effect.

10. In the **Ray Element** rollout, set the values as follows:

    Size: **15**   Intensity: **10.0**   Num: **50**

    Use the default values for other options.

11. To animate rays in the scene, choose the **Toggle Auto Key Mode** button to turn on the animation mode. Next, choose the **Go to Start** button to move the time slider to frame 0. In the **Ray Element** rollout, make sure that the value in the **Angle** spinner is 0.0 at frame 0.

12. Choose the **Go to End** button to move the time slider to frame 1000, and set the value in the **Angle** spinner to **180.0**. The rays appear to be rotating in the final output after rendering.

13. Choose the **Toggle Auto Key Mode** button to turn off the animation mode.

14. In the **Lens Effects Parameters** rollout, select the **Ring** option and then choose the arrow that is pointing toward right; the **Ring** effect becomes available for the omni light at rendering. Also, the **Ring Element** rollout is displayed in the **Environment and Effects** dialog box to modify the parameters of the **Ring** effect.

15. In the **Ring Element** rollout, set the values as follows:

    Size: **3.0**   Intensity: **15.0**

    Use the default values for other options.

16. Close the **Environment and Effects** dialog box and render the Camera001 viewport; the omni light is displayed, refer to Figure 14-46.

> **Note**
> *If you are not able to view the Omni Light in your render, move Camera001 so that you can see the Omni light in your render.*

17. In the Front viewport, select the omni light that is placed just above the *wireframe earth sphere*. Align it to the top of *wireframe earth sphere*, as shown in Figure 14-47. Next, add the **Lens Effects** as described above and set the parameters of different effects in the **Environment and Effects** dialog box as follows:

Glow effect
Size: **3.0** Intensity: **150.0**

Ray effect
Size: **1** Intensity: **30.0** Num: **10**

Star effect
Size: **3** Intensity: **20** Width: **1.0**

Figure 14-46 The effect of the omni light displayed at rendering

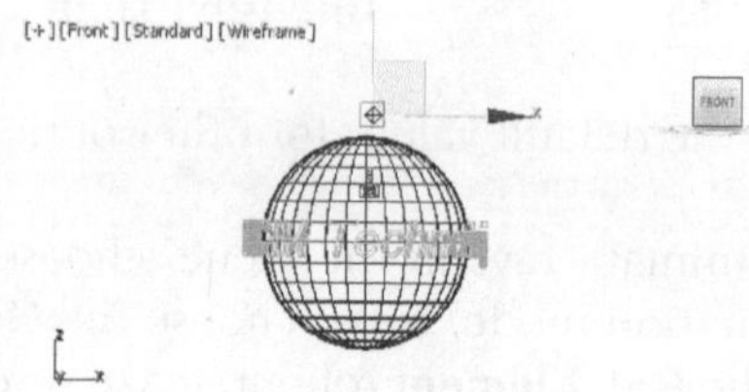

Figure 14-47 The omni light aligned just above the wireframe earth sphere

18. To animate the effects of this omni light in the scene, choose the **Toggle Auto Key Mode** button to turn on the animation mode. Now, choose the **Go to Start** button to move the time slider to frame 0. Also, in the **Star Element** rollout, make sure that the value in the **Angle** spinner is 0.0 at frame 0.

19. Choose the **Go to End** button to move the time slider to frame 1000 and set the value in the **Angle** spinner to **90.0**. The stars appear to be rotating in the final output after rendering.

20. Choose the **Toggle Auto Key Mode** button to turn off the animation mode.

    After applying the effects, the omni light with the lens effect is displayed after rendering, as shown in Figure 14-48.

    Next, you need to add spot lights to the scene.

21. Choose the **Target Spot** tool from **Create > Lights > Standard > Object Type** rollout in the **Command Panel** and then create a spot light in the Front viewport, as shown in Figure 14-49. Also, create another spot light in the Top viewport, as shown in Figure 14-50.

    The spotlights are automatically named as *Spot001* and *Spot002*.

    Next, you need to modify the parameters of the spot lights.

22. Select *Spot001* from the Scene Explorer and choose the **Modify** tab in the **Command Panel**; various rollouts are displayed to modify the parameters of the spotlight.

Figure 14-48 The omini light with lens effect displayed

23. In the **Spotlight Parameters** rollout, set the values as follows:

Hotspot/Beam: **25.3** Falloff/Field: **30.0**

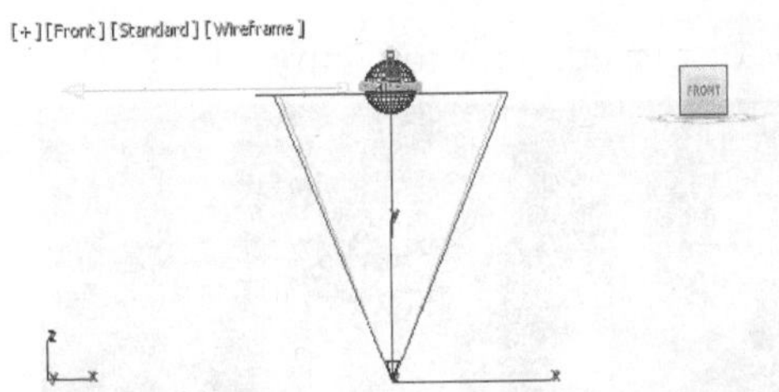

Figure 14-49 Spot light created in the Front viewport

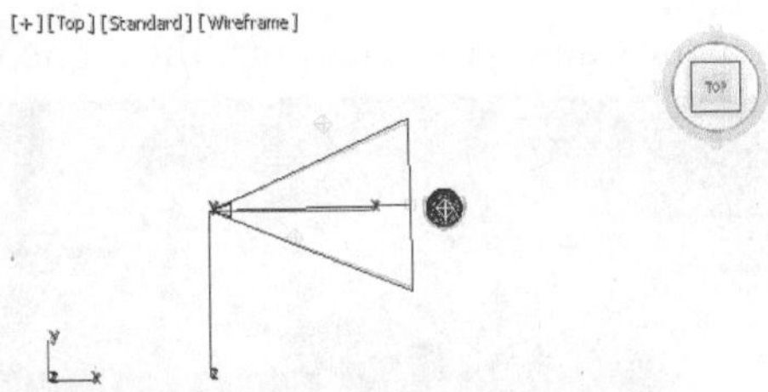

Figure 14-50 Spot light created in the Top viewport

24. In the **Atmospheres & Effects** rollout, add the **Volume Light** effect, select the **Volume Light** option in the rollout, and choose the **Setup** button; the **Environment and Effects** dialog box is displayed. In the **Volume** area of the **Volume Light Parameters** rollout, set the value in the **Density** spinner to **1.5**. Close the **Environment and Effects** dialog box.

25. Render the Camera001 viewport; the scene is displayed, refer to Figure 14-51.

26. In the **Advance Effects** rollout of the Modify panel, select the **Map** check box in the **Projector Map** area. Then, choose the **Projector Map** button labeled as **None** and assign a bitmap image of your choice to this map to give a more realistic effect to the **Volume Light** at rendering, refer to Figure 14-52.

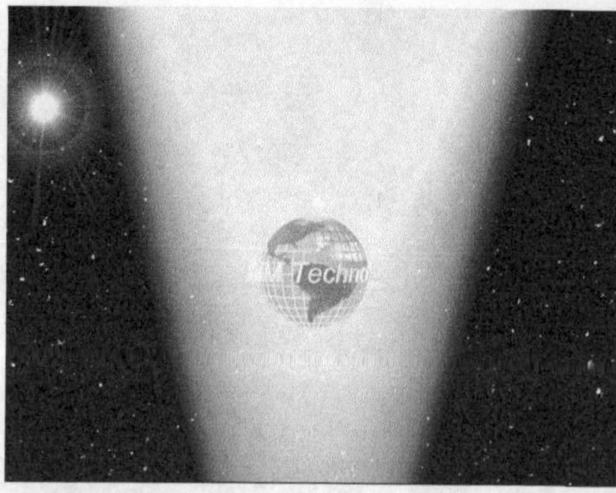

*Figure 14-51 The scene at rendering after applying the **Volume Light** effect in the Spot001 light*

*Figure 14-52 The scene at rendering after assigning a map to **Projector Map***

27. After rendering, you will notice that the **Volume Light** is visible up to the infinite distance. To control the distance of the **Volume Light**, set the parameters in the **Far Attenuation** area in the **Intensity/Color/Attenuation** rollout as follows:

    Select the **Use** and **Show** check boxes.
    Start: **10** End: **850**

Note
*You may need to adjust the values in the **Start** and **End** spinners as the values may differ depending on the placement of the light in the scene.*

28. Render the Camera001 viewport; the scene is displayed, refer to Figure 14-53.

*Figure 14-53 The scene displayed at rendering after setting the parameters in the **Far Attenuation** area*

29. Select *Spot002* in the viewport and choose the **Modify** tab in the **Command Panel**; all the rollouts are displayed to modify the parameters of the selected light.

30. In the **Spotlight Parameters** rollout, set the values as follows:

    Hotspot/Beam: **5.0** Falloff/Field: **7.0**

31. Choose the **Zoom Extents All** tool and align *Spot002 and Spot002.Target* in the viewports, as shown in Figure 14-54.

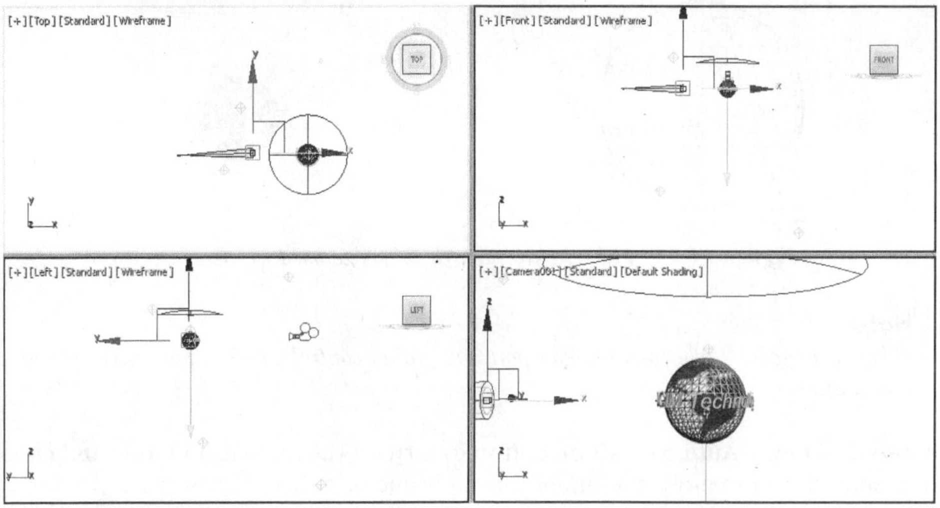

Figure 14-54 *The Spot002 and Spot002.Target light aligned in viewports*

Next, you need to animate *Spot001*.

32. Select *Spot001* and *Spot001.Target* from the Scene Explorer. Next, choose the **Zoom Extents All Selected** tool to view the selected light properly.

33. Choose the **Toggle Auto Key Mode** button to turn on the animation mode and then choose the **Go to Start** button to move the time slider to frame 0.

34. Choose the **Go to End** button to move the time slider to frame 1000 and choose the **Select and Rotate** tool. Next, in the Top viewport, move the cursor over the Z-axis and rotate the *Spot001* and *Spot001.Target* in the clockwise direction until the value in the **Z** spinner becomes **-360** in the coordinate display.

35. Choose the **Toggle Auto Key Mode** button to turn off the animation mode.

Animating Wireframe Earth Sphere and Text

In this section, you will animate *wireframe earth sphere* and *Text001* in the opposite directions.

1. Activate the Top viewport and select *wireframe earth sphere*. Next, choose the **Zoom Extents All Selected** tool; *wireframe earth sphere* is zoomed in all the viewports, as shown in Figure 14-55.

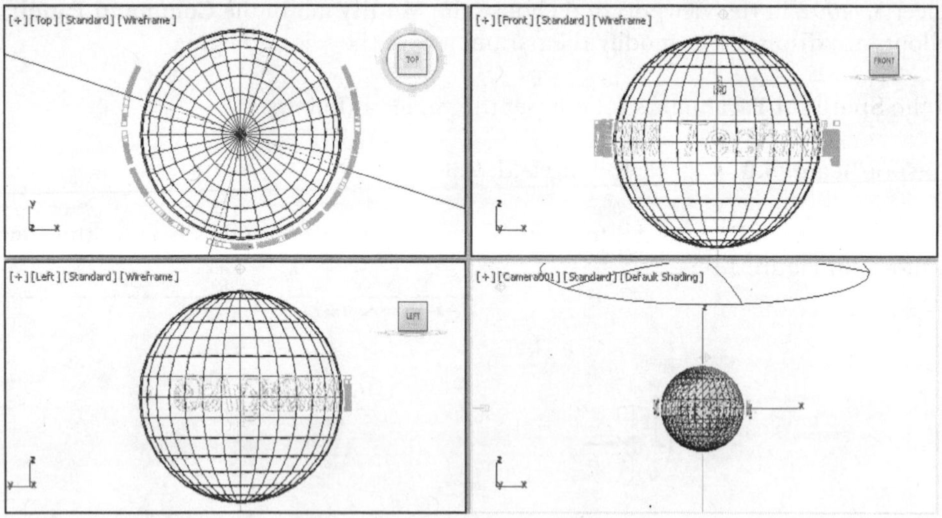

Figure 14-55 *The wireframe earth sphere zoomed in viewports*

Note

When you choose a tool from the viewport navigation controls, it does not affect the Camera001 viewport.

2. Choose the **Toggle Auto Key Mode** button to turn on the animation mode and choose the **Go to Start** button to move the time slider to frame 0.

3. Choose the **Go to End** button to move the time slider to frame 1000 and then choose the **Select and Rotate** tool. In the Top viewport, move the cursor over the X-axis and rotate *wireframe earth sphere* in the counterclockwise direction until the value in the **Z** spinner becomes **360** in the coordinate display.

4. Choose the **Toggle Auto Key Mode** button to turn off the animation mode.

   Next, you need to animate *Text001* around *wireframe earth sphere*.

5. Select *Text001* in the Top viewport and choose the **Hierarchy** tab in the **Command Panel**. In the **Adjust Pivot** rollout, choose the **Affect Pivot Only** button; the pivot point of *Text001* is displayed in the viewport, as shown in Figure 14-56.

6. Align the pivot point of *Text001* at the center of *wireframe earth sphere*, as shown in Figure 14-57. Then, choose the **Affect Pivot Only** button again to deactivate it.

7. Choose the **Select and Rotate** tool and rotate *Text001* in the Top viewport along the Z-axis until the value in the **Z** spinner becomes **-180** in the coordinate display. Next, choose the **Select and Move** tool and align *Text001*, as shown in Figure 14-58.

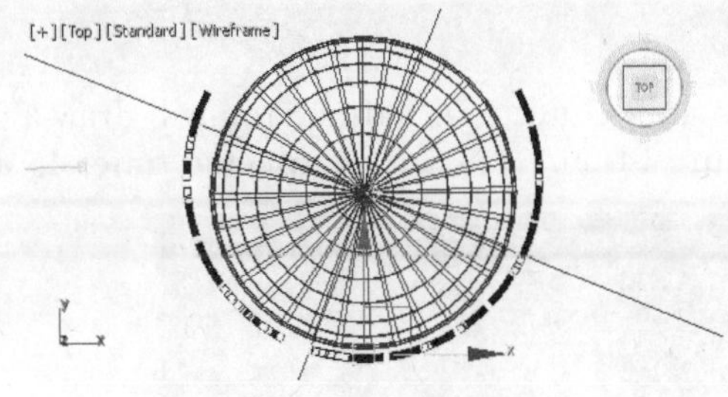

Figure 14-56 The pivot point of the Text001 displayed in the Top viewport

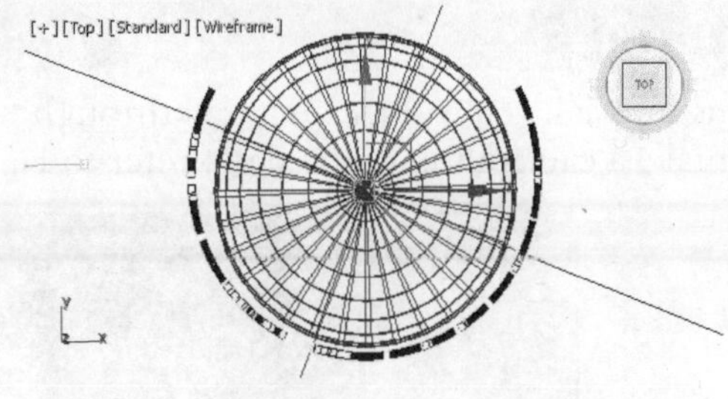

Figure 14-57 The pivot point of the Text001 aligned in the Top viewport

8. Activate the Front viewport. Next, right-click on the **Select and Rotate** tool; the **Rotate Transform Type-In** dialog box is displayed. Enter **10** in the **Z** spinner of the **Offset:Screen** area and press the ENTER key; *Text001* rotates in the Front viewport, as shown in Figure 14-59.

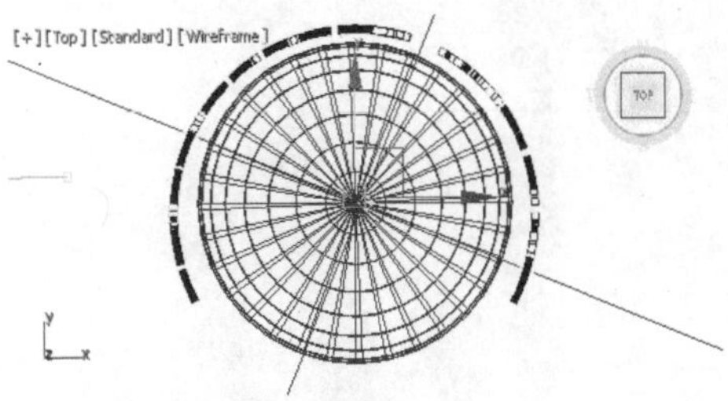

Figure 14-58 The Text001 rotated in the Top viewport

Figure 14-59 The Text001 rotated in the Front viewport

9. Choose the **Toggle Auto Key Mode** button to turn on the animation mode. Choose the **Go to End** button to move the time slider to frame 1000 and make sure that *Text001* is selected. Enter **-360** in the **Y** spinner of the **Offset:Screen** area of the **Rotate Transform Type-In** dialog box and press the ENTER key. Now, close this dialog box.

10. Choose the **Toggle Auto Key Mode** button to turn off the animation mode and choose the **Play Animation** button to view the animation.

Saving and Rendering the Scene

In this section, you will save the scene and then render it. You can also view the final rendered image sequence by downloading the file *c14_3dsmax_2017_rndr.zip* from *www.cadcim.com*. The path of the file is as follows: *Textbooks > Animation and Visual Effects > 3ds Max > Autodesk 3ds Max 2017: A Comprehensive Guide*

1. Choose **Save** from the **Application** menu.

2. To view the final output of the scene that contains all the movements, textures, lights, and animations, you need to render the scene. To do so, follow the procedure described in Tutorial 1 of this chapter.

Tutorial 3

In this tutorial, you will create a walkthrough in an architectural setting. You will draw a path and make a camera follow the path, refer to Figure 14-60. **(Expected time: 45 min)**

Figure 14-60 *The final walkthrough at frame 70*

The following steps are required to complete this tutorial:

a. Create the project folder.
b. Open the file.
c. Create the motion path.
d. Specify the length of the animation.
e. Use the walkthrough assistant.
f. Adjust the head tilt angle.
g. Animate objects in the scene.
h. Preview the animation.
i. Render and save the final animation.

Creating the Project Folder

1. Create a new project folder with the name *c14_tut3* at *\Documents\3dsmax2017* and then save the file with the name *c14tut3*, as discussed in Tutorial 1 of Chapter 2. Open the Windows Explorer and then browse to the *c14_3dsmax_2017_tut* folder. Next, copy *floor.jpeg* and *wall.jpeg* to *\Documents\3dsmax2017\c14_tut3\sceneassets\images.*

Opening the File

1. Choose **Open** from the **Application** menu; the **Open File** dialog box is displayed. In this dialog box, browse to the location *\Documents\c14_3dsmax2017_tut* and select the **c14_tut3_start.max** file from it. Choose the **Open** button to open the file, refer to Figure 14-61.

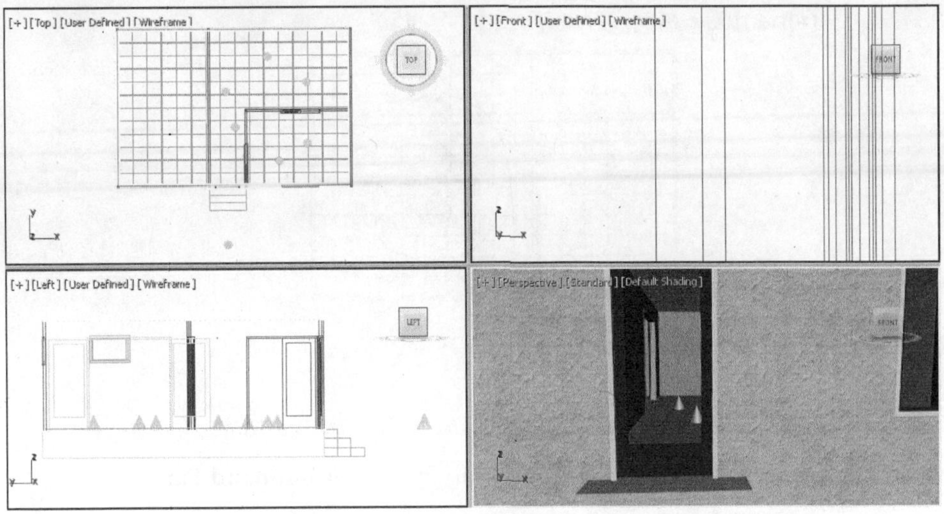

Figure 14-61 The c14_tut3_start file

2. Choose **Save As** from the **Application** menu; the **Save File As** dialog box is displayed. Browse to the location *\Documents\3dsmax2017\c14_tut3\scenes*. Save the file with the name *c14tut3.max* at this location.

Creating the Motion Path

In this section, you will create the motion path by using the **Line** tool. This path needs to have round corners to represent the naturally smooth path a person takes as he walks. Also, the path must not lie too close to any of the walls and must pass through the center of door openings.

1. Activate the Top viewport and maximize it by invoking the **Maximize Viewport Toggle** tool.

2. Invoke the **Zoom Extents All** tool to zoom in the viewports.

3. Choose **Create > Shapes** in the **Command Panel** and make sure **Splines** is selected in the drop-down list below the **Shapes** button, if it is not already selected.

4. Invoke the **Line** tool from the **Object Type** rollout.

5. Select the **Smooth** radio button in the **Initial Type** area from the **Creation Method** rollout.

6. Use the cones as a guide to create a line, starting from the bottom cone, as shown in Figure 14-62.

   The line thus created will be used as a motion path for the camera.

7. Right-click to exit the command. In the **Name and Color** rollout, enter the name of the spline as **Walkthrough-Path**.

   Next, you will refine *Walkthrough-Path*.

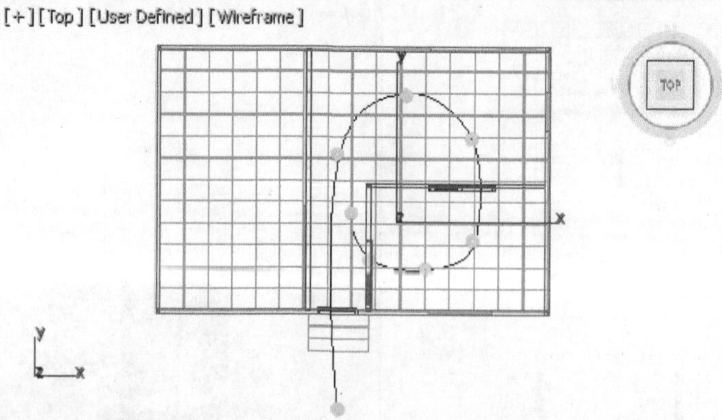

Figure 14-62 *A line created to be used as a path*

8. With the line selected, choose the **Modify** tab from the **Command Panel**.

9. In the **Selection** rollout, choose the **Vertex** button to activate the vertex sub-object mode to display each individual vertex of the path.

10. Choose the **Refine** button from the **Geometry** rollout.

11. Add a new vertex where the path enters the building by clicking on the line at that point; a new vertex appears on the path, as shown in Figure 14-63.

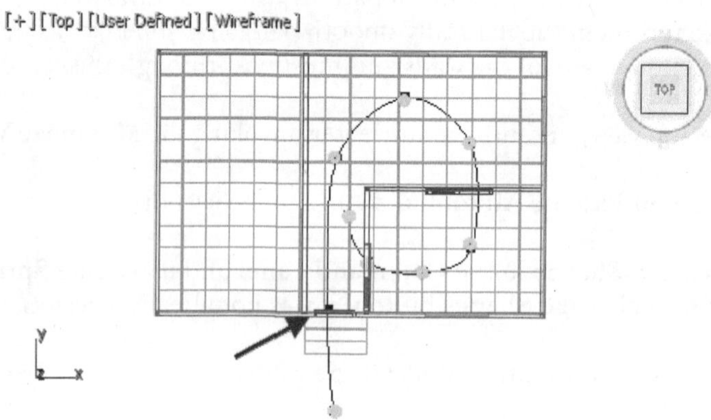

Figure 14-63 *A new vertex added to the path*

12. Invoke the **Select and Move** tool and select the newly added vertex. Now, move it such that it is centered in the doorway.

13. Invoke the **Maximize Viewport Toggle** tool. Activate the Left viewport and maximize it.

14. Move the first vertex down so that it is at the same level as the bottom of the house, as shown in Figure 14-64.

    The motion path is modified such that it follows the stairs into the building.

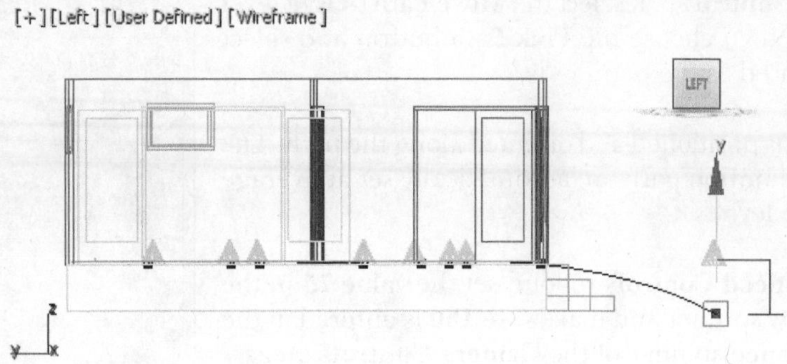

Figure 14-64 The first vertex moved down

15. Choose the **Vertex** button in the **Selection** rollout to exit the **Vertex** sub-object mode.

16. Move *Walkthrough-Path* 66.0 units up on the Y axis.

    The motion path is moved up to the height of an average person's line of sight.

Specifying the Length of the Animation

Walkthrough animations need a large number of frames. If less number of frames are used for the animation, the camera will appear to be turning at the corners very quickly. In addition, it will appear as if the person is running in the scene, instead of walking. Therefore, the more the number of frames in the animation, the smoother will be the final motion created. In this section, you will change the length of animation to increase the number of frames in it.

1. Choose the **Time Configuration** button in the animation controls; the **Time Configuration** dialog box is displayed.

2. Set the value **1000** in the **Length** spinner of the **Animation** area of this dialog box.

   The total number of frames in the animation is set to 1000. This represents a little over 30 seconds of animation.

3. Choose the **OK** button to close the dialog box.

Using the Walkthrough Assistant

The **Walkthrough Assistant** automates the process of creating a camera and makes it follow the path you created. It provides settings for the camera height and head angles.

1. Choose **Animation > Walkthrough Assistant** from the menu bar; the **Walkthrough Assistant** dialog box is displayed, as shown in Figure 14-65. You can activate any viewport in this case.

2. In the **Camera Creation** area of the **Main Controls** rollout, make sure the **Free** radio button is selected. Next, choose the **Create New Camera** button; a free camera is automatically created with the name *Walkthrough_Cam001*. Now, the camera must be moved to the start of the path.

3. In the **Path Control** area, select the **Move Path to Eye level** check box. Next, choose the **Pick Path** button and select the line created as the path.

   The camera is positioned and oriented along the path. The camera and motion path are automatically set at average person's eye level.

4. In the **Advanced Controls** rollout, set the value **75** in the **Field of View** spinner and make sure **160** is entered in the **Target Distance** spinner of the **Camera Controls** area.

   This sets the accurate camera view.

5. Activate the Perspective viewport. Change the display to *Walkthrough_Cam001* view by pressing the C key.

6. Drag the time slider to the right and left to replay the animation of the camera following the motion path.

   If the animation does not seem to be correct, you need to check it and remove the flaw. You may need to close the **Walkthrough Assistant** dialog box and delete the camera. You can then start over again by opening the **Walkthrough Assistant** dialog box and creating a new camera.

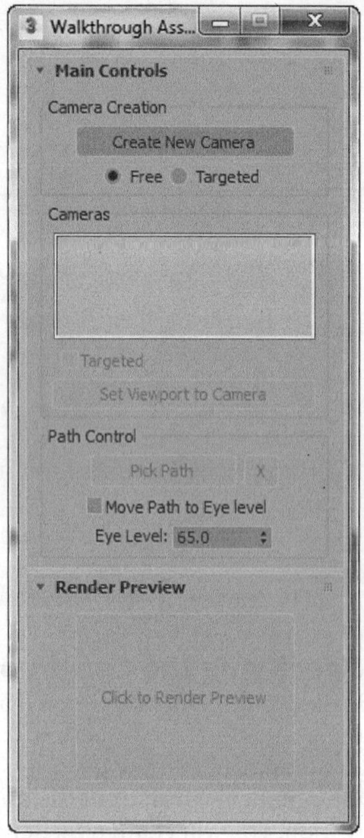

*Figure 14-65 The **Walkthrough Assistant** dialog box*

Adjusting the Head Tilt Angle

As the camera follows the motion path up toward the stairs, it tilts up to follow the path. However, a person walking up to the stairs usually does not tilt his head in this manner. In this section, you will adjust the head tilt angle.

1. Drag the time slider bar to frame 0.

2. Open the **Walkthrough Assistant** dialog box, if it is not already open. Scroll down and set the value **–45** in the **Head Tilt Angle** spinner in the **View Controls** rollout.

   The camera's line of sight is slightly below horizontal in frame 0 of the animation.

3. Choose the **Toggle Auto Key Mode** button to turn on the animation mode.

4. Drag the time slider to the frame in your animation (most probably frame 134) where the camera is halfway through the doorway.

5. Set the value **–10** in the **Head Tilt Angle** spinner.

6. Choose the **Toggle Auto Key Mode** button to turn off the animation mode. Next, drag the time slider bar to frame 0.

7. Make sure the *Walkthrough_Cam001* viewport is activated and then close the **Walkthrough Assistant** dialog box.

8. Choose the **Play Animation** button in the animation playback controls; the animation begins to play in the active viewport.

9. Choose the **Stop Animation** button to stop the animation replay.

Animating Objects in the Scene

In this section, you will animate the entrance door so that it opens when the camera passes through it and closes after some time.

1. Drag the time slider to frame 50.

   This is the frame where the door should begin to open.

2. Choose the **Graph Editors > Track View - Dope Sheet** from the menu bar.

3. Select *Entrance Door* in the viewport. In the **Track View - Dope Sheet** window, click on the plus sign on the left side of *Entrance Door* and then on the **Object (PivotDoor)** to expand the tree.

   The **Track View - Dope Sheet** window displays the **Open (degrees)** track for *Entrance Door*, as shown Figure 14-66.

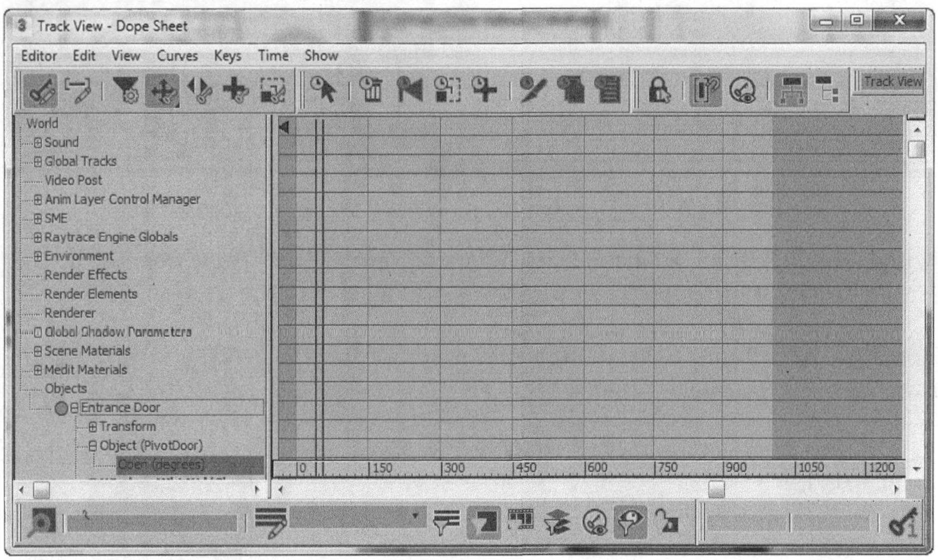

Figure 14-66 *The* **Track View - Dope Sheet** *window*

4. Choose the **Add/Remove Key** button on the top of the **Track View-Dope Sheet** window. 

5. Click on the **Open (degrees)** track at frame 50 for *Entrance Door*.

A key for *Entrance Door* is created at frame 50. The value of this key is 0 which means the door is closed. This key sets the frame where the door begins to open.

6. Close the **Track View-Dope Sheet** window.

7. Drag the time slider to frame 100 and activate the animation mode, if it is not already active.

8. Make sure *Entrance Door* is selected in any viewport.

9. Choose the **Modify** tab in the **Command Panel**.

10. In the **Parameters** rollout, set the value **90** in the **Open** spinner; *Entrance Door* is opened 90 degrees at frame 100, as shown Figure 14-67.

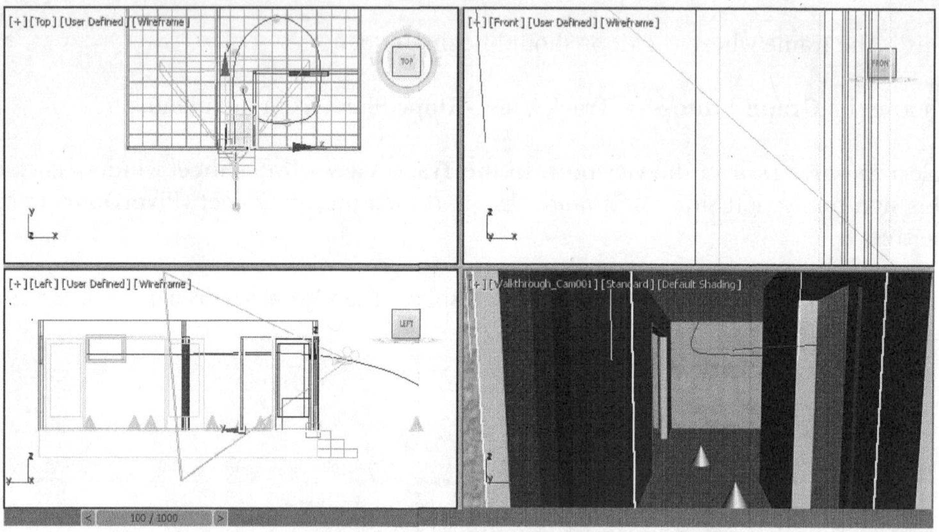

Figure 14-67 *The Entrance Door is opened 90 degrees at frame 100*

11. Choose **Graph Editors > Saved Track Views > Track View - Dope Sheet** from the menu bar; the **Track View - Dope Sheet** window is displayed with the previous settings active.

12. Choose the **Add/Remove Key** button on the top of the **Track View - Dope Sheet** window.

13. Click on the **Open (degrees)** track at frame 224 for *Entrance Door*.

14. Right-click on the new key; the **Entrance Door\ Open(degrees)** dialog box for the new key is displayed, as shown in Figure 14-68.

Figure 14-68 *The* ***Entrance Door\ Open (degrees)*** *dialog box*

15. Make sure 90 is displayed as the value in the **Value** spinner.
The value 90 degrees sets the *Entrance Door* to the fully

open position.

16. Close both the **Entrance Door\Open (degrees)** dialog box as well as the **Track View - Dope Sheet** window.

17. Drag the time slider to frame 275.

18. Make sure the **Toggle Auto Key Mode** button is chosen. Next, set the value **0** in the **Open** spinner in the **Parameters** rollout. The *Entrance Door* is closed at frame 275.

19. Choose the **Toggle Auto Key Mode** button to exit the animation mode.

20. Make sure the Walkthrough_Cam001 viewport is active and then choose the **Play Animation** button in the animation controls to play the animation.

21. Choose the **Stop Animation** button in the animation controls to stop the animation.

Previewing the Animation

Now, you can view the animation you have created by rendering a quick preview. The preview of animation will give you a good idea of whether the animation is working correctly. Before the animation is rendered, hide any object that you do not want to be visible in the preview or the final animation.

1. Invoke the **Select Object** tool from the **Main Toolbar** and select the *Walkthrough-Path* in any viewport; the motion path becomes the active object.

2. Right-click in the viewport to display the quad menu. Choose **Hide Selection** from the upper-right quadrant of this quad menu; the path is hidden and will not be visible in the animation.

3. Choose **Tools > Preview - Grab Viewport > Create Preview Animation** from the menu bar; the **Make Preview** dialog box is displayed.

4. In this dialog box, choose the **Create** button to accept the default settings and render the preview.

   The preview is generated and then played in Windows Media Player.

Rendering the Final Animation

Now that the animation has been completed and verified with the help of its preview, you can render the final animation. The final animation contains all movements and is rendered with colors, textures, and shadows. This process can take some time, depending on the speed of the computer's processor and the length, complexity, and resolution of the animation.

1. Activate the Walkthrough_Cam001 viewport and then invoke the **Render Setup** tool from the **Main Toolbar**; the **Render Setup: NVIDIA mental ray** dialog box is displayed.

2. In the **Time Output** area, select the **Active Time Segment** radio button.

   This sets all the active frames in the animation to be rendered.

3. In the **Output Size** area of the dialog box, choose the **320×240** button.

   This sets the animation to be rendered at a resolution of 320 × 240 pixels. This animation does not need to be of high resolution. The higher the resolution, the longer it will take to render the animation and also the resulting file size will be large.

4. In the **Render Output** area of this dialog box, choose the **Files** button; the **Render Output File** dialog box is displayed. As the project folder is already set, the *renderoutput* folder of this project is displayed in the **Save in** drop-down list.

5. Select **AVI File (*.avi)** from the **Save as type** drop-down list. In the **File name** text box, enter **c14tut3Render** and choose the **Save** button; the path of the file is displayed in the **Render Output** area of the **Render Setup** dialog box.

   The **AVI File Compression Setup** dialog box is displayed, if this file type has not been saved during the current drawing session. This dialog box allows you to adjust the quality and keyframe rate of the animation.

6. Choose the **OK** button to accept the default AVI settings.

Note

*If the **Save File** check box is not selected, the animation will only be rendered on the screen. You will not be able to replay the animation.*

7. Choose the **Render** button in the **Render Setup: NVIDIA mental ray** dialog box; the **Rendered Frame** window and the **Rendering** dialog box are displayed. When the rendering is complete, the **Rendering** dialog box will be closed and the last frame of the animation will be displayed. The animation has been saved to the disk and must be viewed to see the results.

8. Close the **Rendered Frame** window and the **Render Setup: NVIDIA mental ray** dialog box.

9. Choose **Rendering > View Image File** from the menu bar; the **View File** dialog box is displayed. As the project folder is already set, the *renderoutput* folder of this project is displayed in the **Look in** drop-down list.

10. Choose the **Open** button; the animation file is opened and played in Windows Media Player. Now, save the scene.

Self-Evaluation Test

Answer the following questions and then compare them to those given at the end of this chapter:

1. Which of the following buttons is used to turn on the animation mode?

   (a) **Toggle Auto Key Mode** (b) **Toggle Set Key Mode**
   (c) Both a and b (d) None of these

2. Which of the following tools is used to control the animation keys in an animation?

   (a) **Track View** (b) **Key Mode Toggle**
   (c) **Play Animation** (d) **Time Configuration**

3. Which of the following modifiers is used to create morphing in objects?

   (a) **Morph** (b) **Scatter**
   (c) **Mesher** (d) **Terrain**

4. Which of the following options in the **Rendering** pull-down menu is used to add special effects on rendering?

   (a) **Render** (b) **Material Editor**
   (c) **Effects** (d) None of these

5. The _________ button is used to jump between the keyframes directly.

6. The _________ displays the timeline with the frame numbers in it.

7. To render the final animation, you need to choose the _________ tool in the **Main Toolbar**.

8. In the set key animation mode, you need to set the keys for the animation of the selected object by choosing the **Set Keys** button. (T/F)

9. To move the time slider to another frame, you can enter the frame number directly in the **Current Frame (Go to frame)** spinner. (T/F)

10. The **Time Configuration** button is used to set the animation length by defining the number of frames in the **End Time** spinner. (T/F)

Review Questions

Answer the following questions:

1. Which of the following effects can be assigned to the rendered scene from **Rendering > Effects** in the menu bar?

   (a) **Blur** (b) **Lens Effects**
   (c) **Motion Blur** (d) All of these

2. To create the preview of an animation, select the __________ option from the __________ pull-down menu.

3. To save the rendered animation, you need to define a file with the __________ extension in the __________ area of the **Render Setup** dialog box.

4. The __________ button is used to play animation of an object in the viewport.

5. In the **Curve Editor** mode of the track view, the animation is displayed as a spreadsheet of keys. (T/F)

6. The options in the **Frame Rate** area of the **Time Configuration** dialog box are used to define a particular frame rate for animation in frames per second. (T/F)

7. The **Playback** area in the **Time Configuration** dialog box is used to change the speed of the animation. (T/F)

8. To assign the **NVIDIA mental ray** renderer for rendering the animation, you need to choose the **Quick Render (Production)** tool in the **Main Toolbar**. (T/F)

EXERCISES

The rendered output of the scene used in following exercises can be accessed by downloading the *c14_3dsmax_2017_exr.zip* file from *www.cadcim.com*. The path of the file is as follows: *Textbooks > Animation and Visual Effects > 3ds Max > Autodesk 3ds Max 2017: A Comprehensive Guide*

Exercise 1

Create an early morning scene and animate the sea water, refer to Figure 14-69.

(Expected time: 30 min)

Hints:

1. Create an omni light for the sun effect and use the **Lens** effects in it.
2. Create water effect as discussed in Tutorial 1 of this chapter.

Figure 14-69 The morning scene

Exercise 2

Create the solar system using the standard primitives and lights, as shown in Figure 14-70.

(Expected time: 60 min)

Figure 14-70 The solar system

Exercise 3

Extract the contents of *c14_3dsmax_2017_exr.zip* and then open *c14_exr03_start.max*. Create a walkthrough for the lobby, as shown in Figure 14-71. **(Expected time: 30 min)**

Figure 14-71 *Walkthrough for the lobby*

Answers to Self-Evaluation Test

1. c, **2.** a, **3.** a, **4.** c, **5. Key Mode Toggle**, **6.** track bar, **7. Render Production**, **8.** T, **9.** T, **10.** T

15

Systems, Hierarchy, and Kinematics

Learning Objectives

After completing this chapter, you will be able to:
- *Create a Ring Array system*
- *Create a Sunlight system*
- *Create a Daylight system*
- *Understand hierarchy and kinematics*
- *Create a bone system*
- *Understand IK solver, interactive IK, and applied IK*
- *Create a biped system*

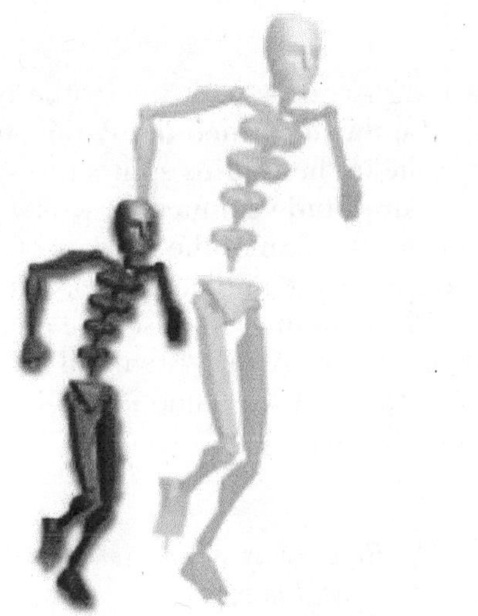

INTRODUCTION

In 3ds Max, Systems is an object set that consists of objects, linkages, and controllers. There are five types of systems: **Bones**, **Ring array**, **Sunlight**, **Daylight**, and **Biped**, refer to Figure 15-1. These systems help you to create complex animations with much ease.

To create the systems, choose **Create > Systems** in the **Command Panel**; the **Standard** option will be displayed in the drop-down list. Also, the **Object Type** rollout will be displayed, as shown in Figure 15-1. There are various tools in the **Object Type** rollout to create systems. In this chapter, you will learn to create and modify different types of systems using these tools.

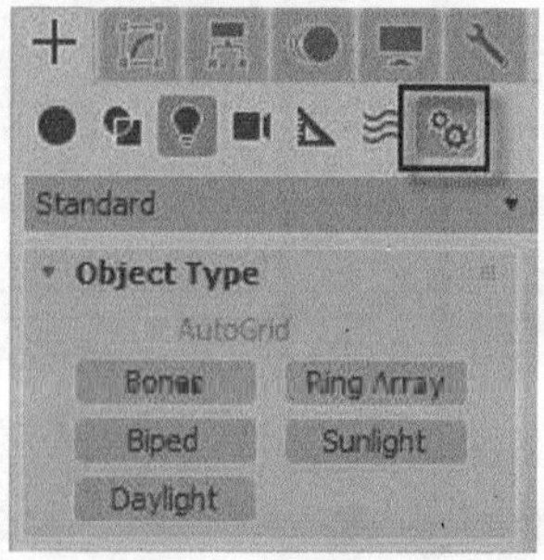

Figure 15-1 The ***Systems*** *in the* ***Command Panel***

Creating a Ring Array System

Command Panel: Create > Systems > Standard > Object Type rollout > Ring Array

A Ring Array system consists of a number of boxes in a circular pattern with a dummy object placed at its center, refer to Figure 15-2.

The dummy object is a wireframe box with a pivot point at its center. The pivot point is used as a center for transformations such as rotation and movement. Note that the dummy object cannot be rendered. You will learn more about the dummy objects in the later chapters.

To create a Ring Array system, choose the **Ring Array** tool from **Create > Systems > Standard > Object Type** rollout in the **Command Panel**; the **Name and Color** and **Parameters** rollouts will be displayed. Next, in the Top viewport, press and hold the left mouse button to specify the center of the Ring Array system, and then drag the cursor to define the radius of the array. Next, release the left mouse button; a dummy object will be created at the center. Also, four boxes will be created in a circular pattern around it, as shown in Figure 15-2. To modify the parameters of the Ring Array system, use the options in the **Parameters** rollout. This rollout is discussed next.

Parameters Rollout

To modify the parameters of a Ring Array system, select one of the boxes in the viewport and choose the **Motion** tab in the **Command Panel**; the **Parameters** rollout will be displayed, as shown in Figure 15-3. Set the value in the **Radius** spinner to specify the radius of the Ring Array system. Set the value in the **Amplitude** spinner to specify the amplitude of ring's sine curve. It is a height offset from the local origin of the dummy object located at the center. Set the value in the **Cycles** spinner to specify the number of peaks in the ring's curve of the Ring Array system. Set the value in the **Phase** spinner to offset the phase of the wave. If you set the whole numbers in this spinner, then the Ring Array system will not be affected, only the decimal values will affect the Ring Array system. Set the value in the **Number** spinner to specify the number of boxes in the Ring Array system.

Note

To modify the parameters of the Ring Array system, you need to choose the ***Motion*** *tab in the* ***Command Panel****. However, if you need to modify the parameters of only the boxes in the Ring Array system, then choose the* ***Modify*** *tab in the* ***Command Panel****.*

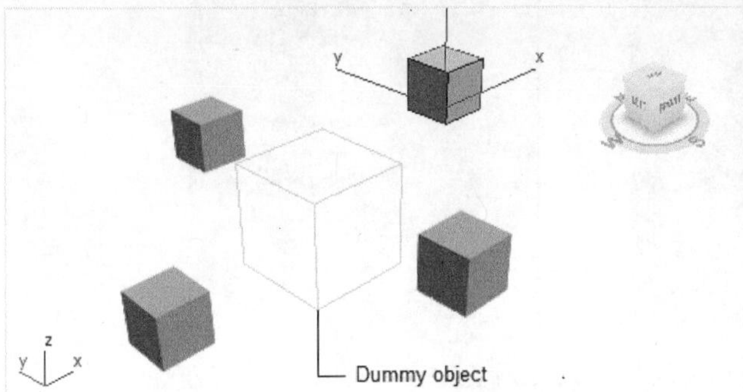

Figure 15-2 The Ring Array system

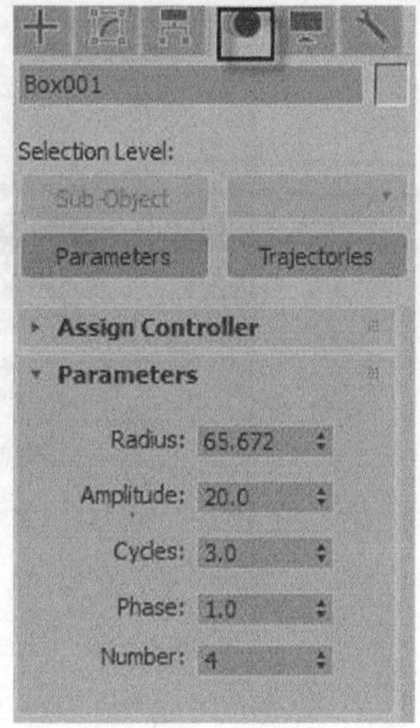

*Figure 15-3 The **Parameters** rollout in the **Motion** tab*

Using Different Objects in a Ring Array System

You can replace the boxes in a Ring Array system with other objects. To do so, first create a Ring Array system and then create an object in the viewport with which you want to replace the boxes in the Ring Array system. Make sure that Ring Array system is selected in the viewport. Next, choose the **Curve Editor (Open)** tool from the **Main Toolbar**; the **Track View - Curve Editor** dialog box will be displayed. The hierarchy tree on the left of this dialog box controls the objects in the viewport. In the hierarchy tree, select the name of the object with which you want to replace the boxes of the Ring Array system, as shown in Figure 15-4, and then right-click on it; a quad menu will be displayed. Choose the **Copy** option from the quad menu. Next, select one of the boxes in the hierarchy tree, as shown in Figure 15-5. Right-click on it and choose the **Paste** option from the quad menu; the **Paste** dialog box will be displayed, as shown in Figure 15-6. Select the **Copy** or **Instance** radio button in the **Paste as** area. Also, select the **Replace all instances** check box in the **Paste Target** area to replace all boxes of the Ring Array system with the same object. Then, choose the **OK** button; the boxes in the Ring Array system will be replaced by the object created in the viewport, as shown in Figure 15-7.

Animating a Ring Array System

You can animate the radius, amplitude, cycles, and phase of a Ring Array system. To do so, choose the **Toggle Auto Key Mode** button from animation playback controls, and then modify the parameters in the **Parameters** rollout at different frames. Choose the **Toggle Auto Key Mode** button again to exit the animation mode.

To apply any transformation such as rotation, move, or scale to the Ring Array system, you need to select the dummy object. Also, you can apply the modifiers to the boxes of the Ring Array system. The modifier that you apply to any one of the boxes will be applied automatically to the other boxes of the Ring Array system.

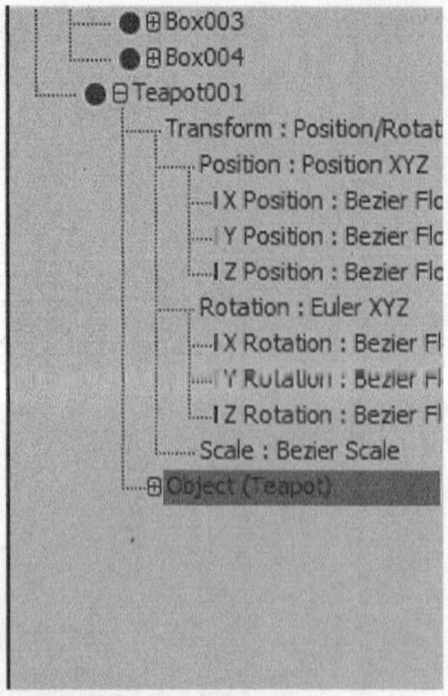

Figure 15-4 The object selected in the hierarchy tree to replace the boxes of the Ring Array system

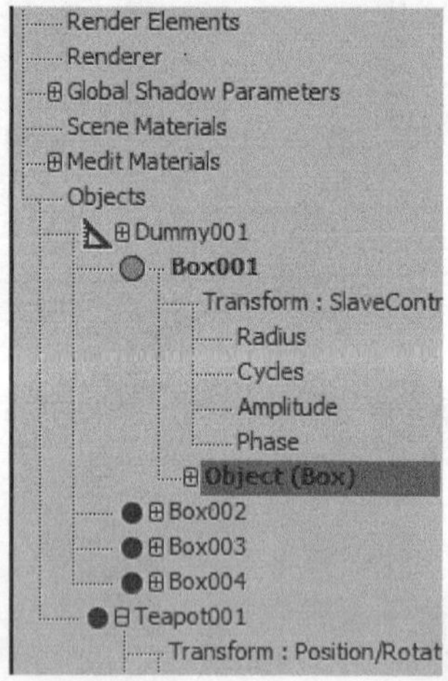

Figure 15-5 The box selected in the hierarchy tree to be replaced with the object

*Figure 15-6 The **Paste** dialog box*

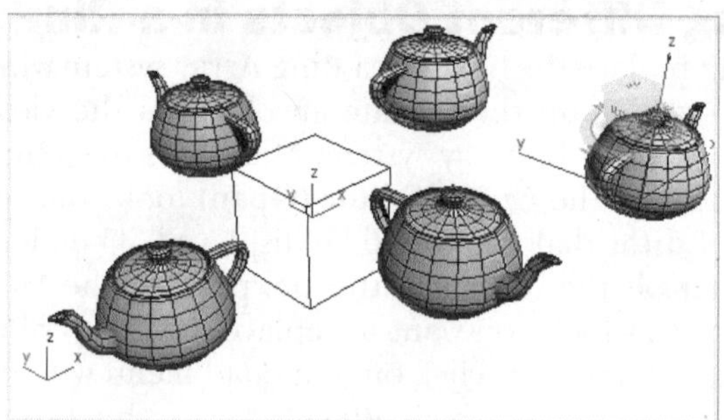

Figure 15-7 The boxes of the Ring Array system replaced with the object (teapot)

Creating a Sunlight System

Command Panel:	Create > Systems > Standard > Object Type rollout > Sunlight

The Sunlight system is used to produce the light effects similar to the geographically accurate effects of the sun over the earth at a particular location, time, and so on, refer to Figures 15-8 and 15-9. You can also animate the position of the sun to get a better idea of the shadows cast by sun at different positions. The Sunlight system uses a directional light.

To create a Sunlight system in the scene, choose the **Sunlight** tool from **Create > Systems > Standard > Object Type** rollout in the **Command Panel**; the **Name and Color** and **Control Parameters** rollouts will be displayed. Next, in the Top viewport, press and hold the left mouse button at the center of the scene to specify the center of the Sunlight system and then drag the cursor to define the radius of the system. Release the left mouse button; a compass rose will be created in the viewports, refer to Figure 15-10. Now, drag the cursor up or down to specify the distance of the directional light from the compass rose and then click on the screen to set the distance; the compass rose and the directional light will be created in the viewports, refer to Figure 15-10. Next, left-click in any of the viewport to exit the **Sunlight** tool.

Figure 15-8 *The scene after creating the Sunlight system*

Figure 15-9 *The scene after changing the position of the sun*

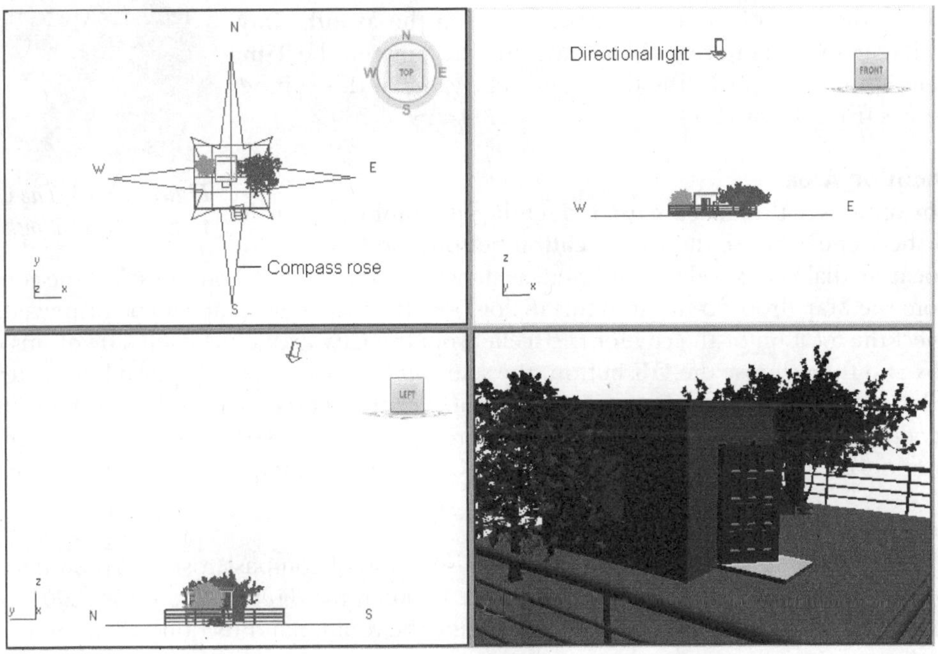

Figure 15-10 *The Sunlight system in all viewports*

By default, the name of the light and the compass rose will be *Sun001* and *Compass001*, respectively. To modify the parameters of the Sunlight system, you need to use the options in the **Control Parameters** rollout. This rollout is discussed next.

Control Parameters Rollout

To modify the parameters of the Sunlight system, select *Sun001* in the viewport and choose the **Motion** tab in the **Command Panel**; the **Control Parameters** rollout will be displayed, as shown in Figure 15-11. The options in this rollout are discussed next.

Note

After selecting Sun001 in the viewport if you choose the ***Modify*** *tab instead of the* ***Motion*** *tab in the* ***Command Panel****, then the rollouts of the directional light will be displayed.*

On selecting the **Motion** tab, the settings of the sun are displayed, refer to Figure 15-11. On the top of this rollout, there are two text boxes: **Azimuth** and **Altitude**. The **Azimuth** text box indicates the compass direction of the sun in degrees. The **Altitude** text box indicates the height of the sun above the horizon in degrees. The values displayed in these text boxes depend on the other settings in the **Control Parameters** rollout. The different areas in this rollout are discussed next.

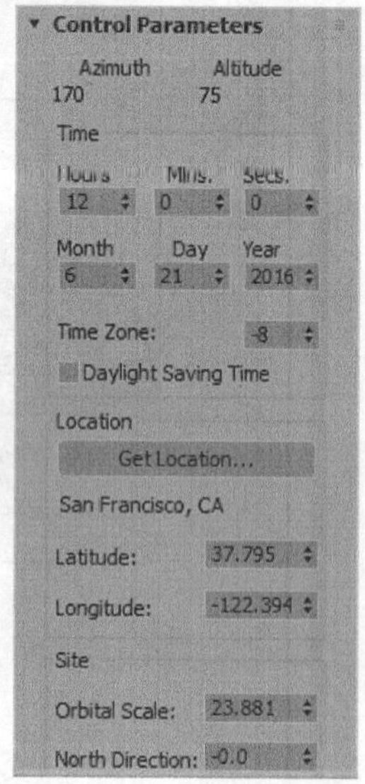

Figure 15-11 *The* ***Control Parameters*** *rollout*

Time Area

The options in this area are used to set the time, date, and time zone. Set the values in the **Hours**, **Mins.**, and **Secs.** spinners to specify the time of the day. Set the values in the **Month**, **Day**, and **Year** spinners to specify the date. Set the value in the **Time Zone** spinner to specify the time zone. The value in this spinner ranges from -12 to 12.

Location Area

The options in this area are used to set the geographical location of the scene. Choose the **Get Location** button; the **Geographic Location** dialog box will be displayed, as shown in Figure 15-12. You can select the continent from the **Map** drop-down list in this dialog box; the respective map will be displayed. Now, select the location or the city for the scene from the **City** area on the left side of this dialog box and then choose the **OK** button; the selected location will be displayed in the text box below the **Get Location** button in the **Control Parameters** rollout. Also, the position of *Sun001* will be changed in the viewport according to the selected location. If you change the location, then the values in the **Latitude** and **Longitude** spinners will also change accordingly.

Site Area

The options in this area are used to set the direction of compass rose. Set the value in the **Orbital Scale** spinner to define the distance between the *Sun001* and *Compass001*. Set the value in the **North Direction** spinner to define the rotational direction of the compass rose in the scene.

To modify the radius of the compass rose, select the *Compass001* in the viewport, and then choose the **Modify** tab; the **Parameters** rollout will be displayed, as shown in Figure 15-13. Next, set the value in the **Radius** spinner; the radius of the compass rose will change.

Creating a Daylight System

Menu bar:	Create > Systems > Daylight system
Command Panel:	Create > Systems > Standard > Object Type rollout > Daylight

The Daylight system is similar to the Sunlight system with the difference that the Daylight system uses a combination of two lights, namely sunlight and skylight. You can use the IES sun light, mr sun light, or target direct light (standard light) as the sunlight in the Daylight system. The IES sky light, mr sky light, or skylight (standard light) can be used as the skylight in the Daylight system.

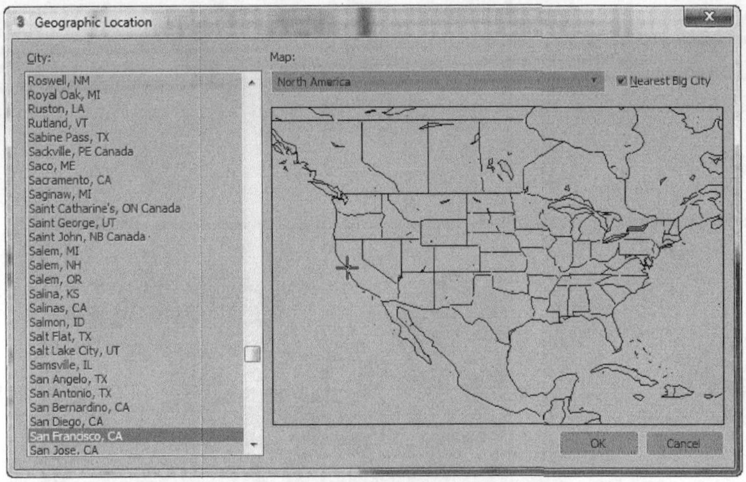

Figure 15-12 *The* ***Geographic Location*** *dialog box*

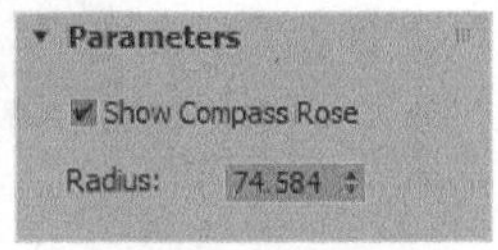

Figure 15-13 *The* ***Parameters*** *rollout*

To create a Daylight system in your scene, choose the **Daylight** tool from **Create > Systems > Standard > Object Type** rollout in the **Command Panel**; the **Daylight System Creation** message box will be displayed. This message box prompts you to use the Logarithmic Exposure Control, as shown in Figure 15-14. Choose the **Yes** button in this message box.

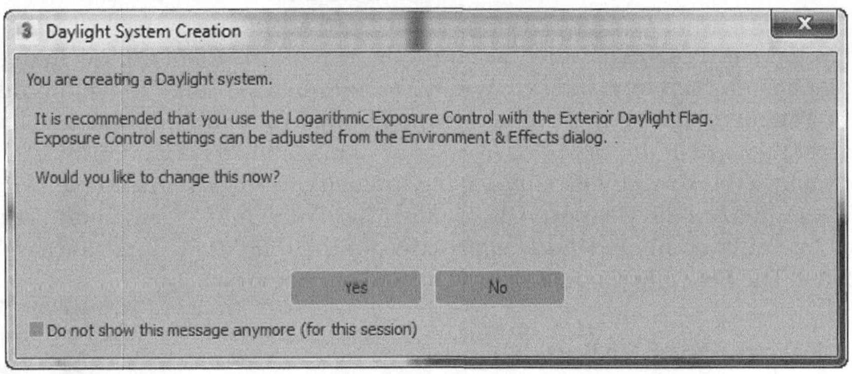

Figure 15-14 *The* ***Daylight System Creation*** *message box*

Next, create the Daylight system using the same method as discussed for the Sunlight system; a compass rose and a combination of the sunlight and skylight will be displayed in the viewports, as shown in Figure 15-15. By default, the name of the light and the compass rose will be *Daylight001* and *Compass001*, respectively. The *Daylight001* light consists of two lights, namely sunlight and skylight. To modify the parameters of the Daylight system, you need to use the options in the **Control Parameters** rollout. This rollout is discussed next.

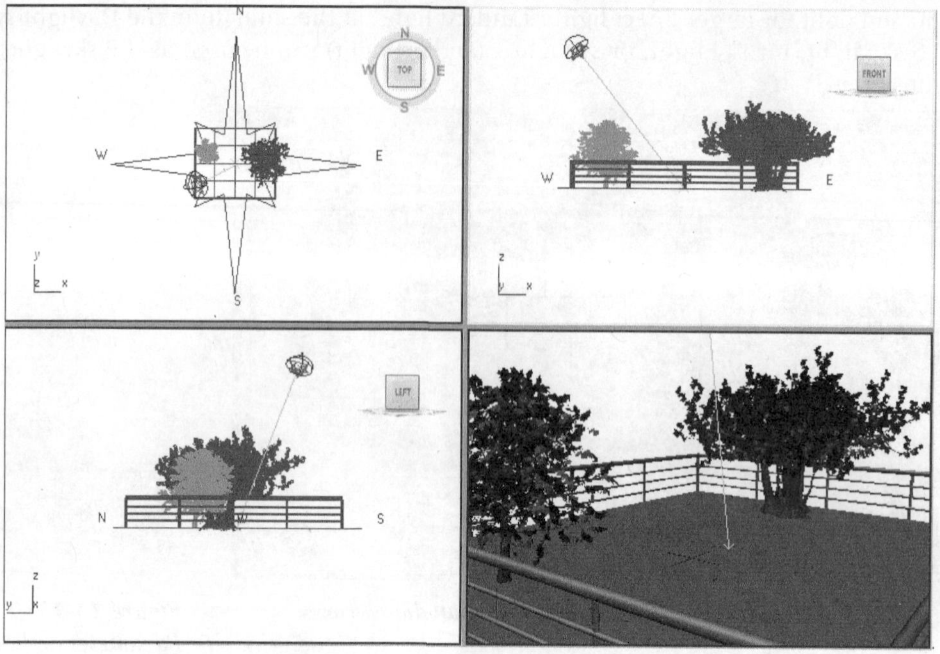

Figure 15-15 The Daylight system created in viewports

Control Parameters Rollout

To modify the parameters of the Daylight system, select the *Daylight001* in the viewport and choose the **Motion** tab in the **Command Panel**; the **Control Parameters** rollout will be displayed. Most of the options in this rollout are the same as those discussed for the Sunlight system.

Additionally, there is a **Manual** radio button on the top of this rollout. By default, this radio button is cleared and therefore, you can modify the parameters using the options displayed in the **Control Parameters** rollout. On selecting the **Manual** radio button, you can manually set the position of the light in the viewport. Also, you can manually set the intensity of the light by setting the value in the **Multiplier** spinner in the **Intensity/Color/Attenuation** rollout. To do so, select the *Daylight001* in the viewport. Choose the **Modify** tab in the **Command Panel**; various rollouts will be displayed in the Modify panel. Most of the rollouts are same as those discussed in Chapter 11. The **Daylight Parameters** rollout is discussed next.

Daylight Parameters Rollout

Figure 15-16 The ***Daylight Parameters*** *rollout*

The options in this rollout are used to select the type of sunlight and the skylight used in the Daylight system, refer to Figure 15-16. The **Active** check box on the right of the **Sunlight** label is selected by default. It is used to turn on the sunlight in the viewport. You can select the light to be used as the sunlight from this drop-down list located below **Sunlight** label.

The **Active** check box on the right of the **Skylight** label is selected by default. It is used to turn on the skylight in the viewport. Select the option to be used as skylight from this drop-down list located below the **Skylight** label.

In the **Position** area, the **Date, Time and Location** radio button is selected by default. It is used to set the time, date, and location of the Daylight system. Choose the **Setup** button; the **Control Parameters** rollout will be displayed in the **Motion** tab, where you can set the time, location, and other parameters of the Daylight system in this rollout. Select the **Manual** radio button in the **Position** area to manually set the position and intensity of the *Daylight001* in the viewport. Select the **Weather Data File** radio button to derive the angle and intensity of the sun from a weather data (EPW) file.

Note
When you select the required sunlight or skylight option from the drop-down list, the corresponding rollouts will also be displayed to modify the selected light.

HIERARCHY AND KINEMATICS

The ability to link objects together to create a chain is known as hierarchy. When you create a complex computer animation then the hierarchy is the most important tool to simplify the animation process. In a hierarchy, the movement, rotation, or scaling of an object is controlled by another object. It creates a parent-child relationship that is very similar to a family tree. The object that is being controlled is known as the child object and the object that controls another object is known as the parent object. The parent object is controlled by a superior parent object, known as the ancestor object of the first child object. The child object that does not have any child is known as the leaf object. The parent object that is superior to all objects in a hierarchy is known as the root object.

When you create an animation by moving, rotating, or scaling the parent object, the transformations will automatically be transferred to its child objects. In this case, there is no need to create separate animation for the child objects. For example, if you have created a car model in which main body of the car is parent object while all other parts of the car are child objects, then transformation applied to main body of the car will automatically be transferred to all other parts of the car.

A hierarchy is basically used to simplify a complex animation. With this feature, you can link a number of objects to a single object and transfer its animation to the linked objects. It is also very useful for creating the character animation. In 3ds Max, there are two methods used for animating the hierarchies namely, forward kinematics (FK) and inverse kinematics (IK). These hierarchies are created by linking the objects. The inverse kinematics is more advanced than the forward kinematics. These kinematics are discussed next.

Forward and Inverse Kinematics

In forward kinematics, the child objects are animated based on the transformations in the parent object. It is a one-way system in which if a parent object moves, then the child objects will also move. But, if the child objects move, then the parent object will not be affected. In other words, you can control the top object of the hierarchy to animate the entire chain. While creating a hierarchy, the forward kinematics is created by default. The inverse kinematics (IK) is just the opposite of the forward kinematics. In inverse kinematics, you can animate the object at the bottom of the hierarchy to control the entire chain. In this kinematics, if you move a child object, then the movement will be transferred to each ancestor in the hierarchy.

Creating a Hierarchy

To create a hierarchy, you need to link the objects that will generate a chain. First, create the objects in the viewport that you need to link together. Then, decide which one of them will be the parent object and which one will be the child object. Next, select one of the child objects in the viewport and then choose the **Select and Link** tool from the **Main Toolbar**. Now, move the cursor over the child object; the cursor will get changed, refer to Figure 15-17. Then, press and hold the left mouse button on the child object and drag the cursor to the parent object; a dotted line will be displayed between the child and parent objects, as shown in Figure 15-17. Next, release the left mouse button over the parent object; the parent object will blink for a second and will be linked to the child object. Next, choose the **Select Object** tool to exit the command. You can link more than one child objects to the parent object using the same procedure. Now, move the parent object in the viewport,

To unlink the child object, select the child object in the viewport and then choose the **Unlink Selection** tool from the **Main Toolbar**.

Hierarchy Tab

The **Hierarchy** tab is used to modify hierarchical linkage between the objects. To do so, select a linkage from the hierarchical linkage in the viewport and choose the **Hierarchy** tab in the **Command Panel**. The **Pivot** button is chosen by default in the **Hierarchy** tab. As discussed in the earlier chapters, the options displayed on choosing the **Pivot** button are used to adjust the pivot point of the object. Choose the **Link Info** button in the **Hierarchy** tab; the **Locks** and **Inherit** rollouts will be displayed, as shown in Figure 15-18.

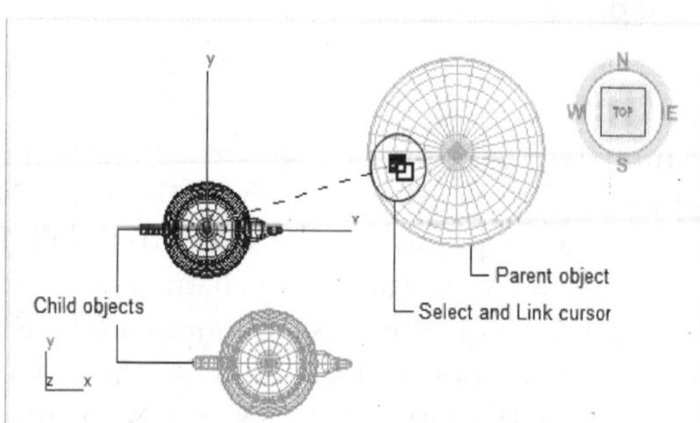

*Figure 15-17 The child object linked to the parent object using the **Select and Link** tool*

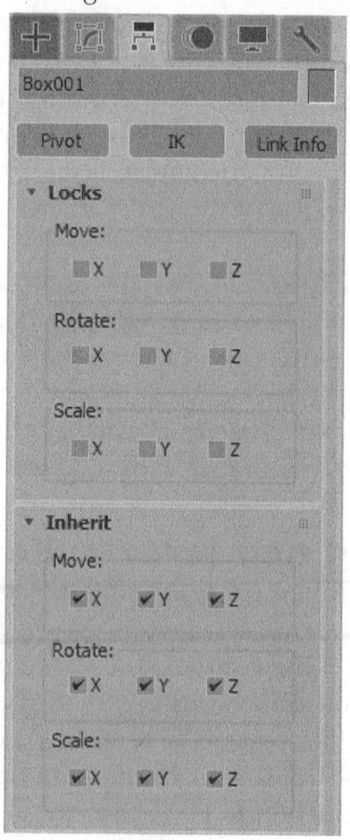

*Figure 15-18 The **Link Info** button chosen in the **Hierarchy** tab*

The options in the **Locks** rollout are used to lock the transformations of an object about any of its local axes. In the **Locks** rollout, there are three areas, **Move**, **Rotate**, and **Scale**. Each area has **X**, **Y**, and **Z** check boxes. To lock a transform, select the corresponding check boxes in these areas. The options in the **Inherit** rollout are used to control the transforms that the child objects inherit from the parent object. In this rollout, there are three areas, **Move**, **Rotate**, and **Scale**. Each area has **X**, **Y**, and **Z** check boxes. By default, all check boxes in each area are selected. As a result, the child object inherits all transforms on all axes. To restrict the child object to inherit the transformation of the parent object, first select the child object and then clear the corresponding check box from the respective area.

Creating Bones System

Command Panel: Create > Systems > Standard > Object Type rollout > Bones

The bones system is created by linking the bones and joints in a hierarchy. You can animate and transform this hierarchy either using the forward kinematics or the inverse kinematics. However, animating the bones system using the inverse kinematics is easier. You can animate any type of the characters as well as the machineries using the bones system. To create bones system, choose the **Bones** tool from **Create > Systems > Standard > Object Type** rollout in the **Command Panel**; the **Name and Color**, **IK Chain Assignment**, and **Bone Parameters** rollouts will be displayed. Next, click any of the viewport to create the base of the hierarchy. Now, move the cursor up or down to define the length of the bone and click in the viewport again to end the creation of the first bone. Similarly, start creating the second bone. Repeat the same process to continue the creation of hierarchy. Next, right-click in the viewport to exit the command; a hierarchy of bones will be created, as shown in Figure 15-19. When you right-click to exit the command, a small bone will be created at the end of the hierarchy. This small bone is used at the time of assigning an IK about which you will learn later in this chapter.

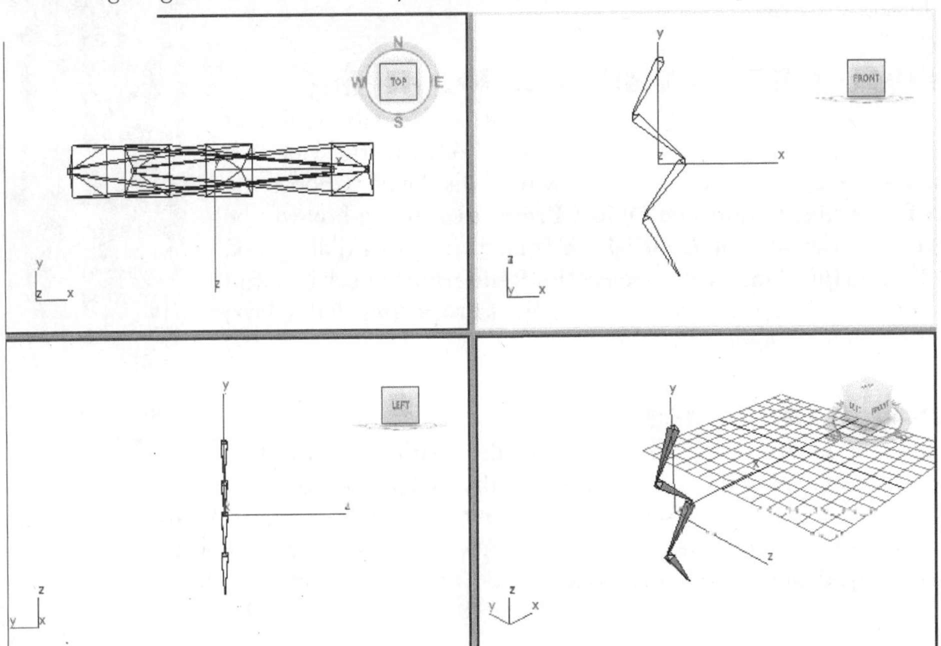

Figure 15-19 The hierarchy of bones created

Note

When you create bones in the viewport, the first bone will be the parent bone and the others will be the child bones of the first bone. The bones created in continuation form a hierarchy of bones. Also, the bone created first will be at the top in the hierarchy and the bone created last will be at the bottom in the hierarchy.

To modify the appearance of bone in the viewport, select the bone in the viewport and then choose the **Modify** tab in the **Command Panel**; the **Bones Parameters** rollout will be displayed. This rollout is discussed next.

Bones Parameters Rollout

There are two areas in this rollout to modify the appearance of bones, refer to Figure 15-20. These areas are discussed next.

Bone Object Area

The **Bone Object** area comprises of some tools. Set the values in the **Width** and **Height** spinners to specify the width and height of the selected bone. Set the value in the **Taper** spinner to specify the taper amount of the bone in percentage.

Bone Fins Area

The options in this area are used to add fins to the bones to increase their thickness, refer to Figure 15-21. Fins help in improving the animation of bulky characters. Select the **Side Fins**, **Front Fin**, and **Back Fin** check boxes to add fins on the sides, front, and back of the bones, respectively. Set the values in the **Size**, **Start Taper**, and **End Taper** spinners to specify the size, start taper, and end taper values of the fins.

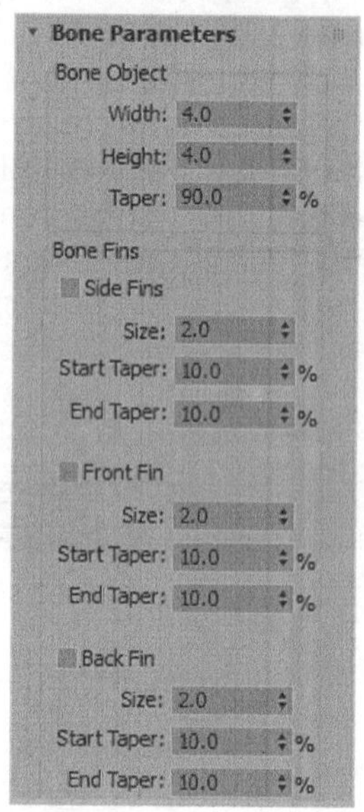

Figure 15-20 The ***Bones Parameters*** *rollout*

Making the Bones Visible on Rendering

By default, the bones created in the viewport will not be visible at rendering. To make them visible, select the bones in the viewport and right-click on them; a quad menu will be displayed. Choose the **Object Properties** option; the **Object Properties** dialog box will be displayed. By default, the **General** tab is chosen in this dialog box. In the **Rendering Control** area, select the **Renderable** check box and then choose the **OK** button to exit the **Object Properties** dialog box; the bones will be visible at rendering.

Modifying the Bones

Generally, the length of the bones is set while creating them in the viewport. After creating them, if you need to edit the length and other properties of the bones, then select the bone in the viewport. Choose **Animation > Bone Tools** from the menu bar; the **Bone Tools** dialog box will be displayed, as shown in Figure 15-22. The rollouts in this dialog box are discussed next.

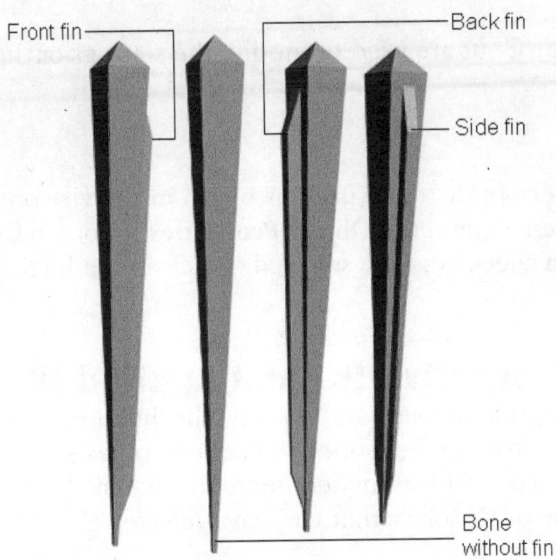

Figure 15-21 The bones with the fins added to them

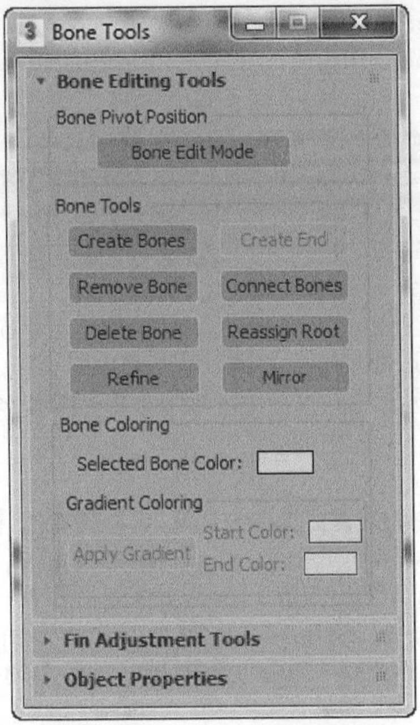

*Figure 15-22 The **Bone Tools** dialog box*

Bone Editing Tools Rollout

The areas in this rollout are used to set the geometry and color of the selected bones. These areas are discussed next.

Bone Pivot Position Area

The **Bone Edit Mode** button in this area is used to edit the length and position of the bone in the viewport. To do so, choose the **Bone Edit Mode** button and then choose the **Select and Move** tool and move the bone along any axes in the viewport.

Bone Tools Area

The **Bone Tools** area consists of different buttons that are used to create, remove, delete, and refine the bones. Choose the **Create Bones** button from this area; the **Bones** tool in the **Command Panel** will be activated, which can be used to create a bone in the viewport. If you choose the **Create End** button, a small bone will be created at the end of the bone system. You can choose the **Remove Bone** button to remove the selected bone. When you remove a bone, its parent bone stretches to cover the pivot point of the removed bone. Choose the **Connect Bones** button to connect the selected bone to another bone in the viewport. Choose the **Delete Bone** button to delete the selected bone and also to remove its parent-child relationship. Choose the **Reassign Root** button; the selected bone will become the parent bone in the hierarchy. To split the selected bone, choose the **Refine** button and then select a bone in the viewport; the bone will split. Choose the **Mirror** button; the **Bone Mirror** dialog box will be displayed. Set the parameters in this dialog box and choose the **OK** button; the selected bone will be mirrored in the viewport.

Bone Coloring Area

The options in this area are used to modify the color of the bone.

Fin Adjustment Tools Rollout

The options in the **Fin Adjustment Tools** rollout are used to modify the settings of the fins of the selected bones in the viewport.

Object Properties Rollout

In this rollout, set the parameters for other objects to be used as bones in the viewport. First, select the hierarchy in the viewport and then expand the **Object Properties** rollout in the **Bone Tools** dialog box. Now, select the **Bone On** check box; the selected objects in the hierarchy will behave as bones.

Understanding IK Solver, Interactive IK, and Applied IK

An IK Solver creates an inverse kinematic solution to rotate and position the links in a hierarchy. It applies an IK controller to each bone for controlling the motion of the child objects in a linkage. The hierarchy to which an IK solver is applied will be animated interactively. The behavior and controls on the linkage depend on the type of IK solver that you have selected.

In an Interactive IK, the IK solution is applied only to the specified keyframes. To apply the Interactive IK, select the end of the hierarchy in the viewport and then choose the **Hierarchy** tab in the **Command Panel**. Next, choose the **IK** button in the **Hierarchy** tab and then choose the **Interactive IK** button in the **Inverse Kinematics** rollout. Next, apply the transforms to the bones in the system.

The Applied IK is used to create the accurate motion in the hierarchy of linked objects. In this case, you need to bind the end of a hierarchy to the animated follow objects. After binding, select any object in your kinematic chain and choose the **Apply IK** button in the **Inverse Kinematics** rollout of the **Hierarchy** tab in the **Command Panel**; the IK solution will be calculated for each frame in the animation and it will create transform keys for every object in the IK chain.

Creating a Bone Hierarchy with an IK Solver

To create a bone system with an IK solver, choose the **Bones** tool from **Create > Systems > Standard > Object Type** rollout in the **Command Panel**; the **Name and Color**, **IK Chain Assignment**, and **Bone Parameters** rollouts will be displayed. In the **IK Chain Assignment** rollout, select the required IK solver from the **IK Solver** drop-down list. Then, select the **Assign To Children** check box, refer to Figure 15-23. Next, create bones in the viewport as discussed earlier; the selected IK solver will automatically be applied to them.

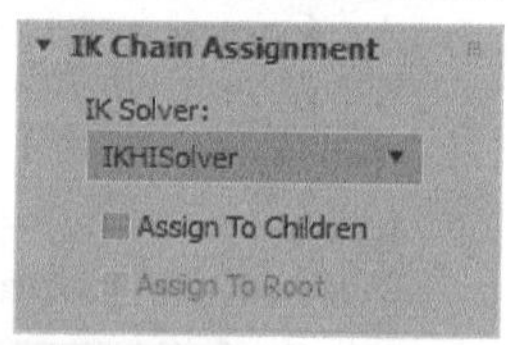

Figure 15-23 The IK Chain Assignment rollout

You can also apply the IK solvers after creating the hierarchy of the bones. To do so, select the bone in the hierarchy and then choose **Animation > IK Solvers** from the menu bar; a cascading menu will be displayed. Now, choose the required IK solver from the cascading menu and then select another bone in the hierarchy in the viewport to define the IK chain.

Creating a Biped System

Command Panel: Create > Systems > Standard > Object Type rollout > Biped

The Biped system is used to create a biped model that has a two-legged figure. It is used to animate the characters such as humans and animals. To create a biped system, choose the **Biped** tool from **Create > Systems > Standard > Object Type** rollout in the **Command Panel**; the **Name and Color** and **Create Biped** rollouts will be displayed. In the Top viewport, press and hold the left mouse button, and then drag the cursor to define the height of the biped model. Release the left mouse button; the biped model will be displayed in all viewports, as shown in Figure 15-24.

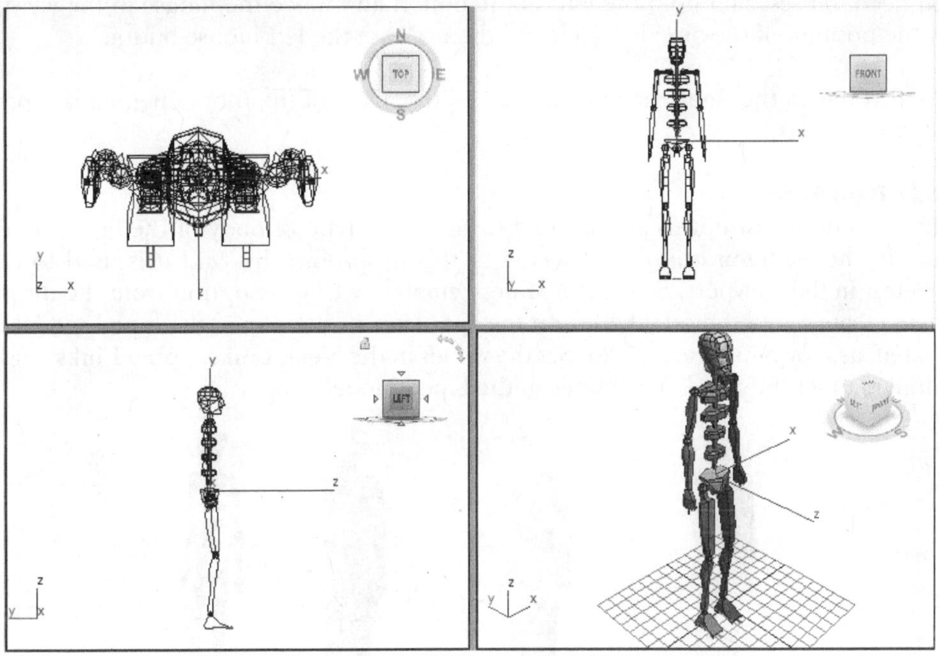

Figure 15-24 The biped model displayed in viewports

Choose the **Select by Name** tool from the **Main Toolbar** to view the names of all bones in the biped system; the **Select From Scene** dialog box will be displayed. Make sure that the **Display Bones** button is chosen in the dialog box to display the names of the biped bones. Among all the bones in a biped system, the *Bip001* bone is the root bone.

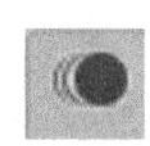

You can modify the biped parameters before creating the biped model using the **Create Biped** rollout displayed on invoking the **Biped** tool. However, to modify the biped model after creating it, select the *Bip001* bone in the biped model. Choose the **Motion** tab in the **Command Panel**; various rollouts will be displayed. In the **Biped** rollout, choose the **Figure Mode** button; the **Structure** rollout will be displayed. Now, expand the **Structure** rollout to modify the parameters of the biped model. Most of the options in the **Structure** rollout are same as in the **Create Biped** rollout. The **Create Biped** rollout is discussed next.

Note

Before creating a biped model, you need to create a character mesh and then, you need to put the biped model in it to animate the character mesh created.

Create Biped Rollout

The options in this rollout are used to define the method of creation of a biped system. You can also modify the number of bones in different parts of the body using this rollout. The areas in this rollout are discussed next.

Creation Method Area

The radio buttons in this area are used to define the method of creation of the biped system. The **Drag Height** radio button is selected by default. It is used to create the biped system as discussed earlier. If you select the **Drag Position** radio button, then to create a biped system, you need to press and hold the left mouse button and move the mouse in the viewport to set the position of the biped model, and then release the left mouse button.

The text box in the **Root Name** area displays the name of the root bone that is superior to all parent bones.

Body Type Area

The drop-down list in this area is used to select the type of body of the biped model. By default, the **Skeleton** option is selected in this drop-down list and it is used to create a skeleton in the viewport. Select the **Male**, **Female**, or **Classic** option from the drop-down list to create a biped model based on the character in the scene; the biped model will be created, as shown in Figure 15-25. Set the values in the **Neck Links**, **Spine Links**, and other spinners to set the number of bones in the biped model.

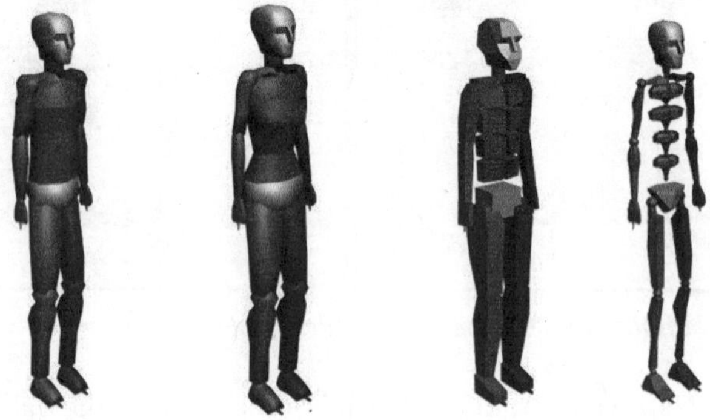

Figure 15-25 *The male, female, classic, and skeleton type biped models*

Note

Biped body parts cannot be removed but you can hide unwanted parts of the biped.

TUTORIALS

Tutorial 1

In this tutorial, you will create an animated scene to study the shadow pattern according to the position of the sun over the earth at a particular location, date, and time. The shadow at one of the frames is shown in Figure 15-26. **(Expected time: 30 min)**

Figure 15-26 The shadow pattern in the scene

The following steps are required to complete this tutorial:

a. Create the project folder.
b. Create a ground and a tree.
c. Create the camera.
d. Create the Sunlight system.
e. Animate the Sunlight system.
f. Save and render the scene.

Creating the Project Folder

Create a new project folder with the name *c15_tut1* at *\Documents\3dsmax2017* and then save the file with the name *c15tut1*, as discussed in Tutorial 1 of Chapter 2.

Creating a Ground and a Tree

In this section, you will create the ground by using the **Plane** tool.

1. Choose the **Plane** tool from **Standard Primitives** and create a plane in the Top viewport, as discussed earlier.

2. Change the name of the plane to *ground*. Also, assign the grass material to it, as discussed in the earlier chapters.

3. Choose the **Foliage** tool from **Create > Geometry > AEC Extended** in the **Command Panel** and create a tree in the Top viewport, as discussed earlier. Set the height of the tree according to *ground*. Align the tree at the center of the ground in all viewports, refer to Figure 15-27.

Creating the Camera

In this section, you will create the camera in the scene by using the **Free** camera tool.

1. Choose the **Free** tool from **Create > Cameras > Standard > Object Type** rollout in the **Command Panel** to create a free camera in the viewport.

2. Create a Free camera in the Front viewport. The camera is automatically named as *Camera001*. Align the *Camera001* in all viewports, refer to Figure 15-27.

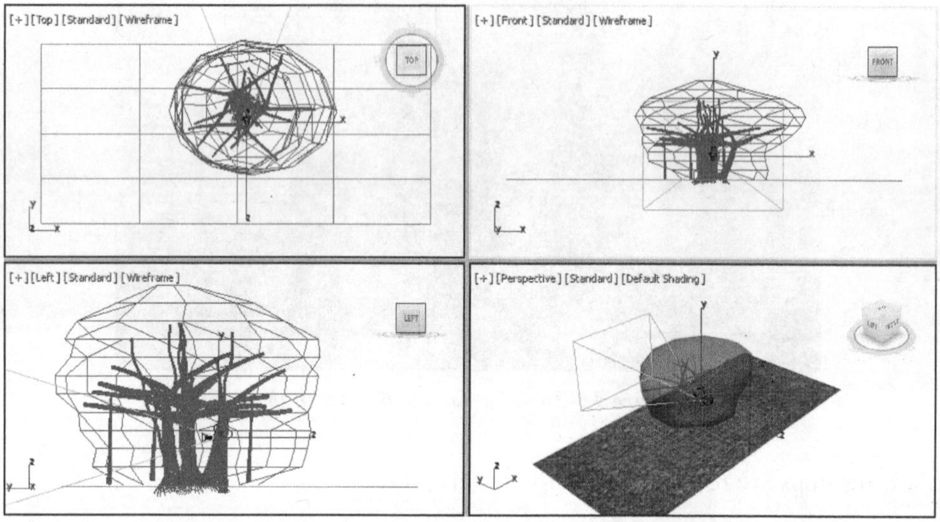

Figure 15-27 *Alignment of the Camera001 in viewports*

You need to press the C key in the Perspective viewport to display the camera view. Adjust the camera view as per your requirements.

Creating the Sunlight System

In this section, you will create the Sunlight system by using the **Sunlight** tool.

1. Choose the **Zoom** tool and zoom out the Top viewport to make room for creating the Sunlight system.

2. Choose **Create > Systems** in the **Command Panel**; various tools are displayed in the **Object Type** rollout. Choose the **Sunlight** tool from the **Object Type** rollout.

3. In the Top viewport, press and hold the left mouse button at the center of the scene to specify the center of the Sunlight system and then drag the cursor to define the radius of the system. Now, release the left mouse button; a compass rose is created. Now, drag the cursor again and click in the viewport to set the distance of the light from the compass rose, as shown in Figure 15-28; the compass rose and the directional light are created in the viewports. Next, right-click in the viewport to exit the command.

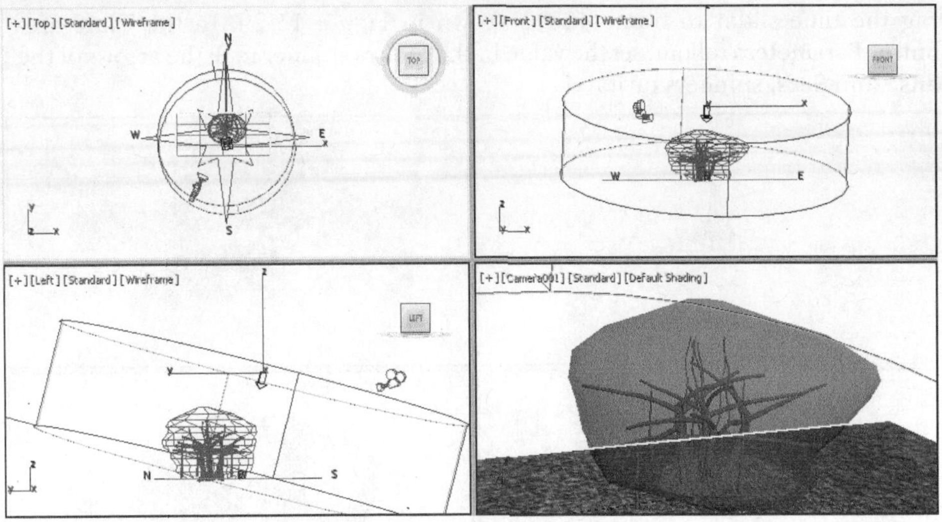

Figure 15-28 The Sunlight system created in viewports

The compass rose and the directional light are automatically named as *Compass001* and *Sun001*, respectively.

4. Choose the **Zoom Extents All** tool to see the objects in every viewport.

Animating the Sunlight System

In this section, you will study the shadow pattern to change the position of *Sun001* at different frames in the time slider.

1. Choose the **Time Configuration** button from the timeline; the **Time Configuration** dialog box is displayed. In the **End Time** spinner of the **Animation** area, set the value to **500**. Now, choose the **OK** button; the total number of frames in the track bar are increased.

2. Select *Sun001* in any viewport and choose the **Motion** tab in the **Command Panel**; the **Control Parameters** rollout is displayed.

   By default, the Sunlight system is placed at the latitude of San Francisco, CA. Also, the sun is set at 12 hours. You can modify the location of the sun in the **Location** area by choosing the **Get Location** button.

   Next, you need to change the position of *Sun001* by modifying the time given in the **Time** area of the **Control Parameters** rollout.

3. Drag the time slider to frame 0. In the **Time** area of the **Control Parameters** rollout, set the value in the **Hours** spinner to **7** and press ENTER.

4. Make sure that *Sun001* is selected in the viewport. Choose the **Toggle Auto Key Mode** button to enter the animation mode; the track bar, the **Toggle Auto Key Mode** button, and the active viewport turn red.

5. Drag the time slider to frame 40, as shown in Figure 15-29. In the **Time** area of the **Control Parameters** rollout, set the value in the **Hours** spinner to **8**; the arrows of the **Hours**, **Mins.**, and **Secs.** spinners turn red.

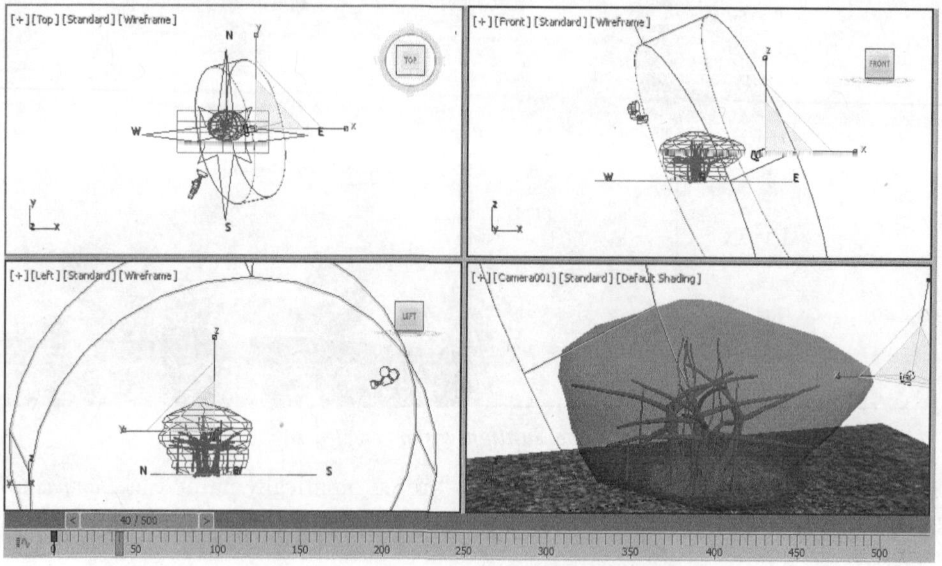

Figure 15-29 The time slider at frame 40

6. Drag the time slider to frame 80. In the **Time** area of the **Control Parameters** rollout, set the value in the **Hours** spinner to **9**.

7. Drag the time slider to 40-frames increments and increase the time in the **Hours** spinner by one hour at each increment. Continue this process until the value in the **Hours** spinner is set to **18**. Note that, at this point the last frame number should be 440.

8. Choose the **Toggle Auto Key Mode** button again to turn off the animation mode.

9. Choose the **Play Animation** button to view the effect of the Sunlight system in Camera viewport.

Saving and Rendering the Scene

In this section, you will save the scene and then render it. You can also view the final rendered image sequence by downloading the *c15_3dsmax_2017_rndr.zip* file from *www.cadcim.com.* The path of the file is as follows:*Textbooks > Animation and Visual Effects > 3ds Max > Autodesk 3ds Max 2017: A Comprehensive Guide*

1. Change the background color of the scene to blue, as discussed in earlier chapters.

2. Choose **Save** from the **Application** menu.

3. For rendering the scene, refer to Tutorial 1 of Chapter 14.

After the completion of the rendering process, the final output of the animation is saved in the *AVI* format at the specified location. You can view the final output of the animation by opening the corresponding *AVI* file.

Tutorial 2

In this tutorial, you will create the footsteps animation of a biped model. The footsteps animation at a frame is shown in Figure 15-30. **(Expected time: 45 min)**

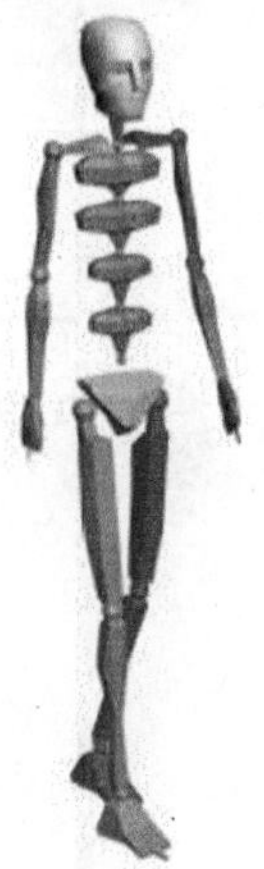

Figure 15-30 *The biped model animation*

The following steps are required to complete this tutorial:

a. Create the project folder.
b. Create a biped model.
c. Create the footsteps animation for the model.
d. Save and render the scene.

Creating the Project Folder

Create a new project folder with the name *c15_tut2* at *\Documents\3dsmax2017* and then save the file with the name *c15tut2*, as discussed in Tutorial 1 of Chapter 2.

Creating a Biped Model

In this section, you will create a biped model by using the **Biped** tool.

1. To create a biped model, first activate the Top viewport. Then, choose the **Biped** tool from **Create > Systems > Standard > Object Type** rollout in the **Command Panel**; various rollouts are displayed.

2. In the **Create Biped** rollout, select the **Drag Position** radio button in the **Creation Method** area and click at the center of the Top viewport; a biped model is displayed in all viewports.

All bones in the biped model are named automatically. The *Bip001* bone is the root bone in the hierarchy and is selected by default after the creation of the model.

3. Choose the **Zoom Extents All** tool; the biped model is displayed in the viewports, as shown in Figure 15-31.

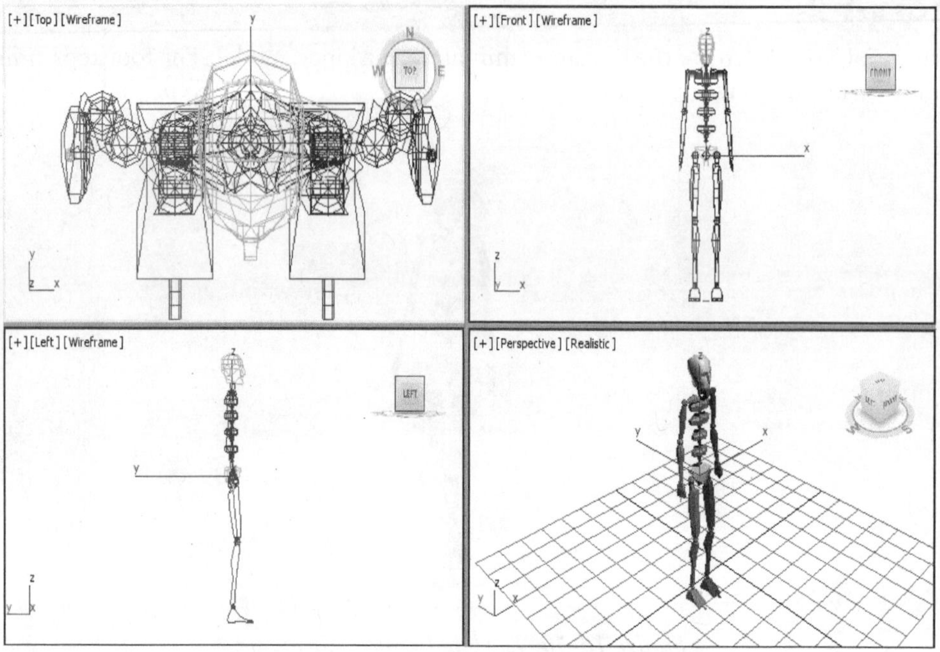

Figure 15-31 The biped model displayed in viewports

Creating the Footsteps Animation for the Model

In this section, you will create the footsteps animation for the biped model.

1. Make sure that *Bip001* is selected in the viewport and choose the **Motion** tab in the **Command Panel**; various rollouts are displayed.

2. Expand the **Biped** rollout and then choose the **Footstep Mode** button; the **Footstep Creation**, **Footstep Operations**, and **Dynamics & Adaptation** rollouts are displayed, as shown in Figure 15-32.

3. Choose the **Zoom** tool and zoom out the Top viewport until one-fourth of the original biped model is visible. Also, set the view of the Top viewport using the **Pan** tool, as shown in Figure 15-33.

4. In the **Footstep Creation** rollout, make sure that the **Walk** button is chosen.

5. Choose the **Create Footsteps (at current frame)** button in theFootstep Creation rollout and then move the cursor over the Top viewport; the shape of the cursor changes. Now, click in the Top viewport to create the footsteps, as shown in Figure 15-34.

6. Choose the **Select and Move** tool and align the footsteps in the Top viewport, as shown in Figure 15-35. Also, rotate some of the footsteps by 45-degree in the clockwise direction, as shown in Figure 15-36.

   Next, you need to create keys for the animation of biped model.

7. In the **Footstep Operations** rollout, choose the **Create Keys for Inactive Footsteps** button; keys are created for the biped animation according to the footsteps.

8. Choose the **Select Object** tool and then choose the **Zoom Extents All** tool.

9. Now, activate the Perspective viewport and choose the **Play Animation** button; the biped model starts moving according to the footsteps created, refer to Figure 15-37.

***Figure 15-32** The rollouts displayed after choosing the **Footstep Mode** button*

10. If you want to add more footsteps in the viewport, then choose the **Select by Name** tool; the **Select From Scene** dialog box is displayed. Now, select *Bip001* bone and choose the **OK** button to close the dialog box.

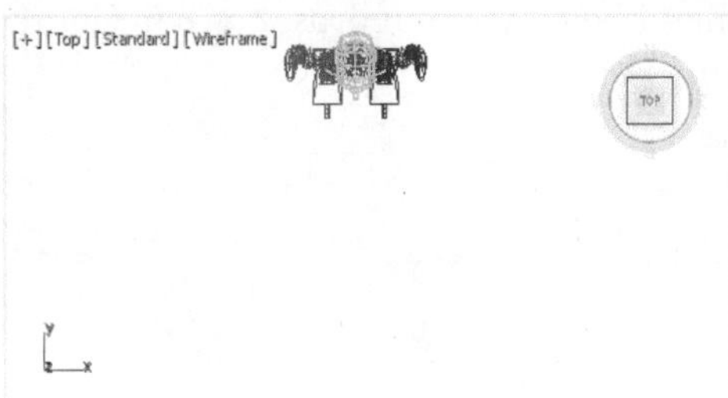

***Figure 15-33** The Top viewport after using the **Zoom** and **Pan** tools*

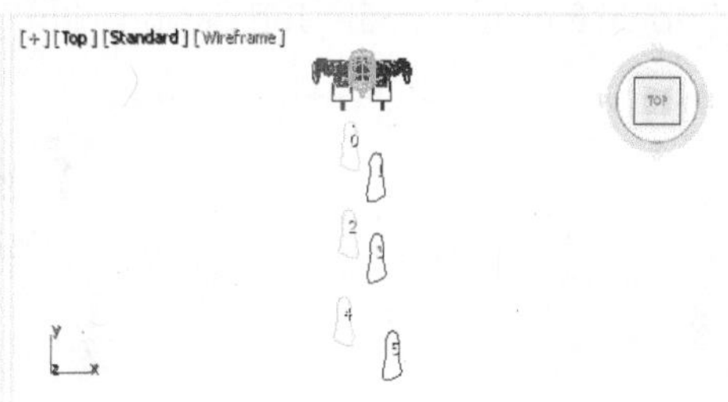

***Figure 15-34** The footsteps created in the Top viewport*

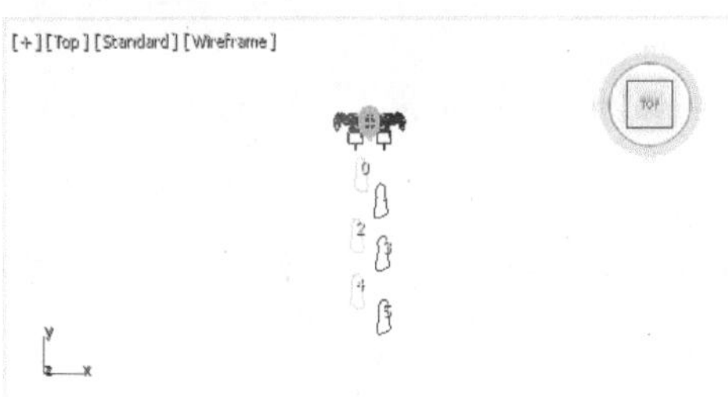

***Figure 15-35** The footsteps aligned using the **Select and Move** tool*

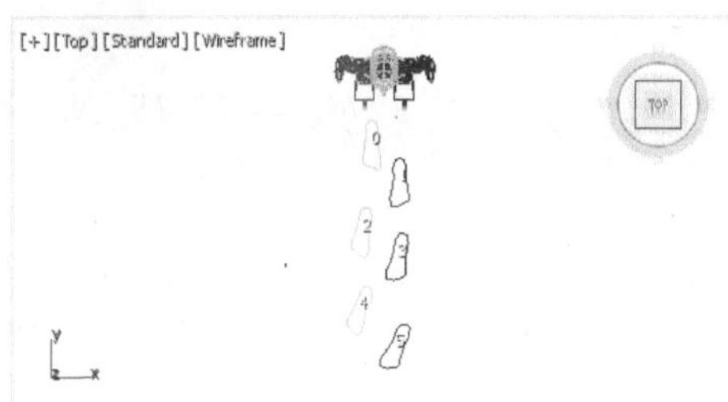

***Figure 15-36** The footsteps after rotating them in the Top viewport*

11. Choose the **Motion** tab in the **Command Panel** if not already chosen and then choose the **Footstep Mode** button in the **Biped** rollout.

12. In the **Footstep Creation** rollout, make sure the **Walk** button is chosen and then choose the **Create Footsteps (append)** button.

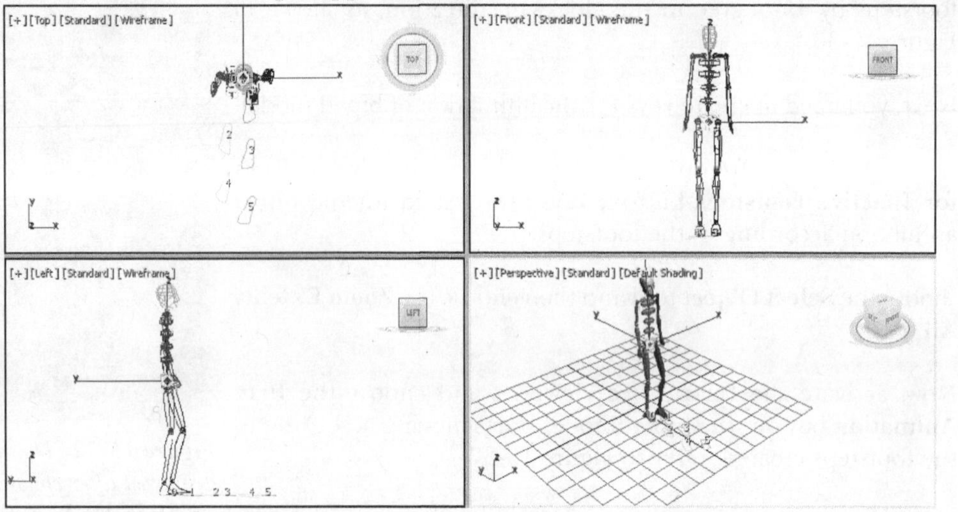

Figure 15-37 The biped model moving after choosing the ***Play Animation*** *button*

13. Move the cursor over the Top viewport; the shape of the cursor changes. Now, create additional footsteps in the Top viewport and align them as required, as shown in Figure 15-38.

Figure 15-38 New footsteps created in the Top viewport

14. In the **Footstep Operations** rollout, choose the **Create Keys for Inactive Footsteps** button; keys are created for the biped animation according to the newly created footsteps.

15. Choose the **Select Object** tool and then the **Zoom Extents All** tool.

16. Activate the Perspective viewport and choose the **Play Animation** button; the biped model starts moving according to the newly created footsteps, as shown in Figure 15-39.

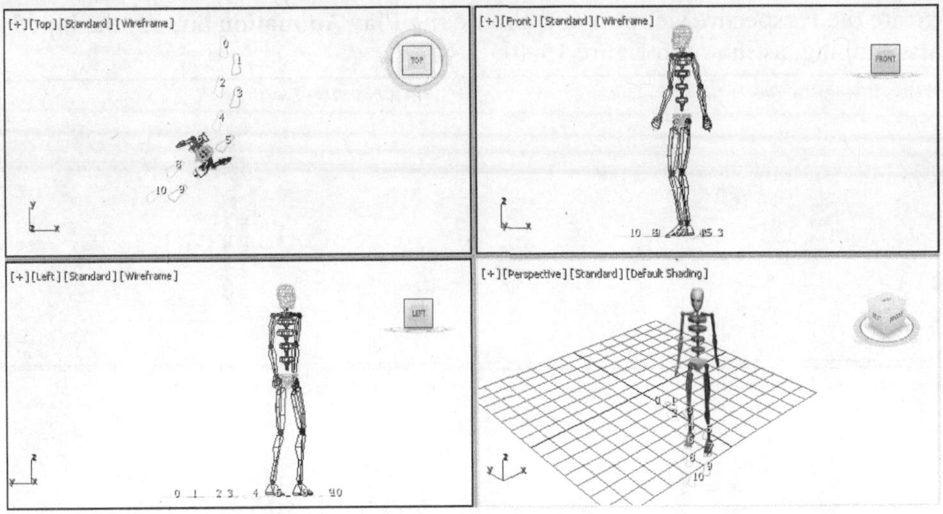

Figure 15-39 The biped model moving according to the newly created footsteps

Next, you will create multiple footsteps automatically.

17. Now, you need to hide the biped model in the scene. To do so, press Ctrl+A to select all bone objects in the scene and then Ctrl+click on *Bip001* Footsteps in the **Scene Explorer**. Right click; a quad-menu is displayed. Select the **Hide Selection** option from the Quad menu.

    Next, create another biped model in the viewport, as discussed in the previous section and then choose the **Zoom Extents All** tool to view it in the viewports.

18. Expand the **Biped** rollout in the **Motion** panel if it is not already expanded. Choose the **Footstep Mode** button in this rollout.

19. In the **Footstep Creation** rollout, choose the **Run** button.

20. Choose the **Create Multiple Footsteps** button in the **Footstep Creation** rollout; the **Create Multiple Footsteps: Run** dialog box is displayed. 

21. In the **General** area of this dialog box, set the value **6** in the **Number of Footsteps** spinner to specify the number of footsteps and then choose the **OK** button. You can also set other parameters in the **Create Multiple Footsteps: Run** dialog box, as required.

    Next, you need to create keys for the biped model.

22. In the **Footstep Operations** rollout, choose the **Create Keys for Inactive Footsteps** button; keys are created for the biped animation.

23. Choose the **Zoom Extents All** tool.

24. Activate the Perspective viewport and choose the **Play Animation** button; the biped model starts running, as shown in Figure 15-40.

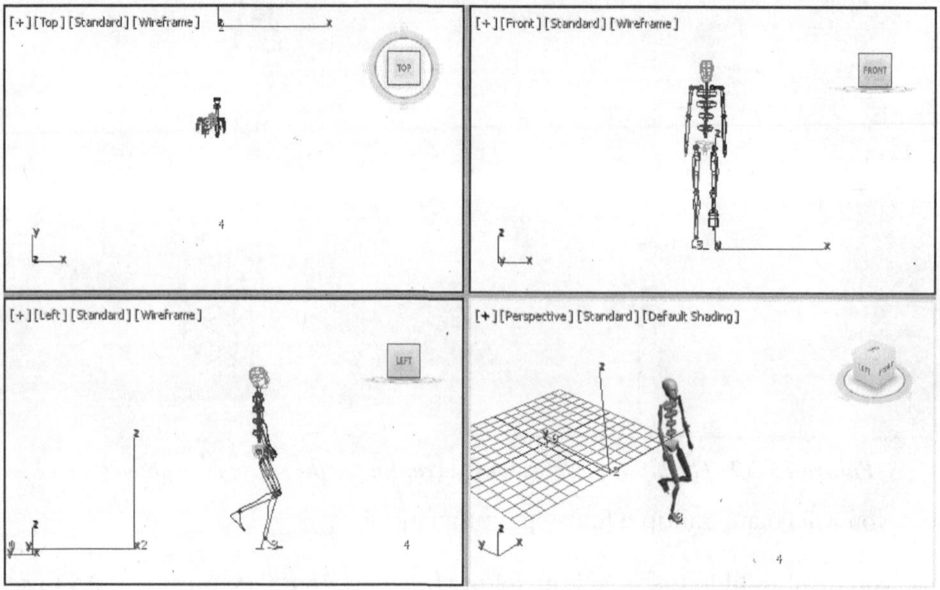

Figure 15-40 *The running biped model in viewports*

Note

*When you create keys for the biped model, various keys are created automatically for each bone in the biped model. Therefore, you can modify the keys created for arms, legs, spine, and head according to the animation you want to create for the biped model. To do so, select a bone in the viewport; the keys created for the selected bone are displayed in the track bar. Now, choose the **Toggle Auto Key Mode** button and modify the bone using the transforms such as move, rotate, and scale on the keys in the track bar.*

25. Make sure that *Bip002* bone of the biped model is selected in the viewport and the **Motion** tab is chosen in the **Command Panel**.

26. Choose the **Save File** button in the **Biped** rollout; the **Save As** dialog box is displayed. Browse to the folder in which you want to save the file. Enter **Run** as the name of the animation file in the **File name** text box and make sure that the **(*.BIP)** option is selected in the **Save as type** drop-down list. 

27. Choose the **Save** button; the animation of the biped model is saved with the name *Run.bip* at the specified location. Now, you can use the same biped animation for another scene.

    Next, you will load the biped animation from the saved *BIP* file.

28. Hide **Bip002** and unhide **Bip001**. Choose the **Select by Name** tool; the **Select From Scene** dialog box is displayed. Now, select *Bip001* bone and choose the **OK** button to close the dialog box.

29. Choose the **Motion** tab in the **Command Panel**. In the **Biped** rollout, choose the **Load File** button; the **Open** dialog box is displayed. Browse to the *Run.bip* file, select the file, and then choose the **Open** button; the animation saved in the *Run.bip* file is loaded into the biped model.

30. Choose the **Play Animation** button; the biped model starts running, as shown in Figure 15-41.

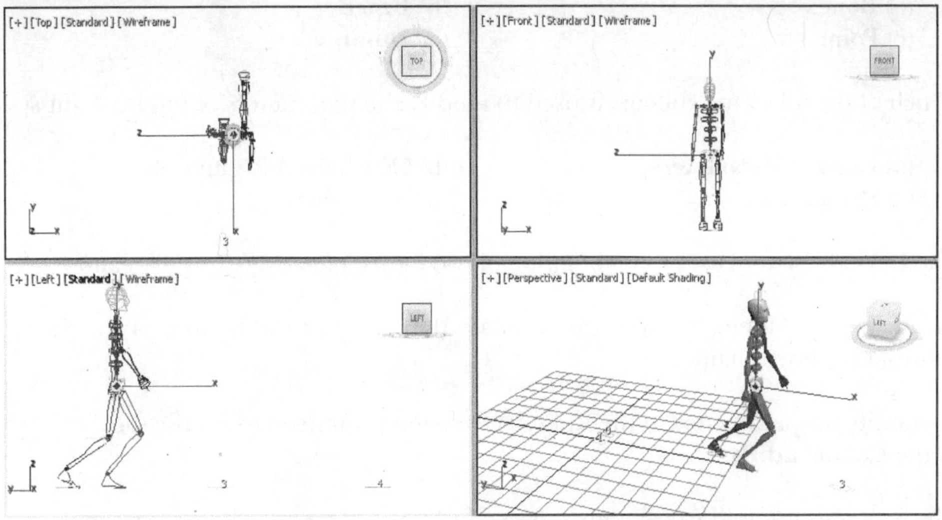

Figure 15-41 The Bip001 in running position after loading the Run.bip file

Saving and Rendering the Scene

In this section, you will save the scene and then render it. You can also view the final rendered image sequence by downloading the file *c15_3dsmax_2017_rndr.zip* from *www.cadcim.com*. The path of the file is as follows: *Textbooks > Animation and Visual Effects > 3ds Max > Autodesk 3ds Max 2017: A Comprehensive Guide*

1. Change the background color of the scene to white, as discussed in Tutorial 1 of Chapter 2.

2. Choose **Save** from the **Application** menu.

3. For rendering, refer to Tutorial 1 of Chapter 14.

Self-Evaluation Test

Answer the following questions and then compare them to those given at the end of this chapter:

1. Which of the following lights can be used as sunlight in the Daylight system?

(a) **IES Sun** (b) **Target Direct**
(c) **mr Sun** (d) All of these

2. Which of the following lights is used as skylight in the Daylight system?

   (a) **IES Sky** (b) **Target Skylight**
   (c) **mr Skylight** (d) All of these

3. Which of the following tools is used to create a bone system in Autodesk 3ds Max?

   (a) **Bones** (b) **Biped**
   (c) **Point** (d) **Dummy**

4. Which of the following rollouts is used to modify the parameters of the Daylight system?

   (a) **Control Parameters** (b) **IK Chain Assignment**
   (c) **Parameters** (d) All of these

5. The Daylight system uses a combination of two lights, namely __________ and __________.

6. In __________ kinematics, you can animate the object at the bottom of the hierarchy to control the entire chain.

7. To modify the parameters of the Ring Array system, you need to choose the __________ tab in the **Command Panel**.

8. The **Systems** are used to combine objects, linkages, and controllers to create an object set that will have all these features. (T/F)

9. A dummy object in the Ring Array system cannot be rendered. (T/F)

10. The ability to link objects together to create a chain is known as hierarchy. (T/F)

Review Questions

Answer the following questions:

1. Which of the following options is used to create an inverse kinematic solution to rotate and position the links in a hierarchy?

   (a) **IK Solver** (b) **Interactive IK**
   (c) **Applied IK** (d) All of these

2. Which of the following options is used to create an inverse kinematic solution only for the specified keyframes?

   (a) **IK Solver** (b) **Interactive IK**
   (c) **Applied IK** (d) All of these

3. Which of the following options is used to create an accurate motion in the hierarchy of linked objects?

(a) **IK Solver** (b) **Interactive IK**
(c) **Applied IK** (d) All of these

4. Which of the following systems is used to create a hierarchical linkage of bones and joints?

(a) Biped system (b) Ring Array system
(c) Sunlight system (d) Daylight system

5. The __________ tab is used to modify the hierarchical linkage between the objects.

6. You can animate and transform the hierarchy of bones using the __________ as well as the __________.

7. The options in the __________ rollout are used to set the fins of the selected bones in the viewport.

8. You cannot replace the boxes in a Ring Array system with other objects. (T/F)

9. You can generate the light effect using a Sunlight system according to the position of the sun over the earth at a particular location, date, and time. (T/F)

10. In forward kinematics, if a parent object moves, then the child objects will also move accordingly. (T/F)

EXERCISE

The rendered output of the scene used in the following exercise can be accessed by downloading the *c15_3dsmax_2017_exr.zip* file from *www.cadcim.com*. The path of the file is as follows: *Textbooks > Animation and Visual Effects > 3ds Max > Autodesk 3ds Max 2017: A Comprehensive Guide*

Exercise 1

Create an animated merry-go-round using the Ring Array system. The position of the swing at different frames is shown in Figures 15-42 and 15-44. **(Expected time: 25 min)**

Figure 15-42 Model to be created in Exercise 1(view 1)

Figure 15-43 Model to be created in Exercise 1(view 2)

Figure 15-44 Model to be created in Exercise 1 (view 3)

Hints:

1. Create the merry-go-round using **Extended Primitives**.

2. Link the parts of the merry-go-round with the dummy objects of the Ring Array system.

3. Replace the boxes of the Ring Array system with the merry-go-round using the **Curve Editor (Open)** tool.

4. Animate the dummy object accordingly.

Answers to Self-Evaluation Test

1. d, **2.** d, **3.** a, **4.** a, **5.** sunlight, skylight, **6.** inverse, **7. Motion**, **8.** T, **9.** T, **10.** T

16

Rigid Body Dynamics and Helpers

Learning Objectives

After completing this chapter, you will be able to:

- *Create static, dynamic, and kinematic rigid bodies*
- *Understand the MassFX interface*
- *Use the mCloth modifier*
- *Understand constraints*
- *Use standard helper objects*
- *Use atmospheric apparatus helper objects*

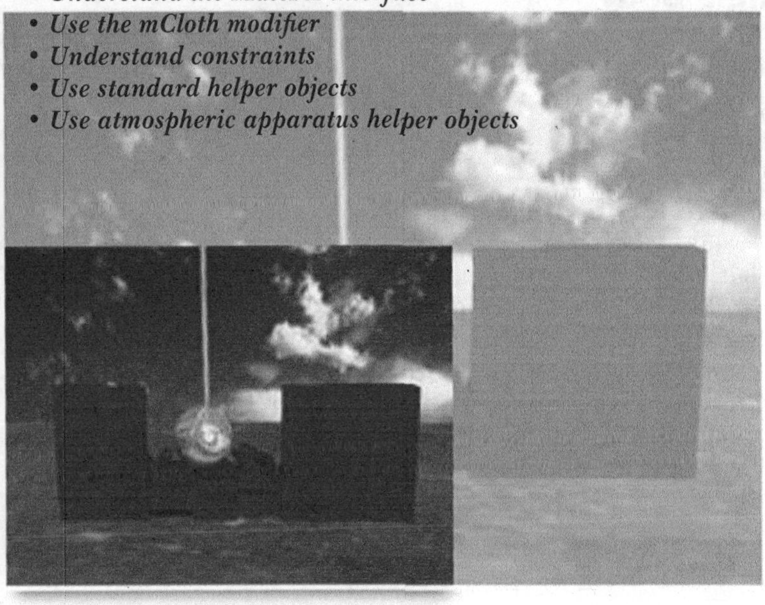

INTRODUCTION

A rigid body is an object which does not deform when it collides with another object. In 3ds Max, you can create three types of rigid bodies by using the **MassFX Toolbar**. This toolbar consists of various types of constraint helpers, simulation controls and also options for converting objects into rigid bodies. You can also simulate cloth objects as Dynamic and Kinematic objects. Conversion of an object into rigid bodies, constraint helpers, and simulation controls will be discussed in detail in this chapter. In addition, the helper objects which are used to support the animation and modeling in a scene will be discussed in this chapter.

TYPES OF RIGID BODIES

Rigid bodies can be classified into three types: Dynamic, Static, and Kinematic. These types are discussed next.

Dynamic Rigid Body

A dynamic rigid body represents an object in the real world. It means that it falls with gravity, can collide with other objects, and can also be pushed by other objects. The motion of the dynamic rigid body is completely controlled by simulation. It cannot be animated by using the standard animation methods.

Kinematic Rigid Body

Unlike a dynamic rigid body, a kinematic rigid body can be animated by using the standard animation methods. It does not fall with gravity and does not get affected by the dynamic rigid body. However, a dynamic rigid body will get affected by a kinematic rigid body. A kinematic rigid body can also act as a stationary object and can be converted into a dynamic rigid body at any point during simulation.

Static Rigid Body

A static rigid body is similar to a kinematic rigid body with the only difference that it cannot be animated. A dynamic rigid body can collide with it and may bounce off when colliding with it, but the static rigid body will not be affected. A static rigid body is used to simulate walls, containers, and so on.

MassFX Toolbar

You can display the **MassFX Toolbar** in the 3ds Max interface. To do so, right-click in the blank area of the **Main Toolbar**; a shortcut menu will be displayed. Choose **MassFX Toolbar** from it; the **MassFX Toolbar** will be displayed in floating state, refer to Figure 16-1. If you double-click on it, it will be docked in the 3ds Max interface.

The **MassFX Toolbar** can be classified into six main categories: MassFX Tools button, Rigid body flyout, Constraint flyout, mCloth flyout, Ragdoll flyout, and Simulation controls. The categories of the **MassFX Toolbar** are discussed next.

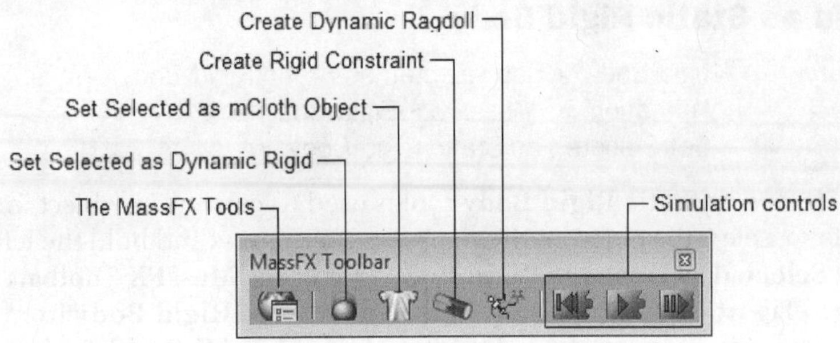

Figure 16-1 The MassFX Toolbar

Rigid Body Flyout

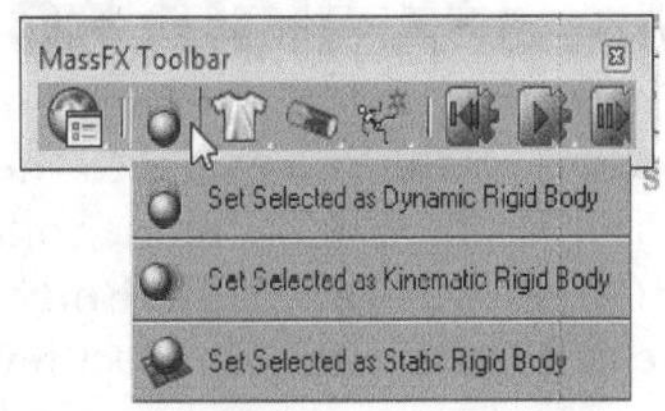

Figure 16-2 Various options displayed in the flyout

The Rigid body flyout consists of three tools: **Set Selected as Dynamic Rigid Body**, **Set Selected as Kinematic Rigid Body**, and **Set Selected as Static Rigid Body**, as shown in Figure 16-2. These tools are used to convert an object into dynamic, static, and kinematic rigid bodies, respectively. These tools are discussed next.

Set Selected as Dynamic Rigid Body

MassFX Toolbar:	Rigid Body > Set Selected as Dynamic Rigid Body
Menu bar:	Animation > MassFX > Rigid Bodies > Set Selected as Dynamic Rigid Body

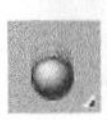

The **Set Selected as Dynamic Rigid Body** tool is used to convert an object into a dynamic rigid body. To do so, select the object in the viewport. Now, click and hold on the **Set Selected as Dynamic Rigid Body** tool in the **MassFX Toolbar**; a flyout will be displayed, refer to Figure 16-2. Choose **Set Selected as Dynamic Rigid Body** from the flyout; the object will be converted into a dynamic rigid body and the **MassFX Rigid Body** modifier will be applied to the object in the modifier stack.

Set Selected as Kinematic Rigid Body

MassFX Toolbar:	Rigid Body > Set Selected as Kinematic Rigid Body
Menu bar:	Animation > MassFX > Rigid Bodies > Set Selected as Kinematic Rigid Body

The **Set Selected as Kinematic Rigid Body** tool is used to convert an object into a kinematic rigid body. To do so, select an object in the viewport. Now, click and hold on the **Set Selected as Dynamic Rigid Body** tool in the **MassFX Toolbar**; a flyout will be displayed, refer to Figure 16-2. Choose **Set Selected as Kinematic Rigid Body** from the flyout; the object will be converted to a kinematic rigid body and the **MassFX Rigid Body** modifier will be applied to the object in the modifier stack.

Set Selected as Static Rigid Body

MassFX Toolbar:	Rigid Body > Set Selected as Static Rigid Body
Menu bar:	Animation > MassFX > Rigid Bodies > Set Selected as Static Rigid Body

The **Set Selected as Static Rigid Body** tool is used to convert an object into a static rigid body. To do so, select the object in the viewport. Next, press and hold the left mouse button on the **Set Selected as Dynamic Rigid Body** tool in the **MassFX Toolbar**; a flyout will be displayed, refer to Figure 16-2. Choose **Set Selected as Static Rigid Body** from the flyout; the object will be converted into a static rigid body and the **MassFX Rigid Body** modifier will be applied to the object in the modifier stack. The **MassFX Rigid Body** modifier is discussed next.

MassFX RIGID BODY MODIFIER

When you convert an object into a dynamic, static, or kinematic rigid body, the **MassFX Rigid Body** modifier is applied to the object, as discussed above. This modifier has different rollouts in the Modify panel. These rollouts will be discussed later. When you click on the **+** sign on the left of the **MassFX Rigid Body** modifier, the **Initial Velocity**, **Initial Spin**, **Center of Mass**, and **Mesh Transform** sub-object levels are displayed. These sub-object levels are discussed next.

Initial Velocity

This sub-object level gives a visual representation of the direction of the initial velocity of the rigid body, refer to Figure 16-3. You can change the direction of velocity by using the **Select and Rotate** tool.

Initial Spin

This sub-object level shows the axis and the direction of the initial spin of a rigid body, refer to Figure 16-4. You can change the axis by using the **Select and Rotate** tool.

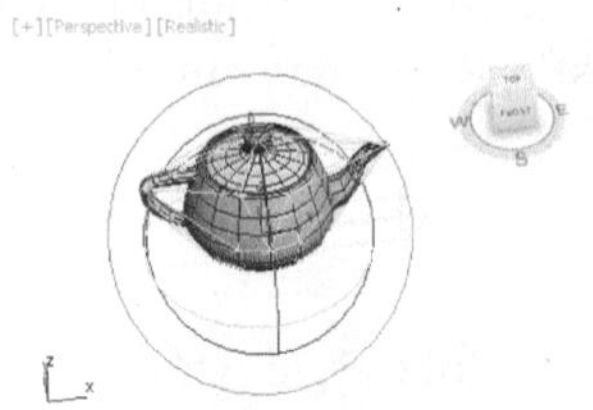

Figure 16-3 *The rigid body with the* ***Initial Velocity*** *sub-object level selected*

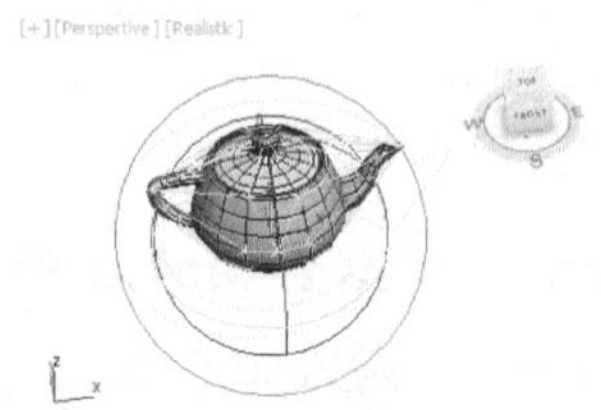

Figure 16-4 *The rigid body with the* ***Initial Spin*** *sub-object level selected*

Center of Mass

This sub-object level gives a visual representation of the location of the center of mass of a rigid body, refer to Figure 16-5. You can change the location of center of mass by using the **Select and Move** tool.

Mesh Transform

This sub-object level is used for positioning and rotating the physical shape of a rigid body. On selecting this level, the physical shape which is in the form of a white wireframe can be transformed in any direction in the viewport, refer to Figure 16-6. You can adjust its placement with respect to the rigid body by using the **Select and Move** and **Select and Rotate** tools.

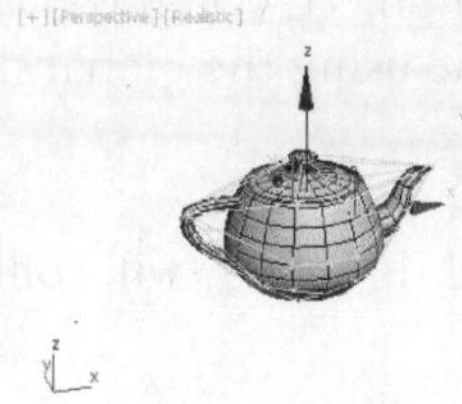

Figure 16-5 The rigid body with the ***Center of Mass*** *sub-object level selected*

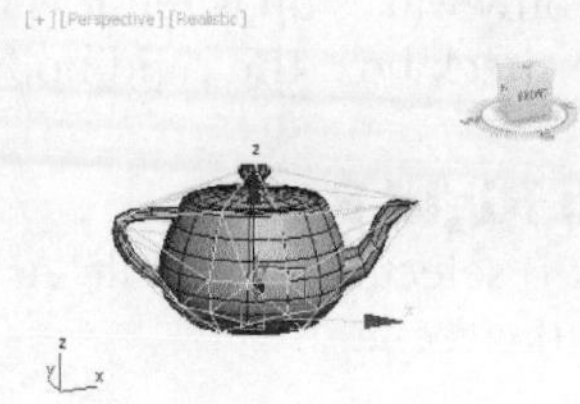

Figure 16-6 The rigid body with the ***Mesh Transform*** *sub-object level selected*

Next, you will learn about various rollouts displayed in the Modify panel of the **MassFX Rigid Body** modifier namely **Rigid Body Properties**, **Physical Material**, **Physical shapes**, and so on.

Rigid Body Properties Rollout

The parameters in the **Rigid Body Properties** rollout are discussed next, refer to Figure 16-7.

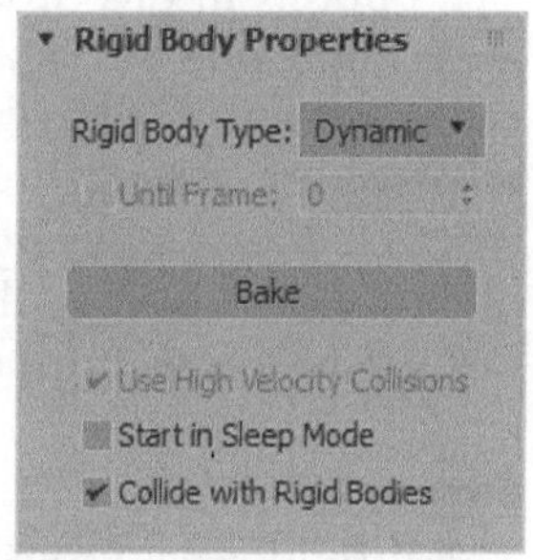

Figure 16-7 The ***Rigid Body Properties*** *rollout*

Rigid Body Type

The options in this drop-down list are used to specify the type of rigid body. The types available in the list are **Dynamic**, **Kinematic**, and **Static**.

Until Frame

By default, this check box and the spinner next to it are inactive. They will be activated only when you select **Kinematic** from the **Rigid Body Type** drop-down list. If you select this check box, then the kinematic rigid body will be converted into a dynamic rigid body at the frame specified in the spinner next to it.

Bake/Unbake

This button gets activated only when the **Dynamic** option is selected in the **Rigid Body Type** drop-down list. When you choose this button, the simulated motion of the selected rigid body is converted into standard animation keyframes for rendering. Once the selected rigid body is baked, this button changes into the **Unbake** button. Choose the **Unbake** button to remove the keyframes and restore to dynamic body.

Use High Velocity Collisions

When this check box is selected, the high velocity collisions settings are applied to the selected rigid body, provided the **Use High Velocity Collisions** check box is selected in the **Scene Settings** rollout of the **World** tab in the **MassFX Tools** dialog box.

Start in Sleep Mode

If a rigid body in a simulation moves slower than a certain rate, it automatically goes in the sleep mode. It only wakes up when it is hit by a non-sleeping object. When you select the **Start in Sleep Mode** check box, the rigid body starts in sleep mode using the global sleep settings.

Collide with Rigid Bodies

This check box is selected by default. As a result, the selected rigid body will collide with other rigid bodies in the scene.

Physical Material Rollout

The parameters in the **Physical Material** rollout are used to control the way the rigid body interacts with the other elements in the scene, refer to Figure 16-8. The parameters in this rollout depend on the type of object used. These parameters are discussed next.

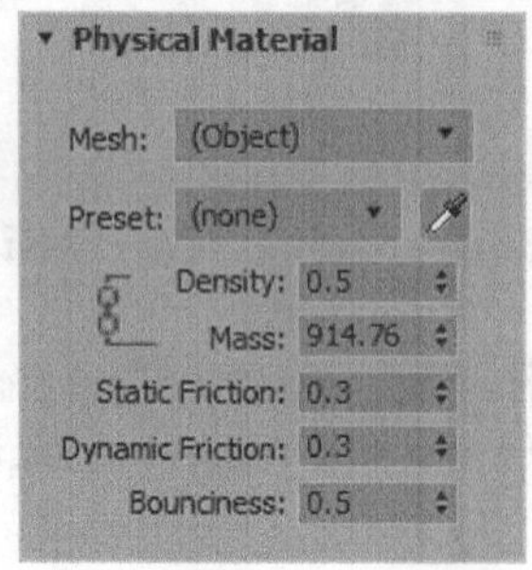

*Figure 16-8 The **Physical Material** rollout*

Mesh

The options in this drop-down list are used to select the physical mesh of the selected rigid body. By default, only the **(Object)** option is displayed in the **Mesh** drop-down list. The other options will be displayed only when the **Override Physical Material** check box is selected in the **Physical Shapes** rollout. To pick settings from a different rigid body in the scene, click the eyedropper icon located next to the **Preset** option and then click a rigid body in the scene.

Preset

This drop-down list consists of options for loading, saving, and creating a preset. Once you create a preset, it gets added in this drop-down list. You can select the preset from this drop-down list to specify physical material properties. It also consists of the **(none)** option. When **(none)** is selected, you can edit the values in the spinners below it. However, on selecting a preset from the list, the values in the spinners cannot be edited.

Density

This spinner is used to specify the density of the selected rigid body in g/cm^3 (gram per cubic centimeter). It is linked with the **Mass** parameter which means that when you change the density, the mass of the rigid body will be calculated automatically.

Mass

This spinner is used to specify the mass of the selected rigid body in kg. If you change this value, density of the rigid body will be calculated automatically.

Static Friction

This spinner is used to specify the static friction value. If the value is 0, it indicates that there is no friction between two rigid bodies. If the value is 1, it indicates full static friction.

Dynamic Friction

This spinner is used to specify the dynamic friction value. If the value is 0, it indicates that there is no dynamic friction between two rigid bodies; if the value is 1, it indicates full dynamic friction.

Bounciness

This spinner is used to set the effective bounciness between the two rigid bodies. It determines the ease and height by which a rigid body will bounce on hitting another rigid body.

Physical Shapes Rollout

The **Physical Shapes** rollout is used to edit the physical meshes assigned to an object in the simulation, refer to Figure 16-9. The parameters in this rollout are discussed next.

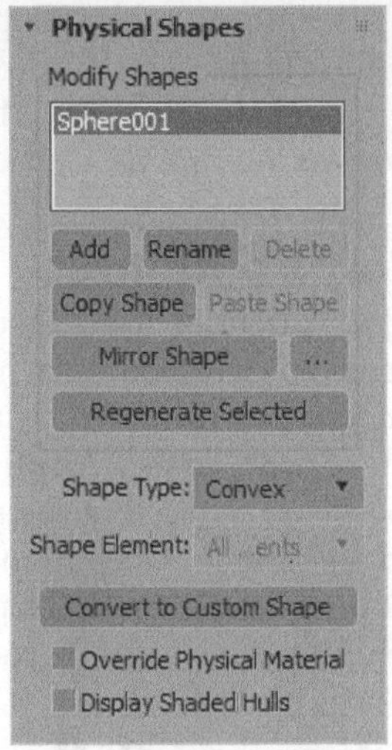

Figure 16-9 The ***Physical Shapes*** *rollout*

Modify Shapes

The list box in this area displays the physical meshes added to a selected rigid body. The **Add** button is used to add a mesh to the selected rigid body. Once you add a mesh, it will be displayed in the list box. You can rename or delete mesh from this list by using the **Rename** or **Delete** button located below this list. Similarly, if you select a mesh and choose the **Copy Shape** button, the selected mesh will get copied to the clipboard. Choose the **Paste Shape** button to paste a mesh to another rigid body.

Shape Type

The options in this drop-down list are used to apply the physical mesh type to the selected physical mesh in the list box in the **Modify Shapes** area. If you change the shape type, a new shape will be generated which will fit around the graphical mesh.

Shape Element

By default, this drop-down list is not active. To activate it, select the **Generate Shape Per Element** check box from the **Rigid Bodies** area of the **Scene Settings** rollout of the **MassFX Tool** dialog box. Also, if this check box is selected, all elements of the mesh will be listed in the **Shape Element** drop-down list. For example, if you convert a **Teapot** primitive to a rigid body, **Element 1**, **Element 2**, **Element 3**, and **Element 4**, which represent **Body**, **Handle**, **Spout**, and **Lid** part. respectively of the teapot, will be displayed in the drop-down list of **Modify Shapes** area.

You can now select the required option from the drop-down list. The selected shape type is molded around the element.

Convert to Custom Shape

When you choose this button, a new editable mesh object will be created from the highlighted physical shape in the list box of the **Modify Shapes** area. The new editable mesh object will be the option that is selected from the **Shape Type** drop-down list. You can edit this mesh using the standard mesh editing tools.

Override Physical Material

By default, material settings specified in the **Override Physical Material** rollout are applied to every physical mesh in the viewport. If a mesh consists of multiple shapes and you require to apply different settings to each individual shape, select the **Override Physical Material** check box in the **Physical Shapes** rollout.

Display Shaded Hulls

If this check box is selected, MassFX renders shapes as shaded solid objects in the viewport when the **Shaded** mode is active.

Physical Mesh Parameters Rollout

The spinners in this rollout vary depending on the option selected in the **Shape Type** drop-down list of the **Physical Shapes** rollout. Figure 16-10 shows the **Physical Mesh Parameters** rollout for the **Convex** mesh type.

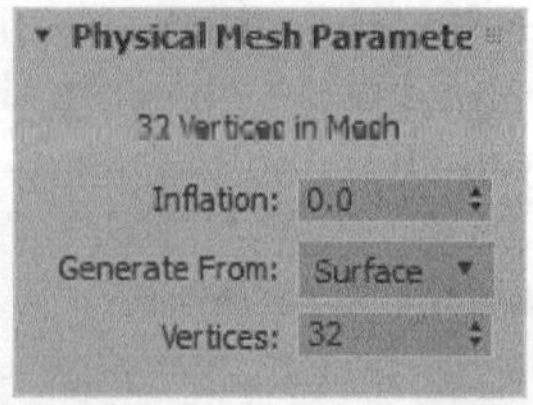

*Figure 16-10 The **Physical Mesh Parameters** rollout for the **Convex** mesh type*

Forces Rollout

This rollout is used to control gravity and apply force space warps to rigid bodies. When the **Use World Gravity** check box is selected, the global gravity setting is applied to the rigid bodies. The **Scene Forces Applied** list box displays the space warps in the scene that affect the selected rigid bodies in the simulation. To add a space warp to the simulation, choose the **Add** button and then click on the space warp icon in the viewport. To prevent a space warp from affecting the simulation, select the desired option in the **Scene Forces Applied** list and then choose the **Remove** button.

Advanced Rollout

The **Advanced** rollout contains **Simulation**, **Contact Shell**, **Initial Motion**, **Center of Mass**, and **Damping** areas, refer to Figure 16-11. The parameters in this rollout depend on the type of object used. The areas in this rollout are discussed next.

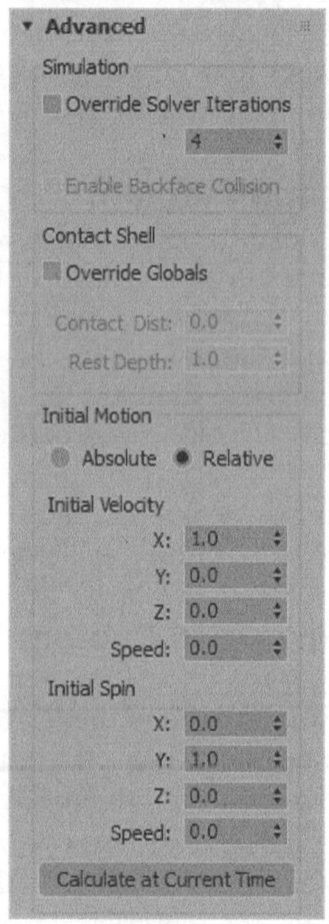

*Figure 16-11 The **Advanced** rollout*

Simulation Area

The options in this area are used to set simulation of objects and are discussed next.

Override Solver Iterations

When this check box is selected, global settings for solver iterations are ignored and value specified for this parameter is used for simulation.

Enable Backface Collision

This check box is only available for the static rigid bodies. When selected, the dynamic objects in simulation collide with the back faces of the static rigid body.

Contact Shell Area

The **Contact Shell** area consists of different options that are used to specify the surrounding volume within which the MassFX will detect collisions between bodies in the simulation. The options in the **Contact Shell** area are discussed next.

Override Globals
On selecting this check box, the MassFX uses the values specified in this area for the collision overlap instead of the global settings value.

Contact Dist
This spinner is used to specify the distance that moving rigid bodies are allowed to overlap.

Rest Depth
This spinner is used to specify the distance that the resting rigid bodies are allowed to overlap.

Initial Motion Area
The options in the **Initial Motion** area are used to set the absolute or relative motion of speed, rotation, and direction at the current frame. The options in the **Initial Motion** area are discussed next.

Absolute
Select this radio button to use the values specified in the **Initial Velocity** and **Initial Spin** spinners instead of the animation-based values. Note that these settings can be applied only to a rigid body which is kinematic at the start of the animation and then turns into a dynamic rigid body at the frame specified in the spinner in the **Rigid Body Properties** rollout.

Relative
This radio button is selected, by default. As a result, the values specified in the **Initial Velocity** and **Initial Spin** spinners are added to the values calculated from the simulation.

Initial Velocity
This option is used to specify the starting direction and speed for a kinematic rigid body (in units per second) when it is converted to a dynamic rigid body. You need to use the **Initial Velocity** sub-object level to see the initial velocity direction. You can use the **Select and Rotate** tool to change the direction of velocity.

Initial Spin
This option is used to specify the starting axis and the rotation speed (in degrees per second) of the kinematic rigid body when it is converted into a dynamic rigid body. You need to use the **Initial Spin** sub-object level to see the initial spin direction. You can use the **Select and Rotate** tool to change the direction of spin.

Calculate at Current Time
The **Calculate at Current Time** button is used to calculate the motion values of an animated kinematic rigid body at a frame other than the one at which it is converted into a dynamic rigid body and then sets those values in the **Initial Velocity** and **Initial Spin** spinners.

Center of Mass Area
The center of mass of an object is a point around which the real physical object rotates unless it is constrained in some way. The options in this area are discussed next.

Calculate from Meshes
By default, this radio button is selected in the **Center of Mass** area. It is used to automatically calculate the center of mass of a rigid body.

Use Pivot
This radio button is used to make the pivot point of the object as its center of mass.

Local Offset
When you select the **Local Offset** radio button, the **X**, **Y**, and **Z** spinners get activated. Set values in these spinners to specify a point as the center of mass. The **Move Pivot to Com** button allows you to relocate the pivot of the object at the center of mass specified by the **Local Offset** XYZ values. This button will be activated only when the **Local Offset** option is selected.

Damping Area
The options in this area are used to slow down the movement of the rigid bodies with the help of forces. The options in the **Damping** area are discussed next.

Linear
The **Linear** spinner is used to specify the amount of force applied to reduce the velocity of a moving rigid body.

Angular
The **Angular** spinner is used to specify the amount of force applied to reduce the speed of rotation of a rigid body.

Note

If you apply the ***MassFX Rigid Body*** *modifier to an object which is already a rigid body, then the existing rigid body will be replaced with the new one and this modifier will remain applied with the change in the rigid body type.*

mCloth MODIFIER
The **mCloth** modifier is a special version of the standard **Cloth** modifier designed to work with the MassFX simulations. When this modifier is applied to any object in the scene, the object either affects the behavior of other objects or it is affected by other objects in the scene. You can create a mCloth object by using the **Set Selected as mCloth Object** tool. To do so, select the object in the viewport and then choose the **Set Selected as mCloth Object** tool from the **MassFX Toolbar**; the **mCloth** modifier and various rollouts to modify the mCloth object will be displayed in the Modify panel, refer to Figure 16-12. These rollouts are discussed next.

mCloth Simulation Rollout
The **mCloth Simulation** rollout is shown in Figure 16-13. The parameters in this rollout are discussed next.

Cloth Behavior
The options in the **Cloth Behavior** drop-down list are used to specify how mCloth object would interact with other simulation bodies. When the **Dynamic** option is selected, the mCloth object

is affected by the motion of other objects in the scene. Also, the mCloth object affects the other objects in the scene. When the **Kinematic** option is selected, the other objects in the scene do not affect the mCloth object. By default, the **Until Frame** check box remains disabled. It is enabled only when **Kinematic** is selected from the **Cloth Behavior** drop-down list and is used to specify the frame number at which the kinematic object will be converted to the dynamic object.

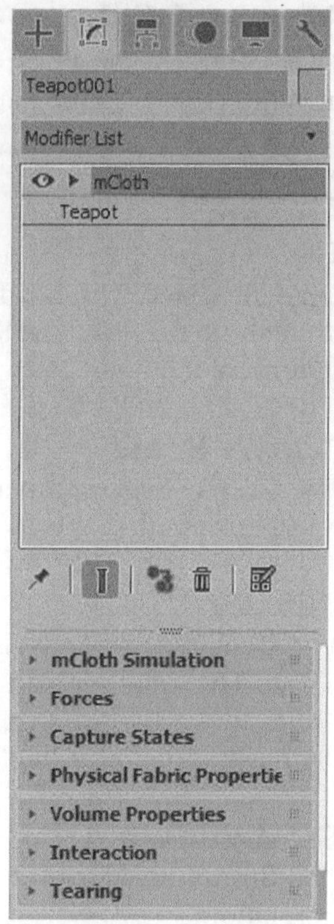

*Figure 16-12 The **mCloth** modifier in the Modify panel*

Bake

The **Bake** button is used to convert the simulated data to the standard animation keys.

Unbake

The **Unbake** button is used to remove the keyframes that are baked using the **Bake** button.

Inherit Velocity

When the **Inherit Velocity** check box is selected, the mCloth simulation begins with the velocity inherited from the preceding animation.

Live Drag

The **Live Drag** button is used to drag or pose the cloth in the viewport. To do so, choose the **Live Drag** button and then drag the cloth in the viewport to pose it or test the behavior of the cloth simulation. Choose the **Live Drag** button again to turn off live drag feature.

*Figure 16-13 The **mCloth Simulation** rollout*

Forces Rollout

The parameters in the **Forces** rollout are same as discussed earlier in this chapter.

Capture States Rollout

The **Capture States** rollout is shown in Figure 16-14. The **Capture Initial State** button in this rollout is used to update the first frame of the cache of the selected mCloth object to the current position. The **Reset Initial State** button is used to restore the state of the selected mCloth object to the state before mCloth in the modifier stack. The **Capture Target State** button is used to capture the current deformation of the mCloth as the target deformation. The **Reset Target State** button is used to reset bend angles to the default values. The **Show** button is used to show the current target state of the cloth.

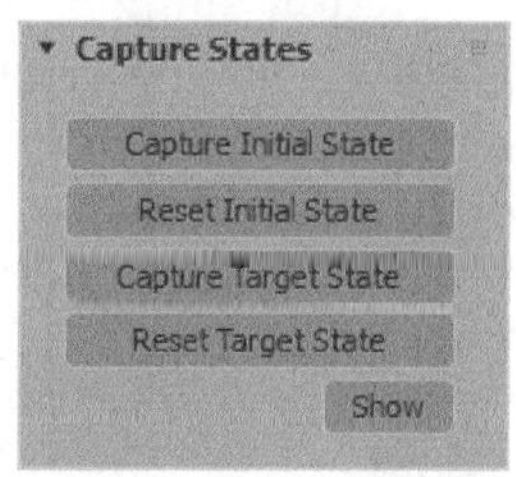

*Figure 16-14 The **Capture States** rollout*

Physical Fabric Properties Rollout

The options in the **Physical Fabric Properties** rollout are shown in Figure 16-15. These parameters are used to control the physical characteristics of the mCloth object and are discussed next.

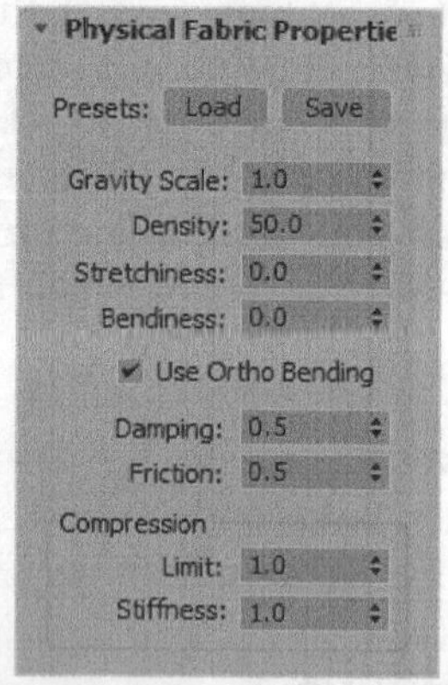

Figure 16-15 The Physical Fabric Properties rollout

Presets

There are two buttons located at the top of the rollout, namely **Load** and **Save**. The **Load** button is used to load a fabric property preset from the disk. The **Save** button is used to save fabric property settings of a fabric.

Gravity Scale

The **Gravity Scale** spinner is used as a multiplier for the gravity. It is used to simulate effects like heavy or wet cloth.

Density

The **Density** spinner is used to specify the weight of the mCloth object. The unit for measurement of the weight is grams per square centimeter. This parameter comes into action when rigid bodies collide. The extent of the effect is determined by ratio of the mass of the mCloth object to the rigid body with which it collides.

Stretchiness

The **Stretchiness** spinner is used to set the extent of stretching of the cloth object during simulation.

Bendiness

The **Bendiness** spinner is used to set the amount of fold of the mCloth object during simulation.

Use Ortho Bending

When the **Use Ortho Bending** check box is selected, MassFX calculates angles instead of springs.

Damping

The **Damping** spinner is used to set the springiness of the cloth and also determines the time that it will take to come to rest when flapping or snapping back.

Friction

The **Friction** spinner is used to specify the extent an mCloth object will slide during self-collision and collision with other objects.

Compression Area

This area is used to specify the compression of the cloth edges. The options in this area are discussed next.

Limit

The **Limit** spinner is used to specify the limit of compression or crumpling of the cloth edges.

Stiffness

The **Stiffness** spinner is used to specify the stiffness to which the cloth edges resist compression or crumpling.

Volume Properties Rollout

The **Volume Properties** rollout is used to the make mCloth object behave like a balloon as if it has enclosed a volume of air, refer to Figure 16-16. The parameters in this rollout are discussed next.

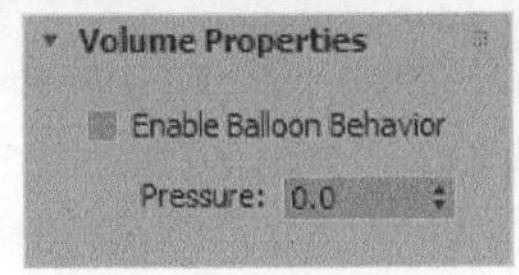

*Figure 16-16 The **Volume Properties** rollout*

Enable Balloon Behavior

When this check box is selected, the mCloth object simulates an enclosed volume.

Pressure

This spinner is used to control the pressure of air inside the inflated mCloth object.

Interaction Rollout

The **Interaction** rollout is shown in Figure 16-17. The parameters in the **Interaction** rollout are used to control the collision behavior. These parameters are discussed next.

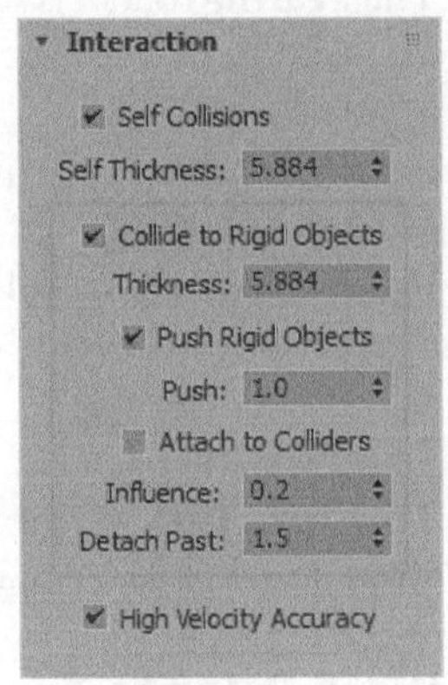

*Figure 16-17 The **Interaction** rollout*

Self Collisions

When this check box is selected, the mCloth object prevents intersection with itself.

Self Thickness

The **Self Thickness** spinner is used to control the thickness of the mCloth object. If the cloth intersects with itself, you can increase the value in this spinner to correct it.

Collide to Rigid Objects

When this check box is selected, the mCloth object can collide with rigid bodies in the simulation.

Thickness

This spinner is used to control the thickness of the mCloth object. It is used when the mCloth object collides with rigid bodies. If other rigid bodies are intersecting the cloth object, increase the value of this parameter to rectify this.

Push Rigid Objects

When this check box is selected, the mCloth object can influence the motion of rigid bodies.

Push

The **Push** spinner is used to set the strength of the force that the mCloth object will exert on the rigid bodies.

Attach to Colliders
When this check box is selected, the mCloth object tries to stick to the objects it collides with.

Influence
The **Influence** spinner is used to control the influence of the mCloth object on the objects it will be attached to.

Detach Past
The **Detach Past** spinner is used to control the extent to which the cloth will stretch before detaching it from the collider.

High Velocity Accuracy
If this check box is selected, the MassFX will use a more accurate collision detection method. As a result, this will slow down the simulation process.

Tearing Rollout
The **Tearing** rollout is shown in Figure 16-18. The parameters in this rollout are used to control the tearing of the mCloth object. These parameters are discussed next.

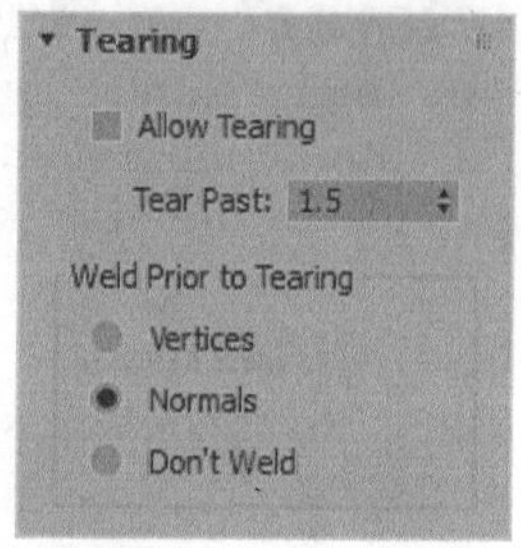

*Figure 16-18 The **Tearing** rollout*

Allow Tearing
If this check box is selected, the predefined splits in the cloth will pull apart when sufficient force is applied to the mCloth object.

Tear Past
The **Tear Past** spinner is used to set the extent to which a cloth can stretch before it tears apart.

Weld Prior to Tearing Area
The radio buttons in this area are used to control the predefined tears before the tearing occurs. These radio buttons are discussed next.

Vertices
The **Vertices** radio button is used to weld the vertices in the predefined tears until they separate. It also changes the topology of the object.

Normals
By default, the **Normals** radio button is selected. As a result, it aligns the normals on the edges along the predefined tears, and then blends them together. It also retains the original topology of the object.

Don't Weld
On selecting this radio button, the torn edges will neither weld nor blend.

Visualize Rollout

The **Visualize** rollout is shown in Figure 16-19. When the **Tension** check box is selected in this rollout, MassFX displays the compression and tension in the mCloth object by vertex coloring. The stretched cloth is shown in red, the compressed cloth in blue, and the neutral area is shown in green color. The spinner on the right of the **Tension** check box gets activated if this check box is selected. You can increase value in this spinner to control the shading. More the values in the slider, more gradual the shading will be.

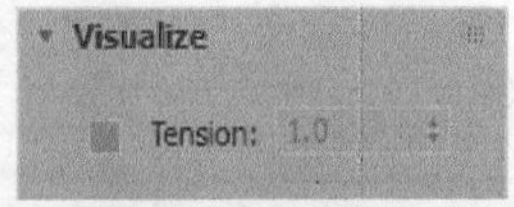

*Figure 16-19 The **Visualize** rollout*

Advanced Rollout

The **Advanced** rollout is shown in Figure 16-20. The parameters in this rollout are discussed next.

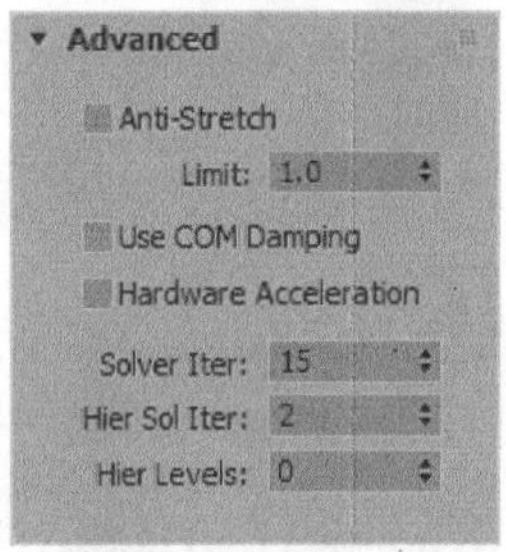

*Figure 16-20 The **Advanced** rollout*

Anti Stretch

If the **Anti Stretch** check box is selected, the MassFX will prevent overstretching of the mcloth by using low solver iterations values.

Limit

The **Limit** spinner is used to set the extent to which overstretching is allowed.

Use COM Damping

If this check box is selected, the damping is set using the center of mass.

Hardware Acceleration

If this check box is selected, MassFX uses the GPU (Graphic Processing Unit) for simulation processing.

Solver Iter

The **Solver Iter** spinner is used to set the number of iterations that the solver will perform per cycle. The higher the value in this spinner, the more stable the cloth will be.

Hier Sol Iter

The **Hier Sol Iter** spinner is used to control the number of iterations for a hierarchical solver. In the MassFX terminology, hierarchy refers to the propagation of forces exerted on a particular vertex to the neighboring vertices.

Hier Levels

The **Hier Levels** spinner is used to control the speed of propagation of force from one vertex to the adjacent vertices. The higher the value in this spinner, the more will be the rate at which forces spread across the cloth instances.

CONSTRAINTS

Constraints are used to restrict the movement of rigid bodies in the simulation. Various types of constraints are available in the **Constraint** flyout, such as rigid constraint, slide constraint, hinge constraint, and so on. These constraints are used to make two rigid bodies work together. A constraint links two rigid bodies together or links a single rigid body to a fixed point in global space. The constraints develop a hierarchical relationship in which the child object must be a dynamic rigid body, while the parent object can be a dynamic or a kinematic rigid body, or can be a point in the global space. The process of creating various constraints given in the **MassFX Toolbar** is discussed next.

Creating the Rigid Constraint

MassFX Toolbar:	Constraints > Create Rigid Constraint
Menu bar:	Animation > MassFX > Constraints > Create Rigid Constraint

You can create a rigid constraint using the **Create Rigid Constraint** tool. To do so, select two objects in the viewport. The object selected first will act as the parent object, which means that it can either be a kinematic or a dynamic rigid body. The second object will act as a child object which means that it must be a dynamic rigid body. Next, choose the **Create Rigid Constraint** tool from the **MassFX Toolbar**; a transparent box will be displayed in the viewport. Move the cursor in the viewport and then click in the viewport when you get the required size of the constraint; a transparent white box representing the constraint will be displayed in the viewport. Also, the **Uconstraint** will be displayed in the modifier stack and various rollouts will be displayed in the Modify panel, as shown in Figure 16-21. If the selected objects are not a rigid body, the **MAXScript** message box will be displayed, as shown in Figure 16-22. Choose the **Yes** button in the message box and then create a rigid body constraint as discussed above. Note that here the **MassFX Rigid Body** modifier will be applied to the selected object and to make it a dynamic rigid body.

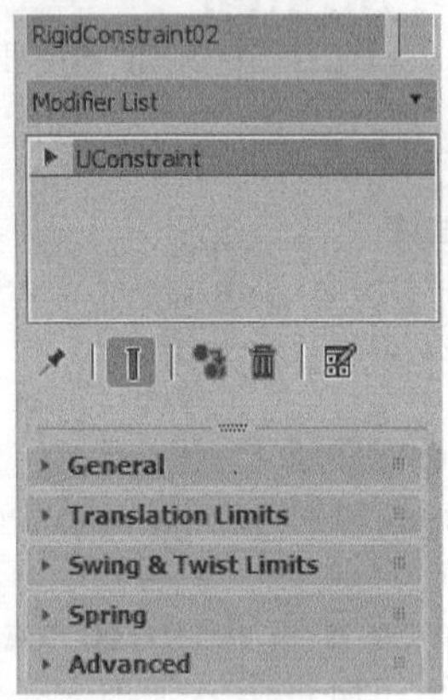

Figure 16-21 *The rollouts of rigid constraint in the Modify panel*

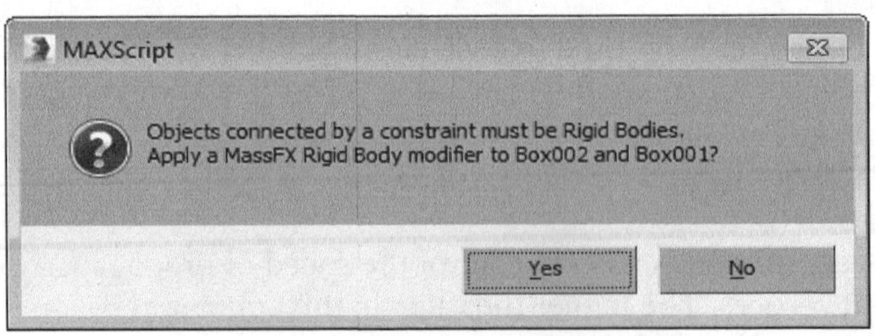

Figure 16-22 *The **MAXScript** message box*

Various rollouts of rigid constraint are discussed next.

General Rollout

The **General** rollout is shown in Figure 16-23. The parameters in this rollout are discussed next.

Connection Area

The groups in the **Connection** area are used to assign constraints to rigid bodies. These groups are discussed next.

Parent

The button located below the **Parent** group is used to specify the parent object in the constraint. To change the parent object, choose this button and select another object in the viewport; the parent object is replaced with the selected object.

Note that the parent object can be a kinematic or a dynamic rigid body. You can choose the **Unchoose the parent rigid body** button located next to it to remove the parent object. On doing so, the button is replaced with the **Undefined** label and the applied constraint is anchored to the global space.

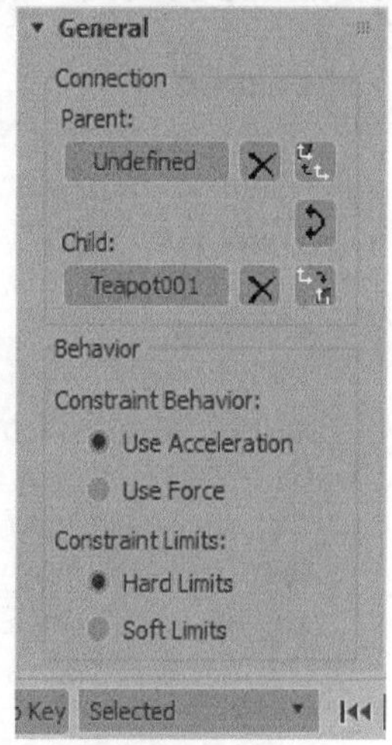

*Figure 16-23 The **General** rollout*

Move to Parent's Pivot

This button is used to set the position of the constraint at the pivot of the parent object.

Switch Parent/Child

This button is used to switch between parent and child objects.

Child

The button located below the **Child** group is used to specify the child object in the constraint. To change the child object, choose this button and select another object in the viewport; the child object is replaced with the selected object. Note that the child object can only be a dynamic rigid body.

Move to Child's Pivot

This button is used to adjust the position of the constraint to be calculated at the pivot of the child object.

Behavior Area

The options in this area are used to specify the behaviour and limit of the constrained bodies. The groups in the **Behavior** area are discussed next.

Constraint Behavior: You can select the radio buttons in this group to determine the constraint behavior using acceleration or forces of the constrained bodies. Select the **Use Acceleration** radio button to use acceleration while performing spring and damping behavior. Similarly, select the **Use Force** radio button to use force to perform spring and damping behavior.

Constraint Limits: The two radio buttons in this group are used to control the constraint behaviour when the child body reaches the limits on using the parameters of the **Translation Limits** rollout and the **Swing & Twist Limits** rollout. If the **Hard Limits** radio button is selected, the child body can bounce off to the limit set in the **Bounce** spinner of the **Translation Limits** rollout. If the **Soft Limits** radio button is selected, the child body can exceed the set limit. When the child body exceeds the limit, the MassFX activates spring and damping behavior to slow down the child or apply force to bring it back into the limit.

Translation Limits Rollout

The parameters in the **Translation Limits** rollout are shown in Figure 16-24. These parameters are discussed next.

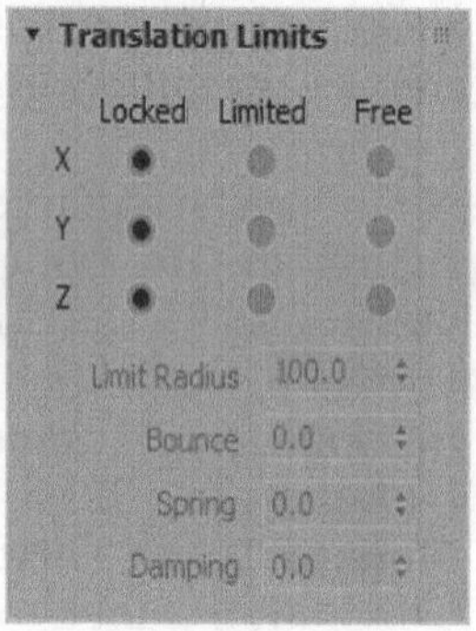

Figure 16-24 The ***Translation Limits*** *rollout*

Locked

If you select the **X**, **Y**, and **Z** radio buttons in the **Locked** column, then the rigid bodies will be prevented from sliding along the respective axes.

Limited

If you select a radio button in the **Limited** column, then the rigid bodies will be able to move along the respective axis by an amount specified in the **Limit Radius** spinner. Note that on selecting a radio button from this column, the **Limit Radius**, **Bounce**, **Spring**, and **Damping** spinners will be activated. If you select more than one radio button in this column, then the motion will be limited radially.

Free

Select the radio buttons in the **Free** column to allow unrestricted motion of the rigid bodies along the axis corresponding to the selected radio button.

Limit Radius

The **Limit Radius** spinner is used to specify the distance that the rigid bodies can move along an axis or axes.

Bounce

The **Bounce** spinner is used to specify the amount by which the rigid bodies will rebound when hit.

Spring

The **Spring** spinner is used to specify the strength of the string which will pull back the rigid bodies to the limit if the limit is exceeded. The larger the values specified in the **Spring** spinner, the greater will be the force applied to the rigid bodies to pull them back to the limit and vice versa.

Damping

The **Damping** spinner is used to specify the amount by which the rigid bodies will move beyond the limit, if the translation exceeds the limit. There will be no damping when the spinner value is set to 0.

Swing & Twist Limits Rollout

The parameters in the **Swing & Twist Limits** rollout are shown in Figure 16-25. The parameters in the **Swing Y** and **Swing Z** areas are related to the rotation of rigid bodies around the local Z and Y axes whereas the parameters in the **Twist** area are related to the rotation of rigid bodies around the local X axis. Most of the parameters in these areas are similar to those discussed in the **Translation Limits** rollout.

Spring Rollout

The parameters in the **Spring** rollout are shown in Figure 16-26. The parameters in the **Spring to Resting Position** area of this rollout are discussed next.

Springiness

The value in the **Springiness** spinner indicates the amount of force which will pull the translation of the parent and child objects back to their initial offset positions.

Damping

The value in the **Damping** spinner indicates the amount of force that would restrict the spring force.

Advanced Rollout

The parameters in the **Advanced** rollout are shown in Figure 16-27. The most commonly used parameters are discussed next.

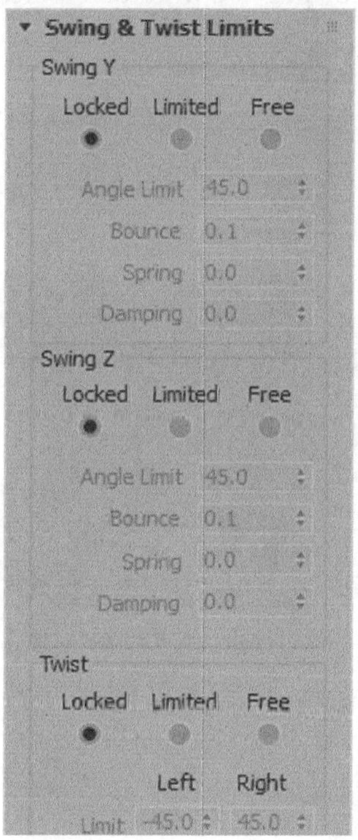

*Figure 16-25 The **Swing & Twist Limits** rollout*

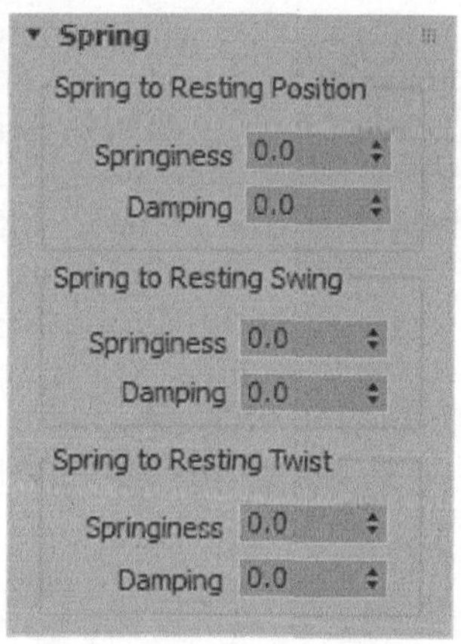

*Figure 16-26 The **Spring** rollout*

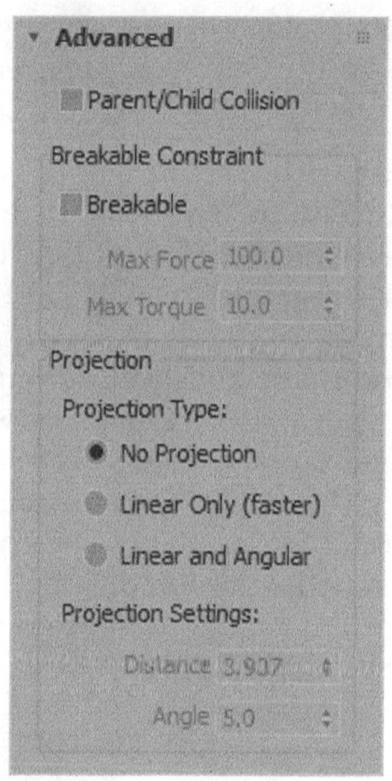

*Figure 16-27 The **Advanced** rollout*

Parent/Child Collision

By default, this check box is cleared. If you select this check box, the parent and child objects will be allowed to collide with each other.

Breakable Constraint Area

This area consists of the **Breakable** check box. If this check box is selected, the constraint is broken during the simulation. On selecting this check box, the **Max Force** and **Max Torque** spinners will be activated. The **Max Force** spinner is used to set the amount of linear force beyond which the constraint will break. The **Max Torque** spinner is used to set the amount of twisting force beyond which the constraint will break.

Projection Area

The options in this area are used to confine the objects within the limits when they violate the limits of the constraint applied to them. By default, the **No Projection** radio button is selected in the **Projection Type** group. As a result, projection of the simulation will not occur in the scene. Select the **Linear Only (faster)** radio button in the **Projection Type** group for linear projections. On selecting the **Linear Only (faster)** radio button, the **Distance** spinner will be activated in the **Projection Settings** group. This spinner is used to specify the distance at which the projection will take place. You can select the **Linear and Angular** radio button in the **Projection Type** group to perform both linear and angular projections. On selecting the **Linear and Angular** radio button, both the **Distance** and **Angle** spinners will be activated in the **Projection Settings** group. The **Angle** spinner is used to specify the minimum angle that the constraint violation must exceed for projection to take place.

Creating the Slide Constraint

MassFX Toolbar:	Constraints > Create Slide Constraint
Menu bar:	Animation > MassFX > Constraints > Create Slide Constraint

You can create the slide constraint by using the **Create Slide Constraint** tool. To do so, select two objects in the viewport as done in the case of rigid constraint. Next, click and hold the cursor on the **Create Rigid Constraint** tool; a flyout will be displayed, as shown in Figure 16-28. Choose **Create Slide Constraint** from the flyout; a connecting line will be displayed in the viewport. Also, **UConstraint** will be displayed in the modifier stack and various rollouts will be displayed in the Modify panel. These rollouts have already been discussed in the **Create Rigid Constraint** section. The slide constraint is similar to the rigid constraint with the only difference that in the slide constraint, the translational motion along **Y** axis is set to **Limited** in the **Translation Limits** rollout by default.

Figure 16-28 Various options in the flyout

Creating the Hinge Constraint

MassFX Toolbar:	Constraints > Create Hinge Constraint
Menu bar:	Animation > MassFX > Constraints > Create Hinge Constraint

You can create the hinge constraint using the **Create Hinge Constraint** tool. To do so, select two objects in the viewport as done in the case of rigid constraint. Next, click and hold the cursor on the **Create Rigid Constraint** tool; a flyout will be displayed. Choose **Create Hinge Constraint** from the flyout; a hinge constraint will be displayed in the viewport. Also, **UConstraint** will be displayed in the modifier stack and various rollouts will be displayed in the Modify panel. These rollouts are same as those discussed in the **Create Rigid Constraint** section. The hinge constraint is similar to the rigid constraint with the only difference that Swing 1 is limited to 100 degrees.

Creating the Twist Constraint

MassFX Toolbar:	Constraints > Create Twist Constraint
Menu bar:	Animation > MassFX > Constraints > Create Twist Constraint

You can create the twist constraint using the **Create Twist Constraint** tool. To do so, select two objects in the viewport as done in case of rigid constraint. Next, click and hold the cursor on the **Create Rigid Constraint** tool; a flyout will be displayed. Choose **Create Twist Constraint** from the flyout; a disc shaped constraint will be displayed in the viewport. Also, **UConstraint** will be displayed in the modifier stack and various rollouts will be displayed in the Modify panel. These rollouts are same as those discussed in the **Create Rigid Constraint** section. Twist constraint is similar to rigid constraint with the only difference that the twist is unlimited.

Creating the Universal Constraint

MassFX Toolbar:	Constraints > Create Universal Constraint
Menu bar:	Animation > MassFX > Constraints > Create Universal Constraint

You can create the universal constraint using the **Create Universal Constraint** tool. To do so, select two objects in the viewport as done in the case of rigid constraint. Next, click and hold the cursor on the **Create Rigid Constraint** tool; a flyout will be displayed. Choose **Create Universal Constraint** from the flyout; a cone-shaped constraint will be displayed in the viewport. Also, **UConstraint** will be displayed in the modifier stack and various rollouts will be displayed in the Modify panel. These rollouts are same as those discussed in the **Create Rigid Constraint** section. The universal constraint is similar to the rigid constraint with the only difference that **Swing 1** and **Swing 2** are limited upto 45 degrees.

Creating the Ball & Socket Constraint

MassFX Toolbar:	Constraints > Create Ball & Socket Constraint
Menu bar:	Animation > MassFX > Constraints > Create Ball & Socket Constraint

You can create the ball & socket constraint using the **Create Ball & Socket Constraint** tool. To do so, select two objects in the viewport as done in the case of rigid constraint. Next, click and hold the cursor on the **Create Rigid Constraint** tool; a flyout will be displayed. Choose **Create Ball & Socket Constraint** from the flyout; a ball and socket constraint will be displayed in the viewport. Also, **Uconstraint** will be displayed in the modifier stack and various rollouts will be displayed in the Modify panel. These rollouts are same as those discussed in the **Create Rigid Constraint** section. The ball & socket constraint is similar to the rigid constraint with the only difference that **Swing 1** and **Swing 2** are limited upto 80 degrees and twist is unlimited.

SIMULATION CONTROLS

Simulation controls are used to control the simulation of rigid bodies. These controls are located on the **MassFX Toolbar**. These controls are discussed next.

Reset Simulation

MassFX Toolbar:	Reset simulation to their original state
Menu bar:	Animation > MassFX > Simulation > Reset Simulation

The **Reset Simulation** button is used to halt the simulation and move the time slider to the first frame. It also resets the transform values of dynamic rigid bodies to their initial values.

Start Simulation

MassFX Toolbar:	Start Simulation
Menu bar:	Animation > MassFX > Simulation > Play Simulation

The **Start Simulation** button is used to start the simulation from the current frame. You can choose the same button to pause the simulation if it is already running.

Start Simulation Without Animation

MassFX Toolbar:	Start Simulation Without Animation

This button is also used to start the simulation with the only difference that the time slider will not move as the simulation runs. It is useful when you want a dynamic rigid body to settle down to a position which can be used as initial transform.

Step Simulation

MassFX Toolbar:	Advance the simulation by one frame
Menu bar:	Animation > MassFX > Simulation > Step Simulation

This button is used to run the simulation for a single frame and move the time slider by a single frame.

The MassFX Tools Dialog Box

MassFX Toolbar:	MassFX Tools
Menu bar:	Animation > MassFX > Utilities > Show MassFX Tools

The **MassFX Tools** button is used to open the **MassFX Tools** dialog box, refer to Figure 16-29. If you choose this button again, the dialog box will close. This dialog box consists of four tabs: **World Parameters**, **Simulation Tools**, **Multi-Object Editor**, and **Display Options**. The options in these tabs are discussed next.

World Parameters

The **World Parameters** tab consists of various rollouts such as **Scene Settings**, **Advanced Settings**, and **Engine**. The parameters in these rollouts provide global settings and controls for creating physical simulations. The most commonly used rollouts in this tab are discussed next.

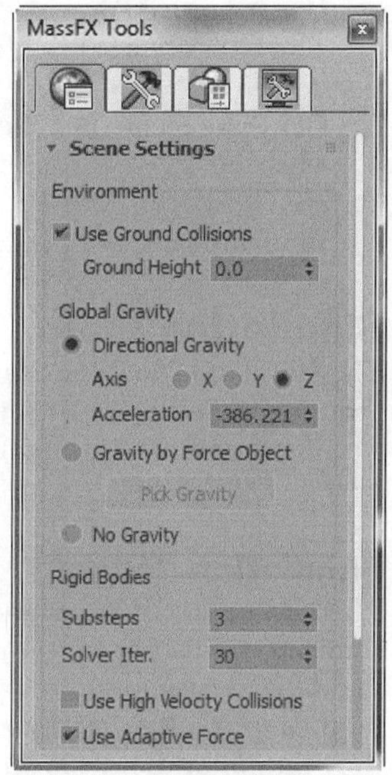

***Figure 16-29** Partial view of the **MassFX Tools** dialog box*

Scene Settings Rollout

This rollout consists of areas that control the settings of the environment and the rigid bodies. The parameters in these areas are discussed next.

Environment Area

The options in this area are used to control ground collisions and gravity. The **Use Ground Collisions** check box is selected in the **Environment** area by default. As a result, the MassFX interface uses an invisible static rigid body that is coplanar with the home grid known as ground rigid body. The **Ground Height** spinner is used to specify the height of the ground rigid body. This spinner is activated only when the **Use Ground Collision** check box is selected. In the **Global Gravity** group, the **Directional Gravity** radio button is selected by default. As a result, a rigid body is subjected to gravity. Select the **X**, **Y**, or **Z** radio button next to the **Axis** group to specify the global axis along which the gravity will be applied. The **Acceleration** spinner is used to specify the force of gravity. A positive value in this spinner will pull the object upward, whereas a negative value will pull the object downward. Select the **Gravity by Force Object** radio button to use a Gravity space warp to add gravity to rigid bodies. On selecting the **No Gravity** radio button, no gravity will be applied to the rigid bodies.

Rigid Bodies Area

The options in this area are used to adjust the settings when collisions and constraint do not work properly. The options in this area are discussed next.

Substeps

The **Substeps** spinner is used to control the number of simulation steps performed between each graphical state. The formula used for the calculation is as follows:

*Simulation per step= (Substeps+1) * Frame Rate*

A frame rate of 30 fps with 1 substep will result in 60 steps per second.

Solver Iter
The **Solver Iter** spinner is used to control the number of times the constraint solver enforces collisions and constraints. It is recommended not to use values higher than 30.

Use High Velocity Collisions
This check box is used to create a simplified collision in a scene carrying fast moving rigid bodies.

Use Adaptive Force
This check box is used to remove jittering in the tightly clustered rigid bodies.

Generate Shape Per Element
This check box is used to create a separate physical mesh for each element. If this check box is cleared, MassFX creates a single physical shape for the entire object. This makes simulation fast but less accurate.

Simulation Tools

The **Simulation Tools** tab consists of three rollouts: **Simulation**, **Simulation Settings**, and **Utilities**, as shown in Figure 16-30. The most commonly used rollouts in this tab are discussed next.

*Figure 16-30 The **Simulation**, **Simulation Settings**, and **Utilities** rollouts in the **Simulation Tools** tab*

Simulation Rollout

The buttons in the **Simulation** rollout are used to control the simulation, bake dynamic transforms to keyframes, and specify the initial transformation stage for a dynamic rigid body. The buttons in the **Playback** area have already been discussed in the **Simulation Controls** section. You can choose a button in the **Simulation Baking** area depending on whether you need to bake the selected object, bake all objects, unbake selected object, or unbake all objects.

Utilities Rollout

The options in the **MassFX Scene** area of this rollout are discussed next.

Explore Scene

When you choose the **Explore Scene** button, the **Scene Explorer - MassFX Explorer** window will be displayed, refer to Figure 16-31. In this window, you can view and change the simulation properties of all rigid bodies and constraints in the scene. If you choose the **Display non-Dynamics Objects** button, all non-dynamic objects will also be displayed in this window.

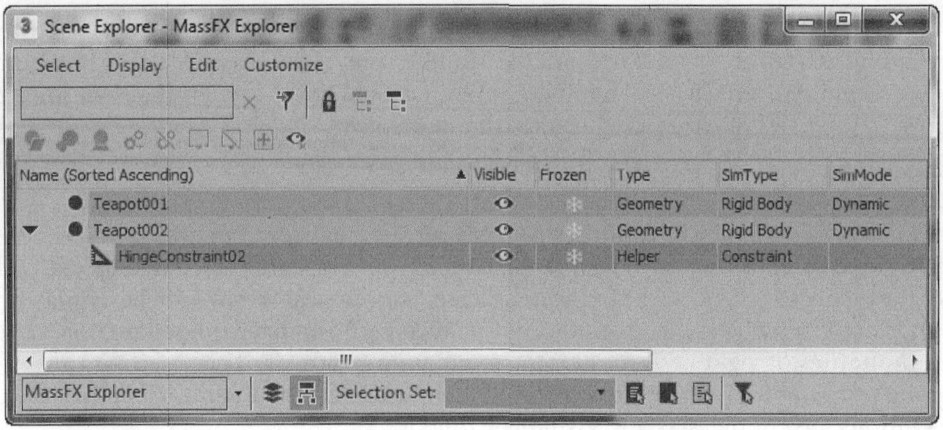

*Figure 16-31 The **Scene Explorer - MassFX Explorer** window*

Validate Scene

When you choose the **Validate Scene** button, the **Validate PhysX Scene** dialog box will be displayed, as shown in Figure 16-32. The **Validate** button in this dialog box is used to check validation of the scene based on the check boxes selected in the dialog box. Green square at the right of the check box indicates that the result is 'valid', red square indicates that the result is 'Fail' and yellow square indicates that you need to take a note of the result.

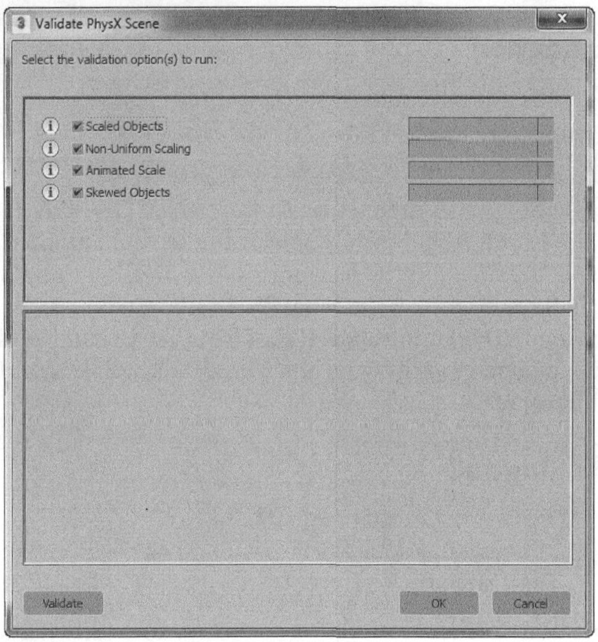

*Figure 16-32 The **Validate PhysX Scene** dialog box*

Export Scene

This button is used to export the MassFX information. On choosing this button, the **Select File to Export** dialog box will be displayed. Browse to the desired location and then enter name of the file in the **File name** edit box. Next, choose the **Save** button to save the file; the **PhysX Export Options** dialog box will be displayed. Choose the desired options from this dialog box. Next, choose the **Export** button to export the scene.

Multi-object Editor

The rollouts in this tab are same as those in the Modify panel of the **MassFX Rigid Body** modifier and have been discussed earlier. The main difference between the two is that by using this tab you can set properties of all selected objects simultaneously.

Display Options

This tab has two rollouts: **Rigid Bodies** and **MassFX Visualizer**. The two check boxes at the top of **Rigid Bodies** rollout are: **Display Physical Meshes** and **Selected Objects Only**. By default, these check boxes are selected and indicate that physical meshes will be displayed in the viewport for selected objects. The options in the **MassFX Visualizer** rollout are used to display various properties of rigid bodies when the simulation proceeds. These settings are used for debugging purposes and will be effective only when you select the **Enable Visualizer** check box in the **Options** area of the **MassFX Visualizer** rollout.

Ragdoll Flyout

The **Ragdoll** flyout is used to control the bones system or character studio biped by using MassFX. Select any bone in the character or an associated skin mesh and then choose the **Ragdoll** command that affects the entire system. The tools available in this flyout are discussed next, as shown in Figure 16-33.

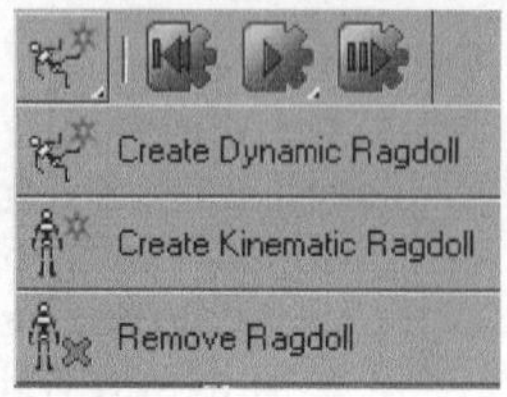

***Figure 16-33** Various options displayed in the **Ragdoll** flyout*

Create Dynamic Ragdoll

MassFX Toolbar:	Ragdoll > Create Dynamic Ragdoll
Menu bar:	Animation > MassFX > Rigid Bodies > Create Dynamic Ragdoll

The **Create Dynamic Ragdoll** tool is used to convert a selected character into a Dynamic ragdoll. Its motion can affect and be affected by other objects in the simulation. To convert a biped into a dynamic ragdoll, select the biped in the viewport. Now, press and hold the left mouse button on the **Create Dynamic Ragdoll** tool in the **MassFX Toolbar**; a flyout will be displayed, refer to Figure 16-33. Choose **Create Dynamic Ragdoll** tool from the flyout; the character studio biped will be converted into a dynamic ragdoll and the **MassFX Ragdoll** modifier will be applied to the biped in the modifier stack.

Create Kinematic Ragdoll

MassFX Toolbar:	Ragdoll > Create Kinematic Ragdoll
Menu bar:	Animation > MassFX > Rigid Bodies > Create Kinematic Ragdoll

The **Create Kinematic Ragdoll** tool is used to convert a selected character into a kinematic ragdoll. Its motion can affect other objects in the simulation but cannot be affected by them. To convert a biped into a kinematic ragdoll, select the character studio biped in the viewport. Press and hold the left mouse button on the **Create Dynamic Ragdoll** tool in the **MassFX Toolbar**; a flyout will be displayed, refer to Figure 16-33. Choose the **Create Kinematic Ragdoll** tool from the flyout; the character studio biped will be converted into a kinematic ragdoll and the **MassFX Ragdoll** modifier will be applied to the character studio biped in the modifier stack.

Remove Ragdoll

MassFX Toolbar:	Ragdoll > Remove Ragdoll
Menu bar:	Animation > MassFX > Rigid Bodies > Remove Ragdoll

The **Remove Ragdoll** tool is used to remove a selected character from the simulation by deleting the Rigid Body modifiers, constraints, and Ragdoll helpers.

HELPERS

The helpers are objects that are used as a supporters, controllers, and so on in the scene. To create helper objects, choose **Create > Helpers** in the **Command Panel**; a drop-down list will be displayed with the **Standard** option selected by default, as shown in Figure 16-34. You can select any other option from this drop-down list. Depending on the option selected, different helpers will be displayed in the **Object Type** rollout. In this section, you will learn about different types of helper objects.

Dummy Helper

Menu bar:	Create > Helpers > Dummy
Command Panel:	Create > Helpers > Standard > Object Type rollout > Dummy

The dummy helper object is a wireframe box, as shown in Figure 16-35. It has a pivot point at its geometric center.

Figure 16-34** The **Helpers** button chosen in the **Command Panel

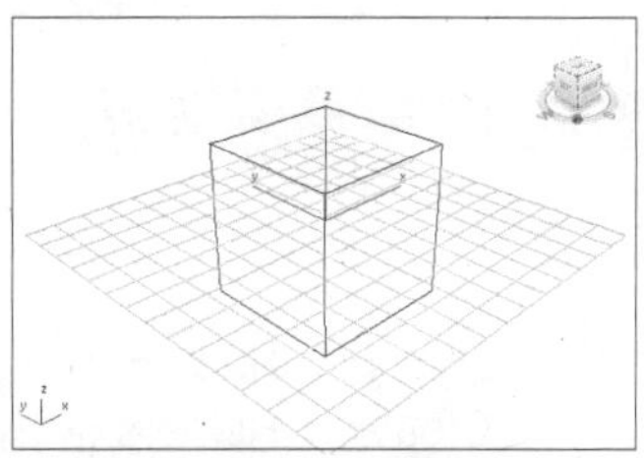

***Figure 16-35** A dummy helper object in the Perspective viewport*

A dummy object helps in animating the objects in a hierarchical linkage. For example, if you link a number of objects to a dummy object and then animate the dummy object, all the linked objects will follow the same animation. You can also use the dummy object to animate the target camera in your scene. To do so, you need to link the camera and its target to the dummy object. Now, if you animate the dummy object, then the camera and its target will follow the same animation.

To create a dummy object, choose **Create > Helpers** in the **Command Panel**; the **Standard** option will be displayed in the drop-down list. Now, invoke the **Dummy** tool from the **Object Type** rollout and then drag the cursor in the viewport from one place to another; a dummy object will be created, refer to Figure 16-35. Note that you cannot modify the shape or size of the dummy object. You can scale it using the scaling tools in the **Main Toolbar**. However, it can create unexpected result if the dummy object is within a hierarchical linkage.

Point Helper

Menu bar:	Create > Helpers > Point
Command Panel:	Create > Helpers > Standard > Object Type rollout > Point

The point helper object is used to create a specific location in 3D space that can be used as a reference in a scene. To create a point helper, choose **Create > Helpers** in the **Command Panel**; the **Standard** option will be displayed in the drop-down list. Invoke the **Point** tool from the **Object Type** rollout; the **Parameters** rollout will be displayed in the Modify panel. Now, press and hold the left mouse button in the viewport and drag the cursor to specify the location of the point. Next, release the mouse button; a point helper object will be displayed, as shown in Figure 16-36. You can modify the shape and size of the point helper object by specifying the parameters in the **Parameters** rollout, refer to Figure 16-37. Select any of the check boxes in the **Display** area to modify the shape of the point helper object in the viewport. Set the value in the **Size** spinner to specify the size of the point helper object. Select the **Constant Screen Size** check box to keep the size of the point helper object constant while zooming the viewport. Select the **Draw On Top** check box to place the point object at the top of the objects in the viewport.

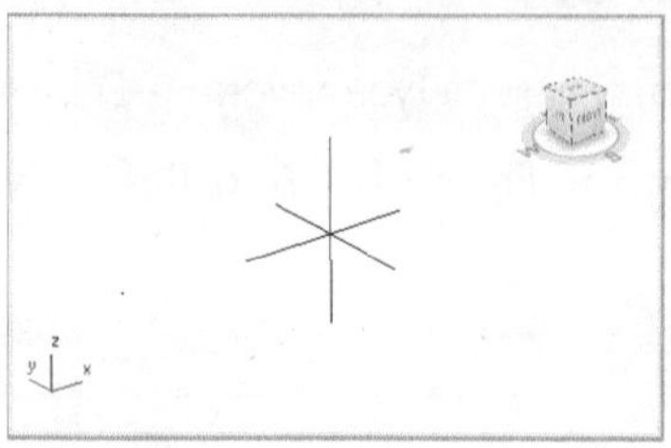

Figure 16-36 A point helper object

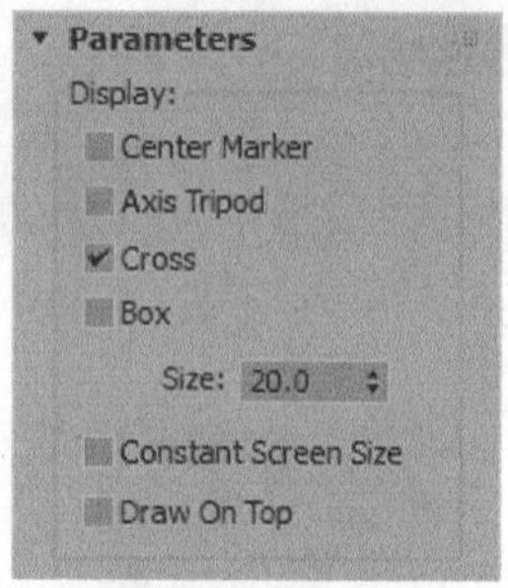

*Figure 16-37 The **Parameters** rollout*

Tape Helper

Menu bar:	Create > Helpers > Tape Measure
Command Panel:	Create > Helpers > Standard > Object Type rollout > Tape

The tape helper is used to create a virtual tape to measure and set on-screen distances. To create a tape measure object, choose **Create > Helpers** in the **Command Panel**; the **Standard** option will be displayed in the drop-down list. Invoke the **Tape** tool from the **Object Type** rollout; the **Parameters** rollout will be displayed in the Modify panel. Now, press and hold the left mouse button in the viewport, drag the cursor from one point to another to place the target of the tape and then release the left mouse button; a tape measure will be created in the viewport, as shown in Figure 16-38. Also, the length of the tape measure object will be displayed in the **Length** spinner of the **Parameters** rollout, as shown in Figure 16-39.

To set specific on-screen distance, select the **Specify Length** check box in the **Parameters** rollout; the **Length** spinner will be activated. Set the value in the **Length** spinner; the length of the tape measure will be modified according to the value specified in the **Length** spinner. Moreover, you can set the position of the target by dragging the target.

Figure 16-38 *A tape measure created in a scene*

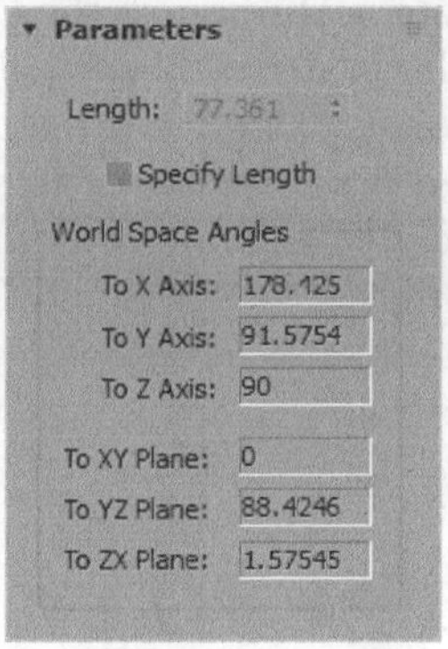

*Figure 16-39 The **Parameters** rollout*

Protractor Helper

Menu bar:	Create > Helpers > Protractor
Command Panel:	Create > Helpers > Standard > Object Type rollout > Protractor

The protractor helper is used to measure the angle between two objects in a scene. To create a protractor for measuring the angle between two objects, choose **Create > Helpers** in the **Command Panel**; the **Standard** option will be displayed in the drop-down list by default. Now, invoke the **Protractor** tool from the **Object Type** rollout; the **Parameters** rollout will be displayed in the Modify panel. Click in the viewport to create the protractor helper, as shown in Figure 16-40. In the **Parameters** rollout, choose the **Pick Object 1** button and select an object in the viewport. Next, choose the **Pick Object 2** button and select another object in the viewport; the angle between the selected objects will be displayed in the **Angle** edit box of the **Parameters** rollout, as shown in Figure 16-41. Also, the connecting lines will be displayed from the protractor object to the other objects in the viewport, refer to Figure 16-40.

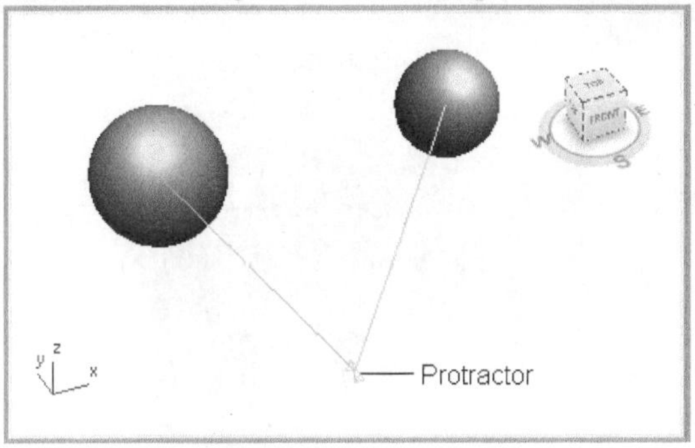

Figure 16-40 A protractor helper object

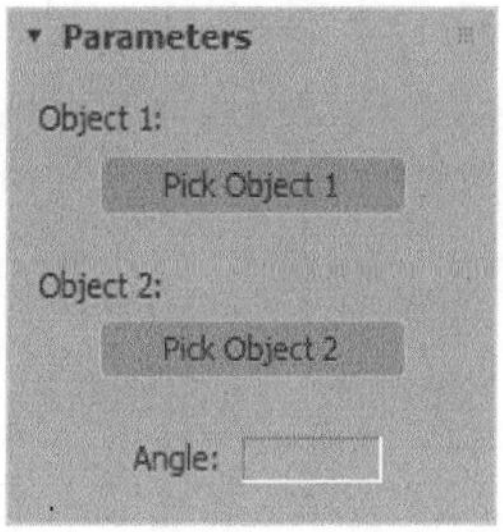

*Figure 16-41 The **Parameters** rollout*

Compass Helper

Menu bar:	Create > Helpers > Compass
Command Panel:	Create > Helpers > Standard > Object Type rollout > Compass

A compass is a part of the sunlight and daylight system and is automatically created with the system. The compass helper is used to create a compass rose in a scene, as shown in Figure 16-42. The compass rose is used to provide directional indicators in a scene. To create a compass rose, choose **Create > Helpers** in the **Command Panel**; the **Standard** option will be displayed in the drop-down list by default. Invoke the **Compass** tool from the **Object Type** rollout; the **Parameters** rollout will be displayed in the Modify panel. Next, press and hold the left mouse button in the viewport and drag the cursor to specify the radius of the compass rose. Next, release the left mouse button; a compass rose will be created. You can also set the value in the **Radius** spinner of the **Parameters** rollout to modify its radius, as shown in Figure 16-43.

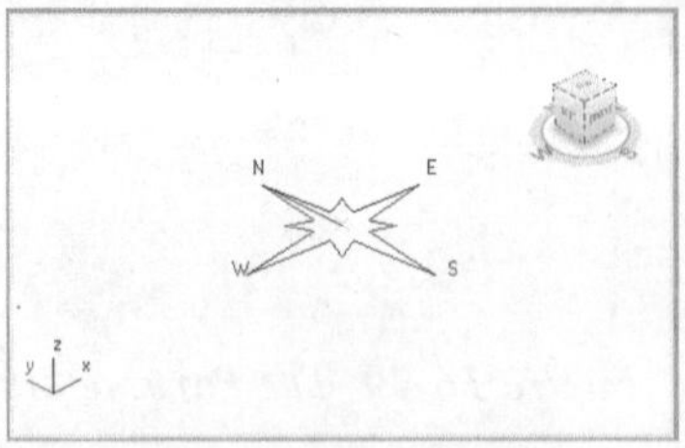

Figure 16-42 A compass rose

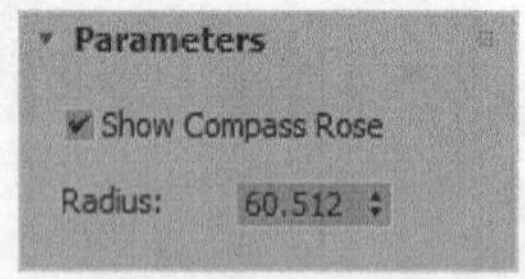

*Figure 16-43 The **Parameters** rollout*

Container Helper

Menu bar:	Create > Helpers > Container
Command Panel:	Create > Helpers > Standard > Object Type rollout > Container

A container is a helper object that is mainly used to organize scene components. On using this helper, the scene components will be organized in a logical group such that they can be handled as a single object. It also helps in reducing the scene complexity. To create a container helper, choose **Create > Helpers** in the **Command Panel**; the **Standard** option will be displayed in the drop-down list by default. Invoke the **Container** tool from the **Object Type** rollout and drag the cursor in the viewport; a container helper will be created, as shown in Figure 16-44. Next, choose the **Modify** tab; various rollouts to modify and set the parameters of the container will be displayed, as shown in Figure 16-45.

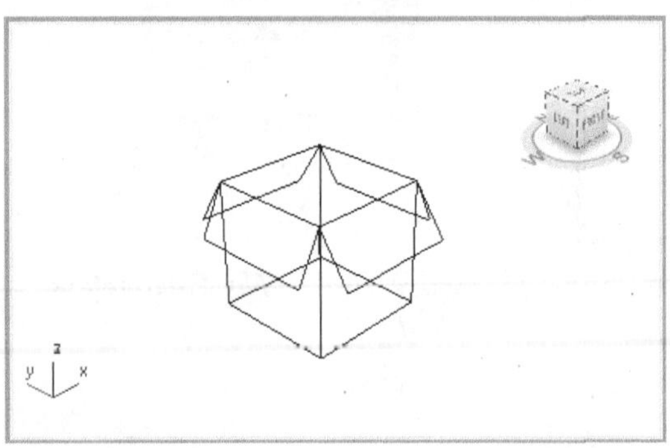

Figure 16-44 A container helper

Figure 16-45 Partial view of various rollouts displayed for the container helper

To add scene components to the container, choose the **Add** button from the **Local Content** rollout; the **Add Container Node** dialog box will be displayed, as shown in Figure 16-46. Select the objects that you want to add to the container and choose the **Add** button in this dialog box; the selected objects will be added to the container. Now, if you transform the container helper by scaling, rotating, or moving, then the added objects will also get transformed in the same way.

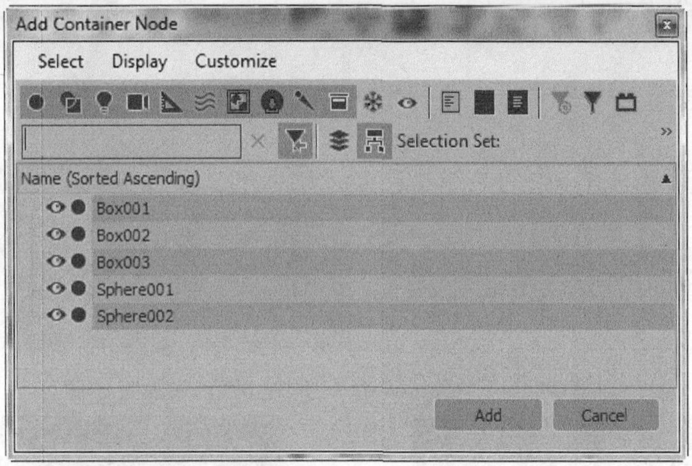

***Figure 16-46** The **Add Container Node** dialog box*

iray Section Helper

Command Panel:	Create > Helpers > Standard > Object Type rollout > iray Section

The iray Section helper is used when iray renderer is selected for rendering a scene. It is used as a cutting plane for iray renderer. When you place the iray Section helper in the scene, either side of the plane (generally closer to the viewing plane) becomes invisible on rendering.

To create a iray Section helper, choose **Create > Helpers** in the **Command Panel**; the **Standard** option will be displayed in the drop-down list by default. Invoke the **iray Section** tool from the **Object Type** rollout; the **iray Section Parameters** rollout will be displayed in the Modify panel, as shown in Figure 16-47. Next, press and hold the left mouse button in the viewport to specify the first corner of the plane and then drag the cursor to define the length and width of the plane. Next, release the left mouse button; the iray section plane will be created, refer to Figure 16-48. This plane will act as a cutting plane in the rendering process. A portion of the scene on one side of the iray section plane will not be visible in rendering. Figure 16-49 shows rendered output before using the iray Section helper and Figure16-50 shows rendered output after using the iray Section helper.

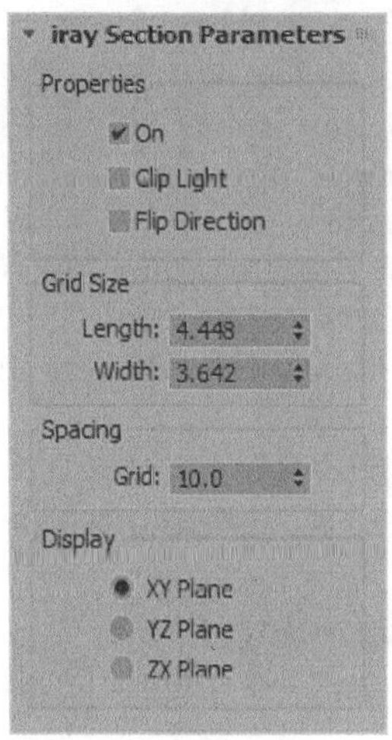

***Figure 16-47** The **iray Section Parameters** rollout*

The areas in the **iray Section Parameters** rollout are discussed next.

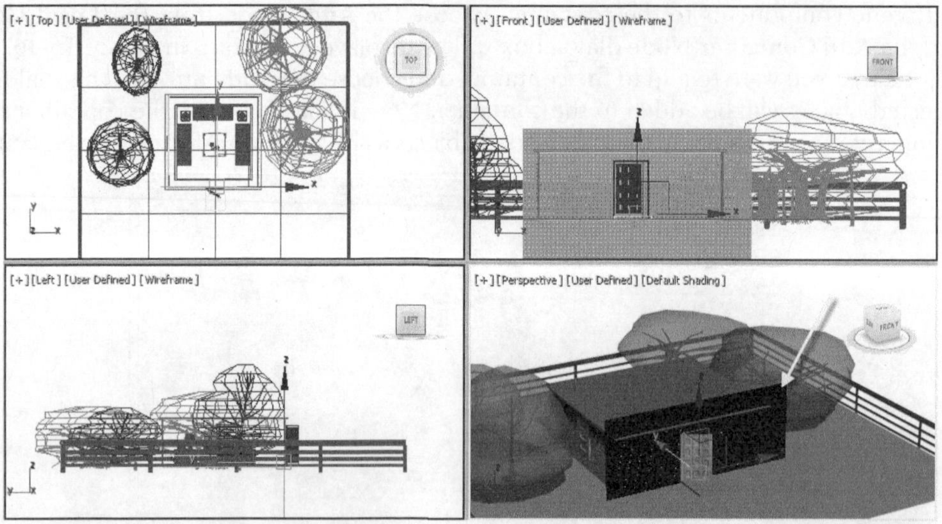

Figure 16-48 The iray section plane created

Figure 16-49 The rendered output before using the iray Section helper

Figure 16-50 The rendered output after using the iray Section helper

Properties Area

In this area, the **On** check box is selected, by default. As a result, the iray section plane is used by the iray renderer. Clear the **On** check box to disable the effect of iray Section helper on rendering. Note that you can also disable the effect of iray Section helper by hiding the iray section plane. The **Clip Light** check box is clear, by default. As a result, lighting is not affected by the use of iray section plane. If you select this check box, lighting is affected by the use of iray section plane. The **Flip Direction** check box is used to toggle the visibility of the scene on either side of the iray section plane at the time of rendering.

Grid Size Area

The **Length** and **Width** spinners are used to set the size of the iray section plane.

Spacing Area

The **Grid** spinner is used to set the grid spacing of the iray section plane.

Display Area

The options in this area are used to set the orientation of the iray section plane.

LightMeter Helper

Command Panel:	Create > Helpers > Standard > Object Type rollout > LightMeter

The LightMeter helper is used to calculate the lighting analysis data (lighting levels) for a scene. To create a LightMeter helper, choose **Create > Helpers** in the **Command Panel**; the **Standard** option will be displayed in the drop-down list by default. Invoke the **LightMeter** tool from the **Object Type** rollout; the **Parameters** and **Display** rollouts will be displayed in the Modify panel, refer to Figure 16-51. Next, press and hold the left mouse button in the viewport to specify the first corner of the grid and then drag the cursor to define the length and width of the grid. Next, release the left mouse button; the LightMeter helper grid will be created. You need to set the values in the **Parameters** rollout to specify dimensions and number of segments of the grid. Each point on the grid represents the sample point. Each sample point displays a value calculated in the lighting analysis.

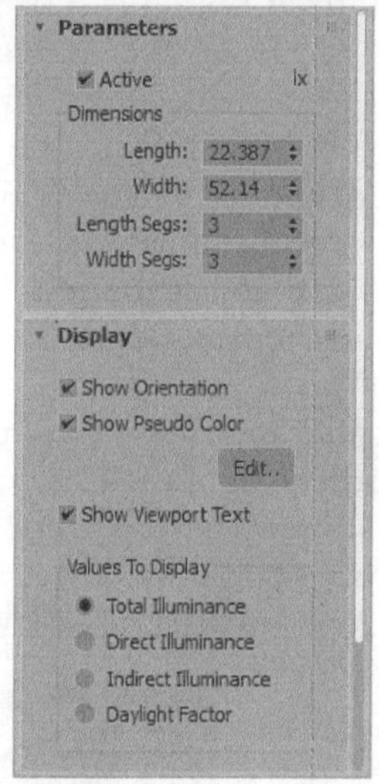

*Figure 16-51 The **Parameters** and **Display** rollouts*

You can calculate the direct illuminance value, indirect illuminance value, total illuminance value, or daylight factor for all sample points. To calculate these values, you need to select the mental ray renderer. After selecting the mental ray renderer, select one of the radio buttons from the **Value To Display** area of the **Display** rollout and then choose the **Calculate All Light Meters** button located below it; the calculated values will be displayed at each sample point in the viewport based on the option selected in the **Value To Display** area.

You can export these calculated values displayed in the viewport to an Excel file in the tabular form by using the **Export To CSV File** button in the **Display** rollout. You can also export these values as an overlay on a rendered image by using the **Lighting Analysis Image Overlay** effect. To add this effect, choose **Rendering > Lighting Analysis > Lighting Analysis - Create > Lighting Analysis Image Overlay** from the menu bar.

Note

*The **Lighting Analysis Image Overlay** effect can also be added using the options in the **Atmospheres & Effects** rollout of the light or by using the options in the **Effects** tab of the **Environment and Effects** dialog box. Various lighting effects are discussed in detail in Chapter 13.*

ATMOSPHERIC APPARATUS

In 3ds Max, there are three types of gizmos that limit the fog or fire effects in a scene. You can create them by using the BoxGizmo, SphereGizmo, and CylGizmo helpers. The BoxGizmo helpers are discussed next.

BoxGizmo Helper

Menu bar:	Create > Helpers > Atmospherics > Box Gizmo
Command Panel:	Create > Helpers > Atmospheric Apparatus > Object Type rollout > BoxGizmo

The BoxGizmo helper is used to create a box-shaped gizmo, as shown in Figure 16-52. To create a BoxGizmo helper object, choose **Create > Helpers** in the **Command Panel**; the **Standard** option will be displayed in the drop-down list by default. Select the **Atmospheric Apparatus** option from the drop-down list. Next, invoke the **BoxGizmo** tool from the **Object Type** rollout; the **Box Gizmo Parameters** rollout will be displayed in the Modify panel. Create a gizmo in the viewport using the same method that was used to create a box. You can adjust the length, width, and height of the gizmo using the **Box Gizmo Parameters** rollout.

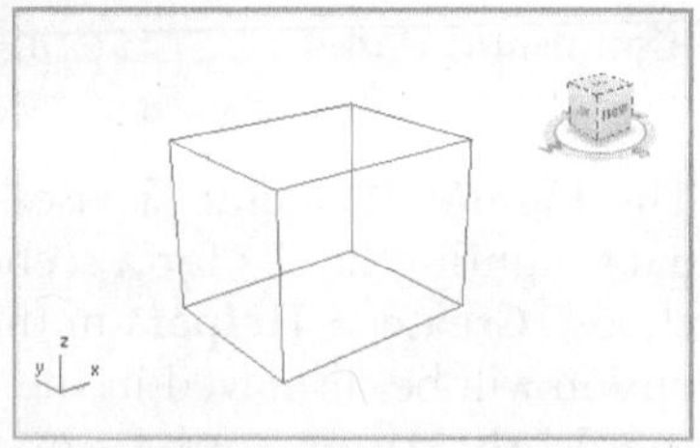

Figure 16-52 *A BoxGizmo helper*

To add an atmosphere to a scene, select the BoxGizmo in the viewport and then choose the **Modify** tab in the **Command Panel**; the **Box Gizmo Parameters** and **Atmospheres & Effects** rollouts will be displayed in the Modify panel, as shown in Figure 16-53. Expand the **Atmospheres & Effects** rollout, if it is not already expanded. Choose the **Add** button; the **Add Atmosphere** dialog box will be displayed, as shown in Figure 16-54.

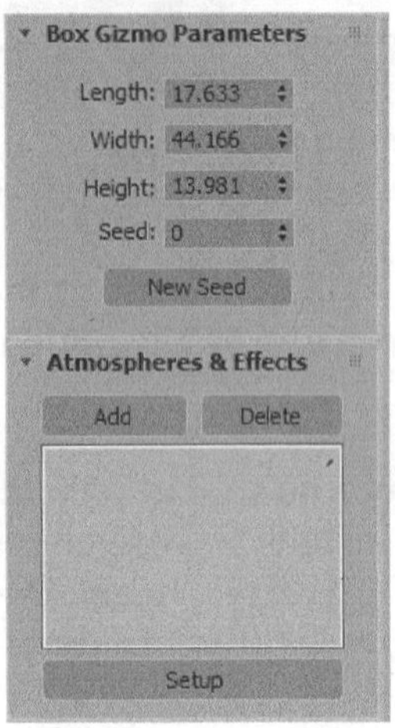

Figure 16-53 *The rollouts for modifying the **BoxGizmo** helper in the Modify panel*

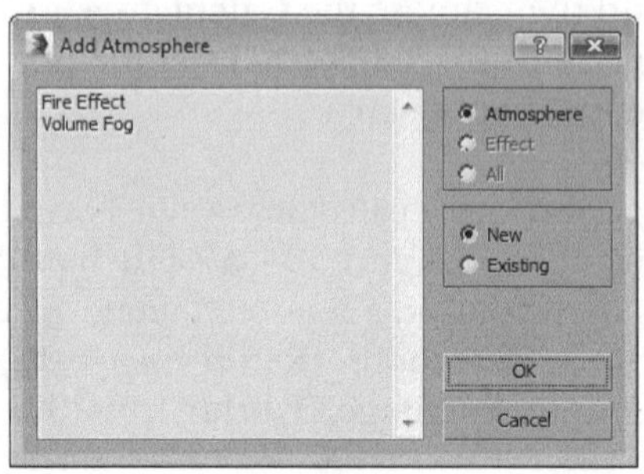

Figure 16-54 *The **Add Atmosphere** dialog box*

Select one of the effects from the text area of the **Add Atmosphere** dialog box and choose the **OK** button; the selected effect will be displayed in the text area of the **Atmospheres & Effects** rollout. Also, when you render the scene, the selected effect will be displayed. To set the parameters of the selected effect, select the name of the effect in the **Atmospheres & Effects** rollout and choose the **Setup** button; the **Environment and Effects** dialog box will be displayed. Set the parameters of the selected effect using the corresponding rollouts in the **Environment and Effects** dialog box.

Note

The SphereGizmo and CylGizmo helpers are the same as the BoxGizmo. The only difference is that the SphereGizmo is spherical and the CylGizmo is cylindrical in shape.

TUTORIALS

Before starting the tutorials, you need to download the *c16_3dsmax_2017_tut.zip* file from *www.cadcim.com*. The path of the file is as follows: *Textbooks > Animation and Visual Effects > 3ds Max > Autodesk 3ds Max 2017: A Comprehensive Guide*

Extract the contents of the zip file and save them in the *Documents* folder.

Tutorial 1

In this tutorial, you will simulate a ball falling on sliders, using the **MassFX Toolbar**, refer to Figure 16-55. **(Expected time: 30 min)**

Figure 16-55 *The ball falling on sliders at frame 42*

The following steps are required to complete this tutorial:

a. Create the project folder.
b. Create sliders and ball.
c. Convert objects into rigid bodies.
d. Play simulation and bake animation of ball.
e. Save and render the scene.

Creating the Project Folder

Create a project folder with the name *c16_tut1* in *3dsmax2017* and then save the file with the name *c16tut1,* as discussed in Tutorial 1 of Chapter 2.

Creating Sliders and Ball

In this section, you will create a ball and a model consisting of back support and six sliders.

1. Activate the Front viewport and choose **Create > Geometry** in the **Command Panel**; the **Standard Primitives** option is displayed in the drop-down list. Next, choose the **Box** tool from the **Object Type** rollout.

2. Expand the **Keyboard Entry** rollout and set the parameters as follows:

   Length: **180** Width: **95** Height: **6**

3. Choose the **Create** button from the **Keyboard Entry** rollout; a box is created.

4. In the **Name and Color** rollout, enter **back support** as the name of the box and press ENTER.

5. Choose the **Select and Move** tool and move *back support* so that it is placed exactly on the grid in the Perspective viewport, as shown in Figure 16-56. This grid acts as a ground plane in the simulation.

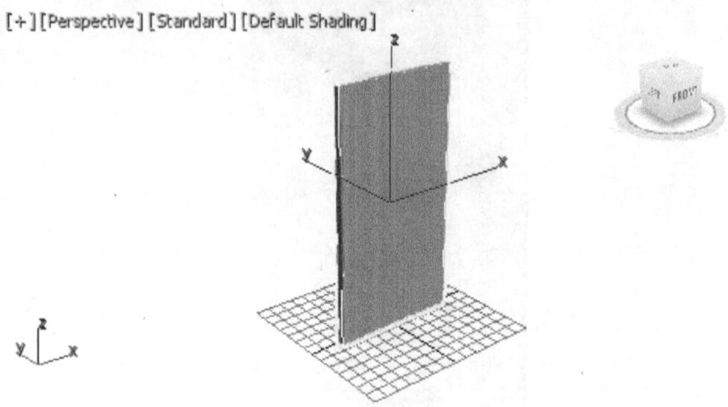

Figure 16-56 Alignment of back support with the grid

Next, you need to create the sliders for the model.

6. Activate the Top viewport. Choose **Create > Geometry > Standard Primitives > Object Type** rollout **> Box** from the **Command Panel**.

7. Expand the **Keyboard Entry** rollout and set the parameters as follows:

   Length: **15** Width: **50** Height: **3**

8. Expand the **Parameters** rollout and set the values as follows:

   Length Segs: **5** Width Segs: **5** Height Segs: **5**

9. Choose the **Create** button from the **Keyboard Entry** rollout; a box is created.

10. In the **Name and Color** rollout, enter **slider1** as the name of the box and then press ENTER.

11. Convert *slider1* into editable poly to modify it at an advanced level.

12. Activate the Front viewport and select the **Polygon** sub-object level and align the left polygons using the **Select and Move** and **Select and Rotate** tools, as shown in Figure 16-57.

13. Select the **Polygon** sub-object level once again to deactivate it. Next, invoke the **Select and Move** tool and move *slider1* at the top of *back support* and rotate it using the **Select and Rotate** tool in the Front viewport, as shown in Figure 16-58.

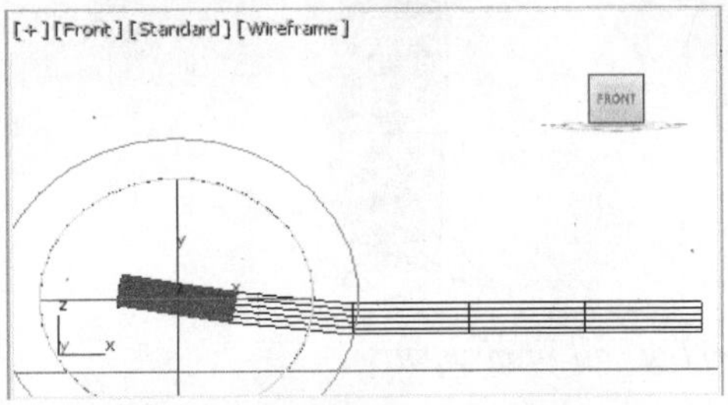

Figure 16-57 *The slider1 geometry after aligning the polygons*

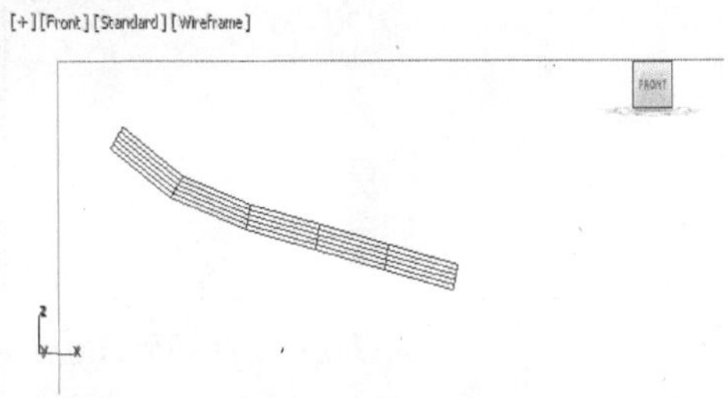

Figure 16-58 *Alignment of the slider1 in the Front viewport*

14. Make sure that *slider1* is selected and the Front viewport is activated. Press and hold the SHIFT key and drag the mouse downward using the left mouse button. Next, release the left mouse button and the SHIFT key when the cursor is approximately at a point above the center of *back support*; the **Clone Options** dialog box is displayed.

15. In the **Clone Options** dialog box, make sure that the **Copy** radio button is selected. Set the value **2** in the **Number of Copies** spinner and choose the **OK** button; two copies of the slider are created and are automatically named as *slider002* and *slider003*.

16. Select *slider1, slider002,* and *slider003*. Choose the **Mirror** tool from the **Main Toolbar** to open the **Mirror Screen Coordinates** dialog box. In this dialog box, select the **Geometry** radio button and then select the **Copy** radio button from the **Clone Selection** area. Next, enter **34** in the **Offset** spinner of the **Mirror Axis** area and then choose the **OK** button to create copies of the selected geometries. Next, align the boxes, refer to Figure 16-59.

    Next, you need to create a ball.

17. Activate the Top viewport. Choose **Create > Geometry > Standard Primitives > Object Type** rollout **> Sphere** from the **Command Panel**.

18. In the **Keyboard Entry** rollout, set the value of the **Radius** spinner to **4** and choose the **Create** button; a sphere is created.

19. Rename the sphere to **ball**. Next, align *ball* in viewports such that it rests on *slider1*, as shown in Figure 16-59.

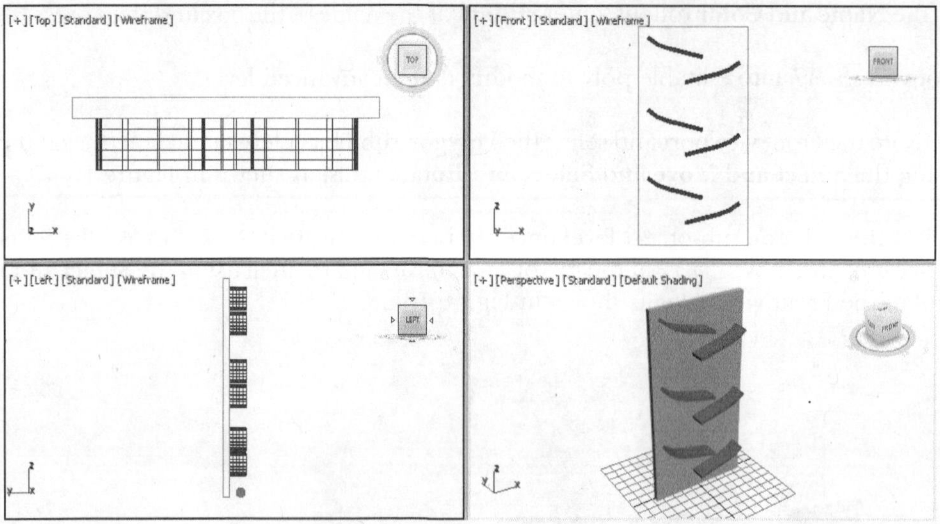

Figure 16-59 Alignment of ball in viewports

Converting Objects into Rigid Bodies

In this section, you need to convert the sliders, ball, and back support into suitable rigid bodies.

1. Select *ball* in the viewport. Make sure that the **MassFX Toolbar** is displayed in the interface.

   If it is not displayed, right-click on the blank space in the **Main Toolbar**; a shortcut menu is displayed. Choose the **MassFX Toolbar** option from the shortcut menu; the **MassFX Toolbar** is displayed.

2. Choose the **Set Selected as Dynamic Rigid Body** tool; the *ball* is converted into a dynamic rigid body and the **MassFX Rigid Body** modifier is applied to it. 

3. Select *back support*. Click and hold on the **Set Selected as Dynamic Rigid Body** tool; a flyout is displayed. Choose the **Set Selected as Static Rigid Body** option from the flyout; *back support* is converted into a static rigid body and the **MassFX Rigid Body** modifier is applied to it. Retain the default settings of the modifier in the Modify panel. 

4. Select all sliders in the viewport. Next, press and hold on the **Set Selected as Dynamic Rigid Body** tool; a flyout is displayed. Choose the **Set Selected as Static Rigid Body** option from the flyout; all sliders are converted into a static rigid body and the **MassFX Rigid Body** modifier is applied to them. 

5. Select *ball* in the viewport and then enter values of the following parameters in the **Physical Material** rollout:

   Mass: **30.92** Bounciness: **0**

6. In the **Physical Shapes** rollout, select **Sphere** from the **Shape Type** drop-down list.

Notice that *ball* now touches the surface of the sliders while sliding.

7. Maximize the Perspective viewport. Next, choose the **Start Simulation** button from the **Simulation** flyout; simulation starts in viewports. 

8. Choose the **Reset Simulation** button to reset the simulation. 

Note

If the ball falls abruptly to the ground midway from any of the sliders, you may need to adjust the rotation angle or position of that slider.

Try changing parameters in the **Physical Material** rollout of *ball* to improve the result.

Baking Animation of Ball

1. Choose the **Start Simulation** button from the **MassFX Toolbar** to start the simulation.

2. Choose the **Reset Simulation** button from the **MassFX Toolbar** to reset the simulation.

   Next, you need to increase the number of frames in the track bar to create the complete animation of the ball as per the simulation.

3. Choose the **Time Configuration** button located at the bottom of the screen; the **Time Configuration** dialog box is displayed. In the **Animation** area of this dialog box, set the value **250** in the **End Time** spinner and press the ENTER key; the number of frames increases in the track bar. Choose the **OK** button to exit the dialog box.

   Next, you need to bake the ball so that the key animation is baked in the track bar.

4. Select *ball* in the viewport and in the **Rigid Body Properties** rollout, choose the **Bake** button; the key animation of *ball* is baked in the track bar, refer to Figure 16-60.

Figure 16-60 *Key animation of ball baked*

Saving and Rendering the Scene

In this section, you will save and render the scene. You can also view the final rendered image of this model by downloading the file *c16_3dsmax_2017_rndr.zip* from *www.cadcim.com*. The path of the file is as follows: *Textbooks > Animation and Visual Effects > 3ds Max > Autodesk 3ds Max 2017: A Comprehensive Guide.*

1. Choose **Save** from the **Application** menu.

2. For rendering, refer to Tutorial 1 of Chapter 14.

Tutorial 2

In this tutorial, you will simulate a scene in which a wall is being broken by a metal ball, as shown in Figure 16-61, using the tools in the **MassFX Toolbar**. **(Expected time: 30 min)**

Figure 16-61 The scene for Tutorial 2

The following steps are required to complete this tutorial:

a. Create the project folder.
b. Open the file.
c. Convert the objects into rigid bodies.
d. Apply constraints to rigid bodies.
e. Play simulation and bake animation.
f. Save and render the scene.

Creating the Project Folder

1. Create a project folder with the name *c16_tut2* in the *3dsmax2017*, as discussed in Tutorial 1 of Chapter 2.

2. Open Windows Explorer and then browse to *\Documents\c16_3dsmax_2017_tut*. Next, copy all jpeg files to *\Documents\3dsmax2017\c16_tut2\sceneassets\images*.

Opening the File

1. Choose **Open** from the **Application** menu; the **Open File** dialog box is displayed. In this dialog box, browse to the location *\Documents\c16_3dsmax_2017_tut* and select the **c16_tut2_start.max** file from it. Choose the **Open** button to open the file, refer to Figure 16-62.

2. Choose **Save As** from the **Application** menu; the **Save File As** dialog box is displayed. Browse to the location *\Documents\3dsmax2017\c16_tut2\scenes*. Save the file with the name *c16tut2.max* at this location.

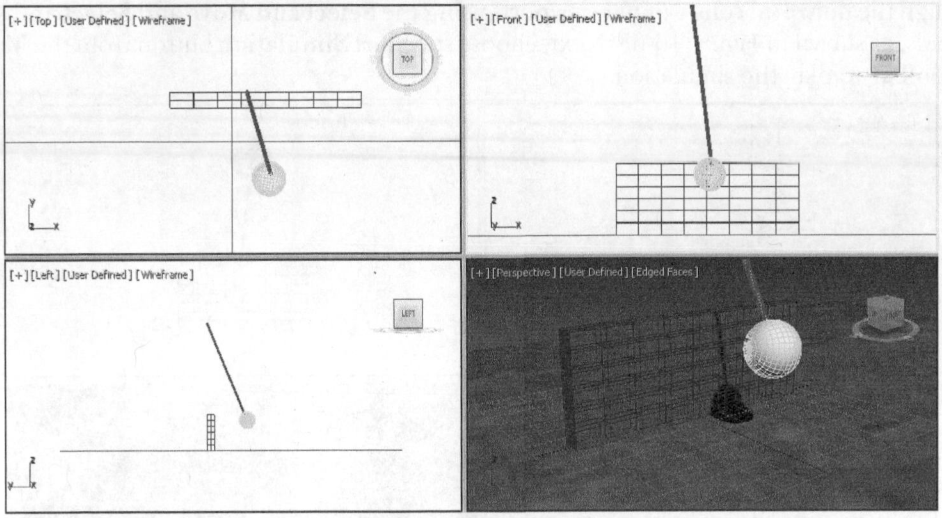

Figure 16-62 The brick wall with a metal ball and metal rod in viewports

Converting the Objects into Rigid Bodies

In this section, you will convert the bricks, metal ball, metal rod, and ground into suitable rigid bodies.

1. Select all bricks in the Left viewport. Click and hold on the **Set Selected as Dynamic Rigid Body** tool; a flyout is displayed. Choose **Set Selected as Dynamic Rigid Body** from the flyout; each brick is converted into a dynamic rigid body and the **MassFX Rigid Body** modifier is applied to it.

2. Similarly, convert *metal ball* and *metal rod* into a dynamic rigid body as done in step 1.

3. Select *ground* in the viewport. Click and hold on the **Set Selected as Dynamic Rigid Body** tool; a flyout is displayed. Choose **Set Selected as Static Rigid Body** from the flyout; *ground* is converted into a static rigid body and the **MassFX Rigid Body** modifier is applied to it.

Applying Constraints to Rigid Bodies

In this section, you will apply a universal constraint and a rigid body constraint to the rigid bodies.

1. Select *metal rod* and *metal ball* in viewport. Click and hold on the **Create Rigid Constraint** tool from the **MassFX Toolbar**; a flyout is displayed. Choose **Create Rigid Constraint** from the flyout; a rigid constraint is displayed in the viewport. Move the cursor and then click in the viewport to specify the size of the constraint.

2. Select *metal ball* from the **Scene Explorer**. Press and hold the left mouse button on the **Create Rigid Constraint** tool from the **MassFX Toolbar**; a flyout is displayed. Choose **Create Universal Constraint** from the flyout. Move the cursor and then click in the viewport to specify the size of the constraint; a universal constraint is displayed in the viewport.

3. Align the universal constraint in viewports using the **Select and Move** and **Select and Rotate** tools, as shown in Figure 16-63. Next, choose the **Start Simulation** button from the **MassFX Toolbar** to play the simulation.

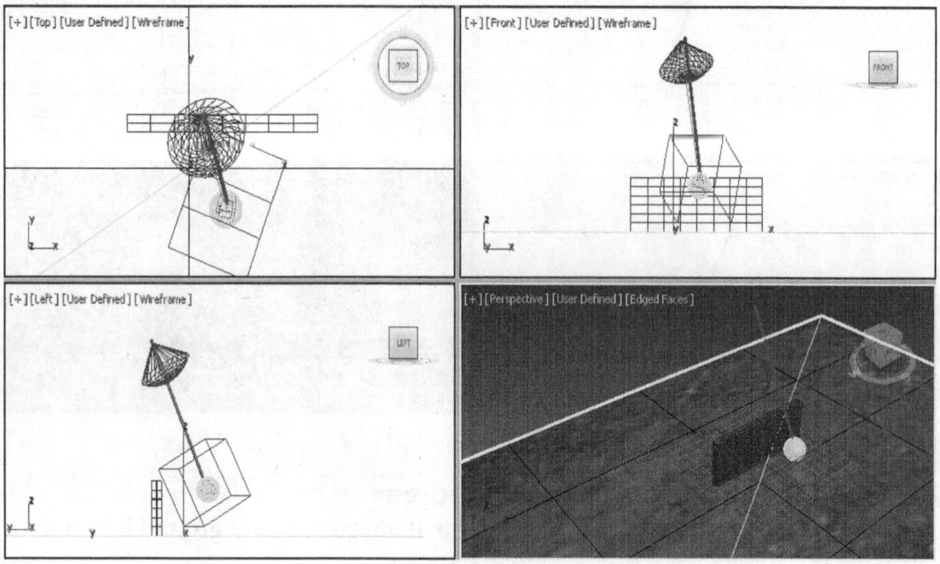

Figure 16-63 Universal constraint aligned in viewports

4. Select all bricks from the **Scene Explorer**. Choose the **MassFX Tools** button from the **Mass FX Toolbar**; the **MassFX Tools** dialog box is displayed. Choose the **Multi-Object Editor** tab from this dialog box and then select **Box** from the **Mesh Type** drop-down list in the **Physical Mesh** rollout. 

5. Select *metal ball* in the viewport and set the drop-down list to **Steel** in the **Preset** group of the **Physical Material** rollout. Next, close the **MassFX Tools** dialog box.

Playing Simulation and Baking Animation

1. Choose the **Start Simulation** button to play the simulation.

   Next, you need to bake the animation in the track bar.

2. Select *metal ball*, *metal rod*, and all bricks from the viewport and choose the **Simulation tools** tab in the **MassFX Tool** dialog box. Next, choose the **Bake all** button in the **Simulation Baking** area of the **Simulation** rollout; the animation is baked in the track bar, refer to Figure 16-64.

Saving and Rendering the Scene

In this section, you will save and render the scene. You can also view the final rendered image of this model by downloading the file *c16_3dsmax_2017_rndr.zip* from *www.cadcim.com*. The path of the file is as follows: *Textbooks > Animation and Visual Effects > 3ds Max > Autodesk 3ds Max 2017: A Comprehensive Guide.*

1. Choose **Save** from the **Application** menu.

2. For rendering, refer to Tutorial 1 of Chapter 14.

Self-Evaluation Test

Answer the following questions and then compare them to those given at the end of this chapter:

1. Which of the following tools is used to help the animation of objects in hierarchical linkage?

   (a) **Dummy** (b) **CylGizmo**
   (c) **Compass** (d) **Tape**

2. Which of the following tools is used to measure the angle between two objects in a scene?

   (a) **Point** (b) **Dummy**
   (c) **Protractor** (d) **Compass**

3. Which of the following is a sub-object level of the **MassFX Rigid Body** modifier?

   (a) **Initial Spin** (b) **Center of Mass**
   (c) **Mesh Transform** (d) **All of the above**

4. A __________ rigid body represents an object in the real world.

5. A __________ is a helper object that is mainly used to organize scene components.

6. The tools of the __________ helpers are used to create the gizmos that limit the fog or fire effects in the scene.

7. __________ are used to restrict the movement of rigid bodies in simulation.

8. The MassFX interface uses an invisible static rigid body that is coplanar with the home grid. (T/F)

9. The helper objects are visible at rendering. (T/F)

10. You can change the type of a rigid body by using the options in the **Rigid Body Type** drop-down list of the **Rigid Body Properties** rollout. (T/F)

Review Questions

Answer the following questions:

1. Which of the following tools is used to create a specific location in the 3D space that can be used as a reference in a specific scene?

   (a) **Point** (b) **Dummy**
   (c) **Protractor** (d) **Compass**

2. Which of the following tools is used to create a virtual tape to measure and set on-screen distances?

   (a) **Dummy** (b) **Point**
   (c) **Compass** (d) **Tape**

3. In the __________ dialog box, you can view and change the simulation properties of all rigid bodies and constraints in the scene.

4. The __________ rollout in the **MassFX Rigid Body** modifier is used to edit the physical meshes assigned to an object in the simulation.

5. When you choose the __________ button, the simulated motion of the selected dynamic rigid body is converted into standard animation keyframes for rendering.

6. The __________ sub-object level displays the axis and the direction of the initial spin for a rigid body.

7. You can use the dummy object to animate the target camera in your scene. (T/F)

8. Static rigid body can be converted into a dynamic rigid body at a frame specified in the **Rigid Body Properties** rollout of the **MassFX Rigid Body** modifier. (T/F)

9. The position of constraints icons affects the behavior of objects in the scene. (T/F)

EXERCISES

The rendered output of the scenes used in the following exercises can be accessed by downloading the *c16_3dsmax_2017_exr.zip* file from *www.cadcim.com*. The path of the file is as follows: *Textbooks > Animation and Visual Effects > 3ds Max > Autodesk 3ds Max 2017: A Comprehensive Guide*

Exercise 1

Create the scene shown in Figure 16-64 using the **SphereGizmo** tool in the **Atmospheric Apparatus** helper. Also, animate the fire effect in the scene. **(Expected time: 15 min)**

Hint:
To animate the fire effect, set the values in the **Phase** and **Drift** spinners in the **Motion** area of the **Fire Effects Parameters** rollout in the **Environment and Effects** dialog box.

Figure 16-64 *Scene for Exercise 1*

Exercise 2

Create a scene showing the simulation of falling balls at different frames from a tray by using the tools in the MassFX interface, refer to Figure 16-65. **(Expected time: 20 min)**

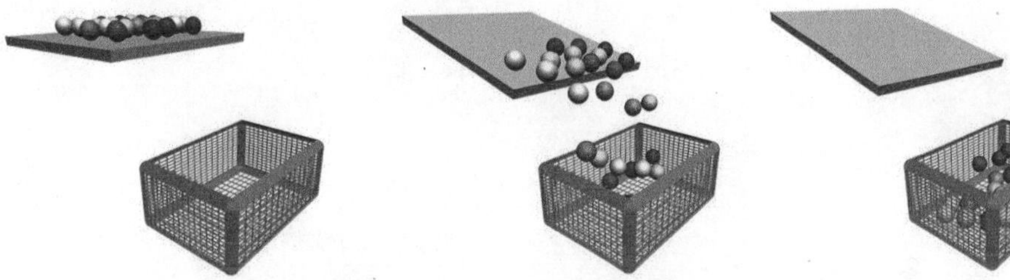

Figure 16-65 *Simulation of falling balls at different frames*

Hint:
Convert the tray into kinematic rigid body and animate so that it tilts. Change the physical mesh of each ball to **Sphere**.

Answers to Self-Evaluation Test

1. a, **2.** c, **3.** d, **4.** dynamic, **5. Container**, **6. Atmospheric Apparatus**, **7.** Constraints, **8.** T, **9.** F, **10.** T

Project 1

Creating a Diner

PROJECT DESCRIPTION

In this project, you will create a scene of the diner, as shown in Figure P1-1. The scene consists of floor, walls, booths, tables with pedestals, and hanging lamps above each table. You will create a window in the wall, a set of blinds in front of the window, and add animation to the blinds to give a scene more realistic look. To add more realistic effect to the scene, you will set up and adjust lights and camera, create glasses and plates on the tables, create text on the window, and assign materials to various objects. You will also set the window background to give more natural effect to the scene. Lastly, you will make necessary adjustments and render the scene for the final output.

Figure P1-1 *The scene of the diner*

Creating the Project Folder

Create a new project folder with the name *Prj_2* at *\Documents\3dsmax2017* and then save the file with the name *Prj2*, as discussed in Tutorial 1 of Chapter 2.

Downloading the Files

Before starting the project, you need to download the *prj1_3dsmax_2017.zip* file from *www.cadcim.com*. The path of the file is as follows: *Textbooks > Animation and Visual Effects > 3ds Max > Autodesk 3ds Max 2017 for Beginners: A Tutorial Approach.*

Extract the contents of the zip file to *Documents*. Open Windows Explorer and then browse to *\Documents\prj1_3dsmax_2017*. Next, copy all files to *\Documents\3dsmax 2017\Prj2\sceneassets\images.*

Creating the Floor

In this section, you will create the floor by using the **Box** tool and then you will apply material to the floor to give it a realistic look.

1. Activate the Top viewport and choose **Create > Geometry** in the **Command Panel**. Then, invoke the **Box** tool from the **Object Type** rollout.

2. Expand the **Keyboard Entry** rollout and set the values in the spinners as given next:

   Length: **100**   Width: **130**   Height: **1**

3. Choose the **Create** button; the floor is created. In the **Name and Color** rollout, enter **Floor**.

4. Choose **Rendering > Material Editor > Compact Material Editor** from the menu bar; the **Material Editor** dialog box is displayed. Select the first material sample slot.

5. Make sure **Blinn** is selected in the drop-down list of the **Shader Basic Parameters** rollout.

6. Expand the **Maps** rollout. Next, choose the **Diffuse Color** button which is currently labeled as **None**; the **Material/Map Browser** dialog box is displayed showing the types of maps that can be added.

7. Select the **Bitmap** map from the **Maps > General** rollout and choose the **OK** button; the **Material/Map Browser** dialog box is closed and the **Select Bitmap Image File** dialog box is displayed. As the project folder is already set, the *images* folder of this project is displayed in the **Look in** drop-down list.

8. Select the file **floor.jpg** and then select the **Override** radio button from the **Gamma** area. Enter the value **2.2** in the spinner located next to it. Now, choose the **Open** button.

Note

1. You need to set gamma override to 2.2 whenever you import a color image map. However, it is not required for the grayscale images used for maps, such as Bump, Noise, and Displacement.

2. Repeat the procedure mentioned in step 8 for all the color images used in this project.

9. In the **Coordinates** rollout, make sure the **Use Real-World Scale** check box is cleared and set the values in the spinners as given next:

   U-Offset: **1.0** V-Offset: **1.0**
   U-Tiling: **4.0** V-Tiling: **4.0** W-Angle: **45**

10. Choose the **Go to Parent** to return back to parent level and then choose the **Assign Material to Selection** tool; the tile material is assigned to *floor.*

11. Choose the **Show Shaded Material in Viewport** tool; the applied material is displayed in the Perspective viewport. Next, rotate the Perspective viewport to set the angle of view, as shown in Figure P1-2.

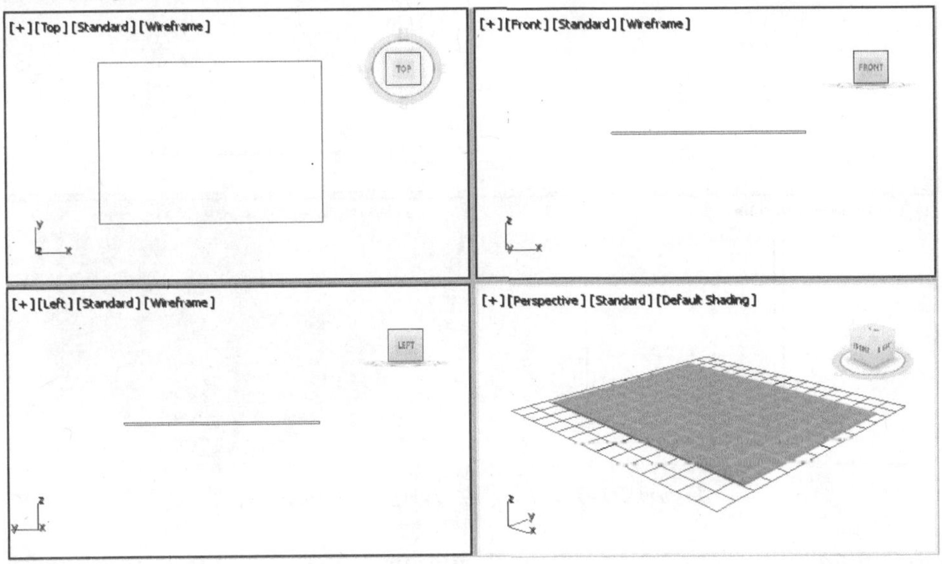

Figure P1-2 Floor created and a material assigned to it

12. Close the **Material Editor** dialog box and choose the **Zoom Extents All** tool to display *floor* to its extent.

Creating Walls

In this section, you will create the walls by using the **Box** tool.

1. Choose the **2D Snap** tool from the **Snaps Toggle** flyout. Next, right-click on it; the **Grid and Snap settings** dialog box is displayed. In this dialog box, select the **Vertex** and the **Edge/Segment** check boxes in the **Snaps** tab and close the dialog box.

2. Activate the Top viewport and then choose **Create > Geometry** in the **Command Panel**. Next, select **AEC Extended** from the drop-down list.

3. Invoke the **Wall** tool from the **Object Type** rollout.

4. Click on the lower left corner of *floor*. Next, drag the cursor to the upper left corner of *floor* and click. Again, drag the cursor to the upper right corner of *floor* and click. Now, right-click in the viewport to exit the tool.

5. In the **Parameters** rollout, make sure 5 is displayed in the **Width** spinner and enter **100** in the **Height** spinner.

6. Enter **wall01** in the **Name and Color** rollout. Figure P1-3 shows *wall01* in the viewport. Next, invoke the **2D Snap** tool again to deactivate it.

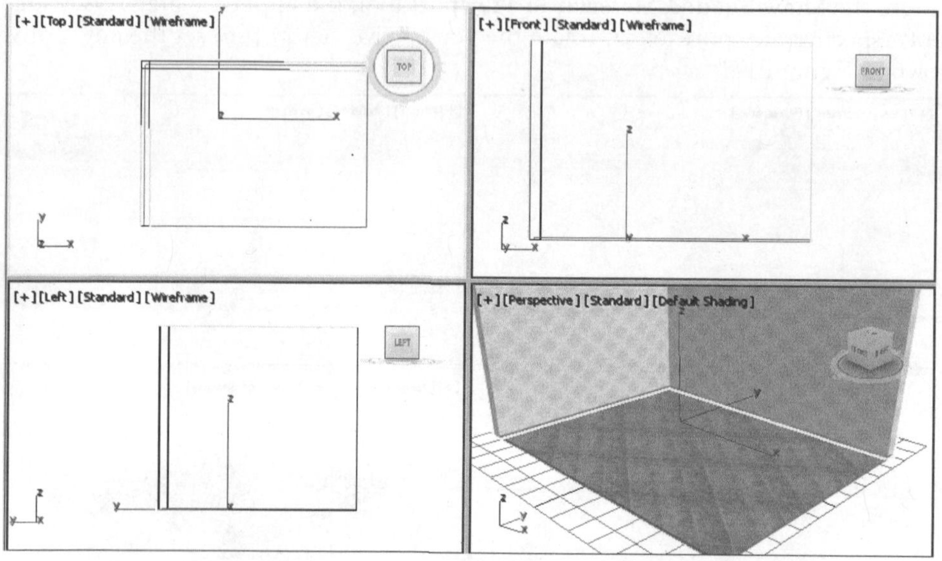

Figure P1-3 *Setting the Perspective viewport*

7. Make sure *wall01* is selected. Next, choose **Rendering > Material Editor > Compact Material Editor** from the menu bar; the **Material Editor** dialog box is displayed. In this dialog box, select the second material sample slot.

8. Make sure **Blinn** is selected in the drop-down list in the **Shader Basic Parameters** rollout, if it is not already selected.

9. Expand the **Maps** rollout. Next, choose the **Diffuse Color** map button which is currently labeled as **None**; the **Material/Map Browser** dialog box is displayed showing the types of maps that can be added.

10. Select the **Bitmap** map from the **Maps > General** rollout and choose the **OK** button; the **Material/Map Browser** dialog box is closed and the **Select Bitmap Image File** dialog box is displayed. As the project folder is already set, the *images* folder of this project is displayed in the **Look in** drop-down list.

11. Select the file **Wall.jpg** and choose the **Open** button.

12. In the **Coordinates** rollout, make sure the **Use Real-World Scale** check box is cleared. Next, set **8** in the **U-Tiling** and **V-Tiling** spinners.

13 In the **Material Editor** dialog box, choose the **Go To Parent** tool to return back to parent level. Now, choose the **Assign Material to Selection** tool to assign the material to the object.

14. Choose the **Show Shaded Material in Viewport** tool to display the assigned material in the viewport, as shown in Figure P1-4. Close the **Material Editor** dialog box.

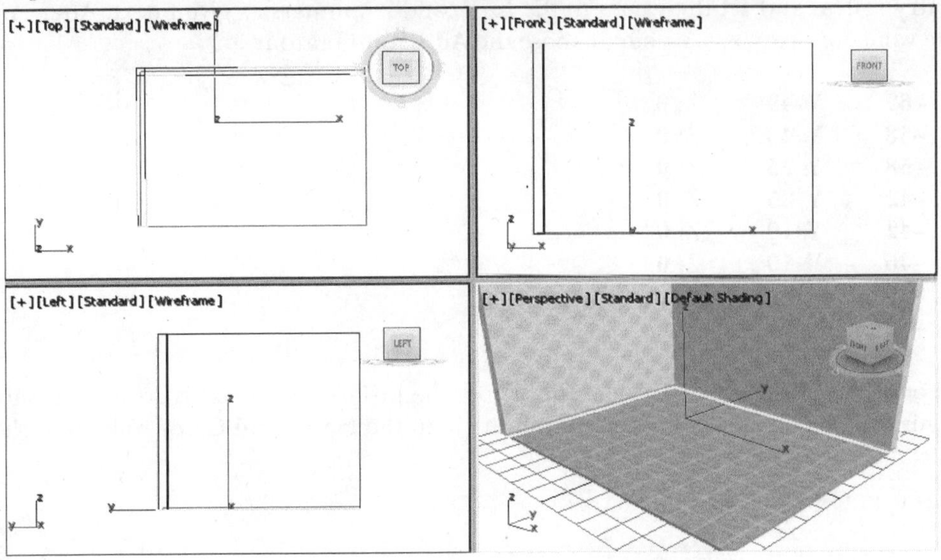

Figure P1-4 *The material assigned to wall01 displayed in the viewport*

Creating the Booth

In this section, you will create the profile of the booth by using the **Line** tool.

1. Right-click on the **Snaps Toggle** tool from the **Main Toolbar**; the **Grid and Snap Settings** dialog box is displayed. In this dialog box, choose the **Home Grid** tab and set the value **2** in the **Grid Spacing** spinner. Next, clear the **Inhibit Grid Subdivision Below Grid Spacing** check box and close the dialog box.

2. Activate the Front viewport and invoke the **Maximize Viewport Toggle** tool to maximize it. Zoom in on the lower-left portion of the viewport.

3. Choose **Create > Shapes** from the **Command Panel**. Choose the **Line** tool from the **Object Type** rollout. Expand the **Keyboard Entry** rollout and set the following values in the **X**, **Y**, and **Z** spinners. After entering the value for every x, y, z point, choose the **Add Point** button:

X: **–64** Y: **1** Z: **0**
X: **–64** Y: **49** Z: **0**
X: **–62** Y: **49** Z: **0**
X: **–62** Y: **21** Z: **0**

X: –46 Y: 21 Z: 0
X: –46 Y: 1 Z: 0

4. Choose the **Close** button; the shape is created. Enter **Booth** as name of the shape; the profile of *Booth* is created. Right-click to exit the tool. Zoom out if you need to see the entire shape. Now, you need to create the seat for *Booth*.

5. Make sure the Front viewport is activated. Choose the **Line** tool again. Expand the **Keyboard Entry** rollout and set the values in the **X**, **Y**, and **Z** spinners as given next. After entering the value for every x, y, z point, choose the **Add Point** button:

X: –62 Y: 49 Z: 0
X: –58 Y: 49 Z: 0
X: –58 Y: 25 Z: 0
X: –42 Y: 25 Z: 0
X: –42 Y: 19 Z: 0
X: –46 Y: 19 Z: 0
X: –46 Y: 21 Z: 0
X: –62 Y: 21 Z: 0

6. Choose the **Close** button to close the shape; the profile of the seat is created, as shown in Figure P1-5. Enter **Seat** as name of the shape in the **Name and Color** rollout. Right-click to exit the tool.

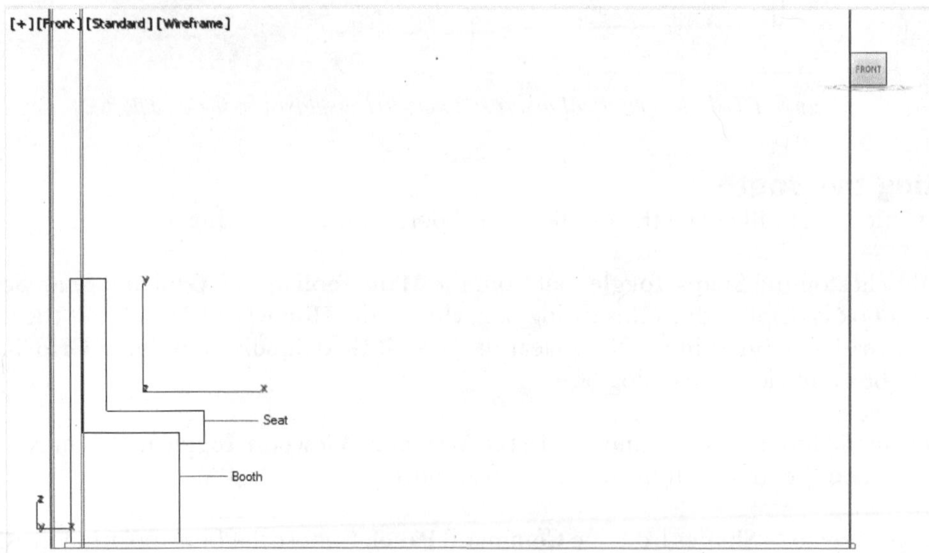

***Figure P1-5** The profile of seat created*

7. Make sure *Seat* is selected. Next, choose the **Modify** tab in the **Command Panel**. In the **Selection** rollout, choose the **Vertex** button; the **Vertex** sub-object mode is activated.

8. Right-click on the top-right vertex of *Seat*; the quad menu is displayed. Select **Bezier** from the upper-left quadrant; the bezier handles are displayed on the vertex and one segment adjoining the vertex is curved.

9. Using the **Select and Move** tool, move the bezier handles to form a curve for the back. Similarly, modify the middle-right vertex of *Seat*, as shown in Figure P1-6. Choose the **Vertex** button in the **Selection** rollout to exit the **Vertex** sub-object mode.

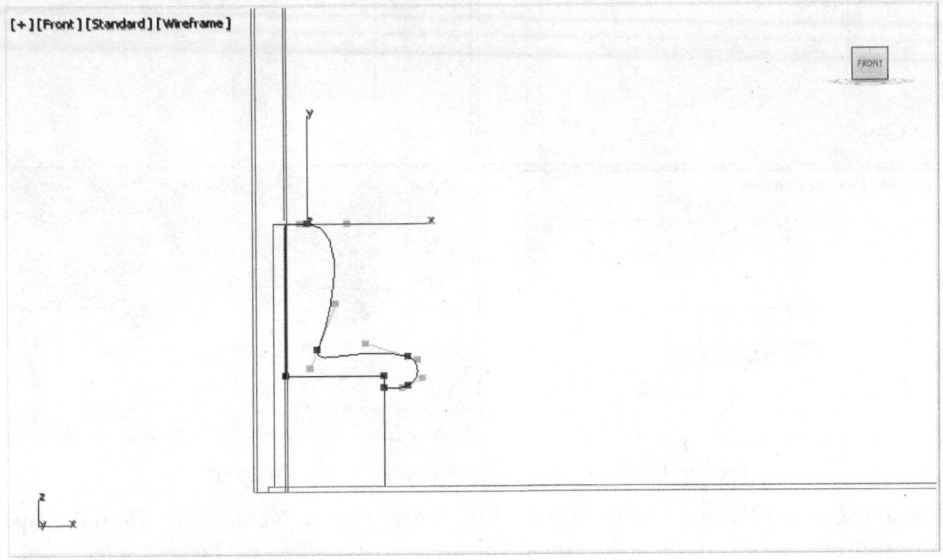

***Figure P1-6** The vertices of Seat modified using the bezier handles*

10. Invoke the **Maximize Viewport Toggle** tool to shift the display back to the four viewport display.

11. Select both *Booth* and *Seat* in any viewport and make sure the **Modify** tab of the **Command Panel** is chosen.

12. In the **Modifier List** drop-down list, select **Extrude** in the **OBJECT-SPACE MODIFIERS** section; the **Extrude** modifier is applied to both the shapes.

13. In the **Parameters** rollout, set the value **40** in the **Amount** spinner; both line profiles are extruded.

14. Activate the Top viewport and move both the extruded objects to the top-left corner of the walls. Next, activate the Perspective viewport and rotate and zoom the *Booth* and *Seat* for better visualization. On doing so, *Booth* and *Seat* are positioned, as shown in Figure P1-7.

15. Select *Booth* and open the **Material Editor** dialog box by pressing the M key. Select the third material sample slot and enter **wood** in the **Material Name** drop-down list.

16. Choose the **Diffuse** button from the **Blinn Basic Parameters** rollout; the **Material/Map Browser** dialog box is displayed.

17. Select the **Bitmap** map from the **Maps > General** rollout and choose the **OK** button. Now, load the map **wood.jpg**, as discussed earlier; the material is displayed in the third sample slot.

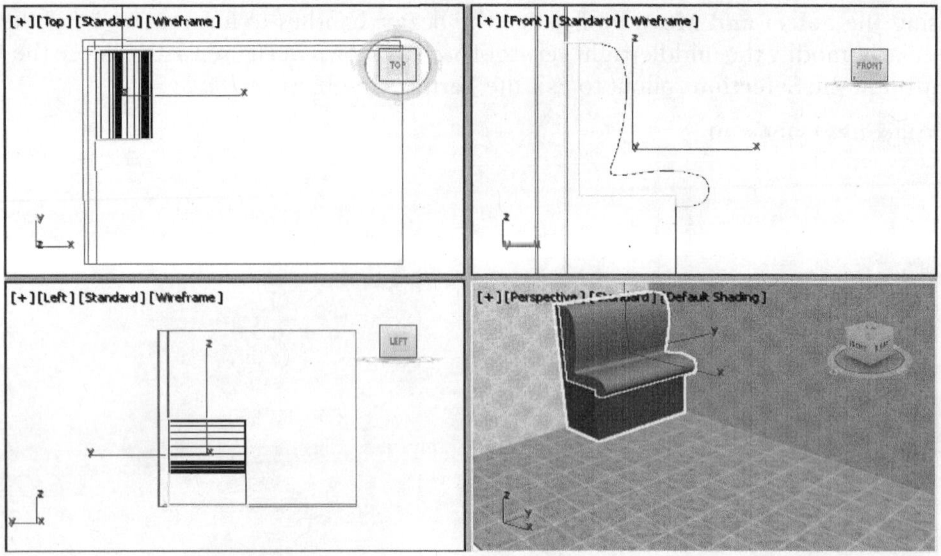

Figure P1-7 Booth and Seat created in the viewport

18. Choose the **Go to Parent** tool to return to the parent level. Next, enter **55** in the **Specular Level** spinner and **31** in the **Glossiness** spinner. Next, make sure *Booth* is selected and then choose the **Assign Material to Selection** and **Show Shaded Material in Viewport** buttons. Close the **Material Editor** dialog box.

19. Choose the **Modify** tab from the **Command Panel**. Next, click on the **Modifier List** drop-down list and select **UVW Map** modifier from it; the **UVW Map** modifier is applied to *Booth*.

20. In the **Parameters** rollout, select the **Box** radio button from the **Mapping** area. Next, select the **Y** radio button and choose the **Fit** button from the **Alignment** area.

21. Select *Seat* and make sure the **Material Editor** dialog box is invoked. Next, select the fourth sample slot in the **Material Editor** dialog box. Next, load the map **FabricPlaid.jpg**, as discussed earlier; the material is displayed in the selected sample slot.

22. In the **Coordinates** rollout, make sure the **Use Real-World Scale** check box is cleared. Next, choose the **Modify** tab in the **Command Panel** and select the **Generate Mapping Coordinate** check box from the **Parameters** rollout.

23. Make sure *Seat* is selected and then choose the **Assign Material to Selection** and **Show Shaded Material in Viewport** tools. Close the **Material Editor** dialog box.

24. Activate the Top viewport and select *Booth* and *Seat*. Choose **Group > Group** from the menu bar; the **Group** dialog box is displayed. In this dialog box, enter **Booth01** in the **Group name** textbox and then choose the **OK** button.

Now, the group can be transformed or modified as a single object.

25. Activate the Front viewport. With the group selected, make sure the **Use Selection Center** tool is invoked in the Pivot Point flyout of the **Main Toolbar**.

26. Invoke the **Mirror** tool from the **Main Toolbar**; the **Mirror: Screen Coordinates** dialog box is displayed. In the **Clone Selection** area of this dialog box, select the **Copy** radio button. In the **Mirror Axis** area, select the **X** radio button and set the value **40** in the **Offset** spinner. Next, choose the **OK** button; a mirror image is created at an offset of 40 units to the right of *Booth01,* as shown in Figure P1-8.

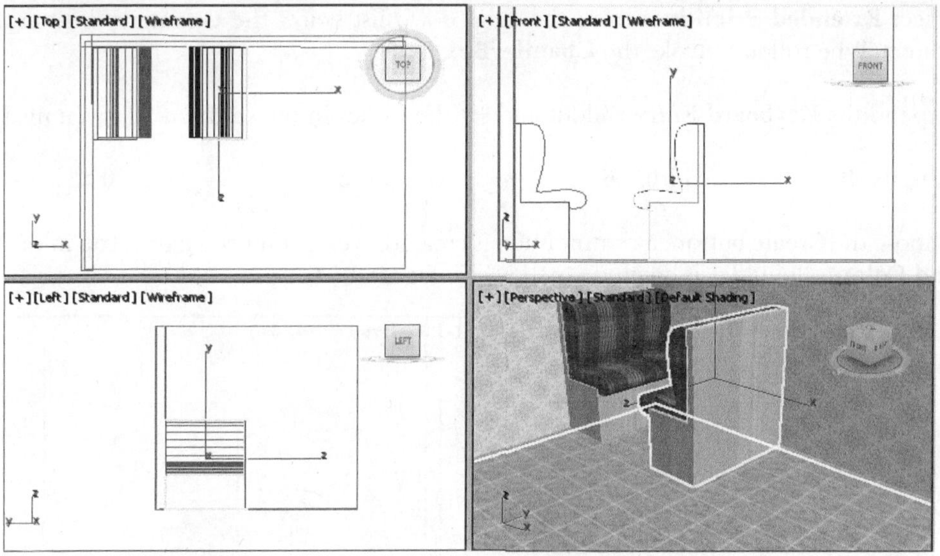

Figure P1-8 *Mirror image created 40 units to the right of Booth01*

27. Enter the name of the mirror image as **Booth02** in the **Name and Color** rollout.

28. Invoke the **Zoom Extents All** tool to zoom the objects to their extents in the viewports.

Creating the Table

In this section, you will create the table. You will also create the base for the table by using the **Cone** tool. Next, you will create the pedestal for the table by using the **Cylinder** tool. The pedestal will be placed on the base of the table. Finally, you will create the table top which will be placed on the top of the pedestal.

1. Activate the Top viewport and then choose **Create > Geometry** in the **Command Panel**. Choose the **Cone** tool from the **Object Type** rollout. Expand the **Keyboard Entry** rollout, and set the values of the parameters as given next.

   Radius 1: **6** Radius 2: **3** Height: **4**

2. Choose the **Create** button. Next, enter the name **Base** in the **Name and Color** rollout; a cone is created, which will become the base of the table.

3. In the **Object Type** rollout, invoke the **Cylinder** tool. In the **Keyboard Entry** rollout, set the value **3** in the **Radius** spinner and **28** in the **Height** spinner.

4. Choose the **Create** button; a cylinder is created. Next, enter the name **Pedestal** in the **Name and Color** rollout.
   Pedestal is created on the base. Now, you will create a tabletop which will be placed on the top of *Pedestal*.

5. Select **Extended Primitives** from the drop-down list below the **Geometry** button. In the **Object Type** rollout, invoke the **ChamferBox** tool.

6. Expand the **Keyboard Entry** rollout and set the values in the spinners as given next:

   Length: **40** Width: **26** Height: **2** Fillet: **0.25**

7. Choose the **Create** button; a chamfer box is created. Next, enter the name **Top** in the **Name and Color** rollout; *Top* is created, as shown in Figure P1-9.

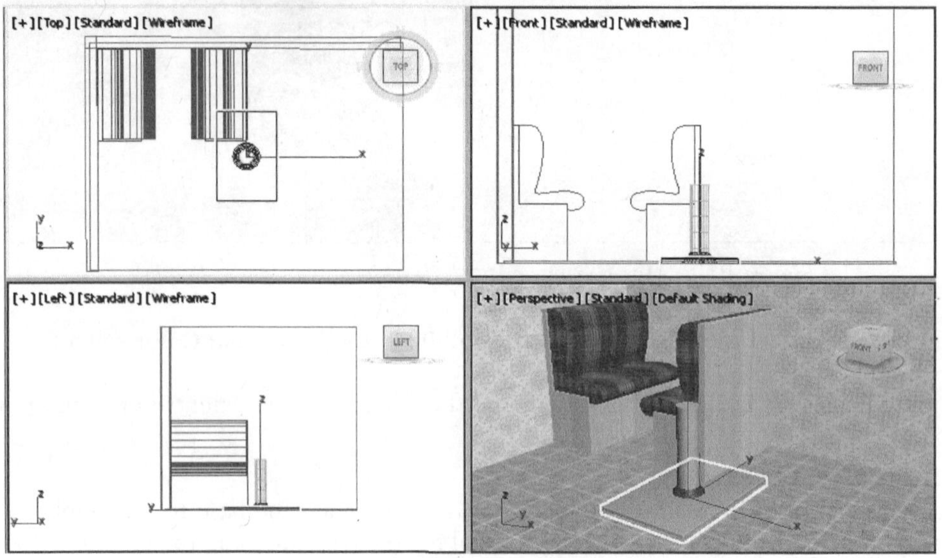

Figure P1-9 *Top created*

8. Maximize the Front viewport and zoom in on the three table objects until the subgrid is displayed. Use the **Select and Move** tool or the **Align** tool to move *Base* so that its lower edge is even with top of *floor*.

9. Select *Pedestal* and use the **Select and Move** tool or the **Align** tool to move it upward so that its lower edge is even with the top edge of *Base*.

10. Select *Top* and use the **Select and Move** tool or the **Align** tool to move it upward so that its lower edge is even with the top edge of *Pedestal*.

11. Restore the four-viewport display. Maximize the Top viewport and zoom in to display the subgrid.

12. Select *Base, Pedestal,* and *Top* and move them such that they are centered between the two booths, as shown in Figure P1-10.

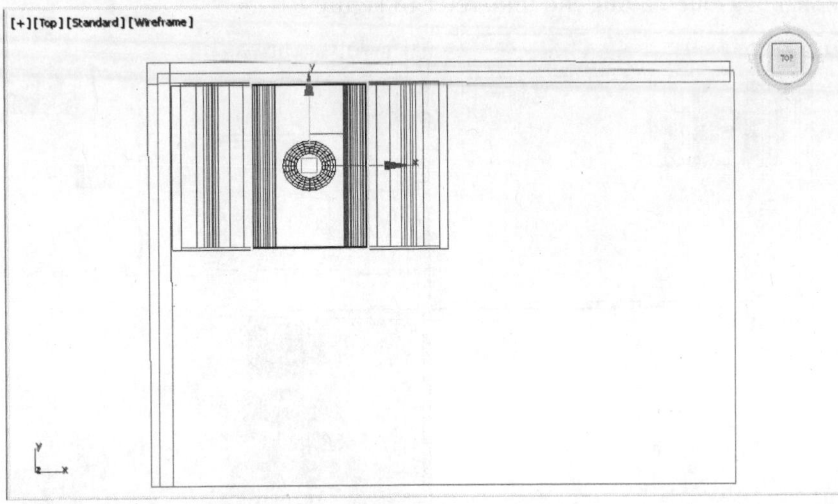

Figure P1-10 *The table components aligned*

13. Select *Top, Base* and *Pedestal* in any viewport and apply the *wood* material to them.

14. Invoke the **Render Setup** tool from the **Main Toolbar**; the **Render Setup: Default Scanline Renderer** dialog box is displayed. In this dialog box, select **NVIDIA mental ray** from the **Renderer** drop-down list; the **Default Scanline Renderer** is changed to **NVIDIA mental ray** renderer. Next, render the Perspective viewport.

Creating the Lamp, Tube, and Target Light

In this section, you will create lights by using the various light tools to illuminate the diner.

1. Activate the Top viewport and then choose **Create > Shapes** in the **Command Panel**. Invoke the **Star** tool from the **Object Type** rollout. In the **Parameters** rollout, set the value **30** in the **Points** spinner.

2. In the **Keyboard Entry** rollout, set the value **4** in the **Radius 1** spinner and **4.8** in the **Radius 2** spinner. Next, choose the **Create** button; a star shape is created in the Top viewport with the name *Star001*. Right-click to exit the tool.

3. Maximize the Front viewport and zoom to display the subgrid. Choose the **Line** tool from the **Object Type** rollout.

4. Draw a vertical line of about 6 units anywhere in the viewport. Right-click to exit the **Line** tool.

5. Make sure the line is selected. Next, choose **Create > Geometry** in the **Command Panel**. Select **Compound Objects** from the drop-down list. Invoke the **Loft** tool from the **Object Type** rollout.

6. In the **Skin Parameters** rollout, set the value **0** in both the **Shape Steps** and the **Path Steps** spinners. In the **Creation Method** rollout, choose the **Get Shape** button and select *Star001*; the star shape is lofted along the line, refer to Figure P1-11.

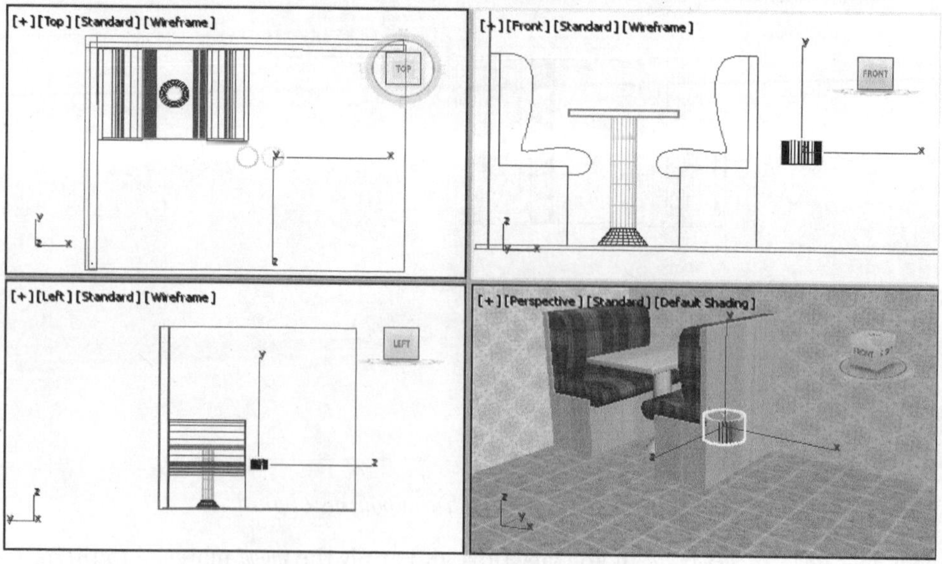

Figure P1-11 The lofted star shape

7. Enter the name **Shade** in the **Name and Color** rollout.

8. Make sure the loft object is selected and then choose the **Modify** tab in the **Command Panel**. Expand the **Deformations** rollout and choose the **Scale** button; the **Scale Deformation(X)** dialog box is displayed.

9. In the **Scale Deformation(X)** dialog box, choose the **Insert Corner Point** button and then insert vertices at points 10 and 90.

   After the vertices are inserted, they can be precisely positioned by entering a value in the text box at the bottom right of the dialog box.

10. Choose the **Move Control Point** button and move the right-hand vertex at point 100 and the vertex at point 90 to 30, as shown in Figure P1-12; the lamp shade is created. Close the **Scale Deformation(X)** dialog box.

11. Choose **Edit > Clone** from the menu bar; the **Clone Options** dialog box is displayed. In this dialog box, select the **Copy** radio button in the **Object** area and enter the name **Shade01** in the **Name** text box. Next, choose the **OK** button.

12. Make sure *Shade01* is selected. Choose the **Hierarchy** tab in the **Command Panel**. Make sure the **Pivot** button is chosen. Next, choose the **Affect Pivot Only** button in the **Move/ Rotate/Scale:** area of the **Adjust Pivot** rollout. Move the pivot point in the Front viewport so that it is aligned with the bottom-middle of *Shade*. Choose the **Affect Pivot Only** button again to exit the pivot adjustment mode.

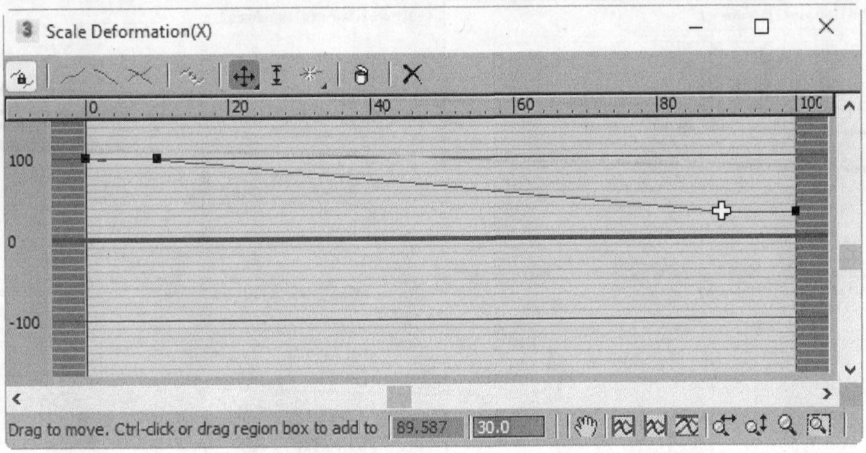

Figure P1-12 *The vertices created and moved in the* ***Scale Deformation****(X) dialog box*

13. Make sure *Shade01* is selected. Next, invoke the **Select and Uniform Scale** and **Use Pivot Point Center** tools. Scale *Shade01* in the Front viewport to 90%, as indicated in the **X**, **Y**, and **Z** text boxes. Alternatively, you can use the **Scale Transformation Type-In** dialog box to scale *Shade01*, which is displayed by right-clicking on the **Select and Uniform Scale** tool.

14. Move *Shade01* slightly downward. Next, select *Shade* from the **Scene Explorer** and then choose **Create > Geometry** in the **Command Panel**. Make sure the **Compound Objects** is selected in the drop-down list.

15. Invoke the **Boolean** tool from the **Object Type** rollout. Choose the **Add Operands** button in the **Boolean Parameters** rollout. Select *Shade01* in any viewport and then choose the **Subtract** button in the **Operand Parameters** rollout; *Shade* is hollowed out.

16. Delete the star and line shapes that were used to create the lamp.

17. Invoke the **Zoom Extents All** tool to view the objects to their extents. In the Top viewport, move *Shade* so that it is centered above the table. In the Front viewport, move and rotate *Shade* to the center of the table, as shown in Figure P1-13.

18. Choose **Rendering > Material Editor > Compact Material Editor** from the menu bar; the **Material Editor** dialog box is displayed. Select the next unused sample slot in it.

19. Choose the material type that is currently labeled as **Standard**; the **Material/Map Browser** dialog box is displayed.

20. Select **Architectural** from the **Materials > Scanline** rollout and then choose the **OK** button; the **Standard** material is replaced by the **Architectural** material. Also, various rollouts are displayed in the **Material Editor** dialog box to modify the **Architectural** material.

21. In the **Templates** rollout, select **Paint-Gloss** from the drop-down list.

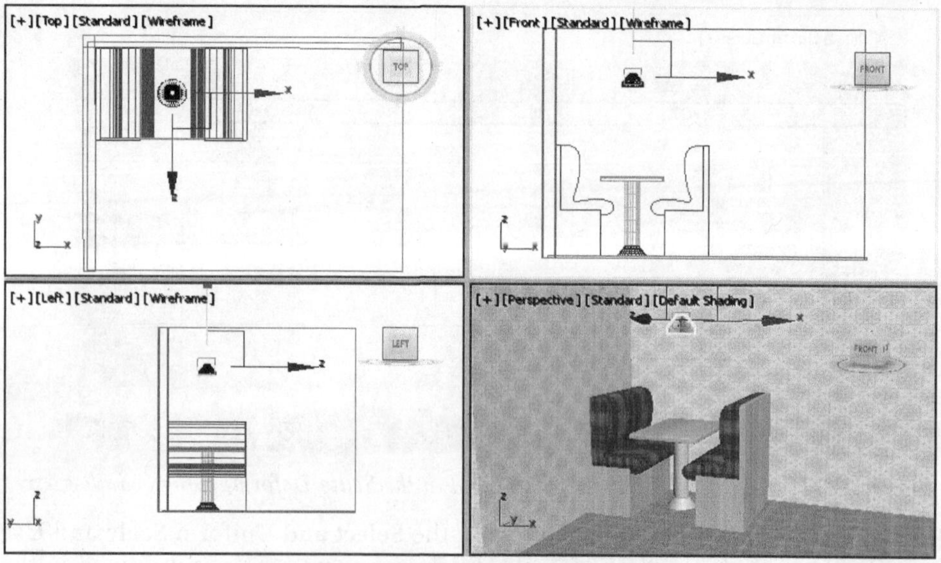

Figure P1-13 Shade moved into position

22. In the **Physical Qualities** rollout, choose the **Diffuse Color** color swatch; the **Color Selector: Diffuse** dialog box is displayed. In this dialog box, set the values as given next:

    Red: **194** Green: **17** Blue: **17**
    Luminance cd/m: **300**

23. Enter the name **Shade** in the **Material name** drop-down list. Choose the **Assign Material to Selection** tool. Next, choose the **Show Shaded Material in Viewport** tool; the material is assigned to *Shade*. Close the **Material Editor** dialog box.

24. Activate the Top viewport and choose **Create > Geometry** in the **Command Panel**. Select **Standard Primitives** in the drop-down list. Invoke the **Cylinder** tool from the **Object Type** rollout.

25. In the **Keyboard Entry** rollout, enter **0.5** in the **Radius** spinner and **15** in the **Height** spinner. Next, choose the **Create** button; a cylinder is created.

26. In the Front viewport, move the cylinder so that its lower edge is aligned with the upper edge of *Shade*. In the Top viewport, place the cylinder at the center of *Shade*, as shown in Figure P1-14.

27. Assign *wood* material to *Cylinder001,* as discussed earlier. Close the **Material Editor** dialog box.

28. Invoke the **Zoom Extents All** tool to zoom the objects to their extents.

29. Choose **Create > Lights** in the **Command Panel**. Select the **Standard** light type in the drop-down list. Next, invoke the **Target Spot** tool from the **Object Type** rollout.

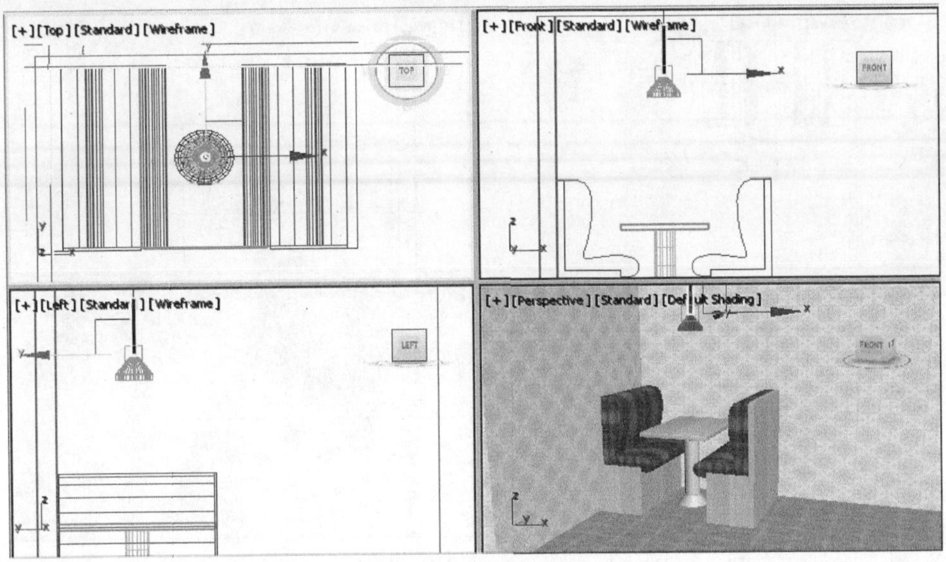

Figure P1-14 A suspension cylinder created

30. In the **Spotlight Parameters** rollout, select the **Show Cone** check box. Also, set the value **60** in the **Hotspot/Beam** spinner and **68** in the **Falloff/Field** spinner.

31. In the **Intensity/Color/Attenuation** rollout, set the value **0.3** in the **Multiplier** spinner and then choose the color swatch located next to it; the **Color Selector: Light Color** dialog box is displayed. In this dialog box, set the values as follows and close the dialog box.

    Red: **254** Green: **255** Blue: **151**

32. In the Front viewport, click at some point in the middle of *Shade*, drag down, and place the target point on the tabletop.

    You may need to zoom in on *Shade* and *Table*. Make sure the light is centered inside *Shade*.

33. In the **Shadows** area of the **General Parameters** rollout, select the **On** check box and then select **Shadow Map** from the drop-down list located below it.

34. In the **Intensity/Color/Attenuation** rollout, select the **Use** check box in the **Far Attenuation** area. Next, set **68** in the **Start** spinner and **70** in the **End** spinner. Now, align both *Spot001* and *Spot001.Target* to the center of *Shade*, as shown in Figure P1-15.

Creating Glasses

In this section, you will create glasses by using the **Cone** tool. These glasses will be placed on the table top.

1. Make sure the Top viewport is active. Next, choose **Create > Geometry** in the **Command Panel**. In the **Object Type** rollout, invoke the **Cone** tool. In the **Parameters** rollout, set the value **1** in the **Height Segments** spinner.

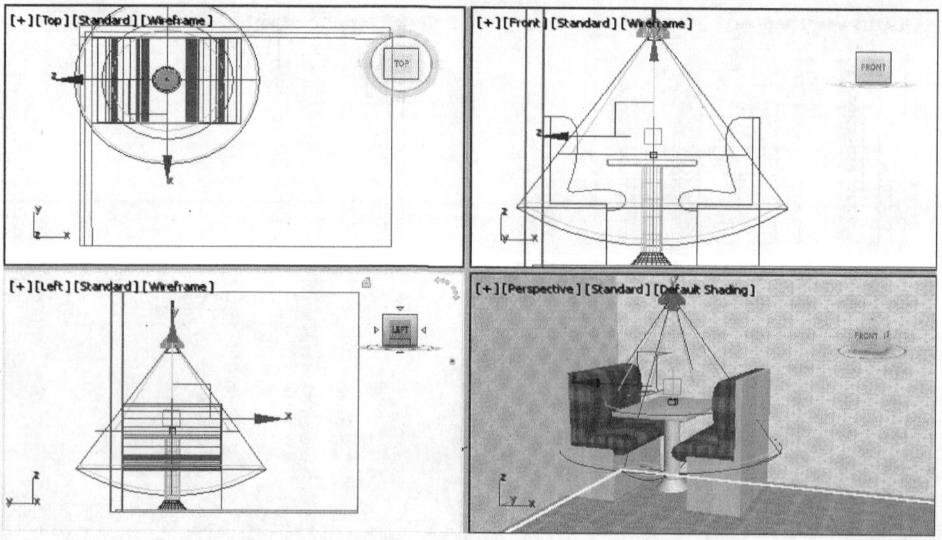

Figure P1-15 A light placed inside the lamp shade

2. Expand the **Keyboard Entry** rollout and enter the values in the spinners as given next:

   Radius 1: **1.5** Radius 2: **2.5** Height: **6**

3. Choose the **Create** button; a cone shape for the glass is created. Enter the name of the shape as **Glass01** in the **Name and Color** rollout and right-click on the viewport to exit the tool.

4. Zoom in on the glass in the Front viewport. Next, choose **Edit > Clone** from the menu bar; the **Clone Options** dialog box is displayed. In this dialog box, make sure the **Copy** radio button is selected in the **Object** area. Enter the name **Glass02** in the **Name** text box. Next, choose the **OK** button.

5. Make sure *Glass02* is selected and then choose the **Hierarchy** tab in the **Command Panel**. Make sure the **Pivot** button is chosen and then choose the **Affect Pivot Only** button. Move the pivot point to the top-center of the cone(*Glass02)* in the Front viewport. Choose the **Affect Pivot Only** button again to exit the pivot adjustment mode.

6. Invoke the **Select and Uniform Scale** tool and scale *Glass02* to 95%, as shown in the **X**, **Y**, and **Z** spinners on the status bar. Next, move *Glass02* slightly upward.

7. Select *Glass01* and then choose **Create > Geometry** in the **Command Panel**. Select **Compound Objects** from the drop-down list.

8. Invoke the **Boolean** tool from the **Object Type** rollout. Choose the **Add Operands** button in the **Boolean Parameters** rollout. Select *Glass02* in any viewport and then choose the **Subtract** button in the **Operand Parameters** rollout; *Glass01* is hollowed out. Now, exit the Boolean operation.

9. Activate the Top viewport. Next, choose **Create > Geometry** in the **Command Panel** and select **Standard Primitives** from the drop-down list. In the **Object Type** rollout, invoke the **Cone** tool.

10. Expand the **Keyboard Entry** rollout and set the values in the spinners as given next:

    Radius 1: **1.4** Radius 2: **2** Height: **4**

11. Choose the **Create** button; the water level effect is created in *Glass01*, as shown in Figure P1-16. Next, enter the name **Water** in the **Name and Color** rollout and right-click on the viewport to exit the tool.

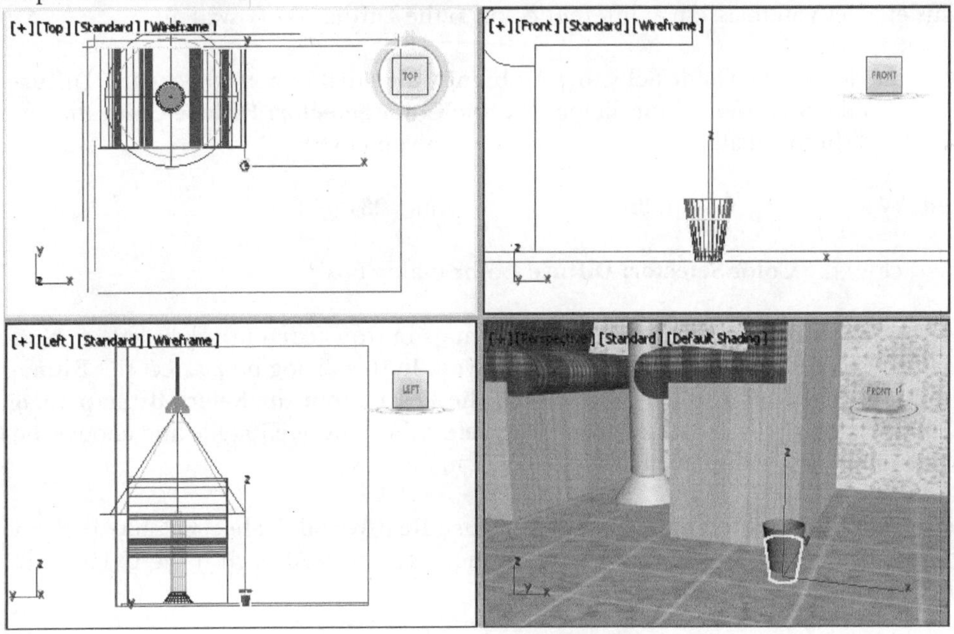

Figure P1-16 A glass with water created

12. Open the **Material Editor** dialog box and select the next unused sample slot. Enter **water** in the **Material Name** drop-down list.

13. In the **Shader Basic Parameters** rollout, select **Blinn** from the drop-down list. Select the **2-Sided** check box. In the **Blinn Basic Parameters** rollout, set the value **25** in the **Opacity** spinner. In the **Specular Highlights** area, set the value **45** in both the **Specular Level** and **Glossiness** spinners.

14. Expand the **Maps** rollout and choose the **Refraction** map button, currently labeled as **None**; the **Material/Map Browser** dialog box is displayed. In this dialog box, select the **Reflect/ Refract** map type from the **Maps > Scanline** rollout and choose the **OK** button. Invoke the **Go to Parent** tool. Assign the *water* material to *Water*. Next align *Water* with *Glass01*.

15. Select *Glass01* in any viewport. In the **Material Editor** dialog box, select the next unused material sample.

16. In the **Shader Basic Parameters** rollout, make sure **Blinn** is selected in the drop-down list and select the **2-Sided** check box. In the **Blinn Basic Parameters** rollout, set the value **25** in the **Opacity** spinner. In the **Specular Highlights** area, set the value **85** in the **Specular Level** spinner and **35** in the **Glossiness** spinner. Choose the **Ambient** color swatch; the **Color Selector: Ambient Color** dialog box is displayed. In this dialog box, set the values as given next:

    Red: **0** Green: **35** Blue: **102**

17. Choose the Lock button between **Ambient** and **Diffuse** to turn it off. 

    This enables you to assign a different color to the **Diffuse** color swatch.

18. Without closing the **Color Selector: Ambient Color** dialog box, choose the **Diffuse** color swatch in the **Material Editor** dialog box; the **Color Selector: Diffuse Color** dialog box is displayed. In this dialog box, set the values as given next:

    Red: **77** Green: **96** Blue: **237**

    Now, close the **Color Selector: Diffuse Color** dialog box.

19. In the **Maps** rollout, choose the **Bump** map button, currently labeled as **None**; the **Material/Map Browser** dialog box is displayed. In this dialog box, select the **Bitmap** from the **Maps > General** rollout and choose the **OK** button; the **Select Bitmap Image File** dialog box is displayed. In this dialog box, select the **concrete.jpg** file and choose the **Open** button; the map is displayed in the selected material slot.

20. In the **Coordinates** rollout, make sure the **Use Real-World Scale** check box is cleared and the value in the **U Tiling** and **V Tiling** spinners is set to **1**. Also, clear the **U Tile** and **V Tile** check boxes.

21. Choose the **Go to Parent** tool to return to the **Maps** rollout. In the **Maps** rollout, set the value **120** in the **Bump** spinner.

22. Enter the name of the material as **Glass** in the **Material Name** drop-down list and assign it to *Glass01*. Close the **Material Editor** dialog box.

23. With *Glass01* selected, choose the **Modify** tab in the **Command Panel**. In the **Modifier List** drop-down list, select **UVW Mapping Add** in the **OBJECT-SPACE MODIFIERS** section and then apply **UVW Map**.

24. In the **Mapping** area of the **Parameters** rollout for the modifier, make sure the **Real-World Map Size** check box is cleared and select the **Cylindrical** radio button.

25. Set the value **5** in the **Length**, **Width**, and **Height** spinners. Also, select the **Z** radio button, if it is not selected and then choose the **Fit** button in the **Alignment** area of the **Parameters** rollout.

26. Select *Glass01* and *Water*. Choose **Group > Group** from the menu bar; the **Group** dialog box is displayed. Enter the name **Drink01** in the **Group** dialog box. Choose the **OK** button; the glass and water are grouped together.

27. Activate the Front viewport and choose the **Zoom Extents** tool. Move *Drink01* to the top of the table so that its bottom edge is aligned with the upper edge of *Top*.

28. In the Top viewport, move *Drink01* upward and toward the left, so that it is placed just to the left of the centerline and 3/4 of the length of the table.

29. Activate the Front viewport and then make sure the **Select and Move** tool is invoked. Press and hold the left mouse button along with the SHIFT key and move *Drink01* toward the right of the table. Now, release the SHIFT key and the left mouse button; the **Clone Options** dialog box is displayed.

30. Make sure the **Copy** radio button is selected in this dialog box and enter **Drink02** in the **Name** textbox. Choose the **OK** button; the dialog box is closed and a copy of *Drink01* is created on the right side of the table. Activate the Top viewport and align *Drink02* so that it is placed at the right of the center line and about ¼th of the length of the table, as shown in Figure P1-17.

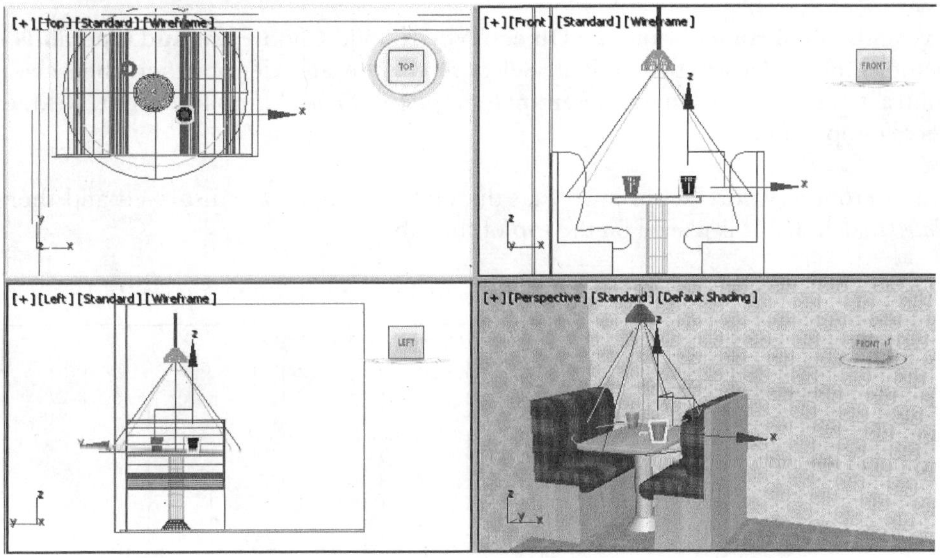

Figure P1-17 Drink02 created and positioned

Creating the Plates

In this section, you will create plates by using the **Cone** tool and then place them on the table top along with glasses.

1. Make sure the Top viewport is activated and then choose **Create > Geometry** in the **Command Panel**. Select **Standard Primitives** in the drop-down list below the **Geometry** button, if it is not selected. Invoke the **Cone** tool from the **Object Type** rollout.

2. In the **Parameters** rollout, make sure the value is set to **1** in the **Height Segments** spinner.
3. Expand the **Keyboard Entry** rollout and set the values in the spinners as given next:

   Radius 1: **2.5** Radius 2: **5.0** Height: **0.75**

4. Choose the **Create** button; a truncated cone is created. Enter the name **Plate01** in the **Name and Color** rollout and right-click on the viewport to exit the tool. Next, *Plate01* will be hollowed out to create a plate.
5. Create a copy of *Plate01,* as discussed earlier and name it as **Plate02**. Zoom in on the plates in the Front viewport.
6. Choose the **Hierarchy** tab in the **Command Panel**. Make sure the **Pivot** button is chosen and then choose the **Affect Pivot Only** button. Move the pivot point to the top-center of *Plate02* and scale *Plate02* from its pivot point to 95% of its original size, as discussed earlier. Next, move *Plate02* slightly upward.
7. Select *Plate01* and choose **Create > Geometry** in the **Command Panel**. Select **Compound Objects** in the drop-down list below the **Geometry** button.
8. Invoke the **Boolean** tool from the **Object Type** rollout. Choose the **Add Operands** button in the **Boolean Parameters** rollout. Select *Plate02* in any viewport and then choose the **Subtract** button in the **Operand Parameters** rollout; *Plate01* is hollowed out. Next, exit the Boolean operation.
9. In the Front viewport, zoom in so that the table and plate are displayed and then move *Plate01* such that it is placed on the top of the table.
10. In the Left viewport, move *Plate01* next to one glass, as shown in Figure P1-18.

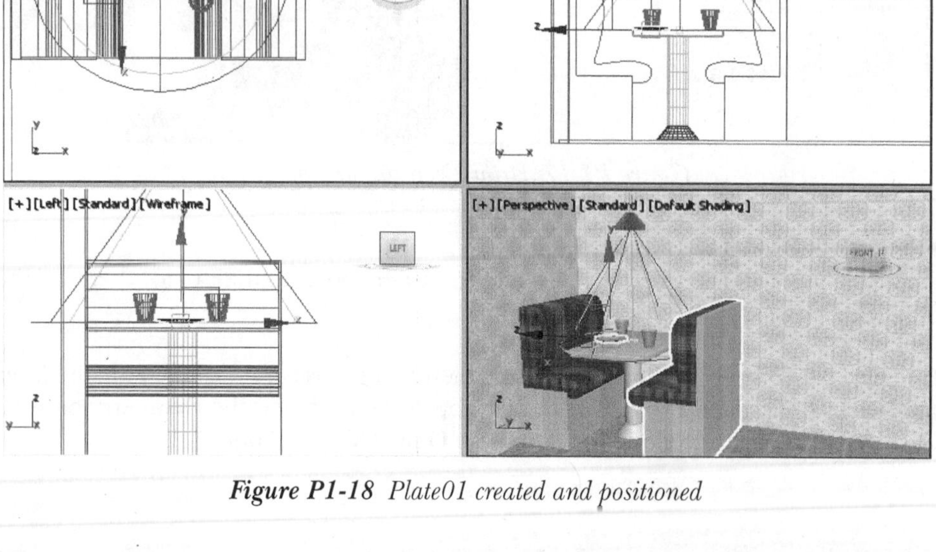

Figure P1-18 *Plate01 created and positioned*

11. Choose **Rendering > Material Editor > Compact Material Editor** from the menu bar; the **Material Editor** dialog box is displayed. Select the next unused sample slot.

12. Choose the **Diffuse Color** color swatch; the **Color Selector: Diffuse Color** dialog box is displayed. In this dialog box, set the values as given next:

    Red: **223** Green: **235** Blue: **233**

13. Choose the **OK** button to close the **Color Selector: Diffuse Color** dialog box. Name the material as **Plate** and assign it to *Plate01*. Close the **Material Editor** dialog box.

Creating the Window

In this section, you will create a window by using the **Fixed** tool. This window will be positioned on the wall next to the diner.

1. Choose the **2D Snap** tool from the **Snaps Toggle** flyout. Next, right-click on it; the **Grid and Snap settings** dialog box is displayed. In this dialog box, make sure the **Edge/Segment** check box is selected in the **Snaps** tab. Close the **Grid and Snap settings** dialog box.

2. Activate the Top viewport and then choose **Create > Geometry** in the **Command Panel**. Next, select **Windows** from the drop-down list.

3. Invoke the **Fixed** tool from the **Object Type** rollout. Next, click on the upper edge of *wall01*, as shown in Figure P1-19 and drag the cursor horizontally to specify the width of the window. Next, release the left mouse button and move the cursor down to specify the depth of the window and click on the lower edge of *wall01*. Now, move the cursor up to define the height of the window and click on the screen; the fixed window is created.

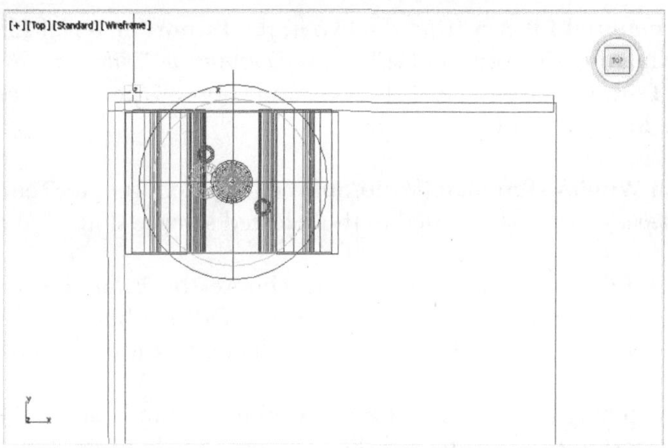

Figure P1-19 *Clicking on the upper edge of wall01*

4. Modify the name of window as *window01*. Next, choose the **2D Snap** tool again to deactivate it.

5. Choose the **Modify** tab from the **Command Panel**. Next, enter **54** in the **Height** spinner, **80** in the **Width** spinner, and **5** in the **Depth** spinner. Now, align *window01* in the viewports, as shown in Figure P1-20.

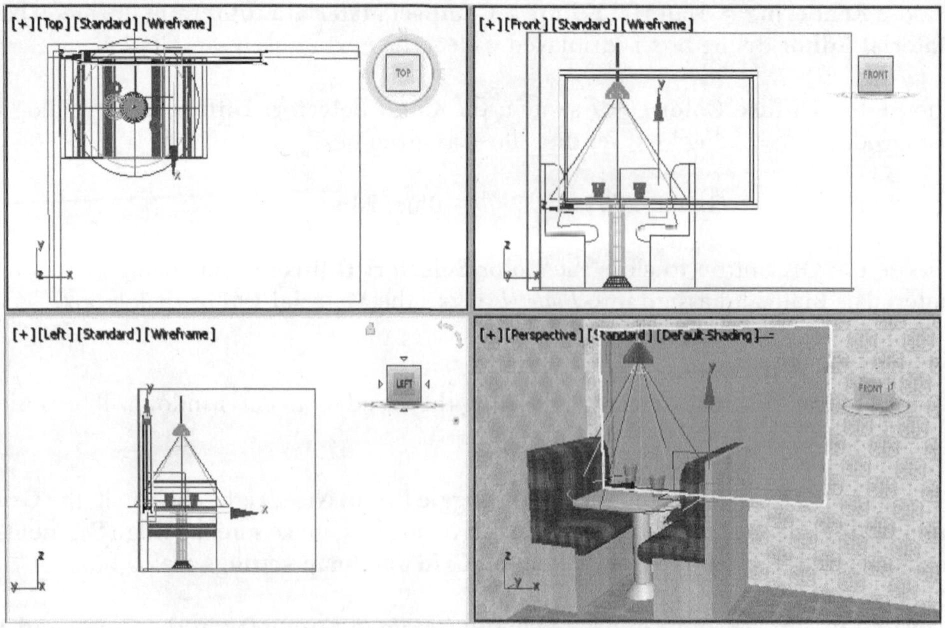

Figure P1-20 window01 aligned in the viewports

6. Choose **Rendering > Material Editor > Compact Material Editor** from the menu bar; the **Material Editor** dialog box is displayed. Select the next unused sample slot.

7. Choose the **Get Material** button; the **Material/Map Browser** dialog box is displayed. In this dialog box, choose the **Material/Map Browser Options** button; a flyout is displayed.

8. Choose **Open material Library** from the flyout; the **Import material Library** dialog box is displayed. Navigate to the location *C:\Program Files\Autodesk\3ds Max 2017\materiallibraries*; and select **AecTemplates** from this dialog box and choose **Open**; the **AecTemplates** library is added in the **Material Editor** dialog box.

9. Double-click on **Window-Template(Multi/Sub-Object)** from the **AecTemplates.mat** rollout; the *Window-Template* material is added to the selected sample slot.

10. In the **Multi/Sub-Object Parameters** rollout, choose the **Front Rails (Standard)** button corresponding to material ID **1**. Next, choose the **Diffuse** button from the **Blinn Basic Parameters** rollout; the **Material/Map Browser** dialog box is displayed.

11. Select the **Bitmap** map from the **Maps > General** rollout and choose the **OK** button. Now, load the map **wood.jpg**, as discussed earlier. Choose the **Go to Parent** tool to return to the previous level.

12. Repeat the process given in steps 10 and 11 for material IDs **2**, **4**, and **5**.

13. Choose the **Panels (Standard)** button for the material ID **3**. Next, choose the **Standard** button on the right of the **Material Name** drop-down list; the **Material/Map Browser** dialog box is displayed. Select the **Architectural** material from the **Materials > Scanline** rollout and

choose **OK**; the **Standard** material is replaced by **Architectural** material in the **Material Editor** dialog box.

14. In the **Material Editor** dialog box, click on the drop-down list in the **Templates** rollout. Next, select **Glass - Clear** from this drop-down list.

15. Choose the **Go to Parent** tool. Next, assign the *Window-Template* material to *window01*.

16. Close the **Material Editor** and the **Material/Map Browser** dialog boxes.

Creating the Text Diner

In this section, you will create the text DINER by using the **Text** tool. This text will be positioned on the outer face of the wall.

1. Activate the Front viewport. Next, choose **Create > Shapes** in the **Command Panel**. Invoke the **Text** tool from the **Object Type** rollout.

2. In the **Parameters** rollout, select **Comic Sans MS Bold** from the **Font** drop-down list. Set the value **20** in the **Size** spinner and in the **Text** area, highlight the current text and type the word **DINER**.

3. Click at a point at the center of *window01* in the Front viewport to place the text, as shown in Figure P1-21.

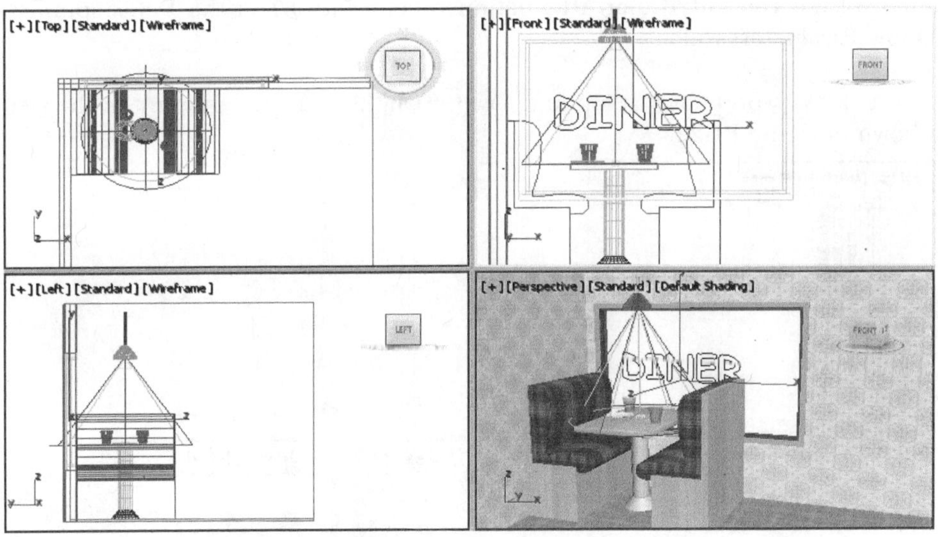

Figure P1-21 The text created

You may need to slightly reposition the text later in the modeling process.

4. Activate the Top viewport and move the DINER text to the outer (top) face of *wall01*.

5. Make sure the text object is selected and then choose the **Modify** tab in the **Command Panel**. In the **Modifier List** drop-down list, select **Extrude** in the **OBJECT-SPACE MODIFIERS** section. In the **Parameters** rollout for the modifier, set the value **0.2** in the **Amount** spinner.

6. Make sure the Top viewport is activated. With the text object selected, invoke the **Mirror** tool; the **Mirror: Screen Coordinates** dialog box is displayed. Next, make sure the **No Clone** and **X** radio buttons are selected and then choose the **OK** button; the text appears reversed so that it can be read from outside the building.

7. Choose **Rendering > Material Editor > Compact Material Editor** from the menu bar; the **Material Editor** dialog box is displayed. Select the next unused sample slot.

8. Choose the **Material Type** button that is currently labeled as **Standard**; the **Material/Map Browser** dialog box is displayed. Select the **Architectural** material from the **Materials > Scanline** rollout and choose the **OK** button; the **Standard** material is replaced by the **Architectural** material.

9. In the **Templates** rollout, select **Metal-Brushed** from the drop-down list under the **Architectural** material type. In the **Physical Qualities** rollout, choose the **Diffuse Color** color swatch and define a color of your choice. Enter the name of the material as **Sign** and assign it to the text object. Close the **Material Editor** and the **Material/Map Browser** dialog boxes.

10. Choose **Create > Lights** in the **Command Panel**. Make sure the **Standard** option is selected in the drop-down list. Next, invoke the **Omni** tool from the **Object Type** rollout. In the **Shadows** area of the **General Parameters** rollout, select the **On** check box and select **Shadow Map** from the drop-down list located below it. Then, set the value **0.3** in the **Multiplier** spinner of the **Intensity/Color/Attenuation** rollout and **0.7** in the **Dens.** spinner of the **Shadow Parameters** rollout.

11. In the Front viewport, click at a point; *Omni001* light is created. Align it in the viewports, as shown in Figure P1-22.

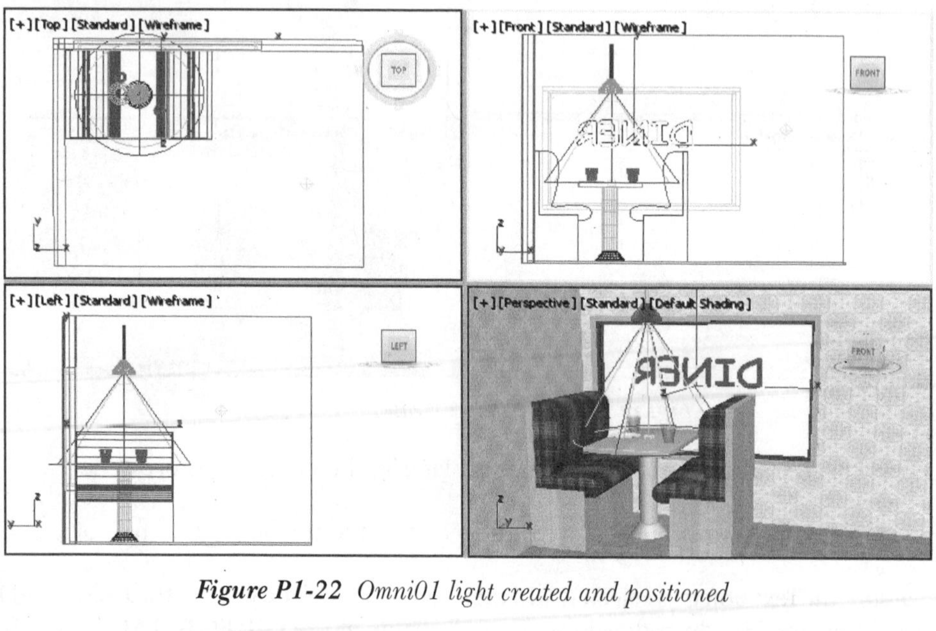

***Figure P1-22** Omni01 light created and positioned*

Creating Blinds

In this section, you will create blinds for the window by using the **Box** tool.

1. Activate the Front viewport and then choose **Create > Geometry** in the **Command Panel** and select **Standard Primitives** from the drop-down list below the **Geometry** button. In the **Object Type** rollout, invoke the **Box** tool.

2. Expand the **Keyboard Entry** rollout and set the values in the spinners as given next:

   Length: **53** Width: **4** Height: **0.125**

3. Choose the **Create** button; a box is created. Enter the name **Blind01** in the **Name and Color** rollout.

4. In the Front viewport, move *Blind01* near the top-left corner of *Window01*. To do so, you may need to zoom into the area around the top-left corner of *Window01*.

5. Activate the Top viewport. Invoke the **Select and Rotate** and **Transform Gizmo Z Constraint** tools. Next, rotate *Blind01* at -20 degrees about the Z axis in the Top viewport.

6. Align *Blind01* in the viewports, as shown in Figure P1-23.

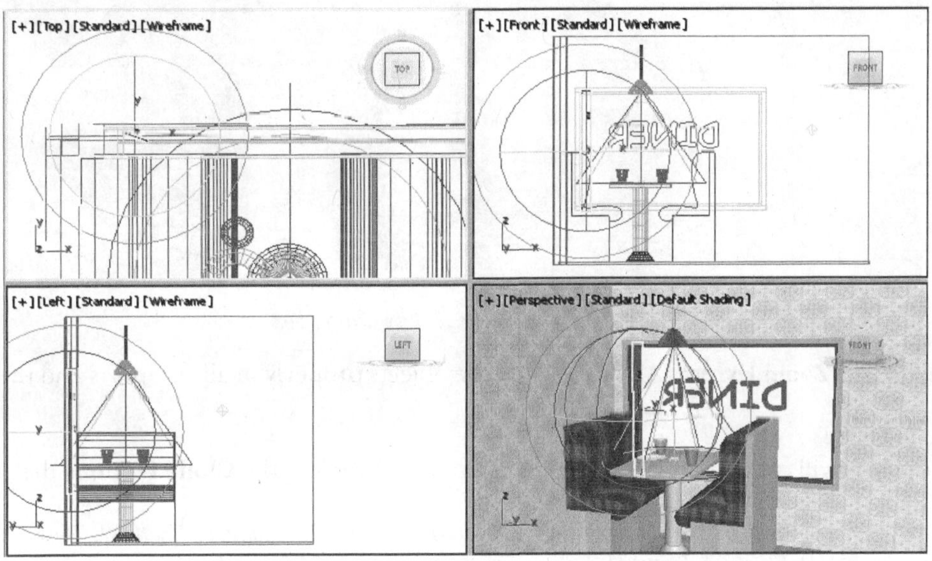

***Figure P1-23** Blind01 created and positioned*

7. Select *Blind01* and then choose **Rendering > Material Editor > Compact Material Editor** from the menu bar, the **Material Editor** dialog box is displayed. Select the next unused sample slot.

8. Choose the **Diffuse** color swatch; the **Color Selector:Diffuse Color** dialog box is displayed. Set the values as given next:

   Red: **255** Green: **244** Blue: **198**

9. Choose the **OK** button to close the **Color Selector:Diffuse Color** dialog box. Enter the name of the material as **Blinds** and assign it to *Blind01*. Next, close the **Material Editor** dialog box.

10. Make sure *Blind01* is selected and choose **Tools > Array** from the menu bar; the **Array** dialog box is displayed, as shown in Figure P1-24. Choose the **Reset All Parameters** button in this dialog box. Set the value **3.6** in the **Incremental X** spinner in the **Move** row. In the **Array Dimensions** area, make sure the **1D** radio button is selected and set the value **22** in the **Count** spinner. Next, select the **Copy** radio button in the **Type of Object** area and choose the **OK** button; 22 blinds are created extending across the window, as shown in Figure P1-25.

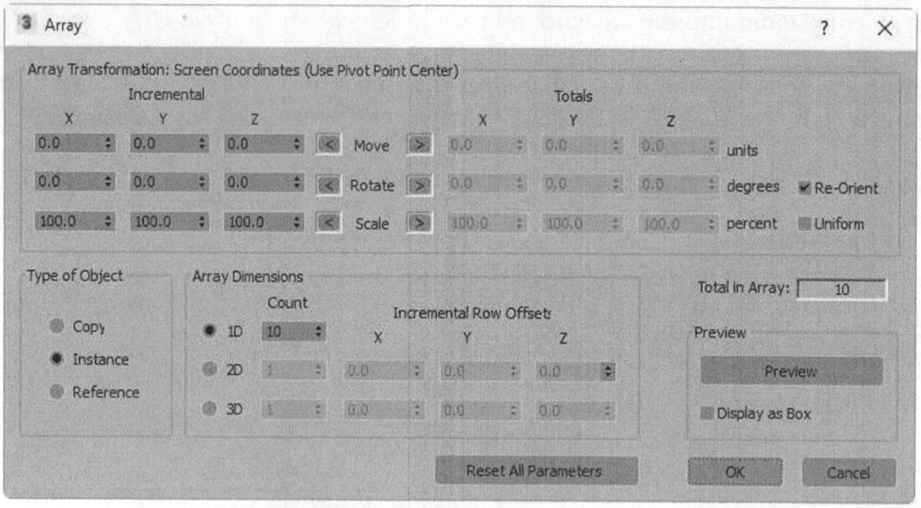

***Figure P1-24** The **Array** dialog box*

11. Invoke the **Zoom Extents All** tool to view the objects properly in all viewports and then save the scene.

    Next, you will create multiple copies of the objects by using the **Clone Options** dialog box.

12. Activate the Front viewport and select *Drink01, Drink02, Booth01, Booth02, Base, Pedestal, Plate01, Shade, Spot001, Spot001.Target, Top*, and *Cylinder001* from the **Scene Explorer**. Group them with the name *Dinerset*.

13. Make sure the **Select and Move** tool is invoked. Then, choose the **Transform Gizmo X Constraint** tool. Press and hold the left mouse button along with the SHIFT key and move the selected objects to the right of the original objects. Release the SHIFT key and the left mouse button when the left edge of the copied booth lines up with the right edge of the original position; the **Clone Options** dialog box is displayed.

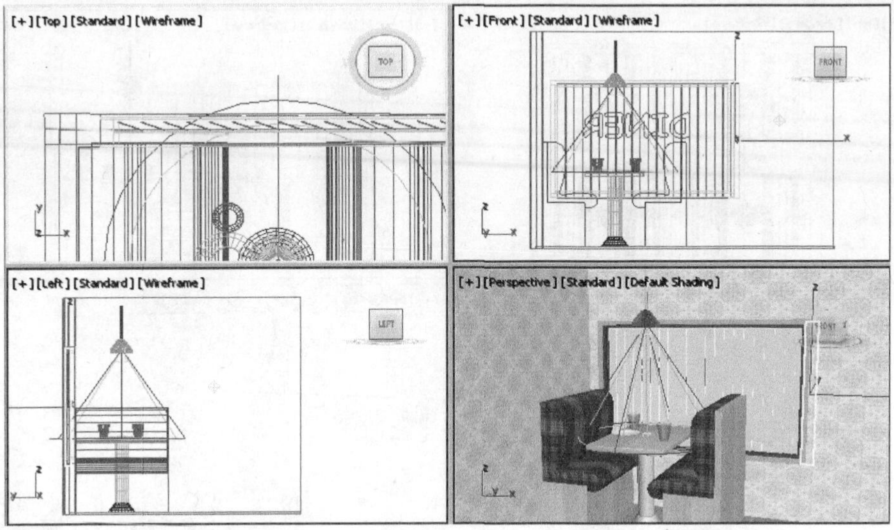

Figure P1-25 The blinds created using the ***Array*** *tool*

14. In this dialog box, enter the name **DinerSet01** in the **Name** text box and select the **Copy** radio button. Now, choose the **OK** button; another set of selected objects is created, as shown in Figure P1-26.

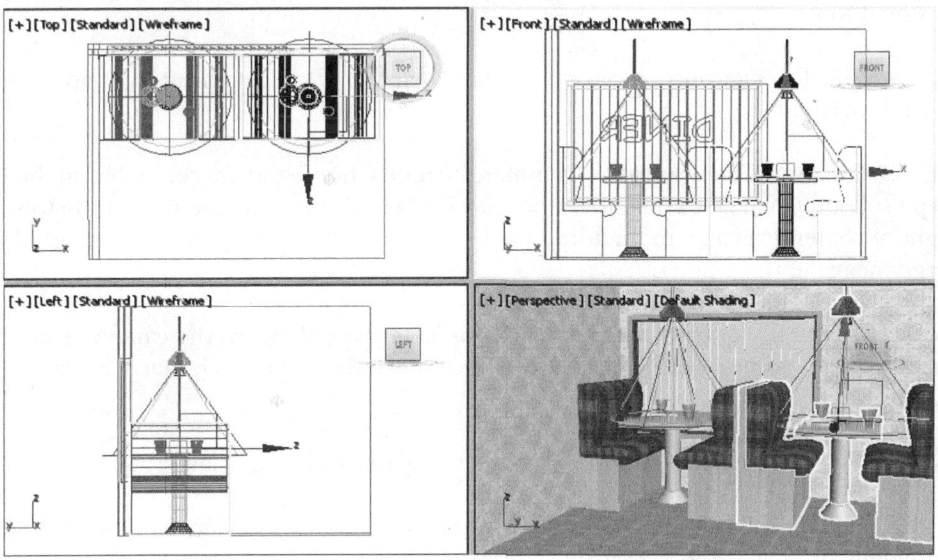

Figure P1-26 The selected objects copied and positioned

15. Select *Dinerset* and *DinerSet01* from the **Scene Explorer** and group them with the name **DinerSet02**.

16. Activate the Top viewport and create a copy of *DinerSet02* with the name **DinerSet03**. Next, align *DinerSet03* in the Top viewport, as shown in Figure P1-27.

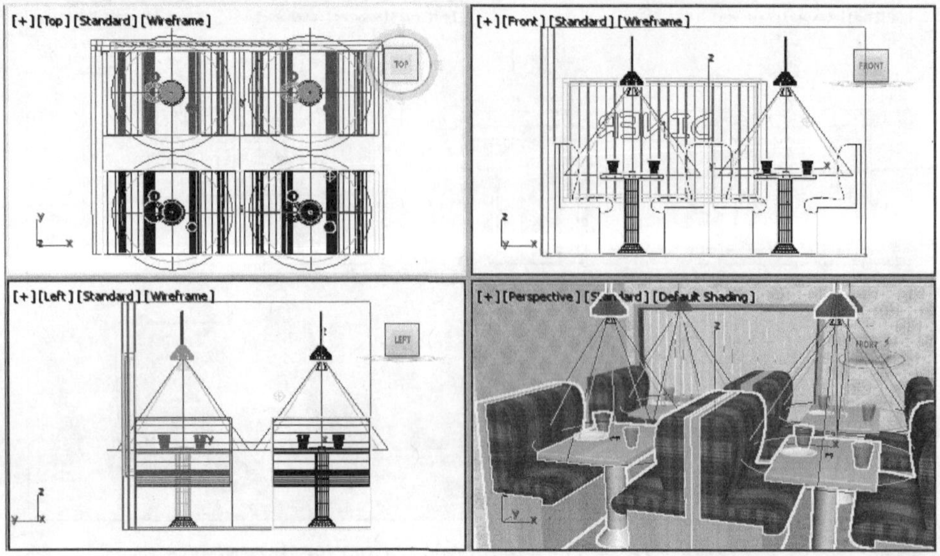

Figure P1-27 DinerSet03 created and aligned in the Top viewport

Adding a Camera

In this section, you will create the camera to apply the angle of direction of the objects by using the **Physical** tool.

1. Activate the Top viewport. Zoom out so that the objects are displayed in almost one-third of their original size.

2. Choose **Create > Cameras** in the **Command Panel**. Choose the **Target** tool from the **Object Type** rollout. Click at a point at the bottom-middle of the viewport and a little toward the right of center. Pressing and holding the left mouse button, drag the cursor and place the target near the right side of *Shade*.

3. Activate the Left viewport. Invoke the **Zoom Extents** tool. Move the camera upward such that it is at the same level as the shades. Next, move the target such that it is placed on the table.

4. Activate the Perspective viewport. Press the C key to display the Camera001 view.

5. Using the **Truck Camera** and **Dolly Camera** tools, adjust the camera in such a way that the edges of *wall01* and *floor* are not visible. Next, align the objects at the center of the PhysCamera001 viewport, refer to Figure P1-28.

Adding More Lights

In this section, you will create lights to illuminate the scene.

1. Choose **Create > Light** in the **Command Panel**. Make sure the **Standard** option is selected in the drop-down list.

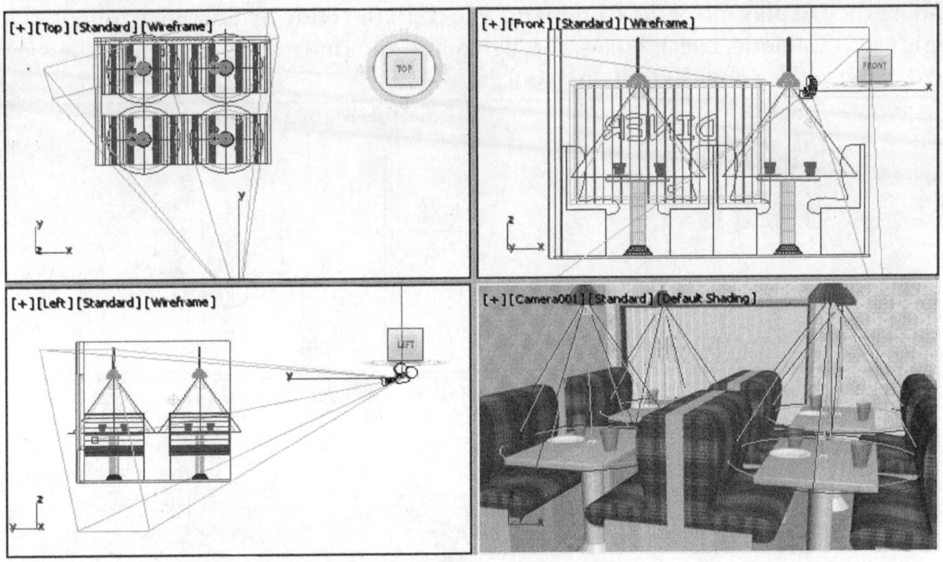

Figure P1-28 *Aligning objects at the center of the PhysCamera001 viewport*

2. Activate the Top viewport and invoke the **Target Spot** tool from the **Object Type** rollout. In the Top viewport, click at a point near the lower-right corner of the viewport and then drag to place the target on the window. In the **Shadows** area of the **General Parameters** rollout, make sure the **On** check box is selected; another spotlight is placed.

3. In the Left viewport, invoke the **Zoom Extents** tool. Next, move spotlight upward so that it is in level with the tabletop or slightly above it. Finally, move spotlight target and place it in the middle of the window, refer to Figure P1-29.

4. Set the value **0.1** in the **Multiplier** spinner of the **Intensity/Color/Attenuation** rollout. Also, set the required values in the **Hotspot/Beam** spinner and the **Falloff/Field** spinner such that the cone created covers the whole room. Next, set **0.7** in the **Dens.** spinner of the **Shadow Parameters** rollout.

Rendering the Still Image

In this section, you will render the still image.

1. Activate the Camera001 viewport. Choose the **Render Production** tool from the **Main Toolbar**; a rendered view of the scene is displayed in the **Rendered Frame** window, as shown in Figure P1-30.

2. Close the **Rendered Frame** window.

3. Make the necessary adjustments in the lights of the scene, if required.

Animating the Scene

In this section, you will animate the scene.

1. Choose the **Display** tab of the **Command Panel**. In the **Hide by Category** rollout, select the **Lights** and **Cameras** check boxes; the lights and the camera are hidden in the viewports. Next, choose the **Zoom Extents All** tool.

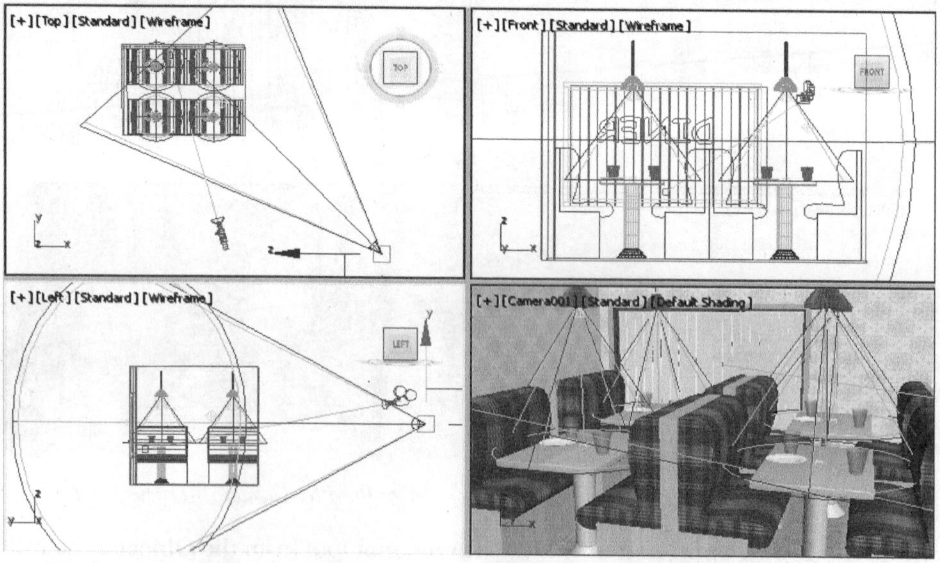

***Figure P1-29** The spotlight target moved and placed in the middle of the window*

***Figure P1-30** The rendered view of the scene*

2. Click on the Shaded viewport label menu; a flyout is displayed. Choose **Wireframe** from the flyout.

   This will improve the system performance when previewing the animation in the viewport.

3. Activate and maximize the Top viewport. Zoom in on the blinds.

4. Choose the **Time Configuration** button to display the **Time Configuration** dialog box. In the **Animation** area, set the value **42** in the **Length** spinner. Choose the **OK** button; the number of frames in the active time segment changes to 42.

5. Select **World** from the **Reference Coordinate System** drop-down list from the **Main Toolbar**.

6. Drag the time slider to frame 0, if it is not at frame one and then choose the **Toggle Auto Key Mode** button to turn it on (red).

7. Select *Blind022* (the farthest-right blind) and right-click on the **Select and Move** tool; the **Move Transform-Type In** dialog box is displayed. In this dialog box, set the value **–2.7** in the **Offset World X** spinner; *Blind022* is moved to the left by 2.7 units. Then, close the **Move Transform Type-In** dialog box.

8. Move the time slider to Frame 1 and select *Blind021* along with *Blind022*. Using the **Move Transform Type-In** dialog box, move these two blinds left by -2.7 units.

9. Move the time slider to Frame 2 and select *Blind020* along with *Blind021* and *Blind022*. Using the **Move Transform Type-In** dialog box, move these three blinds left by -2.7 units.

10. Continue with this pattern until all the blinds are selected and moved except the last one (*Blind01*), as shown in Figure P1-31. The whole process will be completed in 20 frames.

11. Move time slider to Frame 21 and start reversing the above process frame by frame. When you are done, choose the **Toggle Auto Key Mode** button to turn off the animation mode.

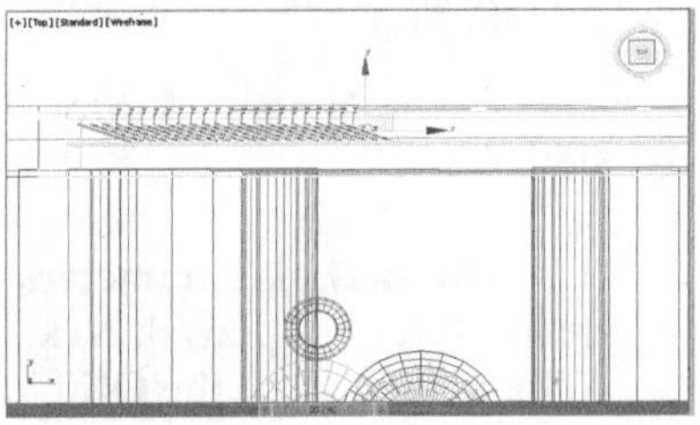

***Figure P1-31** The blinds at the midpoint of the animation*

12. Display the four-viewport configuration and then activate the Camera viewport. Next, choose the **Play Animation** button; the animation is played in the Camera001 viewport.

13. Choose the **Stop Animation** button to stop the playback.

Setting the Background

Now, you need to set the background for the scene.

1. Choose **Create > Geometry** in the **Command Panel**. Invoke the **Plane** tool from the **Object Type** rollout.

2. In the Front viewport, create a plane and align it on the back of *Wall01* in the Left viewport, refer to Figure P1-32.

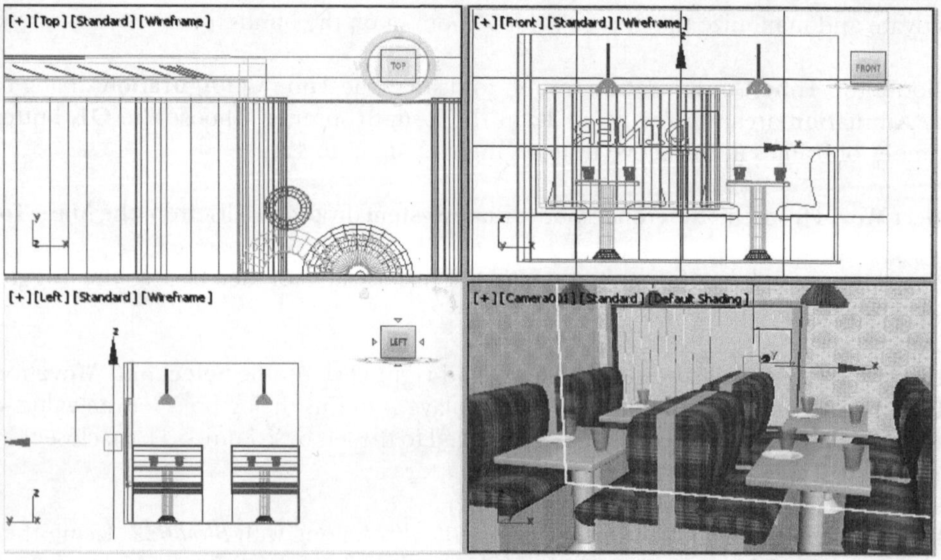

Figure P1-32 The Plane created and aligned on back of Wall02

3. In the **Parameters** rollout, enter **120** in the **Length** spinner and **170** in the **Width** spinner. The proper length and width has been set to the plane.

4. Choose the **Material Editor** dialog box and select the next unused material type sample slot.

5. In the **Blinn Basis Parameters** rollout, choose the **Diffuse** button; the **Material/Map Browser** dialog box is displayed. Next, choose the **Bitmap** map button from the **Maps > General** rollout and choose the **OK** button; the **Select Bitmap Image File** dialog box is displayed.

6. In the **Select Bitmap Image File** dialog box, select the **Sunset.Jpg** file and choose the **Open** button to return to the **Material Editor** dialog box.

7. In the **Coordinates** rollout, make sure the **User Real-World Scale** check box is cleared and **1.0** is set in the **U: Tiling** and **V: Tiling** spinners.

8. Invoke the **Go To Parent** tool to go one level up. Make sure *Plane001* is selected in the viewport and assign this material to *Plane001*.

Rendering the Animation

In this section, you will render the final animation.

1. Activate the Camera001 viewport. Next, choose the **Render Setup** tool; the **Render Setup: NVIDIA mental ray** dialog box is displayed.

2. In the **Time Output** area of the **Common Parameters** rollout, select the **Active Time Segment** radio button. In the **Render Output** area, choose the **Files** button; the **Render Output File** dialog box is displayed.

3. In the **Render Output File** dialog box, select **AVI File (*.avi)** from the **Save as type** drop-down list. In the **File name** text box, enter the name **Project02** and then choose the **Save** button; the **AVI File Compression Setup** dialog box is displayed. Choose the **OK** button in this dialog box.

4. Make sure the **Save File** check box is selected in the **Render Output** area of the **Render Setup** dialog box and then choose the **Render** button in the dialog box.

   It may take several minutes to render the animation frame by frame. After rendering is complete, you need to set some parameters available in the render window to improve the quality of render.

5. Enter **1** in the **FG Bounces** spinner of the **Trace/Bounces Limits** area. Next, set **Final Gather Precision** to **Medium** and **Image Precision (Quality/Noise)** to **Low: Min 1.0 Quality 0.5**.

6. Choose **Rendering > View Image File** from the menu bar; the **View File** dialog box is displayed. Select the **Project02.avi** and choose the **Open** button. The animation is played once in Windows Media Player. Figure P1-33 shows the rendered image at frame 20.

Figure P1-33 *The final animation rendered at frame 20*

Index

D

E

F

G

H

I

K

L

M

N

O

P

Q

R

S

V

W

Z

Other Titles of Interest - BPB/TICKOO SERIES

Publications by BPB/TICKOO SERIES

The following is the list of some of the publications by BPB/TICKOO series:

Autodesk 3ds Max Textbooks

- Autodesk 3ds Max 2017 for Beginners: A Tutorial Approach, 17th Edition

Autodesk Maya Textbooks

- Autodesk Maya 2017: A Comprehensive Guide, 9th Edition

MAXON CINEMA 4D Textbook

- MAXON CINEMA 4D R18 Studio: A Tutorial Approach, 5th Edition

Pixologic ZBrush 4R7 Textbook

- Pixologic ZBrush 4R7: A Comprehensive Guide, 2nd Edition

Programming Textbooks

- Introduction to C++ Programming, 2nd Edition
- Learning Oracle 12c: A PL/SQL Approach, 2nd Edition
- Introduction to Java Programming, 2nd Edition

Autodesk Revit Architecture Textbook

- Exploring Autodesk Revit 2017 for Architecture, 13th Edition

RISA-3D Textbook

- Exploring RISA-3D 14.0

Bentley STAAD.Pro Textbook

- Exploring Bentley STAAD.Pro V8i (SELECTseries 6)

AutoCAD Civil 3D Textbook

- Exploring AutoCAD Civil 3D 2017, 7th Edition

AutoCAD Map 3D Textbook

- Exploring AutoCAD Map 3D 2017, 7th Edition

Autodesk Navisworks Textbook

- Exploring Autodesk Navisworks 2017, 4th Edition

Oracle Primavera Textbook

- Exploring Oracle Primavera P6 v8.4

AutoCAD Raster Design Textbook
- Exploring AutoCAD Raster Design 2017

Autodesk Inventor Textbook
- Autodesk Inventor 2017 for Designers, 17th Edition

AutoCAD MEP Textbook
- AutoCAD MEP 2016 for Designers, 3rd Edition

NX Textbook
- NX 11.0 for Designers, 10th Edition

NX Nastran Textbook
- NX Nastran 9.0 for Designers

SolidWorks Textbook
- SOLIDWORKS 2017 for Designers, 15th Edition

Creo Parametric Textbook
- PTC Creo Parametric 3.0 for Designers, 3rd Edition

Autodesk Alias Textbook
- Learning Autodesk Alias Design 2016, 5th Edition

AutoCAD Electrical Textbook
- AutoCAD Electrical 2017 for Electrical Control Designers, 8th Edition

CATIA Textbook
- CATIA V5-6R2016 for Designers, 14th Edition

Solid Edge Textbook
- Solid Edge ST9 for Designers, 14th Edition

AutoCAD LT Textbook
- AutoCAD LT 2017 for Designers, 12th Edition